For the couple:

_____

In celebration of their marriage on

_____

With warmest congratulations from

_____

CONTENTS

As you start your new life together, you'll find that some of the best memories will be created over meals with each other, and with family and friends. And you'll discover that your kitchen, no matter how tiny or grand, is the heart of your home. So for all of the times you will cook, eat, entertain and share, Betty Crocker will be there to make your time easy and enjoyable.

Cover Photo: The cupcake tier on the cover is made with 36 white cupcakes and an 8-inch white cake on the top. To make the cake and cupcakes, you'll need two white cake mixes or two recipes for Silver White Cake, page 140. Make one recipe of batter and follow the directions for baking a single 8-inch round cake layer; use the rest of the batter to make about 12 cupcakes (see page 142 for cupcake baking directions). Make the second batch of cake batter to make 24 more cupcakes. Frost the cake and cupcakes using a double recipe of Creamy Vanilla Frosting, page 153. Decorate with food-safe fresh roses and edible pearl decors.

OUR FIRST KITCHEN

Whether your first kitchen is small or large, it will hold special memories for the rest of your life. You can arrange it however you like, but here are some tips to get you started with organizing.

EVERYTHING HAS A PLACE

- Store items at point of first use—pans by the stove, spices by where you mix, tableware by where you serve.
- Group items by frequently used and rarely used.
- Use cabinet organizers.
- Install roll-out shelves if you don't already have them.
- Keep things off the counters to free them up for cooking.
- Add hooks to cabinet doors to hang measuring cups and spoons.
- Designate one spot in your kitchen for cookbooks.

Order, Order Please

Tired of searching for that item you just knew that you had but cannot locate? Apply these simple tips to organizing your pantry, refrigerator and freezer and you'll have a good grasp on where everything is located.

- Group Similar Foods Together: Consider the way your family most often uses each item.
- Use Prime Real Estate Well: Reserve the front and center parts of any space for the ingredients you reach for most often. Save hard-to-reach storage areas (both high and low) for foods used only occasionally.
- Label with Abandon: Leave zero question as to what things are and where they are stored. Mark foods carefully with name and include dates.
- Store It: Use containers to keep similar foods together easily and neatly. It's convenient to place sauce and seasoning packets in a box so they are easy to see. A container that holds all of the dry pasta packages makes things tidy.

Incoming Ease

Avoid worrying about food waste and missed expiration dates. Just follow these simple steps when putting away groceries.

- Start Fresh: Before you shop, do a quick cleanup of the refrigerator, freezer and pantry. This also helps refamiliarize you with what is on hand and what needs replacing.
- Strategize Your List: Include ingredients that will help you make use of foods you already have, especially any items that need to be consumed soon.
- Prep Ahead: Make fruits and vegetables ready to use quickly by washing and thoroughly drying them before storing. Consider chopping and dividing them as well.
- Rotate Items: Place newer goods behind older ones. What you see first is what should be used up first, particularly with produce and anything that does not store well.
- Use Trays: Place any raw meats on trays or containers with sides to catch any drips of meat juices. Store these items separately from produce to prevent bacterial contamination.

Containers to Organize

When looking for organizational accessories, first search under your own roof. Leftover food containers, such as butter tubs or small baby food jars, could hold snacks or bulk spices.

Think outside the kitchen, too. That office tote or clear plastic shoe drawer could make a portable snack bin or corral half-used packages of pasta and other dry goods in the pantry. When it comes time to buy, pinpoint the exact function and size of the container you need.

Stocking the Kitchen on a Budget

We all know one sure way to save money is to eat out less often. And while that might mean a few more trips to the grocery store, it also means more time spent at home enjoying the company of family and friends. Making a meal for just the two of you is a chance to share some laughs and stories of the day as well as to save some money.

Check out the Smart Shopping Strategies on page 28, and use these additional tips for navigating the grocery store and saving money.

- Join grocery store clubs that provide members-only savings.

- Buy bulk-size or large packages, then divide and freeze items for later use. This works especially well with meat products. For example, it's quick and convenient to take just two chicken breasts or pork chops out of the freezer and thaw them shortly before cooking.

- Allow enough time to compare prices while you shop.

- Keep a small notebook in your bag filled with the prices and sizes of the items you buy regularly. The next time a "sale" sticker catches your eye, consult your notebook to make sure the deal is real.

- Purchase ingredients that are in season for the best value. For the two of you, buy in small portions so that it's easy to use everything up.

- Choose from the top or bottom shelves because items at eye level are often more expensive. And remember, larger packages are not always the cheapest, especially if you don't use all of it or the product spoils before you can use it. Especially if you're cooking for two, smaller containers are sometimes the best.

- Shop the "reduced section" of the store, being careful to check expiration dates.

- Never shop when you are hungry.

At the Meat Counter

Meats, poultry and fish are a costly part of meals. So here are some strategies to help you save money on these items.

- Watch for specials. If you have planned for salmon, you might find tilapia at a good price instead—be ready to adjust your menu quickly.

- Roast your own whole chicken instead of purchasing a rotisserie chicken (see page 423).

- Instead of buying premade ground beef patties, buy ground beef and make your own. If the beef is on sale, make extra patties and freeze them—individually wrapped patties thaw quickly in the refrigerator.

- Buy bone-in pork chops, which are often cheaper than boneless.

- Instead of boneless chicken breasts, try using thighs or drumsticks; they often cost less per pound.

- Look for inexpensive cuts of meat such as beef chuck roast and pork shoulder that are great for slow cooking in the oven or slow cooker. When you make recipes with larger cuts of meat, divide the cooked food into portions for freezing after you've had your meal.

Money or Time

You decide which is the best buy: bone-in or boneless chicken, whole or shredded carrots, dried or refrigerated pasta? Boneless chicken may be more convenient, but bone-in chicken costs less per pound. And after you remove bones, fat and skin, you'll have the same edible portion as boneless for less money!

Cook for Two Meals

On the next page are two great budget-wise recipes using chicken thighs and pork chops to serve anytime. Leftovers can be used for lunch the next day or frozen for another night.

SKILLET CHICKEN THIGHS WITH BACON AND SPINACH

PREP 15 min **TOTAL** 45 min • **4 servings**

- 8 boneless skinless chicken thighs (3 to 4 oz each)
- 3 slices bacon, chopped
- 2 large carrots, chopped (1½ cups)
- 2 small onions, sliced
- 3 cloves garlic, chopped
- ½ cup chicken broth
- 6 cups fresh baby spinach leaves (8 oz)
- ½ teaspoon salt
- ¼ teaspoon pepper
- 1 tablespoon chopped fresh or ½ teaspoon dried sage leaves
- 1 tablespoon grated lemon peel

1 In 12-inch skillet, cook chicken and bacon over medium-high heat 5 minutes, turning chicken once. Stir in carrots, onions, garlic and broth. Cook uncovered 15 to 20 minutes, turning chicken and stirring frequently, until juice of chicken is clear when thickest part is cut (at least 165°F) and vegetables are tender.

2 Remove pan from heat; add spinach, salt and pepper. Stir mixture about 3 minutes or until spinach wilts. Stir in sage and lemon peel until well blended.

1 Serving: Calories 350; Total Fat 16g (Saturated Fat 5g; Trans Fat 0g); Cholesterol 110mg; Sodium 720mg; Total Carbohydrate 11g (Dietary Fiber 3g); Protein 40g **Exchanges:** 1½ Vegetable, 5½ Lean Meat **Carbohydrate Choices:** 1

PORK CHOPS WITH TARRAGON-ONION GRAVY

PREP 20 min **TOTAL** 20 min • **4 servings**

- 8 boneless center-cut loin pork chops, ¼ inch thick (1 lb)
- ½ teaspoon salt
- ¼ teaspoon pepper
- ¼ cup all-purpose flour
- 1 tablespoon olive oil
- ½ cup thinly sliced onion
- ¾ cup beef-flavored broth (from 32-oz carton)
- 1 tablespoon chopped fresh tarragon leaves

1 Sprinkle pork chops evenly with salt and pepper. Coat pork with flour. In 12-inch skillet, heat oil over medium-high heat. Cook 4 pork chops in oil 1 to 2 minutes on each side or until browned. Remove from skillet to plate. Repeat with remaining 4 pork chops.

2 Reduce heat to medium. Add onion to skillet; cook 3 minutes or until tender. Stir in broth, scraping to loosen browned bits from pan. Return pork and any accumulated juices to skillet. Heat to boiling; reduce heat. Cover; cook 4 minutes or until pork is no longer pink in center. Stir in tarragon.

1 Serving: Calories 240; Total Fat 12g (Saturated Fat 3.5g, Trans Fat 0g); Cholesterol 70mg; Sodium 500mg; Total Carbohydrate 8g (Dietary Fiber 0g); Protein 25g **Exchanges:** ½ Starch, 3½ Lean Meat, ½ Fat **Carbohydrate Choices:** ½

Skillet Chicken Thighs with Bacon and Spinach

DINNER FOR TWO

Here's the perfect menu to share any evening. The beets and dessert can be made ahead so all you need to do is cook the steaks and potatoes, then assemble the salad. Set the table with fresh flowers, turn the lights down low, add some soft music and light the candles to create a romantic dinner just for two. It's time to open the wine!

CHEESY ITALIAN TENDERLOIN STEAKS

PREP 10 min TOTAL 30 min • **2 servings**

  2 beef tenderloin steaks, 1 inch thick (about 4 oz each)
1½ teaspoons olive or vegetable oil
  ¼ teaspoon garlic salt
  1 plum (roma) tomato, seeded, chopped (¼ cup)
  2 tablespoons chopped fresh or 1 teaspoon dried basil leaves
  2 tablespoons shredded mozzarella cheese

1 Set oven control to broil. Place steaks on rack in broiler pan. Brush both sides of steaks with oil; sprinkle with garlic salt.

2 Broil with tops 4 to 6 inches from heat, turning once, until of desired doneness (10 to 15 minutes for medium, 160°F).

3 Remove broiler pan from oven. Sprinkle steaks with tomato, basil and cheese. Broil about 1 minute or just until cheese begins to melt. Serve immediately.

1 Serving: Calories 220; Total Fat 12g (Saturated Fat 4g; Trans Fat 0g); Cholesterol 75mg; Sodium 140mg; Total Carbohydrate 1g (Dietary Fiber 0g); Protein 26g **Exchanges:** ½ Vegetable, 3 Lean Meat, ½ Medium-Fat Meat **Carbohydrate Choices:** 0

Cheesy Italian Tenderloin Steaks

> **Late Night Dinner for Two**
>
> **Cheesy Italian Tenderloin Steaks**
>
> Small red potatoes (page 589) with butter and parsley
>
> Roasted Beet Salad, page 461
>
> Red wine
>
> **Hazelnut Dreamaccinos**

HAZELNUT DREAMACCINOS

The espresso coffee powder is richer and stronger than regular instant coffee powder, making this an intensely coffee-flavored after-dinner treat! For a thicker slushy drink, puree the ice with the other ingredients.

PREP 5 min TOTAL 5 min • **2 servings**

1¼ cups dark chocolate all-natural almond milk
  ⅓ cup water
  2 tablespoons hazelnut-flavored coffee syrup
  1 tablespoon instant espresso powder Ice cubes
  3 tablespoons whipped soy or whipped cream topping (from aerosol can)
  2 teaspoons miniature semisweet chocolate chips or 6 chocolate-covered coffee beans

1 In blender, place milk, water, coffee syrup and espresso powder. Cover; blend until frothy.

2 Pour into glasses over ice. Garnish with whipped topping and chocolate chips.

1 Serving: Calories 150; Total Fat 4.5g (Saturated Fat 2g; Trans Fat 0g); Cholesterol 0mg; Sodium 125mg; Total Carbohydrate 27g (Dietary Fiber 0g); Protein 1g **Exchanges:** 2 Other Carbohydrate, 1 Fat **Carbohydrate Choices:** 2

> ### Just for Fun
>
> About to dial for takeout? Instead, declare it a pantry cook-off night. Each of you gets 5 to 10 minutes to search the pantry, refrigerator and freezer for ingredients—maybe things you have overlooked. Each of you is to come up with a quick dish to serve for dinner—divide the courses so one person has the main dish and the other makes a side dish of some type. You'll have a really creative—and delicious—dinner to share in no time!

QUICK MEAL IDEAS

So you are both busy all day and arrive home wondering, "What's for dinner?" We have the answer! With the following 8 quick dinner ideas at your fingertips and just a few ingredients, you'll be able to quickly assemble and cook a delicious meal in 20 minutes or less.

It's easy to plan ahead to have ingredients on hand or stop at the deli and pick up what you need for these satisfying dishes. Each recipe idea makes about 4 servings, so have your meal, then use leftovers for the next night, pack for lunch or freeze for another meal.

1 Balsamic Chicken and Pasta: In 3-quart saucepan, cook 3 cups bow-tie pasta as directed on package and drain. In the same saucepan, toss the cooked pasta with 2 cups chopped deli rotisserie chicken (or other cooked chicken), ½ cup sliced ripe olives and ½ cup balsamic vinaigrette dressing. Cook over low heat just until hot. Stir in 2 cups baby spinach leaves just until wilted and sprinkle with about 4 ounces herb-seasoned feta cheese crumbles. Serve with crusty Italian bread.

2 Barbecue Beef and Vegetables: In 12-inch skillet, cook 1 pound lean ground beef over medium-high heat about 7 minutes until thoroughly cooked. Stir in 3 cups frozen seasoned chunky-style hash brown potatoes with peppers and 3 cups frozen cut green beans. Cover and cook 8 to 12 minutes or until beans are tender. Stir in 1 cup barbecue sauce. If sauce seems thick, stir in ¼ to ½ cup water. Serve with cantaloupe wedges.

3 Bell Pepper and Olive Pizza: In 10-inch skillet, cook 1 medium diced red bell pepper and ¼ cup sliced green onions in 1 to 2 teaspoons olive oil over medium heat about 3 minutes until tender. Sprinkle prebaked pizza crust with 1½ cups shredded mozzarella cheese, the cooked pepper mixture and ¼ cup sliced ripe olives. Drizzle with ¼ cup marinara sauce. Bake as directed on pizza crust package.

4 Chutney-Topped Turkey Burgers: Cook seasoned turkey patties on the grill as directed on package. Serve in pita bread halves topped with shredded lettuce, sliced roasted bell peppers (from a jar) and mango chutney.

5 Deli Beef and Greens Tossed Salad: In large bowl, toss 1 bag (10 ounces) mixed salad greens, 1 pint (2 cups) deli three bean salad, ¾ cup julienne-cut strips of cooked roast beef (about ¼ pound), 1 cup shredded Swiss cheese and 1 cup grape tomatoes. Serve the salad with bakery breadsticks.

6 Grilled Chicken with Artichokes: Drain 6-ounce jar of marinated artichokes, reserving liquid. Mix liquid with ¼ cup dry white wine or chicken broth. Brush 2 boneless skinless chicken breasts and 1 quartered bell pepper with half of mixture. Place chicken on heated grill over medium heat. Cover and cook 5 minutes. Turn chicken and add pepper to grill. Cover and cook 10 to 15 minutes or until pepper is tender and juice of chicken is clear when center of thickest part is cut (165°F). Heat remaining artichoke marinade mixture and artichokes to boiling; boil 1 minute. Serve with chicken and peppers. Serve chicken with cooked white or brown rice and melon wedges.

7 Last-Minute Shrimp Burritos: In 10-inch skillet, heat ½ cup salsa with ¼ cup chopped bell pepper until hot. Stir in ½ pound uncooked deveined peeled shrimp (thawed if frozen) and cook 3 to 4 minutes until shrimp turn pink. Spoon onto 4 (8-inch) flour tortillas and top each with shredded lettuce, chopped tomato and shredded cheese; roll up. Serve burritos with sliced avocado and refried beans.

8 Turkey with Pesto and Rotini: In 3-quart saucepan, cook 3 cups rotini pasta as directed on package and drain. In the same saucepan, toss the cooked pasta with 2 cups diced cooked turkey, ½ cup basil pesto and ½ cup coarsely chopped roasted red bell peppers. Cook over low heat just until hot. Top each serving with about 1 tablespoon shredded Asiago or Parmesan cheese. Serve with tossed green salad topped with Italian dressing.

EASY ENTERTAINING
Great food and good friends are the ingredients for fabulous times. Always plan for time to enjoy the company of family and friends with a minimum of fuss and muss, and lots of laughter, warmth and the best food. You'll make memories to last a lifetime.

GO BEYOND THE DELI

We all love good food but sometimes there just is not time to make everything. Having a few go-to prepared foods can make planning a party much easier. You can mix and match dishes that you make at home and items that you purchase ready-to-go. The local deli is a good place to start, but there are lots of other locations to check out: Specialty bakeries, gourmet shops, ethnic groceries and organic food stores are all ideal stops in the quest for great party food ideas. The variety of options is almost endless and it's great fun to browse and discover new edibles.

Often you can sample foods at these places before you buy—if not, plan to pick out one new food item each time you venture into a new location. This is a nice way to build a selection of personal party favorites.

Think Ahead

Whether you are entertaining for two or twenty, going formal or staying casual, success depends on great food, lively conversation and an inviting atmosphere. Here are some pointers for great parties:

- Send invitations or call friends as far in advance as possible.
- Consider your comfort level (and available space) for number of guests, type of party, and budget.
- Determine your theme and menu early to allow plenty of time to buy groceries and party supplies.
- Plan to shop a couple of times—once for staples and foods that can be made ahead, and then again for perishables and last minute deli items.
- Write down details—this will help you to make as much as you can ahead of time. Also, make a timetable to help with organizing.

STARTING A COOKING OR GOURMET GROUP

Want a great way to stay in touch with special friends, be creative, eat great food and socialize on a regular basis? Why not start a cooking or gourmet group! Making arrangements with friends who like to cook (and eat) is a perfect way to get started with a project like this. A good goal is to plan for one night per month and rotate homes with others in the group.

The idea is that everyone is responsible for making and bringing one dish to the party. The host, hostess or couple of the month is in charge of designing the menu and delegating what each person is in charge of making. We've included one great menu to get you started and inspire you and your group for future parties!

Gourmet Club Menu for 6 to 8

Bruschetta Eight Ways, page 46
(choose your favorites)

Mixed nuts

White and red wine, sparkling water

Sweet Orange Baked Chicken

Steamed green beans, page 586

Apple-Pecan Salad

No-Knead Basil and Sun-Dried Tomato
Artisan Bread, page 116

Sending E-vites to Friends

It's okay to send e-mail invitations to your friends. Check out websites that help you create personalized invites for any occasion. They are usually free, convenient and, best of all, keep you organized! It's not only easy to send these out, but RSVPs are easy and quick for the guests to send back.

SWEET ORANGE BAKED CHICKEN

PREP 15 min **TOTAL** 55 min • **8 servings**

- 1 box (6.2 oz) fast-cooking long-grain and wild rice mix (with seasoning packet)
- ½ cup sliced almonds, toasted
- 2 tablespoons butter
- 8 boneless skinless chicken breasts (3 lb)
- ½ teaspoon salt
- 1 cup orange marmalade
- ¼ cup honey
- 2 tablespoons Dijon mustard
- 2 teaspoons chopped fresh thyme leaves

1 Heat oven to 425°F. Cook rice as directed on package, omitting butter. Stir in almonds and butter.

2 Spray 15×10×1-inch pan with cooking spray. Cut slit in each chicken breast to form a pocket. Spoon about ¼ cup rice mixture into each pocket. Place chicken in pan; sprinkle evenly with salt.

3 In small bowl, mix marmalade, honey, mustard and thyme until blended. Reserve ½ cup of mixture for serving. Brush remaining marmalade mixture over chicken.

4 Bake 35 to 40 minutes or until juice of chicken is clear when center of thickest part is cut (at least 165°F).

5 Heat reserved marmalade mixture over medium heat and pour evenly over chicken.

1 Serving: Calories 480; Total Fat 12g (Saturated Fat 3.5g; Trans Fat 0g); Cholesterol 115mg; Sodium 610mg; Total Carbohydrate 52g (Dietary Fiber 2g); Protein 42g **Exchanges:** 2 Starch, 1½ Other Carbohydrate, 5 Very Lean Meat, 1½ Fat **Carbohydrate Choices:** 3½

APPLE-PECAN SALAD

PREP 10 min **TOTAL** 10 min • **6 servings**

- 6 cups torn mixed salad greens
- 1 cup chopped Gala apple
- ⅓ cup sweetened dried cranberries
- ⅓ cup candied pecans
- ¼ cup fresh lemon juice
- 3 tablespoons olive oil
- 1 tablespoon honey
- ¼ teaspoon salt
- ½ cup crumbled blue cheese (2 oz)

1 In large bowl, toss salad greens, apple, cranberries and pecans.

2 In small bowl, stir lemon juice, oil, honey and salt with whisk until well blended. Drizzle dressing over salad; toss to coat. Sprinkle with cheese.

1 Serving: Calories 220; Total Fat 12g (Saturated Fat 3g, Trans Fat 0g); Cholesterol 5mg; Sodium 260mg; Total Carbohydrate 26g (Dietary Fiber 2g); Protein 3g **Exchanges:** ½ Starch, ½ Fruit, ½ Other Carbohydrate, 1 Vegetable, 2½ Fat **Carbohydrate Choices:** 2

TIP Although the recipe calls for a Gala apple, any sweet, crisp apple will be just as delicious.

Sweet Orange Baked Chicken

Apple-Pecan Salad

DECORATING WITH FLOWERS

Whether for every day or a special occasion, fresh flowers are a beautiful way to personalize your home. Whatever your style, there is a way to add that floral touch. Use your imagination when it comes to containers and flower combinations—pretty pitchers, individual glasses and bowls can all make interesting flower holders. As long as there's room for water, it can work! And the flower choices are endless, changing from season to season.

There's nothing prettier (or more fragrant) in the spring than a vase of fresh lilacs or a small container filled with lily of the valley. In the fall, a large container of dahlias on the table adds a lovely splash of color. And if you are entertaining, try floating blossoms in a pretty bowl as a centerpiece; any flower will do—the more colorful, the better! When you shop, be ready to purchase what is in season for the best value—any flowers are beautiful.

Don't be afraid to think outside the box when making flower arrangements. Look around your house and use what you have to create interest, beauty and drama. Here are some great ideas to get you started showcasing flowers in your personal decor:

- Cut off most of the stems from flowers and float in a shallow bowl. Use a clear bowl or one where you can see the color of the bowl through the water. Roses, peonies and mums work well for this type of arrangement.

- You don't always need a fancy vase—try using a drinking glass or a canning jar and fill with flowers. If you like, place it in a pretty basket or other container that matches your decor.

- Small juice glasses are perfect for single flowers. Place one or two flowers in each one and line them up or arrange them in the center of the table or on the mantle. Daisies or marigolds are ideal for this.

- For added color and interest, slice lemons, limes or oranges and place in the bottom of clear vases or bowls before adding flowers.

- Use what is in your garden and yard to be creative. Branches or stems of color or just leaves can make a whole arrange-ment, or add interest to flowers. Try add-ing fern leaves, apple blossom branches or hosta leaves to any arrangement.

When you are putting your arrangement together, think about where it will go. If you are making a dining table centerpiece, keep it low so that guests can see over the top of it. Tall arrangements are nice when you are serving from a buffet that is against the wall.

Be sure to keep the flowers a good size in proportion to the serving area and your room. On a coffee table, you'll want to be able to see the flowers from all sides and from the top—which is different from when you are decorating a mantle and only need to see the arrangement from one side.

GO FOR GREAT COCKTAILS AND NIBBLES

Whether it's a casual gathering or something more formal, you always want the food and drink at your party to be memorable. Here are 5 great tips to make your party the best ever!

The Nibbles: Choose appetizers with a variety of flavors and be sure to consider special diets of those attending the party. A great place to start is with a couple of prepared foods. Then try to include a vegetable choice, a bruschetta or crostini with meat or seafood on top, a cheesy dip or spread or sliced cheeses and a salty snack. Check out Cocktails with Friends on page xviii and Creating a Cheese Tray on page 260 for more great ideas.

The Drinks: Select beverages to suit your guests. You might include bottled and sparkling water, juices, red and white wine, coffee or cider and cocktails. See Drink Basics, page 271, for advice on stocking a bar. Then be sure to check out the Shaken Cocktails feature on page 274 for some fun cocktails that are easy to make.

The Shopping: Before you shop, make a detailed list so that you don't miss anything. Put the list in order by stop (grocery store, liquor store, specialty store, and so on) so you are organized and ready to go! If you need any glassware, decorations or paper products, be sure to include those on your list too.

The Setup: Have a specific place to serve the cocktails and nibbles. Think ahead to where the guests might gather and where it is most convenient for everyone. You might want to have the cocktail setup in one area and serve the food in another. A beverage cart, available at furniture and gourmet stores, is a nice place to set up your "mini bar" for convenience when you have guests.

The Decorations: Then decorate! Create a festive party space with simple touches that match your theme. Include colorful centerpieces in your plan.

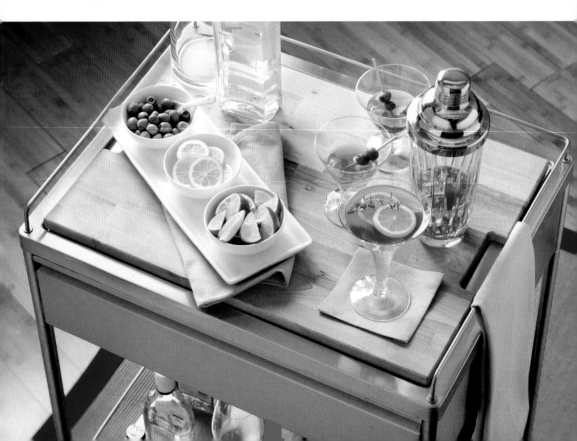

LEMON-THYME COCKTAILS

Add a personal touch to your gathering with a signature cocktail—Lemon-Thyme Cocktails are perfect for this. A simple garnish creates a stunning presentation. The simple syrup is enough for 10 cocktails.

PREP 10 min **TOTAL** 25 min • **2 cocktails**

LEMON-THYME SIMPLE SYRUP (MAKES 1⅓ CUPS)

- 1 cup sugar
- 1 cup water
- 6 sprigs fresh thyme
- 2 tablespoons grated lemon peel (from 2 lemons)

COCKTAIL

- 1 sprig fresh thyme
- 2½ oz vodka
- 3 oz cranberry juice
- 1 oz lemon-thyme simple syrup (above)
- ½ oz orange-flavored liqueur
- Ice

GARNISH

- 1 thin (⅛ inch) lemon slice
- 1 sprig fresh thyme

1 In 1-quart saucepan, heat lemon-thyme simple syrup ingredients over low heat until sugar is dissolved. Let stand 15 minutes. Strain to remove thyme and lemon peel. Use within 2 days.

2 Place 1 sprig fresh thyme in cocktail shaker. Add vodka, cranberry juice, 1 oz of the lemon-thyme simple syrup and liqueur; muddle thyme with back of spoon. Add ice; place lid on shaker, and shake until cold and blended. Strain into 2 martini glasses.

3 Garnish with lemon slice and sprig of thyme.

1 Cocktail: Calories 150; Total Fat 0g (Saturated Fat 0g; Trans Fat 0g); Cholesterol 0mg; Sodium 0mg; Total Carbohydrate 15g (Dietary Fiber 0g); Protein 0g **Carbohydrate Choices:** 1

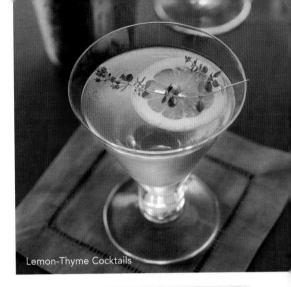

Lemon-Thyme Cocktails

Cocktail Party Basics

Cocktail parties can be a much simpler way to entertain than a dinner party. For small gatherings buy ingredients to make your friends' favorite drinks. For larger parties where you cannot possibly know each person's preference, plan for a larger variety of choices.

- Plan on one drink for each guest per hour.

- Mixers such as mineral water, club soda and soft drinks can work double duty as nonalcoholic drinks.

- Don't skimp on ice. A good rule is to have one pound of ice for each guest; double that in hot weather. Store the ice in an extra cooler, or outside if it's cold enough.

- A 750ml bottle of liquor provides 16 (1.5 ounce) drinks. A 750ml bottle of wine provides 5 (5 ounce) servings. Have both red and white wines available.

Garnishes for Beverages

Some garnishes to have on hand for making drinks include:

- Coarse salt
- Cocktail onions
- Fresh fruit (lemons, oranges, limes, berries)
- Sugar or sugar stirrers
- Maraschino cherries
- Stuffed cocktail olives
- Fresh mint or other herb leaves
- Whole hazelnuts
- Edible flowers

SPECIAL OCCASION MENUS

The key to menu planning is variety—let your creativity be your guide when it comes to compiling a great combination of dishes. Vary the flavors and foods, and try to mix colors and textures. Use the sample menus on the following pages to provide inspiration and get your party planning started!

Cocktails with Friends for 8 to 10

Grilled Antipasti Platter with Lemon Aioli, page 47

Rosemary Pork Sliders

Fig, Red Pepper and Hazelnut Tapenade

Selection of olives (from deli)

Caramelized Onion and Goat Cheese Crostini

Assorted crackers and small breads

Lemon-Thyme Cocktails , page xvii or

Martini Cocktails, page 274 (choose several variations)

Luscious Chocolate Truffles, page 205

Rosemary Pork Sliders

ROSEMARY PORK SLIDERS

Any peppery greens, such as arugula, will work in place of the watercress.

PREP 15 min TOTAL 45 min • **12 sliders**

- 3 tablespoons olive oil
- 1 tablespoon chopped fresh rosemary leaves
- 1 clove garlic, finely chopped
- ½ teaspoon salt
- ¼ teaspoon freshly ground pepper
- 1 pork tenderloin (1¼ lb)
- ½ cup mayonnaise
- 1 tablespoon prepared horseradish
- 1 teaspoon fresh lemon juice
- 12 mini hamburger buns (about 3 inches in diameter)
- 1 cup watercress

1 Heat oven to 425°F. In small bowl, mix 1 tablespoon of the oil, the rosemary, garlic, salt and pepper. Rub mixture over pork.

2 In large ovenproof skillet, heat remaining 2 tablespoons oil over medium-high heat. Add pork; cook 3 minutes on each side or until browned. Place skillet in oven.

3 Bake 18 to 20 minutes or until meat thermometer inserted in center reads at least 145°F. Cover with foil; let stand 3 minutes. Cut pork into 12 (½-inch) slices.

4 In small bowl, mix mayonnaise, horseradish and lemon juice. Spread evenly on cut sides of bun bottoms. Top with pork and watercress; cover with bun tops.

1 Slider: Calories 240; Total Fat 14g (Saturated Fat 2.5g; Trans Fat 0g); Cholesterol 25mg; Sodium 320mg; Total Carbohydrate 16g (Dietary Fiber 0g); Protein 12g **Exchanges:** 1 Starch, ½ Very Lean Meat, 1 Lean Meat, 2 Fat **Carbohydrate Choices:** 1

Fun Party Accessories

Be sure to check out discount, craft and party stores for accessory ideas. Some items that are great for serving include inexpensive plastic or ceramic appetizer plates (often in fun colors), a variety of paper products, decorative picks and forks, and plastic cocktail glasses of all types. Most of these items are not costly and can be used many times.

FIG, RED PEPPER AND HAZELNUT TAPENADE

PREP 15 min TOTAL 15 min • **16 servings**

- 1 cup dried figs
- ⅓ cup water
- ½ cup pitted kalamata olives, chopped
- ½ cup roasted red bell peppers (from a jar), drained, chopped
- 2 tablespoons olive oil
- ¼ cup chopped hazelnuts (filberts)
- 1 tablespoon chopped fresh thyme leaves
  Crisp wheat crackers
- 1 container (8 oz) mascarpone cheese or 1 package (8 oz) cream cheese, softened

1 In small saucepan, heat figs and water to boiling over medium-high heat. Reduce heat; simmer 5 minutes, stirring occasionally, until liquid is absorbed and figs are soft. Cool; chop.

2 In medium serving bowl, place chopped figs and all remaining ingredients except thyme, crackers and cheese; stir well to combine. Sprinkle with thyme. To serve, top each cracker with cheese; spoon fig mixture over cheese.

1 Serving: Calories 190; Total Fat 11g (Saturated Fat 3g; Trans Fat 0g); Cholesterol 10mg; Sodium 210mg; Total Carbohydrate 20g (Dietary Fiber 2g); Protein 2g **Exchanges:** 1 Starch, ½ Other Carbohydrate, 2 Fat **Carbohydrate Choices:** 1

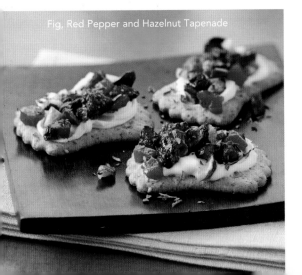

Fig, Red Pepper and Hazelnut Tapenade

CARAMELIZED ONION AND GOAT CHEESE CROSTINI

PREP 1 hr TOTAL 1 hr • **24 crostini**

- 2 tablespoons olive or vegetable oil
- 2 medium sweet onions, thinly sliced (about 2 cups)
- 1 tablespoon packed brown sugar
- 1 tablespoon balsamic vinegar
- 1 teaspoon salt
- 24 slices (¼ inch thick) baguette
  Cooking spray
- 1 package (4 oz) chèvre (goat) cheese, softened
- 1 package (3 oz) cream cheese, softened
- 1 teaspoon chopped fresh thyme or oregano leaves

1 In 12-inch nonstick skillet, heat oil over medium-high heat. Cook onions in oil 10 minutes, stirring every 3 to 4 minutes. Reduce heat to medium-low. Stir in brown sugar, vinegar and salt. Cook 30 to 35 minutes longer, stirring every 5 minutes, until onions are deep golden brown (onions will shrink during cooking). Cool slightly.

2 Heat oven to 325°F. Place baguette slices on ungreased cookie sheet; spray slices lightly with cooking spray. Bake 6 to 9 minutes or until toasted.

3 Meanwhile, in small bowl, mix goat cheese and cream cheese until smooth.

4 Top each toasted baguette slice with 1 teaspoon caramelized onions and 1 rounded teaspoon cheese mixture. Sprinkle with thyme.

1 Crostini: Calories 70; Total Fat 4g (Saturated Fat 2g, Trans Fat 0g); Cholesterol 10mg; Sodium 180mg; Total Carbohydrate 5g (Dietary Fiber 0g); Protein 2g **Exchanges:** ½ Starch, 1 Fat **Carbohydrate Choices:** ½

TIP The caramelized onions can be made ahead. Prepare as directed in step 1, then cover and refrigerate.

Name Tags

For a large group of friends who might not know one another, provide name tags for guests.

Maple-Orange
Sweet Potatoes

MAPLE-ORANGE SWEET POTATOES

PREP 10 min TOTAL 1 hr 25 min • **8 servings**
(⅔ cup each)

- 6 medium-large dark orange sweet potatoes (3 lb)
- ½ cup butter, melted
- ½ cup real maple syrup
- 1 teaspoon grated orange peel
  Juice of 1 medium orange
- ½ teaspoon salt
  Fresh rosemary sprig, if desired

1 Heat oven to 375°F. Line cookie sheet with foil. Place sweet potatoes on cookie sheet; prick several times with fork. Bake 1 hour or until very tender. Let stand 15 minutes.

2 Cut potatoes in half lengthwise; scoop pulp into large bowl. Mash pulp well. Add butter, syrup, orange peel, orange juice and salt; mash well. Garnish with rosemary sprig.

1 Serving: Calories 280; Total Fat 12g (Saturated Fat 7g, Trans Fat 0g); Cholesterol 30mg; Sodium 300mg; Total Carbohydrate 42g (Dietary Fiber 4g); Protein 3g **Exchanges:** ½ Starch, 2 Other Carbohydrate, 1 Vegetable, 2½ Fat **Carbohydrate Choices:** 3

TIP To reduce cook time, microwave sweet potatoes, two at a time, on microwavable paper towels on High 8 to 10 minutes or until tender; proceed to step 2.

BROWN BUTTER PECAN PIE

PREP 30 min TOTAL 5 hr 25 min • **8 servings**

- ½ cup butter (do not use margarine)
- 1 cup sugar
- 1 cup light corn syrup
- 1 teaspoon vanilla bean paste or vanilla
- ¼ teaspoon salt
- 4 eggs, beaten
- 1 refrigerated pie crust, softened as directed on box
- 1¼ cups pecan halves

1 In 2-quart saucepan, melt butter over medium heat, stirring frequently. Cook 2 to 5 minutes, stirring often, until butter stops foaming and browned bits form at bottom of pan. Stir in sugar and corn syrup. Cook over low heat 15 to 18 minutes, stirring frequently, until sugar is dissolved. Cool 1 hour. Add vanilla bean paste, salt and eggs; beat with whisk until well blended.

2 Heat oven to 325°F. Place pie crust in 9-inch glass pie plate as directed on box for One-Crust Filled Pie. Pour filling into crust-lined plate. Arrange pecan halves in concentric circles on top of filling. With fork, gently press pecans into filling to glaze, keeping pecans in circular pattern.

Brown Butter
Pecan Pie

Saturday Brunch for 4 to 6

Croissant Bread Pudding or
Quiche Lorraine, page 81

Pork sausage links or Canadian
bacon slices

Asparagus with Toasted Nuts and Citrus
Zest, page 605

Mango Mimosas, page 276, or
orange juice

Coffee and tea

3 Bake 50 to 55 minutes or until filling is set and crust is golden brown. Cover crust edge with strips of foil after 40 minutes to prevent excessive browning. Cool completely on cooling rack, 3 to 4 hours, before slicing.

1 Serving: Calories 590; Total Fat 31g (Saturated Fat 12g, Trans Fat 0g); Cholesterol 125mg; Sodium 360mg; Total Carbohydrate 72g (Dietary Fiber 1g); Protein 5g **Exchanges:** ½ Starch, 4½ Other Carbohydrate, ½ Medium-Fat Meat, 5½ Fat **Carbohydrate Choices:** 5

CROISSANT BREAD PUDDING

PREP 15 min TOTAL 1 hr 45 min • **6 servings**

- 4 **large croissants (about 2 oz each), cut into 1-inch cubes (about 8 cups)**
- 1 **cup milk**
- 1 **cup half-and-half**
- ½ **cup sugar**
- 1½ **teaspoons ground cinnamon**
- ¼ **teaspoon ground nutmeg**
- 1 **teaspoon vanilla**
- 3 **eggs**
- 1 **cup fresh raspberries**
- ½ **cup real maple syrup, warmed**

1 Heat oven to 350°F. Spray 2½-quart shallow casserole with cooking spray; arrange bread cubes in casserole. Place casserole in 13x9-inch (3-quart) glass baking dish.

2 In large bowl, beat all remaining ingredients, except raspberries and syrup, with whisk until well blended; pour over bread cubes in casserole, pushing down lightly with spoon to soak bread cubes. Let stand 10 minutes; sprinkle with raspberries.

3 Place baking dish with casserole in oven. Pour warm water into baking dish halfway up sides of casserole, being careful not to splash water into casserole.

4 Bake uncovered 1 hour 10 minutes to 1 hour 20 minutes or until knife inserted in center comes out clean. Let stand 10 minutes before serving. Serve warm drizzled with warm syrup.

1 Serving: Calories 520; Total Fat 23g (Saturated Fat 13g; Trans Fat 1g); Cholesterol 170mg; Sodium 140mg; Total Carbohydrate 68g (Dietary Fiber 2g); Protein 10g **Exchanges:** 1 Starch, 3½ Other Carbohydrate, 1 High-Fat Meat, 3 Fat **Carbohydrate Choices:** 4½

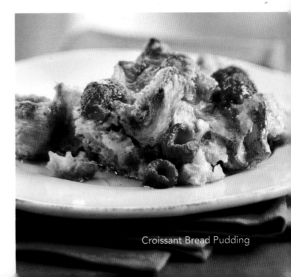

Croissant Bread Pudding

Celebrate New Year's Day for 8 to 10	Taste of Italy Feast for 6 to 8	Festive Holiday Celebration for 6 to 8
Blue Cheese–Apple Tartlets	**Gorgonzola-Stuffed Mushrooms** or	Sangria, page 276 or
Southwestern Spiced Party Nuts, page 45	Olive Tapenade, page 268	Sparkling wine
Selection of bar drinks, soft drinks, juices	Italian red wine	Herb-and-Garlic-Crusted Beef Rib Roast, page 335
Cheese tray selection, page 260 or	Manicotti, page 375 or	Twice-Baked Potatoes, page 599
Greek Layered Dip, page 267	Artichoke-Spinach Lasagna, page 620	Popovers, page 109
Chocolate-Almond Cheesecake Bites	Mixed baby greens with balsamic vinaigrette	Caesar Salad, page 454
	Artisan Asiago Bread, page 117	Olives and pickes
	Tiramisu, page 221	Crème Brûlée, page 225

BLUE CHEESE–APPLE TARTLETS

PREP 15 min TOTAL 25 min • **15 tartlets**

- 1 package (1.9 oz) frozen mini fillo shells (15 shells)
- 1 tablespoon butter
- 1 large Granny Smith apple, peeled, finely chopped
- ¼ cup finely chopped walnuts, toasted Dash ground nutmeg
- ½ cup crumbled blue cheese (2 oz) Fresh thyme leaves, if desired

1 Heat oven to 375°F. On ungreased cookie sheet, place fillo shells.

2 In 10-inch skillet, melt butter over medium-high heat. Cook apple in butter 5 minutes, stirring frequently, until tender. Remove from heat; stir in walnuts and nutmeg. Stir in blue cheese. Divide mixture evenly among fillo shells.

3 Bake 8 minutes or until cheese is melted and tartlets are warm. Garnish with thyme.

1 Tartlet: Calories 60; Total Fat 4g (Saturated Fat 1.5g, Trans Fat 0g); Cholesterol 0mg; Sodium 70mg; Total Carbohydrate 4g (Dietary Fiber 0g); Protein 1g **Exchanges:** ½ Starch, ½ Fat **Carbohydrate Choices:** 0

Blue Cheese-Apple Tartlets

Chocolate-Almond Cheesecake Bites

CHOCOLATE-ALMOND CHEESECAKE BITES

If the chocolate coating cools and starts to get thick, microwave on High for 10 to 15 seconds to soften it.

PREP 50 min **TOTAL** 3 hr 30 min •
48 cheesecake bites

CRUST

16 thin chocolate wafer cookies (from 9-oz package), crushed (1 cup)
¼ cup butter, melted

FILLING

1 package (8 oz) cream cheese, softened
¼ cup sour cream
¼ cup sugar
1 egg
¼ teaspoon almond extract

COATING

2⅓ cups semisweet chocolate chips
3 tablespoons shortening
2 oz vanilla-flavored candy coating (almond bark), chopped
1 teaspoon vegetable oil

1 Heat oven to 300°F. Cut 14×12-inch sheet of foil; line 8-inch square pan with foil so foil extends over sides of pan. Spray foil with cooking spray. In small bowl, mix crust ingredients. Press in bottom of pan.

2 In large bowl, beat cream cheese, sour cream and sugar with electric mixer on medium speed until fluffy. Beat in egg and extract until smooth. Pour over crust.

3 Bake 30 to 40 minutes or until edges are set (center will be soft but will set when cool). Cool on cooling rack 1 hour. Cover; refrigerate 1 hour. Meanwhile, cover 2 cookie sheets with waxed paper.

4 Using foil, lift cheesecake out of pan. Cut into 8 rows by 6 rows, making 48 oblong cheesecake bites. In 1-quart microwavable bowl, microwave chocolate chips and shortening uncovered on Medium (50%) 3 minutes. Stir; microwave in 15-second increments, stirring after each, until melted and smooth.

5 Work with half of bites at a time (24 bites); refrigerate other half until needed. Place 1 bite on fork; and dip into chocolate to coat. Lift fork from chocolate and allow excess chocolate to drain off. Place on cookie sheet. Repeat with remaining bites.

6 In small microwavable bowl, microwave candy coating and oil uncovered on High 1 minute. Stir; microwave in 15-second increments, stirring after each, until melted. Spoon into small food-storage plastic bag. Seal bag; cut tiny hole in corner of bag. Squeeze bag to pipe melted coating over dipped bites. Store in refrigerator.

1 Cheesecake Bite: Calories 100; Total Fat 7g (Saturated Fat 4g, Trans Fat 0g); Cholesterol 15mg; Sodium 40mg; Total Carbohydrate 9g (Dietary Fiber 0g); Protein 1g **Exchanges:** ½ Other Carbohydrate, 1½ Fat **Carbohydrate Choices:** ½

GORGONZOLA-STUFFED MUSHROOMS

PREP 30 min **TOTAL** 50 min •
About 35 mushrooms

1 lb fresh whole mushrooms
⅓ cup crumbled Gorgonzola cheese
¼ cup Italian-style bread crumbs
¼ cup chopped hazelnuts (filberts)
¼ cup finely chopped red bell pepper
4 medium green onions, chopped
½ teaspoon salt

1 Heat oven to 350°F. Remove stems from mushroom caps; reserve caps. Finely chop enough stems to measure about ½ cup. Discard remaining stems.

2 Mix chopped mushroom stems and remaining ingredients in small bowl until well blended. Spoon into mushroom caps, mounding slightly. Place in ungreased 15×10×1-inch pan.

3 Bake 15 to 20 minutes or until thoroughly heated. Serve warm.

1 Mushroom: Calories 15; Total Fat 1g (Saturated Fat 0g, Trans Fat 0g); Cholesterol 0mg; Sodium 65mg; Total Carbohydrate 1g (Dietary Fiber 0g); Protein 1g **Exchanges:** Free **Carbohydrate Choices:** 0

COOKING TOGETHER
Making meals will become an important, necessary part of your life together. But it's not just about the cooking and eating; it's about using the freshest ingredients, making homemade food that is delicious and working together in the kitchen. Exploring local foods, growing herbs, baking bread from scratch and other activities are all delicious ways to start building traditions together as a couple.

EAT LOCAL

Eating local will provide the freshest food possible—be sure to check out our eating local feature on page 242. It's a great primer on what the buzz is all about. Then be ready to experiment with all sorts of great ingredients.

If you join a Community Supported Agriculture Program (CSA), you may get vegetables or fruits that are new to you. Often, trendy new items will be included, like baby vegetables, new varieties of greens or hybrid versions of old favorites. Be sure to give it all a try—you are bound to find some delicious new choices to build great meals on! We've included a couple of recipes to inspire you. Each one is filled with fresh ingredients—maybe you'll discover something new that you have not tried before!

THREE-GRAIN SALAD

PREP 25 min **TOTAL** 3 hr 30 min ●
5 servings (1⅓ cups each)

SALAD
- 5 cups water
- ¾ cup uncooked wheat berries
- ⅓ cup uncooked long-grain brown rice
- ½ cup uncooked hulled or pearl barley
- ½ cup dried cherries or cranberries
- ¼ cup diced carrot
- ¼ cup diced celery
- ¼ cup chopped fresh parsley, if desired
- 1 medium unpeeled apple, chopped (1 cup)
- 4 medium green onions, chopped (¼ cup)

DRESSING
- 3 tablespoons sugar
- 3 tablespoons canola oil
- ⅓ cup cider vinegar
- 2 tablespoons grated red onion
- 1 tablespoon Worcestershire sauce
- 2 cloves garlic, finely chopped

1 In 2-quart saucepan, heat water and wheat berries to boiling. Reduce heat to low. Cover; simmer 10 minutes. Stir in brown rice and barley. Cover; simmer about 50 minutes longer or until grains are tender. Drain if necessary.

2 In small bowl, mix all dressing ingredients. In large bowl, mix cooked grains and remaining salad ingredients. Pour dressing over salad; toss. Cover; refrigerate 1 to 2 hours or until chilled.

1 Serving: Calories 400; Total Fat 9g (Saturated Fat 0.5g; Trans Fat 0g); Cholesterol 0mg; Sodium 210mg; Total Carbohydrate 71g (Dietary Fiber 10g); Protein 7g **Exchanges:** 2½ Starch, 2 Other Carbohydrate, 1½ Fat **Carbohydrate Choices:** 5

Three-Grain Salad

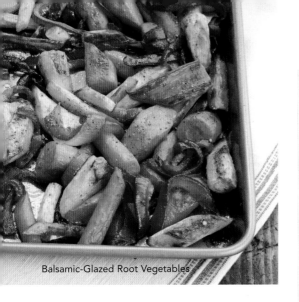
Balsamic-Glazed Root Vegetables

BALSAMIC-GLAZED ROOT VEGETABLES

PREP 20 min **TOTAL** 1 hr •

6 servings (¾ cup each)

1	**lb parsnips, peeled, cut into 2-inch pieces (3 cups)**
1	**lb carrots, cut into 2-inch pieces (3 cups)**
½	**large red onion, thinly sliced, slices cut in half (2 cups)**
3	**tablespoons olive oil**
½	**teaspoon salt**
¼	**teaspoon freshly ground pepper**
⅔	**cup balsamic vinegar**
3	**tablespoons honey**
1	**teaspoon Dijon mustard**

1 Heat oven to 425°F. In large bowl, toss parsnips, carrots, onion, oil, salt and pepper. Arrange vegetables in single layer in ungreased 15×10×1-inch pan.

2 Bake uncovered 35 to 40 minutes, stirring once, until tender and lightly browned.

3 In 1-quart saucepan, heat vinegar, honey and mustard to boiling; cook 6 to 8 minutes, stirring occasionally, until glaze is reduced to ⅓ cup. Remove from heat; drizzle glaze over vegetables.

1 Serving: Calories 220; Total Fat 7g (Saturated Fat 1g; Trans Fat 0g); Cholesterol 0mg; Sodium 280mg; Total Carbohydrate 37g (Dietary Fiber 6g); Protein 2g **Exchanges:** 2 Other Carbohydrate, 1½ Vegetable, 1½ Fat **Carbohydrate Choices:** 2½

Tap into a Community Garden

You may want to check in your area for community gardens—they're a great way to include fresh local produce in your diet, help the community and meet new friends! A community garden is simply a space where plants are grown and maintained by a group of people. These gardens provide opportunities to grow food, share traditions among cultures and generations and build connections. If there is not a garden close by, consider working with some friends or neighbors to start one.

Organization is the key to a successful garden. First determine where your garden will be and who might want to be involved in the project—then start planning. A number of websites are dedicated to starting successful community gardens, but here are some general tips to get you started:

- Organize a meeting of interested people.
- Choose a garden coordinator.
- Choose a name for the garden.
- Determine how large the garden will be.
- Make sure there is a water source for the garden area.
- Determine what you will want to plant and how much of each vegetable or fruit is desired.
- Use a calendar to plan for each necessary task.
- Assign tasks to each of the gardeners.
- Choose dates for harvesting the food.
- Plan for end-of-season cleanup of the garden space.

Host a CSA Dinner

Have some fun with friends and create a meal with the goal of using all of the fruits and vegetables in your CSA package for the week. Plan the meal yourself or ask guests to provide creative input on how to use the different produce items.

Need ideas to start with? You could combine the various greens in a salad and use a new herb in the dressing. Roast vegetables such as beets, carrots, potatoes and peppers using the facing recipe. Slice tomatoes with cucumbers and sprinkle with fresh basil. Turn extra zucchini into Zucchini Bread, page 104. And use fresh fruit in a shortcake, smoothie or crisp, pages 215, 69 and 212.

FARM TO TABLE

When purchasing meats and vegetables, the freshest items will generally appear closest to the farm and be local. Luckily, cutting out the middlemen and buying directly from farms can cut cost too. In the United States, most produce travels nearly 1,500 miles between the farm and your home and approximately 40 percent of our fruit is actually produced overseas. So buying food locally not only means fresher food at its prime, but it also conserves an amazing amount of energy that is used to bring it to us. Follow these tips for unearthing the best in farm-fresh goods.

- Shop close to home—look for farmers' markets and pick-your-own farms. Often you can purchase produce in small amounts at these locations.

- Learn about the seasonal availability of fruits and vegetables in your area.

- Be flexible when you shop so that you can take advantage of items that are seasonal.

- Use reusable shopping bags.

- At the grocery store, look for produce that has been grown in your area.

- Check online for farms that have produce or meats available for purchase.

- Try a local winery if your area has one—it's a great outing for the two of you.

**Harvest Time
Farm to Table Dinner**

Butternut Squash Ravioli

Spinach-Bacon Salad, page 456

Sliced fresh tomatoes drizzled with balsamic vinegar

Apple Crisp, page 212

BUTTERNUT SQUASH RAVIOLI

A small scoop, sometimes used for cookie dough and holding about 1 tablespoon, makes it quick and easy to spoon the squash mixture into the center of the wonton skin.

PREP **1 hr** TOTAL **1 hr 30 min** • **6 servings**

RAVIOLI

- 1 medium butternut squash (about 1½ lb), halved, seeds removed
- 1 tablespoon olive oil
- ½ cup low-fat ricotta cheese
- ¼ cup shredded Parmesan cheese
- ½ teaspoon salt
- ¼ teaspoon pepper
- ¼ teaspoon ground nutmeg
- 36 wonton skins (about 3½-inch square)
- 1 egg
- 2 tablespoons water

BROWNED BUTTER-SAGE SAUCE

- ½ cup butter
- 12 to 15 fresh sage leaves
- 1 clove garlic, finely chopped
- ¼ teaspoon salt
- ¼ teaspoon pepper

TOPPINGS

- 6 tablespoons shredded Parmesan cheese
- 6 fresh sage leaves

1 Heat oven to 400°F. Place squash halves, cut side up, on ungreased cookie sheet. Brush with oil. Roast 30 minutes or until squash is very tender. Cool slightly.

2 When squash is cool enough to handle, use spoon to remove pulp; place in small bowl. Stir in ricotta cheese, ¼ cup Parmesan cheese, ½ teaspoon salt, ¼ teaspoon pepper and the nutmeg.

3 Spoon 1 tablespoon squash mixture onto center of each wonton skin. In another small bowl, beat together egg and water. Brush edges of wonton skins with egg-water mixture. Fold skins tightly over filling, pressing gently to remove any air trapped inside, forming triangles, and sealing filling tightly inside skins. (If filled wonton skins have large air pockets, they can float to surface when boiled, causing them to cook unevenly.)

4 In 1-quart saucepan, heat butter over medium heat about 3 minutes until melted. Add 12 to 15 sage leaves; cook 3 to 4 minutes, watching carefully and stirring frequently, until butter is golden and sage wilts and then crisps. Add garlic; cook 1 minute or until butter is amber in color and garlic is tender. Stir in ¼ teaspoon salt and ¼ teaspoon pepper. Set aside; keep warm.

5 In Dutch oven or large saucepan, heat 4 quarts water to boiling. Slip filled wonton skins into boiling water in batches so as not to crowd them. Boil 3 minutes or until tender. (Do not overcook.) Use slotted spoon to lift ravioli from boiling water; place on serving plates.

6 Drizzle butter mixture evenly over ravioli. Immediately sprinkle each serving with 1 tablespoon Parmesan cheese; garnish each with sage leaf.

1 Serving: Calories 430; Total Fat 24g (Saturated Fat 13g; Trans Fat 0.5g); Cholesterol 95mg; Sodium 910mg; Total Carbohydrate 40g (Dietary Fiber 2g); Protein 13g **Exchanges:** 2½ Starch, 1 Medium-Fat Meat, 3½ Fat **Carbohydrate Choices:** 2½

Butternut Squash Ravioli

GROW FRESH HERBS

Grow some herbs indoors for cooking—it's fun to be able to snip just a little basil to add to a salad when the container is on your windowsill. Or why not have a small pot of rosemary handy—the fragrance is amazing! Other herbs that grow well in small pots include parsley, thyme, mint and chives. Remember to snip and use the herbs often to encourage them to grow. Here are some other tips to get you started:

- Purchase herbs in small pots or plant seeds in sterilized black dirt available at the garden store.

- Keep them in a warm sunny spot away from drafts.

- Water sparingly—herbs do not like wet soil.

- Feed once a month with a fertilizer labeled for use on edibles.

- Most herbs benefit from having the flowers pinched off.

You'll find storage and cooking tips for cut herbs on page 493.

Edible Flowers

Flowers that are edible make a lovely garnish for a variety of foods but they can also be an essential ingredient and add flavor to a dish. Choose flowers that are sold and labeled "edible." They are often available in the produce department. Look for freshness and flowers that are not wilted or discolored. If you are using flowers from a garden, be aware that not all flowers can be eaten. Also, you will want to be sure that they have not ever been treated with a chemical pesticide. Some popular edible flowers include:

- Nasturtium (sweet with a slightly peppery flavor)

- Pansies (very mild and sweet but sometimes a little tart in flavor)

- Roses (sweet with an aromatic flavor that is stronger in roses that are more fragrant)

- Violets (sweet with a nectar-like flavor)

- Chrysanthemums (slightly bitter, pungent)

Many herbs have flowers that can make a colorful garnish or add a little flavor too. Chives, basil, rosemary and thyme are all good choices.

HERBED TOMATO AND POTATO SALAD

PREP 20 min TOTAL 2 hr 45 min • **6 servings**

8	small red potatoes (about 1 lb)
½	cup chopped fresh or 3 tablespoons dried basil leaves
⅓	cup chopped fresh or 2 tablespoons dried sage leaves
⅓	cup chopped fresh or 2 tablespoons dried mint leaves
½	cup olive or vegetable oil
½	cup wine vinegar
5	roma (plum) tomatoes, cut into fourths
1	small onion, finely chopped (¼ cup)

1 Heat 1 inch water (salted if desired) to boiling in 3-quart saucepan. Add potatoes. Cover and heat to boiling; reduce heat. Cook 20 to 25 minutes or until tender; drain and cool. Peel potatoes; cut into ½-inch slices.

2 Gently mix potatoes and remaining ingredients. Cover and refrigerate about 2 hours, stirring occasionally, until chilled.

1 Serving: Calories 240; Total Fat 18g (Saturated Fat 2.5g; Trans Fat 0g); Cholesterol 0mg; Sodium 10mg; Total Carbohydrate 16g (Dietary Fiber 2g); Protein 2g **Exchanges:** 1 Other Carbohydrate, ½ Vegetable, 3½ Fat **Carbohydrate Choices:** 1

Container Gardening

Besides herbs, you may decide to try growing other plants in containers. It's a fun, budget-friendly way to grow some of your own produce, from the few small pots of herbs on the windowsill to tomatoes in a planter on the porch. You can't get any fresher or less expensive than home grown! And although we strive for perfection, just keep in mind that fruits and vegetables are subject to variations in taste, color and quality because of weather conditions. Check local nurseries for varieties that are appropriate for your area and start growing!

COOK FROM SCRATCH

Cooking is an activity that can be enjoyed together—there is nothing more satisfying than creating great food. Why not pick one day or evening per week to try something new? Here is a great homemade bread recipe to get you started.

ORANGE-CARDAMOM ARTISAN ROLLS

A great project to try together is baking your own bread. Artisan breads are typically crafted with few ingredients and are made in small batches—often, they are not kneaded, which makes them pretty easy to make. These rolls are ideal for breakfast or brunch, or as a snack. They are slightly sweet with the characteristic texture of bakery artisan breads and are simply delicious! See pages 116 and 117 for more artisan bread recipes.

PREP 20 min TOTAL 3 hr • **15 rolls**

2	packages regular active dry yeast
1	tablespoon sugar
1½	cups warm water (105°F to 115°F)
½	cup sugar
1	teaspoon salt
1	teaspoon ground cardamom
2	teaspoons grated orange peel
2½	teaspoons vanilla
3½	to 4 cups all-purpose flour
2	tablespoons butter, melted
7½	teaspoons sugar

1 In large bowl, dissolve yeast and 1 tablespoon sugar in warm water. Let stand 10 minutes or until mixture is foamy. Add ½ cup sugar, the salt, cardamom, orange peel and vanilla; stir until well mixed, about 1 minute. Add flour gradually, until mixture begins to pull away from sides of bowl. Mixture will be slightly sticky.

2 Cover bowl loosely with plastic wrap and let rise in warm place about 2 hours or until dough has doubled in size. Refrigerate at least 30 minutes or up to 24 hours.

3 Spray 13×9-inch pan with cooking spray. On lightly floured surface, divide dough evenly into 15 pieces. With floured hands, shape each piece into a ball by stretching surface of dough around to bottom on all 4 sides; pinch bottom to seal. Place in pan.

4 Heat oven to 375°F. Cover pan loosely with plastic wrap and let stand 30 minutes at room temperature. Lightly brush tops of rolls with melted butter; sprinkle ½ teaspoon sugar over each roll.

5 Bake 25 to 30 minutes or until tops are golden brown. Cool 10 minutes; remove from pan to cooling rack. Serve warm.

1 Roll: Calories 160; Total Fat 2g (Saturated Fat 1g; Trans Fat 0g); Cholesterol 0mg; Sodium 170mg; Total Carbohydrate 32g (Dietary Fiber 1g); Protein 3g **Exchanges:** 1 Starch, 1 Other Carbohydrate, ½ Fat **Carbohydrate Choices:** 2

Orange-Cardamom Artisan Rolls

Welcome Spring
Farm to Table Menu
Cherry-Glazed Lamb Chops
New Potatoes and Spring Vegetables
Tossed baby greens with Italian dressing
Baking Powder Biscuits, page 106
Fresh strawberries with ice cream

CHERRY-GLAZED LAMB CHOPS

PREP 15 min TOTAL 15 min • **6 servings**

- 12 lamb rib chops (about 2 lb)
- ½ teaspoon salt
- ½ teaspoon freshly ground pepper
- 1 clove garlic, finely chopped
- 1 teaspoon chopped fresh rosemary leaves
- ⅓ cup balsamic vinegar
- ⅓ cup cherry preserves
  Fresh rosemary sprigs, if desired

1 Set oven control to broil. Spray broiler pan rack with cooking spray; place lamb chops on rack in pan. Sprinkle chops with ¼ teaspoon each of the salt and pepper.

2 In small bowl, mix garlic, chopped rosemary, vinegar, preserves and remaining ¼ teaspoon each salt and pepper. Reserve half of preserves mixture for serving. Brush some of remaining half of the mixture over chops.

3 Broil with tops 5 inches from heat 6 to 7 minutes, turning once and brushing with more preserves mixture, until of desired doneness. Garnish with rosemary sprigs. Serve with reserved preserves mixture.

1 Serving: Calories 170; Total Fat 7g (Saturated Fat 2.5g, Trans Fat 0g); Cholesterol 45mg; Sodium 250mg; Total Carbohydrate 15g (Dietary Fiber 0g); Protein 13g **Exchanges:** ½ Starch, ½ Other Carbohydrate, 1½ Medium-Fat Meat **Carbohydrate Choices:** 1

NEW POTATOES AND SPRING VEGETABLES

PREP 20 min TOTAL 5 hr 40 min • **18 servings** (½ cup each)

- 2 lb small red potatoes
- 2 cups ready-to-eat baby-cut carrots, cut in half lengthwise
- 1 large sweet onion (such as Bermuda, Maui, Spanish or Walla Walla), cut in half, thinly sliced
- 1 teaspoon salt
- 1 lb fresh asparagus spears, cut into 2-inch pieces
- ¼ cup olive or vegetable oil
- 6 tablespoons chopped fresh dill weed
- 1 to 2 teaspoons grated lemon peel
- 2 tablespoons Dijon mustard
- 1 teaspoon salt

1 Cut large potatoes in half as needed to make similar-size pieces. In 5- to 6-quart slow cooker, place carrots. Top with onion and potatoes; sprinkle with 1 teaspoon salt.

2 Cover; cook on Low heat setting 5 to 6 hours.

3 Add asparagus to cooker. Increase heat setting to High; cover and cook 15 to 20 minutes longer or until asparagus is crisp-tender.

4 In small bowl, mix oil, dill weed, lemon peel, mustard and 1 teaspoon salt. Pour over vegetables in cooker; stir to coat. Vegetables will hold on Low heat setting up to 2 hours; stir occasionally.

1 Serving: Calories 80; Total Fat 3.5g (Saturated Fat 0g, Trans Fat 0g); Cholesterol 0mg; Sodium 310mg; Total Carbohydrate 12g (Dietary Fiber 2g); Protein 2g **Exchanges:** ½ Starch, 1 Vegetable, ½ Fat **Carbohydrate Choices:** 1

SPICY PICKLED VEGETABLES

When produce is at its peak, use some tasty vegetables to make this spicy mixture. Jars of these easy-to-make pickled vegetables make delicious gifts or keep them in your refrigerator to serve with any meal. See pages 249–252 for additional pickle recipes.

PREP 15 min **TOTAL** 24 hr 15 min • **24 servings** (¼ cup each)

3 cups white wine vinegar
1½ cups sugar
2 cloves garlic, finely chopped
1 medium head cauliflower (1½ lb), separated into small florets (6 cups)
½ lb fresh green beans, trimmed
2 medium carrots, cut into 3×¼×¼-inch pieces (1½ cups)
2 jalapeño chiles, cut lengthwise into quarters, seeded

1 In medium saucepan, heat vinegar, sugar and garlic over medium heat just until mixture begins to simmer and sugar dissolves; remove from heat. Cool 5 minutes.

2 Meanwhile, in two (1-quart) glass containers, layer all remaining ingredients, dividing evenly between containers. Pour vinegar mixture over vegetables. Cover; refrigerate at least 24 hours before serving but no longer than 2 weeks.

1 Serving: Calories 70; Total Fat 0g (Saturated Fat 0g; Trans Fat 0g); Cholesterol 0mg; Sodium 15mg; Total Carbohydrate 16g (Dietary Fiber 1g); Protein 1g **Exchanges:** 1 Other Carbohydrate, ½ Vegetable **Carbohydrate Choices:** 1

Spicy Pickled Vegetables

DIY Food Projects

Saving a little money is a great reward, but once you start your own do-it-yourself projects, you'll find it's really satisfying to have tasty food on hand and know where the stored food came from. There's a variety of ways to preserve food items. Here are some great ideas to get you started.

- Freeze small amounts of chopped fresh herbs in ice cubes. For flavor, just add a "cube" to whatever you are cooking and it will thaw as it cooks.

- Cut up or chop onions and bell peppers and store in plastic bags in the freezer. Pour out just what you need and keep the rest frozen.

- Dry herbs.

- Freeze meats such as burger patties and pork chops individually.

- Freeze vegetables, pages 240-241.

- Dry tomatoes, page 253.

- Make Greek Yogurt, page 254.

- Freeze pie crust pastry.

- Freeze loaves of bread.

- Make bread, pages 97–128.

- Make jams and jellies, pages 244–247.

- Make pickles, pages 249–252.

- Make canned tomatoes.

- Make salsa, pages 480–481.

- Make granola, page 85.

- Use a food dehydrator to make your own jerky. (See USDA website for jerky safety tips.)

- Grow your own herbs, page xxix.

- Use a meat grinder or food processor to make sausage or ground meat.

- Use a smoker to smoke fish.

- Make basil pesto, page 484.

- Get a popsicle kit and experiment with fruit juice popsicles.

- Make marshmallows, page 208.

- Whip up some salad dressing, pages 474–476.

- Make dried apples or pears.

Betty Crocker
cookbook
1500 recipes for the way you cook today

WILEY

John Wiley & Sons, Inc.

GENERAL MILLS

Editorial Director: Jeff Nowak

Publishing Manager: Christine Gray

Senior Editor: Grace Wells

Editors: Lori Fox and Catherine Swanson

Editorial Assistant: Kelly Gross

Videos and Digital Recipes: Andrea Bidwell, Timothy Boelter and Diane Carlson

Recipe Development and Testing: Betty Crocker Kitchens

Photography: General Mills Photography Studios and Image Library

Photographers: Mike Jensen, Paul Markert, Chuck Nields and Maja Sahlberg

Photo Assistant: Kimberly Whaley

Food Stylists: Nancy Johnson, Stacy LeNeave and Amy Peterson

Food Styling Assistants: Patty Gabbert and Benjamin Plante

JOHN WILEY & SONS, INC.

Publisher: Natalie Chapman

Food Content and Relationship Marketing Director: Geoff Johnson

Food Content Marketing Manager: Susan Klobuchar

Associate Publisher: Jessica Goodman

Executive Editor: Anne Ficklen

Editor: Adam Kowit

Editorial Program Coordinator: Meaghan McDonnell

Production Director: Diana Cisek

Production Manager: Michael Olivo

Senior Production Editors: Alda Trabucchi and Kristi Hart

Production Assistant: Maggie Vernon

Cover Design: Paul DiNovo

Art Director: Tai Blanche

Senior Designer: Holly Wittenberg

Graphics Technician/Imaging: Brent Savage

Manufacturing Manager: Kevin Watt

The Betty Crocker Kitchens seal guarantees success in your kitchen. Every recipe has been tested in America's Most Trusted Kitchens™ to meet our high standards of reliability, easy preparation and great taste.

Find more great ideas at
BettyCrocker.com

Published by John Wiley & Sons, Inc., Hoboken, New Jersey

Published simultaneously in Canada

No part of this publication may be reproduced, stored in a retrieval system, or transmitted in any form or by any means, electronic, mechanical, photocopying, recording, scanning, or otherwise, except as permitted under Section 107 or 108 of the 1976 United States Copyright Act, without either the prior written permission of the Publisher, or authorization through payment of the appropriate per-copy fee to the Copyright Clearance Center, Inc., 222 Rosewood Drive, Danvers, MA 01923, (978) 750-8400, fax (978) 750-4470, or on the web at www.copyright.com. Requests to the Publisher for permission should be addressed to the Permissions Department, John Wiley & Sons, Inc., 111 River Street, Hoboken, NJ 07030, (201) 748-6011, fax (201) 748-6008, or online at http://www.wiley.com/go/permissions.

Trademarks: Wiley and the Wiley logo are trademarks or registered trademarks of John Wiley & Sons and/or its affiliates. Facebook is a registered trademark of Facebook, Inc. Kamut is a registered trademark of Kamut International, Ltd. All other trademarks referred to herein are trademarks of General Mills. John Wiley & Sons, Inc., is not associated with any product or vendor mentioned in this book.

Limit of Liability/Disclaimer of Warranty: While the publisher and author have used their best efforts in preparing this book, they make no representations or warranties with respect to the accuracy or completeness of the contents of this book and specifically disclaim any implied warranties of merchantability or fitness for a particular purpose. No warranty may be created or extended by sales representatives or written sales materials. The advice and strategies contained herein may not be suitable for your situation. You should consult with a professional where appropriate. Neither the publisher nor author shall be liable for any loss of profit or any other commercial damages, including but not limited to special, incidental, consequential, or other damages.

For general information on our other products and services or for technical support, please contact our Customer Care Department within the United States at (800) 762-2974, outside the United States at (317) 572-3993 or fax (317) 572-4002.

Wiley also publishes its books in a variety of electronic formats. Some content that appears in print may not be available in electronic books. For more information about Wiley products, visit our web site at www.wiley.com.

Library of Congress Cataloging-in-Publication Data is available upon request.

ISBN 978-1-118-07223-3

Manufactured in China

10 9 8 7 6 5 4 3 2 1

Cover photos (clockwise from top left of front cover): Sweetened Whipped Cream (page 214); Cherry Pie (page 167); Grilled Barbecue Chicken (page 309); Chili (page 540); vine-ripened tomatoes; cherry tomatoes and mozzarella balls; Cranberry-Orange Muffins (page 98); blood oranges; Classic Shrimp Cocktail (page 294); radishes; Individual Chicken Pot Pies (page 411); strawberries; Red Velvet Cupcakes (page 133).

CONTENTS

Dear Friends,

We've gone through a lot of changes since the first edition of the *Betty Crocker Cookbook* was published in 1950. But change is good, and this 11th edition brings you the best of everything for today's cook—the newest ideas, the tastiest recipes, the prettiest photos and great new features.

The book includes all of the fabulous recipes and information that you expect from America's most trusted kitchen—and more. The 1,100 all-new photos include hundreds of step-by-step images to walk you through a variety of tasks. You'll

delight in the more than 1,500 recipes in all categories of cooking including inspiring variations and creative "mini" recipes for super-easy cooking ideas.

But that's not all! With the new "Learn to Make" feature to guide you through recipes, you'll become an expert in no time. And the "Heirloom Recipe and New Twist" feature brings many classic, cherished dishes to life alongside up-to-date twists that you'll want to try. We've tapped into our online community, too, and shared variations to several of these classic favorites.

As an exciting companion to this cookbook, we're providing you with access to 85 new online cooking videos and 400 bonus recipes designed to enhance and expand on the recipes found within these chapters. Be sure to visit bettycrocker.com/BCcookbook and check it out. If you're in Canada, visit lifemadedelicious.ca/BCcookbook.

This is our best edition ever, and with it you'll be able to create foods that will dazzle family and friends. We've come a long way, but for us, it's still all about providing fabulous recipes and great ideas for the way you cook today—enjoy!

Sincerely,

Betty Crocker

GETTING STARTED

GETTING STARTED
Whatever you are planning to make in your kitchen, you need the correct tools to get started. In this chapter, we provide the basics to get you cooking with ease and confidence.

EQUIPMENT
Look for most of these equipment pieces in department or kitchen specialty stores. There will be a variety of styles of each item available in a range of prices—purchase what your budget will allow, with an eye for quality and durability.

Cutting Boards
It's recommended to have at least two boards—one for raw meats and poultry and one for vegetables and fruit. There are three basic types of cutting boards:

- Plastic, acrylic or glass boards are easy to use and clean; they can be washed in the dishwasher.

- Wood boards will not dull knives as quickly as plastic boards; some can be washed in the dishwasher so check instructions when you purchase.

- Tempered glass boards are the most sanitary, and are durable and heat-resistant. This material is very heavy and the hard surface dulls knife edges quickly.

Food Safety Checklist for Cutting Boards
- Hard plastic or glass cutting boards, because they're less porous than wooden boards, are recommended as the safest for raw poultry, meat, fish and seafood. Also check out the thin, flexible silicone or plastic "cutting boards," which are perfect for transferring foods. Disposable cutting sheets are also available.

- Do not use wooden cutting boards for raw poultry, meat, fish or seafood.

- Avoid cutting cooked foods with the same knife and board used to cut raw foods.

- After each use, wash cutting boards with hot, soapy water. If the board is dishwasher safe, run it through the dishwasher. For added safety, sanitize boards with a mixture of 1 teaspoon chlorine bleach to 1 quart (4 cups) of water. Cover the entire board with the solution and let stand 2 to 3 minutes; rinse thoroughly and air dry or pat dry with paper towels.

- Throw out the cutting board when it becomes worn with deep scratches and cuts. Thoroughly dry boards before storing.

A great cookbook and a few groceries will get you started—now you're cooking!

Knives and Related Tools

Essential for almost anything you do in the kitchen, a good set of knives is an important investment. You'll use them daily so invest in the best quality that you can afford. Wash knives by hand and keep them sharp, and they will last many years. Choose knives that feel good in your hand. There are usually a variety of sizes of each type, so there is something to suit everyone. Look for stainless-steel blades and sturdy, durable handles.

Chef's Knife (8- to 10-inch blade): This knife is used for chopping foods.

Carving or Utility Knife (10-inch blade): Long and thin, this knife is used for carving meat and poultry or slicing cooked meats.

Kitchen Scissors: Great for snipping herbs, cutting up chicken pieces and other tasks.

Paring Knife (3- to 4-inch blade): The short blade of this knife is great for peeling vegetables and fruits, or cutting small amounts of foods.

Serrated Knives: Use a larger knife to cut bread. A smaller knife is great for slicing vegetables like tomatoes.

Sharpening Steel: Use to sharpen knives occasionally by gently scraping each knife back and forth across steel several times.

Steak Knives: Use to cut meat when dining.

Utility Knife (6- to 8-inch blade): There are varieties of this knife, which is usually used for slicing cheeses, fruits, sandwiches and other relatively soft foods.

Peeling Fruit

Using paring knife, cut into top of apple just below the skin, with sharp edge of blade toward you. Turn the apple, carefully peeling off skin in strip(s). Cut off any remaining skin.

Cutting Techniques

Chop: Gather food into close cluster. Hold down top of knife with fingers from one hand while holding knife handle in other hand. Manipulate knife (holding tip of knife on board) up and down over food, until evenly chopped.

Slice: Hold food with fingers of one hand tucking fingers under. Slice with knife held in the other hand.

Julienne: Slice long, thin, uniform strips of food, using slicing method.

Dice or Cube: Hold food with fingers of one hand, tucking fingers under. With knife in other hand, cut into strips; rotate, then cut into small squares.

Using Kitchen Scissors

Snipping: Place small items such as herbs into small cup. Snip with scissors into uniform size.

Cutting: Use scissors to cut small pieces of food into even smaller, similar-shaped pieces.

Photo (at right): 1 Sharpening Steel **2** Chef's Knife **3** Carving or Utility Knife **4** Kitchen Scissors **5** Serrated Knives **6** Paring Knives **7** Steak Knives

Cooking Tools and Handy Gadgets

Having a collection of these tools in your kitchen makes cooking easier and more fun.

Bowls (Large, Medium, Small): Use for mixing, stirring and combining ingredients.

Brushes: A wide variety of sizes and materials are available. Keep brushes used for pastry separate from those used to baste meat.

Can Opener: These are available in handheld types and electric versions.

Citrus Reamer and Juicer: Both remove juice easily from citrus fruits; juicer also keeps the seeds from getting into the juice.

Colanders and Strainers: Use colanders for draining pasta and vegetables. Use strainers to drain liquid from canned goods.

Cooling Racks: To cool foods such as baked goods, so that air can get underneath hot pan or foods.

Fat Separator: Fat rises to the top; with low spout, juices can be poured off, leaving fat behind.

Graters: Look for many styles with a variety of sizes of grating/shredding holes. A handheld plane grater is sharp and has very small holes.

Jar Opener: Aids in opening jars and bottles.

Kitchen Towels: Dish and hand towels should be absorbent. Tea towels are made for drying stemware and cutlery without scratching or leaving lint.

Meat Mallet: Breaks down tough meat fibers for more tender meat. Also used for other tasks.

Offset Metal Spatula: Frosts baked goods while keeping fingers from marking the frosted surface.

Oven Mitt/Pot Holder: Use to remove hot pans from oven or stove-top. Silicone pot holders are also available.

Pastry Blender: Not a must-have but handy when making pastry. You can substitute a fork.

Potato Masher: This handheld tool is for mashing potatoes, cooked vegetables or apples for applesauce.

Photo (at left): 1 Colanders and Strainers **2** Pancake Turner **3** Graters **4** Spoons **5** Timer **6** Kitchen Towel **7** Salad Spinner **8** Cooling Racks **9** Zester **10** Offset Metal Spatula **11** Basting Brushes **12** Whisks **13** Rolling Pin **14** Pastry Blender **15** Jar Opener **16** Ruler **17** Citrus Reamer **18** Scrubbing Brush **19** Silicone Mat **20** Rubber Spatulas **21** Bowls **22** Meat Mallet **23** Potato Masher **24** Silicone Pot Holder

Rolling Pin: Use for rolling cookies and pastry. Look for one that has sturdy, easy-to-hold handles.

Ruler: Use to measure dough and in other recipes requiring food to be shaped to a certain size; also used for determining correct pan sizes.

Salad Spinner: Quickly removes the water from lettuce after washing.

Scrubbing Brush: Aids in pan/dish washing to remove stuck-on food while keeping hands dry.

Silicone Mat: Use as an alternative to waxed paper to keep food from sticking or for rolling out dough.

Silicone or Rubber Spatula or Scraper: A must-have in the kitchen for folding, stirring and scraping. Look for those that are heat resistant.

Spatula and Pancake Turner: Use to turn foods such as burgers or pancakes, remove cookies from pan or serve desserts. Wooden spatulas won't scratch nonstick cookware.

Spoons: Use to stir thick batters and dough. Use wooden spoons for hot items on the stove, such as soups and sauces. Use slotted spoons to drain liquid away from food.

Timer: Lets you know when food is ready.

Tongs: Use to handle raw cuts of meat without touching, for turning foods when cooking or serving lettuce salads or other foods. (Do not let tongs that have touched raw meat contact other foods.)

Vegetable Peeler: Use to peel any vegetable or fruit.

Whisk: Great for beating eggs, sauces and dressings and smoothing lumpy mixtures.

Zester: When pulled across citrus fruit, it removes the peel from the bitter pith below.

Graters

Box Grater: Use to shred or grate larger pieces of cheese, chocolate, citrus peel.

Handheld Plane Grater: Use to grate tiny pieces of citrus peel or whole nutmeg.

Cookware

A variety of cookware is essential in the kitchen. Often, you will be able to purchase sets of cookware with a variety of pieces included. Materials used for cookware include stainless steel, hard-anodized aluminum, cast iron and clad, which is stainless steel bonded with aluminum.

Dutch Ovens: These pots have very thick walls and tight-fitting covers. Sides are shorter than a stockpot. Used for slow-cooking foods, such as roasts, stews and chilies.

Griddle: Large, heavy, flat pan with short (if any) sides, used to cook foods with minimal fat. Great for pancakes, bacon, sandwiches, fried potatoes. Regular griddles are used on the stove-top; electric versions are also available.

Grill Pan: Comes in a variety of shapes; this heavy pan has shallow sides and a ridged cooking surface so fat can drain away from food as it cooks; leaves grill marks on the food. Regular grill pans are used on the stove-top; electric versions are also available.

Saucepans: Come in a range of sizes from 1- to 4-quart and should have tight-fitting lids. Used to cook or reheat foods on the stove-top. Having a variety of sizes will guarantee you have the right size for the job. Using the wrong size pan can be the reason a recipe isn't successful.

Sauté Pans: Similar to skillets, sauté pans generally have sides that are a little higher. Sides can be straight or slightly sloped. In addition to the long handle, these pans typically have a loop handle on the other side so the pan can be easily lifted. Used to brown and cook meats or almost any other kind of food on the stove-top.

Skillets: Usually available in 8-, 10- and 12-inch sizes. Skillets generally have low, gently sloping sides, which allow steam to escape. Used to fry or cook almost any kind of food on the stove-top.

Stockpot: Large pans with tall sides, perfect for making stocks and soups or cooking pasta.

Wok: A round-bottomed pan with high, sloping sides, popular for Asian cooking; for stir-frying, steaming and deep-frying. A ring-shaped stand is usually included for use on a gas stove-top. Special flat-bottomed woks are available for electric stove-tops and electric woks are also available.

Choosing Cookware

Expect prices to vary widely, based upon the materials, thickness and weight. The best heat conductors are copper and aluminum, so buying pans made of one or both of these materials will ensure better cooking results. Consider nonstick coatings, too. Avoid buying uncoated aluminum pans, as the aluminum can react with acidic foods, causing off-flavors in the food as well as discoloring the pans. Also avoid buying stainless steel–only pans, as they can get hot spots when heated, causing food to cook unevenly.

Look for good, all-purpose cookware that conducts heat well, such as:

- Stainless-steel pans with copper bottoms

- Stainless-steel pans with aluminum or copper sandwiched between the steel on the bottom of the pan (also called clad pans)

- Anodized aluminum pans (electrolytically coated to protect the surface, making it dull instead of shiny)

- Solid copper pans, which conduct heat well but are very expensive

- Cast-iron pans, which conduct heat well but are heavy

Also consider:

- **Durability and Price:** Consider how long you want your cookware to look good and last. This will also influence what you pay. Cast iron and copper will last the longest, yet will typically be the most expensive.

- **Maintenance:** How much time do you realistically want to spend making your cookware look good? Copper and cast iron take more work to keep them looking new; while stainless steel is easier to take care of. Nonstick coatings make cleanup easier, but care needs to be taken when cooking and cleaning these pans so the coating won't scratch off.

- **Weight:** Consider weight in pans: Although heavier pans may seem better, they can be hard to lift and handle. Lighter, easier-to-handle pans may work better for you. Heaviness does not necessarily mean better.

Photo (at right): 1 Skillets **2** Saucepans **3** Stockpot **4** Dutch Oven **5** Sauté Pan

Bakeware

Bakeware is available in many materials, including aluminum, glass, ceramic and silicone. For the recipes in this book, *pan* refers to a shiny metal pan and *baking dish* refers to a heat-resistant glass or ceramic dish.

Baking Dishes: Made of heat-resistant glass; usually round, square or rectangular. Use for cakes, desserts and many main dishes.

Baking Pan: This 15x10x1-inch pan is distinguished from a cookie sheet by 1-inch sides on all edges. Used to bake thin, rectangular cakes or bars.

Cake Pans:

- **Angel Food Cake Pan (Tube Pan):** Round, metal pan (10-inch) with a hollow tube in the middle. The bottom is usually remov-able, making it easy to remove the cake from the pan. Use for angel food, chiffon and sponge cakes.

- **Baking Pans:** Available in a variety of sizes of round, square, rectangular and loaf shapes. Use for cakes, breads and desserts.

- **Fluted Tube Cake Pan:** Fluted, round, typically metal pan with center tube. Use for cakes and coffee cakes.

Casseroles: Covered or uncovered, glass or ceramic cookware for baking and serving food.

Cookie Sheets: Flat, rectangular aluminum sheets of various sizes with very short sides on one or more edges. The open sides allow for good air circulation in the oven when baking cookies, biscuits, scones, shortcakes or breads.

Custard Cups: Small, deep, heatproof, individual dishes (6- and 10-ounce) with flat bottoms. Use for baking individual custards and other desserts.

Muffin Pan: One pan with 6 or 12 individual cups for baking muffins or cupcakes. Cups can range in size from miniature to jumbo.

Pie and Tart Pans:

- **Pie Plate or Pan:** A round glass plate with a flared side, designed for baking pies. It pro-duces pie crusts that are flaky, not soggy. A pie pan is the metal version.

- **Tart Pan:** Available in a variety of shapes and sizes, typically with a removable bottom.

Pizza Pan: Round metal pan with no sides, low sides or high sides (deep-dish) for baking pizza. Some are perforated to help crisp the crust.

Popover Pan: One pan with 6 or 12 individual deep cups especially designed for baking popovers.

Silicone Products: Silicone bakeware is flexible, nonstick and safe to use in the oven, microwave, dishwasher and freezer. Look for it in various shapes and sizes. Follow manufacturer's guidelines for maximum baking temperatures.

Soufflé Dish: Round, open dish with high sides, especially designed for making soufflés.

Springform Pan: Round, deep pan of various sizes with removable side. Perfect for cheesecakes and desserts that cannot be turned upside down when removed from pan.

Other Ovenware

Broiler Pan and Rack: Rack has slits to allow fat to drip away from food as it cooks, falling into the pan. For easier cleanup, line pan and rack with foil; cut through foil over rack slits with knife.

Microwavable Cooking Dishes: Specifically made and designated on the label to go in the microwave. Use only dishes labeled "microwave-safe" in the microwave.

Roasting Pan and Rack: Rectangular pan with high sides to prevent spattering; handles make it easy to lift in and out of oven. Rack elevates food to promote fast, even cooking.

Using Silicone Mats

Silicone mats prevent foods from sticking to pans (and no greasing is necessary). Placed in a baking pan on a lower rack in oven, they catch juices bubbling out of pies or casseroles to prevent burning on the bottom of oven. They're also great for rolling dough, since it will release from mat easily.

Photo (at left): 1 Baking Dish **2** Baking Pans **3** Roasting Pan and Rack **4** Muffin Pan **5** Fluted Tube Cake Pan **6** Baking Dish **7** Cookie Sheet **8** Broiler Pan and Rack **9** Pie Plate and Pie Pan **10** Tart Pan **11** Baking Pan

Measuring Correctly

Spoon in dry ingredients, then level off top using a flat-edged utensil such as a knife or metal spatula.

Spoon brown sugar into measuring cup; firmly pack with back of spoon.

Check amount of liquid by looking at it at eye level while cup sits steady on counter.

Dip measuring spoon into food; level off (if dry) or fill to rim (if liquid).

Measuring Utensils

Using the correct measuring equipment can make a difference in a finished recipe. Use glass or liquid measuring cups for liquids, graduated plastic or metal measuring cups for dry ingredients and measuring spoons for small amounts of wet or dry ingredients. Measure accurately following what the recipe indicates. Measuring all of the ingredients before starting a recipe helps to make the process go quickly and efficiently.

Glass Measuring Cups: Pour liquid to desired mark on measuring cup. For accuracy, check the amount by looking at it at eye level.

Measuring Spoons: Use to measure small amounts of liquid and dry ingredients. For dry ingredients, fill and level off. For liquid ingredients, fill to rim.

Plastic and Metal Measuring Cups: Spoon dry ingredient into cup; level off with metal spatula or the flat side of a knife.

Thermometers

Look for a variety of thermometers in department stores and kitchen specialty stores.

Appliance Thermometer: Look for two types: oven thermometers and refrigerator/freezer thermometers.

Candy Thermometer: Use to check temperature of candy while it cooks as well as to check liquid temperature for bread making and deep-frying.

Instant-Read Thermometer: Check a food's temperature quickly, as it will give you a reading in seconds. These are not heat-safe, so they cannot be left in the oven when cooking.

Ovenproof Meat Thermometer: These are heat-safe so they can be left in food in the oven.

How Accurate Are Food Thermometers?

The good news is that most digital and dial thermometers are accurate to within plus or minus 1°F to 2°F. To check a thermometer for accuracy, heat 2 cups water in 1-quart saucepan to boiling. Immerse the stem of the thermometer 2 inches into the boiling water. The thermometer should read 212°F after 30 seconds. If the thermometer is off by a few degrees, calibrate it according to the manufacturer's directions or adjust the temperature you need to allow for the amount the thermometer is off. Check thermometers once or twice a year for accuracy.

Thermometers

Above: 1 Hand Mixer **2** Food Processor **3** Stand Mixer **4** Waffle Maker **5** Mini Chopper **6** Blender

Small Electric Appliances

Often these appliances are not essential for a task but can certainly make things easier. Sometimes it is difficult to make a recipe or perform a task without the correct appliance. Making waffles is not possible without a waffle maker and slow-cooker recipes are designed for the convenience of a slow cooker. So as you think about equipment in the kitchen, consider these items as you might need them.

Blender: Great for blending, liquifying, pureeing and chopping. Immersion blender is a hand-held appliance used to puree soups and sauces in the pan.

Bread Machine: Does all the mixing, kneading, rising and baking of bread or can be used to easily make dough for shaping into other bread products that are then baked in your oven.

Coffee Grinder: Quickly grinds whole coffee beans.

Coffeemaker: Makes coffee automatically. Many models can be set to start coffee before you awake and keep it warm.

Food Processor: Handles a host of cooking tasks quickly: chopping, slicing, crushing, mixing, shredding and pureeing.

Hand Mixer: Use to mix and whip liquid foods quickly. Not good for heavy batters or dough.

Mini Chopper: Much smaller than a food processor; it can chop small amounts of food quickly.

Slow Cooker: An easy way to make meals requiring little preparation, as the food cooks for long periods without much attention. Uses little electricity and doesn't heat up your kitchen. Great for less tender cuts of meat.

Stand Mixer: Preferred by professional chefs for ease of use (hands-free) and is typically more powerful (and quicker) than using a hand mixer, so it can handle thicker, stiffer mixtures, such as bread dough.

Toaster or Toaster Oven: Toaster toasts bread, bagels and English muffins. Toaster oven can be used for the same tasks as well as to heat up, broil or toast foods (such as garlic toast, frozen snacks) quicker and with less energy than if done in the oven.

Waffle Maker: Bakes waffles and is available in a variety of shapes and sizes.

INGREDIENTS

Baking Ingredients

Baking Powder: A leavening mixture made from baking soda, an acid (often cream of tartar) and a moisture absorber. Not interchangeable with baking soda.

Baking Soda: A leavening ingredient that must be mixed with acid such as lemon juice or buttermilk to be effective. Part of baking powder.

Butter: Available unsalted or salted and must contain at least 80% butterfat. Although recipes in this book call for butter only, combinations of butter and margarine are available and can often be used instead of butter. Use only the stick variety of any of these products for baking because the whipped products have air beaten into them and perform differently.

Chocolate: Cocoa beans are made into a thick paste called chocolate liquor, then processed to make various forms of chocolate.

- **Baking Cocoa:** Made from dried chocolate liquor with cocoa butter removed. It is unsweetened.

- **Bittersweet, Sweet (German), Milk and Semisweet Chocolate:** Available in bars and chips (German chocolate in bars only) for baking and eating.

Dark Chocolate

Dark chocolate and minimally processed cocoa powders contain high amounts of antioxidants, which have been shown to reduce blood pressure and the risk of heart disease.

But not all dark chocolate is equal. Look for those with 70% or higher cocoa content, for the most antioxidant benefit. The more bitter the chocolate, the higher the amount of antioxidant-rich cocoa—so avoid chocolate where the first ingredient listed is sugar.

Toasting Coconut

To toast coconut, heat the oven to 350°F. Spread the coconut in an ungreased shallow pan. Bake uncovered 5 to 7 minutes, stirring occasionally, until golden brown. Or sprinkle in an ungreased skillet and cook over medium-low heat 6 to 14 minutes, stirring frequently until browning begins, then stirring constantly until golden brown.

- **Unsweetened Chocolate:** Available in bars, and bitter in flavor; use just for baking.

- **White Chocolate:** Labeled as white baking chips or vanilla baking bar, this product contains no chocolate liquor and so is not true chocolate.

Coconut: Made from the fruit of the coconut palm tree, and available sweetened and unsweetened. Shredded coconut is best for baking, as it is moist. Dry flaked coconut is used mostly for decorating.

Cornstarch: A thickener derived from corn; good for making clear (not opaque) sauces. To substitute for flour, use half as much cornstarch.

Corn Syrup: A sweetener made from corn sugar mixed with acid. Dark and light corn syrups are interchangeable in recipes unless specified.

Cream of Tartar: An acid ingredient that adds stability and volume when beating egg whites.

Eggs: Add richness, moisture and structure to baked goods.

Flour: A primary baking ingredient; comes in many varieties.

- **All-Purpose Flour:** The most common flour; available bleached and unbleached.

- **Bread Flour:** Gives more structure to bread because it is higher in gluten.

- **Cake Flour:** Made from soft wheat; makes tender, fine-textured cakes.

- **Quick-Mixing Flour:** Processed to blend easily; used for sauces and gravies.

- **Self-Rising Flour:** Flour combined with baking powder and salt. Not interchangeable with other flours.

- **Whole Wheat Flour:** Made from the whole grain; gives foods a nutty flavor. Store it in the freezer to prevent rancidity.

Molasses: Made from the sugar-refining process, molasses is available in light and dark varieties. They are interchangeable in recipes unless specified otherwise.

Photo (at right): 1 Brown Sugar **2** Granulated Sugar **3** Egg **4** Yeast **5** White Baking Chips **6** Coconut **7** Sweet Baking (German) Chocolate **8** Baking Cocoa **9** Chocolate Chips **10** Butter **11** Whole Wheat Flour **12** All-Purpose Flour **13** Salt **14** Ground Cinnamon **15** Baking Powder

2

1

4

3

6

5

7

10

8

9

11

14

13

15

12

1/2 tsp [2.5 ml]

1 tsp [5 ml]

1 tsp [5 ml]

Sweeteners

There are several sugar substitutes on the market and more due to be available soon. Although all of them add sweetness, often without calories, they have different uses in cooking. See individual packages for instructions on use.

- Aspartame is great for beverages and cold foods but loses its sweetness when heated so is not good for baking.
- Saccharin is often used with aspartame in beverages and is also used in candies, gums, and some baked goods.
- Stevia comes from an herb and is very sweet. It can be used in beverages (hot and cold) and is an ingredient in many foods.
- Sucralose is heat stable, so can be used in baked products.

Salt: Adds flavor; controls the growth of yeast in breads.

Shortening: Sold in sticks and cans, this solid vegetable oil product is available in regular and butter-flavored varieties. It is hydrogenated and often trans-fat free.

Spices: Add flavor to baked goods. See Spices, page 496.

Sugars: These granular products are made from sugar beets or sugarcane.

- **Brown Sugar:** Light or dark brown in color, and made from white sugar plus molasses. Use either unless specified in a recipe.
- **Coarse, Decorating or Pearl Sugar:** Large-grained; used for decorating.
- **Colored Sugar:** Use for decorating.
- **Granulated:** Look for this sugar in boxes or bags as well as cubes and packets. Superfine sugar dissolves quickly and is great for beverages, meringues and frostings.
- **Powdered Sugar:** Granulated sugar that has been processed to a fine powder and contains a very small amount of cornstarch to keep it from clumping.
- **Raw or Turbinado Sugar:** Popular in restaurants, this is golden brown in color and the granules are larger than granulated sugar.

Yeast: A leavening ingredient used for breads.

- **Bread Machine Yeast:** Use this finely granulated yeast in bread machine recipes.
- **Fast-Acting Dry Yeast:** A dehydrated yeast that allows bread to rise in less time than regular yeast.
- **Regular Active Dry Yeast:** A dehydrated yeast that can be used in most bread recipes. To use instead of bread machine yeast, increase amount to 1 teaspoon for each ¾ teaspoon of yeast used.

Dairy/Refrigerated Ingredients

Butter: See Butter, page 18.

Cheese: See Cheese, page 263.

Cream: Smooth, rich dairy product made from milk. It is churned to make butter and buttermilk, and pasteurized and processed into several forms.

- **Half-and-Half:** Contains 10 to 12% butterfat and does not whip. To save on fat and calories, look for fat-free half-and-half. Although not recommended for baking, it is great for soups and beverages.
- **Sour Cream:** Regular sour cream has 18 to 20% butterfat. Low-fat and fat-free varieties are available and can often be substituted for regular.

Dairy Ingredients

- **Whipping Cream:** Available in light and heavy varieties. It contains 36 to 40% butterfat and doubles in volume when whipped. Ultrapasteurized cream will have a longer shelf life than regular cream.

Eggs: See Egg Basics, page 74.

Margarine: Made with at least 80% fat by weight and usually contains vegetable oil, but has flavoring from dairy products. Margarine can be used in most recipes instead of butter, but use only the stick variety for baking. There are also a variety of "spread" products that have a higher amount of water. These products are not recommended for baking.

Milk: Pasteurized milk is available in many types.

- **Buttermilk:** This fat-free or low-fat product adds a tangy taste to baked goods. It's made from milk with added special bacteria, providing a thick texture and distinctive flavor.

- **Evaporated Milk:** Milk with at least half of the liquid removed. Available in cans near the baked goods, in whole, low-fat and skim varieties.

- **Fat-Free (Skim) Milk:** Contains little or no fat.

- **Low-Fat Milk:** The most popular varieties are 1% (99% of milk fat removed) and 2% (98% of milk fat removed) milk. Recipes in this book were tested with 2% milk.

- **Sweetened Condensed Milk:** A highly sweetened milk product used mostly for baking. Available in cans.

- **Whole Milk:** Contains at least 3.5% milk fat.

Tofu: See Soy Foods, page 618.

Yogurt: Made from milk combined with healthful bacteria. Look for a variety of products with a range of fat content. Some will have fruit and/or sugar added for flavor. Many yogurts are made with added gelatin, giving them a thicker texture. Greek yogurt, page 254, is a very concentrated yogurt with smooth, intense flavor.

Plan Ahead

It's convenient to have certain ingredients on hand for preparing quick meals. Consider the foods you like to make, and keep a running list of items needed for these. When you use something up, mark it on the list for replacement the next time you shop.

Pantry Ingredients

Bouillon/Broth: Available canned, in dehydrated cubes and granulated.

Coffee: Look for a variety of whole beans, ground coffee and instant coffee. See Beverage Basics, page 65.

Gelatin: Colorless powder made from protein and used as a thickener that sets when refrigerated. It is also available in sweetened fruit flavors.

Herbs and Spices: See Herbs, page 495, and Spices, page 496.

Honey: A sweetener produced by bees. Store it at room temperature.

Legumes: See Dried Beans, page 443.

Maple Syrup: Made from maple tree sap. Maple-flavored syrup and pancake syrup are made from corn syrup with some maple syrup or maple flavor added.

Pasta: See Pasta Basics, page 367.

Rice: See Rice, page 429.

Sun-Dried Tomatoes: Available dehydrated and in jars packed in oil. Use the type specified in the recipe.

Tea: Look for a variety of loose tea and tea bags in regular and decaffeinated types. See Beverage Basics, page 65.

Pantry Ingredients

Tortillas: Corn and flour tortillas are often used for sandwich wraps and in recipes.

Vegetable Oil: Look for a variety of oils for cooking and baking. These products contain no cholesterol but do contain fat.

- **Olive Oil:** Has the highest amount of monounsaturated fat of any vegetable oil. Look for extra-virgin, virgin and light olive oil. Fat content will be the same for all of them. Use this oil in salads and cooking.

- **Other Oils:** Often these will be a blend or single oil, such as canola, cottonseed, peanut, safflower or soybean. They can be used interchangeably in recipes.

- **Cooking Spray:** Use to keep foods from sticking.

Condiments, Sauces and Seasonings

Balsamic Vinegar: Slightly sweet vinegar available in regular dark and white varieties. Both types are made from white grapes. Use white vinegar when you don't want to add color to the food. Use both types for salads and in cooking.

Capers: Unopened buds of a Mediterranean plant. They have a very sharp, tangy flavor and are packed in vinegar brine. Use them in appetizers and cooking.

Ketchup: Thick, spicy sauce made from tomatoes, vinegar and seasonings. Use as sauce and in cooking.

Mayonnaise/Salad Dressing: This creamy sauce is used in cooking, for salads and sandwiches. Salad dressing is usually sweeter than mayonnaise.

Mustard: Look for a range of flavors from yellow mustard to darker, more highly flavored varieties. Use to add a sharp flavor to dishes.

Pesto: Italian sauce made from basil, Parmesan cheese, olive oil and pine nuts. Look for pesto in the refrigerated area and in jars near spaghetti sauce. See Basil Pesto, page 484.

Red Pepper Sauce: Spicy sauce made from hot peppers.

Roasted Bell Peppers: Available in red and yellow, and packed in jars for salads, snacking and cooking.

Photo (above): 1 Red Pepper Sauce **2** Worcestershire Sauce **3** Balsamic Vinegar **4** Red Wine Vinegar **5** Mayonnaise **6 and 7** Mustards **8** Salsa **9** Roasted Bell Peppers **10** Pesto **11** Capers

Salsa: Sauce made from tomatoes and a variety of other ingredients. It is available in types that range from mild to spicy. See Salsa, page 480.

Soy Sauce: Asian sauce made from fermented soybeans.

Worcestershire Sauce: Use this highly flavored sauce in stews and meat dishes. It contains a mixture of garlic, soy sauce, onions, molasses and vinegar.

Toasting Nuts and Sesame Seed

To toast nuts, heat the oven to 350°F. Spread nuts in an ungreased shallow pan. Bake uncovered 6 to 10 minutes, stirring occasionally, until light brown. Or, sprinkle in an ungreased skillet. Cook over medium heat 5 to 7 minutes, stirring frequently, until nuts begin to brown, then stirring constantly until nuts are light brown.

To toast sesame seed, sprinkle in ungreased skillet. Cook over medium-low heat 5 to 7 minutes, stirring frequently until browning begins, then stirring constantly until golden brown.

Nuts and Seeds

Great sources of protein, nuts and seeds also contain vitamins, minerals and other components which may contribute to good health. They can be eaten out of hand or added to recipes for texture and crunch. Nuts contain oil, so they may spoil easily. Store them at room temperature up to 1 month, or in an airtight container in the refrigerator for 6 months, or in the freezer up to 1 year.

Almonds: Available in shell, whole (shelled), blanched, sliced or slivered. Also ground into almond flour and meal or made into almond milk.

Brazil Nuts: Actually seeds. Shells are extremely hard; kernels rich, oily. Eat raw or use in trail mixes.

Cashews: Rich, buttery flavor. High fat content; store in refrigerator or freezer only.

Chestnuts: Available fresh, canned (whole or pieces) or as puree. For fresh, choose firm, plump, blemish-free nuts. Store unshelled canned chestnuts in cool, dry place. Refrigerate shelled nuts in airtight container.

Hazelnuts (Filberts): Available whole or chopped. Use in a variety of desserts, salads, main dishes.

Macadamia Nuts: Available shelled, either roasted or raw. Rich, buttery, sweet flavor. High fat content: Store in refrigerator or freezer only.

Pecans: Available shelled (halves or chopped) or unshelled. When buying unshelled, look for blemish- and crack-free nuts. When shaken, the kernels should not rattle.

Pine Nuts: From the pine cones of several varieties of pine trees. Used in pesto; pungent flavor overpowers some foods. High fat content; store in refrigerator or freezer.

Pistachios: Available raw, roasted, salted or unsalted. Buy unshelled pistachios—tan, red (dyed) or white (blanched) shells—partially opened or shelled.

Pumpkin Seeds (Pepitas): Available with or without hulls; raw, roasted, salted. Delicious delicate flavor, common in Mexican cooking.

Sunflower Seeds: Available in or out of shells; dried, roasted, plain or salted. Good for snacking, in salads, sandwiches, baked goods.

Walnuts: English (most common) or black varieties. Buy unshelled walnuts, free from cracks or holes; shelled, crisp, meaty (avoid shriveled nuts).

COOKING TERMS

Cooking has its own vocabulary. This glossary isn't a complete list, but it will help you learn the most common terms if you're a beginning cook, or refresh your memory if you're an experienced one.

Al Dente: Describes doneness of pasta cooked until tender yet firm or somewhat chewy.

Bake: To cook food in an oven with dry heat. Bake food uncovered for a dry and/or crisp top, or covered to keep things moist.

Baste: To spoon, brush or use a bulb baster to add liquid or fat over surface of food during cooking to keep food moist.

Batter: This is an uncooked mixture of flour, eggs, liquid and other ingredients that is thin enough to be spooned or poured.

Beat: To combine ingredients vigorously with spoon, fork, wire whisk, electric mixer or hand beater until smooth. When electric mixer is specified, mixer speed is included.

Blanch: To place food into boiling water for a brief time to preserve color, texture and nutritional value or to remove skin.

Blend: To combine ingredients with spoon, wire whisk or rubber spatula until very smooth, or to combine ingredients in blender or food processor.

Boil: To heat liquid or cook food at a temperature that causes bubbles to rise continuously and break on surface.

Bread or Coat: To coat food by dipping into liquid (beaten egg or milk), then into bread crumbs, cracker crumbs or cornmeal before frying or baking.

Broil: To cook food a measured distance directly under the heat source.

Brown: To cook quickly over high heat, causing surface of food to turn brown while keeping inside moist.

Caramelize Sugar: To melt sugar slowly over low heat until golden brown in color and a syrupy consistency. Or to sprinkle granulated or brown sugar on top of a food, then use a kitchen torch, or place under broiler, until sugar is melted and caramelized.

Basting

Brushing foods with liquid adds flavor to the food while also keeping it moist during cooking.

Boiling and Simmering

Boil liquid or cook food in liquid at a temperature that causes bubbles to rise continuously and break on surface.

Simmer food in liquid at a temperature just below boiling point. Bubbles rise slowly and break just below surface.

Blanching

Immerse food into boiling water to loosen skins, partially cook or brighten color.

Immediately immerse food into ice water to stop the cooking process.

Broiling

Broil food directly under heated broiler element at a specified distance to keep from burning.

Browning

Cook food quickly over heat, causing surface of food to turn brown but keeping interior moist.

Crushing

Place food to be crushed into resealable plastic bag; seal. Roll over bag with rolling pin until food is in small, even pieces.

Coring Fruit

Pierce fruit at stem end with corer; twist into fruit and pull out to remove core.

With paring knife, cut fruit into quarters; cut out core with knife.

Cut In: To work butter, margarine or shortening into dry ingredients. Use pastry blender, lifting up and down with rocking motion, until particles are desired size. Or use fork, or use your fingertips, working quickly so the heat of your fingers doesn't soften fat.

Cut Up: To cut food into small pieces of irregular sizes, using kitchen scissors or knife. Or cut a large food into smaller pieces (whole chicken).

Dash: Refers to less than ⅛ teaspoon of an ingredient.

Deep-Fry: To cook in hot fat that's deep enough to cover and float the food being fried. Sometimes foods are cooked in a shallow amount of oil (about 1 inch). See also Fry, Pan-Broil, Panfry, Sauté.

Deglaze: After food is panfried, excess fat is removed from the skillet, then a small amount of liquid (broth, water, wine) is added and stirred to loosen browned bits of food in skillet. This mixture is used as a base for sauce.

Dice: To cut food with knife into ¼-inch squares.

Dip: To moisten or coat food by submerging into liquid mixture to cover completely.

Chill: To place food in refrigerator until thoroughly cold.

Chop: To cut food into coarse or fine pieces of irregular shapes, using knife, food processor or food chopper.

Cool: To allow hot food to stand at room temperature until it reaches desired temperature. Foods placed on cooling rack cool more quickly.

Core: To remove the center of a fruit (apple, pear, pineapple).

Cover: To place a cover, lid, plastic wrap or foil over container of food.

Crisp-Tender: Describes doneness of cooked vegetables when they retain some crisp texture.

Crush: To press with side of knife blade, or use meat mallet, mortar and pestle or rolling pin to smash into small pieces.

Cube: To cut food with knife into uniform squares, ½ inch or larger.

Deep-Frying

Heat oil to desired temperature.

Drop food carefully into oil; do not crowd.

Drain fried food on paper towel-lined plate.

Drizzling

With spoon, drop glaze over food in thin stream. Cut tiny (⅛-inch) corner from bag of glaze. Squeeze glaze over food in thin stream.

Dissolve: To stir a dry ingredient (gelatin) into a liquid ingredient (boiling water) until dry ingredient disappears.

Dot: To drop small pieces of an ingredient (butter) randomly over another food.

Dough: Refers to a stiff but pliable mixture of flour, liquid and other ingredients that can be dropped from a spoon, rolled or kneaded.

Drain: To pour off liquid by putting food into a colander or strainer. To drain fat from meat, place strainer in disposable container.

Drizzle: To pour in thin stream from spoon, bag, squeeze bottle with tip or liquid measuring cup in uneven pattern over food.

Dust: To sprinkle lightly with flour, granulated sugar, powdered sugar or baking cocoa.

Flake: To break lightly into small, flat pieces using a fork.

Flute: To squeeze pastry with fingers to make decorative edge.

Fold: To gently combine ingredients without decreasing volume. To fold, use rubber spatula to cut down vertically through mixture. Next, slide spatula across bottom of bowl and up other side, carrying some mixture from bottom up and over surface. Repeat, turning bowl ¼ turn after each folding motion.

Fry: To cook in hot fat over medium to high heat. See also Deep-Fry, Pan-Broil, Panfry, Sauté.

Garnish: To decorate food with small amounts of other foods that have distinctive color, flavor or texture (fresh herbs, fresh berries, chocolate curls).

Glaze: To brush, spread or drizzle ingredient on hot or cold food to add thin, glossy coating.

Grate: To rub a hard-textured food across the smallest holes of grater to make tiny particles.

Grease: To coat bottom and sides of pan with shortening, using pastry brush, waxed paper or paper towel to prevent food from sticking. Cooking spray can often be used. Don't use butter or margarine for greasing unless specified in a recipe because foods may stick.

Grease and Flour: After greasing pan with shortening, sprinkle with small amount of flour and shake pan to distribute evenly. Then, turn pan upside down and tap bottom to remove excess flour.

Grill: See Grilling Basics, page 303.

Hull: To remove stem and leaves from strawberries with paring knife or huller.

Husk: To remove leaves and silk from fresh ears of corn.

Julienne: To cut into long, thin slices. Stack slices, then cut into matchlike sticks.

Knead: To work dough on floured surface into smooth, springy mass, using hands or an electric mixer with dough hook. See Making Bread Dough, page 111.

Marinate: To allow food to stand in marinade (savory, acidic liquid) in glass or plastic container for several hours to add flavor. Don't marinate in metal containers because acidic ingredients react with metal to give food an off-flavor.

Melt: To turn a solid into liquid or semiliquid by heating.

Microwave: To cook, reheat or thaw food in a microwave oven. See Microwave Cooking, pages 30 to 31.

Mince: To cut food with knife into very fine pieces that are smaller than chopped, but bigger than crushed.

Hulling

Gently press huller into fruit, around hull. Squeeze while simultaneously twisting and pulling hull away from fruit.

Mix: To combine ingredients in any way that distributes evenly.

Pan-Broil: To cook meat or other food quickly in ungreased or lightly greased skillet. See also Deep-Fry, Fry, Panfry, Sauté.

Panfry: To fry meat or other food in skillet, using small amount of fat and usually pouring off fat from meat during cooking. See also Deep-Fry, Fry, Pan-Broil, Sauté.

Peel: To cut off outer covering with paring knife or vegetable peeler, or remove with fingers.

Poach: To cook in simmering liquid just below the boiling point.

Pound: To flatten boneless cuts of chicken and meat, using meat mallet or rolling pin, until food is uniform thickness.

Process: To use blender, food processor or mini-chopper to liquify, blend, chop, grind or knead food.

Puree: To mash or blend food until smooth, using blender or food processor or forcing food through sieve.

Reduce: To boil liquid, uncovered, to reduce volume to either thicken a mixture or intensify the flavor of remaining liquid.

Roast: To cook meat, poultry or vegetables uncovered in oven. Meat and poultry are often placed on rack in shallow pan without adding liquid; vegetables are usually tossed with oil and spread in single layer on pan.

Roll: To flatten dough into thin, even layer, using rolling pin. Also means to shape food into balls.

Roll Up: To roll a flat food that's spread with filling, or with filling placed at one end. Begin at one end and roll until food is log shaped.

Sauté: Cook food over medium-high heat in a small amount of fat, frequently tossing or turning. See also Deep-Fry, Fry, Pan-Broil, Panfry.

Scald: To heat liquid to just below boiling point until tiny bubbles form at edge. A thin skin will form on top of scalded milk.

Score: To cut shallow lines, about ¼ inch deep through surface of food such as meat or bread to decorate, tenderize or let fat drain away as foods cook or bake.

Pureeing

Place raspberries or other fruit and juice in sieve; with back of spoon press liquid through strainer.

Making Soft and Stiff Peaks

Soft Peaks: Beat just until peaks form but curl over.

Stiff Peaks: Continue beating until peaks stand upright.

Sear: To brown meat, fish or seafood quickly on all sides over high heat to seal in juices.

Season: To add flavor with salt, pepper, herbs, spices or seasoning mixes.

Shred: To push food across a shredding surface to make narrow or fine strips, or to slice very thinly with knife.

Simmer: To cook in liquid just below boiling point while bubbles rise slowly and break just below the surface.

Skim: To remove fat or foam from soup, broth, stock or stew, using spoon, ladle or skimmer (a flat utensil with holes).

Slice: To cut into flat pieces of about the same size.

Smoke: See Smoking Basics, page 324.

Snip: To cut into very small pieces with kitchen scissors.

Soft Peaks: Refers to egg whites or whipping cream beaten until peaks curl when beaters are lifted from bowl. See also Stiff Peaks.

Steam: To cook food by placing in steamer basket, which may be metal or bamboo, over small amount of boiling or simmering water in covered pan.

Stew: To cook slowly in covered pot, pan or casserole in small amount of liquid.

Stiff Peaks: Refers to egg whites or whipping cream beaten until peaks stand up straight when beaters are lifted from bowl. See also Soft Peaks.

Stir: To combine ingredients with circular or figure-eight motion until thoroughly blended.

Stir-Fry: Method of cooking small, similar-size pieces of food in small amount of hot oil in wok or skillet over high heat while stirring constantly.

Strain: To pour mixture or liquid through fine strainer or sieve to remove larger particles.

Tear: To break into pieces with your fingers.

Toast: To brown lightly in toaster, oven, broiler or skillet.

Toss: To gently combine ingredients by lifting and dropping using hands or utensils.

Removing Citrus Peel

Using a sharp paring knife or zester, pull across peel pressing lightly to remove peel, but not the bitter white pith below.

Whip: To beat ingredients to add air and increase volume until ingredients are light and fluffy.

Zest or Peel: Refers to outside colored layer of citrus fruit that contains aromatic oils and flavor. Also refers to action of removing small amounts of peel with knife or citrus zester.

Smart Shopping Strategies

It pays in many ways to be strategic about grocery shopping. First, you will probably save some money—a welcome gift for all of us. But shopping smarter can also mean meals that are better for you, easier to make and tastier. Here are some ideas to start you on the path to more efficient shopping.

Meal Planning

Set aside time for weekly meal planning so there are no more last-minute dinner dashes or takeout splurges.

- Create a chart sectioning off daily meals, including snacks and brown-bag lunches.
- Scan your refrigerator for what needs to be used, such as leftovers or produce that might not last more than a few days. Plan immediate meals around these items.
- Check the pantry to see what is on hand to use for the meals on your chart.
- Fill in the week's meals, adding needed ingredients to a shopping list as you go.
- Take a final assessment, considering the week's activities and the time you'll have to make each meal.

It Pays to Plan Ahead

Make shopping easier and more efficient with these tips:

- Plan time to shop alone so that you are not distracted.
- Bring your own bags. Many stores offer a reusable bag discount.

- Clip coupons ahead of time and read store ads, both print and online.
- Know what your budget is and pay with cash.
- Always shop with a list.
- Have backup ideas in mind in case the store is out of a crucial ingredient that you need.

Super Market Skills

Check out these in-store tactics to help you stick to your list and budget.

- Shop seasonally to get the freshest food at the best prices.
- Shop the perimeter of the store for the most healthful items (dairy, produce, meats).
- Go ahead and check the discount shelves for bargains.
- Buy in bulk those items that you use often.

Do the Math

Good buys start with one key equation: Unit price per ounce. Take the time to make some quick comparison calculations before adding items to your cart. Remember that sale prices and larger packages do not make an automatic bargain. To figure price per ounce: $2.99 ÷ 16 ounces = $.19 per unit.

COOKING AT HIGHER ALTITUDES

For elevations of 3,500 feet or higher, there are unique cooking challenges. Air pressure is lower, so water has a lower boiling point and liquids evaporate faster. That means recipes for conventional and microwave cooking need to be adjusted.

Unfortunately, no set of rules applies to all recipes; sometimes the only way to make improvements is through trial and error. Here are some guidelines to help you with high-altitude cooking challenges:

- Boiling foods such as pasta, rice and vegetables will take longer.

- For microwave cooking, more water may be necessary and foods may need to cook longer. Type and amount of food, the water content of the food and elevation may affect this guideline.

- Cooking meat in boiling liquid or steam takes longer, sometimes as much as 50 to 100 percent. Cooking large meat cuts, such as roasts and turkeys, in the oven also takes longer.

- Grilling foods will take longer.

- Most baked goods made with baking powder or baking soda (but not yeast) can be improved with one or more of the following changes:

    - Increase oven temperature by 25°F.

    - Increase liquid.

    - Decrease baking powder or baking soda.

    - Decrease sugar and/or use a larger pan.

- Very rich recipes, such as pound cakes, will turn out better if you decrease fat. Quick breads and cookies usually don't need as many adjustments.

- Yeast bread dough rises faster at high altitudes and can easily overrise. Let dough rise for a shorter time (just until doubled in size). Flour dries out more quickly at high

altitudes too, so use the minimum amount in the recipe, or decrease the amount by ¼ to ½ cup.

- If you're using a mix, look for specific directions on the package.

Specific Adjustments for Cooking Foods at High Altitudes

- Because water evaporates faster at higher altitudes, boiled candy, cooked frostings and other sugar mixtures concentrate faster. Watch the recipe closely during cooking so it doesn't scorch. You also may want to reduce the recipe temperature by 2°F for every 1,000 feet of elevation. Or use the cold water test for candy (see Testing Candy Temperatures, page 203).

- Deep-fried foods can be too brown on the outside but undercooked on the inside. So that both outside and inside of food are done at same time, reduce temperature of the oil by 3°F for every 1,000 feet of elevation and increase frying time, if necessary.

High-Altitude Experts

If you're new to high-altitude cooking, go to the U.S. Department of Agriculture web site for information: www.fsis.usda.gov/factsheets/high_altitude_cooking_and_food_safety/index.asp.

Or write to Colorado State University, Department of Food Science and Human Nutrition Cooperative Extension, Fort Collins, Colorado.

MICROWAVE COOKING

Convenient to use and great for many tasks, the microwave oven can be a time-saver and is a great appliance to have in any kitchen. Many of us use it just for heating, but it can be a great tool for cooking many food items too. Here, we've provided some helpful tips and a chart for cooking a variety of foods.

Microwaving Tips

- Porous foods like bread and cakes cook quickly. Dense foods like potatoes need to cook longer.

- The colder the food is, the longer it will take to cook.

- Increase cooking time if you increase amount of food.

- Check food at the minimum time to avoid overcooking. Cook longer if necessary.

- Stir food from outer edge to center, so food cooks evenly.

- Foods that contain high amounts of sugar, fat or moisture may cook more quickly.

- For even cooking, arrange food in a circle with thickest parts to outside of dish.

- If food cannot be stirred, and the microwave does not have a turntable, rotate dish ¼ to ½ turn during cooking.

- Small pieces of food cook faster than larger pieces.

- Use standing time to help finish cooking and distribute heat through food.

- For microwaving vegetables, see the Fresh Vegetable Cooking Chart, pages 586 to 590.

Ovens We Use

Recipes in this book that are cooked or heated in the microwave oven were tested in consumer ovens with 700 to 800 watts of power. Your Use and Care Guide will tell you what wattage your oven has. You can adjust your cooking times if the wattage on your oven is less or more than ours.

MICROWAVE COOKING AND HEATING CHART

This chart provides at-a-glance times for cooking, warming and softening many favorite foods. For all items, use microwavable dishes and microwavable paper towels or plastic wrap.

FOOD, UTENSIL AND TIPS	POWER LEVEL	AMOUNT	TIME
Bacon Slices (cook) Place on plate or bacon rack lined with paper towels. Place paper towels between layers; cover with paper towel. Microwave until crisp.	High	1 slice 2 slices 4 slices 6 slices 8 slices	30 seconds to 1½ minutes 1 to 2 minutes 2 to 3 minutes 3 to 5 minutes 4 to 6 minutes
Brown Sugar (soften) Place in glass bowl; cover with damp paper towel, then plastic wrap. Repeat heating once or twice.	High	1 to 3 cups	1 minute; let stand 2 minutes until softened
Butter or Margarine (melt) Remove wrapper. Place in glass bowl; cover with microwavable paper towel.	High	1 to 8 tablespoons ½ to 1 cup	30 to 50 seconds 60 to 75 seconds
Butter or Margarine (soften) Remove wrapper. Place in glass bowl or measuring cup, uncovered.	High	1 to 8 tablespoons ½ to 1 cup	10 to 20 seconds 15 to 30 seconds
Caramels (melt) Remove wrappers. Place in 4-cup glass measuring cup, uncovered.	High	1 bag (14 oz) caramels plus 2 to 4 tablespoons milk	2 to 3 minutes, stirring once or twice
Baking Chocolate (melt) Remove wrappers. Place squares in glass dish or measuring cup, uncovered.	Medium (50%)	1 to 3 oz	1½ to 2½ minutes

MICROWAVE COOKING AND HEATING CHART

FOOD, UTENSIL AND TIPS	POWER LEVEL	AMOUNT	TIME
Chocolate Chips (melt) Place in glass bowl, uncovered. Chips will not change shape.	Medium (50%)	½ to 1 cup	2 to 3 minutes, stirring twice
Coconut (toast) Place in 2-cup glass measuring cup or pie plate, uncovered. Stir every 30 seconds.	High	¼ to ½ cup 1 cup	1½ to 2 minutes 2 to 3 minutes
Cream Cheese (soften) Remove wrapper. Place in glass bowl or leave in plastic tub, uncovered.	Medium (50%)	3-oz package 8-oz package 8-oz tub	45 to 60 seconds 1 to 1½ minutes 45 to 60 seconds
Fruit, Dried (soften) Place in 2-cup glass measuring cup; add ½ teaspoon water for each ½ cup fruit. Cover with plastic wrap, turning back a corner or ¼-inch edge to vent steam.	High	¼ to ½ cup ½ to 1 cup	30 to 45 seconds 45 to 60 seconds; let stand 2 minutes
Fruit, Frozen (thaw) Leave in plastic bag or pouch, or place in glass bowl; thaw until most of ice is gone, stirring or rearranging twice.	Medium (50%)	16-oz bag	3 to 5 minutes
Fruit, Refrigerated (warm) Place on floor of microwave.	High	1 medium 2 medium	15 seconds 20 to 30 seconds; let stand 2 minutes
Honey (dissolve crystals) Leave in jar with lid removed, uncovered. Stir every 20 to 30 seconds or until crystals dissolve.	High	½ to 1 cup	45 seconds to 1½ minutes
Ice Cream (soften) Leave in original container; remove any foil. Let stand 2 to 3 minutes.	Low (10%)	½ gallon	2 to 3 minutes
Muffins or Rolls, Small to Medium (heat) Place on plate, napkin or napkin-lined basket, uncovered.	High	1 2 3 4	5 to 10 seconds 10 to 15 seconds 12 to 20 seconds 20 to 30 seconds
Muffins, Large to Jumbo (heat) Place on plate or napkin, uncovered. Let stand 1 minute.	High	1 2 3 4	10 to 20 seconds 20 to 30 seconds 30 to 40 seconds 40 to 50 seconds
Nuts, Chopped (toast) Place in glass measuring cup, uncovered; add ¼ teaspoon vegetable oil for each ¼ cup nuts. Stir every 30 seconds until light brown.	High	¼ to ½ cup ½ to 1 cup	2½ to 3½ minutes 3 to 4 minutes
Snacks (crisp popcorn, pretzels, corn chips or potato chips) Place in paper towel–lined basket, uncovered.	High	2 cups 4 cups	20 to 40 seconds 40 to 60 seconds
Syrup (heat) Place in glass measuring cup or pitcher, uncovered. Stir every 30 seconds.	High	½ cup 1 cup	30 to 45 seconds 45 to 60 seconds
Water (boil) Place in glass measuring cup uncovered.	High	1 cup	2 to 3 minutes

HEALTH AND NUTRITION

Eating well is about not just eating foods that are good for you, but also enjoying what you eat. Though news reports and headlines may lead you to think some foods are poor choices or that there are quick fixes to feeling great, in reality, common sense and balance are the pillars of good health. Healthy eating can be easy, convenient and include your favorite foods.

The Link between Diet and Health

Thousands of studies have shown that diet has a powerful impact on health, and new research continues to support this connection. The phrase, "You are what you eat," is all telling when you look at just how big an impact diet has on health:

- More than one-third of all cancers can be attributed to diet.

- Three of the five major risk factors for heart disease (that are controllable)—blood cholesterol level, blood pressure and weight—are influenced by food choices.

- Many new research studies are linking certain vitamins, minerals and phytochemicals (naturally occurring substances in plant foods) with a lower risk of disease.

- A poor diet and inactivity result in 300,000 deaths per year in the United States.

- Seventy percent of the diagnosed cases of heart disease may be related to obesity.

This is just the start. Diet and health are connected in many more ways and research continually finds new links. So how do you begin eating healthier for a healthier life?

Make Wise Food Choices a Habit

Don't Skip Meals: When meals are missed, it's harder to maintain blood glucose levels, so you end up overeating at the next meal, potentially eating more than if you had eaten two meals to begin with. Stick to your food plan, and if you don't have time for a meal, have healthy, satisfying snacks on hand.

Plan Meals and Snacks: Planning what you will eat may seem overwhelming at first, but in no time you'll become an expert on what foods keep you satisfied. If you don't plan, your hunger can take control, steering you toward whatever is available, which may not be the best choice. Before you go grocery shopping, decide on healthy meals and snacks to eat at home or take to work or school for the upcoming week, to guide your purchases.

Eat a Variety of Foods: Foods vary in their nutritional makeup so eating a variety of colors and kinds helps to ensure that your body gets all the nutrients it needs for good health. Variety also helps to avoid boredom, which often leads to poor choices.

Choose Low-Fat Foods Often: Health experts recommend that healthy adults reduce their total fat intake to less than 30% of calories per day. Keep in mind that this applies to the entire day's worth of foods—not just a single food or recipe. Whenever you have the choice, choose lower-fat or fat-free versions of foods.

Fat Trimming Tips

- **Eat Fewer High-Fat Foods:** Eat fewer high-fat versions of salad dressing, mayonnaise, sour cream and yogurt. Try reduced-fat products for these foods. Trim visible fat from meat, and remove the skin from chicken and turkey before eating. Cutting back on foods with hidden fat, such as chips, high-fat cheese and many bakery goods, will also reduce your overall fat intake.

- **Eat Smaller Portions:** As portions get bigger, so does the fat content. Skip super-size meals and snacks, and choose normal-size servings.

- **Cook Lean:** Grill, broil, bake, roast, poach, steam, stew or microwave foods whenever possible. You can stir-fry if you use small amounts of unsaturated oils, such as canola or safflower oil. Use nonstick cookware and cooking spray to lessen the amount of fat needed for cooking. Broths and vegetable juices are great nonfat substitutes for oil, shortening or butter, when sautéing.

- **Choose Meatless Meals:** Trading non-meat sources of protein, such as dried beans, peas and grains, for meat, poultry and fish twice a week, in addition to having more vegetables and fruits, will reduce the fat in your diet while increasing fiber and complex carbohydrates.

- **Go for Chicken, Turkey or Fish:** When eating "meat," go for lower-fat choices, such as light-meat chicken and turkey (with skin removed). Most fish is also very lean. Even higher-fat fish, such as salmon, is as lean as or leaner than poultry and lean beef. Some fish also have the added bonus of containing omega-3 fatty acids.

- **Use Low-Fat or Fat-Free Dairy Products:** Many milk products contain a lot of fat, especially if they are made with whole milk or cream. Choose from the many low-fat

and fat-free dairy products available, such as low-fat yogurts, cheese, puddings, milk and ice cream.

Important Nutritional Terms

Here's a basic explanation of many common terms found on food labels:

Carbohydrates: A key source of energy. *Sugars* are simple carbohydrates; *starches* (including breads, cereals and pastas) are complex carbohydrates. *High fructose corn syrup,* chemically similar to table sugar, is the most commonly added sweetener to processed foods and beverages. Research on high fructose corn syrup's impact on health is evolving.

Cholesterol: Dietary cholesterol is a substance found only in animal-based foods. Different types of dietary cholesterol include HDLs (high-density lipoproteins, known as "good cholesterol") that may help protect against heart disease, and LDLs (low-density lipoproteins, known as "bad cholesterol") that may contribute to heart disease.

Dietary Fiber: The part of plant-based foods that isn't broken down or used by our bodies. *Soluble fiber* is found in foods like oats, beans and strawberries and helps lower blood cholesterol levels. *Insoluble fiber* is found in foods like whole-grain breads, cereals, apples and cabbage and helps keep our digestive systems in check.

Minerals: Inorganic elements, like calcium and iron, found in foods and water.

Nutrients: Necessary for life; they build, repair and maintain body cells. Nutrients include protein, carbohydrates, fat, water, vitamins and minerals.

Protein: Provides energy and structural support of body cells and is important for growth.

Vitamins: Essential for controlling body functions. Vitamins are found in small amounts in many foods. Vitamins include vitamin A, B vitamins (such as thiamin, niacin, and riboflavin), vitamin C and folic acid.

Not All Fats Are Equal

Though some fats may be "better" than others for your health, the best advice for eating well is to eat a diet low in all types of fat. Here's the difference between the types of fat:

Saturated Fats: Usually solid at room temperature and found primarily in foods from animal sources. Diets high in saturated fats have been linked to higher levels of blood cholesterol.

Unsaturated Fats: Primarily from plant sources, unsaturated fats may be monounsaturated or polyunsaturated. When unsaturated fats replace saturated fats in the diet, blood cholesterol levels can go down.

Trans Fatty Acids: Formed during the process that changes liquid fats into a more solid and saturated form (hydrogenation), and are found in cookies, snack foods and bakery products. Trans-fats improve shelf life and stability of products.

Omega-3 Fats: Often referred to as fish oils, studies show omega-3s may be helpful for a variety of health reasons. Omega-3 fats can be found in some fish, such as salmon, mackerel, trout and albacore tuna. Flaxseed contains a good amount.

FOOD SAFETY

America's food supply is one of the safest in the world. Farmers, ranchers, food processors, supermarkets and restaurants must follow strict rules and regulations while getting food to you. Once food leaves the grocery store, care must be taken to keep it safe.

Why worry about food safety? Because most illnesses reported from "bad food" are caused by bacterial contamination. Nearly all cases can be linked to improper food handling in our homes, supermarkets and restaurants, meaning they could have been prevented.

Microorganisms are always with us. They're on us and on animals, in the air and water and on raw food. Some bacteria are useful, like those used to create cheese or to ferment beer. But other bacteria cause foods to spoil or cause food poisoning.

The main difference between food-spoiling and food-poisoning bacteria is the temperature at which they survive and grow. Bacteria causing food to spoil can grow at refrigerator temperatures (below 40°F). They usually make the food look or smell bad, raising a red flag that it should be thrown out.

Food-poisoning bacteria *don't* grow at refrigerator temperatures. The best growing temperature for these microorganisms is around 100°F. But the actual temperature varies with the organism and may range from 40°F to 140°F, or the "danger zone." These are pathogens, the type of bacteria that if eaten may lead to illness, disease or even death.

To prevent these bacteria from becoming harmful, they must be stopped from multiplying. Pathogenic bacteria are among the most important organisms to control because of the illness they cause in humans. *The majority are invisible attackers; you can't see, smell or taste them.*

If contaminated food is eaten, people most often get sick within 4 to 48 hours, and it's not always easy to tell if the problem is the flu or food poisoning. Call a doctor or go to a hospital immediately if symptoms are severe, such as vomiting, diarrhea, fever or cramps, or if the victim is very young, elderly, pregnant, has a weakened immune system or is already ill.

Four Basic Food Safety Rules

Proper cleaning, cooking and refrigeration can control most food-poisoning bacteria. Four golden rules apply to preparing food:

1. Keep everything in the kitchen **clean.**

2. Don't **cross-contaminate.**

3. Keep hot foods **hot.**

4. Keep cold foods **cold.**

Cleaning Basics

Wash Your Hands

Your mother was right! Proper hand washing could eliminate nearly half of all cases of food-borne illness. Experts recommend washing hands thoroughly with soap and water for at least 20 seconds before handling food. Twenty seconds is about how long it takes to recite the alphabet or sing happy birthday.

Stay Up to Date with Food Safety

For current information about safe food handling and food-borne illness, contact:

- USDA Meat and Poultry Hotline, 800-674-6845, or visit the web site:

  www.fsis.usda.gov/food_safety_
  education/usda_meat_&_poultry_
  hotline/index.asp

- U.S. Food and Drug Administration's Center for Food Safety and Applied Nutrition Automated Outreach and Information Center, 888-723-3366, or visit the web site:

  www.fda.gov/Food/default.htm

- For general food safety information, browse the following government web site:

  Gateway to Government Food Safety: www.foodsafety.gov

- Your local health department listed online or in the government pages of the phone book.

Always wash hands:

- Before handling food and utensils, or serving and eating food.

- After handling food, especially raw meat, poultry, fish, shellfish and eggs.

- Between jobs like cutting up raw chicken and making a salad.

- After using the bathroom, blowing your nose, changing diapers, touching pets, and handling garbage, dirty dishes, hair, dirty laundry, cigarettes and phones.

- If you have any kind of skin cut or infection on your hands, wear protective plastic or rubber gloves.

- If you sneeze or cough while preparing food, turn your face away and cover your mouth and nose with a tissue; wash your hands afterward.

Keep It Clean

- Wash all utensils and surfaces with hot, soapy water after contact with raw meat, poultry, fish or seafood.

- Use paper towels when working with—and cleaning up after working with—raw poultry, meat, fish or seafood.

- Bleach and commercial kitchen-cleaning agents are the best sanitizers—provided they're diluted according to product directions. They're the most effective at getting rid of bacteria. Hot water and soap does a good job, too, but may not kill all strains of bacteria. Plain water may get rid of visible dirt, but not bacteria.

- Be sure to keep dishcloths and sponges clean because, when wet, these materials harbor bacteria and may promote their growth.

- Clean refrigerator surfaces regularly with hot, soapy water.

- Wash the meat and crisper drawers of the refrigerator often, and keep containers for storing food in the refrigerator very clean.

- Sort through perishable foods each week, tossing out anything past its prime.

Antibacterial Soap

Antibacterial soaps are no more effective than plain soap and water for killing disease-causing germs outside of health-care settings. There is no evidence that antibacterial soaps are more effective than plain soap for preventing infection under most circumstances in the home or in public places. Therefore, plain soap is recommended in public, non-health-care settings and in the home (unless otherwise instructed by your doctor).

- **Do antibacterial soaps promote antibiotic resistance?**

  There is no evidence that antibacterial soaps cause antibiotic resistance, but some scientists believe they may contribute to the development of antibiotic-resistant germs.

- **What about using hand sanitizer?**

  Wash your hands with soap and water when your hands are visibly soiled. If soap and water is not available, use alcohol-based hand sanitizer (wipes or gel).

Credit: Minnesota Department of Health

- Wash sponges and dishcloths often in hot water in the washing machine, and for added safety, sanitize them three times a week by soaking them in a mixture of ¾ cup bleach to 1 gallon (4 quarts) water.

- Keep pets out of the kitchen and away from food.

- Follow guidelines for keeping cutting boards clean on page 7.

Don't Cross-Contaminate

Cross-contamination happens when cooked or ready-to-eat foods pick up bacteria from other foods, hands, cutting boards and utensils. The general rule is to always keep raw meat, poultry, fish, shellfish and eggs separate from other foods. Avoid cross-contamination with these steps:

- Don't chop fresh produce or any food that won't be fully cooked on a cutting board that was used for raw poultry, meat, fish or seafood without cleaning it first as directed above. Wash any knives or utensils that were used in hot, soapy water, too. See page 7 for cutting board and knife guidelines.

- Don't put cooked food on an unwashed plate that was used for raw meat, poultry, fish or seafood.

- Keep raw poultry, meat, fish or seafood separate from cooked and ready-to-eat foods in your grocery cart.

- Prevent leaks by repacking leaky packages and thawing foods in the refrigerator on a tray with sides that's large enough to catch all the juices.

- Wash sinks and sink mats with hot, soapy water if they've come in contact with raw poultry, meat, fish or seafood.

Keep Hot Food Hot

- Bacteria thrive at room temperature or in lukewarm food. Hot foods can't be left at room temperature for more than two hours, including preparation time. Keeping hot foods hot means keeping them at 140°F or higher.

- Don't partially cook perishable foods, then set them aside or refrigerate to finish cooking later. During cooking, the food may not reach a temperature high enough to destroy bacteria. Foods can be partially cooked in the microwave or parboiled only if the cooking process will continue immediately; this usually applies to grilling.

- Don't worry about the safety of the slow cooker. With direct heat from the pot, lengthy cooking times and steam created within the covered pot, harmful bacteria are killed. See also Slow Cooker Safety, page 506.

- Roast meat or poultry at 325°F or above. Lower temperatures can start bacterial growth before cooking is done. Cook meat and poultry completely, following the doneness times and temperatures recommended in this book. A dial or digital thermometer is helpful to make sure meat and poultry are done. See Thermometers, page 16.

Pitch It!
Do not taste leftover food that looks or smells strange to see if it's okay. When in doubt, throw it out!

- Keep cooked food hot, or refrigerate until ready to serve. This includes carryout foods, too.

- Reheat leftovers, stirring often, until steaming hot (165°F). Using a cover while reheating helps leftovers get hot in the center and retains moisture. Heat soups, sauces and gravies to a rolling boil, then boil for 1 minute, stirring constantly, before serving.

Keep Cold Food Cold

- Bacteria thrive at room temperature, so don't allow cold foods to stand at room temperature for more than two hours, including preparation time. Keeping cold foods cold means keeping them at 40°F or lower.

- The most perishable foods are eggs, milk, seafood, fish, meat and poultry or the dishes that contain them, like cream pies or seafood salad. When shopping, put perishables in the cart last. Put packages that can leak into plastic bags to prevent dripping on other foods in your cart.

- Take perishable foods straight home and refrigerate immediately. If the time from the store to home is longer than 30 minutes, bring a cooler with freezer packs or filled with ice and put perishable groceries inside. Making even short stops on the way home during hot weather can cause perishable groceries in a hot car to reach unsafe temperatures very quickly.

- Buy "keep refrigerated" foods only if they are in a refrigerated case and are cold to the touch. Follow the "keep refrigerated," "safe handling" and "use by" labels on these products; this includes carryout foods, too.

- Frozen foods should be frozen solid without lots of ice crystals, which indicates food may have thawed and refrozen.

- Foods will chill faster if there is space between them in the refrigerator or freezer. It also helps to divide large amounts into smaller amounts and store foods in shallow containers.

- Buy an appliance thermometer for all refrigerators and freezers. Refrigerators should register between 35°F and 40°F, and the freezer at 0°F or colder. If your electrical power goes out, keep the refrigerator and freezer doors closed to protect food. Refrigerated foods are safe for 4 to 6 hours. Foods in a fully stocked freezer are safe up to two days, but if half full, for only 24 hours.

- When cleaning your refrigerator or freezer, pack perishables in a cooler with freezer packs or filled with ice.

- Never thaw foods at room temperature—thaw only in the refrigerator or microwave following manufacturer's directions. If food is thawed in the microwave, cook it immediately.

Tips for Keeping Food Safe

Canned Foods: Don't buy or use food in leaking, bulging or badly dented cans, or in jars with cracks or loose or bulging lids. If there is doubt about a can of food, don't taste it! Return it to the store, and report it to your local health department.

Eggs: Store uncooked "do-ahead" recipes with raw eggs in the refrigerator for only up to 24 hours before cooking. Even though it's tempting, don't eat unbaked cookie dough or cake batter containing raw eggs.

Foods made with cooked eggs—cheesecakes, cream fillings, custards, quiches and potato salads—must be served hot or cold, depending on the recipe. Refrigerate leftovers immediately after serving. See also Egg Basics, page 74.

Raw eggs give some dishes, such as frosting, mousse and traditional Caesar salad, a unique texture. When making these recipes, don't use regular raw eggs. Use only pasteurized eggs, pasteurized egg products and substitutes found in the dairy or freezer case. It's also all right to use reconstituted dried eggs or egg whites.

Fruits and Vegetables: Wash with cold running water, using a scrub brush if necessary.

Ground Meat: Don't eat or taste raw ground meat—it's not safe. Cook ground meat thoroughly because being ground exposes more of the meat surface to bacteria. Make sure ground beef dishes like burgers and meatloaf are completely cooked to 160°F in the center of the thickest portion.

Ham: Most hams are fully cooked, but others need cooking. With so many varieties of hams, it can be confusing, so check the label. If you have any doubts, cook it to 165°F.

Luncheon Meats, Hot Dogs: Keep refrigerated, and use within two weeks. If the liquid that forms around hot dogs is cloudy, throw them out. Although hot dogs are fully cooked, reheat them until they're steaming hot all the way through.

Marinades: Marinate foods in a heavy plastic food-storage bag or nonmetal dish in the refrigerator, not at room temperature. Toss out leftover marinades or sauces that have had contact with raw meat, poultry, fish or seafood, or heat them to a rolling boil, then boil 1 minute, stirring constantly, before serving. Another option is to reserve some of the marinade or sauce before marinating; cover and refrigerate it until serving.

Milk: Keep fresh milk products refrigerated. You can store unopened evaporated milk and nonfat dry milk in the cupboard up to several months. Store whole dry milk in the refrigerator because it contains fat, which can become rancid, and use it within a few weeks. Don't drink unpasteurized milk or milk products because they can contain bacteria.

Poultry: Cook all poultry products according to the recipe or package directions. Ground poultry, like ground beef, is susceptible to bacterial contamination and must be cooked to at least 165°F in the center of the thickest portion. See the Poultry chapter for thawing, roasting and stuffing safety.

Safe Buffets

- Serve food at buffets in small dishes. Instead of adding fresh food to a dish that already has had food on it, wash the dish or use a different one.

- Keep foods hot (at least 140°F) with a slow cooker, fondue pot, chafing dish or warming tray. Warming units heated by canned cooking fuel are safe to use, but units heated with candles don't get hot enough to keep foods safe.

- Refrigerate salads made with seafood, poultry, meat and dairy products. Chill both the food and the dish before serving.

- Place containers of cold foods in crushed ice to keep them below 40°F.

- Hot or cold foods should not stand at room temperature for more than 2 hours. If you can't remember how long it's been sitting out, toss it.

- Store leftovers in the refrigerator for the amount of time recommended in the Refrigerator and Freezer Food Storage Chart on page 40.

- At restaurants or potlucks, salad bars and buffets should look clean. Make sure cold foods are cold and hot foods are steaming.

Safe Picnics and Packed Lunches

- Pack lunches in insulated lunch bags or in a small cooler with a freezer pack, frozen juice box or frozen small plastic bottle of water to keep food cold. Keep the bag or cooler out of the sun. Put perishable foods carried in an uninsulated lunch bag in the refrigerator.

- Wash thermal containers and rinse with boiling water after each use. Be sure hot foods are boiling when poured into these containers.

- Wash fruits and vegetables before packing.

- Chill picnic food *before* packing in a freezer-pack or ice-filled cooler. Because beverage coolers will be opened more frequently, use one cooler for beverages and one for perishable foods.

- Tightly wrap raw meat, poultry, fish and seafood, or pack them in a separate cooler, to keep them from dripping onto other foods. Bring along a bottle of instant hand sanitizer, moistened towelettes or a bottle filled with soapy water for washing hands and surfaces after handling raw poultry, meat, fish or seafood.

FOOD STORAGE

Storing Food in the Refrigerator and Freezer

The following tips and time chart are guides for keeping refrigerated and frozen foods safe. Having an appliance thermometer is handy for extra security; check it often to make sure appliances are maintaining proper temperatures.

For all foods, check sell-by and use-by dates on labels carefully. Discard if food is beyond the date shown.

Refrigerator

- Keep refrigerator temperature between 35°F and 40°F. Adjust the temperature to a colder setting after you've added large amounts of room-temperature or warm foods. Readjust to the normal setting after about 8 hours.

- Before putting food in the refrigerator, cover it or close the original container tightly to prevent the food from drying out or transferring odors to other foods. Store produce and strong-flavored foods in tightly covered containers or plastic bags.

- Keep foods in the refrigerator until just before you're ready to use them.

Freezer

- Keep freezer at 0°F or lower.

- Wrap food in plastic wrap, foil or freezer containers labeled for freezer.

- Label and date all packages and containers.

- To prevent freezer burn, remove as much air from packages as possible.

- Store purchased frozen foods in their original packages.

- Use foods that have been in the freezer the longest before using newer foods.

- Always thaw frozen meats, poultry and seafood in the refrigerator—never at room temperature. Or thaw food in your microwave following the manufacturer's directions, then cook immediately.

Refrigerated and Frozen Food Tips

Baked Products: Cool completely, then wrap tightly for storage. Allow frostings to set at room temperature, or freeze frosted baked goods uncovered *before* packaging to set them, then wrap and freeze.

- **Breads:** Refrigerate bread only during hot, humid weather. To thaw frozen bread, loosen wrap and let it stand at room temperature 2 to 3 hours.

- **Cakes:** Refrigerate cakes with custard filling; do not freeze these cakes because filling can separate. Cakes filled and frosted with plain sweetened whipped cream can be frozen. To thaw frozen unfrosted cakes, loosen wrap and let stand at room temperature 2 to 3 hours. To thaw frozen frosted cakes, loosen wrap and place overnight in refrigerator.

- **Cheesecakes:** Thaw frozen cheesecakes, wrapped, in refrigerator 4 to 6 hours.

- **Cookies:** Place delicate frosted or decorated cookies between layers of waxed paper in freezer containers. Thaw most cookies, covered, in container at room temperature 1 to 2 hours. For crisp cookies, remove from container to thaw.

- **Pies:** Many freeze well, but do not freeze custard, cream and unbaked pumpkin pies because they will separate and become watery.

  - **Frozen Unbaked Fruit Pies:** Unwrap and carefully cut slits in top crust. Bake at 425°F for 15 minutes. Reduce oven temperature to 375°F and bake 30 to 45 minutes longer or until crust is golden brown and juice begins to bubble through slits.

  - **Frozen Baked Fruit and Pecan Pies:** Unwrap and thaw at room temperature until completely thawed. Or unwrap and thaw at room temperature 1 hour, then heat in the oven at 375°F for 35 to 40 minutes or until warm.

  - **Frozen Baked Pumpkin Pies:** Unwrap and thaw 3 to 4 hours in the refrigerator.

Dairy Products: Check packages for the use-by or sell-by date, and refrigerate in their original containers.

- **Cream Cheese and Hard Cheese:** If hard cheese is moldy, trim ½ inch from the affected area and rewrap cheese tightly. Thaw frozen cheeses, wrapped, in refrigerator. Because texture becomes crumbly, use cheese that has been frozen only in baked goods such as casseroles, egg dishes, lasagna and pizza.

- **Ice Cream, Sorbet, Frozen Yogurt:** Freeze in original containers. To reduce ice crystals, place foil or plastic wrap directly on surface and cover. For best quality, do not thaw and refreeze.

- **Whipped Cream:** You can freeze both unsweetened and sweetened whipped cream. Drop small mounds of whipped cream onto waxed paper; freeze, then place in airtight container. To thaw, let stand about 15 minutes at room temperature.

Eggs: See Egg Basics, page 74.

Meat Products: Check packages for the use-by or sell-by date. If meat is wrapped in white butcher paper, unwrap and package tightly in plastic wrap, foil or plastic freezer bags.

REFRIGERATOR AND FREEZER FOOD STORAGE CHART

FOODS	REFRIGERATOR (35°F TO 40°F)	FREEZER (0°F OR BELOW)
Baked Products		
Breads, coffee cakes, muffins, quick breads and yeast breads	5 to 7 days	2 to 3 months
Cakes, unfrosted and frosted	3 to 5 days	Unfrosted—3 to 4 months Frosted—2 to 3 months
Cheesecakes, baked	3 to 5 days	4 to 5 months
Cookies, baked	Only if stated in recipe	Unfrosted—up to 12 months Frosted—up to 3 months
Pies—unbaked or baked fruit pies, baked pecan and baked pumpkin pies	Baked pumpkin pies, 3 to 5 days	Unbaked and baked fruit pies—up to 4 months
Dairy Products		
Cottage, and creamy ricotta	Up to 10 days	Not recommended
Hard cheese	3 to 4 weeks	6 to 8 weeks
Buttermilk, cream and milk	Up to 5 days	Not recommended
Sour cream and yogurt	Up to 1 week	Not recommended
Eggs		
Fresh eggs in shell	2 weeks	Not recommended
Cooked eggs in shell	1 week	Not recommended
Fats and Oils		
Butter	No longer than 2 weeks	No longer than 2 months
Margarine and spreads	No longer than 1 month	No longer than 2 months
Mayonnaise and salad dressing	No longer than 6 months	Not recommended
Meats		
Chops, uncooked	3 to 5 days	4 to 6 months
Ground, uncooked	1 to 2 days	3 to 4 months
Roasts and steaks, uncooked	3 to 5 days	6 to 12 months
Cooked	3 to 4 days	2 to 3 months
Cold cuts	Opened—3 to 5 days	Not recommended
	Unopened—2 weeks	Not recommended
Cured bacon	5 to 7 days	No longer than 1 month
Hot dogs	Opened—1 week	1 to 2 months
	Unopened—2 weeks	1 to 2 months
Ham		
Whole or half (cooked)	5 to 7 days	1 to 2 months
Slices (cooked)	3 to 4 days	1 to 2 months
Poultry		
Whole (including game birds, ducks and geese), uncooked	1 to 2 days	No longer than 12 months
Cut up, uncooked	1 to 2 days	No longer than 9 months
Cooked	3 to 4 days	4 months
Seafood		
Uncooked fish	1 to 2 days	3 to 6 months
Cooked and breaded fish	Store in freezer	2 to 3 months
Uncooked shellfish	1 to 2 days	3 to 4 months
Cooked shellfish	3 to 4 days	1 to 2 months

CHAPTER 2

APPETIZERS & BEVERAGES

APPETIZERS

BEVERAGES

CHARTS AND FEATURES

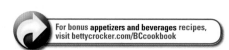

For bonus **appetizers and beverages** recipes,
visit bettycrocker.com/BCcookbook

FAST = Ready in 20 minutes or less LOWER CALORIE = See Helpful Nutrition and Cooking Information, page 685
LIGHTER = 25% fewer calories or grams of fat MAKE AHEAD = Make-ahead directions SLOW COOKER = Slow cooker directions

← Crostini with chopped fresh tomato and basil leaves, Chicken Satay with Peanut Sauce (page 62), Tex-Mex Layered
Dip (page 48), Baked Coconut Shrimp (page 64)

APPETIZER BASICS

Hot-from-the-oven morsels . . . cool and creamy dips . . . sweet or savory snack mixes. The world of appetizers includes a mouthwatering assortment of tastes and textures. Appetizers can be elegant hors d'ouevres suitable for a cocktail party, finger foods for a casual gathering or a snack to tide the family over until dinnertime. No matter the occasion, they're an enticing way to awaken people's taste buds.

ALL KINDS OF APPETIZERS

There are many names given to appetizers, depending on where you live and the specific type of food involved. The appealing array of these tasty treasures includes the following:

Canapés: Small pieces of toast, bread, crackers or baked pastry topped with various cheeses, an anchovy or some type of spread. They can be hot or cold, simple or elaborate.

Charcuterie: French for "cooker of meat." Served as an appetizer platter, this includes thinly sliced meats (often cured), pâtés and rilettes (a paste of meat, poultry or fish cooked in seasoned fat). Often served with pickled vegetables, breads, crostini and mustard.

Crudités: Raw veggies cut into slices, sticks or pieces, usually served with a dip or flavored oil.

Dips and Dunks: Not too thin or too thick, these tasty mixtures are perfect for dipping chips, vegetables and fruit.

Finger Foods: No forks, spoons or knives required. Try Bruschetta, page 46, or Basil-Cheese Triangles, page 57.

First Course: Appetizer served at a sit-down meal. Instead of a traditional appetizer, the first course could be a small serving of a main dish, salad or soup.

Hors d'Oeuvres: French for "outside the work." These are bite-size foods eaten apart from the regular meal, often with cocktails.

Meze (Mezze): Greek name for appetizers or hors d'oeuvres and usually served as a selection of small dishes. These often include hummus, yogurt, cheeses, roasted and pickled vegetables, olives, breads, meats and seafood. These foods can vary widely based on the country of origin.

Salumi: Italian-style cured or preserved meats, including coppa, pancetta and prosciutto. Salumi platters are often served as "antipasto" in contemporary Italian restaurants. Platters may include cheeses and pickled vegetables similar to charcuterie.

Spreads: Unlike dips, spreads are thick, so a knife is needed to spread them on bread or hearty crackers.

Tapas: A popular appetizer style in Spain that consists of small plates of food, often one or two bites each. They can be simple or complex. A collection of these tasty bites can create an entire meal.

A selection of appetizers arranged on a platter

ROASTED GARLIC LOWER CALORIE

Roasting garlic turns it into a sweet and delicious spread. Garlic bulbs (heads of garlic) are made up of as many as 15 sections called cloves.

PREP 10 min **TOTAL** 1 hr • **2 to 8 servings**

- 1 to 4 bulbs garlic
- 2 teaspoons olive or vegetable oil for each bulb garlic
  Salt and pepper to taste
  Sliced French bread, if desired

1 Heat oven to 350°F. Carefully peel paper-like skin from around each bulb of garlic, leaving just enough to hold garlic cloves together. Cut ¼- to ½-inch slice from top of each bulb to expose cloves. Place cut side up on 12-inch square of foil.

2 Drizzle 2 teaspoons oil over each bulb. Sprinkle with salt and pepper. Wrap securely in foil. Place in pie plate or shallow baking pan.

3 Bake 45 to 50 minutes or until garlic is tender when pierced with toothpick or fork. Let stand until cool enough to handle. To serve, gently squeeze soft garlic out of cloves. To serve, spread garlic on bread.

1 Serving: Calories 70; Total Fat 4.5g (Saturated Fat 0.5g; Trans Fat 0g); Cholesterol 0mg; Sodium 300mg; Total Carbohydrate 6g (Dietary Fiber 0g); Protein 1g **Exchanges:** 1 Vegetable, 1 Fat **Carbohydrate Choices:** ½

CINNAMON-SPICE SUGARED NUTS

PREP 10 min **TOTAL** 40 min • **2 cups nuts**

- 1 tablespoon slightly beaten egg white
- 2 cups pecan halves, unblanched whole almonds or walnut halves
- ¼ cup sugar
- 2 teaspoons ground cinnamon
- ¼ teaspoon ground nutmeg
- ¼ teaspoon ground cloves

1 Heat oven to 300°F. In medium bowl, stir egg white and nuts until nuts are coated and sticky.

2 In small bowl, stir remaining ingredients until well mixed; sprinkle over nuts. Stir until nuts are completely coated. In ungreased 15x10x1-inch pan, spread nuts in single layer.

3 Bake uncovered about 30 minutes or until toasted (nut coating becomes crunchy during baking and cooling). Serve slightly warm or cool completely. Store in airtight container at room temperature up to 3 weeks.

¼ Cup: Calories 210; Total Fat 18g (Saturated Fat 1.5g; Trans Fat 0g); Cholesterol 0mg; Sodium 0mg; Total Carbohydrate 10g (Dietary Fiber 3g); Protein 3g **Exchanges:** ½ Other Carbohydrate, ½ High-Fat Meat, 3 Fat **Carbohydrate Choices:** ½

CINNAMON-CARDAMOM MIXED NUTS

Substitute lightly salted mixed nuts for the pecans and ground cardamom for the nutmeg. Omit cloves.

Cutting Garlic

Carefully peel papery skin from around each bulb of garlic, leaving just enough to hold garlic cloves together.

Cut ¼- to ½-inch slice from top of each bulb to expose cloves.

Roasted Garlic

Cinnamon-Spice Sugared Nuts and
Southwestern Spiced Party Nuts

Tomato-Basil Crostini

SOUTHWESTERN SPICED PARTY NUTS FAST

PREP 10 min **TOTAL** 20 min • **2¼ cups nuts**

- 1 can (9.5 to 11.5 oz) salted mixed nuts
- 1 tablespoon butter, melted
- 2 teaspoons chili powder
- ½ teaspoon garlic powder
- ½ teaspoon onion powder
- ¼ teaspoon ground cinnamon
- ¼ teaspoon ground red pepper (cayenne)
- 2 tablespoons sugar

1 Heat oven to 300°F. In medium bowl, mix nuts and butter until nuts are coated. In small bowl, mix remaining ingredients except sugar; sprinkle over nuts. Stir until nuts are completely coated. In ungreased 15x10x1-inch pan, spread nuts in single layer.

2 Bake uncovered about 10 minutes or until nuts are toasted. Return to medium bowl. While nuts are still hot, sprinkle with sugar and toss to coat. Serve warm, or cool completely, about 1 hour. Store in airtight container at room temperature up to 3 weeks.

¼ Cup: Calories 250; Total Fat 21g (Saturated Fat 3.5g; Trans Fat 0g); Cholesterol 0mg; Sodium 240mg; Total Carbohydrate 11g (Dietary Fiber 3g); Protein 6g **Exchanges:** 1 Starch, ½ High-Fat Meat, 3 Fat **Carbohydrate Choices:** 1

SOUTHWESTERN SPICED CASHEWS
Substitute salted whole cashews for the mixed nuts.

TOMATO-BASIL CROSTINI FAST

Capers are the flower buds of the caper bush. Some are not much larger than the end of a cotton swab; others are twice that size. After harvesting they are packed in brine. Look for them in the pickle aisle.

PREP 15 min **TOTAL** 25 min • **12 appetizers**

- 12 slices Italian bread, each ½ inch thick
- ¼ cup olive or vegetable oil
- 1 large tomato, seeded, chopped (1 cup)
- 3 tablespoons chopped fresh basil leaves
- 1 tablespoon large capers or chopped pitted ripe olives
- ½ teaspoon salt
- ½ teaspoon coarsely ground pepper
- 12 slices (1 oz each) regular or fresh mozzarella cheese

1 Heat oven to 375°F. On ungreased cookie sheet, place bread slices in single layer. Drizzle 1 teaspoon oil over each bread slice.

2 In small bowl, mix tomato, basil, capers, salt and pepper. Spread half of tomato mixture over bread slices; top each with cheese slice. Spread remaining tomato mixture over cheese. Bake about 8 minutes or until bread is hot and cheese is melted. Serve hot.

1 Appetizer: Calories 180; Total Fat 11g (Saturated Fat 4.5g; Trans Fat 0g); Cholesterol 15mg; Sodium 390mg; Total Carbohydrate 12g (Dietary Fiber 0g); Protein 9g **Exchanges:** 1 Starch, 1 High-Fat Meat **Carbohydrate Choices:** 1

PROVOLONE-ONION CROSTINI Substitute
a chopped green onion for the capers and provolone cheese for the mozzarella.

BRUSCHETTA EIGHT WAYS

Brush tops of 30 baguette slices with olive oil. Toast in oven at 375°F for 8 to 10 minutes or until lightly browned and crisp.

1 Artichoke Bruschetta: Spread toasted baguette slices with Hot Artichoke Dip (page 51, or purchased dip). Sprinkle with shredded or shaved Asiago or Parmesan cheese. Serve as is, or broil about 1 minute or until cheese is melted. For a different flavor, substitute Spinach Dip (page 47, or purchased dip).

2 Beef Tenderloin Bruschetta: Spread toasted baguette slices with chive-and-onion cream cheese spread thinned with a small amount of milk, or use Creamy Horseradish Sauce (page 483). Top with thinly sliced beef tenderloin or roast beef, thinly sliced or chopped plum (Roma) tomato and chopped fresh parsley.

3 Black Bean Cotija Bruschetta: Spread toasted baguette slices with purchased black bean dip or refried black beans; top with Salsa (page 480, or purchased salsa). Sprinkle with crumbled Cotija cheese or shredded Cheddar and whole or chopped fresh cilantro leaves. For another taste, substitute Guacamole (page 48, or purchased guacamole) for the dip or refried beans.

4 BLT Bruschetta: Spread toasted baguette slices with mayonnaise or salad dressing. Top with shredded lettuce, well-drained chopped seeded tomato and crumbled cooked bacon or bacon bits.

5 Brie, Raspberry and Pear Bruschetta: Lightly spread toasted baguette slices with seedless raspberry preserves. Top with thinly sliced pear and thin slices of Brie cheese. Serve as is, or broil about 1 minute or just until cheese is melted.

6 Caramelized Onion–Gorgonzola Bruschetta: Top toasted baguette slices with Caramelized Onions (page 598). Sprinkle with crumbled Gorgonzola or blue cheese. Serve as is, or broil about 1 minute or just until cheese is melted.

7 Pesto-Mascarpone Bruschetta: Spread toasted baguette slices with mascarpone cheese or softened cream cheese. Spoon Basil, Spinach or Sun-Dried Tomato Pesto (page 484, or purchased pesto) over cheese. Sprinkle with chopped red bell pepper and toasted pine nuts.

8 Smoked Salmon Bruschetta: Arrange thinly sliced smoked salmon on toasted baguette slices. Top with dollop of sour cream or crème fraîche; sprinkle lightly with grated lemon peel and chopped fresh chives or small sprigs of fresh dill.

GRILLED ANTIPASTI PLATTER WITH LEMON AIOLI

PREP 35 min TOTAL 1 hr 45 min • **10 servings**

LEMON AIOLI

1 cup mayonnaise or salad dressing
1 teaspoon grated lemon peel
2 tablespoons fresh lemon juice
1 to 2 cloves garlic, finely chopped

ANTIPASTI

1 medium zucchini, cut into 4-inch sticks
1 medium yellow summer squash or crookneck squash, cut into 4-inch sticks
1 medium red bell pepper, cut into 2-inch pieces
2 cups cherry or grape tomatoes
1 cup small whole mushrooms
1 medium red onion, cut into ½-inch wedges
2 tablespoons olive or vegetable oil
1 teaspoon salt
20 thin slices hard salami (about ¼ lb)
½ lb mozzarella cheese, cut into ½-inch cubes

1 In small bowl, stir all aioli ingredients until well mixed. Cover and refrigerate at least 1 hour before serving.

2 Heat coals or gas grill for direct heat (see Grilling Basics, page 304).

3 In large bowl, toss vegetables with oil and salt. Heat grill basket (grill "wok") on grill until hot. Add vegetables to grill basket. Cover and grill vegetables 6 to 10 minutes, shaking basket or stirring vegetables occasionally, until vegetables are crisp-tender and lightly charred.

4 Arrange salami around edge of large serving platter. Mound grilled vegetables onto center of serving platter. Sprinkle cheese cubes over vegetables. Serve with aioli for dipping.

1 Serving: Calories 320; Total Fat 28g (Saturated Fat 7g; Trans Fat 0g); Cholesterol 35mg; Sodium 670mg; Total Carbohydrate 7g (Dietary Fiber 2g); Protein 10g **Exchanges:** 1 Vegetable, 1 High-Fat Meat, 4 Fat **Carbohydrate Choices:** ½

PROVOLONE-PROSCIUTTO PLATTER

Substitute prosciutto for the salami and cubes of smoked provolone for the mozzarella cheese.

SPINACH DIP LOWER CALORIE

PREP 15 min TOTAL 4 hr 15 min • **3½ cups dip**

1 box (9 oz) frozen chopped spinach, thawed
1 cup mayonnaise or salad dressing
1 cup sour cream
1 package (1.4 oz) vegetable soup and recipe mix
1 can (8 oz) water chestnuts, drained, chopped
1 medium green onion, chopped (1 tablespoon)
1 round uncut loaf bread (about 1 lb), if desired

1 Squeeze thawed spinach to drain; spread on paper towels and pat dry. In large bowl, stir spinach, mayonnaise, sour cream, soup mix (dry), water chestnuts and onion until well mixed. Cover and refrigerate at least 4 hours to blend flavors and soften soup mix.

2 Cut 1- to 2-inch slice from top of bread loaf; hollow out loaf, leaving ½- to 1-inch shell of bread on sides and bottom. Reserve scooped-out bread and top of loaf; cut or tear into pieces to use for dipping. Spoon spinach dip into hollowed-out loaf. Arrange bread pieces around loaf.

1 Tablespoon: Calories 40; Total Fat 4g (Saturated Fat 1g; Trans Fat 0g); Cholesterol 5mg; Sodium 80mg; Total Carbohydrate 1g (Dietary Fiber 0g); Protein 0g **Exchanges:** 1 Fat **Carbohydrate Choices:** 0

LIGHTER **DIRECTIONS** For 2 grams of fat and 30 calories per serving, use reduced-fat mayonnaise and sour cream.

Grilled Antipasti Platter with Lemon Aioli

GUACAMOLE FAST LOWER CALORIE

PREP 20 min TOTAL 20 min • **2 cups dip**

- 1 small jalapeño chile*
- 2 ripe large avocados
- 2 tablespoons fresh lime or lemon juice
- 2 tablespoons finely chopped fresh cilantro
- ¼ to ½ teaspoon salt
  Dash pepper
- 1 small clove garlic, finely chopped
- 1 small tomato, seeded, chopped (½ cup)
- 2 tablespoons finely chopped red onion
  Tortilla chips, if desired

Cutting an Avocado

Cut avocado lengthwise through skin and flesh around pit.

With hands, slowly twist both sides of avocado to separate.

Carefully slide table teaspoon under pit to remove.

With knife, make criss-cross cuts through flesh; remove with spoon.

Guacamole

1 Remove stems, seeds and ribs from chile; chop chile. Cut avocados lengthwise in half; remove pit and peel. In medium glass or plastic bowl, mash avocados with fork. Stir in chile and remaining ingredients except tortilla chips until mixed.

2 Press and smooth plastic wrap directly on surface of guacamole to help prevent discoloration. Serve with tortilla chips.

*1 tablespoon canned chopped green chiles can be substituted for the jalapeño chile.

1 Tablespoon: Calories 15; Total Fat 1g (Saturated Fat 0g; Trans Fat 0g); Cholesterol 0mg; Sodium 15mg; Total Carbohydrate 0g (Dietary Fiber 0g); Protein 0g **Exchanges:** Free **Carbohydrate Choices:** 0

COTIJA GUACAMOLE Stir in ½ cup crumbled Cotija cheese with remaining ingredients in Step 1.

TEX-MEX LAYERED DIP

FAST LOWER CALORIE

Add extra garnishes to the top of this party dip like chopped avocado, sliced olives and fresh cilantro.

PREP 20 min TOTAL 20 min • **32 servings**

- 1 can (15.5 oz) refried black beans with lime juice
- 2 tablespoons chunky-style salsa
- 1½ cups sour cream
- 1 cup Guacamole (above, or purchased guacamole)
- 1 cup shredded Cheddar cheese (4 oz)
- 1 small tomato, seeded, chopped (½ cup)
- 2 medium green onions, chopped (2 tablespoons)
  Tortilla chips

1 In small bowl, mix black beans and salsa. Spoon in thin layer over 12- or 13-inch serving plate.

2 Spoon sour cream over beans, leaving about 1-inch border of beans around edge. Spread guacamole over sour cream, leaving border of sour cream showing.

3 Sprinkle cheese, tomato and onions over guacamole. Serve immediately, or cover with plastic wrap and refrigerate up to 2 hours. Serve with tortilla chips.

1 Serving (2 Tablespoons Dip and 3 Tortilla Chips): Calories 90; Total Fat 6g (Saturated Fat 2.5g; Trans Fat 0g); Cholesterol 10mg; Sodium 140mg; Total Carbohydrate 7g (Dietary Fiber 1g); Protein 3g **Exchanges:** ½ Starch, 1 Fat **Carbohydrate Choices:** ½

Hummus

HUMMUS FAST LOWER CALORIE

Tahini, a thick paste made from ground sesame seed, gives this dip its distinctive flavor. Look for tahini in the condiment, ethnic-foods or pickle aisle.

PREP 5 min TOTAL 5 min • **2 cups dip**

- 1 can (15 to 16 oz) garbanzo beans, drained, ¼ cup liquid reserved
- ½ cup tahini*
- ¼ cup olive oil
- 2 cloves garlic, finely chopped
- 3 tablespoons lemon juice
- 1 teaspoon salt
- ⅛ teaspoon pepper
  Chopped fresh parsley
  Pita bread wedges, crackers or fresh vegetables, if desired

1 In blender or food processor, place beans, reserved bean liquid, tahini, oil, garlic, lemon juice, salt and pepper. Cover and blend on high speed, stopping blender occasionally to scrape sides, until smooth.

2 Spoon into serving dish. Garnish with parsley. Serve with pita bread wedges.

*½ cup sesame seed can be substituted for the tahini, but the hummus will not be smooth.

2 Tablespoons: Calories 60; Total Fat 3g (Saturated Fat 0g; Trans Fat 0g); Cholesterol 0mg; Sodium 85mg; Total Carbohydrate 6g (Dietary Fiber 1g); Protein 2g **Exchanges:** 1 Vegetable, ½ Fat **Carbohydrate Choices:** ½

CUMIN HUMMUS Add ¼ teaspoon ground cumin with the salt and pepper. Omit parsley. Sprinkle with cumin seed if desired.

See how to make **hummus**: Visit bettycrocker.com/BCcookbook

ROASTED GARLIC HUMMUS Stir 1 to 2 tablespoons Roasted Garlic (page 44) into blended mixture.

SUN-DRIED TOMATO HUMMUS Stir ⅓ cup chopped drained sun-dried tomatoes (packed in oil) into blended mixture.

CREAMY FRUIT DIP FAST

PREP 5 min TOTAL 5 min • **1½ cups dip**

- 1 package (8 oz) cream cheese, softened
- 1 jar (7 oz) marshmallow creme
- 1 tablespoon milk

In medium bowl, beat all ingredients with electric mixer on medium speed until smooth and creamy.

2 Tablespoons: Calories 120; Total Fat 7g (Saturated Fat 4g; Trans Fat 0g); Cholesterol 20mg; Sodium 65mg; Total Carbohydrate 14g (Dietary Fiber 0g); Protein 2g **Exchanges:** 1 Starch, 1 Fat **Carbohydrate Choices:** 1

CREAMY CINNAMON FRUIT DIP Add ¼ teaspoon ground cinnamon.

CREAMY GINGERED FRUIT DIP Add 2 tablespoons finely chopped crystallized ginger.

CREAMY LEMON FRUIT DIP Substitute lemon juice for the milk and add 1 teaspoon grated lemon peel.

CREAMY ORANGE FRUIT DIP Substitute orange juice for the milk and add 1 teaspoon grated orange peel.

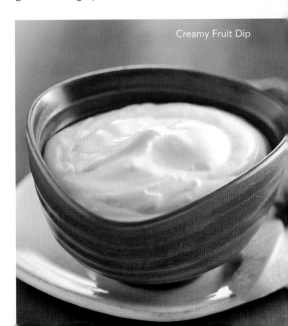

Creamy Fruit Dip

TOP A BLOCK OF CREAM CHEESE

Place an 8-ounce block of cream cheese (or cut in half) on 8-inch serving plate and let stand 15 to 30 minutes at room temperature to soften. Top with any of the following great combinations and serve with assorted crackers.

California-Roll Cream Cheese Spread: Spread thin layer of wasabi sauce or wasabi-flavored mayonnaise (page 287) on top of cream cheese if desired. Top with chopped imitation crabmeat, shredded carrot, chopped cucumber and sliced green onion. Drizzle very lightly with seasoned rice vinegar. Top with diced avocado and toasted sesame seed.

California-Roll Cream Cheese Spread

Chutney–Toasted Coconut Cream Cheese Spread

Chutney–Toasted Coconut Cream Cheese Spread: Top with purchased mango chutney, golden raisins, sliced green onion, fresh cilantro leaves, toasted coconut (page 18) and cashews.

Jalapeño Pepper Jelly Cream Cheese Spread: Top with red or green jalapeño pepper jelly. Any of your favorite jellies, jams or preserves can be substituted.

Lox, Caper and Red Onion Cream Cheese Spread: Top with chopped lox, well-drained small capers, finely chopped red onion and finely chopped Hard-Cooked Egg (page 74).

Olive Tapenade Cream Cheese Spread: Top with purchased olive tapenade, diced salami if desired, diced red, orange or yellow bell pepper and fresh basil or parsley.

Raspberry-Chipotle Cream Cheese Spread: Top with purchased raspberry-chipotle sauce. Or stir finely chopped chipotles in adobo sauce (from 7-ounce can) or ground chipotle powder into raspberry preserves to taste.

CURRIED CHEESE SPREAD FAST

PREP 15 min TOTAL 15 min • **2 cups spread**

- 1 package (8 oz) cream cheese, softened
- 1 cup shredded Havarti or Monterey Jack cheese (4 oz)
- 1 teaspoon curry powder
- 1/8 teaspoon ground red pepper (cayenne)
- 1/8 teaspoon garlic powder
- 2 tablespoons mango chutney
- 1 teaspoon chopped fresh cilantro
- 1 tablespoon sliced almonds, toasted (page 22)
  Assorted crackers or fresh vegetables, if desired

1 In medium bowl, beat cream cheese, Havarti cheese, curry powder, red pepper and garlic powder with electric mixer on medium speed until smooth and well blended.

2 Spread cheese mixture in 6-inch circle, about ½ inch thick, on 8-inch serving plate. Spread chutney over cheese. Sprinkle with cilantro and almonds. Serve with crackers.

2 Tablespoons: Calories 90; Total Fat 8g (Saturated Fat 5g; Trans Fat 0g); Cholesterol 25mg; Sodium 95mg; Total Carbohydrate 1g (Dietary Fiber 0g); Protein 3g **Exchanges:** ½ High-Fat Meat, 1 Fat **Carbohydrate Choices:** 0

LIGHTER **DIRECTIONS** For 4 grams of fat and 55 calories per serving, use reduced-fat cream cheese (Neufchâtel) and substitute reduced-fat Cheddar cheese for the Havarti cheese.

CHEESE BALL

PREP 20 min TOTAL 10 hr 50 min • **16 servings**

- 2 packages (8 oz each) cream cheese
- 3/4 cup crumbled blue, Gorgonzola or feta cheese (4 oz)
- 1 cup shredded sharp Cheddar cheese (4 oz)
- 1 small onion, finely chopped (1/3 cup)
- 1 tablespoon Worcestershire sauce
- 1/2 cup chopped fresh parsley
  Assorted crackers, if desired

1 Place cheeses in medium bowl; let stand at room temperature about 30 minutes or until softened. Beat onion and Worcestershire sauce into cheeses with electric mixer on low speed until mixed. Beat on medium speed 1 to 2 minutes, scraping bowl frequently, until fluffy. Cover and refrigerate at least 8 hours until firm enough to shape into ball.

2 Shape cheese mixture into 1 large ball. Roll in parsley; place on serving plate. Cover and refrigerate about 2 hours or until firm. Serve with crackers.

2 Tablespoons: Calories 160; Total Fat 14g (Saturated Fat 9g; Trans Fat 0g); Cholesterol 45mg; Sodium 240mg; Total Carbohydrate 2g (Dietary Fiber 0g); Protein 6g **Exchanges:** 1 High-Fat Meat, 1 Fat **Carbohydrate Choices:** 0

LIGHTER **DIRECTIONS** For 3 grams of fat and 65 calories per serving, use fat-free cream cheese and reduced-fat Cheddar cheese.

PEPPER JACK CHEESE BALL Substitute ¾ cup shredded pepper jack cheese for the blue cheese. Omit Worcestershire sauce. Substitute cilantro for the parsley.

HOT ARTICHOKE DIP

LOWER CALORIE

To save time, mix ingredients in a microwave-safe casserole. Cover with plastic wrap, folding one edge or corner back ¼ inch to vent steam. Microwave on Medium-High (70%) for 4 to 5 minutes, stirring after 2 minutes, until hot.

PREP 10 min **TOTAL** 35 min • **1½ cups dip**

- ½ cup mayonnaise or salad dressing
- ½ cup grated Parmesan cheese
- 4 medium green onions, chopped (¼ cup)
- 1 can (about 14 oz) artichoke hearts, drained, coarsely chopped
  Crackers or cocktail rye bread, if desired

1 Heat oven to 350°F. In small bowl, stir mayonnaise and cheese until well mixed. Stir in onions and artichoke hearts. Spoon into ungreased 1-quart casserole.

2 Cover and bake 20 to 25 minutes or until hot. Serve warm with crackers.

1 Tablespoon: Calories 50; Total Fat 4.5g (Saturated Fat 1g; Trans Fat 0g); Cholesterol 0mg; Sodium 115mg; Total Carbohydrate 2g (Dietary Fiber 0g); Protein 2g **Exchanges:** 1 Fat **Carbohydrate Choices:** 0

LIGHTER **DIRECTIONS** For 1 gram of fat and 20 calories per serving, use ⅓ cup plain fat-free yogurt and 3 tablespoons reduced-fat mayonnaise for the ½ cup mayonnaise.

HOT ARTICHOKE-SPINACH DIP Increase mayonnaise and Parmesan cheese to 1 cup each. Stir in 1 box (9 oz) frozen chopped spinach, thawed (squeeze thawed spinach to drain; spread on paper towels and pat dry). Spoon into ungreased 1-quart casserole. Bake as directed.

Cheese Ball

Hot Artichoke-Spinach Dip

Learn to Make **Deviled Eggs**

DEVILED EGGS LOWER CALORIE

Deviled eggs are a great appetizer choice, no matter what the occasion. From fresh herbs to assertive wasabi, you can flavor the egg yolk filling in so many ways, appealing to any taste. Knowing how to make hard-cooked eggs with bright, yellow yolks ensures excellent results.

PREP 15 min **TOTAL** 30 min • **12 appetizers**

6 **large eggs**
3 **tablespoons mayonnaise, salad dressing or half-and-half**

1 **teaspoon yellow, Dijon or spicy brown mustard***
⅛ **teaspoon pepper**

1 Place eggs in single layer in 2-quart saucepan. Cover with cold water at least 1 inch above eggs. Cover saucepan; heat to boiling.

2 Immediately remove from heat; let stand covered 15 minutes (12 minutes for medium and 18 minutes for extra-large).

3 Drain. Immediately place eggs in cold water with ice cubes or run cold water over eggs until completely cooled.

4 To peel, gently tap egg on countertop until entire shell is finely crackled. Roll gently between hands to loosen shell. Starting at large end, peel egg under cold running water to help remove shell.

5 Cut lengthwise in half. Slip out yolks into small bowl; mash with fork. To prevent eggs from tipping on the serving plate, cut a thin slice from the bottom of each egg white half before filling. Or, to stand eggs upright, cut

crosswise slice about ⅔ from top of narrow end of egg to remove yolk; cut thin slice from bottom of wide end of egg white to rest on serving platter.

6 Stir mayonnaise, mustard and pepper into yolks. Fill whites with egg yolk mixture, heaping it lightly. Cover and refrigerate up to 24 hours.

*Any flavored prepared mustard can be used or ½ teaspoon ground mustard can be substituted for yellow mustard

1 Appetizer: Calories 60; Total Fat 5g (Saturated Fat 1g; Trans Fat 0g); Cholesterol 110mg; Sodium 75mg; Total Carbohydrate 0g (Dietary Fiber 0g); Protein 3g **Exchanges:** ½ Medium-Fat Meat, ½ Fat **Carbohydrate Choices:** 0

Keys to Success

- **Buy eggs 7 to 10 days ahead of time** for easier peeling. This gives eggs time to take in air, which helps separate the membranes from the shell.

- **Heat just to boiling** to prevent eggs from cracking. If left to boil, the bubbles toss the eggs around in the pan, which can cause their shells to crack.

- **For the easiest peeling,** peel hard-cooked eggs as soon as they are cool enough to handle.

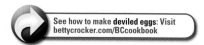
See how to make **deviled eggs:** Visit bettycrocker.com/BCcookbook

MORE DEVILED EGGS

Turn your appetizer platter into a flavor bonanza. Choose one or several of the flavor combinations here and delight your guests.

1 Lighter Deviled Eggs: For 1 gram of fat and 25 calories per serving, mash only 6 yolk halves in Step 5 (reserve remaining yolks for another use or discard). Use fat-free mayonnaise. Stir in ⅓ cup finely chopped zucchini.

2 Bacon-Cheddar Deviled Eggs: Mix 2 to 3 slices crisply cooked crumbled bacon and 2 tablespoons finely shredded Cheddar cheese into yolk mixture. Garnish with additional crumbled bacon or chopped fresh chives or parsley.

3 Blue Cheese Deviled Eggs: Omit mustard. Mix ¼ cup crumbled blue cheese into yolk mixture. Garnish with coarse ground black pepper and small celery leaves.

4 Chipotle Deviled Eggs: Omit mustard. Mix 1½ to 2 teaspoons finely chopped chipotle chiles in adobo sauce (from 7-ounce can), drained, and 1 thinly sliced green onion into yolk mixture. Garnish with whole or chopped cilantro leaves.

5 Curried Deviled Eggs: Omit mustard. Mix 2 tablespoons mango chutney (finely chop larger pieces of fruit if needed) and ¼ teaspoon curry powder into egg yolk mixture. Garnish with cashews or dry-roasted peanuts.

6 Fresh Herb Deviled Eggs: Mix 1 teaspoon each chopped fresh chives, parsley and dill into egg yolk mixture. If desired, substitute basil or marjoram for the dill. Garnish with additional fresh herbs.

7 Ham and Veggie Deviled Eggs: Mix 1 tablespoon each finely chopped red bell pepper, green bell pepper and cooked ham into egg yolk mixture. Garnish with additional chopped bell pepper.

8 Reuben Deviled Eggs: Omit mustard. Substitute Thousand Island salad dressing for the mayonnaise. Stir in 2 tablespoons each finely chopped thinly sliced cooked corned beef and finely chopped sauerkraut (squeezed in paper towel to drain). Garnish with shredded Swiss cheese and caraway seeds.

9 Taco Deviled Eggs: Omit mustard. Increase mayonnaise to ¼ cup. Mix 1 teaspoon dry taco seasoning mix into yolk mixture. Stir in 1 tablespoon well-drained chopped ripe olives, 2 tablespoons well-drained diced seeded tomato and 1 thinly sliced green onion. Garnish with a drizzle of taco sauce or small spoonful of salsa and diced avocado.

10 Wasabi Deviled Eggs: Omit mustard. Mix 1 teaspoon wasabi paste and 1 teaspoon milk into egg yolk mixture. Garnish with thin slices Pickled Gingerroot (page 253), wasabi peas and black sesame seeds.

11 Zesty Deviled Eggs: Mix ½ cup finely shredded cheese, 2 tablespoons chopped fresh parsley and 1 to 2 teaspoons prepared horseradish into egg yolk mixture. Garnish with additional cheese or parsley.

LAYERED PIZZA DIP FAST

PREP 10 min TOTAL 15 min • **16 servings**

- 1 package (8 oz) cream cheese, softened
- ½ cup pizza sauce
- 2 cloves garlic, finely chopped
- ½ cup chopped pepperoni
- 1 can (2.25 oz) sliced ripe olives, drained
- ⅓ cup finely diced red bell pepper
- 5 medium green onions, sliced (⅓ cup)
- ½ cup shredded mozzarella cheese (2 oz)
- ¼ cup shredded fresh basil leaves
  Hard breadsticks or tortilla chips, if desired

1 Set oven control to broil. In small bowl, stir cream cheese, pizza sauce and garlic until well mixed. Spread in thin layer on 12- or 13-inch ovenproof serving plate. Top with pepperoni, olives, bell pepper and onions. Sprinkle with mozzarella cheese.

2 Broil with top 4 inches from heat 1 to 2 minutes or until mozzarella cheese is melted. Sprinkle with basil. Serve immediately with breadsticks.

1 Serving: Calories 90; Total Fat 8g (Saturated Fat 4.5g; Trans Fat 0g); Cholesterol 20mg; Sodium 200mg; Total Carbohydrate 2g (Dietary Fiber 0g); Protein 3g **Exchanges:** ½ High-Fat Meat, 1 Fat **Carbohydrate Choices:** 0

MAKE AHEAD **DIRECTIONS** Assemble this dip on an ovenproof plate up to 24 hours ahead of time; cover tightly with plastic wrap and store in refrigerator. Broil as directed.

Layered Pizza Dip

HOT CRAB DIP LOWER CALORIE

PREP 15 min TOTAL 35 min • **2½ cups dip**

- 1 package (8 oz) cream cheese, softened
- ¼ cup grated Parmesan cheese
- ¼ cup mayonnaise or salad dressing
- ¼ cup dry white wine or nonalcoholic white wine
- 2 teaspoons sugar
- 1 teaspoon ground mustard
- 4 medium green onions, thinly sliced (¼ cup)
- 1 clove garlic, finely chopped
- 1 can (6 oz) crabmeat, drained, cartilage removed and flaked
- ⅓ cup sliced almonds, toasted (page 22)
  Assorted crackers or fresh vegetables, if desired

1 Heat oven to 375°F. In medium bowl, stir all ingredients except crabmeat, almonds and crackers until well blended. Stir in crabmeat.

2 Spread mixture in ungreased 9-inch pie plate or shallow 1-quart casserole. Sprinkle with almonds. Bake uncovered 15 to 20 minutes or until hot and bubbly. Serve with crackers.

1 Tablespoon: Calories 45; Total Fat 4g (Saturated Fat 1.5g; Trans Fat 0g); Cholesterol 10mg; Sodium 50mg; Total Carbohydrate 0g (Dietary Fiber 0g); Protein 2g **Exchanges:** 1 Fat **Carbohydrate Choices:** 0

LIGHTER **DIRECTIONS** For 1 gram of fat and 20 calories per serving, use fat-free cream cheese and mayonnaise. Omit almonds.

CHEESE QUESADILLAS

FAST LOWER CALORIE

PREP 10 min TOTAL 15 min • **18 appetizers**

- 2 cups shredded Cheddar or Colby cheese (8 oz)
- 6 flour tortillas (8 to 10 inch)
- 1 small tomato, seeded, chopped (½ cup)
- 4 medium green onions, chopped (¼ cup)
- 2 tablespoons canned chopped green chiles
  Chopped fresh cilantro or parsley

1 Heat oven to 350°F. Sprinkle ⅓ cup of the cheese evenly over half of each tortilla. Top cheese with remaining ingredients. Fold tortilla over filling. Place on ungreased cookie sheet.

2 Bake about 5 minutes or until hot and cheese is melted. Cut each into 3 wedges, beginning cuts from center of folded side.

1 Appetizer: Calories 70; Total Fat 2g (Saturated Fat 1g; Trans Fat 0g); Cholesterol 0mg; Sodium 190mg; Total Carbohydrate 9g (Dietary Fiber 0g); Protein 4g **Exchanges:** ½ Starch, 1 Fat **Carbohydrate Choices:** ½

LIGHTER **DIRECTIONS** For 1 gram of fat and 45 calories per serving, use reduced-fat cheese and tortillas.

NACHOS FAST

PREP 5 min **TOTAL** 10 min • **4 servings**

- 28 tortilla chips
- 1 cup shredded Monterey Jack or Cheddar cheese (4 oz)
- ¼ cup canned chopped green chiles, if desired
- 2 tablespoons sliced pitted ripe olives
- ⅓ cup sour cream
- ¼ cup salsa

Heat oven to 400°F. Line cookie sheet with foil. Place tortilla chips on cookie sheet. Sprinkle with cheese, chiles and olives. Bake about 4 minutes or until cheese is melted. Top with sour cream and salsa. Serve hot.

1 Serving: Calories 260; Total Fat 18g (Saturated Fat 8g; Trans Fat 0g); Cholesterol 35mg; Sodium 370mg; Total Carbohydrate 15g (Dietary Fiber 1g); Protein 9g **Exchanges:** 1 Starch, 1 High-Fat Meat, 2 Fat **Carbohydrate Choices:** 1

BEEF OR CHICKEN NACHOS Sprinkle 1 cup shredded cooked beef or chicken over tortilla chips. Continue as directed.

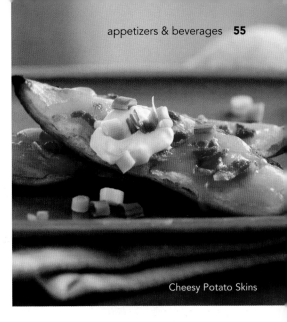
Cheesy Potato Skins

CHEESY POTATO SKINS

PREP 15 min **TOTAL** 2 hr • **8 servings**

- 4 large russet baking potatoes (about 2 lb)
- 2 tablespoons butter, melted
- 1 cup shredded Cheddar cheese or Colby– Monterey Jack cheese blend (4 oz)
- 4 slices bacon, crisply cooked, crumbled (¼ cup)
- ½ cup sour cream
- 8 medium green onions, sliced (½ cup)

1 Heat oven to 375°F. Prick potatoes with fork. Bake potatoes 1 hour to 1 hour 15 minutes or until tender. Let stand until cool enough to handle. Cut potatoes lengthwise into quarters; carefully scoop out pulp, leaving ¼-inch shells. Refrigerate potato pulp for another use.

2 Set oven control to broil. Place potato shells, skin side down, on rack in broiler pan. Brush with butter. Broil with tops 4 to 5 inches from heat 8 to 10 minutes or until crisp and brown. Sprinkle cheese and bacon over potato shells. Broil about 30 seconds longer or until cheese is melted. Serve hot with sour cream and onions.

1 Serving: Calories 280; Total Fat 12g (Saturated Fat 7g; Trans Fat 0g); Cholesterol 35mg; Sodium 230mg; Total Carbohydrate 33g (Dietary Fiber 3g); Protein 9g **Exchanges:** 2 Starch, ½ High-Fat Meat, 1½ Fat **Carbohydrate Choices:** 2

LIGHTER **DIRECTIONS** For 5 grams of fat and 115 calories per serving, decrease cheese to ½ cup; use fat-free sour cream.

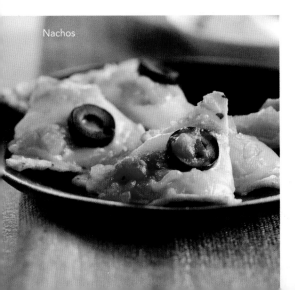
Nachos

SHRIMP EGG ROLLS

Cooked chicken or pork can substituted for the shrimp in this home-cooked version of a favorite take-out food. Thaw frozen egg roll skins at room temperature.

PREP 1 hr 15 min TOTAL 1 hr 15 min • **8 egg rolls**

- 1 teaspoon cornstarch
- ¼ teaspoon five-spice powder
- 4 teaspoons soy sauce
- 1 tablespoon vegetable oil
- 4 cups coleslaw mix (from 16-oz bag)
- 1 cup fresh bean sprouts
- 2 tablespoons sliced green onions
- ½ teaspoon grated gingerroot
- ½ cup finely chopped cooked shrimp
  Vegetable oil for frying
- 8 egg roll skins (from 1-lb package)
- 1 egg, beaten
  Sweet-and-Sour Sauce (page 482, or purchased sauce)

1 In small bowl, combine cornstarch, five-spice powder and soy sauce; blend well. Set aside.

2 In large skillet or wok, heat 1 tablespoon oil over medium-high heat until hot. Add coleslaw mix, bean sprouts, onions and gingerroot; cook and stir 3 to 4 minutes or until tender. Add shrimp and cornstarch mixture; cook and stir 1 to 2 minutes or until mixture is thoroughly coated. Remove from skillet; cool to room temperature.

3 In deep fryer or 4-quart Dutch oven, heat oil (3 to 4 inches) to 350°F.

4 Meanwhile, place 1 egg roll skin on work surface with 1 corner facing you. (Cover remaining skins with damp paper towel to prevent drying out.) Place ¼ cup coleslaw mixture slightly below center of egg roll skin. Fold corner of egg roll skin closest to filling over filling, tucking point under. Fold in and overlap right and left corners. Brush remaining corner with egg; gently roll egg roll toward remaining corner and press to seal. (Cover filled egg roll with damp paper towel to prevent drying out.) Repeat with remaining egg roll skins and coleslaw mixture.

5 Fry egg rolls, a few at a time, in oil 4 to 6 minutes, turning once, until golden brown. Drain on paper towels. Serve with sweet-and-sour sauce.

1 Egg Roll: Calories 220; Total Fat 11g (Saturated Fat 2g, Trans Fat 0g); Cholesterol 60mg; Sodium 220mg; Total Carbohydrate 22g (Dietary Fiber 2g); Protein 8g **Exchanges:** 1½ Starch, ½ Very Lean Meat, 2 Fat **Carbohydrate Choices:** 1½

OVEN-FRIED EGG ROLLS To make in oven, heat oven to 400°F. Spray cookie sheet with cooking spray. Place uncooked egg rolls, seam side down, on cookie sheet. Lightly spray top and sides of egg rolls with cooking spray. Bake 15 to 20 minutes or until golden brown.

Folding Egg Rolls

Fold corner of egg roll skin closest to filling over filling, tucking point under.

Fold in and overlap right and left corners.

Brush remaining corner with egg; gently roll egg roll toward remaining corner and press to seal.

Shrimp Egg Rolls

BASIL-CHEESE TRIANGLES

LOWER CALORIE

Hot tidbits warm up a casual gathering. Make these melt-in-your-mouth appetizers ahead and you'll have more time to enjoy them.

PREP 25 min **TOTAL** 40 min • **72 appetizers**

- 1 lb feta cheese*
- 2 eggs, slightly beaten
- ¼ cup finely chopped fresh or 1 tablespoon dried basil leaves**
- ¼ teaspoon white or black pepper
- 1 package (16 oz) frozen phyllo (filo) sheets (18x14 inches), thawed
- ⅓ cup butter, melted

1 Heat oven to 400°F. Grease cookie sheet. Crumble cheese into small bowl; mash with fork. Stir in eggs, basil and pepper until well mixed.

2 Cut phyllo sheets lengthwise into 2-inch strips. (Cover with plastic wrap then with damp towel to prevent drying out.) Place 1 level teaspoon cheese mixture on end of 1 strip. Fold strip over cheese mixture, end over end in triangular shape, to opposite end. Place on cookie sheet. Repeat with remaining strips and cheese mixture. Brush triangles lightly with butter.

3 Bake 12 to 15 minutes or until puffed and golden brown. Serve warm.

1 Appetizer: Calories 45; Total Fat 2.5g (Saturated Fat 1g; Trans Fat 0g); Cholesterol 10mg; Sodium 105mg; Total Carbohydrate 4g (Dietary Fiber 0g); Protein 2g **Exchanges:** ½ Starch, ½ Fat **Carbohydrate Choices:** 0

Finely shredded Monterey Jack cheese can be substituted.

**Chopped fresh or 1 tablespoon freeze-dried chives can be substituted.*

MAKE AHEAD **DIRECTIONS** Cover and refrigerate unbaked triangles up to 24 hours before baking; bake as directed. Or freeze tightly covered up to 2 months; increase bake time by 5 minutes.

Phyllo Dough

Phyllo (also spelled filo), often used in Greek and Middle Eastern cooking, consists of paper-thin layers of pastry.

For best results, thaw phyllo overnight in the refrigerator and work quickly with each layer. Room-temperature thawing may cause the sheets to stick together. When working with phyllo, be sure to cover sheets with plastic wrap, then with a damp towel to keep them from drying out (do not leave uncovered more than 1 or 2 minutes). Use a soft bristle brush to spread melted butter or oil over dough so it doesn't tear. Unused phyllo can be stored tightly wrapped in the refrigerator for up to 2 weeks or it can be refrozen up to 9 months.

Making Phyllo Pastry Triangles

Cut phyllo sheets lengthwise into 2-inch strips. Place 1 level teaspoon cheese mixture on end of 1 strip.

Fold strip over cheese mixture, end over end in triangular shape.

Fold to opposite end.

Basil-Cheese Triangles

Heirloom Recipe and New Twist

This fabulous appetizer of cheese baked in flaky pastry first appeared in the 10th edition of the cookbook but it has fast become such a favorite that we feel it is a new heirloom recipe. The new twist is similar but is made with phyllo dough instead of puff pastry and has a really fabulous contemporary fig filling. It's a great choice for your next party. Be sure to try the variation submitted by an online Facebook® fan, too.

CLASSIC

BRIE IN PUFF PASTRY WITH CRANBERRY SAUCE

PREP 30 min TOTAL 1 hr 25 min • **12 servings**

CRANBERRY SAUCE*
- 1 **cup fresh cranberries**
- 6 **tablespoons packed brown sugar**
- 1 **tablespoon orange juice**
- ½ **teaspoon grated orange peel**

BRIE IN PASTRY
- 1 **tablespoon butter**
- ⅓ **cup sliced almonds**
- 1 **frozen puff pastry sheet (from 17.3-oz package), thawed**
- 1 **round (14 to 15 oz) Brie cheese**
- 1 **egg, beaten**
  Assorted crackers or sliced fresh fruit, if desired

1 In 1-quart saucepan, stir cranberries, brown sugar and orange juice until well mixed. Heat to boiling, stirring frequently; reduce heat. Simmer uncovered 15 to 20 minutes, stirring frequently, until mixture thickens and cranberries are tender. Stir in orange peel; remove from heat.

2 In 8-inch skillet, melt butter over medium heat. Cook almonds in butter, stirring frequently, until golden brown; remove from heat.

3 Heat oven to 400°F. Spray cookie sheet with cooking spray. Roll pastry into 16x9-inch rectangle on lightly floured surface; cut out one 8½-inch round and one 7-inch round.

4 Remove paper from cheese; leave rind on. Place cheese round on center of 8½-inch round. Spoon cranberry sauce and almonds over cheese. Bring pastry up and press around side of cheese. Brush top edge of pastry with egg. Place 7-inch round on top, pressing around edge to seal. Brush top and side of pastry with egg. Cut decorations from remaining pastry and arrange on top; brush with egg. Place on cookie sheet.

5 Bake 20 to 25 minutes or until golden brown. Cool on cookie sheet on cooling rack 30 minutes before serving. Serve with crackers.

*1 cup purchased whole berry cranberry sauce can be substituted for the cranberry sauce.

1 Serving: Calories 270; Total Fat 19g (Saturated Fat 9g; Trans Fat 1g); Cholesterol 75mg; Sodium 270mg; Total Carbohydrate 17g (Dietary Fiber 0g); Protein 9g **Exchanges:** 1 Starch, 1 High-Fat Meat, 2 Fat **Carbohydrate Choices:** 1

BRIE IN PUFF PASTRY WITH DOUBLE-ORANGE CRANBERRY SAUCE Add 1 tablespoon orange-flavored liqueur or chai-flavored liqueur to the cranberry mixture before cooking. Frozen orange juice concentrate can be substituted for the liqueur.

Contributed by Debbie Arseneault from Scarborough, Ontario

Wrapping Brie in Puff Pastry

Place cheese round on center of 8½-inch round. Spoon cranberry sauce and almonds over cheese. Bring pastry up and press around side of cheese.

Place 7-inch round on top, pressing around edge to seal.

Brush top and sides of pastry with egg.

Cut garnish from pastry scraps; place on top; press lightly.

NEW TWIST

PHYLLO-WRAPPED BRIE WITH FIG PRESERVES AND TOASTED WALNUTS

PREP 25 min TOTAL 45 min • **12 servings**

- 1 **tablespoon butter**
- ⅓ **cup chopped walnuts**
- 3 **sheets frozen phyllo (filo) pastry (18x14 inch), thawed**
- 3 **tablespoons butter, melted**
- 1 **round (14 to 15 oz) Brie cheese**
- ⅓ **cup fig or ginger preserves**
  Assorted crackers or sliced fresh fruit, if desired

1 Heat oven to 400°F. Spray cookie sheet with cooking spray. In 8-inch skillet, melt 1 tablespoon butter over medium heat. Cook walnuts in butter, stirring frequently, until golden brown; remove from heat.

2 Place 1 sheet of phyllo pastry on cutting board; lightly brush with some of the melted butter. Place another sheet of phyllo on top; lightly brush with some of the melted butter. Place remaining sheet of phyllo crosswise over first two sheets; brush lightly with some of the remaining butter.

3 Remove paper from cheese; leave rind on. Place cheese round on center of phyllo sheets. Spoon fig preserves and walnuts over cheese. With both hands, lift phyllo stack toward center and twist in center to make bundle (sheets may tear a little). Brush with remaining butter. Place on cookie sheet. If desired, cut shapes from remaining phyllo dough scraps. Place on top of dough; press lightly to secure.

4 Bake 15 to 20 minutes or until golden brown. Cool on cookie sheet on wire rack 15 minutes before serving. Serve with crackers and additional preserves, if desired.

1 Serving: Calories 220; Total Fat 16g (Saturated Fat 9g; Trans Fat 0g); Cholesterol 45mg; Sodium 270mg; Total Carbohydrate 10g (Dietary Fiber 0g); Protein 8g **Exchanges:** ½ Starch, 1 High-Fat Meat, 1½ Fat **Carbohydrate Choices:** ½

 See how to make **Brie in puff pastry:** Visit bettycrocker.com/BCcookbook

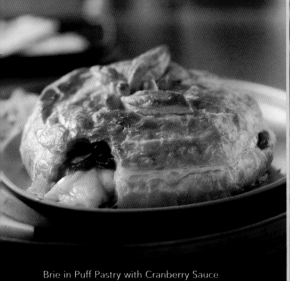
Brie in Puff Pastry with Cranberry Sauce

Phyllo-Wrapped Brie with Fig Preserves and Toasted Walnuts

CHEESE- AND BACON-STUFFED MUSHROOMS LOWER CALORIE

PREP 20 min TOTAL 35 min • **8 servings**

24 fresh whole baby portabella or white mushrooms (1½ to 2 inches in diameter)
2 tablespoons balsamic vinaigrette dressing
4 slices bacon
1½ teaspoons olive oil
½ cup chopped red onion
⅓ cup finely shredded Italian cheese blend
⅓ cup garlic-and-herb spreadable cheese (from 6.5-oz container)
½ teaspoon Dijon mustard
2 tablespoons plain bread crumbs
2 teaspoons chopped fresh Italian (flat-leaf) parsley

1 Heat oven to 350°F. Remove stems from mushrooms; reserve caps. Chop enough stems to measure ¾ cup. Discard remaining stems or reserve for another use. In large bowl, toss mushroom caps with vinaigrette; place stem sides down in ungreased 15x10x1-inch pan.

2 Bake 10 minutes. Let stand until cool enough to handle; drain.

3 Meanwhile, in 10-inch nonstick skillet, cook bacon until crisp; drain on paper towel. Crumble bacon; set aside. Remove and discard drippings from skillet.

4 In same skillet, heat 1 teaspoon of the olive oil over medium heat. Add onion and chopped mushroom stems; cook 4 to 6 minutes, stirring occasionally, until onion is tender.

5 In medium bowl, stir onion mixture, bacon, cheeses and mustard until well blended. Spoon mixture into mushroom caps; place filled sides up in pan. In small bowl, mix bread crumbs and remaining ½ teaspoon olive oil; stir in parsley. Sprinkle bread crumb mixture over filled mushroom caps.

6 Bake 10 to 15 minutes or until thoroughly heated and cheese is melted. Serve warm.

See how to **stuff mushrooms:** Visit bettycrocker.com/BCcookbook

1 Serving: Calories 90; Total Fat 4.5g (Saturated Fat 2g; Trans Fat 0g); Cholesterol 10mg; Sodium 190mg; Total Carbohydrate 6g (Dietary Fiber 1g); Protein 6g **Exchanges:** 1 Vegetable, ½ High-Fat Meat **Carbohydrate Choices:** ½

BUFFALO CHICKEN WINGS

LOWER CALORIE

In our testing we found that coating the wings with flour really helped the sauce cling to the wings.

PREP 20 min TOTAL 55 min • **24 appetizers**

12 chicken wings (about 2 lb)
2 tablespoons butter
½ cup all-purpose flour
½ teaspoon salt
¼ teaspoon pepper
1 cup barbecue sauce (for homemade sauce, see page 309)
1 tablespoon red pepper sauce
½ teaspoon Cajun seasoning
¼ teaspoon ground cumin
1 bottle (8 oz) blue cheese dressing, if desired (for homemade dressing, see page 476)
  Celery, carrot and zucchini sticks, if desired

1 Heat oven to 425°F. Cut each chicken wing at joints to make 3 pieces; discard tip. Cut off and discard excess skin.

2 In 13x9-inch pan, melt butter in oven. In resealable food-storage plastic bag, mix flour, salt and pepper. Add chicken; seal bag tightly. Shake until chicken is completely coated with flour mixture. Place chicken in pan.

3 Bake uncovered 20 minutes. In small bowl, stir barbecue sauce, pepper sauce, Cajun seasoning and cumin until well mixed. Turn chicken. Pour sauce mixture over chicken; toss until evenly coated with sauce.

4 Bake uncovered 10 to 12 minutes longer or until light golden brown on outside and juice of chicken is clear when thickest part is cut

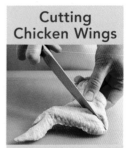

Cutting Chicken Wings

Cut each chicken wing at joints to make 3 pieces; discard tip. Cut off excess skin; discard.

to bone (at least 165°F). Serve with dressing and celery sticks.

1 Appetizer: Calories 80; Total Fat 4.5g (Saturated Fat 1.5g; Trans Fat 0g); Cholesterol 15mg; Sodium 180mg; Total Carbohydrate 6g (Dietary Fiber 0g); Protein 5g **Exchanges:** 1 Medium-Fat Meat **Carbohydrate Choices:** ½

HONEY-MUSTARD CHICKEN WINGS
Substitute honey-mustard barbecue sauce for the plain barbecue sauce. Omit red pepper sauce. Substitute barbecue seasoning for the Cajun seasoning and omit ground cumin. Stir 1 tablespoon mustard seed into sauce mixture.

SALSA CHICKEN WINGS Substitute salsa for the barbecue sauce and chili powder for the Cajun seasoning.

SWEET-SPICY CHICKEN WINGS Substitute sweet-spicy French dressing for the barbecue sauce and Montreal chicken grill seasoning for the Cajun seasoning; omit ground cumin.

MAPLE CHICKEN DRUMMIES
LOWER CALORIE

PREP 15 min TOTAL 1 hr 10 min • **20 appetizers**

  ¼ cup real maple syrup or honey
  ¼ cup chili sauce
  2 tablespoons chopped fresh chives
  1 tablespoon soy sauce
  ½ teaspoon ground mustard
  ¼ teaspoon ground red pepper (cayenne), if desired
  20 chicken wing drummettes (about 2 lb)

1 Heat oven to 375°F. In small bowl, mix all ingredients except chicken. Place chicken in ungreased 15x10x1-inch pan. Pour syrup mixture over chicken; turn chicken to coat.

2 Bake uncovered 45 to 55 minutes, turning once and brushing with sauce after 30 minutes, or until juice of chicken is clear when thickest part is cut to bone (at least 165°F). Serve chicken with sauce.

1 Appetizer: Calories 100; Total Fat 4g (Saturated Fat 1.5g; Trans Fat 0g); Cholesterol 35mg; Sodium 120mg; Total Carbohydrate 3g (Dietary Fiber 0g); Protein 11g **Exchanges:** 1½ Lean Meat **Carbohydrate Choices:** 0

Cheese- and Bacon-Stuffed Mushrooms

Buffalo Chicken Wings

Maple Chicken Drummies

CHICKEN SATAY WITH PEANUT SAUCE LOWER CALORIE

PREP 15 min TOTAL 2 hr 25 min • **8 skewers**

- 3 tablespoons lime juice
- 1 teaspoon curry powder
- 2 teaspoons honey
- ½ teaspoon ground coriander
- ½ teaspoon ground cumin
- ⅛ teaspoon salt
- 2 cloves garlic, finely chopped
- 1 lb boneless skinless chicken breasts, cut into 1-inch cubes
- 1 medium red bell pepper, cut into 1¼-inch pieces
- 4 medium green onions, cut into 2-inch pieces
  Peanut Sauce (page 482) or purchased sauce

1 In small bowl, stir lime juice, curry powder, honey, coriander, cumin, salt and garlic until well mixed. Place chicken in resealable food-storage plastic bag or shallow glass or plastic dish. Add lime-juice mixture; seal bag tightly. Shake or stir to coat chicken with lime-juice mixture. Cover and refrigerate 2 hours, turning bag or stirring occasionally.

2 Set oven control to broil. Spray rack in broiler pan with cooking spray. Remove chicken from marinade; reserve marinade. Thread chicken, bell pepper and onion pieces, leaving space between pieces, on each of 8 (8-inch) metal or bamboo skewers (soak bamboo skewers in water at least 30 minutes to prevent burning). Place skewers on rack in broiler pan.

3 Broil with tops about 3 inches from heat 4 minutes. Turn; brush with marinade. Broil 4 to 5 minutes longer or until chicken is no longer pink in center. Discard any remaining marinade. Serve chicken with peanut sauce.

1 Skewer (1 Skewer and 1 Tablespoon Sauce): Calories 165; Total Fat 8g (Saturated Fat 3g; Trans Fat 0g); Cholesterol 35mg; Sodium 260mg; Total Carbohydrate 8g (Dietary Fiber 1g); Protein 16g **Exchanges:** ½ Other Carbohydrate, 3 Lean Meat, 2 Fat **Carbohydrate Choices:** ½

SPICY LEMON SHRIMP WITH BASIL AIOLI FAST LOWER CALORIE

PREP 10 min TOTAL 15 min • **About 24 appetizers**

- 1 tablespoon grated lemon peel
- 3 tablespoons lemon juice
- ¾ teaspoon crushed red pepper
- ½ teaspoon salt
- 2 cloves garlic, finely chopped
- 3 tablespoons olive or vegetable oil
- 1 lb uncooked deveined peeled large shrimp (about 24), thawed if frozen, tail shells removed
- ½ cup loosely packed fresh basil leaves
- ½ cup mayonnaise or salad dressing

1 Set oven control to broil. In medium glass or plastic bowl, stir lemon peel, lemon juice, red pepper, salt, garlic and 1 tablespoon of the oil until well mixed. Add shrimp; toss to coat.

2 In ungreased 15x10x1-inch pan, place shrimp in single layer. Broil with tops 2 to 3 inches from heat 3 to 5 minutes or until shrimp are pink.

3 In food processor, place basil and remaining 2 tablespoons oil; cover and process until basil is chopped. Add mayonnaise; cover and process until smooth. Serve shrimp with aioli.

1 Appetizer: Calories 60; Total Fat 5g (Saturated Fat 1g; Trans Fat 0g); Cholesterol 30mg; Sodium 105mg; Total Carbohydrate 0g (Dietary Fiber 0g); Protein 3g **Exchanges:** ½ Lean Meat, ½ Fat **Carbohydrate Choices:** 0

MAKE AHEAD DIRECTIONS The shrimp can marinate in the lemon mixture up to 3 hours in the refrigerator before broiling. The basil aioli can be made up to 24 hours ahead; store covered in refrigerator.

Threading Skewers

Thread ingredients on skewers as directed, leaving space between each piece so ingredients cook evenly.

Brush kabobs with marinade.

COLD POACHED SALMON WITH HERB MAYONNAISE

PREP 25 min TOTAL 2 hr 45 min • **12 servings**

SALMON
- 2 cups water
- 1 cup dry white wine, nonalcoholic white wine or apple juice
- 1 teaspoon salt
- ¼ teaspoon dried thyme leaves
- ¼ teaspoon dried oregano leaves
- ⅛ teaspoon ground red pepper (cayenne)
- 1 small onion, sliced
- 4 black peppercorns
- 4 sprigs fresh cilantro
- 2 lb salmon or other medium-firm fish fillet

HERB MAYONNAISE
- ¾ cup mayonnaise or salad dressing
- 1½ tablespoons chopped fresh or 1½ teaspoons dried dill weed or tarragon leaves
- 1 tablespoon chopped fresh chives
- 1 tablespoon chopped fresh parsley
- 1 tablespoon lemon juice
- 1½ teaspoons Dijon mustard
  Dash ground red pepper (cayenne)

GARNISH
Lemon wedges, if desired

1 In 12-inch skillet, heat all ingredients for the salmon except salmon to boiling; reduce heat to low. Cover and simmer 5 minutes.

2 Cut salmon into 6 pieces. Place salmon in skillet; add water to cover if necessary. Heat to boiling; reduce heat to low. Simmer uncovered about 14 minutes or until salmon flakes easily with fork. Carefully remove salmon with slotted spatula; drain on cooling rack. Cover and refrigerate about 2 hours or until chilled.

3 Meanwhile, in small bowl, mix all mayonnaise ingredients; cover and refrigerate until serving. Serve salmon with mayonnaise and lemon wedges.

1 Serving: Calories 220; Total Fat 15g (Saturated Fat 3g; Trans Fat 0g); Cholesterol 55mg; Sodium 370mg; Total Carbohydrate 5g (Dietary Fiber 0g); Protein 16g **Exchanges:** ½ Starch, 2 Lean Meat, 1½ Fat **Carbohydrate Choices:** ½

LEMON-HERB POACHED SALMON Increase water to 3 cups; omit wine. Omit thyme, oregano and ground red pepper. Add 3 to 4 slices lemon, cut in half. Omit cilantro and substitute ¼ cup small sprigs parsley. Continue as directed in Steps 1 and 2. Sprinkle poached salmon with ¼ cup chopped parsley, 2 tablespoons finely chopped red onion, 2 teaspoons capers and 1 teaspoon grated lemon peel. Omit herb mayonnaise.

Cold Poached Salmon with Herb Mayonnaise

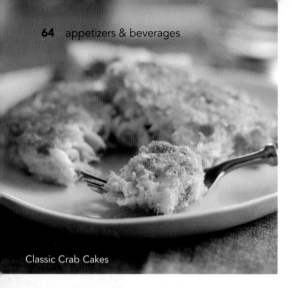

Classic Crab Cakes

CLASSIC CRAB CAKES FAST

PREP 15 min TOTAL 25 min • **6 servings**

- ⅓ cup mayonnaise or salad dressing
- 1 egg
- 1¼ cups soft white bread crumbs (about 2 slices bread)
- 1 teaspoon ground mustard
- ¼ teaspoon salt
- ¼ teaspoon ground red pepper (cayenne), if desired
- ⅛ teaspoon pepper
- 2 medium green onions, chopped
- 1 can (1 lb) or 2 refrigerated containers (8 oz each) pasteurized lump crabmeat, well drained, cartilage removed*
- ¼ cup unseasoned dry bread crumbs
- 2 tablespoons vegetable oil

1 In medium bowl, mix mayonnaise and egg with wire whisk. Gently stir in remaining ingredients except dry bread crumbs and oil so that crabmeat doesn't break apart into small pieces. Shape mixture into 6 patties, about 3 inches in diameter (mixture will be moist). Coat each patty with dry bread crumbs.

2 In 12-inch nonstick skillet, heat oil over medium heat. Cook patties in oil about 10 minutes, gently turning once, until golden brown and hot in center. Reduce heat if crab cakes become brown too quickly.

3 cans (6 oz each) lump crabmeat can be substituted for the 1-lb can or the refrigerated crabmeat.

1 Serving: Calories 330; Total Fat 18g (Saturated Fat 3g; Trans Fat 0g); Cholesterol 120mg; Sodium 690mg; Total Carbohydrate 20g (Dietary Fiber 0g); Protein 22g **Exchanges:** 1 Starch, 3 Lean Meat, 2 Fat **Carbohydrate Choices:** 1

SALMON CAKES Substitute 1 (15-oz) can red salmon, drained, for the lump crabmeat.

BAKED COCONUT SHRIMP

LOWER CALORIE

PREP 30 min TOTAL 40 min • **40 appetizers**

APRICOT SAUCE

- ¾ cup apricot preserves
- 1 tablespoon lime juice
- ½ teaspoon ground mustard

SHRIMP

- ¼ cup all-purpose flour
- 2 tablespoons packed brown sugar
- ¼ teaspoon salt
  Dash ground red pepper (cayenne)
- 1 egg
- 1 tablespoon lime juice
- 1 cup shredded coconut
- 1 lb uncooked deveined peeled small shrimp (40), thawed if frozen, tail shells removed
- 2 tablespoons butter, melted

1 In 1-quart saucepan, stir all sauce ingredients until well mixed. Cook over low heat, stirring occasionally, just until preserves are melted. Refrigerate while making shrimp.

2 Heat oven to 425°F. Spray rack in broiler pan with cooking spray.

3 In shallow bowl, stir flour, brown sugar, salt and red pepper until well mixed. In another shallow bowl, beat egg and lime juice with fork. In third shallow bowl, place coconut.

4 Coat each shrimp with flour mixture. Dip each side of shrimp into egg mixture. Coat well with coconut. Place on rack in broiler pan. Drizzle with butter.

5 Bake 7 to 8 minutes or until shrimp are pink and coating is beginning to brown. Serve with sauce.

1 Appetizer: Calories 50; Total Fat 1.5g (Saturated Fat 1g; Trans Fat 0g); Cholesterol 25mg; Sodium 45mg; Total Carbohydrate 7g (Dietary Fiber 0g); Protein 2g **Exchanges:** ½ Fruit, ½ Fat **Carbohydrate Choices:** ½

BEVERAGE BASICS

Whether it's a mug of hot coffee on a winter morning, a tall glass of iced tea in the summer or a cup of hot chocolate on a cool night, beverages do more than quench our thirst. They also add sparkle to parties, warm weary spirits and add flavor to everyday meals.

BREWING BETTER COFFEE

Ensure that your cup of coffee turns out just right every time!

- Choose the correct grind for your coffee maker. Generally, pre-ground coffee has a medium grind suitable for automatic coffee makers:

  Automatic drip: medium grind
  Espresso maker: fine grind
  Percolator: coarse grind
  Plunger or French press pot: coarse grind

- Use cold tap, filtered or bottled water for best flavor.

- Serve coffee within 15 minutes of brewing. The longer coffee stays in contact with heat, the more harsh and bitter it becomes. If you aren't going to drink it right away and your coffee maker doesn't have a thermal pot, pour it into an insulated carafe.

- Avoid reheating coffee, as its flavor will deteriorate. Instead, brew a fresh pot.

COFFEE AND WATER RATIOS

Strength	Ground Coffee	Water
Regular	1 level tablespoon	¾ cup (6 oz)
Strong	2 level tablespoons	¾ cup (6 oz)

TYPES OF TEA

From afternoon tea in England to Japan's traditional tea ceremony, the consumption of tea is steeped in tradition, making it the most commonly consumed beverage in the world after water. All tea plants belong to the same species. It is how they are processed that determines individual characteristics. Processing variables result in these main types of tea:

- **Black Tea:** Contains the most caffeine, about 50 to 65 percent of the amount in coffee. The color and aroma develop as the leaves ferment or oxidize before being heated and dried. Some familiar varieties are Darjeeling, English Breakfast and Lapsang Souchong. Black tea contains antioxidants.

- **Green Tea:** Pale green in color with a light, fresh flavor. The leaves are steamed and dried but not fermented. Familiar varieties include Gunpowder (so named because it's rolled in little balls that "explode" when they come in contact with water), Tencha and Matcha (which is finely ground Tencha). Green tea contains antioxidants.

The longer the beans are roasted, the darker and stronger flavored the coffee. Most beans are roasted in one of the following styles.

American: Lightest roast with a caramel-like flavor.

Full City: Dark roast with flavors ranging from caramel to chocolate with some hints of a dark roast flavor.

French and Italian: Very dark roasts with strong aroma and bold, strong flavor. The preferred roast for espresso and espresso-based coffee drinks.

- **Oolong Tea:** Partially fermented and a cross between green and black teas. You'll also recognize it as "Chinese restaurant tea." Imperial oolong is prized for its honey flavor, while Formosa oolong tastes a little like peaches.

- **White Tea:** Pale in color with a light, sweet flavor. The leaves are steamed and dried but not fermented. Familiar varieties include Silver Needle and White Peony.

There are literally thousands of tea varieties or herb blends labeled as "tea," including:

- **Blended Tea:** A combination of teas such as English Breakfast and Earl Grey.

- **Decaffeinated Tea:** Almost all of the caffeine is removed during processing.

- **Herb Tea:** Really not a tea because it doesn't contain tea leaves. It is a blend of dried fruits, herbs, flowers and spices in many flavors, such as lemon, orange and peppermint.

TEA EQUIPMENT

A few simple pieces of equipment are all that is needed to produce a soothing cup of tea.

Infuser: Use to hold loose tea leaves. Infusers come in all shapes and sizes.

Tea Kettle: Use to boil water quickly.

Teapot: Use to brew tea. Choose one made of glass, china or earthenware. China pots should have a solid, even glaze inside and out.The lid should stay on while pouring.

Tea Press: Use to brew loose tea leaves. Add very hot or boiling water to a small glass pitcher with plunger or press, which pushes the leaves to the bottom so they don't get into the brewed tea.

Tea Strainer: Handy when you brew loose tea leaves without an infuser. Hold strainer over cup as you pour to catch leaves.

BREWING TEA

1 Fill a tea kettle with cold water. For black or oolong tea, bring water to a boil. For green or white tea, bring water to a temperature between 170°F and 190°F.

2 Warm a clean teapot by filling it with very hot water; drain.

3 Add tea to the warm teapot. Use about 1 teaspoon loose tea or 1 tea bag for every ¾ cup of water. (Use an infuser to hold loose tea leaves.) Pour boiling water over tea, and let steep for 3 to 5 minutes to bring out the full flavor.

4 Instead of color, judge strength of tea by tasting it. Stir tea once to blend evenly. Remove tea bags or infuser, or if loose tea leaves were brewed without an infuser, hold a strainer over cup as you pour to catch leaves. If you prefer weaker tea, add hot water after brewing tea. If desired, serve tea with milk or cream, lemon and sugar.

OVER ICE IS NICE!

For iced tea, brew a pot of tea, using double the amount of tea bags or leaves. Remove the tea bags or strain the tea while pouring it into ice-filled glasses or a pitcher. If you're making tea in advance, let it cool to room temperature before putting it in the refrigerator so it doesn't get cloudy. To sweeten tea, use our Simple Syrup, page 271 or superfine granulated sugar. The sugar is already dissolved so you won't get any sugar settling at the bottom of the glass.

There's More to Milk

It used to be that whole, reduced-fat and fat-free or skim milk were the only kinds of cow's milk available. But over the years, the changing needs and concerns of consumers has led manufacturers to also produce the following milk products. Look for:

- **Organic Milk:** Pesticide, hormone and antibiotic free, organic milk is widely available.

- **Lactaid/Lactose Free Milk:** Manufactured for people with lactose intolerance or sensitivity.

- **Fortified Milk:** Although milk has always been fortified, some brands now include additional calcium or a type of Omega-3 fatty acid called DHA.

- **Ultra Pasteurized Milk:** The newer method to pasteurize milk, called ultra-pasteurization, heats milk to 280°F for just 2 seconds in order to make milk safe to drink.

APPLE-MINT ICED GREEN TEA

LOWER CALORIE

PREP 10 min **TOTAL** 35 min • **6 servings**

> 6   tea bags green tea with mint
> 4   cups boiling water
> 2   cups apple juice
>   Fresh mint sprigs, if desired

1 In large heatproof bowl or pitcher, place tea bags. Pour boiling water over tea bags. Cover; let steep 10 minutes. Remove tea bags. Cool tea 15 minutes.

2 Stir apple juice into tea. Pour over ice. Garnish with mint sprig.

1 Serving: Calories 40; Total Fat 0g (Saturated Fat 0g; Trans Fat 0g); Cholesterol 0mg; Sodium 10mg; Total Carbohydrate 10g (Dietary Fiber 0g); Protein 0g **Exchanges:** ½ Other Carbohydrate **Carbohydrate Choices:** ½

RASPBERRY-GINGER TEA

FAST   LOWER CALORIE

PREP 5 min **TOTAL** 15 min • **6 servings**

> 3   cups brewed tea
> 3   cups cranberry-raspberry or raspberry juice
> 3   slices gingerroot, ¼ inch thick
>   Fresh raspberries and mint sprigs, if desired

1 In 3-quart saucepan, heat all ingredients except raspberries and mint sprigs to boiling over medium-high heat; reduce heat to low.

2 Simmer uncovered 10 minutes, stirring occasionally. Remove gingerroot. Serve warm. Garnish with raspberries and mint sprigs.

1 Serving: Calories 80; Total Fat 0g (Saturated Fat 0g; Trans Fat 0g); Cholesterol 0mg; Sodium 5mg; Total Carbohydrate 21g (Dietary Fiber 0g); Protein 0g **Exchanges:** 1½ Other Carbohydrate **Carbohydrate Choices:** 1½

Apple-Mint Iced Green Tea and Raspberry-Ginger Tea

CHAI FAST LOWER CALORIE

PREP 10 min TOTAL 10 min • **4 servings**

- 2 **cups water**
- ¼ **cup loose Darjeeling tea leaves or 5 tea bags black tea**
- 2 **cups milk**
- ⅛ **teaspoon ground cardamom**
- 2 **whole cloves, crushed**
- 2 **to 4 black peppercorns, crushed Pinch ground cinnamon**
- ¼ **cup sweetened condensed milk or 4 teaspoons sugar**

1 In 2-quart saucepan, heat water to rapid boil over medium-high heat; reduce heat to low. Add tea leaves; simmer 2 to 4 minutes to blend flavors. (If using tea bags, remove and discard.)

2 Stir in remaining ingredients except sweetened condensed milk. Heat just to boiling, but do not let boil over. Stir in sweetened condensed milk. Strain tea through strainer into cups.

1 Serving: Calories 140; Total Fat 6g (Saturated Fat 3.5g; Trans Fat 0g); Cholesterol 25mg; Sodium 85mg; Total Carbohydrate 16g (Dietary Fiber 0g); Protein 6g **Exchanges:** 1 Low-Fat Milk, 1 Fat **Carbohydrate Choices:** 1

HOT SPICED CIDER

LOWER CALORIE

A slow cooker is a great way to keep this cider warm after it's made.

PREP 5 min TOTAL 25 min • **6 servings**

- 6 **cups apple cider**
- ½ **teaspoon whole cloves**
- ¼ **teaspoon ground nutmeg**
- 3 **cinnamon sticks**

In 3-quart saucepan, heat all ingredients to boiling over medium-high heat; reduce heat. Simmer uncovered 10 minutes. Strain cider mixture through strainer into hot-beverage carafe or pitcher to remove cloves and cinnamon if desired. Serve hot.

1 Serving: Calories 120; Total Fat 0g (Saturated Fat 0g; Trans Fat 0g); Cholesterol 0mg; Sodium 5mg; Total Carbohydrate 29g (Dietary Fiber 0g); Protein 0g **Exchanges:** 2 Fruit **Carbohydrate Choices:** 2

HOT BUTTERED RUM–SPICED CIDER Make as directed. For each serving, place 1 tablespoon butter (do not use margarine or vegetable oil spreads), 1 tablespoon packed brown sugar and 2 tablespoons rum in mug. Fill with hot cider.

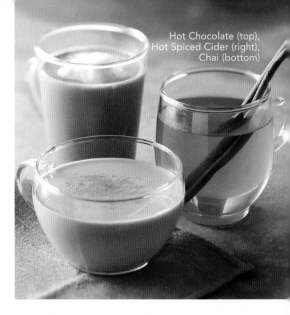

Hot Chocolate (top), Hot Spiced Cider (right), Chai (bottom)

HOT CHOCOLATE FAST

PREP 10 min TOTAL 10 min • **4 servings**

- 2 **tablespoons sugar**
- 2 **tablespoons unsweetened baking cocoa**
- 2½ **cups milk**
- ½ **cup half-and-half**
- ¼ **cup semisweet or dark chocolate chips (1½ oz)**
- ½ **teaspoon vanilla**

1 In 2-quart saucepan, mix sugar and cocoa. Using wire wisk, gradually stir in milk and half-and-half until well blended. Cook and stir over medium heat until thoroughly heated (do not boil). Remove from heat.

2 Add chocolate chips; stir constantly with whisk until chips are melted and mixture is smooth. Stir in vanilla. To serve, pour hot chocolate into 4 cups.

1 Serving (¾ Cup): Calories 230; Total Fat 12g (Saturated Fat 7g; Trans Fat 0g); Cholesterol 25mg; Sodium 75mg; Total Carbohydrate 23g (Dietary Fiber 1g); Protein 6g **Exchanges:** ½ Other Carbohydrate, 1 Milk, 1 Fat **Carbohydrate Choices:** 1½

LIGHTER DIRECTIONS For 4 grams of fat and 160 calories per serving, use fat-free (skim) milk and fat-free half-and-half. Continue as directed in Step 2.

DOUBLE-CHOCOLATE HOT CHOCOLATE Substitute chocolate milk for regular milk.

STRAWBERRY SMOOTHIE

FAST LOWER CALORIE

PREP 5 min **TOTAL** 5 min • **4 servings**

> 1 pint (2 cups) strawberries
> 1 cup milk
> 2 containers (6 oz each) strawberry yogurt (1⅓ cups)

Reserve 4 strawberries for garnish. Cut out the hull, or "cap," from remaining strawberries. In blender, place strawberries, milk and yogurt. Cover and blend on high speed about 30 seconds or until smooth. Pour into 4 glasses. Garnish each with reserved strawberry.

1 Serving (1 Cup): Calories 140; Total Fat 2.5g (Saturated Fat 1g; Trans Fat 0g); Cholesterol 10mg; Sodium 80mg; Total Carbohydrate 24g (Dietary Fiber 2g); Protein 6g **Exchanges:** 1 Fruit, 1 Skim Milk **Carbohydrate Choices:** 1½

PEACH SMOOTHIE Substitute frozen sliced peaches for the strawberries and peach yogurt for the strawberry yogurt.

STRAWBERRY-BANANA SMOOTHIE Substitute 1 medium banana, cut into chunks, for 1 cup of the strawberries.

BLUEBERRY SMOOTHIE FAST

Vanilla soymilk would be a delicious alternative to milk in these antioxidant-rich, vibrant purple smoothies.

PREP 5 min **TOTAL** 5 min • **4 servings**

> 2 cups frozen blueberries
> 2½ cups milk
> 2 containers (6 oz each) blueberry or vanilla yogurt
> Honey or agave nectar, if desired

In blender or food processor, place blueberries, milk and yogurt. Cover and blend on high speed about 1 minute or until smooth. Sweeten to taste with honey. Pour into 4 glasses. Serve immediately.

1 Serving: Calories 210; Total Fat 3.5g (Saturated Fat 1g; Trans Fat 0g); Cholesterol 5mg; Sodium 150mg; Total Carbohydrate 37g (Dietary Fiber 3g); Protein 6g **Exchanges:** ½ Fruit, 1 Other Carbohydrate, 1 Skim Milk, ½ Fat **Carbohydrate Choices:** 2½

RASPBERRY SMOOTHIE Substitute frozen unsweetened raspberries for the blueberries and raspberry yogurt for the blueberry or vanilla yogurt.

Peach Smoothie, Strawberry Smoothie, Blueberry Smoothie

LEMONADE FAST LOWER CALORIE

To get the most juice from a lemon, roll a room-temperature lemon back and forth on the counter with the palm of your hand, pressing down firmly.

PREP 10 min **TOTAL** 10 min • **6 servings**

    3 cups water
    1 cup lemon juice (about 4 lemons)
    ½ cup sugar
       Lemon or orange slices, if desired
       Fresh mint leaves, if desired

In large pitcher, stir water, lemon juice and sugar until sugar is dissolved. Serve lemonade over ice. Garnish with lemon slices and mint.

1 Serving: Calories 80; Total Fat 0g (Saturated Fat 0g; Trans Fat 0g); Cholesterol 0mg; Sodium 10mg; Total Carbohydrate 19g (Dietary Fiber 0g); Protein 0g **Exchanges:** 1 Fruit **Carbohydrate Choices:** 1

LIMEADE Substitute 1 cup lime juice (about 10 limes) for the lemon juice; increase sugar to ¾ cup. Garnish with lime slices and strawberries if desired.

LEMONADE TEA Make lemonade as directed using an 8-cup pitcher. Add 4 cups cold brewed unsweetened iced tea (see directions for making iced tea on page 66) to lemonade. Garnish with fresh mint sprigs if desired. Makes 12 servings

WATERMELON LEMONADE WITH KIWIFRUIT SPLASH

LOWER CALORIE

For a special presentation, moisten the rims of the glasses and dip in coarse sugar crystals. Garnish each drink with slices of watermelon and kiwifruit.

PREP 20 min **TOTAL** 1 hr 20 min • **12 servings**

    4 kiwifruit, peeled, cut into fourths
    1 tablespoon sugar
    8 cups cubed seedless watermelon
    2 cans (12 oz each) frozen lemonade
       concentrate
    4 cups water

1 In blender, place kiwifruit and sugar. Cover; blend on medium speed just until smooth. Freeze 1 to 2 hours or until firm.

2 In blender or food processor, place watermelon (blender will be full until blended). Cover; blend on medium speed until smooth. Place frozen lemonade concentrate and water in large pitcher. Add watermelon mixture; mix well.

3 Pour watermelon lemonade into glasses. Spoon dollop of frozen kiwifruit on top. Serve immediately.

1 Serving (1 Cup): Calories 160; Total Fat 0g (Saturated Fat 0g; Trans Fat 0g); Cholesterol 0mg; Sodium 5mg; Total Carbohydrate 39g (Dietary Fiber 1g); Protein 1g **Exchanges:** 1 Fruit, 1½ Other Carbohydrate **Carbohydrate Choices:** 2½

Watermelon Lemonade with Kiwifruit Splash, Limeade, Lemonade

BREAKFAST & BRUNCH

For bonus **breakfast and brunch** recipes,
visit bettycrocker.com/BCcookbook

FAST = Ready in 20 minutes or less LOWER CALORIE = See Helpful Nutrition and Cooking Information, page 685
LIGHTER = 25% fewer calories or grams of fat MAKE AHEAD = Make-ahead directions SLOW COOKER = Slow cooker directions

← Carton of fresh eggs, Cinnamon French Toast Sticks with Spicy Cider Syrup (page 91), Potato, Bacon and Egg
Scramble (page 76), Baked Apple Oatmeal (page 85)

BREAKFAST AND BRUNCH BASICS

Awake sleepyheads with the enticing aroma of a hearty, wholesome breakfast cooking in the kitchen. A morning meal provides energy to face the busy day. Quick-to-cook options like pancakes and scrambled eggs or grab-and-go ideas are perfect weekday choices. But on the weekend, take time to enjoy special brunch selections like stuffed French toast and omelets. Or get your whole-grain fix with muesli, granola and oatmeal.

FIVE GRAB-AND-GO BREAKFASTS

A busy morning is no excuse to miss breakfast. Pack a portable meal that can be made in minutes. Include a plastic spoon if needed and a napkin to go.

PB & J Bagel-Wich: Spread a split bagel with peanut butter, almond butter or hazelnut spread with cocoa. Sprinkle with chopped fresh or dried fruit. Wrap in foil.

Banana Breakfast Roll-Up: Spread a flour tortilla with plain or flavored cream cheese or equal parts honey and peanut butter. Top with chopped or sliced banana; sprinkle with nuts and dried fruit and roll up. Wrap in foil.

Muesli or Granola Cup: In plastic container with cover, mix equal parts granola or muesli, page 85, and yogurt. Stir in chopped fresh, canned or dried fruit.

Easy Egg Sandwich: Make Hard-Cooked Eggs, page 74; cover and refrigerate up to 1 week. Slice an egg and place over a split English muffin; sprinkle with shredded cheese and bacon bits. Microwave 10 to 20 seconds or until cheese is melted. Wrap in foil.

No-Blend Chunky Smoothie: Place 1 cup yogurt in travel mug; stir in milk until desired thickness. Stir in sweetener if desired and chopped fresh or canned fruit. Add ground flaxseed if desired.

BEST BRUNCH TIPS

Day Before

- Wash and cut all produce except fruits that can discolor (like apples, bananas and pears). Store in separate bags or containers.

- Prepare uncooked egg mixtures; cover and refrigerate. Whisk or stir before using.

- Slice breads for French toast; place in resealable food-storage plastic bags.

- Make juices or bases for beverage mixtures; cover and refrigerate. Don't stir in last-minute additions, such as carbonated beverages or alcohol.

- Prepare the coffeemaker so that it's ready to go in the morning.

- Set the table and gather serving dishes and utensils.

Same Day

- Place hot beverages in thermal carafes or slow cookers.

- Keep pancakes warm until ready to serve by placing uncovered in a single layer on a paper towel–lined cookie sheet in a 200°F oven.

Easy Egg Sandwich, Muesli Cup, Banana Breakfast Roll-Up

EGG BASICS

Eggs are the perfect combination of nutrition and versatility. Packed inside each tasty egg is a good supply of protein, vitamins and minerals. Although eggs contain some fat and cholesterol, they are low in sodium. And 1 large egg has only 80 calories. Here are five basic cooking methods for eggs. Choose your favorite or look for more egg recipes in pages that follow.

EGG TIPS

- Store eggs in refrigerator in original carton on a shelf, not on the door.

- For recipes that call for raw eggs, use pasteurized eggs only. Unpasteurized eggs may contain salmonella bacteria and are unsafe to eat raw.

- Use eggs that have clean, uncracked shells. Don't wash eggs before storing or using.

- Always cook eggs until both yolk and white are firm, not runny. Temperature in center of egg should be 160°F.

- Soft-cooked eggs are not recommended as they do not reach 160°F.

HARD-COOKED (HARD-BOILED) EGGS

Keep hard-cooked eggs on hand for snacks or to use in salads. Or, plan to make Deviled Eggs, page 52.

1 Place 6 large eggs in single layer in 2-quart saucepan. Cover with cold water at least 1 inch above eggs. Cover saucepan; heat to boiling. Immediately remove from heat; let stand covered 15 minutes (12 minutes for medium and 18 minutes for extra-large), then drain. Immediately place eggs in cold water with ice cubes or run cold water over eggs until completely cooled.

2 To peel, gently tap each egg on counter-top until entire shell is finely crackled. Roll gently between hands to loosen shell. Starting at large end, peel egg under cold running water to help remove shell. **6 servings**

SCRAMBLED EGGS

For the fluffiest eggs, try not to stir eggs too often. A rubber spatula or plastic spoon works well to gently stir when necessary.

1 In medium bowl, beat 6 eggs, ⅓ cup water or milk, ¼ teaspoon salt and ⅛ teaspoon pepper thoroughly with fork or wire whisk until well mixed. In 10-inch skillet, heat 1 tablespoon butter over medium heat just until it begins to sizzle.

2 Pour egg mixture into skillet. As mixture begins to set at bottom and side, gently lift cooked portions with pancake turner so that thin, uncooked portion can flow to bottom. Avoid constant stirring. Cook 3 to 4 minutes or until eggs are thickened throughout but still moist. **4 servings**

FRIED EGGS

We call for butter for frying eggs, but you could use margarine or bacon drippings instead.

In 8-inch skillet, melt 1 to 2 tablespoons butter over medium-high heat. Break egg into custard cup; carefully slide into pan from custard cup. Repeat with another egg. Immediately reduce heat to low. Cook 4 to 5 minutes, spooning butter over eggs, until film forms over top and whites and yolks are firm, not runny. **2 servings**

LIGHTER **DIRECTIONS** Omit butter and use a nonstick skillet. Cook eggs over low heat about 1 minute or until edges turn white. Add 4 teaspoons water. Cover and cook about 5 minutes or until film forms over top and whites and yolks are firm, not runny.

POACHED EGGS

Be sure to use a large enough pan so eggs do not touch during cooking.

In skillet or saucepan, heat 2 to 3 inches water to boiling; reduce heat so water is simmering. Break cold egg into custard cup or small glass bowl. Holding cup close to water's surface, carefully slide egg into water. Repeat with another egg. Cook uncovered 3 to 5 minutes or until whites and yolks are firm, not runny. Remove eggs with slotted spoon. **2 servings**

BAKED EGGS

While the eggs are baking, slice some fresh strawberries and pop bread into the toaster to serve along side.

Heat oven to 325°F. Grease 2 custard cups with softened butter. Carefully break 1 egg into each cup. Sprinkle with salt and pepper. Top each with 1 tablespoon milk or half-and-half. Dot with butter. Bake 15 to 18 minutes or until whites and yolks are firm, not runny. **2 servings**

CHEESY BAKED EGGS Instead of dotting with butter, sprinkle each egg with 1 tablespoon shredded Cheddar or Parmesan cheese.

Keeping Eggs Warm

Eggs cool off quickly. To help keep them warm, serve on a warm plate. Use the warming setting on your oven to keep plates warm while making eggs. Or rinse the plates with hot water and dry thoroughly to take off the chill.

SCRAMBLED EGG SCRAMBLERS

Start with Scrambled Eggs and use these ideas to turn them into a complete meal or meal-on-the-go.

Bacon-Blue Cheese Egg Muffin: Scramble eggs with 2 sliced green onions, 2 tablespoons crumbled blue cheese and 4 slices cooked crumbled bacon. Fill split toasted English muffins with eggs; top eggs with thin slices of avocado.

Eggs, Lox and Bagels: Scramble eggs with 3 ounces chopped salmon lox, 1 package (3 ounces) cream cheese, cubed, and ½ teaspoon dried dill weed. Top toasted bagel halves with thin slice of tomato and thin slice of red onion; top with eggs. Serve open-face.

Eggs, Spinach and Ham Croissants: Scramble eggs with chopped ham and baby spinach leaves; stir in shredded Havarti cheese. Fill split croissants with eggs.

Eggs, Spinach and Ham Croissants

Hawaiian Scramble: Scramble eggs with ¼ cup each chopped fresh pineapple, diced Canadian bacon and shredded mozzarella cheese. Serve with toasted Hawaiian bread.

Scrambled Eggs with Caviar and Sour Cream: Place scrambled eggs on slices of toasted Brioche bread; top with a dollop of sour cream and a sprinkle of caviar.

Scrambled Egg Pizzas: Spread 6-inch uncut pita (pocket) breads with thin layer of pizza sauce; top with scrambled eggs, diced green bell pepper and shredded Italian cheese blend. Broil just until cheese is melted.

Scrambled Egg Pizzas

POTATO, BACON AND EGG SCRAMBLE FAST LOWER CALORIE

Pre-cooking the potatoes in boiling water helps them cook faster, turning this scramble into a 20-minute meal.

PREP 10 min TOTAL 20 min • **5 servings**

- 1 **lb small red potatoes (6 or 7), cubed**
- 6 **eggs**
- ⅓ **cup milk**
- ¼ **teaspoon salt**
- ⅛ **teaspoon pepper**
- 2 **tablespoons butter**
- 4 **medium green onions, sliced (¼ cup)**
- 5 **slices bacon, crisply cooked, crumbled**

1 In 2-quart saucepan, heat 1 inch water to boiling. Add potatoes. Cover; heat to boiling. Reduce heat to medium-low. Cook covered 6 to 8 minutes or until potatoes are tender; drain.

2 In medium bowl, beat eggs, milk, salt and pepper with fork or wire whisk until well mixed; set aside.

3 In 10-inch skillet, melt butter over medium-high heat. Cook potatoes in butter 3 to 5 minutes, turning occasionally, until light brown. Stir in onions. Cook 1 minute, stirring constantly.

4 Pour egg mixture into skillet with potatoes and onions. As mixture begins to set at bottom and side, gently lift cooked portions with spatula so that thin, uncooked portion can flow to bottom. Avoid constant stirring. Cook 3 to 4 minutes or until eggs are thickened throughout but still moist. Sprinkle with bacon.

1 Serving: Calories 290; Total Fat 15g (Saturated Fat 6g; Trans Fat 0g); Cholesterol 275mg; Sodium 370mg; Total Carbohydrate 25g (Dietary Fiber 3g); Protein 13g **Exchanges:** 1 Starch, 1 Vegetable, 1 High-Fat Meat, 1 Fat **Carbohydrate Choices:** 1½

MEXICAN SCRAMBLED EGGS Omit bacon. In 8-inch skillet, cook 4 oz fresh crumbled chorizo sausage with ½ cup green bell pepper until sausage is no longer pink; drain. Stir into eggs at end of cook time. Garnish each serving with 1 to 2 tablespoons salsa.

Eggs Benedict

EGGS BENEDICT

As one story goes, Delmonico's restaurant in New York City was the birthplace of this classic brunch dish. When, in the late 1800s, regular patrons, Mr. and Mrs. LeGrand Benedict, complained of nothing new on the lunch menu, the chef created this now-famous dish and named it after them.

PREP 30 min TOTAL 30 min • **6 servings**

- **Hollandaise Sauce (page 487)**
- 3 **English muffins, split, toasted**
- 7 **teaspoons butter, softened**
- 6 **thin slices Canadian bacon or cooked ham**
- 6 **Poached Eggs (page 75)**
- **Paprika, if desired**

1 Keep hollandaise sauce warm.

2 Spread each toasted muffin half with 1 teaspoon of the butter; keep warm.

3 In 10-inch skillet, melt remaining 1 teaspoon butter over medium heat. Cook bacon in butter until light brown on both sides; keep warm.

4 Place 1 slice bacon on each muffin half; top with 1 poached egg. Spoon warm hollandaise sauce over eggs. Sprinkle with paprika.

1 Serving: Calories 410; Total Fat 33g (Saturated Fat 14g; Trans Fat 1.5g); Cholesterol 400mg; Sodium 670mg; Total Carbohydrate 14g (Dietary Fiber 0g); Protein 15g **Exchanges:** 1 Starch, 1½ High-Fat Meat, 4 Fat **Carbohydrate Choices:** 1

SPINACH EGGS BENEDICT Cook 1 (9 oz) box chopped spinach; drain well. Keep warm. Layer spinach under bacon. Continue as directed. Omit bacon if desired.

HUEVOS RANCHEROS

Huevos rancheros is Spanish for "rancher's eggs." When buying tortillas, check for freshness by making sure they are soft and pliable when you bend the package and check that the edges are not dry or cracked.

PREP 1 hr **TOTAL** 1 hr • **6 servings**

- ½ lb bulk uncooked chorizo or pork sausage
  Vegetable oil
- 6 corn tortillas (6 or 7 inch)
- 1¼ cups salsa (for homemade salsa, see page 480)
- 6 Fried Eggs (page 75)
- 1½ cups shredded Cheddar cheese (6 oz)

1 In 8-inch skillet, cook sausage over medium heat 8 to 10 minutes, stirring occasionally, until no longer pink; drain and keep warm.

2 In same skillet, heat ⅛ inch oil over medium heat just until hot. Cook 1 tortilla at a time in oil about 1 minute, turning once, until crisp; drain.

3 In 1-quart saucepan, heat salsa, stirring occasionally, until hot.

4 Spread 1 tablespoon salsa over each tortilla to soften. Place 1 fried egg on each tortilla. Top with salsa, sausage, additional salsa and cheese.

1 Serving: Calories 460; Total Fat 33g (Saturated Fat 14g; Trans Fat 1g); Cholesterol 275mg; Sodium 1100mg; Total Carbohydrate 16g (Dietary Fiber 2g); Protein 25g **Exchanges:** 1 Starch, 3 High-Fat Meat, 2 Fat **Carbohydrate Choices:** 1

BREAKFAST TACOS

FAST LOWER CALORIE

PREP 20 min **TOTAL** 20 min • **6 servings**

- 4 eggs
- ¼ teaspoon garlic salt
- ¼ teaspoon pepper
- ¼ cup chopped green or red bell pepper
- 4 medium green onions, chopped (¼ cup)
- 1 tablespoon butter
- ½ cup shredded pepper Jack cheese (2 oz)
- 6 taco shells
- 1 cup shredded lettuce
- 1 small avocado, pitted, peeled and sliced
- ¼ cup chunky-style salsa

1 In small bowl, beat eggs, garlic salt and pepper thoroughly with fork or wire whisk. Stir in bell pepper and onions.

2 In 8-inch skillet, melt butter over medium heat. Pour egg mixture into skillet. As mixture begins to set at bottom and side, gently lift cooked portions with spatula so that thin, uncooked portion can flow to bottom. Avoid constant stirring. Cook 3 to 4 minutes or until eggs are thickened throughout but still moist. Gently stir in cheese.

3 Heat taco shells as directed on package. Place lettuce in shells. Spoon eggs onto lettuce. Top with avocado and salsa.

1 Serving: Calories 230; Total Fat 16g (Saturated Fat 5g; Trans Fat 1g); Cholesterol 155mg; Sodium 250mg; Total Carbohydrate 13g (Dietary Fiber 3g); Protein 9g **Exchanges:** 1 Starch, 1 High-Fat Meat, 1 Fat **Carbohydrate Choices:** 1

Huevos Rancheros

Breakfast Tacos

Learn to Make **Omelets**

BASIC OMELET

Omelets are a great way to start your day or a natural go-to when it's dinnertime and there aren't many groceries in the refrigerator. We'll show you here how to make omelets that are fluffy and perfectly cooked and how to get them out of the pan—beautifully.

PREP 10 min **TOTAL** 40 min • **4 omelets**

8 **eggs**	8 **teaspoons butter**
Salt and pepper, if desired	

1 For each omelet, in small bowl, beat 2 of the eggs until fluffy. Add salt and pepper to taste. In 8-inch nonstick omelet pan or skillet, heat 2 teaspoons of the butter over medium-high heat just until butter is hot and sizzling. As butter melts, tilt pan to coat bottom.

2 Quickly pour eggs into pan. While rapidly sliding pan back and forth over heat, quickly and continuously stir with spatula to spread eggs over bottom as they thicken. Let stand over heat a few seconds to lightly brown bottom of omelet. Do not overcook; omelet will continue to cook after folding. If desired, add filling (see at right) before folding.

3 To remove from pan, first run spatula under one edge of omelet, folding about one-third of it to the center. Transfer to plate by tilting pan, letting flat, unfolded edge of omelet slide out onto plate. Using edge of pan as a guide, flip folded edge of omelet over flat portion on plate.

4 Repeat with remaining butter and eggs. If desired, omelets can be kept warm on platter in 200°F oven while preparing remaining omelets.

1 Omelet: Calories 220; Total Fat 18g (Saturated Fat 7g; Trans Fat 0g); Cholesterol 445mg; Sodium 170mg; Total Carbohydrate 1g (Dietary Fiber 0g); Protein 13g **Exchanges:** 2 Medium-Fat Meat, 1½ Fat **Carbohydrate Choices:** 0

LIGHTER **DIRECTIONS** For 8 grams of fat and 130 calories per serving, substitute ½ cup fat-free egg product for the omelet (2 eggs).

CHEESE OMELET Before folding omelet, sprinkle with ¼ cup shredded Cheddar, Monterey Jack or Swiss cheese, or ¼ cup crumbled blue cheese.

DENVER OMELET Before adding eggs to pan, cook 2 tablespoons chopped cooked ham, 1 tablespoon finely chopped bell pepper and 1 tablespoon finely chopped onion in butter about 2 minutes, stirring frequently. Continue as directed in Step 2.

HAM AND CHEESE OMELET Before folding omelet, sprinkle with 2 tablespoons shredded Cheddar, Monterey Jack or Swiss cheese and 2 tablespoons finely chopped cooked ham.

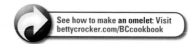

See how to make **an omelet:** Visit bettycrocker.com/BCcookbook

Keys to Success

- **Beat eggs before adding butter to pan.** The butter melts quickly so having the eggs already beaten will prevent the butter from burning.

- **Beat eggs well.** Air beaten into the eggs will result in fluffy omelets.

- **Tilt pan to coat bottom in butter.** This helps prevent the eggs from sticking.

- **Rapidly slide pan back and forth over heat.** Do this while spreading eggs in bottom of pan so they cook quickly but don't overcook.

- **Leave eggs slightly undercooked.** They will continue to cook when folded.

OMELET FILLINGS

Wake up those taste buds with one of these tasty fillings. For cooked fillings, make them first, then keep warm while cooking the omelets. Some fillings are difficult to measure, but in general, for each omelet, plan to use ¼ to ⅓ cup filling. Add filling to one side of omelet; fold remaining side over filling.

1 Avocado, Bacon and Cheddar Filling: Avocado slices, crisply cooked crumbled bacon and shredded Cheddar cheese.

2 Buffalo Chicken and Green Onion Filling: Heat 1 cup cut-up cooked chicken with ⅓ cup bottled buffalo wing sauce until warm. Spoon onto omelets; sprinkle with sliced green onions.

3 Caprese Filling: Tomato slices, thinly sliced fresh mozzarella and fresh basil leaves.

4 Chorizo and Black Bean Salsa Filling: Crumble and cook ½ pound bulk fresh chorizo sausage in skillet; cook and stir until no longer pink. Stir in ¼ cup each drained black beans and salsa; heat through.

5 Crab, Artichoke and Corn Filling: Layer each omelet with about ¼ cup chopped cooked crabmeat or imitation crabmeat pieces, 1 or 2 sliced marinated artichoke hearts from jar, drained, and 2 to 3 tablespoons whole kernel corn from 11-ounce can, drained.

6 Cucumber and Greek Yogurt Filling: Thinly sliced cucumbers, Greek yogurt and chopped fresh or dried dill.

7 Greek Spinach and Feta Filling: Fresh spinach leaves, red onion slices, sliced pitted kalamata olives and crumbled feta cheese.

8 Italian Turkey Sausage and Bell Pepper Filling: Remove casings from 4 Italian turkey sausages. Crumble sausage in skillet and cook with ½ cup each chopped bell pepper and onion until sausage is no longer pink and vegetables are tender.

9 Sun-Dried Tomato and Goat Cheese Filling: Chopped sun-dried tomatoes in oil, drained, crumbled goat cheese and chopped chives.

10 Swiss, Mushroom and Thyme Filling: In small nonstick skillet, melt 1 teaspoon butter over medium heat. Stir in 1½ cups sliced mushrooms and ½ teaspoon dried thyme leaves. Cook 4 to 6 minutes or until tender, stirring occasionally. Spoon onto omelets; sprinkle with shredded Swiss cheese.

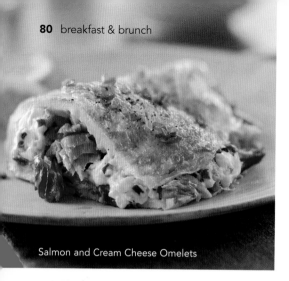

Salmon and Cream Cheese Omelets

SALMON AND CREAM CHEESE OMELETS LOWER CALORIE

PREP **5 min** TOTAL **25 min** • **4 servings**

- 4 teaspoons butter
- 8 eggs, beaten
- ½ cup chives-and-onion cream cheese spread (from 8-oz container)
- 1 cup flaked smoked salmon
  Chopped fresh chives, if desired

1 In omelet pan or 8-inch nonstick skillet, heat 2 teaspoons of the butter over medium-high heat until butter is hot and sizzling.

2 Pour half of the beaten eggs (about 1 cup) into pan. As eggs begin to set at bottom and side, gently lift cooked portions with spatula so that thin, uncooked portion can flow to bottom. Avoid constant stirring. Cook 3 to 4 minutes or until eggs are thickened throughout but still moist.

3 Spoon ¼ cup of the cream cheese in dollops evenly over omelet; sprinkle with ½ cup of the salmon. Tilt pan and slip spatula under omelet to loosen. Remove from heat. Fold omelet in half; let stand 2 minutes. Transfer to serving plate; keep warm.

4 Repeat with remaining ingredients to make second omelet. Cut each omelet crosswise in half to serve; sprinkle with chives.

1 Serving (½ Omelet): Calories 290; Total Fat 22g (Saturated Fat 9g; Trans Fat 0g); Cholesterol 460mg; Sodium 470mg; Total Carbohydrate 4g (Dietary Fiber 0g); Protein 20g **Exchanges:** 3 High-Fat Meat **Carbohydrate Choices:** 0

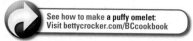

See how to make a **puffy omelet**:
Visit bettycrocker.com/BCcookbook

PUFFY OMELET LOWER CALORIE

PREP **15 min** TOTAL **30 min** • **2 servings**

- 4 eggs, separated
- ¼ cup water
- ¼ teaspoon salt
- ⅛ teaspoon pepper
- 1 tablespoon butter
  Cheese Sauce (page 486), if desired

1 Heat oven to 325°F. In medium bowl, beat egg whites, water and salt with electric mixer on high speed until stiff but not dry. In small bowl, beat egg yolks and pepper on high speed about 3 minutes or until very thick and lemon colored. Fold egg yolks into egg whites.

2 In 10-inch ovenproof skillet, melt butter over medium heat. As butter melts, tilt skillet to coat bottom. Pour egg mixture into skillet. Gently level surface with spatula; reduce heat to low. Cook about 5 minutes or until puffy and bottom is light brown. Carefully lift omelet at edge to see color.

3 Bake uncovered 12 to 15 minutes or until knife inserted in center comes out clean. Tilt skillet and slip pancake turner or metal spatula under omelet to loosen. Fold omelet in half, being careful not to break it. Slip onto warm serving plate. Serve with cheese sauce.

1 Serving (½ Omelet): Calories 200; Total Fat 16g (Saturated Fat 6g; Trans Fat 0g); Cholesterol 440mg; Sodium 460mg; Total Carbohydrate 1g (Dietary Fiber 0g); Protein 13g **Exchanges:** 2 Medium-Fat Meat, 1 Fat **Carbohydrate Choices:** 0

SAVORY ITALIAN FRITTATA

LOWER CALORIE

PREP **10 min** TOTAL **30 min** • **6 servings**

- 8 eggs
- 1 tablespoon chopped fresh or ½ teaspoon dried basil leaves
- 1 tablespoon chopped fresh or ½ teaspoon dried mint leaves
- 1 tablespoon chopped fresh or ½ teaspoon dried sage leaves
- 1 tablespoon freshly grated Parmesan cheese
- ½ teaspoon salt
- ⅛ teaspoon pepper
- ¼ cup diced prosciutto or cooked ham (2 oz)
- 1 tablespoon butter
- 1 small onion, finely chopped (⅓ cup)

1 In medium bowl, beat all ingredients except prosciutto, butter and onion thoroughly with fork or wire whisk until well mixed. Stir in prosciutto.

2 In 10-inch nonstick skillet, melt butter over medium-high heat. Cook onion in butter 4 to 5 minutes, stirring frequently, until crisp-tender; reduce heat to medium-low.

3 Pour egg mixture into skillet. Cover; cook 9 to 11 minutes or until eggs are set around edge and light brown on bottom. Cut into wedges.

1 Serving: Calories 140; Total Fat 10g (Saturated Fat 3.5g; Trans Fat 0g); Cholesterol 295mg; Sodium 450mg; Total Carbohydrate 1g (Dietary Fiber 0g); Protein 11g **Exchanges:** 1½ Medium-Fat Meat, ½ Fat **Carbohydrate Choices:** 0

LIGHTER DIRECTIONS For 3 grams of fat and 80 calories per serving, substitute 2 cups fat-free egg product for the eggs. Substitute cooked turkey ham for the prosciutto.

QUICHE LORRAINE

Quiche Lorraine has a savory custard and is usually flavored with bacon and Swiss or Gruyère cheese. Baking the crust a bit before adding the filling helps to keep it crisp.

PREP 25 min TOTAL 1 hr 40 min • **8 servings**

> **One-Crust Pastry (page 158)**
> 8 **slices bacon, chopped**
> ⅓ **cup finely chopped onion**
> 4 **eggs**
> 2 **cups whipping cream or half-and-half**
> ¼ **teaspoon salt**
> ¼ **teaspoon pepper**
> ⅛ **teaspoon ground red pepper (cayenne)**
> 1 **cup shredded Swiss or Gruyère cheese (4 oz)**

1 Heat oven to 425°F. After folding pastry into fourths, place in 9-inch quiche dish or pie plate. Unfold and ease into dish, pressing firmly against bottom and side. Carefully line pastry with a double thickness of foil, gently pressing foil to bottom and side of pastry. Let foil extend over edge to prevent excessive browning. Bake 10 minutes; carefully remove foil and bake 2 to 4 minutes longer or until pastry just begins to brown and has become set. If crust bubbles, gently push bubbles down with back of spoon.

2 Meanwhile, in 10-inch skillet, cook bacon over medium heat, stirring occasionally, until crisp. Remove bacon with slotted spoon; drain on paper towels. Drain all but 2 teaspoons bacon drippings from skillet. Cook onion in bacon drippings over medium heat 3 to 5 minutes or until light golden brown, stirring occasionally. Set aside.

3 In large bowl, beat eggs slightly with fork or wire whisk. Beat in whipping cream, salt, pepper and red pepper. Sprinkle bacon, onion and cheese into warm pie crust. Gently pour egg mixture into crust.

4 Reduce oven temperature to 325°F. Bake 45 to 50 minutes or until knife inserted in center comes out clean. Let stand 10 minutes before cutting.

1 Serving: Calories 620; Total Fat 52g (Saturated Fat 25g; Trans Fat 3g); Cholesterol 255mg; Sodium 580mg; Total Carbohydrate 20g (Dietary Fiber 0g); Protein 17g **Exchanges:** 1 Starch, 1 Vegetable, 1½ High-Fat Meat, 8 Fat **Carbohydrate Choices:** 1

SEAFOOD QUICHE Substitute 1 cup chopped cooked crabmeat (patted dry), imitation crab-meat, cooked shrimp or salmon for the bacon. Use ⅓ cup finely chopped green onions; increase salt to ½ teaspoon.

SPINACH QUICHE Substitute 1 box (9 oz) frozen chopped spinach, thawed and squeezed to drain, for the bacon. Sprinkle over onion and cheese.

Spinach Quiche

CANADIAN BACON, ASPARAGUS AND POTATO QUICHE LOWER CALORIE

PREP 20 min TOTAL 1 hr 30 min • **8 servings**

One-Crust Pastry (page 158)
4 eggs
1 cup milk
½ teaspoon dried marjoram leaves
¼ teaspoon salt
1 cup frozen country-style shredded hash brown potatoes (from 30-oz bag), thawed
1 cup ½-inch pieces fresh asparagus
1 cup diced Canadian bacon
1½ cups shredded Havarti cheese (6 oz)

1 Heat oven to 425°F. Make pastry; after folding pastry into fourths, place in 9-inch quiche dish or pie plate. Unfold and ease into dish, pressing firmly against bottom and side. Carefully line pastry with a double thickness of foil, gently pressing foil to bottom and side of pastry. Let foil extend over edge to prevent excessive browning.

2 Bake 10 minutes; carefully remove foil and bake 2 to 4 minutes longer or until pastry just begins to brown and has become set. If crust bubbles, gently push bubbles down with back of spoon.

3 In medium bowl, beat eggs, milk, marjoram and salt with fork or wire whisk until well blended. Layer potatoes, asparagus, bacon and cheese in warm pie crust. Gently pour egg mixture into crust.

4 Reduce oven temperature to 375°F. Bake 45 to 50 minutes or until knife inserted in center comes out clean. Let stand 5 minutes before cutting.

1 Serving: Calories 290; Total Fat 19g (Saturated Fat 8g; Trans Fat 2g); Cholesterol 140mg; Sodium 640mg; Total Carbohydrate 15g (Dietary Fiber 1g); Protein 15g **Exchanges:** 1 Starch, 2 High-Fat Meat, ½ Fat **Carbohydrate Choices:** 1

HAM, ASPARAGUS AND POTATO QUICHE

Substitute diced cooked ham or turkey ham for the Canadian bacon and Swiss cheese for the Havarti.

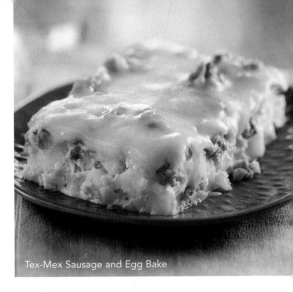
Tex-Mex Sausage and Egg Bake

TEX-MEX SAUSAGE AND EGG BAKE LOWER CALORIE

PREP 20 min TOTAL 9 hr 30 min • **10 servings**

¾ lb bulk uncooked spicy pork sausage
5 cups frozen southern-style diced hash brown potatoes (from 32-oz bag)
1 can (4.5 oz) chopped green chiles, undrained
3 cups shredded Colby–Monterey Jack cheese blend (12 oz)
6 eggs
1½ cups milk
¼ teaspoon salt
1 cup chunky-style salsa (for homemade salsa, see page 480)

1 Spray 13x9-inch (3-quart) glass baking dish with cooking spray. In 10-inch skillet, cook sausage over medium heat 8 to 10 minutes, stirring occasionally, until no longer pink; drain on paper towels.

2 Spread frozen potatoes in baking dish. Sprinkle with sausage, chiles and 1½ cups of the cheese. In medium bowl, beat eggs, milk and salt with fork or wire whisk until well blended. Pour over potato mixture. Sprinkle with remaining 1½ cups cheese. Cover; refrigerate at least 8 hours but no longer than 12 hours.

3 Heat oven to 350°F. Bake uncovered 50 to 60 minutes or until knife inserted in center comes out clean. Let stand 10 minutes before cutting. Serve with salsa.

1 Serving: Calories 350; Total Fat 20g (Saturated Fat 10g; Trans Fat 0g); Cholesterol 175mg; Sodium 1120mg; Total Carbohydrate 25g (Dietary Fiber 3g); Protein 19g **Exchanges:** 1½ Starch, 2 High-Fat Meat, 1 Fat **Carbohydrate Choices:** 1½

HAM AND CHEDDAR STRATA

LOWER CALORIE

PREP 15 min TOTAL 1 hr 35 min • **8 servings**

- 12 slices bread
- 2 cups cut-up cooked smoked ham (about 10 oz)
- 2 cups shredded Cheddar cheese (8 oz)
- 8 medium green onions, sliced (½ cup)
- 6 eggs
- 2 cups milk
- 1 teaspoon ground mustard
- ¼ teaspoon red pepper sauce
  Paprika, if desired

1 Heat oven to 300°F. Spray 13x9-inch (3-quart) glass baking dish with cooking spray.

2 Trim crusts from bread. Arrange 6 slices in baking dish. Layer ham, cheese and onions on bread in dish. Cut remaining slices diagonally in half; arrange on onions.

3 In medium bowl, beat eggs, milk, mustard and pepper sauce with fork or wire whisk; pour evenly over bread. Sprinkle with paprika.

4 Bake uncovered 1 hour to 1 hour 10 minutes or until center is set and bread is golden brown. Let stand 10 minutes before cutting.

1 Serving: Calories 350; Total Fat 19g (Saturated Fat 9g; Trans Fat 0g); Cholesterol 215mg; Sodium 920mg; Total Carbohydrate 20g (Dietary Fiber 0g); Protein 24g **Exchanges:** 1 Starch, 3 Medium-Fat Meat, 1 Fat **Carbohydrate Choices:** 1

Egg, Ham and Swiss Pizza

MAKE AHEAD DIRECTIONS Follow directions through Step 3, then cover and refrigerate up to 24 hours. The casserole may need to bake an additional 5 to 10 minutes.

EGG, HAM AND SWISS PIZZA

Look for the prebaked pizza crusts in the deli or refrigerated section. There are also shelf-stable crusts that can be found near the canned pizza sauce.

PREP 10 min TOTAL 30 min • **6 servings**

- 6 eggs, beaten
- 1 package (10 oz) prebaked thin Italian pizza crust or other 12-inch prebaked pizza crust
- ¼ cup mayonnaise or salad dressing
- 2 tablespoons Dijon mustard
- ½ cup diced cooked ham (4 oz)
- 4 medium green onions, sliced (¼ cup)
- ¼ cup chopped red bell pepper
- 1 cup shredded Swiss cheese (4 oz)

1 Heat oven to 400°F. Heat 10-inch nonstick skillet over medium heat.

2 Pour eggs into skillet. As mixture begins to set at bottom and side, gently lift cooked portions with spatula so that thin, uncooked portion can flow to bottom. Avoid constant stirring. Cook 3 to 4 minutes or until eggs are thickened throughout but still moist.

3 Place pizza crust on ungreased cookie sheet. In small bowl, mix mayonnaise and mustard; spread evenly over crust. Top with eggs, ham, onions, bell pepper and cheese.

4 Bake 10 to 12 minutes or until cheese is melted.

1 Serving: Calories 370; Total Fat 22g (Saturated Fat 8g; Trans Fat 0g); Cholesterol 245mg; Sodium 700mg; Total Carbohydrate 23g (Dietary Fiber 1g); Protein 20g **Exchanges:** 1½ Starch, 2 Medium-Fat Meat, 2 Fat **Carbohydrate Choices:** 1½

LIGHTER DIRECTIONS For 8 grams of fat and 250 calories per serving, substitute 1½ cups fat-free egg product for the eggs. Use 99% fat-free deli ham slices, diced, fat-free mayonnaise and reduced-fat Swiss cheese.

CHILES RELLENOS BAKE

PREP 10 min TOTAL 50 min • **8 servings**

- 8 eggs
- 1 container (8 oz) sour cream
- ¼ teaspoon salt
- 2 drops red pepper sauce
- 2 cups shredded Monterey Jack cheese (8 oz)
- 2 cups shredded Cheddar cheese (8 oz)
- 2 cans (4.5 oz each) chopped green chiles, undrained
- 2 cups salsa (for homemade salsa, see page 480)
- 2 tablespoons chopped fresh cilantro
- ½ cup black beans (from 15-oz can), rinsed, drained
- ½ cup frozen (thawed) or canned (drained) whole kernel corn

1 Heat oven to 350°F. Spray 13x9-inch (3-quart) glass baking dish with cooking spray.

2 In large bowl, beat eggs, sour cream, salt and pepper sauce with wire whisk. Stir in cheeses and chiles. Pour into baking dish.

3 Bake uncovered 40 to 45 minutes or until golden brown and set in center. Meanwhile, in small bowl, mix 1 cup of the salsa and the cilantro. In another small bowl, mix remaining 1 cup salsa, the beans and corn. Serve salsa mixtures with casserole.

1 Serving: Calories 400; Total Fat 29g (Saturated Fat 17g; Trans Fat 0.5g); Cholesterol 285mg; Sodium 870mg; Total Carbohydrate 12g (Dietary Fiber 2g); Protein 23g **Exchanges:** 1 Starch, 3 High-Fat Meat, ½ Fat **Carbohydrate Choices:** 1

CLASSIC CHEESE SOUFFLÉ

LOWER CALORIE

Impress your friends by bringing this golden, puffy cheese soufflé with its heavenly aroma hot out of the oven and straight to the table. Once it's cut, it loses its puffiness, but it still tastes incredibly delicious.

PREP 25 min TOTAL 1 hr 25 min • **4 servings**

- ¼ cup butter
- ¼ cup all-purpose flour
- ½ teaspoon salt
- ¼ teaspoon ground mustard
  Dash ground red pepper (cayenne)
- 1 cup milk
- 1 cup shredded Cheddar cheese (4 oz)
- 3 eggs, separated
- ¼ teaspoon cream of tartar

1 Heat oven to 350°F. Butter 1-quart soufflé dish or casserole. Make a 4-inch-wide band of triple-thickness foil 2 inches longer than circumference of dish. Butter one side of foil. Secure foil band, buttered side in, around top edge of dish.

2 In 2-quart saucepan, melt ¼ cup butter over medium heat. Stir in flour, salt, mustard and red pepper. Cook over medium heat, stirring constantly, until smooth and bubbly; remove from heat. Stir in milk. Heat to boiling, stirring constantly. Boil and stir 1 minute. Stir in cheese until melted; remove from heat.

3 In medium bowl, beat egg whites and cream of tartar with electric mixer on high speed until stiff but not dry; set aside. In small bowl, beat egg yolks on high speed about 3 minutes or until very thick and lemon colored; stir into cheese mixture. Stir about one-fourth of the egg whites into cheese mixture. Fold cheese mixture into remaining egg whites. Carefully pour into soufflé dish.

4 Bake 50 to 60 minutes or until knife inserted halfway between center and edge comes out clean. Carefully remove foil band. Serve immediately by quickly dividing soufflé into sections with two forks.

1 Serving: Calories 330; Total Fat 26g (Saturated Fat 14g; Trans Fat 1g); Cholesterol 225mg; Sodium 620mg; Total Carbohydrate 10g (Dietary Fiber 0g); Protein 15g **Exchanges:** ½ Low-Fat Milk, 1½ High-Fat Meat, 3 Fat **Carbohydrate Choices:** ½

Making Foil Band for Soufflé Dish

Make 4-inch-wide band of triple-thickness foil 2 inches longer than circumference of dish. Grease one side of band with butter. Extend dish by securing band, buttered side in, with masking tape around top outside edge of dish.

TRIPLE-BERRY OATMEAL-FLAX MUESLI LOWER CALORIE

PREP 5 min TOTAL 40 min • **6 servings**

- 2¾ cups old-fashioned oats or rolled barley
- ½ cup sliced almonds
- 2 containers (6 oz each) banana crème or French vanilla low-fat yogurt
- 1½ cups milk
- ¼ cup ground flaxseed or flaxseed meal
- ½ cup fresh blueberries
- ½ cup fresh raspberries
- ½ cup sliced fresh strawberries

1 Heat oven to 350°F. On ungreased cookie sheet, spread oats and almonds. Bake 18 to 20 minutes, stirring occasionally, until light golden brown; cool 15 minutes.

2 In large bowl, mix yogurt and milk until well blended. Stir in oats, almonds and flaxseed. Top each serving with berries.

1 Serving: Calories 320; Total Fat 10g (Saturated Fat 2g; Trans Fat 0g); Cholesterol 5mg; Sodium 60mg; Total Carbohydrate 46g (Dietary Fiber 8g); Protein 13g **Exchanges:** 2 Starch, 1 Other Carbohydrate, 1 High-Fat Meat **Carbohydrate Choices:** 3

GRANOLA LOWER CALORIE

PREP 10 min TOTAL 55 min • **8 servings**

- 3 cups old-fashioned or quick-cooking rolled oats
- 1 cup whole almonds
- 1 teaspoon ground cinnamon
- ⅓ cup real maple syrup or honey
- ½ cup dried cherries
- ½ cup dried blueberries

1 Heat oven to 300°F. Spread oats and almonds evenly in 15x10x1-inch pan. Sprinkle evenly with cinnamon; drizzle with syrup. Toss to coat; spread evenly in pan.

2 Bake 15 minutes. Remove from oven. Stir well to mix so granola dries evenly. Spread mixture evenly in pan. Bake an additional 15 minutes or until mixture is dry and lightly toasted. Cool completely.

3 Place in container with tight-fitting lid or resealable food-storage plastic bag. Add dried fruit; stir to distribute. Cover tightly. Store at room temperature up to 1 month.

1 Serving (½ Cup): Calories 330; Total Fat 11g (Saturated Fat 1g; Trans Fat 0g); Cholesterol 0mg; Sodium 0mg; Total Carbohydrate 50g (Dietary Fiber 7g); Protein 8g **Exchanges:** 2 Starch, 1½ Other Carbohydrate, 2 Fat **Carbohydrate Choices:** 3

Triple-Berry Oatmeal-Flax Muesli

BAKED APPLE OATMEAL

LOWER CALORIE

Steel-cut oats, also known as Scottish or Irish oats, are kernels of the oat sliced lengthwise. They need a longer cooking time, usually 20 minutes on the stove-top. If you can't find them next to regular oats, check the natural- or organic-foods aisle.

PREP 10 min TOTAL 1 hr • **8 servings**

- 2⅔ cups old-fashioned or steel-cut oats
- ½ cup raisins, sweetened dried cranberries or dried cherries
- ⅓ cup packed brown sugar
- 1 teaspoon ground cinnamon
- ¼ teaspoon salt
- 4 cups milk
- 2 medium apples or pears, chopped (2 cups)
- ½ cup chopped walnuts, toasted (page 22) if desired
  Additional milk, if desired

1 Heat oven to 350°F. In 2-quart casserole, mix oats, raisins, brown sugar, cinnamon, salt, 4 cups milk and the apples.

2 Bake uncovered 40 to 50 minutes or until most of the milk is absorbed (a small amount of milk will remain in the center); do not overbake (oats will look chewy). Sprinkle walnuts over top. Serve with additional milk.

1 Serving: Calories 300; Total Fat 9g (Saturated Fat 2.5g; Trans Fat 0g); Cholesterol 10mg; Sodium 130mg; Total Carbohydrate 45g (Dietary Fiber 5g); Protein 10g **Exchanges:** 1½ Starch, 1 Other Carbohydrate, ½ Low-Fat Milk, 1 Fat **Carbohydrate Choices:** 3

Heirloom Recipe and New Twist

This classic pancake recipe has appeared in every Betty Crocker cookbook since 1950. Pancakes are a breakfast tradition and are so easy to make. Our recipe calls for regular milk, but we also give a variation to use buttermilk. Top either version with maple syrup or fresh fruit. Be sure to try our new twist, made with cornmeal, they're hearty and have a delicious buttery syrup on top.

CLASSIC

PANCAKES FAST LOWER CALORIE

PREP 15 min **TOTAL** 15 min • **9 (4-inch) pancakes**

- 1 **egg**
- 1 **cup all-purpose or whole wheat flour**
- 1 **tablespoon sugar**
- 3 **teaspoons baking powder**
- ¼ **teaspoon salt**
- ¾ **cup milk**
- 2 **tablespoons vegetable oil or melted butter**

1 In medium bowl, beat egg with wire whisk until fluffy. Stir in remaining ingredients just until flour is moistened (batter will be slightly lumpy); do not overmix or pancakes will be tough. For thinner pancakes, stir in additional 1 to 2 tablespoons milk.

2 Heat griddle or skillet over medium-high heat (375°F). (To test griddle, sprinkle with a few drops of water. If bubbles jump around, heat is just right.) Brush with vegetable oil if necessary (or spray with cooking spray before heating).

3 For each pancake, pour slightly less than ¼ cup batter onto griddle. Cook 2 to 3 minutes or until bubbly on top and dry around edges. Turn; cook other side until golden brown.

1 Pancake: Calories 110; Total Fat 5g (Saturated Fat 1.5g; Trans Fat 0g); Cholesterol 25mg; Sodium 250mg; Total Carbohydrate 13g (Dietary Fiber 0g); Protein 3g **Exchanges:** 1 Starch, ½ Fat **Carbohydrate Choices:** 1

BERRY PANCAKES Stir ½ cup fresh or frozen (thawed and well drained) blackberries, blueberries or raspberries into batter.

BUTTERMILK PANCAKES Substitute 1 cup buttermilk for the ¾ cup milk. Decrease baking powder to 1 teaspoon. Add ½ teaspoon baking soda.

See how to make **pancakes**: Visit bettycrocker.com/BCcookbook

WHOLE-GRAIN STRAWBERRY PANCAKES Make pancakes with whole wheat flour. Top each serving with ¼ cup strawberry yogurt and ½ cup sliced fresh strawberries.

ORANGE-CRANBERRY PANCAKES Substitute orange juice for the milk. Stir in ¼ cup dried cranberries and ¼ cup chopped dried apples after mixing ingredients in Step 1.

Contributed by Mary Nuzum-Osborn from Carson, Iowa

Turning Pancakes

Pancakes are ready to turn when they are puffed and bubbles form on top.

Pancakes

CORNBREAD PANCAKES WITH BUTTER-PECAN SYRUP

For this recipe, make the syrup first, then the pancakes, so breakfast is all warm at the same time.

PREP 30 min **TOTAL** 30 min • **8 servings**

BUTTER-PECAN SYRUP

- 2 tablespoons butter
- ⅓ cup chopped pecans
- ¾ cup real maple syrup or maple-flavored syrup

PANCAKES

- 1¼ cups all-purpose flour
- ¾ cup cornmeal
- ¼ cup sugar
- 2 teaspoons baking powder
- ½ teaspoon salt
- 1⅓ cups milk
- ¼ cup vegetable oil
- 1 egg, beaten

1 In 1-quart saucepan, melt butter over medium heat. Add pecans; cook, stirring frequently, 2 to 3 minutes, or until browned. Stir in syrup; heat until hot. Remove from heat.

2 Heat griddle or skillet over medium-high heat (375°F). Brush with vegetable oil if necessary (or spray with cooking spray before heating).

3 In large bowl, mix flour, cornmeal, sugar, baking powder and salt. Stir in milk, oil and egg just until blended.

4 For each pancake, pour about ¼ cup batter onto griddle. Cook 2 to 3 minutes or until bubbly on top and dry around edges. Turn; cook other side until golden brown. Serve with syrup.

1 Serving: Calories 380; Total Fat 15g (Saturated Fat 3.5g; Trans Fat 0g); Cholesterol 35mg; Sodium 350mg; Total Carbohydrate 57g (Dietary Fiber 2g); Protein 6g **Exchanges:** 1 Starch, 3 Other Carbohydrate, 3 Fat **Carbohydrate Choices:** 4

Pancake Tips

- Mix pancake batter in a measuring cup or bowl with handle and spout. Then you can easily pour batter onto griddle.

- For the most tender pancakes, mix just until dry ingredients are moistened. There may still be lumps in the batter.

- Keep pancakes warm in a single layer on paper towel-lined cookie sheet in a 200°F oven.

Cornbread Pancakes with Butter-Pecan Syrup

PUFFY OVEN PANCAKE

LOWER CALORIE

More like a popover than a pancake, this oven pancake puffs up high around the edges when it's done. Serve it quickly, before it sinks.

PREP 10 min **TOTAL** 40 min • **4 servings**

- 2 tablespoons butter
- 2 eggs
- ½ cup all-purpose flour
- ¼ teaspoon salt
- ½ cup milk
  Lemon juice and powdered sugar or cut-up fruit, if desired

1 Heat oven to 400°F. In 9-inch glass pie plate, melt butter in oven; brush butter over bottom and side of plate.

2 In medium bowl, beat eggs slightly with wire whisk. Stir in flour, salt and milk just until flour is moistened (do not overbeat or pancake may not puff). Pour into pie plate.

3 Bake 25 to 30 minutes or until puffy and deep golden brown. Serve immediately sprinkled with lemon juice and powdered sugar or topped with fruit.

1 Serving: Calories 160; Total Fat 9g (Saturated Fat 5g; Trans Fat 0g); Cholesterol 125mg; Sodium 230mg; Total Carbohydrate 14g (Dietary Fiber 0g); Protein 5g **Exchanges:** 2 Starch, 1 Fat **Carbohydrate Choices:** 1

APPLE OVEN PANCAKE Make pancake as directed, except sprinkle 2 tablespoons packed brown sugar and ¼ teaspoon ground cinnamon evenly over melted butter in pie plate. Arrange 1 cup thinly sliced peeled baking apple (1 medium) over sugar. Pour batter over apple. Bake 30 to 35 minutes.

Immediately loosen edge of pancake and turn upside down onto heatproof serving plate.

DOUBLE OVEN PANCAKE Melt ⅓ cup butter in 13x9-inch pan. Use 4 eggs, 1 cup all-purpose flour, ¼ teaspoon salt and 1 cup milk. Bake 30 to 35 minutes.

CREPES **LOWER CALORIE**

Crepe is French for "pancake." But crepes are much thinner than pancakes and cook very quickly.

PREP 10 min **TOTAL** 35 min • **12 crepes**

- 1½ cups all-purpose flour
- 1 tablespoon granulated sugar
- ½ teaspoon baking powder
- ½ teaspoon salt
- 2 cups milk
- 2 tablespoons butter, melted
- ½ teaspoon vanilla
- 2 eggs
  Applesauce, sweetened berries, jelly or jam, if desired
  Powdered sugar, if desired

1 In medium bowl, mix flour, granulated sugar, baking powder and salt. Stir in milk, 2 tablespoons butter, the vanilla and eggs. Beat with wire whisk just until smooth.

2 Lightly butter 6- to 8-inch skillet or crepe pan. Heat over medium heat until bubbly. For each crepe, pour slightly less than ¼ cup batter into skillet. Immediately tilt and rotate skillet so thin layer of batter covers bottom. Cook until light brown. Run wide spatula around edge to loosen; turn and cook other side until light brown. Repeat with remaining batter, buttering skillet as needed.

3 Stack crepes, placing waxed paper between each; keep covered. Spread applesauce, sweetened berries, jelly or jam thinly over each warm crepe; roll up. (Be sure to fill crepes so when rolled the more attractive side is on the outside.) Sprinkle with powdered sugar.

1 Crepe: Calories 140; Total Fat 8g (Saturated Fat 3.5g; Trans Fat 0g); Cholesterol 55mg; Sodium 190mg; Total Carbohydrate 15g (Dietary Fiber 0g); Protein 4g **Exchanges:** 1 Starch, 1½ Fat **Carbohydrate Choices:** 1

See how to make **crepes:** Visit bettycrocker.com/BCcookbook

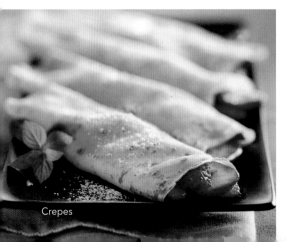

Crepes

MAKE AHEAD DIRECTIONS Make crepes as directed and cool completely; do not fill. Stack crepes with plastic wrap between each; wrap tightly and freeze up to 2 months.

WAFFLES

PREP 5 min TOTAL 35 min • **6 (7-inch) round waffles**

- 2 **eggs**
- 2 **cups all-purpose or whole wheat flour**
- 1 **tablespoon sugar**
- 4 **teaspoons baking powder**
- ¼ **teaspoon salt**
- 1¾ **cups milk**
- ½ **cup vegetable oil or melted butter**
  Fresh berries, if desired

1 Heat waffle iron. (Waffle irons without a nonstick coating may need to be brushed with vegetable oil or sprayed with cooking spray before batter for each waffle is added.)

2 In large bowl, beat eggs with wire whisk until fluffy. Beat in remaining ingredients except berries just until smooth.

3 Pour slightly less than ¾ cup batter onto center of hot waffle iron. (Check manufacturer's directions for recommended amount of batter.) Close lid of waffle iron.

4 Bake about 5 minutes or until steaming stops. Carefully remove waffle. Serve immediately. Top with fresh berries. Repeat with remaining batter.

1 Waffle: Calories 380; Total Fat 22g (Saturated Fat 4g; Trans Fat 0g); Cholesterol 75mg; Sodium 480mg; Total Carbohydrate 38g (Dietary Fiber 1g); Protein 9g **Exchanges:** 2½ Starch, 4 Fat **Carbohydrate Choices:** 2½

Waffles

LIGHTER DIRECTIONS For 7 grams of fat and 255 calories per serving, substitute ½ cup fat-free egg product for the eggs, use fat-free (skim) milk and decrease oil to 3 tablespoons.

FRENCH TOAST LOWER CALORIE

If you've got bread left over from a meal, save it to make this breakfast dish. Day-old or firm bread makes the best French toast.

PREP 5 min TOTAL 25 min • **8 slices**

- 3 **eggs**
- ¾ **cup milk**
- 1 **tablespoon sugar**
- ¼ **teaspoon vanilla**
- ⅛ **teaspoon salt**
- 8 **slices firm-textured sandwich bread, Texas toast or 1-inch-thick slices French bread**

1 In medium bowl, beat eggs, milk, sugar, vanilla and salt with wire whisk until well mixed. Pour into shallow bowl.

2 Heat griddle or skillet over medium heat or to 375°F. (To test griddle, sprinkle with a few drops of water. If bubbles jump around, heat is just right.) Grease griddle with vegetable oil if necessary (or spray with cooking spray before heating).

3 Dip bread into egg mixture. Place on griddle. Cook about 4 minutes on each side or until golden brown.

1 Slice: Calories 230; Total Fat 3.5g (Saturated Fat 1g, Trans Fat 0g); Cholesterol 80mg; Sodium 490mg; Total Carbohydrate 39g (Dietary Fiber 1g); Protein 10g **Exchanges:** 2 Starch, ½ Other Carbohydrate, ½ Medium-Fat Meat **Carbohydrate Choices:** 2½

LIGHTER DIRECTIONS For 2 grams of fat and 95 calories per serving, substitute 1 egg and 2 egg whites for the 3 eggs and use ⅔ cup fat-free (skim) milk. Increase vanilla to ½ teaspoon.

OVEN FRENCH TOAST Heat oven to 450°F. Generously butter 15x10x1-inch pan. Heat pan in oven 1 minute; remove from oven. Arrange dipped bread in hot pan. Drizzle any remaining egg mixture over bread. Bake 5 to 8 minutes or until bottoms are golden brown; turn bread. Bake 2 to 4 minutes longer or until golden brown.

PANCAKE AND FRENCH TOAST TOPPERS

Need to add some dazzle to your breakfast table? These toppings can be served over Pancakes (page 86), French Toast (page 89) or Waffles (page 89). Move over maple syrup and butter!

1 Apple-Rum Butter: Beat ½ cup softened butter with electric mixer until light and fluffy. Gradually beat in ½ cup Apple Butter (page 247, or purchased) and 1 teaspoon rum or ¼ teaspoon rum extract to taste.

2 Blackberry-Lime Sauce: In small saucepan, combine 2 cups blackberries or raspberries, ¼ cup water, ¼ cup sugar and 1 tablespoon fresh lime juice. Simmer sauce for 10 to 15 minutes until berries break down and sauce slightly thickens; stir in 1 teaspoon grated lime peel.

3 Cherry and Granola Topping: Top with about ¼ cup vanilla yogurt and ¼ cup frozen (thawed) sweet cherries; sprinkle with 2 tablespoons granola.

4 Maple Yogurt Topping with Candied Nuts and Bananas: Stir ⅓ cup real maple syrup into 8 ounces plain Greek yogurt; top pancakes or French toast with maple yogurt; sprinkle with purchased candied or regular walnuts or pecans and sliced bananas.

5 Red, White and Blueberries Topping: Melt ¼ cup raspberry preserves in small saucepan; add about 1 tablespoon orange liqueur or orange juice. Serve sauce with pancakes or French toast, fresh blueberries and ½ cup crème fraîche or sour cream mixed with 1 tablespoon sugar.

6 Super Sundae Topping: Drizzle pancakes or French toast with warm Chocolate Sauce (page 234) or chocolate syrup; top with sliced bananas, fresh strawberries, chopped toasted pecans, Sweetened Whipped Cream (page 214) and a maraschino cherry.

CINNAMON FRENCH TOAST STICKS WITH SPICY CIDER SYRUP

FAST   LOWER CALORIE

PREP 10 min TOTAL 20 min • **10 servings**

SPICY CIDER SYRUP

 1 cup sugar
 3 tablespoons all-purpose flour
 ¼ teaspoon ground cinnamon
 ¼ teaspoon ground nutmeg
 2 cups apple cider
 2 tablespoons lemon juice
 ¼ cup butter, cut into 8 pieces

FRENCH TOAST

 ½ cup all-purpose flour
 2 teaspoons ground cinnamon
1¼ cups milk
 1 teaspoon vanilla
 2 eggs
10 slices firm-textured sandwich bread,
     cut into thirds

1 In 2-quart saucepan, mix sugar, 3 tablespoons flour, ¼ teaspoon cinnamon and nutmeg. Stir in cider and lemon juice. Cook over medium heat, stirring constantly, until mixture thickens and boils. Boil and stir 1 minute; remove from heat. Stir in butter; keep warm.

2 In small bowl, beat all French toast ingredients except bread with fork until smooth. Heat griddle or skillet over medium-high heat or to 375°F.

3 Dip sticks of bread into batter; drain excess batter back into bowl. Place bread on griddle. Cook about 4 minutes on each side or until golden brown. Serve with syrup.

1 Serving: Calories 270; Total Fat 7g (Saturated Fat 3g; Trans Fat 0g); Cholesterol 55mg; Sodium 190mg; Total Carbohydrate 46g (Dietary Fiber 0g); Protein 5g **Exchanges:** 2 Starch, 1 Fruit, 1 Fat **Carbohydrate Choices:** 3

APRICOT-STUFFED FRENCH TOAST **LOWER CALORIE**

PREP 15 min TOTAL 1 hr 10 min • **6 servings**

 1 loaf (8 oz) or ½ loaf (1-lb size) day-old
     French bread
 1 package (3 oz) cream cheese, softened
 3 tablespoons apricot preserves
 ¼ teaspoon grated lemon peel
 3 eggs
 ¾ cup half-and-half or milk
 2 tablespoons granulated sugar
 1 teaspoon vanilla
 ⅛ teaspoon salt
 ⅛ teaspoon ground nutmeg, if desired
 2 tablespoons butter, melted
     Powdered sugar, if desired

1 Spray 13x9-inch pan with cooking spray. Cut bread crosswise into 12 (1-inch) slices. Cut a horizontal slit in the side of each bread slice, cutting to—but not through—the other edge.

2 In medium bowl, beat cream cheese, preserves and lemon peel with electric mixer on medium speed about 1 minute or until well mixed. Spread about 2 teaspoons of cream cheese mixture inside the slit in each bread slice. Place stuffed bread slices in pan.

3 In medium bowl, beat eggs, half-and-half, granulated sugar, vanilla, salt and nutmeg with fork or wire whisk until well mixed. Pour egg mixture over bread slices in pan, and turn slices carefully to coat. Cover and refrigerate at least 30 minutes but no longer than 24 hours.

4 Heat oven to 425°F. Uncover French toast; drizzle with butter. Bake 20 to 25 minutes or until golden brown. Sprinkle with powdered sugar.

1 Serving (2 Slices): Calories 310; Total Fat 16g (Saturated Fat 8g; Trans Fat 1g); Cholesterol 145mg; Sodium 380mg; Total Carbohydrate 32g (Dietary Fiber 1g); Protein 9g **Exchanges:** 1 Starch, 1 Other Carbohydrate, 1 High-Fat Meat, 1½ Fat **Carbohydrate Choices:** 2

Apricot-Stuffed French Toast

STRAWBERRY CREAM BRUNCH CAKE

PREP 20 min TOTAL 1 hr 35 min • **16 servings**

CREAM CHEESE FILLING

- 1 **package (8 oz) cream cheese, softened**
- ¼ **cup sugar**
- 2 **tablespoons all-purpose flour**
- 1 **egg**

CAKE

- 2¼ **cups all-purpose flour**
- ¾ **cup sugar**
- ¾ **cup cold butter**
- ½ **teaspoon baking powder**
- ½ **teaspoon baking soda**
- ¼ **teaspoon salt**
- ¾ **cup sour cream**
- 1 **teaspoon almond extract**
- 1 **egg**
- ½ **cup strawberry or raspberry preserves**
- ½ **cup sliced almonds**

1 Heat oven to 350°F. Grease bottom and side of 10-inch springform pan or 11x7-inch (2-quart) glass baking dish with shortening; lightly flour.

2 In small bowl, mix filling ingredients until smooth; set aside.

3 In large bowl, mix 2¼ cups flour and ¾ cup sugar. Cut in butter, using pastry blender or fork, until mixture looks like coarse crumbs. Reserve 1 cup of the crumb mixture. Stir baking powder, baking soda, salt, sour cream, almond extract and egg into remaining crumb mixture. Spread batter over bottom and 2 inches up side (about ¼ inch thick) of pan.

4 Pour filling over batter. Carefully spoon preserves evenly over filling. Mix almonds and reserved crumb mixture; sprinkle over preserves.

5 Bake springform pan 50 to 60 minutes, 11x7-inch dish 35 to 45 minutes, or until filling is set and crust is deep golden brown. Cool 15 minutes; remove side of springform pan. Serve warm if desired. Store covered in refrigerator.

1 Serving: Calories 320; Total Fat 18g (Saturated Fat 10g; Trans Fat 0.5g); Cholesterol 70mg; Sodium 220mg; Total Carbohydrate 35g (Dietary Fiber 1g); Protein 4g **Exchanges:** 1½ Starch, 1 Other Carbohydrate, 3½ Fat **Carbohydrate Choices:** 2

MAKE AHEAD **DIRECTIONS** Cool cake completely, then wrap tightly and freeze up to 1 month. To thaw, let stand at room temperature several hours before serving.

Strawberry Cream Brunch Cake

LEMON CURD–FILLED BUTTER CAKE

A classic lemon curd is the filling in this buttery-rich dense yellow cake. If you want to save time, use a jar of purchased lemon curd.

PREP 25 min **TOTAL** 2 hr 40 min • **12 servings**

LEMON CURD

- ¼ cup granulated sugar
- 2 tablespoons cornstarch
- ¾ cup cold water
- 3 egg yolks
- 1 tablespoon grated lemon peel
- 3 tablespoons lemon juice

CAKE

- 1 cup butter, softened
- 1 cup granulated sugar
- 5 eggs
- 1¾ cups all-purpose flour
- 2 teaspoons grated lemon peel
- 1½ teaspoons baking powder
- 1 teaspoon vanilla
- ⅓ cup slivered almonds, toasted (page 22)
- ½ teaspoon powdered sugar, if desired

1 In 1-quart saucepan, mix ¼ cup granulated sugar and the cornstarch. Stir in water and egg yolks with wire whisk until well mixed and no lumps remain. Heat to boiling over medium heat, stirring constantly, until mixture begins to thicken. Cook and stir 1 minute; remove from heat. Stir in 1 tablespoon lemon peel and the lemon juice. Refrigerate uncovered 20 minutes, stirring once, until room temperature.

2 Heat oven to 350°F. Grease bottom and side of 9-inch springform pan with shortening; lightly flour. In large bowl, beat butter and 1 cup granulated sugar with electric mixer on medium speed about 1 minute or until smooth.

3 Beat in eggs, one at a time, until just blended, then continue beating on medium speed 2 minutes, scraping bowl once. On low speed, beat in flour, 2 teaspoons lemon peel, the baking powder and vanilla about 30 seconds or until just blended.

Lemon Curd–Filled Butter Cake

4 Spread half of cake batter (about 2 cups) in bottom of pan. Spoon lemon curd evenly onto batter, spreading to ½ inch from edge. Drop remaining batter by tablespoonfuls around edge of curd and pan; spread batter evenly and toward center to cover curd. Sprinkle almonds over top.

5 Bake 45 to 55 minutes or until center is set, cake is firm to the touch and top is golden brown. Cool in pan on cooling rack at least 1 hour (center will sink slightly). Run thin knife around side of cake; remove side of pan. Sprinkle with powdered sugar before serving. Store covered in refrigerator.

1 Serving: Calories 360; Total Fat 20g (Saturated Fat 9g; Trans Fat 1g); Cholesterol 180mg; Sodium 190mg; Total Carbohydrate 37g (Dietary Fiber 0g); Protein 6g **Exchanges:** 1 Starch, 1½ Other Carbohydrate, 4 Fat **Carbohydrate Choices:** 2½

Lemon Curd

Originally a British specialty, lemon curd is an intensely rich, very sweet blend of sugar, egg yolks and lemon. It's used here as a filling but can also be used as a spread or dessert topping.

SOUR CREAM COFFEE CAKE

PREP 30 min **TOTAL** 2 hr • **16 servings**

BROWN SUGAR FILLING

- ½ cup packed brown sugar
- ½ cup finely chopped nuts
- 1½ teaspoons ground cinnamon

COFFEE CAKE

- 3 cups all-purpose or whole wheat flour
- 1½ teaspoons baking powder
- 1½ teaspoons baking soda
- ¾ teaspoon salt
- 1½ cups granulated sugar
- ¾ cup butter, softened
- 1½ teaspoons vanilla
- 3 eggs
- 1½ cups sour cream

GLAZE

- ½ cup powdered sugar
- ¼ teaspoon vanilla
- 2 to 3 teaspoons milk

1 Heat oven to 350°F. Grease bottom and side of 10-inch angel food (tube) cake pan, 12-cup fluted tube cake pan or two 9x5-inch loaf pans with shortening or cooking spray.

2 In small bowl, stir filling ingredients until well mixed; set aside. In large bowl, stir flour, baking powder, baking soda and salt until well mixed; set aside.

3 In another large bowl, beat granulated sugar, butter, 1½ teaspoons vanilla and eggs with electric mixer on medium speed 2 minutes, scraping bowl occasionally. Beat about one-fourth of the flour mixture and sour cream at a time alternately into sugar mixture on low speed until blended.

4 For angel food or fluted tube cake pan, spread one-third of the batter (about 2 cups) in pan, then sprinkle with one-third of the filling; repeat twice. For loaf pans, spread one-fourth of the batter (about 1½ cups) in each pan, then sprinkle each with one-fourth of the filling; repeat once.

5 Bake angel food or fluted tube cake pan about 1 hour, loaf pans about 45 minutes, or until toothpick inserted near center comes out clean. Cool 10 minutes in pan on cooling rack.

6 Remove from pan to cooling rack. Cool 20 minutes. In small bowl, stir glaze ingredients until smooth and thin enough to drizzle. Drizzle glaze over coffee cake. Serve warm if desired.

1 Serving: Calories 360; Total Fat 16g (Saturated Fat 8g; Trans Fat 0.5g); Cholesterol 75mg; Sodium 360mg; Total Carbohydrate 49g (Dietary Fiber 1g); Protein 5g **Exchanges:** 2 Starch, 1 Other Carbohydrate, 3 Fat **Carbohydrate Choices:** 3

Removing Coffee Cake from Pan

Slide narrow metal spatula between cake and tube along side of pan. For 2-piece pan, push up from bottom to release. Slide spatula between cake and base to release bottom of cake.

Sour Cream Coffee Cake

QUICK BREADS

YEAST BREADS

CHARTS AND FEATURES

For bonus **breads** recipes, visit
bettycrocker.com/BCcookbook

FAST = Ready in 20 minutes or less LOWER CALORIE = See Helpful Nutrition and Cooking Information, page 685
LIGHTER = 25% fewer calories or grams of fat MAKE AHEAD = Make-ahead directions SLOW COOKER = Slow cooker directions

← Containers of baking ingredients, Jumbo Upside-Down Date-Bran Muffins (page 101), Cornbread (page 105),
Fresh Herb Batter Bread (page 115)

QUICK BREAD BASICS
Quick breads include loaves, muffins, scones and biscuits. Because they're leavened with baking powder or baking soda instead of yeast, the preparation time is shorter. So novice and accomplished bakers alike can offer fresh-from-the-oven goodies in no time.

SELECTING PANS

Use only the pan size specified in the recipe.

For golden brown color and tender crusts, use shiny pans and cookie sheets, which reflect heat.

If using dark or nonstick pans, reduce oven temperature by 25°F. These pans absorb heat more easily than shiny pans, causing baked goods to brown more quickly.

Insulated pans often require slightly longer baking times and result in baked goods that may be less brown.

BEFORE YOU BEGIN

- Check expiration dates on leavening packages for freshness.
- Chop, mash or shred fruits, vegetables or nuts so that they're ready to be added to batter.
- For best results, use butter. If you choose to use margarine, be sure the product has at least 65 percent fat. Do not use reduced-fat butter or whipped products.

TIPS FOR PERFECT QUICK BREADS

- Overmixing makes quick breads tough. Mix batter for loaves and muffins with a spoon, not an electric mixer, just until dry ingredients are moistened.
- To prevent gummy, soggy or heavy loaves, don't increase amount of fruit or vegetables called for in recipe.
- Grease bottom only of loaf or muffin pans, unless otherwise specified; this prevents a lip or hard, dry edge from forming.
- Allow at least 2 inches of space around pans for heat circulation.
- Cracks will form on top of quick breads. This is caused by leavening action during baking and is normal.
- Cool loaves completely for about 2 hours to prevent crumbling when slicing. For easy slicing and better flavor, store loaves tightly covered for 24 hours.
- Cut loaves with serrated knife, using a light sawing motion.
- Wrap completely cooled loaves tightly in plastic wrap or foil and refrigerate up to 1 week. Tightly wrapped loaves placed in freezer plastic bags can be frozen for 3 months.

Use a shiny cookie sheet for the best results and cut scones into wedges before baking.

Learn to Make **Muffins**

BLUEBERRY MUFFINS LOWER CALORIE

Homemade blueberry muffins burst with fresh flavor that store-bought can never duplicate—and it doesn't take rocket science to make them great. Overmixing leads to peaked tops, tough interiors and dry muffins, so follow these simple steps and your muffins will be beautiful and delicious!

PREP 10 min **TOTAL** 40 min • **12 muffins**

¾ cup milk
¼ cup vegetable oil or melted butter
1 egg
2 cups all-purpose flour
½ cup granulated sugar
2 teaspoons baking powder

½ teaspoon salt
1 cup fresh, canned (drained) or frozen blueberries
2 tablespoons coarse sugar or additional granulated sugar, if desired

1 Heat oven to 400°F. Grease bottoms only of 12 regular-size muffin cups with shortening or cooking spray, or line with paper baking cups.

2 In large bowl, beat milk, oil and egg with fork or wire whisk until well mixed. Stir in flour, granulated sugar, baking powder and salt all at once just until flour is moistened (batter will be lumpy). Fold in blueberries. Divide batter evenly among muffin cups; sprinkle each with ½ teaspoon coarse sugar.

3 Bake 20 to 25 minutes or until golden brown and toothpick inserted in center comes out clean. If baked in greased pan, let stand about 5 minutes in pan, then remove from pan to cooling rack; if baked in paper baking cups, immediately remove from pan to cooling rack. Serve warm if desired.

1 Muffin: Calories 170; Total Fat 6g (Saturated Fat 1g; Trans Fat 0g); Cholesterol 20mg; Sodium 190mg; Total Carbohydrate 27g (Dietary Fiber 0g); Protein 3g **Exchanges:** 1 Starch, 1 Fruit, 1 Fat **Carbohydrate Choices:** 2

APPLE-CINNAMON MUFFINS Omit blueberries. Stir in 1 cup chopped peeled apple (about 1 medium) and ½ teaspoon ground cinnamon with the flour. Bake 25 to 30 minutes.

BANANA MUFFINS Omit blueberries. Decrease milk to ⅓ cup. Beat in 1 cup mashed very ripe bananas (2 medium) with the milk. Use packed brown sugar instead of granulated sugar in the muffins.

CRANBERRY-ORANGE MUFFINS Omit blueberries. Beat in 1 tablespoon grated orange peel with the milk. Fold 1 cup coarsely chopped cranberries into batter.

STREUSEL-TOPPED BLUEBERRY MUFFINS Make muffin batter as directed, omitting the 2 tablespoons coarse sugar. In medium bowl, mix ¼ cup all-purpose flour, ¼ cup packed brown sugar and ¼ teaspoon ground cinnamon. Cut in 2 tablespoons firm butter, using pastry blender or fork, until crumbly. Divide batter evenly among muffin cups. Sprinkle each with about 1 tablespoon streusel.

Blueberry Muffins

See how to make **blueberry muffins:**
Visit bettycrocker.com/BCcookbook

SPECIALTY MUFFINS TIMES AND TEMPERATURES

Use this chart to convert a 12-muffin recipe to mini or jumbo muffins or muffin tops. Check at the minimum time to see if muffins are done, then check every minute or two until done.

Muffin batters with large pieces of nuts, fruit or chocolate work better for jumbo muffins; for mini muffins, use miniature chips and small pieces of fruit and nuts.

Pans for baking muffin tops often have a dark nonstick surface; check the manufacturer's instructions to see if reducing the oven temperature by 25°F is recommended.

Muffin Size	Muffin Cup Size	Oven Temperature	Bake Time	Yield
MUFFINS				
Mini	1¾ x 1 inch (small)	400°F	10 to 17 minutes	24
Jumbo	3½ x 1¾ inches (large)	375°F	25 to 35 minutes	4
MUFFIN TOPS				
Regular	2¾ x ⅜ inch	400°F	8 to 10 minutes	18
Jumbo	4 x ½ inch	400°F	15 to 20 minutes	6

Keys to Success

- **Grease bottoms** only of muffin cups. Muffins will rise higher in the cups if they can "grab" onto the sides.

- **Beat wet ingredients first** before adding dry ingredients. This will prevent the batter from being overmixed.

- **Stir in dry ingredients** all at once, just until moistened, to prevent overmixing.

- **Fold in blueberries gently** to prevent blueberries from releasing juice into the batter and turning the batter gray.

Muffin Fix-Ups

The best muffins should be golden brown, slightly rounded with bumpy tops, tender, moist, even textured and easy to remove from the pan. Here are some things that can happen, with solutions to help.

- Pale—the oven was not hot enough.

- Peaked or smooth on top—too much mixing.

- Tough and heavy—too much flour or mixing.

- Dry—too much flour, oven too hot or baked too long.

- Tunnels—too much mixing.

- Sticks to pan—pan not greased correctly.

Learn with Betty | MUFFINS

Perfect Muffin: This muffin is slightly rounded with bumpy top.

Overmixed Muffin: This muffin has a peaked, smooth top.

Overbaked Muffin: This muffin is dry with a rough top and is too brown.

Glorious Morning Muffins

ALMOND–POPPY SEED MUFFINS LOWER CALORIE

Look for poppy seed in small jars in the spice section of the grocery store, or small packages in the produce area.

PREP 15 min **TOTAL** 30 min • **12 muffins**

- ½ cup sugar
- ⅓ cup vegetable oil
- 1 egg
- ½ teaspoon almond extract
- ½ cup sour cream
- ¼ cup milk
- 1⅓ cups all-purpose flour
- ½ teaspoon baking powder
- ½ teaspoon salt
- ¼ teaspoon baking soda
- 2 tablespoons poppy seed
- 1 tablespoon sugar
- 2 tablespoons sliced almonds

1 Heat oven to 375°F. Place paper baking cup in each of 12 regular-size muffin cups, or grease bottoms only with shortening or cooking spray.

2 In large bowl, stir ½ cup sugar, oil, egg and almond extract. Beat in sour cream and milk with spoon until blended. Stir in flour, baking powder, salt, baking soda and poppy seed until well blended. Divide batter evenly among muffin cups. Sprinkle with 1 tablespoon sugar and the almonds.

3 Bake 14 to 17 minutes or until toothpick inserted in center comes out clean. Remove from pan to cooling rack. Serve warm if desired.

1 Muffin: Calories 180; Total Fat 10g (Saturated Fat 2.5g, Trans Fat 0g); Cholesterol 25mg; Sodium 160mg; Total Carbohydrate 21g (Dietary Fiber 0g); Protein 3g **Exchanges:** 1 Starch, ½ Other Carbohydrate, 1½ Fat **Carbohydrate Choices:** 1½

Serving Muffins

The traditional bread basket lined with a clean paper or cloth napkin is still the ideal way to serve warm-from-the-oven muffins. The napkin holds in some warmth while the open weave of the basket lets steam escape, which could otherwise condense and make the muffins soggy.

GLORIOUS MORNING MUFFINS

PREP 20 min **TOTAL** 50 min • **18 muffins**

- 2 eggs
- ¾ cup vegetable oil
- ¼ cup milk
- 2 teaspoons vanilla
- 2 cups all-purpose flour
- 1 cup packed brown sugar
- 2 teaspoons baking soda
- 2 teaspoons ground cinnamon
- ½ teaspoon salt
- 1½ cups shredded carrots (2 to 3 medium)
- 1 cup shredded peeled apple (1 medium)
- ½ cup coconut
- ½ cup raisins
- ¾ cup sliced almonds

1 Heat oven to 350°F. Line 18 regular-size muffin cups with paper baking cups, or grease with shortening or cooking spray.

2 In large bowl, beat eggs, oil, milk and vanilla with wire whisk until well blended. Add flour, brown sugar, baking soda, cinnamon and salt; stir just until dry ingredients are moistened. Stir in carrots, apple, coconut, raisins and ½ cup of the almonds. Divide batter evenly among muffin cups. Sprinkle remaining ¼ cup almonds over batter.

3 Bake 20 to 25 minutes or until toothpick inserted in center comes out clean. Cool 5 minutes in pan; remove from pan to cooling rack. Serve warm if desired.

1 Muffin: Calories 250; Total Fat 13g (Saturated Fat 2.5g; Trans Fat 0g); Cholesterol 25mg; Sodium 230mg; Total Carbohydrate 29g (Dietary Fiber 2g); Protein 3g **Exchanges:** 1 Starch, 1 Other Carbohydrate, 2½ Fat **Carbohydrate Choices:** 2

JUMBO UPSIDE-DOWN DATE-BRAN MUFFINS

This muffin batter was intentionally developed to be thick. The dense batter forms a sticky layer similar to caramel roll topping, and it also prevents the topping from bubbling up and running over the edge of the pan. You end up with moist bakery-style muffins with delicious sticky tops.

PREP 20 min TOTAL 40 min • **6 muffins**

MUFFINS

1 cup Fiber One® cereal
1 cup buttermilk
¼ cup vegetable oil
1 teaspoon vanilla
1 egg
1¼ cups whole wheat flour
¾ cup chopped dates
½ cup packed brown sugar
1 teaspoon baking soda
¼ teaspoon salt

TOPPING

3 tablespoons packed brown sugar
2 tablespoons butter, melted
1 tablespoon light corn syrup

1 Heat oven to 400°F. Grease bottoms and sides of 6 jumbo muffin cups with shortening or cooking spray (do not use paper baking cups).

2 In blender or food processor, place cereal, buttermilk, oil, vanilla and egg. Cover; let stand 10 minutes. Meanwhile, in small bowl, stir all topping ingredients until well mixed. Place 2 teaspoons of the topping in bottom of each muffin cup.

3 Blend cereal mixture on medium speed until smooth; set aside. In medium bowl, stir flour, dates, ½ cup brown sugar, the baking soda and salt until well mixed. Pour cereal mixture over flour mixture; stir just until moistened (batter will be thick). Divide batter evenly among muffin cups.

4 Bake 14 to 18 minutes or until tooth-pick inserted in center comes out clean. Immediately place cookie sheet upside down on muffin pan; turn cookie sheet and pan over to remove muffins. Serve warm if desired.

1 Muffin: Calories 230; Total Fat 8g (Saturated Fat 2g; Trans Fat 0g); Cholesterol 25mg; Sodium 220mg; Total Carbohydrate 36g (Dietary Fiber 5g); Protein 4g **Exchanges:** 1 Starch, 1½ Other Carbohydrate, 1½ Fat **Carbohydrate Choices:** 2½

UPSIDE-DOWN DATE-BRAN MUFFINS

Grease bottoms and sides of 12 regular-size muffin cups with shortening or cooking spray (do not use paper baking cups). Place 1 teaspoon of the topping in each cup before adding batter. Bake as directed. Due to the thickness of the batter, the bake time range will be the same for both sizes of muffins.

BEST-EVER OATMEAL-FLAX BREAD LOWER CALORIE

Oats, whole wheat flour and flaxseed is a winning combination for a deliciously moist bread that's even better toasted the next day. The flaxseed in this recipe replaces eggs and much of the oil that is used in other quick breads.

PREP 10 min TOTAL 3 hr 10 min • **1 loaf (16 slices)**

1½ cups whole wheat flour
1 cup all-purpose flour
⅔ cup packed dark brown sugar
½ cup old-fashioned oats
⅓ cup ground flaxseed or flaxseed meal
1 teaspoon baking soda
1 teaspoon salt
1⅔ cups buttermilk
1 tablespoon old-fashioned oats

1 Heat oven to 350°F. Spray 8x4-inch loaf pan with cooking spray.

2 In large bowl, mix flours, brown sugar, ½ cup oats, the flaxseed, baking soda and salt. Stir in buttermilk just until mixed. Pour batter into pan. Sprinkle with 1 tablespoon oats.

3 Bake 45 to 55 minutes or until toothpick inserted in center comes out clean. Cool in pan on cooling rack 5 minutes. Remove from pan to cooling rack. Cool completely, about 2 hours, before slicing.

1 Slice: Calories 140; Total Fat 2g (Saturated Fat 0g; Trans Fat 0g); Cholesterol 0mg; Sodium 250mg; Total Carbohydrate 27g (Dietary Fiber 3g); Protein 4g **Exchanges:** 1 Starch, 1 Other Carbohydrate **Carbohydrate Choices:** 2

Heirloom Recipe and New Twist

Although the true origin of banana bread is not known, this enduring favorite has been around at least since the 1930s. Our version of banana bread has appeared in all editions of the Betty Crocker Cookbook. The Cranberry-Sweet Potato Bread is a great new flavor combination that is rich with sweet potato, sweet spices and cranberries. Either recipe is a great, easy choice to make any time.

CLASSIC

BANANA BREAD LOWER CALORIE

Don't throw away those bananas that are turning brown and soft. Turn them into banana bread.

PREP 15 min **TOTAL** 3 hr 25 min • **2 loaves** (12 slices each)

- 1¼ cups sugar
- ½ cup butter, softened
- 2 eggs
- 1½ cups mashed very ripe bananas (3 medium)
- ½ cup buttermilk
- 1 teaspoon vanilla
- 2½ cups all-purpose flour
- 1 teaspoon baking soda
- 1 teaspoon salt
- 1 cup chopped nuts, if desired

1 Heat oven to 350°F. Grease bottoms only of 2 (8x4-inch) loaf pans or 1 (9x5-inch) loaf pan.

2 In large bowl, stir sugar and butter until well mixed. Stir in eggs until well mixed. Stir in bananas, buttermilk and vanilla; beat with spoon until smooth. Stir in flour, baking soda and salt just until moistened. Stir in nuts. Divide batter evenly between 8-inch pans or pour into 9-inch pan.

3 Bake 8-inch loaves about 1 hour, 9-inch loaf about 1 hour 15 minutes, or until toothpick inserted in center comes out clean. Cool 10 minutes in pans on cooling rack.

4 Loosen sides of loaves from pans; remove from pans and place top side up on cooling rack. Cool completely, about 2 hours, before slicing. Wrap tightly and store at room temperature up to 4 days, or refrigerate.

1 Slice: Calories 150; Total Fat 4.5g (Saturated Fat 2.5g; Trans Fat 0g); Cholesterol 30mg; Sodium 190mg; Total Carbohydrate 24g (Dietary Fiber 0g); Protein 2g **Exchanges:** ½ Starch, 1 Other Carbohydrate, 1 Fat **Carbohydrate Choices:** 1½

See how to make banana bread: Visit bettycrocker.com/BCcookbook

BLUEBERRY-BANANA BREAD Omit nuts. Stir 1 cup fresh or frozen (thawed) and drained blueberries into batter.

Quick Bread Fix-Ups

The best quick bread has a golden brown rounded top with a lengthwise crack. It has a thin, tender crust, moist texture with small even holes and any fruit or nuts evenly distributed. Here are some things that can happen with solutions to help.

- Did not rise—too much mixing or leavening was old.
- Tunnels—too much mixing.
- Compact—too much flour, not enough leavening.
- Tough—too much mixing.
- Rims around edges—sides of pan were greased.

MAKING MINI LOAVES

Bake quick bread batters in miniature loaf pans, muffin pans or small cake molds in special shapes. To determine how much batter to use for a pan, fill with water, then pour the water into a measuring cup. See below for how much batter to use for your pan size.

Approximate Pan Size	Amount of Batter	Approximate Bake Time at 350°F
⅓ cup	¼ cup	15 to 20 minutes
½ cup	⅓ cup	15 to 20 minutes
⅔ to ¾ cup	½ cup	25 to 35 minutes
1 cup	¾ cup	35 to 40 minutes

CRANBERRY–SWEET POTATO BREAD

PREP 20 min **TOTAL** 2 hr • **2 loaves (12 slices each)**

2⅓	cups sugar
⅔	cup water
⅔	cup vegetable oil
1	teaspoon vanilla
2	cups mashed cooked dark-orange sweet potatoes (about 1¼ lb)*
4	eggs
3⅓	cups all-purpose flour
2	teaspoons baking soda
1½	teaspoons salt
1	teaspoon ground cinnamon
½	teaspoon baking powder
½	teaspoon ground nutmeg
1	cup sweetened dried cranberries
1	cup chopped pecans, if desired

1 Heat oven to 350°F. Grease and flour 2 (8x4-inch) loaf pans or 1 (9x5-inch) loaf pan. In large bowl, mix sugar, water, oil, vanilla, sweet potatoes and eggs until well blended.

2 In medium bowl, mix flour, baking soda, salt, cinnamon, baking powder and nutmeg. Add to sweet potato mixture; stir just until dry ingredients are moistened. Stir in cranberries and pecans. Divide batter evenly between 8-inch pans or spoon into 9-inch pan.

3 Bake 60 to 70 minutes or until toothpick inserted in center comes out clean. Cool 15 minutes in pans on cooling rack.

4 Loosen sides of loaves from pans; remove from pans and place top side up on cooling rack. Cool completely, about 2 hours, before slicing. Wrap tightly and store at room temperature up to 4 days, or refrigerate.

*1 can (23 oz) sweet potatoes in syrup, drained and mashed can be substituted for the fresh sweet potatoes.

1 Slice: Calories 240; Total Fat 7g (Saturated Fat 1.5g; Trans Fat 0g); Cholesterol 35mg; Sodium 280mg; Total Carbohydrate 41g (Dietary Fiber 1g); Protein 3g **Exchanges:** 1 Starch, 1½ Other Carbohydrate, 1½ Fat **Carbohydrate Choices:** 3

Banana Bread

Cranberry–Sweet Potato Bread

ZUCCHINI BREAD LOWER CALORIE

You don't need to peel the zucchini if it is very fresh and green. Older, larger zucchini may require peeling before shredding. The peel adds little green flecks to the bread.

PREP 15 min **TOTAL** 3 hr 25 min • **2 loaves (12 slices each)**

- 3 **cups shredded zucchini (2 to 3 medium)**
- 1⅔ **cups sugar**
- ⅔ **cup vegetable oil**
- 2 **teaspoons vanilla**
- 4 **eggs**
- 3 **cups all-purpose or whole wheat flour**
- 2 **teaspoons baking soda**
- 1 **teaspoon salt**
- 1 **teaspoon ground cinnamon**
- ½ **teaspoon baking powder**
- ½ **teaspoon ground cloves**
- ½ **cup chopped nuts**
- ½ **cup raisins, if desired**

1 Heat oven to 350°F. Grease bottoms only of 2 (8x4-inch) loaf pans or 1 (9x5-inch) loaf pan with shortening or cooking spray.

2 In large bowl, stir zucchini, sugar, oil, vanilla and eggs until well mixed. Stir in remaining ingredients except nuts and raisins. Stir in nuts and raisins. Divide batter evenly between 8-inch pans or pour into 9-inch pan.

3 Bake 8-inch loaves 50 to 60 minutes, 9-inch loaf 1 hour 10 minutes to 1 hour 20 minutes, or until toothpick inserted in center comes out clean. Cool 10 minutes in pans on cooling rack.

4 Loosen sides of loaves from pans; remove from pans and place top side up on cooling rack. Cool completely, about 2 hours, before slicing. Wrap tightly and store at room temperature up to 4 days, or refrigerate up to 10 days.

1 Slice: Calories 200; Total Fat 9g (Saturated Fat 1.5g; Trans Fat 0g); Cholesterol 35mg; Sodium 230mg; Total Carbohydrate 27g (Dietary Fiber 1g); Protein 3g **Exchanges:** 1 Starch, 1 Other Carbohydrate, 1½ Fat **Carbohydrate Choices:** 1

CRANBERRY BREAD Omit zucchini, cinnamon, cloves and raisins. Stir in ½ cup milk and 2 teaspoons grated orange peel with the oil. Stir 3 cups fresh or frozen (thawed and drained) cranberries into batter. Bake 1 hour to 1 hour 10 minutes.

ORANGE ZUCCHINI BREAD Stir in 2 teaspoons grated orange peel with the flour mixture. When loaf is cooled, drizzle with Orange Glaze (page 156). Let stand until set.

PUMPKIN BREAD Substitute 1 can (15 oz) pumpkin (not pumpkin pie mix) for the zucchini.

Cranberry Bread

Brown Bread with Raisins

BROWN BREAD WITH RAISINS

LOWER CALORIE

Created in colonial times and also called Boston brown bread, this authentic dark bread is made with cornmeal and molasses. Originally, it called for rye meal, which was available at the time. If you like the flavor of rye, substitute ½ cup rye flour for ½ cup of the whole wheat flour.

PREP 15 min **TOTAL** 1 hr 45 min • **1 loaf (32 slices)**

- 1 cup all-purpose flour
- 1 cup whole wheat flour
- 1 cup whole-grain cornmeal
- 1 cup raisins
- 2 cups buttermilk
- ¾ cup molasses
- 2 teaspoons baking soda
- 1 teaspoon salt

1 Heat oven to 325°F. Grease 2-quart casserole with shortening or cooking spray.

2 In large bowl, beat all ingredients with electric mixer on low speed 30 seconds, scraping bowl constantly. Beat on medium speed 30 seconds, scraping bowl constantly. Pour batter into casserole.

3 Bake uncovered about 1 hour or until toothpick inserted in center comes out clean. Immediately loosen sides of bread with metal spatula and unmold bread; cool 30 minutes on cooling rack before slicing. Serve warm.

1 Slice: Calories 90; Total Fat 0.5g (Saturated Fat 0g; Trans Fat 0g); Cholesterol 0mg; Sodium 170mg; Total Carbohydrate 19g (Dietary Fiber 0g); Protein 2g **Exchanges:** 1 Starch **Carbohydrate Choices:** 1

STEAMED BROWN BREAD Remove labels from four 4¼x3-inch cans (15- to 16-oz vegetable cans). Grease cans or heatproof 7-inch tube mold with shortening or cooking spray. Make batter as directed. Fill cans about two-thirds full. Cover tightly with foil. Place cans on rack in Dutch oven or steamer; pour boiling water into pan to level of rack. Cover pan. Keep water boiling over low heat about 3 hours or until toothpick inserted in center comes out clean. (Add boiling water during steaming if necessary.)

CORNBREAD **LOWER CALORIE**

PREP 10 min **TOTAL** 35 min • **12 servings**

- 1 cup milk
- ¼ cup butter, melted
- 1 egg
- 1¼ cups yellow, white or blue cornmeal
- 1 cup all-purpose flour
- ½ cup sugar
- 1 tablespoon baking powder
- ½ teaspoon salt

1 Heat oven to 400°F. Grease bottom and side of 9-inch round pan or 8-inch square pan with shortening or cooking spray.

2 In large bowl, beat milk, butter and egg with wire whisk. Stir in remaining ingredients all at once just until flour is moistened (batter will be lumpy). Pour into pan.

3 Bake 20 to 25 minutes or until golden brown and toothpick inserted in center comes out clean. Serve warm.

1 Serving: Calories 170; Total Fat 5g (Saturated Fat 2.5g; Trans Fat 0g); Cholesterol 30mg; Sodium 260mg; Total Carbohydrate 29g (Dietary Fiber 0g); Protein 4g **Exchanges:** 1 Starch, 1 Other Carbohydrate, 1 Fat **Carbohydrate Choices:** 2

BACON CORNBREAD Make cornbread as directed. Stir 4 slices cooked, crumbled bacon into batter before pouring into pan.

CORN MUFFINS Grease bottoms only of 12 regular-size muffin cups with shortening or cooking spray, or line with paper baking cups. Fill cups about three-quarters full. Bake as directed in Step 3.

BAKING POWDER BISCUITS

LOWER CALORIE

PREP 10 min **TOTAL** 25 min • **12 biscuits**

- 2 **cups all-purpose or whole wheat flour**
- 1 **tablespoon sugar**
- 3 **teaspoons baking powder**
- 1 **teaspoon salt**
- ½ **cup shortening or cold butter, cut into 8 pieces**
- ¾ **cup milk**

1 Heat oven to 450°F. In medium bowl, mix flour, sugar, baking powder and salt. Cut in shortening, using pastry blender or fork, until mixture looks like fine crumbs. Stir in milk until dough leaves side of bowl (dough will be soft and sticky).

2 Place dough on lightly floured surface. Knead lightly 10 times. Roll or pat until ½ inch thick. Cut with floured 2- to 2¼-inch biscuit cutter. On ungreased cookie sheet, place biscuits about 1 inch apart for crusty sides, touching for soft sides.

3 Bake 10 to 12 minutes or until golden brown. Immediately remove from cookie sheet to cooling rack. Serve warm.

1 Biscuit: Calories 160; Total Fat 9g (Saturated Fat 2.5g; Trans Fat 1.5g); Cholesterol 0mg; Sodium 330mg; Total Carbohydrate 18g (Dietary Fiber 0g); Protein 3g **Exchanges:** 1 Starch, 2 Fat **Carbohydrate Choices:** 1

BUTTERMILK BISCUITS Decrease baking powder to 2 teaspoons; add ¼ teaspoon baking soda with the sugar. Substitute buttermilk for the milk. (If buttermilk is thick, use slightly more than ¾ cup.)

DROP BISCUITS Grease cookie sheet with shortening. Increase milk to 1 cup. Drop dough by 12 spoonfuls about 2 inches apart onto cookie sheet.

Tips for Perfect Biscuits

- The uniform distribution of shortening into the flour mixture helps create flaky biscuits. A pastry blender is the best tool for cutting shortening into the flour mixture but you can use a fork, too. Use the fork to break up pieces so that they are very small.

- Dip the biscuit cutter in flour before each cut to prevent sticking. Push the cutter straight down through dough. If you twist as you cut, biscuits will be uneven. Make cuts as close together as possible to yield the most biscuits.

- If you don't have a biscuit cutter, use the open end of a clean narrow can or glass. For fun shapes, use cookie cutters.

- To rework trimmings, lightly press (don't knead) dough together. Roll or pat to ½-inch thickness and cut. (Note these baked biscuits may be uneven.)

Making Baking Powder Biscuits

Cut shortening into flour mixture until the mixture looks like fine crumbs.

Stir in milk until dough leaves side of bowl (dough will be soft and sticky).

Drop Biscuits

EASY CREAM BISCUITS

LOWER CALORIE

These biscuits are absolutely delicious. The whipping cream replaces shortening or butter, making them super tender and rich.

PREP 10 min TOTAL 35 min • **12 biscuits**

1¾ cups all-purpose flour
2½ teaspoons baking powder
½ teaspoon salt
About 1¼ cups whipping cream

1 Heat oven to 450°F. In large bowl, mix flour, baking powder and salt. Stir in just enough whipping cream so dough leaves side of bowl and forms a ball. (If dough is too dry, mix in 1 to 2 teaspoons more whipping cream.)

2 Place dough on lightly floured surface; gently roll in flour to coat. Knead lightly 10 times, sprinkling with flour if dough is too sticky. Roll or pat until ½ inch thick. Cut with floured 2 to 2¼-inch biscuit cutter. On ungreased cookie sheet, place biscuits about 1 inch apart.

3 Bake 10 to 12 minutes or until golden brown. Immediately remove from cookie sheet to cooling rack. Serve warm.

1 Biscuit: Calories 140; Total Fat 8g (Saturated Fat 5g; Trans Fat 0g); Cholesterol 30mg; Sodium 210mg; Total Carbohydrate 15g (Dietary Fiber 0g); Protein 2g **Exchanges:** 1 Other Carbohydrate, 1½ Fat **Carbohydrate Choices:** 1

CINNAMON-RAISIN CREAM BISCUITS Stir in 2 tablespoons sugar, 1 teaspoon ground cinnamon and ⅓ cup raisins or dried currants with the flour. Drizzle Vanilla Glaze (page 156) over warm biscuits if desired.

Easy Cream Biscuits

CHOCOLATE CHIP CREAM BISCUITS Stir in 1 tablespoon sugar and ¼ cup miniature chocolate chips with the flour. Drizzle with Chocolate Glaze (page 156) if desired.

CRANBERRY CREAM BISCUITS Stir in 2 tablespoons sugar, ¼ teaspoon ground nutmeg and ½ cup dried cranberries with the flour.

HERBED CREAM BISCUITS Stir in ½ teaspoon dried Italian seasoning with the flour.

Biscuit Fix-Ups

The best biscuits should be light golden brown, high with fairly smooth level tops, tender and flaky. Here are some things that can happen with solutions to help.

- Not high—not enough baking powder or too much mixing.
- Dark bottom crust—oven too hot or oven rack too low.
- Not tender or flaky—not enough shortening, too much mixing or too much flour.

Learn with Betty | BISCUITS

Perfect Biscuit: This biscuit is light golden brown and high with fairly smooth sides. It will be tender and light.

Underleavened Biscuit: This biscuit did not have enough leavening and was mixed too much. It will be tough and not flaky.

Overbaked Biscuit: This biscuit was overbaked and the oven was too hot. It will be hard and crumbly.

SCONES

PREP 15 min TOTAL 35 min • **8 scones**

1¾ cups all-purpose flour
3 tablespoons granulated sugar
2½ teaspoons baking powder
½ teaspoon salt
⅓ cup cold butter, cut into 8 pieces
1 egg, beaten
½ teaspoon vanilla
4 to 6 tablespoons whipping cream
Additional whipping cream
Coarse sugar or additional granulated sugar

1 Heat oven to 400°F.

2 In large bowl, mix flour, granulated sugar, baking powder and salt. Cut in butter, using pastry blender or fork, until mixture looks like fine crumbs. Stir in egg, vanilla and just enough of the 4 to 6 tablespoons whipping cream so dough leaves side of bowl.

3 Place dough on lightly floured surface; gently roll in flour to coat. Knead lightly 10 times. On ungreased cookie sheet, roll or pat dough into 8-inch round. Cut into 8 wedges with sharp knife that has been dipped in flour, but do not separate wedges. Brush with additional whipping cream; sprinkle with coarse sugar.

4 Bake 14 to 16 minutes or until light golden brown. Immediately remove from cookie sheet; carefully separate wedges. Serve warm.

1 Scone: Calories 240; Total Fat 11g (Saturated Fat 6g; Trans Fat 0.5g); Cholesterol 55mg; Sodium 360mg; Total Carbohydrate 31g (Dietary Fiber 0g); Protein 4g **Exchanges:** 1 Starch, 1 Other Carbohydrate, 2 Fat **Carbohydrate Choices:** 2

CHERRY–CHOCOLATE CHIP SCONES Stir in ½ cup each dried cherries and miniature semisweet chocolate chips with the egg, vanilla and whipping cream.

CHOCOLATE CHIP SCONES Stir in ½ cup miniature semisweet chocolate chips with the egg, vanilla and whipping cream.

CRANBERRY-ORANGE SCONES Stir in ½ cup dried cranberries and 1 teaspoon grated orange peel with the egg, vanilla and whipping cream.

CURRANT SCONES Stir in ½ cup dried currants or raisins with the egg, vanilla and whipping cream.

LEMON-CHERRY SCONES Stir in ½ cup dried cherries and 2 teaspoons grated lemon peel with the egg, vanilla and whipping cream.

RASPBERRY–WHITE CHOCOLATE SCONES Substitute almond extract for the vanilla; increase whipping cream to ½ cup. Stir in ¾ cup frozen unsweetened raspberries (do not thaw) and ⅔ cup white vanilla baking chips with the egg, almond extract and whipping cream. Omit kneading step; pat dough into 8-inch circle on ungreased cookie sheet. Continue as directed—except bake 18 to 23 minutes. Raspberries will color the dough a little bit.

Making Scones

Roll or pat dough into 8-inch circle on ungreased cookie sheet.

Cut into 8 wedges with sharp knife or pizza cutter dipped in flour; do not separate.

Cherry–Chocolate Chip Scones

Popovers

POPOVERS LOWER CALORIE

Popovers get their name because they pop up high out of their baking cups in the oven. Serve them hot with butter or try one of the sweet or savory butters (page 501).

PREP 10 min **TOTAL** 45 min • **6 popovers**

- 2 **eggs**
- 1 **cup all-purpose flour**
- 1 **cup milk**
- ½ **teaspoon salt**

1 Heat oven to 450°F. Generously grease 6-cup popover pan with shortening. Heat popover pan in oven 5 minutes.

2 Meanwhile, in medium bowl, beat eggs slightly with fork or wire whisk. Beat in remaining ingredients just until smooth (do not overbeat or popovers may not puff as high). Fill cups about half full.

3 Bake 20 minutes. Reduce oven temperature to 325°F. Bake 10 to 15 minutes longer or until deep golden brown. Immediately remove from cups. Serve hot.

1 Popover: Calories 120; Total Fat 3g (Saturated Fat 1g; Trans Fat 0g); Cholesterol 75mg; Sodium 240mg; Total Carbohydrate 18g (Dietary Fiber 0g); Protein 6g **Exchanges:** 1 Starch, 1 Fat **Carbohydrate Choices:** 1

MAKE AHEAD **DIRECTIONS** After baking the popovers, pierce each popover with the point of a sharp knife to let the steam out; cool completely on cooling rack. When it's time to eat, just reheat uncovered on an ungreased cookie sheet at 350°F for 5 minutes.

DUMPLINGS LOWER CALORIE

Many cultures have some type of dumpling recipe; these dumplings are similar to biscuits. Drop them on top of Beef Stew (page 340) or Burgundy Stew (page 508).

PREP 10 min **TOTAL** 30 min • **10 dumplings**

- 1½ **cups all-purpose flour**
- 1 **tablespoon parsley flakes, if desired**
- 2 **teaspoons baking powder**
- ½ **teaspoon salt**
- 3 **tablespoons shortening or cold butter, cut into 6 pieces**
- ¾ **cup milk**

1 In medium bowl, mix flour, parsley flakes, baking powder and salt. Cut in shortening, using pastry blender or fork, until mixture looks like fine crumbs. Stir in milk.

2 Drop dough by 10 spoonfuls onto hot meat or vegetables in boiling stew (do not drop directly into liquid or dumplings may break apart from the bubbling and become soggy). Cook uncovered 10 minutes. Cover and cook 10 minutes longer.

1 Dumpling: Calories 110; Total Fat 4.5g (Saturated Fat 1g; Trans Fat 0.5g); Cholesterol 0mg; Sodium 220mg; Total Carbohydrate 15g (Dietary Fiber 0g); Protein 3g **Exchanges:** 1 Starch, ½ Fat **Carbohydrate Choices:** 1

HERB DUMPLINGS Substitute 2 teaspoons chopped fresh herbs or 1 teaspoon dried herbs (such as basil, sage or thyme leaves or celery seed) for the parsley flakes.

See how to make **popovers**: Visit bettycrocker.com/BCcookbook

POPOVER TIPS

For the popovers that pop up beautifully:

- Make sure oven is heated to 450°F.
- Heat the popover pan in the hot oven.
- Use room-temperature eggs and milk if possible.
- Use a popover pan (not a muffin pan).
- Bake until deep golden brown so popovers don't fall.

YEAST BREAD BASICS
The tried-and-true recipes in this section make it easy for anyone to try his or her hand at baking yeast breads that are sure to be ideal for any occasion.

YEAST BREAD INGREDIENTS

Flour: All-purpose and bread flours are both high-gluten flours and can be used interchangeably in these recipes. The gluten (an elastic protein) is developed when dough is kneaded, making these two flours ideal for bread baking.

Whole wheat and rye flours have less gluten and should be combined with all-purpose or bread flour. Up to half of a recipe's all-purpose or bread flour can be replaced with whole wheat or rye flour, with equally good results.

Yeast: Yeast is temperature sensitive—too much heat will kill it while too little prevents growth. Check the package expiration date before use.

There are two ways to activate yeast. In the **traditional mixing method,** yeast is dissolved in warm water (105°F to 115°F) and then combined with other ingredients. In the **quick-mix method,** yeast and other dry ingredients are combined, then very warm liquid (120°F to 130°F) is beaten in. Follow the method and temperature guidelines given in the recipe.

With fast-acting dry yeast, rising times may be shorter. Check package directions for best results.

Liquid: Water gives bread a crisp crust, while milk results in a softer crust plus added nutrients.

English Muffin Toasting Bread (page 113)

Sweetener: Sugar, honey and molasses feed yeast to help it grow, add flavor and help brown crust. Don't use artificial sweeteners because they won't feed yeast.

Salt: Salt adds flavor, provides structure to dough by strengthening the gluten and controls yeast growth by preventing dough from rising too much. Never omit salt if specified in recipe.

Fat: Butter, margarine, shortening and vegetable or olive oil make bread tender, and moist and add flavor.

Eggs: Eggs add flavor, richness and color, and promote a fine texture and tender crust.

STORING AND SERVING YEAST BREADS

- Cool breads and rolls completely.

- Breads should not be frosted or glazed before freezing.

- Store soft-crust breads and rolls in resealable food-storage plastic bags or airtight containers in a cool, dry place up to 7 days.

- Store unsliced crisp-crust breads unwrapped at room temperature up to 3 days. Once sliced, place in closed paper bag and use within 1 day or freeze.

- Because refrigeration causes bread to dry out more quickly, only refrigerate breads containing perishable ingredients like cheese or meat.

- To freeze, wrap bread tightly in plastic wrap or foil; place in resealable food-storage plastic bag and freeze up to 3 months.

- To thaw, partially unwrap bread to let moisture escape; let stand at room temperature 2 to 3 hours.

- To reheat thawed breads or rolls, wrap in foil and bake at 350°F (10 to 15 minutes for rolls and 15 to 20 minutes for loaves). For a crisper crust, unwrap during the last 5 minutes.

Making Bread Dough

After the first addition of flour has been beaten in, dough will be very soft and fall in "sheets" off rubber spatula.

To knead, fold dough toward you. With heels of your hands, push dough away from you with short rocking motion. Rotate dough a quarter turn; repeat. Dough will feel springy and smooth.

Dough should rise until doubled in size. Press fingertips about ½ inch into dough. If indentations remain, dough has risen enough.

Gently push fist into dough to deflate. This releases large air bubbles to produce a finer texture in traditional loaves.

Bread Machine Tips

If you use an electric bread machine, there are some special techniques to know about.

- Follow the directions in the manual that comes with your machine and add ingredients in the order that they suggest.
- Carefully measure the ingredients with standard measuring cups and spoons. Even little variations can affect the finished bread.
- Use bread machine yeast; finer granulation disperses more thoroughly during mixing and kneading.
- Opening the machine during rising or baking can cause the loaf to collapse so don't check progress except during mixing and kneading.
- When using the delay cycle, be sure the yeast does not come in contact with liquid. Don't use the delay cycle with recipes using eggs, fresh dairy products (except butter), honey, meats or fresh fruits and vegetables because bacteria can grow during this cycle.
- Keep the area around the bread machine open for good ventilation.

Shaping Traditional Yeast Bread Loaves

Flatten dough with hands or rolling pin into 18x9-inch rectangle.

Tightly roll dough up toward you, beginning at 9-inch side.

Making Free-Form Loaves

Shape dough into smooth ball by stretching surface of dough around to bottom on all four sides; pinch bottom to seal.

Place on cookie sheet; carefully slash tic-tac-toe pattern on each loaf top with serrated knife.

FRENCH BREAD LOWER CALORIE

The traditional flavor and texture of French bread is developed by making a sponge and by refrigerating the shaped loaves before baking. The sponge is a bread-dough mixture made in the first step with yeast and some of the flour and water. Spraying the loaves with water and adding a water pan to the oven help to make a crust. Crispy French bread is best the day you bake it.

PREP 25 min TOTAL 8 hr • **2 loaves**
(16 slices each)

- 1½ cups all-purpose flour
- 1 package regular active dry yeast (2¼ teaspoons)
- 1 cup very warm water (120°F to 130°F)
- 1 teaspoon salt
- 1⅓ to 1⅔ cups all-purpose or bread flour

1 In large bowl, mix 1½ cups all-purpose flour and yeast. Add warm water. Beat with wire whisk or electric mixer on low speed 1 minute, scraping bowl frequently, until batter is very smooth. Cover tightly with plastic wrap and let stand about 1 hour or until bubbly.

2 Stir in salt and enough flour, ½ cup at a time, until a soft dough forms. Place dough on lightly floured surface. Knead 5 to 10 minutes or until dough is smooth and springy (dough will be soft). Grease large bowl with shortening. Place dough in bowl, turning dough to grease all sides. Cover bowl loosely with plastic wrap and let rise in warm place 1 hour to 1 hour 15 minutes or until dough has doubled in size. Dough is ready if indentation remains when touched.

3 Grease uninsulated cookie sheet with shortening or cooking spray. Place dough on lightly floured surface, forming into an oval-shaped mound. Sprinkle top of dough with flour. With a straight-edged knife, press straight down on dough lengthwise to divide into 2 equal parts (the parts will be elongated in shape). Gently shape each part into narrow loaf, about 16 inches long, stretching top of loaf slightly to make it smooth. Place loaves, smooth sides up, about 4 inches apart on cookie sheet.

4 Cover loaves loosely, but airtight, with plastic wrap. (Loaves will expand slightly in the refrigerator.) Refrigerate at least 4 hours but no longer than 24 hours. (This step can be omitted, but refrigerating develops the flavor and texture of the bread. If omitted, continue with next step.)

5 Uncover loaves; spray with cool water; let rise in warm place about 1 hour or until refrigerated loaves have come to room temperature.

6 Place 8- or 9-inch square pan on bottom rack of oven; add hot water to pan until about ½ inch from top. Heat oven to 450°F.

7 With serrated knife, carefully cut ¼-inch-deep slashes diagonally across loaves at 2-inch intervals. Spray loaves with cool water. Place loaves in oven and spray again.

8 Bake 18 to 20 minutes or until loaves are deep golden brown with crisp crust and sound hollow when tapped. Remove from cookie sheet to cooling rack; cool.

1 Slice: Calories 40; Total Fat 0g (Saturated Fat 0g; Trans Fat 0g); Cholesterol 0mg; Sodium 75mg; Total Carbohydrate 9g (Dietary Fiber 0g); Protein 1g **Exchanges:** ½ Starch **Carbohydrate Choices:** ½

CHEESY HERBED FRENCH BREAD Stir in ¼ cup grated Parmesan cheese and 1 teaspoon dried basil leaves with the flour in Step 2.

GARLIC BREAD Heat oven to 400°F. In small bowl, stir ¼ teaspoon garlic powder with ⅓ cup softened butter. Slice 1 loaf French bread into 1-inch slices. Spread each slice with butter mixture. Wrap in foil. Bake 10 to 15 minutes or until hot.

Freezing French Bread

It's great to have an extra loaf of French bread on hand in the freezer. Wrap the cooled loaf tightly in foil and place in freezer plastic bag. If the bread is too long to fit, cut the loaf in half. Freeze up to 3 months. Thaw at room temperature, about 2 hours.

Making French Bread

Mix batter until very smooth. Cover batter in bowl tightly with plastic wrap; let stand 1 hour or until bubbly.

Add flour, ½ cup at a time, until soft dough forms. Knead 5 to 10 minutes until smooth and springy.

Shape each dough half into narrow loaf, about 16 inches long, stretching top to make smooth.

With serrated knife, carefully cut ¼-inch-deep slashes diagonally across loaves at 2-inch intervals.

French Bread

ENGLISH MUFFIN TOASTING BREAD LOWER CALORIE

The open, porous texture of English muffin bread is what allows it to get so nice and crisp when it's toasted. Serve slices of the bread as you would English muffins, with butter, honey and marmalade or another favorite jam.

PREP 15 min TOTAL 3 hr 45 min • **1 loaf (16 slices)**

Cornmeal, if desired
1   cup milk
¼   cup water
1   tablespoon butter
3   cups all-purpose or bread flour
1   tablespoon sugar
1   teaspoon salt
¼   teaspoon baking soda
1   package regular active or fast-acting dry yeast (2¼ teaspoons)
Butter, melted, if desired

1 Grease bottom and sides of 8x4-inch loaf pan with shortening or cooking spray; sprinkle with cornmeal. In 1-quart saucepan, heat milk, water and 1 tablespoon butter over medium heat until very warm (120°F to 130°F).

2 In large bowl, mix 1½ cups of the flour, the sugar, salt, baking soda and yeast. Stir in milk mixture. Beat with electric mixer on low speed 1 minute, scraping bowl frequently. Beat on medium speed 1 minute, scraping bowl frequently. Stir in remaining 1½ cups flour.

3 Pat dough evenly in pan with floured fingers. Cover loosely with plastic wrap sprayed with cooking spray. Let rise in warm place 45 to 60 minutes. Dough is ready if indentation remains when touched.

4 Heat oven to 400°F. Bake 22 to 27 minutes or until golden brown. Remove from pan to cooling rack. For softer crust, brush top of loaf with melted butter while on cooling rack. Cool completely, about 2 hours.

1 Slice: Calories 110; Total Fat 1.5g (Saturated Fat 0.5g; Trans Fat 0g); Cholesterol 0mg; Sodium 180mg; Total Carbohydrate 21g (Dietary Fiber 0g); Protein 3g **Exchanges:** 1½ Starch **Carbohydrate Choices:** 1½

CLASSIC WHITE BREAD

LOWER CALORIE

There's something soothing about homemade bread and the aroma while these delicious loaves bake is amazing! Serve slices topped with your favorite preserves or honey, or make sandwiches.

PREP 35 min **TOTAL** 2 hr 55 min • **2 loaves (16 slices each)**

- 6 to 7 cups all-purpose or bread flour
- 3 tablespoons sugar
- 1 tablespoon salt
- 2 tablespoons shortening or softened butter
- 2 packages regular active or fast-acting dry yeast (4½ teaspoons)
- 2¼ cups very warm water (120°F to 130°F)
- 2 tablespoons butter, melted, if desired

1 In large bowl, stir 3½ cups of the flour, the sugar, salt, shortening and yeast until well mixed. Add warm water. Beat with electric mixer on low speed 1 minute, scraping bowl frequently. Beat on medium speed 1 minute, scraping bowl frequently. Stir in enough remaining flour, 1 cup at a time, to make dough easy to handle.

2 Place dough on lightly floured surface. Knead about 10 minutes or until dough is smooth and springy. Grease large bowl with shortening. Place dough in bowl, turning dough to grease all sides. Cover bowl loosely with plastic wrap and let rise in warm place 40 to 60 minutes or until dough has doubled in size. Dough is ready if indentation remains when touched.

3 Grease bottoms and sides of 2 (8x4- or 9x5-inch) loaf pans with shortening or cooking spray.

4 Gently push fist into dough to deflate. Divide dough in half. Flatten each half with hands or rolling pin into 18x9-inch rectangle on lightly floured surface. Roll dough up tightly, beginning at 9-inch side. (See Shaping Traditional Yeast Bread Loaves, page 111.) Press with thumbs to seal after each turn. Pinch edge of dough into roll to seal. Pinch each end of roll to seal. Fold ends under loaf. Place loaves seam side down in pans. Brush loaves lightly with 1 tablespoon of the melted butter. Cover loosely with plastic wrap and let rise in warm place 35 to 50 minutes or until dough has doubled in size.

5 Move oven rack to low position so that tops of pans will be in center of oven. Heat oven to 425°F. Bake 25 to 30 minutes or until loaves are deep golden brown and sound hollow when tapped. Remove from pans to cooling rack. Brush loaves with remaining 1 tablespoon melted butter; cool.

1 Slice: Calories 100; Total Fat 1g (Saturated Fat 0g; Trans Fat 0g); Cholesterol 0mg; Sodium 220mg; Total Carbohydrate 21g (Dietary Fiber 0g); Protein 3g **Exchanges:** 1 Starch **Carbohydrate Choices:** 1½

Classic White Bread

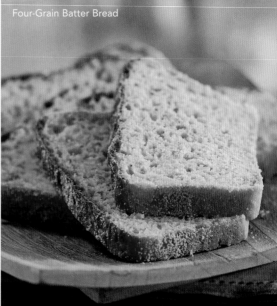
Four-Grain Batter Bread

FOUR-GRAIN BATTER BREAD

Homemade bread doesn't get much easier than this! It's called batter bread because the dough is soft and doesn't require kneading. Just mix it, put it in the pan, let it rise and bake.

PREP 15 min TOTAL 1 hr 10 min • **2 loaves (16 slices each)**

Cornmeal
4½ to 4¾ cups all-purpose or bread flour
2 tablespoons sugar
1 teaspoon salt
¼ teaspoon baking soda
2 packages regular active or fast-acting dry yeast (4½ teaspoons)
2 cups milk
½ cup water
½ cup whole wheat flour
½ cup wheat germ
½ cup quick-cooking oats

1 Grease bottoms and sides of 2 (8x4-inch) loaf pans with shortening or cooking spray; sprinkle with cornmeal.

2 In large bowl, mix 3½ cups of the all-purpose flour, the sugar, salt, baking soda and yeast. In 1-quart saucepan, heat milk and water over medium heat, stirring occasionally, until very warm (120°F to 130°F). Add milk mixture to flour mixture. Beat with electric mixer on low speed until moistened. Beat on medium speed 3 minutes, scraping bowl occasionally.

3 Stir in whole wheat flour, wheat germ, oats and enough remaining all-purpose flour to make a stiff batter. Divide batter evenly between pans. Round tops of loaves by patting with floured hands. Sprinkle with cornmeal. Cover loosely with plastic wrap and let rise in warm place about 30 minutes or until batter is about 1 inch below tops of pans.

4 Heat oven to 400°F. Bake about 25 minutes or until tops of loaves are light brown. Remove from pans to cooling rack; cool.

1 Slice: Calories 100; Total Fat 1g (Saturated Fat 0g; Trans Fat 0g); Cholesterol 0mg; Sodium 90mg; Total Carbohydrate 19g (Dietary Fiber 1g); Protein 4g **Exchanges:** 1 Starch **Carbohydrate Choices:** 1

WHOLE WHEAT–RAISIN BATTER BREAD
Increase whole wheat flour to 2 cups. Omit wheat germ and oats. Stir in 1 cup raisins with the second addition of all-purpose flour.

FRESH HERB BATTER BREAD

PREP 10 min TOTAL 1 hr 35 min • **1 loaf (20 slices)**

3 cups all-purpose flour
1 tablespoon sugar
1 teaspoon salt
1 package regular active or fast-acting dry yeast (2¼ teaspoons)
1¼ cups very warm water (120°F to 130°F)
2 tablespoons chopped fresh parsley
2 tablespoons shortening or softened butter
1½ teaspoons chopped fresh or ½ teaspoon dried rosemary leaves
½ teaspoon chopped fresh or ¼ teaspoon dried thyme leaves
Butter, melted, if desired

1 Grease bottom and sides of 8x4- or 9x5-inch loaf pan with shortening or cooking spray.

2 In large bowl, mix 2 cups of the flour, the sugar, salt and yeast. Add warm water, parsley, shortening, rosemary and thyme. Beat with electric mixer on low speed 1 minute, scraping bowl frequently. Beat on medium speed 1 minute, scraping bowl frequently. Stir in remaining 1 cup flour until smooth.

3 Spread batter evenly in pan. Round top of loaf by patting with floured hands. Cover loosely with plastic wrap lightly sprayed with cooking spray; let rise in warm place about 40 minutes or until dough has doubled in size.

4 Heat oven to 375°F. Bake 40 to 45 minutes or until loaf sounds hollow when tapped. Immediately remove from pan to cooling rack. Brush top of loaf with melted butter; sprinkle with additional chopped fresh herbs if desired. Cool.

1 Slice: Calories 80; Total Fat 1.5g (Saturated Fat 0g; Trans Fat 0g); Cholesterol 0mg; Sodium 120mg; Total Carbohydrate 15g (Dietary Fiber 0g); Protein 2g **Exchanges:** 1 Starch **Carbohydrate Choices:** 1

NO-KNEAD ARTISAN BREAD

LOWER CALORIE

PREP 10 min **TOTAL** 4 hr • **2 (6-inch) loaves (12 slices each)**

    3   to 3½ cups all-purpose flour
    1   tablespoon sugar
    1½ teaspoons salt
    1   package regular active dry yeast
        (2¼ teaspoons)
    1¼ cups very warm water (120°F to 130°F)
    1   tablespoon olive oil
        Cornmeal

1 In large bowl, mix 2 cups of the flour, the sugar, salt and yeast. Stir in water and oil until well mixed, about 1 minute. Beat with wooden spoon 2 minutes.

2 Stir in 1 cup flour. Stir in additional flour, 2 tablespoons at a time, until dough leaves side of bowl, flour is incorporated and dough is not sticky. Cover tightly with plastic wrap; refrigerate at least 2 hours but no longer than 24 hours.

3 Grease large cookie sheet with shortening or cooking spray; sprinkle with cornmeal, shaking off excess. Divide dough in half.

4 With floured hands, shape each half of dough into smooth ball by stretching surface of dough around to bottom on all 4 sides; pinch bottom to seal. (See Making Free-Form Loaves, page 111.) Place dough balls on cookie sheet about 5 inches apart. Cover loosely with plastic wrap lightly sprayed with cooking spray; let rise in warm place about 1½ hours or until dough has doubled in size.

5 Heat oven to 375°F. Place 8- or 9-inch pan on bottom rack of oven; add hot water until about ½ inch from top. Uncover dough; carefully slash tic-tac-toe pattern on each loaf top with serrated knife. Bake 15 to 20 minutes or until loaves are dark golden brown and bread sounds hollow when tapped. Remove from cookie sheet to cooling rack; cool.

1 Slice: Calories 70; Total Fat 1g (Saturated Fat 0g; Trans Fat 0g); Cholesterol 0mg; Sodium 150mg; Total Carbohydrate 15g (Dietary Fiber 0g); Protein 2g **Exchanges:** 1 Starch **Carbohydrate Choices:** 1

See how to make **no-knead artisan bread:** Visit bettycrocker.com/BCcookbook

NO-KNEAD BASIL AND SUN-DRIED TOMATO BREAD Fold ¼ cup well-drained sun-dried tomatoes in oil (from 7-oz jar), and 1 tablespoon fresh basil leaves (or 1 teaspoon dried basil leaves) into each dough half with hands in Step 3 before shaping. Continue as directed.

NO-KNEAD KALAMATA OLIVE–ROSEMARY BREAD Fold ¼ cup pitted and sliced kalamata olives and 1 tablespoon chopped fresh rosemary leaves (or 1 teaspoon dried rosemary leaves) into each dough half with hands in Step 3 before shaping. Continue as directed.

NO-KNEAD SEMOLINA, FENNEL AND RAISIN BREAD Substitute 1 cup semolina flour for the 1 cup all-purpose flour in Step 2. Stir in 1 tablespoon fennel seed and 1 cup golden raisins with the semolina flour. (Raisins will turn deep golden brown when baked.)

What Is Artisan Bread?

Baked in small batches, artisan breads are made with age-old bread-baking techniques. They are crafted with few ingredients, sometimes as few as five. The texture of artisan bread is firm and moist but crusty outside.

This no-knead version of artisan bread was developed to be very much like a bakery bread. It's simply delicious!

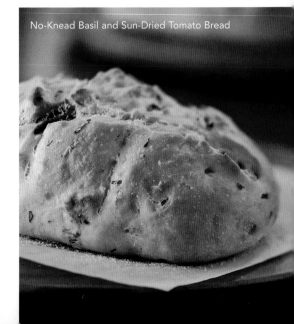
No-Knead Basil and Sun-Dried Tomato Bread

Artisan Asiago Bread

ARTISAN ASIAGO BREAD

LOWER CALORIE

This large, flour-dusted loaf looks and tastes like it came from a bakery. When you slice it, you'll find pockets of cheese scattered throughout.

PREP 25 min **TOTAL** 4 hr 15 min • **1 large loaf (24 slices)**

- 3½ to 3¾ cups bread flour
- 1 teaspoon sugar
- 1 package regular active or fast-acting dry yeast (2¼ teaspoons)
- 1¼ cups very warm water (120°F to 130°F)
- 2 tablespoons olive or vegetable oil
- 2 teaspoons dried rosemary or thyme leaves, if desired
- 1 teaspoon salt
- 1¼ cups diced Asiago, Swiss or other firm cheese

1 In large bowl, mix 1½ cups of the flour, the sugar and yeast. Add warm water. Beat with wire whisk or electric mixer on low speed 1 minute, scraping bowl frequently. Cover tightly with plastic wrap; let stand about 1 hour or until bubbly.

2 Stir in oil, rosemary and salt. Stir in enough remaining flour, ½ cup at a time, until a soft, smooth dough forms. Let stand 15 minutes.

3 Place dough on lightly floured surface. Knead 5 to 10 minutes or until dough is smooth and springy. Knead in 1 cup of the cheese. Grease large bowl with shortening. Place dough in bowl, turning dough to grease all sides. Cover bowl tightly with plastic wrap; let rise in warm place 45 to 60 minutes or until dough has doubled in size. Dough is ready if indentation remains when touched.

4 Lightly grease uninsulated cookie sheet with shortening or cooking spray. Place dough on lightly floured surface. Gently shape into football-shaped loaf, about 12 inches long, by stretching sides of dough downward to make a smooth top. (See Making Free-Form Loaves, page 111.) Place loaf with smooth side up on cookie sheet. Coat loaf generously with flour. Cover loosely with plastic wrap; let rise in warm place 45 to 60 minutes or until dough has almost doubled in size.

5 Place 8- or 9-inch square pan on bottom rack of oven; add hot water to pan until about ½ inch from the top. Heat oven to 450°F.

6 Spray loaf with cool water; sprinkle with flour. With serrated knife, carefully cut ½-inch-deep slash lengthwise down center of loaf. Sprinkle remaining ¼ cup cheese into slash.

7 Bake 10 minutes. Reduce oven temperature to 400°F. Bake 20 to 25 minutes longer or until loaf is deep golden and sounds hollow when tapped. Remove from cookie sheet to cooling rack; cool.

1 Slice: Calories 110; Total Fat 3g (Saturated Fat 1.5g; Trans Fat 0g); Cholesterol 5mg; Sodium 115mg; Total Carbohydrate 16g (Dietary Fiber 0g); Protein 4g **Exchanges:** 1 Starch, ½ Fat **Carbohydrate Choices:** 1

RICH EGG BREAD LOWER CALORIE

PREP 30 min TOTAL 3 hr 5 min • 1 loaf (16 slices)

     3   to 3¼ cups all-purpose or bread flour
     ¼   cup sugar
     1½ teaspoons salt
     1   package regular active or fast-acting
         dry yeast (2¼ teaspoons)
     1   cup very warm water (120°F to 130°F)
     2   tablespoons vegetable oil
     1   egg
         Butter, melted, if desired

1 In large bowl, mix 1½ cups of the flour, the sugar, salt and yeast. Add warm water and oil. Beat with electric mixer on low speed 1 minute, scraping bowl frequently. Beat on medium speed 1 minute, scraping bowl frequently. Add egg; beat until smooth. Stir in enough remaining flour, ¼ cup at a time, to make dough easy to handle.

2 Place dough on lightly floured surface. Knead about 10 minutes or until dough is smooth and springy. Grease large bowl with shortening. Place dough in bowl, turning dough to grease all sides. Cover bowl loosely with plastic wrap; let rise in warm place about 1 hour or until dough has doubled in size. (At this point, dough can be refrigerated up to 24 hours.) Dough is ready if indentation remains when touched.

3 Grease bottom and sides of 9x5- or 8x4-inch loaf pan with shortening or cooking spray. Gently push fist into dough to deflate.

Flatten dough with hands or rolling pin into 18x9-inch rectangle on lightly floured surface. Roll up tightly, beginning at 9-inch side. (See Shaping Traditional Yeast Bread Loaves, page 111.) Pinch edge of dough into roll to seal. Pinch each end of roll to seal. Fold ends under loaf. Place loaf seam side down in pan. Cover loosely with plastic wrap lightly sprayed with cooking spray and let rise in warm place about 1 hour or until dough has doubled in size.

4 Move oven rack to low position so that top of pan will be in center of oven. Heat oven to 375°F. Bake 30 to 35 minutes or until loaf is deep golden brown and sounds hollow when tapped. Remove from pan to cooling rack. Brush loaf with melted butter; cool.

1 Slice: Calories 120; Total Fat 2.5g (Saturated Fat 0g; Trans Fat 0g); Cholesterol 15mg; Sodium 230mg; Total Carbohydrate 21g (Dietary Fiber 0g); Protein 3g **Exchanges:** 1½ Starch **Carbohydrate Choices:** 1½

CHALLAH BRAID Make dough as directed in recipe. Lightly grease cookie sheet with shortening or spray with cooking spray. After pushing fist into dough, divide into 3 equal parts. Roll each part into 14-inch rope. Place ropes close together on cookie sheet. Braid ropes gently and loosely, starting in middle; do not stretch. Pinch ends; tuck ends under braid securely. Brush with vegetable oil. Cover loosely with plastic wrap; let rise in warm place 40 to 50 minutes or until dough has doubled in size. Heat oven to 375°F. In small bowl, mix 1 egg yolk and 2 tablespoons water; brush over braid. Sprinkle with poppy seed. Bake 25 to 30 minutes or until golden brown.

Braiding Challah

Braid ropes gently and loosely, starting at middle; do not stretch.

Challah Braid

SPREADS FOR BREADS

Here are some easy and delicious spreads for sweet breads, yeast breads, toast or crostini. All of these can be made ahead and refrigerated for up to one week.

1 Date-Nut Butter: Combine ½ cup softened butter, 1 tablespoon granulated sugar and ½ teaspoon vanilla until smooth; stir in ¼ cup finely chopped pitted dates and 2 tablespoons finely chopped toasted pecans.

2 Feta and Dill Cream Cheese Spread: In food processor, combine ¼ cup each softened cream cheese and crumbled feta cheese (thin with a little milk for desired consistency); process until smooth. Stir in chopped fresh dill weed to taste.

3 Ginger Butter: Combine ½ cup softened butter and 3 tablespoons brown sugar until smooth; stir in 3 tablespoons finely chopped crystallized ginger.

4 Gorgonzola, Walnut and Cranberry Spread: In food processor, combine ¼ cup each crumbled Gorgonzola or blue cheese and softened butter; process until smooth. Stir in 1 tablespoon each finely chopped toasted walnuts and dried cranberries.

5 Herbed Goat Cheese Spread: Combine 8 ounces room-temperature goat cheese with ¼ cup finely chopped fresh herbs such as basil, parsley, chives or tarragon; stir until smooth. Stir in lemon-pepper seasoning to taste.

6 Peanut Butter–Maple Butter: Combine ¼ cup each softened butter, creamy peanut butter and real maple syrup until smooth.

7 Strawberry Butter: In food processor, combine ½ cup softened butter, ½ cup sliced fresh strawberries, 1 tablespoon powdered sugar and ½ teaspoon grated orange peel; process until almost smooth.

8 Tomato–Red Pepper Spread: In food processor, combine 6-ounce can tomato paste, 2 tablespoons olive oil, ¼ cup jarred, drained, coarsely chopped roasted red peppers, 1 garlic clove, chopped, and ¼ cup torn fresh basil leaves; process until smooth.

Learn to Make Caramel Rolls

CARAMEL STICKY ROLLS

Mmm! The aroma of homemade sticky rolls baking in the oven is too much for even the sleepiest to resist. Here you'll find the simple tricks to ensure your irresistible rolls will rise and bake beautifully.

PREP 40 min **TOTAL** 3 hr 15 min ● **15 rolls**

ROLLS

- 3½ to 4 cups all-purpose or bread flour
- ⅓ cup granulated sugar
- 1 teaspoon salt
- 2 packages regular active or fast-acting dry yeast (4½ teaspoons)
- 1 cup very warm milk (120°F to 130°F)
- ¼ cup butter, softened
- 1 egg

CARAMEL TOPPING

- 1 cup packed brown sugar
- ½ cup butter, softened
- ¼ cup light corn syrup
- 1 cup pecan halves, if desired

FILLING

- ½ cup chopped pecans or raisins, if desired
- ¼ cup granulated sugar or packed brown sugar
- 1 teaspoon ground cinnamon
- 2 tablespoons butter, softened

1 In large bowl, mix 2 cups of the flour, ⅓ cup granulated sugar, the salt and yeast. Add warm milk, ¼ cup butter and egg. Beat with electric mixer on low speed 1 minute, scraping bowl frequently. Beat on medium speed 1 minute, scraping bowl frequently. Stir in enough remaining flour, ½ cup at a time, to make dough easy to handle.

2 Place dough on lightly floured surface. Knead about 5 minutes or until dough is smooth and springy. Grease large bowl with shortening. Place dough in bowl, turning dough to grease all sides. Cover bowl loosely with plastic wrap; let rise in warm place about 1 hour 30 minutes or until dough has doubled in size. Dough is ready if indentation remains when touched.

3 In 2-quart saucepan, heat brown sugar and ½ cup butter to boiling, stirring constantly; remove from heat. Stir in corn syrup. Pour into 13x9-inch pan. Sprinkle with pecan halves.

4 In small bowl, mix all filling ingredients except 2 tablespoons butter; set aside.

5 Gently push fist into dough to deflate. Flatten dough with hands or rolling pin into 15x10-inch rectangle on lightly floured surface. Spread with 2 tablespoons butter; sprinkle with filling. Roll rectangle up tightly, beginning at 15-inch side. Pinch edge of dough into roll to seal. With fingers, shape until even. With dental floss or a serrated knife, cut roll into 15 (1-inch) slices.

6 Place slices slightly apart in pan. Cover loosely with plastic wrap; let rise in warm place about 30 minutes or until dough has doubled in size.

7 Heat oven to 350°F. Bake 30 to 35 minutes or until golden brown. Let stand 2 to 3 minutes. Place heatproof tray or serving plate upside down onto pan; immediately turn tray and pan over. Let pan remain 1 minute so caramel can drizzle over rolls; remove pan. Serve warm.

1 Roll: Calories 320; Total Fat 12g (Saturated Fat 6g; Trans Fat 0.5g); Cholesterol 45mg; Sodium 250mg; Total Carbohydrate 50g (Dietary Fiber 1g); Protein 4g **Exchanges:** 1 Starch, 2½ Other Carbohydrate, 2 Fat **Carbohydrate Choices:** 3

LIGHTER **CARAMEL STICKY ROLLS** For 4 grams of fat and 255 calories per serving, make recipe as directed—except omit caramel topping and pecan halves. Line pan with foil; spray with cooking spray. Drizzle 1 cup caramel ice-cream topping over foil (heat topping slightly if it is stiff). Continue as directed—except omit chopped pecans from filling.

MAKE AHEAD **CARAMEL STICKY ROLLS** After placing slices in pan, cover tightly with plastic wrap or foil; refrigerate 4 to 24 hours. Before baking, remove from refrigerator; remove plastic wrap or foil and cover loosely with plastic wrap. Let rise in warm place about 2 hours or until dough has doubled in size. If some rising has occurred in refrigerator, rising time may be less than 2 hours. Bake as directed.

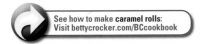
See how to make **caramel rolls:** Visit bettycrocker.com/BCcookbook

CINNAMON ROLLS Omit caramel topping and pecan halves. Grease bottom and sides of 13x9-inch pan with shortening or cooking spray. Place dough slices in pan. Let rise and bake as directed in Steps 6 and 7—except do not turn pan upside down. Remove rolls from pan to cooling rack. Cool 10 minutes. Drizzle with Vanilla Glaze (page 150) if desired.

Keys to Success

- **Heat milk to temperature within range** indicated in recipe for yeast to grow properly and the dough to rise correctly.
- **Knead dough until smooth and springy,** so the dough develops correctly.
- **Let dough rise in a warm, draft-free area,** so it will rise properly.
- **Let dough rise just until doubled** because if not allowed to rise long enough, the rolls may not rise as high. If allowed to rise too long, the rolls may collapse while baking.
- **Stretch and shape dough until even** to get uniformly sized rolls.
- **Cut dough with dental floss** or serrated knife so rolls keep their shape and do not flatten during cutting.

Caramel Sticky Rolls

Cinnamon Rolls

S'More Swirl Bread

S'MORE SWIRL BREAD

LOWER CALORIE

PREP 20 min **TOTAL** 2 hr 40 min • **1 loaf (16 slices)**

FILLING

- ¼ cup finely crushed graham crackers (4 squares)
- 2 teaspoons sugar
- ¾ cup miniature marshmallows
- 1½ bars (1.55 oz each) milk chocolate candy, finely chopped

BREAD

- 2 cups whole wheat flour
- 1 cup all-purpose flour
- ⅓ cup sugar
- 1 teaspoon salt
- 1 package regular active or fast-acting dry yeast (2¼ teaspoons)
- 1¼ cups very warm milk (120°F to 130°F)
- 2 tablespoons vegetable oil
- 1 egg
- 2 teaspoons butter, melted

1 Grease bottom and sides of 9x5- or 8x4-inch loaf pan with shortening or cooking spray. In small bowl, mix graham cracker crumbs and 2 teaspoons sugar. Reserve 2 teaspoons mixture for topping baked bread.

2 In large bowl, mix flours, ⅓ cup sugar, the salt and yeast. Add warm milk, oil and egg; stir until flour is completely moistened and stiff batter forms. Spoon half of batter into pan, spreading completely to sides of pan.

3 In the following order, sprinkle batter with marshmallows, graham cracker mixture and chocolate, keeping at least a ½-inch border of uncovered batter on all sides. Spoon remaining batter as evenly as possible over filling;

carefully and gently spread batter to sides of pan. Cover loosely with plastic wrap lightly sprayed with cooking spray; let rise in warm place 1 hour to 1 hour 10 minutes or until dough has doubled in size.

4 Heat oven to 350°F. Bake 35 to 40 minutes or until top of loaf is deep golden brown and loaf sounds hollow when tapped. Immediately remove from pan to cooling rack. Brush top of loaf with melted butter; sprinkle with reserved 2 teaspoons graham cracker mixture. Cool 30 minutes.

1 Slice: Calories 170; Total Fat 4.5g (Saturated Fat 1.5g; Trans Fat 0g); Cholesterol 15mg; Sodium 180mg; Total Carbohydrate 28g (Dietary Fiber 2g); Protein 4g **Exchanges:** ½ Starch, 1½ Other Carbohydrate, 1 Fat **Carbohydrate Choices:** 2

HONEY–WHOLE WHEAT BREAD

LOWER CALORIE

PREP 35 min **TOTAL** 3 hr 10 min • **2 loaves (16 slices each)**

- 3 cups whole wheat flour
- ⅓ cup honey or real maple syrup
- ¼ cup shortening or softened butter
- 3 teaspoons salt
- 2 packages regular active or fast-acting dry yeast (4½ teaspoons)
- 2¼ cups very warm water (120°F to 130°F)
- 3 to 4 cups all-purpose or bread flour
- 2 tablespoons butter, melted, if desired

1 In large bowl, beat whole wheat flour, honey, shortening, salt and yeast with electric mixer on low speed until well mixed. Add warm water. Beat on low speed 1 minute, scraping bowl frequently. Beat on medium speed 1 minute, scraping bowl frequently. Stir in enough all-purpose flour, 1 cup at a time, to make dough easy to handle.

2 Place dough on lightly floured surface. Knead about 10 minutes or until dough is smooth and springy. Grease large bowl with shortening. Place dough in bowl, turning dough to grease all sides. Cover bowl loosely with plastic wrap; let rise in warm place 40 to 60 minutes or until dough has doubled in size. Dough is ready if indentation remains when touched.

3 Grease bottoms and sides of 2 (8x4- or 9x5-inch) loaf pans with shortening or cooking spray.

4 Gently push fist into dough to deflate. Divide dough in half. Flatten each half with hands or rolling pin into 18x9-inch rectangle on lightly floured surface. Roll dough up tightly, beginning at 9-inch side. (See Shaping Traditional Yeast Bread Loaves, page 111.) Press with thumbs to seal after each turn. Pinch edge of dough into roll to seal. Pinch each end of roll to seal. Fold ends under loaf. Place loaves seam side down in pans. Brush loaves with1 tablespoon of the melted butter. Cover loosely with plastic wrap and let rise in warm place 35 to 50 minutes or until dough has doubled in size.

5 Move oven rack to low position so that tops of pans will be in center of oven. Heat oven to 375°F. Bake 40 to 45 minutes or until loaves are deep golden brown and sound hollow when tapped. Remove from pans to cooling rack. Brush loaves with remaining 1 tablespoon melted butter; cool.

1 Slice: Calories 120; Total Fat 2g (Saturated Fat 0g; Trans Fat 0g); Cholesterol 0mg; Sodium 220mg; Total Carbohydrate 22g (Dietary Fiber 2g); Protein 3g **Exchanges:** 1½ Starch **Carbohydrate Choices:** 1½

SUNFLOWER-HERB WHOLE WHEAT BREAD
Add 1 tablespoon dried basil leaves and 2 teaspoons dried thyme leaves with the salt. Stir in 1 cup unsalted sunflower nuts with the all-purpose flour.

CINNAMON, RAISIN AND WALNUT WHEAT BREAD

LOWER CALORIE

PREP 25 min TOTAL 3 hr 20 min • **1 large loaf (24 slices)**

- 2 **cups whole wheat flour**
- 1 **package regular active or fast-acting dry yeast (2¼ teaspoons)**
- 2 **cups very warm water (120°F to 130°F)**
- 2 **tablespoons packed brown sugar**
- 2 **tablespoons olive or vegetable oil**
- 2 **teaspoons salt**
- 2 **teaspoons ground cinnamon**
- 2 **to 2½ cups bread flour**
- 1 **cup coarsely chopped walnuts, toasted if desired**
- 1 **cup raisins, dried cherries or dried cranberries**
  Cornmeal

1 In large bowl, mix whole wheat flour and yeast. Add warm water. Beat with wire whisk or electric mixer on low speed 1 minute, scraping bowl frequently. Cover tightly with plastic wrap and let stand 15 minutes.

2 Stir in brown sugar, oil, salt, cinnamon, and 1 cup of the bread flour; beat until smooth. Stir in enough remaining bread flour, ½ cup at a time, until a soft, smooth dough forms.

3 Place dough on lightly floured surface. Knead 5 to 10 minutes or until dough is smooth and springy. Knead in walnuts and raisins. Grease large bowl with shortening. Place dough in bowl, turning dough to grease all sides. Cover bowl loosely with plastic wrap; let rise in warm place about 1 hour or until dough has doubled in size. Dough is ready if indentation remains when touched.

4 Grease uninsulated cookie sheet with shortening or cooking spray; sprinkle with cornmeal. Place dough on lightly floured surface. Gently shape into an even, round ball, without releasing all of the bubbles in dough. Stretch sides of dough downward to make a smooth top. (See Making Free-Form Loaves, page 111.) Place loaf with smooth side up on cookie sheet. Spray loaf with cool water. Cover loosely with plastic wrap; let rise in warm place 45 to 60 minutes or until dough has almost doubled in size.

5 Heat oven to 375°F. Spray loaf with cool water. With serrated knife, carefully cut ¼-inch-deep slashes in tic-tac-toe pattern on top of loaf.

6 Place in oven; spray with cool water. Bake 35 to 40 minutes or until loaf is dark brown and sounds hollow when tapped. Remove from cookie sheet to cooling rack; cool.

1 Slice: Calories 150; Total Fat 4.5g (Saturated Fat 0.5g; Trans Fat 0g); Cholesterol 0mg; Sodium 200mg; Total Carbohydrate 24g (Dietary Fiber 2g); Protein 4g **Exchanges:** 1 Starch, ½ Other Carbohydrate, ½ Fat **Carbohydrate Choices:** 1½

APPLE-PECAN BREAD Substitute chopped pecans for the walnuts and chopped dried apples for the raisins.

FRUIT AND ALMOND BREAD Omit cinnamon. Substitute chopped almonds for the walnuts and diced dried fruit for the raisins.

SOURDOUGH BREAD

LOWER CALORIE

PREP 30 min **TOTAL** 11 hr 45 min • **2 loaves (16 slices each)**

- 1 cup Sourdough Starter (at right)
- 2½ cups all-purpose or bread flour
- 2 cups warm water (105°F to 115°F)
- 3¾ to 4¼ cups all-purpose or bread flour
- 3 tablespoons sugar
- 1 teaspoon salt
- 3 tablespoons vegetable oil

1 In 3-quart glass bowl, mix sourdough starter, 2½ cups of the flour and the warm water with wooden spoon until smooth. Cover and let stand in warm, draft-free place 8 hours.

2 Add 3¾ cups flour, the sugar, salt and oil to mixture in bowl. Stir with wooden spoon until dough is smooth and flour is completely absorbed. (Dough should be just firm enough to gather into ball. If necessary, add remaining ½ cup flour gradually, stirring until all flour is absorbed.)

3 On heavily floured surface, knead dough about 10 minutes or until smooth and springy. Grease large bowl with shortening. Place dough in bowl, turning to grease all sides. Cover and let rise in warm place about 1 hour 30 minutes or until dough has doubled in size. Dough is ready if indentation remains when touched.

4 Grease large cookie sheet with shortening. Gently push fist into dough several times to remove air bubbles. Divide dough in half. Shape each half into a round, slightly flat loaf. Do not tear dough by pulling. Place loaves on opposite corners on cookie sheet. With sharp serrated knife, make three ¼-inch-deep slashes in top of each loaf. Cover and let rise about 45 minutes or until dough has doubled in size.

5 Heat oven to 375°F. Brush loaves with cold water. Place in middle of oven. Bake 35 to 45 minutes, brushing occasionally with water, until loaves sound hollow when tapped. Remove from cookie sheet to cooling rack. Cool completely, about 1 hour.

1 Slice: Calories 110; Total Fat 2.5g (Saturated Fat 0g; Trans Fat 0g); Cholesterol 0mg; Sodium 220mg; Total Carbohydrate 20g (Dietary Fiber 0g); Protein 3g **Exchanges:** 1½ Starch **Carbohydrate Choices:** 1

Sourdough Bread

Sourdough Starter

- 1 teaspoon regular active dry yeast
- ¼ cup warm water (105°F to 115°F)
- ¾ cup milk
- 1 cup all-purpose flour

1 In 3-quart glass bowl, dissolve yeast in warm water. Stir in milk. Gradually stir in flour; beat until smooth. Cover with towel or cheesecloth; let stand in warm, draft-free place (80°F to 85°F) about 24 hours or until starter begins to ferment (bubbles will appear on surface of starter). If starter has not begun fermentation after 24 hours, discard and begin again. If fermentation has begun, stir well; cover tightly with plastic wrap and return to warm, draft-free place. Let starter stand 2 to 3 days or until foamy.

2 When starter has become foamy, stir well; pour into 1-quart crock or glass jar with tight-fitting cover. Store in refrigerator. Starter is ready to use when a clear liquid has risen to top. Stir before using. Use 1 cup starter in Sourdough Bread recipe; reserve remaining starter. To remaining starter, add ¾ cup milk and ¾ cup flour. Store covered at room temperature about 12 hours or until bubbles appear; refrigerate.

3 Use starter regularly, every week or so. If the volume of the breads you bake begins to decrease, dissolve 1 teaspoon active dry yeast in ¼ cup warm water. Stir in ½ cup milk, ¾ cup flour and the remaining starter.

FOCACCIA LOWER CALORIE

PREP 30 min TOTAL 1 hr 50 min • **2 breads**
(12 slices each)

- 2½ to 3 cups all-purpose or bread flour
- 2 tablespoons chopped fresh or
  1 tablespoon dried rosemary
  leaves, crumbled
- 1 tablespoon sugar
- 1 teaspoon salt
- 1 package regular active or fast-acting
  dry yeast (2¼ teaspoons)
- 3 tablespoons olive or vegetable oil
- 1 cup very warm water (120°F to 130°F)
- 2 tablespoons olive or vegetable oil
- ¼ cup grated Parmesan cheese

1 In large bowl, mix 1 cup of the flour, rosemary, sugar, salt and yeast. Add 3 tablespoons oil and warm water. Beat with electric mixer on medium speed 3 minutes, scraping bowl frequently. Stir in enough remaining flour until dough is soft and leaves side of bowl.

2 Place dough on lightly floured surface. Knead 5 to 8 minutes or until smooth and springy. Grease large bowl with shortening. Place dough in bowl, turning dough to grease all sides. Cover bowl loosely with plastic wrap; let rise in warm place about 30 minutes or until dough has almost doubled in size. Dough is ready if indentation remains when touched.

3 Grease 2 cookie sheets or 12-inch pizza pans with small amount of oil or spray with cooking spray. Gently push fist into dough to deflate. Divide dough in half. Shape each half into a flattened 10-inch round on cookie sheet. Cover loosely with plastic wrap lightly sprayed with cooking spray; let rise in warm place about 30 minutes or until dough has doubled in size.

4 Heat oven to 400°F. Gently make ½-inch-deep depressions about 2 inches apart in dough with fingers. Carefully brush with 2 tablespoons oil; sprinkle with cheese. Bake 15 to 20 minutes or until golden brown. Serve warm if desired.

1 Slice: Calories 80; Total Fat 3.5g (Saturated Fat 0.5g; Trans Fat 0g); Cholesterol 0mg; Sodium 120mg; Total Carbohydrate 12g (Dietary Fiber 0g); Protein 2g **Exchanges:** 1 Starch **Carbohydrate Choices:** 1

ONION FOCACCIA Make dough as directed in recipe— except omit rosemary, 2 tablespoons oil and Parmesan cheese. In 10-inch skillet, heat ⅓ cup olive oil over medium heat. Stir in 4 cups thinly sliced onions and 4 cloves garlic, finely chopped. Cook uncovered 10 minutes, stirring every 3 to 4 minutes. Reduce heat to medium-low. Cook 30 to 40 minutes longer, stirring well every 5 minutes, until onions are light golden brown. Continue and bake as directed in recipe—except do not brush dough with oil; after second rising, carefully spread onion mixture over breads.

BREADSTICKS Make dough as directed in recipe. After kneading, cover loosely with plastic wrap; let rest 30 minutes. Grease 2 cookie sheets with shortening or cooking spray; sprinkle with cornmeal. Divide dough into 12 pieces. Roll and shape each piece into 12-inch rope, sprinkling with flour if dough is too sticky. Place ½ inch apart on cookie sheets. Brush with oil and sprinkle with grated Parmesan cheese or coarse salt if desired. Cover loosely with plastic wrap, and let rise in warm place about 20 minutes or until dough has almost doubled in size. Heat oven to 425°F. Bake 10 to 12 minutes or until golden brown. Makes 1 dozen breadsticks

Making Impressions in Focaccia Dough

Gently make ½-inch-deep depressions about 2 inches apart with fingertips.

Focaccia

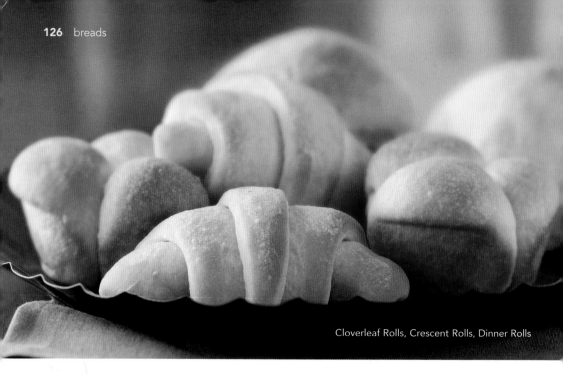

Cloverleaf Rolls, Crescent Rolls, Dinner Rolls

DINNER ROLLS LOWER CALORIE

PREP 30 min TOTAL 2 hr 15 min • **15 rolls**

3½ to 3¾ cups all-purpose or bread flour
¼ cup sugar
¼ cup butter, softened
1 teaspoon salt
1 package regular active or fast-acting dry yeast (2¼ teaspoons)
½ cup very warm water (120°F to 130°F)
½ cup very warm milk (120°F to 130°F)
1 egg
Butter, melted, if desired

1 In large bowl, stir 2 cups of the flour, the sugar, ¼ cup butter, the salt and yeast until well mixed. Add warm water, warm milk and egg. Beat with electric mixer on low speed 1 minute, scraping bowl frequently. Beat on medium speed 1 minute, scraping bowl frequently. Stir in enough remaining flour, ¼ cup at a time, to make dough easy to handle.

2 Place dough on lightly floured surface. Knead about 5 minutes or until dough is smooth and springy. Grease large bowl with shortening. Place dough in bowl, turning dough to grease all sides. Cover bowl loosely with plastic wrap; let rise in warm place about 1 hour or until dough has doubled in size. Dough is ready if indentation remains when touched.

3 Grease bottom and sides of 13x9-inch pan with shortening or cooking spray.

4 Gently push fist into dough to deflate. Divide dough into 15 equal pieces. Shape each piece into a ball; place in pan. Brush with melted butter. Cover loosely with plastic wrap; let rise in warm place about 30 minutes or until dough has doubled in size.

5 Heat oven to 375°F. Bake 12 to 15 minutes or until golden brown. Serve warm if desired.

1 Roll: Calories 160; Total Fat 4g (Saturated Fat 2g; Trans Fat 0g); Cholesterol 25mg; Sodium 190mg; Total Carbohydrate 26g (Dietary Fiber 1g); Protein 4g **Exchanges:** 2 Starch **Carbohydrate Choices:** 2

MAKE AHEAD DIRECTIONS After placing rolls in pan, cover tightly with foil and refrigerate 4 to 24 hours. Before baking, remove from refrigerator; remove foil and cover loosely with plastic wrap. Let rise in warm place about 2 hours or until dough has doubled in size. If some rising has occurred in the refrigerator, rising time may be less than 2 hours. Bake as directed.

Learn with Betty | YEAST BREAD

Perfect Yeast Bread: This loaf is high and evenly shaped and golden brown with an even texture.

Underrisen Yeast Bread: This loaf did not rise because the yeast got too hot and dough was not kneaded enough.

Overrisen Yeast Bread: This loaf was kneaded too much and contained too much flour.

CLOVERLEAF ROLLS Grease bottoms and sides of 24 regular-size muffin cups with shortening or cooking spray. Make dough as directed in recipe—except after pushing fist into dough, divide dough into 72 equal pieces. (To divide, cut dough in half, then continue cutting pieces in half until there are 72 pieces.) Shape each piece into a ball. Place 3 balls in each muffin cup. Brush with melted butter. Cover loosely with plastic wrap and let rise in warm place about 30 minutes or until dough has doubled in size. Bake as directed. Makes 24 rolls

CRESCENT ROLLS Grease cookie sheets with shortening or cooking spray. Make dough as directed in recipe—except after pushing fist into dough, cut dough in half. Roll each half into 12-inch circle on floured surface. Spread with softened butter. Cut each circle into 16 wedges. Roll up each wedge, beginning at rounded edge.

Place rolls, with points underneath, on cookie sheets and curve slightly. Brush with melted butter. Cover loosely with plastic wrap and let rise in warm place about 30 minutes or until dough has doubled in size. Bake as directed. Makes 32 rolls

Yeast Bread Fix-Ups

The best yeast breads and rolls are high and evenly shaped, are golden or dark brown and have an even texture. Here are some things that can happen, with solutions to help.

- Not high—water too hot for yeast, too little flour, not enough kneading, pan too large.
- Coarse texture—rose too long, too little flour, not enough kneading, oven too cool.
- Yeasty flavor—rose too long, temperature too high during rise time.
- Large air pockets—dough not rolled tightly when loaf was shaped.
- Dry and crumbly—too much flour, not enough kneading.

NAAN

If you have never seen the way naan breads are made, take a peek the next time you are at an Indian restaurant: The chef slaps a piece of dough between his hands, stretching it into that familiar teardrop shape. Working quickly, he reaches into the tandoor (clay-lined oven) and slaps the dough against its inner wall. Within seconds, the dough puffs up and forms brown spots. He peels the bread away from the wall with a flat-edged skewer and brushes it with clarified butter.

PREP 10 min **TOTAL** 1 hr 20 min • **4 breads (8 servings)**

    3 cups all-purpose flour
    1 tablespoon sugar
    2 teaspoons baking powder
    1 teaspoon salt
    ½ teaspoon baking soda
    ½ cup milk, slightly warmed
    2 tablespoons vegetable oil
      About ¼ cup warm water
    2 tablespoons butter, melted*

1 In large bowl, sift together flour, sugar, baking powder, salt and baking soda. Mix warm milk and oil; stir into flour mixture. Stir in warm water, 2 tablespoons at a time, until dough leaves side of bowl and forms a fairly stiff ball. The dough should not be sticky or dry.

2 Knead dough in bowl or on lightly floured surface 2 to 3 minutes or until dough becomes smooth and pliable. Brush dough lightly with some of the melted butter and cover with plastic wrap; set aside 30 minutes. (At this point, dough can be covered and refrigerated up to 24 hours. When ready to roll, let dough stand at room temperature 30 minutes so it becomes soft and easy to handle.)

3 Heat oven to 450°F. Place round or square pizza stone in oven to heat.

4 Divide dough into 4 equal pieces. Shape each into a ball; brush each lightly with some of the butter. Cover and let stand 20 to 30 minutes.

5 Working with one piece of dough at a time, roll into 8-inch circle or teardrop shape, about ¼ inch thick, on lightly floured surface, taking care not to tear dough. Repeat with remaining dough.

6 Place dough on hot pizza stone and bake 3 to 4 minutes or until brown spots form and bubbles start to appear on surface. Turn; bake 7 to 8 minutes. Remove bread with spatula; brush lightly with remaining butter.

7 Wrap cooked breads in foil to keep warm while cooking remaining dough. Cut each bread in half to serve.

*Clarified Butter (page 490) can be substituted for the melted butter.

1 Serving (½ Bread): Calories 240; Total Fat 7g (Saturated Fat 2.5g; Trans Fat 0g); Cholesterol 10mg; Sodium 520mg; Total Carbohydrate 38g (Dietary Fiber 1g); Protein 5g **Exchanges:** 2 Starch, ½ Other Carbohydrate, 1 Fat **Carbohydrate Choices:** 2½

Making Naan

Roll one piece of dough at a time into 8-inch circle or teardrop shape, about ¼ inch thick.

Place dough on hot pizza stone; bake 3 to 4 minutes or until brown spots form and bubbles start to appear on surface. Turn; bake 7 to 8 minutes.

Naan

CAKES, PIES & TARTS

CAKES

PIES AND PASTRY

CHARTS AND FEATURES

 For bonus cakes, pies and tarts recipes, visit bettycrocker.com/BCcookbook

---

FAST = Ready in 20 minutes or less   LOWER CALORIE = See Helpful Nutrition and Cooking Information, page 685
LIGHTER = 25% fewer calories or grams of fat   MAKE AHEAD = Make-ahead directions   SLOW COOKER = Slow cooker directions

← Apples being prepared for a pie, Sour Cream Spice Cake (page 146), Starlight Yellow Cake (page 141) with Creamy Chocolate Frosting (page 152), Cherry Pie (page 167) with Classic Lattice Top Crust (page 161)

CAKE BASICS
With our easy-to-follow directions, you'll be sweetly surprised at how simple it is to make a tender, moist and delicious cake. In the chapter, you'll find a variety of cakes to choose from, and tips and tricks to make you an expert in no time.

PICKING CAKE PANS

- Use the pan size called for in the recipe. If the size is not printed on the bottom of the pan, measure the length and width from inside edge to inside edge. Too small a pan may allow batter to overflow. Too large a pan may result in a flat cake.

- For tender, light cakes, use shiny pans, which reflect heat. Dark pans or pans with nonstick coating absorb heat faster than shiny pans and can cause cakes to brown too quickly.

- Fill cake pans half full with batter. This is important for a novelty or shaped pan (such as a heart or star shape), which can be an odd size.

STORING CAKES

- Cool cakes completely before wrapping and storing.

- Refrigerate any cake that contains dairy products in the filling or frosting.

- Store layer or tube cakes under a cake cover or improvise with an inverted mixing bowl.

- Serve cakes with fluffy frosting as soon as possible because cake will tend to absorb the frosting. Store under a cake cover but slip a knife under the edge so it is not airtight.

- Freeze frosted or unfrosted cakes unwrapped on a plate. When frozen, wrap in plastic wrap or foil and freeze up to 6 months.

- Cakes with cream or fruit filling or whipped cream frosting do not freeze well.

- Thaw unfrosted cakes wrapped at room temperature. Unwrap frosted cakes before thawing.

Tips for Perfect Cakes

- For testing, we used handheld electric mixers. If you have a stand mixer, follow the manufacturer's directions for speed settings.

- Heat the oven to the correct temperature. If the oven is too cold, cake will not rise; if the oven is too hot, the cake may overbake.

- Measure ingredients accurately and add them in the order listed in the recipe. With cakes, accuracy is important. If ingredients are over or under measured, or the order of ingredients and beating times are not followed, the cake may not rise or bake properly.

- Use butter for the best results. If you choose to substitute margarine, use those with at least 65% fat. Do not use reduced-fat butter or whipped products.

- Follow instructions for cake cooling and pan removal. If a cake is left in the pan for too long and sticks, try reheating it in the oven for 1 minute.

- Cool cakes on cooling racks to allow for air circulation.

Remove cakes from pans and place on cooling racks to cool.

ABOUT BUTTER CAKES

Sometimes called shortening cakes, these are made with butter, shortening or margarine, flour, eggs, liquid and baking powder or baking soda.

- Avoid overmixing batter, which can cause tunnels or a sunken center in the cake.

- Bake cakes on center oven rack.

- Arrange round cake pans in oven so there is at least 1 inch of space between them.

- If baking three layers but not all three fit in the oven, refrigerate one pan of batter until others are baked and then bake remaining layer separately.

- Grease pans with solid shortening, not butter or margarine. Use cooking spray if the recipe calls for it.

- To remove cake from pan, insert knife between cake and pan, then slide around the edge to loosen it. Place wire rack upside down over cake. Invert carefully so cake is on rack and remove the pan. Invert onto another rack and flip cake right side up.

- Cut cake with thin, sharp knife in gentle sawing motion.

ABOUT FOAM CAKES

Foam cakes, such as angel food, sponge and chiffon, depend on beaten egg whites for their light and airy texture.

Angel food cakes contain no added leavening, no fat and no egg yolks. They have a high proportion of beaten egg whites to flour.

Sponge cakes use both egg whites and egg yolks and sometimes a little leavening but do not contain added fat.

Chiffon cakes are a cross between foam and butter cakes because they are made with some leavening, vegetable oil or shortening and egg yolks, as well as beaten egg whites.

- Use a clean, dry bowl and beaters to beat egg whites so they will whip properly. Even a speck of fat from egg yolk can keep them from whipping up.

- Do not grease and flour pans unless directed in recipe. During baking, batter needs to cling to and climb up sides of pans.

- For any tube pan cake, move oven rack to lowest position in oven so cake will bake completely without browning too much.

Foam Cake Fix-Ups

The best foam cakes are high, golden brown with cracks in the surface, soft, moist and delicate. Here are some things that can happen, with solutions to help.

- Low and compact—underbeaten, overmixed or overfolded batter, incorrect cooling or underbaking.

- Coarse and not tender—underbeaten egg whites or underfolded batter.

Learn with Betty | FOAM CAKES

Perfect Cake: This cake is high, golden brown with feathery, light texture.

Underrisen Cake: This cake is compact because of underbeating or very overbeaten egg whites, overfolded batter or underbaking.

Overbaked Cake: This cake is too brown and crumbly from batter not being properly folded or underbeaten egg whites and overbaking.

RED VELVET CAKE

The origins of red velvet cake are a mystery, but it's been popular in the southern United States since the early 1900s. The smooth-as-silk and buttery-rich frosting is extra delicious.

PREP 15 min TOTAL 2 hr • **12 servings**

CAKE

- 2½ cups all-purpose flour
- 1½ cups sugar
- 2 tablespoons unsweetened baking cocoa
- 1 tablespoon baking powder
- 1 teaspoon salt
- 1½ cups vegetable oil
- 1 cup buttermilk
- 1 teaspoon vanilla
- 1 bottle (1 oz) red food color
- 2 eggs

FROSTING

- ½ cup all-purpose flour
- 1½ cups milk
- 1½ cups sugar
- 1½ cups butter, softened
- 1 tablespoon vanilla

1 Heat oven to 350°F. Grease bottoms and sides of 3 (8- or 9-inch) round pans with shortening; lightly flour.

2 In large bowl, beat all cake ingredients with electric mixer on low speed 30 seconds, scraping bowl constantly. Beat 2 minutes on medium speed, scraping bowl occasionally. Pour into pans.

3 Bake 25 to 35 minutes or until toothpick inserted in center comes out clean. Cool 10 minutes; remove from pans to cooling rack. Cool completely, about 1 hour.

4 In medium saucepan, mix ½ cup flour and 1½ cups milk with whisk until smooth. Cook over medium heat until mixture is very thick, stirring constantly. Remove from heat; cool 10 minutes. In large bowl, beat 1½ cups sugar and the butter with electric mixer on medium speed until light and fluffy. Gradually add flour mixture by tablespoonfuls; beat on high speed until smooth. Beat in vanilla. Fill and frost cake, using 1 cup frosting between layers. Store covered in refrigerator.

1 Serving: Calories 800; Total Fat 52g (Saturated Fat 20g; Trans Fat 1g); Cholesterol 100mg; Sodium 510mg; Total Carbohydrate 76g (Dietary Fiber 1g); Protein 5g **Exchanges:** 1½ Starch, 3½ Other Carbohydrate, 10½ Fat **Carbohydrate Choices:** 5

RED VELVET CUPCAKES Place a paper baking cup in each of 24 regular-size muffin cups. Heat oven and make cake batter as directed in recipe. Spoon batter evenly into muffin cups, filling each about ⅔ full. Bake 20 to 22 minutes or until toothpick inserted in center comes out clean. Remove cupcakes from pan to cooling rack. Cool completely, about 30 minutes. Frost with red velvet cake frosting (above) or Fluffy White Frosting, page 154.

Red Velvet Cake

Making Red Velvet Cake Frosting

Cook frosting in saucepan over medium heat, stirring constantly, until very thick.

Gradually add flour mixture by tablespoonfuls, beating on high speed until smooth and thick.

Learn to Make **Layer Cake**

CHOCOLATE LAYER CAKE

Homemade chocolate cake layered with frosting is impressive but certainly not hard to achieve. To make great cakes, just remember that baking is more precise than cooking. You need to use the right pans, measure ingredients accurately and follow directions carefully.

PREP 20 min **TOTAL** 2 hr 15 min • **12 servings**

2¼ cups all-purpose flour or 2½ cups
    cake flour
1⅔ cups sugar
 ⅔ cup unsweetened baking cocoa
1¼ teaspoons baking soda
 1 teaspoon salt
 ¼ teaspoon baking powder

1¼ cups water
 ¾ cup butter, softened
 2 eggs
 1 teaspoon vanilla
    Fudge Frosting (page 152) or Fluffy
    White Frosting (page 154), if desired

1 Heat oven to 350°F. Grease bottom and sides of 2 (8- or 9-inch) round pans, 3 (8-inch) round pans or 13x9-inch pan with shortening; lightly flour.

2 In large bowl, beat all ingredients except frosting with electric mixer on low speed 30 seconds, scraping bowl constantly. Beat on high speed 3 minutes, scraping bowl occasionally. Pour into pan(s).

3 Bake round pans 30 to 35 minutes or 13x9-inch pan 40 to 45 minutes, or until toothpick inserted in center comes out clean. Cool rounds 10 minutes; remove from pans to cooling racks. Cool 13x9-inch cake in pan on cooling rack. Cool completely, about 1 hour.

4 Fill and frost round layers or frost top of 13x9-inch cake with frosting.

1 Serving: Calories 330; Total Fat 13g (Saturated Fat 6g; Trans Fat 0.5g); Cholesterol 65mg; Sodium 430mg; Total Carbohydrate 48g (Dietary Fiber 2g); Protein 5g **Exchanges:** 2 Starch, 1 Other Carbohydrate, 2½ Fat **Carbohydrate Choices:** 3

Keys to Success

- Pick the right pan. (See Picking Cake Pans, page 131.)

- **Grease pans well with shortening; lightly flour.** Shortening works the best for cakes with high, straight sides.

- **Measure ingredients accurately.** (See Measuring Correctly, page 16.)

- **Bake cakes on center rack,** leaving space between pans and sides of oven.

- **Cool cakes completely** and brush off loose crumbs before frosting.

- **Frost cake first with very thin layer of frosting** to seal in crumbs, then frost again with remaining frosting.

Preparing Cake Pans

Here's how to ensure your cakes come out of the pans cleanly:

1 Brush shortening on bottom and sides of pan using a pastry brush, making sure to cover all areas.

2 Sprinkle a tablespoon or two of all-purpose flour into the pan.

3 Tap and rotate side of pan, working over the sink or trash can, to coat all greased areas with flour.

4 Discard any loose flour left in the pan; tap inverted pan to discard any excess flour.

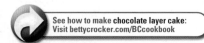

See how to make chocolate layer cake:
Visit bettycrocker.com/BCcookbook

Simple Ways to Make a Cake Look Fabulous

Turn a plain frosted cake into a masterpiece with one of these easy toppers:

- Fresh fruit such as berries or slices of kiwifruit or starfruit added just before serving adds a pop of color. Or top with chocolate-covered strawberries or other fruit (page 211), to take it to another level.

- Candies such as fruit slices, gummy candies and marzipan are just a few of the choices.

- Cookies such as frosted animal crackers, pirouette cookies or mini sandwich cookies add interest without much work. Add them just before serving, so they don't get soft.

- Sprinkles or decors, available in a wide variety at your supermarket specialty food store or cake-decorating supply stores.

- Edible flowers, candied violets or rose petals grown without pesticides so they can be eaten.

- Nuts such as pecans, cashews, or walnut halves, or try chocolate-covered nuts.

- Chocolate Curls (page 211).

- Coconut either shredded or flaked, plain or toasted (page 18).

Creating a Foil Tent

If you want to cover a frosted cake with foil, place several toothpicks partway into the top of the cake. The foil will rest on the toothpicks and not touch the frosting.

Frosting a Layer Cake

Brush any loose crumbs from cooled cake layer. Place 4 strips of waxed paper around edge of plate. Place layer, rounded side down, on plate.

Spread ⅓ to ½ cup frosting over top of first layer to within about ¼ inch of edge.

Place second cake layer, rounded side up, on frosted first layer. Coat side of cake with a very thin layer of frosting to seal in crumbs.

Frost side of cake in swirls, making a rim about ¼ inch high above top of cake. Spread remaining frosting on top, just to the built-up rim. Carefully remove waxed-paper strips.

Chocolate Layer Cake with Fudge Frosting

CHOCOLATE SNACK CAKE

Adding more chocolate to a recipe does not necessarily provide more chocolate flavor. The best way to enhance chocolate flavor is to increase the other flavors present in chocolate. Chocolate contains subtle hints of coffee, vanilla, spice and even smoke. By adding these flavors to your recipe, such as the coffee in this cake, you make it more chocolaty.

PREP 10 min TOTAL 1 hr • **9 servings**

- 1½ **cups all-purpose flour**
- 1 **cup sugar**
- ¼ **cup unsweetened baking cocoa**
- 1 **teaspoon baking soda**
- ½ **teaspoon salt**
- ⅓ **cup vegetable oil**
- 1 **teaspoon white or cider vinegar**
- ½ **teaspoon vanilla**
- 1 **cup cold strong brewed coffee or cold water**
  Ice cream or whipped cream, if desired

1 Heat oven to 350°F. Grease bottom and side of 9-inch round pan or 8-inch square pan with shortening; lightly flour.

2 In medium bowl, mix flour, sugar, cocoa, baking soda and salt. In small bowl, stir oil, vinegar and vanilla until well mixed. Vigorously stir oil mixture and coffee into flour mixture about 1 minute or until well blended. Immediately pour into pan.

3 Bake 30 to 35 minutes or until toothpick inserted in center comes out clean. Cool 15 minutes. Serve warm or cool with ice cream.

Chocolate Snack Cake

1 Serving: Calories 250; Total Fat 9g (Saturated Fat 1.5g; Trans Fat 0g); Cholesterol 0mg; Sodium 270mg; Total Carbohydrate 39g (Dietary Fiber 1g); Protein 3g **Exchanges:** 1 Starch, 1½ Other Carbohydrate, 2 Fat **Carbohydrate Choices:** 2½

CHOCOLATE CHIP SNACK CAKE Make batter as directed and pour into pan. Sprinkle with ⅓ cup miniature semisweet chocolate chips and 3 tablespoons sugar. Bake as directed.

DATE–CHOCOLATE CHIP CAKE

Because this cake has a delicious rich topping, you really don't need to add anything else. Look for dates that are already chopped at the grocery store. If you have whole pitted dates, use a kitchen scissors to snip them into small pieces.

PREP 20 min TOTAL 3 hr 15 min • **12 servings**

- 1¼ **cups boiling water**
- 1 **cup chopped pitted dates**
- 1 **teaspoon baking soda**

  TOPPING
- ½ **cup semisweet chocolate chips (3 oz)**
- ¼ **cup packed brown sugar**
- ¼ **cup all-purpose flour**
- 1 **tablespoon butter, softened**

  CAKE
- 1¾ **cups all-purpose flour**
- ½ **cup granulated sugar**
- ½ **cup packed brown sugar**
- 1 **teaspoon baking soda**
- ½ **teaspoon salt**
- ⅔ **cup vegetable oil**
- 1 **teaspoon vanilla**
- 2 **eggs**

1 In large bowl, pour boiling water over dates. Stir in 1 teaspoon baking soda. Cool about 15 minutes or until lukewarm. In small bowl, mix all topping ingredients; set aside.

2 Heat oven to 350°F. Stir all cake ingredients into date mixture. Pour into ungreased 9-inch square pan. Sprinkle with topping.

3 Bake 50 to 55 minutes or until toothpick inserted in center comes out clean. Cool completely, about 2 hours.

1 Serving: Calories 380; Total Fat 17g (Saturated Fat 4.5g; Trans Fat 0g); Cholesterol 40mg; Sodium 340mg; Total Carbohydrate 53g (Dietary Fiber 2g); Protein 4g **Exchanges:** 1 Starch, ½ Fruit, 2 Other Carbohydrate, 3½ Fat **Carbohydrate Choices:** 3½

GERMAN CHOCOLATE CAKE

Samuel German, an employee of the Baker's Chocolate Company, developed a sweet chocolate in 1852. Over a hundred years later, in 1957, a reader of a Dallas newspaper submitted her recipe for this now-famous three-tiered cake with coconut-pecan frosting. Sales of sweet chocolate soared, and the rest is delicious history!

PREP 30 min **TOTAL** 2 hr 20 min • **12 servings**

- 4 oz sweet baking chocolate, chopped
- ½ cup water
- 2¼ cups all-purpose flour or 2½ cups cake flour
- 1 teaspoon baking soda
- 1 teaspoon salt
- 2 cups sugar
- 1 cup butter, softened
- 4 eggs, separated
- 1 teaspoon vanilla
- 1 cup buttermilk
  Coconut-Pecan Filling and Topping (below)

1 Heat oven to 350°F. Grease bottoms and sides of 3 (8- or 9-inch) round pans with shortening. Line pan bottoms with waxed paper or cooking parchment paper; grease again.

2 In 1-quart saucepan, heat chocolate and water over low heat, stirring frequently, until chocolate is completely melted; cool.

3 In medium bowl, mix flour, baking soda and salt; set aside. In another medium bowl, beat sugar and butter with electric mixer on high speed until light and fluffy. Beat in egg yolks, one at a time. Beat in chocolate and vanilla on low speed. Beat flour mixture into sugar mixture alternately with buttermilk on low speed, beating after each addition just until smooth.

4 Wash and dry mixer beaters. In small bowl, beat egg whites on high speed until stiff; fold into batter. Pour into pans. If all pans won't fit in oven at one time, refrigerate batter in third pan and bake separately.

5 Bake 8-inch pans 35 to 40 minutes and 9-inch pans 30 to 35 minutes, or until toothpick inserted in center comes out clean. Cool 10 minutes; remove from pans to cooling racks. Remove waxed paper. Cool completely, about 1 hour.

German Chocolate Cake

6 Fill layers and frost top of cake with filling and topping, leaving side of cake unfrosted. Store covered in refrigerator.

1 Serving: Calories 440; Total Fat 20g (Saturated Fat 10g; Trans Fat 1g); Cholesterol 110mg; Sodium 450mg; Total Carbohydrate 58g (Dietary Fiber 1g); Protein 6g **Exchanges:** 2 Starch, 2 Other Carbohydrate, 3½ Fat **Carbohydrate Choices:** 4

COCONUT-PECAN FILLING AND TOPPING

In 2-quart saucepan, stir 1 cup granulated or packed brown sugar, ½ cup butter, 1 cup evaporated milk or half-and-half, 1 teaspoon vanilla and 3 egg yolks until well mixed. Cook over medium heat about 12 minutes, stirring frequently, until thickened and bubbly. Stir in 1⅓ cups flaked coconut and 1 cup chopped pecans (toasted if desired, page 22). Cool about 30 minutes, beating occasionally with spoon, until spreadable.

Sweet Baking Chocolate

Sweet baking chocolate is the same as German sweet chocolate. It's 48% cacao and is rich and creamy with a mild chocolate flavor.

CHOCOLATE-HAZELNUT TRUFFLE TORTE

PREP 25 min TOTAL 2 hr • **12 servings**

TORTE

- 1 **cup semisweet chocolate chips (6 oz)**
- ½ **cup butter, cut into pieces**
- ½ **cup all-purpose flour**
- 4 **eggs, separated**
- ½ **cup sugar**
- ⅔ **cup hazelnuts (filberts), toasted (page 22), finely chopped**
  Whole or chopped hazelnuts, if desired

CHOCOLATE TRUFFLE FILLING AND FROSTING

- 2 **cups semisweet chocolate chips (12 oz)**
- ¼ **cup butter, cut into pieces**
- ½ **cup whipping cream or hazelnut-flavored liquid nondairy creamer**

1 Heat oven to 325°F. Grease bottoms and sides of 2 (9-inch) round pans with shortening. Line pan bottoms with waxed paper or cooking parchment paper.

2 In 2-quart saucepan, melt chocolate chips and butter over medium heat, stirring constantly; cool 5 minutes. Stir in flour until smooth. Stir in egg yolks until well blended.

3 In large bowl, beat egg whites with electric mixer on high speed until foamy. Beat in sugar, 1 tablespoon at a time, until soft peaks form. Fold chocolate mixture into egg whites. Fold in ⅔ cup hazelnuts. Spread in pans.

4 Bake 25 minutes or until tops of cakes appear dry and toothpick inserted in center comes out clean. Cool 5 minutes. Run knife around side of each cake to loosen; remove from pans to cooling racks. Remove waxed paper. Cool completely, about 1 hour.

5 In 2-quart saucepan, melt 2 cups chocolate chips and ¼ cup butter over low heat, stirring constantly; remove from heat. Stir in whipping cream. Refrigerate 30 to 40 minutes, stirring frequently, just until thick enough to mound and hold its shape when dropped from a spoon. (If filling becomes too thick, microwave on High 10 to 15 seconds to soften.)

6 Spread ⅔ cup of the filling on bottom cake layer. Top with other layer. Frost top of cake with remaining filling. Garnish with hazelnuts.

1 Serving: Calories 490; Total Fat 34g (Saturated Fat 18g; Trans Fat 0.5g); Cholesterol 115mg; Sodium 110mg; Total Carbohydrate 41g (Dietary Fiber 3g); Protein 5g **Exchanges:** 1½ Starch, 1 Other Carbohydrate, 6½ Fat **Carbohydrate Choices:** 3

Folding in Chocolate

With rubber spatula, fold chocolate mixture into egg whites just until well blended. Overmixing will reduce egg white volume, so fold gently.

Chocolate-Hazelnut Truffle Torte

MOLTEN CHOCOLATE CAKES

Molten cakes or lava cakes, made popular by restaurants, are easy to make at home. The batter can even be made a day ahead of time—perfect for entertaining. Be sure to grease the custard cups with shortening, dust the cups with cocoa and bake the cakes at the correct oven temperature for the right time. These steps are critical to the success of this recipe. If the centers are too cakelike in texture, bake a few minutes less the next time; if they're too soft, bake a minute or two longer.

PREP 20 min TOTAL 40 min • **6 servings**

   Unsweetened baking cocoa
 6 **oz semisweet baking chocolate, chopped**
 ½ **cup plus 2 tablespoons butter**
 3 **whole eggs**
 3 **egg yolks**
 1½ **cups powdered sugar**
 ½ **cup all-purpose flour**
   Additional powdered sugar, if desired

1 Heat oven to 450°F. Grease bottoms and sides of 6 (6-oz) custard cups with shortening; dust with cocoa.

2 In 2-quart saucepan, melt chocolate and butter over low heat, stirring frequently. Cool slightly.

3 In large bowl, beat whole eggs and egg yolks with wire whisk or hand beater until well blended. Beat in 1½ cups powdered sugar. Beat in melted chocolate mixture and flour. Divide batter evenly among custard cups. Place cups on cookie sheet with sides.

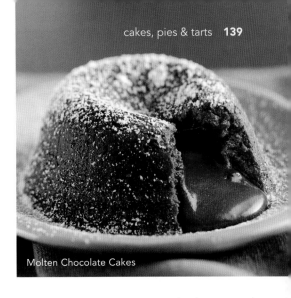

Molten Chocolate Cakes

4 Bake 12 to 14 minutes or until sides are set and centers are still soft (tops will be puffed and cracked). Let stand 3 minutes. Run small knife or metal spatula around side of each cake to loosen. Immediately place heatproof serving plate upside down onto each cup; turn plate and cup over and remove cup. Sprinkle with additional powdered sugar. Serve warm.

1 Serving: Calories 550; Total Fat 33g (Saturated Fat 16g; Trans Fat 1g); Cholesterol 265mg; Sodium 170mg; Total Carbohydrate 56g (Dietary Fiber 2g); Protein 7g **Exchanges:** 2 Starch, 2 Other Carbohydrate, 6 Fat **Carbohydrate Choices:** 4

MAKE AHEAD **DIRECTIONS** Batter can be made up to 24 hours ahead. After pouring batter into custard cups, cover with plastic wrap and refrigerate up to 24 hours. You may need to bake the cakes 1 to 2 minutes longer.

Learn with Betty | MOLTEN CHOCOLATE CAKE

Perfect Cake: This cake has a flowing chocolate center. There are no problems.

Underbaked Cake: This cake is too runny because it was not baked long enough.

Overbaked Cake: This cake is completely cooked through because it was baked too long.

SILVER WHITE CAKE

PREP 10 min **TOTAL** 2 hr 5 min • **12 servings**

- 2¼ cups all-purpose flour or 2½ cups cake flour
- 1⅔ cups sugar
- 3½ teaspoons baking powder
- 1 teaspoon salt
- ⅔ cup shortening
- 1¼ cups milk
- 1 teaspoon vanilla or almond extract
- 5 egg whites
  Fluffy White Frosting (page 154) or Creamy Chocolate Frosting (page 152), if desired

1 Heat oven to 350°F. Grease bottom and sides of 13x9-inch pan or 2 (9-inch) or 3 (8-inch) round pans with shortening; lightly flour.

2 In large bowl, beat all ingredients except egg whites and frosting with electric mixer on low speed 30 seconds, scraping bowl constantly. Beat on high speed 2 minutes, scraping bowl occasionally.

3 Beat in egg whites on high speed 2 minutes, scraping bowl occasionally. Pour into pan(s).

4 Bake 13x9-inch pan 40 to 45 minutes, 9-inch pans 30 to 35 minutes, 8-inch pans 23 to 28 minutes, or until toothpick inserted in center comes out clean or until cake springs back when touched lightly in center. Cool 13x9-inch cake in pan on cooling rack. Cool rounds 10 minutes; remove from pans to cooling racks. Cool completely, about 1 hour.

5 Frost 13x9-inch cake or fill and frost round layers with frosting.

1 Serving: Calories 320; Total Fat 12g (Saturated Fat 3g; Trans Fat 2g); Cholesterol 0mg; Sodium 370mg; Total Carbohydrate 47g (Dietary Fiber 0g); Protein 5g **Exchanges:** 2 Starch, 1 Other Carbohydrate, 2 Fat **Carbohydrate Choices:** 3

CHOCOLATE CHIP CAKE Fold ½ cup miniature or finely chopped regular semisweet chocolate chips into batter just before pouring into pans.

COOKIES 'N CREAM CAKE Stir 1 cup crushed chocolate cream sandwich cookies into batter after beating in egg whites. Bake as directed. Frost with fluffy white frosting; garnish with chocolate cream sandwich cookies.

MARBLE CAKE Before pouring batter into pan(s), remove 1¾ cups of the batter; reserve. Pour remaining batter into pan(s). Stir 3 tablespoons unsweetened baking cocoa and ⅛ teaspoon baking soda into reserved batter. Drop chocolate batter by tablespoonfuls randomly onto white batter. Cut through batters with knife for marbled design. Bake and cool as directed in Step 4.

Marbling Batter

Drop chocolate batter by tablespoonfuls randomly over white batter. Cut through batters with knife.

Marble Cake with Fluffy White Frosting

STARLIGHT YELLOW CAKE

PREP 10 min **TOTAL** 2 hr • **12 servings**

- 2¼ cups all-purpose flour
- 1½ cups sugar
- 3½ teaspoons baking powder
- 1 teaspoon salt
- ½ cup butter, softened
- 1¼ cups milk
- 1 teaspoon vanilla
- 3 eggs
  Creamy Chocolate Frosting (page 152) or Peanut Butter Frosting (page 153), if desired

1 Heat oven to 350°F. Grease bottom and sides of 13x9-inch pan or 2 (9-inch) or 3 (8-inch) round pans with shortening; lightly flour.

2 In large bowl, beat all ingredients except frosting with electric mixer on low speed 30 seconds, scraping bowl constantly. Beat on high speed 3 minutes, scraping bowl occasionally. Pour into pan(s).

3 Bake 13x9-inch pan 35 to 40 minutes, 9-inch pans 25 to 30 minutes, 8-inch pans 30 to 35 minutes, or until toothpick inserted in center comes out clean or cake springs back when touched lightly in center. Cool 13x9-inch cake in pan on cooling rack. Cool rounds 10 minutes; remove from pans to cooling racks. Cool completely, about 1 hour.

4 Frost 13x9-inch cake or fill and frost round layers with frosting.

1 Serving: Calories 290; Total Fat 10g (Saturated Fat 4.5g; Trans Fat 0g); Cholesterol 75mg; Sodium 420mg; Total Carbohydrate 45g (Dietary Fiber 0g); Protein 5g **Exchanges:** 2 Starch, 1 Other Carbohydrate, 1½ Fat **Carbohydrate Choices:** 3

STARLIGHT CHERRY CAKE Stir in ½ cup dried cherries after beating batter in Step 2. Frost with Cherry-Nut Frosting (page 155).

STARLIGHT PEANUT BUTTER CAKE Substitute peanut butter for the butter. Frost with Fudge Frosting (page 152), if desired.

Butter Cake Fix-Ups

The best butter cakes are high, golden brown, slightly rounded on top, fine-grained, moist and tender.

Here are some things that can happen, with solutions to help.

- Did not rise enough—too much liquid or fat or the oven was too cool.
- Peaked with cracks on top—too much flour and oven too hot.
- Rim or ridge around top—pan sprayed with cooking spray.
- Coarse-grained and crumbly—too much butter or sugar, not enough egg or underbeaten.
- Heavy and wet—too much liquid or butter or not enough flour.
- Sticks to pan—pan not greased and/or floured or the cake was left in the pan too long before being removed.

Learn with Betty | BUTTER CAKES

Perfect Cake: This cake is high and golden brown with a slightly rounded top. The texture is soft, velvety and tender.

Underrisen Cake: This cake did not rise and is pale in color because of too much liquid or fat, not enough leavening or pan was too large.

Overbaked Cake: This cake is too brown and sunk in the middle because of too much leavening, too much liquid or was baked too long.

CARAMEL SNICKERDOODLE CAKE

PREP 20 min TOTAL 2 hr 40 min • **16 servings**

1¾ cups plus 2 tablespoons sugar
  2 teaspoons ground cinnamon
2½ cups all-purpose flour
  2 teaspoons baking soda
  1 teaspoon salt
  1 can (5 oz) evaporated milk
  1 cup sour cream
 ½ cup butter, melted
  1 teaspoon vanilla
  2 eggs, beaten
 10 caramels, unwrapped

1 Heat oven to 350°F. Grease 12-cup fluted tube cake pan with shortening. In small bowl, mix 2 tablespoons of the sugar and 1 teaspoon of the cinnamon. Sprinkle mixture over inside of pan, turning to evenly coat. Shake out any excess.

2 In large bowl, mix remaining 1¾ cups sugar, remaining 1 teaspoon cinnamon, the flour, baking soda and salt. Reserve 1 tablespoon of the evaporated milk for the topping. Stir remaining evaporated milk, sour cream, butter, vanilla and eggs into dry ingredients until well blended. Pour into pan.

3 Bake 40 to 50 minutes or until toothpick inserted in center comes out clean. Let stand 30 minutes; remove from pan to cooling rack. Cool completely, about 1 hour.

4 In small microwavable bowl, microwave caramels with reserved evaporated milk uncovered on High 1 to 2 minutes, stirring every 30 seconds, until caramels are melted and mixture is smooth. Drizzle over cooled cake.

1 Serving: Calories 340; Total Fat 11g (Saturated Fat 6g; Trans Fat 0g); Cholesterol 50mg; Sodium 420mg; Total Carbohydrate 54g (Dietary Fiber 0g); Protein 4g **Exchanges:** 1½ Starch, 2 Other Carbohydrate, 2 Fat **Carbohydrate Choices:** 3½

Three Basic Cupcakes

For cupcakes, place paper baking cups in each of 24 regular-size muffin cups. Follow directions for specific cupcake:

- **Starlight Yellow Cupcakes:** To make batter, follow directions for Starlight Yellow Cake (page 141).

- **Silver White Cupcakes:** To make batter, follow directions for Silver White Cake (page 140).

- **Chocolate Cupcakes:** To make batter, follow directions for Chocolate Layer Cake (page 134).

Pour batter into muffin cups. Bake 20 to 25 minutes or until toothpick inserted in center comes out clean. Cool completely on cooling rack, 30 minutes.

Caramel Snickerdoodle Cake

CUPCAKES EIGHT WAYS

1 Chili-Chocolate Cupcakes: Make, bake and cool Chocolate Cupcakes (at left), stirring 3 teaspoons ancho chili powder or regular chili powder and ¼ teaspoon ground cinnamon into batter before filling muffin cups. Make Creamy Chocolate Frosting (page 152), adding 2 teaspoons espresso coffee powder and ¼ ground cinnamon before mixing. Frost cupcakes with frosting. Garnish with Chocolate Curls (page 211), if desired.

2 Confetti Cupcakes: Coarsely chop ½ cup candy coated chocolate candies. Make, bake and cool Starlight Yellow Cupcakes (at left), stirring chopped candies into batter before filling muffin cups. Frost with Fudge Frosting (page 152); sprinkle each cupcake with 1 to 2 teaspoons candy-coated chocolate candies.

3 Malted Milk Ball Cupcakes: Make Starlight Yellow Cupcakes (at left), adding ¼ cup original-flavor malted milk powder to batter before mixing. Stir in 1 cup crushed malted milk balls. Bake and cool as directed. Make Creamy Chocolate Frosting (page 152), stirring in 2 tablespoons malted milk powder before mixing. Frost cupcakes; sprinkle each with about 2 teaspoons crushed malted milk balls.

4 Orange-Chocolate Cupcakes: Make, bake and cool Chocolate Cupcakes (at left), adding 2 tablespoons grated orange peel to batter. Frost with Orange Frosting (page 153). Cut 6 orange slice candies into small pieces. Top each cupcake with candy pieces.

5 Raspberry–Cream Cheese Cupcakes: Make Starlight Yellow Cupcakes (at left); spoon batter evenly into muffin cups. Cut 1 (3-ounce) package cream cheese into 24 pieces. Place 1 piece cream cheese on top of each cupcake; press into batter slightly. Spoon ¼ teaspoon raspberry preserves on top of cream cheese in each cupcake. Bake and cool cupcakes as directed. Frost with Cream Cheese Frosting (page 154).

6 Snickerdoodle Cupcakes: Make, bake and cool Silver White Cupcakes (at left) adding 1 teaspoon ground cinnamon to batter. Make Creamy Vanilla Frosting (page 153), adding 1 teaspoon ground cinnamon when mixing. Frost cupcakes; sprinkle lightly with ground cinnamon.

7 Toasty Almond Cupcakes: Spread 1 cup sliced almonds in shallow pan. Bake at 350°F for 5 to 7 minutes or until golden brown, stirring occasionally. Make, bake and cool Starlight Yellow Cupcakes (at left), adding 1 teaspoon almond extract to batter. Frost with Caramel Frosting (page 154). Sprinkle each cupcake with toasted almonds.

8 Whoopie Pie Cupcakes: Make, bake and cool Chocolate Cupcakes (at left). Make ½ recipe Fluffy White Frosting (page 154), stirring in ¾ cup marshmallow creme after beating to stiff peaks. Cut each cupcake in half crosswise. Spread frosting on bottom half of each; top with cupcake tops. Press together slightly.

Heirloom Recipe and New Twist

In 1895, Sperry Flour Company (a firm that joined General Mills) produced a recipe booklet called "Easy Cooking for Little Cooks." Included in this booklet was a recipe for pound cake, given its name because the primary ingredients were one pound each of butter, sugar and flour. This recipe has been a favorite ever since. The new twist takes the simple pound cake to a new level and includes a layer of ginger flavor and an incredible browned butter glaze. Be sure to check out the variations from Facebook fans too—we love the flavors they added.

CLASSIC

POUND CAKE

PREP 20 min **TOTAL** 4 hr • **24 servings**

- 3 **cups all-purpose flour**
- 1 **teaspoon baking powder**
- ¼ **teaspoon salt**
- 2½ **cups granulated sugar**
- 1 **cup butter, softened**
- 1 **teaspoon vanilla or almond extract**
- 5 **eggs**
- 1 **cup milk or evaporated milk**
  Powdered sugar, if desired

1 Heat oven to 350°F. Generously grease bottom, side and tube of 10-inch angel food (tube) cake pan, 12-cup fluted tube cake pan or 2 (9x5-inch) loaf pans with shortening; lightly flour.

2 In medium bowl, mix flour, baking powder and salt; set aside. In large bowl, beat granulated sugar, butter, vanilla and eggs with electric mixer on low speed 30 seconds, scraping bowl constantly. Beat on high speed 5 minutes, scraping bowl occasionally. Beat flour mixture into sugar mixture alternately with milk on low speed, beating just until smooth after each addition. Pour into pan(s).

3 Bake angel food or fluted tube cake pan 1 hour 10 minutes to 1 hour 20 minutes, loaf pans 55 to 60 minutes, or until toothpick inserted in center comes out clean. Cool 20 minutes; remove from pan(s) to cooling rack. Cool completely, about 2 hours. Sprinkle with powdered sugar.

1 Serving: Calories 230; Total Fat 9g (Saturated Fat 4.5g; Trans Fat 0g); Cholesterol 65mg; Sodium 115mg; Total Carbohydrate 33g (Dietary Fiber 0g); Protein 3g **Exchanges:** 1 Starch, 1 Other Carbohydrate, 2 Fat **Carbohydrate Choices:** 2

LEMON–POPPY SEED POUND CAKE Substitute 1 teaspoon lemon extract for the vanilla. Fold 1 tablespoon grated lemon peel and ¼ cup poppy seed into batter. Drizzle with Lemon Glaze (page 156) if desired.

ORANGE-COCONUT POUND CAKE Fold 1⅓ cups coconut and 2 tablespoons grated orange peel into batter. Drizzle with Orange Glaze (page 156) if desired.

TOASTED ALMOND POUND CAKE Substitute almond extract for the vanilla. Fold 1½ cups slivered almonds, toasted (page 22), into batter. Drizzle with Chocolate Glaze (page 156) or Vanilla Glaze (page 156) if desired.

CRANBERRY-ORANGE POUND CAKE Stir in ½ cup coarsely chopped fresh cranberries or dried cranberries and 1 teaspoon grated orange peel before pouring into pan. Bake as directed.

> **Contributed by Tara Kehoe from El Paso, Texas**

RASPBERRY-TOPPED POUND CAKE Make Raspberry Sauce (page 235). Spoon sauce over servings of pound cake. Top with Sweetened Whipped Cream (page 214).

> **Contributed by Kathy Salazar O'Brien from Comstock Park, Michigan**

Serving Pound Cakes

Either of these cakes is perfect for any special occasion. For a pretty serving presentation, place the cake on a serving plate or platter. Surround with fresh fruit such as strawberries, raspberries or blueberries. Tuck in an edible flower or two and it's ready for the party!

See how to make **pound cake**:
Visit bettycrocker.com/BCcookbook

TRIPLE-GINGER POUND CAKE

PREP 20 min **TOTAL** 4 hr • **24 servings**

- 3 cups all-purpose flour
- 2 teaspoons ground ginger
- 1 teaspoon baking powder
- ¼ teaspoon salt
- 2½ cups sugar
- 1 cup butter, softened
- 1 tablespoon grated gingerroot
- 1 teaspoon vanilla
- 5 eggs
- 1 cup milk or evaporated milk
- ½ cup finely chopped crystallized ginger
  Browned Butter Glaze (page 156)

1 Heat oven to 350°F. Generously grease bottom, side and tube of 10-inch angel food (tube) cake pan, 12-cup fluted tube cake pan or 2 (9x5-inch) loaf pans with shortening; lightly flour.

2 In medium bowl, mix flour, ground ginger, baking powder and salt; set aside. In large bowl, beat sugar, butter, gingerroot, vanilla and eggs with electric mixer on low speed 30 seconds, scraping bowl constantly. Beat on high speed 5 minutes, scraping bowl occasionally. Beat flour mixture into sugar mixture alternately with milk on low speed, beating just until smooth after each addition. Fold in crystallized ginger. Pour into pan(s).

3 Bake angel food or fluted tube cake pan 1 hour 10 minutes to 1 hour 20 minutes, loaf pans 55 to 60 minutes, or until toothpick inserted in center comes out clean. Cool 20 minutes; remove from pan(s) to cooling rack. Cool completely, about 2 hours. Drizzle with glaze.

1 Serving: Calories 300; Total Fat 12g (Saturated Fat 7g; Trans Fat 0g); Cholesterol 70mg; Sodium 135mg; Total Carbohydrate 46g (Dietary Fiber 0g); Protein 3g **Exchanges:** 1 Starch, 2 Other Carbohydrate, 2½ Fat **Carbohydrate Choices:** 3

Grating Gingerroot

With ginger grater or handheld plane grater, grate peeled gingerroot.

Pound Cake

Triple-Ginger Pound Cake

Tres Leches Cake

TRES LECHES CAKE

In Spanish, tres leches *means "three milks."*

PREP 30 min TOTAL 4 hr 15 min • **15 servings**

Starlight Yellow Cake (page 141) or
Silver White Cake (page 140)
2 cups whipping cream
1 cup whole milk
1 can (14 oz) sweetened condensed milk
(not evaporated)
⅓ cup rum or 1 tablespoon rum extract
plus enough water to measure ⅓ cup
2 tablespoons rum or 1 teaspoon
rum extract
½ teaspoon vanilla
½ cup chopped pecans, toasted (page 22)

1 Heat oven to 350°F. Grease bottom only of
13x9-inch pan with shortening. Pour desired
cake batter into pan. Bake 35 to 40 minutes
for yellow cake or 40 to 45 minutes for white
cake, or until toothpick inserted in center
comes out clean or cake springs back when
touched lightly in center. Let stand 5 minutes.

2 Pierce top of hot cake every ½ inch with
long-tined fork, wiping fork occasionally to
reduce sticking. In large bowl, stir 1 cup of the
whipping cream, the whole milk, condensed
milk and ⅓ cup rum until well mixed. Carefully
pour milk mixture evenly over top of cake.
Cover and refrigerate about 3 hours or until
chilled and most of milk mixture has been
absorbed into cake (when cutting cake to
serve, you may notice some of the milk
mixture on the bottom of the pan).

3 In chilled large deep bowl, beat remaining
1 cup whipping cream, 2 tablespoons rum and
the vanilla with electric mixer on low speed
until mixture begins to thicken. Gradually
increase speed to high and beat just until
soft peaks form, lifting beaters occasionally
to check thickness. Frost cake with whipped
cream mixture. Sprinkle with pecans. Store
covered in refrigerator.

1 Serving: Calories 480; Total Fat 24g (Saturated Fat 12g; Trans Fat
1g); Cholesterol 110mg; Sodium 400mg; Total Carbohydrate 57g
(Dietary Fiber 0g); Protein 8g **Exchanges:** 2 Starch, 2 Other
Carbohydrate, 4½ Fat **Carbohydrate Choices:** 4

TROPICAL TRES LECHES CAKE Make cake
as directed through Step 3 — except omit
pecans. Sprinkle with 1 cup coconut, toasted
(page 18), and ½ cup chopped macadamia
nuts, toasted (page 22).

SOUR CREAM SPICE CAKE

PREP 20 min TOTAL 2 hr 5 min • **16 servings**

2¼ cups all-purpose flour
1½ cups packed brown sugar
2 teaspoons ground cinnamon
1¼ teaspoons baking soda
1 teaspoon baking powder
¾ teaspoon ground cloves
½ teaspoon salt
½ teaspoon ground nutmeg
1 cup raisins, chopped
1 cup sour cream
½ cup chopped walnuts
¼ cup butter, softened
¼ cup shortening
½ cup water
2 eggs
Browned Butter Frosting (page 153),
if desired

1 Heat oven to 350°F. Grease bottom and
sides of 13x9-inch pan or 2 (8- or 9-inch)
round pans with shortening; lightly flour.

2 In large bowl, beat all ingredients except
frosting with electric mixer on low speed
30 seconds, scraping bowl constantly. Beat
on high speed 3 minutes, scraping bowl
occasionally. Pour into pan(s).

Testing Cakes for Doneness

Insert wooden cake tester or toothpick into center of cake.

When you remove cake tester, it should be clean, maybe with some dry crumbs on it. If there is wet batter, the cake is not done.

3 Bake 13x9-inch pan 40 to 45 minutes, round pans 30 to 35 minutes, or until toothpick inserted in center comes out clean. Cool 13x9-inch cake in pan on cooling rack. Cool rounds 10 minutes; remove from pans to cooling racks. Cool completely, about 1 hour.

4 Frost 13x9-inch cake or fill and frost round layers with frosting.

1 Serving: Calories 290; Total Fat 12g (Saturated Fat 4.5g; Trans Fat 1g); Cholesterol 45mg; Sodium 240mg; Total Carbohydrate 42g (Dietary Fiber 1g); Protein 4g **Exchanges:** 1 Starch, 2 Other Carbohydrate, 2 Fat **Carbohydrate Choices:** 3

CARROT CAKE

Here's one of our favorite carrot cakes, featuring pineapple and coconut. It's rich and moist and has an incredible cream cheese frosting.

PREP 20 min **TOTAL** 2 hr 5 min • **12 servings**

- 1½ cups sugar
- 1 cup vegetable oil
- 3 eggs
- 2 cups all-purpose flour
- 2 teaspoons ground cinnamon
- 1 teaspoon baking soda
- ½ teaspoon salt
- 1 teaspoon vanilla
- 3 cups shredded carrots (4 medium)
- 1 can (8 oz) crushed pineapple in juice, drained (½ cup)
- 1 cup chopped nuts
- ½ cup coconut
  Cream Cheese Frosting (page 154), if desired

1 Heat oven to 350°F. Grease bottom and sides of 13x9-inch pan or 2 (8- or 9-inch) round pans with shortening; lightly flour.

2 In large bowl, beat sugar, oil and eggs with electric mixer on low speed about 30 seconds or until blended. Add flour, cinnamon, baking soda, salt and vanilla; beat on medium speed 1 minute. Stir in carrots, pineapple, nuts and coconut (batter will be thick). Pour into pan(s).

3 Bake 13x9-inch pan 40 to 45 minutes, round pans 30 to 35 minutes, or until toothpick inserted in center comes out clean. Cool 13x9-inch cake in pan on cooling rack. Cool rounds 10 minutes; remove from pans to cooling racks. Cool completely, about 1 hour.

4 Frost 13x9-inch cake or fill and frost round layers with frosting. Store covered in refrigerator.

1 Serving: Calories 470; Total Fat 28g (Saturated Fat 6g; Trans Fat 0g); Cholesterol 55mg; Sodium 240mg; Total Carbohydrate 47g (Dietary Fiber 3g); Protein 5g **Exchanges:** 1 Starch, 2 Other Carbohydrate, ½ Vegetable, 5½ Fat **Carbohydrate Choices:** 3

LIGHTER DIRECTIONS For 10 grams of fat and 280 calories per serving, substitute ½ cup unsweetened applesauce for ½ cup of the oil and 1 egg plus 4 egg whites for the eggs. Omit nuts.

APPLE CAKE Substitute 3 cups chopped peeled tart apples (3 medium) for the carrots.

ZUCCHINI CAKE Substitute 3 cups shredded zucchini (2 to 3 medium) for the carrots.

Carrot Cake

BANANA CAKE

PREP 15 min TOTAL 2 hr 15 min • **12 servings**

2½ cups all-purpose flour
1¼ cups sugar
1½ teaspoons baking soda
 1 teaspoon salt
 1 teaspoon baking powder
1½ cups mashed very ripe bananas
    (3 medium)
 ½ cup butter, softened
 ½ cup buttermilk
 2 eggs
 ⅔ cup chopped nuts, if desired
    Cream Cheese Frosting (page 154),
    if desired

1 Heat oven to 350°F. Grease bottom and
sides of 13x9-inch pan or 2 (8- or 9-inch)
round pans with shortening; lightly flour.

2 In large bowl, beat all ingredients except
nuts and frosting with electric mixer on low
speed 30 seconds, scraping bowl constantly.
Beat on high speed 3 minutes, scraping bowl
occasionally. Stir in nuts. Pour into pan(s).

3 Bake 13x9-inch pan 45 to 50 minutes, round
pans 40 to 45 minutes, or until toothpick
inserted in center comes out clean. Cool
rectangle in pan on cooling rack. Cool rounds
10 minutes; remove from pans to cooling rack.
Cool completely, about 1 hour.

4 Frost 13x9-inch cake or fill and frost round
layers with frosting.

1 Serving: Calories 340; Total Fat 13g (Saturated Fat 4.5g; Trans
Fat 0g); Cholesterol 55mg; Sodium 470mg; Total Carbohydrate 49g
(Dietary Fiber 2g); Protein 5g **Exchanges:** 2 Starch, 1 Other
Carbohydrate, 2½ Fat **Carbohydrate Choices: 3**

APPLESAUCE CAKE Substitute 1½ cups
unsweetened applesauce for the bananas
and ½ cup water for the buttermilk. Add
1½ teaspoons pumpkin pie spice; decrease
baking powder to ¾ teaspoon. Stir in 1 cup
raisins with the nuts. Frost with Maple-Nut
Frosting (page 153) or cream cheese frosting.

GANACHE-TOPPED BANANA CAKE Grease
and lightly flour bottom and side of 9-inch
springform pan. Make batter as directed
in recipe; pour into pan. Wrap bottom of
pan with foil to prevent spills. Bake 55 to 60
minutes or until toothpick inserted in center

comes out clean. Cool 10 minutes. Carefully
run knife around side of cake to loosen. Remove
side of pan. Cool completely about 1 hour.
Top with Chocolate Ganache (page 155).

JEWELED FRUITCAKE

LOWER CALORIE

PREP 15 min TOTAL 1 day 2 hr • **32 servings**

 2 cups pitted dates (12 oz)
 2 cups dried apricots (12 oz)
1½ cups nuts (8 oz)
 1 cup red and green maraschino cherries
    (12 oz), drained
 1 cup red and green candied pineapple
    (7 oz), chopped*
 ¾ cup all-purpose flour
 ¾ cup sugar
 ½ teaspoon baking powder
 ½ teaspoon salt
1½ teaspoons vanilla
 3 eggs
    Light corn syrup, if desired

1 Heat oven to 300°F. Line 9x5- or 8x4-inch
loaf pan with foil; grease foil with shortening.

2 In large bowl, stir all ingredients except
corn syrup until well mixed. Spread in pan.

3 Bake about 1 hour 45 minutes or until
toothpick inserted in center comes out clean. If
necessary, cover with foil during last 30 minutes
of baking to prevent excessive browning.

4 Remove fruitcake from pan (with foil) to
cooling rack. For a glossy top, immediately
brush with corn syrup. Allow loaf to cool
completely and become firm before cutting,
about 24 hours. Wrap tightly and store in
refrigerator no longer than 2 months.

*Dried cherries or cranberries can be substituted for the
candied pineapple.*

1 Serving: Calories 200; Total Fat 6g (Saturated Fat 0.5g; Trans Fat
0g); Cholesterol 20mg; Sodium 70mg; Total Carbohydrate 36g (Dietary
Fiber 3g); Protein 2g **Exchanges:** 1 Starch, 1 Fruit, 1 Fat **Carbohydrate
Choices:** 2½

MINI JEWELED FRUITCAKE LOAVES
Generously grease bottoms and sides of
8 miniature loaf pans (4½x2½x1½ inches) with
shortening, or line with foil and grease with
shortening. Divide batter evenly among pans
(about 1 cup each). Bake 55 to 60 minutes or
until toothpick inserted in center comes out

Jelly Roll

clean. Remove from pans to cooling rack. Allow loaves to cool completely and become firm before cutting, about 24 hours. Makes 8 mini loaves

JELLY ROLL LOWER CALORIE

If you tried to roll a regular layer cake, it would crack. This special kind of cake, called a sponge cake, is soft and flexible so that it can be rolled up.

PREP 30 min **TOTAL** 1 hr 15 min • **10 servings**

> 3 **eggs**
> 1 **cup granulated sugar**
> ⅓ **cup water**
> 1 **teaspoon vanilla**
> ¾ **cup all-purpose flour**
> 1 **teaspoon baking powder**
> ¼ **teaspoon salt**
>   **Powdered sugar**
>   **About ⅔ cup jelly or jam**

1 Heat oven to 375°F. Line 15x10x1-inch pan with waxed paper, foil or cooking parchment paper; generously grease waxed paper or foil with shortening.

2 In medium bowl, beat eggs with electric mixer on high speed about 5 minutes or until very thick and lemon colored. Gradually beat in granulated sugar. Beat in water and vanilla on low speed. Gradually add flour, baking powder and salt, beating just until batter is smooth. Pour into pan, spreading to corners.

3 Bake 12 to 15 minutes or until toothpick inserted in center comes out clean. Immediately loosen cake from sides of pan and turn upside down onto towel generously sprinkled with powdered sugar. Carefully remove paper. Trim off stiff edges of cake if necessary. While cake is hot, carefully roll cake and towel from narrow end. Cool on cooling rack at least 30 minutes.

4 Unroll cake and remove towel. Beat jelly slightly with fork to soften; spread over cake. Roll up cake. Sprinkle with powdered sugar.

1 Serving: Calories 200; Total Fat 1.5g (Saturated Fat 0.5g; Trans Fat 0g); Cholesterol 65mg; Sodium 135mg; Total Carbohydrate 42g (Dietary Fiber 0g); Protein 3g **Exchanges:** 1 Starch, 2 Other Carbohydrate **Carbohydrate Choices:** 3

CHOCOLATE CAKE ROLL Increase eggs to 4. Beat in ¼ cup unsweetened baking cocoa with the flour. If desired, fill cake with ice cream instead of jelly or jam. Spread 1 to 1½ pints (2 to 3 cups) slightly softened ice cream over cooled cake. Roll up cake; wrap in plastic wrap. Freeze about 4 hours or until firm.

LEMON CURD JELLY ROLL Make jelly roll cake as directed adding 2 teaspoons grated lemon peel to batter with flour. Omit jelly and spread cake with ⅔ cup purchased lemon curd or make Lemon Curd (page 492). Roll as directed. Store covered in refrigerator.

WHIPPED CREAM JELLY ROLL Make jelly roll cake as directed substituting ½ teaspoon almond extract for the vanilla. In small bowl, whip ⅓ cup whipping cream, 2 teaspoons powdered sugar and ¼ teaspoon almond extract to stiff peaks. Spread over cake and roll as directed. Store covered in refrigerator.

Angel Food Cake

ANGEL FOOD CAKE   LOWER CALORIE

What to do with the leftover egg yolks from this recipe? One idea would be to make some Lemon Curd or Lime Curd, page 492.

PREP 20 min TOTAL 3 hr 25 min • **12 servings**

- 1½ **cups egg whites (about 12)**
- 1½ **cups powdered sugar**
- 1 **cup cake flour**
- 1½ **teaspoons cream of tartar**
- 1 **cup granulated sugar**
- 1½ **teaspoons vanilla**
- ½ **teaspoon almond extract**
- ¼ **teaspoon salt**
    Chocolate Glaze (page 156) or Vanilla Glaze (page 156), if desired

1 Let egg whites stand at room temperature for 30 minutes. Room temperature egg whites will have more volume when beaten than cold egg whites. Move oven rack to lowest position. Heat oven to 375°F.

2 In medium bowl, mix powdered sugar and flour; set aside. In large, clean, dry bowl, beat egg whites and cream of tartar with electric mixer on medium speed until foamy. Beat in granulated sugar, 2 tablespoons at a time, on high speed, adding vanilla, almond extract and salt with the last

addition of sugar. Continue beating until stiff and glossy. Do not underbeat.

3 Sprinkle powdered sugar–flour mixture, ¼ cup at a time, over egg white mixture, folding in with rubber spatula just until sugar-flour mixture disappears. Push batter into ungreased 10-inch angel food (tube) cake pan. Cut gently through batter with metal spatula or knife to break air pockets.

4 Bake 30 to 35 minutes or until cracks feel dry and top springs back when touched lightly. Immediately turn pan upside down onto heatproof bottle or funnel. Let hang about 2 hours or until cake is completely cool.

5 Loosen side of cake with knife or long metal spatula; remove from pan. Spread or drizzle glaze over top of cake.

1 Serving: Calories 180; Total Fat 0g (Saturated Fat 0g; Trans Fat 0g); Cholesterol 0mg; Sodium 100mg; Total Carbohydrate 41g (Dietary Fiber 0g); Protein 4g **Exchanges:** 1½ Starch, 1 Other Carbohydrate **Carbohydrate Choices: 3**

CHERRY ANGEL FOOD CAKE Gently fold ⅓ cup chopped, very well-drained maraschino cherries into batter in Step 3. Continue as directed.

CHOCOLATE-CHERRY ANGEL FOOD CAKE Stir 2 oz grated semisweet baking chocolate into powdered sugar and flour in Step 2. Continue as directed. Gently fold ⅓ cup

Making Angel Food Cake

Beat egg whites and sugar until stiff and glossy.

To fold, cut down vertically through center of egg whites, across bottom of bowl and up side, turning egg whites over. Rotate bowl one-fourth turn and repeat. Continue folding just until ingredients are blended.

Use a metal spatula to cut through batter, pushing batter gently against side of pan and tube, to break large air pockets.

chopped, very well-drained maraschino cherries into batter in Step 3. Continue as directed.

CHOCOLATE CONFETTI ANGEL FOOD CAKE Stir 2 oz grated semisweet baking chocolate into powdered sugar and flour in Step 2. Continue as directed.

ESPRESSO ANGEL FOOD CAKE Stir 2 tablespoons instant espresso coffee powder or granules into powdered sugar and flour in Step 2. Continue as directed.

LEMON CHIFFON CAKE

Here's the cake that serves up the best of both worlds—the lightness of angel food and the richness of a layer cake.

PREP 20 min **TOTAL** 3 hr 35 min • **12 servings**

- 2 **cups all-purpose flour or 2¼ cups cake flour**
- 1½ **cups sugar**
- 3 **teaspoons baking powder**
- 1 **teaspoon salt**
- ¾ **cup cold water**
- ½ **cup vegetable oil**
- 2 **teaspoons vanilla**
- 1 **tablespoon grated lemon peel**
- 7 **egg yolks (if using all-purpose flour) or 5 egg yolks (if using cake flour)**
- 1 **cup egg whites (about 8)**
- ½ **teaspoon cream of tartar**
  Lemon Glaze (page 156), if desired

1 Move oven rack to lowest position. Heat oven to 325°F.

2 In large bowl, mix flour, sugar, baking powder and salt. Beat in water, oil, vanilla, lemon peel and egg yolks with electric mixer on low speed until smooth.

3 Wash and dry mixer beaters. In large bowl, beat egg whites and cream of tartar with electric mixer on high speed until stiff peaks form. Gradually pour egg yolk mixture over beaten egg whites, folding in with rubber spatula just until blended. Pour into ungreased 10-inch angel food (tube) cake pan.

4 Bake about 1 hour 15 minutes or until top springs back when touched lightly. Immediately turn pan upside down onto

heatproof bottle or funnel. Let hang about 2 hours or until cake is completely cool.

5 Loosen side of cake with knife or long metal spatula; remove from pan. Spread glaze over top of cake, allowing some to drizzle down side.

1 Serving: Calories 300; Total Fat 12g (Saturated Fat 2.5g; Trans Fat 0g); Cholesterol 125mg; Sodium 360mg; Total Carbohydrate 42g (Dietary Fiber 0g); Protein 6g **Exchanges:** 2 Starch, 1 Other Carbohydrate, 1 Fat **Carbohydrate Choices:** 3

ORANGE CHIFFON CAKE Omit vanilla. Substitute 2 tablespoons grated orange peel for the lemon peel. Spread with Orange Glaze (page 156), if desired.

PEPPERMINT CHIFFON CAKE Omit vanilla; add ½ teaspoon peppermint extract with water and oil in Step 2. Spread with Vanilla, Chocolate or Dark Chocolate Glaze (page 156), if desired.

SPICED CHIFFON CAKE Add 1 teaspoon ground cinnamon and ¼ teaspoon each ground nutmeg, allspice and cloves with flour and sugar in Step 2. Spread with Vanilla or Browned Butter Glaze (page 156), if desired.

Cooling a Foam Cake

Immediately turn pan upside down onto heatproof bottle or funnel (plastic funnel can be wrapped with foil to make it heatproof).

Lemon Chiffon Cake

FUDGE FROSTING

PREP 10 min TOTAL 55 min • **12 servings**
(3½ cups frosting)

  2 **cups granulated sugar**
  1 **cup unsweetened baking cocoa**
  1 **cup milk**
  ½ **cup butter, cut into pieces**
  ¼ **cup light corn syrup**
  ¼ **teaspoon salt**
  2 **teaspoons vanilla**
  2½ **to 3 cups powdered sugar**

1 In 3-quart saucepan, mix granulated sugar and cocoa. Stir in milk, butter, corn syrup and salt. Heat to boiling, stirring frequently. Boil 3 minutes, stirring occasionally. Cool 45 minutes.

2 Beat in vanilla and enough powdered sugar for spreading consistency.

3 Frost 13x9-inch cake, or fill and frost 8- or 9-inch two-layer cake. Leftover frosting can be tightly covered and refrigerated up to 5 days or frozen up to 1 month. Let stand 30 minutes at room temperature to soften; stir before using.

1 Serving: Calories 550; Total Fat 14g (Saturated Fat 7g; Trans Fat 0.5g); Cholesterol 35mg; Sodium 180mg; Total Carbohydrate 103g (Dietary Fiber 4g); Protein 3g **Exchanges:** 1 Starch, 6 Other Carbohydrate, 2½ Fat **Carbohydrate Choices:** 7

Frosting Toppers

Make your favorite frosting, then add a special ingredient to top off your cake or cupcakes.

- **Pearl Sugar:** White sugar granules add interest for special occasions like showers.
- **Crystal and Sanding Sugar:** Sprinkle this glistening, colorful sugar on top of frosting.
- **Food Writer Pens:** Use as you would ink markers to add dazzling color.
- **Decorating Spray:** Spray on cupcakes; it dries to form a powdery coating. The look is similar to a technique used by bakeries.
- **Colored Sprinkles:** Look for an amazing array of colored shapes for topping frosting.

CREAMY CHOCOLATE FROSTING FAST

PREP 15 min TOTAL 15 min • **12 servings**
(2 cups frosting)

  ⅓ **cup butter, softened**
  3 **oz unsweetened baking chocolate, melted and cooled at least 5 minutes**
  3 **cups powdered sugar**
  2 **teaspoons vanilla**
  3 **to 4 tablespoons milk**

1 In large bowl, beat butter and chocolate with spoon or electric mixer on low speed until blended. Gradually beat in powdered sugar on low speed until blended.

2 Gradually beat in vanilla and just enough milk to make frosting smooth and spreadable. If frosting is too thick, beat in more milk, a few drops at a time. If frosting becomes too thin, beat in a small amount of powdered sugar.

3 Frost 13x9-inch cake, or fill and frost 8- or 9-inch two-layer cake. Leftover frosting can be tightly covered and refrigerated up to 5 days or frozen up to 1 month. Let stand 30 minutes at room temperature to soften; stir before using.

NOTE: To fill and frost an 8-inch three-layer cake, use ½ cup butter, 4 oz chocolate, 4½ cups powdered sugar, 1 tablespoon vanilla and about ¼ cup milk.

1 Serving: Calories 210; Total Fat 9g (Saturated Fat 5g; Trans Fat 0g); Cholesterol 15mg; Sodium 35mg; Total Carbohydrate 32g (Dietary Fiber 1g); Protein 0g **Exchanges:** ½ Starch, 2 Other Carbohydrate, 1½ Fat **Carbohydrate Choices:** 2

CREAMY COCOA FROSTING Substitute ⅓ cup unsweetened baking cocoa for the chocolate.

MOCHA FROSTING Add 2½ teaspoons instant coffee granules or crystals with the powdered sugar.

WHITE CHOCOLATE FROSTING Substitute 2 oz white chocolate baking squares or bars, melted and cooled at least 5 minutes, for the chocolate. Do not use white vanilla baking chips because they will add a grainy texture.

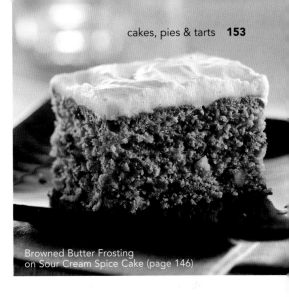

Browned Butter Frosting
on Sour Cream Spice Cake (page 146)

CREAMY VANILLA FROSTING

FAST

PREP 10 min TOTAL 10 min • **12 servings**
(1¾ cups frosting)

> 3 cups powdered sugar
> ⅓ cup butter, softened
> 1½ teaspoons vanilla
> 1 to 2 tablespoons milk

1 In large bowl, mix powdered sugar and butter with spoon or electric mixer on low speed until blended. Stir in vanilla and 1 tablespoon of the milk.

2 Gradually beat in just enough remaining milk to make frosting smooth and spreadable. If frosting is too thick, beat in more milk, a few drops at a time. If frosting becomes too thin, beat in a small amount of powdered sugar.

3 Frost 13x9-inch cake, or fill and frost 8- or 9-inch two-layer cake. Leftover frosting can be tightly covered and refrigerated up to 5 days or frozen up to 1 month. Let stand 30 minutes at room temperature to soften; stir before using.

NOTE: To fill and frost an 8-inch three-layer cake, use 4½ cups powdered sugar, ½ cup butter, 2 teaspoons vanilla and about 3 table-spoons milk.

1 Serving: Calories 170; Total Fat 5g (Saturated Fat 2.5g; Trans Fat 0g); Cholesterol 15mg; Sodium 35mg; Total Carbohydrate 30g (Dietary Fiber 0g); Protein 0g **Exchanges:** 2 Other Carbohydrate, 1 Fat **Carbohydrate Choices:** 2

BROWNED BUTTER FROSTING In 1-quart saucepan, heat ⅓ cup butter (do not use margarine or vegetable oil spreads) over medium heat just until light brown, stirring constantly. Watch carefully because butter can brown and then burn quickly. Cool butter. Use browned butter instead of softened butter in recipe.

LEMON FROSTING Omit vanilla. Substitute lemon juice for the milk. Stir in 1 teaspoon grated lemon peel.

MAPLE-NUT FROSTING Omit vanilla. Substitute 1 to 2 tablespoons real maple syrup or maple-flavored syrup for the milk. Stir in ¼ cup finely chopped nuts.

ORANGE FROSTING Omit vanilla. Substitute orange juice for the milk. Stir in 1 teaspoon grated orange peel.

PEANUT BUTTER FROSTING Substitute creamy peanut butter for the butter. Increase milk to about ¼ cup, adding more if necessary, a few drops at a time.

Learn with Betty | BROWNED BUTTER

Perfectly Browned Butter: This butter is golden brown.

Underbrowned Butter: This butter is not browned enough.

Overbrowned Butter: This butter is scorched and too brown.

CREAM CHEESE FROSTING FAST

This is the perfect frosting for carrot cake and spice or applesauce cakes. Be sure to refrigerate the frosted cake since cream cheese is perishable.

PREP 10 min **TOTAL** 10 min • **12 servings**
(2½ cups frosting)

> 1 **package (8 oz) cream cheese, softened**
> ¼ **cup butter, softened**
> 2 **to 3 teaspoons milk**
> 1 **teaspoon vanilla**
> 4 **cups powdered sugar**

1 In large bowl, beat cream cheese, butter, milk and vanilla with electric mixer on low speed until smooth.

2 Gradually beat in powdered sugar, 1 cup at a time, on low speed until frosting is smooth and spreadable.

3 Frost 13x9-inch cake, or fill and frost 8- or 9-inch two-layer cake. Leftover frosting can be tightly covered and refrigerated up to 5 days or frozen up to 1 month. Let stand 30 minutes at room temperature to soften; stir before using.

1 Serving: Calories 260; Total Fat 10g (Saturated Fat 6g; Trans Fat 0g); Cholesterol 30mg; Sodium 80mg; Total Carbohydrate 40g (Dietary Fiber 0g); Protein 2g **Exchanges:** 1 Starch, 1½ Other Carbohydrate, 2 Fat **Carbohydrate Choices:** 2½

CHOCOLATE CREAM CHEESE FROSTING

Add 2 oz unsweetened baking chocolate, melted and cooled 10 minutes, with the butter.

CARAMEL FROSTING

For a richer frosting, use whole milk or half-and-half.

PREP 10 min **TOTAL** 40 min • **12 servings**
(2 cups frosting)

> ½ **cup butter**
> 1 **cup packed brown sugar**
> ¼ **cup milk**
> 2 **cups powdered sugar**

1 In 2-quart saucepan, melt butter over medium heat. Stir in brown sugar. Heat to boiling, stirring constantly; reduce heat to low. Boil and stir 2 minutes. Stir in milk. Heat to boiling; remove from heat. Cool to lukewarm, about 30 minutes.

2 Gradually stir in powdered sugar. Place saucepan of frosting in bowl of cold water.

Beat with spoon until frosting is smooth and spreadable. If frosting becomes too stiff, stir in additional milk, 1 teaspoon at a time, or heat over low heat, stirring constantly.

3 Frost 13x9-inch cake, or fill and frost 8- or 9-inch two-layer cake. Leftover frosting can be tightly covered and refrigerated up to 5 days or frozen up to 1 month. Let stand 30 minutes at room temperature to soften; stir before using.

1 Serving: Calories 220; Total Fat 8g (Saturated Fat 4g; Trans Fat 0g); Cholesterol 20mg; Sodium 60mg; Total Carbohydrate 38g (Dietary Fiber 0g); Protein 0g **Exchanges:** 2½ Other Carbohydrate, 1½ Fat **Carbohydrate Choices:** 2½

FLUFFY WHITE FROSTING

LOWER CALORIE

This frosting got its name because its large white peaks hold up long after it's beaten. It's sometimes called White Mountain Frosting.

PREP 25 min **TOTAL** 55 min • **12 servings**
(3 cups frosting)

> 2 **egg whites**
> ½ **cup sugar**
> ¼ **cup light corn syrup**
> 2 **tablespoons water**
> 1 **teaspoon vanilla**

1 Let egg whites stand at room temperature for 30 minutes. Room temperature egg whites will have more volume when beaten than cold egg whites. In medium bowl, beat egg whites with electric mixer on high speed just until stiff peaks form.

2 In 1-quart saucepan, stir sugar, corn syrup and water until well mixed. Cover and heat to rolling boil over medium heat. Uncover and boil 4 to 8 minutes, without stirring, to 242°F on candy thermometer or until small amount of mixture dropped into cup of very cold water forms a firm ball that holds its shape until pressed (see Testing Candy Temperature, page 203). For an accurate temperature reading, tilt the saucepan slightly so mixture is deep enough for thermometer.

3 Pour hot syrup very slowly in thin stream into egg whites, beating constantly on medium speed. Add vanilla. Beat on high speed about 10 minutes or until stiff peaks form.

4 Frost 13x9-inch cake, or fill and frost 8- or 9-inch two-layer cake. Leftover frosting can be tightly covered and refrigerated up to 2 days; do not freeze. Let stand 30 minutes at room temperature to soften; do not stir.

1 Serving: Calories 60; Total Fat 0g (Saturated Fat 0g; Trans Fat 0g); Cholesterol 0mg; Sodium 15mg; Total Carbohydrate 14g (Dietary Fiber 0g); Protein 0g **Exchanges:** 1 Other Carbohydrate **Carbohydrate Choices:** 1

BUTTERSCOTCH FROSTING Substitute packed brown sugar for the sugar. Decrease vanilla to ½ teaspoon.

CHERRY-NUT FROSTING Stir in ¼ cup chopped candied cherries, ¼ cup chopped nuts and, if desired, 6 to 8 drops red food color.

PEPPERMINT FROSTING Stir in ⅓ cup coarsely crushed hard peppermint candies or ½ teaspoon peppermint extract.

CHOCOLATE GANACHE FAST

Ganache is a very rich chocolate glaze made with semisweet chocolate and heavy cream. If you glaze the cake on a cooling rack with waxed paper underneath the rack, the ganache will drip over the side of the cake and the extra drips will fall onto the waxed paper. When the ganache hardens, just slide the cake—easily and neatly—onto your serving plate.

PREP 5 min **TOTAL** 10 min • **12 servings** (**1¼ cups ganache**)

- ⅔ **cup whipping cream**
- 6 **oz semisweet baking chocolate, chopped**

1 In 1-quart saucepan, heat whipping cream over low heat until hot but not boiling; remove from heat.

2 Stir in chocolate until melted. Let stand about 5 minutes. Ganache is ready to use when it mounds slightly when dropped from a spoon. It will become firmer the longer it cools.

3 Glaze 13x9-inch cake or top and side of 8- or 9-inch two-layer cake. Pour ganache carefully onto top center of cake; spread with large spatula so it flows evenly over top and down to cover side of cake. Leftover glaze can be tightly covered and refrigerated up to 5 days; do not freeze. Let stand 30 minutes at room temperature to soften; stir before using.

1 Serving: Calories 120; Total Fat 8g (Saturated Fat 5g; Trans Fat 0g); Cholesterol 15mg; Sodium 5mg; Total Carbohydrate 9g (Dietary Fiber 0g); Protein 0g **Exchanges:** ½ Other Carbohydrate, 1½ Fat **Carbohydrate Choices:** ½

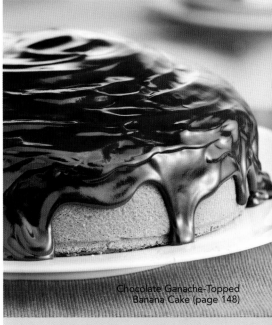

Chocolate Ganache-Topped Banana Cake (page 148)

Using Ganache

Ganache is ready to use when it is fairly thick and mounds slightly when dropped from a spoon.

Pour ganache carefully onto center of cake; spread to cover top and down side of cake.

CHOCOLATE GLAZE

FAST LOWER CALORIE

The corn syrup in this glaze not only adds sweetness but also gives it the glossy sheen. This recipe can easily be doubled.

PREP 5 min **TOTAL** 15 min • **12 servings** (½ cup glaze)

- ½ cup semisweet chocolate chips (3 oz)
- 2 tablespoons butter
- 2 tablespoons light corn syrup
- 1 to 2 teaspoons hot water

1 In 1-quart saucepan, heat chocolate chips, butter and corn syrup over low heat, stirring frequently, until chocolate chips are melted. Cool about 10 minutes.

2 Stir in hot water, 1 teaspoon at a time, until glaze is smooth and has the consistency of thick syrup.

3 Glaze one 12-cup fluted tube cake, 10-inch angel food or chiffon cake or top of an 8- or 9-inch layer cake. Leftover glaze can be tightly covered and refrigerated up to 5 days; do not freeze. Let stand 30 minutes at room temperature to soften; stir before using.

1 Serving: Calories 70; Total Fat 4g (Saturated Fat 2g; Trans Fat 0g); Cholesterol 5mg; Sodium 20mg; Total Carbohydrate 7g (Dietary Fiber 0g); Protein 0g **Exchanges:** ½ Other Carbohydrate, 1 Fat **Carbohydrate Choices:** ½

DARK CHOCOLATE GLAZE Substitute dark chocolate chips for the semisweet chocolate chips.

MILK CHOCOLATE GLAZE Substitute milk chocolate chips for the semisweet chocolate chips.

MINT CHOCOLATE GLAZE Substitute mint-flavored chocolate chips for the semisweet chocolate chips.

WHITE CHOCOLATE GLAZE Substitute white vanilla baking chips for the semisweet chocolate chips.

VANILLA GLAZE **FAST**

PREP 5 min **TOTAL** 5 min • **12 servings** (1 cup glaze)

- ⅓ cup butter
- 2 cups powdered sugar
- 1½ teaspoons vanilla
- 2 to 4 tablespoons hot water

1 In 1½-quart saucepan, melt butter over low heat; remove from heat. Stir in powdered sugar and vanilla.

2 Stir in hot water, 1 tablespoon at a time, until glaze is smooth and has the consistency of thick syrup.

3 Glaze one 12-cup fluted tube cake, 10-inch angel food or chiffon cake or top of an 8- or 9-inch layer cake. Leftover glaze can be tightly covered and refrigerated up to 5 days; do not freeze. Let stand 30 minutes at room temperature to soften; stir before using.

1 Serving: Calories 130; Total Fat 5g (Saturated Fat 3g; Trans Fat 0g); Cholesterol 15mg; Sodium 35mg; Total Carbohydrate 20g (Dietary Fiber 0g); Protein 0g **Exchanges:** 1½ Other Carbohydrate, 1 Fat **Carbohydrate Choices:** 1

BROWNED BUTTER GLAZE Brown the butter as directed in Browned Butter Frosting (page 153). Continue as directed in Step 1.

LEMON GLAZE Stir 1 teaspoon grated lemon peel into melted butter. Omit vanilla. Substitute lemon juice, heated, for the hot water.

ORANGE GLAZE Stir 1 teaspoon grated orange peel into melted butter. Omit vanilla. Substitute orange juice, heated, for the hot water.

Making and Drizzling Glaze

Glaze should be consistency of thick syrup.

With spoon, drizzle glaze over top of cake.

PIE AND PASTRY BASICS

Don't turn your back on that pie cooling on the counter. With its flaky pastry and delicious filling, a generous slice of homemade pie is hard to resist. Using the information here, you'll be able to make any pie with confidence, so get ready for oohs, aahs and requests for seconds.

PICKING PIE PANS

Use the size pie plate or pan called for in the recipe.

Use a heat-resistant glass pie plate or dull aluminum pie pan. Shiny or disposable pie pans reflect heat and prevent crusts from browning. Dark pans absorb heat, causing overbrowning. Nonstick pans can cause an unfilled crust to shrink excessively.

It is not necessary to grease the pan as pastry is high in fat.

FREEZING PIE PASTRY

Unbaked and baked pie pastry (without filling) can be frozen for up to 2 months.

- For rounds of pastry dough, wrap tightly in plastic wrap and freeze. Thaw in refrigerator before rolling and filling.
- For unbaked pastry crust in a pan, wrap tightly in foil or place in a freezer plastic bag. There's no need to thaw before baking.
- For baked pastry crust in a pan, wrap tightly in foil or place in a freezer plastic bag. Thaw before using.

FREEZING FILLED PIES

Filled unbaked and baked pies can be frozen for up to 2 months.

- Completely cool baked pies before freezing.
- Do not freeze cream, custard and meringue-topped pies. The filling and the meringue will break down and become watery.
- Fruit pies can be frozen unbaked or baked. Pecan and pumpkin pies need to be baked before freezing.
- Thaw unbaked frozen pies in the refrigerator before baking.
- To serve baked frozen pies, unwrap and bake at 325°F for 45 minutes or until thawed and warm.

Tips for Perfect Pie Pastry

- Use ice water to make the crusts—add an ice cube to the water to keep it cold.
- Use a pastry blender to mix the shortening and flour. A fork will work, too.
- Overworking the pastry dough will make it tough, so handle it as little as possible.
- Refrigerate pastry for 45 minutes; this helps it roll more easily.
- Use a floured pastry cloth or board to roll pastry to the size indicated in the recipe.

Bake pie crust until light brown and place on cooling rack to cool.

MAKING PIE PASTRY

Flaky, tender pie crust is the secret to any pie, and there is no mystery behind making it. Here you'll find the basic pastry recipes for pies and tarts. There are recipes for both one- and two-crust pies. On the following pages, you'll find baking methods for pie-crust and tart shells.

You'll also find a variety of decorative crust ideas, from creating a pretty pie edge to a beautiful and easy lattice top. Finally, turn to page 164 for all you need to make a great two-crust apple pie, with tips for getting great results the first time.

ONE-CRUST PASTRY

This pastry recipe is perfect for making any pie or tart. You can bake the pastry before filling for a variety of cooked or fresh fillings, or fill and then bake. Individual recipes will indicate which method to use and how to bake.

PREP 20 min TOTAL 1 hr 5 min • **8 servings**

- 1 **cup plus 1 tablespoon all-purpose flour**
- ½ **teaspoon salt**
- ⅓ **cup cold shortening**
- 3 **to 5 tablespoons ice-cold water**

1 In medium bowl, mix flour and salt. Cut in shortening, using pastry blender or fork, until mixture forms coarse crumbs the size of small peas. Sprinkle with the water, 1 tablespoon at a time, tossing with fork until all flour is moistened and pastry almost leaves side of bowl (1 to 2 teaspoons more water can be added if necessary).

2 Gather pastry into a ball. Shape into flattened round on lightly floured surface. Wrap flattened round in plastic wrap and refrigerate 45 minutes or until dough is firm and cold, yet pliable. This allows the shortening to become slightly firm, which helps make the

baked pastry flaky. If refrigerated longer, let pastry soften slightly at room temperature before rolling.

3 Using floured rolling pin, roll pastry on lightly floured surface (or pastry board with floured pastry cloth) into round 2 inches larger than upside-down 9-inch glass pie plate or 3 inches larger than 10- or 11-inch tart pan. Fold pastry into fourths and place in pie plate or roll pastry loosely around rolling pin and transfer to pie plate or tart pan. Unfold or unroll pastry and ease into plate or pan, pressing firmly against bottom and side and being careful not to stretch pastry, which will cause it to shrink when baked.

4 For pie, trim overhanging edge of pastry 1 inch from rim of pie plate. Fold edge under to form standing rim; flute edges (see Decorative Crust Ideas, page

161). For tart, trim overhanging edge of pastry even with top of tart pan. Fill and bake as directed in desired pie or tart recipe.

1 Serving: Calories 140; Total Fat 9g (Saturated Fat 2g, Trans Fat 0g); Cholesterol 0mg; Sodium 150mg; Total Carbohydrate 13g (Dietary Fiber 0g); Protein 1g **Exchanges:** 1 Starch, 1½ Fat **Carbohydrate Choices:** 1

BUTTER CRUST Substitute cold butter, cut into ½-inch pieces, for half of the shortening.

TWO-CRUST PASTRY

Use this pastry recipe for any pie where the filling is cooked between two crusts, such as a fruit pie. For convenience, you could also use just half of the pastry dough for a one-crust pie and freeze the other round of pastry, wrapped tightly in plastic wrap, for another pie.

PREP 20 min TOTAL 1 hr 5 min • **8 servings**

- **2 cups plus 2 tablespoons all-purpose flour**
- **1 teaspoon salt**
- **⅔ cup cold shortening**
- **6 to 8 tablespoons ice-cold water**

1 In medium bowl, mix flour and salt. Cut in shortening, using pastry blender or fork, until mixture forms coarse crumbs the size of small peas. Sprinkle with the water, 1 tablespoon at a time, tossing with fork until all flour is moistened and pastry almost leaves side of bowl (1 to 2 teaspoons more water can be added if necessary).

2 Gather pastry into a ball. Divide pastry in half and shape into 2 rounds on lightly floured surface. Wrap flattened rounds in plastic wrap and refrigerate 45 minutes or until dough is firm and cold, yet pliable. This allows the shortening to become slightly firm, which helps make the baked pastry flaky. If refrigerated longer, let pastry soften slightly at room temperature before rolling.

3 Using floured rolling pin, roll one round of pastry on lightly floured surface (or pastry board with floured pastry cloth) into round 2 inches larger than upside-down 9-inch glass pie plate. Fold pastry into fourths and place in pie plate or roll pastry loosely around rolling pin and transfer to pie plate. Unfold or unroll pastry and ease into plate, pressing firmly against bottom and side and being careful not to stretch pastry, which will cause it to shrink when baked.

4 Spoon desired filling into bottom crust. Trim over-hanging edge of bottom crust ½ inch from rim of plate.

5 Roll other round out. Fold into fourths and place over filling; or roll loosely around rolling pin and place over filling. Unfold or unroll pastry over filling. Cut slits in pastry so steam can escape.

6 Trim overhanging edge of top pastry 1 inch from rim of plate. Fold edge of top crust under bottom crust, pressing on rim to seal; flute edges (see Decorative Crust Ideas, page 161). Bake as directed in desired pie recipe.

1 Serving: Calories 280; Total Fat 18g (Saturated Fat 3g, Trans Fat 0g); Cholesterol 0mg; Sodium 300mg; Total Carbohydrate 26g (Dietary Fiber 0g); Protein 2g **Exchanges:** 1½ Starch, 2 Fat **Carbohydrate Choices**: 2

BUTTER CRUST Substitute cold butter, cut into ½-inch pieces, for half of the shortening.

Making Pie Crust in a Food Processor

1 Measure 2 tablespoons ice-cold water for One-Crust Pastry or 4 tablespoons ice-cold water for Two-Crust Pastry into liquid measuring cup; set aside.

2 Place flour, salt and shortening in food processor. Cover and process, using quick on-and-off motions, until particles are the size of small peas.

3 With food processor running, pour water all at once through feed tube just until dough leaves side of bowl (dough should not form a ball). Continue as directed in Step 2 of pastry recipes.

BAKING METHODS FOR PIE CRUST

For many pies (such as apple pie and pecan pie), the filling is added to the unbaked pastry. Then the pie is baked so that the crust and filling bake together. For other pies the crust is either partially baked or completely baked before filling is added; this is done to help prevent the crust from becoming soggy or when the filling does not need to be baked.

PARTIALLY BAKED ONE-CRUST PIE

Use, if recipe directs, to prevent bottom crust from becoming soggy.

1 Heat oven to 425°F. Carefully line pastry with a double thickness of foil, gently pressing foil to bottom and side of pastry. Let foil extend over edge to prevent excessive browning.

2 Bake 10 minutes; carefully remove foil and bake 2 to 4 minutes longer or until pastry just begins to brown and has become set. If crust bubbles, gently push bubbles down with back of spoon.

3 Fill and bake as directed in pie or tart recipe, changing oven temperature if necessary.

BAKED ONE-CRUST PIE

Use for one-crust pies and tarts baked completely before filling is added, such as banana cream or lemon meringue pie.

1 Heat oven to 475°F. For pie, trim overhanging edge of pastry 1 inch from rim of pie plate. For tart, trim overhanging edge of pastry even with top of tart pan. Prick bottom and side of pastry thoroughly with fork.

2 Bake 8 to 10 minutes or until light brown; cool on cooling rack.

BAKED TART SHELLS AND INDIVIDUAL PIE CRUSTS

Make pastry as directed for One-Crust Pastry (page 158)—except roll pastry into 13-inch round. Cut into 8 (4½-inch) rounds, rerolling pastry scraps if necessary.

1 Heat oven to 475°F. Fit rounds over backs of regular-size muffin cups or 6-oz custard cups, making pleats so pastry will fit snugly against the cups. (If using individual pie pans or tart pans, cut pastry rounds 1 inch larger than upside-down pans; fit into pans.) Prick pastry thoroughly with fork to prevent puffing. Place on cookie sheet.

2 Bake 8 to 10 minutes or until light brown; cool before removing from cups. Fill each shell with ⅓ to ½ cup of your favorite filling, pudding, fresh fruit or ice cream.

Decorative Cut-Outs

For an extra-pretty pie, make decorative cut-outs on the top of a two-crust pie. Use a small cookie cutter, and cut shapes from the top crust before placing it on the filling. Place cut-outs on top of the pie crust, attaching with a little cold water. Sprinkle with coarse sugar.

DECORATIVE CRUST IDEAS

Fluting the edge of a crust not only adds a decorative touch but also helps keep the filling from bubbling over. Start by forming a stand-up rim of pastry that is even thickness on edge of pie plate, pressing edges together. This seals pastry and makes fluting easier.

SCALLOPED EDGE

Place thumb and index finger about 1 inch apart on outside of raised edge. With other index finger, push pastry toward outside to form scalloped edge.

ROPE OR PINCHED EDGE

Place side of thumb on pastry rim at angle. Pinch pastry by pressing knuckle of index finger down into pastry toward thumb.

FORKED OR HERRINGBONE EDGE

Dip fork tines in flour, then press fork diagonally onto edge without pressing through pastry. Rotate tines 90 degrees and press next to first set of marks. Continue around edge of pastry rotating tines back and forth.

Cutting Pies

Cut cooled pies with a sharp, thin-bladed knife. For meringue or ice cream pies, dip the knife into warm water and wipe clean before cutting. Use a pie cutter or wedge-shaped spatula to remove each slice.

See how to make **a lattice pie crust**: Visit bettycrocker.com/BCcookbook

LATTICE TOP CRUSTS

A lattice top crust adds a nice touch to a two-crust pie, letting the filling peak through. For an easy "wow," try one of these methods for the top pastry of your pie. Using a pastry wheel adds a decorative touch to a lattice crust.

EASY LATTICE TOP

Make pastry for Two-Crust Pastry, except trim overhanging edge of bottom crust 1 inch from rim of plate. Place filling in crust. After rolling pastry for top crust, cut into ½-inch-wide strips. Place half of strips about ½ inch apart on filling. Place remaining strips ½ inch apart crosswise over first strips. Trim strips evenly with edge of overhanging crust. Fold edge up, forming high, stand-up ridge; flute edges as desired.

CLASSIC LATTICE TOP

Make pastry for Two-Crust Pastry, except trim overhanging edge of bottom crust 1 inch from rim of plate. Place filling in crust. After rolling pastry for top crust, cut into ½-inch-wide strips. Place half of strips about ½ inch apart on filling. Weave remaining strips over and under first strips. Trim strips evenly with edge of overhanging crust. Fold edge up, forming high, stand-up ridge; flute edges as desired.

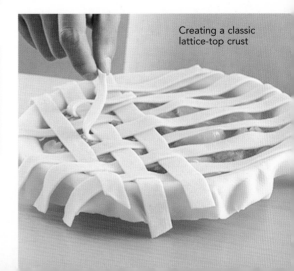

Creating a classic lattice-top crust

EASY BUTTERMILK PASTRY `FAST`

This pastry is a dream to work with because it's extra easy to roll and handle, and the baked crust is very flaky.

PREP 15 min **TOTAL** 15 min • **Two 9-inch crusts (8 servings each)**

- 2 cups all-purpose flour
- 1 teaspoon salt
- ⅔ cup cold shortening
- 3 tablespoons cold butter
- ⅓ cup buttermilk
- 2 teaspoons vegetable oil

1 In medium bowl, mix flour and salt. Cut in shortening and butter, using pastry blender or fork, until mixture forms coarse crumbs the size of small peas.

2 Mix in buttermilk and oil with fork until all flour is moistened and pastry leaves side of bowl. Divide in half; shape each half into a ball. If making one-crust pie, wrap second ball of pastry and freeze for later use.

3 Roll pastry as directed in Step 3 of One-Crust Pastry (page 158). Fill and bake as directed in pie recipe. Or to bake before filling is added, heat oven to 475°F. Prick bottom and side of pastry thoroughly with fork. Bake 8 to 10 minutes or until light brown; cool on cooling rack.

1 Serving (For One Crust): Calories 160; Total Fat 11g (Saturated Fat 3.5g; Trans Fat 1.5g); Cholesterol 5mg; Sodium 170mg; Total Carbohydrate 12g (Dietary Fiber 0g); Protein 2g **Exchanges:** 1 Starch, 2 Fat **Carbohydrate Choices:** 1

PRESS-IN-THE-PAN OIL PASTRY

No rolling is needed for this crust! Use it for pies that have only a bottom crust. Try it for Pumpkin Pie, page 172, as well as for pie crusts that are baked before being filled.

PREP 10 min **TOTAL** 25 min • **One 9-inch crust (8 servings)**

- 1⅓ cups all-purpose flour
- ½ teaspoon salt
- ⅓ cup vegetable oil
- 2 tablespoons ice-cold water

1 In medium bowl, stir flour, salt and oil until all flour is moistened. Sprinkle with cold water, 1 tablespoon at a time, tossing with fork until all water is absorbed. Gather pastry into a ball. Press firmly and evenly against bottom and up side of 9-inch glass pie plate; flute (see Decorative Crust Ideas, page 161).

2 Fill and bake as directed in pie recipe. Or to bake before filling is added, heat oven to 475°F. Prick bottom and side of pastry thoroughly with fork. Bake 10 to 12 minutes or until light brown; cool on cooling rack.

1 Serving: Calories 150; Total Fat 9g (Saturated Fat 1.5g; Trans Fat 0g); Cholesterol 0mg; Sodium 150mg; Total Carbohydrate 16g (Dietary Fiber 0g); Protein 2g **Exchanges:** 1 Starch, 1½ Fat **Carbohydrate Choices:** 1

Banana Cream Pie (page 169) with Easy Buttermilk Pastry

Caramel Chocolate Pie Supreme (page 174) with Press-in-the-Pan Oil Pastry

PRESS-IN-THE-PAN TART PASTRY FAST

PREP 10 min TOTAL 20 min • **One 11-inch crust (8 servings)**

- 1¼ cups all-purpose flour
- ½ cup butter, softened
- 2 tablespoons packed brown sugar
- 1 egg

1 In medium bowl, stir all ingredients until soft dough forms. Using lightly floured fingers, press firmly and evenly against bottom and side of ungreased 11-inch tart pan.

2 Fill and bake as directed in tart recipe. Or to bake before filling is added, heat oven to 475°F. Bake 8 to 10 minutes or until light brown; cool on cooling rack.

1 Serving: Calories 200; Total Fat 12g (Saturated Fat 6g; Trans Fat 0.5g); Cholesterol 55mg; Sodium 85mg; Total Carbohydrate 18g (Dietary Fiber 0g); Protein 3g **Exchanges:** 1 Starch, 2½ Fat **Carbohydrate Choices:** 1

EASY NUT CRUST FAST

PREP 10 min TOTAL 20 min • **One 9-inch crust (8 servings)**

- 1 cup all-purpose flour
- ½ cup butter, softened
- ¼ cup finely chopped nuts

1 In medium bowl, mix all ingredients until soft dough forms. Using lightly floured fingers, press firmly and evenly against bottom and side of 9-inch glass pie plate.

2 Fill and bake as directed in pie recipe. Or to bake before filling is added, heat oven to 475°F. Bake 7 to 8 minutes or until light brown; cool on cooling rack.

1 Serving: Calories 190; Total Fat 14g (Saturated Fat 8g; Trans Fat 0g); Cholesterol 30mg; Sodium 80mg; Total Carbohydrate 12g (Dietary Fiber 0g); Protein 2g **Exchanges:** 1 Starch, 2½ Fat **Carbohydrate Choices:** 1

GRAHAM CRACKER CRUST FAST

PREP 10 min TOTAL 20 min • **One 9-inch crust (8 servings)**

- 1½ cups finely crushed regular or cinnamon graham crackers (24 squares)
- ⅓ cup butter, melted
- 3 tablespoons sugar

1 Heat oven to 350°F. In medium bowl, stir all ingredients until well mixed. Reserve 3 tablespoons crumb mixture for garnishing top of pie before serving, if desired. Press remaining mixture firmly and evenly against bottom and side of 9-inch glass pie plate.

2 Bake about 10 minutes or until light brown; cool on cooling rack. Fill as directed in pie recipe.

1 Serving: Calories 160; Total Fat 9g (Saturated Fat 5g; Trans Fat 0g); Cholesterol 20mg; Sodium 150mg; Total Carbohydrate 17g (Dietary Fiber 0g); Protein 1g **Exchanges:** ½ Starch, ½ Other Carbohydrate, 2 Fat **Carbohydrate Choices:** 1

COOKIE CRUMB CRUST Substitute 1½ cups finely crushed chocolate wafer cookies (24 cookies), vanilla wafer cookies (35 cookies) or gingersnaps (30 cookies) for the graham crackers. Decrease butter to ¼ cup; omit sugar.

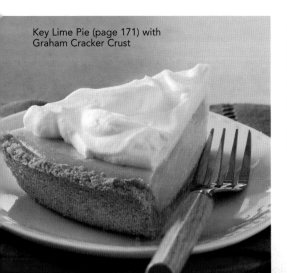

Key Lime Pie (page 171) with Graham Cracker Crust

Making Graham Cracker Crust

Mix crumbs until butter is combined and mixture is crumbly.

Press crumb mixture firmly against side and bottom of pie plate.

Learn to Make **Apple Pie**

CLASSIC APPLE PIE

Once you've had homemade apple pie, nothing else will ever compare. What sets it apart is a tender, flaky crust that can only be achieved when made by hand. Here's how to make perfectly baked apple pie, with a flaky crust filled with juicy fresh apples.

PREP 30 min **TOTAL** 3 hr 20 min • **8 servings**

Two-Crust Pastry (page 159)
or Easy Buttermilk Pastry (page 162)
½ cup sugar
¼ cup all-purpose flour
¾ teaspoon ground cinnamon
¼ teaspoon ground nutmeg

Dash salt
6 cups thinly sliced (⅛ inch thick) peeled tart apples (6 medium)
2 tablespoons cold butter, if desired
2 teaspoons water
1 tablespoon sugar

1 Heat oven to 425°F. Place pastry in 9-inch glass pie plate.

2 In large bowl, mix ½ cup sugar, the flour, cinnamon, nutmeg and salt. Stir in apples. Spoon into pastry-lined pie plate. Cut butter into small pieces; sprinkle over apples. Cover with top pastry; cut slits in pastry. Seal and flute (see Decorative Crust Ideas, page 161).

3 Brush top crust with 2 teaspoons water; sprinkle with 1 tablespoon sugar. Cover edge with pie crust shield ring or 2- to 3-inch strip of foil to prevent excessive browning; remove shield or foil during last 15 minutes of baking.

1 Serving: Calories 420; Total Fat 21g (Saturated Fat 7g; Trans Fat 2g); Cholesterol 10mg; Sodium 330mg; Total Carbohydrate 53g (Dietary Fiber 3g); Protein 4g **Exchanges:** 1½ Starch, 2 Fruit, 4 Fat **Carbohydrate Choices:** 3½

FRENCH APPLE PIE Heat oven to 400°F. Make pastry and place in 9-inch glass pie plate. Spoon apple mixture into pastry-lined pie plate. Omit butter, 2 teaspoons water and 1 tablespoon sugar. In small bowl, mix 1 cup all-purpose flour and ½ cup packed brown sugar. Cut in ½ cup cold butter with fork until crumbly. Sprinkle over apple mixture. Bake 35 to 40 minutes or until golden brown. Cover top with foil during last 10 to 15 minutes of baking, if necessary, to prevent excessive browning. Serve warm.

4 Bake 40 to 50 minutes or until crust is golden brown and juice begins to bubble through slits in crust. Cool on cooling rack at least 2 hours.

See how to make **apple pie**: Visit
bettycrocker.com/BCcookbook

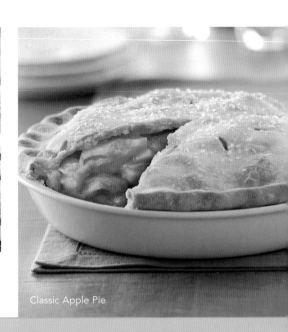
Classic Apple Pie

Keys to Success

- **Choose local apples if available.** They will vary depending on season and location but will often be the freshest and juiciest.

- **Mix 2 to 3 varieties of apples** for best taste and texture.

- **Cut apples thinly** to ensure they cook all the way through.

- **Spoon loose flour mixture evenly over apples** to evenly thicken juices.

- **Seal pastry** so juices cannot escape from edge of pie and cut slits in top to let steam escape.

- **Cover edge** to prevent overbrowning.

- **Prevent juices that escape** from burning on bottom of oven by placing a pan lined with foil on oven rack below the pie.

- **Bake until crust is golden brown** and juice bubbles through crust to ensure fruit is tender.

- **Cover crust loosely** with small pieces of foil on areas that are darkening too quickly.

- **Cool pie on cooling rack** to prevent bottom crust from getting soggy.

Showstopping Top Crusts

Adding a gourmet touch is simple when you use one of these methods before baking:

- **Shiny crust:** Brush crust with milk.

- **Sugary crust:** Brush crust lightly with water or milk; sprinkle with granulated sugar or white coarse sugar crystals.

- **Glazed crust:** Brush crust lightly with beaten egg or egg yolk mixed with a teaspoon of water.

These pie crusts may brown more quickly. If this happens, put a sheet of foil loosely on top of the pie to slow the browning.

You can also add a glaze after baking.

- **Glaze for baked pie crust:** In small bowl, stir together ½ cup powdered sugar, 2 to 3 teaspoons milk, orange juice or lemon juice and, if desired, 2 teaspoons grated orange peel or lemon peel. Brush or drizzle over warm baked pie crust, but do not let glaze run over the edge of the pie.

PICKING APPLES						
Variety	Flavor	Texture	Eating and Salads	Baking	Pies	Sauce
Braeburn	Sweet-Tart	Crisp	X	X	X	X
Cortland	Slightly Tart	Slightly Crisp	X	X	X	X
Crispin/Mutsu	Sweet	Crisp	X	X	X	X
Fuji/Gala	Sweet	Crisp	X			
Golden Delicious	Sweet	Crisp	X	X	X	X
Granny Smith	Tart	Crisp	X	X	X	X
Haralson	Tart	Crisp	X	X	X	X
Honeycrisp	Sweet	Crisp	X	X		X
Jonathan	Slightly Tart	Tender	X		X	X
McIntosh	Sweet-Tart	Tender	X			X
Prairie Spy	Slightly Sweet	Crisp	X	X	X	X
Red Delicious	Sweet	Crisp	X			
Rome	Slightly Tart	Slightly Crisp		X	X	X

Easy Apple Tart

EASY APPLE TART

There's no pie plate required for this recipe. The filling is partially wrapped in a pastry crust and baked on a cookie sheet.

PREP 40 min TOTAL 2 hr 15 min • **8 servings**

   One-Crust Pastry (page 158) or
   Easy Buttermilk Pastry (page 162)
⅔ cup packed brown sugar
⅓ cup all-purpose flour
4 cups thinly sliced (⅛ inch thick) peeled tart apples (4 medium)
1 tablespoon cold butter
   Granulated sugar, if desired

1 Heat oven to 425°F. Make pastry as directed—except roll into 13-inch circle. Place on ungreased large cookie sheet. Cover with plastic wrap to keep pastry moist while making filling.

2 In large bowl, mix brown sugar and flour. Stir in apples. Mound apple mixture on center of pastry to within 3 inches of edge. Cut butter into small pieces; sprinkle over apples. Fold edge of pastry over apples, making pleats so it lays flat on apples (pastry will not cover apples in center). Sprinkle pastry with sugar.

3 Bake 30 to 35 minutes or until crust is light golden brown. To prevent excessive browning, cover center of pie with 5-inch square of foil during last 10 to 15 minutes of baking. Cool on cookie sheet on cooling rack 1 hour, or serve warm if desired.

1 Serving: Calories 290; Total Fat 12g (Saturated Fat 3.5g; Trans Fat 2g); Cholesterol 0mg; Sodium 160mg; Total Carbohydrate 43g (Dietary Fiber 2g); Protein 2g **Exchanges:** 1 Starch, 1 Fruit, 1 Other Carbohydrate, 2 Fat **Carbohydrate Choices:** 3

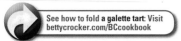

See how to fold **a galette tart**: Visit bettycrocker.com/BCcookbook

BLUEBERRY PIE

PREP 30 min TOTAL 3 hr 15 min • **8 servings**

   Two-Crust Pastry (page 159) or
   Easy Buttermilk Pastry (page 162)
1¼ cups sugar
½ cup cornstarch
½ teaspoon ground cinnamon, if desired
6 cups fresh blueberries
1 tablespoon lemon juice
1 tablespoon cold butter, if desired

1 Heat oven to 425°F. Place pastry in 9-inch glass pie plate.

2 In large bowl, mix sugar, cornstarch and cinnamon. Stir in blueberries. Spoon into pastry-lined pie plate. Sprinkle with lemon juice. Cut butter into small pieces; sprinkle over blueberries. Cover with top pastry that has slits cut in it; seal and flute (see Decorative Crust Ideas, page 161). Cover edge with pie crust shield ring or 2- to 3-inch strip of foil to prevent excessive browning (page 164); remove shield or foil during last 15 minutes of baking.

3 Bake 35 to 45 minutes or until crust is golden brown and juice begins to bubble through slits in crust. Cool on cooling rack at least 2 hours.

1 Serving: Calories 410; Total Fat 19g (Saturated Fat 4.5g; Trans Fat 3g); Cholesterol 0mg; Sodium 270mg; Total Carbohydrate 57g (Dietary Fiber 4g); Protein 4g **Exchanges:** 1 Starch, 1 Fruit, 2 Other Carbohydrate, 3½ Fat **Carbohydrate Choices:** 4

BLACKBERRY, BOYSENBERRY, LOGANBERRY OR RASPBERRY PIE

Substitute any of these fresh berries for the blueberries; omit lemon juice.

Blueberry Pie

BLUEBERRY-PEACH PIE Substitute 2½ cups sliced peeled fresh peaches for 4 cups of the blueberries; omit lemon juice. Place blueberries in pastry-lined pie plate; sprinkle with half of the sugar mixture. Top with peaches; sprinkle with remaining sugar mixture. Cover with top pastry; continue as directed in Step 2.

QUICK BLUEBERRY PIE Substitute 6 cups frozen unsweetened blueberries, thawed and drained, for the fresh blueberries.

CHERRY PIE

The two types of cherries, sweet and sour, are great for different uses. Sour cherries, also called pie cherries, tart cherries or tart red cherries, make wonderful pies. Sweet cherries are great for eating fresh, but not good for pies. Top the pie with a lattice crust (page 161) and dazzle everyone!

PREP 40 min **TOTAL** 3 hr 25 min • **8 servings**

> Two-Crust Pastry (page 159) or
> Easy Buttermilk Pastry (page 162)
> 1⅓ cups sugar
> ½ cup all-purpose flour
> 6 cups fresh sour cherries, pitted
> 2 tablespoons cold butter, if desired

1 Heat oven to 425°F. Place pastry in 9-inch glass pie plate.

2 In large bowl, mix sugar and flour. Stir in cherries. Spoon into pastry-lined pie plate. Cut butter into small pieces; sprinkle over cherries. Cover with top pastry that has slits cut in it; seal and flute (see Decorative Crust Ideas, page 161). Cover edge with pie crust shield ring or 2- to 3-inch strip of foil to prevent excessive browning (page 164); remove shield or foil during last 15 minutes of baking.

3 Bake 35 to 45 minutes or until crust is golden brown and juice begins to bubble through slits in crust. Cool on cooling rack at least 2 hours.

1 Serving: Calories 540; Total Fat 22g (Saturated Fat 5g; Trans Fat 3.5g); Cholesterol 0mg; Sodium 300mg; Total Carbohydrate 81g (Dietary Fiber 4g); Protein 5g **Exchanges:** 2 Starch, 1 Fruit, 2 Other Carbohydrate, 4 Fat **Carbohydrate Choices:** 5½

QUICK CHERRY PIE Substitute 6 cups frozen unsweetened pitted tart red cherries, thawed and drained, or 3 cans (14.5 oz each) pitted tart red cherries, drained, for the fresh cherries.

PEACH PIE

PREP 45 min **TOTAL** 3 hr 30 min • **8 servings**

> Two-Crust Pastry (page 159) or
> Easy Buttermilk Pastry (page 162)
> ⅔ cup sugar
> ⅓ cup all-purpose flour
> ¼ teaspoon ground cinnamon
> 6 cups sliced peeled fresh peaches (6 to 8 medium)
> 1 teaspoon lemon juice
> 1 tablespoon cold butter, if desired

1 Heat oven to 425°F. Place pastry in 9-inch glass pie plate.

2 In large bowl, mix sugar, flour and cinnamon. Stir in peaches and lemon juice. Spoon into pastry-lined pie plate. Cut butter into small pieces; sprinkle over peaches. Cover with top pastry that has slits cut in it; seal and flute (see Decorative Crust Ideas, page 161). Cover edge with pie crust shield ring or 2- to 3-inch strip of foil to prevent excessive browning (page 164); remove shield or foil during last 15 minutes of baking.

3 Bake about 45 minutes or until crust is golden brown and juice begins to bubble through slits in crust. Cool on cooling rack at least 2 hours.

1 Serving: Calories 440; Total Fat 21g (Saturated Fat 5g; Trans Fat 3.5g); Cholesterol 0mg; Sodium 300mg; Total Carbohydrate 59g (Dietary Fiber 5g); Protein 5g **Exchanges:** 2 Starch, 1 Fruit, 1 Other Carbohydrate, 3 Fat **Carbohydrate Choices:** 4

APRICOT PIE Substitute 6 cups fresh apricot halves for the peaches.

QUICK PEACH PIE Substitute 6 cups frozen sliced peaches, partially thawed and drained, for the fresh peaches.

Peach Pie

RHUBARB PIE

Rhubarb is very tart, so there's a lot of sugar in this pie. Use the lower amount of sugar for young, thin rhubarb stalks.

PREP 35 min TOTAL 3 hr 30 min • **8 servings**

 Two-Crust Pastry (page 159) or
 Easy Buttermilk Pastry (page 162)
 2 to 2⅓ cups sugar
 ⅔ cup all-purpose flour
 1 teaspoon grated orange peel, if desired
 6 cups chopped (½-inch pieces) fresh rhubarb
 1 tablespoon cold butter, if desired

1 Heat oven to 425°F. Place pastry in 9-inch glass pie plate.

2 In large bowl, mix sugar, flour and orange peel. Stir in rhubarb. Spoon into pastry-lined pie plate. Cut butter into small pieces; sprinkle over rhubarb. Cover with top pastry that has slits cut in it; seal and flute (see Decorative Crust Ideas, page 161). Cover edge with pie crust shield ring or 2- to 3-inch strip of foil to prevent excessive browning (page 164); remove shield or foil during last 15 minutes of baking.

3 Bake 50 to 55 minutes or until crust is golden brown and juice begins to bubble through slits in crust. Cool on cooling rack at least 2 hours.

1 Serving: Calories 540; Total Fat 21g (Saturated Fat 5g; Trans Fat 3.5g); Cholesterol 0mg; Sodium 300mg; Total Carbohydrate 84g (Dietary Fiber 3g); Protein 5g **Exchanges:** 2 Starch, 1 Fruit, 2½ Other Carbohydrate, 3 Fat **Carbohydrate Choices:** 5½

QUICK RHUBARB PIE Substitute 2 bags (16 oz each) frozen unsweetened rhubarb, thawed and drained, for the fresh rhubarb.

STRAWBERRY-RHUBARB PIE Substitute 3 cups sliced fresh strawberries for 3 cups of the rhubarb. Use 2 cups sugar.

MIXED BERRY CRUMBLE TART

PREP 40 min TOTAL 1 hr 25 min • **8 servings**

 One-Crust Pastry (page 158)
 1½ cups sliced fresh strawberries
 1½ cups fresh blueberries
 1 cup fresh raspberries
 ⅔ cup sugar
 2 tablespoons cornstarch
 ¾ cup all-purpose flour
 ½ cup sugar
 1 teaspoon grated orange peel
 ⅓ cup butter, melted

1 Heat oven to 425°F. Make pastry as directed—except roll into 13-inch circle. Fold pastry into fourths and place in 10- or 11-inch tart pan; unfold and press against bottom and side of pan. Trim overhanging edge of pastry even with top of pan.

2 In large bowl, gently toss berries with ⅔ cup sugar and the cornstarch. Spoon into pastry-lined pan.

3 In small bowl, stir flour, ½ cup sugar, the orange peel and butter with fork until crumbly. Sprinkle evenly over berries. Bake 35 to 45 minutes or until fruit bubbles in center. Remove tart from side of pan. Serve warm.

1 Serving: Calories 420; Total Fat 18g (Saturated Fat 6g; Trans Fat 2g); Cholesterol 20mg; Sodium 200mg; Total Carbohydrate 60g (Dietary Fiber 3g); Protein 3g **Exchanges:** 1 Starch, 3 Fruit, 3½ Fat **Carbohydrate Choices:** 4

Rhubarb Pie

Mixed Berry Crumble Tart

BANANA CREAM PIE

PREP 30 min TOTAL 2 hr 30 min • **8 servings**

One-Crust Pastry (page 158),
Easy Buttermilk Pastry (page 162) or
Press-in-the-Pan Oil Pastry (page 162)
4 egg yolks
⅔ cup sugar
¼ cup cornstarch
½ teaspoon salt
3 cups milk
2 tablespoons butter, softened
2 teaspoons vanilla
2 large ripe but firm bananas
1 cup Sweetened Whipped Cream
(page 214)

1 Bake pastry as directed for Baked
One-Crust Pie (page 160).

2 In medium bowl, beat egg yolks with fork;
set aside. In 2-quart saucepan, mix sugar,
cornstarch and salt. Gradually stir in milk. Cook
over medium heat, stirring constantly, until
mixture thickens and boils. Boil and stir 1 minute.

3 Immediately stir at least half of the hot
mixture gradually into egg yolks, then stir
back into hot mixture in saucepan. Boil and
stir 1 minute; remove from heat. Stir in butter
and vanilla; cool filling slightly. Slice bananas
into pie crust; pour warm filling over bananas.
Press plastic wrap on filling to prevent a tough
layer from forming on top. Refrigerate at least
2 hours until set.

4 Remove plastic wrap. Top pie with whipped
cream. Cover and refrigerate cooled pie until
serving. Store covered in refrigerator.

1 Serving: Calories 410; Total Fat 22g (Saturated Fat 8g; Trans Fat 2g);
Cholesterol 135mg; Sodium 370mg; Total Carbohydrate 46g (Dietary
Fiber 1g); Protein 7g **Exchanges:** 1 Starch, 1 Fruit, ½ Other
Carbohydrate, ½ Low-Fat Milk, 4½ Fat **Carbohydrate Choices:** 3

BUTTERSCOTCH CREAM PIE Substitute dark
or light brown sugar for the granulated sugar.
Omit bananas.

CHOCOLATE-BANANA CREAM PIE Make
Chocolate Cream Pie filling. Cool filling slightly.
Slice 2 large ripe but firm bananas and evenly
distribute over bottom of crust; pour warm
filling over bananas. Continue as directed.

CHOCOLATE CREAM PIE Increase sugar to
1½ cups and cornstarch to ⅓ cup; omit butter
and bananas. Stir in 2 oz unsweetened baking
chocolate, chopped, after stirring in milk.

COCONUT CREAM PIE Increase cornstarch
to ⅓ cup. Substitute 1 can (14 oz) coconut
milk (not cream of coconut) and milk to equal
3 cups for the milk. Stir in ¾ cup flaked coconut,
toasted (page 18), with the butter. Omit
bananas. Refrigerate pie 3 hours until set.
Top with whipped cream; sprinkle with ¼ cup
flaked coconut, toasted.

CARAMEL CREAM PIE

PREP 30 min TOTAL 2 hr 30 min • **8 servings**

Easy Nut Crust (page 163)
⅔ cup sugar
3 cups half-and-half
4 egg yolks
¼ cup cornstarch
¼ teaspoon salt
2 tablespoons butter, softened
1 teaspoon vanilla
1 cup Sweetened Whipped Cream
(page 214)

1 Bake crust as directed.

2 In 2-quart saucepan, heat sugar over medium
heat until sugar begins to melt. Stir until sugar
is completely dissolved and becomes deep
golden brown to amber colored. Remove
from heat; gradually stir in 2¾ cups of the half-
and-half (mixture will boil and splatter at first).
Heat over low heat, stirring frequently, until
any hardened sugar bits dissolve. (See Making
Caramel, page 206.) Remove from heat.

3 Meanwhile, in small bowl, beat egg yolks,
cornstarch, salt and remaining ¼ cup half-and-
half with fork until well blended; set aside.
Gradually whisk egg yolk mixture into half-and-
half mixture until well blended. Cook over
medium heat, stirring constantly, until mixture
thickens and boils. Boil and stir 1 minute.

4 Remove from heat. Stir in butter and vanilla;
cool filling slightly. Pour warm filling into crust.
Press plastic wrap on filling to prevent a tough
layer from forming on top. Refrigerate at least
2 hours until set.

5 Remove plastic wrap. Top pie with whipped
cream. Cover and refrigerate cooled pie until
serving. Store covered in refrigerator.

1 Serving: Calories 500; Total Fat 35g (Saturated Fat 20g, Trans Fat 1g);
Cholesterol 195mg; Sodium 220mg; Total Carbohydrate 38g (Dietary
Fiber 0g); Protein 6g **Exchanges:** 1 Starch, 1½ Other Carbohydrate,
½ Medium-Fat Meat, 6½ Fat **Carbohydrate Choices:** 2½

LEMON MERINGUE PIE

Be sure to save the egg whites to make the meringue when you separate the eggs. To speed up the beating, let the egg whites warm up to room temperature (about 30 minutes).

PREP 50 min TOTAL 3 hr 5 min • **8 servings**

> One-Crust Pastry (page 158),
> **Easy Buttermilk Pastry (page 162) or**
> **Press-in-the-Pan Oil Pastry (page 162)**
> **Meringue for 9-inch pie (below)**
> 3 **egg yolks (reserve whites**
> **for meringue)**
> 1½ **cups sugar**
> ⅓ **cup plus 1 tablespoon cornstarch**
> 1½ **cups water**
> 3 **tablespoons butter**
> 2 **teaspoons grated lemon peel**
> ½ **cup lemon juice**
> 2 **drops yellow food color, if desired**

1 Bake pastry as directed for Baked One-Crust Pie (page 160).

2 Make sugar mixture for meringue. While sugar mixture for meringue is cooling, in small bowl, beat egg yolks with fork; set aside. In 2-quart saucepan, mix sugar and cornstarch. Gradually stir in water. Cook over medium heat, stirring constantly, until mixture thickens and boils. Boil and stir 1 minute.

3 Immediately stir at least half of the hot mixture gradually into egg yolks, then stir back into hot mixture in saucepan. Boil and stir

2 minutes or until very thick. (Do not boil less than 2 minutes or filling may stay too soft or become runny.) Remove from heat. Stir in butter, lemon peel, lemon juice and food color. Press plastic wrap on filling to prevent a tough layer from forming on top.

4 Heat oven to 350°F. Make the meringue. Pour hot lemon filling into pie crust. Spoon meringue onto hot lemon filling. Spread over filling, carefully sealing meringue to edge of crust to prevent shrinking or weeping.

5 Bake 12 to 15 minutes or until meringue is light brown. Cool away from draft 2 hours. Refrigerate cooled pie until serving. Store covered in refrigerator.

1 Serving: Calories 450; Total Fat 17g (Saturated Fat 6g; Trans Fat 1.5g); Cholesterol 95mg; Sodium 250mg; Total Carbohydrate 70g (Dietary Fiber 0g); Protein 5g **Exchanges:** 2 Starch, 2½ Other Carbohydrate, 3 Fat **Carbohydrate Choices:** 4½

MERINGUE FOR 9-INCH PIE In 1-quart saucepan, mix ½ cup sugar and 4 teaspoons cornstarch. Stir in ½ cup cold water. Cook over medium heat, stirring constantly, until mixture thickens and boils. Boil and stir 1 minute; remove from heat. Cool completely while making filling for pie recipe. (To cool more quickly, place in freezer about 10 minutes.) In large bowl, beat 4 egg whites and ⅛ teaspoon salt with electric mixer on high speed just until soft peaks begin to form. Very gradually, beat in sugar mixture until stiff peaks form.

Spreading Meringue over Pie

Spread meringue evenly over hot filling, sealing to edge of crust to help keep meringue from shrinking.

Lemon Meringue Pie

Pecan Pie

KEY LIME PIE

Key limes, found in the Florida Keys, are smaller and rounder than the more familiar Persian limes and can be difficult to find. The good news is that bottled Key lime juice is available in most large supermarkets.

PREP 20 min TOTAL 2 hr 50 min • **8 servings**

  Graham Cracker Crust (page 163)
 4 egg yolks
 2 cans (14 oz each) sweetened condensed
  milk (not evaporated)
 ¾ cup bottled or fresh Key lime juice or
  regular lime juice
 1 or 2 drops green food color, if desired
 1½ cups Sweetened Whipped Cream
  (page 214)

1 Make crust as directed, except do not bake. Heat oven to 375°F.

2 In medium bowl, beat egg yolks, condensed milk, lime juice and food color with electric mixer on medium speed about 1 minute or until well blended. Pour into unbaked crust.

3 Bake 14 to 16 minutes or until center is set. Cool on cooling rack 15 minutes. Cover and refrigerate until chilled, at least 2 hours but no longer than 3 days. Spread with whipped cream. Store covered in refrigerator.

1 Serving: Calories 430; Total Fat 23g (Saturated Fat 13g; Trans Fat 1g); Cholesterol 165mg; Sodium 230mg; Total Carbohydrate 48g (Dietary Fiber 0g); Protein 7g **Exchanges:** ½ Starch, 2½ Other Carbohydrate, 1 High-Fat Meat, 3 Fat **Carbohydrate Choices:** 3

PECAN PIE

PREP 20 min TOTAL 1 hr 10 min • **8 servings**

  One-Crust Pastry (page 158),
  Easy Buttermilk Pastry (page 162) or
  Press-in-the-Pan Oil Pastry (page 162)
 ⅔ cup sugar*
 ⅓ cup butter, melted
 1 cup light or dark corn syrup
 3 eggs
 1 cup pecan halves or broken pecans

1 Heat oven to 375°F. Place pastry in 9-inch glass pie plate.

2 In medium bowl, beat sugar, butter, corn syrup and eggs with wire whisk until well blended. Stir in pecans. Pour into pastry-lined pie plate.

3 Bake 40 to 50 minutes or until center is set. Serve warm or cold.

⅓ cup packed light or dark brown sugar can be used for half of the sugar.

1 Serving: Calories 530; Total Fat 29g (Saturated Fat 8g; Trans Fat 2g); Cholesterol 100mg; Sodium 420mg; Total Carbohydrate 62g (Dietary Fiber 2g); Protein 5g **Exchanges:** 2 Starch, 2 Other Carbohydrate, 6 Fat **Carbohydrate Choices:** 4

KENTUCKY PECAN PIE Add 2 tablespoons bourbon or 1 teaspoon brandy extract with the corn syrup. Stir in 1 cup semisweet chocolate chips (6 oz) with the pecans.

Storing Pecans

Because of their high fat content, store pecans in the refrigerator up to 3 months or in the freezer up to 6 months.

PUMPKIN PIE

Be sure to use canned pumpkin, not pumpkin pie mix, in this recipe. The mix has sugar and spices already in it, so if you have purchased the pumpkin pie mix, follow the directions on that label. Or if you like, use 1½ cups cooked fresh pumpkin.

PREP 20 min TOTAL 3 hr 35 min • **8 servings**

    One-Crust Pastry (page 158)
 2 eggs
 ½ cup sugar
 1 teaspoon ground cinnamon
 ½ teaspoon salt
 ½ teaspoon ground ginger
 ⅛ teaspoon ground cloves
 1 can (15 oz) pumpkin (not pumpkin pie mix)
 1 can (12 oz) evaporated milk
    Sweetened Whipped Cream (page 214), if desired

1 Heat oven to 425°F. Place pastry in 9-inch glass pie plate. After fluting edge of pastry in pie plate (see Decorative Crust Ideas, page 161), carefully line pastry with a double thickness of foil, gently pressing foil to bottom and side of pastry. Let foil extend over edge to prevent excessive browning. Bake 10 minutes; carefully remove foil. Bake 2 to 4 minutes longer or until pastry just begins to brown and has become set. If crust bubbles, gently push bubbles down with back of spoon.

2 In medium bowl, beat eggs slightly with wire whisk. Beat in remaining ingredients except whipped cream.

3 Cover edge of pie crust with pie crust shield ring or 2- to 3-inch strip of foil to prevent excessive browning; remove shield or foil during last 15 minutes (page 164) of baking. To prevent spilling the filling, place pie plate on oven rack before pouring filling into hot crust.

4 Bake 15 minutes. Reduce oven temperature to 350°F. Bake about 45 minutes longer or until knife inserted in center comes out clean. Cool on cooling rack 1 hour; refrigerate uncovered until completely chilled. Cover loosely and store in refrigerator. Serve with whipped cream.

1 Serving: Calories 300; Total Fat 15g (Saturated Fat 5g; Trans Fat 2g); Cholesterol 65mg; Sodium 360mg; Total Carbohydrate 33g (Dietary Fiber 2g); Protein 7g **Exchanges:** 1 Starch, 1 Fruit, 3 Fat **Carbohydrate Choices:** 2

PRALINE PUMPKIN PIE Make pie as directed—except decrease second bake time to 35 minutes. Mix ⅓ cup packed brown sugar, ⅓ cup chopped pecans and 1 tablespoon butter, softened. Sprinkle over pie. Bake about 10 minutes longer or until knife inserted in center comes out clean.

Testing Pumpkin Pie for Doneness

Bake until knife inserted in center comes out clean.

Pumpkin Pie

CREAMY THREE-BERRY TART

PREP 30 min TOTAL 3 hr • **10 servings**

CINNAMON CRUST

1½ cups finely crushed graham crackers (24 squares)
⅓ cup butter, melted
3 tablespoons sugar
1 teaspoon ground cinnamon

FILLING

1 package (8 oz) cream cheese, room temperature
½ cup sugar
2 tablespoons lemon juice
1 cup whipping cream
1 cup fresh blueberries
1 cup fresh blackberries
1 cup fresh raspberries
¼ cup strawberry jam
1 tablespoon orange juice

1 Heat oven to 350°F. In medium bowl, mix crust ingredients until well mixed. Using fingers, press mixture firmly and evenly against bottom and up side of ungreased 9-inch tart pan with removable bottom. Bake 8 to 12 minutes or until golden brown. Cool completely on cooling rack, about 20 minutes.

2 In large bowl, beat cream cheese, ½ cup sugar and the lemon juice with an electric mixer on low speed until blended. Add whipping cream; beat on high speed 3 to 5 minutes or until light and fluffy. Spread mixture evenly in tart shell. Refrigerate at least 2 hours.

3 If necessary, use a thin-bladed knife to loosen side of pan from any places where it sticks to the crust. Remove tart from side of pan before topping with berries. Arrange berries on filling.

4 In small microwavable bowl, microwave jam uncovered on High about 20 seconds or until warm. Stir in orange juice with fork; mix well. Gently brush glaze over berries.

1 Serving: Calories 380; Total Fat 23g (Saturated Fat 14g; Trans Fat 1g); Cholesterol 70mg; Sodium 220mg; Total Carbohydrate 39g (Dietary Fiber 2g); Protein 3g **Exchanges:** 1 Starch, ½ Fruit, 1 Other Carbohydrate, 4½ Fat **Carbohydrate Choices:** 2½

CREAMY BLUEBERRY, BLACKBERRY OR RASPBERRY TART Three cups of all blueberries, blackberries or raspberries can be used instead of the three different berries.

> ### Removing Tart from Pan
>
> Place the pan on a wide, short can and pull down the side of the pan to remove it. If you don't have a can, hold the tart in both hands and push the bottom up and let the side of the pan slip onto your arm.

CLASSIC FRENCH SILK PIE

Use only pasteurized eggs in this recipe to prevent the risk of food poisoning that can result from eating raw eggs.

PREP 30 min TOTAL 3 hr • **10 servings**

One-Crust Pastry (page 158) or Easy Buttermilk Pastry (page 162)
1 cup butter, softened*
1½ cups sugar
1 tablespoon vanilla
3 oz unsweetened baking chocolate, melted and cooled
5 pasteurized eggs
1½ cups Sweetened Whipped Cream (page 214)
Chocolate Curls (page 211), if desired

1 Bake pastry as directed for Baked One-Crust Pie (page 160). Cool completely.

2 In medium bowl, beat butter with electric mixer on medium speed until creamy. Gradually beat in sugar until light and fluffy and sugar begins to dissolve, 3 to 5 minutes. Beat in vanilla and chocolate. Beat in eggs, one at a time, on high speed, beating well after each addition and until light and fluffy, about 3 minutes. Beat until light and fluffy and sugar is completely dissolved. Pour into pie crust. Refrigerate until set, at least 4 hours.

3 Spread with whipped cream. Garnish with chocolate curls. Store covered in refrigerator.

*Do not use margarine or vegetable oil spreads because filling will be curdled instead of smooth and creamy.

1 Serving: Calories 420; Total Fat 29g (Saturated Fat 13g; Trans Fat 2g); Cholesterol 35mg; Sodium 250mg; Total Carbohydrate 35g (Dietary Fiber 2g); Protein 4g **Exchanges:** 1 Starch, 1 Other Carbohydrate, 6 Fat **Carbohydrate Choices:** 2

MOCHA FRENCH SILK PIE Beat in 1½ teaspoons instant coffee granules or crystals with the baking chocolate.

CARAMEL CHOCOLATE PIE SUPREME

PREP 30 min TOTAL 2 hr 45 min • **12 servings**

> Easy Nut Crust (page 163)
> 30 caramels (from 14-oz bag), unwrapped
> 2 tablespoons butter
> 2 tablespoons water
> ½ cup chopped pecans, toasted (page 22)
> 2 packages (3 oz each) cream cheese, softened
> ⅓ cup powdered sugar
> 4 oz sweet baking chocolate, chopped
> 3 tablespoons hot water
> 1 teaspoon vanilla
> 2 cups whipping cream
> 2 tablespoons powdered sugar
> Chocolate Curls (page 211), if desired

1 Bake crust as directed. In 2-quart saucepan, heat caramels, butter and 2 tablespoons water over medium heat, stirring frequently, until caramels are melted. Pour into pie crust. Sprinkle with pecans. Refrigerate about 1 hour or until chilled.

2 In small bowl, beat cream cheese and ⅓ cup powdered sugar with spoon until smooth. Spread over caramel layer; refrigerate.

3 In 1-quart saucepan, heat chocolate and 3 tablespoons hot water over low heat, stirring constantly, until chocolate is melted. Cool to room temperature. Stir in vanilla.

4 In chilled large, deep bowl, beat whipping cream and 2 tablespoons powdered sugar with electric mixer on low speed until mixture begins to thicken. Gradually increase speed to high and beat until stiff peaks form. Reserve 1½ cups.

5 Fold chocolate mixture into remaining whipped cream. Spread over cream cheese mixture. Garnish with reserved whipped cream and chocolate curls. Cover and refrigerate at least 1 hour until firm but no longer than 48 hours. Store covered in refrigerator.

1 Serving: Calories 520; Total Fat 39g (Saturated Fat 21g; Trans Fat 1g); Cholesterol 85mg; Sodium 190mg; Total Carbohydrate 38g (Dietary Fiber 2g); Protein 6g **Exchanges:** 1½ Starch, 1 Other Carbohydrate, 7½ Fat **Carbohydrate Choices:** 2½

GRASSHOPPER PIE

PREP 30 min TOTAL 4 hr 50 min • **8 servings**

> Cookie Crumb Crust (page 163)
> ½ cup milk
> 32 large marshmallows (from 10-oz bag)
> ¼ cup green or white crème de menthe
> 3 tablespoons white crème de cacao
> 1½ cups whipping cream
> Few drops green food color, if desired
> Grated semisweet baking chocolate, if desired

1 Bake crust using chocolate wafer cookies. Reserve about 2 tablespoons crumbs to sprinkle over top of pie if desired.

2 In 3-quart saucepan, heat milk and marshmallows over low heat, stirring constantly, just until marshmallows are melted. Refrigerate about 20 minutes, stirring occasionally, until mixture mounds slightly when dropped from a spoon. (If mixture becomes too thick, place saucepan in bowl of warm water and stir mixture until proper consistency.) Gradually stir in crème de menthe and crème de cacao.

3 In chilled large, deep bowl, beat whipping cream with electric mixer on low speed until mixture begins to thicken. Gradually increase speed to high and beat until stiff peaks form.

4 Fold marshmallow mixture into whipped cream. Fold in food color. Spread in crust. Sprinkle with reserved cookie crumbs and grated chocolate. Refrigerate about 4 hours or until set. Store covered in refrigerator.

1 Serving: Calories 410; Total Fat 23g (Saturated Fat 13g; Trans Fat 1.5g); Cholesterol 65mg; Sodium 200mg; Total Carbohydrate 46g (Dietary Fiber 0g); Protein 3g **Exchanges:** 1 Starch, 2 Other Carbohydrate, 4½ Fat **Carbohydrate Choices:** 3

CAFÉ LATTE PIE Substitute water for the milk; add 1 tablespoon instant espresso coffee powder or granules with the water. Substitute coffee liqueur for the crème de menthe and Irish whiskey for the crème de cacao.

IRISH CREAM PIE Substitute ⅓ cup Irish cream liqueur for the crème de menthe and crème de cacao.

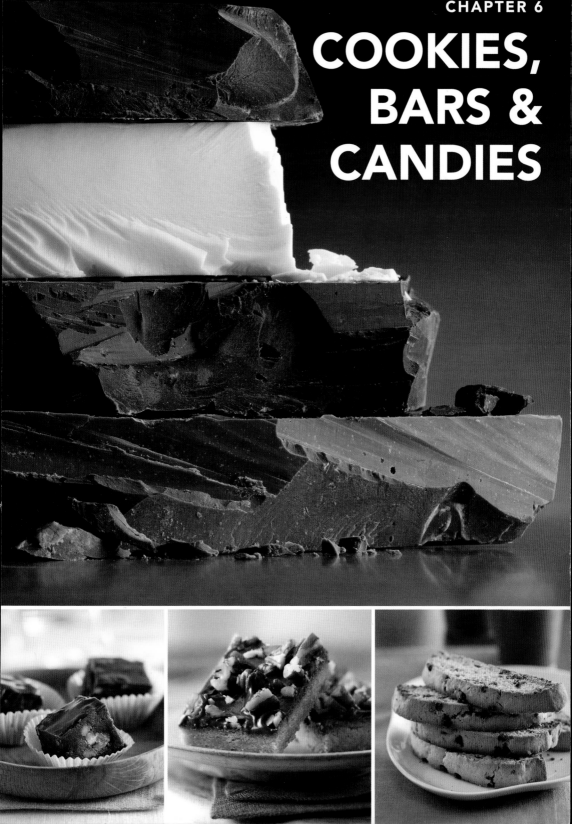

COOKIES, BARS & CANDIES

COOKIES AND BARS

For bonus **cookies, bars and candies** recipes,
visit bettycrocker.com/BCcookbook

FAST = Ready in 20 minutes or less LOWER CALORIE = See Helpful Nutrition and Cooking Information, page 685
LIGHTER = 25% fewer calories or grams of fat MAKE AHEAD = Make-ahead directions SLOW COOKER = Slow cooker directions

← Blocks of chocolate, Chocolate Fudge (page 203), Toffee Bars (page 200), Banana–Chocolate Chip Biscotti (page 197)

COOKIE AND BAR BASICS

Homemade cookies and bars are just the best, and with great recipes and some tips and tricks, you'll be baking some up in no time. Whether chock-full of chocolate and nuts or sweet and buttery, there's a favorite for everyone.

COOKIE SHEETS

Choosing the right cookie sheet makes all the difference in the finished product.

- Choose sheets that are at least 2 inches smaller than the inside of your oven to allow heat to circulate.

- The sheet may be open on one to three sides. If the sheet has four sides, cookies may not brown as evenly.

- Having at least 2 cookie sheets is helpful. When one batch of cookies is finished baking, another batch is ready to go.

Here are the three basic types of cookie sheets and how cookies bake on each one:

- The best cookie sheets are shiny aluminum with a smooth surface. They reflect heat, letting cookies bake evenly and brown properly. The recipes in this book were tested using shiny aluminum cookie sheets.

- Insulated cookie sheets help prevent cookies from turning too dark on the bottom. Cookies baked on these sheets may take longer to bake; the bottoms will be light colored and cookies may not brown as much overall. Cookies may be difficult to remove from these cookie sheets because the bottoms of the cookies are more tender.

- Nonstick and dark-surface cookie sheets may result in cookies that are smaller in diameter and more rounded. The tops and especially the bottoms will be more browned, and the bottoms may be hard. Check cookies at the minimum bake time so they don't get too brown or burn. Follow the manufacturer's directions; some recommend reducing the oven temperature by 25°F.

BAKING PANS FOR BARS

Use the exact size of pan called for in a recipe when baking bars. Bars made in pans that are too big become hard and overcooked, and those made in pans that are too small can be doughy in the center and hard on the edges.

Shiny metal pans are recommended for baking bars. They reflect the heat and prevent the bottom from getting too brown and hard. Follow the manufacturer's directions when using dark, nonstick or glass baking pans; they may recommend you reduce the oven temperature by 25°F. Check for doneness 3 to 5 minutes before the minimum bake time given in the recipe.

Quick Pan Cleanup

Lining baking pans for bars with foil means quicker cleanup and also makes it easier to cut bars. To line baking pans with foil, turn the pan upside down. Tear off a piece of foil longer than the pan. Smooth the foil around the pan bottom and then remove. Flip the pan over, and gently fit the shaped foil into the pan. When the bars or brownies are cool, lift them out of the pan by the foil "handles," peel back the foil and cut the bars as directed.

Line the pan for bars with foil for easy removal and cutting.

Greasing Pans

- Grease only when a recipe calls for it. Grease cookie sheets and baking pans with shortening or cooking spray. Unless the recipe directs, do not use butter, margarine or oil because the area between the cookies might burn during baking.

- Don't grease nonstick cookie sheets. Even if a recipe calls for greasing; the cookies may spread too much.

- As an alternative to greasing, line pans or sheets with parchment paper or use a silicone baking mat.

CHOOSING THE RIGHT INGREDIENTS

Flours: Bleached or unbleached all-purpose flour is recommended for cookies and bars. Whole wheat flour also can be used, but only substitute it for one-third to one-half the amount of all-purpose flour to keep cookies from becoming too dry. Don't use bread and cake flours. Bread flour causes cookies and bars to become tough and cake flour causes the cookies to be too delicate and fragile. For more information on flour and how to measure it, see Flour, and Measuring Correctly, page 16.

Sweeteners: In addition to adding sweetness to cookies and bars, sugars also help brown and add tenderness to baked goods.

Leavenings: Cookies usually call for baking soda or baking powder, which are not interchangeable. For more information, see Baking Soda, page 18, and Baking Powder, page 18.

Fats and Oils: Fats add tenderness and flavor to cookies and bars, but they are not all equal. For best results, use butter or, if the recipe calls for it, shortening. If you choose to use margarine, use only products with at least 65% fat. Any other spreads or reduced-fat products contain more water, resulting in cookies that are soft, tough and puffy.

Eggs: Eggs add richness, moisture and structure to cookies and bars. All the recipes in this book have been tested with large eggs. Egg product substitutes, made of egg whites, can be substituted for whole eggs, but the baked cookies and bars may be dry.

Liquids: Liquids like water, fruit juice, cream and milk tend to make cookies crisper by causing them to spread more. Add only as much liquid as the recipe calls for.

Oats: Quick-cooking and old-fashioned oats are interchangeable unless a recipe calls for a specific type. Instant oatmeal products are not the same as quick-cooking oats and should not be used for baking.

Nuts, Peanuts and Almond Brickle Chips: When nuts are called for in a recipe, you can substitute any variety of nut or peanuts. Nuts can easily become rancid, giving them an unpleasant, strong flavor that can ruin the taste of cookies. To prevent rancidity, store nuts and peanuts tightly covered in the refrigerator or freezer up to 2 years. Do not freeze cashews because they can become soggy. Almond brickle baking chips can also become rancid. To prevent rancidity, store them in the refrigerator or freezer up to 6 months. Always taste items before adding to a recipe; if they don't taste fresh, throw them out.

Bake a Test Cookie

If you're new to cookie baking or are trying a new recipe, bake just one cookie as directed in the recipe to see how it performs. This is a great way to make adjustments before baking a whole sheet of cookies. If the cookie spreads too much, add 1 to 2 tablespoons of flour to the dough, or refrigerate the dough 1 to 2 hours before baking. If it's too round or hard, add 1 to 2 tablespoons of milk to the dough.

Use a Plastic Knife

Pans can sometimes get scratched when bars are cut with a metal knife, so try a plastic knife. In fact, a plastic knife works best for cutting brownies and soft, sticky bars such as Lemon Bars, page 201.

Learn with Betty | SOFTENING BUTTER

Perfectly Softened: Butter is soft (leaves a slight indentation when touched lightly) yet still holds its shape.

Too Soft: Butter is overly softened and doesn't hold its shape.

Partially Melted: Butter is overly softened and has started to melt.

Softening Butter: Let butter soften at room temperature for 30 to 45 minutes. You can also soften it in the microwave; see Microwave Cooking and Heating chart, pages 30 to 31. If the butter is too soft, the dough will be too soft and will cause the cookies to spread too much.

MIXING

An electric mixer or spoon can be used for mixing the dough in most of the recipes in this book. The sugars, fats and liquids are usually beaten together first until well mixed. Flour and other dry ingredients are almost always stirred in by hand to avoid overmixing the dough, which can result in tough cookies. When the recipes in this book were tested, there were no significant differences in the appearance or texture of cookies mixed with an electric mixer and those mixed with a spoon.

Beating Butter and Sugar

Butter and sugar have been beaten long enough when mixture is light and fluffy and light in color.

TIPS FOR PERFECT COOKIES

- Use completely cooled cookie sheets. Cookies will spread too much if put on a hot or warm cookie sheet.
- Make all cookies the same size so they bake evenly. (See Cookie Scoops, page 181).
- When baking bars, use the pan size specified in the recipe.
- Bake cookies and bars on the middle oven rack. For even baking, we recommend baking one sheet at a time. If you do bake two sheets at once, position oven racks as close to the middle as possible and switch sheets halfway through baking.
- Check cookies and bars at the minimum bake time, baking longer if needed.
- Using a flat, thin metal spatula, remove cookies from the baking sheet and cool as directed.
- Cool bars and brownies in the pan on a wire cooling rack.

Removing Stuck Cookies

If cookies were left to cool too long on the cookie sheet and are difficult to remove, put the cookies back in the oven for 1 to 2 minutes, and then remove them from the sheet; they should come off easily.

STORING COOKIES AND BARS

- Store crisp cookies at room temperature in loosely covered containers.

- Keep chewy and soft cookies at room temperature in resealable food-storage plastic bags or tightly covered containers.

- Let frosted or decorated cookies set or harden before storing; place them between layers of parchment or waxed paper, plastic wrap or foil.

- Put crisp cookies and chewy, soft cookies in separate containers to prevent the crisp cookies from becoming soft.

- Store cookies with different flavors in separate containers, or they will pick up the flavors of the other cookies.

- Most bars can be stored tightly covered, but check the recipe to be sure; some may need to be loosely covered and others may need to be refrigerated.

- To freeze cookies and bars, tightly wrap and label. Freeze unfrosted cookies up to 1 year and frosted cookies up to 3 months. Do not freeze meringue, custard-filled or cream-filled cookies. To freeze delicate frosted or decorated cookies, place in single layers in freezer containers and cover with waxed paper before adding another layer.

- Thaw most cookies, covered, in the container at room temperature for 1 to 2 hours. For crisp cookies, remove from the container to thaw.

Cookie Scoops

A spring-handled cookie or ice-cream scoop makes quick work of forming cookie dough into equal portions (see photo on page 182). Scoops come in various sizes referred to by number. (The larger the number, the smaller the scoop.) For instance, a #16 scoop yields ¼ cup and a #70 scoop equals 1 level tablespoon. Scoops can vary by manufacturer, so measure the volume of the scoop with water first to make sure it equals the amount called for.

Types of Baking Cocoa

When a recipe calls for "cocoa," use unsweetened baking cocoa, not hot chocolate mix products, which are sweetened and have additional ingredients. Two types of baking cocoa are available: nonalkalized (regular) and alkalized ("Dutch" or "European"). Alkalized cocoa goes through a "Dutching" process to neutralize natural acids found in cocoa. The result is a darker cocoa with a more mellow chocolate flavor than regular cocoa. The two types of cocoa can be used interchangeably, but baked goods made with Dutch cocoa will be darker in color and a bit milder in flavor.

Learn with Betty | MELTING CHOCOLATE

Perfectly Melted: This chocolate was melted perfectly; it is smooth and creamy.

Too Melted or Seized: This chocolate has either been melted over too high a heat or has come in contact with a small amount of liquid, causing it to seize.

Correcting Seized Chocolate: To make chocolate smooth again, use a whisk to beat in at least 1 tablespoon melted butter, vegetable oil or melted vegetable shortening. Heat over very low heat, if necessary, stirring constantly.

OATMEAL-RAISIN COOKIES

LOWER CALORIE

Quick-cooking and old-fashioned rolled oats are interchangeable unless a recipe calls for a specific type. Instant oatmeal products are not the same and should not be used for baking—you will have mushy cookies.

PREP 45 min TOTAL 45 min • **3 dozen cookies**

- ⅔ cup granulated sugar
- ⅔ cup packed brown sugar
- 1 teaspoon baking soda
- 1 teaspoon ground cinnamon
- ½ teaspoon baking powder
- ½ teaspoon salt
- ½ cup butter, softened
- ½ cup shortening
- 1 teaspoon vanilla
- 2 eggs
- 3 cups quick-cooking or old-fashioned oats
- 1 cup all-purpose flour
- 1 cup raisins, chopped nuts or semisweet chocolate chips, if desired

1 Heat oven to 375°F. In large bowl, beat all ingredients except oats, flour and raisins with electric mixer on medium speed, or mix with spoon, until well blended. Stir in oats, flour and raisins.

2 On ungreased cookie sheets, drop dough by rounded tablespoonfuls about 2 inches apart.

3 Bake 9 to 11 minutes or until light brown. Immediately remove from cookie sheets to cooling racks.

1 Cookie: Calories 120; Total Fat 6g (Saturated Fat 2g; Trans Fat 0.5g); Cholesterol 20mg; Sodium 95mg; Total Carbohydrate 15g (Dietary Fiber 0g); Protein 2g **Exchanges:** 1 Starch, 1 Fat **Carbohydrate Choices:** 1

LIGHTER DIRECTIONS For 3 grams of fat and 95 calories per serving, substitute unsweetened applesauce for the shortening and ½ cup fat-free egg product for the eggs. Increase cinnamon and vanilla to 1½ teaspoons each.

OATMEAL-CRANBERRY COOKIES Substitute 1 cup dried cranberries for the raisins.

WHITE CHOCOLATE CHUNK– MACADAMIA COOKIES

LOWER CALORIE

PREP 35 min TOTAL 35 min • **2½ dozen cookies**

- 1 cup packed brown sugar
- ½ cup granulated sugar
- ½ cup butter, softened
- ½ cup shortening
- 1 teaspoon vanilla
- 1 egg
- 2¼ cups all-purpose flour
- 1 teaspoon baking soda
- ¼ teaspoon salt
- 6 oz white chocolate baking bar, cut into ¼- to ½-inch chunks
- 1 jar (3.25 oz) macadamia nuts, coarsely chopped

1 Heat oven to 350°F. In large bowl, beat sugars, butter, shortening, vanilla and egg with electric mixer on medium speed, or mix with spoon, until light and fluffy. Stir in flour, baking soda and salt (dough will be stiff). Stir in white chocolate chunks and nuts.

2 On ungreased cookie sheets, drop dough by rounded tablespoonfuls about 2 inches apart.

3 Bake 10 to 12 minutes or until light brown. Cool 1 to 2 minutes; remove from cookie sheets to cooling racks.

1 Cookie: Calories 190; Total Fat 11g (Saturated Fat 4g; Trans Fat 1g); Cholesterol 15mg; Sodium 100mg; Total Carbohydrate 21g (Dietary Fiber 0g); Protein 2g **Exchanges:** 1 Starch, ½ Other Carbohydrate, 2 Fat **Carbohydrate Choices:** 1½

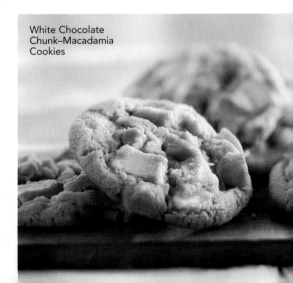

White Chocolate Chunk–Macadamia Cookies

Learn to Make **Chocolate Chip Cookies**

CHOCOLATE CHIP COOKIES LOWER CALORIE

Homemade chocolate chip cookies are hard to resist—especially when they are perfectly soft and chewy on the inside with a golden brown, slightly crusty exterior. The secret to these gems is a combination of fresh ingredients, correct measuring and a good baking technique.

PREP 55 min **TOTAL** 55 min ● **4 dozen cookies**

¾ cup granulated sugar
¾ cup packed brown sugar
1 cup butter, softened
1 teaspoon vanilla
1 egg
2¼ cups all-purpose flour

1 teaspoon baking soda
½ teaspoon salt
1 bag (12 oz) semisweet or dark chocolate chips (2 cups)
1 cup coarsely chopped nuts, if desired

1 Heat oven to 375°F. In large bowl, beat sugars, butter, vanilla and egg with electric mixer on medium speed, or mix with spoon, until well blended. Stir in flour, baking soda and salt (dough will be stiff). Stir in chocolate chips and nuts.

2 On ungreased cookie sheets, drop dough by rounded tablespoonfuls about 2 inches apart. For perfectly sized and shaped cookies, use a #70 cookie scoop.

3 Bake 8 to 10 minutes or until light brown (centers will be soft). Cool 1 to 2 minutes; remove from cookie sheets to cooling racks.

1 Cookie: Calories 140; Total Fat 8g (Saturated Fat 3.5g; Trans Fat 0g); Cholesterol 15mg; Sodium 80mg; Total Carbohydrate 16g (Dietary Fiber 0g); Protein 1g **Exchanges:** 1 Other Carbohydrate, 1½ Fat
Carbohydrate Choices: 1

LIGHTER CHOCOLATE CHIP COOKIES
For 5 grams of fat and 90 calories per serving, decrease butter to ¾ cup and omit nuts. Substitute 1 cup miniature semisweet chocolate chips for the 12-oz bag of chocolate chips.

CANDY COOKIES Substitute 2 cups candy-coated chocolate candies for the chocolate chips.

CHOCOLATE CHIP BARS Press dough into ungreased 13x9-inch pan. Bake 15 to 20 minutes or until golden brown. Cool in pan on cooling rack. Makes 48 bars.

JUMBO CHOCOLATE CHIP COOKIES Drop dough by ¼ cupfuls or #16 cookie scoop about 3 inches apart onto ungreased cookie sheets. Bake 12 to 15 minutes or until edges are set (centers will be soft). Cool 1 to 2 minutes; remove from cookie sheets to cooling racks. Makes 1½ dozen cookies.

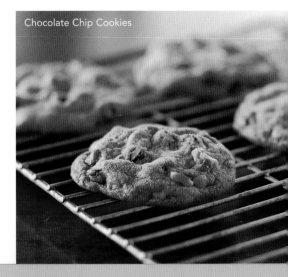
Chocolate Chip Cookies

Keys to Success

- **Measure ingredients accurately.** Dough that is the right consistency will make cookies that have great shape and texture. (See Measuring Correctly, page 16.)

- **Use softened butter.** Do not melt butter, or the dough will be too soft and may result in oddly shaped cookies. (See Softening Butter, page 179).

- **Use a cookie scoop** to make cookies the perfect size and shape if desired.

- **Place dough on completely cooled cookie sheets.** Warm cookie sheets can be cooled quickly by placing in the freezer for a few minutes or running under cold running water and wiping dry.

- **Let baked cookies rest on cookie sheet** a couple minutes. This allows them to firm up a little so that they are easy to remove from the sheet.

- **Cool cookies until chips are firm** before storing, to prevent melted chocolate from getting over all the cookies.

- **Freeze individual unbaked cookies on cookie sheets.** When frozen, place in container or freezer plastic bag; label and freeze up to 6 months. Bake the frozen cookies a little longer than the bake time.

Cookies for Gifts

Sharing a gift of homemade chocolate chip cookies or other homemade goodies can be the perfect way to spread a little good cheer, whether delivered by hand or mailed. Here are tips for giving any cookies, bars or candies to ensure they stay fresh and intact.

- Keep containers on hand for when you want to give homemade items as a gift:
  - Look for inexpensive plates or serving containers in the dollar section of your discount store.
  - Wash and keep to-go containers from take-out meals.
  - Look for inexpensive decorative tins or paper containers in craft stores or import stores.

- Cushion items by first placing a paper towel or napkin in the bottom of the container. If you stack items, place layers of waxed paper between layers.

- Cover tightly with plastic wrap or foil if container doesn't have a lid.

- If baking in advance and freezing, let frozen cookies thaw directly in gift container for maximum freshness.

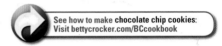

See how to make **chocolate chip cookies**:
Visit bettycrocker.com/BCcookbook

Learn with Betty | CHOCOLATE CHIP COOKIES

Perfect Cookie: It is slightly rounded on top and evenly golden brown.

Flat Cookie: The butter was too soft or partially melted, the flour was under measured or the cookie sheet was too hot.

Round or Hard Cookie: Too much flour was used and cookie was overbaked.

GLUTEN-FREE CHOCOLATE CHIP COOKIES LOWER CALORIE

The Betty Crocker Kitchens staff hovered around these cookies when they were fresh and warm, giving them two thumbs up. Nobody missed the wheat flour. They bake up chewy with crisp edges, and the brown rice flour gives them a pleasant bit of grittiness that will remind you of cornmeal.

PREP 55 min **TOTAL** 55 min • **4 dozen cookies**

- 1 cup packed brown sugar
- ¾ cup granulated sugar
- 1 cup butter, softened*
- 1 teaspoon vanilla
- 1 egg
- 2½ cups brown rice flour
- ¼ cup cornstarch
- 2 tablespoons tapioca flour
- 1 teaspoon xanthan gum
- 1 teaspoon baking soda
- ½ teaspoon salt
- 1 bag (12 oz) semisweet or dark chocolate chips (2 cups)
- 1 cup chopped nuts, toasted (page 22), if desired

1 Heat oven to 375°F. In large bowl, beat sugars, butter and vanilla with electric mixer on low speed, or mix with spoon, until well blended. Beat in egg until mixture becomes light and fluffy; do not underbeat.

2 In small bowl, measure brown rice flour, cornstarch and tapioca flour by lightly spooning into measuring cup or spoon; level off with straight edge of knife or spatula. (Careful measuring of dry ingredients is important for successful gluten-free baking results.) Stir in xanthan gum, baking soda and salt until thoroughly blended (you may need to rub any clumps between your fingers to break apart). Stir flour mixture into butter mixture. Stir in chocolate chips and nuts.

3 On ungreased cookie sheets, drop dough by heaping tablespoonfuls about 2 inches apart.

4 Bake 8 to 10 minutes or until light brown (centers will be soft). Cool 1 to 2 minutes; remove from cookie sheets to cooling racks. Store in tightly covered container (gluten-free baked goods dry out more quickly than wheat flour–based baked goods).

Do not use light butter or vegetable oil spreads in this recipe.

1 Cookie: Calories 140; Total Fat 6g (Saturated Fat 4g; Trans Fat 0g); Cholesterol 15mg; Sodium 80mg; Total Carbohydrate 19g (Dietary Fiber 1g); Protein 1g **Exchanges:** ½ Starch, 1 Other Carbohydrate, 1 Fat **Carbohydrate Choices:** 1

Always read labels to make sure each recipe ingredient is gluten free. Products and ingredient sources can change.

CHOCOLATE CRINKLES

LOWER CALORIE

PREP 1 hr **TOTAL** 4 hr • **6 dozen cookies**

- 2 cups granulated sugar
- ½ cup vegetable oil
- 2 teaspoons vanilla
- 4 oz unsweetened baking chocolate, melted and cooled
- 4 eggs
- 2 cups all-purpose flour
- 2 teaspoons baking powder
- ½ teaspoon salt
- 1 cup powdered sugar

1 In large bowl, stir granulated sugar, oil, vanilla and chocolate until well mixed. Stir in eggs, one at a time. Stir in flour, baking powder and salt. Cover and refrigerate at least 3 hours.

2 Heat oven to 350°F. Grease cookie sheets with shortening or cooking spray, or line with cooking parchment paper or silicone baking mats.

Chocolate Crinkles

3 In small bowl, place powdered sugar. Drop dough by teaspoonfuls into powdered sugar; roll around to coat. Shape into balls. On cookie sheets, place balls about 2 inches apart.

4 Bake 10 to 12 minutes or until almost no indentation remains when touched in center. Immediately remove from cookie sheets to cooling racks.

1 Cookie: Calories 70; Total Fat 2.5g (Saturated Fat 1g; Trans Fat 0g); Cholesterol 10mg; Sodium 35mg; Total Carbohydrate 10g (Dietary Fiber 0g); Protein 0g **Exchanges:** ½ Starch, ½ Fat **Carbohydrate Choices:** ½

PUMPKIN COOKIES WITH BROWNED BUTTER FROSTING

LOWER CALORIE

PREP 55 min **TOTAL** 1 hr 40 min • **2½ dozen cookies**

COOKIES

- ⅔ cup granulated sugar
- ⅔ cup packed brown sugar
- ¾ cup butter, softened
- 1 teaspoon vanilla
- ½ cup (from 15-oz can) pumpkin (not pumpkin pie mix)
- 2 eggs
- 2¼ cups all-purpose flour
- 1 teaspoon baking soda
- 1 teaspoon ground cinnamon
- ½ teaspoon salt

BROWNED BUTTER FROSTING

- 3 cups powdered sugar
- 1 teaspoon vanilla
- 3 to 4 tablespoons milk
- ⅓ cup butter*

1 Heat oven to 375°F. In large bowl, beat granulated sugar, brown sugar, ¾ cup butter and 1 teaspoon vanilla with electric mixer on medium speed, scraping bowl occasionally, until well blended. Beat in pumpkin and eggs until well mixed. On low speed, beat in flour, baking soda, cinnamon and salt.

2 On ungreased cookie sheets, drop dough by heaping tablespoonfuls about 2 inches apart.

3 Bake 10 to 12 minutes or until almost no indentation remains when touched in center. Immediately remove from cookie sheets to

Pumpkin Cookies with Browned Butter Frosting

cooling racks. Cool completely, about 45 minutes.

4 In medium bowl, place powdered sugar, 1 teaspoon vanilla and 3 tablespoons milk. In 1-quart saucepan, heat ⅓ cup butter over medium heat, stirring constantly, just until light brown.

5 Pour browned butter over powdered sugar mixture. Beat on low speed about 1 minute or until smooth. Gradually add just enough of the remaining 1 tablespoon milk to make frosting creamy and spreadable. Generously frost cooled cookies. Store in tightly covered container.

Do not use margarine or vegetable oil spreads in the frosting; it will burn.

1 Cookie: Calories 190; Total Fat 7g (Saturated Fat 4.5g; Trans Fat 0g); Cholesterol 30mg; Sodium 135mg; Total Carbohydrate 29g (Dietary Fiber 0g); Protein 2g **Exchanges:** ½ Starch, 1½ Other Carbohydrate, 1½ Fat **Carbohydrate Choices:** 2

SPICY PUMPKIN COOKIES WITH BROWNED BUTTER FROSTING Spice up these cookies by adding ⅛ teaspoon each ground cloves and ground ginger with the flour.

WHOOPIE PIES

PREP 45 min TOTAL 1 hr 25 min • **1½ dozen sandwich cookies**

COOKIES

- 1 **cup granulated sugar**
- ½ **cup butter, softened**
- ½ **cup buttermilk**
- 2 **teaspoons vanilla**
- 1 **egg**
- 2 **oz unsweetened baking chocolate, melted and cooled**
- 1¾ **cups all-purpose flour**
- ½ **teaspoon baking soda**
- ½ **teaspoon salt**

CREAMY MARSHMALLOW FILLING

- 3 **cups powdered sugar**
- 1 **jar (7 oz) marshmallow creme**
- ¾ **cup butter, softened**
- 6 **to 7 teaspoons milk**

1 Heat oven to 400°F. Grease cookie sheets with shortening or cooking spray, or line with cooking parchment paper or silicone baking mats.

2 In large bowl, beat granulated sugar, ½ cup butter, the buttermilk, vanilla, egg and chocolate with electric mixer on medium speed, or mix with spoon, until well blended. Stir in flour, baking soda and salt. On cookie sheets, drop dough by rounded tablespoonfuls about 2 inches apart.

3 Bake 8 to 10 minutes or until almost no indentation remains when touched in center. Immediately remove from cookie sheets to cooling racks. Cool completely, about 30 minutes.

4 In large bowl, beat all filling ingredients on medium speed about 2 minutes or until light and fluffy. Place flat sides of 2 cookies together with scant 3 tablespoons filling, sandwich style. Store in tightly covered container.

1 Sandwich Cookie: Calories 350; Total Fat 15g (Saturated Fat 9g; Trans Fat 0.5g); Cholesterol 45mg; Sodium 210mg; Total Carbohydrate 50g (Dietary Fiber 1g); Protein 2g **Exchanges:** 1 Starch, 2½ Other Carbohydrate, 3 Fat **Carbohydrate Choices:** 3

CHOCOLATE CHIP WHOOPIE PIES Fold ½ cup miniature semisweet chocolate chips into filling.

PINK PEPPERMINT WHOOPIE PIES Add 6 drops red food color to filling ingredients. Once cookies are assembled, sprinkle edges of filling with crushed peppermint candies or candy canes.

TOFFEE WHOOPIE PIES Fold ½ cup chocolate-covered toffee bits into filling.

Making Whoopie Pies

Bake cookies until almost no indentation remains when touched lightly in center.

Place flat sides of 2 cookies together with filling, sandwich style.

Pink Peppermint Whoopie Pies

COOKIE SANDWICHES

Bake and cool a batch of your favorite cookies and spread with delicious filling (bottom sides together) to create fun-to-eat cookie sandwiches.

Peanut Butter–Chocolate Cookies: Mix ½ cup creamy peanut butter with 3 tablespoons softened butter, 1 cup powdered sugar, and 2 to 3 tablespoons half-and-half. Spread 1 teaspoon mixture on 1 chocolate chip cookie (page 182) and top with a second cookie to form sandwich.

Mint Chocolate Chip Ice Cream Sandwiches: Place small scoop of slightly softened mint chip ice cream on 1 chocolate chip cookie (page 182) and top with second cookie; press together slightly. Roll sides in chocolate sprinkles. Wrap in plastic wrap and freeze at least 2 hours.

Mint Chocolate Chip Ice Cream Sandwiches

Peanut Butter and Jelly Cookies: Spread 1 teaspoon strawberry jam on 1 peanut butter cookie (page 188) and spread 1 teaspoon of ready-to-spread vanilla frosting on second cookie; press cookies together to form sandwich.

Peanut Butter–Maple Cream Cookies: Mix until fluffy 1 package (8 ounces) softened cream cheese, ¼ cup softened butter, 1 cup powdered sugar and ¼ cup maple syrup. Spread 1 teaspoon of mixture on 1 peanut butter cookie (page 188); top with second cookie to form sandwich.

Chocolate–Hazelnut Cookies: Spread 1 teaspoon hazelnut spread with cocoa on 1 sugar cookie (page 192); top with a second cookie to form sandwich.

Lemon-Raspberry Cookie Sandwiches

Lemon–Raspberry Cookie Sandwiches: Spread 1 teaspoon lemon curd on 1 sugar cookie (page 192); spread 1 teaspoon raspberry jam on second cookie; press cookies together to form sandwich. Dust with powdered sugar.

GINGERSNAPS LOWER CALORIE

After baking, these spicy cookies have a crackly and sugary top. Serve them with ice cream, fresh fruit, sorbet or coffee.

PREP 45 min **TOTAL** 45 min • **4 dozen cookies**

1	cup packed brown sugar
¾	cup shortening
¼	cup molasses
1	egg
2¼	cups all-purpose flour
2	teaspoons baking soda
1	teaspoon ground cinnamon
1	teaspoon ground ginger
½	teaspoon ground cloves
¼	teaspoon salt
	Granulated sugar

1 Heat oven to 375°F. Lightly grease cookie sheets with shortening or cooking spray, or line with cooking parchment paper or silicone baking mats.

2 In large bowl, beat brown sugar, shortening, molasses and egg with electric mixer on medium speed, or mix with spoon, until well blended. Stir in remaining ingredients except granulated sugar.

3 Shape dough by rounded teaspoonfuls into balls. Dip tops into granulated sugar. On cookie sheets, place balls, sugared sides up, about 3 inches apart.

4 Bake 10 to 12 minutes or just until set. Immediately remove from cookie sheets to cooling racks.

1 Cookie: Calories 80; Total Fat 3.5g (Saturated Fat 1g; Trans Fat 0.5g); Cholesterol 0mg; Sodium 70mg; Total Carbohydrate 11g (Dietary Fiber 0g); Protein 0g **Exchanges:** 1 Other Carbohydrate, ½ Fat **Carbohydrate Choices:** 1

Gingersnaps

Heirloom Recipe and New Twist

This chewy, sweet cookie recipe has been a favorite of the Betty Crocker Kitchens for decades. They are easy to make, pack well in lunches or for gifts and can be frozen for snacks later. Our new twist gives you a true flavor change—switching out the peanut butter for hazelnut spread with cocoa. The yummy filling is a nice surprise. And check out the two tasty variations from our Facebook fans too—more great choices!

CLASSIC

PEANUT BUTTER COOKIES

LOWER CALORIE

Although we call for creamy peanut butter, you could use the chunky variety instead. Or, add ½ to ¾ cup chopped honey-roasted peanuts after the flour is mixed in.

PREP 45 min **TOTAL** 45 min • **2½ dozen cookies**

- ½ cup granulated sugar
- ½ cup packed brown sugar
- ½ cup peanut butter
- ½ cup butter, softened
- 1 egg
- 1¼ cups all-purpose flour
- ¾ teaspoon baking soda
- ½ teaspoon baking powder
- ¼ teaspoon salt
  Additional granulated sugar

1 Heat oven to 375°F. In large bowl, beat ½ cup granulated sugar, the brown sugar, peanut butter, butter and egg with electric mixer on medium speed, or mix with spoon, until well blended. Stir in flour, baking soda, baking powder and salt.

2 Shape dough into 1¼-inch balls. On ungreased cookie sheets, place balls about 3 inches apart. Flatten in crisscross pattern with fork dipped in additional granulated sugar.

3 Bake 9 to 10 minutes or until light brown. Cool 5 minutes; remove from cookie sheets to cooling racks.

1 Cookie: Calories 110; Total Fat 6g (Saturated Fat 1.5g; Trans Fat 0g); Cholesterol 10mg; Sodium 95mg; Total Carbohydrate 13g (Dietary Fiber 0g); Protein 2g **Exchanges:** 1 Starch, 1 Fat **Carbohydrate Choices:** 1

RICH PEANUT BUTTER CHIP COOKIES Omit ½ cup granulated sugar; increase brown sugar to 1 cup. After stirring in flour, baking soda, baking powder and salt, stir in 1 cup peanut butter chips. Shape dough into balls as directed. Dip tops of balls into granulated sugar, but do not flatten. Bake as directed.

CHOCOLATE-FROSTED PEANUT BUTTER COOKIES Frost   cookies with Creamy Chocolate Frosting, page 152. Let stand until set.

Contributed by Susan Howren-Worsham **from Katy, Texas**

TRIPLE DELIGHT COOKIES After mixing in Step 1, stir in ⅓ cup each peanut butter chips, white vanilla baking chips and semisweet chocolate chips. Bake as directed.

Contributed by Melissa Prejean **from Old Orchard Beach, Maine**

Making Peanut Butter Cookies

Shape dough into 1¼-inch balls; place on cookie sheet about 3 inches apart.

Flatten in crisscross pattern with fork dipped in sugar.

Peanut Butter Cookies

STUFFED HAZELNUT COOKIES

PREP 1 hr **TOTAL** 1 hr • **2 dozen cookies**

FILLING

- ½ cup hazelnut spread with cocoa
- ½ cup powdered sugar
- ¼ cup chopped hazelnuts (filberts)

COOKIES

- 1 cup granulated sugar
- ½ cup hazelnut spread with cocoa
- ½ cup butter, softened
- 1 egg
- 1½ cups all-purpose flour
- ¾ teaspoon baking soda
- ½ teaspoon baking powder
- ¼ teaspoon salt
  Additional granulated sugar

GLAZE

- 1 cup dark chocolate chips
- 2 teaspoons shortening
- 6 teaspoons finely chopped hazelnuts (filberts), if desired

1 Heat oven to 375°F. In small bowl, mix ½ cup hazelnut spread, powdered sugar and ¼ cup chopped hazelnuts. Shape into 24 (1-inch) balls.

2 In large bowl, beat 1 cup granulated sugar, ½ cup hazelnut spread, the butter and egg with electric mixer on medium speed, or mix with spoon, until well blended. Stir in flour, baking soda, baking powder and salt.

3 Divide dough into 24 (1½-inch) balls. Flatten each ball into 2½-inch round. Shape 1 cookie dough round around 1 hazelnut ball, covering completely. Repeat with remaining dough and hazelnut balls. On ungreased cookie sheets, place filled dough rounds about 3 inches apart.

4 Bake 9 to 10 minutes or until edges are set. Cool 5 minutes; remove from cookie sheets to cooling racks.

5 In small microwavable bowl, heat chocolate chips and shortening in microwave on High 30 seconds; stir. Microwave about 30 seconds longer or until mixture can be stirred smooth. Drizzle over cooled cookies; sprinkle each with ¼ teaspoon finely chopped hazelnuts. Let cookies stand until glaze sets.

1 Cookie: Calories 220; Total Fat 11g (Saturated Fat 4.5g; Trans Fat 0g); Cholesterol 20mg; Sodium 110mg; Total Carbohydrate 29g (Dietary Fiber 1g); Protein 2g **Exchanges:** ½ Starch, 1½ Other Carbohydrate, 2 Fat **Carbohydrate Choices:** 2

Hazelnuts

These sweet, rich nuts are often called filberts or cobnuts. They grow in clusters on hazelnut (filbert) trees in many parts of the world. Hazelnut production has recently increased in Oregon and the state of Washington. Versatile and sweet, hazelnuts are a great addition to a variety of foods from sweet desserts and pastries to salads and main dishes. These tasty morsels are available whole or chopped and often in flavors for snacking.

To remove the bitter brown papery skin, bake them at 350°F for 10 to 12 minutes, stirring once or twice. Then rub them with a clean kitchen towel to remove the skins.

See how to make **peanut butter cookies:** Visit bettycrocker.com/BCcookbook

Stuffed Hazelnut Cookies

SNICKERDOODLES LOWER CALORIE

This favorite, whimsically named cookie originated in New England in the 1800s. It's traditionally rolled in cinnamon-sugar before baking.

PREP 40 min TOTAL 40 min • **4 dozen cookies**

- 1¾ cups sugar
- ½ cup butter, softened
- ½ cup shortening
- 2 eggs
- 2¾ cups all-purpose flour
- 2 teaspoons cream of tartar
- 1 teaspoon baking soda
- ¼ teaspoon salt
- 1 tablespoon ground cinnamon

1 Heat oven to 400°F. In large bowl, beat 1½ cups of the sugar, the butter, shortening and eggs with electric mixer on medium speed, or mix with spoon, until well blended. Stir in flour, cream of tartar, baking soda and salt.

2 Shape dough into 1¼-inch balls. In small bowl, mix remaining ¼ cup sugar and the cinnamon. Roll balls in cinnamon-sugar mixture. On ungreased cookie sheets, place balls 2 inches apart.

3 Bake 8 to 10 minutes or just until set. Immediately remove from cookie sheets to cooling racks.

1 Cookie: Calories 90; Total Fat 4.5g (Saturated Fat 1.5g; Trans Fat 0g); Cholesterol 15mg; Sodium 55mg; Total Carbohydrate 13g (Dietary Fiber 0g); Protein 1g **Exchanges:** 1 Other Carbohydrate, 1 Fat **Carbohydrate Choices:** 1

THUMBPRINT COOKIES

LOWER CALORIE

PREP 50 min TOTAL 50 min • **3 dozen cookies**

- ¼ cup packed brown sugar
- ¼ cup shortening
- ¼ cup butter, softened
- ½ teaspoon vanilla
- 1 egg, separated
- 1 cup all-purpose flour
- ¼ teaspoon salt
- 1 cup finely chopped nuts
  About 6 tablespoons jelly or jam (any flavor)

1 Heat oven to 350°F. In medium bowl, beat brown sugar, shortening, butter, vanilla and egg yolk with electric mixer on medium speed, or mix with spoon. Stir in flour and salt.

2 Shape dough into 1-inch balls. In small bowl, beat egg white slightly with fork. Place nuts in small bowl. Dip each ball into egg white; roll in nuts. On ungreased cookie sheets, place balls about 1 inch apart. Press thumb into center of each cookie to make indentation, but do not press all the way to cookie sheet.

3 Bake 8 to 10 minutes or until light brown. Quickly remake indentations with end of wooden spoon if necessary. Immediately remove from cookie sheets to cooling racks. Fill each with about ½ teaspoon of the jelly.

1 Cookie: Calories 70; Total Fat 4.5g (Saturated Fat 1g; Trans Fat 0g); Cholesterol 10mg; Sodium 30mg; Total Carbohydrate 7g (Dietary Fiber 0g); Protein 0g **Exchanges:** ½ Starch, ½ Fat **Carbohydrate Choices:** ½

HAZELNUT THUMBPRINT COOKIES Roll balls of dough into finely chopped hazelnuts. Instead of jelly, fill indentations with hazelnut spread with cocoa.

LEMON-ALMOND THUMBPRINT COOKIES Roll balls of dough into finely chopped slivered almonds. Instead of jelly, fill indentations with Lemon Curd (page 93).

PEANUT-FUDGE THUMBPRINT COOKIES Roll balls of dough into finely chopped dry-roasted peanuts. Instead of jelly, fill indentations with hot fudge topping (look for the thick topping, not the pourable or syrup variety).

Left to right: Lemon-Almond Thumbprint Cookies, Thumbprint Cookies, Hazelnut Thumbprint Cookies

See how to make **thumbprint cookies:** Visit bettycrocker.com/BCcookbook

BROWN SUGAR REFRIGERATOR COOKIES LOWER CALORIE

Also called icebox cookies, these crisp cookies are very easy to make. The dough can be frozen tightly wrapped for up to 2 months, then sliced and baked when you want. Just add 1 or 2 minutes to the baking time when the dough comes straight from the freezer.

PREP 20 min TOTAL 2 hr 55 min • **6 dozen cookies**

1	**cup packed brown sugar**
1	**cup butter, softened**
1	**teaspoon vanilla**
1	**egg**
3	**cups all-purpose flour**
1½	**teaspoons ground cinnamon**
½	**teaspoon baking soda**
½	**teaspoon salt**
⅓	**cup finely chopped nuts**

1 In large bowl, beat brown sugar, butter, vanilla and egg with electric mixer on medium speed, or mix with spoon, until well blended. Stir in remaining ingredients except nuts. Stir in nuts.

2 On plastic wrap, shape dough into 10x3-inch rectangle. Wrap and refrigerate about 2 hours or until firm but no longer than 24 hours.

3 Heat oven to 375°F. Cut rectangle into ⅛-inch slices. On ungreased cookie sheets, place slices 2 inches apart.

4 Bake 6 to 8 minutes or until light brown. Cool 1 to 2 minutes; remove from cookie sheets to cooling racks.

1 Cookie: Calories 60; Total Fat 3g (Saturated Fat 1.5g; Trans Fat 0g); Cholesterol 10mg; Sodium 45mg; Total Carbohydrate 7g (Dietary Fiber 0g); Protein 0g **Exchanges:** ½ Starch, ½ Fat **Carbohydrate Choices:** ½

CITRUS–BROWN SUGAR REFRIGERATOR COOKIES Add 1 tablespoon grated lemon or orange peel with the flour.

MAPLE–BROWN SUGAR REFRIGERATOR COOKIES Substitute 2 teaspoons maple flavor for the vanilla.

TOASTED COCONUT–BROWN SUGAR REFRIGERATOR COOKIES Add 1 cup toasted coconut (page 18) with the flour.

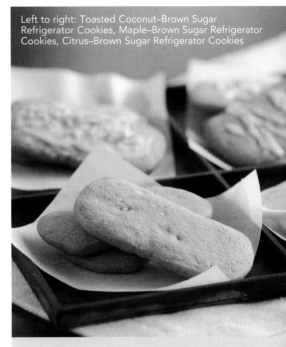

Left to right: Toasted Coconut–Brown Sugar Refrigerator Cookies, Maple–Brown Sugar Refrigerator Cookies, Citrus–Brown Sugar Refrigerator Cookies

Making Refrigerator Cookies

Beat cookie mixture with electric mixer or with spoon; stir in nuts.

Shape dough on plastic wrap into 10x3-inch rectangle.

Wrap; refrigerate about 2 hours or until firm.

Unwrap; cut rectangle into ⅛-inch slices.

SUGAR COOKIES LOWER CALORIE

PREP 55 min **TOTAL** 2 hr 55 min • **5 dozen 2-inch cookies**

- 1½ cups powdered sugar
- 1 cup butter, softened
- 1 teaspoon vanilla
- ½ teaspoon almond extract
- 1 egg
- 2½ cups all-purpose flour
- 1 teaspoon baking soda
- 1 teaspoon cream of tartar
  Granulated sugar or Colored Sugar (at right)

1 In large bowl, beat powdered sugar, butter, vanilla, almond extract and egg with electric mixer on medium speed, or mix with spoon, until well blended. Stir in flour, baking soda and cream of tartar. Cover and refrigerate at least 2 hours.

2 Heat oven to 375°F. Lightly grease cookie sheets with shortening or cooking spray, or line with cooking parchment paper or silicone baking mats.

3 Divide dough in half. Roll each half on lightly floured surface until ¼ inch thick. Cut into desired shapes with 2- to 2½-inch cookie cutters. Sprinkle with granulated sugar. On cookie sheets, place cutouts about 2 inches apart.

4 Bake 7 to 8 minutes or until edges are light brown. Remove from cookie sheets to cooling racks.

1 Cookie: Calories 60; Total Fat 3g (Saturated Fat 1.5g; Trans Fat 0g); Cholesterol 10mg; Sodium 45mg; Total Carbohydrate 8g (Dietary Fiber 0g); Protein 0g **Exchanges:** ½ Starch, ½ Fat **Carbohydrate Choices:** ½

COLORED SUGAR Place ½ cup granulated sugar in resealable food-storage plastic bag. Add liquid food color to tint as desired. Seal bag. Squeeze and rub sugar in bag until it becomes evenly colored. Homemade colored sugar might clump; if it does, just break apart until clumps are gone.

FROSTED AND DECORATED SUGAR COOKIES Omit granulated sugar. Frost cooled cookies with Creamy Vanilla Frosting (page 153) tinted with food color if desired. Decorate with colored sugar, small candies, candied fruit or nuts if desired.

PAINTBRUSH SUGAR COOKIES Omit granulated sugar. Cut rolled dough into desired shapes with cookie cutters. (Cut no more than 12 cookies at a time to keep them from drying out.) Mix 1 egg yolk and ¼ teaspoon water. Divide mixture among several custard cups. Tint each with a different food color to make bright colors. (If paint thickens while standing, stir in a few drops water.) Paint designs on cookies with small paintbrushes. Bake as directed in Step 4.

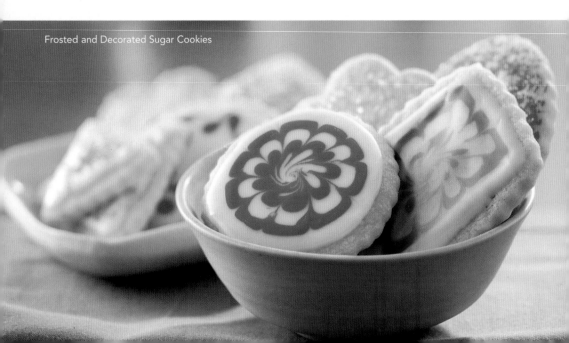

Frosted and Decorated Sugar Cookies

ROLLING COOKIES

On lightly floured surface, shape refrigerated dough (½ at a time) into flattened round without cracks.

Using ruler or sticks as guide, roll dough ¼ inch thick.

Using cookie cutters dipped in flour, cut desired shapes.

USING A DECORATING BAG

Insert coupler inside disposable pastry bag. (Cut end if necessary so coupler will reach tip of bag.)

Attach tip with ring; open bag, pulling opening far over hand and fill with frosting.

Squeeze and twist with even pressure to pipe frosting onto cookies.

DECORATING COOKIES

Colored Sugar: Sprinkle cookies with decorating sugar or decors before baking.

Frosted: Frost cookies and top with nuts, decorating sugar or decors. Or frost and drizzle dots of colored frosting or gel food color on top; use a toothpick to make designs.

Painted: Make egg yolk paints and paint cookies before baking.

SHORTBREAD COOKIES

LOWER CALORIE

Serve these meltingly tender, buttery cookies plain, or dip the edges in melted chocolate.

PREP 20 min **TOTAL** 40 min • **2 dozen 1½-inch cookies**

- ¾ cup butter, softened
- 5 tablespoons sugar
- 2 cups all-purpose flour

1 Heat oven to 350°F. In large bowl, stir butter and 4 tablespoons of the sugar until well mixed. Stir in flour. (If dough is crumbly, mix in 1 to 2 tablespoons more softened butter.)

2 Roll dough on lightly floured surface until ½ inch thick; sprinkle with remaining 1 tablespoon sugar. Cut into small shapes with knife or use cookie cutters. On ungreased cookie sheets, place shapes ½ inch apart.

3 Bake about 20 minutes or until set. Immediately remove from cookie sheets to cooling racks.

1 Cookie: Calories 100; Total Fat 6g (Saturated Fat 3g; Trans Fat 0g); Cholesterol 15mg; Sodium 40mg; Total Carbohydrate 10g (Dietary Fiber 0g); Protein 1g **Exchanges:** ½ Starch, 1 Fat **Carbohydrate Choices:** ½

SHORTBREAD COOKIE WEDGES Make dough as directed. On ungreased cookie sheet, pat dough into 8-inch round. Sprinkle with 1 table-spoon sugar. Bake 20 to 24 minutes or until set.

Cool 10 minutes on cookie sheet on cooling rack. Using sharp knife, cut into 24 wedges.

CHERRY-SHORTBREAD COOKIES Stir in ½ cup chopped dried cherries, cranberries or blueberries with the flour.

GINGER-SHORTBREAD COOKIES Stir in 3 tablespoons chopped crystallized ginger with the flour.

SHORTBREAD-NUT COOKIES Stir in ½ cup finely chopped hazelnuts, macadamia nuts, pecans, pistachio nuts or slivered almonds, toasted if desired (page 22), with the flour.

TOFFEE-SHORTBREAD COOKIES Stir in ½ cup toffee bits with the flour.

Dipping Cookies in Chocolate

Heat 1 cup chocolate chips and 1 teaspoon oil until mixture can be stirred smooth.

Dip cookies; wipe excess on edge of bowl. Place on waxed paper to set.

Shortbread Cookies and variations

SOFT NO-ROLL SUGAR COOKIES

LOWER CALORIE

PREP 50 min TOTAL 2 hr 50 min • **3½ dozen cookies**

- 1½ cups granulated sugar
- 1 cup powdered sugar
- 1 cup butter, softened
- ¾ cup vegetable oil
- 2 tablespoons milk
- 3 teaspoons vanilla
- 2 eggs
- 4¼ cups all-purpose flour
- 1 teaspoon baking soda
- 1 teaspoon cream of tartar
- ½ teaspoon salt

1 In large bowl, beat 1 cup of the granulated sugar, the powdered sugar, butter, oil, milk, vanilla and eggs with electric mixer on medium speed, or mix with spoon, until well blended. Stir in flour, baking soda, cream of tartar and salt. Cover and refrigerate about 2 hours or until firm.

2 Heat oven to 350°F. Shape dough into 1½-inch balls. In small bowl, place remaining ½ cup granulated sugar. Roll balls in sugar. On ungreased cookie sheets, place balls about 3 inches apart. Press bottom of drinking glass on each ball until about ¼ inch thick. Sprinkle each cookie with a little additional sugar.

3 Bake 13 to 15 minutes or until set and edges just begin to turn brown. Immediately remove from cookie sheets to cooling racks.

1 Cookie: Calories 160; Total Fat 9g (Saturated Fat 3g; Trans Fat 0g); Cholesterol 20mg; Sodium 90mg; Total Carbohydrate 20g (Dietary Fiber 0g); Protein 2g **Exchanges:** 1 Starch, ½ Other Carbohydrate, 1½ Fat **Carbohydrate Choices:** 1

CHOCOLATE CHIP, CHERRY AND PISTACHIO SOFT NO-ROLL SUGAR COOKIES
Stir in 1 cup semisweet chocolate chips, ½ cup dried cherries and ½ cup pistachio nuts after mixing in the flour mixture.

GLAZED SOFT NO-ROLL SUGAR COOKIES
After cooling, drizzle Chocolate Glaze (page 156) over cookies. Let stand until set.

SPRITZ COOKIES LOWER CALORIE

PREP 45 min TOTAL 45 min • **5 dozen cookies**

- 1 cup butter, softened*
- ½ cup sugar
- 2¼ cups all-purpose flour
- 1 egg
- 1 teaspoon almond extract or vanilla
- ½ teaspoon salt
  Few drops red or green food color, if desired

1 Heat oven to 400°F. In large bowl, beat butter and sugar with electric mixer on medium speed, or mix with spoon, until well blended. Stir in remaining ingredients.

2 Place dough in cookie press. On ungreased cookie sheets, form desired shapes.

3 Bake 6 to 9 minutes or until set but not brown. Immediately remove from cookie sheets to cooling racks.

Do not use margarine or vegetable oil spreads in this recipe.

1 Cookie: Calories 50; Total Fat 3g (Saturated Fat 1.5g; Trans Fat 0g); Cholesterol 10mg; Sodium 40mg; Total Carbohydrate 5g (Dietary Fiber 0g); Protein 0g **Exchanges:** ½ Other Carbohydrate, ½ Fat **Carbohydrate Choices:** ½

CHOCOLATE BUTTERY SPRITZ COOKIES
Stir 2 oz unsweetened baking chocolate, melted and cooled, into butter-sugar mixture.

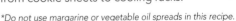

Making Spritz Cookies

Place desired design disc in cookie press. Place dough in press; press dough through press onto cookie sheet.

Spritz Cookies

Gingerbread Cookies

GINGERBREAD COOKIES

LOWER CALORIE

PREP 1 hr 40 min TOTAL 3 hr 40 min • **5 dozen 2½-inch cookies**

COOKIES
½ cup packed brown sugar
½ cup butter, softened
½ cup molasses
⅓ cup cold water
3½ cups all-purpose flour
2 teaspoons baking soda
2 teaspoons ground ginger
½ teaspoon ground allspice
½ teaspoon ground cinnamon
¼ teaspoon ground cloves
¼ teaspoon salt

DECORATOR'S FROSTING
2 cups powdered sugar
2 tablespoons water or milk
½ teaspoon vanilla
Food color, colored sugars and small candies, if desired

1 In large bowl, beat brown sugar, butter, molasses and water with electric mixer on medium speed, or mix with spoon, until well blended. Stir in remaining cookie ingredients until mixed. Cover; refrigerate at least 2 hours.

2 Heat oven to 350°F. Grease cookie sheets with shortening or cooking spray, or line with cooking parchment paper or silicone baking mats.

3 Divide dough in half. Roll each half on lightly floured surface until ¼ inch thick. Cut with floured gingerbread boy or girl cookie cutter or other shaped cutter. On cookie sheets, place cutouts about 2 inches apart. After cutting as many cookies as possible, lightly press scraps of dough together; reroll dough and cut additional cookies.

4 Bake 10 to 12 minutes or until no indentation remains when touched in center. Immediately remove from cookie sheets to cooling racks. Cool cookie sheets 10 minutes between batches. Let cookies stand about 30 minutes until completely cooled.

5 Meanwhile, in medium bowl, mix powdered sugar, water and vanilla with spoon until smooth and spreadable. Stir in food color, one drop at a time, until frosting is desired color. (For intense, vivid color, use paste food color. You would have to use too much liquid food color to get a vivid color, and the frosting will begin to separate and look curdled.) Cover and set aside.

6 When ready to decorate, place frosting in small resealable food-storage plastic bag. Seal bag; push frosting down in one corner. With scissors, snip off corner of bag. Squeeze bag to pipe frosting onto cookies and make desired design. Or spread over cookies with small metal spatula. Decorate as desired with colored sugars and candies.

1 Cookie: Calories 60; Total Fat 1.5g (Saturated Fat 1g; Trans Fat 0g); Cholesterol 0mg; Sodium 65mg; Total Carbohydrate 10g (Dietary Fiber 0g); Protein 0g **Exchanges:** ½ Other Carbohydrate, ½ Fat **Carbohydrate Choices:** ½

HAZELNUT BISCOTTI

LOWER CALORIE

PREP 25 min TOTAL 1 hr 50 min • **40 cookies**

1 cup hazelnuts (filberts), coarsely chopped
1 cup sugar
½ cup butter, softened
1 teaspoon almond extract
1 teaspoon vanilla
2 eggs
3½ cups all-purpose flour
1 teaspoon baking powder
½ teaspoon baking soda

1 Heat oven to 350°F. Spread hazelnuts in ungreased shallow pan. Bake uncovered about 10 minutes, stirring occasionally, until golden brown; cool.

2 In large bowl, beat sugar, butter, almond extract, vanilla and eggs with electric mixer on medium speed, or mix with spoon, until well blended. Stir in flour, baking powder and baking soda. Stir in hazelnuts. Place dough on lightly floured surface. Gently knead 2 to 3 minutes or until dough holds together and hazelnuts are evenly distributed.

3 Divide dough in half. On large ungreased cookie sheet, shape each half into 10x3-inch rectangle, rounding edges slightly.

4 Bake about 25 minutes or until center is firm to the touch. Cool on cookie sheet 15 minutes; move to cutting board. Using sharp knife, cut each rectangle crosswise into ½-inch slices.

5 Place slices, cut side down, on cookie sheet. Bake about 15 minutes or until crisp and light brown. Immediately remove from cookie sheet to cooling rack.

1 Cookie: Calories 100; Total Fat 4.5g (Saturated Fat 1.5g; Trans Fat 0g); Cholesterol 15mg; Sodium 45mg; Total Carbohydrate 14g (Dietary Fiber 0g); Protein 2g **Exchanges:** 1 Starch, ½ Fat **Carbohydrate Choices:** 1

ALMOND BISCOTTI Substitute 1 cup slivered almonds for the hazelnuts.

Making Biscotti

On cookie sheet, shape each dough half into 10x3-inch rectangle, rounding edges slightly.

Cool baked rectangles 15 minutes; cut into ½-inch slices. Place cut side down on same cookie sheet. Bake until crisp and golden brown.

BANANA–CHOCOLATE CHIP BISCOTTI LOWER CALORIE

PREP 30 min TOTAL 1 hr 35 min • **40 cookies**

- 1 **cup sugar**
- ½ **cup butter, softened***
- ½ **cup mashed very ripe banana (1 medium)**
- 1 **teaspoon vanilla**
- 2 **eggs**
- 3 **cups all-purpose flour**
- 3 **teaspoons baking powder**
- ¼ **teaspoon salt**
- ½ **cup miniature semisweet chocolate chips**

1 Heat oven to 350°F. Grease large cookie sheet with shortening or cooking spray, or line with cooking parchment paper or silicone baking mat.

2 In large bowl, beat sugar and butter with electric mixer on medium speed, or mix with spoon, until well blended. Beat in banana, vanilla and eggs until smooth. Stir in flour, baking powder and salt. Stir in chocolate chips.

3 Divide dough in half. On cookie sheet, shape each half into 10x3-inch rectangle with greased hands (dough will be sticky).

4 Bake about 25 minutes or until toothpick inserted in center comes out clean. Cool on cookie sheet 15 minutes; move to cutting board. Using sharp knife, cut each rectangle crosswise into ½-inch slices.

5 Place slices, cut side down, on cookie sheet. Bake 10 to 12 minutes or until golden brown and dry on top. Turn cookies. Bake about 10 minutes longer or until golden brown. Immediately remove from cookie sheet to cooling rack.

*Do not use vegetable oil spreads in this recipe.

1 Cookie: Calories 90; Total Fat 3.5g (Saturated Fat 2g; Trans Fat 0g); Cholesterol 15mg; Sodium 70mg; Total Carbohydrate 14g (Dietary Fiber 0g); Protein 1g **Exchanges:** ½ Starch, ½ Other Carbohydrate, ½ Fat **Carbohydrate Choices:** 1

CHOCOLATE BROWNIES

If you like chewy, fudgy, chocolaty brownies, this is your recipe. We really like the walnuts in the recipe, but you could use pecans or cashews instead. Or, make the brownies without nuts—they're delicious any way you make them.

PREP 25 min **TOTAL** 3 hr 10 min • **16 brownies**

- ⅔ cup butter
- 5 oz unsweetened baking chocolate, chopped
- 1¾ cups sugar
- 2 teaspoons vanilla
- 3 eggs
- 1 cup all-purpose flour
- ½ cup chopped walnuts, toasted if desired (page 22)
  Creamy Chocolate Frosting or Mocha Frosting (one-half recipe, page 152), if desired

1 Heat oven to 350°F. Grease bottom and sides of 9-inch square pan with shortening.

2 In 1-quart saucepan, melt butter and chocolate over low heat, stirring constantly. Cool 5 minutes.

3 In medium bowl, beat sugar, vanilla and eggs with electric mixer on high speed 5 minutes. Beat in chocolate mixture on low speed, scraping bowl occasionally. Beat in flour just until blended, scraping bowl occasionally. Stir in walnuts. Spread in pan.

4 Bake 40 to 45 minutes or just until brownies begin to pull away from sides of pan. Cool completely in pan on cooling rack, about 2 hours. Frost with creamy chocolate frosting. Cut into 4 rows by 4 rows.

1 Brownie: Calories 310; Total Fat 18g (Saturated Fat 8g; Trans Fat 0g); Cholesterol 60mg; Sodium 65mg; Total Carbohydrate 31g (Dietary Fiber 2g); Protein 4g **Exchanges:** 1 Starch, 1 Other Carbohydrate, 3½ Fat **Carbohydrate Choices: 2**

CHOCOLATE BROWNIE PIE Grease bottom and side of 10-inch glass pie plate with shortening. Spread batter in pie plate. Bake 35 to 40 minutes or until center is set. Cool completely in pan on cooling rack. Cut into wedges. Omit frosting. Serve with ice cream and Hot Fudge Sauce (page 233) if desired. Makes 12 servings

CHOCOLATE–PEANUT BUTTER BROWNIES Substitute ⅓ cup crunchy peanut butter for ⅓ cup of the butter. Omit walnuts. Before baking, arrange 16 miniature chocolate-covered peanut butter cup candies, unwrapped, over top. Press into batter so tops of cups are even with top of batter.

DOUBLE CHOCOLATE BROWNIES Stir in ½ cup semisweet or dark chocolate chips after adding the flour in Step 3.

Determining Brownie Doneness

Brownies will start to pull away from sides of pan when done.

Chocolate–Cream Cheese Brownies, Chocolate Brownies

CHOCOLATE–CREAM CHEESE BROWNIES LOWER CALORIE

PREP 25 min TOTAL 3 hr 15 min • **48 brownies**

CREAM CHEESE FILLING

2 packages (8 oz each) cream cheese, softened
½ cup sugar
2 teaspoons vanilla
1 egg

BROWNIES

1 cup butter, cut into pieces
4 oz unsweetened baking chocolate, chopped
2 cups sugar
2 teaspoons vanilla
4 eggs
1½ cups all-purpose flour
½ teaspoon salt
1 cup coarsely chopped nuts, toasted if desired (page 22)

1 Heat oven to 350°F. Grease bottom and sides of 13x9-inch pan with shortening.

2 In medium bowl, beat all filling ingredients with electric mixer on medium speed until smooth; set aside.

3 In 1-quart saucepan, melt butter and chocolate over low heat, stirring frequently. Remove from heat; cool 5 minutes.

4 In large bowl, beat chocolate mixture, sugar, vanilla and eggs with electric mixer on medium speed 1 minute, scraping bowl occasionally. Beat in flour and salt on low speed 30 seconds, scraping bowl occasionally. Beat on medium speed 1 minute. Stir in nuts. Spread 1¾ cups of batter in pan. Spread filling over batter. Drop remaining batter in mounds randomly over filling to make spreading easier; carefully spread, using short strokes, to cover cream cheese layer (this helps prevent mixing cream cheese layer into brownie batter).

5 Bake 45 to 50 minutes or until toothpick inserted in center comes out clean. Cool completely in pan on cooling rack, about 2 hours. Cut into 8 rows by 6 rows. Store covered in refrigerator.

1 Brownie: Calories 160; Total Fat 11g (Saturated Fat 5g; Trans Fat 0g); Cholesterol 45mg; Sodium 85mg; Total Carbohydrate 15g (Dietary Fiber 0g); Protein 2g **Exchanges:** 1 Starch, 2 Fat **Carbohydrate Choices:** 1

LIGHTER DIRECTIONS For 6 grams of fat and 120 calories per serving, use softened reduced-fat cream cheese (Neufchâtel) in the filling. For brownies, substitute ½ cup unsweetened applesauce for ½ cup of the butter and 2 eggs plus 4 egg whites for the 4 eggs. Decrease nuts to ½ cup.

BLONDIES LOWER CALORIE

Blondies are just brownies without chocolate. This version is buttery and flavored with brown sugar—they come out rich and chewy. When completely cooled, dress up the bars with a sprinkle of powdered sugar or a drizzle of Browned Butter Glaze (page 156), Chocolate Glaze (page 156) or Vanilla Glaze (page 156).

PREP 15 min TOTAL 45 min • **16 bars**

¼ cup butter
1 cup packed brown sugar
1 teaspoon vanilla
2 tablespoons milk
1 egg
1 cup all-purpose flour
½ cup chopped nuts, if desired
1 teaspoon baking powder
½ teaspoon salt

1 Heat oven to 350°F. Grease bottom and sides of 8-inch square pan with shortening.

2 In 1½-quart saucepan, melt butter over low heat; remove from heat. Stir in brown sugar, vanilla, milk and egg. Stir in remaining ingredients. Spread in pan.

3 Bake about 25 minutes or until golden brown. Cool 5 minutes in pan on cooling rack. Cut into 4 rows by 4 rows while warm.

1 Bar: Calories 110; Total Fat 3.5g (Saturated Fat 1.5g; Trans Fat 0g); Cholesterol 20mg; Sodium 135mg; Total Carbohydrate 20g (Dietary Fiber 0g); Protein 1g **Exchanges:** 1 Other Carbohydrate, 1 Fat **Carbohydrate Choices:** 1

TOFFEE BARS LOWER CALORIE

PREP 20 min TOTAL 1 hr 25 min • **32 bars**

- 1 cup butter, softened
- 1 cup packed brown sugar
- 1 teaspoon vanilla
- 1 egg yolk
- 2 cups all-purpose flour
- ¼ teaspoon salt
- ⅔ cup milk chocolate chips or 3 bars (1.55 oz each) milk chocolate candy, unwrapped, chopped
- ½ cup chopped nuts

1 Heat oven to 350°F. In large bowl, stir butter, brown sugar, vanilla and egg yolk until well mixed. Stir in flour and salt (dough will be stiff). Press dough in ungreased 13x9-inch pan.

2 Bake 25 to 30 minutes or until very light brown (crust will be soft, do not overbake). Immediately sprinkle chocolate chips over hot crust. Let stand about 5 minutes or until chips are soft; spread evenly. Sprinkle with nuts. Cool 30 minutes in pan on cooling rack. For easiest cutting, cut into 8 rows by 4 rows while warm.

1 Bar: Calories 140; Total Fat 8g (Saturated Fat 3.5g; Trans Fat 0g); Cholesterol 25mg; Sodium 65mg; Total Carbohydrate 15g (Dietary Fiber 0g); Protein 1g **Exchanges:** 1 Other Carbohydrate, 1½ Fat **Carbohydrate Choices:** 1

DOUBLE-TOFFEE BARS Stir in ½ cup toffee bits with the flour and salt.

DATE BARS LOWER CALORIE

PREP 30 min TOTAL 1 hr 5 min • **36 bars**

    DATE FILLING
- 3 cups chopped pitted dates (1 lb)
- 1½ cups water
- ¼ cup granulated sugar

    BARS
- 1 cup packed brown sugar
- 1 cup butter, softened
- 1¾ cups all-purpose or whole wheat flour
- 1½ cups quick-cooking oats
- ½ teaspoon baking soda
- ½ teaspoon salt

1 In 2-quart saucepan, cook filling ingredients over low heat about 10 minutes, stirring constantly, until thickened. Cool 5 minutes.

2 Heat oven to 400°F. Grease bottom and sides of 13x9-inch pan with shortening.

3 In large bowl, stir brown sugar and butter until well mixed. Stir in flour, oats, baking soda and salt until crumbly. Press half of the crumb mixture evenly in bottom of pan. Spread with filling. Top with remaining crumb mixture; press lightly.

4 Bake 25 to 30 minutes or until light brown. Cool 5 minutes in pan on cooling rack. Cut into 6 rows by 6 rows while warm.

1 Bar: Calories 160; Total Fat 5g (Saturated Fat 2.5g; Trans Fat 0g); Cholesterol 15mg; Sodium 85mg; Total Carbohydrate 25g (Dietary Fiber 2g); Protein 2g **Exchanges:** 1 Starch, ½ Other Carbohydrate, 1 Fat **Carbohydrate Choices:** 1½

FIG BARS Substitute 3 cups chopped dried figs for the dates.

CHEWY RASPBERRY-ALMOND BARS

If you don't have baking spray with flour, grease the pan with cooking spray and dust lightly with flour.

PREP 20 min TOTAL 2 hr • **16 bars**

- 1½ cups quick-cooking oats
- 1½ cups all-purpose flour
- ¾ cup packed light brown sugar
- ½ teaspoon salt
- ¾ cup cold butter
- 1 egg, beaten
- ¾ cup seedless red raspberry jam
- 1 cup fresh raspberries (6 oz)
- ½ cup sliced almonds

1 Heat oven to 375°F. Spray 9-inch square pan with baking spray with flour.

2 In large bowl, mix oats, flour, brown sugar and salt. Cut in butter, using pastry blender or fork, until mixture looks like coarse crumbs. Reserve 1 cup mixture for topping. To remaining mixture, stir in egg until just moistened.

3 Press dough firmly and evenly into bottom of pan, using fingers or bottom of measuring cup. Spread with jam. Arrange raspberries over jam. Stir almonds into reserved crumb mixture; sprinkle evenly over raspberries.

4 Bake 30 to 35 minutes or until light brown. Cool completely in pan on cooling rack, about 1 hour. Cut into 4 rows by 4 rows.

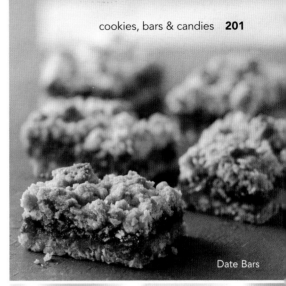

1 Bar: Calories 260; Total Fat 11g (Saturated Fat 6g; Trans Fat 0g); Cholesterol 35mg; Sodium 150mg; Total Carbohydrate 36g (Dietary Fiber 2g); Protein 3g **Exchanges:** 2 Starch, ½ Other Carbohydrate, 1½ Fat **Carbohydrate Choices:** 2½

CHEWY BLUEBERRY-ALMOND BARS

Substitute blueberry preserves for the raspberry jam and fresh blueberries for the raspberries.

LEMON BARS LOWER CALORIE

PREP 10 min TOTAL 2 hr • **25 bars**

- 1 **cup all-purpose flour**
- ½ **cup butter, softened**
- ¼ **cup powdered sugar**
- 2 **eggs**
- 1 **cup granulated sugar**
- 2 **teaspoons grated lemon peel**
- 2 **tablespoons lemon juice**
- ½ **teaspoon baking powder**
- ¼ **teaspoon salt**
  Additional powdered sugar

1 Heat oven to 350°F. In medium bowl, mix flour, butter and ¼ cup powdered sugar with spoon, until well mixed. Press in ungreased 8- or 9-inch square pan, building up ½-inch edges.

2 Bake crust 20 minutes; remove from oven. In medium bowl, beat remaining ingredients except additional powdered sugar with electric mixer on high speed about 3 minutes or until light and fluffy. Pour over hot crust.

3 Bake 25 to 30 minutes or until no indentation remains when touched lightly in center. Cool completely in pan on cooling rack, about 1 hour. Dust with powdered sugar. Cut into 5 rows by 5 rows.

1 Bar: Calories 100; Total Fat 4g (Saturated Fat 2g; Trans Fat 0g); Cholesterol 25mg; Sodium 65mg; Total Carbohydrate 14g (Dietary Fiber 0g); Protein 1g **Exchanges:** 1 Other Carbohydrate, 1 Fat **Carbohydrate Choices:** 1

LEMON-COCONUT BARS

Stir ½ cup flaked coconut into egg mixture in Step 2.

LIME BARS

Substitute lime peel and lime juice for the lemon peel and juice.

Date Bars

Chewy Raspberry-Almond Bars

Pressing Crust in Pan

Using fingertips, press dough in pan; build up ½-inch edges.

Lemon Bars

CANDY BASICS

Are you hesitant to try your hand at candy making? Begin by making a few fast, no-fuss confections, and then tackle a more traditional candy recipe. With a little practice and the tips here, you'll be a candy maker in no time.

SELECTING AND PREPARING PANS

Use the exact size of saucepan specified or cooking time will be affected.

The right size baking pan is needed so the candy will have the right thickness, set up properly and have the desired texture.

Grease the pan with butter or line it with foil so the candy can be easily removed.

MIXING, COOKING AND COOLING

- For best results, use butter. If you choose to use margarine, it needs to contain at least 65% fat. Do not use vegetable oil spreads or reduced-calorie, reduced-fat or tub products.

- Be sure to butter the side of the saucepan if directed. This will prevent crystals from forming. Crystals can result in grainy candy.

- Don't double the recipe. Increasing the amount of ingredients changes the cooking time, so the resulting candy may not set up properly. Make two batches instead.

- A cool, dry day is best for making candy. Some candies, like pralines, won't turn out when made on a humid day.

Wrap Caramels (page 206) or other candies in small squares of waxed paper to store.

- Unless otherwise directed, do not stir the candy mixture while cooling. Stirring during cooling can cause the mixture to crystallize, creating candy that is grainy. Follow recipes exactly, stirring when indicated.

Using a Candy Thermometer

Here are a few tips for using a candy thermometer:

- To check the candy thermometer for accuracy, put the thermometer in water and bring water to a boil. The thermometer should read 212°F. If the reading is higher or lower, make the necessary adjustment when making the candy.

- If you live in a high-altitude area (above 3,500 feet), refer to an altitude table to find out the boiling point and adjust the cooking time if necessary.

- To get an accurate reading, the thermometer should stand upright in the candy mixture. The bulb, or tip, of the thermometer shouldn't rest on the bottom of the pan. Read the thermometer at eye level. Watch the temperature closely—after 200°F, it goes up very quickly.

- If you don't have a candy thermometer, you can do a cold-water test. With a clean spoon, drop a small amount of candy mixture into a cupful of very cold water (see Testing Candy Temperatures at right).

CHOCOLATE FUDGE

This traditional fudge recipe is perfect to make for gifts or to serve on a dessert tray.

PREP 35 min **TOTAL** 2 hr 35 min • **64 candies**

    4 cups sugar
  1⅓ cups milk or half-and-half
    ¼ cup light corn syrup
    ¼ teaspoon salt
    4 oz unsweetened baking chocolate, chopped, or ⅔ cup unsweetened baking cocoa
    ¼ cup butter, cut into pieces
    2 teaspoons vanilla
    1 cup chopped nuts, if desired

1 Check the accuracy of your candy thermometer before starting (see Using a Candy Thermometer, at left). Grease bottom and sides of 8-inch square pan with butter.

2 In 3-quart saucepan, cook sugar, milk, corn syrup, salt and chocolate over medium heat, stirring constantly, until chocolate is melted and sugar is dissolved. Cook, stirring occasionally, to 234°F on candy thermometer or until small amount of mixture dropped into cup of very cold water forms a soft ball that flattens when removed from water; remove from heat. Stir in butter.

3 Cool mixture without stirring to 120°F, about 1 hour. (Bottom of saucepan will be lukewarm.) Add vanilla. Beat vigorously and continuously with wooden spoon 5 to 10 minutes or until mixture is thick and no longer glossy. (Mixture will hold its shape when dropped from a spoon.)

4 Quickly stir in nuts. Spread in pan. Let stand about 1 hour or until firm. Cut into 1-inch squares. Store in airtight container.

1 Candy: Calories 80; Total Fat 2g (Saturated Fat 1g; Trans Fat 0g); Cholesterol 0mg; Sodium 20mg; Total Carbohydrate 14g (Dietary Fiber 0g); Protein 0g **Exchanges:** 1 Other Carbohydrate, ½ Fat **Carbohydrate Choices:** 1

CHEWY CHOCOLATE FUDGE Stir in ½ cup dried cherries with the nuts.

PENUCHE Substitute 2 cups packed brown sugar for 2 cups of the granulated sugar; omit chocolate.

Testing Candy Temperatures

Thread stage (230°F to 233°F): Fine, thin, 2-inch thread falls off spoon when removed from hot mixture.

Soft-ball stage (234°F to 240°F): When dropped into very cold water, forms a soft ball that flattens between fingers.

Firm-ball stage (242°F to 248°F): When dropped into very cold water, forms a firm ball that holds its shape until pressed.

Hard-ball stage (250°F to 268°F): When dropped into very cold water, forms a hard ball that holds its shape but is still pliable.

Soft-crack stage (270°F to 290°F): When dropped into very cold water, separates into hard but pliable threads.

Hard-crack stage (300°F to 310°F): When dropped into very cold water, separates into hard, brittle threads that break easily.

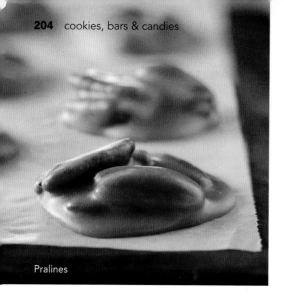

Pralines

NO-COOK CHOCOLATE FUDGE

You won't need a thermometer for this recipe. Sweetened condensed milk is the secret ingredient that makes this creamy fudge super-easy to make.

PREP 10 min TOTAL 1 hr 40 min • **64 candies**

1 can (14 oz) sweetened condensed milk (not evaporated)
1 bag (12 oz) semisweet chocolate chips (2 cups)
1 oz unsweetened baking chocolate, if desired
1½ cups chopped nuts, if desired
1 teaspoon vanilla

1 Grease bottom and sides of 8-inch square pan with butter.

2 In 2-quart saucepan, heat condensed milk, chocolate chips and unsweetened chocolate over low heat, stirring constantly, until chocolate is melted and mixture is smooth; remove from heat.

3 Quickly stir in nuts and vanilla. Spread in pan. Refrigerate about 1 hour 30 minutes or until firm. Cut into 1-inch squares. Store in airtight container.

1 Candy: Calories 60; Total Fat 2.5g (Saturated Fat 1.5g; Trans Fat 0g); Cholesterol 0mg; Sodium 10mg; Total Carbohydrate 8g (Dietary Fiber 0g); Protein 0g **Exchanges:** ½ Starch, ½ Fat **Carbohydrate Choices:** ½

CHERRY-ALMOND NO-COOK CHOCOLATE FUDGE Toast ¾ cup slivered almonds (page 22); cool completely. In Step 3, quickly stir in toasted almonds and ¾ cup dried cherries or coarsely chopped maraschino cherries, very well drained (pat dry with paper towels), with the vanilla.

ROCKY ROAD NO-COOK CHOCOLATE FUDGE Reduce nuts to ¾ cup. In Step 3, quickly stir in the nuts and ¾ cup miniature marshmallows with the vanilla.

PRALINES

Pronounced prah-LEEN *or* PRAY-leen, *this confection originated in Louisiana, where brown sugar and pecans are abundant.*

PREP 25 min TOTAL 1 hr 15 min • **3 dozen candies**

1½ cups granulated sugar
1½ cups packed light brown sugar
1 cup half-and-half
2 tablespoons light corn syrup
⅛ teaspoon salt
2 tablespoons butter
1 teaspoon vanilla
1¾ cups pecan halves

1 Check the accuracy of your candy thermometer before starting (see Using a Candy Thermometer, page 202). In 3-quart saucepan, mix sugars, half-and-half, corn syrup and salt. Heat to boiling, stirring constantly. Reduce heat to medium. Cook uncovered about 6 minutes, without stirring, to 236°F on candy thermometer or until small amount of mixture dropped into cup of very cold water forms a soft ball that flattens when removed from water; remove from heat. Drop butter into hot mixture (do not stir in). Cool uncovered 10 minutes without stirring.

2 Add vanilla and pecan halves. Beat with spoon about 2 minutes or until mixture is thickened and just begins to lose its gloss. On waxed paper, quickly drop mixture by heaping tablespoonfuls, dividing pecans equally; spread slightly. Let stand uncovered 30 minutes or until candies are firm.

3 Wrap candies individually in waxed paper or plastic wrap. Store in airtight container.

1 Candy: Calories 120; Total Fat 5g (Saturated Fat 1g, Trans Fat 0g); Cholesterol 0mg; Sodium 20mg; Total Carbohydrate 19g (Dietary Fiber 0g); Protein 0g **Exchanges:** 1½ Other Carbohydrate, 1 Fat **Carbohydrate Choices:** 1

LUSCIOUS CHOCOLATE TRUFFLES

PREP 20 min TOTAL 1 hr 15 min • **24 truffles**

- 1 **bag (12 oz) semisweet dark or milk chocolate chips (2 cups)**
- 2 **tablespoons butter, softened**
- ¼ **cup whipping cream**
- 2 **tablespoons liqueur (almond, cherry, coffee, hazelnut, Irish cream, orange, raspberry, or other flavor), if desired**
- 1 **tablespoon shortening**
  Finely chopped nuts, if desired
- ¼ **cup powdered sugar, if desired**
- ½ **teaspoon milk, if desired**

1 In 2-quart saucepan, melt 1 cup of the chocolate chips over low heat, stirring constantly; remove from heat. Stir in butter. Stir in whipping cream and liqueur. Refrigerate 10 to 15 minutes, stirring frequently, just until thick enough to hold a shape.

2 Line cookie sheet with foil. On cookie sheet, drop chocolate mixture by teaspoonfuls; shape into balls. (If mixture is too sticky, refrigerate until firm enough to shape.) Freeze 30 minutes.

3 In 1-quart saucepan, heat shortening and remaining 1 cup chocolate chips over low heat, stirring constantly, until chocolate is melted and mixture is smooth; remove from heat. Using fork, dip truffles, one at a time, into chocolate. Return to foil-covered cookie sheet. Immediately sprinkle some of the truffles with nuts. Refrigerate about 10 minutes or until coating is set.

4 In small bowl, stir powdered sugar and milk until smooth; drizzle over some of the truffles. Refrigerate just until set. Store in airtight container in refrigerator. Serve truffles at room temperature by removing from refrigerator about 30 minutes before serving.

1 Truffle: Calories 160; Total Fat 10g (Saturated Fat 6g; Trans Fat 0g); Cholesterol 10mg; Sodium 15mg; Total Carbohydrate 14g (Dietary Fiber 1g); Protein 1g **Exchanges:** ½ Other Carbohydrate, 1½ Fat **Carbohydrate Choices:** 1

TOFFEE TRUFFLES Stir in 3 tablespoons chopped toffee bits candy with the whipping cream.

WHITE CHOCOLATE–CHOCOLATE TRUFFLES Stir in 3 tablespoons chopped white chocolate with the whipping cream.

Luscious Chocolate Truffles

Making Truffles

Refrigerate truffle mixture just until thick enough to hold a shape.

Using fork, dip truffles one at a time into chocolate, covering completely.

CARAMELS

Cut little rectangles of waxed paper ahead of time, so you're ready to wrap when it's time. Here's another secret—cutting the caramels with a kitchen scissors is quicker and easier than using a knife.

PREP 40 min **TOTAL** 2 hr 40 min • **64 candies**

- 2 **cups sugar**
- ½ **cup butter, cut into pieces**
- 2 **cups whipping cream**
- ¾ **cup light corn syrup**

1 Check the accuracy of your candy thermometer before starting (page 202). Line 8- or 9-inch square pan with foil, leaving 1 inch of foil hanging over on 2 opposite sides of pan; grease foil with butter.

2 In 3-quart saucepan, heat all ingredients to boiling over medium heat, stirring constantly. Boil uncovered about 35 minutes, stirring frequently, to 245°F on candy thermometer or until small amount of mixture dropped into cup of very cold water forms a firm ball that holds its shape until pressed. Immediately spread in pan. Cool completely, about 2 hours.

3 Using foil, lift caramels out of pan; place on cutting board. Peel foil from caramels. Cut into 1-inch squares. Wrap individually in waxed paper or plastic wrap; store in airtight container at room temperature.

1 Candy: Calories 70; Total Fat 4g (Saturated Fat 2g; Trans Fat 0g); Cholesterol 10mg; Sodium 15mg; Total Carbohydrate 9g (Dietary Fiber 0g); Protein 0g **Exchanges:** ½ Other Carbohydrate, 1 Fat **Carbohydrate Choices:** ½

CHOCOLATE CARAMELS Heat 2 oz unsweetened baking chocolate, chopped, with the sugar mixture.

CHOCOLATE-TOPPED SEA SALT CARAMELS After spreading caramel mixture into pan in Step 2, refrigerate about 1 hour or until completely cooled. In small microwavable bowl, microwave ½ cup semisweet chocolate chips and ½ teaspoon vegetable oil on High 30 to 45 seconds, stirring every 10 seconds, until chocolate is melted. Using spatula, spread chocolate evenly over caramel layer. Sprinkle with 1 teaspoon coarse sea salt or any coarse salt. Refrigerate about 30 minutes or until chocolate is set. Continue as directed in Step 3.

Making Caramels

Lift caramels from pan; peel foil from caramels. Cut into 1-inch squares.

Left to right: Chocolate Caramels, Chocolate-Topped Sea Salt Caramels, Caramels

PEANUT BRITTLE

PREP 1 hr 55 min TOTAL 1 hr 55 min • **6 dozen candies**

- 1½ teaspoons baking soda
- 1 teaspoon water
- 1 teaspoon vanilla
- 1½ cups sugar
- 1 cup water
- 1 cup light corn syrup
- 3 tablespoons butter, cut into pieces
- 1 lb unsalted raw Spanish peanuts (3 cups)

Peanut Brittle

1 Check the accuracy of your candy thermometer before starting (see Using a Candy Thermometer, page 202). Heat oven to 200°F. Grease two 15x10x1-inch pans with butter; keep warm in oven. (Keeping the pans warm allows the candy to be spread ¼ inch thick without it setting up.) Grease long metal spatula with butter; set aside.

2 In small bowl, mix baking soda, 1 teaspoon water and the vanilla; set aside. In 3-quart saucepan, mix sugar, 1 cup water and the corn syrup. Cook over medium heat about 25 minutes, stirring occasionally, to 240°F on candy thermometer or until small amount of mixture dropped into cup of very cold water forms a soft ball that flattens when removed from water.

3 Stir in butter and peanuts. Cook over medium heat about 13 minutes, stirring constantly, to 300°F or until small amount of mixture dropped into cup of very cold water separates into hard, brittle threads. (Watch carefully so mixture does not burn.) Immediately remove from heat. Quickly stir in baking soda mixture until light and foamy.

4 Pour half of the candy mixture onto each cookie sheet and quickly spread about ¼ inch thick with buttered spatula. Cool completely, at least 1 hour. Break into pieces. Store in airtight container at room temperature up to 2 weeks.

1 Candy: Calories 70; Total Fat 3.5g (Saturated Fat 0.5g; Trans Fat 0g); Cholesterol 0mg; Sodium 35mg; Total Carbohydrate 9g (Dietary Fiber 0g); Protein 2g **Exchanges:** ½ Starch, 1 Fat **Carbohydrate Choices:** ½

MICROWAVE METHOD Prepare cookie sheets as directed. Omit all water. In 8-cup microwavable measuring cup, mix sugar, corn syrup and peanuts. Microwave uncovered on High 10 to 12 minutes, stirring every 5 minutes, until peanuts are light brown. Stir in vanilla and butter thoroughly. Microwave uncovered on High 4 to 6 minutes to 300°F on microwave candy thermometer or until small amount of mixture dropped into cup of very cold water separates into hard, brittle threads. Quickly stir in baking soda until mixture is light and foamy. Continue as directed in Step 4.

ALMOND OR CASHEW BRITTLE Substitute unsalted almonds or cashews for the peanuts.

RUM BALLS

PREP 20 min TOTAL 24 hr 20 min • **5 dozen rum balls**

- 1 package (9 oz) thin chocolate wafer cookies, finely crushed (2⅓ cups)
- 2 cups finely chopped almonds, pecans or walnuts
- 2 cups powdered sugar
- ¼ cup light rum
- ¼ cup light corn syrup
  Additional powdered sugar

1 In large bowl, mix cookies, almonds and 2 cups powdered sugar. Stir in rum and corn syrup.

2 Shape mixture into 1-inch balls. Roll in additional powdered sugar. Cover tightly and refrigerate at least 24 hours before serving to blend flavors.

1 Rum Ball: Calories 60; Total Fat 2g (Saturated Fat 0g; Trans Fat 0g); Cholesterol 0mg; Sodium 25mg; Total Carbohydrate 9g (Dietary Fiber 0g); Protein 0g **Exchanges:** ½ Starch, ½ Fat **Carbohydrate Choices:** ½

BOURBON BALLS Substitute ¼ cup bourbon for the rum.

BRANDY BALLS Substitute ¼ cup brandy for the rum.

PEPPERMINT MARSHMALLOWS

LOWER CALORIE

PREP 50 min **TOTAL** 8 hr 50 min • **77 marshmallows**

- ⅓ cup powdered sugar
- 2½ tablespoons unflavored gelatin
- ½ cup cold water
- 1½ cups granulated sugar
- 1 cup corn syrup
- ¼ teaspoon salt
- ½ cup water
- 1 teaspoon peppermint extract
- 8 to 10 drops red food color

1 Check the accuracy of your candy thermometer before starting (page 202). Generously grease bottom and sides of 11x7-inch (2-quart) glass baking dish with butter; dust with 1 tablespoon of the powdered sugar. In bowl of stand mixer, sprinkle gelatin over ½ cup cold water to soften; set aside.

2 In 2-quart saucepan, heat granulated sugar, corn syrup, salt and ½ cup water over low heat, stirring constantly, until sugar is dissolved. Heat to boiling; cook uncovered about 30 minutes without stirring, to 240°F on candy thermometer or until small amount of mixture dropped into cup of very cold water forms a soft ball that flattens between fingers; remove from heat.

3 Slowly pour syrup into softened gelatin while beating on low speed. Increase speed to high; beat 8 to 10 minutes or until mixture is white and has almost tripled in volume. Add peppermint extract; beat on high speed 1 minute. Pour into baking dish, patting lightly with wet hands. Drop food color randomly onto top of marshmallow mixture. Pull table knife through food color to create swirl pattern over top. Let stand uncovered at least 8 hours or overnight.

4 Dust cutting board with about 1 tablespoon powdered sugar. Place remaining powdered sugar in small bowl. To remove marshmallow mixture, loosen sides from dish and gently lift in one piece onto cutting board. Using sharp knife greased with butter, cut into 1-inch squares (11 rows by 7 rows). Dust bottom and sides of each marshmallow by dipping into bowl of powdered sugar. Store in airtight container at room temperature up to 3 weeks.

1 Marshmallow: Calories 35; Total Fat 0g (Saturated Fat 0g; Trans Fat 0g); Cholesterol 0mg; Sodium 10mg; Total Carbohydrate 8g (Dietary Fiber 0g); Protein 0g **Exchanges:** ½ Other Carbohydrate **Carbohydrate Choices:** ½

Making Marshmallows

Beat syrup-gelatin mixture until almost tripled in volume; beat in peppermint extract.

Drop food color randomly on marshmallow mixture; pull table knife through to swirl pattern.

Peppermint Marshmallows

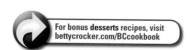
For bonus desserts recipes, visit
bettycrocker.com/BCcookbook

FAST = Ready in 20 minutes or less LOWER CALORIE = See Helpful Nutrition and Cooking Information, page 685
LIGHTER = 25% fewer calories or grams of fat MAKE AHEAD = Make-ahead directions SLOW COOKER = Slow cooker directions

← Chocolate Ice Cream (page 230), Chocolate–Sour Cream Fondue (page 230), Layered Pumpkin Cheesecake (page 220), Gingerbread (page 216)

DESSERT BASICS

From comforting cobblers, refreshing ice creams and creamy puddings to elegant cheesecakes, airy meringues and attractive trifles, this chapter offers an assortment of delectable desserts perfect for any occasion. For a fun and festive finishing touch, add some sparkle to any dessert with one of our easy ideas below.

Chocolate-Covered Confections: Melt chocolate (below). Dip dried apricots, fresh strawberries, pretzels, marshmallows or whole nuts three-fourths of the way into chocolate. Place on cookie sheet lined with waxed paper. Refrigerate 10 minutes to set; chill until serving.

Chocolate Swirls and Filigree: Melt chocolate (below). Place chocolate in resealable plastic bag; seal bag. Cut off tiny corner of bag. Squeeze bag to pipe swirls inside clear serving bowl or in stemware. Refrigerate 10 minutes to set; chill until serving. For filigree, pipe designs (such as stars, trees, letters, numbers or random patterns) onto cookie sheet lined with waxed paper. Refrigerate until chocolate is set. Gently remove designs from paper; chill until serving.

Chocolate Curls: Let milk chocolate stand at room temperature about 15 minutes. (Semisweet chocolate can also be used but curls will be smaller.) Pull swivel vegetable peeler or thin, sharp knife across block, using long, thin strokes. (To make chocolate shavings, use shorter strokes.) Use toothpick to lift curls and arrange them on the dessert.

Pretty Rims: Dip rims of glasses or small serving bowls in water, then in colored or white decorator sugar crystals, granulated sugar or edible glitter. Or melt chocolate (at left). Dip rims in chocolate and then in chopped nuts, chopped candies or sprinkles if desired. Refrigerate 10 minutes to harden; chill until serving.

Sugared Herbs: Lightly brush woody herb sprigs like rosemary, thyme or sage with corn syrup; sprinkle with granulated or decorator sugar crystals. Let stand uncovered up to 1 hour or until dry.

Candy Brittle: Line 15x10x1-inch pan with foil; spray with cooking spray. Place hard candy, such as peppermint, in plastic bag. Finely crush candies with flat side of meat mallet. Spread evenly in pan. Bake at 350°F for 6 to 8 minutes or until melted. Cool; break into pieces.

Making Chocolate Curls

Pull swivel peeler across chocolate bar or block, using long, thin strokes.

Melting Chocolate

In 1-quart saucepan, heat 1 cup semisweet or dark chocolate chips with 1 teaspoon shortening over low heat, stirring constantly until melted; remove from heat.

Sugared Herbs (rosemary) and Chocolate-Covered Confections (marshmallows, dried apricots, strawberries and pretzels)

APPLE CRISP

PREP 20 min TOTAL 1 hr • **6 servings**

> 6 medium tart cooking apples (Granny Smith or Rome), peeled, sliced (about 6 cups)
> ¾ cup packed brown sugar
> ½ cup all-purpose flour
> ½ cup quick-cooking or old-fashioned oats
> 1 teaspoon ground cinnamon
> ½ teaspoon ground nutmeg
> ⅓ cup cold butter
> Cream or ice cream, if desired

1 Heat oven to 375°F. Spray bottom and sides of 8-inch square (2-quart) glass baking dish with cooking spray.

2 Spread apples in baking dish. In medium bowl, mix brown sugar, flour, oats, cinnamon and nutmeg. Cut in butter, using pastry blender or fork, until mixture is crumbly. Sprinkle evenly over apples.

3 Bake 35 to 40 minutes or until topping is golden brown and apples are tender when pierced with fork. Serve warm with cream.

1 Serving: Calories 330; Total Fat 11g (Saturated Fat 7g; Trans Fat 0g); Cholesterol 25mg; Sodium 85mg; Total Carbohydrate 55g (Dietary Fiber 4g); Protein 3g **Exchanges:** 1 Starch, 1 Fruit, 1½ Other Carbohydrate, 2 Fat **Carbohydrate Choices:** 3½

BLUEBERRY CRISP Substitute 6 cups fresh or frozen (thawed and drained) blueberries for the apples.

CARAMEL APPLE CRISP Toss apples with ½ cup butterscotch caramel topping before spreading in pan.

RHUBARB CRISP Substitute 6 cups chopped fresh or frozen (thawed and drained) rhubarb for the apples. Sprinkle ½ cup granulated sugar over rhubarb; stir to combine. Continue as directed in Step 2.

BAKED APPLES LOWER CALORIE

Often overlooked, baked apples make a perfect last-minute dessert for entertaining or family dinners. Use the larger amount of brown sugar for very tart apples.

PREP 10 min TOTAL 50 min • **4 servings**

> 4 large unpeeled tart cooking apples (Granny Smith or Rome)
> 2 to 4 tablespoons packed brown sugar
> 4 teaspoons butter
> ½ teaspoon ground cinnamon

1 Heat oven to 375°F. Core apples to within ½ inch of bottom. Remove 1-inch strip of peel from around middle of each apple, or peel upper half of each apple to prevent splitting. Place apples in ungreased 8-inch square (2-quart) glass baking dish.

2 In center of each apple, place 1½ teaspoons to 1 tablespoon sugar, 1 teaspoon butter and ⅛ teaspoon cinnamon. Sprinkle with additional cinnamon. Pour water into baking dish until ¼ inch deep.

3 Bake 30 to 40 minutes or until apples are tender when pierced with fork. (Time will vary depending on size and variety of apple.) Spoon syrup in dish over apples several times during baking if desired.

1 Serving: Calories 200; Total Fat 4.5g (Saturated Fat 2g; Trans Fat 0g); Cholesterol 10mg; Sodium 25mg; Total Carbohydrate 39g (Dietary Fiber 5g); Protein 0g **Exchanges:** 2 Fruit, ½ Other Carbohydrate, ½ Fat **Carbohydrate Choices:** 2½

Microwaving Baked Apples

You can make baked apples in minutes in your microwave oven. Make apples as directed; place each apple in 10-ounce custard cup or individual microwavable casserole or bowl. Do not add water to cups. Microwave uncovered on High 5 to 10 minutes, rotating cups ½ turn after 3 minutes, until apples are tender when pierced with fork.

Apple Crisp

APPLE DUMPLINGS

This recipe for apple dumplings was available free in Gold Medal® flour bags, as noted in a 1938 advertisement, and has also been included in many of the company's cookbooks over the years, beginning with the 1904 Christmas Edition of the Gold Medal Flour Cook Book.

PREP 55 min TOTAL 1 hr 35 min • **6 dumplings**

- **Two-Crust Pastry (page 159)**
- 6 **small cooking apples (Golden Delicious, Braeburn, Rome), about 3 inches in diameter***
- 3 **tablespoons raisins, dried cranberries or dried cherries, if desired**
- 3 **tablespoons chopped nuts, if desired**
- 2½ **cups packed brown sugar**
- 1⅓ **cups water**
- 2 **tablespoons butter, softened**
- ¼ **teaspoon ground cinnamon**
- **Cream or Sweetened Whipped Cream (page 214), if desired**

1 Heat oven to 425°F. Make pastry as directed—except roll two-thirds of the pastry into 14-inch square; cut into four 7-inch squares. Roll remaining pastry into 14x7-inch rectangle; cut into two 7-inch squares.

2 Peel and core apples; place 1 apple on each pastry square. Mix raisins and nuts; fill apples with mixture. Moisten corners of pastry squares. Bring 2 opposite corners up over apple and pinch together. Repeat with remaining corners, and pinch edges of pastry to seal.

3 Place dumplings in ungreased 13x9-inch (3-quart) glass baking dish. In 2-quart saucepan, heat brown sugar, water, butter and cinnamon to boiling over high heat, stirring frequently. Carefully pour syrup around dumplings.

4 Bake about 40 minutes, spooning syrup over dumplings 2 or 3 times, until crust is golden and apples are tender when pierced with a small knife or toothpick. Serve warm or cool with cream.

*Dough squares will not be large enough to seal larger apples.

1 Dumpling: Calories 680; Total Fat 32g (Saturated Fat 9g; Trans Fat 5g); Cholesterol 10mg; Sodium 450mg; Total Carbohydrate 94g (Dietary Fiber 4g); Protein 5g **Exchanges:** 2 Starch, 4 Other Carbohydrate, 6 Fat **Carbohydrate Choices:** 6

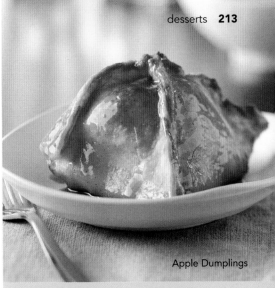

Apple Dumplings

Making Apple Dumplings

Moisten corners of pastry squares. Bring 2 opposite corners up over apple and pinch together.

Repeat with remaining corners; pinch edges of pastry to seal.

LIGHTER DIRECTIONS For 5 grams of fat and 320 calories per serving, omit Two-Crust Pastry. Place 6 sheets (18x14 inches) of frozen (thawed) phyllo dough on cutting board. Cut into 14-inch square. Discard remaining strips of phyllo. Divide square into 3 stacks of 2 sheets each. Set aside one stack; cover remaining stacks with plastic wrap and then a damp towel to prevent drying. Take uncovered stack and spray top with butter-flavored cooking spray. Fold in half; spray top. Cut in half, forming 2 squares. Repeat with remaining stacks to form a total of 6 squares, covering standing squares as directed above until each dumpling is assembled. Continue as directed in Step 2, omitting nuts.

Learn to Make **Strawberry Shortcake**

STRAWBERRY SHORTCAKE

Loved by folks of all ages, shortcake is a sure bet to please your family or guests. The best shortcake is tender and flaky, then topped with juicy fresh strawberries or other fruit and freshly whipped cream. Here's our version of this favorite dessert with easy-to-follow directions for making it just right.

PREP 15 min **TOTAL** 2 hr • **6 servings**

2 pints (4 cups) fresh strawberries, sliced	½ cup cold butter, cut into pieces
1 cup sugar	⅔ cup milk
2 cups all-purpose flour	1 egg, slightly beaten
3 teaspoons baking powder	Sweetened Whipped Cream (below), if desired
½ teaspoon salt	

1 In large bowl, stir strawberries and ½ cup of the sugar until well mixed. Let stand 1 hour so strawberry juice forms.

2 Heat oven to 375°F. Grease bottom and side of 8- or 9-inch round cake pan with shortening; lightly flour.

3 In medium bowl, mix flour, remaining ½ cup sugar, the baking powder and

salt. Cut in butter, using pastry blender or fork, until mixture looks like coarse crumbs. Stir in milk and egg just until blended. Spoon into pan; spread evenly.

4 Bake 30 to 35 minutes or until toothpick inserted in center comes out clean. Cool 10 minutes.

5 Place cooling rack upside down on pan; turn rack and pan over and remove pan. Carefully invert shortcake onto serving plate, right side up. Cut shortcake into 6 wedges. If desired, split each horizontally in half. Fill and top with strawberries and whipped cream.

1 Serving: Calories 490; Total Fat 18g (Saturated Fat 8g; Trans Fat 1g); Cholesterol 80mg; Sodium 570mg; Total Carbohydrate 75g (Dietary Fiber 4g); Protein 7g **Exchanges:** 2 Starch, 1 Fruit, 2 Other Carbohydrate, 3½ Fat **Carbohydrate Choices:** 5

DROP SHORTCAKES Heat oven to 425°F. Make dough as directed; drop dough to form 6 shortcakes about 2 inches apart onto ungreased cookie sheet. Bake 12 to 14 minutes or until golden brown.

SWEETENED WHIPPED CREAM Chill bowl and beaters in freezer or refrigerator 10 to 20 minutes. In chilled medium bowl, beat ½ cup whipping cream, 1 tablespoon powdered or granulated sugar and ½ teaspoon vanilla on low speed of electric mixer until mixture begins to thicken. Gradually increase speed to high and beat just until soft peaks form. Do not overbeat or mixture will curdle. Makes 1 cup. Double ingredients to make 2 cups.

Keys to Success

- **Wash and cut fruit** just before making the shortcake.

- **Mix fruit with sugar** and let stand so it draws out juice and makes a fruit syrup to spoon over the shortcake.

- **Cut in butter** until mixture looks like coarse crumbs, so butter will be evenly distributed, for flaky shortcake.

- **Stir just until blended** so that dough isn't overmixed, which can make shortcake tough.

- **Beat whipping cream only until soft peaks form** so that it holds a loose shape when spooned onto the shortcake.

See how to make **strawberry shortcake**: Visit bettycrocker.com/BCcookbook

MORE SHORTCAKES

Shortcake is the perfect way to showcase fruit that's in season! Try these mouthwatering combinations or make up your own flavor mix with what you have on hand.

1 Blueberry-Lime Shortcake: Omit strawberries and ½ cup sugar added to fruit. Mix 1 tablespoon grated lime peel into the flour. Fill and top shortcake wedges, using 1 cup lime or lemon curd (from 10-ounce jar), 4 cups blueberries and whipped cream.

3 Raspberries, Peaches 'n Cream Shortcake: Omit strawberries, reduce sugar added to fruit to ⅓ cup and omit whipped cream. In medium bowl, combine 2 cups fresh raspberries and ⅓ cup sugar, crushing a few berries with back of spoon. Let stand 1 hour so juice is formed. Add 2 peaches, peeled and sliced; stir gently. Fill each shortcake wedge with ½ cup vanilla ice cream, 1 tablespoon warmed seedless raspberry jam and ½ cup of the fruit. Serve immediately.

2 Caribbean Fruit Shortcake: Omit strawberries, ½ cup sugar added to fruit and whipped cream. 1 cup each chopped papaya and mango mix (1 medium papaya and 1 medium mango) and 3 kiwifruit, peeled and sliced, with ½ cup sugar. Let stand 30 minutes. Mix ⅓ cup sour cream and 2 tablespoons packed brown sugar; refrigerate 30 minutes. Fill and top shortcake wedges with fruit. Top with sour cream mixture.

4 Strawberry Shortcake: (at left).

5 Triple Berry Shortcake: Decrease strawberries to 1 pint (2 cups) and sugar added to fruit to ⅓ cup. Toss strawberries and ⅓ cup sugar with 1 cup each fresh raspberries and blueberries, and ¼ cup raspberry- or orange-flavored liqueur or orange juice. Fill and top as directed.

PEACH COBBLER

PREP 25 min **TOTAL** 1 hr 5 min • **6 servings**

- ½ cup sugar
- 1 tablespoon cornstarch
- ¼ teaspoon ground cinnamon
- 4 cups sliced peeled fresh peaches (6 medium)*
- 1 teaspoon lemon juice
- 1 cup all-purpose flour
- 1 tablespoon sugar
- 1½ teaspoons baking powder
- ½ teaspoon salt
- 3 tablespoons cold butter
- ½ cup milk
- 2 tablespoons sugar, if desired
  Cream, if desired

1 Heat oven to 400°F. In 2-quart saucepan, mix ½ cup sugar, the cornstarch and cinnamon. Stir in peaches and lemon juice. Cook over medium-high heat 4 to 5 minutes, stirring constantly, until mixture thickens and boils. Boil and stir 1 minute. Pour into ungreased 2-quart casserole; keep peach mixture hot in oven.

2 In medium bowl, mix flour, 1 tablespoon sugar, the baking powder and salt. Cut in butter, using pastry blender or fork, until mixture looks like fine crumbs. Stir in milk. Drop dough in 6 spoonfuls onto hot peach mixture. Sprinkle 2 tablespoons sugar over dough.

3 Bake 25 to 30 minutes or until topping is golden brown. Serve warm with cream.

*4 cups frozen sliced peaches (from two 16-oz bags), thawed and drained, can be substituted for the fresh peaches.

1 Serving: Calories 300; Total Fat 13g (Saturated Fat 7g; Trans Fat 0.5g); Cholesterol 40mg; Sodium 240mg; Total Carbohydrate 44g (Dietary Fiber 4g); Protein 3g **Exchanges:** 1½ Starch, 1½ Fruit, 1 Fat **Carbohydrate Choices:** 3

APPLE COBBLER Substitute 4 cups sliced peeled apples for baking (Granny Smith or Rome) for the peaches.

FRESH BLUEBERRY COBBLER Substitute 4 cups blueberries for the peaches. Omit cinnamon.

FRESH CHERRY COBBLER Substitute 4 cups pitted tart red or sweet cherries for the peaches. Increase sugar in cherry mixture to 1¼ cups for tart cherries and 1 cup for sweet cherries, and cornstarch to 3 tablespoons. Substitute ¼ teaspoon almond extract for the lemon juice.

RASPBERRY-PEACH COBBLER Substitute 2 cups fresh raspberries for 1 cup of the peaches.

GINGERBREAD

PREP 10 min **TOTAL** 1 hr 5 min • **9 servings**

- 2⅓ cups all-purpose flour
- 1 teaspoon baking soda
- 1 teaspoon ground ginger
- 1 teaspoon ground cinnamon
- ½ teaspoon salt
- ½ cup butter, softened, or shortening
- ⅓ cup sugar
- 1 cup molasses
- ¾ cup hot water
- 1 egg
  Lemon Sauce (page 235), if desired
  Sweetened Whipped Cream (page 214), if desired

1 Heat oven to 325°F. Grease bottom and sides of 9-inch square pan with shortening; lightly flour.

2 In large bowl, beat all ingredients except lemon sauce and whipped cream with electric mixer on low speed 30 seconds, scraping bowl constantly. Beat on medium speed 3 minutes, scraping bowl occasionally. Pour into pan.

Peach Cobbler

3 Bake 50 to 55 minutes or until toothpick inserted in center comes out clean. Serve warm with lemon sauce and whipped cream.

1 Serving: Calories 370; Total Fat 12g (Saturated Fat 3g; Trans Fat 2g); Cholesterol 25mg; Sodium 360mg; Total Carbohydrate 60g (Dietary Fiber 1g); Protein 4g **Exchanges:** 1 Starch, 3 Other Carbohydrate, 2 Fat **Carbohydrate Choices:** 4

DOUBLE-CHOCOLATE HOT FUDGE SUNDAE CAKE

PREP 20 min TOTAL 1 hr 5 min • **9 servings**

- 1 cup all-purpose flour
- ¾ cup granulated sugar
- 2 tablespoons unsweetened baking cocoa
- 2 teaspoons baking powder
- ¼ teaspoon salt
- ½ cup chocolate or regular milk
- 2 tablespoons butter, melted, or vegetable oil
- 1 teaspoon vanilla
- ½ cup semisweet chocolate chips
- ½ cup chopped walnuts or pecans, toasted (page 22), if desired
- 1 cup packed brown sugar
- ¼ cup unsweetened baking cocoa
- 1¾ cups hot strong brewed coffee or hot water
  Ice cream, if desired

1 Heat oven to 350°F. In ungreased 9-inch square pan, mix flour, granulated sugar, 2 tablespoons cocoa, the baking powder and salt. Mix in milk, butter and vanilla with fork until smooth. Stir in chocolate chips and nuts.

2 Spread batter in pan. Sprinkle with brown sugar and ¼ cup cocoa. Pour hot coffee evenly over batter.

3 Bake 35 to 40 minutes or until top is dry. Cool 10 minutes. Spoon warm cake into dessert dishes. Top with ice cream. Spoon sauce from pan onto each serving.

1 Serving: Calories 260; Total Fat 4g (Saturated Fat 1g; Trans Fat 0g); Cholesterol 0mg; Sodium 190mg; Total Carbohydrate 54g (Dietary Fiber 2g); Protein 3g **Exchanges:** 2 Starch, 1 Fat **Carbohydrate Choices:** 3½

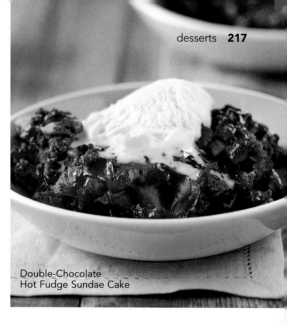

Double-Chocolate
Hot Fudge Sundae Cake

LEMON PUDDING CAKE

LOWER CALORIE

This great dessert has a yummy layer of cake topped with creamy lemon.

PREP 15 min TOTAL 50 min • **6 servings**

- 3 eggs, separated
- ½ cup fat-free (skim) milk
- ¼ cup fresh lemon juice
- 1 teaspoon grated lemon peel
- ½ cup sugar
- ⅓ cup all-purpose flour
- ⅛ teaspoon salt

1 Heat oven to 350°F. Grease 1-quart casserole or soufflé dish. In small bowl, beat egg yolks. Stir in milk, lemon peel and lemon juice. Add sugar, flour and salt; beat until smooth. In another small bowl, beat egg whites with electric mixer on high speed until stiff peaks form. Gently fold yolk mixture into beaten egg whites. Do not overmix. Pour into casserole. Place casserole in 13x9-inch pan; pour hot water into pan until 1 inch deep.

2 Bake 25 to 35 minutes or until light golden brown. Serve warm or cool.

1 Serving (½ Cup): Calories 140; Total Fat 3g (Saturated Fat 1g; Trans Fat 0g); Cholesterol 105mg; Sodium 90mg; Total Carbohydrate 24g (Dietary Fiber 0g); Protein 4g **Exchanges:** 1 Starch, ½ Other Carbohydrate, ½ Fat **Carbohydrate Choices:** 1½

Learn to Make **Cheesecake**

NEW YORK CHEESECAKE

Cheesecake can take any meal to a whole new level. It seems so special and decadent to your guests—they'll think it was hard to make and that you went all out. But don't say a word. We've worked hard to find the secrets to a perfectly-baked crust and a creamy rich filling—now you will know them, too.

PREP 45 min **TOTAL** 15 hr 45 min • **16 servings**

CRUST
- 1 cup all-purpose flour
- ½ cup butter, softened
- ¼ cup sugar
- 1 egg yolk

CHEESECAKE
- 5 packages (8 oz each) cream cheese, softened
- 1¾ cups sugar
- 3 tablespoons all-purpose flour
- 1 tablespoon grated orange peel, if desired
- 1 tablespoon grated lemon peel, if desired
- ¼ teaspoon salt
- 5 whole eggs
- 2 egg yolks
- 1 cup whipping cream, divided
- ⅓ cup slivered almonds, toasted (page 22), or fresh fruit, if desired

1 Heat oven to 400°F. Grease bottom and side of 9-inch springform pan with cooking spray; remove bottom. In medium bowl, mix all crust ingredients using pastry blender or fork until dough forms; gather into a ball. Press one-third of the dough evenly on bottom of pan. Place on cookie sheet. Bake 8 to 10 minutes or until light golden brown; cool 10 minutes.

2 Assemble bottom and side of pan; secure side. Press remaining dough 2 inches up side of pan. Wrap outside bottom and side of pan with foil to prevent leaking.

3 Increase oven temperature to 450°F. In large bowl, beat cream cheese, 1¾ cups sugar, 3 tablespoons flour, the orange peel, lemon peel and salt with electric mixer on medium speed about 1 minute or until smooth. On low speed, beat in eggs, egg yolks and ¼ cup of the whipping cream just until blended. Pour into crust.

4 Bake 15 minutes. Reduce oven temperature to 200°F. Bake 1 hour 25 minutes to 1 hour 40 minutes longer or until set at least 2 inches from edge of pan but center still jiggles slightly when moved and surface is golden brown (it will become firm during refrigeration). Do not insert knife into cheesecake because the hole may cause cheesecake to crack. Turn off oven; leave cheesecake in oven 30 minutes longer. Remove from oven and cool in pan on cooling rack away from drafts 30 minutes.

5 Without releasing side of pan, run knife around side of pan carefully to loosen cheesecake. Refrigerate uncovered about 3 hours or until chilled; cover and continue refrigerating at least 9 hours or overnight before serving.

6 Run knife around side of pan to loosen cheesecake again; remove side of pan. Leave cheesecake on pan bottom to serve. In chilled medium deep bowl, beat remaining ¾ cup whipping cream with electric mixer on low speed until mixture begins to thicken. Gradually increase speed to high and beat until stiff peaks form. Spread whipped cream over top of cheesecake. Sprinkle with almonds. Store covered in refrigerator. To cut cheesecake, use long, thin-bladed, non-serrated knife. Dip knife into hot water after each cut, cleaning it off with towel.

1 Serving: Calories 520; Total Fat 38g (Saturated Fat 22g; Trans Fat 1g); Cholesterol 215mg; Sodium 310mg; Total Carbohydrate 35g (Dietary Fiber 0g); Protein 9g **Exchanges:** 2½ Other Carbohydrate, 1 High-Fat Meat, 6 Fat **Carbohydrate Choices:** 2

LIGHTER DIRECTIONS For 19 grams of fat and 330 calories per serving, omit crust. Move oven rack to lowest position. Heat oven to 425°F. Lightly grease side only of 9-inch springform pan with shortening. Mix ¾ cup graham cracker crumbs, 2 tablespoons butter, melted, and 2 tablespoons sugar; press evenly in bottom of pan. Use reduced-fat cream cheese (Neufchâtel); increase flour to ¼ cup. Substitute 1¼ cups fat-free egg product for the 5 eggs. Omit ¼ cup whipping cream. Continue as directed in Steps 3 and 4. Omit ¾ cup whipping cream and almonds. Serve with fresh fruit if desired.

CHOCOLATE CHIP NEW YORK CHEESECAKE
Fold 1 cup miniature semisweet chocolate chips into cheese mixture before pouring into crust.

Using a Springform Pan

This 2-piece pan has a side band that unlatches and loosens, so it can be removed from the bottom. To re-attach the pieces, put the bottom inside the opened band; re-latch the buckle so the bottom connects to the side (in the small groove that's near the bottom edge).

Keys to Success

- **Soften cream cheese** to room temperature (to use the microwave, see page 31). If cold, filling will be lumpy.

- **Check doneness at minimum time.** Most cheesecakes are done when small area in center seems soft or jiggles slightly when pan is shaken. The hot cheesecake will continue to finish cooking as it cools. Don't insert knife—it may cause a crack to form.

- **Loosen cheesecake from side of pan.** Cheesecakes shrink while cooling, loosening it will allow it to shrink without pulling and will prevent large cracks from forming. After cooling 30 minutes, run a metal spatula or table knife between side of pan and cake to loosen (but don't release or remove side). Repeat again before releasing and removing side.

- **Refrigerate uncovered** at least 3 hours or until completely chilled before covering. This prevents condensation from dripping on top of cheesecake.

- **Refrigerate at least 9 hours** or overnight so cheesecake is completely set and firm. This allows for easier cutting and serving.

- **Freeze cheesecake up to 2 months.** Thaw in refrigerator before serving.

See how to make **New York cheesecake**: Visit bettycrocker.com/BCcookbook

New York Cheesecake

TURTLE CHEESECAKE

PREP 30 min TOTAL 4 hr 20 min • **12 servings**

- 1½ cups finely crushed vanilla wafer cookies (about 40 cookies)
- ¼ cup butter, melted
- 2 packages (8 oz each) cream cheese, softened
- ½ cup sugar
- 2 teaspoons vanilla
- 2 eggs
- ¼ cup hot fudge topping
- 1 cup caramel topping
- ½ cup coarsely chopped pecans, toasted (page 22), if desired

1 Heat oven to 350°F. In medium bowl, mix cookie crumbs and butter. Press crumb mixture firmly against bottom and side of 9-inch glass pie plate.

2 In large bowl, beat cream cheese, sugar, vanilla and eggs with electric mixer on low speed until smooth. Pour half of mixture into pie plate.

3 Add hot fudge topping to remaining cream cheese mixture in bowl; beat on low speed until smooth. Spoon over vanilla mixture in pie plate. Swirl mixtures slightly with tip of knife.

4 Bake 40 to 50 minutes or until center is set. Cool 1 hour. Refrigerate at least 2 hours until chilled. Serve with caramel topping and pecans. Store covered in refrigerator.

1 Serving: Calories 390; Total Fat 24g (Saturated Fat 12g; Trans Fat 1g); Cholesterol 85mg; Sodium 310mg; Total Carbohydrate 39g (Dietary Fiber 1g); Protein 6g **Exchanges:** 1½ Starch, 1 Other Carbohydrate, 4½ Fat **Carbohydrate Choices:** 2½

LAYERED PUMPKIN CHEESECAKE

PREP 40 min TOTAL 9 hr 35 min • **16 servings**

- 2 cups crushed gingersnap cookies (about 32 cookies)
- ¼ cup butter, melted
- 4 packages (8 oz each) cream cheese, softened
- 1½ cups sugar
- 4 eggs
- 1 cup canned pumpkin (not pumpkin pie mix)
- 1½ teaspoons ground ginger
- 1 teaspoon ground cinnamon
- ¼ teaspoon ground nutmeg

1 Heat oven to 300°F. Grease 9-inch springform pan with shortening or cooking spray. Wrap foil around pan to catch drips. In small bowl, mix cookie crumbs and butter. Press crumb mixture in bottom and 1 inch up side of pan. Bake 8 to 10 minutes or until set. Cool 5 minutes.

2 In large bowl, beat cream cheese with electric mixer on medium speed just until smooth and creamy; do not overbeat. On low speed, gradually beat in sugar. On low speed, beat in eggs, one at a time, just until blended. Spoon 3 cups of the cream cheese mixture into pan; spread evenly.

3 Stir pumpkin, ginger, cinnamon and nutmeg into remaining cream cheese mixture; mix with wire whisk until smooth. Spoon over mixture in pan.

4 Bake 1 hour 25 minutes to 1 hour 30 minutes or until edges are set but center of cheesecake still jiggles slightly when moved.

5 Turn oven off; open oven door at least 4 inches. Leave cheesecake in oven 30 minutes longer. Remove from oven; place on cooling rack. Without releasing side of pan, run knife around side of pan to loosen cheesecake. Cool in pan on cooling rack 30 minutes. Cover loosely; refrigerate at least 6 hours but no longer than 24 hours.

6 Run knife around side of pan to loosen cheesecake again; carefully remove side of pan. Place cheesecake on serving plate. Store covered in refrigerator.

Turtle Cheesecake

Tiramisu

1 Serving: Calories 390; Total Fat 26g (Saturated Fat 15g; Trans Fat 1g); Cholesterol 125mg; Sodium 290mg; Total Carbohydrate 34g (Dietary Fiber 0g); Protein 7g **Exchanges:** 2 Other Carbohydrate, 1 Medium-Fat Meat, 4½ Fat **Carbohydrate Choices:** 2

TIRAMISU

Mascarpone is a rich double or triple cream cheese that originated in the Lombardy region of Italy. It has a delicate, buttery flavor with just a hint of sweetness. Look for it in the cheese case in large supermarkets, specialty cheese shops or gourmet food stores.

PREP 35 min TOTAL 5 hr 35 min • **8 servings**

- 6 **egg yolks**
- ¾ **cup sugar**
- ⅔ **cup milk**
- 1 **lb mascarpone cheese or 2 packages (8 oz each) cream cheese, softened**
- 1¼ **cups whipping cream**
- ½ **teaspoon vanilla**
- ¼ **cup cold brewed espresso or very strong coffee**
- 2 **tablespoons rum***
- 2 **packages (3 oz each) ladyfingers (24 ladyfingers)****
- 1½ **teaspoons unsweetened baking cocoa**

1 In 2-quart saucepan, beat egg yolks and sugar with wire whisk until well mixed. Beat in milk. Heat to boiling over medium heat, stirring constantly; reduce heat to low. Boil and stir 1 minute; remove from heat. Pour into medium bowl; place plastic wrap directly onto surface of custard mixture. Refrigerate about 1 hour or until chilled.

2 Add cheese to custard mixture. Beat with electric mixer on medium speed until smooth; set aside. Wash and dry beaters from mixture. In chilled large, deep bowl, beat whipping cream and vanilla with electric mixer on low speed until mixture begins to thicken. Gradually increase speed to high and beat until stiff peaks form; set aside.

3 In small bowl, mix espresso and rum. Separate ladyfingers horizontally.

4 In ungreased 11x7-inch (2-quart) glass baking dish, arrange half of ladyfingers in single layer. Brush with espresso mixture (do not soak). Spread half of cheese mixture over ladyfingers; spread with half of whipped

Making Tiramisu

Separate ladyfingers horizontally; brush with espresso mixture.

Spread half of cheese mixture over ladyfingers; spread with half of whipped cream.

cream. Repeat layers with remaining ladyfingers, brushing with espresso mixture, cheese mixture and whipped cream. Sprinkle with cocoa. Refrigerate at least 4 hours to develop flavors but no longer than 24 hours. Store covered in refrigerator.

*⅛ teaspoon rum extract mixed with 2 tablespoons water can be substituted for the rum.

**2 packages (10.75 oz each) frozen (thawed) pound cake can be substituted for the ladyfingers. Place each pound cake on its side; carefully cut each lengthwise into 3 slices (to total 6 slices). Brush each slice with espresso mixture. Arrange 3 slices crosswise in baking dish. Spread half of cheese mixture over cake; spread with half of whipped cream. Repeat layers with remaining pound cake, cheese mixture and whipped cream.

1 Serving: Calories 540; Total Fat 38g (Saturated Fat 22g; Trans Fat 1.5g); Cholesterol 270mg; Sodium 260mg; Total Carbohydrate 39g (Dietary Fiber 0g); Protein 9g **Exchanges:** 2 Starch, ½ Other Carbohydrate, 7½ Fat **Carbohydrate Choices:** 2½

ENGLISH TRIFLE

PREP 30 min TOTAL 3 hr 50 min • **10 servings**

- ½ **cup sugar**
- 3 **tablespoons cornstarch**
- ¼ **teaspoon salt**
- 3 **cups milk**
- ½ **cup dry sherry or other dry white wine or white grape juice**
- 3 **egg yolks, beaten**
- 3 **tablespoons butter, softened**
- 1 **tablespoon vanilla**
- 2 **packages (3 oz each) ladyfingers (24 ladyfingers)***
- ½ **cup strawberry preserves**
- 1 **pint (2 cups) fresh strawberries, sliced, or 1 box (10 oz) frozen sliced strawberries, thawed, drained**
- 1 **cup whipping cream**
- 2 **tablespoons sugar**
- 2 **tablespoons slivered almonds, toasted (page 22)**

1 In 3-quart saucepan, mix ½ cup sugar, the cornstarch and salt. Gradually stir in milk and sherry. Heat to boiling over medium heat, stirring constantly. Boil and stir 1 minute.

2 Gradually stir at least half of the hot mixture into egg yolks, then stir back into hot mixture in saucepan. Boil and stir 1 minute; remove from heat. Stir in butter and vanilla. Press plastic wrap on surface of pudding to prevent tough layer from forming on top. Refrigerate about 3 hours or until chilled.

3 Split ladyfingers horizontally in half. Spread cut sides with preserves. In 2-quart serving bowl or trifle bowl, layer one-fourth of ladyfingers, cut sides up, half of strawberries and half of pudding; repeat layers. Arrange remaining ladyfingers around edge of bowl in upright position with cut sides toward center. (It may be necessary to gently ease ladyfingers down into pudding about 1 inch so they remain upright.) Cover; refrigerate.

4 In chilled large, deep bowl, beat whipping cream and 2 tablespoons sugar with electric mixer on low speed until mixture begins to thicken. Gradually increase speed to high and beat until stiff peaks form. Spread over dessert. Sprinkle with almonds. Cover; refrigerate until serving. Store covered in refrigerator.

*2 packages (10.75 oz each) frozen (thawed) pound cake can be substituted for the ladyfingers. Place each pound cake on its side; carefully cut each lengthwise into 3 slices (to total 6 slices). Cut each of the 6 slices into 4 slices (to total 24 slices). Spread one side of each slice with preserves and layer as directed.

1 Serving: Calories 360; Total Fat 16g (Saturated Fat 8g; Trans Fat 1g); Cholesterol 110mg; Sodium 180mg; Total Carbohydrate 46g (Dietary Fiber 1g); Protein 6g **Exchanges:** 2 Starch, 1 Other Carbohydrate, 3 Fat **Carbohydrate Choices:** 3

CREAM PUFFS

PREP 30 min TOTAL 2 hr 40 min • **12 cream puffs**

PUFFS

- ½ **cup butter, cut into pieces**
- 1 **cup water**
- 1 **cup all-purpose flour**
- 4 **eggs**

CREAM FILLING

- ⅓ **cup granulated sugar**
- 2 **tablespoons cornstarch**
- 2 **cups milk**
- 2 **egg yolks, slightly beaten**
- 2 **tablespoons butter, softened**
- 2 **teaspoons vanilla**
  Powdered sugar, if desired

1 Heat oven to 400°F. In 2-quart saucepan, heat ½ cup butter and the water over high heat stirring occasionally, until boiling rapidly. Stir in flour; reduce heat to low. With wooden spoon, beat vigorously over low heat about 1 minute or until mixture forms a ball; remove from heat.

2 Beat in 1 egg at a time, beating vigorously after each addition until mixture is smooth and glossy.* Onto ungreased cookie sheet, drop dough by slightly less than ¼ cupfuls in mounds about 3 inches apart.

3 Bake 35 to 40 minutes or until puffed and golden. Remove from cookie sheet to cooling rack; prick side of each puff with the tip of sharp knife to release steam. Cool away from drafts 30 minutes.

4 In 2-quart saucepan, stir granulated sugar and cornstarch until mixed. Gradually stir in milk with wire whisk. Cook over medium heat, stirring constantly, until mixture thickens and boils. Boil and stir 1 minute. Gradually stir at least half of the hot mixture into egg yolks, then stir back into hot mixture in saucepan. Boil and stir 1 minute; remove from heat. Stir in 2 tablespoons butter and the vanilla. Press plastic wrap on surface of filling to prevent a tough layer from forming on top. Refrigerate at least 1 hour or until cool.

5 Using sharp knife, cut off top third of each puff; reserve tops. Pull out any strands of soft dough from puffs. Just before serving, fill bottom of each puff with about 2 rounded tablespoons filling; replace tops. Sprinkle with powdered sugar. Store cream puffs covered in refrigerator.

*Or beat in eggs with electric mixer on medium speed. Beat 1 minute after adding each egg.

1 Cream Puff: Calories 210; Total Fat 13g (Saturated Fat 7g; Trans Fat 0g); Cholesterol 135mg; Sodium 140mg; Total Carbohydrate 17g (Dietary Fiber 0g); Protein 6g **Exchanges:** 1 Starch, ½ Medium-Fat Meat, 2 Fat **Carbohydrate Choices:** 1

ECLAIRS Shape eclairs as directed below. Fill each eclair with cream filling. Drizzle with Vanilla Glaze (page 156).

ICE CREAM PUFFS Omit cream filling and fill cream puffs with your favorite flavor of ice cream. Cover and freeze until serving. Serve with Hot Fudge Sauce (page 233) or Caramel Sauce (page 234).

PROFITEROLES Fill cream puffs with cream filling or ice cream. Drizzle with Chocolate Sauce (page 234).

WHIPPED-CREAM PUFFS Omit cream filling. Make Sweetened Whipped Cream (page 214), using 2 cups whipping cream and ¼ cup granulated or powdered sugar and a large deep bowl. Fill puffs with cream.

Making Cream Puffs and Eclairs

Beat vigorously with wooden spoon after adding the flour until mixture forms a ball.

To shape cream puffs, drop dough by slightly less than ¼ cupfuls in mounds about 3 inches apart.

To shape eclairs, shape each mound into finger shape, 4½ x 1½ inch with metal spatula.

Cut off top third of each cooked puff; pull out any strands of soft dough.

Profiteroles

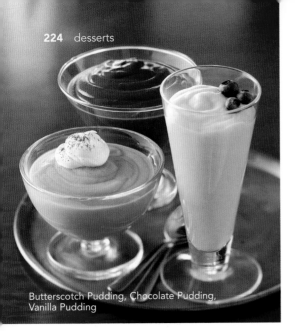

Butterscotch Pudding, Chocolate Pudding, Vanilla Pudding

VANILLA PUDDING

PREP 10 min TOTAL 1 hr 20 min • **4 servings**

⅓ cup sugar
2 tablespoons cornstarch
⅛ teaspoon salt
2 cups milk
2 egg yolks, slightly beaten
2 tablespoons butter, softened
2 teaspoons vanilla

1 In 2-quart saucepan, mix sugar, cornstarch and salt. Gradually stir in milk. Cook over medium heat, stirring constantly, until mixture thickens and boils. Boil and stir 1 minute.

2 Gradually stir at least half of hot mixture into egg yolks, then stir back into hot mixture in saucepan. Boil and stir 1 minute; remove from heat. Stir in butter and vanilla.

3 Pour pudding into 4 dessert dishes. Cover; refrigerate about 1 hour or until chilled. Store covered in refrigerator.

1 Serving: Calories 220; Total Fat 11g (Saturated Fat 5g; Trans Fat 0g); Cholesterol 130mg; Sodium 170mg; Total Carbohydrate 26g (Dietary Fiber 0g); Protein 5g **Exchanges:** 1½ Other Carbohydrate, 1 Low-Fat Milk, 2 Fat **Carbohydrate Choices: 2**

BUTTERSCOTCH PUDDING Substitute ⅔ cup packed dark or light brown sugar for the granulated sugar; decrease vanilla to 1 teaspoon.

CHOCOLATE PUDDING Increase sugar to ½ cup; stir ⅓ cup unsweetened baking cocoa into sugar mixture. Omit butter.

PANNA COTTA

If you don't want to unmold the ramekins, pour the custard into four parfait glasses instead, making sure to leave room at the top for the sauce.

PREP 10 min TOTAL 4 hr 20 min • **4 servings**

2 cups half-and-half
1½ teaspoons unflavored gelatin
¼ cup sugar
1 teaspoon vanilla
Dash salt
Raspberry Sauce (page 235), if desired

1 Pour half-and-half into 1½-quart saucepan. Sprinkle gelatin evenly over half-and-half. Let stand 10 minutes.

2 Heat mixture over medium-high heat 5 to 7 minutes, stirring constantly, until gelatin is dissolved and mixture is just beginning to simmer (do not boil). Remove from heat. Stir in sugar, vanilla and salt until sugar is dissolved.

3 Pour mixture into 4 (6-oz) ramekins or custard cups. Cover tightly with plastic wrap; refrigerate about 4 hours or until set.

4 When ready to serve, run thin knife around edge of each panna cotta. Dip bottom of each ramekin into bowl of very hot water for 5 seconds. Immediately place serving plate upside down onto each ramekin; turn plate and ramekin over and remove ramekin. Serve with raspberry sauce.

1 Serving: Calories 210; Total Fat 14g (Saturated Fat 9g; Trans Fat 0g); Cholesterol 45mg; Sodium 125mg; Total Carbohydrate 18g (Dietary Fiber 0g); Protein 4g **Exchanges:** 1 Other Carbohydrate, ½ High-Fat Meat, 2 Fat **Carbohydrate Choices: 1**

Panna Cotta

CRÈME BRÛLÉE

PREP 20 min TOTAL 7 hr • **4 servings**

- 2 **cups whipping cream**
- ⅓ **cup sugar**
- 1 **teaspoon vanilla**
- 6 **egg yolks, slightly beaten**
  Boiling water
- 8 **teaspoons sugar**

1 Heat oven to 350°F. In large bowl, stir whipping cream, ⅓ cup sugar and the vanilla until well mixed. Add egg yolks; beat with wire whisk until evenly colored and well blended.

2 In 13x9-inch pan, place 4 (6-oz) ceramic ramekins.* Pour cream mixture evenly into ramekins. Carefully place pan in oven. Pour enough boiling water into pan, being careful not to splash water into ramekins, until water covers two-thirds of the height of the ramekins.

3 Bake 30 to 40 minutes or until tops are light golden brown and sides are set (centers will be jiggly). Carefully transfer ramekins to cooling rack, using tongs or grasping tops of ramekins with pot holder. Cool 2 hours or until room temperature. Cover tightly with plastic wrap; refrigerate until chilled, at least 4 hours but no longer than 2 days.

4 Uncover ramekins; gently blot any condensation on custards with paper towel. Sprinkle 2 teaspoons sugar over each custard. Holding kitchen torch 3 to 4 inches from custard, caramelize sugar by heating with torch about 2 minutes, moving flame continuously over sugar in circular motion, until sugar is melted and light golden brown. (Or caramelize under broiler; see below.) Serve immediately, or refrigerate up to 8 hours before serving. If served immediately, custard will be softer.

BROILING DIRECTIONS Sprinkle 2 teaspoons brown sugar over each chilled custard. (Brown sugar melts more evenly under broiler.) Place ramekins in 15x10x1-inch pan or on cookie sheet with sides. Broil with tops 4 to 6 inches from heat 5 to 6 minutes or until sugar is melted and forms a glaze.

Do not use glass custard cups or glass pie plates; they cannot withstand the heat from the kitchen torch or broiler and may break.

1 Serving: Calories 540; Total Fat 45g (Saturated Fat 25g; Trans Fat 1g); Cholesterol 450mg; Sodium 50mg; Total Carbohydrate 29g (Dietary Fiber 0g); Protein 7g **Exchanges:** 2 Other Carbohydrate, 1 High-Fat Meat, 7½ Fat **Carbohydrate Choices:** 2

See how to caramelize crème brûlée: Visit bettycrocker.com/BCcookbook

Caramelizing Crème Brûlée

Gently blot any condensation on custards with paper towel.

Holding kitchen torch 3 to 4 inches from custard, caramelize sugar on each custard moving flame continuously over sugar in circular motion. The sugar is partially melted at this point.

Keep moving flame continuously over sugar in circular motion 1 to 2 minutes until sugar is melted and light golden brown.

Crème Brûlée

BAKED CUSTARD LOWER CALORIE

PREP 15 min TOTAL 1 hr 30 min • **6 servings**

- 3 **eggs, slightly beaten**
- ⅓ **cup sugar**
- 1 **teaspoon vanilla**
  Dash salt
- 2½ **cups very warm milk, or half-and-half (120°F to 130°F)**
  Ground nutmeg

1 Heat oven to 350°F. In medium bowl, beat eggs, sugar, vanilla and salt with wire whisk or fork. Gradually stir in milk.

2 Pour mixture into 6 (6-oz) ramekins or custard cups. Sprinkle with nutmeg. Place cups in 13x9-inch pan; place pan in oven. Carefully pour very hot water into pan to within ½ inch of tops of cups.

3 Bake about 45 minutes or until knife inserted halfway between center and edge comes out clean. Carefully transfer cups from water using tongs or grasping tops of cups with pot holder. Cool about 30 minutes. Serve warm or cool. If desired, unmold custard cups onto individual serving plates. Store covered in refrigerator.

1 Serving: Calories 130; Total Fat 5g (Saturated Fat 2g; Trans Fat 0g); Cholesterol 115mg; Sodium 120mg; Total Carbohydrate 16g (Dietary Fiber 0g); Protein 7g **Exchanges:** 1 Low-Fat Milk, 1 Fat **Carbohydrate Choices:** 1

CARAMEL CUSTARD (CRÈME CARAMEL)

Before making custard, in 1-quart saucepan, heat ½ cup sugar over low heat 10 to 15 minutes, stirring constantly with wooden spoon, until sugar is melted and golden brown (sugar becomes very hot and could melt a plastic spoon). Immediately divide syrup among 6 (6-oz) custard cups before it hardens in saucepan; carefully tilt cups to coat bottoms (syrup will be extremely hot). Let syrup harden in cups about 10 minutes. Make custard as directed in Step 1; pour over syrup in cups. Bake as directed in Steps 2 and 3. Cool completely. Cover; refrigerate until serving or up to 48 hours.

To unmold, carefully loosen side of custard with knife or small spatula. Place dessert dish on top of cup and, holding tightly, turn dish

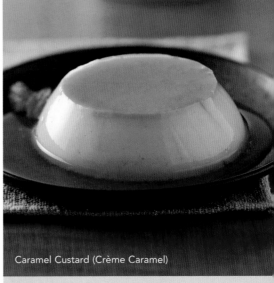

Caramel Custard (Crème Caramel)

Unmolding Custard

Run thin knife around edge of each baked custard; dip bottom of each cup into hot water for about 5 seconds.

Immediately place serving plate upside-down onto each cup; hold both cup and plate firmly. Turn cup upside down onto plate; remove ramekin.

and cup upside down. Shake cup gently to loosen custard. Caramel syrup will drizzle over custard, forming a sauce.

Water Bath Cooking

Why is custard or crème brûlée baked in a pan of water? The water bath method helps custard bake gently and evenly. Without the hot water, the edges of the custard cook too quickly. Put the custard cups in the empty pan, put the pan in the oven, then carefully pour hot water into the pan. When the custards are done, remove the cups from the water or they will keep cooking.

CHOCOLATE MOUSSE

What more can you say—chocolate and cream delivered in airy billows. Sublime, but for a special touch, garnish with fresh fruit or chocolate curls.

PREP 20 min **TOTAL** 2 hr 20 min • **8 servings**

- 4 **egg yolks**
- ¼ **cup sugar**
- 2½ **cups whipping cream**
- 8 **oz semisweet or dark baking chocolate, chopped**

1 In small bowl, beat egg yolks with electric mixer on high speed 3 minutes or until thick and lemon colored. Slowly beat in sugar.

2 In 2-quart saucepan, heat 1 cup of the whipping cream over medium heat just until hot. Gradually stir at least half of the hot cream into egg yolk mixture, then stir back into hot cream in saucepan. Cook over low heat about 5 minutes, stirring constantly, until mixture thickens (do not boil).

3 Stir in chocolate until melted. Cover; refrigerate 2 hours, stirring occasionally, until chilled.

4 In chilled large, deep bowl, beat remaining 1½ cups whipping cream with electric mixer on low speed until mixture begins to thicken. Gradually increase speed to high and beat until stiff peaks form. Fold chocolate mixture into whipped cream.

5 Pipe or spoon mixture into 8 dessert dishes or stemmed glasses. Refrigerate until serving. Store covered in refrigerator.

1 Serving: Calories 460; Total Fat 41g (Saturated Fat 24g; Trans Fat 0.5g); Cholesterol 190mg; Sodium 35mg; Total Carbohydrate 17g (Dietary Fiber 4g); Protein 6g **Exchanges:** ½ Starch, ½ Other Carbohydrate, ½ Medium-Fat Meat, 7½ Fat **Carbohydrate Choices:** 1

LIGHTER DIRECTIONS For 14 grams of fat and 255 calories per serving, substitute 2 whole eggs for the 4 egg yolks, half-and-half for 1 cup of the whipping cream and 3 cups frozen (thawed) fat-free whipped topping for the whipped 1½ cups whipping cream.

RICE PUDDING LOWER CALORIE

Leftover cooked rice can be used in this recipe. Use 1½ cups cooked rice and increase the bake time by about 5 minutes because the rice will be cold.

PREP 30 min **TOTAL** 1 hr 30 min • **8 servings**

- ½ **cup uncooked regular long-grain white rice**
- 1 **cup water**
- 2 **whole eggs or 4 egg yolks**
- ½ **cup sugar**
- ½ **cup raisins or chopped dried apricots**
- 2½ **cups milk**
- 1 **teaspoon vanilla**
- ¼ **teaspoon salt**
  Ground cinnamon or nutmeg
  Raspberry Sauce (page 235) if desired
  Sweetened Whipped Cream (page 214), if desired

1 In 1½-quart saucepan, heat rice and water to boiling, stirring once or twice; reduce heat to low. Cover; simmer 14 minutes (do not lift cover or stir). All water should be absorbed; if not, drain excess water.

2 Heat oven to 325°F. In ungreased 1½-quart casserole, beat eggs with wire whisk or fork. Stir in sugar, raisins, milk, vanilla, salt and hot rice. Sprinkle with cinnamon.

3 Bake uncovered 45 minutes, stirring every 15 minutes. Top of pudding will be very wet and not set (overbaking may cause pudding to curdle).

4 Stir well; let stand 15 minutes. Enough liquid will be absorbed while standing to make pudding creamy. Serve warm, or cover and refrigerate about 3 hours or until chilled. Serve with raspberry sauce and whipped cream. Store covered in refrigerator.

1 Serving: Calories 180; Total Fat 3g (Saturated Fat 1g; Trans Fat 0g); Cholesterol 60mg; Sodium 125mg; Total Carbohydrate 33g (Dietary Fiber 0g); Protein 5g **Exchanges:** 2 Starch, ½ Fat **Carbohydrate Choices:** 2

ALMOND-CHERRY RICE PUDDING

Substitute dried cherries for the raisins and ½ teaspoon almond extract for the 1 teaspoon vanilla. Omit raspberry sauce.

Heirloom Recipe and New Twist

Versions of bread pudding have appeared in every edition of Betty Crocker Cookbook since 1950, a mark of how timeless bread pudding is. In the new twist recipe, we've taken bread pudding to a new place, with flavors of cherry and chocolate. The croissants add flaky texture to the dessert. Be sure to try the variation from one of our Facebook fans included with the classic recipe.

CLASSIC

BREAD PUDDING WITH WHISKEY SAUCE

PREP 25 min **TOTAL** 2 hr 20 min • **12 servings**

BREAD PUDDING

   4 whole eggs
   1 egg yolk
 ¾ cup sugar
2½ cups milk
2½ cups whipping cream
   1 tablespoon vanilla
1½ teaspoons ground cinnamon
  12 oz French or other firm bread, cut into ½-inch slices, then cut into 1½-inch pieces (10 cups)
 ½ cup raisins, if desired
   2 tablespoons sugar
   2 tablespoons butter, melted

WHISKEY SAUCE

 ½ cup butter, cut into pieces
   2 tablespoons water
   1 egg
   1 cup sugar
   2 tablespoons whiskey or bourbon or 1 teaspoon brandy extract

1 Heat oven to 325°F. Grease bottom and sides of 13x9-inch (3-quart) glass baking dish with shortening or cooking spray.

2 In large bowl, beat 4 eggs, 1 egg yolk and ¾ cup sugar with wire whisk until well blended. Beat in milk, whipping cream, vanilla and 1 teaspoon of the cinnamon until well blended. Stir in 7 cups of the bread pieces and the raisins. Let stand 20 minutes. Pour into baking dish. Lightly press remaining 3 cups bread pieces on top of mixture.

3 In small bowl, stir 2 tablespoons sugar and remaining ½ teaspoon cinnamon until well blended. Brush top of bread mixture with melted 2 tablespoons butter; sprinkle with cinnamon-sugar. Bake uncovered 55 to 65 minutes or until top is puffed and light golden brown (center will jiggle slightly). Cool 30 minutes.

4 Meanwhile, in 1-quart saucepan, melt ½ cup butter over low heat; do not allow to simmer. Remove from heat; cool 10 minutes. Mix water and 1 egg in small bowl; stir into butter until blended. Stir in 1 cup sugar. Cook over medium-low heat, stirring constantly, until sugar is dissolved and mixture begins to boil; remove from heat. Stir in whiskey. Cool at least 10 minutes before serving.

5 Serve sauce over warm bread pudding. Store bread pudding and sauce covered in refrigerator.

1 Serving: Calories 500; Total Fat 30g (Saturated Fat 16g; Trans Fat 1.5g); Cholesterol 190mg; Sodium 300mg; Total Carbohydrate 50g (Dietary Fiber 0g); Protein 8g **Exchanges:** 2 Starch, 1½ Other Carbohydrate, 5½ Fat **Carbohydrate Choices:** 3

LIGHTER **DIRECTIONS** For 7 grams of fat and 300 calories per serving, substitute 4 cups fat-free (skim) milk and 1 cup half-and-half for the milk and whipping cream. Substitute 2 eggs and ½ cup fat-free egg product for the 4 eggs and 1 egg yolk. Instead of whiskey sauce, stir 1 tablespoon bourbon or 1 teaspoon brandy extract into 1 cup fat-free caramel topping; heat if desired.

BREAD PUDDING WITH LEMON CURD

Make bread pudding as directed, but omit whiskey sauce. Make Lemon Curd (page 492) or purchase lemon curd. Serve the lemon curd over warm bread pudding.

See how to make **bread pudding:** Visit bettycrocker.com/BCcookbook

Contributed by **Sandy Paxton Combs** from Sherman, Texas

CHOCOLATE-CHERRY CROISSANT BREAD PUDDING

PREP 25 min **TOTAL** 2 hr 20 min • **12 servings**

BREAD PUDDING

- 4 whole eggs
- 1 egg yolk
- ¾ cup sugar
- 2½ cups milk
- 2½ cups whipping cream
- 1 tablespoon vanilla
- 7 large (5½x4½ inches) croissants, cut into 1½-inch pieces (10 cups)
- 1 cup dark chocolate chips
- 2 tablespoons butter, melted
- 2 tablespoons sugar
- ½ cup dried cherries

CHERRY SAUCE

- ¼ cup sugar
- 1 tablespoon cornstarch
- ½ cup water
- 1 bag (16 oz) frozen dark sweet cherries
- ½ teaspoon vanilla

1 Heat oven to 325°F. Grease bottom and sides of 13x9-inch (3-quart) glass baking dish with shortening or cooking spray. In large bowl, beat 4 whole eggs, 1 egg yolk and ¾ cup sugar with wire whisk until well blended. Beat in milk, whipping cream and vanilla until well blended. Stir in 7 cups of the croissant pieces. Let stand 20 minutes. Pour into baking dish. Sprinkle with chocolate chips. Lightly press remaining 3 cups croissant pieces on top of mixture. Brush top of croissant pieces with butter; sprinkle with 2 tablespoons sugar. Sprinkle with dried cherries.

2 Bake uncovered 55 to 65 minutes or until top is light golden brown (center will jiggle slightly). Cool 30 minutes.

3 Meanwhile, in 2-quart saucepan, mix ¼ cup sugar, the cornstarch and water until blended. Stir in frozen cherries. Cook over medium-high heat, stirring constantly, until mixture boils and thickens. Boil and stir 1 minute. Remove from heat; stir in vanilla. Cool at least 10 minutes before serving.

4 Serve sauce over warm bread pudding. Store bread pudding and sauce covered in refrigerator.

1 Serving: Calories 600; Total Fat 37g (Saturated Fat 22g; Trans Fat 1g); Cholesterol 200mg; Sodium 120mg; Total Carbohydrate 57g (Dietary Fiber 2g); Protein 9g **Exchanges:** 1 Starch, ½ Fruit, 2 Other Carbohydrate, ½ Milk, 6½ Fat **Carbohydrate Choices:** 4

Bread Pudding with Whiskey Sauce

Chocolate-Cherry Croissant Bread Pudding

CHOCOLATE–SOUR CREAM FONDUE FAST

Dip, dunk or dredge goodies into this heavenly chocolate fondue. It's a divine dessert!

PREP 20 min **TOTAL** 20 min • **12 servings**

- 24 oz milk chocolate or semisweet chocolate chips, or sweet baking chocolate
- 1 cup sour cream
- ½ cup half-and-half
- 1 tablespoon instant coffee granules or crystals, or ½ teaspoon ground cinnamon
- 4 cups cut-up fresh fruit
- 4 cups cubed angel food cake or pound cake

1 In 2-quart saucepan, heat chocolate, sour cream, half-and-half and coffee granules over low heat, stirring constantly, until chocolate is melted and mixture is smooth; remove from heat.

2 Pour chocolate mixture into fondue or chafing dish to keep warm. Spear fruit and cake with fondue forks; dip and swirl in fondue with stirring motion. If mixture becomes too thick, stir in small amount of half-and-half.

1 Serving: Calories 410; Total Fat 22g (Saturated Fat 13g; Trans Fat 0g); Cholesterol 25mg; Sodium 180mg; Total Carbohydrate 48g (Dietary Fiber 3g); Protein 6g **Exchanges:** 1 Starch, 2 Other Carbohydrate, 4½ Fat **Carbohydrate Choices:** 3

VANILLA ICE CREAM

PREP 10 min **TOTAL** 2 hr 40 min • **1 quart**

- 3 egg yolks, slightly beaten
- ½ cup sugar
- 1 cup milk
- ¼ teaspoon salt
- 2 cups whipping cream
- 1 tablespoon vanilla

1 In 2-quart saucepan, stir egg yolks, sugar, milk and salt until well mixed. Cook over medium heat just until mixture comes to a boil, stirring constantly (do not allow mixture to continue to boil or it will curdle). Immediately remove from heat.

2 Pour milk mixture into chilled bowl. Refrigerate uncovered 2 to 3 hours, stirring occasionally, until room temperature. At this point, mixture can be refrigerated up to 24 hours before completing recipe if desired.

3 Stir whipping cream and vanilla into milk mixture. Pour into 1-quart ice-cream freezer and freeze according to manufacturer's directions.

1 Serving (½ Cup): Calories 270; Total Fat 21g (Saturated Fat 12g; Trans Fat 0.5g); Cholesterol 150mg; Sodium 110mg; Total Carbohydrate 16g (Dietary Fiber 0g); Protein 3g **Exchanges:** 1 Starch, 4 Fat **Carbohydrate Choices:** 1

CHOCOLATE ICE CREAM Increase sugar to 1 cup. Beat 2 oz unsweetened baking chocolate, melted and cooled, into milk mixture before cooling. Decrease vanilla to 1 teaspoon.

EGGNOG ICE CREAM Add 1 teaspoon rum extract with vanilla. Stir in ¼ teaspoon nutmeg with sugar.

FRESH BLUEBERRY ICE CREAM Decrease vanilla to 1 teaspoon. Mash 2 cups fresh blueberries and an additional ⅓ cup sugar with potato masher or process in food processor until slightly chunky (not pureed); stir into milk mixture after adding vanilla.

FRESH PEACH ICE CREAM Decrease vanilla to 1 teaspoon. Mash 4 or 5 fresh peeled peaches with potato masher or process in food processor until slightly chunky (not pureed) to make 2 cups; stir into milk mixture after adding vanilla.

FRESH RASPBERRY ICE CREAM Substitute ½ teaspoon almond extract for the vanilla. Mash 1 pint (2 cups) frest raspberries with potato masher or process in food processor until slightly chunky (not pureed); stir into milk mixture after adding almond extract.

FRESH STRAWBERRY ICE CREAM Decrease vanilla to 1 teaspoon. Mash 1 pint (2 cups) fresh strawberries and an additional ½ cup sugar with potato masher or process in food processor until slightly chunky (not pureed); stir into milk mixture after adding vanilla. Stir in a few drops of red food color if desired.

ICE CREAM GLAMOUR

Make any frozen dessert special with one of the following delicious ideas. Making your own ice cream and sauces is a great starting point, but if you are rushed, go ahead and use purchased ice cream and ready-made sauces instead.

1 Blueberry-Pomegranate Bonanza: Top Fresh Blueberry Ice Cream (at left) with scoops of fresh blueberries. Drizzle with bottled pomegranate juice; garnish with fresh pomegranate seeds.

2 Cake 'n Ice Cream: Make, bake and cool Pound Cake (page 145), or purchase frozen pound cake. Cut cake into 1-inch squares. Serve in dessert dishes with Chocolate Ice Cream (at left). Drizzle with Raspberry Sauce (page 235); garnish with fresh raspberries.

3 Caramel-Brownie Sundaes: Cut Chocolate Brownies (page 198) into small squares. Layer in dessert dishes with Caramel Ice Cream (page 232) and Chocolate Sauce (page 234).

4 Caramel-Pecan Topper: Drizzle Caramel Sauce (page 234) over Vanilla Ice Cream (at left). Sprinkle with pecan halves and chopped dark chocolate (from candy bars).

5 Fresh Berry Topper: In medium bowl, mix about 1 cup each fresh blueberries, raspberries and boysenberries. Sprinkle with 2 tablespoons orange juice; let stand about 1 hour, stirring gently occasionally. Serve over Vanilla Ice Cream (at left) or Lemonade Sorbet (page 232).

6 Melon Mania: Top Cantaloupe Granita (page 233) with cantaloupe, honeydew and watermelon balls. Drizzle with fresh lime juice; garnish with grated lime peel.

7 Peach and Granola Parfaits: Layer Fresh Peach Ice Cream (at left) with granola and thinly sliced peaches or nectarines in parfait or dessert dishes.

8 Peanuts and Ice Cream: Top Vanilla or Chocolate Ice Cream (at left) with coarsely chopped honey roasted peanuts. Add small scoops of peanut butter and Hot Fudge Sauce (page 233).

9 Strawberries 'n Cream Topper: Top Fresh Strawberry Ice Cream (at left), with sliced fresh strawberries and sliced bananas. Dollop with whipped cream.

CARAMEL ICE CREAM

PREP 15 min TOTAL 2 hr 40 min • **1 quart**

- ½ cup sugar
- 2 cups whipping cream
- 1 cup milk
- 3 egg yolks, slightly beaten
- ¼ teaspoon salt
- 2 teaspoons vanilla

1 In 2-quart saucepan, heat sugar over medium heat until sugar begins to melt. Stir until sugar is completely dissolved and becomes deep golden brown to amber in color. Remove from heat; gradually stir in 1 cup of the whipping cream (mixture will boil and splatter at first). Heat over low heat, stirring frequently, until any hardened sugar bits dissolve; remove from heat.

2 With whisk, stir in remaining 1 cup whipping cream, the milk, egg yolks, salt and vanilla until well mixed. Cook over medium heat just until mixture comes to a boil, stirring constantly (do not allow mixture to continue to boil or it will curdle). Immediately remove from heat.

3 Pour milk mixture into chilled bowl. Refrigerate uncovered 2 to 3 hours, stirring occasionally, until room temperature. At this point, mixture can be refrigerated up to 24 hours before completing recipe if desired.

4 Pour into 1-quart ice-cream freezer and freeze according to manufacturer's directions.

1 Serving (½ Cup): Calories 300; Total Fat 25g (Saturated Fat 15g; Trans Fat 1g); Cholesterol 160mg; Sodium 110mg; Total Carbohydrate 16g (Dietary Fiber 0g); Protein 3g **Exchanges:** 1 Other Carbohydrate, ½ Medium-Fat Meat, 4½ Fat **Carbohydrate Choices:** 1

Heat sugar in saucepan over medium heat until sugar begins to melt.

Stir until sugar is completely dissolved and is deep golden brown to amber colored.

Gradually stir in whipping cream.

Heat over low heat, stirring frequently, until hardened sugar bits dissolve.

LEMONADE SORBET LOWER CALORIE

PREP 10 min TOTAL 4 hr 10 min • **4 servings**

- 1½ cups cold water
- 1 cup frozen (thawed) lemonade concentrate (from 12-oz can)
- 3 tablespoons honey
  Lemon slices, if desired
  Blueberries, if desired

1 In blender or food processor, place water, lemonade concentrate and honey. Cover; blend on low speed about 30 seconds or until smooth. Pour into 8-inch square (2-quart) glass baking dish.

2 Freeze about 4 hours until firm, stirring several times to keep mixture smooth. Garnish with lemon slices and blueberries.

1 Serving: Calories 190; Total Fat 0g (Saturated Fat 0g; Trans Fat 0g); Cholesterol 0mg; Sodium 0mg; Total Carbohydrate 47g (Dietary Fiber 0g); Protein 0g **Exchanges:** 1 Fruit, 2 Other Carbohydrate **Carbohydrate Choices:** 3

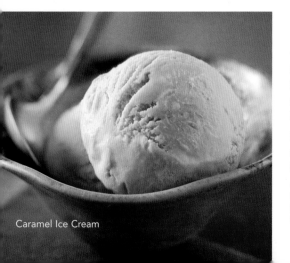

Caramel Ice Cream

Caramelizing Sugar for Ice Cream

CRANBERRY-RASPBERRY SORBET Substitute cranberry-raspberry concentrate for the lemonade concentrate.

LIMEADE SORBET Substitute limeade concentrate for the lemonade concentrate.

ORANGE SORBET Substitute orange juice concentrate for the lemonade concentrate.

PINEAPPLE SORBET Substitute pineapple juice concentrate for the lemonade concentrate.

CANTALOUPE GRANITA

LOWER CALORIE

Granita is the Italian term for an "ice" or frozen dessert made with fruit or fruit juice. Be sure to use ripe cantaloupe or honeydew for the best flavor.

PREP 15 min TOTAL 3 hr 15 min • **10 servings**

- 2 **cups cubed cantaloupe or honeydew melon**
- 2 **cups soymilk or milk**
- 3 **tablespoons honey**
- ¾ **teaspoon ground ginger**

1 Place all ingredients in blender or food processor. Cover; blend on high speed about 30 seconds or until smooth. Pour into 8- or 9-inch square (2-quart) glass baking dish.

2 Freeze 30 minutes. When ice crystals begin to form at edges of dish, stir mixture with fork. Freeze 2 hours 30 minutes to 3 hours longer, stirring every 30 minutes, until firm.

1 Serving (½ Cup): Calories 50; Total Fat 0.5g (Saturated Fat 0g; Trans Fat 0g); Cholesterol 0mg; Sodium 35mg; Total Carbohydrate 10g (Dietary Fiber 0g); Protein 2g **Exchanges:** 1 Other Carbohydrate **Carbohydrate Choices:** ½

GRANITA SLUSH Make recipe as directed; spoon into 10 serving glasses. Gently stir ¼ cup sparkling mineral water or ginger ale into each glass.

HOT FUDGE SAUCE

PREP 5 min TOTAL 40 min • **3 cups sauce**

- 1 **can (12 oz) evaporated milk**
- 1 **bag (12 oz) semisweet or dark chocolate chips (2 cups)**
- ½ **cup sugar**
- 1 **tablespoon butter, softened**
- 1 **teaspoon vanilla**

Cantaloupe Granita

Lemonade Sorbet

1 In 2-quart saucepan, heat milk, chocolate chips and sugar to boiling over medium heat, stirring constantly; remove from heat.

2 Stir in butter and vanilla until mixture is smooth and creamy. Cool about 30 minutes or until sauce begins to thicken. Serve warm. Store sauce covered in refrigerator up to 4 weeks. Sauce becomes firm when refrigerated; heat slightly before serving (sauce will become thin if overheated).

1 Tablespoon: Calories 60; Total Fat 2.5g (Saturated Fat 1.5g; Trans Fat 0g); Cholesterol 0mg; Sodium 10mg; Total Carbohydrate 7g (Dietary Fiber 0g); Protein 0g **Exchanges:** ½ Starch, ½ Fat **Carbohydrate Choices:** ½

CHOCOLATE SAUCE

FAST

PREP 15 min TOTAL 15 min • **1½ cups sauce**

1½ cups light corn syrup
3 oz unsweetened baking chocolate, chopped
1 tablespoon butter, softened
¾ teaspoon vanilla

1 In 1-quart saucepan, heat corn syrup and chocolate over low heat, stirring frequently, until chocolate is melted; remove from heat.

2 Stir in butter and vanilla. Serve warm or cool. Store covered in refrigerator up to 10 days. Reheat slightly before serving if desired.

1 Tablespoon: Calories 90; Total Fat 2.5g (Saturated Fat 1.5g; Trans Fat 0g); Cholesterol 0mg; Sodium 30mg; Total Carbohydrate 17g (Dietary Fiber 0g); Protein 0g **Exchanges:** 1 Other Carbohydrate, ½ Fat **Carbohydrate Choices:** 1

CARAMEL SAUCE

PREP 5 min TOTAL 45 min • **2½ cups sauce**

1 cup light corn syrup
1¼ cups packed brown sugar
¼ cup butter, cut into pieces
1 cup whipping cream

1 In 2-quart saucepan, heat corn syrup, brown sugar and butter to boiling over low heat, stirring constantly. Boil 5 minutes, stirring occasionally.

2 Stir in whipping cream; heat to boiling, stirring constantly. Cool about 30 minutes. Serve warm. Store covered in refrigerator up to 10 days. Reheat slightly before serving if desired.

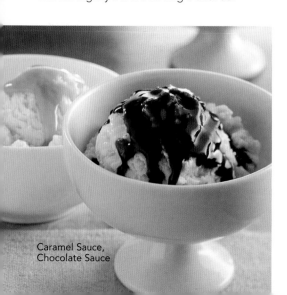

Caramel Sauce,
Chocolate Sauce

1 Tablespoon: Calories 80; Total Fat 3g (Saturated Fat 1.5g; Trans Fat 0g); Cholesterol 10mg; Sodium 20mg; Total Carbohydrate 13g (Dietary Fiber 0g); Protein 0g **Exchanges:** 1 Other Carbohydrate, ½ Fat **Carbohydrate Choices:** 1

BUTTERSCOTCH SAUCE

PREP 10 min TOTAL 35 min • **1¾ cups sauce**

½ cup granulated sugar
½ cup packed brown sugar
6 tablespoons butter, cut into pieces
½ cup whipping cream
½ cup light corn syrup
½ teaspoon salt
1 teaspoon vanilla

1 In 2-quart saucepan, stir all ingredients except vanilla. Cook over low heat, stirring constantly, until butter is melted and sugars are dissolved.

2 Increase heat to medium. Heat to boiling, stirring constantly. Boil gently 5 minutes, stirring occasionally; remove from heat. Cool 20 minutes.

3 Stir in vanilla. Serve warm or cool. Store covered in refrigerator up to 10 days. Sauce becomes firm when refrigerated; heat slightly before serving (sauce will become thin if overheated).

1 Tablespoon: Calories 80; Total Fat 4g (Saturated Fat 2g; Trans Fat 0g); Cholesterol 10mg; Sodium 70mg; Total Carbohydrate 12g (Dietary Fiber 0g); Protein 0g **Exchanges:** 1 Other Carbohydrate, ½ Fat **Carbohydrate Choices:** 1

ORANGE SAUCE

LOWER CALORIE

PREP 10 min TOTAL 25 min • **2⅓ cups sauce**

1 cup sugar
2 tablespoons cornstarch
1 tablespoon all-purpose flour
¼ teaspoon salt
1¼ cups orange juice
½ cup water
¼ cup lemon juice
1 tablespoon butter, softened
1 teaspoon grated orange peel
1 teaspoon grated lemon peel

1 In 1½-quart saucepan, mix sugar, cornstarch, flour and salt. Gradually stir in orange juice, water and lemon juice. Cook over medium heat, stirring constantly, until mixture thickens and boils (mixture will become translucent during cooking). Boil and stir 3 minutes; remove from heat.

2 Stir in remaining ingredients. Serve warm. Store covered in refrigerator up to 10 days.

1 Tablespoon: Calories 35; Total Fat 0g (Saturated Fat 0g; Trans Fat 0g); Cholesterol 0mg; Sodium 20mg; Total Carbohydrate 8g (Dietary Fiber 0g); Protein 0g **Exchanges:** ½ Fruit **Carbohydrate Choices:** ½

LEMON SAUCE FAST LOWER CALORIE

PREP 5 min TOTAL 15 min • **1¼ cups sauce**

- ½ cup sugar
- 2 tablespoons cornstarch
- ¾ cup water
- 1 tablespoon grated lemon peel
- ¼ cup lemon juice
- 2 tablespoons butter, softened

1 In 1-quart saucepan, mix sugar and cornstarch. Gradually stir in water. Cook over medium heat, stirring constantly, until mixture thickens and boils. Boil and stir 1 minute; remove from heat.

2 Stir in remaining ingredients. Serve warm or cool. Store covered in refrigerator up to 10 days.

1 Tablespoon: Calories 35; Total Fat 1g (Saturated Fat 0.5g; Trans Fat 0g); Cholesterol 0mg; Sodium 10mg; Total Carbohydrate 6g (Dietary Fiber 0g); Protein 0g **Exchanges:** ½ Fruit **Carbohydrate Choices:** ½

RASPBERRY SAUCE

FAST LOWER CALORIE

PREP 5 min TOTAL 10 min • **1 cup sauce**

- 3 tablespoons sugar
- 2 teaspoons cornstarch
- ⅓ cup water
- 1 box (10 oz) frozen raspberries in syrup, thawed, undrained

1 In 1-quart saucepan, mix sugar and cornstarch. Stir in water and raspberries with syrup. Cook over medium heat, stirring constantly, until mixture thickens and boils (mixture will become translucent during cooking). Boil and stir 1 minute.

Raspberry Sauce

Making Raspberry Sauce

Stir water and raspberries into sugar and cornstarch.

Cook, stirring constantly until mixture thickens and boils, and becomes translucent.

2 Strain sauce through strainer into bowl to remove seeds if desired. Serve warm or cool. Store covered in refrigerator up to 10 days.

1 Tablespoon: Calories 30; Total Fat 0g (Saturated Fat 0g; Trans Fat 0g); Cholesterol 0mg; Sodium 0mg; Total Carbohydrate 7g (Dietary Fiber 0g); Protein 0g **Exchanges:** ½ Fruit **Carbohydrate Choices:** ½

STRAWBERRY SAUCE Substitute frozen strawberries in syrup for the raspberries.

MERINGUE SHELL LOWER CALORIE

A meringue shell bakes up crisp yet melts in your mouth when you bite into it. Just before serving, fill with fresh fruit, ice cream, Chocolate Mousse (page 227), Lemon Curd (page 492) or Vanilla Pudding (page 224).

PREP 15 min **TOTAL** 4 hr 45 min • **8 servings**

- 3 **egg whites**
- ¼ **teaspoon cream of tartar**
- ¾ **cup sugar**

1 Heat oven to 275°F. Line cookie sheet with cooking parchment paper.

2 In medium bowl, beat egg whites and cream of tartar with electric mixer on high speed until foamy. Beat in sugar, 1 tablespoon at a time; continue beating until stiff peaks form and mixture is glossy. Do not underbeat. On cookie sheet, shape meringue into 9-inch circle with back of spoon, building up side.

3 Bake 1 hour 30 minutes. Turn off oven; leave meringue in oven with door closed 1 hour. Finish cooling at room temperature, about 2 hours.

1 Serving: Calories 80; Total Fat 0g (Saturated Fat 0g; Trans Fat 0g); Cholesterol 0mg; Sodium 20mg; Total Carbohydrate 19g (Dietary Fiber 0g); Protein 1g **Exchanges:** 1 Starch **Carbohydrate Choices:** 1

INDIVIDUAL MERINGUE SHELLS Drop meringue by ⅓ cupfuls onto paper-lined cookie sheet. Shape into circles, building up sides. Bake 1 hour. Turn off oven; leave meringues in oven with door closed 1 hour. Finish cooling at room temperature, about 2 hours. Makes 8 to 10 meringues.

CHOCOLATE MERINGUE SHELL After beating egg white mixture, sprinkle 2 tablespoons unsweetened baking cocoa through sieve over top. Fold cocoa into mixture. Bake as directed.

Meringue Shell Tips

- Bake a meringue shell until it's completely dry to prevent it from becoming soft.

- Cool meringue in the oven, with heat turned off, for as long as recipe suggests so they are dry and crisp.

- Store meringue tightly covered.

- Fill meringue just before serving to keep it crisp.

Shaping Indvidual Meringue Shells

Shape each meringue with back of spoon into desired shape, building up side.

Individual Meringue Shells filled with Lemon Curd (page 492)

DO IT YOURSELF

For bonus do it yourself recipes,
visit bettycrocker.com/BCcookbook

FAST = Ready in 20 minutes or less LOWER CALORIE = See Helpful Nutrition and Cooking Information, page 685
LIGHTER = 25% fewer calories or grams of fat MAKE AHEAD = Make-ahead directions SLOW COOKER = Slow cooker directions

← Peaches being prepared for freezing, Cranberry-Grape Jelly (page 246), Pickled Gingerroot (page 253), Brownie
Mix (page 255)

DO-IT-YOURSELF BASICS

Why make your own pickles, jelly or taco mix when you can easily get these at your grocery store? Homemade versions of these items make great, inexpensive yet thoughtful gifts, and when you use produce picked at the peak of ripeness and combine it with other fresh ingredients, the taste is incomparable. Also, the homemade versions don't have the preservatives that the store-bought varieties may contain, and because you are in control, any seasoning mix can be salt free or adjusted to your liking.

CHOOSING CONTAINERS

When making your own foods, it's important to think about the containers you want to store them in. Follow these general guidelines, then see individual recipes for specific requirements and sizes.

Freezer Jam: Choose plastic containers that are meant to go in the freezer or use glass preserving jars with no curves under the neck of the jar. Be sure to choose a size that will leave enough room for expansion.

Canned Jelly: Choose glass preserving jars (regular or wide mouth) with lids and bands.

Fruit Butter: Choose wide-mouthed glass preserving jars or plastic containers with tight-fitting lids.

Chutney: For chutney that will be frozen, choose plastic containers that are meant to go in the freezer or use glass preserving jars with no curves under the neck of the jar. Be sure to choose a size that will leave enough

room for expansion. For chutney that will be refrigerated only, choose wide-mouthed glass preserving jars or plastic containers with tight-fitting lids.

Pickle Slices: Choose glass preserving jars (regular or wide mouth) with lids and bands.

Whole Pickles: Choose wide-mouthed glass preserving jars with lids and bands.

Pickled Vegetables: Choose nonreactive covered containers.

Dried Vegetables: Choose tightly covered containers.

Seasoning Mixes: Choose small containers with tight-fitting lids.

Dessert Mixes: Choose food-safe glass jars with screw-on lids to show off the layers.

Beverage Mixes: Choose food-safe glass jars with screw-on lids to show off the layers or plastic containers with tight-fitting lids.

Great Reasons for Gifting Food

Naturally, homemade foods make great holiday gifts, but gifts of food are perfect for so many other reasons as well:

- As a thank you
- To cheer a sick friend
- To welcome a new neighbor
- As a hostess gift when attending a party
- As a birthday or anniversary gift

For freezer jam, choose plastic containers that are freezer safe.

CANNING AND PRESERVING BASICS

HOME CANNING

With rising grocery prices and the growing desire to know what is in food and where it comes from, home canning is making a comeback. Plus there's something satisfying about looking at a row of jellies, tomatoes or peaches that you've just "put up," or canned yourself, with produce from your garden or local farmers' market.

Home canning isn't hard, but you have to be careful so the food you preserve is safe from bacterial contamination. To destroy spoilage organisms such as molds, yeast and bacteria, food must be processed for a sufficient amount of time at a high enough temperature. The acidity of the food will determine which canning method you use.

A **pressure canner** is a large heavy pot with a rack for holding canning jars and has a tight-fitting lid with a vent petcock and a dial or weighted pressure gauge and safety fuse. This method must be used for low-acid foods, such as meat, poultry, seafood and vegetables.

A **boiling water canner** is a large kettle with a lid and rack to hold canning jars. This method

is recommended for all acidic foods, such as fruits, tomatoes with added acid, jams, jellies and pickled vegetables.

The open kettle method of canning, which uses no lid, is not recommended because temperatures never get hot enough to kill bacteria.

If you are unsure about the safety of certain home-canned foods, boiling the food for 10 minutes at altitudes below 1,000 feet will destroy these toxins. Boil an additional minute for every 1,000 feet of additional elevation.

FREEZING FOODS

There's a big movement sweeping not only the nation but many other countries as well to eat local food. Freezing is a simple, time-saving way to preserve in-season food. When foods are frozen at their peak of freshness, much of the nutrient value is left in the food, making it a great way to have fresh-tasting, nutritious food all year long. For both fruits and vegetables, use freezer plastic bags or clean plastic containers with tight-fitting lids. Produce will freeze faster and be easier to thaw

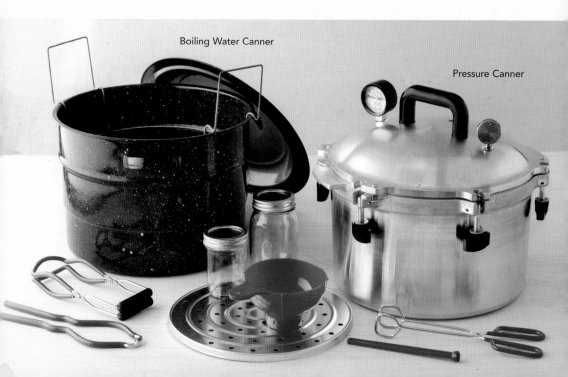

Boiling Water Canner

Pressure Canner

Stay Up to Date with Home Canning

For current information about safe home canning, check out these resources:

- National Center for Home Food Preservation:
  www.uga.edu/nchfp
  The University of Georgia
  208 Hoke Smith Annex
  Athens, GA 30602-4356
  FAX: 706-542-1979

- The USDA Complete Guide to Home Canning (Agriculture Information Bulletin 539)
  www.uga.edu/nchfp/publications/publications_usda.html
  Copies of this book can be ordered at https://mdc.itap.purdue.edu/item.asp?itemID=19265

- Local USDA Extension Service office listed in the phone book under "Government Offices"

Is It Still Good?

Before eating your home-canned foods (or commercially packaged foods), it's important to inspect them closely for any signs of spoilage. For commercially packaged foods, you can check for spoilage while at the store and again at home before using. If any of the signs are present, do not eat. Discard the food in such a way that children and pets won't accidentally eat it either. Look for these signs of spoilage:

- Lid is loose and is no longer vacuum sealed or lid swells.

- Gas bubbles are present inside jar.

- Liquid spurts out when container is opened.

- Mold, cloudiness, yeast growth or fermentation is present.

- Container is leaking.

- Disagreeable odor is present when container is opened.

if containers are not too large. Most fruits and vegetables can be frozen for up to 1 year.

Vegetables

Most vegetables benefit from blanching before freezing because it stops the enzyme actions, which can cause loss of flavor, color and texture. This process also retards the loss of vitamins, brightens the color and softens vegetables for easier packing.

Boiling water blanching is the preferred method. To do this, bring 1 gallon of water per pound of cleaned vegetables to a boil. Add the vegetables and let the water return to boiling.

Boil using the following guidelines:

- 2 minutes for green peas and turnips or parsnips (cubed)

- 3 minutes for asparagus (medium stalks), broccoli florets, Brussels sprouts (small), bell pepper halves, cauliflower florets, green or yellow wax beans and okra

- 5 minutes for asparagus (large stalks), Brussels sprouts (large), carrots (baby), edamame pods and corn on the cob (small to

medium ears)—cut kernels from cob after boiling and cooling. After boiling, immediately remove the vegetables from the water and plunge into cold water to cool quickly.

Fruits

To freeze fruits, sort, wash and drain fruits carefully. Prepare fruits as you would for serving, removing stems, coring, peeling and slicing as needed. Frozen fruit will retain much of the nutritional value but will be softer after freezing. Small whole fruits such as berries and cherries can be frozen individually, then placed in bags for use in salads and desserts.

Some fruits such as apples, peaches, nectarines and pears might need added acid to freeze well and keep their color. Ascorbic acid products are available for this. Be sure to follow the package directions carefully. Citric acid or lemon juice can also be used by placing ¼ teaspoon in a quart of cold water. Place sliced fruit in the mixture for 1 to 2 minutes. Drain and freeze in resealable food-storage plastic bags, or pack with sugar, water or fruit juice as directed in individual recipes.

EATING LOCAL

WHY BUY LOCAL?

There are many advantages to eating locally grown or produced food. Locally grown food can be more nutritious and flavorful because it's often fresher than most food in the supermarket, which may have traveled from other countries before it arrived in your store. Many times local food is grown without the chemicals that large-scale producers use.

Buying local connects the community to those who grew or produced the food; the local economy benefits because buying directly from family farmers helps them stay in business. It also has a smaller environmental impact because the food doesn't need to be transported as far.

FINDING LOCALLY GROWN PRODUCE

- **Farmers' Markets:** Small farms supply nearby farmers' markets as a way to get their fresh produce directly to consumers. You can find markets in many church and store parking lots. Or look for farmers' markets in your area at www.localharvest.org by typing in your zip code.

- **U-Picks:** These are farms that allow members of the community to come during harvest time and pick their own produce. Look for ads in local newspapers or search for u-picks also online.

- **Farm Stands:** Farms set up stands along the side of the road or in the parking lots of local merchants to sell fresh produce brought in daily from their farms.

- **Food Co-ops:** These are grocery stores, usually specializing in natural foods and often local and organic foods. They are set up as a cooperative owned and controlled by the members, although typically you don't have to be a member to shop at a co-op.

- **Community Supported Agriculture (CSA) Program:** CSAs are becoming more and more popular as a way to get the freshest produce directly from farmers. Consumers buy a "share" of a local farmer's produce in advance. Members then receive a weekly portion of the farmer's products throughout the growing season, typically June through November. CSAs not only link consumers directly with local farms for produce or other products, such as flowers, meat, eggs, bread or cheese, but they also help support the farm (as well as share in the risks related to a bad harvest). Consumers get the freshest foods available, which means great taste and more nutrients. They also develop a relationship with the farmer who grows their food and are often able to visit the farm so they know what farming practices are used for the food they will be eating. To learn more about CSAs, visit www.localharvest.org/csa.

- **Grocery Stores:** Often local stores will feature produce from local growers when it is in season.

Seasonality of Produce

Fresh produce eaten shortly after being picked has the best flavor and most nutrients. Buying locally grown produce ensures that it's as fresh as you can get. Plus, produce in season will taste the best and also will usually be the cheapest.

To learn about the peak seasons for produce grown in your area, see How to Shop at a Farmers' Market below, or click on your state on either of these web sites:

- www.fieldtoplate.com/guide.php
- localfoods.about.com/od/searchbystate/State_Seasonal_Produce_Guides.htm

How to Shop at a Farmers' Market

Here's all you need to know to get the most from your farmers' market experience:

- **Buy in bulk for a discount.** Consider polling your neighbors before you go to see if there's an item that many would want—maybe several neighbors would like fresh corn. If you buy in bulk, you can typically get a discount off the price.

- **Bring a large reusable bag.** Use it to place all your purchases in while you shop, and if it has a shoulder strap, it will leave your hands free.

- **Bring a cooler and ice for hot days.** If it's a hot day and you are a long way from home, have a cooler with ice in the car to store the produce in so it will stay fresh during the ride.

- **Bring cash.** Having the right change makes your transactions quicker and easier.

- **Plan your arrival time depending on what you want.** For the freshest produce and best selection, go early. For the best deals and lowest prices on what's left, go at the end.

- **Know what's in season.** See Seasonality of Produce, above. Peak-season produce will not only taste the best but also may be less expensive than at other times of the year, helping to keep your food budget in check.

- **Walk around first before buying.** Survey the market first to get an idea of what is available and to see if one farmer's prices are better than another's.

- **Ask questions and meet the growers.** You can find out about how their products were grown and many times get free samples to try before you buy.

- **Find out what will be sold in weeks to come.** Ask what growers will be selling in the upcoming weeks so you can be prepared to stock up on those foods, taking advantage of lower prices.

- **Buy items other than produce.** Many markets offer items you might not realize would be available at a farmers' market—from fresh bouquets of flowers and gift items, such as honeys, jams, sauces and seasonings, to handmade selections such as dolls and blankets, or even vegetables, herbs and flowers you can plant and grow at home.

- **Eat and enjoy.** Many markets offer food choices that are ready to eat. You can enjoy breakfast or lunch as you stroll past the vendors.

- **Ask questions.** Not everything at a farmers' market is necessarily locally grown. If you're unsure whether or not an item is locally grown, just ask.

Heirloom Recipe and New Twist

Freezer jams have become very popular not only because of their fresh, just-picked flavor but also because they are easy to make. Strawberry Freezer Jam is a favorite for us and was first printed in the 1995 edition of this cookbook. Triple Berry–Pomegranate Freezer Jam is a wonderful, unique flavor combination sure to get rave reviews, so be sure to try it next time you have a bounty of fresh berries on hand.

CLASSIC

STRAWBERRY FREEZER JAM

LOWER CALORIE

PREP 20 min **TOTAL** 24 hr 30 min • **5 half-pints jam**

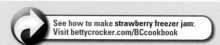

See how to make **strawberry freezer jam:**
Visit bettycrocker.com/BCcookbook

- 1 **quart (4 cups) strawberries, cut in half**
- 4 **cups sugar**
- ¾ **cup water**
- 1 **package (1¾ oz) powdered fruit pectin**

1 In large bowl, mash strawberries with potato masher, or process in food processor until slightly chunky (not pureed) to make 2 cups crushed strawberries. Stir sugar into strawberries in large bowl; mix well. Let stand at room temperature 10 minutes, stirring occasionally.

2 In 1-quart saucepan, mix water and pectin until pectin is dissolved. Heat to boiling, stirring constantly. Boil and stir 1 minute. Pour hot pectin mixture over strawberry mixture; stir constantly until sugar is completely dissolved, about 3 minutes.

3 Immediately pour mixture into hot, sterilized jars or freezer containers, leaving ½ inch at top for expansion during freezing; cover. Let stand at room temperature about 24 hours or until set.

4 Store in freezer up to 12 months or in refrigerator up to 3 weeks. Thaw frozen jam in refrigerator and stir before serving.

1 Tablespoon: Calories 45; Total Fat 0g (Saturated Fat 0g; Trans Fat 0g); Cholesterol 0mg; Sodium 0mg; Total Carbohydrate 11g (Dietary Fiber 0g); Protein 0g **Exchanges:** ½ Other Carbohydrate **Carbohydrate Choices:** 1

BLUEBERRY FREEZER JAM Substitute 2 pints (4 cups) blueberries, crushed (2½ cups crushed) for the strawberries. Decrease sugar to 3 cups. Add 1 teaspoon grated lemon or orange peel if desired. Decrease water to ½ cup.

RASPBERRY FREEZER JAM Substitute 3 pints (6 cups) raspberries, crushed (3 cups crushed) for the strawberries. Increase sugar to 5¼ cups.

Strawberry Freezer Jam

Triple Berry–Pomegranate Freezer Jam

Apple-Pepper Jelly

NEW TWIST

TRIPLE BERRY–POMEGRANATE FREEZER JAM LOWER CALORIE

PREP 25 min **TOTAL** 24 hr 35 min • **6 half-pints jam**

- 1 pint (2 cups) strawberries, cut in half
- 1 pint (2 cups) raspberries
- ½ pint (1 cup) blueberries
- 4¼ cups sugar
- ¾ cup pomegranate juice
- 1 package (1¾ oz) powdered fruit pectin

1 In large bowl, mash berries with potato masher, or process in food processor until slightly chunky (not pureed) to make 2½ cups crushed berries. Stir sugar into berries in large bowl; mix well. Let stand at room temperature 10 minutes, stirring occasionally.

2 In 1-quart saucepan, mix juice and pectin. Heat to boiling, stirring constantly. Boil and stir 1 minute. Pour hot pectin mixture over berry mixture; stir constantly until sugar is completely dissolved, about 3 minutes.

3 Immediately pour mixture into hot, sterilized jars or freezer containers, leaving ½ inch at top for expansion during freezing; cover. Let stand at room temperature about 24 hours or until set.

4 Store in freezer up to 12 months or in refrigerator up to 3 weeks. Thaw frozen jam in refrigerator and stir before serving.

1 Tablespoon: Calories 40; Total Fat 0g (Saturated Fat 0g; Trans Fat 0g); Cholesterol 0mg; Sodium 0mg; Total Carbohydrate 10g (Dietary Fiber 0g); Protein 0g **Exchanges:** ½ Other Carbohydrate **Carbohydrate Choices:** ½

Dissolving Pectin

In saucepan, mix water and pectin until pectin is dissolved. Heat to boiling, stirring constantly.

Pour hot pectin mixture over strawberry mixture; stir constantly until sugar is completely dissolved.

APPLE-PEPPER JELLY LOWER CALORIE

PREP 20 min **TOTAL** 24 hr 20 min • **4 half-pints jelly**

- 2 cups water
- 1 can (6 oz) frozen apple juice concentrate, thawed
- 1 package (1¾ oz) powdered fruit pectin
- 3¾ cups sugar
  Few drops red food color, if desired
- 1 to 2 tablespoons crushed red pepper flakes

1 In 3-quart saucepan, mix water, apple juice concentrate and pectin until pectin is dissolved. Heat to boiling, stirring constantly. Stir in sugar. Heat to rolling boil, stirring constantly; remove from heat. Stir in food color. Quickly skim off foam. Stir in pepper flakes.

2 Immediately pour into hot, sterilized jars or freezer containers, leaving ½ inch at top for expansion during freezing; cover. Let stand at room temperature about 24 hours or until set. Store covered in refrigerator up to 1 month or in freezer up to 2 months. Thaw jelly in refrigerator before serving.

1 Tablespoon: Calories 50; Total Fat 0g (Saturated Fat 0g; Trans Fat 0g); Cholesterol 0mg; Sodium 0mg; Total Carbohydrate 14g (Dietary Fiber 0g); Protein 0g **Exchanges:** 1 Other Carbohydrate **Carbohydrate Choices:** 1

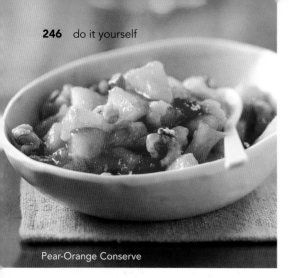

Pear-Orange Conserve

PEAR-ORANGE CONSERVE

LOWER CALORIE

Usually served as a spread for toast, biscuits, scones and bread, conserves differ from single-fruit preserves in that they have two or more fruits and some type of nut. The orange flavor of this conserve makes it a perfect match for grilled meats or even holiday turkey or ham.

PREP 20 min **TOTAL** 4 hr 20 min • **4 cups conserve**

- 5 **medium pears, cored and diced (6 cups)**
- 1 **medium seedless orange, unpeeled, chopped**
- 1½ **cups sugar**
- ½ **cup chopped well-drained maraschino cherries or dried cherries**
- ½ **cup chopped walnuts or slivered almonds**

1 In 2-quart saucepan, mix pears, orange and sugar. Heat to boiling, stirring frequently. Reduce heat to low, cook 15 minutes, stirring occasionally. Add cherries and walnuts; cook 5 to 10 minutes, stirring occasionally.

2 Spoon into glass or plastic containers. Cover and store in refrigerator up to 3 weeks.

1 Tablespoon: Calories 40; Total Fat 0.5g (Saturated Fat 0g; Trans Fat 0g); Cholesterol 0mg; Sodium 0mg; Total Carbohydrate 8g (Dietary Fiber 0g); Protein 0g **Exchanges:** ½ Other Carbohydrate **Carbohydrate Choices:** ½

SLOW COOKER DIRECTIONS Mix pears, orange and sugar in 2- to 3½-quart slow cooker. Cover and cook on High heat setting 2 hours. Stir mixture. Cook uncovered on High heat setting 1½ to 2 hours or until very thick. Stir in cherries and walnuts. Cool about 2 hours. Spoon conserve into glass or plastic container. Cover and store in refrigerator up to 3 weeks.

CRANBERRY-GRAPE JELLY

LOWER CALORIE

This pretty jelly can be made any time of the year with readily available fruit juices. It's delicious on toast or paired with peanut butter in a sandwich.

PREP 30 min **TOTAL** 1 hr 10 min • **5 half-pints jelly**

- 5 **(½ pint) glass preserving jars with lids and bands**
- 2 **cups cranberry juice cocktail**
- ¾ **cup grape juice**
- 1 **package (1¾ oz) powdered fruit pectin**
- ½ **teaspoon butter, if desired**
- 3¼ **cups sugar**

1 Fill boiling water canner half full with water; heat until water is simmering. Wash jars as directed in Preparing Jars for Canning (page 251).

2 In 3-quart saucepan, mix cranberry juice cocktail, grape juice, pectin and butter (which helps to reduce foaming) until blended. Heat to boiling over high heat, stirring constantly. Stir in sugar all at once. Return to boiling, stirring constantly. Boil and stir 1 minute; remove from heat.

3 Quickly skim off foam. Immediately pour into jars, leaving ¼-inch headspace. Drain flat lids well. Wipe rims and threads of jars. Place flat lids on jars and screw bands on tightly to seal. Place jars on elevated rack in canner; lower rack into canner. To process jelly safely, water must cover jars by 1 to 2 inches; add additional boiling water if necessary. Cover. Heat to boiling; continue boiling 10 minutes.

4 Carefully remove jars with canning jar lifter or heavy-duty tongs and place upright on towel. Cool completely. After 24 hours, check seal on cooled jars by pressing middles of lids with finger. If the lids spring back, jars are not sealed and must be stored in the refrigerator. Store completely sealed, unopened jars in a cool, dry place up to 1 year. Once opened, store in refrigerator up to 3 weeks.

1 Tablespoon: Calories 20; Total Fat 0g (Saturated Fat 0g; Trans Fat 0g); Cholesterol 0mg; Sodium 0mg; Total Carbohydrate 5g (Dietary Fiber 0g); Protein 0g **Exchanges:** Free **Carbohydrate Choices:** ½

APPLE BUTTER LOWER CALORIE

PREP 30 min TOTAL 4 hr 30 min • **4 cups apple butter**

   12 medium Granny Smith or other cooking apples (4 lb), peeled, cut into quarters
  1½ cups packed brown sugar
    1 tablespoon ground cinnamon
    1 teaspoon ground allspice
    1 teaspoon ground nutmeg
    ½ teaspoon ground cloves
  1¼ cups apple juice
    1 tablespoon lemon juice

1 In 4-quart Dutch oven or saucepan, mix all ingredients. Heat to boiling, stirring occasionally; reduce heat. Cover; simmer 1 hour.

2 Mash apples with potato masher or large fork. Simmer uncovered about 1 hour longer, stirring occasionally, until mixture is very thick. Cool about 2 hours.

3 Spoon into glass or plastic containers. Cover and store in refrigerator up to 3 weeks.

1 Tablespoon: Calories 40; Total Fat 0g (Saturated Fat 0g; Trans Fat 0g); Cholesterol 0mg; Sodium 0mg; Total Carbohydrate 9g (Dietary Fiber 0g); Protein 0g **Exchanges:** ½ Fruit **Carbohydrate Choices:** ½

SLOW COOKER DIRECTIONS Decrease apple juice to ½ cup. Spray 5- to 6-quart slow cooker with cooking spray. In slow cooker, mix all ingredients. Cover; cook on Low heat setting 8 to 10 hours or until apples are very tender. Mash apples with potato masher or large fork. Cook uncovered on Low heat setting 1 to 2 hours longer, stirring occasionally, until very thick.

SPICED APRICOT-GINGER PRESERVES FAST LOWER CALORIE

PREP 10 min TOTAL 10 min • **1 cup preserves**

    1 cup apricot or peach preserves
    1 tablespoon finely chopped crystallized ginger
    1 tablespoon orange-flavored liqueur or orange juice
    ¼ teaspoon ground nutmeg

1 In 1-quart saucepan, mix all ingredients. Heat to boiling; boil 1 minute, stirring frequently.

2 Spoon into glass or plastic container. Cover and store in refrigerator up to 2 months.

1 Tablespoon: Calories 60; Total Fat 0g (Saturated Fat 0g; Trans Fat 0g); Cholesterol 0mg; Sodium 5mg; Total Carbohydrate 15g (Dietary Fiber 0g); Protein 0g **Exchanges:** 1 Other Carbohydrate **Carbohydrate Choices:** 1

Apple Butter

Spiced Apricot-Ginger Preserves

APPLE-CRANBERRY CHUTNEY

Serve the chutney with roast turkey, ham or pork. Or for a quick appetizer, spoon chutney over a block of cream cheese and serve with crackers.

PREP 15 min TOTAL 3 hr • **2 cups chutney**

- 2 medium cooking apples, chopped (2 cups)
- 2 cups fresh or frozen cranberries
- 1 medium red bell pepper, chopped (1 cup)
- 1 small onion, finely chopped (⅓ cup)
- ¾ cup packed brown sugar
- ½ cup golden raisins, dried cranberries or dried cherries
- ½ cup white vinegar
- 1½ teaspoons finely chopped gingerroot
- 1 clove garlic, finely chopped

1 In 2-quart saucepan, mix all ingredients. Heat to boiling, stirring occasionally; reduce heat. Cover; simmer 30 minutes.

2 Uncover; simmer about 15 minutes longer, stirring occasionally, until mixture has thickened and fruit is tender. Cool about 2 hours.

3 Spoon into glass or plastic container. Cover and store in refrigerator up to 2 weeks or in freezer up to 2 months.

¼ Cup: Calories 150; Total Fat 0g (Saturated Fat 0g; Trans Fat 0g); Cholesterol 0mg; Sodium 10mg; Total Carbohydrate 36g (Dietary Fiber 2g); Protein 0g **Exchanges:** 1 Fruit, 1½ Other Carbohydrate **Carbohydrate Choices:** 2½

Crunchy Veggie Relish

CRUNCHY VEGGIE RELISH

LOWER CALORIE

PREP 20 min TOTAL 24 hr 20 min • **6 cups relish**

- 6 cups finely chopped green cabbage
- 2 medium cucumbers, peeled, shredded (3 cups)
- 1 medium red bell pepper, chopped (1 cup)
- 1 cup sugar
- 1½ teaspoons salt
- 1 teaspoon mustard seed
- ½ teaspoon celery seed
- ½ cup white or cider vinegar

In large bowl, mix all ingredients. Spoon into 1-quart and 1-pint jars or plastic containers. Cover; refrigerate at least 24 hours before serving. Store covered in refrigerator up to 2 weeks.

¼ Cup: Calories 45; Total Fat 0g (Saturated Fat 0g; Trans Fat 0g); Cholesterol 0mg; Sodium 150mg; Total Carbohydrate 10g (Dietary Fiber 0g); Protein 0g **Exchanges:** ½ Other Carbohydrate, 1 Vegetable **Carbohydrate Choices:** ½

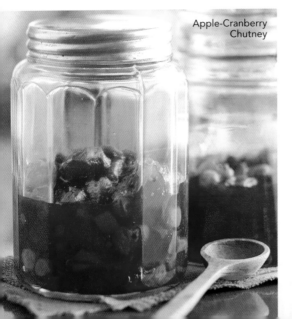
Apple-Cranberry Chutney

Spooning Relish into Jars

Spoon into containers and cover.

See how to make **chutney:** Visit bettycrocker.com/BCcookbook

CORN RELISH LOWER CALORIE

Try this relish on hot dogs, brats and burgers, or spoon it on grilled chicken or pork. Black or brown mustard seed can be used instead of the more readily available yellow mustard seed.

PREP 15 min TOTAL 4 hr 15 min • **2 cups relish**

- 2 cups frozen whole kernel corn or 1 can (15.25 oz) whole kernel corn, drained
- 2 tablespoons chopped green bell pepper
- 1 tablespoon finely chopped onion
- 1 jar (2 oz) diced pimientos, drained
- ½ cup sugar
- ½ teaspoon celery seed
- ¼ teaspoon salt
- ¼ teaspoon mustard seed
- ½ cup cider or white vinegar
- ¼ teaspoon red pepper sauce

1 If using frozen corn, cook and drain as directed on package. In medium heatproof glass or plastic bowl, mix corn, bell pepper, onion and pimientos.

2 In 1-quart saucepan, heat remaining ingredients to boiling, stirring occasionally. Boil 2 minutes. Pour over corn mixture; stir.

3 Spoon into glass or plastic containers. Cover; refrigerate at least 4 hours before serving. Store covered in refrigerator up to 5 days.

2 Tablespoons: Calories 45; Total Fat 0g (Saturated Fat 0g; Trans Fat 0g); Cholesterol 0mg; Sodium 40mg; Total Carbohydrate 11g (Dietary Fiber 0g); Protein 0g **Exchanges:** 2 Vegetable **Carbohydrate Choices:** 1

EASY REFRIGERATOR PICKLES

LOWER CALORIE

When choosing cucumbers for pickles, pick out the smaller ones, and pickle them soon after buying or harvesting.

PREP 10 min TOTAL 24 hr 10 min • **6 cups pickles**

- 6 cups thinly sliced unpeeled unwaxed cucumbers
- 2 small onions, sliced
- 1 medium carrot, thinly sliced (½ cup)
- 1¾ cups sugar
- 2 tablespoons salt
- 1 tablespoon chopped fresh or 1 teaspoon dried dill weed
- 1 cup white or cider vinegar

1 In 2½- or 3-quart glass container, layer cucumbers, onions and carrot.

2 In medium bowl, stir remaining ingredients until sugar is dissolved; pour over vegetables.

3 Spoon into glass or plastic containers. Cover; refrigerate at least 24 hours before serving. Store covered in refrigerator up to 2 weeks.

¼ Cup: Calories 70; Total Fat 0g (Saturated Fat 0g; Trans Fat 0g); Cholesterol 0mg; Sodium 590mg; Total Carbohydrate 16g (Dietary Fiber 0g); Protein 0g **Exchanges:** 1 Other Carbohydrate **Carbohydrate Choices:** 1

EASY BELL PEPPER–GARLIC REFRIGERATOR PICKLES Cut 1 small red bell pepper into thin strips; layer with cucumbers, onions and carrot in container. Add 1 whole clove of garlic, peeled, with remaining ingredients.

Corn Relish

Easy Refrigerator Pickles

Learn to Make **Pickles**

BREAD AND BUTTER PICKLES LOWER CALORIE

It's rewarding to take a jar of pickles out of your pantry, months after the cucumbers were picked, knowing how delicious they will be. Great homemade pickles are simpler to make than you think. Follow our recipe and tips to learn how to process pickles correctly to make a delicious homemade treat.

PREP 4 hr 20 min **TOTAL** 1 wk 5 hr • **6 quarts pickles**

- 5 **quarts (20 cups) thinly sliced unpeeled unwaxed medium cucumbers**
- 6 **medium onions, thinly sliced**
- 3 **cloves garlic, peeled**
- ⅓ **cup pickling or canning salt**
  Ice cubes
- 6 **(1 quart) glass preserving jars with lids and bands**

- 4½ **cups sugar**
- 2 **cups white vinegar**
- 2 **tablespoons mustard seed**
- 1 **tablespoon coriander seed**
- 1½ **teaspoons ground turmeric**

1 In large nonreactive container, mix cucumbers, onions and garlic. Sprinkle with pickling salt and cover with layer of ice cubes; mix lightly. Let stand 3 hours.

2 Meanwhile, fill boiling water canner half full with water; heat until water is simmering. Wash jars as directed in Preparing Jars for Canning, at right.

3 Drain cucumber mixture well; discard garlic. Pack cucumber and onion slices loosely into jars. In 3-quart saucepan, mix sugar, vinegar, seeds and turmeric. Heat to boiling. Fill jars with vinegar mixture, leaving ½-inch headspace.

4 Drain flat lids well. Wipe rims and threads of jars. Place flat lids on jars and screw bands on tightly to seal. Place jars on elevated rack

in canner; lower rack into canner. To process pickles safely, water must cover jars by 1 to 2 inches; add additional boiling water if necessary. Cover. Heat to boiling; continue boiling 10 minutes.

5 Carefully remove jars with canning jar lifter or heavy-duty tongs and place upright on towel. Cool completely. After 24 hours, check

seal on cooled jars by pressing middles of lids with finger. If the lids spring back, jars are not sealed and must be stored in the refrigerator. Store completely sealed unopened jars in a cool, dry place up to 1 year (let stand at least 1 week to blend flavors before serving). Once opened, store in refrigerator up to 3 weeks.

1 Serving (½ Cup): Calories 50; Total Fat 0g (Saturated Fat 0g; Trans Fat 0g); Cholesterol 0mg; Sodium 300mg; Total Carbohydrate 11g (Dietary Fiber 1g); Protein 0g **Exchanges:** ½ Other Carbohydrate, ½ Vegetable **Carbohydrate Choices:** 1

See how to make **bread and butter pickles**: Visit bettycrocker.com/BCcookbook

Other Uses for Pickles

Here are some great ways to include pickles in your everyday menu:

- Add pickles to sandwiches, green salads and pasta salads.

- Finely chop into a relish to use on hamburgers or hot dogs.

- Add to your vegetable or antipasto platters.

- Eat pickles as a low-calorie snack. They can suppress your appetite until the next meal.

- Use to make Tartar Sauce, page 483, for use on fish, salmon burgers and salmon or crab cakes—or even French fries!

Preparing Jars for Canning

Wash preserving jars and screw bands with hot soapy water; rinse well with warm water. Place flat lids in 2-quart saucepan on unheated burner or other heatproof surface; pour boiling water over lids. Let stand in hot water until ready to use.

Keys to Success

- **Use a nonreactive container.** This means plastic, ceramic, glass, stainless steel—not other metals that can react with the ingredients used to make the pickles.

- **Use only fresh, blemish-free cucumbers and onions.**

- **Use pickling or canning salt.** Look for it near the canning supplies in most grocery stores. Table salt can cause the brine to become cloudy and darken the pickles.

- **Toss cucumbers with salt.** Let them stand so the salt will draw the water out of the cucumbers and raise the acidity. Higher acidity means they can be kept for a longer time.

- **Wash jars; rinse and dry as directed.** (See Preparing Jars for Canning, at left.) It is essential to remove any bacteria or other contaminants (including water) that can later spoil the food if not removed first.

- **Loosely pack the vegetables.** Leave ample space for the vinegar mixture to surround the vegetables to preserve them properly.

- **Heat vinegar mixture to boiling.** This will kill off any potential bacteria present.

- **Leave ½-inch headspace in jars.** This is so that liquid won't overflow the jars and prevent the lids from sealing during processing.

- **Process pickles safely.** Use an elevated rack to prevent the jars from cracking. Use enough boiling water to cover the jars by 1 to 2 inches.

- **Retighten bands after 24 hours.** Lids can loosen during the processing.

- **Check lids for seal.** If they pop back when pressed, the jars need to be refrigerated and used within 3 weeks. Properly processed jars will have lids that don't spring back. They can be stored in a cool, dark, dry place up to 1 year.

Bread and Butter Pickles

GARLIC DILL PICKLES

LOWER CALORIE

PREP 1 hr 20 min TOTAL 1 wk 2 hr • **4 quarts pickles**

- 4 (1 quart) glass preserving jars with lids and bands
- 7 pints (3-inch) unwaxed pickling cucumbers (about 24 to 30 cucumbers)
- 12 to 16 sprigs fresh dill weed
- 12 cloves garlic, peeled
- 4 slices onion, ½ inch thick
- 4 teaspoons mustard seed
- 4 cups water
- 2 cups cider or white vinegar
- 2 tablespoons pickling or canning salt*

1 Fill boiling water canner half full with water; heat until water is simmering. Wash jars as directed in Preparing Jars for Canning (page 251).

2 Wash cucumbers; cut off stems and blossom ends. Pack cucumbers loosely in jars. To each jar, add 3 or 4 dill weed sprigs, 3 garlic cloves, 1 onion slice and 1 teaspoon mustard seed. In large saucepan, heat water, vinegar and salt to boiling. Fill jars, leaving ½-inch headspace.

3 Drain flat lids well. Wipe rims and threads of jars. Place flat lids on jars and screw bands on tightly to seal. Place jars on elevated rack in canner; lower rack into canner. To process pickles safely, water must cover jars by 1 to 2 inches; add additional boiling water if necessary. Cover. Heat to boiling; continue boiling 10 minutes.

4 Carefully remove jars with canning jar lifter or heavy-duty tongs and place upright on

towel. Cool completely. After 24 hours, check seal on cooled jars by pressing middles of lids with finger. If the lids spring back, jars are not sealed and must be stored in the refrigerator. Store completely sealed unopened jars in a cool, dry place up to 1 year (let stand at least 1 week to blend flavors before serving). Once opened, store in refrigerator up to 3 weeks.

Pickling or canning salt, available in most grocery stores, is preferred for making pickles. Table salt can cause the brine to become cloudy and darken the pickles.

1 Pickle: Calories 5; Total Fat 0g (Saturated Fat 0g; Trans Fat 0g); Cholesterol 0mg; Sodium 220mg; Total Carbohydrate 1g (Dietary Fiber 0g); Protein 0g **Exchanges:** Free **Carbohydrate Choices:** 0

PICKLED TARRAGON–BABY CARROTS LOWER CALORIE

PREP 20 min TOTAL 24 hr 20 min • **14 servings**

- 1 bag (16 oz) ready-to-eat baby-cut carrots
- ½ cup tarragon vinegar
- 1 tablespoon chopped fresh or 1 teaspoon dried tarragon leaves
- 1 tablespoon olive or vegetable oil
- ¼ teaspoon coarse ground black pepper

1 In 3-quart saucepan, heat 2 quarts water to boiling. Add carrots; cook 3 minutes. Meanwhile, in large bowl, mix remaining ingredients. Drain carrots; immediately stir into mixture in bowl.

2 Cover tightly; refrigerate 24 hours to blend flavors, stirring once, before serving. Store covered in refrigerator up to 3 months.

1 Serving (¼ Cup): Calories 25; Total Fat 1g (Saturated Fat 0g; Trans Fat 0g); Cholesterol 0mg; Sodium 25mg; Total Carbohydrate 3g (Dietary Fiber 1g); Protein 0g **Exchanges:** ½ **Carbohydrate Choices:** 0

Packing Cucumbers

Wash cucumbers; cut off stems and blossom ends.

Pack cucumbers loosely in jars. Add dill, garlic, onion and mustard seed to jars.

Pickled Tarragon–Baby Carrots

PICKLED GINGERROOT

LOWER CALORIE

Boldly flavor foods with either the ginger slices or the pickling liquid. In addition to serving with sushi, try thin strips of the ginger with grilled meats and vegetables or tossed into a marinade or stir-fry.

PREP 15 min **TOTAL** 24 hr 30 min • **½ cup gingerroot slices and 1½ cups liquid**

- ¼ **cup sugar**
- 1 **cup chicken broth (for homemade broth, see page 528)**
- ½ **cup seasoned or unseasoned rice vinegar**
- 2 **tablespoons dry sherry or mirin (rice wine)**
- ¼ **lb gingerroot, peeled, very thinly sliced**

1 In 1-quart saucepan, heat sugar, broth, vinegar and sherry to boiling, stirring frequently, until sugar is dissolved. Stir in gingerroot; remove from heat. Cool 15 minutes.

2 Pour into nonreactive container. Cover; refrigerate at least 24 hours before serving. Store covered in refrigerator up to 3 months.

1 Serving (2 Slices): Calories 10; Total Fat 0g (Saturated Fat 0g; Trans Fat 0g); Cholesterol 0mg; Sodium 25mg; Total Carbohydrate 2g (Dietary Fiber 0g); Protein 0g **Exchanges:** Free **Carbohydrate Choices:** 0

Drying Vegetables

We've included one recipe for drying tomatoes, but you may want to try drying other vegetables. Successful drying depends on the amount of heat and air circulation. For more information, go to www.ext.colostate.edu/pubs/foodnut/09308.html.

OVEN-DRIED TOMATOES

LOWER CALORIE

Plum or Roma tomatoes work best for drying because they are thick-fleshed with few seeds. Regular tomatoes can be used but may take longer to dry because they contain more liquid and seeds.

PREP 10 min **TOTAL** 12 hr 10 min • **12 servings**

- 24 **plum (Roma) tomatoes**

1 Heat oven to 200°F. Rinse tomatoes under cold running water and remove stems; drain on paper towels. Cut each tomato in half lengthwise. Using small spoon, scoop out and discard seeds.

2 Place tomato halves in single layer, cut side down, on broiler rack. Place larger halves on outer edges of rack for even cooking.

3 Dry in oven 6 to 12 hours or until tomatoes are shriveled, dry to the touch and very chewy in texture, turning once after 4 hours. Edges may be crisp, but tomatoes should not be crisp in center; they should be somewhat pliable. Check after 6 hours and remove any smaller tomatoes that have dried. Tomatoes will be dark red and some piees may have brown or dark spots.

4 Remove from oven and cool completely. Store in tightly covered container in cool dark location. To rehydrate, place tomatoes in small bowl. Cover with hot or boiling water. Let stand 15 to 30 minutes or until softened.

1 Serving (2 Tomatoes): Calories 20; Total Fat 0g (Saturated Fat 0g; Trans Fat 0g); Cholesterol 0mg; Sodium 5mg; Total Carbohydrate 4g (Dietary Fiber 1g); Protein 1g **Exchanges:** Free **Carbohydrate Choices:** 0

Drying Tomatoes

Cut each tomato in half lengthwise; remove seeds with small spoon.

Place tomato halves, cut side down, on broiler rack.

Oven-Dried Tomatoes

GREEK YOGURT LOWER CALORIE

Sometimes called yogurt cheese, Greek yogurt is concentrated yogurt with a silky, smooth texture. Do not start with yogurt that contains gelatin. The gelatin prevents the liquid from draining from the yogurt.

PREP 5 min **TOTAL** 9 hr • **8 servings**

2 **cups regular or fat-free plain yogurt (1 lb)**

1 Line medium colander with cheesecloth or muslin. Place colander in bowl. Place yogurt in lined colander; drain 1 hour.

2 Loosely cover colander and bowl. Refrigerate 6 to 8 hours or until texture of yogurt is smooth and silky. Transfer yogurt from cheesecloth to medium bowl; set aside. Discard whey (liquid) in bowl. Store yogurt in refrigerator.

1 Serving (¼ Cup): Calories 35; Total Fat 0g (Saturated Fat 0g, Trans Fat 0g); Cholesterol 0mg; Sodium 45mg; Total Carbohydrate 5g (Dietary Fiber 0g); Protein 3g **Exchanges:** ½ Skim Milk **Carbohydrate Choices:** ½

CARDAMOM-SCENTED YOGURT CHEESE

Make yogurt as directed in recipe. Stir ¼ teaspoon saffron threads into 1 tablespoon hot milk. Let stand 1 to 2 minutes or until milk is a rich, golden yellow-orange color. Stir milk mixture, ¼ cup chopped unsalted pistachios, ⅛ teaspoon ground nutmeg and ⅛ teaspoon ground cardamom into yogurt. Cover and refrigerate about 2 hours or until chilled.

Straining Yogurt

Spoon yogurt into cheesecloth.

Drain until very thick.

SALT-FREE HERB MIX

FAST   LOWER CALORIE

This super-versatile salt-free seasoning is great to sprinkle on meats, poultry, fish and vegetables. Or, toss hot cooked pasta with olive oil or melted butter and some of this blend, then sprinkle with shredded cheese.

PREP 5 min **TOTAL** 5 min • **¼ cup mix**

1 **tablespoon onion powder**
1 **tablespoon garlic powder**
1 **tablespoon parsley flakes**
1 **teaspoon dried basil leaves**
1 **teaspoon dried thyme leaves**
1 **teaspoon dried marjoram leaves**
1 **teaspoon coarse ground black pepper**

In small container with tight-fitting lid, mix all ingredients until well blended; cover. Store in cool, dry place up to 6 months. Stir or shake well before each use.

1 Teaspoon: Calories 5; Total Fat 0g (Saturated Fat 0g; Trans Fat 0g); Cholesterol 0mg; Sodium 0mg; Total Carbohydrate 1g (Dietary Fiber 0g); Protein 0g **Exchanges:** Free **Carbohydrate Choices:** 0

SALT-FREE TACO SEASONING MIX FAST   LOWER CALORIE

Use this homemade taco seasoning in any recipe calling for the store-bought version. The beauty of this mix is you can add your own salt to taste. Twelve teaspoons of this mix is equal to a 1-ounce package of purchased taco seasoning mix.

PREP 5 min **TOTAL** 5 min • **½ cup mix**

2 **tablespoons chili powder**
1 **tablespoon onion powder**
5 **teaspoons ground cumin**
5 **teaspoons paprika**
2½ **teaspoons garlic powder**
⅛ **to ¼ teaspoon ground red pepper (cayenne)**

In small container with tight-fitting lid, mix all ingredients until well blended; cover. Store in cool, dry place up to 6 months. Stir or shake well before each use.

1 Teaspoon: Calories 10; Total Fat 0g (Saturated Fat 0g; Trans Fat 0g); Cholesterol 0mg; Sodium 10mg; Total Carbohydrate 1g (Dietary Fiber 0g); Protein 0g **Exchanges:** Free **Carbohydrate Choices:** 0

SMOKY SALT-FREE TACO SEASONING MIX

Substitute 2 teaspoons smoked paprika for 2 teaspoons of the regular paprika.

BROWNIE MIX

An impressive layered brownie mix makes the perfect gift from your kitchen to someone you love. Include a note with instructions to complete the brownies.

PREP 15 min **TOTAL** 1 hr 35 min • **1 jar mix (16 brownies)**

DRY BROWNIE MIX

 1 cup semisweet or dark chocolate chips
 ½ cup plus 2 tablespoons all-purpose flour
 ½ teaspoon salt
 ½ cup unsweetened baking cocoa
 ½ cup all-purpose flour*
 ⅔ cup granulated sugar
 ⅔ cup packed brown sugar
 ½ cup white vanilla baking chips
 ½ cup chopped pecans or walnuts, if desired

TO COMPLETE BROWNIES

 ⅔ cup butter, melted
 3 eggs, beaten
 1 teaspoon vanilla

1 In 1-quart jar with tight-fitting lid, layer all brownie mix ingredients in order given; cover.

2 Give with gift card that reads: To make brownies, heat oven to 350°F. Grease 8- or 9-inch square pan with shortening or cooking spray. In large bowl, place contents of jar, butter, eggs and vanilla. (If brown sugar has become slightly firm, break up with fork.) Using spoon, beat about 30 strokes until well blended. Spoon and spread in pan. Bake 35 to 40 minutes or until set. Cool completely, about 45 minutes. Cut into 4 rows by 4 rows.

*Two separate measurements of flour are listed in order to create an extra layer.

1 Brownie: Calories 290; Total Fat 14g (Saturated Fat 9g; Trans Fat 0g); Cholesterol 60mg; Sodium 160mg; Total Carbohydrate 37g (Dietary Fiber 2g); Protein 3g **Exchanges:** 1 Starch, 1½ Other Carbohydrate, 2½ Fat **Carbohydrate Choices:** 2½

Layering Dessert Mixes

Layer ingredients in jar in order given.

CONFETTI COOKIE MIX

LOWER CALORIE

PREP 50 min **TOTAL** 50 min • **1 jar mix (3 dozen cookies)**

DRY COOKIE MIX

 1 cup sugar
 ¾ cup all-purpose flour
 ½ teaspoon baking soda
 ¼ teaspoon salt
 ⅓ cup unsweetened baking cocoa
 1½ cups quick-cooking or old-fashioned oats
 1 cup miniature candy-coated milk chocolate baking bits

TO COMPLETE COOKIES

 ½ cup softened butter
 2 tablespoons water
 ½ teaspoon vanilla
 3 eggs

1 In medium bowl, mix sugar, flour, cocoa, baking soda and salt. In 1-quart jar with tight-fitting lid, place flour mixture then cocoa; tap lightly to pack. Top with oats and baking bits; cover.

2 Give with gift card that reads: To make cookies, heat oven to 350°F. In large bowl, place contents of jar, butter, water, vanilla and egg. Stir 30 seconds with spoon or until combined. On ungreased cookie sheets, spoon dough by rounded teaspoonfuls 2 inches apart. Bake 10 to 12 minutes or until edges are set. Cool 5 minutes; remove to cooling racks.

1 Cookie: Calories 100; Total Fat 4.5g (Saturated Fat 2.5g; Trans Fat 0g); Cholesterol 15mg; Sodium 60mg; Total Carbohydrate 14g (Dietary Fiber 1g); Protein 1g **Exchanges:** ½ Starch, ½ Other Carbohydrate, 1 Fat **Carbohydrate Choices:** 1

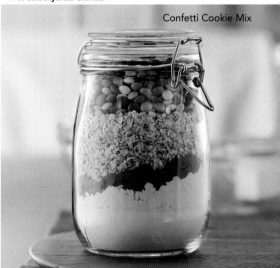

Confetti Cookie Mix

CHAI MIX FAST

Chai is the Hindi name for tea made with milk and spices such as cardamom, cinnamon, cloves, ginger, nutmeg and pepper. Give a jar of this chai mix with a lovely mug and cinnamon sticks for stirring.

PREP 10 min TOTAL 10 min • **1 jar mix**

- 1 **cup instant nonfat dry milk**
- ½ **cup powdered vanilla-flavored nondairy creamer**
- ¼ **cup plus 2 tablespoons powdered sugar**
- ½ **cup dry unsweetened instant tea**
- 2 **teaspoons ground cinnamon**
- 1 **teaspoon ground cardamom**
- ½ **teaspoon ground cloves**

1 In small bowl, mix dry milk, creamer and powdered sugar. In another small bowl, mix dry tea and spices. Into 1-pint jar with tight-fitting lid, alternately spoon milk and tea mixtures, packing lightly; cover.

2 Give with gift card that reads: For each serving, place ¼ cup Chai Mix in cup or mug. Fill with 1 cup very hot water. For creamier chai, use half milk and half water.

1 Serving (¼ Cup): Calories 110; Total Fat 3.5g (Saturated Fat 3g; Trans Fat 0g); Cholesterol 0mg; Sodium 65mg; Total Carbohydrate 17g (Dietary Fiber 0g); Protein 4g **Exchanges:** 1 Other Carbohydrate, ½ Skim Milk, ½ Fat **Carbohydrate Choices:** 1

COFFEE SHOP MOCHA MIX

FAST

PREP 10 min TOTAL 10 min • **12 servings**

- 1½ **cups dry nondairy creamer**
- 1 **cup packed brown sugar**
- ⅓ **cup dark unsweetened baking cocoa**
- ¼ **cup instant espresso coffee granules or powder**

1 In medium bowl, mix all ingredients, breaking any large lumps with spoon. Store in airtight container.

2 Give with a gift card that reads: For each serving, place ¼ cup Coffee Shop Mocha Mix in cup or mug. Add ¾ cup boiling water or very hot milk; stir until mix is dissolved. If desired, garnish with whipped cream and a pinch of cocoa. Serve immediately.

1 Serving (¼ Cup): Calories 150; Total Fat 4.5g (Saturated Fat 4g, Trans Fat 0g); Cholesterol 0mg; Sodium 25mg; Total Carbohydrate 27g (Dietary Fiber 1g); Protein 1g **Exchanges:** 2 Other Carbohydrate, 1 Fat **Carbohydrate Choices:** 2

SPICED COFFEE SHOP MOCHA MIX Add 1 teaspoon ground cinnamon and ½ teaspoon ground nutmeg with dry ingredients in Step 1. Continue as directed.

Chai Mix

ENTERTAINING

FEATURES AND GLOSSARIES

For bonus entertaining recipes,
visit bettycrocker.com/BCcookbook

FAST = Ready in 20 minutes or less LOWER CALORIE = See Helpful Nutrition and Cooking Information, page 685
LIGHTER = 25% fewer calories or grams of fat MAKE AHEAD = Make-ahead directions SLOW COOKER = Slow cooker directions

◀ Margaritas (page 273), Smoked Salmon Cheesecake (page 269), Greek Layered Dip (page 267), Mango Mimosas (page 276)

ENTERTAINING BASICS
Holiday celebrations . . . dinner parties . . . backyard cookouts . . . birthday meals. The reasons to gather with friends and family throughout the year are endless. A beautifully set table and a menu of fabulous foods makes each occasion even more special. Entertaining can be fun and easy with the tips provided here.

SETTING THE DINING TABLE

If remembering how to set a table is a bit fuzzy, follow these time-tested guidelines.

- Be creative with placemats and napkins, centerpieces and serving pieces. Not everything needs to be a perfect match. As long as colors, patterns or themes coordinate, an eclectic mix can be fun.
- Allow enough elbow room for each person.
- Place flatware 1 inch from the edge of the table.

For a casual place setting, place a fork to the left of the plate, a knife to the right (blade side toward plate) with the spoon to the right of the knife.

For a formal place setting, arrange pieces to be used first farthest from the plate. Place first-course salad or soup plate on top of main-course plate.

- Place the bread plate above the forks, with the butter knife across the plate.
- Place the salad plate to the left of the forks when served with the main course.
- Place the water glass at the tip of the knife and wine or other glasses to the right.
- Place the coffee or tea cup slightly above and to the right of the spoons, or bring with dessert.
- Place dessert flatware above the dinner plate, or bring with dessert.
- Place the napkin in the center of the plate, to the left of the forks or tuck inside an empty glass.
- Before dessert, clear the table of all items that won't be used with dessert.

SETTING A BUFFET TABLE

Buffets are a great option when the gathering is less formal or you're short on table space. Follow these tips when planning a buffet.

- Buffets can be set up on a variety of surfaces, including a center island or counter, dining room table, sideboard, picnic table or folding table. Allow ample room for people to move around the serving area.
- Arrange buffet items starting with the main course and then the side dishes, salad, condiments, bread, flatware, with glasses and napkins last.
- Make cutlery bundles for easier carrying.
- If people will be standing to eat, skip paper plates and use dishes or plastic plates. If you must use paper, make sure they are heavy-duty. Avoid serving foods that require cutting.

Formal place setting

CREATING A CHEESE TRAY

Whether served as an appetizer or a dessert, a cheese tray is easy to assemble and sure to please. A cheese tray can be simple and inexpensive or an impressive show-stopper.

- You want to serve at least three types of cheese on a tray. For larger groups or buffets, offer more.

- Plan on at least 2 ounces of cheese per person.

- When selecting cheese, aim for variety so people can taste different flavors and textures. Try mixing textures (soft, semisoft, hard and very hard) and flavors (mellow and sharp). Many specialty grocery stores offer countless types and can provide suggestions.

- Cheese is easier to slice when it is cold but tastes best at room temperature. Remove from the refrigerator and unwrap; cover with a cheese dome or upside-down bowl and let stand 30 to 60 minutes.

- Arrange cheese on a cheese board or platter. Sets of cheese knives include spreaders for soft cheese, a curved blade for hard cheese, a cheese plane or wide blade for semihard cheese and a thin blade for semihard cheeses. Butter knives also work well.

- Cheese is wonderful on its own with crackers or bread. Other accompaniments can include dried or fresh fruits, nuts, olives, preserves, chutney and honey (for drizzling) and fig cake and quince paste, available in specialty cheese departments.

- Wine is a perfect partner for cheese. Ask your wine and cheese shop for suggestions.

Cheese Plate Ideas

Mix cheese textures and flavors with other items to make interesting cheese plates.

- Flavored Cheddar, like chipotle, queso blanco and pepper Jack with grapes, pickled chiles, dates, grape tomatoes.

- Gruyère, Havarti and blue or Gorgonzola with apple and pear slices, dried apricots, olive assortment.

- Chèvre (goat cheese), Colby, cream cheese with chives, crackers, breads, chutney.

Cheese tray arrangement with a variety of items

MENUS TO CELEBRATE
Whether you want to put together a special-occasion meal, a casual get-together or a formal sit-down gathering, the *Betty Crocker Cookbook* can help. With over 1,500 recipes in the book to choose from, you're sure to find some irresistible favorites to use all year long. Here are some great ideas to get you started.

Classic Thanksgiving Dinner
Roast Turkey, page 416
Bread Stuffing, page 418
Mashed Potatoes, page 602,
    and Pan Gravy, page 418
Candied Sweet Potatoes, page 604
Cranberry Sauce, page 58
Pumpkin Pie, page 172
Pecan Pie, page 171

Merry Christmas Dinner
Pomegranate Martinis, page 274
Fresh vegetables, dip and crackers
Glazed Baked Ham, page 356, or Pork Crown
    Roast with Fruited Stuffing Supreme,
    page 352
Scalloped Potatoes, page 600
Mandarin Salad with Sugared Almonds,
    page 458
Red Velvet Cake, page 133, or English Trifle,
    page 222

Ring in the New Year
Champagne
Phyllo-Wrapped Brie with Fig Preserves and
    Toasted Walnuts, page 59
Lemon- and Parmesan-Crusted Salmon,
    page 288
Classic Risotto, page 433
Tossed salad
Chocolate–Sour Cream Fondue, page 230

Cocktails and Appetizers
Martini, Manhattan, or Gin and Tonic
    Cocktails, pages 273–275
Wine and beer
Hot and Saucy Cocktail Meatballs, page 270
Cheese- and Bacon-Stuffed Mushrooms,
    page 60
Brie in Puff Pastry with Cranberry Sauce,
    page 58

Roasted Vegetable Dip with Baked Pita
    Crisps, page 268
Cold Poached Salmon with Herbed
    Mayonnaise, page 63

Make It Vegetarian
Margaritas, page 273
Hummus, page 49
Guacamole, page 48
Baked Chimichangas, page 635
Spanish Rice, page 432

Game Night
Original Chex® Party Mix, page 266
Tangy Italian Beef Sandwiches, page 511
Chili, page 540
Tortilla and potato chips
Chocolate Brownies, page 198

Backyard Bash
Watermelon Lemonade with Kiwifruit Splash,
    page 70
Apple-Mint Green Iced Tea, page 67
Tex-Mex Layered Dip, page 48
Grilled Barbecue Chicken, page 308
Creamy Potato Salad, page 464
Chocolate Layer Cake, page 134

"Kiddo's" Birthday Celebration
Creamy Fruit Dip, page 49
Nachos, page 55
Sloppy Joes, page 545
Fresh vegetables and chips
Cupcakes, page 143

Casual Supper for Friends
Layered Pizza Dip, page 54
Pecan-Maple Chicken, page 406
Rice Pilaf, page 430
Tossed salad with Italian Dressing, page 475
Ice cream with Hot Fudge Sauce, page 233

262

Jarlsberg

Emmentaler

Gouda

Queso
Fresco

Chipotle
Cheddar

Gruyère

Smoked
Gouda

Manchego

Horseradish
Havarti

Cotija

Cotija
Añejo

Cottage Cheese

Smoked
Cheddar

Tomato-Basil
Cheddar

Havarti

Queso Blanco

Ricotta

Mascarpone

Sharp
Cheddar

Colby

Dill Havarti

Edam

Blueberry
Cheddar

Blue

Gorgonzola

Fontina

Mozzarella

Cream Cheese
with Chives

Havarti

Cream Cheese

Roquefort

Romano

Pearl Mozzarella

Feta

Brie

Parmesan

Curds

Asiago

Chèvre
(Goat)

CHEESE

Very Hard (Grating)

Asiago: Mild when young; nutty and semisharp when aged. Melts best when grated. Use with pasta, potatoes, rice salads, vegetables.

Cotija: Firm, dry, crumbly. Salty, sharp flavor. Cotija añejo (aged) is firmer and harder than regular Cotija. Both will soften but do not change shape when heated. Crumble over salads, tacos, refried beans or other Mexican dishes.

Parmesan: Sharp, savory, salty. Flavor intensifies with age. Melts best when grated. Use in salads, cooked dishes, casseroles, or as a pizza topping.

Romano: Sharp, robust. Similar to but richer than Parmesan. Pecorino Romano is made from sheep's milk. Melts best when grated. Use in pasta, soups, salads, egg dishes, stuffings or on pizza.

Hard

Cheddar: Rich, nutty flavor ranging from mild to full-bodied with a bite in sharp Cheddar. Smoked Cheddar contains smoked hardwood flavor. Other ingredients may be added.

Edam: Mildly salty, nutty. Melts best when shredded. Use in sandwiches, salads, soups, snacks.

Emmentaler: Similar to Swiss. Mild, slightly nutty, buttery. Melts well. Use in sandwiches, sauces, snacks.

Gouda: Mellow, rich caramel flavor. Smoked Gouda contains smoked hardwood flavor. Melts best when shredded. Use in sandwiches, soups, salads, snacks.

Gruyère: Mellow, buttery, nutty. Melts well. Use in fondues, baked dishes, onion soup.

Jarlsberg: Similar to Swiss. Slightly sweet, nutty. Use in baked dishes, sandwiches, snacks.

Manchego: Creamy, mildly nutty. Melts well. Use as any meal course or in sandwiches, salads, baked dishes, snacks.

Swiss: Mellow, buttery, slightly nutty. Melts well. Use in baked dishes, fondues, sandwiches or salads.

Semisoft

Blue: Rich, robust, salty with lingering tang. Melts best when crumbled. Use in vegetable, fruit and pasta salads, spreads, dressings, dips or with grilled meats.

Curds: Mild, milky; with a rubbery texture. Use as a snack or as a topping.

Feta: Very sharp, salty flavor. Melts best in sauces. Use in salads, Greek or hot or cold pasta or egg dishes.

Fontina: Delicate, nutty with a hint of honey flavor. Melts well. Use in sandwiches, baked dishes, snacks.

Gorgonzola: Robust, spicy. Melts best when crumbled. Use in salads, pasta, soufflés, spreads, dressings, dips.

Havarti: Buttery, mild yet tangy. Melts best when shredded. Use in sandwiches, egg dishes, salads or on baked potatoes. Other ingredients may be added.

Queso Blanco: Fresh (unripened) with a crumbly, curdy texture. Commonly fried. Softens but holds its shape when heated. Use in soups, salads, stuffings, snacks.

Roquefort: Rich, melt-in-your-mouth texture with a clean, sharp, lingering tang. Use in vegetable, fruit and pasta salads, spreads, dressings, dips or with grilled meats.

Soft

Brie: Rich, buttery. Softens and flows when heated. Use for party trays, sandwiches, snacks.

Chèvre (Goat): Creamy, fresh, mildly tangy. Made with goat's milk. Softens but holds its shape when heated. Use in appetizers, salads, baked dishes, sauces.

Cottage Cheese (Dry or Creamed): Mild, milky. Use in baked dishes or salads.

Cream Cheese: Rich, slightly tangy. Melts best in sauces. Use in baked dishes, cheesecakes, fruit or gelatin salads, snacks, spreads. Other ingredients may be added.

Fresh Mozzarella: Creamy, soft texture with a delicate, milky flavor. Use in salads, sandwiches, as an appetizer or pizza topping.

Mascarpone: Very soft, sweet, mild with a buttery texture. Melts best in sauces. Use in fillings, toppings, dips, spreads, sauces.

Queso Fresco: Spongy, fresh (unripened) with a grainy texture. Slightly acidic flavor. Softens but holds its shape when heated. Crumble over enchiladas or refried beans.

Ricotta: Mild, slightly sweet. Use in fillings, stuffings, spreads, cheesecakes.

AMARETTO CHEESE-FILLED APRICOTS LOWER CALORIE

These filled apricots would be a beautiful addition to a cheese, fruit and nut platter.

PREP 30 min TOTAL 1 hr 30 min • **30 apricots**

- 4 oz cream cheese (half of 8-oz package), softened
- ⅓ cup slivered almonds, toasted (page 22), chopped
- ¼ cup chopped dried cherries or sweetened dried cranberries
- 2 tablespoons amaretto or orange juice
- 30 soft whole dried apricots

1 In small bowl, mix cream cheese, ¼ cup of the almonds, the cherries and amaretto with spoon. Spoon into small resealable food-storage plastic bag. Cut ½ inch off a corner of bag.

2 With fingers, open apricots along one side so they look like partially open clamshells. Pipe about 1 teaspoon cheese mixture into each apricot.

3 Finely chop remaining almonds. Dip cheese edge of apricots into almonds. Refrigerate 1 hour before serving.

1 Apricot: Calories 45; Total Fat 2g (Saturated Fat 1g; Trans Fat 0g); Cholesterol 0mg; Sodium 10mg; Total Carbohydrate 6g (Dietary Fiber 0g); Protein 0g **Exchanges:** ½ Fruit, ½ Fat **Carbohydrate Choices:** ½

FIG- AND BLUE CHEESE–FILLED APRICOTS

Omit cherries and amaretto. Mix cream cheese with ¼ cup crumbled blue cheese, 2 tablespoons chopped dried figs and 1 tablespoon milk. Fill and dip apricots as directed.

ASIAN CHICKEN LETTUCE WRAPS FAST LOWER CALORIE

PREP 15 min TOTAL 15 min • **24 appetizers**

- 2 cups finely chopped cooked chicken
- 4 medium green onions, sliced diagonally (¼ cup)
- 1 can (8 oz) sliced water chestnuts, drained, finely chopped
- ½ cup Peanut Sauce (page 482) or purchased spicy peanut sauce
- 1 tablespoon chopped fresh mint leaves
- ¼ teaspoon crushed red pepper flakes
- 24 small (about 3 inch) leaves Bibb lettuce (about 1½ heads), breaking larger leaves into smaller size if necessary
- ½ cup chopped salted roasted peanuts

1 In medium bowl, mix all ingredients except lettuce and peanuts.

2 Spoon about 2 tablespoons chicken mixture onto each lettuce leaf. Sprinkle with peanuts.

1 Appetizer: Calories 60; Total Fat 3.5g (Saturated Fat 1g; Trans Fat 0g); Cholesterol 10mg; Sodium 35mg; Total Carbohydrate 3g (Dietary Fiber 0g); Protein 5g **Exchanges:** ½ Lean Meat, ½ Fat **Carbohydrate Choices:** 0

SHRIMP SUMMER ROLLS WITH DIPPING SAUCE LOWER CALORIE

Chili paste and chili sauce are not the same thing. Chili paste is made of fermented fava beans, flour, red chiles and sometimes garlic. You can find it in the ethnic-foods section of your supermarket.

PREP 40 min TOTAL 40 min • **24 appetizers**

DIPPING SAUCE

- 1 jar (7¼ oz) hoisin sauce (⅔ cup)
- 1 cup water
- 2 teaspoons roasted red chili paste (from 4-oz jar)
- ½ teaspoon crushed red pepper flakes

SUMMER ROLLS

- 4 oz dried thin rice noodles or rice vermicelli (from 8.8-oz package)
- 2 cups shredded romaine lettuce
- ½ cup fresh cilantro leaves
- ½ cup shredded carrot (1 medium)
- 10 oz frozen cooked salad shrimp (about 1¾ cups), thawed, drained
- 12 round rice paper wrappers (about 8 inch; from 12-oz package)

Amaretto Cheese-Filled Apricots

Asian Chicken Lettuce Wraps

Shrimp Summer Rolls with Dipping Sauce

1 In medium bowl, mix dipping sauce ingredients. Cover; refrigerate while continuing with recipe.

2 Cook and drain noodles as directed on package. Meanwhile, in large bowl, mix lettuce, cilantro, carrot and shrimp.

3 Sprinkle water over 1 paper towel; place on cutting board. Fill a 10-inch pie plate with water. Place 1 rice paper wrapper in water 45 to 60 seconds or until pliable but not completely softened. Gently remove wrapper from water, shaking to drain excess water; place on damp paper towel.

4 Starting close to 1 edge of wrapper, form a row of about ¼ cup noodles. On noodles, arrange about ⅓ cup of the lettuce mixture. Starting with edge covered with fillings, roll up wrapper over fillings, stopping after first turn to tuck in sides. Continue to roll up, tucking in sides. Repeat with remaining wrappers.

5 Place rolls, seam sides down and without touching, on platter. (If rolls touch, they will stick together.) Cut each roll in half diagonally. Serve immediately with sauce.

1 Appetizer (½ Roll): Calories 70; Total Fat 0g (Saturated Fat 0g; Trans Fat 0g); Cholesterol 25mg; Sodium 230mg; Total Carbohydrate 12g (Dietary Fiber 0g); Protein 3g **Exchanges:** ½ Starch, ½ Other Carbohydrate **Carbohydrate Choices:** 1

MAKE AHEAD DIRECTIONS Make as directed; cover with moist paper towels and refrigerate up to 2 hours.

See how to roll **summer rolls:**
Visit bettycrocker.com/BCcookbook

SEAFOOD SALAD TARTLETS

FAST   LOWER CALORIE

PREP 15 min **TOTAL** 15 min • **30 tartlets**

- 1 **can (6 oz) crabmeat, drained, cartilage removed and flaked**
- 1 **jar (6 to 7 oz) marinated artichoke hearts, well drained, finely chopped (about 1 cup)**
- ¼ **cup chives-and-onion cream cheese spread (from 8-oz container)**
- 2 **tablespoons mayonnaise or salad dressing**
- 2 **tablespoons chopped red onion**
- ½ **teaspoon seafood seasoning (from 6-oz container)**
- 2 **packages (2.1 oz each) frozen mini phyllo shells (30 shells)**
- 30 **tiny shrimp (from 4-oz can), rinsed, patted dry**
     Fresh parsley sprigs

1 In medium bowl, mix crabmeat, artichokes, cream cheese spread, mayonnaise, onion and seafood seasoning.

2 Just before serving, spoon slightly less than 1 tablespoon crabmeat mixture into each phyllo shell. Garnish each tartlet with shrimp and parsley.

1 Tartlet: Calories 35; Total Fat 1.5g (Saturated Fat 0.5g; Trans Fat 0g); Cholesterol 10mg; Sodium 80mg; Total Carbohydrate 3g (Dietary Fiber 0g); Protein 2g **Exchanges:** ½ Medium-Fat Meat **Carbohydrate Choices:** 0

MAKE AHEAD DIRECTIONS Pat crabmeat and artichokes with paper towels (to help prevent filling from getting too moist during storage). Make filling as directed in Step 1. Cover; refrigerate up to 8 hours. Just before serving, fill shells as directed in Step 2.

Heirloom Recipe and New Twist

Originally published as a cereal box in 1952, this recipe is probably one of our all-time most requested recipes. It is so popular, it was made into a ready-to-eat snack product available at most grocery stores. The new twist is a sweet and spicy change of pace that could be served for any gathering. Be sure to also try the variations from online Facebook fans.

CLASSIC

ORIGINAL CHEX® PARTY MIX

PREP 10 min **TOTAL** 1 hr 25 min • **24 servings**

LOWER CALORIE

- 6 **tablespoons butter**
- 2 **tablespoons Worcestershire sauce**
- 1½ **teaspoons seasoned salt**
- ¾ **teaspoon garlic powder**
- ½ **teaspoon onion powder**
- 3 **cups Corn Chex® cereal**
- 3 **cups Rice Chex® cereal**
- 3 **cups Wheat Chex® cereal**
- 1 **cup mixed nuts**
- 1 **cup small pretzel twists**
- 1 **cup miniature garlic-flavor bagel chips or regular-size bagel chips, broken into 1-inch pieces**

1 Heat oven to 250°F. In ungreased large roasting pan, melt butter in oven. Stir in seasonings. Gradually stir in remaining ingredients until evenly coated.

2 Bake uncovered 1 hour, stirring every 15 minutes. Spread on paper towels; cool completely about 15 minutes. Store in airtight container.

1 Serving (½ Cup): Calories 140; Total Fat 6g (Saturated Fat 2.5g; Trans Fat 0g); Cholesterol 10mg; Sodium 330mg; Total Carbohydrate 17g (Dietary Fiber 2g); Protein 3g **Exchanges:** 1 Starch, 1 Fat **Carbohydrate Choices:** 1

MICROWAVE DIRECTIONS In large microwavable bowl, microwave butter uncovered on High about 40 seconds or until melted. Stir in seasonings. Gradually stir in remaining ingredients until evenly coated. Microwave uncovered on High 5 to 6 minutes, stirring thoroughly every 2 minutes. Spread on paper towels; cool about 15 minutes. Store in airtight container.

LIGHTER **DIRECTIONS** For 90 calories and 2 grams of fat per serving, decrease butter to 3 tablespoons, omit mixed nuts and use fat-free bagel chips.

MAKE AHEAD **DIRECTIONS** Make recipe as directed and cool completely. Store in airtight container in refrigerator up to 2 weeks.

SMOKED ALMOND AND PISTACHIO CHEX® MIX Substitute about ½ cup each hickory smoked almonds and pistachios for the mixed nuts.

Contributed by Melinda McKinney Kerbs from North Bend, Washington

DRIED CRANBERRY AND CHOCOLATE CHEX® MIX Add about ½ cup each dried cranberries and dark chocolate chips after cooling mixture.

Contributed by Jenny Durbin from Cincinnati, Ohio

Make Your Own Chex® Mix

This party mix is very versatile and you can change it many ways. Why not try using all one type of nut such as almonds, peanuts or cashews? Or, use just one or two varieties of cereal instead of all three. We love the pretzel twists and bagel chips but tiny cheese crackers or small corn chips are nice substitutes.

Original Chex® Party Mix

CHEX® MOROCCAN CRUNCH

PREP 10 min **TOTAL** 1 hr 25 min • **21 servings**

- ⅓ cup butter
- 1 teaspoon seasoned salt
- 1 teaspoon ground cumin
- 1 teaspoon ground coriander
- ½ teaspoon ground cinnamon
- 1 teaspoon dried mint leaves, if desired
- 8 cups Corn Chex®, Rice Chex® or Wheat Chex® cereal (or any combination)
- 2 cups almonds
- 1 cup chopped dried mixed fruit or raisins
- ¼ cup finely chopped crystallized ginger
- 3 tablespoons honey, if desired

1 Heat oven to 250°F. In ungreased large roasting pan, melt butter in oven. Stir in seasonings. Gradually stir in cereal and almonds until evenly coated.

2 Bake uncovered 1 hour, stirring every 15 minutes. Stir in dried fruits and ginger. Drizzle with honey. Cool completely, about 15 minutes. Store in airtight container.

1 Serving (½ Cup): Calories 180; Total Fat 10g (Saturated Fat 2.5g; Trans Fat 0g); Cholesterol 10mg; Sodium 200mg; Total Carbohydrate 18g (Dietary Fiber 3g); Protein 4g **Exchanges:** 1 Other Carbohydrate, ½ High-Fat Meat, 1½ Fat **Carbohydrate Choices:** 1

See how to make Chex® mix:
Visit bettycrocker.com/BCcookbook

Chex® Moroccan Crunch

GREEK LAYERED DIP FAST

True Greek yogurt is thicker and has a creamier consistency than regular plain yogurt because much of the liquid whey has been removed. Gelatin or other thickeners are not used, making it richly flavored and very smooth.

PREP 20 min **TOTAL** 20 min • **12 servings**

- 2 whole wheat pita (pocket) breads (6 inch) Cooking spray
- 1 container (8 oz) plain hummus (for homemade hummus, see page 49)
- 1 container (6 oz) Greek plain yogurt (for homemade Greek yogurt, see page 254)
- 1 tablespoon chopped fresh parsley
- 1 teaspoon lemon juice
- ⅛ teaspoon pepper
- 1 medium plum (Roma) tomato, seeded, chopped
- ⅓ cup pitted kalamata or ripe olives, quartered
- ⅓ cup finely chopped seeded cucumber
- 1 cup crumbled feta cheese (4 oz)
- 4 medium green onions, chopped (¼ cup)
- 1 tablespoon olive oil
- ½ medium cucumber, sliced
- 1 medium green or red bell pepper, cut into strips

1 Heat oven to 350°F. Split each pita bread horizontally to make 2 rounds. Cut each round into 6 wedges. Place on ungreased cookie sheet, rough surface up. Spray with cooking spray. Bake 8 to 10 minutes or until golden brown and crisp; cool.

2 Meanwhile, spread hummus on shallow serving platter or in pie plate. In small bowl, mix yogurt, parsley, lemon juice and pepper; spread evenly over hummus. Top with tomato, olives, chopped cucumber, cheese and onions. Drizzle with oil. Serve with pita chips, sliced cucumber and bell pepper strips.

1 Serving (¼ Cup Dip, 2 Chips and 4 Veggies): Calories 100; Total Fat 4.5g (Saturated Fat 1g; Trans Fat 0g); Cholesterol 5mg; Sodium 270mg; Total Carbohydrate 12g (Dietary Fiber 2g); Protein 4g **Exchanges:** ½ Starch, ½ Skim Milk, ½ Fat **Carbohydrate Choices:** 1

LIGHTER DIRECTIONS For 100 calories and 4.5 grams of fat per serving, use fat-free Greek plain yogurt. Reduce feta cheese to ½ cup and olive oil to 1 teaspoon.

ROASTED VEGETABLE DIP WITH BAKED PITA CRISPS LOWER CALORIE

If you don't feel like making the homemade pita crisps, you can purchase bags of pita chips.

PREP 15 min TOTAL 45 min • **6 servings**

BAKED PITA CRISPS

- 2 pita (pocket) breads (6 inch)
- 1 tablespoon olive oil or melted butter
- 1¼ teaspoons dried basil leaves
- 3 tablespoons grated Parmesan cheese

ROASTED VEGETABLE DIP

- 1 medium zucchini, sliced (2 cups)
- 1 medium yellow summer squash, sliced (1½ cups)
- 1 medium red bell pepper, sliced
- 1 medium red onion, thinly sliced
- 2 cloves garlic, peeled
  Cooking spray
- ½ teaspoon salt
- ¼ teaspoon ground red pepper (cayenne)

1 Heat oven to 375°F. Split each pita bread horizontally to make 2 rounds. Cut each round into 6 wedges. Lightly brush oil over smooth surface of pita; sprinkle with basil and cheese. Place on ungreased cookie sheet, basil and cheese side up. Bake 6 to 8 minutes or until golden brown and crisp; cool completely.

2 Increase oven temperature to 400°F. In 15x10x1-inch pan, spread zucchini, yellow squash, bell pepper, onion and garlic in single layer. Spray vegetables with cooking spray. Sprinkle with salt and red pepper.

3 Bake about 30 minutes, turning vegetables once, until tender and light brown.

4 Place vegetables in food processor or blender. Cover; blend on high speed about 1 minute, stopping blender occasionally to scrape sides, until smooth. Spoon into serving bowl. Serve warm, or refrigerate at least 2 hours until chilled. Serve with pita crisps.

1 Serving (¼ Cup Dip and 4 Chips): Calories 25; Total Fat 0g (Saturated Fat 0g; Trans Fat 0g); Cholesterol 0mg; Sodium 170mg; Total Carbohydrate 5g (Dietary Fiber 1g); Protein 1g **Exchanges:** 1 Vegetable **Carbohydrate Choices:** ½

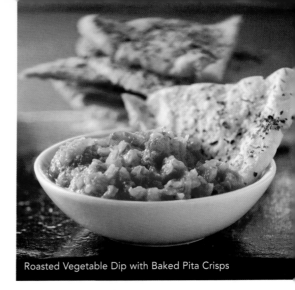

Roasted Vegetable Dip with Baked Pita Crisps

OLIVE TAPENADE

FAST LOWER CALORIE

Tapenade is a French condiment often served with vegetables, fish and meat. The flavor is tangy, rich and strong. Fresh rosemary is delicious in this version but you could use parsley instead.

PREP 10 min TOTAL 10 min • **14 servings**

- 1½ cups pitted kalamata or ripe olives
- ¼ cup chopped walnuts
- 3 tablespoons olive oil
- 3 tablespoons capers, drained
- 1½ teaspoons fresh rosemary leaves
- 1 teaspoon Italian seasoning
- 2 cloves garlic, peeled
  Chopped red bell pepper, if desired
  Assorted crackers, if desired

1 In food processor or blender, place all ingredients except bell pepper and crackers. Cover; process with quick on-and-off motions, until slightly coarse.

2 Spoon into serving dish. Sprinkle with bell pepper. Serve with crackers.

1 Serving (2 Tablespoons): Calories 60; Total Fat 6g (Saturated Fat 1g; Trans Fat 0g); Cholesterol 0mg; Sodium 190mg; Total Carbohydrate 2g (Dietary Fiber 0g); Protein 0g **Exchanges:** 1 Fat **Carbohydrate Choices:** 0

TOMATO AND ONION TART

LOWER CALORIE

PREP 35 min TOTAL 2 hr • **12 servings**

- 1 tablespoon olive or vegetable oil
- 1 tablespoon butter
- 1 large sweet onion (such as Maui or Walla Walla), quartered, thinly sliced
  One-Crust Pastry (page 158)
- ¼ cup grated Parmesan cheese
- 2 medium plum (Roma) tomatoes, thinly sliced
- ½ small zucchini, thinly sliced
- ¼ cup whipping cream
- 1 egg
- ¾ cup shredded Gruyère or Swiss cheese (3 oz)
- 4 medium green onions, thinly sliced (¼ cup)

1 In 10-inch skillet, heat oil and butter over medium-high heat. Add onion; cook 5 minutes, stirring occasionally, until onion begins to brown. Reduce heat to medium-low; cook 20 to 25 minutes, stirring frequently, until brown and tender.

2 Heat oven to 450°F. Unroll pie pastry on work surface. Roll pie crust with rolling pin to 12 inches in diameter. Gently press crust in bottom and up side of ungreased 10-inch tart pan with removable bottom. Trim off excess crust. Prick bottom and side of crust with fork. Bake 10 minutes. Remove from oven. Reduce oven temperature to 400°F.

3 Sprinkle bottom of partially baked crust with 2 tablespoons of the Parmesan cheese. Using slotted spoon, spoon onion evenly over crust. Top with tomatoes and zucchini, arranging a circle of tomato slices around outside edge, a circle of zucchini slices next to the tomatoes and a circle of tomato slices in center.

4 In small bowl, beat whipping cream and egg with wire whisk. Pour over vegetables. Top with Gruyère cheese and remaining 2 tablespoons Parmesan cheese.

5 Bake 15 minutes. Top with green onions; bake 10 to 15 minutes longer or until filling is set and crust is golden brown. Cool 5 minutes before removing side of pan.

1 Serving: Calories 160; Total Fat 11g (Saturated Fat 5g; Trans Fat 0g); Cholesterol 35mg; Sodium 160mg; Total Carbohydrate 10g (Dietary Fiber 0g); Protein 4g **Exchanges:** ½ Starch, ½ High-Fat Meat, 1½ Fat **Carbohydrate Choices:** ½

QUICKER TOMATO AND ONION TART Omit pastry and substitute 1 pie crust from box of refrigerated pie crusts, softened as directed. Continue as directed.

SMOKED SALMON CHEESECAKE LOWER CALORIE

PREP 30 min TOTAL 4 hr 20 min • **36 servings**

- 1 cup crushed buttery crackers (about 24 crackers)
- 3 tablespoons butter, melted
- 2 packages (8 oz each) cream cheese, softened
- ¼ cup whipping cream
- 2 eggs
- ¼ teaspoon salt
- 1½ cups shredded Gouda cheese (6 oz)
- ¼ cup sliced green onions (4 medium)
- 1 package (4½ oz) smoked salmon, flaked
- 2 tablespoons sliced green onions (2 medium), if desired
- 2 tablespoons red caviar, if desired
  Pumpernickel crackers, if desired

1 Heat oven to 375°F. In small bowl, stir crackers and butter until well mixed. Press evenly in bottom of 9-inch springform pan. Bake about 8 minutes or until golden brown.

2 Reduce oven temperature to 325°F. In large bowl, beat cream cheese with electric mixer on medium speed until smooth. Add whipping cream, eggs and salt; beat until smooth. Stir in Gouda cheese, ¼ cup onions and salmon until well mixed. Spoon evenly over crust.

3 Bake 45 to 50 minutes or until center is set. Run knife around edge of pan to loosen cheesecake. Cool completely at room temperature, about 1 hour. Cover and refrigerate at least 2 hours but no longer than 48 hours.

4 Remove side of pan. Place cheesecake on serving platter. Top with 2 tablespoons onions and the caviar. Cut into wedges. Serve with crackers.

1 Serving: Calories 90; Total Fat 8g (Saturated Fat 4.5g; Trans Fat 0g); Cholesterol 35mg; Sodium 150mg; Total Carbohydrate 2g (Dietary Fiber 0g); Protein 3g **Exchanges:** ½ Medium-Fat Meat, 1 Fat **Carbohydrate Choices:** 0

HOT AND SAUCY COCKTAIL MEATBALLS LOWER CALORIE

Handle meatballs as little as possible when forming them so they are moist and tender.

PREP 30 min **TOTAL** 1 hr 20 min • **6 dozen meatballs**

2 lb lean (at least 80%) ground beef
1 cup dry bread crumbs (any flavor)
⅔ cup finely chopped onion
½ cup milk
2 tablespoons chopped fresh parsley
2 teaspoons salt
1 teaspoon Worcestershire sauce
⅛ teaspoon pepper
2 eggs
2 bottles (12 oz each) chili sauce
2½ cups grape jelly

1 Heat oven to 400°F. In medium bowl, mix all ingredients except chili sauce and jelly. Shape into 1-inch meatballs. Place in ungreased 13x9-inch pan or on rack in broiler pan.

2 Bake uncovered about 20 minutes or until thoroughly cooked and no longer pink in center.

3 In Dutch oven, heat chili sauce and jelly over medium heat, stirring constantly, until jelly is melted. Stir in meatballs until coated. Simmer uncovered 30 minutes. Serve hot with toothpicks.

1 Meatball: Calories 60; Total Fat 1.5g (Saturated Fat 0.5g, Trans Fat 0g); Cholesterol 15mg; Sodium 210mg; Total Carbohydrate 9g (Dietary Fiber 0g); Protein 3g **Exchanges:** ½ Other Carbohydrate, ½ Lean Meat **Carbohydrate Choices:** ½

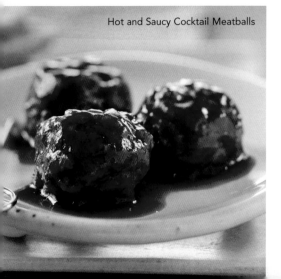

Hot and Saucy Cocktail Meatballs

CHEESE FONDUE

Gruyère is a rich, smooth, firm cheese named for the Gruyère valley in Fribourg, Switzerland. It has a mild, nutty, slightly sharp flavor that is stronger than Swiss cheese, and it melts into creamy smoothness.

PREP 10 min **TOTAL** 40 min • **5 servings**

2 cups shredded Swiss cheese (8 oz)
2 cups shredded Gruyère or Swiss cheese (8 oz)
2 tablespoons all-purpose flour
1 clove garlic, cut in half
1 cup dry white wine or nonalcoholic white wine
1 tablespoon lemon juice
3 tablespoons kirsch, dry sherry, brandy or nonalcoholic white wine
1 loaf (1 lb) French bread, cut into 1-inch pieces
   Apple and pear slices, if desired

1 In resealable food-storage plastic bag, place cheeses and flour. Shake until cheese is coated with flour; let stand 30 minutes at room temperature.

2 Rub garlic on bottom and side of fondue pot, saucepan or skillet; discard garlic. Add wine. Heat over simmer setting on fondue pot or over low heat just until bubbles rise to surface (do not boil). Stir in lemon juice.

3 Gradually add cheese mixture, about ½ cup at a time, gently stirring constantly with wire whisk over low heat until melted. If the mixture is stirred too vigorously, the cheese could become stringy. (To keep fondue creamy and smooth, it's important to make sure all cheese is melted before each new addition of cheese.)

4 Stir in kirsch. Keep warm over simmer setting. If made in saucepan or skillet, pour into a fondue pot or heatproof serving bowl and keep warm over low heat. Fondue must be served over heat to maintain its smooth, creamy texture. Spear bread and fruit with fondue forks; dip and swirl in fondue with stirring motion. If fondue becomes too thick, stir in ¼ to ½ cup heated dry white wine or nonalcoholic white wine.

1 Serving (2 Tablespoons Fondue and 4 Bread Pieces): Calories 610; Total Fat 30g (Saturated Fat 17g; Trans Fat 1.5g); Cholesterol 90mg; Sodium 800mg; Total Carbohydrate 50g (Dietary Fiber 3g); Protein 35g **Exchanges:** 3 Starch, 3½ High-Fat Meat **Carbohydrate Choices:** 3

DRINK BASICS
You don't need to have one of everything for a well-stocked bar. Start with a few liquors, beers and wines, then build from there. Keep nonalcoholic beverages on hand, too. Other items useful to have are below.

- **Mixers:** Club soda, tonic water, ginger ale, Bloody Mary mix (or tomato juice), fruit juices, sweetened lime juice, margarita mix and soda (regular and diet colas and lemon-lime).

- **Garnishes:** Celery stalks, cucumber and pickle spears, fresh fruit, fresh herb sprigs, lemon and lime wedges, maraschino cherries, mint leaves, olives, coarse salt and pepper, granulated and decorator sugar.

- **Gizmos and Gadgets:** Blender, bottle opener, coasters, cocktail napkins, corkscrew, ice bucket, ice tongs, pitcher, martini shaker, shot glass, mini measure, muddler, stirring sticks and straws.

LIQUORS AND LIQUEURS

- Liquors (spirits, hard liquor) are distilled alcoholic beverages made from a fermented mash of ingredients such as grains or plants. Favorites include bourbon, brandy, gin, rum, tequila, vodka and whiskey.

- Liqueurs are sweetened flavored liquors made with ingredients such as barks, flowers, fruits, herbs, leaves, nuts, roots, seeds and spices. Liqueurs include amaretto, coffee-flavored liqueur (Kahlua), crème de men-the, and Irish cream liqueur. They are used sparingly, so purchase small bottles.

Simple Syrup
To use this syrup to sweeten drinks, add 1 teaspoon per drink instead of 1 teaspoon sugar (add more for a sweeter drink). In 2-quart saucepan, stir 2 cups sugar and 2 cups water. Heat over medium heat, stirring frequently, until sugar dissolves. Store covered in refrigerator up to 1 month. Makes 3 cups

ALL ABOUT BEER

Basic beer ingredients are water, malted barley (or other grains such as corn, rye or wheat), hops and yeast. Hundreds of styles of beer are crafted using these building blocks.

Types of Beer

Ale: The fermenting yeast in ale tends to gather on the surface for several days before sinking to the bottom. Ale is usually fuller, more complex and higher in alcohol than lager.

Lager: The fermenting yeast in lager sinks to the bottom, with the resulting brew being lighter in color, less complex in flavor and lower in alcohol than an ale. Pilsners, porters and stouts are lagers. Lager is the most common style of beer sold in the United States. Lagers are best served around 45°F; colder temperatures can make the beer cloudy and might dull the flavor.

Specialty Beer: These beers include ales, lagers or a hybrid of the two and contain other ingredients that don't fit neatly into those two styles. Nuances can include ingredients like fruit, vegetables, herbs, coffee, nuts, chocolate and the processing of the malt over a fire for a smoky flavor. Serve specialty beers at about 55°F so the complex flavors can be fully enjoyed.

Bar equipment

THE WORLD OF WINE

Wine has been enjoyed across the globe for centuries. Three things determine the flavor of wine: the type of grapes, where the grapes were grown and how the grapes were crafted into wine. Picking out a bottle of wine doesn't have to be intimidating. Wine stores can offer great selection guidance and advice. For in-depth knowledge, look to the bookstore or online. In the end, the only thing that matters is what you like!

Varietal Wine

Varietal is a term describing wines primarily made from one variety of grape. The most common white and red varietals, along with some of their common aromas and flavors, are listed below. Generic wines are made from a blend of grapes.

White Varietals

- Chardonnay: apple, buttery, creamy, lemon, melon, nutty, oaky, pear, pineapple
- Chenin Blanc: fruity, peach, spicy
- Pinot Gris or Pinot Grigio: apple, crisp, pear
- Riesling: apple, grapefruit, green grapes, melon, peach/nectarine, orange
- Sauvignon Blanc or Fumé Blanc: citrus, herbaceous, grassy, melon

Red Varietals

- Cabernet Sauvignon: black currant, blackberry, black cherry, chocolate, fig, plum
- Merlot: blackberry, black cherry, chocolate, plum, vanilla
- Pinot Noir: berries, blackberry, black cherry, currant, spicy
- Sangiovese: blackberry, cherry, plum, spice

Sparkling Spritzers

To make wine spritzers, mix 2 cups chilled dry white wine or nonalcoholic wine, 1 cup chilled cranberry-apple juice drink and 1 cup chilled sparkling water. Serve over ice. Garnish with fresh fruit or mint leaves, if desired. Makes 6 servings (about ⅔ cup each).

- Syrah (Shiraz): blackberry, chocolate, plum, pepper, spicy
- Zinfandel: berries, cherry, earthy, pepper, spicy

Other Wines

- Sparkling Wines are effervescent wines, such as Asti Spumante and Champagne.
- Fortified Wines have added liquor, such as brandy; they include Madeira, Marsala, port and sherry
- Aromatic Wines, inluding vermouth, are wines flavored with ingredients, such as herbs and spices

Pairing Wine and Food

No hard and fast rules exist, but the general philosophy is to serve like with like. Light-bodied, light-tasting white wines pair well with mild-flavored foods such as chicken and fish. Full-bodied, full-flavored red wines pair well with rich, robust foods like lasagna or steak. Pairings can cross over because both white and red wines have lighter to more full-bodied varieties. Look for pairing suggestions on labels.

Storing and Serving Wine

- Store wine in a cool, dry location away from light. Lay bottles on their sides, not upright, so corks don't dry out and shrink, which can allow air to enter and spoil the wine.
- Serve white and sparkling wines at about 45°F to 55°F and reds at 55°F to 60°F. If served too cold, wine has little flavor.
- Wine glasses are specifically designed with shapes that maximize the aromas and flavors of individual wines. A set of all-purpose glasses for both red and white wines is a good starting point.
- To store leftover wine, push the cork back into the bottle or seal using a vacuum-pump device (rubber corks are included). Wine stores also sell canned nitrogen or argon; sprayed into the wine bottle, the gas replaces oxygen, thereby preserving the wine. It doesn't affect the flavor and isn't harmful.

MARGARITAS FAST

PREP 15 min TOTAL 15 min • **8 servings**

    Margarita salt or kosher (coarse) salt
2 cups cracked ice
2½ cups sweet-and-sour drink mix or
    nonalcoholic margarita drink mix
1⅓ cups tequila
1⅓ cups fresh lime juice*
  ¾ cup orange-flavored liqueur
    (such as Cointreau or Triple Sec)

Rub rims of 8 stemmed glasses with water; dip rims of glasses into salt. Place ice in pitcher. Add drink mix, tequila, lime juice and liqueur; shake or stir until blended. Pour into glasses, straining out ice.

*¾ cup frozen (thawed) limeade concentrate can be substituted.

1 Serving (½ Cup): Calories 180; Total Fat 0g (Saturated Fat 0g; Trans Fat 0g); Cholesterol 0mg; Sodium 0mg; Total Carbohydrate 11g (Dietary Fiber 0g); Protein 0g

---

Frozen Strawberry Margaritas

In blender, place 6 ounces frozen limeade concentrate and 1 box (10 oz) frozen strawberries. Blend until smooth. Add 3 cups water and ¾ cup tequila; blend until smooth. Pour into freezer container. Freeze until slushy, at least 24 hours. To serve, stir and spoon ⅔ cup into each glass and fill with ⅓ cup lemon-lime carbonated beverage.

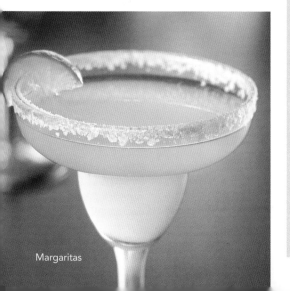

Margaritas

CLASSIC COCKTAILS

Bloody Mary: In tall glass, mix 3 ounces tomato juice, 2 ounces vodka, 1 ounce lemon juice, dash Worcestershire sauce, dash celery salt and pepper. Mix well and add hot pepper sauce to taste. Add ice to fill glass. Garnish with celery stalk and lime or lemon wedge.

Gibson: In shaker, mix 2½ ounces gin and ½ ounce dry vermouth. Add ice cubes and shake; strain into cocktail glass. Garnish with 1 to 3 cocktail onions.

Gimlet: In cocktail glass, mix 1 ounce lime juice, 1½ ounces gin or vodka and crushed ice to fill glass. Garnish with hazelnut or lime wedge.

Gin and Tonic: In tall glass over ice, mix 2 ounces gin with 3 ounces tonic water. Garnish with lime wedge.

Mimosa: In tall glass over ice, mix 3 ounces orange juice and 3 ounces champagne. Garnish with orange wedge.

Mojito: In cocktail glass, mix ½ ounce lime juice and 1 teaspoon sugar until dissolved. Rub about 6 mint leaves over inside of glass and discard leaves. Fill glass with 2 ounces rum, 2 ounces club soda and crushed ice. Garnish with mint sprig.

Mojito

Old-Fashioned: In cocktail glass, mix 3 ounces brandy, 2 to 3 dashes aromatic bitters, 1 teaspoon sugar and dash lemon juice. Add crushed ice to fill glass. Garnish with lemon peel.

Screwdriver: In tall glass over ice, mix 1½ ounces vodka or gin and 6 ounces orange juice. Garnish with orange wedge.

Sidecar: Coat rim of cocktail glass with sugar. In shaker, mix 2 ounces cognac, 1 ounce orange-flavored liqueur, such as Triple Sec and 1 ounce lemon juice. Add ice cubes and shake; strain into glass. Garnish with lemon wedge.

Sidecar

Tom Collins: In tall glass, mix 2 ounces gin, 1 ounce lemon juice and 1 teaspoon superfine sugar until blended. Add club soda and ice to fill glass. Garnish with maraschino cherry and lemon slice.

Learn to Make **Shaken Cocktails**

The best shaken cocktails are always served refreshingly cold with a very thin layer of ice floating on the surface. Equally important are the garnishes—they add flavor as well as make the drinks look special. Here's all you need to know to mix up cocktails so delicious they just might make you legendary.

MARTINI COCKTAILS FAST

PREP 10 min **TOTAL** 10 min • **2 or 4 servings**

Ingredients	To Serve 2	To Serve 4
Pimiento-stuffed green olives or lemon twists	2	4
Small ice cubes or shaved ice	¼ cup	½ cup
Gin	⅓ cup	⅔ cup
Dry vermouth	⅓ cup	⅔ cup
Aromatic bitters	2 dashes	4 dashes (⅛ to ¼ teaspoon)

1 Chill 2 or 4 (3-oz) stemmed glasses in freezer.

2 Place olive in each chilled glass. Place ice in martini shaker or pitcher. Add gin, vermouth and bitters; shake or stir to blend and chill. Pour into glasses, straining out ice.

1 Serving (⅓ Cup): Calories 150; Total Fat 0.5g (Saturated Fat 0g; Trans Fat 0g); Cholesterol 0mg; Sodium 65mg; Total Carbohydrate 5g (Dietary Fiber 0g); Protein 0g

BACON MARTINI COCKTAILS Omit all ingredients except ice. Heat oven to 400°F. Line 15x10x1-inch pan with foil. Coat both sides of 4 slices bacon with 2 teaspoons brown sugar, pressing into bacon. Place on pan. Bake 10 to 15 minutes or until bacon is crisp and sugar is bubbly. Cool on cooling rack. Add ½ cup vodka, ⅓ cup apple-flavored brandy, ⅓ cup apple cider and 2 tablespoons real maple syrup to ice in martini shaker; shake or stir and pour as directed. Garnish each with a piece of bacon and an apple slice.

CHOCOLATE MARTINI COCKTAILS Omit all ingredients except ice. Swirl about 1 tablespoon chocolate syrup on inside of each chilled glass. To serve, add ⅓ cup chocolate-flavored liqueur, ⅓ cup Irish cream liqueur, ⅓ cup vanilla-flavored vodka and ⅓ cup creme de cacao to ice in martini shaker; shake or stir and pour over swirled chocolate in each glass.

COCONUT-RUM MARTINI COCKTAILS Omit all ingredients except ice. Add ½ cup pineapple juice, ½ cup coconut rum and ⅓ cup dark rum to ice in martini shaker; shake or stir and pour as directed. Garnish each with a pineapple wedge and a maraschino cherry.

GREEN TEA MARTINI COCKTAILS Omit all ingredients except ice. Add ½ cup citrus-flavored vodka, ½ cup chilled brewed green tea and ⅓ cup sweet tea-flavored vodka or regular vodka to ice in martini shaker; shake or stir and pour as directed.

MANGO MARTINI COCKTAILS Omit all ingredients except ice. Puree 5 slices mango and 5 tablespoons syrup from

Making a Citrus Twist

With vegetable peeler or small knife, cut strip of orange or lemon peel; twist as desired.

Coating the Edge of a Glass

Wet rim of glass with citrus wedge or dip into lemon or lime juice or water on small plate; shake off excess.

Dip wet rim into sugar, coarse (kosher) salt, decorator sugar or chocolate candy sprinkles on small plate.

one jar (24 oz) refrigerated mango slices in extra light syrup to make about ½ cup puree. Add ½ cup mango puree, ½ cup peach-flavored vodka, ¼ cup orange-flavored liqueur and 2 tablespoons fresh lime juice to ice in martini shaker; shake or stir and pour as directed. Garnish each with a slice of mango and a slice of lime if desired.

MARGATINI COCKTAILS Omit all ingredients except ice. If desired, wet rim of each glass by dipping in frozen limeade concentrate. Dip into coarse salt. In 1 cup measure, mix ½ cup frozen limeade concentrate and enough water to equal ⅔ cup. Add concentrate mixture, ⅓ cup vodka and ⅓ cup tequila to ice in martini shaker; shake or stir and pour as directed. Garnish each with a slice of lime if desired.

POMEGRANATE MARTINI COCKTAILS Omit all ingredients except ice. Wet rim of each glass by rubbing with lime wedge; dip into colored sugar. Add 1 cup pomegranate juice, 3 tablespoons citrus-flavored vodka, 2 tablespoons orange-flavored liqueur and 1 tablespoon fresh lime juice to ice in martini shaker; shake or stir and pour as directed.

SWEET MARTINI COCKTAILS Substitute sweet vermouth for the dry vermouth.

MANHATTAN COCKTAILS FAST

PREP 10 min **TOTAL** 10 min • **2 or 4 servings**

Ingredients	To Serve 2	To Serve 4
Small ice cubes or shaved ice	¼ cup	½ cup
Bourbon or whiskey	⅓ cup	⅔ cup
Sweet vermouth	⅓ cup	⅔ cup
Aromatic bitters	2 dashes	4 dashes (⅛ to ¼ teaspoon)
Maraschino cherries	2	4

1 Chill 2 or 4 (3-oz) stemmed glasses in freezer.

2 Place cherry in each chilled glass. Place ice in martini shaker or pitcher. Add bourbon, vermouth and bitters; shake or stir to blend. Pour into glasses, straining out ice.

1 Serving (⅓ Cup): Calories 130; Total Fat 0g (Saturated Fat 0g; Trans Fat 0g); Cholesterol 0mg; Sodium 0mg; Total Carbohydrate 4g (Dietary Fiber 0g); Protein 0g

Keys to Success

- **Chill glasses in freezer.** This will help chill drinks without diluting them.

- **For the coldest drinks,** use a martini shaker or a plastic shaker bottle with a strainer insert to really move the drink around the ice cubes, chilling it well.

- **Strain drink immediately after mixing** so that the ice will chill the drink but not dilute it.

- **Serve immediately.** Ice-cold drinks taste better than ones that are less chilled.

Chocolate Martini

Bacon Martini

Martini

Coconut-Rum Martini

Pomegranate Martini

See how to make shaken cocktails: Visit bettycrocker.com/BCcookbook

EGGNOG

The holidays seem a bit more cheery with a cup of nog. For food safety, our eggnog is made with a cooked egg custard instead of raw eggs.

PREP 35 min TOTAL 2 hr 35 min • **10 servings**

CUSTARD

- 3 eggs, slightly beaten
- ⅓ cup granulated sugar
  Dash salt
- 2½ cups milk
- 1 teaspoon vanilla

EGGNOG

- 1 cup whipping cream
- 2 tablespoons powdered sugar
- ½ teaspoon vanilla
- ½ cup light rum*
  Ground nutmeg

1 In heavy 2-quart saucepan, stir eggs, granulated sugar and salt until well mixed. Gradually stir in milk. Cook over medium heat 10 to 15 minutes, stirring constantly, until mixture just coats a metal spoon; remove from heat. Stir in 1 teaspoon vanilla. Place saucepan in cold water until custard is cool. (If custard curdles, beat vigorously with hand beater until smooth.) Cover and refrigerate at least 2 hours but no longer than 24 hours.

2 Just before serving, in chilled medium bowl, beat whipping cream, powdered sugar and ½ teaspoon vanilla with electric mixer on high speed until stiff. Gently stir 1 cup of the whipped cream and rum into custard.

3 Pour custard mixture into small punch bowl. Drop remaining whipped cream in mounds onto custard mixture. Sprinkle with nutmeg. Serve immediately. Store covered in refrigerator up to 2 days.

*2 tablespoons rum extract and ⅓ cup milk can be substituted for the rum.

1 Serving: Calories 160; Total Fat 10g (Saturated Fat 6g; Trans Fat 0g); Cholesterol 95mg; Sodium 70mg; Total Carbohydrate 12g (Dietary Fiber 0g); Protein 4g **Exchanges:** ½ Other Carbohydrate, ½ Low-Fat Milk, 1½ Fat **Carbohydrate Choices:** 1

LIGHTER **DIRECTIONS** For 3 grams of fat and 120 calories per serving, for the custard, substitute 2 eggs plus 2 egg whites for the 3 eggs and 2¼ cups fat-free (skim) milk for the milk. For the eggnog, substitute 2 cups frozen (thawed) reduced-fat whipped topping for the beaten whipping cream, powdered sugar and vanilla.

SANGRIA FAST

Sangria is also lovely made with white or rosé (blush) wine. Try adding fresh peach or plum slices instead of the lemon and orange.

PREP 10 min TOTAL 10 min • **8 servings**

- ⅔ cup lemon juice
- ⅓ cup orange juice
- ¼ cup sugar
- 1 lemon, cut into thin slices
- 1 orange, cut into thin slices
- 1 bottle (750 mL) dry red wine or nonalcoholic red wine

1 In half-gallon glass pitcher, mix juices and sugar until sugar is dissolved. Add lemon and orange slices to pitcher.

2 Stir wine into juice mixture. Add ice if desired.

1 Serving: Calories 100; Total Fat 0g (Saturated Fat 0g; Trans Fat 0g); Cholesterol 0mg; Sodium 10mg; Total Carbohydrate 10g (Dietary Fiber 0g); Protein 0g **Exchanges:** ½ Other Carbohydrate, 1 Fat **Carbohydrate Choices:** ½

WHITE SANGRIA Substitute dry white wine such as Chardonnay or Sauvignon Blanc for the dry red wine.

MANGO MIMOSAS FAST

PREP 5 min TOTAL 5 min • **12 servings**

- 2 cups orange juice, chilled
- 2 cups mango nectar, chilled*
- 1 bottle (750 mL) regular or nonalcoholic dry champagne or sparkling white wine, chilled

In 1½-quart pitcher, mix orange juice and mango nectar. Pour champagne into glasses until half full. Fill glasses with juice mixture.

*Apricot or peach nectar can be substituted.

1 Serving (⅔ Cup): Calories 100; Total Fat 0g (Saturated Fat 0g; Trans Fat 0g); Cholesterol 0mg; Sodium 10mg; Total Carbohydrate 11g (Dietary Fiber 0g); Protein 0g **Exchanges:** ½ Fruit, 1 Fat **Carbohydrate Choices:** 1

PINEAPPLE MIMOSAS Substitute pineapple juice for the mango nectar. Garnish with a pineapple wedge.

FISH & SHELLFISH

FISH

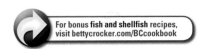

For bonus **fish and shellfish recipes,**
visit bettycrocker.com/BCcookbook

FAST = Ready in 20 minutes or less **LOWER CALORIE** = See Helpful Nutrition and Cooking Information, page 685
LIGHTER = 25% fewer calories or grams of fat **MAKE AHEAD** = Make-ahead directions **SLOW COOKER** = Slow cooker directions

← Shrimp Scampi (page 295), Pan-Seared Tilapia with Orange-Cream Sauce (page 285), Beer-Batter Fried Fish (page 284), Crab-Stuffed Shrimp (page 297)

FISH BASICS

People are eating fish more than ever because it is delicous, is healthful and can be fixed in many ways. Farm-raised fish, like catfish, salmon and trout, whether fresh or freshly frozen, is available almost everywhere. Fish is naturally rich in high-quality protein, yet is low in fat, saturated fat, cholesterol and calories. Follow our basics guide for all the information you need about buying, storing and cooking fish.

BUYING FISH

Fresh Fillets, Steaks or Whole Fish

- Flesh should be shiny, firm and spring back when touched. Avoid fish with dark edges or brown or yellowish discoloration.

- The contents should smell fresh and mild, not fishy or like ammonia.

- Be sure to use the fish by the package sell-by date.

- Eyes should be bright, clear and slightly bulging. Only a few fish, like walleye, have naturally cloudy eyes.

- Gills should be bright pink to red with no slime.

- Scales should be bright and shiny and should cling tightly to the skin.

Frozen Fish

- The package should be tightly wrapped, with few or no ice crystals and no freezer burn (which appears as dry or dark spots).

- The package should be odor free.

CHOOSING FISH BY FLAVOR AND TEXTURE

Fish can be categorized by flavor and texture, making it easy to substitute one fish for another within a category.

Mild Flavor	Moderate Flavor	Full Flavor
Delicate to Medium Texture		
Alaskan Pollock	Hake/Whiting	Herring/Sardines
Flounder	Lingcod	Smelt
Orange Roughy	Walleye	
Skate	Whitefish	
Sole		
Medium-Firm Texture		
Catfish	Black Sea Bass	Butterfish/Pompano
Cod	Char	Mackerel
Cusk	Chilean Sea Bass	Sablefish/Black Cod
Haddock	Drum	Salmon
Red Snapper	Lake Perch	Snapper
Tilapia	Mahi Mahi	Vermillion Snapper
Tilefish	Porgy/Scup	Wahoo
	Rainbow Trout	
	Redfish	
	Rockfish/Ocean Perch	
	Sea Bass	
	Shad	
Firm Texture		
Grouper	Shark	Marlin
Halibut	Sturgeon	Swordfish
Monkfish		Tuna (Albacore, Bluefin, Yellowfin/Ahi)
Striped Bass		

Selection of fresh fish steaks and fillets

Red Snapper   Tuna   Tilapia   Salmon

STORING FRESH FISH

- Store fresh fish in its original packaging in the meat compartment or coldest part of your refrigerator. Use within 2 days.

- Fish packaged in clear plastic wrap on a tray can be frozen as it is. Other fish should be tightly wrapped in butcher paper, foil or freezer plastic bags. Freeze for up to 6 months; thaw overnight in refrigerator.

COOKING FISH

Fish is naturally delicate and tender; overcooking makes it dry. Use the "10-minute rule" for cooking moist, flaky fish:

- Measure the fish at its thickest point. If it will be stuffed or rolled, measure it before stuffing or rolling.

- Fish fillets will often have skin on one side. Cook the fish, skin side down. The skin helps to hold the fish together and is easy to remove after cooking.

- Cook 10 minutes per inch of thickness. Turn over halfway through cooking time only if specified. Fillets less than ½ inch thick usually need no turning. Cook frozen fish 20 minutes per inch. Add 5 minutes to the total cooking time if the fish is cooked in foil or in a sauce.

- Cook just until the fish flakes easily with a fork. Insert a fork gently into the thickest part of the fish and twist slightly. The flesh should begin to separate along the natural lines.

FISH POUNDS PER SERVING

The number of servings per pound varies depending on the form of fish.

Type of Fish	Pounds per Serving
Fillets or Steaks	⅓ to ½
Pan-Dressed (often scaled with internal organs, head, tail and fins removed)	½
Drawn (whole with head and tail; only internal organs removed)	½ to ¾
Whole (right from the water)	¾ to 1

- Marinate fish no longer than 30 minutes. Fish will become mushy if it is in an acid marinade longer than that.

Removing Bones and Skin from Fish Fillets

Not all purchased fish fillets will have bones or skin, but if they do, follow these steps.

Place fish fillet, skin side down, on cutting board. Run fingertips along surface of fillet to feel for bones. Remove bones with needle-nose pliers or fingers (use a paper towel to help grasp the slippery bones).

Starting at tail end of fillet, work edge of boning knife between flesh and skin to separate. Grasp skin with paper towel and hold as you run knife down length of fillet.

TIMETABLE FOR COOKING FISH IN A MICROWAVE

- Arrange fish fillets or steaks in single layer in shallow microwavable dish with thickest parts to the outside edge. Fold thin ends of fillets under for even thickness or loosely roll up thin fillets.
- Cover with plastic wrap, folding one edge or corner back about ¼ inch to vent steam.
- Microwave on High as directed below, rotating dish once if the microwave has no turntable, until thermometer inserted into thickest portion reads 170°F and the fish flakes easily with a fork. Let stand as directed before serving.

Form of Fish	Approximate Weight in Pounds	Microwave Time in Minutes	Stand Time in Minutes
Fillets	1	5 to 7	2
	1½	7 to 9	3
Steaks (1 inch thick)	1	5 to 7	3
	1½	8 to 10	3

BUTTERY BROILED FISH STEAKS

FAST

Here's one of the easiest and simplest ways to cook fresh fish. Serve with wedges of fresh lemon to drizzle over the cooked fish.

PREP 5 min TOTAL 20 min • **4 servings**

4 small salmon, tuna, halibut or other medium-firm to firm fish steaks, about ¾ inch thick (6 oz each)
Salt and pepper to taste
2 tablespoons butter, melted

1 Set oven control to broil. Sprinkle both sides of fish with salt and pepper. Place fish on rack in broiler pan. Brush with 1 tablespoon of the butter.

2 Broil with tops about 4 inches from heat 5 minutes. Carefully turn fish; brush with remaining 1 tablespoon butter. Broil 4 to 6 minutes longer or until fish flakes easily with fork.

1 Serving: Calories 280; Total Fat 15g (Saturated Fat 6g; Trans Fat 0g); Cholesterol 125mg; Sodium 340mg; Total Carbohydrate 0g (Dietary Fiber 0g); Protein 36g **Exchanges:** 5 Lean Meat **Carbohydrate Choices:** 0

BROILED FISH FILLETS Substitute 1 lb fish fillets, cut into 4 serving pieces, for the fish steaks. Broil with tops about 4 inches from heat 5 to 6 minutes or until fish flakes easily with fork (do not turn).

LEMON-BUTTER BAKED FISH FILLETS LOWER CALORIE

PREP 5 min TOTAL 25 min • **4 servings**

1 lb sole, orange roughy or other delicate- to medium-texture fish fillets, ½ to ¾ inch thick
2 tablespoons butter, melted
1 tablespoon fresh lemon juice
¼ teaspoon salt
¼ teaspoon paprika

1 Heat oven to 375°F. Spray 13x9-inch pan with cooking spray.

2 Remove skin from fish if present, if desired. Cut fish into 4 serving pieces; place in pan (if fish has skin, place skin side down). Tuck under any thin ends for more even cooking.

3 In small bowl, mix remaining ingredients; drizzle over fish. Bake uncovered 15 to 20 minutes or until fish flakes easily with fork. Remove skin from fish before serving if desired.

1 Serving: Calories 140; Total Fat 7g (Saturated Fat 3g; Trans Fat 0g); Cholesterol 70mg; Sodium 270mg; Total Carbohydrate 0g (Dietary Fiber 0g); Protein 19g **Exchanges:** 2½ Lean Meat **Carbohydrate Choices:** 0

OVEN-FRIED FISH LOWER CALORIE

PREP 15 min TOTAL 25 min • **4 servings**

1 lb skinless cod, haddock or other medium-firm fish fillets, about ¾ inch thick
¼ cup cornmeal
¼ cup unseasoned dry bread crumbs
¾ teaspoon chopped fresh or ¼ teaspoon dried dill weed
½ teaspoon paprika
¼ teaspoon salt
⅛ teaspoon pepper
¼ cup milk
3 tablespoons butter, melted

1 Move oven rack to position slightly above middle of oven. Heat oven to 450°F.

2 Cut fish into four 2x1½-inch pieces. In shallow dish, mix cornmeal, bread crumbs, dill, paprika, salt and pepper. Place milk in another shallow dish. Dip fish into milk, then coat with cornmeal mixture.

3 Place fish in ungreased 13x9-inch pan. Drizzle butter over fish. Bake uncovered about 12 minutes or until fish flakes easily with fork.

1 Serving: Calories 240; Total Fat 11g (Saturated Fat 5g; Trans Fat 0.5g); Cholesterol 85mg; Sodium 360mg; Total Carbohydrate 12g (Dietary Fiber 0g); Protein 24g **Exchanges:** 1 Starch, 3 Lean Meat **Carbohydrate Choices:** 1

Learn to Make **Panfried Fish**

PANFRIED FISH `LOWER CALORIE`

Panfried fish is quick and easy enough for weeknight meal but is also a great choice for a special occasion. You want it to be tender and flaky on the inside and golden brown and crispy on the outside. Follow our easy instructions and you'll be an expert in no time.

PREP 10 min **TOTAL** 30 min • **6 servings**

Vegetable oil or shortening
1½ lb perch, snapper or other medium-firm fish fillets (½ to ¾ inch thick)
¾ teaspoon salt
¼ teaspoon pepper

1 egg
1 tablespoon water
⅔ cup all-purpose flour, cornmeal or dry bread crumbs

---

1 Pour about ⅛ inch oil into 12-inch skillet. Heat over medium heat. Cut fish into 6 serving pieces. Sprinkle both sides with salt and pepper.

2 In small bowl, beat egg and water with fork or wire whisk until blended. Place flour in shallow dish. Dip fish into egg, then coat with flour.

3 Fry fish in oil 6 to 8 minutes, turning once, until fish flakes easily with fork and is brown on both sides. (Fish cooks very quickly, especially the thinner tail sections; be careful not to overcook.) Remove with slotted spatula; drain on paper towels.

1 Serving: Calories 200; Total Fat 7g (Saturated Fat 1.5g; Trans Fat 0g); Cholesterol 95mg; Sodium 230mg; Total Carbohydrate 11g (Dietary Fiber 0g); Protein 24g **Exchanges:** 1 Starch, 3 Very Lean Meat, ½ Fat **Carbohydrate Choices:** 1

BROWN-BUTTER PANFRIED FISH Omit oil. Use flour for coating. Heat ¼ cup butter in skillet over medium heat 3 to 4 minutes, stirring constantly, until light brown. Add fish; cook as directed.

GARLIC-BUTTER PANFRIED FISH Omit salt. Substitute crushed garlic-butter–flavored croutons for the flour. (Place croutons in resealable food-storage plastic bag and crush with rolling pin.) Continue as directed in Step 2.

PARMESAN-HERB AND LEMON PANFRIED FISH Omit salt and pepper. Substitute Italian-style panko crispy bread crumbs for flour and decrease to ⅓ cup. Mix bread crumbs, ⅓ cup grated Parmesan cheese and 1 teaspoon grated lemon peel; continue as directed in Step 2.

Keys to Success

- Use vegetable oil or shortening for frying fish. Other oils can smoke before they get hot enough to cook the fish, resulting in a burned flavor.

- Dip in egg, then in flour. The wetness of the egg helps hold the flour on the fish. During cooking, the protein in the egg binds the flour to the fish to help keep the coating attached.

- Check for doneness. When the fish is done, the outside will be golden brown with no parts that are dark brown, and the inside will be firm but flake easily with a fork.

See how to make **panfried fish**:
Visit bettycrocker.com/BCcookbook

TOPPERS FOR PANFRIED FISH

Moist and tender freshly cooked fish is a wonderful canvas for just about any flavor. Here are some tasty offerings (4 to 6 servings) to spread on just-cooked fillets.

1 Avocado-Kiwi Salsa: Gently toss 1 cup avocado cubes, ½ cup peeled chopped kiwifruit, 3 tablespoons sliced green onions, 1 tablespoon finely chopped seeded jalapeño chile, 2 tablespoons lime juice, 2 tablespoons chopped fresh cilantro and ¼ teaspoon salt.

3 Sweet Pea-Mint Pesto: Place 1 cup cooked cold sweet peas, 2 tablespoons chopped fresh mint leaves, 1 garlic clove, ¼ teaspoon each coarse black pepper and salt, and ¼ cup each olive oil and shredded Parmesan cheese in food processor. Process just until blended.

2 Honey-Pecan Sauce: Mix 3 tablespoons honey, 2 tablespoons melted butter, 2 tablespoons chopped toasted pecans (page 22), 2 teaspoons fresh lemon juice and 1 teaspoon coarse-grained mustard.

4 Tomato-Basil Butter: Mix ½ cup softened butter, 3 tablespoons tomato paste and 1 tablespoon chopped fresh basil until well blended.

BEER-BATTER FRIED FISH

The batter on this fish cooks up light, puffy and very crisp.

PREP 15 min TOTAL 25 min • **4 servings**

Vegetable oil for frying
1 lb skinless walleye, sole or other delicate- to medium-texture fish fillets, about ½ inch thick
3 to 4 tablespoons all-purpose flour
1 cup all-purpose flour
½ cup regular or nonalcoholic beer
1 egg
½ teaspoon salt
Tartar Sauce (page 483), if desired

1 In deep fryer or 4-quart Dutch oven, heat oil (1½ inches) to 350°F. Cut fish into 8 serving pieces. Lightly coat fish with 3 to 4 tablespoons flour.

2 In medium bowl, mix remaining ingredients except tartar sauce with wooden spoon until smooth. (If batter is too thick, stir in additional beer, 1 tablespoon at a time, until desired consistency.) Dip fish into batter, letting excess drip into bowl.

3 Fry batches of fish in oil about 4 minutes, turning once, until golden brown (tail sections may cook more quickly). Remove with slotted spoon; drain on paper towels. Serve hot with tartar sauce.

1 Serving: Calories 390; Total Fat 17g (Saturated Fat 3g; Trans Fat 0.5g); Cholesterol 115mg; Sodium 410mg; Total Carbohydrate 30g (Dietary Fiber 1g); Protein 27g **Exchanges:** 2 Starch, 3 Very Lean Meat, 3 Fat **Carbohydrate Choices:** 2

PECAN-CRUSTED FISH FILLETS

PREP 15 min TOTAL 25 min • **4 servings**

1 cup finely chopped pecans (not ground)
¼ cup dry unseasoned bread crumbs
2 teaspoons grated lemon peel
1 egg
1 tablespoon milk
1 lb skinless sole, orange roughy, walleye or other delicate- to medium-texture fish fillets, about ½ inch thick
½ teaspoon salt
¼ teaspoon pepper
2 tablespoons vegetable oil
Lemon wedges

1 In shallow dish, mix pecans, bread crumbs and lemon peel. In another shallow dish, beat egg and milk with fork or wire whisk until blended.

2 Cut fish into 4 serving pieces. Sprinkle both sides of fish with salt and pepper. Dip fish into egg mixture, then coat well with pecan mixture, pressing lightly into fish.

3 In 12-inch nonstick skillet, heat oil over medium heat. Add fish. Reduce heat to medium-low. Cook 6 to 10 minutes, carefully turning once with 2 pancake turners, until fish flakes easily with fork and is brown. Serve with lemon wedges.

1 Serving: Calories 350; Total Fat 25g (Saturated Fat 3g; Trans Fat 0g); Cholesterol 105mg; Sodium 450mg; Total Carbohydrate 9g (Dietary Fiber 3g); Protein 24g **Exchanges:** ½ Starch, 3 Lean Meat, 3 Fat **Carbohydrate Choices:** ½

Seafood Sustainability

Many chefs, restaurateurs and consumers ask for sustainable seafood. It's sustainable when the population of a fish species is managed to provide for today's needs without damaging the ability of the species to reproduce. If you buy fish managed under a U.S. fishery management plan, it meets 10 national standards that ensure fish stocks are maintained, over-fishing is eliminated, and the long-term socioeconomic benefits are achieved.

For more information, go to www.nmfs.noaa.gov/fishwatch

Pecan-Crusted Fish Fillets

PAN-SEARED TILAPIA WITH ORANGE-CREAM SAUCE

PREP 30 min TOTAL 30 min • **4 servings**

SAUCE
½ cup dry white wine or chicken broth
¼ cup orange juice
3 tablespoons finely chopped shallots or onion
¾ cup whipping cream
1 teaspoon grated orange peel
¼ cup cold butter, cut into 4 pieces
¼ teaspoon salt
⅛ teaspoon white pepper

TILAPIA
1 tablespoon vegetable oil
4 skinless tilapia or other medium-firm fish fillets (1½ lb)
¼ teaspoon salt

GARNISH
¼ cup chopped hazelnuts (filberts) or almonds, toasted (page 22)

1 In 2-quart saucepan, heat wine, orange juice and shallots to boiling over medium-high heat. Boil uncovered 4 minutes, stirring occasionally, until liquid is reduced by half. Add whipping cream; heat to boiling, stirring occasionally. Boil uncovered 6 minutes, stirring occasionally, until sauce is thickened and reduced to about ½ cup.

2 Remove from heat; add orange peel. Beat in butter, 1 piece at a time, with whisk, adding the next piece only after the first has been completely beaten in and melted. When all of the butter has been beaten in, add ¼ teaspoon salt and the white pepper. Cover to keep warm.

3 In 12-inch nonstick skillet, heat oil over medium-high heat until hot. Sprinkle fish with ¼ teaspoon salt. Cook fish in oil 6 minutes, turning once, or until edges begin to brown and fish flakes easily with fork. To serve, spoon sauce over fish and sprinkle with nuts.

1 Serving: Calories 460; Total Fat 35g (Saturated Fat 16g; Trans Fat 1g); Cholesterol 160mg; Sodium 510mg; Total Carbohydrate 4g (Dietary Fiber 1g); Protein 31g **Exchanges:** 4½ Medium-Fat Meat, 2½ Fat **Carbohydrate Choices:** 0

ROASTED TILAPIA AND VEGETABLES LOWER CALORIE

PREP 15 min TOTAL 40 min • **4 servings**

8 oz fresh asparagus spears
2 small zucchini, cut in half lengthwise, then cut into ½-inch pieces
1 medium bell pepper, cut into ½-inch strips
1 large onion, cut into ½-inch wedges, separated
2 tablespoons olive oil
2 teaspoons Montreal steak grill seasoning
4 skinless tilapia or other medium-firm fish fillets (6 oz each)
1 tablespoon butter, melted
½ teaspoon paprika

1 Heat oven to 450°F. Snap off tough ends of asparagus; cut each spear in half. In large bowl, mix asparagus, zucchini, bell pepper, onion and oil. Sprinkle with 1 teaspoon of the grill seasoning; toss to coat. Spread vegetables in ungreased 15x10x1-inch pan. Place on lowest oven rack; bake 5 minutes.

2 Meanwhile, spray 13x9-inch (3-quart) glass baking dish with cooking spray. Pat tilapia fillets dry with paper towels. Brush fish with butter; sprinkle with paprika and remaining 1 teaspoon grill seasoning. Place in baking dish.

3 Place baking dish on middle oven rack. Bake fish and vegetables uncovered 17 to 18 minutes or until fish flakes easily with fork and vegetables are tender.

1 Serving: Calories 290; Total Fat 12g (Saturated Fat 3.5g; Trans Fat 0g); Cholesterol 100mg; Sodium 520mg; Total Carbohydrate 10g (Dietary Fiber 3g); Protein 34g **Exchanges:** 2 Vegetable, 4 Lean Meat, ½ Fat **Carbohydrate Choices:** ½

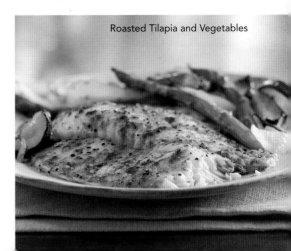
Roasted Tilapia and Vegetables

SOLE AMANDINE LOWER CALORIE

A French term, amandine means "garnished with almonds" and is often misspelled as "almondine." If you own a gratin dish (a shallow oval-shaped ovenproof baking dish), use it to bake this classic dish.

PREP 15 min TOTAL 35 min • **6 servings**

- 1½ **lb skinless sole, orange roughy or other delicate- to medium-texture fish fillets, ½ to ¾ inch thick**
- ½ **cup sliced almonds**
- ¼ **cup butter, softened**
- 2 **tablespoons grated lemon peel**
- ½ **teaspoon salt**
- ½ **teaspoon paprika**
- 2 **tablespoons fresh lemon juice**
  Chopped fresh parsley, if desired

1 Heat oven to 375°F. Spray 11x7-inch (2-quart) glass baking dish with cooking spray.

2 Cut fish into 6 serving pieces. Place in baking dish (if fish has skin, place skin side down). Tuck under any thin ends for more even cooking.

3 In small bowl, mix almonds, butter, lemon peel, salt and paprika; spoon over fish. Sprinkle with lemon juice.

4 Bake uncovered 15 to 20 minutes or until fish flakes easily with fork. Sprinkle with parsley.

1 Serving: Calories 210; Total Fat 13g (Saturated Fat 4.5g; Trans Fat 0g); Cholesterol 75mg; Sodium 330mg; Total Carbohydrate 2g (Dietary Fiber 1g); Protein 21g **Exchanges:** 3 Very Lean Meat, 2½ Fat **Carbohydrate Choices:** 0

LIGHTER DIRECTIONS For 6 grams of fat and 140 calories per serving, decrease both almonds and butter to 2 tablespoons.

ORANGE SOLE AMANDINE Substitute orange peel for the lemon peel and orange juice for the lemon juice. Garnish with fresh basil leaves.

Baking, Broiling or Grilling Fish with the Skin On

Baking, broiling or grilling skin-on fish helps to hold the delicate flesh together. Removing skin after cooking is easier than before cooking. When done, carefully insert a metal spatula between the skin and the flesh, starting at the tail end if present (if no tail end, start at any edge). While holding onto a small piece of skin, slide the fish off.

Sole Amandine

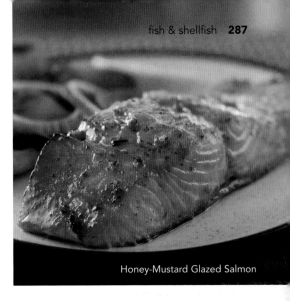

Honey-Mustard Glazed Salmon

ASIAN TUNA WITH WASABI AIOLI

Wasabi, also called Japanese horseradish, has sharp, pungent, fiery flavors. It comes in both powder and paste forms and is available in the ethnic-foods aisle of large supermarkets. If you can't find it, regular prepared horseradish makes a great substitute.

PREP 10 min **TOTAL** 2 hr 25 min • **8 servings**

TUNA

- 2 lb tuna steaks, ¾ to 1 inch thick
- ½ cup vegetable oil
- ⅓ cup soy sauce
- 2 tablespoons packed brown sugar
- 2 teaspoons sesame oil
- 2 teaspoons grated gingerroot
- 2 cloves garlic, finely chopped

WASABI AIOLI

- ½ cup mayonnaise or salad dressing
- 1 teaspoon wasabi powder or prepared horseradish

GARNISH

- 2 teaspoons sesame seed, toasted (page 22) if desired

1 If tuna steaks are large, cut into 8 serving pieces. In shallow glass or plastic dish or resealable food-storage plastic bag, mix vegetable oil, soy sauce, brown sugar, sesame oil, gingerroot and garlic. Add tuna; turn to coat with marinade. Cover dish or seal bag; refrigerate, turning once, at least 2 hours but no longer than 4 hours.

2 Meanwhile, in small bowl, mix aioli ingredients. Cover and refrigerate until serving.

3 Set oven control to broil. Remove tuna from marinade; reserve marinade. Place tuna on rack in broiler pan. Broil with top 4 to 6 inches from heat 10 to 15 minutes, brushing 2 to 3 times with marinade and turning once, until fish flakes easily with fork and is slightly pink in center. Discard any remaining marinade. Sprinkle sesame seed over tuna. Serve with aioli.

1 Serving: Calories 350; Total Fat 27g (Saturated Fat 4.5g; Trans Fat 0g); Cholesterol 75mg; Sodium 600mg; Total Carbohydrate 4g (Dietary Fiber 0g); Protein 22g **Exchanges:** 3 Medium-Fat Meat, 2½ Fat **Carbohydrate Choices:** 0

HONEY-MUSTARD GLAZED SALMON LOWER CALORIE

PREP 5 min **TOTAL** 35 min • **4 servings**

- 1 salmon fillet (1 lb)
- 1 tablespoon packed brown sugar
- 1 tablespoon butter, melted
- 1 tablespoon olive or vegetable oil
- 1 tablespoon honey
- 1 tablespoon soy sauce
- 1 tablespoon Dijon mustard
- 1 clove garlic, finely chopped

1 Place salmon, skin side down, in shallow glass or plastic dish. In small bowl, mix remaining ingredients; pour over salmon. Cover; refrigerate at least 15 minutes but no longer than 1 hour.

2 Set oven control to broil. Remove salmon from marinade; reserve marinade. Place salmon, skin side down, on rack in broiler pan. Broil with top 4 to 6 inches from heat 10 to 15 minutes, brushing 2 to 3 times with marinade, until fish flakes easily with fork. Discard any remaining marinade.

1 Serving: Calories 230; Total Fat 11g (Saturated Fat 3.5g; Trans Fat 0g); Cholesterol 80mg; Sodium 320mg; Total Carbohydrate 7g (Dietary Fiber 0g); Protein 24g **Exchanges:** ½ Starch, 3 Lean Meat **Carbohydrate Choices:** ½

LEMON- AND PARMESAN-CRUSTED SALMON

This excellent salmon is easy, elegant and impressive. Serve with steamed or grilled asparagus spears and buttered small red potatoes.

PREP 10 min TOTAL 35 min • **4 servings**

- 1 salmon fillet (1¼ lb)
- 2 tablespoons butter, melted
- ¼ teaspoon salt
- ¾ cup medium- to firm-textured bread crumbs (about 1 slice bread)*
- ¼ cup grated Parmesan cheese
- 2 medium green onions, thinly sliced (2 tablespoons)
- 2 teaspoons grated lemon peel
- ¼ teaspoon dried thyme leaves

1 Heat oven to 375°F. Spray shallow baking pan with cooking spray. Pat salmon dry with paper towels. Place salmon, skin side down, in pan. Brush with 1 tablespoon of the butter. Sprinkle with salt.

2 In small bowl, mix bread crumbs, cheese, onions, lemon peel and thyme. Stir in remaining 1 tablespoon butter. Press bread crumb mixture evenly on salmon.

3 Bake uncovered 15 to 25 minutes or until fish flakes easily with fork. Serve immediately.

*Soft-textured bread is not recommended because it's too moist and won't create a crisp crumb topping.

1 Serving: Calories 290; Total Fat 16g (Saturated Fat 6g; Trans Fat 0g); Cholesterol 115mg; Sodium 420mg; Total Carbohydrate 4g (Dietary Fiber 0g); Protein 33g **Exchanges:** 5 Lean Meat, ½ Fat **Carbohydrate Choices:** 0

Salmon Burgers with Sour Cream-Dill Sauce

SALMON BURGERS WITH SOUR CREAM–DILL SAUCE

PREP 20 min TOTAL 30 min • **4 servings**

SOUR CREAM–DILL SAUCE

- ⅓ cup sour cream
- 3 tablespoons mayonnaise or salad dressing
- ¾ teaspoon dried dill weed

BURGERS

- 1 egg
- 2 tablespoons milk
- 1 can (14¾ oz) salmon, drained, skin and bones removed, flaked
- 2 medium green onions, chopped (2 tablespoons)
- 1 cup soft bread crumbs (about 1½ slices bread)
- ¼ teaspoon salt
- 1 tablespoon vegetable oil

1 In small bowl, stir sauce ingredients until well mixed. Cover; refrigerate until serving.

2 In medium bowl, beat egg and milk with fork or wire whisk. Stir in remaining ingredients except oil. Shape mixture into 4 patties, about 4 inches in diameter.

3 In 10-inch nonstick skillet, heat oil over medium heat. Cook patties in oil about 8 minutes, turning once, until golden brown. Serve with sauce.

1 Serving: Calories 300; Total Fat 22g (Saturated Fat 6g; Trans Fat 0g); Cholesterol 120mg; Sodium 750mg; Total Carbohydrate 6g (Dietary Fiber 0g); Protein 20g **Exchanges:** ½ Starch, 2½ Lean Meat, 3 Fat **Carbohydrate Choices:** ½

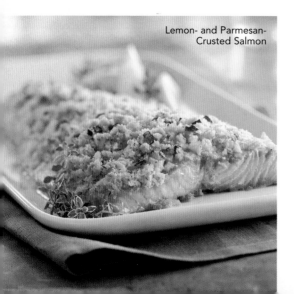

Lemon- and Parmesan-Crusted Salmon

SHELLFISH BASICS

Compared to fish, shellfish have a slightly salty flavor that is still mild enough to have wide appeal. Shellfish are grouped into two main categories: crustaceans and mollusks. Crustaceans have long bodies with soft, jointed shells and include crabs, crayfish, lobsters and shrimp. Mollusks have soft bodies covered by a shell and no spinal column and include abalone, clams, mussels, octopus, oysters, scallops and squid (calamari).

BUYING SHELLFISH

Most supermarkets carry both fresh and frozen shellfish. Keep the following tips in mind when purchasing:

Clams, Mussels and Oysters: Clam varieties include *hard shell* (cherrystone and littleneck) and *softshell* (razor and steamers). Clams, mussels and oysters in shells should be purchased alive. Look for tightly closed shells that are not cracked, chipped or broken. They should have a mild odor. The shells may open naturally but will close if lightly tapped, indicating they are still alive. If shells do not close, throw them out. Clams and mussels should be cleaned before using; see specific recipes on page 297 and 298.

Shucked Clams, Mussels and Oysters (No Shells): These should be plump and surrounded by a clear, slightly milky or light gray liquid.

Scallops: Varieties include *sea scallops* (1½ to 2 inches wide) and tiny *bay scallops* (½ inch wide). Scallops should look moist and have a mild, sweet smell. They should not be standing in liquid or stored on ice. They are usually creamy white and may be tinted light orange, light tan or pink.

Live Crabs and Lobsters: These will show some leg movement, and lobsters will curl their tails under when picked up. Crabs and lobsters must be cooked live or killed immediately before cooking; throw out any that are dead. Crabmeat is available in a pasteurized fresh form, and both crab and lobster meat are available frozen and canned.

Shrimp: Shrimp are sold in a variety of ways: raw ("green") with the heads on; raw in the shell without the heads; raw, peeled and deveined; cooked in the shell; or cooked, peeled and deveined. Shrimp should have a clean sea odor. If they smell like ammonia, they're spoiled and should be discarded.

Squid (Calamari): Squid ranges in color from cream with reddish brown spots to light pink. Buy fresh squid that's whole with clear eyes and a fresh sea odor. Cleaned squid is also available; it should be in juices, and the meat should be firm.

Imitation Seafood Products

Imitation seafood products, like crab legs or pieces or lobster pieces, are usually made from pollock and are less expensive than shellfish but similar in taste and texture to the real thing. To enhance flavor, some real shellfish, a shellfish extract or artificial shellfish flavoring is added. Check labels carefully if you have a shellfish allergy.

Cook clams until they open; discard any that do not open.

Lobster

Snow Crab

Brown Shrimp

Tiger Shrimp

King
Crab

Salad Shrimp

Laughing Bird Shrimp

Crayfish

Cherrystone
Clams

Soft-Shell Crab

Hard-Shell
Blue Crab

Countneck
Clams

Littleneck
Clams

Sea Scallops

Lantern Bay Scallops

Blue Point Oysters

Squid (Calamari)

Prince Edward Island (P. E. I.) Mussels

Manila Clams

STORING SHELLFISH

- Live crabs (hard- or soft-shell) and lobsters should be cooked the same day they're purchased. Put them on a tray with sides, cover with a damp cloth and refrigerate until ready to cook.

- Raw scallops, shrimp, squid and shucked shellfish should be stored in a leakproof bag or plastic container with a lid. Cook scallops, shrimp and squid within 2 days. Shucked shellfish should be used within 7 days.

- Live clams, mussels and oysters should be refrigerated in a container covered with a clean, damp cloth, **not with an airtight lid or in a plastic bag, which will cause suffocation.** Live clams, mussels and oysters may open their shells even when refrigerated. Give the shells a tap—they will close if alive; if not, throw them out. Cook within 2 days.

SHELLFISH PER SERVING

The amount of shellfish you need per person depends on the type you're preparing.

Type of Shellfish	Amount per Serving
Clams, Mussels or Oysters	
In shell	3 large hard-shell clams
	6 small hard-shell clams
	18 soft-shell clams
	18 mussels
	6 oysters
Shucked	¼ lb
Crab (Hard-Shell) or Lobster	1¼ lb live or ¼ lb cooked
Crab (Soft-Shell)	2 crabs
Shrimp	
With head, unpeeled	1 lb
Without head, unpeeled	½ lb
Without head, peeled	¼ lb
Squid	
Whole	½ lb
Cleaned	¼ lb

SUCCESSFULLY COOKING SHELLFISH

Cooked shellfish should be moist and slightly chewy; overcooking makes it tough and rubbery. Follow these guidelines to determine when shellfish is done:

- Crabs and lobsters turn bright red.

- Scallops turn milky white or opaque and get firm.

- Raw shrimp turns pink and gets firm.

- Live clams, oysters and mussels open their shells.

- Shucked clams, oysters and mussels get plump and opaque. Oyster edges start to curl.

- To cook in a skillet (panfry), heat about 1 tablespoon oil over medium-high heat. Cook the shellfish as directed below.

- To boil, bring water to a boil in large saucepan. Add shellfish and cook as directed below.

- To broil, place shellfish on broiler rack. Broil 7 to 9 inches from heat as directed below.

TIMETABLE FOR COOKING SHELLFISH

Shellfish can be cooked in a variety of ways. Keep in mind the cooking time varies depending on the method of preparation.

Type of Shellfish	Amount in Pounds (about 4 servings)	Method and Cook Time
Scallops, bay or sea	1	Panfry 3 to 6 minutes
		Boil 2 to 3 minutes
		Broil 3 to 5 minutes
Shrimp, peeled and deveined	1	Panfry 3 to 6 minutes
		Boil 2 to 3 minutes
		Broil 3 to 5 minutes
Shrimp in the shell	1	Boil 4 to 6 minutes
Clams or Oysters in shell	4	Boil or steam 5 to 7 minutes
Mussels in shell	2	Boil or steam 5 to 7 minutes
Squid	1	Panfry 2 to 3 minutes

TIMETABLE FOR COOKING SHRIMP OR SCALLOPS IN A MICROWAVE

- Pat scallops dry with paper towels; if large, cut in half. Rinse shrimp. Arrange in circle in shallow microwavable dish that's large enough to hold shellfish in a single layer.
- Cover with plastic wrap, folding one edge or corner back about ¼ inch to vent steam.
- Microwave on High as directed below, rotating the dish once if the microwave has no turntable, until scallops are white and shrimp are pink and firm. Let stand as directed before serving.

Type of Shellfish	Approximate Weight in Pounds	Microwave Time in Minutes	Stand Time in Minutes
Scallops (bay or sea)	1	4 to 5	2
Shrimp, peeled and deveined	1	6 to 8, stirring after 3 minutes	3
Shrimp in the shell	1	5 to 7, stirring after 3 minutes	3

HEATING COOKED CRAB LEGS

Most crab legs available for purchase are already cooked. Follow these steps to heat them before serving.

1. Cut crab legs to fit 8-inch square microwavable dish.

2. Cover with plastic wrap, folding one edge or corner back about ¼ inch to vent steam.

3. Microwave on Medium-High (70%) as directed below, rotating dish once if the microwave has no turntable, until hot. Let stand as directed before serving.

Type of Shellfish	Approximate Weight in Pounds	Microwave Time in Minutes	Stand Time in Minutes
Cooked Crab Legs, thawed if frozen	2	5 to 6	5

UNDERSTANDING SHRIMP COUNT

Fresh and frozen shrimp are sold by a descriptive size name like *jumbo* or *large,* and by "count," or number per pound. The larger the shrimp, the lower the count. Size and count vary throughout the United States.

Common Shrimp Size Market Name	Count (Approximate Number) per Pound
Colossal	Fewer than 10
Jumbo	11 to 15
Extra Large	16 to 20
Large	21 to 30
Medium	31 to 35
Small	36 to 45
Miniature or Tiny	About 100

Soft-Shell Crabs

Soft-shell crabs are the same species as Atlantic hard-shell blue crabs, except soft-shell crabs have been caught immediately after shedding their old hard shells. They stay soft for only a couple of hours before their shells harden again. Like all live crabs, they should be cooked the same day they're purchased.

Note: For more information about shellfish handling, safety and nutrition, call the FDA's Center for Food Safety and Applied Nutrition, 1-888-SAFEFOOD (723-3366). Recorded information is available 24 hours a day, or you can speak to an information specialist by calling Monday through Friday, 10 a.m. to 4 p.m. Eastern Standard Time. Or check the FDA's web site at www.fda.gov

DEEP-FRIED SHRIMP

PREP 40 min TOTAL 40 min • **4 servings**

Vegetable oil for frying
½ cup all-purpose flour
1 teaspoon salt
½ teaspoon pepper
2 eggs
¾ cup dry bread crumbs
1 lb uncooked medium shrimp, thawed if frozen, peeled (with tail shells left on), deveined

1 In deep fryer or 4-quart Dutch oven, heat oil (2 to 3 inches) to 350°F.

2 In shallow dish, mix flour, salt and pepper. In another shallow dish, beat eggs slightly with fork or wire whisk. In third shallow dish, place bread crumbs. Pat shrimp dry with paper towels. Coat shrimp with flour mixture; dip into egg, then coat with bread crumbs.

3 Fry 4 or 5 shrimp at a time in oil about 1 minute, turning once, until golden brown. Drain on paper towels.

1 Serving: Calories 300; Total Fat 14g (Saturated Fat 2.5g; Trans Fat 0g); Cholesterol 215mg; Sodium 920mg; Total Carbohydrate 27g (Dietary Fiber 0g); Protein 19g **Exchanges:** 2 Starch, 2 Lean Meat, 1 Fat **Carbohydrate Choices:** 2

DEEP-FRIED OYSTERS OR CLAMS Substitute ¾ lb shucked oysters or clams, drained, for the shrimp.

DEEP-FRIED SEA SCALLOPS Substitute ¾ lb sea scallops, drained, for the shrimp. Fry 3 to 4 minutes or until golden brown. Bay scallops, which are smaller, will cook more quickly.

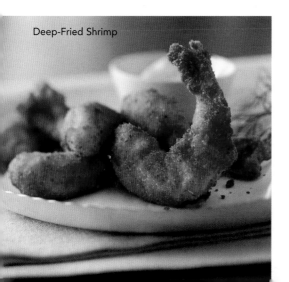
Deep-Fried Shrimp

EASY AIOLI

Made in minutes, these flavor-packed sauces jazz up any plain cooked fish. Start by placing 1 cup of regular, reduced-fat or fat-free mayonnaise in a small bowl to make any of the following flavors (for homemade mayonnaise, see page 483):

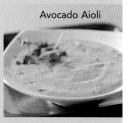
Avocado Aioli

Avocado Aioli: Place mayonnaise, 1 cup ripe avocado cubes, 1 tablespoon fresh lime juice and ¼ to ½ teaspoon red pepper sauce in food processor; process until smooth. Stir in 2 tablespoons chopped fresh cilantro.

Caper-Peppercorn Aioli: Add 2 tablespoons small well-drained capers and ½ to ¾ teaspoon coarse ground fresh pepper to mayonnaise.

Honey-Basil Aioli: Add 2 tablespoons chopped fresh basil, ½ teaspoon lemon pepper and 1 teaspoon honey to mayonnaise.

Orange-Chive Aioli: Add 2 tablespoons chopped fresh chives or green onion tops and 2 teaspoons grated orange peel to mayonnaise.

Sesame-Ginger Aioli: Add 2 tablespoons purchased teriyaki baste and glaze, 2 tablespoons finely chopped green onions, 2 teaspoons honey, 2 teaspoons toasted sesame seed, (page 22), and 2 teaspoons grated gingerroot to mayonnaise.

Smoked Paprika Aioli: Add 1 tablespoon lemon juice, ½ teaspoon grated lemon peel and 1 teaspoon smoked paprika to mayonnaise.

Sun-Dried Tomato Aioli: In food processor, place mayonnaise, ½ cup drained julienne-cut sun-dried tomatoes in oil and herbs (from jar), 1 tablespoon lemon juice and 1 clove garlic; process until blended.

Sun-Dried Tomato Aioli

Heirloom Recipe and New Twist

This cocktail sauce was in the first Betty Crocker Cookbook in 1950, along with the shrimp in another chapter. Because it is such a party and restaurant favorite, we thought it was time to pair the two recipes together. Bloody Mary Shrimp Cocktail is our new twist. Why not make both recipes for your next party?

CLASSIC

CLASSIC SHRIMP COCKTAIL

LOWER CALORIE

Use the freshest shrimp available for this classic recipe.

PREP 30 min **TOTAL** 35 min • **6 servings**

COCKTAIL SAUCE
- 1 **cup ketchup**
- 4 **to 6 teaspoons prepared horseradish**
- 1 **teaspoon Worcestershire sauce**
- 2 **or 3 drops red pepper sauce**

SHRIMP
- 4 **cups water**
- 1½ **lb uncooked large shrimp in shells, thawed if frozen, peeled, deveined, tails left on**

1 In small bowl, mix all sauce ingredients, stirring in 1 to 2 teaspoons additional horseradish if you like a hotter sauce.

2 In 3-quart saucepan, heat water to boiling. Add shrimp. Cover and return to boiling; reduce heat. Simmer uncovered 3 to 5 minutes or until shrimp are pink; drain. Serve shrimp with sauce.

1 Serving: Calories 100; Total Fat 0.5g (Saturated Fat 0g; Trans Fat 0g); Cholesterol 105mg; Sodium 770mg; Total Carbohydrate 11g (Dietary Fiber 0g); Protein 12g **Exchanges:** ½ Starch, 1½ Very Lean Meat **Carbohydrate Choices:** 1

Classic Shrimp Cocktail

Deveining Shrimp

Using a small, pointed knife or shrimp deveiner, make a shallow cut along the center back of each shrimp and wash out vein.

See how to make **shrimp cocktail:**
Visit bettycrocker.com/BCcookbook

Bloody Mary Shrimp Cocktail

NEW TWIST

BLOODY MARY SHRIMP COCKTAIL LOWER CALORIE

For a special presentation, place shrimp in an oversized martini glass (about 12 to 14 inches in diameter), pour cocktail sauce mixture over shrimp and garnish like a Bloody Mary with a skewer of colossal olives, small lime wedge and a celery stick.

PREP 30 min **TOTAL** 2 hr 40 min • **6 servings**

- 1½ lb cooked deveined peeled medium shrimp (60), thawed if frozen
- ½ cup tomato juice
- ¼ cup vodka, if desired
- ½ teaspoon red pepper sauce
- ½ teaspoon sugar
- ½ teaspoon celery salt
- 2 tablespoons chopped fresh parsley
- 1 cup cocktail sauce
- ¼ cup finely chopped pitted green olives

1 Arrange shrimp in single layer in 11x7-inch (2-quart) glass baking dish.

2 Heat tomato juice, vodka and pepper sauce to boiling in 1-quart saucepan over medium-high heat. Stir in sugar; reduce heat. Simmer uncovered 5 minutes, stirring occasionally. Stir in celery salt and parsley; pour over shrimp. Cover and refrigerate 2 to 3 hours.*

3 Mix cocktail sauce and olives; pour into small serving bowl. Remove shrimp from marinade with slotted spoon; arrange on serving platter. Serve shrimp with sauce.

*Don't marinate the shrimp more than 3 hours; a longer time in the tomato juice will toughen the shrimp.

1 Serving: Calories 170; Total Fat 2.5g (Saturated Fat 0g; Trans Fat 0g); Cholesterol 220mg; Sodium 1040mg; Total Carbohydrate 13g (Dietary Fiber 0g); Protein 24g **Exchanges:** ½ Starch, ½ Other Carbohydrate, 3 Very Lean Meat **Carbohydrate Choices:** 1

Bloody Mary Shrimp Shooters

For a fun appetizer, serve the shrimp and sauce in decorative shot glasses. Place about a tablespoon of the sauce in each shot glass, and top with one or two cooked shrimp. Garnish with a little chopped fresh parsley or celery leaves.

SHRIMP SCAMPI LOWER CALORIE

Serve these succulent shrimp over a bed of hot fettuccine or angel hair pasta and sprinkle with chopped fresh parsley.

PREP 35 min **TOTAL** 35 min • **6 servings**

- 2 tablespoons olive or vegetable oil
- 1½ lb uncooked medium shrimp, thawed if frozen, peeled, deveined
- 2 medium green onions, thinly sliced (2 tablespoons)
- 2 tablespoons fresh lemon juice
- 1 tablespoon chopped fresh parsley
- 2 cloves garlic, finely chopped
- ¼ teaspoon salt
    Grated or shredded Parmesan cheese, if desired

In 10-inch skillet, heat oil over medium heat. Cook shrimp and remaining ingredients except cheese in oil 2 to 3 minutes, stirring frequently, until shrimp are pink. Remove from heat; sprinkle with cheese.

1 Serving: Calories 90; Total Fat 4g (Saturated Fat 0.5g; Trans Fat 0g); Cholesterol 105mg; Sodium 220mg; Total Carbohydrate 1g (Dietary Fiber 0g); Protein 12g **Exchanges:** 2 Very Lean Meat, ½ Fat **Carbohydrate Choices:** 0

Shrimp Scampi

PANFRIED PEANUT-GINGER SHRIMP LOWER CALORIE

PREP 15 min TOTAL 45 min • **4 servings**

- 2 tablespoons soy sauce
- 2 teaspoons grated gingerroot
- ¼ teaspoon red pepper sauce
- 1 clove garlic, finely chopped
- ½ lb uncooked deveined peeled medium shrimp, thawed if frozen
- 3 tablespoons vegetable oil
- 1 cup hot cooked vermicelli or spaghetti (page 367)
- 4 green onions, cut into 1-inch pieces
- 6 oz fresh or frozen (partially thawed) snow pea pods (1½ cups)
- 2 tablespoons creamy peanut butter
- ¼ cup chopped peanuts

1 In large resealable food-storage plastic bag, mix soy sauce, gingerroot, pepper sauce and garlic. Add shrimp; seal bag. Let stand 15 minutes.

2 Meanwhile, in 10-inch skillet or wok, heat 2 tablespoons of the oil over medium-high heat. Cook and stir vermicelli, onions and pea pods in oil until onions are crisp-tender. Remove mixture from skillet.

3 In same skillet, heat remaining 1 tablespoon oil. Cook and stir shrimp in oil until pink. Stir in vermicelli mixture. Stir in peanut butter until mixture is coated; cook until hot. Sprinkle with peanuts.

1 Serving: Calories 320; Total Fat 20g (Saturated Fat 3.5g; Trans Fat 0g); Cholesterol 80mg; Sodium 590mg; Total Carbohydrate 19g (Dietary Fiber 3g); Protein 17g **Exchanges:** 1 Starch, 1 Vegetable, 1½ Lean Meat, 3 Fat **Carbohydrate Choices:** 1

SHRIMP CREOLE LOWER CALORIE

This traditional dish from Louisiana is a slightly spicy mixture of spices with tomatoes and shrimp. It's similar to gumbo but thicker.

PREP 30 min TOTAL 1 hr • **6 servings**

- ¼ cup butter
- 3 medium onions, chopped (1½ cups)
- 2 medium green bell peppers, finely chopped (2 cups)
- 2 medium stalks celery, finely chopped (1 cup)
- 2 cloves garlic, finely chopped
- 1 can (15 oz) tomato sauce
- 1 cup water
- 2 teaspoons chopped fresh parsley
- 1½ teaspoons salt
- ¼ teaspoon ground red pepper (cayenne)
- 2 dried bay leaves
- 2 lb uncooked medium shrimp, thawed if frozen, peeled, deveined
- 6 cups hot cooked rice (page 429)

1 In 3-quart saucepan, melt butter over medium heat. Cook onions, bell peppers, celery and garlic in butter about 10 minutes, stirring occasionally, until onions are tender. Stir in remaining ingredients except shrimp and rice. Heat to boiling; reduce heat to low. Simmer uncovered 10 minutes.

2 Stir in shrimp. Heat to boiling; reduce heat to medium. Cover and cook 4 to 6 minutes, stirring occasionally, until shrimp are pink. Remove bay leaves. Serve shrimp mixture over rice.

1 Serving: Calories 400; Total Fat 9g (Saturated Fat 4.5g; Trans Fat 0g); Cholesterol 160mg; Sodium 1860mg; Total Carbohydrate 57g (Dietary Fiber 3g); Protein 22g **Exchanges:** 3½ Starch, 1 Vegetable, 1½ Very Lean Meat, 1 Fat **Carbohydrate Choices:** 4

Panfried Peanut-Ginger Shrimp

Shrimp Creole

CRAB-STUFFED SHRIMP

LOWER CALORIE

PREP 45 min TOTAL 1 hr 20 min • **4 servings**

- 16 uncooked extra-large shrimp (about 1 lb), thawed if frozen, peeled (with tail shells left on), deveined
- 1 tablespoon butter
- 2 tablespoons finely chopped onion
- 2 tablespoons finely chopped celery
- 1 clove garlic, finely chopped
- 2 tablespoons dry white wine or nonalcoholic white wine
- ½ cup soft bread crumbs (about 1 slice bread)
- 1 tablespoon chopped fresh parsley
- ¼ teaspoon salt
- 2 tablespoons whipping cream
- 1 can (6 oz) crabmeat, drained, flaked
- 2 tablespoons grated Parmesan cheese
- ⅛ teaspoon paprika

1 Heat oven to 375°F. Leaving the tail intact, cut slit on inside curve of each shrimp without cutting all the way through. Press open to butterfly.

2 In 10-inch skillet, melt butter over medium heat. Cook onion, celery and garlic in butter about 2 minutes, stirring occasionally, until softened. Stir in wine; cook about 30 seconds or until bubbly.

3 In medium bowl, stir vegetable mixture, bread crumbs, parsley, salt, whipping cream and crabmeat until well mixed. Mound slightly less than 1 tablespoon of stuffing onto each butterflied shrimp, pressing to shape.

4 In ungreased 15x10x1-inch pan, place shrimp with stuffing sides up. Sprinkle cheese and paprika over stuffing. Bake about 30 minutes or until shrimp are pink and stuffing is starting to brown.

1 Serving (4 Shrimp): Calories 190; Total Fat 8g (Saturated Fat 4g; Trans Fat 0g); Cholesterol 210mg; Sodium 550mg; Total Carbohydrate 3g (Dietary Fiber 0g); Protein 26g **Exchanges:** 3½ Very Lean Meat, 1½ Fat **Carbohydrate Choices:** 0

STEAMED CLAMS **LOWER CALORIE**

PREP 10 min TOTAL 50 min • **4 servings**

- 4 lb cherrystone, littleneck or steamer clams in shells
- 6 cups water
- ⅓ cup white vinegar
- ½ cup boiling water, chicken broth or white wine
  Melted butter or Clarified Butter (page 490), if desired

1 Discard any broken-shell or open (dead) clams that do not close when tapped. Place remaining clams in large container. Cover with 6 cups water and the vinegar. Let stand 30 minutes; drain. Scrub clams in cold water.

2 In steamer*, place clams and boiling water. Cover; steam 5 to 8 minutes or until clam shells open at least 1 inch, removing clams as they open. Discard any unopened clams.

3 Serve hot clams in shells with butter.

*If steamer is not available, place clams in 6-quart Dutch oven. Add 1 inch boiling water; cover tightly.

1 Serving: Calories 50; Total Fat 0.5g (Saturated Fat 0g; Trans Fat 0g); Cholesterol 25mg; Sodium 40mg; Total Carbohydrate 2g (Dietary Fiber 0g); Protein 9g **Exchanges:** 1 Lean Meat **Carbohydrate Choices:** 0

Buying Clams

In the fish market, you might find a variety of clams and names for them. Littleneck (topnecks) are the smallest hard-shell clams, with cherrystone (quahogs or chowder clams) being a little bigger. Steamer clams are soft-shell clams but can be cooked in the same way as hard-shell clams.

See how to select and prepare **clams**: Visit bettycrocker.com/BCcookbook

Opening Raw Clams

Hold clam with hinged side against heavy cloth or oven mitt. Insert oyster knife or blunt-tipped knife between shell halves.

Gently twist knife to pry open the shell and release juices. Be sure to work over bowl or plate to catch juices.

Holding clam firmly, move sharp knife around clam, cutting muscle at hinge. Gently twist knife to pry open shell. Cut clam meat from shell.

STEAMED MUSSELS IN WINE SAUCE LOWER CALORIE

Serve these succulent mussels with a crisp green salad dressed with a vinaigrette and topped with shavings of Parmesan cheese. Add slices of crusty Italian bread for soaking up all the delicious garlic-flavored wine sauce.

PREP 20 min TOTAL 30 min • **4 servings**

24 large fresh mussels in shells (about 2 lb)
2 tablespoons olive oil
½ cup chopped fresh parsley
4 cloves garlic, finely chopped
2 plum (Roma) tomatoes, chopped
1 cup dry white wine or chicken broth
½ teaspoon salt
½ teaspoon freshly ground pepper

1 Discard any broken-shell or open (dead) mussels that do not close when tapped. Scrub remaining mussels in cold water, removing any barnacles with a dull paring knife. If there are beards, remove them by tugging away from shells.

2 Place mussels in large container. Cover with cool water. Agitate water with hand, then drain and discard water. Repeat several times until water runs clear; drain.

3 In 12-inch skillet, heat oil over medium-high heat. Cook parsley and garlic in oil, stirring frequently, until garlic is lightly golden. Add mussels, tomatoes, wine, salt and pepper. Cover; cook about 10 minutes or until mussel shells open.

4 Discard any unopened mussels. Spoon liquid from skillet over each serving.

1 Serving (6 Mussels): Calories 170; Total Fat 8g (Saturated Fat 1g; Trans Fat 0g); Cholesterol 40mg; Sodium 640mg; Total Carbohydrate 6g (Dietary Fiber 0g); Protein 16g **Exchanges:** 1 Vegetable, 2 Lean Meat, ½ Fat **Carbohydrate Choices:** ½

BOILED LOBSTERS LOWER CALORIE

PREP 20 min TOTAL 35 min • **2 servings**

2 to 4 quarts water
2 live lobsters (about 1 lb each)
 Melted butter or Clarified Butter (page 490), if desired
 Lemon wedges, if desired

1 Fill 6-quart Dutch oven or stockpot one-third full with water. Heat to boiling. Plunge lobsters head first into water. Cover; heat to boiling. Reduce heat to low. Simmer 10 to 12 minutes or until lobsters turn bright red; drain.

2 To remove meat, follow directions below. Serve with butter and lemon wedges. Serve green tomalley (liver) and coral roe (only in females) if desired.

1 Serving: Calories 100; Total Fat 0.5g (Saturated Fat 0g; Trans Fat 0g); Cholesterol 75mg; Sodium 400mg; Total Carbohydrate 1g (Dietary Fiber 0g); Protein 21g **Exchanges:** 3 Very Lean Meat **Carbohydrate Choices:** 0

Determining Spoiled Mussels

After cooking mussels, discard those that do not open; they are spoiled.

Removing Lobster Meat

Separate tail from body by breaking shell in half where tail and body meet.

Cut away membrane on tail to expose meat. Discard vein that runs through tail and sac near head of lobster.

Twist large claws away from body of lobster. Use nutcracker to break open claws. Remove meat from claws, tail and body.

Boiled Hard-Shell Blue Crabs

Pan-Seared Parmesan Scallops

BOILED HARD-SHELL BLUE CRABS LOWER CALORIE

Blue crab is the most familiar hard-shell crab. It is usually four to six inches in diameter and often has red claw tips.

PREP 20 min **TOTAL** 1 hr • **4 servings**

- 4 **quarts water**
- 16 **live hard-shell blue crabs**
  Melted butter or Clarified Butter (page 490), if desired
  Cocktail Sauce (page 294), if desired

1 In stockpot, heat water to boiling. Drop 4 crabs at a time into water. Cover; heat to boiling. Reduce heat to low. Simmer 10 minutes; drain. Repeat with remaining crabs.

2 To remove meat, follow directions below. Serve with butter and cocktail sauce.

1 Serving (4 Crabs): Calories 100; Total Fat 2g (Saturated Fat 0g; Trans Fat 0g); Cholesterol 105mg; Sodium 290mg; Total Carbohydrate 0g (Dietary Fiber 0g); Protein 21g **Exchanges:** 3 Very Lean Meat **Carbohydrate Choices:** 0

PAN-SEARED PARMESAN SCALLOPS FAST LOWER CALORIE

Tender seared scallops are simple to make and delightful to eat. Serve them with Risotto, page 433, Polenta, page 438, or your favorite hot cooked pasta and grilled asparagus spears or steamed green beans.

PREP 10 min **TOTAL** 20 min • **4 servings**

- 16 **large sea scallops (about 1¼ lb)**
- ½ **cup grated Parmesan cheese**
- 1 **tablespoon olive or vegetable oil**
- 1 **tablespoon butter**
  Coarse ground black pepper
  Chopped fresh chives or parsley

1 Pat scallops dry with paper towels. Place cheese in shallow dish or resealable food-storage plastic bag. Coat scallops with cheese. Discard any remaining cheese.

2 Heat oil and butter in 12-inch nonstick skillet over medium-high heat. Cook half of scallops at a time in oil 3 to 6 minutes, turning once, until golden brown on outside and white and opaque inside. Sprinkle with pepper and chives.

1 Serving: Calories 170; Total Fat 11g (Saturated Fat 4.5g; Trans Fat 0g); Cholesterol 50mg; Sodium 410mg; Total Carbohydrate 0g (Dietary Fiber 0g); Protein 19g **Exchanges:** 2 Very Lean Meat, ½ Lean Meat, 1½ Fat **Carbohydrate Choices:** 0

PAN-SEARED ASIAGO SCALLOPS Substitute Asiago cheese for the Parmesan.

Removing Crabmeat

Place crab on its back. Using thumb, pry up tail flap, twist off and discard. Turn right side up; pry up top shell. Pull it away from body and discard.

Using small knife (or fingers), cut the gray-white gills from both sides of crab. Discard gills and internal organs.

Twist off claws and legs; use nutcracker to crack shells at joints. Remove meat with cocktail fork or nutpick. Break body in half; remove remaining meat.

COQUILLES SAINT-JACQUES

LOWER CALORIE

Coquilles is French for "shell."

PREP 45 min **TOTAL** 1 hr 5 min • **6 servings**

- 1½ lb bay scallops*
- 1 cup dry white wine or chicken broth
- ¼ cup chopped fresh parsley
- ½ teaspoon salt
- 5 tablespoons butter
- 6 oz mushrooms, sliced (2 cups)
- 2 shallots or green onions, chopped
- 3 tablespoons all-purpose flour
- ½ cup half-and-half
- ½ cup shredded Swiss cheese (2 oz)
- 1 cup soft bread crumbs (about 1½ slices bread)
- 2 tablespoons butter, melted

1 Lightly grease 6 (4-inch) baking shells or ceramic ramekins** with butter. Place in 15x10x1-inch pan. Drain scallops well; pat dry with paper towels.

2 In 3-quart saucepan, place scallops, wine, parsley and salt. Add just enough water to cover scallops; heat to boiling. Reduce heat to low. Simmer uncovered about 6 minutes or until scallops are white and opaque. Remove scallops with slotted spoon; reserve liquid. Heat reserved liquid to boiling. Boil until reduced to 1 cup. Strain and reserve.

3 In same saucepan, melt 2 tablespoons of the butter over medium heat. Cook mushrooms and shallots in butter 5 to 6 minutes, stirring occasionally, until mushrooms are tender. Remove from saucepan.

4 In same saucepan, melt 3 tablespoons of the butter over medium heat. Stir in flour. Cook, stirring constantly, until smooth and bubbly; remove from heat. Gradually stir in reserved liquid. Heat to boiling, stirring constantly; cook and stir 1 minute. Stir in half-and-half, scallops, mushroom mixture and ¼ cup of the cheese; heat through.

5 In small bowl, toss bread crumbs and 2 tablespoons melted butter. Divide scallop mixture among baking shells. Sprinkle with remaining ¼ cup cheese and the bread crumb mixture.

6 Set oven control to broil. Broil baking shells with tops 5 inches from heat 3 to 5 minutes or until crumbs are toasted.

*2 packages (12 oz each) frozen scallops, thawed, can be substituted for the fresh scallops.
**Do not use glass custard cups or baking dishes; they cannot withstand the heat from the broiler and may break.

1 Serving: Calories 340; Total Fat 20g (Saturated Fat 10g; Trans Fat 1g); Cholesterol 80mg; Sodium 630mg; Total Carbohydrate 19g (Dietary Fiber 1g); Protein 20g **Exchanges:** 1 Starch, 1 Vegetable, 2 Lean Meat, 3 Fat **Carbohydrate Choices:** 1

HEARTY SEAFOOD STEW

LOWER CALORIE

PREP 20 min **TOTAL** 1 hr • **6 servings**

- 2 tablespoons vegetable oil
- 2 medium carrots, thinly sliced (1 cup)
- 2 medium stalks celery, sliced (1 cup)
- 1 large onion, chopped (1 cup)
- 1 clove garlic, finely chopped
- 1 can (14.5 oz) stewed tomatoes, undrained
- 2 cups water
- 1 tablespoon beef bouillon granules
- 1 medium potato, cut into ½-inch pieces
- 1 lb cod or other medium-firm fish fillets, cut into 1-inch pieces
- ½ lb uncooked medium shrimp, thawed if frozen, peeled, deveined
- 1 can (15.5 oz) great northern beans, rinsed, drained
- 1 small zucchini, cut in half lengthwise, then cut crosswise into slices (1 cup)
- 1 teaspoon chopped fresh or ¼ teaspoon dried thyme leaves
- ½ teaspoon pepper
  Chopped fresh parsley, if desired

1 In 4-quart Dutch oven, heat oil over medium-high heat. Cook carrots, celery, onion and garlic in oil about 5 minutes, stirring frequently, until vegetables are tender. Stir in tomatoes, water, bouillon and potato. Heat to boiling; reduce heat. Cover; simmer 20 minutes, stirring occasionally.

2 Stir in cod, shrimp, beans, zucchini, thyme and pepper. Heat to boiling; reduce heat. Cover; simmer 6 to 10 minutes or until fish flakes easily with fork and shrimp are pink. Serve topped with parsley.

1 Serving: Calories 290; Total Fat 6g (Saturated Fat 1g; Trans Fat 0g); Cholesterol 75mg; Sodium 740mg; Total Carbohydrate 32g (Dietary Fiber 7g); Protein 26g **Exchanges:** 2 Starch, 1 Vegetable, 2½ Very Lean Meat, ½ Fat **Carbohydrate Choices:** 2

GRILLING & SMOKING

GRILLING

For bonus grilling and smoking recipes,
visit bettycrocker.com/BCcookbook

FAST = Ready in 20 minutes or less LOWER CALORIE = See Helpful Nutrition and Cooking Information, page 685
LIGHTER = 25% fewer calories or grams of fat MAKE AHEAD = Make-ahead directions SLOW COOKER = Slow cooker directions

← Pork Ribs with Smoky Barbecue Sauce (page 318), Flank Steak with Smoky Honey-Mustard Sauce (page 310),
Grilled Fish Tacos (page 320), Grilled Herbed New Potatoes (page 323)

GRILLING BASICS

No matter the time of year, folks are firing up their grills for a sizzling selection of main courses showcasing beef, poultry, pork, seafood and more. Grilling is a quick-cooking option that infuses dishes with a sensational smoky flavor friends and family can't resist.

TYPES OF GRILLS

There are three basic types of grills: gas, charcoal and electric. The type of grill you choose depends on your personal needs and preferences. Follow the manufacturer's directions for whatever type of grill you use.

Gas: Fueled by propane, gas grills usually heat up in 5 to 10 minutes. It is easy to control the temperature of gas grills. They are more costly than charcoal grills, but cleanup is quick and easy.

Charcoal: Briquettes are heated by mounding in a pyramid shape and lighting by using a chimney starter (at right). It can take close to half an hour for the coals to get hot. Charcoal grills are a cost-friendly option.

Electric: Outdoor electric grills are great for people living in apartments or condominiums where charcoal and gas grills are prohibited. Like gas grills, they are quick to light and fairly easy to clean.

Mound charcoal in a pyramid shape in the grill.

Starting a Charcoal Grill

- **Pyramid Style:** Place the briquettes in the grill, arranging them into a pyramid. Pour lighter fluid over the top; light the briquettes. NEVER USE GASOLINE OR KEROSENE TO START A FIRE. In addition to lighter fluid, briquettes can be lit with electric starters, fire starter gels or paraffin starters. Or look for instant-lighting briquettes that don't require lighter fluid.

- **Charcoal Chimney Starter:** A charcoal chimney starter is a vented, cylindrical canister with a large, easy-to-grasp handle. It's great for starting coals quickly and evenly. To use, set the canister on the bottom of the charcoal grill. Stuff crumpled newspaper down inside the bottom of the canister; fill to the top of the canister with briquettes. Light the paper. When the coals are ready, remove the chimney and spread out the hot coals.

When Are Coals Ready?

After lighting briquettes, leave them in the mounded shape until they are glowing red, about 20 minutes, then spread them in a single layer. In daylight, coals are ready when coated with a light gray ash; after dark, coals are ready when they have an even red glow.

Check the temperature of the coals by holding the palm of your hand near the grill rack and timing how long you can comfortably keep it there.

2 seconds=high heat
3 seconds=medium-high heat
4 seconds=medium heat
5 seconds=low heat

Controlling the Temperature

- If the coals are too hot, spread them out or close the air vents halfway. For a gas or electric grill, use a lower burner setting.

- If the coals are too cool, move them closer together and knock off the ashes by tapping them with long-handled tongs, or open the air vents. For a gas or electric grill, use a higher setting.

PREVENTING FLARE-UPS

Fats and liquids dripping through the grill rack can cause flare-ups, which can burn the food. Here are some ways to prevent flare-ups.

- Trim excess fat from meats.
- Don't line the bottom of the grill with foil because grease needs to drain into the catch pan.
- Keep the grill bottom and grease catch pan clean and free of debris.
- Brush on sugary or tomato-based sauces during the last 10 to 15 minutes to prevent them from burning.
- After cooking on a gas grill, turn the heat setting to high for 10 to 15 minutes with the cover closed. This burns off any residue on the grill rack and lava rock or ceramic briquettes.
- Clean grill rack with a brass bristle brush after each use.

Follow these tips if a flare-up does occur:

- Cover the grill and move food to a different area of the grill rack.
- Spread coals farther apart or, if necessary, remove food from the grill and spritz the flames with water from a spray bottle. When flames are gone, return food to the grill.
- For a gas or electric grill, turn all burners off. NEVER USE WATER TO EXTINGUISH FLAMES ON A GAS OR ELECTRIC GRILL. When flames are gone, light the grill again.

FOOD SAFETY TIPS FOR GRILLING

- If you brush raw meat with sauce, wash the brush in hot, soapy water before using on cooked meat, or use a clean brush. To keep your hands away from heat, use a brush with a long handle.
- Always place cooked food on a clean plate, not on the same plate that carried raw food.
- Boil marinades used when cooking meats for 1 minute before serving. Better yet, set aside some marinade to use for serving, and discard marinade used for basting.

DIRECT AND INDIRECT HEAT

Follow grill manufacturer's directions for both methods.

Direct-Heat Grilling: Food is cooked on the grill rack directly over heat. This method is best for foods that cook in less than 25 minutes, like burgers, chops and steaks.

Indirect-Heat Grilling: Food is cooked on the grill rack but not directly over heat; heat comes from the sides. This method is best for foods that take longer than 25 minutes to cook, like ribs, whole chickens or turkeys and roasts.

Setting Up Grill for Direct Heat

For charcoal grill, evenly spread hot, white coals over firebox of grill.

For gas grill, heat all burners on high for 10 to 15 minutes; then reduce heat as needed.

Setting Up Grill for Indirect Heat

For charcoal grill, move hot, white coals to edge of firebox, leaving area in middle free of coals; place drip pan in open area. Grill food over drip pan.

For gas grill, heat all burners on high for 10 to 15 minutes. Turn off center burner and place drip pan in center. Grill food over drip pan. Adjust temperature of ignited burners as needed. If grill only has two burners, turn off one and set drip pan on that side.

TIMETABLE FOR GRILLING POULTRY

The times below are based on medium direct heat. Grill poultry until the internal temperature is at least 165°F, or until juice is clear when center of thickest part is cut; for whole chickens and turkeys, measure temperature in thigh, not touching bone. Turn chicken breasts and turkey breasts and parts once halfway though grilling. Turn chicken parts two or three times.

Cut	Weight in Pounds	Grilling Time in Minutes
CHICKEN		
Cut-Up Broiler-Fryer	3 to 3½	35 to 40
Bone-In Split Breasts (Breast Halves)	2½ to 3	20 to 25
Boneless Skinless Breasts	1¼	15 to 20
TURKEY		
Tenderloins	1 to 1½	8 to 12
Breast Slices	1 to 1½	6 to 7

Making Grill Marks

Start with a hot grill. Use high heat to make the marks and quickly sear the steaks to form a crust on the outside.

Place steaks on grill; do not move. Grill steaks 3 to 5 minutes, or until grill marks are visible on bottom of steaks. Do not move steaks during this time.

Rotate steaks one-quarter turn. Rotate steaks and grill again, following same method above, to form crosshatch marks.

Repeat on other side. Make marks on other side, using same method above.

Finish cooking steaks over medium heat. Reduce gas grill to medium or move steaks over coals with medium heat. Finish cooking steaks as directed, turning once. Grill time may be slightly less, due to searing process.

TIMETABLE FOR GRILLING BEEF, VEAL, PORK AND LAMB

The cooking times below are based on medium direct heat, unless otherwise specified. For beef and lamb cuts, the internal temperature should be 145°F (medium-rare), 160°F (medium) or 170°F (well-done). For veal cuts, cook to 160°F (medium) or 170°F (well-done). For pork cuts, cook to 145°F; let stand at least 3 minutes.* For ground beef, veal, lamb and pork, the temperature should reach 160°F (medium). Turn foods once halfway through grilling (turn beef and pork tenderloins two or three times).

Cut	Thickness or Weight in Pounds	Grilling Time in Minutes
Beef Rib Eye Steak	¾ inch	6 to 8
	1 inch	11 to 14
Beef Porterhouse/ T-Bone Steak	¾ inch	10 to 12
	1 inch	14 to 16
Beef Top Loin or Strip Steak	¾ inch	10 to 12
	1 inch	15 to 18
Beef Tenderloin Steak	1 inch	13 to 15
	1½ inch	14 to 16
Beef Top Sirloin	¾ inch	13 to 16
	1 inch	17 to 21
	1½ inch	22 to 26
Beef Top Round Steak (marinated)	¾ inch	8 to 9
	1 inch	16 to 18
Beef Flank Steak (marinated)	1 to 1½ lb	17 to 21
Ground Beef Patties (4 per pound)	½ inch (4-inch diameter)	10 to 12
(4 per 1½ pounds)	¾ inch (4-inch diameter)	12 to 15
Veal Chop, Loin or Rib	¾ to 1 inch	14 to 16
Veal Chop (bone-in or boneless)	¾ to 1 inch	9 to 12
	1½ inch	12 to 16
Pork Tenderloin	1 to 1½ lb	15 to 25
Pork Loin Back Ribs or Spareribs (use indirect heat)	2 to 4 lb	1½ to 2 hours
Ground Pork Patties	½ inch (4-inch diameter)	8 to 10
Lamb Chop, Loin or Rib	1 inch	10 to 15
Lamb Chop, Sirloin	1 inch	12 to 15

The USDA recommends pork be cooked to 145°F with a 3-minute resting period. If you prefer pork more well done, cook to 160°F.

Grilling Vegetables

See Fresh Vegetable Grilling Chart, page 322.

HONEY-MUSTARD CHICKEN SANDWICHES LOWER CALORIE

PREP 30 min TOTAL 30 min • **4 sandwiches**

- ¼ cup Dijon mustard
- 2 tablespoons honey
- 1 teaspoon dried oregano leaves
- ⅛ to ¼ teaspoon ground red pepper (cayenne)
- 4 boneless skinless chicken breasts (about 1¼ lb)
- 4 whole-grain sandwich buns, split
- 4 slices tomato
  Leaf lettuce

1 Heat gas or charcoal grill. In small bowl, mix mustard, honey, oregano and red pepper. Brush half of mixture on chicken.

2 Place chicken on grill over medium heat. Cover grill; cook 15 to 20 minutes, brushing frequently with mustard mixture and turning occasionally, until juice of chicken is clear when center of thickest part is cut (at least 165°F). Discard any remaining mustard mixture. Serve chicken in buns with tomato and lettuce.

1 Sandwich: Calories 290; Total Fat 7g (Saturated Fat 1.5g; Trans Fat 0g); Cholesterol 85mg; Sodium 400mg; Total Carbohydrate 24g (Dietary Fiber 3g); Protein 36g **Exchanges:** 1 Starch, ½ Other Carbohydrate, 5 Very Lean Meat, ½ Fat **Carbohydrate Choices:** 1½

GRILLED CRANBERRY-ALMOND CHICKEN SALAD

PREP 40 min TOTAL 40 min • **6 servings**

CREAMY POPPY SEED DRESSING
- ¾ cup mayonnaise or salad dressing
- ⅓ cup sugar
- 2 tablespoons cider vinegar
- 2 teaspoons poppy seed

SALAD
- 6 boneless skinless chicken breasts (about 1¾ lb)
  Cooking spray
- ½ teaspoon salt
- 3 cups bite-size pieces iceberg lettuce
- 3 cups bite-size pieces romaine lettuce
- ½ cup crumbled Gorgonzola cheese (2 oz)
- ½ cup dried cranberries
- 6 tablespoons slivered almonds, toasted (page 22)

1 Heat gas or charcoal grill. In small bowl, mix all dressing ingredients with wire whisk. Reserve ¾ cup dressing for salad.

2 Spray chicken with cooking spray; sprinkle with salt. Place chicken on grill over medium heat. Cover grill; cook 15 to 20 minutes, turning once and brushing occasionally with remaining dressing, until juice is clear when center of thickest part is cut (at least 165°F). Discard any remaining dressing used for brushing.

3 Divide lettuces among 6 plates. Cut chicken into ½-inch slices; place on lettuce. Drizzle with reserved ¾ cup dressing. Sprinkle with cheese, cranberries and almonds.

1 Serving: Calories 530; Total Fat 34g (Saturated Fat 7g; Trans Fat 0g); Cholesterol 100mg; Sodium 580mg; Total Carbohydrate 24g (Dietary Fiber 2g); Protein 32g **Exchanges:** 1 Other Carbohydrate, 2 Vegetable, 4 Lean Meat, 4½ Fat **Carbohydrate Choices:** 1½

THREE-HERB CHICKEN

PREP 55 min TOTAL 1 hr 25 min • **4 servings**

- ½ cup vegetable oil
- ½ cup lime juice
- 2 tablespoons chopped fresh or 2 teaspoons dried basil leaves
- 2 tablespoons chopped fresh or 2 teaspoons dried oregano leaves
- 2 tablespoons chopped fresh or 2 teaspoons dried thyme leaves
- 1 teaspoon onion powder
- ¼ teaspoon lemon-pepper seasoning
- 4 chicken thighs (about 1 lb)
- 4 chicken drumsticks (about 1 lb)

1 In shallow glass dish, mix all ingredients except chicken pieces. Add chicken pieces; turn to coat. Cover; refrigerate at least 30 minutes but no longer than 24 hours, turning occasionally.

2 Heat gas or charcoal grill. Remove chicken from marinade; reserve marinade. Place chicken skin side down on grill over medium heat. Cover grill; cook 8 to 10 minutes. Turn chicken; brush with marinade. Cover grill; cook 25 to 35 minutes longer, turning occasionally and brushing with marinade, until juice of chicken is clear when thickest part is cut to bone (165°F). Discard any remaining marinade.

1 Serving: Calories 430; Total Fat 33g (Saturated Fat 7g; Trans Fat 0g); Cholesterol 100mg; Sodium 95mg; Total Carbohydrate 1g (Dietary Fiber 0g); Protein 31g **Exchanges:** 4 Medium-Fat Meat, 3 Fat **Carbohydrate Choices:** 0

Mediterranean Chicken Packets

MEDITERRANEAN CHICKEN PACKETS

PREP 20 min TOTAL 45 min • **4 servings**

- 1 **package (4 oz) crumbled tomato-basil feta cheese***
- 2 **tablespoons grated lemon peel**
- 1 **teaspoon dried oregano leaves**
- 4 **boneless skinless chicken breasts (about 1¼ lb)**
- 4 **plum (Roma) tomatoes, each cut into 3 slices**
- 1 **small red onion, finely chopped (¼ cup)**
- 20 **pitted kalamata olives**

1 Heat gas or charcoal grill. In small bowl, mix cheese, lemon peel and oregano.

2 Cut four 18x12-inch sheets of heavy-duty foil. On one side of each sheet of foil, place 1 chicken breast, 3 tomato slices, ¼ cup onion and 5 olives. Spoon one-fourth of cheese mixture over chicken and vegetables on each sheet.

3 Bring 2 sides of foil up over chicken and vegetables so edges meet. Seal edges, making tight ½-inch fold; fold again, allowing space for heat circulation and expansion. Fold other sides to seal.

4 Place foil packets on grill over medium heat. Cover grill; cook 20 to 25 minutes or until juice of chicken is clear when center of thickest part is cut (at least 165°F). To serve, cut large X across top of each packet; carefully fold back foil to allow steam to escape.

*1 package (4 oz) regular crumbled feta cheese can be substituted for the flavored feta cheese.

1 Serving: Calories 260; Total Fat 12g (Saturated Fat 6g; Trans Fat 0g); Cholesterol 100mg; Sodium 560mg; Total Carbohydrate 7g (Dietary Fiber 2g); Protein 31g **Exchanges:** 1 Vegetable, 4 Lean Meat **Carbohydrate Choices:** ½

GRILLED BUFFALO CHICKEN STICKS LOWER CALORIE

PREP 30 min TOTAL 1 hr 10 min • **10 servings**

- 2 **tablespoons butter, melted**
- ¼ **cup red pepper sauce**
- 1 **tablespoon honey**
- ½ **teaspoon celery seed**
- ½ **teaspoon salt**
- 1 **lb uncooked chicken breast tenders (not breaded)**
- ½ **cup blue cheese dressing (for homemade dressing, see page 476)**

1 In medium bowl, mix butter, pepper sauce, honey, celery seed and salt. Remove 2 tablespoons sauce mixture; set aside. Add chicken to remaining sauce mixture; stir to coat. Cover; refrigerate at least 30 minutes but no longer than 2 hours. Meanwhile, soak 10 (10- to 12-inch) bamboo skewers in water 30 minutes.

2 Heat gas or charcoal grill. Remove chicken from marinade; discard marinade. Thread each chicken tender on a skewer.

3 Carefully brush oil on grill rack. Place kabobs on grill over medium heat. Cover grill; cook 8 to 10 minutes, turning once and brushing frequently with reserved sauce mixture, until chicken is no longer pink in center. Discard any remaining sauce mixture. Serve chicken with blue cheese dressing.

1 Serving: Calories 140; Total Fat 9g (Saturated Fat 2g; Trans Fat 0g); Cholesterol 35mg; Sodium 270mg; Total Carbohydrate 4g (Dietary Fiber 0g); Protein 11g **Exchanges:** 1½ Very Lean Meat, 2 Fat **Carbohydrate Choices:** 0

Pitting Olives

Place olive in olive pitter. Press through pitter, removing pit.

BEER CAN CHICKEN

The steam from the beer and the savory rub make this chicken very moist and flavorful.

PREP 10 min **TOTAL** 1 hr 55 min • **6 servings**

BASIC BARBECUE RUB
- 1 **tablespoon paprika**
- 2 **teaspoons salt**
- ½ **teaspoon garlic powder**
- ½ **teaspoon onion powder**
- ½ **teaspoon pepper**

CHICKEN
- 1 **whole chicken (4 to 4½ lb)**
- 1 **can (12 oz) beer or nonalcoholic beer**

1 In small bowl, mix rub ingredients. Fold wings of chicken across back with tips touching. Sprinkle rub inside cavity and all over outside of chicken; rub with fingers.

2 Pour out ½ cup of beer from can. Holding chicken upright with larger opening of body cavity downward; insert beer can into larger cavity. Insert ovenproof meat, grilling or digital thermometer so tip is in thickest part of inside thigh and does not touch bone.

3 Heat gas or charcoal grill for indirect cooking. For two-burner gas grill, heat one burner to medium; place chicken with beer can upright on unheated side. For one-burner gas grill, place chicken with beer can upright on grill over low heat. For charcoal grill, move medium coals to edge of firebox; place chicken with beer can upright on grill rack over drip pan.

4 Cover grill; cook 1 hour 15 minutes to 1 hour 30 minutes or until thermometer reads at least 165°F and legs move easily when lifted or twisted. Using tongs, carefully lift chicken to 13x9-inch pan, holding large metal spatula under beer can for support. Let stand 15 minutes before carving. Remove beer can; discard.

1 Serving: Calories 300; Total Fat 18g (Saturated Fat 5g; Trans Fat 0.5g); Cholesterol 115mg; Sodium 700mg; Total Carbohydrate 0g (Dietary Fiber 0g); Protein 36g **Exchanges:** 5 Lean Meat, 1 Fat **Carbohydrate Choices:** 0

Making Beer Can Chicken

Sprinkle rub inside cavity of chicken and rub all over outside.

Insert open beer can into cavity of chicken.

Using tongs, carefully lift finished chicken to pan, holding metal spatula under beer can for support.

Beer Can Chicken

GRILLED BARBECUE CHICKEN

PREP 10 min TOTAL 55 min • **6 servings**

BARBECUE SAUCE

1 medium onion, finely chopped (½ cup)
1 cup ketchup or 1 can (8 oz) tomato sauce
½ cup hot water
⅓ cup lemon juice
1 tablespoon Worcestershire sauce
2 teaspoons paprika
1 teaspoon salt
1 teaspoon sugar
½ teaspoon pepper

CHICKEN

1 teaspoon salt
1 teaspoon paprika
¼ teaspoon pepper
1 cut-up whole chicken (3 to 3½ lb)

1 Heat gas or charcoal grill. In 1-quart saucepan, heat sauce ingredients over medium heat until boiling, stirring occasionally.

2 In small bowl, mix 1 teaspoon salt, 1 teaspoon paprika and ¼ teaspoon pepper. Sprinkle both sides of chicken with salt mixture.

3 Carefully brush grill rack with vegetable oil. Place chicken, skin side up, on grill over medium heat. Cover grill; cook 15 minutes.

4 Turn chicken; brush with barbecue sauce. Cover grill; cook 20 to 25 minutes longer, turning and brushing with sauce, until juice of chicken is clear when thickest piece is cut to bone (at least 165°F).

1 Serving: Calories 380; Total Fat 13g (Saturated Fat 3.5g; Trans Fat 0g); Cholesterol 155mg; Sodium 1410mg; Total Carbohydrate 14g (Dietary Fiber 1g); Protein 51g **Exchanges:** 1 Other Carbohydrate, 7 Very Lean Meat, 2 Fat **Carbohydrate Choices:** 1

GRILLED BARBECUE CHICKEN BREASTS

Substitute 6 bone-in chicken breasts for the cut-up whole chicken.

Use Tongs to Turn

For moist grilled chicken, use a pair of tongs instead of a fork to turn the pieces. A fork might pinch the flesh, letting too much of the juice out.

TURKEY ON THE GRILL

PREP 30 min TOTAL 12 hr 45 min • **12 servings**

LEMON-GARLIC MARINADE

1 cup chicken broth (for homemade broth, see page 528)
¼ cup olive or vegetable oil
2 tablespoons fresh lemon juice
¼ cup chopped fresh basil leaves
¼ cup chopped fresh parsley or cilantro
½ teaspoon salt
¼ teaspoon pepper
2 cloves garlic, finely chopped

TURKEY

1 whole turkey (12 lb), thawed if frozen
2 tablespoons Cajun seasoning

1 In blender, place all marinade ingredients. Cover and blend until smooth. If turkey has plastic leg holder, remove and discard before grilling. Inject marinade into turkey using poultry injector, following directions that came with injector (or place turkey on large tray with 1-inch sides or in large glass dish and pour marinade over turkey).

2 Sprinkle Cajun seasoning inside cavity and over outside of turkey. Fasten neck skin to back of turkey with skewer. Fold wings across back of turkey so tips are touching. Tuck legs under band of skin at tail. Place turkey on large tray with 1-inch sides or in large glass dish. Cover; refrigerate 8 hours but no longer than 24 hours.

3 Insert ovenproof meat, grilling or digital thermometer in turkey so tip is in thickest part of inside thigh and does not touch bone. Heat gas or charcoal grill for indirect cooking. For two-burner gas grill, heat one burner to medium; place turkey, breast side up, on unheated side. For one-burner gas grill, place turkey, breast side up, on grill over low heat. For charcoal grill, move medium coals to edge of firebox; place turkey, breast side up, on grill rack over drip pan.

4 Cover grill; cook 3 to 4 hours or until thermometer reads at least 165°F and legs move easily when lifted or twisted. Let stand 15 minutes before carving.

1 Serving: Calories 430; Total Fat 22g (Saturated Fat 6g; Trans Fat 0g); Cholesterol 155mg; Sodium 360mg; Total Carbohydrate 0g (Dietary Fiber 0g); Protein 56g **Exchanges:** 8 Lean Meat **Carbohydrate Choices:** 0

TURKEY BREAST WITH CHILI-CUMIN RUB

Whole turkey breasts grill beautifully. Because they're available in different sizes, adjust the grilling time as needed and check the meat thermometer for doneness.

PREP 10 min TOTAL 2 hr 50 min ● **8 servings**

CHILI-CUMIN RUB

- 2 **tablespoons packed brown sugar**
- 2 **teaspoons paprika**
- 1 **teaspoon chili powder**
- 1 **teaspoon ground cumin**
- ½ **teaspoon ground mustard**
- ½ **teaspoon ground ginger**
- ½ **teaspoon garlic-pepper blend**
- ½ **teaspoon salt**

TURKEY

- 1 **bone-in whole turkey breast (5 to 6 lb), thawed if frozen**
- 2 **tablespoons cold butter**

1 In small bowl, mix rub ingredients. Loosen skin on turkey breast in 4 or 5 places. Cut butter into small slices; place randomly under skin of turkey. Sprinkle rub over entire outside of turkey; rub with fingers. Insert ovenproof meat, grilling or digital thermometer so tip is in thickest part of breast and does not touch bone.

2 Heat gas or charcoal grill for indirect cooking. For two-burner gas grill, heat one burner to medium; place turkey, breast side up, on unheated side. For one-burner gas grill, place turkey, breast side up, on grill over low heat. For charcoal grill, move medium coals to edge of firebox; place turkey, breast side up, on grill rack over drip pan filled with ½ inch water.

3 Cover grill; cook 30 minutes. Turn turkey. Cover grill; cook 1 hour 30 minutes to 2 hours longer or until thermometer reads at least 165°F. Remove turkey from grill; cover with foil. Let stand 10 minutes before slicing.

1 Serving: Calories 390; Total Fat 18g (Saturated Fat 6g; Trans Fat 0g); Cholesterol 155mg; Sodium 290mg; Total Carbohydrate 4g (Dietary Fiber 0g); Protein 54g **Exchanges:** 7½ Very Lean Meat, 3 Fat **Carbohydrate Choices:** 0

FLANK STEAK WITH SMOKY HONEY-MUSTARD SAUCE

The flavor of this easy steak is simply delicious, and it's easy to make. Add avocado and tomato slices when you serve it.

PREP 30 min TOTAL 30 min ● **6 servings**

HONEY-MUSTARD SAUCE

- ¼ **cup honey mustard dressing**
- 1 **tablespoon frozen (thawed) orange juice concentrate**
- 1 **tablespoon water**
- 1 **small clove garlic, finely chopped**
- 1 **chipotle chile in adobo sauce (from 7-oz can), finely chopped**

STEAK

- 1 **beef flank steak (about 1½ lb)**
- 6 **flour tortillas (9 or 10 inch)**

1 Heat gas or charcoal grill. In small bowl, mix sauce ingredients. In both sides of beef, make cuts about ½ inch apart and ⅛ inch deep in diamond pattern. Brush 2 tablespoons of the sauce on both sides of beef.

2 Place beef on grill over medium heat. Cover grill; cook 17 to 20 minutes, turning once, until desired doneness. Cut beef across grain into thin slices. Serve with remaining sauce and tortillas.

1 Serving: Calories 360; Total Fat 16g (Saturated Fat 4.5g; Trans Fat 1.5g); Cholesterol 55mg; Sodium 460mg; Total Carbohydrate 22g (Dietary Fiber 0g); Protein 31g **Exchanges:** 1½ Starch, 4 Lean Meat, ½ Fat **Carbohydrate Choices:** 1½

SIRLOIN STEAK WITH SMOKY HONEY-MUSTARD SAUCE Substitute lean boneless beef top sirloin steak for the flank steak.

Slicing Flank Steak

Using sharp knife, cut steak across grain, cutting at a slight angle.

BEEF FAJITAS

PREP 1 hr TOTAL 9 hr • **6 servings**

- 1 **boneless beef top sirloin steak, 1½ inches thick (1½ lb), trimmed of excess fat**
    Fajita Marinade (page 498)
- 2 **large onions, sliced**
- 2 **medium green or red bell peppers, cut into ¼-inch strips**
- 2 **tablespoons vegetable oil**
- 12 **flour tortillas (9 or 10 inch)**
- 1 **jar (8 oz) picante sauce (1 cup)**
- 1 **cup shredded Cheddar or Monterey Jack cheese (4 oz)**
- 1½ **cups guacamole (for homemade guacamole, see page 48)**
- ¾ **cup sour cream**

1 Pierce beef with fork in several places. Place in resealable food-storage plastic bag or shallow glass or plastic dish. Pour marinade over beef; turn to coat. Cover and refrigerate at least 8 hours but no longer than 24 hours, turning occasionally.

2 Heat gas or charcoal grill. In large bowl, toss onions and bell peppers with oil; place in grill basket (grill "wok"). Set aside.

3 Remove beef from marinade; reserve marinade. Place beef on grill over medium heat. Cover grill; cook 22 to 26 minutes for medium-rare (145°F) to medium doneness (160°F), turning once and brushing occasionally with reserved marinade. Add vegetables to grill for last 6 to 8 minutes of cooking, shaking basket or stirring vegetables once or twice, until crisp-tender.

4 Meanwhile, heat oven to 325°F. Wrap tortillas in foil. Heat in oven about 15 minutes or until warm. Remove tortillas from oven; keep wrapped.

5 Discard any remaining marinade. Cut beef across grain into very thin slices. For each fajita, place a few slices of beef, some of the onion mixture, 1 heaping tablespoonful each picante sauce and cheese, 2 tablespoons guacamole and 1 tablespoon sour cream on center of tortilla. Fold 1 end of tortilla up about 1 inch over filling; fold right and left sides over folded end, overlapping. Fold remaining end down.

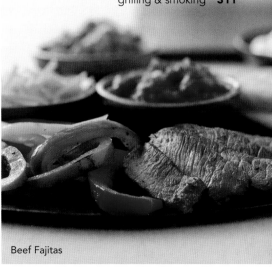

Beef Fajitas

1 Serving: Calories 710; Total Fat 33g (Saturated Fat 12g; Trans Fat 1.5g); Cholesterol 100mg; Sodium 910mg; Total Carbohydrate 63g (Dietary Fiber 7g); Protein 38g **Exchanges:** 3½ Starch, ½ Other Carbohydrate, 4 Medium-Fat Meat, 2 Fat **Carbohydrate Choices:** 4

LIGHTER DIRECTIONS For 11 grams of fat and 520 calories per serving, omit vegetable oil; spray onions and bell peppers with cooking spray and toss before placing in grill basket. Use fat-free tortillas and reduced-fat cheese and sour cream. Omit guacamole.

CHICKEN FAJITAS Substitute 1 lb boneless skinless chicken breast for the beef. Marinate 2 hours. Cook chicken on grill over medium heat 15 to 20 minutes, turning occasionally. Cut chicken into thin slices.

SHRIMP FAJITAS Substitute 1 lb uncooked medium shrimp, peeled, deveined, for the beef. Marinate 1 hour. Cook shrimp in grill basket (grill "wok") 4 to 6 minutes over medium heat until pink, turning occasionally.

Fajitas

Fajitas are often made with skirt steak, but sirloin is an easy alternative. The accompaniments are what make them so tasty. Other options include shredded lettuce, sliced tomatoes, chopped green onions and refried beans.

Learn to Make Grilled Steak

TEXAS T-BONES LOWER CALORIE

Why go to a fancy restaurant when you can achieve the same results at home? A perfectly grilled steak, done just how you like it, is easy when you follow these tips. You'll grill steaks like a pro with our tips for checking doneness and pumping up the flavor with marinades, rubs and toppings. You can grill other steak cuts the same way using the Timetable for Grilling Beef, Veal, Pork and Lamb on page 305.

PREP 25 min **TOTAL** 55 min • **4 servings**

STEAKS

- 4 beef T-bone steaks, about ¾ inch thick (10 to 12 oz each)
- 2 cloves garlic, cut in half
- 4 teaspoons black peppercorns, crushed
  Salt and pepper to taste, if desired

MUSTARD BUTTER

- ¼ cup butter, softened
- 1 tablespoon Dijon mustard
- ½ teaspoon Worcestershire sauce
- ¼ teaspoon lime juice

1 Heat gas or charcoal grill. Trim fat from steaks to ¼-inch thickness. Rub garlic on beef. Press peppercorns into beef. Let steaks stand for 30 minutes to reach room temperature. In small bowl, mix mustard butter ingredients; set aside.

1 Serving: Calories 390; Total Fat 25g (Saturated Fat 10g; Trans Fat 1g); Cholesterol 140mg; Sodium 270mg; Total Carbohydrate 1g (Dietary Fiber 0g); Protein 40g **Exchanges:** 6 Lean Meat, 1½ Fat **Carbohydrate Choices:** 0

2 Place beef on grill over medium heat. Cover grill; cook 10 to 12 minutes for medium doneness (160°F), turning once. Sprinkle with salt and pepper. Serve with mustard butter.

Keys to Success

- **Crush peppercorns** in resealable food-storage plastic bag using rolling pin or meat mallet.

- **Let steaks stand at room temperature** 30 minutes before grilling. Cold steaks will contract and can become tough.

- **Prepare grill for medium heat** (see Grilling Basics, page 303).

- **To grill other steak cuts,** such as tenderloin, top loin steak or rib steak, see Timetable for Grilling Beef, Veal, Pork and Lamb (page 305) for correct times.

See how to make **T-bone steaks**: Visit bettycrocker.com/BCcookbook

Learn with Betty | BEEF STEAK DONENESS

Medium-Rare (145°F): Steak is very pink in the center and slightly brown toward the exterior.

Medium (160°F): Steak is light pink in the center and brown toward the exterior.

Well Done (170°F): Steak is uniformly brown throughout.

Bring on the Flavor!

Add even more flavor to your steaks with marinades, rubs and toppings. Use any of these instead of the mustard butter in the main recipe.

Toppings: Add a punch of flavor to your steak with one of the following toppings.

Béarnaise Sauce: (page 487). This makes a luxurious topping for steak.

Blue Cheese Butter: Mix ½ cup butter, softened, with ¼ cup crumbled blue cheese.

Horseradish–Sour Cream: Mix ½ cup sour cream with ¼ cup creamy horseradish sauce.

Savory Butter: Top each steak with a pat of Savory Butter or any variation (page 501).

Southwestern Butter: Mix ½ cup butter, softened, with ½ teaspoon chili powder, ¼ teaspoon ground cumin and 2 tablespoons salsa.

Marinades: Letting steaks marinate in highly seasoned liquid adds flavor and moistness. See ideas for marinades on pages 309 and 498 to 499.

Rubs: These highly seasoned mixtures are literally rubbed into the surface. Rubs can be dry (seasonings or herbs mixed with salt or sugar) or wet (seasonings with added liquid such as oil, mustard or wine, that form a paste). See ideas for rubs on pages 308, 310, 318, 325 and 326. Sprinkle the rub mixture on both sides of steaks; rub in with fingers. Let stand about 30 minutes before cooking.

Top Loin (Strip) Steak
with Savory Herb Butter
(page 501)

T-Bone Steak with
Mustard Butter
(page 310)

Tenderloin Steak with
Bearnaise Sauce (page 487)

BURGER BASH

Step out of the ketchup, mustard, and pickle routine to create your own signature burgers. Choose from the selections below or get creative and whip up a burger of your own. Use our Timetable for Grilling Beef, Veal, Pork and Lamb (page 305) or Timetable for Grilling Poultry (page 305) for basic cooking directions. There's no end to the world of burgers!

1 Bavarian-Style Burgers: Spread thin layer of hot sweet mustard on split onion buns. Top grilled ground beef patties with Emmentaler cheese slices after turning. Place on buns and top with Caramelized Onions (page 598).

2 Caprese Burgers: Mix equal parts mayonnaise and Basil Pesto (page 485, or purchased) and spread on split Italian rolls. Top grilled ground beef patties with thick slices of fresh mozzarella cheese and sliced tomatoes; sprinkle with coarse ground pepper.

3 Chicago Burgers: Sprinkle 1 pound ground beef with celery salt. Shape into patties and grill as directed in timetable (page 305). Place on poppy seed buns and top with yellow mustard, sweet pickle relish, chopped onions, tomato wedges and jarred green sport peppers (made famous on Chicago-style hot dogs) or banana pepper rings.

4 Chicken Avocado BLT Burgers: Spread thin layer of mayonnaise on buns. Top grilled ground chicken patties with sliced avocado, crisp bacon, lettuce leaves and tomato slices.

5 Hawaiian Burgers: Top grilled ground beef patties with mozzarella cheese slices after turning. Place on buns and top with smoky barbecue sauce and grilled pineapple slices.

6 Pepper Jack–Jalapeño Burgers: Spread thin layer of chipotle mayonnaise on buns. Top grilled ground beef patties with pepper Jack cheese slices after turning. Place on buns and top with well-drained sliced pickled jalapeño peppers.

7 Tex-Mex Burgers: Sprinkle 1 pound ground beef with 1 ounce package fajita seasoning mix and ¼ cup finely chopped onion. Shape into patties and grill as directed in timetable (page 305). Place on buns and top with Guacamole (page 48, or purchased) and Salsa (page 480).

8 Turkey Reuben Burgers: Spread toasted rye bread or buns with Thousand Island dressing (page 475, or purchased). Top grilled ground turkey patties with Swiss cheese slices after turning. Place on toasted bread slices or buns and top with well-drained sauerkraut; serve with additional dressing if desired.

SWEET ONION–TOPPED CAESAR BURGERS

PREP 30 min TOTAL 30 min • **4 sandwiches**

1	lb lean (at least 80%) ground beef
2	tablespoons chopped fresh parsley
½	cup Caesar dressing
½	teaspoon peppered seasoned salt
1	small sweet onion (Bermuda, Maui, Spanish or Walla Walla), cut into ¼- to ½-inch slices
1½	cups shredded romaine lettuce
2	tablespoons shredded Parmesan cheese
4	burger buns, split

1 Heat gas or charcoal grill. In medium bowl, mix beef, parsley, 2 tablespoons of the dressing and the peppered seasoned salt. Shape mixture into 4 patties, about ½ inch thick.

2 Place patties on grill over medium heat. Cover grill; cook 10 to 12 minutes, turning once, until meat thermometer inserted in center of patties reads 160°F. Add onion slices to side of grill for last 8 to 10 minutes of cooking, brushing with 2 tablespoons of the dressing and turning once, until crisp-tender.

3 In small bowl, toss romaine, cheese and remaining ¼ cup dressing. Layer romaine mixture, patties and onion in buns.

1 Sandwich: Calories 500; Total Fat 33g (Saturated Fat 9g; Trans Fat 1g); Cholesterol 75mg; Sodium 840mg; Total Carbohydrate 25g (Dietary Fiber 2g); Protein 26g **Exchanges:** 1½ Starch, 1 Vegetable, 3 High-Fat Meat, 1 Fat **Carbohydrate Choices:** 1½

BLUE CHEESE BURGERS Substitute blue cheese dressing for the Caesar dressing and blue cheese for the Parmesan cheese.

GRILLED LEMON-PEPPER PORK TENDERLOIN LOWER CALORIE

PREP 30 min TOTAL 40 min • **6 servings**

1	teaspoon grated lemon peel
½	teaspoon seasoned salt
½	teaspoon coarse ground black pepper
½	teaspoon paprika
¼	teaspoon dried thyme or marjoram leaves
2	teaspoons olive or vegetable oil
2	pork tenderloins (about ¾ lb each)

1 Heat gas or charcoal grill. In small bowl, mix all ingredients except oil and pork. Brush oil over all sides of pork. Rub lemon peel mixture over pork.

2 Place pork on grill over medium-low heat. Cover grill; cook 15 to 20 minutes, turning occasionally, until pork has slight blush of pink in center and meat thermometer inserted in center reads 145°F.

3 Remove pork from grill; cover with foil. Let stand at least 3 minutes before slicing.

1 Serving: Calories 160; Total Fat 6g (Saturated Fat 1.5g; Trans Fat 0g); Cholesterol 70mg; Sodium 160mg; Total Carbohydrate 0g (Dietary Fiber 0g); Protein 26g **Exchanges:** 3½ Very Lean Meat, 1 Fat **Carbohydrate Choices:** 0

Removing Silverskin from Pork Tenderloin

Slide long, narrow knife under silverskin; hold silverskin tightly with one hand while slicing under membrane.

Sweet Onion–Topped Caesar Burgers

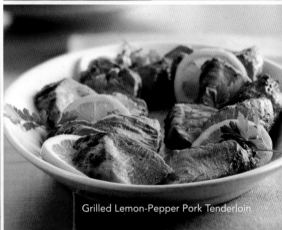

Grilled Lemon-Pepper Pork Tenderloin

Heirloom Recipe and New Twist

This classic recipe was inspired by decadent restaurant sandwiches. Topped with onions and Swiss cheese, it's simply delicious. Our new twist takes the open-faced burger to a spicy new place. You'll enjoy the chorizo sausage and the roasted chile mayonnaise with a touch of cilantro.

CLASSIC

PATTY MELTS WITH SMOTHERED ONIONS

PREP 35 min **TOTAL** 35 min • **4 sandwiches**

- 1 lb lean (at least 80%) ground beef
- ½ teaspoon salt
- ¼ teaspoon dried thyme leaves
- ¼ teaspoon dried oregano leaves
- ⅛ teaspoon pepper
- 2 teaspoons Dijon mustard
- 1 clove garlic, finely chopped
- 1 teaspoon olive or vegetable oil
- 2 medium red onions, thinly sliced, separated into rings
- ⅛ teaspoon salt
   Dash pepper
- 8 slices rye bread
- 4 slices (¾ oz each) Swiss cheese

1 Heat gas or charcoal grill. In medium bowl, mix beef, ½ teaspoon salt, the thyme, oregano, ⅛ teaspoon pepper, the mustard, and the garlic. Shape mixture into 4 patties, about ¾ inch thick.

2 In 8-inch skillet, heat oil over medium-high heat. Cook onions in oil 8 to 10 minutes, stirring frequently, until tender. Stir in ⅛ teaspoon salt and dash pepper; keep warm.

3 Place patties on grill over medium heat. Cover grill; cook 13 to 15 minutes, turning once, until meat thermometer inserted in center of patties reads 160°F. Add bread slices to side of grill for last 5 minutes of cooking, turning once, until lightly toasted.

4 Top patties with cheese. Cover grill; cook about 1 minute longer or until cheese is melted. Place patties on bread; top with onions and remaining bread.

1 Sandwich: Calories 440; Total Fat 22g (Saturated Fat 9g; Trans Fat 1g); Cholesterol 90mg; Sodium 880mg; Total Carbohydrate 31g (Dietary Fiber 3g); Protein 31g **Exchanges:** 2 Starch, 4 Medium-Fat Meat, 1 Fat **Carbohydrate Choices:** 2

Mix It Up

Although patty melts are usually made with ground beef, you could also make them with ground turkey or a mixture of ground pork and beef. Varying the cheese is a nice option. Why not try Cheddar or mozzarella to top the patties?

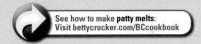

See how to make **patty melts**: Visit bettycrocker.com/BCcookbook

Learn with Betty | HAMBURGERS

Perfect Hamburger: The center of this hamburger has reached a safe 160°F and is no longer pink.

Undercooked Hamburger: The center of this hamburger has not reached a safe temperature of 160°F and is too pink.

Overcooked Hamburger: This burger has been overcooked and is hard and dry.

BEEF AND CHORIZO BURGERS WITH ROASTED CHILE MAYONNAISE

Chorizo comes in two forms—fresh and cured. The fresh chorizo used in this recipe is a common ingredient in Mexican dishes, while the cured, which comes completely cooked, is more often found in Spanish cuisine.

PREP 40 min **TOTAL** 45 min • **4 sandwiches**

ROASTED CHILE MAYONNAISE

- ¼ cup mayonnaise or salad dressing
- 2 teaspoons lime juice
- 1 clove garlic, finely chopped
- 1 tablespoon chopped fresh cilantro
- 1 small poblano chile

BURGERS

- 1 lb lean (at least 80%) ground beef
- ½ lb bulk chorizo sausage or Italian pork sausage, crumbled
- ¾ teaspoon salt
- ¼ teaspoon pepper
- 4 slices (1 oz each) Monterey Jack cheese
- 4 burger buns, split or 8 slices bread
- 1 medium tomato, coarsely chopped

1 Heat gas or charcoal grill. In small bowl, mix mayonnaise, lime juice, garlic and cilantro. Cover; refrigerate.

2 Remove stem, seeds and membranes from chile; cut chile lengthwise into quarters. Place skin side down on grill over medium heat. Cover grill; cook about 10 minutes or until skin is blackened and blistered. Immediately place chile in bowl. Cover tightly with plastic wrap; cool 5 minutes. Peel blackened skin from chile; rinse chile with water. Set aside.

3 In large bowl, mix beef, chorizo, salt and pepper. Shape into 4 patties, ½ inch thick.

4 Place patties on grill over medium heat. Cover grill; cook 11 to 13 minutes, turning once, until meat thermometer inserted in center of patties reads 160°F. During last 2 minutes of cooking, top each patty with cheese and place buns, cut sides down, on grill. Cook until cheese is melted and buns are toasted. Remove burgers and buns from grill; cover to keep warm.

5 Finely chop roasted chile; stir into mayonnaise mixture. Spread 1 tablespoon mixture on cut sides of buns. Place burgers on bottom halves of buns; top with tomato. Cover with top halves of buns.

1 Sandwich: Calories 560; Total Fat 35g (Saturated Fat 14g; Trans Fat 1.5g); Cholesterol 125mg; Sodium 1580mg; Total Carbohydrate 27g (Dietary Fiber 1g); Protein 36g **Exchanges:** 1½ Starch, ½ Vegetable, 4 High-Fat Meat, ½ Fat **Carbohydrate Choices:** 2

Patty Melts with Smothered Onions

Beef and Chorizo Burgers with Roasted Chile Mayonnaise

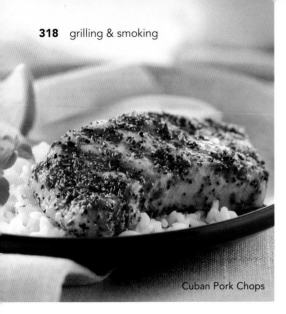

Cuban Pork Chops

CUBAN PORK CHOPS FAST

Serve these flavor-packed pork chops with corn on the cob and cooked rice tossed with black beans.

PREP 15 min TOTAL 15 min • **4 servings**

CUBAN RUB

- 2 tablespoons grated lime peel
- 1 tablespoon cracked black pepper
- 1 tablespoon cumin seed
- 2 tablespoons olive or vegetable oil
- ½ teaspoon salt
- 1 clove garlic, finely chopped

PORK

- 4 boneless pork loin or rib chops, about 1 inch thick (about 2 lb), trimmed of excess fat
  Mango slices, if desired

1 Heat gas or charcoal grill. In small bowl, mix rub ingredients; rub evenly on both sides of pork chops.

2 Place pork chops on grill over medium heat. Cover grill; cook 8 to 10 minutes, turning frequently, until pork is no longer pink and meat thermometer inserted in center reads 145°F. Let stand at least 3 minutes. Garnish with mango slices.

1 Serving: Calories 330; Total Fat 16g (Saturated Fat 4g; Trans Fat 0g); Cholesterol 95mg; Sodium 400mg; Total Carbohydrate 2g (Dietary Fiber 1g); Protein 45g **Exchanges:** 6½ Very Lean Meat, 2½ Fat **Carbohydrate Choices:** 0

PORK RIBS WITH SMOKY BARBECUE SAUCE

PREP 30 min TOTAL 1 hr 40 min • **4 servings**

RIBS

- 2 racks (2 lb each) pork back ribs (not cut into serving pieces)
- 1 tablespoon vegetable oil
- 4 teaspoons chopped fresh or 1½ teaspoons dried thyme leaves

SMOKY BARBECUE SAUCE

- ½ cup ketchup
- ¼ cup water
- 3 tablespoons packed brown sugar
- 2 tablespoons white vinegar
- 2 teaspoons celery seed
- ¼ teaspoon liquid smoke
- ¼ teaspoon red pepper sauce

1 Brush meaty side of ribs with oil; sprinkle with thyme. Heat gas or charcoal grill for indirect cooking. For two-burner gas grill, heat one burner to medium; place pork, meaty side up, on unheated side. For one-burner gas grill, place pork, meaty side up, on grill over low heat. For charcoal grill, move medium coals to edge of firebox; place pork, meaty side up, on grill rack over drip pan.

2 Cover grill; cook 1 hour to 1 hour 10 minutes or until tender and no longer pink next to bones. Meanwhile, in 1-quart saucepan, mix sauce ingredients; heat to boiling. Reduce heat; simmer uncovered 15 minutes, stirring occasionally. Brush sauce over pork 2 or 3 times during last 15 minutes of grilling. Heat any remaining sauce to boiling; boil and stir 1 minute. Cut pork into 4 serving pieces. Serve with sauce.

1 Serving: Calories 960; Total Fat 70g (Saturated Fat 25g; Trans Fat 0g); Cholesterol 265mg; Sodium 550mg; Total Carbohydrate 18g (Dietary Fiber 0g); Protein 64g **Exchanges:** 1 Other Carbohydrate, 9 Medium-Fat Meat, 5 Fat **Carbohydrate Choices:** 1

SOUTHWEST PORK RIBS WITH SMOKY BARBECUE SAUCE Omit oil and thyme. Use Southwest Rub (at right).

SLOW COOKER DIRECTIONS Cut ribs into 4 serving pieces. Omit oil and thyme. Spray 5- to 6-quart slow cooker with cooking spray. Place ribs in slow cooker. Cover; cook on Low heat setting 6 hours. Brush ribs with sauce. Place on grill over medium heat. Cover grill; cook about 15 minutes.

GRILLED ROSEMARY LAMB CHOPS

In this easy recipe, we call for French-cut lamb chops which are small and very tender. If these chops are not available, the recipe can also be made with lamb loin or sirloin chops. Both of these cuts will be a little meatier, so allow one chop per serving.

PREP 25 min TOTAL 25 min • **2 servings**

- 1 tablespoon country-style Dijon mustard
- 1 tablespoon chopped fresh rosemary
- 2 teaspoons honey
- 1 clove garlic, finely chopped
- ½ teaspoon salt
- ¼ teaspoon coarse ground black pepper
- 6 French-cut baby lamb chops (1 to 1¼ inches thick)

1 Heat gas or charcoal grill. In small bowl, mix all ingredients except lamb. Spread mixture on one side of each lamb chop.

2 Place lamb on grill, coated side up, over medium heat. Cover grill; cook 12 to 15 minutes or until thermometer inserted in center reads 160°F.

1 Serving (3 chops): Calories 330; Total Fat 14g (Saturated Fat 5g; Trans Fat 0.5g); Cholesterol 140mg; Sodium 880mg; Total Carbohydrate 7g (Dietary Fiber 0g); Protein 43g **Exchanges:** ½ Other Carbohydrate, 6 Very Lean Meat, 2 Fat **Carbohydrate Choices:** ½

Grilled Rosemary Lamb Chops

RUB IN FLAVOR

Dry rubs are easy to make and add a big punch of instant flavor to meats, poultry, fish and seafood. Store unused rub mixtures in airtight containers in a cool, dark location for up to 6 months. Rub mixture generously on all sides of meat, poultry or fish.

Caribbean Rub: Mix 1 tablespoon packed brown sugar, 1½ teaspoons ground allspice, 1 teaspoon each ground ginger and ground cinnamon, ½ teaspoon dried thyme leaves, ¼ teaspoon each salt and ground red pepper (cayenne).

Espresso Steak Rub: Mix 2 tablespoons each instant espresso coffee powder, ancho chile pepper powder, paprika and brown sugar with 1 tablespoon unsweetened baking cocoa, 1 teaspoon ground red pepper (cayenne) and ⅛ teaspoon ground cinnamon.

Espresso Steak Rub

Smoke 'n Spice Rub: Mix 2 tablespoons each ground chipotle chile pepper powder, regular chili powder, smoked paprika, salt and brown sugar.

Southwest Rub

Southwest Rub: Mix 2 tablespoons each regular chili powder or ancho chile pepper powder, ground cumin, smoked or regular paprika, garlic powder, salt and brown sugar.

Tandoori Rub: Mix 2 tablespoons each ground ginger, ground cumin, ground coriander, paprika, ground turmeric and salt with 1 tablespoon ground red pepper (cayenne).

Spicy Herb Rub: Mix together 3 tablespoons dried Italian seasoning, 1 tablespoon brown sugar, ½ teaspoon each salt and garlic powder, ¼ teaspoon each black pepper and ground red pepper (cayenne).

GRILLED FISH FAST LOWER CALORIE

This is a very versatile recipe that you can vary by using a different type of fish each time you make it. You could also sprinkle the fish with a little garlic powder or a favorite herb like dried basil or thyme. Or see the flavor rubs on page 319.

PREP 20 min TOTAL 20 min • **4 servings**

1½ lb fish steaks or 1 lb fish fillets (halibut, lake trout, mahi mahi, marlin, red snapper, salmon, swordfish or tuna), about ¾ inch thick
2 tablespoons butter, melted
1 teaspoon salt
¼ teaspoon pepper
1 lemon, cut into 4 wedges

1 Heat gas or charcoal grill. Cut fish into 4 serving pieces. Brush fish with 1 tablespoon of the butter; sprinkle with salt and pepper.

2 Carefully brush oil on grill rack. Place fish on grill over medium heat (if fish fillets have skin, place skin side down). Cover grill; cook 10 to 14 minutes, brushing 2 or 3 times with remaining 1 tablespoon butter, until fish flakes easily with fork. Serve with lemon wedges.

1 Serving: Calories 210; Total Fat 8g (Saturated Fat 4g; Trans Fat 0g); Cholesterol 105mg; Sodium 770mg; Total Carbohydrate 1g (Dietary Fiber 0g); Protein 32g **Exchanges:** 4½ Very Lean Meat, 1 Fat **Carbohydrate Choices:** 0

HERBED GRILLED FISH Sprinkle fish with 1 teaspoon dried Italian seasoning with the salt and pepper. Substitute olive oil for butter.

HONEY-DIJON GRILLED FISH Mix 2 tablespoons each honey and Dijon mustard. Brush mixture on fish before grilling. Omit salt and butter.

Removing Skin from Cooked Fish

Grab skin from tail end with tongs or fingers and gently peel off.

GRILLED FISH TACOS

FAST LOWER CALORIE

PREP 20 min TOTAL 20 min • **8 tacos**

1 lb sea bass, red snapper or other medium-firm fish fillets
1 tablespoon olive or vegetable oil
1 teaspoon ground cumin or chili powder
½ teaspoon salt
¼ teaspoon pepper
8 soft corn tortillas (6 inch)
¼ cup sour cream
Toppers (shredded lettuce and chopped avocado, tomato, onion and fresh cilantro), if desired
½ cup salsa (for homemade salsa, see page 480)
Fresh lime wedges, if desired

1 Heat gas or charcoal grill. Brush fish with oil; sprinkle with cumin, salt and pepper.

2 Carefully brush additional oil on grill rack. Place fish on grill over medium heat. Cover grill; cook 5 to 7 minutes, turning once, until fish flakes easily with fork.

3 Heat tortillas as directed on package. Spread sour cream on tortillas. Add fish, toppers and salsa. Serve with lime wedges.

1 Taco: Calories 140; Total Fat 4.5g (Saturated Fat 1.5g; Trans Fat 0g); Cholesterol 35mg; Sodium 310mg; Total Carbohydrate 12g (Dietary Fiber 2g); Protein 12g **Exchanges:** 1 Starch, 1½ Lean Meat **Carbohydrate Choices:** 1

Create a Taco Bar

For a large gathering, double or triple the fish taco recipe, grilling two or three types of fish. Offer soft corn tortillas and hard taco shells. Serve with toppings for guests to choose from:

- Shredded lettuce
- Chopped tomatoes
- Chopped avocado
- Chopped fresh cilantro
- Shredded cheeses
- Sliced olives
- Cooked corn
- Cooked black beans
- Sour cream
- Salsa

Spicy Coconut-Curry Grilled Shrimp

GINGER-TERIYAKI GRILLED SALMON WITH HONEY-MANGO SALSA LOWER CALORIE

PREP 30 min TOTAL 1 hr 30 min • **4 servings**

HONEY-MANGO SALSA

1 teaspoon grated lime peel
2 tablespoons lime juice
1 tablespoon honey
  Dash red pepper sauce
2 ripe medium mangoes, seed removed, peeled and diced (1 cup)
2 tablespoons finely chopped red onion

SALMON

3 tablespoons teriyaki baste and glaze (from 12-oz bottle)
1 tablespoon grated gingerroot
1 salmon fillet (1 lb)

1 In small bowl, mix lime peel, lime juice, honey and pepper sauce. Add mangoes and onion; toss. Cover; refrigerate 1 hour.

2 Heat gas or charcoal grill. In shallow glass or plastic dish, mix teriyaki glaze and gingerroot. Cut salmon into 4 serving pieces; place, skin side up, in marinade. Let stand 15 minutes.

3 Remove salmon from marinade; discard marinade. Carefully brush oil on grill rack. Place salmon, skin side up, on grill over medium heat. Cover grill; cook 2 minutes. Turn salmon. Cover grill; cook 5 to 10 minutes longer or until fish flakes easily with fork. Serve with salsa.

1 Serving: Calories 230; Total Fat 7g (Saturated Fat 2g; Trans Fat 0g); Cholesterol 75mg; Sodium 590mg; Total Carbohydrate 17g (Dietary Fiber 1g); Protein 25g **Exchanges:** ½ Fruit, ½ Other Carbohydrate, 3 Lean Meat **Carbohydrate Choices:** 1

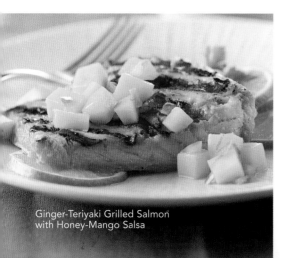

Ginger-Teriyaki Grilled Salmon with Honey-Mango Salsa

SPICY COCONUT-CURRY GRILLED SHRIMP LOWER CALORIE

PREP 20 min TOTAL 45 min • **6 servings**

18 bamboo skewers (6 inch)
¾ cup canned coconut milk (not cream of coconut)
2 teaspoons curry powder
2 teaspoons cornstarch
1 teaspoon honey
¼ teaspoon salt
54 uncooked medium shrimp (about 2 lb), thawed if frozen, peeled, deveined
2 tablespoons olive or vegetable oil
1 teaspoon red pepper sauce

1 Soak skewers in water at least 30 minutes before using to prevent burning. Meanwhile, heat gas or charcoal grill. In small microwavable bowl, mix coconut milk, curry powder, cornstarch, honey and salt. Microwave uncovered on High about 2 minutes, stirring every 30 seconds, until mixture bubbles and thickens; set aside.

2 In large bowl, place shrimp. Drizzle with oil and pepper sauce; toss to coat. Thread 3 shrimp on each skewer, leaving space between each.

3 Place kabobs on grill over medium heat. Cover grill; cook 4 to 6 minutes, turning once, until shrimp are pink. Serve with coconut-curry mixture.

1 Serving (3 Kabobs and 4 Teaspoons Sauce): Calories 210; Total Fat 11g (Saturated Fat 5g; Trans Fat 0g); Cholesterol 215mg; Sodium 370mg; Total Carbohydrate 5g (Dietary Fiber 1g); Protein 24g **Exchanges:** ½ Other Carbohydrate, 3½ Lean Meat **Carbohydrate Choices:** ½

EASY GRILLED VEGETABLES

LOWER CALORIE

PREP 25 min **TOTAL** 1 hr 25 min • **6 servings**

  12 pattypan squash (about 1 inch in diameter) or 2 medium zucchini cut into 1-inch pieces
   2 medium red or green bell peppers, each cut into 6 pieces
   1 large red onion, cut into ½-inch slices
  ⅓ cup Italian dressing
      Freshly ground pepper, if desired

1 In 13x9-inch (3-quart) glass baking dish, place squash, bell peppers and onion. Pour dressing over vegetables. Cover; let stand 1 hour to blend flavors.

2 Heat gas or charcoal grill. Remove vegetables from marinade; reserve marinade. Place squash and bell peppers in grill basket (grill "wok"). Place grill basket on grill over medium heat. Cover grill; cook 5 minutes.

3 Add onion to grill basket. Cover grill; cook 5 to 10 minutes longer, turning and brushing vegetables with marinade 2 or 3 times, until tender. Sprinkle with pepper.

1 Serving: Calories 110; Total Fat 6g (Saturated Fat 0.5g; Trans Fat 0g); Cholesterol 0mg; Sodium 120mg; Total Carbohydrate 11g (Dietary Fiber 3g); Protein 2g **Exchanges:** ½ Other Carbohydrate, 1 Vegetable, 1 Fat **Carbohydrate Choices:** 1

FRESH VEGETABLE GRILLING CHART

Grill vegetables in a grill basket (grill "wok") for time indicated over medium heat.

Vegetable	Form	Minutes
Asparagus Spears	Whole	8 to 10
Bell Peppers	Cut into ½-inch strips	5 to 10
Broccoli Florets	Cut in half lengthwise	15 to 20
Carrots, Baby-Cut	Whole	20 to 25
Cauliflower Florets	Cut in half lengthwise	10 to 15
Cherry Tomatoes	Whole	5 to 10
Corn on the Cob (husked and wrapped in foil)	Whole	12 to 18
Green Beans	Whole	10 to 15
Mushrooms, White	Whole with stems removed	8 to 10
Mushrooms, Portabella	Whole with stems removed	8 to 10
Onions	Cut into ½-inch slices	10 to 15
Potatoes, Russet or Idaho	Cut into quarters lengthwise	15 to 20
Potatoes, Small Red	Cut into quarters	10 to 15
Zucchini, Small	Cut in half lengthwise	10 to 15

See how to use a **grill basket**: Visit bettycrocker.com/BCcookbook

Easy Grilled Vegetables

Grilled Corn with Herb Butter

GRILLED CORN WITH HERB BUTTER

If you've run out of heavy-duty foil, layer two sheets of standard foil to make your packet.

PREP 30 min TOTAL 30 min • **6 servings**

- ¼ cup butter
- 2 tablespoons chopped fresh chives
- ½ teaspoon garlic salt
- 6 ears fresh sweet corn, husks removed, cleaned
- ¼ cup grated Parmesan cheese

1 Heat gas or charcoal grill. Cut 30x18-inch sheet of heavy-duty foil. In small microwavable bowl, place butter, chives and garlic salt. Microwave uncovered on High 15 to 20 seconds or until butter is melted.

2 Brush butter mixture over each ear of corn. Place corn on center of foil. Pour any remaining butter mixture over corn. Sprinkle with cheese. Bring 2 sides of foil up over corn so edges meet. Seal edges, making tight ½-inch fold; fold again, allowing space for heat circulation and expansion. Fold other sides to seal.

3 Place packet on grill over low heat. Cover grill; cook 12 to 18 minutes, rotating packet ½ turn after every 6 minutes, until corn is tender. To serve, cut large X across top of packet; carefully fold back foil to allow steam to escape.

1 Serving: Calories 210; Total Fat 10g (Saturated Fat 6g; Trans Fat 0g); Cholesterol 25mg; Sodium 220mg; Total Carbohydrate 25g (Dietary Fiber 4g); Protein 5g **Exchanges:** 1½ Starch, 2 Fat **Carbohydrate Choices:** 1½

Making Foil Packets for Grill

Fold top over twice to prevent leakage from packet, leaving room for heat circulation and expansion.

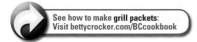

See how to make **grill packets**: Visit bettycrocker.com/BCcookbook

Using a Grill Basket

Spray basket with cooking spray (away from grill flame to prevent flare-up). Place food in basket; place basket directly on grill. Shake or stir food in basket for even cooking.

GRILLED HERBED NEW POTATOES

With their creamy sauce, these grilled potatoes go great with grilled beef tenderloin or tuna steaks.

PREP 25 min TOTAL 25 min • **4 servings**

SOUR CREAM SAUCE

- ⅓ cup sour cream
- 1 tablespoon chopped fresh or ½ teaspoon dried rosemary leaves, crumbled
- ¼ teaspoon lemon-pepper seasoning
- ⅛ teaspoon garlic powder

POTATOES

- 2 tablespoons olive or vegetable oil
- 1 tablespoon chopped fresh or ½ teaspoon dried parsley flakes
- 1 tablespoon chopped fresh or ½ teaspoon dried rosemary leaves, crumbled
- ½ teaspoon lemon-pepper seasoning
- ¼ teaspoon salt
- 8 small red potatoes, cut into quarters

1 Heat gas or charcoal grill. In small bowl, mix sauce ingredients. Cover; refrigerate until serving.

2 In large bowl, mix remaining ingredients except potatoes. Add potatoes; toss to coat. Place potatoes in grill basket (grill "wok").

3 Place grill basket on grill over medium heat. Cover grill; cook 10 to 15 minutes, shaking basket or stirring potatoes occasionally, until tender. Serve potatoes with sauce.

1 Serving: Calories 270; Total Fat 11g (Saturated Fat 3.5g; Trans Fat 0g); Cholesterol 15mg; Sodium 240mg; Total Carbohydrate 40g (Dietary Fiber 4g); Protein 5g **Exchanges:** 2 Starch, ½ Other Carbohydrate, 2 Fat **Carbohydrate Choices:** 2½

SMOKING BASICS

Smoking is an almost effortless style of outdoor cooking that doesn't require frequent tending, turning or basting and infuses an unforgettable flavor into every bite! Smoking foods at home is easy with these tips.

TYPES OF SMOKERS

Smokers are tall and cylindrical and consist of a firebox, water pan, one or two grill racks and a dome-shaped cover. The most common smokers are charcoal water smokers and electric water smokers (generally considered more reliable than charcoal water smokers for maintaining a consistent temperature inside).

The food is placed on a grill rack high above the heat. A pan of water or other liquid (beer, fruit juice, wine, soda) rests between the heat source and the food. Aromatic wood chunks, chips or shreds, which have been soaked in water, are added for smoke and flavor. Foods cook very slowly in a dense cloud of smoke and steam, infusing the characteristic flavor, moisture and tenderness smoked meats are known for. Foods best suited to smoking include ribs, beef brisket, roasts, poultry and fish. Follow smoker manufacturer's directions.

SAFETY TIPS FOR SMOKING

It's best to follow the manufacturer's directions, but here are some basic safety tips to ensure successful results:

- Use only completely thawed meats, poultry, fish or seafood because the heat inside a smoker is too low to thaw and cook frozen food safely.

- It's best to smoke foods when the outdoor temperature is 65°F or higher and there is little or no wind. Below 55°F, the smoker and food will not get hot enough and may result in an additional 2 to 3 hours of cooking.

- Monitor the temperature inside the smoker with an ovenproof meat thermometer to ensure the heat stays between 225°F and 300°F throughout the cooking process.

- To gauge the temperature of the food, use a digital oven-cord thermometer. It can stay in the food in the smoker and sounds an alarm when the food has reached the correct temperature. Using an analog ovenproof thermometer is another option; however, you must lift the cover to check for doneness (at the minimum time given in the recipe), which releases heat and increases the cooking time. Note that some smoked foods will remain pink even when fully cooked, so using a thermometer to determine doneness is very important. See Thermometers, page 16, for more information.

Smoking on a Grill

If you have a grill but want smoked flavor, here is how to do it.

- Cover 1 to 2 cups wood chips or shreds or 2 or 3 wood chunks with water, and soak at least 30 minutes; drain.

- Put soaked wood onto a piece of heavy-duty foil; seal tightly to form a pouch. Poke 6 to 8 slits in top of pouch with a sharp knife.

- Put pouch on grill rack or follow manufacturer's directions for adding wood chips. Cover grill and let pouch get hot enough to start smoking, about 10 minutes. Add food, leaving the pouch in the grill during cooking.

Wood chips for smoking clockwise from top left: hickory chips, mesquite chips, apple chips, cedar chips

HOT AND SPICY RIBS

PREP 15 min TOTAL 5 hr 15 min • **6 servings**

RIBS

4 cups hickory wood chips
5 pounds pork spareribs (not cut into 16 serving pieces)
Barbecue sauce, if desired

HOT AND SPICY RUB

1 tablespoon garlic powder
1 tablespoon paprika
2 teaspoons ground red pepper (cayenne)
2 teaspoons dried thyme leaves, crumbled
1 teaspoon salt
1 teaspoon pepper

1 In large bowl, cover wood chips with water; soak 30 minutes.

2 Drain wood chips. Prepare and heat smoker using wood chips and adding water to water pan following manufacturer's directions.

3 In small bowl, mix rub ingredients. Cut rack of pork in half to fit on smoker rack if necessary. Rub spice mixture into pork.

4 Place pork on rack in smoker. Cover and smoke 4 hours 30 minutes to 5 hours or until tender and no longer pink next to bones. If smoking stops, add additional wood chips through side door of smoker. Serve pork with barbecue sauce.

1 Serving: Calories 580; Total Fat 45g (Saturated Fat 16g; Trans Fat 0g); Cholesterol 180mg; Sodium 530mg; Total Carbohydrate 2g (Dietary Fiber 0g); Protein 43g **Exchanges:** 6 Medium-Fat Meat, 3 Fat **Carbohydrate Choices:** 0

Removing Silverskin from Pork Ribs

Slide knife under silverskin; lift and loosen until you can grab it with a paper towel. Pull it off in one piece if possible.

Hot and Spicy Ribs

CAJUN CHICKEN

PREP 15 min **TOTAL** 3 hr 15 min • **6 servings**

CHICKEN

- 2 cups hickory wood chips
- 1 cut-up whole chicken (3 to 3½ lb)
- 1 tablespoon vegetable oil

CAJUN SPICE RUB

- 1 teaspoon black pepper
- ½ teaspoon white pepper
- ½ teaspoon ground red pepper (cayenne)
- ½ teaspoon salt
- ½ teaspoon ground cumin
- ½ teaspoon ground nutmeg

1 In large bowl, cover wood chips with water; soak 30 minutes.

2 Drain wood chips. Prepare and heat smoker using wood chips.

3 In small bowl, mix rub ingredients. Brush chicken with oil. Rub mixture into all sides of chicken.

4 Place chicken, skin side up, on rack in smoker. Cover and smoke 2 hours 30 minutes to 3 hours or until juice is clear when thickest part is cut to the bone (at least 165°F).

1 Serving: Calories 340; Total Fat 15g (Saturated Fat 4g; Trans Fat 0g); Cholesterol 155mg; Sodium 340mg; Total Carbohydrate 0g (Dietary Fiber 0g); Protein 50g **Exchanges:** 6½ Very Lean Meat, ½ Lean Meat, 2 Fat **Carbohydrate Choices:** 0

SMOKED BRINED SALMON

Serve this deliciously moist salmon with grilled vegetables and French bread.

PREP 10 min **TOTAL** 3 hr 10 min • **6 servings**

- ½ cup sugar
- ¼ cup salt
- 1 tablespoon grated orange peel (from 1 small orange)
- 1 teaspoon black peppercorns
- 1 medium onion, sliced
- 4 cups water
- 1 skin-on salmon fillet (2½ to 3 lb)
- 4 to 6 wood chunks (hickory, mesquite or apple)*
- 2 tablespoons vegetable oil
- ½ teaspoon paprika
- ¼ teaspoon pepper

1 In 1-gallon resealable food-storage plastic bag, mix sugar, salt, orange peel, peppercorns, onion, and 4 cups water. Seal bag and squeeze to mix until sugar and salt have dissolved. Place salmon in brine; seal bag. Refrigerate at least 3 hours but no longer than 4 hours.

2 In large bowl, cover wood chunks with water; soak 30 minutes. Drain. Prepare and heat smoker using wood chunks and adding water to water pan following manufacturer's directions.

3 Remove salmon from brine; discard brine. Blot salmon dry with paper towels. Brush both sides of salmon with oil.

4 Place salmon, skin side down, on top grill rack in smoker. Sprinkle with paprika and pepper. Cover and smoke about 1 hour or until fish flakes easily with fork. If smoking stops, add additional wood chunks through side door of smoker.

5 Place salmon, skin side up, on foil. Peel skin from fish and discard. Use foil to turn fish onto serving platter.

*2 cups hickory, mesquite or apple wood chips can be substituted.

1 Serving: Calories 270; Total Fat 13g (Saturated Fat 3g; Trans Fat 0g); Cholesterol 105mg; Sodium 490mg; Total Carbohydrate 4g (Dietary Fiber 0g); Protein 34g **Exchanges:** 5 Lean Meat **Carbohydrate Choices:** 0

Smoked Brined Salmon

MEATS

CHARTS, FEATURES AND TIMETABLES

For bonus **meats** recipes, visit
bettycrocker.com/BCcookbook

FAST = Ready in 20 minutes or less **LOWER CALORIE** = See Helpful Nutrition and Cooking Information, page 685
LIGHTER = 25% fewer calories or grams of fat **MAKE AHEAD** = Make-ahead directions **SLOW COOKER** = Slow cooker directions

← Herb- and Garlic-Crusted Beef Rib Roast (page 335), Brandy-Herb Pan Steaks (page 334), Cornbread-Topped
Sausage Pie (page 357), Beef Stroganoff (page 342)

MEAT BASICS

Standing in front of the meat case at your local grocery store does not need to be overwhelming. There are many cuts of meat to choose from, and the information in this chapter will help you be a savvy meat shopper.

TIPS FOR BUYING FRESH MEAT

- Choose packages without any tears, holes or leaks. There should be little or no liquid in the bottom of the tray.

- Packages should be cold and feel firm. Avoid packages that are stacked too high in the meat case because they may not have been kept cold enough.

- Check the sell-by date and use within 2 days of the date.

- Put packages of meat in plastic bags before putting them in your grocery cart. This way, any bacteria in the juices won't drip on and contaminate other foods, especially those that won't be cooked.

- Don't buy or use meat that has turned gray or has an off odor.

- Refrigerate meat as soon as you get home from shopping. If it will take longer than 30 minutes to get it home, keep meat cold in a cooler with ice packs.

READING A MEAT LABEL

Labels include the following information to help you make the right choice for your recipe and even to help you know how the meat should be cooked. Labels indicate:

- The kind of meat: beef, pork, veal or lamb.

- The primal or wholesale cut (where it comes from on the animal): chuck, rib or loin, for example.

- The retail cut of meat: chuck pot roast, rib-eye steak or loin chops, for example.

- The weight, price per pound, total price and sell-by date.

Knowing how you are going to cook the meat will help you decide what cut to purchase. (See retail cut charts for beef, veal, pork and lamb on pages 330, 331, 348 and 349.) The most tender cuts are from the rib and loin sections because they are exercised the least. The least tender cuts are from those muscles that are exercised the most—which also makes them very flavorful. See pages 359 to 364 to help you determine which cooking method is best for which cut.

SERVINGS PER POUND

The number of servings per pound varies depending on the type of meat and the amount of bone and fat present. The average serving is based on 2½ to 3½ ounces of cooked meat per person, but you can always plan for more.

The little streaks of white fat running through the lean of meat is called marbling. The more marbling, the more tender and juicy the meat will be when cooked. Here, the top steak has more marbling so will be more tender.

Type of Meat	Servings per Pound
Boneless Cuts (ground, boneless chops, loin, tenderloin)	3 to 4
Bone-In Cuts (rib roasts, pot roasts, country-style ribs)	2 to 3
Very Bony Cuts (back ribs, spareribs, short ribs, shanks)	1 to 1½

RETAIL BEEF CUTS

A variety of cuts is available in the marketplace. The information and images here should help you choose the right cut for your recipe needs.

Diagram: 1 Chuck **2** Rib **3** Loin **4** Sirloin **5** Round **6** Brisket **7** Shank **8** Plate **9** Flank

Stew Meat

Beef Brisket Roast

Beef Chuck Shoulder Pot Roast (boneless)

Beef Chuck Top Blade Steak

Beef Rib Roast (bone-in; small end)

Beef Short Ribs

Beef Rib-Eye Roast (rolled)

Beef Rib-Eye Steak

Beef Chuck 7-Bone Pot Roast (bone-in)

Beef Tri-Tip Roast

Beef Round Tip Roast

Beef Rump Roast or Bottom Round (boneless)

Beef Flank Steak

Beef Top Sirloin Steak (boneless)

Beef Skirt Steak

Beef Eye of Round Steak

Beef Top Round Steak

Porterhouse Steak

Beef Tenderloin Steak

Beef Tenderloin Roast

Beef T-Bone Steak

VEAL CUTS

Here are some of the more commonly used cuts of veal that you might find called for in recipes.

Veal Rib Chop (bone-in)

Veal Loin Chop

Veal Cross-Cut Shank

Beef Top Loin Steak

Veal Leg Cutlets

Veal Top Round Steak (boneless)

STORING MEAT

- Meat wrapped in butcher paper should be repackaged tightly in plastic wrap, foil or freezer plastic bags.

- Meat packaged in clear plastic wrap on a plastic or Styrofoam tray doesn't need to be repackaged.

- Store meat in the meat compartment or coldest part of your refrigerator, or freeze it as soon as possible. Ground meat is more perishable than other cuts, so use it within 2 days.

- Cook or freeze meat within 2 days of the sell-by date.

- If meat was purchased frozen or was frozen right after purchasing, keep it in the refrigerator after thawing for the number of days listed in the Timetable for Storing Meat, below. If the meat was refrigerated several days before freezing, use it the same day you thaw it.

Handling Raw Meat

Cooking meat to the recommended doneness destroys any bacteria. To avoid any cross-contamination when preparing raw meat for cooking, follow the tips in Don't Cross-Contaminate, page 35.

Cutting Raw Meat

Need to cut raw meat into cubes, thin slices or strips? Put the meat in the freezer first. Leave the meat in the freezer until it's firm but not frozen, about 30 to 60 minutes, depending on the size of the piece. It'll be easy to slice, even paper thin.

TIMETABLE FOR STORING MEAT

Cut of Meat	Refrigerator (36°F to 40°F)	Freezer (0°F or Colder)
Ground Meats		
Beef	1 to 2 days	3 to 4 months
Veal	1 to 2 days	2 to 3 months
Pork	1 to 2 days	1 to 3 months
Steaks and Roasts		
Beef	3 to 4 days	6 to 12 months
Veal	1 to 2 days	6 to 9 months
Pork	2 to 4 days	3 to 6 months
Lamb	3 to 5 days	6 to 9 months
Cubes and Slices	2 to 3 days	6 to 12 months
Leftover Cooked Meats	3 to 4 days	2 to 3 months
Cured, Smoked and Ready-to-Serve Meat Products		
Corned Beef	1 week	2 weeks
Hot Dogs	3 to 5 days	1 month
Bacon	5 to 7 days	1 month

THAWING MEAT

Thaw meat slowly in the refrigerator in a dish or baking pan with sides or in a resealable food-storage plastic bag to catch any drips during thawing. Don't thaw meat on the countertop because bacteria thrive at room temperature.

Amount of Frozen Meat	Thawing Time in Refrigerator*
Large Roast (4 lb or larger)	4 to 7 hours per lb
Small Roast (under 4 lb)	3 to 5 hours per lb
Steak or Chops (1 inch thick)	12 to 14 hours total
Ground Beef or Beef Pieces (1- to 1½-lb package)	24 hours total
Ground Beef Patties (½ to ¾ inch thick)	12 hours total

*To thaw meat in the microwave, follow manufacturer's directions.

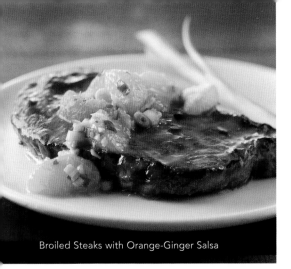

Broiled Steaks with Orange-Ginger Salsa

BROILED STEAKS WITH ORANGE-GINGER SALSA

PREP 30 min TOTAL 1 hr 30 min • **4 servings**

- 1 **can (11 oz) mandarin orange segments, drained**
- 2 **tablespoons packed brown sugar**
- 2 **tablespoons sliced green onions**
- 2 **tablespoons chopped fresh cilantro**
- 1 **tablespoon finely chopped gingerroot**
- 3 **tablespoons lime juice**
- 1 **teaspoon chili puree with garlic**
- 4 **beef rib-eye steaks, ½ inch thick (6 oz each)**
- ½ **cup hoisin sauce**
  Pepper

1 In medium bowl, mix orange segments, brown sugar, onions, cilantro, gingerroot, lime juice and chili puree. Cover and refrigerate at least 1 hour to blend flavors.

2 Set oven control to broil. Spray broiler pan rack with nonstick cooking spray. Place beef steaks on rack in broiler pan. Brush hoisin sauce on tops and sides of beef; sprinkle with pepper. Broil with tops 3 to 5 inches from heat 10 minutes. Turn beef; brush with hoisin sauce and sprinkle with pepper. Broil about 10 minutes longer for medium doneness (160°F). Serve with orange mixture.

1 Serving: Calories 420; Total Fat 13g (Saturated Fat 5g; Trans Fat 0.5g); Cholesterol 80mg; Sodium 620mg; Total Carbohydrate 32g (Dietary Fiber 2g); Protein 43g **Exchanges:** 1 Starch, 1 Other Carbohydrate, 5½ Very Lean Meat, 2 Fat **Carbohydrate Choices:** 2

LEMON-DIJON PAN STEAK

FAST **LOWER CALORIE**

Also known as Steak Diane, this classic restaurant dish is often made tableside from a tidy service cart that is draped with a crisp white tablecloth. It's quite a showstopper that is easy to make at home right on top of the stove.

PREP 10 min TOTAL 20 min • **4 servings**

- 1 **lb boneless beef top sirloin steak, about ¾ inch thick**
- ¼ **teaspoon coarse ground black pepper**
- 1 **cup beef broth (for homemade broth, see page 530)**
- 1 **tablespoon all-purpose flour**
- 2 **teaspoons Dijon mustard**
- 2 **teaspoons Worcestershire sauce**
- ½ **teaspoon grated lemon peel**
- 2 **tablespoons chopped fresh chives**

1 Cut beef into 4 serving pieces. Spray 12-inch skillet with cooking spray; heat over medium heat. Sprinkle both sides of beef with pepper. Cook beef in skillet 9 to 11 minutes for medium doneness (160°F), turning once. Remove beef from skillet; keep warm.

2 In small bowl, mix remaining ingredients except chives until smooth; add to skillet. Heat to boiling. Boil 1 minute, stirring constantly. Stir in chives. Serve over beef.

1 Serving: Calories 170; Total Fat 4.5g (Saturated Fat 1.5g; Trans Fat 0g); Cholesterol 75mg; Sodium 390mg; Total Carbohydrate 2g (Dietary Fiber 0g); Protein 30g **Exchanges:** 4 Very Lean Meat, ½ Fat **Carbohydrate Choices:** 0

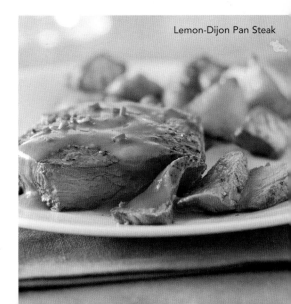

Lemon-Dijon Pan Steak

BRANDY-HERB PAN STEAKS

LOWER CALORIE

PREP 10 min TOTAL 30 min • **4 servings**

  1 teaspoon cracked or coarse ground
     black pepper
  ¾ teaspoon chopped fresh or ¼ teaspoon
     dried basil leaves
  ¾ teaspoon chopped fresh or ¼ teaspoon
     dried rosemary leaves
  ½ teaspoon coarse (kosher or sea) salt
  4 boneless beef tenderloin steaks, 1 inch
     thick (4 to 6 oz each)
  1 tablespoon butter
  ¼ cup beef broth
  2 tablespoons brandy or beef broth

1 In small bowl, mix pepper, basil, rosemary and salt. Rub mixture into both sides of each steak.

2 In 12-inch skillet, melt butter over medium heat. Cook steaks in butter 6 to 8 minutes, turning once, until medium-rare to medium (145°F to 160°F). Remove beef from skillet; keep warm.

3 Add broth and brandy to skillet. Heat to boiling, stirring to loosen browned bits from bottom of skillet; reduce heat. Simmer uncovered 3 to 4 minutes or until slightly thickened. Serve with steaks.

1 Serving: Calories 200; Total Fat 5g (Saturated Fat 2g; Trans Fat 0g); Cholesterol 90mg; Sodium 110mg; Total Carbohydrate 0g (Dietary Fiber 0g); Protein 37g **Exchanges:** 5 Very Lean Meat, ½ Fat **Carbohydrate Choices:** 0

Making a Pan Sauce

Remove cooked meat from skillet; add liquid, stirring to loosen browned bits from bottom of skillet.

Simmer uncovered until mixture is slightly thickened.

MUSHROOM BRANDY-HERB PAN STEAKS

Remove beef from skillet as directed in Step 2. Add 1 tablespoon additional butter and 1 cup sliced fresh mushrooms to skillet. Cook and stir 2 to 3 minutes or until tender. Leave mushrooms in skillet and make sauce as directed in Step 3.

SWISS STEAK LOWER CALORIE

PREP 15 min TOTAL 1 hr 55 min • **6 servings**

  1 boneless beef round, tip or chuck steak,
     about ¾ inch thick (1½ lb)
  3 tablespoons all-purpose flour
  1 teaspoon ground mustard
  ½ teaspoon salt
  2 tablespoons vegetable oil
  1 can (14.5 oz) diced tomatoes, undrained
  2 cloves garlic, finely chopped
  1 cup water
  1 large onion, cut in half, sliced
  1 large green bell pepper, sliced

1 Cut beef into 6 serving pieces. In small bowl, mix flour, mustard and salt. Sprinkle half of the flour mixture over one side of beef; pound in with meat mallet. Turn beef; pound in remaining flour mixture.

2 In 10-inch skillet, heat oil over medium heat. Cook beef in oil about 15 minutes, turning once, until brown.

3 Stir in tomatoes and garlic. Heat to boiling; reduce heat. Cover; simmer about 1 hour 15 minutes, occasionally spooning sauce over beef, until beef is tender.

4 Add water, onion and bell pepper. Heat to boiling; reduce heat. Cover; simmer 5 to 8 minutes longer or until vegetables are tender.

1 Serving: Calories 210; Total Fat 8g (Saturated Fat 2g; Trans Fat 0g); Cholesterol 60mg; Sodium 340mg; Total Carbohydrate 10g (Dietary Fiber 2g); Protein 24g **Exchanges:** 2 Vegetable, 3 Lean Meat **Carbohydrate Choices:** ½

SLOW COOKER DIRECTIONS Omit water. Cut beef into 6 serving pieces. Coat beef with flour mixture (do not pound in). Brown beef in oil as directed in Step 2. Spray 3½- to 6-quart slow cooker with cooking spray. In slow cooker, place beef, onion and bell pepper. Mix tomatoes and garlic; pour over beef and vegetables. Cover; cook on Low heat setting 7 to 9 hours or until beef and vegetables are tender.

HERB- AND GARLIC-CRUSTED BEEF RIB ROAST

When buying the roast, look for it under several names: beef rib roast, standing rib roast or prime rib roast.

PREP 15 min TOTAL 3 hr • **8 servings**

    1 beef rib roast, small end (4 to 6 lb)
    2 teaspoons dried basil leaves
    2 teaspoons dried thyme leaves
    1 teaspoon coarse (kosher or sea) salt
    1 teaspoon garlic powder
    ¼ teaspoon coarse ground black pepper

1 Heat oven to 350°F. For easy cleanup, line shallow roasting pan with foil. Place beef, fat side up, in pan. In small bowl, mix basil, thyme, salt, garlic powder and pepper; sprinkle and press onto all surfaces of roast. Insert ovenproof meat thermometer so tip is in thickest part of beef and does not rest in fat or touch bone. (Do not add water to pan.)

2 For medium-rare, roast uncovered 1 hour 45 minutes to 2 hours 15 minutes or until thermometer reads 135°F. (Temperature will continue to rise about 10°F, and beef will be easier to carve.) Remove from oven. Cover beef loosely with foil; let stand 10 to 15 minutes until thermometer reads 145°F. For medium, roast 2 hours 15 minutes to 2 hours 45 minutes or until thermometer reads 150°F. Cover beef loosely with foil; let stand 15 to 20 minutes or until thermometer reads 160°F.

3 Remove beef from pan onto carving board; carve beef. Serve with pan drippings if desired.

1 Serving: Calories 340; Total Fat 17g (Saturated Fat 7g; Trans Fat 0.5g); Cholesterol 140mg; Sodium 390mg; Total Carbohydrate 13g (Dietary Fiber 0g); Protein 32g **Exchanges:** 1 Starch, 4 Lean Meat, 1 Fat **Carbohydrate Choices:** 1

BEEF RIB ROAST WITH OVEN-BROWNED POTATOES About 1 hour 30 minutes before beef is done, prepare and boil 8 medium potatoes as directed on page 589. For decorative potatoes, make crosswise cuts almost through whole potatoes to make thin slices and decrease boiling time to 10 minutes. Place potatoes in beef drippings in pan, turning to coat completely; or brush potatoes with melted butter and place on rack with beef. Continue cooking about 1 hour 15 minutes, turning potatoes once, until golden brown. Sprinkle with salt and pepper if desired.

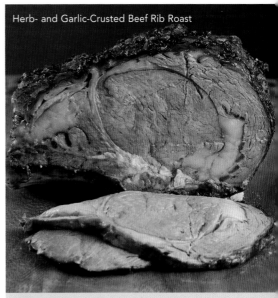

Herb- and Garlic-Crusted Beef Rib Roast

Carving a Beef Rib Roast

With roast on cutting board, carefully cut bone portion away from meat.

Turn roast bone side down. Cut slices evenly and toward bone side of roast.

Learn to Make Beef Tenderloin

HERB ROASTED BEEF TENDERLOIN

Beef tenderloin is hands-down a terrific choice for entertaining—its fabulous flavor and impressive look make it seem like it would be difficult to prepare, but it's really quite simple. Knowing how to cook it to perfection is easy when you follow the great tips here.

PREP 15 min **TOTAL** 1 hr 25 min • **6 servings**

1 beef tenderloin (about 2½ lb)	½ teaspoon dried marjoram leaves
1 tablespoon olive or vegetable oil	¼ teaspoon coarse (kosher or sea) salt
½ teaspoon coarse ground black pepper	

1 Heat oven to 425°F. Turn small end of beef under about 6 inches. Tie beef with kitchen string at about 1½-inch intervals. Place in shallow roasting pan. Brush with oil. Sprinkle with pepper, marjoram and salt. Insert ovenproof meat thermometer so tip is in thickest part of beef.

2 For medium-rare, roast 35 to 40 minutes or until thermometer reads 135°F. (Temperature will continue to rise about 10°F, and beef will be easier to carve.) Cover beef loosely with foil; let stand 15 to 20 minutes until thermometer reads 145°F. For medium, roast uncovered 45 to 50 minutes or until thermometer reads 150°F. Cover beef loosely with foil; let stand 10 to 15 minutes until thermometer reads 160°F. Remove string from beef before carving.

1 Serving: Calories 300; Total Fat 16g (Saturated Fat 5g; Trans Fat 0.5g); Cholesterol 110mg; Sodium 190mg; Total Carbohydrate 0g (Dietary Fiber 0g); Protein 41g **Exchanges:** 5½ Lean Meat **Carbohydrate Choices:** 0

BACON-WRAPPED HERB ROASTED BEEF TENDERLOIN After sprinkling tenderloin with pepper, marjoram and salt, place 6 bacon slices (don't use thick-sliced) over top of beef, tucking ends under bottom. Continue as directed.

Keys to Success

- **Turn under small end of tenderloin** to make the meat uniform thickness so it will cook evenly.

- **Tie beef with kitchen string** to maintain shape and prevent turned-under portion from separating during cooking.

- **Use meat thermometer** to check for doneness. This prevents having to cut into meat to check, which causes juices to escape.

- **Roast to 10°F below desired end temperature,** as tenderloin continues to cook while it rests.

- **Cover loosely and let stand** so juices can resettle and meat will be easier to carve.

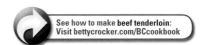
See how to make **beef tenderloin:** Visit bettycrocker.com/BCcookbook

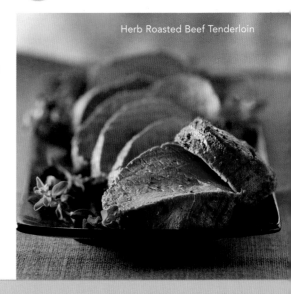

Herb Roasted Beef Tenderloin

GORGONZOLA- AND MUSHROOM-STUFFED BEEF TENDERLOIN WITH MERLOT SAUCE

Use the directions in the Herb Roasted Beef Tenderloin as a guide when making this elegant entree.

1 To butterfly tenderloin for stuffing, place tenderloin on cutting board. Hold long knife parallel to cutting board. Cut horizontally through long side of tenderloin, halfway up side of meat, stopping approximately ½ inch from other side.

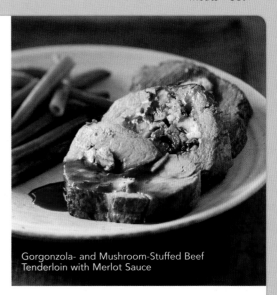

Gorgonzola- and Mushroom-Stuffed Beef Tenderloin with Merlot Sauce

2 Open beef as if opening a book. Cover with plastic wrap. Pound beef with flat end of meat mallet or rolling pin until uniformly ¼ inch thick.

3 In 10-inch skillet, cook ¾ cup sliced mushrooms in 1 tablespoon butter over medium-high heat until tender. Stir in ¾ cup soft bread crumbs, ½ cup crumbled Gorgonzola cheese (2 oz) and ¼ cup chopped fresh parsley. Spread mixture over beef to within 1 inch of edges; tightly roll beginning with long side. Turn small end under about 6 inches.

4 Tie beef with kitchen string at 1½-inch intervals. Bake as directed in main recipe. In 1-quart saucepan, heat ½ cup currant jelly, ½ cup Merlot or

nonalcoholic red wine, ¼ cup beef broth and 1 tablespoon butter to boiling, stirring occasionally; reduce heat to low. Simmer uncovered 35 to 40 minutes, stirring occasionally, until sauce is slightly reduced and syrupy. Serve sauce with beef.

Doneness Variations

What do you do when some guests like their beef medium-rare and others like it medium-well? Cook the tenderloin as directed for medium-rare. The ends will be more done than the center, so serve end slices to those who like their beef cooked more, and serve the center slices to those who like it cooked less.

Savory Sauces

Beef tenderloin is fabulous as is, but make it really special by adding one of these sauces as an accompaniment:

- Béarnaise Sauce (page 487)*
- Creamy Horseradish Sauce (page 483)**
- Mornay Sauce (page 487)
- Peppery Red-Wine Sauce (page 488)*

*can be made ahead and reheated
**can be made ahead

POT ROAST

Spreading a layer of horseradish all over the outside of the meat is the secret to making this pot roast. Contrary to what you might think, the horseradish doesn't add a hot or spicy flavor. Instead, it mellows during cooking, leaving behind a delicious flavor you can't quite put your finger on.

PREP 30 min **TOTAL** 4 hr • **8 servings**

- 1 **boneless beef chuck, arm, shoulder or blade pot roast (4 lb)***
- 1 **teaspoon salt**
- 1 **teaspoon pepper**
- 1 **jar (8 oz) prepared horseradish**
- 1 **cup water**
- 8 **small potatoes, cut in half**
- 8 **medium carrots or parsnips, peeled, cut into quarters**
- 8 **small whole onions, peeled**
- ½ **cup cold water**
- ¼ **cup all-purpose flour**

1 In 4-quart Dutch oven, cook beef over medium heat until brown on all sides; reduce heat to low.

2 Sprinkle beef with salt and pepper. Spread horseradish over all sides of beef. Add 1 cup water to Dutch oven. Heat to boiling; reduce heat. Cover; simmer 2 hours 30 minutes.

3 Add potatoes, carrots and onions to Dutch oven. Cover; simmer about 1 hour longer or until beef and vegetables are tender.

4 Remove beef and vegetables to warm platter; keep warm. Skim excess fat from broth in Dutch oven. Add enough water to broth to measure 2 cups. In tightly covered container, shake ½ cup cold water and the flour; gradually stir into broth. Heat to boiling, stirring constantly. Boil and stir 1 minute. Serve gravy with beef and vegetables.

*3-lb beef bottom round, rolled rump, tip or chuck eye roast can be substituted; decrease salt to ¾ teaspoon.

1 Serving: Calories 370; Total Fat 11g (Saturated Fat 4g; Trans Fat 0g); Cholesterol 85mg; Sodium 470mg; Total Carbohydrate 32g (Dietary Fiber 5g); Protein 35g **Exchanges:** 1½ Starch, 2 Vegetable, 4 Very Lean Meat, 1 Fat **Carbohydrate Choices:** 2

SLOW COOKER DIRECTIONS In 12-inch skillet, cook beef over medium heat until brown on all sides. Spray 4- to 6-quart slow cooker with cooking spray. In slow cooker, place potatoes, carrots and onions. Place beef on vegetables. In small bowl, mix horseradish, salt and pepper; spread evenly over beef. Pour water into slow cooker. Cover; cook on Low heat setting 8 to 10 hours or until beef and vegetables are tender.

BARBECUE POT ROAST Decrease pepper to ½ teaspoon. Omit horseradish and water. Make Smoky Barbecue Sauce (page 318). After browning beef in Step 1, pour barbecue sauce over beef. After removing beef and vegetables in Step 4, skim fat from sauce. Omit water and flour. Serve sauce with beef and vegetables.

CONFETTI POT ROAST Omit potatoes and horseradish. Sprinkle beef with ½ teaspoon dried Italian seasoning. Add 8 oz fresh green beans and 1 cup frozen corn with carrots in Step 3. Continue as directed. Serve with mashed potatoes.

CREAM GRAVY POT ROAST Substitute 1 can (10½ oz) condensed beef broth for the 1 cup water. For the gravy, add enough half-and-half or milk, instead of water, to the broth (from the roast) to measure 2 cups. Substitute ½ cup half-and-half or milk for the ½ cup cold water.

GARLIC-HERB POT ROAST Decrease pepper to ½ teaspoon. Omit horseradish. After browning beef in Step 1, sprinkle with 1 tablespoon chopped fresh or 1 teaspoon dried marjoram leaves, 1 tablespoon chopped fresh or 1 teaspoon dried thyme leaves, 2 teaspoons chopped fresh or ½ teaspoon dried oregano leaves and 4 cloves garlic, finely chopped. Substitute 1 can (10½ oz) condensed beef broth for the 1 cup water.

Pot Roast Cuts

Less-tender, inexpensive cuts of meat are usually used for pot roast. Chuck or round cuts are the most common cuts used to make this hearty dish. It's often referred to as Yankee pot roast when vegetables are added partway through the cooking process.

BRAISED BRISKET OF BEEF

LOWER CALORIE

Enjoy classic brisket of beef boldly flavored and traditionally served with new potatoes and steamed carrots.

PREP 20 min TOTAL 11 hr 30 min • **12 servings**

- 1 **fresh beef brisket (not corned beef), 3 lb**
- 1½ **cups white wine vinegar**
- 1 **bottle (12 oz) chili sauce**
- ¼ **cup packed brown sugar**
- 1 **teaspoon dried basil leaves**
- ½ **teaspoon salt**
- 2 **medium onions, thinly sliced**
  Chopped parsley, if desired

1 Place beef in resealable food-storage plastic bag or 3-quart casserole, cutting beef in half if necessary to fit. In medium bowl, stir vinegar, chili sauce, brown sugar, basil and salt until well blended. Pour over beef; turn to coat. Seal bag or cover casserole; refrigerate at least 8 hours but no longer than 24 hours, turning beef once.

2 Heat oven to 325°F. Place beef and marinade in 4-quart ovenproof Dutch oven or 3-quart casserole. Place onions over top; cover. Roast 2 hours, brushing beef twice with marinade.

3 Remove cover; roast 1 hour longer, brushing beef frequently with marinade, until beef is tender. Cover and let stand 10 minutes.

4 To serve, cut beef across grain into thin slices; arrange on serving platter. With slotted spoon, place onions over beef. Sprinkle with parsley. Discard cooking liquid.

1 Serving: Calories 210; Total Fat 7g (Saturated Fat 2.5g; Trans Fat 0g); Cholesterol 45mg; Sodium 510mg; Total Carbohydrate 12g (Dietary Fiber 2g); Protein 25g **Exchanges:** ½ Other Carbohydrate, ½ Vegetable, 3 Lean Meat **Carbohydrate Choices:** 1

MAKE AHEAD DIRECTIONS Marinating the brisket the night before saves time in the morning—and the unattended cooking leaves you more time to prepare the rest of the dinner and to visit with your guests.

BRAISED BRISKET OF BEEF WITH CARROTS
In Step 3, after removing corn, add 2 cups julienne carrots (1½ x ½ x ½ inch). Turn to coat with pan liquid. Continue as directed.

Pot Roast

Barbecue Pot Roast

Braised Brisket of Beef

BEEF STEW `LOWER CALORIE`

Look for beef stew meat, already trimmed and cut into ½- to 1-inch pieces, in the meat department.

PREP 15 min TOTAL 3 hr 45 min • **8 servings**

- 1 **lb beef stew meat, cut into ½-inch pieces**
- 1 **medium onion, cut into 8 wedges**
- 1 **bag (8 oz) ready-to-eat baby-cut carrots (about 30)**
- 1 **can (14.5 oz) diced tomatoes, undrained**
- 1 **can (10½ oz) condensed beef broth**
- 1 **can (8 oz) tomato sauce**
- ⅓ **cup all-purpose flour**
- 1 **tablespoon Worcestershire sauce**
- 1 **teaspoon salt**
- 1 **teaspoon sugar**
- 1 **teaspoon dried marjoram leaves**
- ¼ **teaspoon pepper**
- 12 **small red potatoes (1½ lb), cut into quarters**
- 2 **cups sliced fresh mushrooms (about 5 oz) or 1 package (about 3.5 oz) fresh shiitake mushrooms, sliced**

1 Heat oven to 325°F. In 4-quart ovenproof Dutch oven, mix all ingredients except potatoes and mushrooms. Cover; bake 2 hours, stirring once.

2 Stir in potatoes and mushrooms. Cover; bake 1 hour to 1 hour 30 minutes longer or until beef and vegetables are tender.

1 Serving: Calories 310; Total Fat 7g (Saturated Fat 2.5g; Trans Fat 0g); Cholesterol 35mg; Sodium 820mg; Total Carbohydrate 43g (Dietary Fiber 6g); Protein 18g **Exchanges:** 2 Starch, 2 Vegetable, 1 Medium-Fat Meat, ½ Fat **Carbohydrate Choices:** 3

`SLOW COOKER` **DIRECTIONS** Chop onion (½ cup). Omit tomato sauce. Increase flour to ½ cup. Spray 3½- to 6-quart slow cooker with cooking spray. In slow cooker, mix all ingredients except beef. Add beef (do not stir). Cover; cook on Low heat setting 8 to 9 hours. Stir well.

CHUNKY TOMATO-PEPPER BEEF STEW Add 1 cup diced bell pepper with the onion; omit mushrooms. Substitute 1 additional can (14.5 oz) diced tomatoes for the tomato sauce.

CONFETTI BEEF STEW Omit potatoes. Bake 2 hours. Add 1 cup frozen cut green beans and 1 cup frozen corn in Step 2.

BEEF SHORT RIBS CARBONNADE `LOWER CALORIE`

Popular beef short ribs combine with the classic flavors of carbonnade à la flamande, a Belgian beef stew hailing from Flanders. Serve with mashed potatoes or one of its many flavor variations on page 602.

PREP 30 min TOTAL 3 hr 10 min • **8 servings**

- 3 **tablespoons vegetable oil**
- 4 **lb beef short ribs**
- 2 **large onions, sliced**
- 3 **tablespoons all-purpose flour**
- 1 **can (14 oz) beef broth (for homemade broth, see page 530)**
- 1 **teaspoon balsamic vinegar**
- 1 **tablespoon packed brown sugar**
- 1 **teaspoon dried thyme leaves**
- 1 **teaspoon salt**
- ¼ **teaspoon pepper**
- 1 **can or bottle (12 oz) beer or nonalcoholic beer**

1 Heat oven to 325°F. In 12-inch skillet, heat 1 tablespoon of the oil over high heat. Cook ribs in oil about 10 minutes, turning frequently, until brown on all sides. Discard drippings. Place ribs in large roasting pan. Cover; bake 1 hour.

2 Meanwhile, in same skillet, heat remaining 2 tablespoons oil over medium-high heat. Cook onions in oil 10 to 15 minutes, stirring frequently, until tender and brown. Stir in flour, coating well. Stir in broth, vinegar, sugar, thyme, salt and pepper.

Beef Stew

Beef Short Ribs Carbonnade

1 In 4-quart Dutch oven or 12-inch skillet, heat oil over medium heat. Cook beef in oil about 15 minutes, stirring occasionally, until brown; drain.

2 Stir in remaining ingredients except water, flour and noodles. Heat to boiling; reduce heat. Cover; simmer about 1 hour 15 minutes, stirring occasionally, until beef is tender.

3 In tightly covered container, shake water and flour until mixed; gradually stir into beef mixture. Heat to boiling, stirring constantly. Boil and stir 1 minute. Serve over noodles.

1 Serving: Calories 510; Total Fat 18g (Saturated Fat 6g; Trans Fat 0.5g); Cholesterol 125mg; Sodium 850mg; Total Carbohydrate 53g (Dietary Fiber 5g); Protein 33g **Exchanges:** 3 Starch, 2 Vegetable, 3 Medium-Fat Meat **Carbohydrate Choices:** 3½

LIGHTER DIRECTIONS For 7 grams of fat and 335 calories per serving, omit vegetable oil; spray Dutch oven with cooking spray before heating. Decrease beef to 1 lb. Use noodles made without egg yolks.

SLOW COOKER DIRECTIONS In 12-inch skillet, cook beef in oil 5 to 7 minutes or just until brown. Spray 2½- to 3½-quart slow cooker with cooking spray. In slow cooker, mix beef and remaining ingredients except water, flour and noodles. Cover; cook on Low heat setting 8 to 9 hours or until beef is tender. In tightly covered container, shake water and flour until mixed; stir into beef mixture. Increase heat setting to High. Cover; cook 10 to 20 minutes or until thickened. Serve over noodles.

3 Drain drippings from roasting pan. Pour onion mixture over ribs. Add beer. Cover; bake about 1 hour 30 minutes longer or until ribs are tender. Serve ribs with pan juices.

1 Serving: Calories 270; Total Fat 18g (Saturated Fat 6g; Trans Fat 0.5g); Cholesterol 50mg; Sodium 570mg; Total Carbohydrate 9g (Dietary Fiber 1g); Protein 18g **Exchanges:** ½ Starch, 2½ Medium-Fat Meat, 1 Fat **Carbohydrate Choices:** ½

HUNGARIAN GOULASH

All paprika is made from ground sweet peppers and ranges in flavor from sweet to mild or hot. Look for Hungarian paprika for a fuller, sweet flavor or for hot paprika if you prefer a bite.

PREP 30 min TOTAL 2 hr 10 min • **6 servings**

- 1 tablespoon vegetable oil or bacon drippings
- 1½ lb boneless beef chuck, tip or round roast or boneless pork shoulder, cut into ¾-inch cubes
- ½ cup beef broth (for homemade broth, see page 530)
- 3 tablespoons paprika
- 1½ teaspoons salt
- ½ teaspoon caraway seed
- ¼ teaspoon pepper
- 3 large onions, chopped (3 cups)
- 2 cloves garlic, finely chopped
- 1 can (14.5 oz) diced tomatoes, undrained
- ¼ cup cold water
- 2 tablespoons all-purpose flour
- 6 cups hot cooked egg noodles (page 367)

Hungarian Goulash

BEEF STROGANOFF LOWER CALORIE

PREP 20 min TOTAL 50 min • **6 servings**

- 1½ **lb beef tenderloin or boneless top loin steak**
- 2 **tablespoons butter**
- 1½ **cups beef broth (for homemade broth, see page 530)**
- 2 **tablespoons ketchup**
- 1 **teaspoon salt**
- 1 **small clove garlic, finely chopped**
- 3 **cups sliced fresh mushrooms (8 oz)**
- 1 **medium onion, chopped (½ cup)**
- ¼ **cup all-purpose flour**
- 1 **cup sour cream or plain yogurt (8 oz)**
   Hot cooked noodles (page 367) or rice (page 429), if desired

1 Cut beef across grain into 1½x½-inch strips (beef is easier to cut if partially frozen). In 12-inch skillet, melt butter over medium-high heat. Cook beef in butter, stirring occasionally, until brown.

2 Reserve ⅓ cup of the broth. Stir remaining broth, the ketchup, salt and garlic into beef. Heat to boiling; reduce heat. Cover; simmer about 10 minutes or until beef is tender.

3 Stir in mushrooms and onion. Heat to boiling; reduce heat. Cover; simmer about 5 minutes longer or until onion is tender.

4 In tightly covered container, shake reserved ⅓ cup broth and the flour until mixed; gradually stir into beef mixture. Heat to boiling, stirring constantly. Boil and stir 1 minute; reduce heat to low. Stir in sour cream; heat until hot. Serve over noodles.

1 Serving: Calories 330; Total Fat 20g (Saturated Fat 10g; Trans Fat 1g); Cholesterol 100mg; Sodium 810mg; Total Carbohydrate 10g (Dietary Fiber 1g); Protein 28g **Exchanges:** 2 Vegetable, 3½ Lean Meat, 1 Fat **Carbohydrate Choices:** ½

SLOW COOKER DIRECTIONS Substitute boneless beef bottom round steak for the tenderloin; cut and cook in butter as directed in Step 1. Reserve ⅓ cup of the broth. Spray 3- to 4-quart slow cooker with cooking spray. In slow cooker, mix beef, remaining broth, ketchup, salt, garlic, mushrooms and onion. Cover; cook on Low heat setting 8 to 9 hours or until beef is tender. In tightly covered container, shake reserved ⅓ cup broth and the flour until mixed; stir into beef mixture.

Increase heat setting to High. Cover; cook 15 to 20 minutes or until thickened. Stir in sour cream; heat until hot. Serve over noodles.

GROUND BEEF STROGANOFF Substitute 1 lb lean (at least 80%) ground beef for the tenderloin; omit butter. In 12-inch skillet, cook ground beef, stirring occasionally, until brown; drain. Continue as directed in Step 2.

KOREAN BARBECUED BEEF

Bulgogi, or marinated beef, is one of the most popular dishes in Korea. Whether you grill it, broil it or cook it on the stove-top, the distinctive sweet-salty marinade with a hint of sesame brings a unique flavor to an easy main dish. If you're adventurous, add a side of kimchi, a super-spicy cabbage condiment you can find in many supermarkets.

PREP 10 min TOTAL 45 min • **4 servings**

- 1 **lb boneless beef top loin or sirloin steak**
- ¼ **cup soy sauce**
- 3 **tablespoons sugar**
- 2 **tablespoons sesame or vegetable oil**
- ¼ **teaspoon pepper**
- 3 **medium green onions, finely chopped (3 tablespoons)**
- 2 **cloves garlic, chopped**
   Hot cooked rice (page 429), if desired

1 Cut beef diagonally across grain into ⅛-inch slices (beef is easier to cut if partially frozen). In medium glass or plastic bowl, mix remaining ingredients except rice. Add beef; stir until well coated. Cover; refrigerate 30 minutes.

2 Drain beef; discard marinade. Heat 10-inch skillet over medium heat. Cook beef in skillet 2 to 3 minutes, stirring frequently, until brown. Serve beef with rice.

1 Serving: Calories 280; Total Fat 11g (Saturated Fat 2.5g; Trans Fat 0g); Cholesterol 80mg; Sodium 940mg; Total Carbohydrate 12g (Dietary Fiber 0g); Protein 33g **Exchanges:** 1 Other Carbohydrate, 4½ Very Lean Meat, 1½ Fat **Carbohydrate Choices:** 1

MEATBALLS

Shape meatballs fast by using an ice-cream scoop. Or instead, pat the mixture into a 9x3-inch rectangle in an ungreased 13x9-inch pan. Cut into squares, and separate slightly. Bake uncovered 25 to 30 minutes.

PREP 15 min TOTAL 40 min • **4 servings**

- 1 lb lean (at least 80%) ground beef
- ½ cup unseasoned dry bread crumbs
- ¼ cup milk
- ½ teaspoon salt
- ½ teaspoon Worcestershire sauce
- ¼ teaspoon pepper
- 1 small onion, finely chopped (⅓ cup)
- 1 egg

1 Heat oven to 400°F. In large bowl, mix all ingredients. Shape mixture into 20 (1½-inch) balls. Place in ungreased 13x9-inch pan or on rack in broiler pan.

2 Bake uncovered 20 to 25 minutes or until no longer pink in center and meat thermometer inserted in center of meatball reads 160°F.

1 Serving (5 Meatballs): Calories 280; Total Fat 15g (Saturated Fat 6g; Trans Fat 1g); Cholesterol 125mg; Sodium 490mg; Total Carbohydrate 12g (Dietary Fiber 0g); Protein 24g **Exchanges:** 1 Starch, 3 Medium-Fat Meat **Carbohydrate Choices:** 1

MINI MEATBALLS Shape beef mixture into 1-inch balls. Bake 15 to 20 minutes. Makes 3 dozen appetizers

SKILLET MEATBALLS In 10-inch skillet, cook meatballs over medium heat about 20 minutes, turning occasionally, until no longer pink in center and meat thermometer inserted in center of meatball reads 160°F.

TURKEY OR CHICKEN MEATBALLS
Substitute 1 lb ground turkey or chicken for the ground beef. (If using ground chicken, decrease milk to 2 tablespoons.) To bake, spray 13x9-inch pan with cooking spray before adding meatballs; bake until no longer pink in center and meat thermometer inserted in center reads at least 165°F. To cook in skillet, heat 1 tablespoon vegetable oil over medium heat before adding meatballs; cook until no longer pink in center and meat thermometer inserted in center of meatball reads at least 165°F.

FIESTA TACO CASSEROLE

Have a flavor fiesta with classic taco ingredients baked into a casserole.

PREP 15 min TOTAL 45 min • **4 servings**

- 1 lb lean (at least 80%) ground beef
- 1 can (15 to 16 oz) spicy chili beans in sauce, undrained
- 1 cup chunky-style salsa
- 2 cups coarsely broken tortilla chips
- 4 medium green onions, sliced (¼ cup)
- 1 medium tomato, chopped (¾ cup)
- 1 cup shredded Cheddar or Monterey Jack cheese (4 oz)
  Tortilla chips, if desired
  Shredded lettuce, if desired
  Additional chunky-style salsa, if desired

1 Heat oven to 350°F. In 10-inch skillet, cook beef over medium heat 8 to 10 minutes, stirring occasionally, until brown; drain. Stir in beans and 1 cup salsa. Heat to boiling, stirring occasionally.

2 In ungreased 2-quart casserole, place broken tortilla chips. Top with beef mixture. Sprinkle with onions, tomato and cheese.

3 Bake uncovered 20 to 30 minutes or until hot and bubbly. Arrange tortilla chips around edge of casserole. Serve with lettuce and additional salsa.

1 Serving: Calories 530; Total Fat 27g (Saturated Fat 11g; Trans Fat 1g); Cholesterol 100mg; Sodium 1540mg; Total Carbohydrate 36g (Dietary Fiber 7g); Protein 35g **Exchanges:** 2 Starch, ½ Other Carbohydrate, 4 Medium-Fat Meat, 1 Fat **Carbohydrate Choices:** 2½

Fiesta Taco Casserole

Heirloom Recipe and New Twist

If you have not tried this classic meat loaf—one of our most requested recipes—here is your chance. And if you are in the mood for a new idea, be sure to sample our new Italian-inspired twist with its wonderful cheesy filling and topping. Also, be sure to check out the variation contributed by a Facebook fan.

CLASSIC

MEAT LOAF

PREP 20 min **TOTAL** 1 hr 40 min • **6 servings**

- 1½ lb lean (at least 80%) ground beef
- 1 cup milk
- 1 tablespoon Worcestershire sauce
- 1 teaspoon chopped fresh or ¼ teaspoon dried sage leaves
- ½ teaspoon salt
- ½ teaspoon ground mustard
- ¼ teaspoon pepper
- 1 clove garlic, finely chopped, or ⅛ teaspoon garlic powder
- 1 egg
- 3 slices bread, torn into small pieces*
- 1 small onion, finely chopped (⅓ cup)
- ½ cup ketchup, chili sauce or barbecue sauce

1 Heat oven to 350°F. In large bowl, mix all ingredients except ketchup. Spread mixture in ungreased 8x4- or 9x5-inch loaf pan, or shape into 9x5-inch loaf in ungreased 13x9-inch pan. Spread ketchup over top.

2 Insert ovenproof meat thermometer so tip is in center of loaf. Bake uncovered 1 hour to 1 hour 15 minutes or until beef is no longer pink in center and thermometer reads 160°F. (See also Ground Beef, at right.) Drain meat loaf. Let stand 5 minutes; remove from pan.

*½ cup dry bread crumbs or ¾ cup quick-cooking oats can be substituted for the 3 slices bread.

1 Serving: Calories 290; Total Fat 15g (Saturated Fat 6g; Trans Fat 1g); Cholesterol 110mg; Sodium 610mg; Total Carbohydrate 15g (Dietary Fiber 0g); Protein 24g **Exchanges:** ½ Starch, ½ Other Carbohydrate, 3 Medium-Fat Meat **Carbohydrate Choices:** 1

LIGHTER **DIRECTIONS** For 7 grams of fat and 240 calories per serving, substitute ground turkey breast for the ground beef and ¼ cup fat-free egg product for the egg. Use fat-free (skim) milk. Bake uncovered 1 hour to 1 hour 15 minutes or until turkey is no longer pink in center and thermometer reads at least 165°F.

MINI MEAT LOAVES Spray 12 regular-size muffin cups with cooking spray. Divide beef mixture evenly among cups (cups will be very full). Brush tops with about ¼ cup ketchup. Place muffin pan on cookie sheet to catch any spillover. Bake about 30 minutes or until loaves are no longer pink in center and thermometer reads 160°F when inserted in center of loaves in middle of muffin pan (outer loaves will be done sooner). Immediately remove from cups.

MEXICAN MEAT LOAF Omit sage. Substitute ⅔ cup milk and ⅓ cup salsa for the 1 cup milk. Stir in ½ cup shredded Colby-Monterey Jack cheese blend (2 oz) and 1 can (4.5 oz) chopped green chiles, drained, in Step 1. Substitute ⅔ cup salsa for the ketchup.

HORSERADISH MEAT LOAF Omit sage. Stir 1 to 2 tablespoons cream-style prepared horseradish with ingredients in Step 1.

Contributed by Sharon Mynatt from Kansas City, Missouri

Ground Beef

Always purchase ground beef that looks very fresh and has a sell-by date on the package. The beef should have bright pink color with no signs of brown. Beef that is 80 percent lean means that there is about 20 percent fat in the product. If you like leaner ground beef, look for 85 or 90 percent lean.

Because of food safety concerns, always cook ground beef thoroughly and follow recipes for specified cooking times. We recommend using a thermometer to be sure the center of the food reaches 160°F.

See how to make **meat loaf:** Visit bettycrocker.com/BCcookbook

CHEESY STUFFED MEAT LOAF

PREP 20 min **TOTAL** 1 hr 15 min • **6 servings**

MEAT LOAF

- 1 lb lean (at least 90%) ground turkey
- ½ lb bulk Italian pork sausage
- ¼ cup shredded Asiago or Parmesan cheese
- ½ cup dry bread crumbs
- 1 small onion, finely chopped (⅓ cup)
- 2 tablespoons chopped fresh or 2 teaspoons dried basil leaves
- ½ teaspoon salt
- ½ teaspoon ground mustard
- ¼ teaspoon pepper
- 1 clove garlic, finely chopped
- ½ cup milk
- 1 tablespoon Worcestershire sauce
- 1 egg
- 8 oz mozzarella cheese, cut into ½-inch cubes

TOPPING

- ⅔ cup chili sauce, tomato pasta sauce or pizza sauce
- ¼ cup shredded Asiago or Parmesan cheese
- 2 tablespoons chopped fresh or 2 teaspoons dried basil leaves
- ¼ teaspoon pepper

1 Heat oven to 350°F. In large bowl, mix all ingredients except topping. Line ungreased 13x9-inch pan with foil. Shape meat loaf mixture into 9x5-inch loaf on foil in pan. In small bowl, mix all topping ingredients; spread over top and sides of loaf.

2 Insert ovenproof meat thermometer so tip is in center of loaf. Bake uncovered 45 to 50 minutes or until meat is no longer pink in center and thermometer reads 165°F. Let stand 5 minutes; remove from pan.

1 Serving: Calories 450; Total Fat 25g (Saturated Fat 11g; Trans Fat 0g); Cholesterol 130mg; Sodium 1390mg; Total Carbohydrate 18g (Dietary Fiber 2g); Protein 37g **Exchanges:** ½ Starch, ½ Other Carbohydrate, ½ Vegetable, 3½ Lean Meat, 1½ High-Fat Meat, ½ Fat **Carbohydrate Choices:** 1

Meat Loaf

Cheesy Stuffed Meat Loaf

VEAL PARMIGIANA

PREP 1 hr 5 min TOTAL 1 hr 40 min • **6 servings**

> 1 egg
> 2 tablespoons water
> ⅔ cup unseasoned dry bread crumbs
> ⅓ cup grated Parmesan cheese
> 1½ lb veal leg cutlets, ¼ inch thick*
> ¼ cup olive or vegetable oil
> 2 cups tomato pasta sauce
> (for homemade Italian tomato pasta
> sauce, see page 370)
> 2 cups shredded mozzarella cheese (8 oz)

1 Heat oven to 350°F. In small bowl, beat egg and water. In shallow dish, mix bread crumbs and Parmesan cheese. Dip veal into egg mixture, then coat with bread crumb mixture.

2 In 12-inch skillet, heat oil over medium heat. Cook half of the veal in oil about 5 minutes, turning once, until light brown; drain. Repeat with remaining veal, adding 1 or 2 tablespoons oil if necessary.

3 In ungreased 11x7-inch (2-quart) glass baking dish, place half of the veal, overlapping slices slightly. Spoon 1 cup of the tomato sauce over veal. Sprinkle with 1 cup of the mozzarella cheese. Repeat with remaining veal, sauce and cheese.

4 Bake uncovered about 25 minutes or until sauce is bubbly and cheese is light brown.

1½ lb veal round steak can be substituted for the veal leg cutlets. Cut veal into 12 pieces. Place each piece between sheets of plastic wrap or waxed paper. Pound with flat side of meat mallet until ¼ inch thick.

1 Serving: Calories 450; Total Fat 24g (Saturated Fat 9g; Trans Fat 0g); Cholesterol 135mg; Sodium 890mg; Total Carbohydrate 26g (Dietary Fiber 1g); Protein 34g **Exchanges:** 1 Starch, 2 Vegetable, 4 Medium-Fat Meat **Carbohydrate Choices:** 2

CHICKEN PARMIGIANA Substitute

8 boneless skinless chicken breasts (about 2 lb) for the veal. Place each chicken breast between sheets of plastic wrap or waxed paper. Pound with flat side of meat mallet until ¼ inch thick. In Step 3, cook chicken until no longer pink in center.

SALTIMBOCCA

The translation of this dish's name, "jump in the mouth," is a whimsical description of how the flavors spring to life when you take a bite of the savory combination of veal, prosciutto and sage.

PREP 15 min TOTAL 25 min • **4 servings**

> 8 veal top round steaks, ¼ inch thick
> (about 1½ lb)
> ½ cup all-purpose flour
> 8 thin slices prosciutto or cooked ham
> 8 thin slices (1 oz each) mozzarella cheese
> 8 fresh sage leaves
> ¼ cup butter
> ½ cup dry white wine or chicken broth
> ½ teaspoon salt
> ¼ teaspoon pepper

1 Pound each veal steak with flat side of meat mallet to tenderize and flatten slightly. Coat veal with flour; shake off excess. On each veal slice, layer 1 slice each prosciutto and cheese and 1 sage leaf. Roll up veal; tie with kitchen string or secure with toothpicks.

2 In 10-inch skillet, melt butter over medium heat. Cook veal rolls in butter about 5 minutes, turning occasionally, until brown. Add wine; sprinkle rolls with salt and pepper. Cover; cook over medium-high heat about 5 minutes or until veal is no longer pink in center.

1 Serving: Calories 560; Total Fat 32g (Saturated Fat 18g; Trans Fat 1g); Cholesterol 185mg; Sodium 970mg; Total Carbohydrate 15g (Dietary Fiber 0g); Protein 47g **Exchanges:** 1 Starch, 6 Medium-Fat Meat, ½ Fat **Carbohydrate Choices:** 1

Saltimbocca

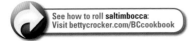

See how to roll **saltimbocca**:
Visit bettycrocker.com/BCcookbook

OSSO BUCO

These braised veal shanks, featuring white wine, beef broth and a touch of lemon peel, are very tender. Instead of serving osso buco with mashed potatoes or pasta, try Classic Risotto (make 1½ times the recipe, page 433).

PREP 40 min **TOTAL** 3 hr 10 min • **6 servings**

- 6 **veal or beef shank cross cuts, 2 to 2½ inches thick (3 to 3½ lb)**
- ½ **teaspoon salt**
- ¼ **teaspoon pepper**
- ¼ **cup all-purpose flour**
- 2 **tablespoons olive or vegetable oil**
- ⅓ **cup dry white wine or apple juice**
- 1 **can (10½ oz) condensed beef broth (for homemade broth, see page 530)**
- 1 **clove garlic, finely chopped**
- 1 **dried bay leaf**
- 2 **tablespoons chopped fresh parsley**
- 1 **teaspoon grated lemon peel**
  Shredded Parmesan or Asiago cheese, if desired
- 6 **cups hot cooked mashed potatoes (page 602) or spaghetti (page 367)**

1 Sprinkle veal with salt and pepper; coat with flour. In 4-quart Dutch oven, heat oil over medium heat. Cook veal in oil about 20 minutes, turning occasionally, until brown on all sides.

2 Stir in wine, broth, garlic and bay leaf. Heat to boiling; reduce heat. Cover; simmer 1 hour 30 minutes to 2 hours or until veal is tender.

3 Remove veal; place on serving platter. Skim fat from broth; remove bay leaf. Pour broth over veal; sprinkle with parsley, lemon peel and cheese. Serve with mashed potatoes.

1 Serving: Calories 700; Total Fat 30g (Saturated Fat 9g; Trans Fat 4g); Cholesterol 255mg; Sodium 1090mg; Total Carbohydrate 41g (Dietary Fiber 4g); Protein 68g **Exchanges:** 2½ Starch, 7 Lean Meat, 1 Fat **Carbohydrate Choices:** 3

Beef and Veal Liver

For the best flavor, look for calf's liver. Although the price may be a bit higher than for beef, the liver will be from a younger animal and so more tender.

Osso Buco

LIVER AND ONIONS

LOWER CALORIE

Serve this classic dish sprinkled with crumbled crisply cooked bacon, and add mashed potatoes on the side.

PREP 10 min **TOTAL** 25 min • **4 servings**

- 3 **tablespoons butter**
- 2 **medium onions, thinly sliced**
- 1 **lb beef or veal liver, ½ to ¾ inch thick**
  All-purpose flour
- 3 **tablespoons vegetable oil or shortening**
  Salt and pepper to taste

1 In 10-inch skillet, melt butter over medium-high heat. Cook onions in butter 4 to 6 minutes, stirring frequently, until light brown. Remove onions from skillet; keep warm.

2 Coat liver with flour. In same skillet, heat oil over medium heat. Cook liver in oil 2 to 3 minutes on each side or until brown on outside and slightly pink in center, returning onions to skillet during last minute of cooking. Don't overcook or liver could become tough. Sprinkle with salt and pepper.

1 Serving: Calories 310; Total Fat 21g (Saturated Fat 7g; Trans Fat 0.5g); Cholesterol 325mg; Sodium 310mg; Total Carbohydrate 10g (Dietary Fiber 1g); Protein 20g **Exchanges:** 2 Vegetable, 3 Medium-Fat Meat, 1 Fat **Carbohydrate Choices:** ½

LIGHTER DIRECTIONS For 8 grams of fat and 200 calories per serving, omit butter and decrease oil to 1 tablespoon. Use nonstick skillet. Spray skillet with cooking spray before cooking onions in Step 1.

RETAIL PORK CUTS

Here are many pork cuts available at the market. They will have different names in different regions of the country, but this chart should help you identify what you are purchasing.

Diagram: 1 Shoulder Butt **2** Loin **3** Picnic Shoulder **4** Side **5** Leg

Pork Center Cut Rib Chop (bone-in)

Pork Center Rib Roast (bone-in)

Pork Sirloin Chop (bone-in)

Pork Loin Boneless Rolled Roast (double)

Pork Crown Roast (bone-in)

Pork Tenderloin

Pork Loin Chop (bone-in)

Pork Spareribs

Pork Loin Back Ribs

Pork Loin Center Cut Boneless Roast and Chops

Pork Blade Steak (bone-in)

Pork Blade Roast (bone-in)

Pork Ham (bone-in/ shank half)

Pork Center-Cut Ham Steak

Pork Loin Country-Style Ribs

Pork Smoked Picnic

RETAIL LAMB CUTS

These cuts of lamb are what is available at grocery stores. For specific cuts, ask a butcher to provide it for you because lamb is not as readily available as pork or beef.

Diagram: 1 Shoulder **2** Rib **3** Loin and Sirloin
4 Leg and Hind Shank **5** Breast and Foreshank

Lamb Stew Meat

Lamb Boneless Shoulder Roast

Lamb Loin Chops

Lamb Blade Chop (bone-in)

Lamb Loin Roast (bone-in)

Lamb Foreshank

Lamb Arm Chop (bone-in)

Lamb Loin Roast (boneless)

Lamb Spareribs

Lamb Sirloin Chop (bone-in)

Lamb Leg sirloin (half of leg bone-in)

Lamb Rib Roast (bone-in)

Lamb Frenched Chops

Lamb Leg Roast (bone-in sirloin half of leg)

Lamb Leg Roast (boned and tied)

Lamb Rib Chops (bone-in)

PANFRIED PORK CHOPS WITH CIDER SAUCE LOWER CALORIE

PREP 30 min TOTAL 30 min • **4 servings**

- 4 boneless pork loin chops, ½ to ¾ inch thick (4 oz each), trimmed of fat
- ¼ teaspoon seasoned salt
- ¼ teaspoon dried thyme leaves
- ⅛ teaspoon garlic powder
- ⅛ teaspoon pepper
- 1 tablespoon vegetable oil
- ½ cup apple cider
- ¼ cup brandy or apple cider
- 1 tablespoon butter

1 Sprinkle both sides of pork chops with seasoned salt, thyme, garlic powder and pepper. In 12-inch skillet, heat oil over medium-high heat. Add pork chops; cook uncovered about 5 minutes until bottom sides of pork chops are brown.

2 Turn pork chops; reduce heat to medium-low. Cook uncovered 5 to 10 minutes longer or until pork is no longer pink in center. Remove from skillet to serving platter; cover with foil to keep warm while preparing sauce.

3 Add cider and brandy to skillet. Heat to boiling, stirring constantly to loosen browned bits from bottom of skillet; reduce heat to low. Add butter, simmer uncovered, stirring frequently, 1 to 3 minutes or until slightly thickened. Serve sauce over chops.

1 Serving: Calories 250; Total Fat 15g (Saturated Fat 5g; Trans Fat 0g); Cholesterol 75mg; Sodium 150mg; Total Carbohydrate 4g (Dietary Fiber 0g); Protein 24g **Exchanges:** ½ Starch, 3 Lean Meat, 1 Fat **Carbohydrate Choices:** 0

BONE-IN PORK CHOPS WITH CIDER SAUCE Substitute 4 bone-in pork loin chops, ½ inch thick, for the boneless chops. Cook pork chops uncovered about 5 minutes on each side or until brown. Reduce heat to low. Cover and cook about 10 minutes longer or until pork is no longer pink in center.

PORK CHOPS WITH MUSTARD-CHIVE CREAM SAUCE Make pork chops and keep warm as directed above. Add ¼ cup dry sherry to skillet. Heat to boiling, stirring constantly to loosen browned bits from bottom of skillet. Stir in ½ cup whipping cream, 1 tablespoon country-style Dijon mustard, 2 teaspoons chopped chives, ⅛ teaspoon salt and

⅛ teaspoon pepper. Simmer uncovered, stirring frequently, 3 minutes or until slightly thickened. Serve sauce over chops.

SPICY SOUTHWESTERN PORK CHOPS Omit all ingredients except pork chops. In small bowl, mix 1 teaspoon chili powder, 1 teaspoon chipotle chile pepper powder, ½ teaspoon ground cumin, ¼ teaspoon each salt, ground red pepper (cayenne) and garlic powder and ⅛ teaspoon black pepper; rub on both sides of chops. Cook as directed above. (Pork chops will get very dark from the spice coating.)

PORK CHOPS WITH GREEN CHILE CORN

PREP 15 min TOTAL 30 min • **4 servings**

- 1 tablespoon vegetable oil
- 4 bone-in pork loin chops, ¾ inch thick (about 1½ lb)
- ½ teaspoon seasoned salt
- ½ cup chopped red onion
- 1½ cups frozen whole kernel corn
- 1 can (4.5 oz) chopped green chiles, undrained
- ¼ cup water
- 1 tablespoon Worcestershire sauce
- ½ teaspoon dried thyme leaves
- 1 medium tomato, seeded, chopped

1 In 12-inch nonstick skillet, heat oil over medium-high heat. Sprinkle pork chops with seasoned salt. Cook pork in oil 3 to 4 minutes or until brown on both sides. Remove pork from skillet.

2 Add onion, corn and green chiles to skillet. Cook 2 to 3 minutes over medium heat, stirring occasionally, just until mixture is thoroughly heated.

3 Stir in water, Worcestershire sauce and thyme. Place pork in skillet, pressing into vegetable mixture. Cover; cook 10 to 15 minutes, turning pork and stirring vegetables occasionally, until pork is no longer pink when cut near bone and meat thermometer reads 145°F. Remove pork from skillet. Stir tomato into corn mixture; cook and stir 1 minute. Serve corn mixture with pork.

1 Serving: Calories 290; Total Fat 13g (Saturated Fat 4g, Trans Fat 0g); Cholesterol 75mg; Sodium 380mg; Total Carbohydrate 17g (Dietary Fiber 2g); Protein 29g **Exchanges:** 1 Starch, 3½ Lean Meat, ½ Fat **Carbohydrate Choices:** 1

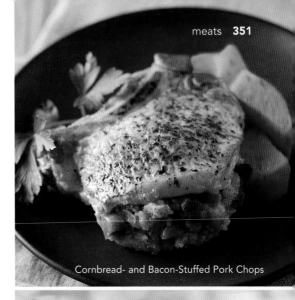
Cornbread- and Bacon-Stuffed Pork Chops

CORNBREAD- AND BACON-STUFFED PORK CHOPS

PREP 30 min TOTAL 1 hr 30 min • **6 servings**

- 6 bone-in pork rib or loin chops, 1 to 1¼ inches thick (about 4 lb)
- 4 slices bacon, cut into ½-inch pieces
- 1 medium onion, chopped (½ cup)
- 1 small green bell pepper, chopped (½ cup)
- 1 cup cornbread stuffing mix
- ½ cup water
- ½ cup shredded Cheddar cheese (2 oz)
- ½ teaspoon seasoned salt
- ½ teaspoon dried marjoram leaves
- ¼ teaspoon pepper

1 Heat oven to 350°F. Make a pocket in each pork chop by cutting into side of chop toward the bone.

2 In 12-inch skillet, cook bacon over medium heat, stirring occasionally, until crisp. Stir in onion and bell pepper. Cook 2 to 3 minutes, stirring occasionally, until vegetables are crisp-tender; remove from heat. Drain. Stir in stuffing crumbs and water until well mixed. Stir in cheese.

3 Sprinkle both sides of pork chops with seasoned salt, marjoram and pepper. Fill pockets with about ⅓ cup stuffing. In same skillet, cook pork over medium heat, turning once, until brown.

4 Place pork chops in 13x9-inch pan. Cover tightly with foil; bake 45 minutes. Uncover; bake about 15 minutes longer or until pork is no longer pink and meat thermometer inserted in center reads 145°F.

1 Serving: Calories 600; Total Fat 30g (Saturated Fat 11g; Trans Fat 0g); Cholesterol 210mg; Sodium 540mg; Total Carbohydrate 9g (Dietary Fiber 1g); Protein 73g **Exchanges:** ½ Starch, 9½ Very Lean Meat, ½ High-Fat Meat, 4 Fat **Carbohydrate Choices:** ½

Cutting Pocket in a Pork Chop

With sharp knife, make pocket in side of pork chop, cutting toward bone.

Spicy Southwestern Pork Chops

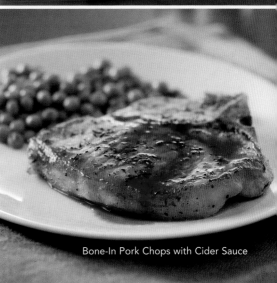
Bone-In Pork Chops with Cider Sauce

Pork Crown Roast with
Fruited Stuffing Supreme

PORK CROWN ROAST WITH FRUITED STUFFING SUPREME

PREP 20 min TOTAL 4 hr 15 min • **16 servings**

PORK ROAST

1 **pork crown roast, about 16 to 18 ribs (8 to 10 lb)***
2 **teaspoons salt**
1 **teaspoon pepper**

STUFFING

1 **lb bulk pork sausage**
¼ **cup butter**
4 **medium stalks celery, chopped (2 cups)**
¾ **cup chopped onion (about 1 large)**
1 **cup chicken broth (for homemade broth, see page 528)**
1 **teaspoon dried sage leaves, crushed**
1 **teaspoon poultry seasoning**
6½ **cups unseasoned stuffing cubes (16 oz)**
1 **can (8 oz) crushed pineapple in juice, undrained**
1 **cup applesauce**
1 **cup orange marmalade**

1 Heat oven to 325°F. Sprinkle pork with salt and pepper. On rack in shallow roasting pan, place roast with bone ends up. Wrap bone ends in foil to prevent excessive browning. Insert ovenproof meat thermometer so tip is in thickest part of pork and does not touch

bone or rest in fat. Place small heatproof bowl or crumpled foil in crown to hold shape of roast evenly. Do not add water.

2 Roast uncovered 2 hours 40 minutes to 3 hours 20 minutes. Meanwhile, in 10-inch skillet, cook sausage over medium heat 8 to 10 minutes, stirring occasionally, until no longer pink; drain well and set aside. In same skillet, melt butter over medium-high heat. Cook celery and onion in butter about 5 minutes, stirring occasionally, until vegetables are crisp-tender. Stir in broth, sage and poultry seasoning. In very large bowl, mix stuffing cubes, sausage, pineapple, applesauce and marmalade. Add vegetable mixture; stir until well blended.

3 About 1 hour before pork is done, remove bowl and fill center of crown with stuffing. (Remaining stuffing can be baked in 1½-quart covered casserole.) Cover stuffing with foil for first 30 minutes of roasting, then remove foil and finish roasting.

4 Remove pork from oven when thermometer reads 145°F. Cover loosely with foil; let stand at least 3 minutes.

5 Remove foil wrapping; place paper frills on bone ends if desired. To serve, spoon stuffing into bowl and cut pork between ribs.

A 4-lb boneless pork loin can be substituted. Place in roasting pan. Insert ovenproof meat thermometer so tip is in thickest part. Bake uncovered about 1 hour 20 minutes. Remove pork from oven when thermometer reads 145°F. Cover loosely with foil; let stand at least 3 minutes. Make stuffing as directed and bake in covered casserole.

1 Serving: Calories 580; Total Fat 24g (Saturated Fat 9g; Trans Fat 0.5g); Cholesterol 135mg; Sodium 1020mg; Total Carbohydrate 44g (Dietary Fiber 2g); Protein 46g **Exchanges:** 2 Starch, 5 Lean Meat, 1 Fat **Carbohydrate Choices:** 3

Carving a Pork Crown Roast

Place roast on carving board or serving platter. Insert meat fork into roast to keep it from moving; cut slices between ribs.

CARIBBEAN PORK ROAST

Serve this special spicy roast with hot cooked rice or couscous.

PREP 20 min TOTAL 6 hr • **8 servings**

- 1 boneless pork center loin roast (2 to 2½ lb)
- 1 cup orange juice
- ½ cup lime juice
- 1½ teaspoons ground cumin
- 1½ teaspoons red pepper sauce
- ¾ teaspoon ground allspice
- 1 medium bell pepper (any color), cut into 8 pieces
- 1 medium onion, quartered
- 4 cloves garlic, finely chopped
  Salt and pepper, if desired
- 1½ teaspoons sugar
- ½ teaspoon salt

1 Trim fat from pork. Pierce pork deeply in several places with meat fork or skewer; place in resealable food-storage plastic bag.

2 In blender or food processor, place remaining ingredients except salt and pepper, sugar and ½ teaspoon salt. Cover and blend on medium speed until smooth. Pour blended mixture over pork. Seal bag; place in dish. Refrigerate at least 4 hours but no longer than 24 hours, turning bag occasionally.

3 Heat oven to 325°F. Remove pork from marinade; refrigerate marinade. Sprinkle pork with salt and pepper; place on rack in shallow roasting pan. Bake uncovered 1 hour to 1 hour 30 minutes or until meat thermometer inserted into center of pork reads 145°F. Remove from oven; cover with foil and let stand at least 3 minutes.

4 Meanwhile, in 1½-quart saucepan, mix marinade, sugar and ½ teaspoon salt. Heat to boiling; reduce heat. Simmer uncovered about 5 minutes, stirring occasionally, until mixture is slightly thickened. Slice pork; serve with sauce.

1 Serving: Calories 240; Total Fat 10g (Saturated Fat 3.5g; Trans Fat 0g); Cholesterol 80mg; Sodium 210mg; Total Carbohydrate 8g (Dietary Fiber 0g); Protein 29g **Exchanges:** ½ Other Carbohydrate, 4 Lean Meat **Carbohydrate Choices:** ½

PORK TENDERLOIN WITH ROASTED VEGETABLES

PREP 10 min TOTAL 55 min • **6 servings**

- 2 pork tenderloins (about ¾ lb each)
- 1 bag (16 oz) ready-to-eat baby-cut carrots
- 2 lb small red potatoes (16 to 20), cut in half
- 1 medium onion, cut into wedges
- 6 whole cloves garlic
- 1 tablespoon olive or vegetable oil
- 2 teaspoons dried rosemary leaves, crushed
- 1 teaspoon dried sage leaves, crushed
- ¼ teaspoon salt
- ¼ teaspoon pepper

1 Heat oven to 450°F. Spray shallow roasting pan with cooking spray. Place pork in pan. Insert ovenproof meat thermometer so tip is in thickest part of pork. Place carrots, potatoes, onion and garlic around pork. Drizzle with oil; sprinkle with rosemary, sage, salt and pepper.

2 Roast uncovered 25 to 30 minutes or until thermometer reads 145°F. Remove pork from pan. Stir vegetables; roast 5 to 10 minutes longer or until tender. Serve pork with vegetables and garlic.

1 Serving: Calories 320; Total Fat 7g (Saturated Fat 2g; Trans Fat 0g); Cholesterol 50mg; Sodium 220mg; Total Carbohydrate 38g (Dietary Fiber 5g); Protein 26g **Exchanges:** 2 Starch, 1½ Vegetable, 2½ Very Lean Meat, 1 Fat **Carbohydrate Choices:** 2½

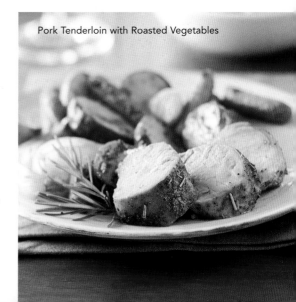
Pork Tenderloin with Roasted Vegetables

Learn to Make **Ribs**

SAUCY RIBS

Tender, lip-smacking ribs with great sauce are about as American as apple pie. Here, you get to choose the type of ribs and sauce that you like. Then, follow our directions and tips, and you'll have tasty, delicious ribs in no time.

PREP 20 min **TOTAL** 2 hr 50 min • **6 servings**

4½ lb pork loin back ribs, pork spareribs, beef short ribs or 3 lb pork country-style ribs (choose one type of ribs)
Salt and pepper to taste

1 recipe Spicy Barbecue Sauce, Sweet-Savory Sauce or Molasses-Mustard Sauce (at right)

1 Heat oven as directed in chart below.

2 Make sauce. Cover and refrigerate if not using immediately.

3 Cut ribs into 6 serving pieces using a knife or scissors. Place meat side up in pan listed in chart. Sprinkle with salt and pepper.

4 Cook as directed in chart until tender, brushing or covering with sauce as directed.

1 Serving (Pork Loin Back Ribs): Calories 730; Total Fat 60g (Saturated Fat 23g; Trans Fat 0.5g); Cholesterol 225mg; Sodium 220mg; Total Carbohydrate 1g (Dietary Fiber 0g); Protein 48g **Exchanges:** 7 High-Fat Meat, 1 Fat **Carbohydrate Choices:** 0

SLOW COOKER DIRECTIONS Cut ribs into 2- or 3-rib portions. Place ribs in 5- to 6-quart slow cooker. Sprinkle with ½ teaspoon salt and ¼ teaspoon pepper. Pour ½ cup water into slow cooker. Cover and cook on Low heat setting 8 to 9 hours. Remove ribs. Drain and discard liquid from slow cooker. Make desired sauce; pour into bowl. Dip ribs into sauce to coat. Place ribs in slow cooker. Pour any remaining sauce over ribs. Cover and cook on Low heat setting 1 hour.

See how to make ribs: Visit bettycrocker.com/BCcookbook

SAUCY RIBS COOKING CHART				
Ribs	**Oven Temperature**	**Pan**	**Directions**	**Serving Tips**
Pork Loin Back Ribs	325°F	Rack in roasting pan or 13x9-inch pan	Bake covered 1 hour 45 minutes; brush with sauce. Bake uncovered about 45 minutes longer, brushing frequently with sauce.	Heat remaining sauce to boiling; boil and stir 1 minute.*
Pork Spareribs	325°F	Rack in roasting pan or 13x9-inch pan	Bake covered 1 hour 15 minutes; brush with sauce. Bake uncovered about 45 minutes longer, brushing frequently with sauce.	Heat remaining sauce to boiling; boil and stir 1 minute.*
Pork Country-Style Ribs	350°F	13x9-inch pan	Cover; bake about 2 hours; drain. Pour sauce over ribs. Bake uncovered 30 minutes longer.	Spoon sauce from pan over ribs.
Beef Short Ribs	350°F	13x9-inch pan	Pour sauce over ribs. Cover; bake about 2 hours 30 minutes.	Spoon sauce from pan over ribs.

*Heat remaining sauce to boiling before serving with ribs to kill any bacteria from the uncooked ribs that might have gotten into the sauce.

SPICY BARBECUE SAUCE

- ⅓ cup butter
- 2 tablespoons white or cider vinegar
- 2 tablespoons water
- 1 teaspoon sugar
- ½ teaspoon garlic powder
- ½ teaspoon onion powder
- ½ teaspoon pepper
  Dash ground red pepper (cayenne)

In 1-quart saucepan, heat all ingredients over medium heat, stirring frequently, until butter is melted.

SWEET-SAVORY SAUCE

- 1 cup chili sauce
- ¾ cup grape jelly
- 1 tablespoon plus 1½ teaspoons dry red wine or beef broth
- 1 teaspoon Dijon mustard

In 1-quart saucepan, heat all ingredients over medium heat, stirring occasionally, until jelly is melted.

MOLASSES-MUSTARD SAUCE

- ½ cup molasses
- ⅓ cup Dijon mustard
- ⅓ cup cider or white vinegar

In small bowl, mix molasses and mustard. Stir in vinegar.

Keys to Success

- Remove membrane (silverskin) from back of ribs. See Removing Silverskin from Pork Ribs (page 325).
- Cut ribs into serving pieces between bones, using sharp knife or kitchen scissors, so ribs are easier to work with when cooking.
- Place ribs meaty side up in pan, so fat can drip away into bottom of roasting pan or into 13x9-inch pan to drain later.
- Add sauce toward end of cooking time so it doesn't burn.
- Cook ribs as directed until tender. Cook a little longer if you like the meat falling off the bone.

Pork Loin Back Ribs with Spicy Barbecue Sauce

Pork Spareribs with Sweet-Savory Sauce

Pork Country-Style Ribs with Molasses-Mustard Sauce

GLAZED BAKED HAM `LOWER CALORIE`

PREP 10 min TOTAL 1 hr 55 min ● **10 servings**

- 1 **cooked smoked bone-in ham (6 lb)**
- 1 **cup packed brown sugar**
- 1 **tablespoon cornstarch**
- ¼ **teaspoon salt**
- 1 **can (8 oz) crushed pineapple, undrained**
- 2 **tablespoons lemon juice**
- 1 **tablespoon yellow or Dijon mustard**

1 Heat oven to 325°F. Place ham on rack in shallow roasting pan. Insert ovenproof meat thermometer in ham so tip is in center of thickest part of meat and does not touch bone or rest in fat. Bake uncovered 1 hour 30 minutes or until thermometer reads at least 140°F.

2 Meanwhile, in 1-quart saucepan, mix brown sugar, cornstarch and salt. Stir in pineapple, lemon juice and mustard. Cook over medium heat, stirring constantly, until mixture thickens and boils. Boil and stir 1 minute. Brush glaze over ham during last 45 minutes of baking.

3 Remove ham from oven. Cover loosely with foil; let stand 10 to 15 minutes for easier carving.

1 Serving: Calories 140; Total Fat 3.5g (Saturated Fat 1g; Trans Fat 0g); Cholesterol 35mg; Sodium 830mg; Total Carbohydrate 14g (Dietary Fiber 0g); Protein 14g **Exchanges:** 1 Other Carbohydrate, 4 Lean Meat **Carbohydrate Choices:** 1

HAM WITH BROWN SUGAR–ORANGE GLAZE Omit all ingredients exept ham. Bake ham as directed. In small bowl, mix ½ cup packed brown sugar, 2 tablespoons orange juice and ½ teaspoon ground mustard. Brush glaze over ham during last 45 minutes of baking.

All About Hams

Whatever kind of ham you choose, they all come from cured pork leg meat. Curing gives ham its distinctive sweet-smoky and salty flavor. Hams are usually either wet or dry cured. Most supermarket hams, including the convenient spiral-cut hams, are wet cured, meaning they have been processed with a brine of water, salt, sugar and spices. Brining keeps the meat moist and tender.

Dry-cured hams are rubbed with salt, sugar and spices, then aged anywhere from several weeks to more than a year. These hams, referred to as country hams, are often named for the city in which they are processed. Dry-cured hams are very salty, so follow package directions for using.

Carving Ham

Place ham on carving board or platter fat side up, bone facing you. Cut in half next to bone.

Place boneless side of ham fat side up; cut slices. Cut slices from bone-in portion, cutting away bone.

Glazed Baked Ham

Greek Lamb Chops

CORNBREAD-TOPPED SAUSAGE PIE

This is a delicious recipe to serve family or friends. The topping is a wonderful homemade cornbread.

PREP 15 min TOTAL 55 min • **6 servings**

SAUSAGE PIE

- 1 lb bulk Italian sausage
- 1 medium onion, chopped (½ cup)
- 1 small bell pepper (any color), chopped (½ cup)
- 2 cloves garlic, finely chopped
- 1 can (15 oz) tomato sauce
- 1 box (9 oz) frozen whole kernel corn, thawed
- 1 jar (4.5 oz) sliced mushrooms, drained

CORNBREAD TOPPING

- ⅔ cup cornmeal
- ⅓ cup all-purpose flour
- 1 tablespoon sugar
- 2 teaspoons baking powder
- ¼ teaspoon salt
- ½ cup milk
- 2 tablespoons vegetable oil
- 1 egg
- ¼ cup shredded pepper Jack cheese

1 Heat oven to 400°F.

2 In 10-inch skillet, cook sausage, onion, bell pepper and garlic over medium heat 8 to 10 minutes, stirring frequently, until sausage is no longer pink; drain. Stir in tomato sauce, corn and mushrooms. Heat to boiling; remove from heat.

3 In medium bowl, stir all topping ingredients except cheese. Beat vigorously with spoon 30 seconds. Stir in cheese.

4 Spoon sausage mixture into ungreased 2-quart casserole. Pour topping over hot sausage mixture, spreading evenly.

5 Bake uncovered 20 to 25 minutes or until topping is golden brown.

1 Serving: Calories 430; Total Fat 22g (Saturated Fat 7g; Trans Fat 0g); Cholesterol 85mg; Sodium 1320mg; Total Carbohydrate 39g (Dietary Fiber 4g); Protein 19g **Exchanges:** 2 Starch, 2 Vegetable, 1 High-Fat Meat, 2½ Fat **Carbohydrate Choices:** 2½

GREEK LAMB CHOPS

PREP 15 min TOTAL 40 min • **4 servings**

- 4 lamb shoulder, arm or loin chops, about ½ inch thick (6 oz each)
- 1 teaspoon dried oregano leaves
- ¼ teaspoon salt
- ¼ teaspoon pepper
- 4 cloves garlic, finely chopped (1 tablespoon)
- 1 tablespoon olive or vegetable oil
- ½ cup chicken broth (for homemade broth, see page 528)
- 1 tablespoon lemon juice
- 1 tablespoon butter
- ¼ cup sliced pitted kalamata or ripe olives
- 2 tablespoons chopped fresh parsley
- 2 tablespoons crumbled feta cheese

1 Sprinkle both sides of lamb with oregano, salt and pepper. Press garlic into lamb.

2 In 12-inch skillet, heat oil over medium-high heat. Cook lamb in oil 4 to 6 minutes, turning once, until brown.

3 Add broth to skillet; reduce heat to medium-low. Cover and cook 8 to 10 minutes, turning once, until lamb is tender. Remove lamb from skillet; keep warm.

4 Heat liquid in skillet to boiling. Boil 1 to 2 minutes or until slightly reduced. Stir in lemon juice and butter. Cook and stir just until slightly thickened. Stir in olives and parsley. Spoon sauce over lamb. Top with cheese.

1 Serving: Calories 270; Total Fat 17g (Saturated Fat 6g; Trans Fat 1g); Cholesterol 95mg; Sodium 490mg; Total Carbohydrate 2g (Dietary Fiber 0g); Protein 27g **Exchanges:** 4 Lean Meat, 1 Fat **Carbohydrate Choices:** 0

HERB AND GARLIC ROAST LEG OF LAMB

PREP 15 min TOTAL 2 hr 50 min • **10 servings**

- ¼ cup finely chopped fresh parsley
- 1 tablespoon chopped fresh or 1 teaspoon dried rosemary leaves, crushed
- 1 tablespoon chopped fresh or 1 teaspoon dried thyme leaves, crushed
- 2 teaspoons kosher (coarse) salt
- ½ teaspoon pepper
- 2 cloves garlic, finely chopped
- 3 tablespoons olive or vegetable oil
- 1 boneless leg of lamb (5 to 6 lb)

1 Heat oven to 325°F. In small bowl, stir all ingredients except lamb until well mixed.

2 Place lamb in shallow roasting pan (keep netting or string on lamb). Spread herb mixture over entire surface of lamb. Insert meat thermometer so tip is in thickest part of lamb and does not rest in fat.

3 Roast uncovered 2 hours 5 minutes to 2 hours 15 minutes for medium-rare or until thermometer reads 140°F. For medium doneness, roast until thermometer reads 155°F. (Temperature will continue to rise about 5°F, and lamb will be easier to carve.)

4 Remove from oven. Cover lamb loosely with foil; let stand 10 to 15 minutes or until thermometer reads 145°F (or 160°F for medium doneness). Remove netting or string before carving. Serve lamb with pan juices if desired.

1 Serving: Calories 370; Total Fat 20g (Saturated Fat 6g; Trans Fat 1g); Cholesterol 155mg; Sodium 590mg; Total Carbohydrate 0g (Dietary Fiber 0g); Protein 48g **Exchanges:** 7 Lean Meat **Carbohydrate Choices:** 0

MOROCCAN LAMB STEW

LOWER CALORIE

PREP 15 min TOTAL 1 hr • **6 servings**

- 1 pound boneless lamb shoulder
- 1½ cups chicken broth (for homemade broth, see page 528)
- 1 large onion, chopped (1 cup)
- 3 cloves garlic, finely chopped
- 1 tablespoon all-purpose flour
- 1 cup dry red wine or chicken broth
- 1 cup dried apricots
- ¼ cup pitted dried plums
- ¼ cup raisins
- 1 teaspoon paprika
- 1 can (14.5 oz) whole peeled tomatoes, undrained
- ⅓ cup chopped fresh parsley
- 3 cups hot cooked couscous

1 Trim fat from lamb; cut into cubes. Spray Dutch oven with cooking spray; heat over medium-high heat. Cook lamb in Dutch oven, stirring frequently, until brown. Remove lamb from Dutch oven.

2 Add ½ cup of the broth to Dutch oven; heat to boiling. Stir in onion and garlic. Cook 3 minutes, stirring frequently. Stir in flour. Cook 1 minute, stirring constantly.

3 Stir in the lamb, remaining 1 cup broth, the wine, apricots, plums, raisins, paprika and tomatoes, breaking up tomatoes. Heat to boiling; reduce heat. Cover and simmer 45 minutes. Stir in parsley. Serve over couscous.

1 Serving: Calories 350; Total Fat 6g (Saturated Fat 2g; Trans Fat 0g); Cholesterol 50mg; Sodium 480mg; Total Carbohydrate 49g (Dietary Fiber 5g); Protein 23g **Exchanges:** 2 Starch, 1½ Other Carbohydrate, 2 Very Lean Meat, ½ Lean Meat, ½ Fat **Carbohydrate Choices:** 3

Herb and Garlic Roast Leg of Lamb

Moroccan Lamb Stew

ROASTING MEAT

Roasting is a great method for cooking large, tender cuts of meat. *Roasting* simply means cooking in the oven, uncovered without liquid, at a constant temperature throughout the cooking process to achieve juicy, evenly cooked meat.

Let meat stand at room temperature 15 to 30 minutes before roasting. Place meat fat side up on a rack in a shallow roasting pan.

(Bone-in roasts don't need a rack.) Insert ovenproof meat thermometer so tip is in center of thickest part of meat and does not touch bone or rest in fat. Don't add water or liquid; don't cover. Roast at the oven temperature given in the chart below for the time listed and until thermometer reaches the remove-from-oven temperature. Remove meat from oven; cover loosely with foil and let stand as directed below before carving.

TIMETABLE FOR ROASTING AND BAKING MEAT

Cut of Meat	Weight in Pounds	Approximate Total Roasting Time in Hours (unless noted otherwise)	Remove from Oven When Internal Temperature Reaches	Final Doneness Temperature (after standing time)
BEEF				
Rib-Eye Roast (boneless) Roast at 350°F. Let stand 10 to 15 minutes.	3 to 4	1½ to 2	135°F	145°F medium-rare
		1¾ to 2	150°F	160°F medium
	4 to 6	2 to 2½	135°F	145°F medium-rare
		2 to 2¼	150°F	160°F medium
	6 to 8	2½ to 2¾	135°F	145°F medium-rare
			150°F	160°F medium
Rib Roast (bone-in) Roast at 350°F. Let stand 10 to 15 minutes.	4 to 6 (2 ribs)	1¾ to 2¼	135°F	145°F medium-rare
		2¼ to 2¾	150°F	160°F medium
	6 to 8 (2 to 4 ribs)	2¼ to 2½	135°F	145°F medium-rare
		2¾ to 3	150°F	160°F medium
	8 to 10 (4 to 5 ribs)	2½ to 3	135°F	145°F medium-rare
		3 to 3½	150°F	160°F medium
Tenderloin Roast Roast at 425°F. Let stand 10 to 15 minutes.	2 to 3	35 to 40 minutes	135°F	145°F medium-rare
		45 to 50 minutes	150°F	160°F medium
	4 to 5	50 to 60 minutes	135°F	145°F medium-rare
		60 to 70 minutes	150°F	160°F medium
Tri-Tip Roast Roast at 425°F. Let stand 10 to 15 minutes.	1½ to 2	30 to 40 minutes	135°F	145°F medium-rare
		40 to 45 minutes	150°F	160°F medium
Round Tip Roast Roast at 325°F. Let stand 10 to 15 minutes.	3 to 4	1¾ to 2	140°F	145°F medium-rare
		2¼ to 2½	155°F	160°F medium
	4 to 6	2 to 2½	140°F	145°F medium-rare
		2½ to 3	155°F	160°F medium
	6 to 8	2½ to 3	140°F	145°F medium-rare
		3 to 3½	155°F	160°F medium
Rump Roast Roast at 325°F. Let stand 10 to 15 minutes.	3 to 4	1½ to 2	135°F	145°F medium-rare
Bottom Round Roast Roast at 325°F. Let stand 10 to 15 minutes.	3 to 4	1½ to 2	135°F	145°F medium-rare

TIMETABLE FOR ROASTING AND BAKING MEAT continued

Cut of Meat	Weight in Pounds	Approximate Total Roasting Time in Hours (unless noted otherwise)	Remove from Oven When Internal Temperature Reaches	Final Doneness Temperature (after standing time)
Eye Round Roast Roast at 325°F. Let stand 10 to 15 minutes.	2 to 3	1½ to 1¾	135°F	145°F medium-rare
Brisket, Fresh Bake at 325°F. Let stand 10 to 15 minutes.	2½ to 4	2½ to 3 (must be cooked with liquid to partially cover)	———	170°F well done
Brisket, Corned Bake at 325°F. Let stand 10 to 15 minutes.	2½ to 3½ 3½ to 5	2½ to 3½ 3½ to 4½	Follow package directions.	170°F well done; follow package directions.
VEAL				
Loin Roast (bone-in) Roast at 325°F.	3 to 4	1¾ to 2¼	155°F	160°F medium
Rib Roast (bone-in) Roast at 325°F.	4 to 5	1½ to 2¼	155°F	160°F medium
PORK*				
Loin Roast (bone-in or boneless) Roast at 325°F.	2 to 5	20 minutes per lb	145°F	Let stand at least 3 minutes.
Crown Roast Roast at 325°F.	6 to 10	20 minutes per lb	145°F	Let stand at least 3 minutes.
Shoulder Roast/Butt Roast at 325°F.	3 to 6	20 minutes per lb	145°F	Let stand at least 3 minutes.
Ribs (back, spareribs) Bake at 325°F.	———	Cover and cook 1 hour 15 minutes, uncover and cook 45 minutes longer.	Tender	No standing time
Ribs (country-style) Bake at 350°F.	———	Cover and cook 2 hours, uncover and cook 30 minutes longer.	Tender	No standing time
Tenderloin Roast at 425°F to 450°F.	¾ to 1	20 to 30 minutes	145°F	Let stand at least 3 minutes.
Ham, Fully Cooked (bone-in or boneless) Roast at 325°F.	———	15 to 20 minutes per lb	140°F	No standing time
Fresh Leg/Uncured Ham, Cook Before Eating (bone-in) Roast at 325°F.	———	15 to 20 minutes per lb	145°F	Let stand at least 3 minutes.

*The USDA recommends pork be cooked to 145°F with a 3-minute resting period. If you prefer pork more well done, cook to 160°F.

TIMETABLE FOR ROASTING AND BAKING MEAT continued

Cut of Meat	Weight in Pounds	Approximate Total Roasting Time in Hours (unless noted otherwise)	Remove from Oven When Internal Temperature Reaches	Final Doneness Temperature (after standing time)
LAMB				
Leg Roast (whole, bone-in)	5 to 7	20 to 25 minutes per lb	140°F	145°F medium-rare
Roast at 325°F. Let stand 10 to 15 minutes.		25 to 30 minutes per lb	155°F	160°F medium
	7 to 9	15 to 20 minutes per lb	140°F	145°F medium-rare
		20 to 25 minutes per lb	155°F	160°F medium
Leg Roast (whole, boneless)	4 to 7	25 to 30 minutes per lb	140°F	145°F medium-rare
Roast at 325°F. Let stand 10 to 15 minutes.		30 to 35 minutes per lb	155°F	160°F medium
Shoulder Roast or Shank Leg Half (bone-in)	3 to 4	30 to 35 minutes per lb	140°F	145°F medium-rare
Roast at 325°F. Let stand 10 to 15 minutes.		40 to 45 minutes per lb	155°F	160°F medium

Cooking Ham

The most popular hams are fully cooked and ready to eat. Packaged cooked hams should be cooked to at least 140°F. If you are not sure what kind of ham you have, or the cooked ham has been repackaged, it must be heated to an internal temperature of at least 165°F. Raw fresh ham should be cooked to at least 145°F and allowed to stand or rest at least 3 minutes.

BRAISING MEAT

Braising (or pot roasting) is great for large, less tender cuts of meat, such as those coming from the chuck, shank, brisket or round. These cuts are generally less expensive than more tender cuts. The meat is browned first to add depth of flavor, then covered and cooked slowly with a small amount of liquid to make the meat very tender.

STEWING MEAT

Stewing is great for less tender cuts of meat. It's similar to braising except typically uses enough liquid to cover the meat. Any cut from the chuck or round (except top round) can be used for stews. Stew meat (precut pieces from the chuck or round) can be purchased in most grocery stores.

BROILING MEAT

Broiling is a great method for cooking smaller cuts of meat quickly without fat. It's done in the oven, with the control set to "broil," so the meat is cooked directly under high heat. Broiling enhances the flavor of smaller cuts by caramelizing the surface of the meat, creating a flavorful "crust" and sealing in the juices. Set the oven control to broil; heat 10 minutes. Check the oven's use-and-care manual for whether the oven door should be partially opened or closed during broiling. Place the meat on a rack in the broiler pan; season to taste with salt and pepper. For cuts less than 1 inch thick, broil 2 to 3 inches from the heat. For cuts 1 to 1½ inches thick, broil 3 to 4 inches from the heat unless the timetable below gives a different distance. Broil for the time listed, turning once.

TIMETABLE FOR BROILING MEAT

Cut of Meat	Thickness in Inches	Approximate Cooking Time in Minutes	Final Doneness Temperature
BEEF			
Rib Eye Steak	¾	8 to 12	145°F medium-rare to 160°F medium
	1	14 to 18	
	1½	21 to 27	
Porterhouse/T-Bone Steak	¾	9 to 12	145°F medium-rare to 160°F medium
	1	13 to 17	
	1½	24 to 31	
Top Loin (Strip) Steak	¾	9 to 11	145°F medium-rare to 160°F medium
	1	13 to 17	
	1½	19 to 23	
Top Blade Chuck Steak	8 oz each	15 to 20	145°F medium-rare to 160°F medium
Tenderloin Steak	1	13 to 16 (broil 2 to 3 inches from heat)	145°F medium-rare to 160°F medium
	1½	18 to 22	
Top Sirloin Steak (boneless)	¾	9 to 12	145°F medium-rare to 160°F medium
	1	16 to 21	
	1½	26 to 31	
	2	34 to 39	
Ground Patties			
4 per lb	½ (4-inch diameter)	10 to 12	160°F medium
4 per 1½ lb	¾ (4-inch diameter)	12 to 14	160°F medium
VEAL			
Chop, Loin or Rib	¾ to 1	14 to 16	160°F medium
PORK*			
Chop (bone-in or boneless)	¾ to 1	9 to 12	Let stand at least 3 minutes. 145°F medium
	1½	12 to 16	145°F medium
Ground Patties	½	8 to 10	160°F medium
LAMB			
Chop, Loin or Rib	1	10 to 15	160°F medium
Chop, Sirloin	1	12 to 15	160°F medium

*The USDA recommends pork be cooked to 145°F with a 3-minute resting period. If you prefer pork more well done, cook to 160°F.

GRILLING MEAT

See Timetable for Grilling Beef, Veal, Pork and Lamb, page 305.

PANFRYING MEAT

Panfrying (also known as pan broiling) is a great method for cooking tender cuts of meat without liquid and is faster than oven broiling, if you're in a hurry. It's important not to overcook meat with this method, or it can become tough and dry.

Use a nonstick skillet, or lightly coat a regular skillet with vegetable oil or cooking spray. Heat the skillet over medium heat (unless otherwise noted) for 5 minutes. Season meat as desired. Add the meat to the skillet. Don't add water, liquids or fats; don't cover. Cook for the time listed until the thermometer reaches the final doneness temperature, turning once. If the meat browns too quickly, reduce heat to medium-low.

TIMETABLE FOR PANFRYING MEAT

Cut of Meat	Thickness in Inches	Approximate Cooking Time in Minutes	Final Doneness Temperature
BEEF			
Rib Eye Steak	¾	8 to 10	145°F medium-rare to 160°F medium
	1	12 to 15	
Porterhouse/T-Bone Steak	¾	11 to 13	145°F medium-rare to 160°F medium
	1	14 to 17	
Top Loin (Strip) Steak	¾	10 to 12	145°F medium-rare to 160°F medium
	1	12 to 15	
Top Blade Chuck Steak	8 oz each	13 to 15	145°F medium-rare to 160°F medium
Tenderloin Steak (use medium-high heat for ½-inch thickness)	½	3 to 5	145°F medium-rare to 160°F medium
	¾	7 to 9	
	1	10 to 13	
Top Sirloin Steak (boneless)	¾	10 to 13	145°F medium-rare to 160°F medium
	1	15 to 20	
Top Round Steak (best when marinated before cooking)	¾	11 to 12	145°F medium-rare to 160°F medium
	1	15 to 16	
Cubed Steak (use medium-high heat)	——	3 to 5	145°F medium-rare to 160°F medium
Ground Patties			
4 per lb	½ (4-inch diameter)	10 to 12	160°F medium
4 per 1½ lb	¾ (4-inch diameter)	12 to 15	160°F medium
VEAL			
Chop, Loin or Rib (use medium-high heat)	¾ to 1	10 to 14	160°F medium
Cutlet (use medium-high heat)	¼	4 to 6	160°F medium
Ground Patties (use medium-high heat)	½	9 to 12	160°F medium

TIMETABLE FOR PANFRYING MEAT_{continued}

Cut of Meat	Thickness in Inches	Approximate Cooking Time in Minutes	Final Doneness Temperature
PORK*			
Chop, Loin or Rib (bone-in or boneless)	¾ to 1	8 to 12	145°F medium
Cutlets (bone-in or boneless)	¼	3 to 4	Tender
Tenderloin Medallions	¼ to ½ ½	4 to 8 8 to 10	Tender 145°F medium (let stand at least 3 minutes)
Ground Patties	½	8 to 10	160°F medium
Ham Slice, Cooked Ham Steak, Cooked	½ 1	6 to 8 8 to 10	140°F medium 140°F medium
LAMB			
Chop, Loin or Rib	1	9 to 11	160°F medium
Ground Patties	½	9 to 12	160°F medium

*The USDA recommends pork be cooked to 145°F with a 3-minute resting period. If you prefer pork more well done, cook to 160°F.

PASTA

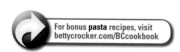
For bonus **pasta** recipes, visit
bettycrocker.com/BCcookbook

FAST = Ready in 20 minutes or less LOWER CALORIE = See Helpful Nutrition and Cooking Information, page 685
LIGHTER = 25% fewer calories or grams of fat MAKE AHEAD = Make-ahead directions SLOW COOKER = Slow cooker directions

← Herb Pasta (page 391) before cooking, Cheesy Baked Rigatoni (page 379), Spaghetti Carbonara (page 382), Potato
Gnocchi (page 392)

PASTA BASICS
Whether mixed in a comforting casserole or simply topped with a sensational sauce, the meal possibilities using dried, fresh, frozen and homemade pasta are endless . . . but always enjoyable.

POINTERS FOR PURCHASING PASTA

- **Dried Pasta:** Avoid broken pasta or pasta that looks cracked. It may fall apart during cooking. Check the expiration dates on packages.

- **Fresh Pasta:** Avoid packages with moisture droplets or liquid; the pasta may be moldy or mushy. The pasta should be smooth and evenly colored without broken or crumbly pieces. Look for "sell by dates," too.

- **Frozen Pasta:** Avoid packages that are frozen as a solid block and those with ice crystals or freezer burn (dry, white spots).

STORING PASTA

Dried Pasta: Label, date and store tightly covered in a cool, dry location up to 1 year.

Fresh Pasta: Refrigerate; use by package expiration date. Store opened, uncooked pasta in tightly covered container up to 3 days.

Frozen Pasta: Freeze unopened fresh pasta in its original package up to 9 months. Leftover uncooked pasta can be frozen in airtight container up to 3 months and homemade fresh pasta up to 1 month.

Cooked Pasta: To prevent from sticking during storage, toss cooked pasta with 1 to 2 teaspoons vegetable or olive oil (per pound) after draining. Refrigerate tightly covered up to 5 days or freeze up to 2 months.

COOKING PASTA TO PERFECTION

- Use 1 quart (4 cups) water for every 4 ounces of pasta. Once the water has boiled vigorously, add pasta gradually and stir frequently during cooking to prevent it from sticking together.

- To add flavor, use ½ teaspoon salt for every 8 ounces of pasta. Stir in just as the water starts to boil and make sure it dissolves before adding pasta.

- Follow package directions for cook times. For baked recipes, slightly undercook pasta because it will continue to cook during baking.

- Cooked pasta should be al dente, or tender but firm to the bite, without any raw flavor. Overcooked pasta is mushy, waterlogged and bland.

- Unless specified, do not rinse pasta after draining or sauces won't cling. Pasta is usually only rinsed for cold salads.

PASTA YIELDS

- Plan on ½ to ¾ cup cooked pasta per side dish or appetizer serving and 1 to 1½ cups per main-dish serving.

- To easily measure 4 ounces of dried spaghetti, make a circle with your thumb and index finger (about the size of a quarter) and fill it with pasta.

Type of Pasta	Uncooked	Cooked	Servings
Short Pastas Penne, Rotini, Shells, Wagon Wheels	6 to 7 oz	4 cups	4 to 6
Long Pastas Capellini, Linguine, Spaghetti, Vermicelli	7 to 8 oz	4 cups	4 to 6
Egg Noodles	8 oz	4 to 5 cups	4 to 6

Toss your favorite pasta with olive oil and chopped fresh herbs, such as basil or parsley.

Spinach Fettuccine

Ditalini

Rigatoni

Ziti

Lasagnotte

Couscous

Gnocchi

Mini Gnocchi

Cellophane Noodles

Couscous (large)

Cheese Ravioletti

Fusilli Bucati

Cheese Ravioli

Spinach Cheese Tortellini

Sausage Ravioli

Cheese Tortellini

Long Ziti

Orzo

Mafalde

Lasagna

Acini de Pepe

Vermicelli

Angel Hair

Spaghetti

Brown Rice Gluten Free Spaghetti

Linguine

Elbow Macaroni

Gemelli

Tri Color Rotini

Rotelle

Pappardelle

Radiatore

Campanelle

Fusilli Bucati

Trivelli

Angel Hair Nests

Tagliatelle

Wagon Wheels

Orecchiette

Farfalle (Bow Ties)

Egg Bows

Mezze Penne

Penne

Garganelli

Mostaccioli

Beet Rotini

Casarecci

Fine Egg Noodles

Conchiglioni

Gnocchi

Dumpling Egg Noodles

Maccheroni

Chiocciole

Manicotti

Lumache

Whole Wheat Elbows Macaroni

Extra Wide Egg Noodles

Whole Wheat Gobbetti

Whole Wheat Penne

Fettuccini

Bucatini

Tagliatelle

Rice Bran Pad Thai

Whole Wheat Linguine

ITALIAN TOMATO SAUCE

LOWER CALORIE

A great tomato pasta sauce can be one of your best go-to dinner ideas. Make a batch or two and freeze it in portion sizes that work for you. Use it as is, or toss in some pepperoni, cooked Italian sausage and mushrooms or olives.

PREP 15 min TOTAL 1 hr 5 min • **4 cups sauce**

- 2 tablespoons olive or vegetable oil
- 1 large onion, chopped (1 cup)
- 1 small green bell pepper, chopped (½ cup)
- 2 large cloves garlic, finely chopped
- 1 can (28 oz) whole tomatoes, undrained
- 2 cans (8 oz each) tomato sauce
- 2 tablespoons chopped fresh or 2 teaspoons dried basil leaves
- 1 tablespoon chopped fresh or 1 teaspoon dried oregano leaves
- ½ teaspoon salt
- ½ teaspoon fennel seed
- ¼ teaspoon pepper

1 In 3-quart saucepan, heat oil over medium heat. Cook onion, bell pepper and garlic in oil 2 minutes, stirring occasionally.

2 Stir in remaining ingredients, breaking up tomatoes with fork. Heat to boiling; reduce heat. Simmer uncovered 45 minutes.

3 Use sauce immediately, or cover and refrigerate up to 2 weeks or freeze up to 1 year.

½ **Cup:** Calories 90; Total Fat 3.5g (Saturated Fat 0g; Trans Fat 0g); Cholesterol 0mg; Sodium 670mg; Total Carbohydrate 11g (Dietary Fiber 2g); Protein 2g **Exchanges:** 2 Vegetable, ½ Fat **Carbohydrate Choices:** 1

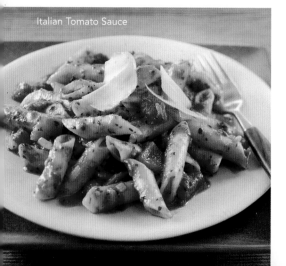
Italian Tomato Sauce

SLOW COOKER **Directions** Use 1 medium onion, chopped (½ cup). Substitute 1 can (28 oz) diced tomatoes, undrained, for the whole tomatoes. Use 1 can (8 oz) tomato sauce. Spray 3½- to 6-quart slow cooker with cooking spray. In slow cooker, mix all ingredients. Cover; cook on Low heat setting 8 to 10 hours.

BOLOGNESE LOWER CALORIE

A staple of Northern Italy, bolognese is a hearty, thick meat sauce with canned tomatoes, wine and milk or cream. Think of it as a meat sauce with tomato versus a tomato sauce with meat.

PREP 15 min TOTAL 1 hr 15 min • **6 cups sauce**

- 2 tablespoons olive or vegetable oil
- 1 tablespoon butter
- 2 medium carrots, finely chopped (1 cup)
- 1 medium stalk celery, finely chopped (½ cup)
- 1 medium onion, chopped (½ cup)
- 2 cloves garlic, finely chopped
- 1 lb lean (at least 80%) ground beef
- ¼ cup chopped pancetta or bacon
- ½ cup dry red wine, nonalcoholic red wine or beef broth
- 3 cans (28 oz each) whole tomatoes, drained, chopped
- 1 teaspoon dried oregano leaves
- ½ teaspoon pepper
- ½ cup milk or whipping cream

1 In 12-inch skillet, heat oil and butter over medium-high heat. Cook carrots, celery, onion and garlic in oil mixture, stirring frequently, until crisp-tender. Stir in beef and pancetta. Cook 8 to 10 minutes, stirring occasionally, until beef is thoroughly cooked; drain.

2 Stir in wine. Heat to boiling; reduce heat to low. Simmer uncovered until wine has evaporated. Stir in tomatoes, oregano and pepper. Heat to boiling; reduce heat to low. Cover; simmer 45 minutes, stirring occasionally. Remove from heat; stir in milk.

3 Use sauce immediately, or cover and refrigerate up to 48 hours or freeze up to 2 months.

½ **Cup:** Calories 100; Total Fat 4g (Saturated Fat 1g; Trans Fat 0g); Cholesterol 25mg; Sodium 360mg; Total Carbohydrate 8g (Dietary Fiber 2g); Protein 9g **Exchanges:** 1½ Vegetable, 1 Medium-Fat Meat **Carbohydrate Choices:** ½

MARINARA SAUCE LOWER CALORIE

Classic marinara sauces vary from region to region and from cook to cook, with everyone claiming a favorite. Our version is layered with the flavors of Italian herbs and a nice hint of garlic.

PREP 15 min **TOTAL** 45 min • **6 cups sauce**

> 2 cans (28 oz each) crushed tomatoes with basil, undrained
> 1 can (6 oz) tomato paste
> 1 large onion, chopped (1 cup)
> 8 cloves garlic, finely chopped
> 1 tablespoon olive or vegetable oil
> 2 teaspoons sugar
> 1½ teaspoons dried basil leaves
> 1 teaspoon dried oregano leaves
> 1 teaspoon pepper
> ½ teaspoon salt

1 In 3-quart saucepan, stir all ingredients until well mixed. Heat to boiling; reduce heat to low. Cover; simmer 30 minutes to blend flavors.

2 Use sauce immediately, or cover and refrigerate up to 2 weeks or freeze up to 1 year.

½ Cup: Calories 130; Total Fat 2g (Saturated Fat 0g; Trans Fat 0g); Cholesterol 0mg; Sodium 900mg; Total Carbohydrate 24g (Dietary Fiber 4g); Protein 4g **Exchanges:** ½ Starch, 1 Other Carbohydrate, ½ Vegetable, ½ Fat **Carbohydrate Choices:** 1½

Pasta Sauce Fix-Ups

Take a jar of your favorite pasta sauce and add one or more of the following ingredients to make it your own. Then simmer and serve it over your favorite pasta.

- Cooked crumbled ground beef, Italian sausage or turkey sausage
- Diced pepperoni or cooked meatballs
- Cooked shrimp or crabmeat
- Sliced ripe olives
- Sliced fresh mushrooms
- Diced bell pepper or green onions
- Frozen white kernel corn
- Chopped fresh basil or oregano
- Chopped fresh tomato
- Sliced green onions
- Sliced canned artichoke hearts
- Sliced roasted bell peppers (from a jar)

Creamy Tomato-Vodka Sauce

CREAMY TOMATO-VODKA SAUCE LOWER CALORIE

The vodka in this sauce adds complexity and depth to the overall flavor, but doesn't leave behind a vodka taste.

PREP 10 min **TOTAL** 30 min • **3 cups sauce**

> 1 tablespoon olive or vegetable oil
> 1 small onion, chopped (⅓ cup)
> 2 cloves garlic, finely chopped
> 1 can (28 oz) crushed tomatoes with basil, undrained
> ½ cup vodka or chicken broth
> 1 teaspoon sugar
> ¼ teaspoon coarse (kosher or sea) salt
> ⅛ teaspoon pepper
> ½ cup whipping cream

1 In 10-inch skillet, heat oil over medium heat. Cook onion and garlic in oil 3 to 4 minutes, stirring constantly, until crisp-tender.

2 Stir in tomatoes, vodka, sugar, salt and pepper. Heat to boiling. Reduce heat to low; simmer 20 minutes, stirring occasionally. Stir in whipping cream. Heat just until hot.

½ Cup: Calories 130; Total Fat 9g (Saturated Fat 4g; Trans Fat 0g); Cholesterol 20mg; Sodium 270mg; Total Carbohydrate 8g (Dietary Fiber 1g); Protein 2g **Exchanges:** 1 Vegetable, 2 Fat **Carbohydrate Choices:** ½

FRESH TOMATO SAUCE

FAST   LOWER CALORIE

PREP 20 min TOTAL 20 min • **4 cups sauce**

- 1 can (28 oz) whole tomatoes, drained
- 2 cloves garlic, finely chopped
- 1 tablespoon chopped fresh or 1 teaspoon dried basil leaves
- 1 tablespoon chopped fresh parsley or 1 teaspoon parsley flakes
- 1 teaspoon grated Parmesan cheese
- 1 teaspoon olive or vegetable oil
- ½ teaspoon salt
- ½ teaspoon pepper
- 6 medium ripe tomatoes, diced (about 4½ cups)
- ¾ cup pitted kalamata or ripe olives, cut in half
- 1 tablespoon capers, if desired

1 In food processor or blender, place all ingredients except diced tomatoes, olives and capers. Cover and process until smooth. Pour into large glass or plastic bowl. Stir in tomatoes, olives and capers. Serve warm or cool.

2 Use sauce immediately, or cover and refrigerate up to 2 weeks or freeze up to 1 year.

½ **Cup:** Calories 70; Total Fat 2.5g (Saturated Fat 0g; Trans Fat 0g); Cholesterol 0mg; Sodium 430mg; Total Carbohydrate 10g (Dietary Fiber 3g); Protein 2g **Exchanges:** 2 Vegetable **Carbohydrate Choices:** ½

ROASTED TOMATO SAUCE Cut 6 to 8 plum (Roma) tomatoes into quarters. Toss with 2 tablespoons olive oil. Spread on shallow pan. Bake at 450°F for 10 to 12 minutes. Substitute for the 6 ripe tamotes. Substitute 2 cans (14.5 oz each) fire-roasted diced tomatoes for the can of whole tomatoes.

SPAGHETTI AND MEATBALLS

PREP 1 hr 45 min TOTAL 2 hr 15 min • **6 servings**

- Italian Tomato Sauce (page 370)
- Meatballs (page 343)
- 4 cups hot cooked spaghetti (page 367)
- Grated or shredded Parmesan cheese, if desired

1 Make tomato sauce and meatballs.

2 Stir meatballs into sauce. Simmer uncovered over low heat 30 minutes, stirring occasionally. Serve over spaghetti. Serve with cheese.

1 Serving: Calories 430; Total Fat 16g (Saturated Fat 4.5g; Trans Fat 0.5g); Cholesterol 85mg; Sodium 1320mg; Total Carbohydrate 49g (Dietary Fiber 6g); Protein 23g **Exchanges:** 2 Starch, ½ Other Carbohydrate, 2 Vegetable, 2 Medium-Fat Meat, 1 Fat **Carbohydrate Choices:** 3

CHICKEN SPAGHETTI Omit meatballs. In 10-inch skillet, cook 1 lb ground chicken, 1 large onion, chopped (1 cup), and 2 cloves garlic, finely chopped, over medium heat 8 to 10 minutes, stirring occasionally, until chicken is no longer pink; drain. Stir chicken mixture into sauce. Simmer as directed in Step 2.

SPAGHETTI AND MEAT SAUCE Omit meatballs. In 10-inch skillet, cook 1 lb lean (at least 80%) ground beef or bulk Italian pork sausage, 1 large onion, chopped (1 cup), and 2 cloves garlic, finely chopped, over medium heat 8 to 10 minutes, stirring occasionally, until meat is thoroughly cooked; drain. Stir meat mixture into sauce. Simmer as directed in Step 2.

Fresh Tomato Sauce

Spaghetti and Meatballs

THREE-INGREDIENT PASTA SAUCES

Start with your favorite hot cooked plain or filled pasta and one of these easy three-ingredient flavor-packed sauces. Top with grated, shredded or shaved Asiago or Parmesan cheese, if desired. You might also like to offer freshly ground black pepper and crushed red pepper flakes as a final garnish.

1 Artichoke, Olive and Sun-Dried Tomato Sauce: Heat 1 can (14 ounces) undrained marinated artichoke hearts, coarsely chopped, ¼ cup sliced drained sun-dried tomatoes in oil and 2 tablespoons sliced pitted kalamata olives; toss with pasta.

2 Bacon Alfredo Sauce: Heat 10 ounces refrigerated Alfredo sauce with 2 slices crisply cooked crumbled bacon or bacon bits and ¼ cup chopped fresh Italian parsley; toss with pasta.

3 Cheesy Cheddar and Meatballs: Heat 1 jar (14 to 16 ounces) double Cheddar or roasted garlic pasta sauce, 8 ounces hot cooked Italian meatballs (cut in half or quarters) and 2 tablespoons chopped fresh basil; toss with pasta.

4 Margherita Pasta: Heat 1 can (14.5 ounces) undrained diced tomatoes with 2 tablespoons basil, garlic and oregano and toss with hot cooked pasta; gently stir in fresh mozzarella cheese cut into ¼-inch cubes.

5 Pepperoni and Olive Sauce: Heat 1 cup tomato pasta sauce or pizza sauce with 4 cups chopped pepperoni and 2 tablespoons sliced ripe olives. Toss with or serve over hot cooked pasta.

6 Shrimp Marinara Sauce: Heat 10 ounces refrigerated marinara sauce with 8 ounces cooked medium shrimp, 2 tablespoons chopped fresh basil and crushed red pepper flakes, if desired. Toss with or serve over hot cooked pasta.

Italian Sausage with Tomatoes and Penne

ITALIAN SAUSAGE WITH TOMATOES AND PENNE

PREP 25 min TOTAL 25 min • **4 servings**

- 3 cups uncooked penne pasta (9 oz)
- 1 lb uncooked Italian sausage links, cut crosswise into ¼-inch slices
- ½ cup beef broth (for homemade broth, see page 530)
- 1 medium yellow summer squash, cut in half lengthwise, then cut crosswise into ¼-inch slices
- 2 cups grape or cherry tomatoes, cut in half lengthwise
- ¼ cup chopped fresh or 1 tablespoon dried basil leaves
- 6 green onions, cut into ½-inch pieces
- 2 tablespoons extra-virgin olive oil
  Shaved Parmesan cheese, if desired

1 Cook and drain pasta as directed on package.

2 Meanwhile, spray 12-inch skillet with cooking spray; heat over medium-high heat. Cook sausage in skillet 4 to 6 minutes, stirring frequently, until brown. Stir in broth; reduce heat to medium. Cover and cook 5 minutes.

3 Stir in squash, tomatoes and 2 tablespoons of the basil. Heat to boiling; reduce heat to low. Cover and simmer 5 minutes, stirring occasionally. Stir in onions. Simmer uncovered 1 minute.

4 Toss pasta, oil and remaining 2 tablespoons basil. Divide pasta among individual bowls. Top with sausage mixture and cheese.

1 Serving: Calories 490; Total Fat 31g (Saturated Fat 9g; Trans Fat 0g); Cholesterol 70mg; Sodium 1140mg; Total Carbohydrate 30g (Dietary Fiber 3g); Protein 21g **Exchanges:** 1 Starch, ½ Other Carbohydrate, 2 Vegetable, 2 High-Fat Meat, 3 Fat **Carbohydrate Choices:** 2

GARDEN VEGETABLE SPAGHETTI

PREP 10 min TOTAL 25 min • **6 servings**

- 1 package (16 oz) spaghetti
- 2 tablespoons olive or vegetable oil
- 2 medium carrots, sliced (1 cup)
- 1 medium onion, diced (½ cup)
- 2 medium zucchini, cut into ½-inch slices (4 cups)*
- 2 cloves garlic, finely chopped
- 3 medium tomatoes, cut into 1-inch pieces
- ½ cup frozen sweet peas (from 12-oz bag), cooked, drained
- 1 tablespoon chopped fresh or 1 teaspoon dried basil leaves
- ½ teaspoon salt
- ¼ teaspoon pepper
- ⅔ cup grated Parmesan cheese

1 Cook and drain spaghetti as directed on package.

2 Meanwhile, in 10-inch skillet, heat oil over medium-high heat. Cook carrots, onion, zucchini and garlic in oil, stirring frequently, until vegetables are crisp-tender.

3 Stir in remaining ingredients except cheese; cook until hot. Serve vegetable mixture over spaghetti. Sprinkle with cheese.

1 small eggplant (about 12 oz), peeled and diced (3½ cups), can be substituted for the zucchini.

1 Serving: Calories 440; Total Fat 10g (Saturated Fat 3g; Trans Fat 0g); Cholesterol 10mg; Sodium 430mg; Total Carbohydrate 71g (Dietary Fiber 7g); Protein 17g **Exchanges:** 4 Starch, 2 Vegetable, 1½ Fat **Carbohydrate Choices:** 5

Garden Vegetable Spaghetti

MANICOTTI

PREP 40 min TOTAL 1 hr 35 min • **7 servings**

- 14 uncooked manicotti pasta shells
- 1 lb lean (at least 80%) ground beef
- 1 cup sliced fresh mushrooms (3 oz)*
- 1 large onion, chopped (1 cup)
- 2 cloves garlic, finely chopped
- 1 jar (24 to 28 oz) tomato pasta sauce (for homemade sauce, see page 370)
- 2 boxes (9 oz each) frozen chopped spinach, thawed
- 2 cups small-curd cottage cheese
- ⅓ cup grated Parmesan cheese
- ¼ teaspoon ground nutmeg
- ¼ teaspoon pepper
- 2 cups shredded mozzarella cheese (8 oz)
- 2 tablespoons grated Parmesan cheese

1 Cook and drain pasta shells as directed on package, using minimum cook time (to help prevent shells from tearing while filling).

2 Meanwhile, in 10-inch skillet, cook beef, mushrooms, onion and garlic over medium heat 8 to 10 minutes, stirring occasionally, until beef is thoroughly cooked; drain. Stir in pasta sauce.

3 Heat oven to 350°F. Spray 13x9-inch (3-quart) glass baking dish with cooking spray.

4 Squeeze thawed spinach to drain; spread on paper towels and pat dry. In medium bowl, mix spinach, cottage cheese, ⅓ cup Parmesan cheese, nutmeg and pepper.

5 In baking dish, spread 1 cup of the beef mixture. Fill pasta shells with spinach mixture; place on beef mixture in dish. Pour remaining beef mixture evenly over shells, covering completely. Sprinkle with mozzarella cheese and 2 tablespoons Parmesan cheese.

6 Cover; bake 30 minutes. Uncover; bake 20 to 25 minutes longer or until hot and bubbly.

1 can (4 oz) mushrooms pieces and stems, drained, can be substituted for the fresh mushrooms.

1 Serving: Calories 570; Total Fat 21g (Saturated Fat 10g; Trans Fat 0.5g); Cholesterol 70mg; Sodium 1360mg; Total Carbohydrate 55g (Dietary Fiber 6g); Protein 39g **Exchanges:** 2½ Starch, 1 Other Carbohydrate, 4½ Lean Meat, 1 Fat **Carbohydrate Choices:** 3½

Filling Manicotti Shells

Spoon filling into resealable food-storage plastic bag; seal bag.

With scissors, make ½ inch cut from from one corner of bag.

Insert tip of bag into each manicotti shell; gently squeeze filling into each shell.

Or use teaspoon to fill shells.

Manicotti

Heirloom Recipe and New Twist

Identical to the recipe included in the 1995 edition of the Betty Crocker Cookbook, this lasagna continues as a favorite and is often requested. For the new twist, we've included a great shortcut make-ahead lasagna-flavored casserole perfect for families or entertaining.

CLASSIC

ITALIAN SAUSAGE LASAGNA

PREP 1 hr **TOTAL** 2 hr • **8 servings**

- 1 lb bulk Italian sausage or lean (at least 80%) ground beef
- 1 medium onion, chopped (½ cup)
- 1 clove garlic, finely chopped
- 3 tablespoons chopped fresh parsley
- 1 tablespoon chopped fresh or 1 teaspoon dried basil leaves
- 1 teaspoon sugar
- 1 can (15 oz) tomato sauce
- 1 can (14.5 oz) whole tomatoes, undrained
- 8 uncooked lasagna noodles
- 1 container (15 to 16 oz) ricotta cheese or small-curd cottage cheese
- ½ cup grated Parmesan cheese
- 1 tablespoon chopped fresh or 1½ teaspoons dried oregano leaves
- 2 cups shredded mozzarella cheese (8 oz)

1 In 10-inch skillet, cook sausage, onion and garlic over medium heat 8 to 10 minutes, stirring occasionally, until sausage is no longer pink; drain.

2 Stir in 2 tablespoons of the parsley, the basil, sugar, tomato sauce and tomatoes, breaking up tomatoes with a fork. Heat to boiling, stirring occasionally; reduce heat. Simmer uncovered about 45 minutes or until slightly thickened.

3 Heat oven to 350°F. Cook and drain noodles as directed on package. Meanwhile, in small bowl, mix ricotta cheese, ¼ cup of the Parmesan cheese, the oregano and remaining 1 tablespoon parsley.

4 In ungreased 13x9-inch (3-quart) glass baking dish, spread half of the sausage mixture (about 2 cups). Top with 4 noodles. Spread half of the cheese mixture (about 1 cup) over noodles. Sprinkle with half of the mozzarella cheese. Repeat layers, ending with mozzarella. Sprinkle with remaining ¼ cup Parmesan cheese.

5 Cover; bake 30 minutes. Uncover; bake about 15 minutes longer or until hot and bubbly. Let stand 15 minutes before cutting.

1 Serving: Calories 430; Total Fat 23g (Saturated Fat 11g; Trans Fat 0g); Cholesterol 70mg; Sodium 1110mg; Total Carbohydrate 28g (Dietary Fiber 3g); Protein 28g **Exchanges:** 2 Starch, 3 Medium-Fat Meat, 1 Fat **Carbohydrate Choices:** 2

MAKE AHEAD DIRECTIONS Cover unbaked lasagna with foil; refrigerate no longer than 24 hours or freeze up to 2 months. Bake covered 45 minutes, then bake uncovered 15 to 20 minutes longer (35 to 45 minutes if frozen). Check the center and bake a little longer if necessary until hot and bubbly.

EASY ITALIAN SAUSAGE LASAGNA

Substitute 4 cups (from two 26- to 28-oz jars) tomato pasta sauce with meat for the first 8 ingredients. Omit Steps 1 and 2.

Lasagna Noodles

There are a variety of brands of lasagna noodles. Cook the noodles in boiling water, following the directions on the package, just until tender or al dente. If the noodles are overcooked, they might fall apart while you are layering the lasagna. After cooking the noodles, place them in cold water until you're ready to layer. This keeps them from sticking together.

See how to make **lasagna**: Visit bettycrocker.com/BCcookbook

RAVIOLI SAUSAGE LASAGNA

PREP 20 min **TOTAL** 9 hr 30 min • **8 servings**

- 1¼ **lb bulk regular or spicy Italian pork sausage**
- 3½ **cups Marinara Sauce (page 371) or Italian Tomato Sauce (page 370)***
- 1 **bag (25 to 27½ oz) frozen beef, cheese, chicken and herb, sausage or butternut squash–filled ravioli**
- 2½ **cups shredded mozzarella cheese (10 oz)**
- ½ **cup shredded Asiago or Parmesan cheese**
- 2 **tablespoons grated Parmesan cheese**

1 In 10-inch skillet, cook sausage over medium heat, stirring occasionally, until no longer pink; drain.

2 In ungreased 13x9-inch (3-quart) glass baking dish, spread ½ cup of the pasta sauce. Arrange single layer of frozen ravioli over sauce; evenly pour 1 cup pasta sauce over ravioli. Sprinkle evenly with 1½ cups sausage, 1 cup of the mozzarella and ¼ cup of the Asiago cheese. Repeat layers with remaining ravioli, pasta sauce and sausage.

3 Cover tightly with foil; refrigerate at least 8 hours but no longer than 24 hours.

4 Heat oven to 350°F. Bake covered 45 minutes. Remove foil; sprinkle with remaining 1½ cups mozzarella and ¼ cup Asiago cheeses and the grated Parmesan cheese. Bake 15 to 20 minutes longer or until cheese is melted and lasagna is hot in center. Let stand 10 minutes before serving.

1 jar (26 to 28 oz) tomato pasta sauce (any variety) can be substituted.

1 Serving: Calories 440; Total Fat 23g (Saturated Fat 11g; Trans Fat 0g); Cholesterol 65mg; Sodium 870mg; Total Carbohydrate 34g (Dietary Fiber 2g); Protein 25g **Exchanges:** 2 Starch, ½ Other Carbohydrate, 1 Lean Meat, ½ Medium-Fat Meat, 1 High-Fat Meat, 1½ Fat **Carbohydrate Choices:** 2

RAVIOLI SAUSAGE LASAGNA WITH OLIVES AND SUN-DRIED TOMATOES Stir in 1 can (2¼ oz) sliced ripe olives, drained, and ¼ cup julienne-cut sun-dried tomatoes in oil and herbs, drained (from 8-oz jar) into drained sausage in Step 1. Continue as directed.

RAVIOLI SAUSAGE-MUSHROOM LASAGNA Cook 1½ cups sliced fresh mushrooms with the sausage in Step 1. Continue as directed.

Italian Sausage Lasagna

Ravioli Sausage Lasagna

CREAMY SEAFOOD LASAGNA

PREP 20 min **TOTAL** 1 hr 20 min • **8 servings**

- 9 uncooked lasagna noodles
- ¼ cup butter
- 1 medium onion, finely chopped (½ cup)
- 2 cloves garlic, finely chopped
- ¼ cup all-purpose flour
- 2 cups half-and-half
- 1 cup chicken broth (for homemade broth, see page 528)
- ⅓ cup dry sherry or chicken broth
- ½ teaspoon salt
- ¼ teaspoon pepper
- 1 container (15 oz) ricotta cheese
- ½ cup grated Parmesan cheese
- 1 egg, slightly beaten
- ¼ cup chopped fresh parsley
- 2 packages (8 oz each) frozen salad-style imitation crabmeat, thawed, drained and chopped
- 2 packages (4 oz each) frozen cooked salad shrimp, thawed, drained
- 3 cups shredded mozzarella cheese (12 oz)
- 1 tablespoon chopped fresh parsley, if desired

1 Heat oven to 350°F. Cook and drain noodles as directed on package.

2 Meanwhile, in 3-quart saucepan, melt butter over medium heat. Cook onion and garlic in butter 2 to 3 minutes, stirring occasionally, until onion is crisp-tender. Stir in flour; cook and stir until bubbly. Gradually stir in half-and-half, broth, sherry, salt and pepper. Heat to boiling, stirring constantly. Boil and stir 1 minute; remove from heat.

Creamy Seafood Lasagna

3 In medium bowl, mix ricotta cheese, Parmesan cheese, egg and ¼ cup parsley.

4 In ungreased 13x9-inch (3-quart) glass baking dish, spread ¾ cup of the sauce. Top with 3 noodles. Spread half of the imitation crabmeat and shrimp over noodles; spread with ¾ cup of the sauce. Sprinkle with 1 cup of the mozzarella cheese; top with 3 noodles. Spread ricotta mixture over noodles; spread with ¾ cup of the sauce. Sprinkle with 1 cup of the mozzarella cheese; top with remaining noodles. Spread with remaining imitation crabmeat, shrimp and sauce. Sprinkle with remaining 1 cup mozzarella cheese.

5 Bake uncovered 40 to 45 minutes or until cheese is light golden brown. Let stand 15 minutes before cutting. Sprinkle with 1 tablespoon parsley.

1 Serving: Calories 560; Total Fat 29g (Saturated Fat 17g; Trans Fat 1g); Cholesterol 180mg; Sodium 1400mg; Total Carbohydrate 33g (Dietary Fiber 2g); Protein 41g **Exchanges:** 2 Starch, 5 Medium-Fat Meat, ½ Fat **Carbohydrate Choices:** 2

LIGHTER DIRECTIONS For 11 grams of fat and 430 calories per serving, decrease butter to 2 tablespoons; use fat-free half-and-half, fat-free ricotta cheese, reduced-fat Parmesan cheese and reduced-fat mozzarella cheese.

CHEESY PIZZA CASSEROLE

PREP 20 min **TOTAL** 55 min • **6 servings**

- 3 cups uncooked rigatoni pasta (9 oz)
- ½ lb lean (at least 80%) ground beef
- ½ cup chopped pepperoni
- ¼ cup sliced pitted ripe olives
- 2 jars or cans (14 to 15 oz each) pizza sauce
- 1 cup shredded mozzarella cheese (4 oz)

1 Heat oven to 350°F. Cook and drain pasta as directed on package.

2 Meanwhile, in 10-inch skillet, cook beef over medium heat 8 to 10 minutes, stirring occasionally, until thoroughly cooked; drain. In ungreased 2½-quart casserole, mix pasta, beef, pepperoni, olives and pizza sauce.

3 Cover; bake about 30 minutes or until hot and bubbly. Sprinkle with cheese. Bake uncovered about 5 minutes longer or until cheese is melted.

1 Serving: Calories 430; Total Fat 13g (Saturated Fat 4.5g; Trans Fat 0g); Cholesterol 35mg; Sodium 850mg; Total Carbohydrate 58g (Dietary Fiber 5g); Protein 19g **Exchanges:** 4 Starch, 1½ Medium-Fat Meat **Carbohydrate Choices:** 4

CHEESY BAKED RIGATONI

PREP 25 min TOTAL 1 hr 5 min • **8 servings**

  3 **cups uncooked rigatoni pasta (9 oz)**
  1 **lb bulk Italian pork sausage**
  1 **can (28 oz) crushed tomatoes, undrained**
  3 **cloves garlic, finely chopped**
  ¼ **cup chopped fresh or 1 tablespoon dried basil leaves**
  1 **package (8 oz) sliced fresh mushrooms (3 cups)**
  1 **jar (7 oz) roasted red bell peppers, drained, chopped**
  1 **cup shredded Parmesan cheese (4 oz)**
  2½ **cups shredded mozzarella cheese (10 oz)**

1 Heat oven to 375°F. Spray 13x9-inch (3-quart) glass baking dish with cooking spray. Cook and drain pasta as directed on package, using minimum cooking time.

2 Meanwhile, in 10-inch skillet, cook sausage over medium heat 8 to 10 minutes, stirring occasionally, until no longer pink; drain. In medium bowl, mix tomatoes, garlic and basil.

3 In baking dish, layer half each of the pasta, sausage, mushrooms, roasted peppers, Parmesan cheese, tomato mixture and mozzarella cheese. Repeat layers.

4 Bake uncovered 35 to 40 minutes or until hot in center and cheese is golden brown.

1 Serving: Calories 410; Total Fat 20g (Saturated Fat 10g; Trans Fat 0g); Cholesterol 55mg; Sodium 730mg; Total Carbohydrate 33g (Dietary Fiber 3g); Protein 26g **Exchanges:** 1½ Starch, ½ Other Carbohydrate, 3 Medium-Fat Meat, 1 Fat **Carbohydrate Choices:** 2

MEATLESS CHEESY BAKED RIGATONI Omit sausage. Stir 1 can (15 oz) white or red kidney beans in with the tomato mixture in Step 2. Bake as directed.

TUNA-NOODLE CASSEROLE

PREP 20 min TOTAL 50 min • **6 servings**

  1¼ **cups uncooked medium egg noodles, medium pasta shells or elbow macaroni (3 to 4 oz)**
  2 **tablespoons butter**
  2 **tablespoons all-purpose flour**
  ¾ **teaspoon salt**
  2 **cups milk**
  1 **cup shredded American or process sharp Cheddar cheese (4 oz)**
  1 **cup frozen sweet peas, thawed***
  1 **can (12 oz) tuna in water, drained**
  ⅔ **cup dry bread crumbs****
  1 **tablespoon butter, melted**

1 Heat oven to 350°F. Cook and drain noodles as directed on package.

2 Meanwhile, in 1½-quart saucepan, melt 2 tablespoons butter over low heat. Stir in flour and salt. Cook over medium heat, stirring constantly, until smooth and bubbly; remove from heat. Gradually stir in milk. Heat to boiling, stirring constantly. Boil and stir 1 minute. Stir in cheese until melted. Add noodles, peas and tuna; mix well.

3 Spoon into ungreased 2-quart casserole. Cover; bake about 25 minutes or until hot and bubbly.

4 In small bowl, mix bread crumbs and 1 tablespoon butter. Sprinkle over casserole. Bake uncovered about 5 minutes longer or until topping is toasted.

*2 cups fresh broccoli florets, cooked until crisp-tender and drained, can be substituted for the peas. Or, use frozen broccoli florets, thawed and drained (do not cook).

**1 cup broken or crushed regular or sour cream and onion–flavored potato chips can be substituted for the bread crumbs. Omit butter.

1 Serving: Calories 380; Total Fat 15g (Saturated Fat 8g; Trans Fat 0.5g); Cholesterol 55mg; Sodium 910mg; Total Carbohydrate 37g (Dietary Fiber 3g); Protein 25g **Exchanges:** 2 Starch, 1 Vegetable, 2 Medium-Fat Meat, 1 Fat **Carbohydrate Choices:** 2½

SALMON-NOODLE CASSEROLE Substitute 1 can (14¾ oz) red or pink salmon, drained, skin and bones removed, flaked, for the tuna.

CHICKEN TETRAZZINI

PREP 20 min TOTAL 50 min • **6 servings**

- 1 package (7 oz) spaghetti, broken into thirds
- ¼ cup butter
- ¼ cup all-purpose flour
- ½ teaspoon salt
- ¼ teaspoon pepper
- 1 cup chicken broth (for homemade broth, see page 528)
- 1 cup whipping cream
- 2 tablespoons dry sherry or water
- 2 cups cubed cooked chicken or turkey
- 1 jar (4.5 oz) sliced mushrooms, drained
- ½ cup grated Parmesan cheese

1 Heat oven to 350°F. Cook and drain spaghetti as directed on package.

2 Meanwhile, in 2-quart saucepan, melt butter over low heat. Stir in flour, salt and pepper. Cook, stirring constantly, until flour mixture is smooth and bubbly; remove from heat. Stir in broth and whipping cream. Heat to boiling, stirring constantly. Boil and stir 1 minute.

3 Stir spaghetti, sherry, chicken and mushrooms into sauce. Spoon into ungreased 2-quart casserole. Sprinkle with cheese. Bake uncovered about 30 minutes or until bubbly in center.

1 Serving: Calories 470; Total Fat 27g (Saturated Fat 14g; Trans Fat 1g); Cholesterol 110mg; Sodium 810mg; Total Carbohydrate 33g (Dietary Fiber 2g); Protein 23g **Exchanges:** 2 Starch, 2½ Medium-Fat Meat, 2½ Fat **Carbohydrate Choices:** 2

CHICKEN- AND SPINACH-STUFFED SHELLS

PREP 30 min TOTAL 1 hr 10 min • **6 servings**

- 18 large pasta shells (from 16-oz package)
- 1 container (15 oz) whole-milk ricotta cheese
- 1 egg, slightly beaten
- ¼ cup grated Parmesan cheese
- 2 cups frozen cut-leaf spinach, thawed, squeezed to drain
- 1 cup chopped cooked chicken
- 1 jar (26 oz) tomato pasta sauce (for homemade sauce, see page 370)
- 2 cups shredded Italian cheese blend (8 oz)

1 Heat oven to 350°F. Cook and drain pasta as directed on package. Rinse with cool water; drain.

2 Meanwhile, in medium bowl, mix ricotta cheese, egg, Parmesan cheese, spinach and chicken.

3 Spread 1 cup of the pasta sauce in bottom of ungreased 13x9-inch (3-quart) glass baking dish. Spoon about 2 tablespoons ricotta mixture into each pasta shell. Arrange shells, filled sides up, on sauce in baking dish. Spoon remaining sauce over stuffed shells.

4 Cover dish with foil; bake 30 minutes. Sprinkle with Italian cheese blend. Bake uncovered 5 to 10 minutes longer or until cheese is melted.

Filling Pasta Shells

Using teaspoon, spoon filling into each cooked pasta shell.

Chicken- and Spinach-Stuffed Shells

1 Serving: Calories 570; Total Fat 28g (Saturated Fat 15g; Trans Fat 0.5g); Cholesterol 120mg; Sodium 1330mg; Total Carbohydrate 48g (Dietary Fiber 4g); Protein 33g **Exchanges:** 3 Starch, 1 Vegetable, 3 Medium-Fat Meat, 2 Fat **Carbohydrate Choices:** 3

MAKE AHEAD **DIRECTIONS** Make as directed through Step 3. Cover tightly and refrigerate up to 24 hours. Add 5 to 10 minutes to the first bake time before topping with cheese.

SHRIMP AND SNAP PEA CASSEROLE

PREP 15 min TOTAL 40 min • **6 servings**

3 cups uncooked penne pasta (9 oz)
2 cups fresh sugar snap peas*
½ cup butter
2 cups sliced fresh mushrooms (about 5 oz)
2 cloves garlic, finely chopped
½ cup all-purpose flour
½ teaspoon salt
¼ teaspoon pepper
2 cups milk
2 tablespoons sherry or dry white wine, if desired
1 can (14 oz) chicken broth (for homemade broth, see page 528)
¾ cup shredded fontina or Swiss cheese (3 oz)
1 lb cooked deveined peeled medium shrimp, thawed if frozen, tail shells removed
⅓ cup shredded Parmesan cheese
⅓ cup sliced almonds

1 Heat oven to 350°F. Spray 13x9-inch (3-quart) glass baking dish with cooking spray.

2 Cook pasta as directed on package, adding peas to the cooking water with the pasta during the last 5 minutes of cooking. Drain.

3 Meanwhile, in 4-quart saucepan or Dutch oven, melt butter over low heat. Cook mushrooms and garlic in butter, stirring occasionally, until mushrooms are tender. Stir in flour, salt and pepper. Cook over medium heat, stirring constantly, until mixture is smooth and bubbly. Gradually stir in milk, sherry and broth until smooth. Heat to boiling, stirring constantly. Stir in fontina cheese until melted; remove from heat.

4 Stir pasta, peas and shrimp into mushroom mixture. Pour into baking dish. Sprinkle with Parmesan cheese and almonds.

5 Bake uncovered 20 to 25 minutes or until cheese is golden brown.

2 cups frozen sugar snap pea pods (from 1-lb bag), thawed and drained, can be substituted. Do not add to pasta cooking water; stir into pasta, shrimp and mushroom mixture in Step 4.

1 Serving: Calories 590; Total Fat 27g (Saturated Fat 13g; Trans Fat 1g); Cholesterol 215mg; Sodium 980mg; Total Carbohydrate 51g (Dietary Fiber 5g); Protein 35g **Exchanges:** 3 Starch, 1 Vegetable, 3½ Medium-Fat Meat, 1½ Fat **Carbohydrate Choices:** 3½

SPINACH FETTUCCINE WITH CHICKEN AND BACON

PREP 20 min TOTAL 50 min • **4 servings**

1 package (9 oz) refrigerated spinach fettuccine
3 tablespoons butter
3 tablespoons all-purpose flour
1 can (14 oz) chicken broth (for homemade broth, see page 528)
½ cup half-and-half
1½ cups cubed cooked chicken
½ cup oil-packed sun-dried tomatoes, drained, cut into thin strips
2 slices bacon, crisply cooked, crumbled (2 tablespoons)
3 tablespoons shredded Parmesan cheese

1 Heat oven to 350°F. Spray 8-inch square (2-quart) glass baking dish with cooking spray.

2 Cook and drain fettuccine as directed on package.

3 Meanwhile, in 2-quart saucepan, melt butter over medium heat. Stir in flour. Gradually stir in broth. Heat to boiling, stirring constantly; remove from heat. Stir in half-and-half. Stir in chicken, tomatoes and bacon. Add fettuccine; toss gently to mix well.

4 Spoon into baking dish. Sprinkle with cheese. Bake uncovered about 30 minutes or until hot in center.

1 Serving: Calories 540; Total Fat 24g (Saturated Fat 10g; Trans Fat 1g); Cholesterol 140mg; Sodium 740mg; Total Carbohydrate 51g (Dietary Fiber 3g); Protein 30g **Exchanges:** 3 Starch, 1 Vegetable, 3 Medium-Fat Meat, 1 Fat **Carbohydrate Choices:** 3½

SPAGHETTI CARBONARA

Carbonara is a simple Italian dish made with eggs, cheese and bacon. Because the eggs are just tossed with the hot pasta and just slightly cooked to help thicken the sauce, be sure to use pasteurized eggs for the recipe.

PREP 10 min TOTAL 25 min • **6 servings**

- 1 package (16 oz) spaghetti
- 1 clove garlic, finely chopped
- 6 slices bacon, cut into 1-inch pieces
- 3 pasteurized eggs*, beaten, or ¾ cup fat-free egg product
- 1 tablespoon olive or vegetable oil
- ½ cup freshly grated Parmesan cheese
- ½ cup freshly grated Romano cheese
- 2 tablespoons chopped fresh parsley
- ¼ teaspoon pepper
  Additional freshly grated Parmesan cheese, if desired
  Freshly ground pepper, if desired

1 In 4-quart Dutch oven or saucepan, cook and drain spaghetti as directed on package; return to Dutch oven.

2 Meanwhile, in 10-inch skillet, cook garlic and bacon over medium heat, stirring occasionally, until bacon is crisp; drain.

3 In small bowl, mix eggs, oil, ½ cup Parmesan cheese, Romano cheese, parsley and ¼ teaspoon pepper.

4 Add bacon mixture and egg mixture to hot cooked spaghetti. Cook over low heat, tossing mixture constantly, until egg mixture coats spaghetti; remove from heat. Serve with additional Parmesan cheese and freshly ground pepper.

Pasteurized eggs are uncooked eggs that have been heat-treated to kill bacteria which can cause food poisoning and gastrointestinal distress. Because the eggs in this recipe are not cooked, be sure to use pasteurized eggs. They can be found in the dairy case at large supermarkets. Fat-free egg product is also pasteurized.

1 Serving: Calories 450; Total Fat 13g (Saturated Fat 5g; Trans Fat 0g); Cholesterol 25mg; Sodium 450mg; Total Carbohydrate 62g (Dietary Fiber 5g); Protein 22g **Exchanges:** 4 Starch, ½ Medium-Fat Meat **Carbohydrate Choices:** 4

CHICKEN AND SPAGHETTI CARBONARA

Add 2 cups cut-up cooked chicken in Step 4 before heating.

PASTA WITH PROSCIUTTO AND ASIAGO CHEESE FAST LOWER CALORIE

PREP 10 min TOTAL 20 min • **4 servings**

- 2 cups uncooked fusilli (corkscrew) pasta (6 oz)
- 2 tablespoons olive or vegetable oil
- 1 package (8 oz) sliced fresh mushrooms (3 cups)
- 6 medium green onions, cut into ½-inch pieces
- 1 medium red bell pepper, coarsely chopped (1 cup)
- 1 clove garlic, finely chopped
- 1 package (3 oz) thinly sliced prosciutto, cut into thin strips*
- 1 tablespoon chopped fresh or ½ teaspoon dried basil leaves
- 2 teaspoons chopped fresh or ¼ teaspoon dried oregano leaves
- ¼ teaspoon salt
- ¼ cup shredded Asiago cheese (1 oz)

1 Cook and drain pasta as directed on package.

2 Meanwhile, in 10-inch nonstick skillet, heat 1 tablespoon of the oil over medium-high heat. Cook mushrooms, onions, bell pepper and garlic in oil 2 to 3 minutes, stirring occasionally, until vegetables are tender.

3 Stir in prosciutto, basil, oregano and salt. Stir in pasta and remaining 1 tablespoon oil; toss. Sprinkle with cheese.

Half of a 6-oz package thinly sliced cooked ham may be substituted for the prosciutto.

1 Serving: Calories 320; Total Fat 12g (Saturated Fat 3g; Trans Fat 0g); Cholesterol 20mg; Sodium 560mg; Total Carbohydrate 39g (Dietary Fiber 4g); Protein 15g **Exchanges:** 2 Starch, 2 Vegetable, 1 Lean Meat, 1½ Fat **Carbohydrate Choices:** 2½

Pasta with Prosciutto and Asiago Cheese

SPANISH CLAMS, SAUSAGE AND LINGUINE

PREP 15 min TOTAL 40 min • **6 servings**

- ½ lb bulk hot Italian pork sausage
- 3 medium onions, chopped (1½ cups)
- 2 medium carrots, chopped (1 cup)
- 3 cloves garlic, finely chopped
- 1 can (28 oz) crushed tomatoes, undrained
- 2 cans (14.5 oz each) diced tomatoes with roasted garlic, undrained
- ½ cup dry red wine or clam juice
- 1½ teaspoons ground cumin
- 1 teaspoon dried rosemary leaves, crumbled
- ½ cup small pimiento-stuffed olives, coarsely chopped
- 24 unopened littleneck clams (about 2 lb), scrubbed*
- 12 oz uncooked linguine
  Grated Romano or Parmesan cheese, if desired

1 In 4-quart Dutch oven, cook sausage, onions, carrots and garlic over medium-high heat 5 to 7 minutes, stirring frequently, until sausage is no longer pink; drain.

2 Stir in remaining ingredients except clams, linguine and cheese. Heat to boiling; reduce heat to medium-low. Partially cover and simmer 10 minutes.

3 Meanwhile, cook and drain linguine as directed on package; keep warm.

4 Add clams to sausage mixture. Cover and cook over medium-high heat 5 to 7 minutes or until clams open. Discard any unopened clams. Serve clam sauce over linguine. Serve with cheese.

3 cans (10 oz each) whole clams, drained, can be substituted for the fresh clams.

1 Serving: Calories 440; Total Fat 11g (Saturated Fat 3g; Trans Fat 0g); Cholesterol 35mg; Sodium 870mg; Total Carbohydrate 65g (Dietary Fiber 8g); Protein 21g **Exchanges:** 3 Starch, 4 Vegetable, ½ Medium-Fat Meat, 1 Fat **Carbohydrate Choices:** 4

SPANISH CLAMS, CHORIZO AND PENNE

Substitute chorizo sausage for the Italian sausage and penne for the linguine. Use dried basil instead of rosemary.

SPAGHETTI WITH WHITE CLAM SAUCE

PREP 10 min TOTAL 25 min • **4 servings**

- 1 package (7 oz) spaghetti
- ¼ cup butter or olive oil
- 2 cloves garlic, finely chopped
- 2 tablespoons chopped fresh parsley
- 2 cans (6½ oz each) minced clams, undrained
- ½ cup grated Parmesan cheese
  Additional chopped fresh parsley

1 Cook and drain spaghetti as directed on package.

2 Meanwhile, in 1½-quart saucepan, melt butter over medium heat. Cook garlic in butter about 3 minutes, stirring occasionally, until light golden. Stir in 2 tablespoons parsley and the clams. Heat to boiling; reduce heat. Simmer uncovered 3 to 5 minutes.

3 In large bowl, toss spaghetti and clam sauce. Sprinkle with cheese and additional parsley.

1 Serving: Calories 480; Total Fat 18g (Saturated Fat 8g, Trans Fat 1g); Cholesterol 100mg; Sodium 410mg; Total Carbohydrate 45g (Dietary Fiber 3g); Protein 36g **Exchanges:** 3 Starch, 3 Medium-Fat Meat, ½ Fat **Carbohydrate Choices:** 3

LINGUINI WITH WHITE CLAM SAUCE AND BASIL

Substitute linguini pasta for the spaghetti and use chopped basil instead of the parsley. Continue as directed.

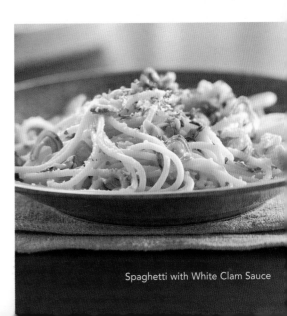

Spaghetti with White Clam Sauce

PAD THAI WITH SHRIMP

Pad Thai is Thailand's most well-known noodle dish, which you'll find on almost all Thai restaurant menus in America. Look for the traditional Asian ingredients in the ethnic-foods aisle.

PREP 35 min TOTAL 40 min • **4 servings**

- 1 **package (6 to 8 oz) linguine-style stir-fry rice noodles***
- 3 **tablespoons fresh lime juice**
- 3 **tablespoons packed brown sugar**
- 2 **tablespoons fish sauce or soy sauce**
- 2 **tablespoons soy sauce**
- 1 **tablespoon rice vinegar or white vinegar**
- ¾ **teaspoon ground red pepper (cayenne)**
- 3 **tablespoons vegetable oil**
- 3 **cloves garlic, finely chopped**
- 1 **medium shallot, finely chopped, or ¼ cup finely chopped onion**
- 2 **eggs, beaten**
- 1 **package (12 oz) frozen cooked deveined peeled medium shrimp, thawed**
- ¼ **cup finely chopped dry-roasted peanuts**
- 3 **cups fresh bean sprouts**
- 4 **medium green onions, thinly sliced (¼ cup)**
- ¼ **cup firmly packed fresh cilantro leaves**

1 In 3-quart saucepan, heat 4 cups water to boiling. Remove from heat; add noodles (push noodles into water with back of spoon if necessary to cover completely with water). Soak 3 to 5 minutes or until noodles are soft but firm. Drain; rinse noodles with cold water.

2 In small bowl, stir lime juice, brown sugar, fish sauce, soy sauce, vinegar, red pepper and 1 tablespoon of the oil until well mixed; set aside.

3 In nonstick wok or 12-inch skillet, heat remaining 2 tablespoons oil over medium heat. Cook garlic and shallot in oil about 30 seconds, stirring constantly, until starting to brown. Add eggs. Cook about 2 minutes, stirring gently and constantly, until scrambled but still moist.

4 Stir in noodles and lime juice mixture. Increase heat to high. Cook about 1 minute, tossing constantly with 2 wooden spoons, until sauce begins to thicken. Add remaining ingredients except cilantro. Cook 2 to 3 minutes, tossing with 2 wooden spoons, until bean sprouts are no longer crisp and noodles are tender.

5 Place noodle mixture on serving platter. Sprinkle with cilantro. Garnish with additional chopped dry-roasted peanuts and green onions if desired.

*Thin or thick rice stick noodles can be substituted for the linguine-style stir-fry rice noodles.

1 Serving: Calories 560; Total Fat 23g (Saturated Fat 4g; Trans Fat 0g); Cholesterol 240mg; Sodium 1310mg; Total Carbohydrate 59g (Dietary Fiber 4g); Protein 29g **Exchanges:** 3 Starch, ½ Other Carbohydrate, 1 Vegetable, 2½ Lean Meat, 2½ Fat **Carbohydrate Choices:** 4

PAD THAI WITH CHICKEN Substitute 2 cups chopped cooked chicken for the shrimp.

PAD THAI WITH PORK Substitute 2 cups shredded cooked pork for the shrimp.

Pad Thai with Shrimp

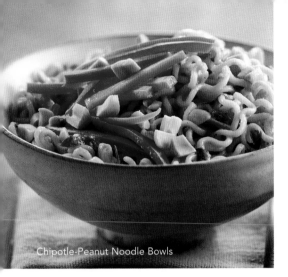

Chipotle-Peanut Noodle Bowls

CHIPOTLE-PEANUT NOODLE BOWLS

PREP 15 min TOTAL 30 min • **4 servings**

- ½ cup creamy peanut butter
- ½ cup apple juice
- 2 tablespoons soy sauce
- 2 chipotle chiles in adobo sauce (from 7-oz can), seeded, chopped
- 1 teaspoon adobo sauce from can of chiles
- ¼ cup chopped fresh cilantro
- 2 medium carrots, cut into julienne strips
- 1 medium red bell pepper, cut into julienne strips
- 1 package (8 to 10 oz) Chinese curly noodles
- 2 tablespoons chopped peanuts

1 In large bowl, mix peanut butter, apple juice, soy sauce, chiles and adobo sauce until smooth. Stir in cilantro; set aside.

2 In 2-quart saucepan, heat 4 cups water to boiling. Add carrots and bell pepper; cook 1 minute. Remove from water with slotted spoon. Add noodles to water; cook and drain as directed on package.

3 Add noodles to peanut butter mixture; toss. Divide noodles among 4 bowls; top with carrots and bell pepper. Sprinkle with peanuts.

1 Serving: Calories 590; Total Fat 36g (Saturated Fat 6g; Trans Fat 0g); Cholesterol 0mg; Sodium 980mg; Total Carbohydrate 51g (Dietary Fiber 7g); Protein 15g **Exchanges:** 3 Starch, 1 Vegetable, ½ High-Fat Meat, 6 Fat **Carbohydrate Choices:** 3½

FETTUCCINE ALFREDO

Here's our version of the famous dish created in the early 1900s by restaurateur Alfredo di Lello in Rome. It is just as rich with butter, cream and cheese as the original was then. The combination of whipping cream and Parmesan cheese is the secret to thickening the sauce.

PREP 10 min TOTAL 25 min • **4 servings**

- 8 oz uncooked fettuccine

  ALFREDO SAUCE
- ½ cup butter, cut into pieces
- ½ cup whipping cream
- ¾ cup grated Parmesan cheese
- ½ teaspoon salt
  Dash pepper

  GARNISH
  Chopped fresh parsley, if desired

1 Cook and drain fettuccine as directed on package.

2 Meanwhile, in 10-inch skillet, heat butter and whipping cream over medium heat, stirring frequently, until butter is melted and mixture starts to bubble; reduce heat to low. Simmer 6 minutes, stirring frequently, until slightly thickened; remove from heat. Stir in cheese, salt and pepper.

3 In large bowl, toss fettuccine with sauce until well coated. Sprinkle with parsley.

1 Serving: Calories 570; Total Fat 40g (Saturated Fat 21g; Trans Fat 2g); Cholesterol 155mg; Sodium 810mg; Total Carbohydrate 38g (Dietary Fiber 2g); Protein 15g **Exchanges:** 2½ Starch, 1 High-Fat Meat, 5½ Fat **Carbohydrate Choices:** 2½

LIGHTER DIRECTIONS For 17 grams of fat and 370 calories per serving, decrease butter to ¼ cup and Parmesan cheese to ½ cup; substitute evaporated milk for the whipping cream.

CHICKEN FETTUCCINE ALFREDO Stir in 1½ cups diced cooked chicken with the cheese, salt and pepper.

See how to make **Alfredo sauce:** Visit bettycrocker.com/BCcookbook

Keeping Pasta Hot

If you're using a serving bowl, warm it before adding the pasta. Fill the bowl with hot water and pour out the water just before serving, then spoon pasta into the bowl.

Learn to Make **Macaroni and Cheese**

MACARONI AND CHEESE

Once you've tasted the depth of flavor in our homemade mac and cheese, you'll see why it's the perfect choice for the entire family. Don't even try to compare it to the box variety—it's in a league of its own.

PREP 25 min **TOTAL** 50 min • **4 servings**

1 **package (7 oz) elbow macaroni (2½ cups)**	¼ **teaspoon ground mustard**
¼ **cup butter**	¼ **teaspoon Worcestershire sauce**
¼ **cup all-purpose flour**	2 **cups milk or half-and-half**
½ **teaspoon salt**	2 **cups shredded sharp Cheddar cheese (8 oz)**
¼ **teaspoon pepper**	

1 Heat oven to 350°F. Cook and drain macaroni as directed on package.

2 Meanwhile, in 3-quart saucepan, melt butter over low heat. Stir in flour, salt, pepper, mustard and Worcestershire sauce. Cook over low heat, stirring constantly, until mixture is smooth and bubbly; remove from heat.

3 Stir in milk. Heat to boiling, stirring constantly. Boil and stir 1 minute; remove from heat. Stir in cheese until melted.

4 Gently stir macaroni into cheese sauce. Pour into ungreased 2-quart casserole. Bake uncovered 20 to 25 minutes or until bubbly.

1 Serving (1 Cup): Calories 610; Total Fat 34g (Saturated Fat 19g; Trans Fat 1g); Cholesterol 100mg; Sodium 980mg; Total Carbohydrate 51g (Dietary Fiber 3g); Protein 26g **Exchanges:** 3 Starch, ½ Low-Fat Milk, 2 High-Fat Meat, 2½ Fat **Carbohydrate Choices:** 3½

STOVE-TOP METHOD Make as directed up to stirring in cheese in Step 3. Serve immediately.

LIGHTER **DIRECTIONS** For 10 grams of fat and 390 calories per serving, decrease butter to 2 tablespoons. Use fat-free (skim) milk and 1½ cups reduced-fat Cheddar cheese (6 oz).

BACON MACARONI AND CHEESE Stir in ⅔ cup cooked, crumbled bacon with macaroni in Step 4.

CARAMELIZED ONION MACARONI AND CHEESE Stir in 1 cup Caramelized Onions (page 507) with macaroni in Step 4.

FIRE-ROASTED TOMATO MACARONI AND CHEESE Stir in ½ teaspoon smoked paprika with flour in Step 2. Add 1 can (14.5 oz) fire-roasted diced tomatoes, drained, with macaroni in Step 4.

LOBSTER MACARONI AND CHEESE Add ⅛ teaspoon each ground red pepper (cayenne) and ground nutmeg with flour in Step 2. Substitute ¾ cup each shredded fontina and Gruyère cheese for 1½ cups of the Cheddar. Stir in 2 cups cooked lobster pieces or lump crabmeat with macaroni in Step 4.

SOUTHWEST MACARONI AND CHEESE Omit ground mustard and Worcestershire sauce. Add 2 teaspoons ground ancho chile pepper or chili powder, ½ teaspoon ground cumin and ¼ teaspoon garlic powder with flour in Step 2. Stir in 1 can (4 oz) diced green chiles, ¼ cup thinly sliced green onions, ¼ cup diced bell pepper and ¼ cup chopped fresh cilantro with macaroni in Step 4. Top with coarsely crushed corn chips before serving.

See how to make **macaroni and cheese:** Visit bettycrocker.com/BCcookbook

MACARONI AND CHEESE TOPPINGS

For a little something extra, add one or more of the following on top.

Sprinkle on before baking:

- Mix ½ cup fresh or dried bread crumbs with 2 tablespoons melted butter or olive oil
- One-half cup crushed plain potato chips (flavored chips tend to get too brown if added before baking)
- One-half cup French-fried onions

Add just before removing from oven:

- One-half cup additional shredded cheese (bake 3 to 5 minutes or until cheese is melted)

Sprinkle on about ¼ cup of any of the following after baking—or serve alongside:

- Crushed plain or flavored croutons
- Crushed crackers, flavored potato chips or snack chips
- Chopped fresh parsley or other herbs
- Sliced or cubed avocado
- Thinly sliced or chopped tomatoes
- Salsa or sour cream
- Diced bell peppers
- Sliced olives

Keys to Success

- **Cook pasta before mixing with sauce.** It will not get tender if added uncooked.
- **Cook flour mixture until smooth and bubbly.**
- **Stir constantly while making sauce,** so that the flour mixture thickens the milk evenly.
- **Serve immediately** so pasta will be creamy and not continue to soak up the sauce.

Swap the Cheese

Use any of the following cheeses in place of all or part of the Cheddar in the recipe.

- Asiago or Parmesan (up to 1 cup)
- Blue or Gorgonzola crumbled (up to 1 cup)
- Brie crumbled (up to 1 cup)
- Cheddar (white or smoked)
- Colby
- Edam
- Fontina
- Gouda (regular or smoked)
- Gruyère
- Havarti
- Jarlsberg
- Manchego
- Monterey Jack or pepper Jack
- Swiss

Macaroni and Cheese topped with fresh bread crumbs

PASTA PRIMAVERA

Serve this creamy, vegetable-filled primavera with warm sliced French bread.

PREP 15 min **TOTAL** 35 min • **4 servings**

- 8 oz uncooked fettuccine or linguine
- 1 tablespoon olive or vegetable oil
- 1 cup fresh broccoli florets
- 1 cup fresh cauliflower florets
- 2 medium carrots, thinly sliced (1 cup)
- 1 cup frozen sweet peas, thawed
- 1 small onion, chopped (⅓ cup)
  Alfredo Sauce (page 385) or 1 cup purchased sauce
- 1 tablespoon grated Parmesan cheese

1 Cook and drain fettuccine as directed on package.

2 Meanwhile, in 12-inch skillet, heat oil over medium-high heat. Cook broccoli, cauliflower, carrots, peas and onion in oil 6 to 8 minutes, stirring frequently, until vegetables are crisp-tender. Remove from heat; keep warm.

3 Stir Alfredo sauce into vegetable mixture. Stir in fettuccine; heat through. Sprinkle with cheese.

1 Serving: Calories 530; Total Fat 28g (Saturated Fat 14g; Trans Fat 1g); Cholesterol 115mg; Sodium 520mg; Total Carbohydrate 47g (Dietary Fiber 5g); Protein 20g **Exchanges:** 3 Starch, 1 Vegetable, ½ High-Fat Meat, 4 Fat **Carbohydrate Choices:** 3

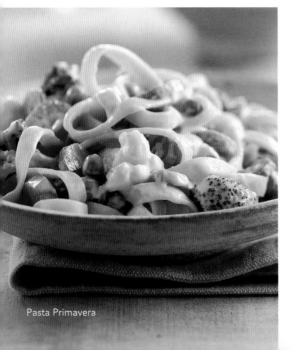

Pasta Primavera

MIXED ROASTED VEGETABLES AND PASTA

PREP 25 min **TOTAL** 1 hr 10 min • **6 servings**

- 1 medium green or yellow bell pepper, cut into 1-inch pieces
- 1 medium red bell pepper, cut into 1-inch pieces
- 1 medium onion, cut into 8 wedges, separated
- 2 medium zucchini, cut into 1-inch pieces
- 1 package (8 oz) fresh whole mushrooms
- 3 tablespoons olive or vegetable oil
- 2 tablespoons red wine vinegar
- 2 teaspoons Italian seasoning
- ½ teaspoon salt
- ¼ teaspoon pepper
- 2 cups uncooked cavatappi or gemelli pasta (about 5 oz)
- 2 medium tomatoes, seeded, cut into 2-inch pieces
- ⅓ cup chopped fresh or 2 tablespoons dried basil leaves
- 2 cups shredded Italian cheese blend (8 oz)

1 Heat oven to 450°F. In 15x10x1-inch pan or shallow 3-quart casserole, place bell peppers, onion, zucchini and mushrooms.

2 In small bowl, mix oil, vinegar, Italian seasoning, salt and pepper; drizzle evenly over vegetables. Bake uncovered 25 to 30 minutes. Meanwhile, cook and drain pasta as directed on package.

3 Reduce oven temperature to 350°F. Add tomatoes, basil and pasta to vegetable mixture; toss to coat. Sprinkle with cheese. Bake uncovered about 15 minutes longer or until vegetables are tender and cheese is melted.

1 Serving: Calories 370; Total Fat 16g (Saturated Fat 6g; Trans Fat 0g); Cholesterol 20mg; Sodium 410mg; Total Carbohydrate 41g (Dietary Fiber 5g); Protein 18g **Exchanges:** 2 Starch, 2 Vegetable, 1 High-Fat Meat, 1 Fat **Carbohydrate Choices:** 3

OLIVES AND PORTABELLA ROASTED VEGETABLES AND PASTA Substitute baby portabella mushrooms for the whole mushrooms and add ½ cup sliced pitted ripe olives with the tomatoes.

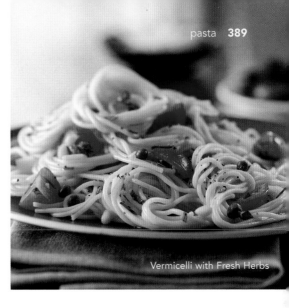

Vermicelli with Fresh Herbs

VERMICELLI WITH FRESH HERBS

FAST

PREP 10 min TOTAL 20 min • **6 servings**

- 1 package (16 oz) vermicelli
- 1 tablespoon capers
- ¼ cup olive or vegetable oil
- 2 tablespoons chopped pine nuts
- 1 tablespoon chopped fresh parsley
- 2 teaspoons chopped fresh rosemary leaves
- 2 teaspoons chopped fresh sage leaves
- 1 teaspoon chopped fresh basil leaves
- 1 pint (2 cups) cherry or grape tomatoes, cut into quarters
  Freshly ground pepper, if desired

1 Cook and drain vermicelli as directed on package.

2 Meanwhile, coarsely chop capers if they are large. In medium bowl, mix capers and remaining ingredients except tomatoes and pepper.

3 In large bowl, toss vermicelli and herb mixture. Stir in tomatoes. Sprinkle with pepper.

1 Serving: Calories 410; Total Fat 12g (Saturated Fat 1.5g; Trans Fat 0g); Cholesterol 0mg; Sodium 45mg; Total Carbohydrate 64g (Dietary Fiber 6g); Protein 11g **Exchanges:** 4 Starch, 1 Vegetable, 1 Fat **Carbohydrate Choices:** 4

VERMICELLI WITH FRESH HERBS AND CANNELLINI Stir in can (15 oz) cannellini beans, rinsed with hot water and drained, with vermicelli in Step 3.

VERMICELLI WITH FRESH HERBS, OLIVES AND FRESH MOZZARELLA Add ½ cup coarsely chopped pitted kalamata olives and 1 cup ciliegini or bocconcini (small fresh mozzarella cheese balls), cut in half, with vermicelli in Step 3.

VERMICELLI WITH FRESH HERBS AND SHRIMP Stir in 12 oz cooked medium shrimp with tomatoes in Step 3.

VERMICELLI WITH FRESH HERBS, SPINACH AND BACON Toss 1 cup firmly packed thinly sliced fresh spinach leaves with vermicelli in Step 3. Sprinkle with 6 slices crisply cooked crumbled bacon, 2 tablespoons shredded Parmesan cheese and pepper.

PUTTANESCA

The ladies of the night in Naples, Italy, are credited, according to one of many theories, with creating this spicy pasta dish. It uses just a few ingredients, so it's fast and easy to cook.

PREP 15 min TOTAL 40 min • **4 servings**

- ⅓ cup olive or vegetable oil
- 2 cloves garlic, cut in half
- 1 tablespoon capers
- 4 flat anchovy fillets in oil, drained, finely chopped
- 2 cans (28 oz each) whole tomatoes, drained, chopped
- 1 small jalapeño chile, seeded, finely chopped
- 1 package (16 oz) spaghetti
- ½ cup sliced pitted kalamata or ripe olives

1 In 4-quart Dutch oven or saucepan, heat oil over medium-high heat. Cook garlic in oil, stirring frequently, until golden. Remove garlic and discard.

2 Stir capers, anchovy fillets, tomatoes and chile into oil in Dutch oven. Heat to boiling; reduce heat to low. Simmer uncovered 15 minutes.

3 Meanwhile, cook and drain spaghetti as directed on package. Stir spaghetti and olives into tomato mixture; cook until thoroughly heated.

1 Serving: Calories 750; Total Fat 24g (Saturated Fat 3.5g, Trans Fat 0g); Cholesterol 0mg; Sodium 790mg; Total Carbohydrate 112g (Dietary Fiber 9g); Protein 22g **Exchanges:** 6 Starch, ½ Other Carbohydrate, 2½ Vegetable, 4 Fat **Carbohydrate Choices:** 7½

Sesame Noodle Salad

GREEK PASTA SALAD

LOWER CALORIE

PREP 25 min TOTAL 25 min • **12 servings**

- 3 cups uncooked rainbow rotini pasta (9 oz)
- 1 large green bell pepper, cut into strips
- 1 large orange or yellow bell pepper, cut into strips
- 1 can (14 oz) artichoke hearts, drained
- 1 cup crumbled feta cheese (4 oz)
- ⅔ cup pitted kalamata olives
- ½ cup sun-dried tomatoes in oil, drained, chopped
- 1 cup Greek vinaigrette or Italian dressing
- ¼ teaspoon coarse ground black pepper
  Chopped fresh parsley, if desired

1 Cook and drain pasta as directed on package. Rinse with cold water; drain.

2 In large bowl, mix remaining ingredients except parsley. Add pasta; toss. Sprinkle with parsley.

1 Serving (¾ Cup): Calories 230; Total Fat 12g (Saturated Fat 3g; Trans Fat 0g); Cholesterol 10mg; Sodium 430mg; Total Carbohydrate 26g (Dietary Fiber 3g); Protein 5g **Exchanges:** 1½ Starch, ½ Vegetable, 2 Fat **Carbohydrate Choices:** 2

MAKE AHEAD **DIRECTIONS** Make salad as directed—except leave out green bell pepper. It will lose its bright green color. Cover salad and refrigerate up to 24 hours. Just before serving, stir in reserved green bell pepper.

Greek Pasta Salad

SESAME NOODLE SALAD

LOWER CALORIE

Light-colored sesame oil has a delicate, nutty flavor while dark sesame oil has a stronger, robust flavor.

PREP 15 min TOTAL 25 min • **12 servings**

SESAME DRESSING
- 3 tablespoons vegetable oil
- 3 tablespoons soy sauce
- 1 tablespoon balsamic or rice vinegar
- 1 tablespoon dark sesame oil
- 4½ teaspoons sugar
- 1½ teaspoons grated gingerroot
- ½ teaspoon garlic powder
- ⅛ teaspoon ground red pepper (cayenne)

SALAD
- 8 oz uncooked soba (buckwheat) noodles or angel hair pasta
- 2 medium carrots, shredded (1 cup)
- 1 small cucumber, cut lengthwise in half, then cut crosswise into thin slices
- 2 medium green onions, thinly sliced
- 1 tablespoon sesame seed, toasted (page 22)

1 In small bowl, stir all dressing ingredients until well mixed; set aside.

2 In 4-quart Dutch oven or saucepan, heat 2 quarts water to boiling. Cook noodles in boiling water 6 to 8 minutes or until tender (if using angel hair pasta, cook as directed on package); drain and rinse with cold water.

3 In large bowl, toss noodles, dressing and remaining salad ingredients. Cover; refrigerate until serving time.

1 Serving: Calories 120; Total Fat 5g (Saturated Fat 1g; Trans Fat 0g); Cholesterol 0mg; Sodium 230mg; Total Carbohydrate 16g (Dietary Fiber 2g); Protein 3g **Exchanges:** 1 Starch, 1 Fat **Carbohydrate Choices:** 1

HOMEMADE PASTA LOWER CALORIE

Use a large wooden board or laminated counter-top for rolling out pasta. Avoid cold surfaces like granite, metal or marble because the dough tends to stick.

PREP 30 min TOTAL 1 hr 55 min • **8 servings**

- 2 **cups all-purpose flour**
- ½ **teaspoon salt**
- 2 **eggs**
- ¼ **cup water**
- 1 **tablespoon olive or vegetable oil**

1 In medium bowl, mix flour and salt. Make a well in center of flour mixture. Add eggs, water and oil to well; mix thoroughly. (If dough is too dry, mix in enough water to make dough easy to handle. If dough is too sticky, gradually add flour when kneading.)

2 Gather dough into a ball. On lightly floured surface, knead 5 to 10 minutes or until smooth and springy. Cover with plastic wrap or foil; let stand 15 minutes.

3 Divide dough into 4 equal parts. On lightly floured surface, roll one-fourth of dough at a time into rectangle, ¹⁄₁₆ to ⅛ inch thick (keep remaining dough covered; if using pasta machine, pass dough through machine until ¹⁄₁₆ inch thick). Loosely fold rectangle lengthwise into thirds. Cut crosswise into 2-inch strips for lasagna, ¼-inch strips for fettuccine or ⅛-inch strips for linguine. Unfold and gently shake out strips. Hang pasta on pasta drying rack or arrange in single layer on lightly floured towels; let stand 30 minutes or until dry.

4 In 6- to 8-quart saucepan, heat 4 quarts water (salted if desired) to boiling; add pasta. Boil uncovered 2 to 5 minutes, stirring occasionally, until firm but tender. Begin testing for doneness when pasta rises to surface of water; drain.

1 Serving: Calories 150; Total Fat 3.5g (Saturated Fat 0.5g; Trans Fat 0g); Cholesterol 55mg; Sodium 160mg; Total Carbohydrate 24g (Dietary Fiber 0g); Protein 5g **Exchanges:** 1½ Starch, ½ Fat **Carbohydrate Choices:** 1½

HERB PASTA Add 1 tablespoon chopped fresh or 1 teaspoon dried crumbled herb leaves to flour mixture before adding eggs.

Cutting Homemade Pasta

On lightly floured surface, roll one-fourth of dough at a time into rectangle, ¹⁄₁₆ to ⅛ inch thick (keep remaining dough covered).

Loosely fold rectangle lengthwise into thirds.

Cut pasta crosswise into 2-inch strips for lasagna, ¼-inch strips for fettuccine or ⅛-inch strips for linguine.

Unfold and gently shake out strips. Hang strips on pasta drying rack or arrange in single layer on lightly floured towels.

Homemade Pasta

SPAETZLE LOWER CALORIE

The word spaetzle *is German for "little sparrow," which is what the shape of these tiny noodles or dumplings resembles. Serve them as a side dish tossed with a little melted butter—as you would serve potatoes or rice—or topped with a creamy sauce or gravy. If you want to make them quickly, look for a spaetzle maker in kitchenware stores.*

PREP 10 min TOTAL 25 min • **6 servings**

> 2 **eggs, beaten**
> ¼ **cup milk or water**
> 1 **cup all-purpose flour**
> ¼ **teaspoon salt**
> **Dash pepper**
> 1 **tablespoon butter**

1 Fill 4-quart Dutch oven or saucepan half full with water; heat to boiling. In medium bowl, mix eggs, milk, flour, salt and pepper with fork (batter will be thick).

2 Press a few tablespoons of the batter at a time through colander with ¼-inch holes, or spaetzle maker, into boiling water. Stir once or twice to prevent sticking. Cook 2 to 5 minutes or until spaetzle rise to surface and are tender; drain. Toss with butter.

1 Serving: Calories 120; Total Fat 4g (Saturated Fat 1.5g; Trans Fat 0g); Cholesterol 75mg; Sodium 135mg; Total Carbohydrate 17g (Dietary Fiber 0g); Protein 5g **Exchanges:** 1 Starch, 1 Fat **Carbohydrate Choices:** 1

LIGHTER **DIRECTIONS** For 2 grams of fat and 100 calories per serving, substitute ½ cup fat-free egg product for the eggs.

POTATO GNOCCHI

Potato gnocchi are small dumplings made from potatoes; their flavor and texture are similar to fresh pasta. Serve with your favorite pasta sauce or toss with melted butter.

PREP 10 min TOTAL 50 min • **6 servings**

> 2 **medium baking potatoes (6 oz each)**
> 1 **teaspoon salt**
> 2 **eggs**
> 2 **to 2⅓ cups all-purpose flour**
> 4 **quarts water**
> 1 **tablespoon salt**

1 In 4-quart Dutch oven or saucepan, heat potatoes and enough water to cover to boiling. Cover and boil about 30 minutes or until tender; drain and cool slightly. Peel potatoes and mash in large bowl until smooth; cool.

2 Stir 1 teaspoon salt, the eggs and enough of the flour into mashed potatoes to make a stiff dough. Shape into 1-inch oval balls.

3 Heat 4 quarts water and 1 tablespoon salt to boiling in 6- to 8-quart Dutch oven or saucepan. Add about ¼ of the gnocchi. After gnocchi rise to surface, boil uncovered 4 minutes. Remove with slotted spoon; drain. Repeat with remaining gnocchi.

1 Serving: Calories 220; Total Fat 2g (Saturated Fat 0.5g; Trans Fat 0g); Cholesterol 70mg; Sodium 470mg; Total Carbohydrate 43g (Dietary Fiber 2g); Protein 7g **Exchanges:** 3 Starch, **Carbohydrate Choices:** 3

Making Spaetzle

Press a few tablespoons batter at a time through spaetzle maker or colander with ¼-inch holes into boiling water.

Cook until spaetzle rise to surface and are tender.

Shaping Potato Gnocchi

To make traditional ridges in gnocchi, roll each 1-inch oval ball over gnocchi ridger.

Or, make ridges by pulling the tines of a table fork over each 1-inch oval ball.

POULTRY

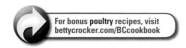

For bonus **poultry** recipes, visit
bettycrocker.com/BCcookbook

FAST = Ready in 20 minutes or less LOWER CALORIE = See Helpful Nutrition and Cooking Information, page 685
LIGHTER = 25% fewer calories or grams of fat MAKE AHEAD = Make-ahead directions SLOW COOKER = Slow cooker directions

◀ Herb Roasted Chicken and Vegetables (page 396), Chicken and Dumplings (page 402), Thai-Style Coconut Chicken
(page 407), Feta-Topped Chicken (page 409)

POULTRY BASICS
From fast-to-fix stir-fries and classic stews to roasted whole birds, poultry offers appealing options for everyday cooking as well as for special occasions.

BUYING FRESH POULTRY

- Look for tightly wrapped packages without tears, holes or leaks and with little or no liquid.

- Check for a fresh odor. If it doesn't smell right, don't buy it.

- Choose cold packages and stay away from those stacked above the top of the meat case, which may not be cold enough.

- Don't buy any packages if the sell-by date has already passed.

- Whole birds and cut-up pieces should be plump and meaty with smooth, moist-looking skin and no traces of feathers.

- Boneless skinless products should look plump and moist.

- Chicken skin color can vary from yellow to white and doesn't indicate quality; turkey skin should be cream-colored.

- Cut ends of the bones should be pink to red in color.

- Place packages in plastic bags so juices don't drip and contaminate other foods.

- Place poultry in refrigerator as soon as you get home. If you're shopping on a hot day or will be longer than 30 minutes, store it in an ice-packed cooler.

STORING POULTRY

- Poultry packaged in clear, sealed plastic wrap on a plastic tray doesn't need to be repackaged.

- Poultry wrapped in butcher paper should be repackaged in plastic wrap, foil or resealable plastic freezer bags.

- Store in the meat compartment or coldest part of refrigerator, or freeze as soon as possible.

- Cook or freeze poultry within 2 days of the sell-by date.

- If poultry was purchased frozen or was frozen at home, keep it in the refrigerator after thawing for the number of days listed in the Timetable for Storing Poultry (below). If it was refrigerated several days before freezing, use it the same day you thaw it.

TIMETABLE FOR STORING POULTRY

Type of Poultry	Refrigerator (36°F to 40°F)	Freezer (0°F or colder)
Uncooked Poultry, whole or in parts	1 to 2 days	12 months (whole chicken or turkey)
		9 months (chicken or turkey pieces, whole turkey breasts)
Uncooked Ground Poultry	1 to 2 days	3 to 4 months
Cooked Poultry	2 days	4 months

Serve Oven-Fried Chicken Fingers (page 398) in a basket with a choice of dipping sauces.

Learn to Make **Roast Chicken**

HERB ROASTED CHICKEN AND VEGETABLES

It's a satisfying moment when you bring your beautifully roasted chicken surrounded with lovely vegetables to the table. Here's how to make that perfect whole roasted chicken—one you'll be proud to serve.

PREP 20 min **TOTAL** 2 hr 5 min • **6 servings**

¼ cup olive or vegetable oil	¼ teaspoon coarse ground black pepper
2 tablespoons chopped fresh or 1 teaspoon dried thyme leaves	1 lemon
2 tablespoons chopped fresh or 1 teaspoon dried marjoram leaves	1 whole chicken (4 to 5 lb)
½ teaspoon salt	6 small red potatoes, cut in half
	1 cup ready-to-eat baby-cut carrots
	8 oz fresh green beans, trimmed

1 Heat oven to 375°F. In small bowl, mix oil, thyme, marjoram, salt and pepper. Grate 1 teaspoon peel from lemon; stir peel into oil mixture. Cut lemon into quarters; place in cavity of chicken.

2 Fold wings across back of chicken so tips are touching. Skewer or tie legs together. On rack in shallow roasting pan or 13x9-inch pan fitted with rack, place chicken, breast side up. Brush some of the oil mixture on chicken. Insert ovenproof meat thermometer so tip is in thickest part of thigh but does not touch bone.

3 Roast uncovered 45 minutes. Arrange potatoes, carrots and green beans around chicken; brush remaining oil mixture on chicken and veg-

etables. Roast uncovered 30 to 45 minutes longer or until thermometer reads at least 165°F, legs move easily when lifted or twisted and vegetables are tender. Cover loosely with foil; let stand 15 to 20 minutes for easiest carving.

See how to make roast chicken: Visit bettycrocker.com/BCcookbook

4 Remove lemon and discard. Place chicken on platter; arrange vegetables around chicken. Serve with pan drippings.

1 Serving: Calories 480; Total Fat 27g (Saturated Fat 6g; Trans Fat 0.5g); Cholesterol 115mg; Sodium 320mg; Total Carbohydrate 23g (Dietary Fiber 4g); Protein 38g **Exchanges:** 1 Starch, 2 Vegetable, 4½ Lean Meat **Carbohydrate Choices:** 1½

BUTTERY ROSEMARY-HONEY ROASTED CHICKEN Omit all ingredients except chicken. Place chicken on rack in shallow roasting pan as directed in Step 2. Arrange 1½ lb buttercup or acorn squash, seeded, cut into ½-inch rings or slices, then cut in half crosswise, and 2 medium onions, cut into 1-inch wedges, around chicken. In small bowl, mix ½ cup melted butter, ¼ cup lemon juice, 2 tablespoons honey, 2 teaspoons dried rosemary, crushed, and 1 clove garlic, finely chopped. Brush half of mixture on chicken

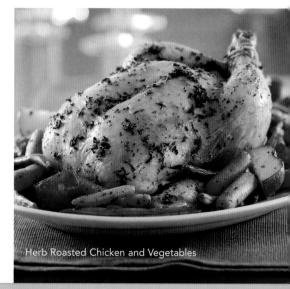

Herb Roasted Chicken and Vegetables

and vegetables. Insert thermometer as directed in Step 2. Roast uncovered 1 hour. Brush chicken and vegetables with remaining butter mixture. Cover loosely with foil. Roast 45 to 55 minutes longer. Continue as directed.

GARLIC BUTTER–HERB ROASTED CHICKEN AND VEGETABLES Omit olive oil and lemon. Make Garlic Butter (page 501) but do not chill. Starting at leg end of chicken, gently separate skin (do not peel back) from chicken breast using fingers, being careful not to tear or puncture skin. Rub ¼ cup of the garlic butter under skin to cover entire chicken breast; gently replace skin. Melt remaining garlic butter; stir in thyme, marjoram, salt and pepper. Continue as directed, brushing melted garlic butter on chicken and vegetables after roasting 45 minutes.

PROVENÇAL ROASTED CHICKEN Heat oven to 400°F. Reduce olive oil to 1 teaspoon. Omit remaining ingredients except chicken, ground pepper and lemon. Place chicken on rack in shallow roasting pan as directed in Step 2. In small bowl, mix grated peel and juice of the lemon and the oil. Drizzle half of lemon mixture over chicken. Pat pepper and 1 tablespoon herbes de Provence on skin of chicken. Place squeezed lemon halves inside chicken cavity. In large bowl, toss 8 small red potatoes (1½ lb), cut into quarters, 2 medium zucchini, cut into 1½-inch pieces, 1 can (14.5 oz) diced tomatoes with basil, garlic and oregano, drained, ½ cup chopped pitted kalamata olives and remaining lemon mixture. Arrange vegetables around chicken in pan. Insert thermometer as directed in Step 2. Roast 1 hour 45 minutes to 2 hours. Continue as directed.

Keys to Success

- **Place lemon in cavity to add flavor** to the entire chicken. Discard lemon after cooking.

- **Brush with oil** to help keep chicken moist and make the outside of chicken deliciously crusty.

- **Cover darker spots** (such as wings or top of breast) with small pieces of foil if chicken is browning unevenly.

- **Use an ovenproof meat thermometer** to check for doneness. An instant-read thermometer can be used to check temperature when you remove the chicken from the oven but cannot be used in oven.

- **Let chicken rest** for 15 to 20 minutes prior to carving to give the juices time to redistribute and make the meat easier to slice.

Carving a Whole Chicken

Place chicken, breast up, on cutting board. Remove ties or skewers.

When holding drumstick, cut through joint between thigh and body. Separate drumstick and thigh by cutting through connecting joint.

Remove wing from body by cutting through wing joint.

Just to right of breast bone, cut down through meat to remove; slice breast meat.

SKILLET-FRIED CHICKEN

PREP 10 min TOTAL 40 min • **6 servings**

- ½ cup all-purpose flour
- 1 tablespoon paprika
- 1½ teaspoons salt
- ½ teaspoon pepper
- 1 cut-up whole chicken (3 to 3½ b)
  Vegetable oil

1 In shallow dish, mix flour, paprika, salt and pepper. Coat chicken with flour mixture.

2 In 12-inch nonstick skillet, heat oil (¼ inch) over medium-high heat. Cook chicken in oil, skin side down, about 10 minutes or until light brown on all sides; reduce heat to low. Turn chicken skin side up.

3 Simmer uncovered about 20 minutes, without turning, until juice of chicken is clear when thickest piece is cut to bone (at least 165°F).

1 Serving: Calories 330; Total Fat 20g (Saturated Fat 4.5g; Trans Fat 0g); Cholesterol 85mg; Sodium 670mg; Total Carbohydrate 9g (Dietary Fiber 0g); Protein 28g **Exchanges:** ½ Starch, 4 Medium-Fat Meat **Carbohydrate Choices:** ½

LIGHTER DIRECTIONS For 11 grams of fat and 250 calories per serving, remove skin from chicken before cooking. Use 2 tablespoons oil in Step 2.

BUTTERMILK FRIED CHICKEN Increase flour to 1 cup. Dip chicken into 1 cup buttermilk before coating with flour mixture.

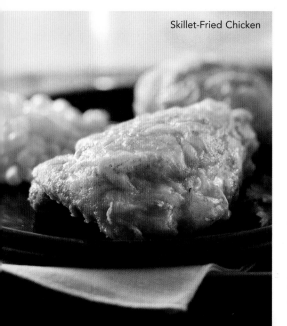

Skillet-Fried Chicken

OVEN-FRIED CHICKEN

PREP 10 min TOTAL 1 hr • **6 servings**

- ¼ cup butter
- ½ cup all-purpose flour
- 1 teaspoon seasoned salt
- 1 teaspoon paprika
- ½ teaspoon garlic powder
- ¼ teaspoon pepper
- 1 cut-up whole chicken (3 to 3½ lb)

1 Heat oven to 425°F. In 13x9-inch pan, melt butter in oven. In shallow dish, mix flour, seasoned salt, paprika, garlic powder and pepper. Coat chicken with flour mixture. Place chicken, skin side down, in pan.

2 Bake uncovered 30 minutes. Turn chicken; bake about 20 minutes longer or until juice is clear when thickest piece is cut to bone (at least 165°F).

1 Serving: Calories 330; Total Fat 21g (Saturated Fat 8g; Trans Fat 1g); Cholesterol 105mg; Sodium 330mg; Total Carbohydrate 8g (Dietary Fiber 0g); Protein 28g **Exchanges:** ½ Starch, 4 Lean Meat, 1½ Fat **Carbohydrate Choices:** ½

LIGHTER DIRECTIONS For 11 grams of fat and 240 calories per serving, remove skin from chicken before cooking. Do not melt butter in pan; spray pan with cooking spray. Decrease butter to 2 tablespoons; drizzle melted butter over chicken after turning in Step 2.

CRUNCHY OVEN-FRIED CHICKEN Remove skin from chicken if desired. Substitute 1 cup corn flake crumbs or panko crispy bread crumbs for the ½ cup flour. Dip chicken into ¼ cup melted butter before coating with crumb mixture.

OVEN-FRIED CHICKEN FINGERS Substitute 1½ lb boneless skinless chicken breasts, cut crosswise into 1½-inch strips, for the cut-up whole chicken. Decrease butter to 2 tablespoons. After coating chicken with flour mixture in Step 1, toss with melted butter in pan. Bake uncovered 15 minutes. Turn strips; bake 10 to 15 minutes longer or until no longer pink in center.

Checking Doneness

Cut into chicken piece to make sure that juices run clear and are no longer pink.

Cutting Up a Whole Chicken

Cut off each leg by cutting skin between thigh and body; continue cutting through meat between tail and hip joint, cutting as closely as possible to backbone. Bend leg back until hip joint pops out as shown.

Separate thigh and drumstick by cutting about ⅛ inch from the fat line toward the drumstick as shown. (A thin white fat line runs crosswise at joint between drumstick and thigh.)

Remove each wing from body by cutting into wing joint with sharp knife, rolling knife to let the blade follow through at the curve of joint as shown.

Separate back from breast by holding body, neck end down, and cutting downward along each side of backbone.

Bend breast halves back to pop out the keel bone. Remove keel bone as shown in Boning Chicken Breasts, below.

Boning Chicken Breasts

Loosen keel bone and white cartilage by running tip of index finger around both sides. Pull out bone in one or two pieces.

Insert tip of knife under long rib bone. Resting knife against bones, use steady, even pressure to gradually trim meat away from bones. Cut rib cage away from breast, cutting through shoulder joint to remove entire rib cage. Repeat on other side.

Slip knife under white tendons on either side of breast; loosen and pull out tendons (grasp end of tendons with paper towel if tendons are slippery). Remove skin if desired. Cut breast lengthwise in half.

COQ AU VIN

This classic French chicken-and-vegetable stew simmers in red wine. This recipe calls for small whole onions (pearl onions), which you can buy fresh or frozen. The frozen ones are super-easy to use because there are no skins to peel.

PREP 10 min **TOTAL** 1 hr 20 min • **6 servings**

- ½ cup all-purpose flour
- 1 teaspoon salt
- ¼ teaspoon pepper
- 1 cut-up whole chicken (3 to 3½ lb)
- 8 slices bacon
- ¾ cup frozen small whole onions (from 1-lb bag)
- 3 cups sliced fresh mushrooms (8 oz)
- 1 cup chicken broth (for homemade broth, see page 528)
- 1 cup dry red wine or nonalcoholic red wine
- 4 medium carrots, cut into 2-inch pieces
- 1 clove garlic, finely chopped
- ½ teaspoon salt
  Bouquet garni*

1 In shallow dish, mix flour, 1 teaspoon salt and the pepper. Coat chicken with flour mixture.

2 In 12-inch skillet, cook bacon over medium heat 8 to 10 minutes, turning once, until crisp. Remove bacon with slotted spoon and drain on paper towels; set aside. Cook chicken in bacon drippings over medium heat about 15 minutes, turning occasionally, until brown on all sides.

3 Move chicken to one side of skillet; add onions and mushrooms to other side. Cook uncovered over medium-high heat about 6 minutes, stirring occasionally, until mushrooms are tender. Drain drippings from skillet.

4 Crumble bacon. Stir bacon and remaining ingredients into vegetables. Heat to boiling; reduce heat. Cover; simmer about 35 minutes or until juice of chicken is clear when thickest part is cut to bone (at least 165°F). Remove bouquet garni; skim off excess fat.

Tie ½ teaspoon dried thyme leaves, 2 large sprigs fresh parsley and 1 dried bay leaf in cheesecloth bag or place in tea ball.

1 Serving: Calories 350; Total Fat 19g (Saturated Fat 6g; Trans Fat 0g); Cholesterol 95mg; Sodium 1020mg; Total Carbohydrate 12g (Dietary Fiber 1g); Protein 33g **Exchanges:** 1 Starch, 2 Vegetable, 4 Lean Meat, ½ Fat **Carbohydrate Choices:** 1

SLOW COOKER DIRECTIONS Remove skin from chicken. Decrease flour to ⅓ cup. Cut carrots into ½-inch pieces. Cook, drain and crumble bacon; refrigerate. Brown chicken as directed. Spray 3½- to 6-quart slow cooker with cooking spray. In slow cooker, place carrots and chicken. Mix remaining ingredients except mushrooms and bacon; pour over chicken. Cover; cook on Low heat setting 4 to 6 hours. Stir in mushrooms and bacon. Increase heat setting to High. Cover; cook 30 minutes. Remove bouquet garni; skim off excess fat.

Coq au Vin

Chicken Tagine

CHICKEN TAGINE

PREP 15 min TOTAL 1 hr • **6 servings**

1 tablespoon olive or vegetable oil
1 cut-up whole chicken (3 to 3½ lb)
1 medium onion, sliced
2 cloves garlic, finely chopped
¼ cup chopped fresh cilantro
1 teaspoon ground cumin
1 teaspoon ground turmeric
1 teaspoon ground ginger
1 teaspoon salt
1 cinnamon stick (2 inch)
1 cup chicken broth (for homemade broth, see page 528)
1 can (14.5 oz) diced tomatoes, undrained
1 cup pitted dried plums, cut into bite-size pieces
½ cup pitted green olives
1 small lemon, cut into quarters
 Hot cooked couscous or rice (page 429), if desired

1 In 4-quart Dutch oven, heat oil over medium-high heat. Place chicken, skin side down, in hot oil; add onion and garlic. Cook uncovered 6 to 10 minutes, turning chicken occasionally, until chicken is brown on all sides.

2 Reduce heat to medium. Sprinkle cilantro, cumin, turmeric, ginger and salt over chicken. Add cinnamon stick; pour broth and tomatoes over chicken. Turn chicken several times to coat evenly. Add plums, olives and lemon, pressing into liquid around chicken. Reduce heat to low. Cover; simmer about 30 minutes or until juice of chicken is clear when thickest piece is cut to bone (at least 165°F).

3 Place chicken on deep serving platter; cover to keep warm. Increase heat to high; boil sauce uncovered about 5 minutes, stirring occasionally, until thickened. Pour sauce over chicken. Garnish with additional chopped fresh cilantro if desired. Serve over couscous.

1 Serving: Calories 370; Total Fat 18g (Saturated Fat 4.5g; Trans Fat 0g); Cholesterol 85mg; Sodium 920mg; Total Carbohydrate 23g (Dietary Fiber 4g); Protein 29g **Exchanges:** ½ Fruit, 2 Vegetable, 3½ Medium-Fat Meat, ½ Fat **Carbohydrate Choices:** 1½

HONEY-MUSTARD CHICKEN

PREP 5 min TOTAL 1 hr 5 min • **6 servings**

1 cut-up whole chicken (3 to 3½ lb)
⅓ cup country-style Dijon mustard
3 tablespoons honey
1 tablespoon mustard seed
½ teaspoon freshly ground pepper

1 Heat oven to 375°F. In ungreased 13x9-inch pan, place chicken, skin side down. In small bowl, mix remaining ingredients. Brush some of the mustard mixture on chicken.

2 Cover; bake 30 minutes. Turn chicken; brush with remaining mustard mixture. Bake uncovered about 30 minutes longer or until juice of chicken is clear when thickest piece is cut to bone (at least 165°F). If chicken begins to brown too quickly, cover with foil.

1 Serving: Calories 280; Total Fat 15g (Saturated Fat 4g; Trans Fat 0g); Cholesterol 85mg; Sodium 410mg; Total Carbohydrate 10g (Dietary Fiber 0g); Protein 28g **Exchanges:** ½ Other Carbohydrate, 4 Lean Meat, 1 Fat **Carbohydrate Choices:** ½

CHICKEN AND DUMPLINGS

PREP 20 min **TOTAL** 3 hr 5 min • **4 servings**

- 1 cut-up whole chicken (3 to 3½ lb)
- 4 medium stalks celery (with leaves), chopped (about 2 cups)
- 1 large onion, chopped (1 cup)
- 1 medium carrot, sliced (½ cup)
- ¼ cup chopped fresh parsley or 1 tablespoon parsley flakes
- 1 teaspoon salt
- ⅛ teaspoon pepper
- 5 cups water
- 2 cups all-purpose flour
- 1 tablespoon dried parsley flakes, if desired
- 2 teaspoons baking powder
- ½ teaspoon salt
- 3 tablespoons cold butter or shortening
- ¾ cup milk

1 Remove excess fat from chicken. In 4-quart Dutch oven, place chicken, celery, onion, carrot, parsley, 1 teaspoon salt, the pepper and water. Heat to boiling; reduce heat. Cover; simmer about 2 hours or until juice of chicken is clear when thickest piece is cut to bone (at least 165°F).

2 Remove chicken and vegetables from Dutch oven. Skim ½ cup fat from broth; reserve. Transfer broth to large bowl; reserve 4 cups. (Save remaining broth for another use.)

3 In Dutch oven, heat reserved ½ cup fat over low heat. Stir in ½ cup of the flour. Cook, stirring constantly, until mixture is smooth and bubbly; remove from heat. Stir in reserved 4 cups broth. Heat to boiling, stirring constantly. Boil and stir 1 minute. Add chicken and vegetables; reduce heat to low. Heat about 20 minutes or until hot.

4 In medium bowl, mix the remaining 1½ cups flour, the parsley flakes, baking powder and ½ teaspoon salt. Cut in butter, using pastry blender (or fork), until mixture looks like fine crumbs. Stir in milk. Drop dough by spoonfuls onto hot chicken mixture (do not drop directly into liquid or dumplings may become soggy). Cook uncovered over low heat 10 minutes. Cover; cook 10 minutes longer.

1 Serving: Calories 820; Total Fat 55g (Saturated Fat 16g; Trans Fat 2.5g); Cholesterol 120mg; Sodium 1770mg; Total Carbohydrate 48g (Dietary Fiber 1g); Protein 34g **Exchanges:** 3 Starch, 3½ Medium-Fat Meat, 6 Fat **Carbohydrate Choices:** 3

QUICKER CHICKEN AND DUMPLINGS

Omit all dumpling ingredients in Step 4. In Step 3, stir in ½ cup Original Bisquick® mix instead of the flour. Continue as directed in Step 3. In Step 4, in medium bowl, stir 2 cups Bisquick and ⅔ cup milk with fork or wire whisk until soft dough forms. Drop dough by spoonfuls as directed. Cook uncovered over low heat 10 minutes. Cover; cook 10 minutes longer.

CHICKEN CACCIATORE

PREP 20 min **TOTAL** 1 hr 20 min • **6 servings**

- 1 cut-up whole chicken (3 to 3½ lb)
- ½ cup all-purpose flour
- ¼ cup vegetable oil
- 2 medium onions
- 1 medium green bell pepper
- 1 can (14.5 oz) diced tomatoes, undrained
- 1 can (8 oz) tomato sauce
- 1 cup sliced fresh mushrooms (3 oz)
- 1½ teaspoons chopped fresh or ½ teaspoon dried oregano leaves
- 1 teaspoon chopped fresh or ¼ teaspoon dried basil leaves
- ½ teaspoon salt
- 2 cloves garlic, finely chopped
  Grated Parmesan cheese, if desired

1 Coat chicken with flour. In 12-inch skillet, heat oil over medium-high heat. Cook chicken in oil 15 to 20 minutes or until brown on all sides; drain.

2 Cut onions and bell pepper in half; cut each half crosswise into quarters. Stir onions, bell pepper and remaining ingredients except cheese into chicken in skillet.

3 Heat to boiling; reduce heat. Cover; simmer 30 to 40 minutes or until juice of chicken is clear when thickest piece is cut to bone (at least 165°F). Serve with cheese.

1 Serving: Calories 400; Total Fat 23g (Saturated Fat 5g; Trans Fat 0g); Cholesterol 85mg; Sodium 630mg; Total Carbohydrate 19g (Dietary Fiber 3g); Protein 30g **Exchanges:** 3 Vegetable, 3 Medium-Fat Meat, 2 Fat **Carbohydrate Choices:** 1

SLOW COOKER DIRECTIONS Remove skin from chicken. Decrease flour to ⅓ cup. Decrease oil to 2 tablespoons; omit tomato sauce. Substitute 1 jar (4.5 oz) sliced mushrooms, drained, for the fresh mushrooms. Brown chicken as directed. Cut onions and bell pepper as directed. Spray 3½- to 6-quart slow cooker with cooking spray. In slow cooker, place half of chicken. Mix onions, bell pepper and remaining ingredients except cheese; spoon half of mixture over chicken. Add remaining chicken; top with remaining vegetable mixture. Cover; cook on Low heat setting 4 to 6 hours. Serve with cheese.

CHICKEN MARSALA

PREP 10 min **TOTAL** 35 min • **4 servings**

   4   **boneless skinless chicken breasts (about 1¼ lb)**
   ½   **cup all-purpose flour**
   ¼   **teaspoon salt**
   ¼   **teaspoon pepper**
   2   **tablespoons olive or vegetable oil**
   2   **cloves garlic, finely chopped**
   1   **cup sliced fresh mushrooms (3 oz)**
   ¼   **cup chopped fresh parsley or 1 tablespoon parsley flakes**
   ½   **cup Marsala wine or chicken broth Hot cooked pasta (page 367), if desired**

1 Between sheets of plastic wrap or waxed paper, flatten each chicken breast to ¼-inch thickness. In shallow dish, mix flour, salt and pepper. Coat chicken with flour mixture.

2 In 10-inch skillet, heat oil over medium-high heat. Cook garlic, mushrooms and parsley in oil 5 minutes, stirring frequently. Add chicken to skillet. Cook about 8 minutes, turning once, until brown. Add wine. Cook 8 to 10 minutes longer or until chicken is no longer pink in center. Serve with pasta.

1 Serving: Calories 280; Total Fat 8g (Saturated Fat 2g; Trans Fat 0g); Cholesterol 85mg; Sodium 230mg; Total Carbohydrate 17g (Dietary Fiber 0g); Protein 34g **Exchanges:** 1 Starch, 4 Very Lean Meat, 1 Fat **Carbohydrate Choices:** 1

Browning Chicken

Use medium-high heat to brown chicken. For the best browning, the skillet should be hot when you add the chicken. Let the chicken cook on one side without turning. When it is properly browned, it should release from the pan without sticking so the other side can be cooked.

Chicken Marsala

CHICKEN NIÇOISE LOWER CALORIE

Niçoise is a French term meaning "as prepared in Nice," referring to dishes made in the Riviera coastal region of France.

PREP 10 min TOTAL 35 min • **4 servings**

- 1¼ cups dry white wine or chicken broth
- 4 boneless skinless chicken thighs (about 1 lb)
- 3 cloves garlic, finely chopped
- ½ cup frozen small whole onions (from 1-lb bag)
- 1 tablespoon Italian seasoning
- 2 medium bell peppers, sliced
- 6 pitted kalamata olives, chopped
- 2 cups hot cooked rice (page 429)

1 In 10-inch nonstick skillet, heat ¼ cup of the wine to boiling. Cook chicken in wine about 5 minutes, turning once, until outside of chicken is white. Remove chicken from skillet; keep warm.

2 Add garlic, onions, Italian seasoning, bell peppers, olives and remaining 1 cup wine to skillet. Heat to boiling; boil 5 minutes.

3 Return chicken to skillet; reduce heat to medium. Cook 10 to 15 minutes or until juice of chicken is clear when center of thickest part is cut (at least 165°F). Serve over rice.

1 Serving: Calories 320; Total Fat 10g (Saturated Fat 3g; Trans Fat 0g); Cholesterol 70mg; Sodium 125mg; Total Carbohydrate 30g (Dietary Fiber 2g); Protein 27g **Exchanges:** 2 Starch, 3 Lean Meat **Carbohydrate Choices:** 2

CHICKEN PICCATA FAST

PREP 10 min TOTAL 20 min • **6 servings**

- 6 boneless skinless chicken breasts (about 1½ lb)
- 1 egg, slightly beaten
- 1 tablespoon water
- ½ cup dry bread crumbs (any flavor)
- ½ teaspoon salt
- ¼ teaspoon pepper
- ⅛ teaspoon garlic powder
- ¼ cup all-purpose flour
- 2 tablespoons butter
- 2 tablespoons vegetable oil
- 2 tablespoons lemon juice
- 2 tablespoons dry white wine or chicken broth
  Chopped fresh parsley, if desired
  Lemon wedges, if desired

1 Between sheets of plastic wrap or waxed paper, flatten each chicken breast to ¼-inch thickness. In small bowl, mix egg and water. In shallow bowl, mix bread crumbs, salt, pepper and garlic powder. Coat chicken with flour. Dip into egg mixture; coat with bread crumb mixture.

2 In 12-inch skillet, heat butter and oil over medium heat. Cook chicken in butter mixture 8 to 10 minutes, turning once, until chicken is no longer pink in center. Remove chicken from skillet; keep warm.

3 Stir lemon juice and wine into drippings in skillet. Heat to boiling; pour over chicken. Sprinkle with parsley and serve with lemon wedges.

1 Serving: Calories 290; Total Fat 14g (Saturated Fat 4.5g; Trans Fat 0g); Cholesterol 115mg; Sodium 370mg; Total Carbohydrate 11g (Dietary Fiber 0g); Protein 28g **Exchanges:** ½ Starch, 4 Very Lean Meat, 2½ Fat **Carbohydrate Choices:** 1

Flattening Chicken Breasts

Place chicken breast, smooth side up, between pieces of plastic wrap or waxed paper. Using flat side of meat mallet or rolling pin, gently pound chicken breasts, working from center out, until ¼ inch thick.

Or using the heel of your hand, apply firm pressure (pounding lightly if necessary) to chicken breasts, pressing until ¼ inch thick.

Chicken Piccata

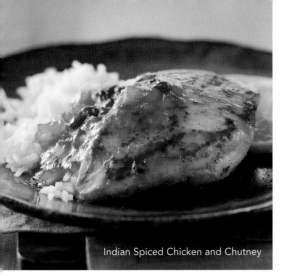

Indian Spiced Chicken and Chutney

CHICKEN KORMA

PREP 15 min TOTAL 1 hr 30 min • **4 servings**

- 1 lb boneless skinless chicken breasts, cut crosswise into ½-inch strips
- ¼ cup whipping cream
- 2 tablespoons finely chopped gingerroot
- 5 medium cloves garlic, finely chopped
- 1 tablespoon finely chopped fresh cilantro
- 1 teaspoon coriander seed, ground
- ½ teaspoon cumin seed, ground
- ½ teaspoon salt
- ¼ teaspoon ground red pepper (cayenne)
- 2 tablespoons Clarified Butter (page 490) or butter
- ½ cup tomato sauce
- ¼ cup finely chopped fresh or 2 tablespoons crumbled dried fenugreek leaves (méthi)*

1 In medium bowl, mix all ingredients except clarified butter, tomato sauce and fenugreek. Cover; refrigerate at least 1 hour but no longer than 24 hours.

2 In 10-inch skillet, heat clarified butter over medium heat. Add chicken mixture and tomato sauce. Cook about 5 minutes, stirring frequently, or until chicken is partially cooked.

3 Stir in fenugreek; reduce heat. Cover; simmer about 10 minutes longer or until chicken is no longer pink in center.

Watercress leaves or fresh parsley can be substituted, but flavor will be milder.

1 Serving: Calories 270; Total Fat 15g (Saturated Fat 8g; Trans Fat 0g); Cholesterol 100mg; Sodium 570mg; Total Carbohydrate 7g (Dietary Fiber 2g); Protein 28g **Exchanges:** ½ Starch, 3½ Lean Meat, 1 Fat **Carbohydrate Choices:** ½

INDIAN SPICED CHICKEN AND CHUTNEY LOWER CALORIE

PREP 5 min TOTAL 1 hr 25 min • **4 servings**

SPICY YOGURT MARINADE

- ½ cup plain yogurt
- 1 tablespoon lemon juice
- 2 teaspoons grated gingerroot
- ½ teaspoon paprika
- ½ teaspoon ground coriander
- ½ teaspoon salt
- ¼ teaspoon ground red pepper (cayenne)
- ⅛ teaspoon ground cloves

CHICKEN AND CHUTNEY

- 4 boneless skinless chicken breasts (about 1¼ lb)
- ½ cup purchased mango chutney
  Hot cooked basmati rice or regular long-grain white rice (page 429), if desired

1 In small bowl, mix all marinade ingredients. Place chicken in resealable food-storage plastic bag or shallow glass or plastic dish. Pour marinade over chicken; turn to coat. Seal bag or cover dish; refrigerate 1 hour.

2 In 12-inch skillet, cook chicken and marinade over medium-high heat 15 to 20 minutes, turning once, until juice of chicken is clear when center of thickest part is cut (at least 165°F). Top with chutney. Serve with rice.

1 Serving: Calories 230; Total Fat 5g (Saturated Fat 1.5g; Trans Fat 0g); Cholesterol 85mg; Sodium 410mg; Total Carbohydrate 13g (Dietary Fiber 0g); Protein 33g **Exchanges:** 1 Fruit, 4½ Very Lean Meat, ½ Fat **Carbohydrate Choices:** 1

Chicken Korma

EASY CHICKEN PANFRIES

With just a few ingredients and less than 20 minutes, you can have great-tasting chicken on the table—it's that easy and that quick.

· Start with 4 boneless skinless chicken breasts.

· Flatten to ¼-inch thickness between plastic wrap or waxed paper (see Flattening Chicken Breasts, page 404).

· Use a 12-inch nonstick skillet and follow directions below using medium heat; chicken is done when juice of chicken is clear when center of thickest part is cut (at least 165°F).

1 Buffalo Chicken: Heat 1 tablespoon vegetable oil in skillet. Add chicken; brown both sides. Pour ½ cup buffalo-chicken-wing–flavored hot sauce evenly over chicken; turn to coat. Cook about 8 minutes, turning once. During last 2 to 3 minutes of cooking; sprinkle each breast with about 2 teaspoons crumbled blue cheese; cover skillet to melt cheese.

2 Caesar-Feta Chicken: Heat ¼ cup vinaigrette-style Caesar dressing in skillet. Add chicken; cook about 10 minutes, turning once. During last 2 to 3 minutes of cooking, sprinkle chicken with 1 cup cut-up seeded tomato and ½ cup crumbled feta cheese; cover skillet to soften cheese.

3 Fresh Herb Chicken: Heat 1 tablespoon butter in skillet. Add chicken; brown both sides. Add ¼ cup dry white wine or chicken broth, 1 tablespoon each chopped fresh basil, chives and dill and ¼ teaspoon garlic salt. Cook about 8 minutes, turning once.

4 Italian Chicken and Peppers: Heat ¼ cup vinaigrette-style Italian dressing in skillet. Add chicken; cook about 10 minutes, turning once. During last 5 minutes of cooking, add 2 small bell peppers (any color), cut into strips, stirring once or twice.

5 Pecan-Maple Chicken: Melt 2 tablespoons butter with ½ teaspoon salt in skillet. Add chicken; brown both sides. Add 2 tablespoons pure maple syrup and ½ cup pecan halves. Cook about 8 minutes, turning chicken once and pecans twice.

6 Ranch Chicken: Heat 2 tablespoons vegetable oil in skillet. Brush chicken with ¼ cup ranch dressing; coat evenly with ⅓ cup Italian style panko crispy bread crumbs. Cook about 10 minutes, turning once.

THAI-STYLE COCONUT CHICKEN

Instead of takeout, make this dish with global flavors in your own kitchen. If you like your Thai food hot, just add another chile or two.

PREP 25 min TOTAL 35 min • **4 servings**

- 1 tablespoon vegetable oil
- 1 lb boneless skinless chicken breasts, cut into bite-size pieces
- 1 teaspoon grated lime peel
- 1 teaspoon grated gingerroot
- 1 clove garlic, finely chopped
- 2 serrano chiles or 1 jalapeño chile, seeded, finely chopped
- ¼ cup finely chopped fresh cilantro
- 1 can (14 oz) coconut milk (not cream of coconut)
- 1 teaspoon packed brown sugar
- ½ teaspoon salt
- 1 tablespoon soy sauce
- 1 cup fresh sugar snap peas
- 1 medium green bell pepper, cut into 1-inch pieces
- 1 medium tomato, seeded, chopped (¾ cup)
- 1 tablespoon chopped fresh basil leaves
  Hot cooked jasmine rice (page 429), if desired

1 In nonstick wok or 12-inch skillet, heat oil over medium-high heat. Add chicken; cook and stir 2 to 3 minutes or until chicken is no longer pink in center. Add lime peel, gingerroot, garlic, chiles and cilantro; cook and stir 1 minute.

2 Pour coconut milk over chicken. Stir in brown sugar, salt, soy sauce, peas and bell pepper. Reduce heat to medium. Simmer uncovered 3 to 5 minutes, stirring occasionally, until vegetables are crisp-tender. Stir in tomato.

3 Spoon into shallow serving bowls; top with basil. Serve with rice.

1 Serving: Calories 430; Total Fat 26g (Saturated Fat 17g; Trans Fat 0g); Cholesterol 85mg; Sodium 650mg; Total Carbohydrate 14g (Dietary Fiber 4g); Protein 35g **Exchanges:** ½ Starch, 1 Vegetable, 5 Lean Meat, 2 Fat **Carbohydrate Choices:** 1

CASHEW CHICKEN AND BROCCOLI

PREP 40 min TOTAL 45 min • **4 servings**

- 3 tablespoons soy sauce
- 2 teaspoons grated gingerroot
- 1 teaspoon sugar
- 1 teaspoon sesame oil, if desired
- 1 lb boneless skinless chicken breasts, cut into bite-size pieces
- ¾ cup chicken broth (for homemade broth, see page 528)
- 1½ teaspoons cornstarch
- 1 tablespoon vegetable oil
- 3 cups fresh broccoli florets
- 2 green onions, sliced (2 tablespoons)
- 1 cup salted roasted cashews
- 2 cups hot cooked rice (page 429)

1 In large bowl, mix soy sauce, gingerroot, sugar and sesame oil. Stir in chicken until coated; let stand 15 minutes to marinate.

2 In small bowl, stir ¼ cup of the broth and the cornstarch until cornstarch is dissolved; set aside.

3 In 12-inch skillet, heat vegetable oil over high heat. Remove chicken from marinade and add to heated oil in skillet; reserve any remaining marinade. Cook chicken about 3 minutes, stirring frequently, until no longer pink in center.

4 Stir broccoli and remaining ½ cup broth into chicken in skillet; cover and cook 1 minute. Stir in onions and cashews.

5 Stir reserved marinade into cornstarch mixture. Stir into chicken mixture; cook and stir 1 to 2 minutes or until mixture boils and sauce thickens slightly. Serve over rice.

1 Serving: Calories 590; Total Fat 23g (Saturated Fat 4.5g; Trans Fat 0g); Cholesterol 70mg; Sodium 1590mg; Total Carbohydrate 58g (Dietary Fiber 3g); Protein 37g **Exchanges:** 3 Starch, ½ Other Carbohydrate, 1½ Vegetable, 3½ Lean Meat, 2 Fat **Carbohydrate Choices:** 4

COFFEE CHICKEN WITH QUICK MOLE SAUCE

PREP 45 min TOTAL 2 hr 45 min • **6 servings**

CHICKEN

4 cups water
⅓ cup salt
⅓ cup packed dark brown sugar
1 tablespoon cumin seed
1 tablespoon chili powder
1 lime, thinly sliced
1 cup strong brewed coffee
6 boneless skinless chicken breasts (about 1¾ lb)
2 tablespoons vegetable oil

MOLE SAUCE

1 medium onion, thinly sliced
2 cloves garlic, finely chopped
1 can (28 oz) crushed tomatoes, undrained
1¼ cups chicken broth (for homemade broth, see page 528)
1 tablespoon creamy peanut butter
1 teaspoon granulated sugar
½ teaspoon ground cumin
Dash ground cinnamon
1 oz unsweetened baking chocolate
2 chipotle chiles in adobo sauce (from 7-oz can), chopped

1 In 2-quart saucepan, heat water, salt, brown sugar, cumin seed, chili powder and lime slices over medium heat, stirring occasionally, until salt and brown sugar are dissolved. Remove from heat; stir in coffee. Cool to room temperature.

Coffee Chicken with Quick Mole Sauce

2 Place chicken in 1-gallon resealable food-storage plastic bag or large bowl; pour cooled coffee mixture over chicken. Seal bag or cover bowl; refrigerate 2 to 3 hours.

3 In 12-inch skillet, heat oil over medium heat. Remove chicken from marinade; discard marinade. Pat chicken dry with paper towels. Cook chicken in oil 5 to 6 minutes, turning once, until golden brown. Remove from skillet; set aside.

4 In same skillet, cook onion over medium heat 5 minutes, stirring occasionally, until soft and lightly browned. Add garlic; cook 30 seconds or until fragrant. Add remaining sauce ingredients. Cook uncovered 3 minutes, stirring occasionally, until mixture simmers and peanut butter and chocolate are melted.

5 Reduce heat to medium-low; arrange chicken in sauce. Cook uncovered 15 to 20 minutes, stirring occasionally, until sauce thickens and juice of chicken is clear when center of thickest part is cut (at least 165°F).

1 Serving: Calories 320; Total Fat 14g (Saturated Fat 4g; Trans Fat 0g); Cholesterol 80mg; Sodium 2130mg; Total Carbohydrate 15g (Dietary Fiber 3g); Protein 33g **Exchanges:** ½ Starch, ½ Other Carbohydrate, 4½ Lean Meat **Carbohydrate Choices:** 1

MOROCCAN SPICED CHICKEN

LOWER CALORIE

PREP 10 min TOTAL 30 min • **4 servings**

1 tablespoon paprika
½ teaspoon salt
½ teaspoon ground cumin
¼ teaspoon ground allspice
¼ teaspoon ground cinnamon
4 boneless skinless chicken breasts (about 1¼ lb)
1 tablespoon vegetable oil
1 small papaya, peeled, seeded and sliced
Hot cooked couscous, if desired

1 In small bowl, mix paprika, salt, cumin, allspice and cinnamon. Coat both sides of chicken with spice mixture.

2 In 10-inch skillet, heat oil over medium heat. Cook chicken in oil 15 to 20 minutes, turning once, until juice of chicken is clear when center of thickest part is cut (at least 165°F). Serve chicken with papaya and couscous.

Moroccan Spiced Chicken

1 Serving: Calories 240; Total Fat 8g (Saturated Fat 2g; Trans Fat 0g); Cholesterol 85mg; Sodium 380mg; Total Carbohydrate 8g (Dietary Fiber 2g); Protein 32g **Exchanges:** ½ Fruit, 4½ Very Lean Meat, 1 Fat **Carbohydrate Choices:** ½

FETA-TOPPED CHICKEN

LOWER CALORIE

PREP 10 min TOTAL 25 min • **4 servings**

- 4 **boneless skinless chicken breasts (about 1¼ lb)**
- 2 **tablespoons balsamic vinaigrette dressing**
- 1 **teaspoon Italian seasoning**
- ¼ **teaspoon seasoned pepper blend**
- 1 **large plum (Roma) tomato, cut into 8 slices**
- ¼ **cup crumbled feta cheese (1 oz)**

1 Set oven control to broil. Spray rack of broiler pan with cooking spray. Brush both sides of chicken with dressing; sprinkle with Italian seasoning and seasoned pepper blend.

2 Place chicken on rack in pan. Broil with tops 4 inches from heat about 10 minutes, turning once, until juice of chicken is clear when center of thickest part is cut (at least 165°F).

3 Top each chicken breast with 2 slices tomato and 1 tablespoon cheese. Broil 2 to 3 minutes longer or until cheese is light brown.

1 Serving: Calories 220; Total Fat 8g (Saturated Fat 2.5g; Trans Fat 0g); Cholesterol 90mg; Sodium 260mg; Total Carbohydrate 3g (Dietary Fiber 0g); Protein 33g **Exchanges:** 4½ Very Lean Meat, 1 Fat **Carbohydrate Choices:** 0

See how to roll **chicken cordon bleu:** Visit bettycrocker.com/BCcookbook

OVEN CHICKEN CORDON BLEU

LOWER CALORIE

PREP 20 min TOTAL 50 min • **4 servings**

- 4 **boneless skinless chicken breasts (about 1¼ lb)**
- 2 **teaspoons Dijon mustard**
- 4 **teaspoons chopped fresh chives**
- 4 **very thin slices lean cooked ham (about ¾ oz each)**
- 4 **very thin slices reduced-fat Swiss cheese (about ¾ oz each)**
- 1 **egg white**
- 1 **tablespoon water**
- ⅓ **cup finely crushed corn flakes or bran flakes cereal**
- ¼ **teaspoon paprika**

1 Heat oven to 375°F. Spray 8-inch square (2 quart) glass baking dish with cooking spray. Between sheets of plastic wrap or waxed paper, flatten each chicken breast to ¼-inch thickness (see page 404).

2 Spread each chicken breast with ½ teaspoon mustard; sprinkle with 1 teaspoon chives. Cut ham and cheese slices to fit chicken. Top each chicken breast with ham and cheese slice. Roll up, tucking ends inside.

3 In shallow bowl, combine egg white and water; beat slightly. Place cereal crumbs in shallow dish. Coat chicken rolls with egg white mixture; roll in crumbs. Place in baking dish; sprinkle with paprika.

4 Bake 25 to 30 minutes, or until chicken is no longer pink in center.

1 Serving: Calories 150; Total Fat 4g (Saturated Fat 1.5g; Trans Fat 0g); Cholesterol 60mg; Sodium 440mg; Total Carbohydrate 2g (Dietary Fiber 0g); Protein 25g **Exchanges:** 3 Lean Meat, **Carbohydrate Choices:** 1

Oven Chicken Cordon Bleu

Heirloom Recipe and New Twist

This classic pot pie has appeared in some form in most editions of Betty Crocker Cookbook throughout the years. It's still a favorite of many and an excellent dinner choice. Our new twist has similar flavors but is made in individual casseroles and topped with tender puff pastry. We have also included two Facebook fan recipe variations for you to sample.

CLASSIC

CHICKEN POT PIE

Pot pie for dinner is possible even if you're busy. Just pick up refrigerated pie crusts instead of making them yourself. You'll cut your preparation time in half.

PREP 40 min **TOTAL** 1 hr 15 min • **6 servings**

- ⅓ **cup butter**
- ⅓ **cup all-purpose flour**
- ⅓ **cup chopped onion**
- ½ **teaspoon salt**
- ¼ **teaspoon pepper**
- 1¾ **cups chicken broth (for homemade broth, see page 528)**
- ⅔ **cup milk**
- 2½ **to 3 cups cut-up cooked chicken or turkey**
- 1 **box (10 oz) frozen peas and carrots***
  Two-Crust Pastry (page 159)

1 In 2-quart saucepan, melt butter over medium heat. Stir in flour, onion, salt and pepper. Cook, stirring constantly, until mixture is bubbly; remove from heat. Stir in broth and milk. Heat to boiling, stirring constantly. Boil and stir 1 minute. Stir in chicken and peas and carrots; remove from heat.

2 Heat oven to 425°F. Roll two-thirds of pastry into 13-inch square. Ease into ungreased 9-inch (2-quart) glass baking dish. Pour chicken mixture into pastry-lined dish.

3 Roll remaining pastry into 11-inch square. Cut out designs with 1-inch cookie cutter. Place square over chicken mixture. Arrange cutouts on pastry. Turn edges of pastry under and flute (see Decorative Crust Ideas, page 161). Bake about 35 minutes or until golden brown.

*About 1½ cups of any frozen vegetable combination can be substituted. (Smaller vegetable pieces will be distributed more evenly throughout the filling.)

See how to make chicken pot pie:
Visit bettycrocker.com/BCcookbook

1 Serving: Calories 670; Total Fat 43g (Saturated Fat 14g; Trans Fat 5g); Cholesterol 80mg; Sodium 1050mg; Total Carbohydrate 44g (Dietary Fiber 3g); Protein 25g **Exchanges:** 3 Starch, 2½ Lean Meat, 6½ Fat **Carbohydrate Choices:** 3

LIGHTER DIRECTIONS For 22 grams of fat and 425 calories per serving, decrease butter to 2 tablespoons, increase flour to ½ cup, decrease broth to 1½ cups and use fat-free (skim) milk. After melting butter in Step 1, stir in milk, onion, salt and pepper; stir in flour. Cook, stirring constantly, until mixture is bubbly; remove from heat. Stir in broth. Continue as directed—except use One-Crust Pastry for top crust in Step 3. Spray 9-inch square baking dish or pan with cooking spray. Pour chicken mixture into dish (not pastry-lined). Bake 25 to 35 minutes or until golden brown.

TUNA POT PIE Substitute 1 can (12 oz) tuna in water, drained, for the chicken.

CHICKEN DIVAN POT PIE Substitute 1 box (9 oz) broccoli cuts for the frozen sweet peas and carrots. Stir 1 teaspoon curry powder and a few drops hot pepper sauce into flour mixture before cooking. Continue as directed.

Contributed by **Mary Nester Allard** from Haverford, PA

PORTABELLA CHICKEN POT PIE Add 1½ cups sliced baby portabella mushrooms to flour mixture before cooking in Step 1. Spoon cranberry sauce into small bowl; stir well. Continue as directed.

Contributed by **Alison Thode** from Brentwood, California

NEW TWIST

INDIVIDUAL CHICKEN POT PIES

This twist on pot pie is easy to make and easy to serve. It's also lower in calories, so it's easy on the diet, too.

PREP 35 min **TOTAL** 1 hr 15 min • **8 servings**

- 1 tablespoon olive oil
- 1 cup diced unpeeled red potatoes
- 1 medium carrot, thinly sliced (½ cup)
- 1 medium stalk celery, thinly sliced (½ cup)
- 1 medium onion, chopped (½ cup)
- 2 cloves garlic, finely chopped
- 2 cans (10¾ oz each) condensed 98% fat-free cream of chicken soup with 45% less sodium
- 1 cup fat-free or regular half-and-half
- ½ cup dry sherry, nonalcoholic wine or chicken broth
- ¾ cup water
- 1½ teaspoons parsley flakes
- 1 teaspoon poultry seasoning
- 2 cups cubed cooked chicken breast
- 1 cup frozen sweet peas, thawed
- 1 package (17.3 oz) frozen puff pastry sheets, thawed

1 Heat oven to 400°F. Lightly spray 8 (8-oz) individual baking dishes (ramekins) with cooking spray.

2 In 3-quart saucepan, heat oil. Cook potatoes, carrot, celery, onion and garlic over medium heat about 10 minutes, stirring occasionally, until vegetables are tender. Stir in soup, half-and-half, sherry, water, 1 teaspoon of the parsley, the poultry seasoning, chicken and peas; heat to boiling. Remove from heat.

3 Cut 8 (4-inch) squares from puff pastry.

4 Place ramekins on cookie sheet. Divide chicken mixture evenly among ramekins. Top each ramekin with puff pastry square. Sprinkle with remaining ½ teaspoon parsley.

5 Bake 30 to 35 minutes or until pastry is puffed and golden brown. Cool 5 minutes before serving.

1 Serving: Calories 540; Total Fat 29g (Saturated Fat 7g, Trans Fat 6g); Cholesterol 35mg; Sodium 530mg; Total Carbohydrate 48g (Dietary Fiber 2g); Protein 18g **Exchanges:** 3 Starch, ½ Vegetable, 1 Very Lean Meat, 5½ Fat **Carbohydrate Choices:** 3

Chicken Pot Pie

Individual Chicken Pot Pies

Chicken Enchiladas

CHICKEN DIVAN LOWER CALORIE

PREP 35 min TOTAL 40 min • **6 servings**

- 2 lb fresh broccoli
- ¼ cup butter
- ¼ cup all-purpose flour
- ⅛ teaspoon ground nutmeg
- 1½ cups chicken broth (for homemade broth, see page 528)
- 1 cup grated or shredded Parmesan cheese (4 oz)
- ½ cup whipping cream
- 2 tablespoons dry white wine or chicken broth
- 6 large slices cooked chicken or turkey breast, ¼ inch thick (¾ lb)

1 Cut broccoli lengthwise into ½-inch florets. In 2-quart saucepan, heat 1 inch water (salted if desired) to boiling. Add broccoli. Heat to boiling. Boil uncovered 5 minutes; drain and keep warm.

2 In same saucepan, melt butter over medium heat. Stir in flour and nutmeg. Cook, stirring constantly, until smooth and bubbly; remove from heat. Stir in broth. Heat to boiling, stirring constantly. Boil and stir 1 minute; remove from heat. Stir in ½ cup of the cheese, the whipping cream and wine.

3 Set oven control to broil. Place warm broccoli in ungreased 11x7-inch (2-quart) ovenproof baking dish.* Top with chicken. Pour cheese sauce over chicken. Sprinkle with remaining ½ cup cheese. Broil with top 3 to 5 inches from heat about 3 minutes or until cheese is bubbly and light brown.

Do not use a glass baking dish; it cannot withstand the heat from the broiler and may break.

1 Serving: Calories 350; Total Fat 22g (Saturated Fat 12g; Trans Fat 1g); Cholesterol 105mg; Sodium 690mg; Total Carbohydrate 9g (Dietary Fiber 3g); Protein 29g **Exchanges:** 2 Vegetable, 3 Lean Meat, 2 Fat **Carbohydrate Choices:** ½

Chicken Divan

CHICKEN ENCHILADAS

LOWER CALORIE

PREP 25 min TOTAL 50 min • **6 servings**

- 1 cup Salsa Verde (page 480) or Salsa (page 481)
- ¼ cup cilantro sprigs
- ¼ cup parsley sprigs
- 1 tablespoon lime juice
- 2 cloves garlic
- 2 cups chopped cooked chicken
- ¾ cup shredded mozzarella cheese (3 oz)
- 6 flour tortillas (7 or 8 inches)
- 1 medium lime, cut into wedges

1 Heat oven to 350°F. Spray 11x7-inch (2-quart) glass baking dish with cooking spray. Place salsa verde, cilantro sprigs, parsley sprigs, lime juice and garlic in blender or food processor. Cover and blend on high speed about 30 seconds or until smooth. Reserve half of mixture.

2 Mix remaining sauce mixture, the chicken and ¼ cup of the cheese. Spoon about ¼ cup chicken mixture onto each tortilla. Roll tortilla around filling; place seam side down in baking dish.

3 Pour reserved sauce mixture over enchiladas. Sprinkle with remaining ½ cup cheese. Bake uncovered 20 to 25 minutes or until hot. Serve with lime wedges.

1 Serving: Calories 290; Total Fat 10g (Saturated Fat 3.5g; Trans Fat 0.5g); Cholesterol 50mg; Sodium 540mg; Total Carbohydrate 29g (Dietary Fiber 2g); Protein 21g **Exchanges:** 2 Starch, 2 Very Lean Meat, 1½ Fat **Carbohydrate Choices:** 2

COUNTRY FRENCH CHICKEN AND RICE LOWER CALORIE

PREP 25 min TOTAL 3 hr 25 min • **8 servings**

- ¼ cup chopped sun-dried tomatoes in oil, drained
- 2 tablespoons herbes de Provence
- 2 tablespoons olive oil
- 2 tablespoons lemon juice
- 1 tablespoon finely chopped garlic
- 1 teaspoon salt
- 8 bone-in chicken thighs (about 2 lb), skin and fat removed
- 1½ cups sliced fresh mushrooms (4 oz)
- 1 cup uncooked regular long-grain white rice
- 1 medium carrot, shredded (½ cup)
- 2 cups boiling water
- 1 tablespoon chopped fresh Italian (flat-leaf) parsley
- 2 teaspoons grated lemon peel

1 In 1-gallon resealable food-storage plastic bag, mix tomatoes, herbes de Provence, oil, lemon juice, garlic and ½ teaspoon of the salt. Add chicken thighs and mushrooms; seal bag. Turn to coat thighs and mushrooms in marinade. Refrigerate at least 2 hours but no longer than 24 hours.

2 Heat oven to 375°F. Spray 13x9-inch (3-quart) glass baking dish with cooking spray. In baking dish, place rice, carrot and remaining ½ teaspoon salt; stir in boiling water. Pour chicken thighs, mushrooms and marinade evenly over rice mixture.

3 Cover with foil. Bake 50 to 60 minutes or until liquid is absorbed and juice of chicken is clear when thickest part is cut to bone (at least 165°F). Sprinkle with parsley and lemon peel.

1 Serving: Calories 260; Total Fat 10g (Saturated Fat 2.5g; Trans Fat 0g); Cholesterol 45mg; Sodium 360mg; Total Carbohydrate 23g (Dietary Fiber 1g); Protein 18g **Exchanges:** 1½ Starch, 2 Lean Meat, ½ Fat **Carbohydrate Choices:** 1½

EASY COOKED CHICKEN IDEAS

Start with cubed or shredded cooked chicken (home-cooked or rotisserie) to make very tasty meals. See Cooked Poultry Yields, page 424, as a guide.

Cherry-Chicken Pitas: Mix 2 cups chopped cooked chicken, ½ cup dried cherries, ½ cup toasted chopped slivered almonds or walnuts, ⅔ cup mayonnaise and dash pepper. Line each of 6 pita (pocket) bread halves with lettuce; fill with chicken mixture.

Chicken-Cashew Wraps: Mix 2 cups shredded cooked chicken, ½ cup cashew pieces, ½ cup sliced celery, 2 tablespoons sliced green onions and ⅓ cup honey mustard dressing. Spoon mixture into 4 flour tortillas (7 or 8 inch) to within 1 inch of edges. Top each with ¼ cup shredded lettuce and 1 tablespoon diced bell pepper; roll up.

Chicken-Cashew Wraps

Chicken-Tortellini Salad: Toss 1 package (9 ounces) cooked cheese-filled tortellini, 6 cups assorted salad greens, 3 cups cubed cooked chicken and ½ cup creamy Italian dressing; sprinkle with shredded Parmesan cheese.

Chicken-Tortellini Salad

Pesto Chicken and Pasta: Toss 4 cups hot cooked pasta with 2 cups shredded cooked chicken, ½ cup Basil Pesto (page 485, or purchased pesto), ½ cup coarsely chopped roasted red bell peppers, drained, (from 7-ounce jar) and ¼ cup sliced pitted ripe olives.

Thai-Broccoli Chicken Peanut Salad: Mix 4 cups broccoli slaw mix (from 16-ounce bag) with 2 cups shredded cooked chicken and ⅓ to ½ cup Peanut Sauce (page 482, or purchased sauce). Sprinkle with dry-roasted peanuts and cilantro leaves.

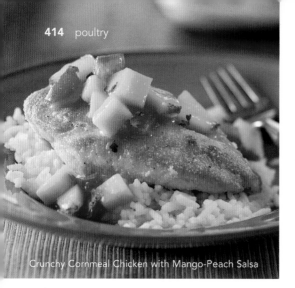

Crunchy Cornmeal Chicken with Mango-Peach Salsa

CRUNCHY CORNMEAL CHICKEN WITH MANGO-PEACH SALSA

PREP 10 min TOTAL 30 min • **4 servings**

MANGO-PEACH SALSA

- 3 medium peaches, peeled, chopped (1½ cups)*
- 1 ripe large mango, seed removed, peeled and chopped (1½ cups)**
- 1 large tomato, seeded, chopped (1 cup)
- ¼ cup chopped fresh cilantro
- 3 tablespoons vegetable oil
- 2 tablespoons white vinegar
- ¼ teaspoon salt

CHICKEN

- ½ cup yellow cornmeal
- ½ teaspoon salt
- ¼ teaspoon pepper
- 4 boneless skinless chicken breasts (about 1¼ lb)
- 2 tablespoons vegetable oil

1 In large bowl, mix all salsa ingredients. Cover; refrigerate until serving.

2 In shallow dish, mix cornmeal, ½ teaspoon salt and the pepper. Coat chicken with cornmeal mixture.

3 In 10-inch skillet, heat oil over medium-high heat. Cook chicken in oil 15 to 20 minutes, turning once, until juice of chicken is clear when center of thickest part is cut (at least 165°F). Serve with salsa.

3 cups chopped frozen (thawed) sliced peaches can be substituted for the fresh peaches.

**Jarred mango slices, well drained, can be substituted for the fresh mango.*

1 Serving: Calories 450; Total Fat 22g (Saturated Fat 4g; Trans Fat 0g); Cholesterol 85mg; Sodium 520mg; Total Carbohydrate 30g (Dietary Fiber 5g); Protein 34g **Exchanges:** 2 Fruit, 5 Lean Meat, 1 Fat **Carbohydrate Choices:** 2

SAGE CHICKEN AND POTATOES

LOWER CALORIE

PREP 15 min TOTAL 1 hr 15 min • **4 servings**

- 4 boneless skinless chicken breasts (about 1¼ lb)
- 3 medium russet potatoes, unpeeled, cut into ¾-inch pieces (3 cups)
- 1½ cups ready-to-eat baby-cut carrots
- 1 jar (12 oz) home-style chicken gravy
- 2 tablespoons Worcestershire sauce
- 1 teaspoon dried sage leaves
- ½ teaspoon garlic-pepper blend

1 Heat oven to 400°F. Spray 13x9-inch (3-quart) glass baking dish with cooking spray.

2 In baking dish, arrange chicken, potatoes and carrots. In small bowl, mix remaining ingredients; pour over chicken and vegetables.

3 Spray sheet of foil with cooking spray; place sprayed side down over baking dish. Bake 50 to 60 minutes or until vegetables are tender and juice of chicken is clear when center of thickest part is cut (at least 165°F).

1 Serving: Calories 320; Total Fat 9g (Saturated Fat 2.5g; Trans Fat 0g); Cholesterol 75mg; Sodium 680mg; Total Carbohydrate 30g (Dietary Fiber 4g); Protein 31g **Exchanges:** 2 Starch, 3½ Very Lean Meat, 1 Fat **Carbohydrate Choices:** 2

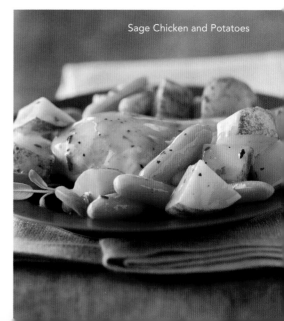

Sage Chicken and Potatoes

ZESTY ROASTED CHICKEN AND POTATOES

PREP 10 min TOTAL 45 min • **6 servings**

  6 **boneless skinless chicken breasts (about 1¾ lb)**
  1 **lb small red potatoes, cut into quarters**
  ⅓ **cup mayonnaise or salad dressing**
  3 **tablespoons Dijon mustard**
  ½ **teaspoon pepper**
  2 **cloves garlic, finely chopped**
     Chopped fresh chives, if desired

1 Heat oven to 350°F. Spray 15x10x1-inch pan with cooking spray.

2 Place chicken and potatoes in pan. In small bowl, mix remaining ingredients except chives; brush over chicken and potatoes.

3 Roast uncovered 30 to 35 minutes or until potatoes are tender and juice of chicken is clear when center of thickest part is cut (at least 165°F). Sprinkle with chives.

1 Serving: Calories 380; Total Fat 23g (Saturated Fat 5g; Trans Fat 0g); Cholesterol 95mg; Sodium 340mg; Total Carbohydrate 14g (Dietary Fiber 2g); Protein 28g **Exchanges:** 1 Starch, 4 Lean Meat **Carbohydrate Choices:** 1

APPLE-MAPLE BRINED TURKEY BREAST

PREP 25 min TOTAL 14 hr 25 min • **8 servings**

BRINE AND TURKEY

  ½ **gallon (64 oz) apple cider**
  1 **cup real maple syrup or maple-flavored syrup**
  ½ **cup kosher (coarse) salt**
  ¼ **cup chopped fresh or 1 tablespoon rubbed sage leaves**
  1 **tablespoon dried marjoram leaves**
  5 **cloves garlic, finely chopped**
  1 **bone-in whole turkey breast (5 to 6 lb), thawed if frozen**

BASTING SAUCE AND GRAVY

  ¼ **cup butter, cut into pieces**
  1½ **teaspoons chopped fresh or ½ teaspoon rubbed sage leaves**
  ½ **teaspoon salt**
  ¼ **teaspoon dried marjoram leaves**
  ¼ **teaspoon coarse ground black pepper**
  ¼ **cup all-purpose flour**

1 Reserve 1 cup apple cider for basting; cover and refrigerate. In 6-quart nonreactive bowl (glass or stainless steel) or stockpot (stainless steel), stir remaining cider, the syrup, salt, ¼ cup fresh sage, 1 tablespoon marjoram and garlic until salt is dissolved. Add turkey breast. Cover; refrigerate 12 hours. Do not brine turkey for more than 12 hours or it will become too salty.

2 Heat oven to 325°F. Remove turkey from brine; discard brine. Thoroughly rinse turkey under cool running water, gently rubbing outside and inside of turkey to release salt. Pat skin and cavity dry with paper towels.

3 Place turkey, skin side up, on rack in large shallow roasting pan. Insert ovenproof meat thermometer so tip is in thickest part of breast and does not touch bone. Roast uncovered 1 hour.

4 In 1-quart saucepan, heat reserved cider, the butter, 1½ teaspoons fresh sage, ½ teaspoon salt, ¼ teaspoon marjoram and pepper over medium heat until butter is melted and mixture is hot. Roast turkey about 1 hour longer or until thermometer reads at least 165°F, basting generously with cider mixture and pan juices every 15 minutes.

5 Remove turkey from oven. Cover loosely with foil; let stand 15 to 20 minutes for easiest carving. Meanwhile, pour pan drippings and scrapings into measuring cup; let stand 5 minutes. Skim 4 tablespoons fat from top of drippings and place in 2-quart saucepan; skim and discard any remaining fat. Add enough water to remaining drippings to measure 2 cups; set aside.

6 Stir flour into fat in saucepan, using wire whisk. Cook over medium heat, stirring constantly, until mixture is smooth and bubbly; remove from heat. Gradually stir in reserved 2 cups drippings. Heat to boiling, stirring constantly. Boil and stir about 1 minute or until mixture thickens. Serve with turkey.

1 Serving: Calories 470; Total Fat 21g (Saturated Fat 8g; Trans Fat 0.5g); Cholesterol 165mg; Sodium 2080mg; Total Carbohydrate 17g (Dietary Fiber 0g); Protein 55g **Exchanges:** 1 Other Carbohydrate, 7½ Lean Meat **Carbohydrate Choices:** 1

Learn to Make **Roast Turkey**

ROAST TURKEY

Think roasting a turkey is out of your league? Not a chance! Here you can easily learn how to roast and carve a beautiful bird with confidence.

PREP 20 min **TOTAL** 4 hr 20 min • **12 servings**

1 whole turkey (12 to 15 lb), thawed if frozen*	3 tablespoons butter, melted, or vegetable oil

1 Heat oven to 325°F. Discard giblets and neck or reserve for another use.

2 Fold wings across back of turkey so tips are touching. If turkey doesn't have an ovenproof plastic leg band holding legs together, tuck legs under band of skin at tail (if present), or tie legs together with kitchen string, then tie to tail if desired. Place turkey, breast side up, on rack in roasting pan. Brush butter over turkey. Insert ovenproof meat thermometer so tip is in thickest part of thigh but does not touch bone. (Do not add water or cover turkey.)

3 Roast uncovered 3 hours to 3 hours 45 minutes. After roasting about 2 hours, remove leg band, cut band of skin or remove string holding legs to allow the inside of the thighs to cook thoroughly and evenly. Place tent of foil loosely over turkey to prevent excessive browning.

4 Turkey is done when thermometer reads at least 165°F and legs move easily when lifted or twisted. Place turkey on warm platter and cover with foil to keep warm. Reserve drippings if making gravy (see page 418). Let turkey stand 15 to 20 minutes for easiest carving.

1 Serving: Calories 600; Total Fat 27g (Saturated Fat 8g; Trans Fat 0.5g); Cholesterol 250mg; Sodium 210mg; Total Carbohydrate 0g (Dietary Fiber 0g); Protein 88g **Exchanges:** 6 Lean Meat, 1 Fat **Carbohydrate Choices:** 0

*For optimal food safety and even doneness, the USDA recommends cooking stuffing separately. However, if you choose to stuff poultry or game birds, it's necessary to use an accurate food thermometer to make sure the center of the stuffing reaches a safe minimum temperature of 165°F. Cooking home-stuffed poultry or game birds is riskier than cooking those that are not stuffed. Even if the poultry or game bird itself has reached the safe minimum internal temperature of 165°F, the stuffing may not have reached same temperature. Bacteria can survive in stuffing that has not reached 165°F, possibly resulting in food-borne illness. Do not stuff poultry or game birds that will be grilled, smoked, fried or microwaved, because it will never get hot enough in the center to be safe.

BRINED WHOLE TURKEY In large clean bucket or stainless steel stockpot, mix 2 gallons cold water and 2 cups kosher (coarse) salt until salt is dissolved. Add turkey (brine should cover bird). Cover; refrigerate 8 to 12 hours. Remove turkey from brine; thoroughly rinse under cool water, gently rubbing inside and outside of turkey to release salt. Pat dry inside and out with paper towels. Follow directions for roast turkey to prepare turkey for roasting. In medium bowl, toss 1 quartered medium onion, 1 coarsely chopped carrot, 1 coarsely chopped stalk celery, 1 teaspoon dried thyme leaves and 1 tablespoon of the melted butter. Spoon into turkey cavity. Place turkey in roasting pan and add thermometer as directed in recipe. Brush all sides of turkey with remaining melted butter. Roast turkey as directed in recipe. Remove turkey from oven. Remove vegetables from cavity.

See how to make **roast turkey**: Visit bettycrocker.com/BCcookbook

Keys to Success

- Allow enough time to thaw turkey. Refer to the Timetable for Thawing Poultry (at right).

- **Rinse turkey well** with cold water and be sure to remove anything inside the turkey cavity such as neck, giblets and liver.

- **Make sure you have a roaster that the turkey will fit in.** The turkey should not touch sides of pan and there should be a little space all around the turkey in the pan for proper roasting.

- **Roast turkey on a rack** to ensure even doneness and allow juices to drain into pan.

- **Use an ovenproof meat thermometer** to check for doneness. Some turkeys have pop-up timers, but they are not always accurate.

- **Cover dark spots with small pieces of foil** if turkey is roasting unevenly. Remove foil before carving.

- **Allow roasted turkey to stand** loosely covered with foil for 15 to 20 minutes before carving so juices can redistribute throughout meat and keep turkey moist.

TIMETABLE FOR THAWING POULTRY

For food safety reasons, never thaw poultry at room temperature. Cook poultry the same day it's thawed. **Refrigerator Thawing:** Place poultry in a pan with sides or in a resealable food-storage plastic bag to catch drips. Allow about 24 hours for every 4 to 5 pounds. **Cold Water Thawing:** Submerge the packaged poultry in cold water, changing the water every 30 minutes. Allow 30 minutes per pound.

Type of Poultry	Weight in Pounds	Refrigerator Thawing Time (days)	Cold-Water Thawing Time (hours)
Chicken, Whole	3 to 4	1	2 to 2½
Turkey, Whole	8 to 12	2 to 3	4 to 6
	12 to 16	3 to 4	6 to 8
	16 to 20	4 to 5	8 to 10
	20 to 24	5 to 6	10 to 12
Cut-Up Pieces	Up to 4	3 to 9 hours	1½ to 2

Carving Roast Turkey

Place turkey, breast up, on cutting board. Remove ties or skewers. While gently pulling leg away from body, cut through joint between thigh and body. Separate drumstick and thigh by cutting through connecting joint.

Serve drumsticks and thighs whole or carved. To carve, remove meat from drumstick by slicing at an angle, and slice thigh by cutting even slices parallel to the bone.

Carefully cut down through breast meat next to bone, removing one side of breast.

Cut turkey breast into slices.

Roast Turkey

Learn to Make Gravy and Stuffing

Here, you'll learn to make lump-free gravy and moist, flavorful stuffing with ease. It's easy to double either recipe for more servings.

PAN GRAVY FAST LOWER CALORIE

PREP 5 min TOTAL 10 min • **1 cup gravy**

> **Drippings from roast turkey or other cooked meat**
> 2 **tablespoons all-purpose flour**
> 1 **cup liquid (turkey or meat juices, broth, water)**
> **Few drops browning sauce, if desired**
> **Salt and pepper to taste**

1 After removing turkey from pan, pour drippings (turkey juices and fat) into fat separator or glass measuring cup, leaving browned particles in pan. The fat will rise to the top. With spoon, return 2 tablespoons of the fat to the pan. Pour or spoon off and discard any remaining fat; reserve remaining drippings.

2 Stir flour into fat in cooking pan. Cook over low heat, stirring constantly and scraping up browned bits, until mixture is smooth and bubbly; remove from heat.

3 Gradually stir in reserved drippings plus enough broth or water to equal 1 cup. Heat to boiling, stirring constantly. Boil and stir 1 minute. Stir in browning sauce if a darker color is desired. Stir in salt and pepper.

1 Tablespoon: Calories 20; Total Fat 1.5g (Saturated Fat 0.5g, Trans Fat 0g); Cholesterol 0mg; Sodium 65mg; Total Carbohydrate 0g (Dietary Fiber 0g); Protein 0g **Exchanges: Free Carbohydrate Choices:** 0

PAN CREAM GRAVY Substitute half-and-half or whole milk for the liquid.

THIN GRAVY Decrease meat drippings and flour to 1 tablespoon each.

BREAD STUFFING

PREP 15 min TOTAL 1 hr • **10 servings**

> ¾ **cup butter**
> 2 **large stalks celery (with leaves), chopped (1½ cups)**
> 1 **large onion, chopped (1 cup)**
> 9 **cups soft bread cubes (about 15 slices bread)**
> 1½ **teaspoons chopped fresh or ½ teaspoon dried thyme leaves**
> 1½ **teaspoons chopped fresh or ½ teaspoon dried sage leaves or ¼ teaspoon ground sage**
> 1 **teaspoon salt**
> ¼ **teaspoon pepper**

1 Heat oven to 350°F. Spray 13x9-inch (3-quart) glass baking dish with cooking spray.

2 In 4-quart Dutch oven or saucepan, melt butter over medium-high heat. Add celery and onion; cook 4 to 6 minutes, stirring occasionally, until tender. Add remaining ingredients; stir gently to mix well. Spoon into baking dish.

3 Cover with foil; bake 25 minutes. Remove foil; bake 10 to 15 minutes longer or until center is hot and edges are beginning to brown.

1 Serving (½ Cup): Calories 230; Total Fat 15g (Saturated Fat 7g; Trans Fat 1g); Cholesterol 35mg; Sodium 530mg; Total Carbohydrate 19g (Dietary Fiber 1g); Protein 3g **Exchanges:** 1 Starch, 3 Fat **Carbohydrate Choices:** 1

LIGHTER DIRECTIONS For 6 grams of fat and 135 calories per serving, decrease butter to ¼ cup. In 4-quart Dutch oven, heat butter and ½ cup chicken broth to boiling over medium-high heat. Cook celery and onion in broth mixture until tender.

See how to make gravy and stuffing: Visit bettycrocker.com/BCcookbook

MORE STUFFINGS

Cornbread Stuffing: Substitute cornbread cubes for the soft bread cubes. For Cornbread-Sausage Stuffing, omit salt; add ½ lb cooked crumbled pork or chorizo sausage (see Sausage Stuffing below) and 1 cup chopped toasted pecans with remaining stuffing ingredients.

Giblet Stuffing: Place giblets, but not liver, and neck from turkey or chicken in 2-quart saucepan. Add enough water to cover; season with salt and pepper. Simmer uncovered over low heat 1 to 2 hours or until tender. Drain giblets. Remove meat from neck and finely chop with giblets; add with the remaining stuffing ingredients.

Oyster Stuffing: Add 2 cans (8 ounces each) whole oysters, drained and chopped, with the remaining stuffing ingredients.

Sausage Stuffing: Omit salt. In 10-inch skillet, cook 1 lb bulk pork or fresh chorizo sausage over medium heat, stirring occasionally, until no longer pink; drain, reserving drippings. Substitute drippings for part of the butter. Add cooked sausage with the remaining stuffing ingredients.

Wild Rice Stuffing: Mix 3 cups cooked wild rice, ¼ cup melted butter, 1 cup orange juice, 1 medium apple, peeled and cut into chunks, 1 cup dry bread crumbs and ½ cup each raisins and walnuts in ungreased 2-quart casserole. Cover; bake at 325°F for 55 to 60 minutes or until apple is tender.

Keys to Success for Stuffing

- **Choose soft-textured bread** for soft, moist stuffing or firm-textured bread for firmer, drier stuffing.

- **Toss stuffing ingredients** enough to mix evenly but gently so as not to break up the bread pieces.

- **Spoon stuffing lightly into baking dish;** do not pack.

- **Cook stuffing** until center is hot and edges begin to brown.

Oyster Stuffing

Cornbread Stuffing

Wild Rice Stuffing

Bread Stuffing

DIJON AND HERB TURKEY BREAST WITH MUSHROOM GRAVY

PREP 25 min **TOTAL** 3 hr 10 min • **8 servings**

- 1 tablespoon Dijon mustard
- 1 tablespoon butter, softened
- ½ teaspoon dried thyme leaves
- ½ teaspoon dried marjoram leaves
- ½ teaspoon salt
- ¼ teaspoon coarse ground black pepper
- 1 bone-in whole turkey breast (5 to 6 lb), thawed if frozen
- 1 can (14 oz) chicken broth (for homemade broth, see page 528)
- 1 package (8 oz) small fresh whole mushrooms
- 1 medium onion, cut into 12 wedges
- ¼ cup all-purpose flour
- ¼ cup cold water
   Salt and pepper to taste, if desired

1 Heat oven to 325°F. In small bowl, mix mustard, butter, thyme, marjoram, ½ teaspoon salt and ¼ teaspoon pepper.

2 In shallow roasting pan, place turkey breast, skin side up. Brush with mustard mixture. Pour ½ cup of the broth into bottom of pan; refrigerate remaining broth. Insert ovenproof meat thermometer so tip is in thickest part of breast and does not touch bone. Spray sheet of foil with cooking spray; cover turkey. (Foil does not need to tightly cover turkey; secure foil to each end of pan.)

3 Roast 1 hour. Add mushrooms and onion to pan; spoon pan drippings over top. Roast uncovered 1 hour to 1 hour 30 minutes longer or until thermometer reads at least 165°F. Place turkey on warm platter; cover with foil. Let stand 15 to 20 minutes for easiest carving.

4 Meanwhile, pour pan drippings (without vegetables) into measuring cup; reserve vegetables. Add remaining broth to drippings to equal 1½ cups; pour into 2-quart saucepan. In small bowl, mix flour and water until smooth; stir into drippings in saucepan. Heat to boiling over medium-high heat, stirring constantly with wire whisk. Boil and stir about 1 minute or until mixture thickens. Stir in reserved vegetables. Simmer 5 minutes,

stirring occasionally. Stir in salt and pepper to taste. Serve with turkey.

1 Serving: Calories 400; Total Fat 17g (Saturated Fat 5g; Trans Fat 0g); Cholesterol 150mg; Sodium 550mg; Total Carbohydrate 6g (Dietary Fiber 0g); Protein 56g **Exchanges:** ½ Starch, 7½ Very Lean Meat, 2½ Fat **Carbohydrate Choices:** ½

DUCKLING WITH ORANGE SAUCE

Piercing the duck skin lets much of the unwanted fat drain away. Using a fork, pierce the skin all over, especially at the breast, but don't pierce the flesh.

PREP 20 min **TOTAL** 3 hr 5 min • **4 servings**

- 1 whole duckling (4 to 5 lb), thawed if frozen
- 2 teaspoons grated orange peel
- ½ cup orange juice
- ¼ cup currant jelly
- 1 tablespoon lemon juice
- ⅛ teaspoon ground mustard
- ⅛ teaspoon salt
- 1½ teaspoons cornstarch
- 1 tablespoon cold water
- 1 medium orange, peeled, sectioned
- 1 tablespoon orange-flavored liqueur, if desired

1 Heat oven to 350°F. Fasten neck skin to back of duckling with skewer. Fold wings across back of duckling so tips are touching. On rack in shallow roasting pan, place duckling, breast side up. Pierce skin all over with fork. Loosely tie legs to the tail, if desired, to better hold an even shape during cooking. Insert ovenproof meat thermometer so tip is in thickest part of inside thigh and does not touch bone.

2 Roast uncovered about 2 hours 30 minutes or until thermometer reads at least 165°F and legs move easily when lifted or twisted. If necessary, place tent of foil loosely over breast during last hour to prevent excessive browning. Place duckling on warm platter; cover and let stand 15 to 20 minutes for easiest carving.

3 Meanwhile, in 1-quart saucepan, heat orange peel, orange juice, jelly, lemon juice, mustard and salt to boiling. In small bowl, mix cornstarch and water; stir into sauce. Cook over medium heat, stirring constantly, until mixture thickens and boils. Boil and stir 1 minute. Stir in orange sections and liqueur. Brush duckling with some of the sauce. Serve with remaining sauce.

1 Serving: Calories 490; Total Fat 24g (Saturated Fat 7g; Trans Fat 1g); Cholesterol 155mg; Sodium 230mg; Total Carbohydrate 20g (Dietary Fiber 1g); Protein 49g **Exchanges:** 1 Starch, 6½ Lean Meat, 1 Fat **Carbohydrate Choices:** 1

ORANGE-ROASTED PHEASANTS

It may seem like you are cooking a lot when you cook a couple of pheasants, but there is not much meat to the amount of bone. With two pheasants, you'll have four nice servings.

PREP 20 min TOTAL 1 hr 30 min • **4 servings**

- ½ cup butter, softened
- 2 teaspoons grated orange peel
- 1 teaspoon salt
- ¼ teaspoon pepper
- 2 tablespoons honey
- 4 medium green onions, sliced (¼ cup)
- 2 pheasants (2½ to 3 lb each), thawed if frozen
- ½ cup orange-flavored liqueur or orange juice
- 1 cup chicken broth (for homemade broth, see page 528)

1 Heat oven to 350°F. In small bowl, stir butter, orange peel, salt, pepper, honey and onions until well mixed.

2 In shallow roasting pan, place pheasants, breast sides up. Starting at the back opening, gently separate skin from breast of each pheasant, using fingers. Spread butter mixture under skin. Secure skin to flesh with toothpick if necessary. Insert ovenproof meat thermometer so tip is in thickest part of inside thigh and does not touch bone.

3 Roast uncovered about 50 to 60 minutes or until thermometer reads at least 165°F and legs move easily when lifted or twisted. Remove pheasants to warm platter; cover loosely with foil.

4 Pour liqueur and broth into roasting pan, scraping up browned bits from pan; pour mixture into 1-quart saucepan. Heat to boiling, stirring occasionally; boil about 15 minutes, stirring occasionally, until liquid is reduced to 1 cup. Serve sauce with pheasants.

1 Serving: Calories 670; Total Fat 45g (Saturated Fat 18g; Trans Fat 2g); Cholesterol 220mg; Sodium 1170mg; Total Carbohydrate 10g (Dietary Fiber 0g); Protein 56g **Exchanges:** ½ Starch, 8 Medium-Fat Meat **Carbohydrate Choices:** ½

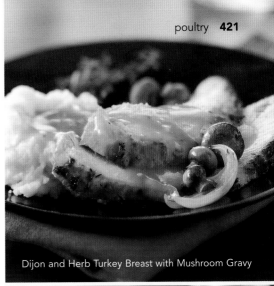

Dijon and Herb Turkey Breast with Mushroom Gravy

Duckling with Orange Sauce

Orange-Roasted Pheasants

ROAST GOOSE WITH APPLE STUFFING

PREP 1 hr 30 min TOTAL 5 hr 25 min • **8 servings**

- 1 **whole goose (8 to 10 lb), thawed if frozen**
- ¼ **cup butter**
- 2 **medium stalks celery (with leaves), chopped (1 cup)**
- 1 **medium onion, chopped (½ cup)**
- 6 **cups soft bread crumbs (about 9 slices bread)**
- 3 **medium unpeeled tart apples, chopped (3 cups)**
- 1½ **teaspoons chopped fresh or ½ teaspoon rubbed sage leaves***
- ¾ **teaspoon chopped fresh or ¼ teaspoon dried thyme leaves**
- ½ **teaspoon salt**
- ¼ **teaspoon pepper**
  Pan Gravy (page 418)**, if desired

1 Heat oven to 350°F. Discard giblets and neck or reserve for another use. Remove excess fat from goose.

2 On rack in shallow roasting pan, place goose breast side up. Fasten neck skin to back of goose with skewer. Fold wings across back of goose so tips are touching. Pierce skin all over with fork so fat can drain. Insert ovenproof meat thermometer so tip is in thickest part of inside thigh and does not touch bone. (Do not add water or cover goose.)

3 Roast uncovered 3 hours to 3 hours 30 minutes (if necessary, place tent of foil loosely over goose during last hour to prevent excessive browning), removing excess fat from pan occasionally. Meanwhile, spray 2-quart casserole with cooking spray. In 3-quart saucepan, melt butter over medium-high heat. Cook celery and onion in butter, stirring occasionally, until tender; remove from heat. Stir in remaining ingredients except gravy. Spoon into casserole. Cover and refrigerate until baking time.

4 Bake stuffing covered alongside goose for last 35 to 45 minutes of roasting time, removing foil during last 10 minutes of baking, until center is hot and edges are beginning to brown. Goose is done when thermometer reads at least 165°F and legs move easily when lifted or twisted. Reserve drippings if making gravy. Let stand 15 to 20 minutes for easiest carving.

*½ teaspoon ground sage can be substituted.

**Pan Gravy recipe makes 1 cup. Increase, if needed, for desired amount.

1 Serving: Calories 820; Total Fat 54g (Saturated Fat 18g; Trans Fat 1.5g); Cholesterol 210mg; Sodium 630mg; Total Carbohydrate 26g (Dietary Fiber 2g); Protein 57g **Exchanges:** 1 Starch, ½ Fruit, 8 Medium-Fat Meat, 2 Fat **Carbohydrate Choices:** 2

Roast Goose with Apple Stuffing

TIMETABLE FOR ROASTING POULTRY

Roasting times are general guidelines. Also check turkey labels for timing recommendations.

Begin checking turkey doneness about 1 hour before the end of recommended roasting time. For purchased stuffed turkeys, follow package directions instead of this timetable.

Type of Poultry	Weight in Pounds	Oven Temperature	Roasting Time in Hours
CHICKEN			
Whole Chicken (not stuffed)*	3 to 3½	375°F	1¾ to 2
TURKEY			
Whole Turkey (not stuffed)*	8 to 12	325°F	2¾ to 3
	12 to 14	325°F	3 to 3¾
	14 to 18	325°F	3¾ to 4¼
	18 to 20	325°F	4¼ to 4½
	20 to 24	325°F	4½ to 5
Whole Turkey Breast (bone-in)	2 to 4	325°F	1½ to 2
	3 to 5	325°F	1½ to 2½
	5 to 7	325°F	2 to 2½
GAME			
Whole Duck	3½ to 4	350°F	2
	5 to 5½	350°F	3
Whole Goose	7 to 9	350°F	2½ to 3
	9 to 11	350°F	3 to 3½
	11 to 13	350°F	3½ to 4
Whole Pheasant	2 to 3	350°F	1 to 1¼
Whole Rock Cornish Hen	1 to 1½	350°F	1 to 1¼

*For optimal food safety and even doneness, the USDA recommends cooking stuffing separately. However, if you choose to stuff poultry or game birds, it's necessary to use an accurate food thermometer to make sure the center of the stuffing reaches a safe minimum temperature of 165°F. Cooking home-stuffed poultry or game birds is riskier than cooking those that are not stuffed. Even if the poultry or game bird itself has reached the safe minimum internal temperature of 165°F, the stuffing may not have reached same temperature. Bacteria can survive in stuffing that has not reached 165°F, possibly resulting in food-borne illness. Do not stuff poultry or game birds that will be grilled, smoked, fried or microwaved, because it will never get hot enough in the center to be safe.

Substituting Chicken Pieces

You can substitute any chicken pieces for a cut-up chicken by using the same weight in breasts, thighs, legs or wings. If you use all breasts or thighs, which are thicker and meatier, you may need to increase cooking time.

The Chicken Skin Myth

Cooking chicken with the skin on adds to the flavor, not the fat. Research has found that the fat doesn't soak into the meat during cooking. Leaving the skin on also helps keep juices in, creating meat that is more moist and tender. It's the skin itself that has the fat, calories and cholesterol, so discard it after cooking.

TIMETABLE FOR BROILING POULTRY

Cook poultry right from refrigerator. Set the oven control to broil. Check the owner's manual for whether the oven door should be partially opened or closed during broiling. Place poultry on a rack in the broiler pan. Broil for the time listed, turning once, until a thermometer reaches at least 165°F or until the juice is clear when centers of thickest pieces are cut.

Cut of Poultry	Weight in Pounds	Broiling Time
CHICKEN		
Cut Up	3 to 3½	Skin side down 30 minutes; turn. Broil 15 to 25 minutes longer (7 to 9 inches from heat)
Bone-In Split Breasts	2½ to 3	25 to 35 minutes (7 to 9 inches from heat)
Boneless Skinless Breasts	1¼	15 to 20 minutes (4 to 6 inches from heat)
Wings	2 to 2½	10 minutes (5 to 7 inches from heat)
TURKEY		
Tenderloins	1 to 1½	8 to 12 minutes (4 to 6 inches from heat)
Breast Slices	1 to 1½	7 minutes (4 to 6 inches from heat)

COOKED POULTRY YIELDS

Remove the uncertainty of wondering if you will have enough cooked poultry for your favorite recipe by using this handy chart.

Type of Poultry	Weight in Pounds	Yield of Chopped, Cubed or Shredded Cooked Poultry in Cups
CHICKEN		
Whole Chicken	3 to 3½	2½ to 3
Bone-In Split Breast	1½	2
Boneless Skinless Breasts	1½	3
Legs (thighs and drumsticks)	1½	1¾
TURKEY		
Whole Turkey	6 to 8	7 to 10
Bone-In Breast	3 to 9	5 to 13
Tenderloins	1½	3

RICE, GRAINS & BEANS

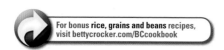

For bonus **rice, grains and beans** recipes, visit bettycrocker.com/BCcookbook

FAST = Ready in 20 minutes or less LOWER CALORIE = See Helpful Nutrition and Cooking Information, page 685
LIGHTER = 25% fewer calories or grams of fat MAKE AHEAD = Make-ahead directions SLOW COOKER = Slow cooker directions

← Cooking brown rice, Caribbean Black Beans (page 448), Red Harvest Quinoa (page 441), Classic Risotto with Peas (page 433)

RICE AND GRAIN BASICS

Cultivated for centuries, grains appear in every cultural cuisine, in an array of dishes and even in beverages. Not only are grains budget friendly, but they also have many nutritional benefits. They are low in fat, have no cholesterol, and are high in fiber. Pair grains with vegetables, pasta and meat for flavorful and filling foods.

COOKING RICE AND GRAINS

Before using wild rice and quinoa, rinse thoroughly to remove any dirt. To cook rice and grains, bring water to a boil; stir in the grain or rice. Unless otherwise indicated, return to a boil; cover and reduce heat to low. Cook for the specified time or until tender. Follow package directions if they differ from this method. When ready to serve cooked rice and grains, fluff with a fork.

STORING AND REHEATING RICE AND GRAINS

Store uncooked rice and grains up to 6 months at room temperature in a cool, dry place or up to 1 year in the freezer. Store cooked rice and grains tightly covered in the refrigerator up to 5 days or freeze in airtight containers up to 6 months.

Reheat plain or seasoned rice and grains using one of these methods (frozen grains will take longer):

- In a microwavable container, add 2 tablespoons water for every 1 cup of cooked grains. Tightly cover and microwave on High for 1 to 2 minutes.

- In a covered saucepan, add 2 tablespoons water for every 1 cup of cooked grains; heat over low heat 5 to 10 minutes.

Different Types of Grains

A **whole grain** is the entire seed of a grass plant containing all parts of its kernel, including the fiber-rich outer coating of bran, the energy-dense middle layer called the endosperm and the nutrient-packed germ. If any part of the grain is removed, it's not considered whole. Whole grains contain essential vitamins, minerals, healthy fats, antioxidants and phytonutrients. Examples of whole grains are barley, quinoa, wheat and wild rice.

In contrast, a **refined grain** has been through the milling process, which removes the bran and germ. This process gives the grain a finer texture, but it also removes important fiber and vitamins. Most refined grains are labeled as being "enriched," meaning some iron and B vitamins have been added back in after processing. Examples of refined grains and foods made from refined grains include white rice, white bread and white flour.

Store whole grains in tightly covered containers.

Sushi

Organic Sweet
Brown

Bamboo

Colusari
Red

Basmati

Jasmine

Wild

Arborio

White

Brown

RICE

Rice is a food staple for almost half of the world's population. It is incredibly versatile and can add flavor and texture to meals. White rice comes in many forms: Regular rice (long, medium and short grain) is the longest-cooking variety. Converted rice is partially cooked and takes a little less time to cook. When you are really in a hurry, instant rice is the fastest, cooking in about 5 minutes. Instant or precooked brown rice is also quick to make but takes just a bit longer, about 10 minutes. It's also a great last-minute choice. To cook rice, bring rice and water to a boil; reduce heat to low, cover and follow the specific directions for each kind of rice.

Arborio: Contains a high proportion of starch that gives risotto its characteristic creamy texture.

Bamboo: White rice infused with fresh bamboo juice, which imparts a pale jade color when cooked and a fragrance similar to jasmine tea. A very moist, sticky rice.

Basmati: Long grains stay separate (not sticky) when cooked. Subtle flavor and aromatic.

Brown: White rice without the outer brown hull removed, so it's considered a whole grain. It contains more nutrients and fiber than white rice.

Colusari Red: Burgundy-colored whole-grain rice. It has a light, nutty, popcorn-like flavor and chewy texture that blends well with other rice or grains.

Jasmine: Fragrant white rice with a subtle nutty flavor that differs from basmati. Less sticky than other forms of rice.

Organic Sweet Brown: Sweeter and more glutinous than regular brown rice with the benefits of whole grain.

Sushi: The right proportion of starches allow the grains to stick together and therefore help hold sushi together.

White: White rice includes three main types, with different characteristics:

> **Long-grain:** Grains stay separate and fluffier when cooked; good for side dishes.
>
> **Medium-grain:** Plumper and shorter; good for paella or as a substitute for Arborio in risotto.
>
> **Short-grain:** The shortest and most moist; good for puddings and molded salads.

Wild: Not actually rice but seeds from a semiaquatic grass with the benefits of whole grain. Somewhat chewy with a nutty flavor, wild rice is significantly higher in protein than regular white rice and is a good source of fiber.

TIMETABLE FOR COOKING RICE

To cook rice, bring rice and water to a boil; reduce heat to low, cover and follow the specific directions for each kind of rice.

Type of Rice (1 Cup)	Amount of Water in Cups	Cooking Directions	Yield in Cups
Basmati White	1½	Simmer 15 to 20 minutes.	3
Jasmine	1¾	Simmer 15 to 20 minutes.	3
Long-Grain White	2	Simmer 15 minutes.	3
Parboiled (Converted) White	2½	Simmer 20 to 25 minutes. Let stand 5 minutes.	3 to 4
Precooked (Instant) White	1	After stirring in rice, cover and remove from heat; let stand 5 minutes.	2
Long-Grain Brown (Regular and Basmati)	2¾	Simmer 45 to 50 minutes.	4
Precooked (Instant) Brown	1¼	Simmer 10 minutes.	2
Wild	2½	Simmer 40 to 50 minutes.	3

Learn to Make Rice Pilaf

RICE PILAF

Rice pilaf can be a new dish each time you make it just by using different ingredients. The secret to the flavor is browning the rice in butter until it is golden brown before adding the liquid to the pan. If you want to make plain cooked rice, see Timetable for Cooking Rice, page 429.

PREP 10 min **TOTAL** 35 min • **4 servings**

2 tablespoons butter
1 small onion, chopped (⅓ cup)
1 cup uncooked regular long-grain white rice

2 cups chicken broth (for homemade broth, see page 528)
¼ teaspoon salt

1 In 3-quart saucepan, melt butter over medium heat. Cook onion in butter about 3 minutes, stirring occasionally, until tender.

2 Stir in rice. Cook 5 minutes, stirring frequently, until rice is golden brown. Stir in broth and salt.

3 Heat to boiling, stirring once or twice; reduce heat to low. Cover; simmer 15 minutes (do not lift cover or stir). Remove from heat; let stand covered 5 minutes.

1 Serving: Calories 260; Total Fat 7g (Saturated Fat 3g; Trans Fat 0g); Cholesterol 15mg; Sodium 700mg; Total Carbohydrate 42g (Dietary Fiber 0g); Protein 7g **Exchanges:** 2 Starch, 1 Other Carbohydrate, 1 Fat **Carbohydrate Choices:** 3

Keys to Success

- **Cook rice in butter until golden brown.** This adds a toasted flavor and ensures the pilaf will be fluffy, as the butter coats the individual grains to keep them from sticking together.

- **Cook in chicken broth rather than water.** It adds extra flavor to the pilaf.

- **Stir only once or twice, then do not lift cover or stir.** This lets the rice cook up fluffy, not sticky or starchy.

- **Let rice stand covered after cooking** so it can absorb any remaining liquid and become fluffy. Move pan to a cool burner so the rice doesn't burn.

- **If there is still liquid in the pan, cook it uncovered** over low heat for a few minutes, until the liquid is gone.

Ways to Use Cooked Rice

Rice is a great way to make a variety of dishes more filling. Next time you make Rice Pilaf or other rice for dinner, consider making a double-batch, so you'll already have rice on hand to add to other foods. See Storing and Reheating Rice and Grains, page 427. Try one of these creative ways to use cooked rice:

- Stir some into hot soup, just until the rice is heated through.

- Use as a filling for omelets—reheat before spooning into the omelet. (See Basic Omelet, page 78.)

- Make up your own fried rice concoction. Brown the rice in a small amount of oil, then stir in chopped or shredded cooked meat or chicken, or any vegetables you have on hand.

- Use as a filling for tacos or burritos—reheat before adding with your other favorite fillings.

- Make a rice salad by tossing cold pilaf or plain cooked rice with your favorite vinaigrette or salad dressing; add finely chopped vegetables for color and crunch.

See how to make **rice pilaf**: Visit bettycrocker.com/BCcookbook

MORE RICE PILAFS

Pilafs can be made using other kinds of rice, such as basmati or jasmine, or other grains (see Bulgur Pilaf, page 439, and Lemon-Millet Pilaf, page 440). See Timetable for Cooking Rice on page 429 or Timetable for Cooking Common Grains on page 437 for the cooking times for specific grains and rice varieties.

1 Brown Rice Pilaf: Substitute uncooked regular brown rice for the white rice. Make as directed—except in Step 3, increase simmer time to 45 to 50 minutes.

2 Cashew Pilaf: Stir ¼ cup coarsely chopped cashews and 2 tablespoons chopped fresh parsley into cooked pilaf.

3 Curry Pilaf: Stir in ½ cup diced dried fruit and raisin mixture, ¼ teaspoon ground allspice, ¼ teaspoon ground turmeric and ¼ teaspoon curry powder with the broth and salt in Step 2.

4 Mushroom Pilaf: Cook 1 cup sliced fresh mushrooms, or 1 can (4 ounces) mushrooms pieces and stems, drained, with onion in Step 1.

5 Orange and Cranberry Pilaf: Add ½ teaspoon grated orange peel with the broth and salt in Step 2. Stir ¼ cup sweetened dried cranberries into cooked pilaf.

6 Pine Nut and Green Onion Pilaf: Cook ½ cup sliced green onions and ¼ cup pine nuts with the rice in Step 2.

7 Prosciutto, Parmesan and Pea Pilaf: Cook 3 ounces chopped prosciutto ham with the rice in Step 2. Stir ¼ cup frozen sweet peas (thawed) and ¼ cup shredded Parmesan cheese into cooked pilaf.

8 Rice, Cherry and Pistachio Pilaf: Substitute uncooked wild and whole-grain brown rice blend for the white rice. Make as directed—except in Step 3, increase simmer time to 45 to 50 minutes. Stir ¼ cup each dried cherries and chopped pistachios into cooked pilaf.

PARMESAN RICE AND PEAS WITH BACON LOWER CALORIE

PREP 10 min TOTAL 45 min • **8 servings**

- 2 slices bacon, chopped
- 1 medium onion, chopped (½ cup)
- 1 cup uncooked regular long-grain rice
- 1 can (14 oz) chicken broth (for homemade broth, see page 528)
- ½ cup water
- 1 cup frozen baby sweet peas, thawed
- ¾ cup grated Parmesan cheese
- ⅛ teaspoon pepper

1 In 2-quart saucepan, cook bacon over medium heat 3 to 4 minutes, stirring occasionally, until crisp. Stir in onion. Cook about 1 minute, stirring occasionally, until onion is tender.

2 Stir in rice until well coated with bacon drippings. Stir in broth and water. Heat to boiling; reduce heat to low. Cover and simmer about 20 minutes or until rice is tender and broth is absorbed.

3 Gently stir in peas. Cover and cook 1 to 2 minutes or until peas are hot; remove from heat. Stir in cheese and pepper.

1 Serving: Calories 160; Total Fat 4.5g (Saturated Fat 2g; Trans Fat 0g); Cholesterol 10mg; Sodium 430mg; Total Carbohydrate 24g (Dietary Fiber 1g); Protein 8g **Exchanges:** 1½ Starch, ½ High-Fat Meat **Carbohydrate Choices:** 1½

CONFETTI BROWN RICE

LOWER CALORIE

PREP 15 min TOTAL 1 hr 10 min • **6 servings**

- 1 tablespoon butter
- ½ cup uncooked regular brown rice
- 1½ cups sliced fresh mushrooms (4 oz)
- 2 medium green onions, thinly sliced (2 tablespoons)
- 1¼ cups water
- ½ teaspoon salt
- ¼ teaspoon pepper
- 2 cups frozen broccoli, corn and red peppers (from 1-lb bag), cooked and drained
- 1 tablespoon lemon juice

1 In 10-inch nonstick skillet, melt butter over medium heat. Cook rice, mushrooms and onions in butter about 3 minutes, stirring occasionally, until onions are tender. Stir in water, salt and pepper. Heat to boiling, stirring occasionally; reduce heat.

2 Cover and simmer about 50 minutes or until rice is tender. Stir in vegetables and lemon juice. Heat uncovered, stirring occasionally, until hot and liquid is absorbed.

1 Serving: Calories 90; Total Fat 2.5g (Saturated Fat 0g; Trans Fat 0g); Cholesterol 0mg; Sodium 220mg; Total Carbohydrate 14g (Dietary Fiber 3g); Protein 2g **Exchanges:** 1 Starch, ½ Fat **Carbohydrate Choices:** 1

SPANISH RICE LOWER CALORIE

PREP 10 min TOTAL 40 min • **10 servings**

- 2 tablespoons vegetable oil
- 1 cup uncooked regular long-grain white rice
- 1 medium onion, chopped (½ cup)
- 2½ cups water
- 1½ teaspoons salt
- ¾ teaspoon chili powder
- ⅛ teaspoon garlic powder
- 1 small green bell pepper, chopped (½ cup)
- 1 can (8 oz) tomato sauce
- 1 large tomato, seeded, chopped (1 cup)

1 In 10-inch skillet, heat oil over medium heat. Cook rice and onion in oil about 5 minutes, stirring frequently, until rice is golden brown and onion is crisp-tender.

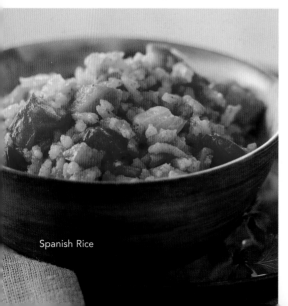

Spanish Rice

2 Stir in remaining ingredients except tomato. Heat to boiling; reduce heat. Cover; simmer 20 minutes, stirring occasionally. Stir in tomato. Cover; simmer about 5 minutes longer or until rice is tender.

1 Serving (½ Cup): Calories 120; Total Fat 3g (Saturated Fat 0g; Trans Fat 0g); Cholesterol 0mg; Sodium 500mg; Total Carbohydrate 20g (Dietary Fiber 1g); Protein 2g **Exchanges:** 1 Starch, ½ Fat **Carbohydrate Choices:** 1

SPANISH RICE WITH BACON Omit oil. Cut 6 slices bacon into 1-inch pieces. In 10-inch skillet, cook bacon over medium heat, stirring occasionally, until crisp. Remove from skillet with slotted spoon and drain on paper towels. Drain all but 2 tablespoons bacon drippings from skillet. Cook rice and onion in drippings over medium heat about 5 minutes, stirring frequently, until rice is golden brown and onion is crisp-tender. Continue as directed in Step 2. Stir in bacon just before serving.

CLASSIC RISOTTO

PREP 10 min TOTAL 35 min • **4 servings**

- 2 **tablespoons olive or vegetable oil**
- 1 **tablespoon butter**
- 1 **small onion, thinly sliced**
- 1 **tablespoon chopped fresh parsley**
- 1 **cup uncooked short-grain Arborio rice or regular long-grain white rice**
- ½ **cup dry white wine or chicken broth**
- 3 **cups chicken broth, warmed (for homemade broth, see page 528)**
- ½ **cup freshly grated Parmesan cheese**
- ¼ **teaspoon coarse ground black pepper**

1 In 10-inch nonstick skillet or 3-quart saucepan, heat oil and butter over medium-high heat until butter is melted. Cook onion and parsley in oil mixture about 5 minutes, stirring frequently, until onion is tender.

2 Stir in rice. Cook, stirring occasionally, until edges of kernels are translucent. Stir in wine. Cook about 3 minutes, stirring constantly, until wine is absorbed.

3 Reduce heat to medium. Stir in 1 cup of the warm broth. Cook uncovered about 5 minutes, stirring frequently, until broth is absorbed. Repeat, adding another 1 cup of broth. Stir in remaining 1 cup broth. Cook about 8 minutes, stirring frequently, until rice is just tender and mixture is creamy. Stir in cheese and pepper.

1 Serving: Calories 360; Total Fat 15g (Saturated Fat 5g; Trans Fat 0g); Cholesterol 15mg; Sodium 1020mg; Total Carbohydrate 43g (Dietary Fiber 0g); Protein 13g **Exchanges:** 3 Starch, 2½ Fat **Carbohydrate Choices:** 3

CLASSIC RISOTTO WITH BUTTERNUT SQUASH Stir in 1 cup mashed cooked butternut squash or sweet potato with the first cup of the broth in Step 3. Continue as directed.

CLASSIC RISOTTO WITH PEAS Just before serving, stir in 1 box (9 oz) frozen baby sweet peas, cooked and drained.

CLASSIC RISOTTO WITH SHRIMP Stir in 8 oz cooked medium shrimp during last 3 to 5 minutes of cooking

See how to cook **risotto:** Visit bettycrocker.com/BCcookbook

Learn with Betty COOKING RISOTTO

Perfect Risotto: This risotto is thickened and creamy.

Undercooked Risotto: This risotto was not cooked long enough and is soupy or watery instead of creamy.

Overcooked Risotto: This risotto was cooked too long and is dried out and no longer creamy.

CHEESY BROCCOLI-RICE BAKE

PREP 15 min TOTAL 50 min • **8 servings**

- 2 **tablespoons butter**
- 1 **large onion, chopped (1 cup)**
- 1 **loaf (16 oz) prepared cheese product, cut into cubes**
- 1 **can (10¾ oz) condensed cream of mushroom soup**
- ⅔ **cup milk**
- ¼ **teaspoon pepper, if desired**
- 2 **cups fresh small broccoli florets**
- 3 **cups cooked rice (page 429)**
- 1 **cup fine soft bread crumbs (about 1½ slices bread)**
- 2 **tablespoons butter, melted**

1 Heat oven to 350°F. Spray 13x9-inch (3-quart) glass baking dish with cooking spray.

2 In 10-inch skillet, melt 2 tablespoons butter over medium-high heat. Cook onion in butter, stirring occasionally, until crisp-tender; reduce heat to medium. Stir in cheese, soup, milk and pepper. Cook, stirring frequently, until cheese is melted.

3 Stir broccoli and rice into cheese mixture. Spoon into baking dish. In small bowl, mix bread crumbs and 2 tablespoons melted butter; sprinkle over rice mixture.

4 Bake uncovered 30 to 35 minutes or until light brown on top and bubbly around edges.

1 Serving: Calories 370; Total Fat 21g (Saturated Fat 12g; Trans Fat 1g); Cholesterol 65mg; Sodium 1420mg; Total Carbohydrate 31g (Dietary Fiber 2g); Protein 13g **Exchanges:** 1½ Starch, ½ Other Carbohydrate, 1 High-Fat Meat, 2½ Fat **Carbohydrate Choices:** 2

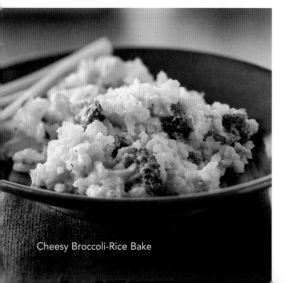

Cheesy Broccoli-Rice Bake

LIGHTER DIRECTIONS For 9 grams of fat and 275 calories per serving, omit the first 2 tablespoons butter; spray skillet with cooking spray. Use reduced-fat prepared cheese product, condensed 98% fat-free cream of mushroom soup and fat-free (skim) milk. Mix bread crumbs with 1 tablespoon butter.

PORK FRIED RICE

Using cold cooked rice is best so the grains stay separated during frying.

PREP 15 min TOTAL 25 min • **4 servings**

- 1 **cup fresh bean sprouts**
- 2 **tablespoons vegetable oil**
- 1 **cup sliced fresh mushrooms (3 oz)**
- 3 **cups cold cooked regular long-grain white rice (page 429)**
- 1 **cup cut-up cooked pork**
- 2 **medium green onions, sliced (2 tablespoons)**
- 2 **eggs, slightly beaten**
- 3 **tablespoons soy sauce**
  Dash white pepper

1 Rinse bean sprouts with cold water; drain and set aside.

2 In 10-inch skillet, heat 1 tablespoon of the oil over medium heat; rotate skillet until oil covers bottom. Cook mushrooms in oil about 1 minute, stirring frequently, until coated.

3 Add bean sprouts, rice, pork and onions to skillet. Cook over medium heat about 5 minutes, stirring and breaking up rice, until sprouts are thoroughly cooked and no longer crisp and mixture is hot.

4 Move rice mixture to side of skillet. Add remaining 1 tablespoon oil to other side of skillet. Cook eggs in oil over medium heat, stirring constantly, until eggs are thickened throughout but still moist. Stir eggs into rice mixture. Stir in soy sauce and pepper.

1 Serving: Calories 360; Total Fat 14g (Saturated Fat 3.5g; Trans Fat 0g); Cholesterol 135mg; Sodium 1190mg; Total Carbohydrate 37g (Dietary Fiber 1g); Protein 20g **Exchanges:** 2½ Starch, 2 Lean Meat, 1 Fat **Carbohydrate Choices:** 2½

LIGHTER DIRECTIONS For 3 grams of fat and 240 calories per serving, decrease pork to ½ cup and finely chop. Use nonstick skillet and omit oil in Step 4. Substitute ½ cup fat-free egg product for the eggs.

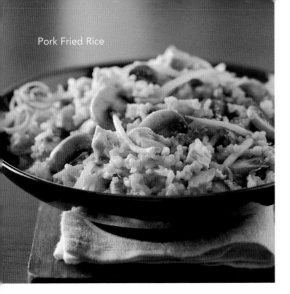
Pork Fried Rice

CHICKEN FRIED RICE Substitute 1 cup shredded cooked chicken for the pork and add 1 cup cooked frozen sweet peas with chicken mixture in Step 3.

SHRIMP FRIED RICE Substitute 1 cup frozen cooked salad shrimp, thawed, for the pork.

Wild Rice

Native to the Great Lakes area, wild rice is not rice at all. It's a long-grain marsh grass that in the past was harvested by local residents. Now it is cultivated commercially in many states, so it is much more available than previously. Nutty and chewy, wild rice has a wonderful texture and flavor. It is a whole grain that contains a good amount of protein and fiber, is low in fat and contains no gluten. To make wild rice, follow these tips:

- One cup of uncooked rice will make 3 cups cooked.

- Rinse thoroughly under cold water to remove debris.

- Use the correct amount of water: 2½ cups water for 1 cup uncooked wild rice.

- Remember that it takes longer than white or brown rice to cook—up to 1 hour.

- Cook until the kernels "pop." Overcooked rice will be mushy.

CRANBERRY–WILD RICE BAKE

LOWER CALORIE

Make this your next dish to take along and share. If you're anticipating feeding a crowd, double the recipe and bake in a 13x9-inch baking dish or 3-quart casserole.

PREP 45 min **TOTAL** 2 hr 20 min • **8 servings**

- 1 cup uncooked wild rice
- 2½ cups water
- 1 tablespoon butter
- 1 medium onion, chopped (½ cup)
- 1 cup sliced mushrooms (3 oz)
- 2½ cups chicken broth, heated (for homemade broth, see page 528)
- ¼ teaspoon salt
- 2 cloves garlic, finely chopped
- 1 cup dried cranberries

1 Heat oven to 350°F. Grease 8-inch square (2-quart) glass baking dish.

2 In 2-quart saucepan, heat wild rice and water to boiling, stirring occasionally; reduce heat to low. Cover and simmer 30 minutes; drain.

3 In 10-inch skillet, melt butter over medium heat. Cook onion and mushrooms in butter, stirring occasionally, until onion is tender. Mix wild rice and onion mixture in baking dish. Mix broth, salt and garlic; pour over rice mixture.

4 Cover and bake 1 hour 15 minutes. Stir in cranberries. Cover and bake 15 to 20 minutes or until liquid is absorbed.

1 Serving: Calories 170; Total Fat 2.5g (Saturated Fat 1g; Trans Fat 0g); Cholesterol 0mg; Sodium 410mg; Total Carbohydrate 31g (Dietary Fiber 2g); Protein 5g **Exchanges:** 1 Starch, 1 Other Carbohydrate, ½ Fat **Carbohydrate Choices:** 2

Cranberry–Wild Rice Bake

436

Rye Berries

Buckwheat

Bulgur

Gold Quinoa

Red Quinoa

Spelt

Pearled Barley

Wheat Berries

Rolled Rye Flakes

Millet

Teff

Hulled Barley

Oat Groats

Coarse-Ground Cornmeal

Blue Cornmeal

Steel-Cut Oats

Kamut®

Flaxseed

Kasha

Amaranth

OTHER GRAINS

Look for these grains in your grocery or health-food store:

Amaranth: High in protein and gluten free, it's used in baked goods.

Barley: Pearled barley has some of the hull removed, so it isn't considered a whole grain, like hulled barley. Substitute rolled barley flakes for old-fashioned oats.

Buckwheat: High in protein and gluten free, ideal for people who struggle with wheat allergies and can't tolerate gluten.

Bulgur: Boiled, dried and cracked wheat kernels.

Cornmeal: Ground whole-grain, whole corn kernels. Available in white, yellow, and blue forms. For cooking directions, see Polenta, page 438.

Flaxseed: While not actually a grain, its nutritional profile is similar to that of whole grains. Add to baked goods.

Kamut®: Trademarked name of organically grown grain resembling wheat kernels.

Kasha: Generic for any crushed grain, commonly buckwheat kernels.

Millet: Mild-flavored, mixes well with other foods and is delicious toasted.

Oats: Oats are a healthful grain with several types available:

    Quick-Cooking and Old-Fashioned Oats: Both are whole grain with bran and germ still intact.

    Oat Groats: Whole oats (before being steamed and rolled), so they have the highest nutritional value of all oat products.

    Steel-Cut Oats: Groats cut into smaller pieces; they are chewier and nuttier than quick-cooking or old-fashioned oats.

Quinoa: Quick-cooking grain perfect for a light, fluffy side dish or to add to soups and salads.

Rye: Fibrous grain with a deep, rich flavor. Substitute rolled rye flakes for old-fashioned oats.

Spelt: Nutty-flavored, higher protein variety of wheat.

Teff: A whole grain with a sweet, molasses-like flavor typically used to make Ethiopia's spongy flatbread *injera*.

Wheat Berries: Chewy, nutty, whole wheat kernels for main or side dishes or for adding to salads.

TIMETABLE FOR COOKING COMMON GRAINS

Check packages of products for additional information.

Type of Grain (1 cup)	Amount of Water in Cups	Cooking Directions	Yield in Cups
Barley, Regular	4	Simmer for 45 to 50 minutes.	4
Barley, Quick-Cooking	2	Simmer for 10 to 12 minutes. Let stand 5 minutes.	3
Bulgur	3	Bring water to boil, then add bulgur; cover and remove from the heat. Let stand 30 to 60 minutes. Drain if needed. Or cook as directed on package.	3
Kasha	2	Bring water to boil, then add Kasha; cover and let stand 10 to 15 minutes. Drain if needed. Or cook as directed on package.	4
Millet	2½	Simmer for 15 to 20 minutes.	4
Oats, Steel-Cut	4	Bring water to boil, then add oats. Simmer uncovered 25 to 30 minutes.	1
Quinoa	2	Simmer for 15 minutes.	3 to 4
Wheat Berries	2½	Simmer for 50 to 60 minutes.	2¾ to 3

POLENTA LOWER CALORIE

Polenta is a staple in northern Italy and Eastern European countries, but we know it as cornmeal mush. It's very versatile, showing up for breakfast with maple syrup, nestled next to a grilled pork chop or topped with pasta sauce.

PREP 10 min TOTAL 30 min • **6 servings**

   1 **cup yellow cornmeal**
   4 **cups water**
1½ **teaspoons salt**
   1 **tablespoon butter or olive oil**

1 In 2-quart saucepan, mix cornmeal and ¾ cup of the water (this helps to prevent clumping). Stir in remaining 3¼ cups water and the salt. Cook over medium heat 8 to 10 minutes, stirring constantly, until mixture thickens and boils; reduce heat.

2 Cover; simmer about 10 minutes, stirring occasionally, until very thick; remove from heat. Add butter; stir until polenta is smooth.

1 Serving (¾ Cup): Calories 80; Total Fat 0g (Saturated Fat 0g; Trans Fat 0g); Cholesterol 0mg; Sodium 590mg; Total Carbohydrate 18g (Dietary Fiber 0g); Protein 2g **Exchanges:** 1 Starch **Carbohydrate Choices:** 1

FRIED POLENTA Spray 9x5-inch loaf pan with cooking spray. After simmering polenta 10 minutes in Step 2, spread in loaf pan. Cover; refrigerate at least 12 hours until firm. Turn pan upside down to unmold. Cut into ½-inch slices. Coat slices with flour. In 10-inch skillet, melt 2 tablespoons butter over low heat. Cook slices in butter about 5 minutes on each side or until brown.

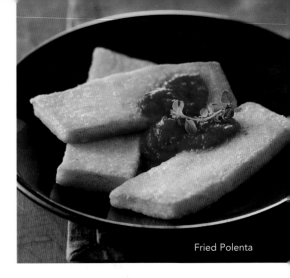

Fried Polenta

FASTER FRIED POLENTA Spread polenta in sprayed 13x9-inch pan; refrigerate uncovered about 3 hours or until firm. Cut into 6 squares. (Cut squares diagonally into triangles if desired.) Cook in butter as directed for Fried Polenta.

PARMESAN POLENTA Make Polenta or Rich and Creamy Polenta as directed—except stir in ½ cup shredded Parmesan cheese with butter in Step 2.

RICH AND CREAMY POLENTA Substitute half-and-half for 1½ cups of the water. Continue as directed.

VEGETABLE POLENTA Stir in 1½ cups frozen mixed vegetables in Step 2 before simmering 5 minutes.

Learn with Betty | COOKING POLENTA

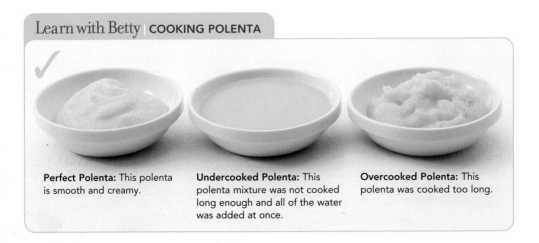

Perfect Polenta: This polenta is smooth and creamy.

Undercooked Polenta: This polenta mixture was not cooked long enough and all of the water was added at once.

Overcooked Polenta: This polenta was cooked too long.

CHEESE GRITS

Coarsely ground dried corn kernels called hominy grits are a treasured tradition in many families. A bowl of steaming-hot grits, topped with a pat of butter, is a breakfast favorite. The cheese can be left out if you prefer.

PREP 20 min TOTAL 1 hr 10 min • **8 servings**

- 2 cups milk
- 2 cups water
- ½ teaspoon salt
- ¼ teaspoon pepper
- 1 cup uncooked quick-cooking corn grits
- 1½ cups shredded Cheddar cheese (6 oz)
- 2 medium green onions, sliced (2 tablespoons)
- 2 eggs, slightly beaten
- 1 tablespoon butter
- ¼ teaspoon paprika

1 Heat oven to 350°F. Spray 1½-quart casserole with cooking spray.

2 In 2-quart saucepan, heat milk, water, salt and pepper to boiling. Gradually add grits, stirring constantly; reduce heat. Simmer uncovered about 5 minutes, stirring frequently, until thickened. Stir in cheese and onions.

3 Stir 1 cup of the grits mixture into eggs, then stir back into remaining grits in saucepan. Pour into casserole. Cut butter into small pieces; sprinkle over grits. Sprinkle with paprika.

4 Bake uncovered 35 to 40 minutes or until set. Let stand 10 minutes before serving.

1 Serving: Calories 220; Total Fat 11g (Saturated Fat 6g; Trans Fat 0g); Cholesterol 85mg; Sodium 340mg; Total Carbohydrate 19g (Dietary Fiber 0g); Protein 11g **Exchanges:** 1 Starch, 1 High-Fat Meat, ½ Fat **Carbohydrate Choices:** 1

LIGHTER DIRECTIONS For 1 gram of fat and 125 calories per serving, use fat-free (skim) milk and 1 cup reduced-fat Cheddar cheese, and substitute ½ cup fat-free egg product for the eggs. Omit butter.

BACON AND CHEESE GRITS Stir in 4 slices cooked and crumbled bacon just before pouring into casserole. Bake as directed.

BULGUR PILAF

Bulgur comes from wheat berries (wheat kernels) that have been steamed, dried and crushed. With its mild flavor and chewy texture, bulgur is a great stand-in for rice in nearly any recipe.

PREP 15 min TOTAL 35 min • **6 servings**

- 2 tablespoons butter
- ½ cup slivered almonds
- 1 medium onion, chopped (½ cup)
- 1 medium carrot, chopped (½ cup)
- 1 can (14 oz) chicken broth (for homemade broth, see page 528)
- 1 cup uncooked bulgur
- ¼ teaspoon lemon-pepper seasoning salt or black pepper
- ¼ cup chopped fresh parsley

1 In 12-inch skillet, melt 1 tablespoon of the butter over medium-high heat. Cook almonds in butter 2 to 3 minutes, stirring constantly, until golden brown. Remove almonds from skillet and set aside.

2 Add remaining 1 tablespoon butter, the onion and carrot to skillet. Cook about 3 minutes, stirring occasionally, until vegetables are crisp-tender.

3 Stir in broth, bulgur and lemon-pepper seasoning salt. Heat to boiling; reduce heat. Cover; simmer about 15 minutes or until bulgur is tender and liquid is absorbed. Stir in almonds and parsley.

1 Serving: Calories 200; Total Fat 9g (Saturated Fat 2.5g; Trans Fat 0g); Cholesterol 10mg; Sodium 330mg; Total Carbohydrate 23g (Dietary Fiber 6g); Protein 7g **Exchanges:** 1 Starch, 1 Vegetable, 1½ Fat **Carbohydrate Choices:** 1½

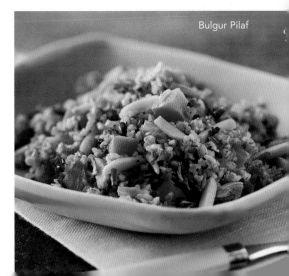

Bulgur Pilaf

LEMON MILLET PILAF

LOWER CALORIE

PREP 10 min **TOTAL** 30 min • **6 servings**

- 1 can (14 oz) chicken broth (for homemade broth, see page 528)
- ⅓ cup water
- ¼ teaspoon onion powder
- ½ cup uncooked millet
- ½ cup uncooked regular long-grain white rice
- ½ cup frozen whole kernel corn (from 12-oz bag)
- ½ cup coarsely chopped fresh parsley
- 1 teaspoon grated lemon peel

1 In 2-quart saucepan, heat broth, water and onion powder to boiling. Stir in millet, rice and corn; reduce heat.

2 Cover; simmer 15 to 20 minutes or until millet and rice are tender and liquid is absorbed. Stir in parsley and lemon peel. Serve immediately.

1 Serving: Calories 150; Total Fat 1.5g (Saturated Fat 0g; Trans Fat 0g); Cholesterol 0mg; Sodium 300mg; Total Carbohydrate 29g (Dietary Fiber 2g); Protein 5g **Exchanges:** 1 Starch, 1 Other Carbohydrate **Carbohydrate Choices:** 2

KASHA AND BOW-TIE PILAF

LOWER CALORIE

To find kasha, also called roasted buckwheat kernels or groats, you may need to look in the health-food, cereal or kosher-food section of your supermarket. If you haven't tried kasha before, we think you will enjoy its toasty, nutty flavor.

PREP 10 min **TOTAL** 35 min • **12 servings**

- 3 tablespoons butter
- 1 large onion, coarsely chopped (1 cup)
- 1 medium red bell pepper, coarsely chopped (1 cup)
- 1 cup sliced fresh mushrooms (3 oz)
- 1 cup uncooked buckwheat kernels or groats (kasha)
- 1 egg, beaten
- 2 cups chicken broth (for homemade broth, see page 528)
- ½ teaspoon salt
- ¼ teaspoon pepper
- 1 cup uncooked bow-tie (farfalle) pasta (2 oz)
- ½ cup chopped fresh parsley

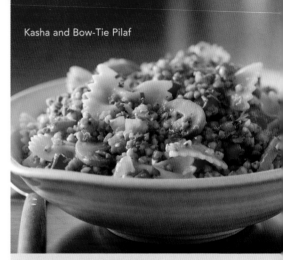

Kasha and Bow-Tie Pilaf

Cooking Kasha

Cook kasha mixed with egg over medium heat about 3 minutes, stirring constantly, until browned and dry.

Cover and simmer in broth 10 to 15 minutes or until broth is absorbed and kasha is tender.

1 In 12-inch nonstick skillet, melt butter over medium heat. Cook onion, bell pepper and mushrooms in butter 3 to 4 minutes, stirring occasionally, until tender. Remove from skillet and set aside.

2 In small bowl, stir kasha and egg, coating well. In same skillet, cook kasha over medium heat about 3 minutes, stirring constantly, until browned and dry.

3 Return vegetables to skillet; stir in broth, salt and pepper. Heat to boiling; reduce heat to low. Cover; simmer 10 to 15 minutes or until broth is absorbed and kasha is tender.

4 Meanwhile, cook and drain pasta as directed on package. Stir cooked pasta and parsley into kasha mixture.

1 Serving: Calories 100; Total Fat 4g (Saturated Fat 1.5g; Trans Fat 0g); Cholesterol 25mg; Sodium 300mg; Total Carbohydrate 13g (Dietary Fiber 2g); Protein 4g **Exchanges:** 1 Starch, ½ Fat **Carbohydrate Choices:** 1

RED HARVEST QUINOA

Quinoa, pronounced KEEN-wah, was a staple grain of the Incas of South America. It's very mild in flavor and loaded with nutrients. Before cooking, it needs to be thoroughly rinsed to remove its natural bitter coating.

PREP 20 min TOTAL 45 min • **8 servings**

- 1 cup uncooked red or white quinoa
- 1 tablespoon butter
- ½ cup coarsely chopped apple
- ⅓ cup chopped celery
- ¼ cup chopped red onion
- 1½ cups roasted vegetable stock (from 32-oz carton) or chicken broth (for homemade broth, see page 528)
- ½ cup orange juice
- ½ cup sweetened dried cranberries or cherries
- 1 jar (1¾ oz) pine nuts (about ⅓ cup), toasted (page 22)*
- ¼ cup shredded Parmesan cheese (1 oz)
- ¼ teaspoon salt
- 2 tablespoons finely chopped fresh parsley

1 Rinse quinoa thoroughly by placing in a fine-mesh strainer and holding under cold running water until water runs clear; drain well.

2 In 2-quart saucepan, melt butter over medium heat. Cook apple, celery, onion and quinoa in butter 5 minutes, stirring occasionally.

3 Stir in vegetable stock and orange juice. Heat to boiling; reduce heat. Cover; simmer 15 to 20 minutes or until all liquid is absorbed and quinoa is tender. Fluff with fork; stir in cranberries, pine nuts, cheese and salt. Sprinkle with parsley.

*Chopped walnuts or pecans can be substituted.

1 Serving (½ Cup): Calories 190; Total Fat 8g (Saturated Fat 2g; Trans Fat 0g); Cholesterol 5mg; Sodium 340mg; Total Carbohydrate 26g (Dietary Fiber 2g); Protein 5g **Exchanges:** 1½ Starch, 1½ Fat **Carbohydrate Choices:** 2

Quinoa

Tiny and bead-shaped, quinoa cooks quickly and expands to four times its volume. The flavor is delicate and similar to couscous. Look for it at most supermarkets and in health-food stores.

CREAMY QUINOA PRIMAVERA

PREP 10 min TOTAL 35 min • **6 servings**

- 1½ cups uncooked white quinoa
- 3 cups chicken broth (for homemade broth, see page 528)
- 1 package (3 oz) cream cheese, cut into cubes
- 1 tablespoon chopped fresh or 1 teaspoon dried basil leaves
- 2 teaspoons butter
- 2 cloves garlic, finely chopped
- 5 cups thinly sliced or bite-size pieces assorted uncooked vegetables (asparagus, broccoli, carrot or zucchini)
- 2 tablespoons grated Romano cheese

1 Rinse quinoa thoroughly by placing in a fine-mesh strainer and holding under cold running water until water runs clear; drain well.

2 In 2-quart saucepan, heat quinoa and broth to boiling; reduce heat. Cover; simmer 15 to 20 minutes or until all broth is absorbed. Stir in cream cheese and basil.

3 In 10-inch nonstick skillet, melt butter over medium-high heat. Cook garlic in butter about 30 seconds, stirring frequently, until golden. Stir in vegetables. Cook 2 to 4 minutes, stirring frequently, until vegetables are crisp-tender. Add quinoa mixture; toss. Sprinkle with Romano cheese.

1 Serving: Calories 280; Total Fat 10g (Saturated Fat 4.5g; Trans Fat 0g); Cholesterol 20mg; Sodium 630mg; Total Carbohydrate 36g (Dietary Fiber 5g); Protein 12g **Exchanges:** 2 Starch, 1 Vegetable, ½ Medium-Fat Meat, 1 Fat **Carbohydrate Choices:** 2½

Creamy Quinoa Primavera

TOASTED BARLEY WITH MIXED VEGETABLES **LOWER CALORIE**

Barley is a good source of protein, and it tastes good, too.

PREP 10 min **TOTAL** 1 hr 20 min • **6 servings**

- ½ cup uncooked hulled barley
- 1 can (14 oz) chicken broth (for homemade broth, see page 528)
- 2 large onions, chopped (2 cups)
- 2 packages (8 oz each) sliced fresh mushrooms (6 cups)
- 4 medium carrots, cut into julienne strips (2 cups)
- 1 large red bell pepper, coarsely chopped (1½ cups)
- 2 tablespoons chopped fresh or 1 tablespoon dried dill weed
- ½ teaspoon pepper
- 4 medium green onions, chopped (¼ cup)

1 Spray 12-inch skillet with cooking spray. Cook barley in skillet over medium heat 6 to 8 minutes, stirring frequently until barley begins to brown, then stirring constantly until golden brown. Reduce heat to low; add broth. Cover; simmer 40 minutes.

2 Stir in remaining ingredients except green onions. Heat to boiling over high heat; reduce heat to low. Cover; simmer 20 minutes longer or until vegetables are tender. Sprinkle with green onions.

1 Serving (1 Cup): Calories 140; Total Fat 1g (Saturated Fat 0g; Trans Fat 0g); Cholesterol 0mg; Sodium 320mg; Total Carbohydrate 26g (Dietary Fiber 6g); Protein 6g **Exchanges:** 1 Starch, ½ Other Carbohydrate, 1 Vegetable **Carbohydrate Choices:** 2

Barley

Cultivated since the Stone Age, this hearty grain can be used in many ways. It's great in side dishes, for soups or in main dishes. It's often mixed with other grains and adds lots of texture. Toasting barley helps to bring out the wonderful nutty flavor of this hearty grain.

Toasting Barley

Cook barley over medium heat 6 to 8 minutes, stirring frequently until barley begins to brown.

Then cook stirring constantly, until golden brown.

Toasted Barley with Mixed Vegetables

BEAN BASICS

Available dried, canned and frozen, beans are extremely versatile and, with their mild flavor, pair well with countless seasonings. They also make an excellent substitute for meat. Beans, along with peanuts, lentils, soybeans and peas, are considered legumes.

STORING BEANS

Uncooked (Dried): Store up to 1 year at room temperature in a cool, dry location in tightly covered container with a label and date.

Cooked: Cover and store in the refrigerator 2 to 3 days or freeze in airtight container up to 6 months.

PREPARING BEANS FOR COOKING

Before cooking dried beans, sort through to remove any shriveled, small or damaged ones and to remove stones; rinse and drain. With the exception of black-eyed peas, lentils and splits peas, dried legumes need to be soaked before cooking to soften and plump them. Because they rehydrate to triple their dry size, choose a pot that's big enough. There are two methods for soaking beans:

- **Quick-Soak Method:** Place dried beans in a large saucepan; add enough water to cover. Heat to boiling; boil 2 minutes. Remove from heat, cover and let stand for at least 1 hour. Drain, then cook in fresh, cold water.

- **Long-Soak Method:** Place dried beans in a large saucepan or bowl; add enough cold water to cover. Let stand 8 to 24 hours. Drain then cook in fresh, cold water.

COOKING BEANS

Soak 1 cup dried beans using one of the methods described above in a 3- to 4-quart saucepan; drain and add fresh water to cover. Heat to boiling; boil uncovered 2 minutes. Reduce heat to low. Cover and simmer (do not boil or beans will burst), stirring occasionally, for the time indicated in the Timetable for Cooking Dried Beans, page 444, or until tender. Beans continue to dry with age, so you may need to add a little more water and cook longer if beans have absorbed all the water but aren't quite tender. Very old beans may never soften completely.

DRIED BEANS AND LENTILS

There are many types of beans and lentils available, and here is some information on the more unusual varieties.

Adzuki Beans: Mild, nutty flavor, similar to kidney beans and interchangeable with them.

Fava Beans: Large, flat beans; earthy flavor. Appear brown and wrinkled when dried. *Habas* are dried favas with skins removed. Used in Mediterranean and Middle Eastern dishes, such as falafel.

French Green Lentils: Considered to be the most flavorful lentils. They don't get mushy as fast as other varieties, making them a good choice in recipes requiring firmer lentils.

Mayocoba (Peruano) Beans: Light, buttery taste; soft, creamy texture. Common in Latin American and northern Mexican cooking.

Mung Beans: Sweet flavor; popular in India and China. Interchangeable with lentils or peas in recipes. Called *grams*, or when hulled, *moong dal.*

Peas (Green, Yellow): Field peas grown for drying. Available whole, hulled and split. Yellow peas milder than green; split peas are sweeter, less starchy than whole peas.

Pink Beans: Interchangeable with pinto beans. Popular in southwestern cooking.

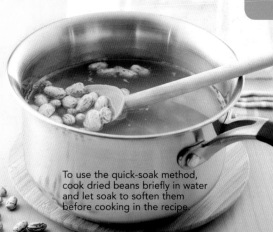

To use the quick-soak method, cook dried beans briefly in water and let soak to soften them before cooking in the recipe.

Pink Beans

Great Northern Beans

Kidney Beans

Adzuki Beans

Split Mung Beans

Mung Beans

Red Beans

Small Red Beans

Pinto Beans

Black Beans

Bayo Bea

Mayocoba (Peruano)

Fava Beans

Lentils

Whole Lentils

Lima Beans

Baby Limas

Red Lentils

Broad Beans

Soybeans

Navy Beans

French Green Lentils

Green Split Peas

Yellow Split Peas

Whole Green Peas

Garbanzo Beans (Chickpeas)

TIMETABLE FOR COOKING DRIED BEANS

Place beans in a large saucepan; add enough water to cover, and soak if needed using one of the methods described on page 443. Drain and add fresh water to cover. Bring to a boil; reduce heat to low; then cover and simmer, stirring occasionally, for the amount of time specified below.

Type of Bean (⅔ Cup)	Simmer Time	Yield in Cups
Adzuki Beans Lentils	30 to 45 minutes	2 to 3
Mung Beans Split Peas	45 to 60 minutes	2 to 2¼
Black-Eyed Peas, Butter Beans, Cannellini Beans, Great Northern Beans, Lima Beans, Navy Beans, Pinto Beans	1 to 1½ hours	2 to 2½
Anasazi Beans, Black Beans, Fava Beans, Kidney Beans	1 to 2 hours	2
Garbanzo Beans (Chickpeas)	2 to 2½ hours	2
Soybeans	3 to 4 hours	2

CANNELLINI WITH TOMATOES AND SAGE FAST

Cannellini are simply large white kidney beans. You could use red kidney beans if you like for this dish.

PREP 15 min TOTAL 15 min • **4 servings**

- 1 tablespoon olive or vegetable oil
- 2 cloves garlic, finely chopped
- 1 can (14.5 oz) diced tomatoes, undrained
- 1 can (15 or 19 oz) cannellini beans, drained, rinsed
- 1 tablespoon finely chopped fresh or ½ teaspoon dried sage leaves
- ¼ teaspoon coarse (kosher or sea) salt
- ⅛ teaspoon pepper

1 In 10-inch skillet, heat oil over medium heat. Add garlic; cook 1 to 2 minutes, stirring constantly, until light golden brown.

2 Stir in tomatoes, beans and sage. Heat to boiling. Reduce heat; simmer uncovered 5 to 7 minutes or until most of the liquid has evaporated. Stir in salt and pepper.

1 **Serving:** Calories 190; Total Fat 4g (Saturated Fat 0.5g; Trans Fat 0g); Cholesterol 0mg; Sodium 280mg; Total Carbohydrate 28g (Dietary Fiber 7g); Protein 10g **Exchanges:** 1½ Starch, 1 Vegetable, ½ Very Lean Meat, ½ Fat **Carbohydrate Choices:** 2

RED BEANS AND RICE

PREP 10 min TOTAL 2 hr • **8 servings**

- 1 cup dried kidney beans (8 oz), sorted, rinsed*
- 3 cups water
- 2 oz salt pork (with rind), diced, or 3 slices bacon, cut up
- 1 medium green bell pepper, chopped (1 cup)
- 1 medium onion, chopped (½ cup)
- 1 cup uncooked regular long-grain white rice
- 1 teaspoon salt

1 In 3-quart saucepan, heat beans and water to boiling. Boil uncovered 2 minutes; reduce heat. Cover; simmer 1 hour to 1 hour 15 minutes or until tender (do not boil or beans will fall apart). Drain beans, reserving liquid.

2 In 10-inch skillet, cook salt pork over medium heat, stirring occasionally, until crisp. Stir in bell pepper and onion. Cook, stirring occasionally, until onion is tender.

3 Add enough water to bean liquid, if necessary, to measure 2 cups. Add bean liquid, salt pork mixture, rice and salt to beans in 3-quart saucepan. Heat to boiling, stirring once or twice; reduce heat. Cover; simmer 14 minutes (do not lift cover or stir). Remove from heat. Fluff with fork. Cover; let steam 5 to 10 minutes.

1 can (15 to 15.5 oz) red kidney beans, drained and liquid reserved, can be substituted for the dried kidney beans. Omit water and skip Step 1.

1 **Serving (¾ Cup):** Calories 210; Total Fat 4.5g (Saturated Fat 1.5g; Trans Fat 0g); Cholesterol 0mg; Sodium 360mg; Total Carbohydrate 35g (Dietary Fiber 4g); Protein 7g **Exchanges:** 2 Starch, 1 Vegetable, ½ Fat **Carbohydrate Choices:** 2

SLOW COOKER **DIRECTIONS** Increase water to 3¼ cups. Use 1⅓ cups uncooked instant white rice. Spray 3½- to 6-quart slow cooker with cooking spray. In slow cooker, mix all ingredients except rice. Cover; cook on High heat setting 3 hours 30 minutes to 4 hours 30 minutes or until beans are tender. Stir in rice. Cover; cook 15 minutes longer. Stir well.

HOPPIN' JOHN Substitute 1 cup dried black-eyed peas for the kidney beans. Omit bell pepper.

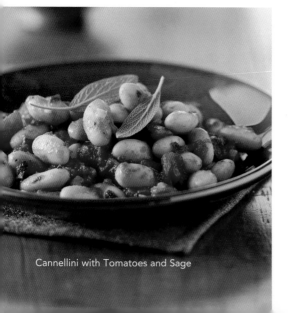

Cannellini with Tomatoes and Sage

Heirloom Recipe and New Twist

You know you have a popular recipe when it shows up again and again, no matter where you are or what the occasion. And so it is with this terrific casserole that's perfect for potlucks and other gatherings. This recipe has been printed in many of our cookbooks over the years and is an often-requested favorite. The new twist spices it up a bit and has a great combination of beans for a new look and taste.

CLASSIC

THREE-BEAN CASSEROLE

PREP 10 min **TOTAL** 1 hr 5 min • **8 servings**

- **1** lb lean (at least 80%) ground beef
- **2** medium stalks celery, sliced (1 cup)
- **1** medium onion, chopped (½ cup)
- **1** large clove garlic, finely chopped
- **2** cans (16 oz each) baked beans (any variety), undrained
- **1** can (15 to 16 oz) lima or butter beans, drained, rinsed
- **1** can (15 to 15.5 oz) kidney beans, drained, rinsed
- **1** cup barbecue sauce
- **1** tablespoon ground mustard
- **2** tablespoons honey or packed brown sugar
- **1** tablespoon white or cider vinegar
- **¼** teaspoon red pepper sauce

1 Heat oven to 400°F. In 10-inch skillet, cook beef, celery, onion and garlic over medium heat 8 to 10 minutes, stirring occasionally, until beef is no longer pink; drain.

2 In ungreased 3-quart casserole, mix beef mixture and remaining ingredients. Bake uncovered about 45 minutes, stirring once, until hot and bubbly.

1 Serving (1⅓ Cups): Calories 420; Total Fat 10g (Saturated Fat 3g; Trans Fat 0g); Cholesterol 20mg; Sodium 1400mg; Total Carbohydrate 62g (Dietary Fiber 16g); Protein 22g **Exchanges:** 4 Starch, 1 Fat **Carbohydrate Choices:** 4

SLOW COOKER **DIRECTIONS** Cook beef and vegetables as directed in Step 1. Spray 3½- to 6-quart slow cooker with cooking spray. In slow cooker, mix beef mixture and remaining ingredients. Cover; cook on High heat setting 2 hours to 2 hours 30 minutes to blend flavors.

PORK THREE-BEAN CASSEROLE Substitute 1 lb bulk pork sausage for the ground beef and 1 can (8 oz) tomato sauce for the barbecue sauce.

Three-Bean Casserole

Italian Three-Bean and Sausage Casserole

ITALIAN THREE-BEAN AND SAUSAGE CASSEROLE

We like the spicy pork sausage in this new recipe, but you could use mild or sweet sausage, or why not try turkey Italian sausage for another twist?

PREP 10 min **TOTAL** 1 hr 5 min • **6 servings**

- 1 lb bulk spicy Italian pork sausage
- 1 large red bell pepper, chopped (1½ cups)
- 1 medium onion, chopped (½ cup)
- 1 large clove garlic, finely chopped
- 2 cans (15 oz each) cannellini beans, drained, rinsed
- 1 can (15.5 oz) great northern beans, drained, rinsed
- 1 can (15 to 16 oz) garbanzo beans, drained, rinsed
- 1 jar (1 lb 10 oz) tomato pasta sauce with basil and garlic
- 1½ teaspoons chopped fresh or ½ teaspoon dried basil leaves
   Additional chopped fresh basil

1 Heat oven to 400°F. In 10-inch skillet, cook sausage, bell pepper, onion and garlic over medium heat 8 to 10 minutes, stirring occasionally, until sausage is no longer pink; drain.

2 In ungreased 3-quart casserole, mix sausage mixture and remaining ingredients. Bake uncovered about 45 minutes, stirring once, until hot and bubbly. Garnish with additional basil.

1 Serving (1⅓ Cups): Calories 530; Total Fat 14g (Saturated Fat 3.5g; Trans Fat 0g); Cholesterol 30mg; Sodium 1230mg; Total Carbohydrate 70g (Dietary Fiber 17g); Protein 30g **Exchanges:** 3 Starch, 1½ Other Carbohydrate, 1½ Very Lean Meat, 1½ High-Fat Meat **Carbohydrate Choices:** 4½

See how to make **three-bean casserole:** Visit bettycrocker.com/BCcookbook

Homemade Baked Beans

HOMEMADE BAKED BEANS

PREP 20 min **TOTAL** 6 hr 35 min • **10 servings**

- 1 bag (16 oz) dried navy beans (2 cups), sorted, rinsed
- 10 cups water
- ½ cup packed brown sugar
- ¼ cup light or dark molasses
- 1 teaspoon salt
- 6 slices bacon, crisply cooked, crumbled (about ⅓ cup)
- 1 medium onion, chopped (½ cup)
- 3 cups water

1 Heat oven to 350°F. In ovenproof 4-quart Dutch oven, heat beans and 10 cups water to boiling. Boil uncovered 2 minutes.

2 Stir in remaining ingredients except 3 cups water. Cover; bake 4 hours, stirring occasionally.

3 Stir in 3 cups water. Bake uncovered 2 hours to 2 hours 15 minutes longer, stirring occasionally, until beans are tender and desired consistency.

1 Serving (½ Cup): Calories 240; Total Fat 3g (Saturated Fat 1g; Trans Fat 0g); Cholesterol 0mg; Sodium 320mg; Total Carbohydrate 43g (Dietary Fiber 6g); Protein 10g **Exchanges:** 2 Starch, 2 Vegetable **Carbohydrate Choices:** 3

SLOW COOKER DIRECTIONS Spray 3½- to 6-quart slow cooker with cooking spray. In slow cooker, place beans and 5 cups water. Cover; cook on High heat setting 2 hours. Turn off heat; let stand 8 to 24 hours. Stir in brown sugar, molasses, salt, bacon and onion. Cover; cook on Low heat setting 10 to 12 hours or until beans are very tender and most of liquid is absorbed.

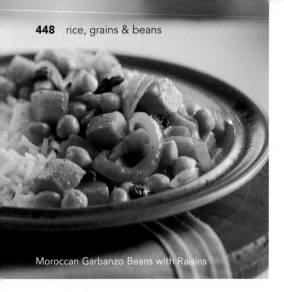

Moroccan Garbanzo Beans with Raisins

CARIBBEAN BLACK BEANS

PREP 15 min TOTAL 1 hr 10 min • **5 servings**

4½ cups water
1½ cups dried black beans (10 oz)*
 2 teaspoons vegetable oil
 1 medium papaya or mango, peeled, seeded and diced (about 1½ cups)
 1 medium red bell pepper, finely chopped (1 cup)
½ cup finely chopped red onion (about 1 medium)
½ cup orange juice
¼ cup lime juice
 2 tablespoons chopped fresh cilantro
½ teaspoon ground red pepper (cayenne)
 2 cloves garlic, finely chopped
 5 cups hot cooked rice (page 429)

1 In 2-quart saucepan, heat water and beans to boiling. Boil uncovered 2 minutes; reduce heat. Cover; simmer about 45 minutes, stirring occasionally, until beans are tender. Drain.

2 In 10-inch skillet, heat oil over medium heat. Cook remaining ingredients except rice in oil about 5 minutes, stirring occasionally, until bell pepper is crisp-tender. Stir in beans. Cook about 5 minutes or until hot. Serve over rice.

2 cans (15 oz each) black beans, drained and rinsed, can be substituted for the dried black beans. Omit water and Step 1.

1 Serving: Calories 450; Total Fat 3g (Saturated Fat 0.5g; Trans Fat 0g); Cholesterol 0mg; Sodium 10mg; Total Carbohydrate 89g (Dietary Fiber 14g); Protein 17g **Exchanges:** 4 Starch, 2 Fruit **Carbohydrate Choices:** 6

MOROCCAN GARBANZO BEANS WITH RAISINS FAST

Garbanzo, chickpea, ceci. This bean with many names shares culinary history in Mediterranean, Middle Eastern, Indian and Mexican cultures. Unlike most cooked legumes, this nutty-flavored bean has a firm texture.

PREP 20 min TOTAL 20 min • **4 servings**

1⅓ cups uncooked regular long-grain white rice
2⅔ cups water
 1 tablespoon olive or vegetable oil
 1 large onion, sliced
 1 medium onion, chopped (½ cup)
 1 clove garlic, finely chopped
 1 cup diced seeded peeled acorn or butternut squash
¼ cup raisins
 1 cup chicken broth (for homemade broth, see page 528)
 1 teaspoon ground turmeric
 1 teaspoon ground cinnamon
½ teaspoon ground ginger
 1 can (15 to 16 oz) garbanzo beans, drained, rinsed

1 Cook rice in water as directed on package.

2 Meanwhile, in 3-quart saucepan, heat oil over medium heat. Cook sliced onion, chopped onion and garlic in oil about 7 minutes, stirring occasionally, until onions are tender. Stir in remaining ingredients except garbanzo beans.

3 Heat to boiling; reduce heat. Cover; simmer about 8 minutes, stirring occasionally, until squash is tender. Stir in beans; heat thoroughly. Serve over rice.

1 Serving: Calories 470; Total Fat 6g (Saturated Fat 1g; Trans Fat 0g); Cholesterol 0mg; Sodium 860mg; Total Carbohydrate 88g (Dietary Fiber 11g); Protein 14g **Exchanges:** 5 Starch, ½ Fruit, ½ Other Carbohydrate, ½ Fat **Carbohydrate Choices:** 6

Beans

Switching beans in a recipe is often a great way to change the flavor. It's an easy switch with canned beans. For dried beans, check the package label or the Timetable for Cooking Dried Beans on page 444 to be sure they cook in the same time as your recipe.

SALADS & SALAD DRESSINGS

SALADS

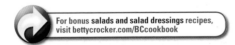

For bonus **salads and salad dressings** recipes,
visit bettycrocker.com/BCcookbook

FAST = Ready in 20 minutes or less **LOWER CALORIE** = See Helpful Nutrition and Cooking Information, page 685
LIGHTER = 25% fewer calories or grams of fat **MAKE AHEAD** = Make-ahead directions **SLOW COOKER** = Slow cooker directions

← Rinsing salad greens, Classic Tabbouleh (page 469), Asparagus-Strawberry Salad with Lemon-Honey Dressing (page 462), Seven-Layer Salad (page 462)

SALAD BASICS
From mixed greens and fresh fruit to tender pasta and crisp vegetables, salad ingredients span a range of flavors and textures. In this chapter, you'll find a selection of side salads that complement other recipes on your menu, as well as salads that can stand alone as a main course. Or make the featured homemade dressings and take basic tossed salads from simple to spectacular.

SELECTING, STORING AND HANDLING SALAD GREENS

- Choose fresh, crisp greens with no bruising, discoloration or wilting.
- Remove roots and stems, if necessary, and any brown or wilted spots.
- Store unwashed greens in a paper towel–lined sealed plastic bag or a tightly covered container with damp (not wet) paper towels; refrigerate up to 5 days.
- Rinse greens under cold water and shake off excess moisture before using.
- Salad greens should be as dry as possible when using so dressings cling and don't get watery.
    - Dry greens with a salad spinner or put on a clean kitchen towel or several layers of paper towels, pat dry.
    - Gently roll up washed and dried greens in a towel or paper towels; place in a plastic bag and refrigerate for 3 to 5 days.

Store greens in a paper towel–lined bag.

Drying Lettuce

Salad Spinner: Place washed leaves in basket of spinner; cover spinner and spin until lettuce is dry.

Towel Dry: Place washed leaves on clean kitchen towel or in several layers of paper towels and pat dry.

MILD GREENS

Butterhead Lettuce (Bibb, Boston): Small rounded heads of soft, tender, buttery leaves; delicate, mild flavor.

Iceberg Lettuce (Crisphead): Solid, compact heads with leaves ranging in color from medium green outer leaves to pale green inner ones; very crisp, mild flavor.

Leaf Lettuce (Green, Red, Oak): Tender, crisp leaves in loose heads. Mildly flavored but stronger than iceberg lettuce.

Mâche (Corn Salad): Spoon-shaped medium- to dark-green leaves with velvety texture; mild, subtly sweet and nutty.

Mesclun (Field or Wild Greens): A mixture of young, tender, small greens often including arugula, chervil, chickweed, dandelion, frisée, mizuna and oak leaf lettuce.

Mixed Salad Greens (Prepackaged): These prewashed greens come in many varieties, some with dressing, croutons or cheese.

Romaine Lettuce (Cos): Narrow, elongated, dark green, crisp leaves with tips sometimes tinged with red. The broad white center rib is especially crunchy.

Butterhead Lettuce (Boston)

Mesclun

Escarole

Mâche

Spinach

Frisée

Romaine Lettuce

Arugula

Watercress

Radicchio

Curly Endive

Iceberg Lettuce

Leaf Lettuce (Red and Green)

Belgian Endive

Collard
Greens

Dandelion
Greens

Mustard
Greens

Beet
Greens

Chard

BOLD GREENS AND CABBAGE

Arugula (Rocket): Small, slender, dark green leaves similar to radish leaves; slightly bitter, peppery mustard flavor.
Pick smaller leaves for milder flavor.

Belgian Endive (French): Narrow, cupped, cream-colored leaves tinged with green or red; slightly bitter flavor.

Cabbage: Comes in several distinctly flavored varieties. Green and red cabbage are most common; look for compact heads of waxy, tightly wrapped leaves. Savoy cabbage has crinkled leaves and Chinese (or napa) cabbage has long, crisp leaves.

Curly Endive: Frilly, narrow, slightly prickly leaves; slightly bitter taste.

Escarole: Broad, wavy, medium-green leaves; slightly bitter flavor but milder than Belgian or curly endive.

Frisée: Slender, curly leaves ranging in color from yellow-white to yellow-green; slightly bitter flavor.

Greens (Beet, Chard, Collard, Dandelion, Mustard): All have a strong, sharp flavor. Young greens are milder and more tender for tossed salads; older greens are more bitter and should be cooked for best flavor.

Kale: Firm dark green leaves with frilly edges tinged with shades of blue and purple; mild cabbage taste. Pick young, small leaves for best flavor.

Radicchio: Looks like a small, loose-leaf cabbage with smooth, tender leaves; slightly bitter flavor. The two most common radicchios in the United States are a ruby red variety with broad white veins and one with leaves speckled in shades of pink, red and green.

Sorrel (Sour Grass): Resembles spinach, but with smaller leaves; sharp, lemony flavor.

Spinach: Smooth, tapered, dark green leaves, sometimes with crumpled edges; slightly bitter flavor. Baby spinach leaves are smaller and milder in flavor than regular spinach leaves.

Watercress: Small, crisp, dark green, coin-size leaves; strong peppery flavor.

Learn to Make Caesar Salad

CAESAR SALAD

This classic salad is the perfect go-to recipe to accompany most any meal. It's not hard to whip up, but knowing how to make a great dressing and crisp croutons turns a ho-hum Caesar into a specialty salad that folks will ask you to make again and again.

PREP 15 min **TOTAL** 15 min • **6 servings**

1 clove garlic, cut in half
8 anchovy fillets, cut up*
⅓ cup olive oil
3 tablespoons fresh lemon juice
1 teaspoon Worcestershire sauce
¼ teaspoon salt
¼ teaspoon ground mustard

Freshly ground pepper
1 large or 2 small bunches romaine lettuce, torn into bite-size pieces (10 cups)
1 cup Garlic Croutons (at right)
⅓ cup freshly grated Parmesan cheese

1 Rub large salad bowl with cut clove of garlic for extra flavor if desired. Chop garlic and place in bowl.

2 In salad bowl, using wire whisk, mix anchovies, oil, lemon juice, Worcestershire sauce, salt, mustard and pepper.

3 Add romaine; toss until coated. Sprinkle with croutons and cheese; toss. Serve immediately.

*2 teaspoons anchovy paste can be substituted. If you prefer, anchovies can be omitted.

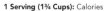

1 Serving (1¾ Cups): Calories 190; Total Fat 16g (Saturated Fat 3g; Trans Fat 0g); Cholesterol 10mg; Sodium 500mg; Total Carbohydrate 7g (Dietary Fiber 2g); Protein 6g **Exchanges:** 1½ Vegetable, ½ High-Fat Meat, 2½ Fat **Carbohydrate Choices:** ½

CHICKEN CAESAR SALAD Broil or grill 6 boneless skinless chicken breasts (pages 305 and 424); slice diagonally and arrange on salads. Serve chicken warm or chilled.

SHRIMP CAESAR SALAD Broil or grill 1 lb deveined peeled large shrimp (page 291); arrange on salads. Serve shrimp warm or chilled.

Keys to Success

- **Rub bowl with garlic** to impart a light garlic flavor to lettuce when tossed if desired.

- **Chop garlic pieces** to add more garlic flavor to salad.

- **Use whisk to mix** all dressing ingredients together so that oil is suspended (emulsified) with other ingredients.

- **Toss salad by scooping up lettuce,** croutons and dressing with salad utensils or tongs in batches to get dressing onto lettuce gently without bruising or breaking leaves.

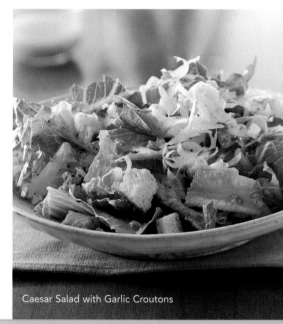

Caesar Salad with Garlic Croutons

Juicing Lemons

Before squeezing, roll lemon back and forth on counter several times with palm of hand, using firm pressure, to help burst the cells holding the juice.

Cut lemon in half crosswise. Using citrus reamer, press into center of cut side of lemon and twist to squeeze out juice. Strain juice through small mesh strainer to remove seeds.

Fresh Lemon Juice

Room-temperature lemons (and limes) yield more juice. Microwave whole lemons on High for about 20 seconds to warm them up.

Other ways to juice lemons are:

- **Lemon Juicer:** To use lemon juicer, press cut side of lemon over center of juicer to squeeze out juice.

- **Hands:** Lemon halves can also be squeezed over cupped palm of hand to catch seeds while juice goes between fingers into a bowl below.

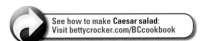

See how to make **Caesar salad:** Visit bettycrocker.com/BCcookbook

CROUTONS

PREP 10 min **TOTAL** 55 min • **16 servings**

- 10 slices (½ inch thick) firm white or whole-grain bread
- ½ cup butter, melted*

1 Heat oven to 300°F. Cut bread slices into ½-inch cubes. Spread in single layer in 15x10x1-inch pan. Drizzle butter evenly over bread cubes; toss to coat.

2 Bake 30 to 35 minutes, stirring occasionally, or until golden brown, dry and crisp. Cool completely. Store tightly covered at room temperature up to 2 days.

*Olive oil can be substituted. After drizzling bread cubes with oil, sprinkle evenly with ½ teaspoon salt; toss to coat.

1 Serving (¼ Cup): Calories 90; Total Fat 6g (Saturated Fat 4g, Trans Fat 0g); Cholesterol 15mg; Sodium 150mg; Total Carbohydrate 8g (Dietary Fiber 0g); Protein 1g **Exchanges:** ½ Starch, 1 Fat **Carbohydrate Choices:** ½

GARLIC CROUTONS Add 3 cloves garlic, very finely chopped, or ¼ teaspoon garlic powder to butter before drizzling over bread cubes.

HERBED CROUTONS Drizzle bread cubes with olive oil instead of butter. Sprinkle with 2 teaspoons Italian seasoning and ½ teaspoon salt; toss to coat.

PUMPERNICKEL OR RYE CROUTONS Substitute pumpernickel or rye bread. Bake as directed or until pumpernickel cubes are dry and crisp and rye cubes are light golden brown, dry and crisp.

Greek Salad

GREEK SALAD FAST LOWER CALORIE

PREP 20 min TOTAL 20 min • **8 servings**

LEMON DRESSING

¼ cup olive oil
2 tablespoons fresh lemon juice
1½ teaspoons Dijon mustard
½ teaspoon sugar
¼ teaspoon salt
⅛ teaspoon pepper

SALAD

5 cups fresh baby spinach leaves
1 head Boston lettuce, torn into bite-size pieces (4 cups)
1 cup crumbled feta cheese (4 oz)
24 pitted kalamata or Greek olives*
4 medium green onions, sliced (¼ cup)**
3 medium tomatoes, cut into wedges
1 medium cucumber, sliced

In tightly covered container, shake all dressing ingredients. In large bowl, toss salad ingredients and dressing. Serve immediately.

Extra-large pitted ripe olives can be substituted.

**Chopped red onion can be substituted.*

1 Serving (1¾ Cups): Calories 140; Total Fat 11g (Saturated Fat 3.5g; Trans Fat 0g); Cholesterol 15mg; Sodium 680mg; Total Carbohydrate 6g (Dietary Fiber 2g); Protein 4g **Exchanges:** 1 Vegetable, 2½ Fat **Carbohydrate Choices:** ½

SPINACH-BACON SALAD

LOWER CALORIE

A little bit sweet, a little bit salty—this classic salad is delicious. Look for bags of prewashed spinach to get this on the table faster.

PREP 20 min TOTAL 20 min • **6 servings**

4 slices bacon, cut into ½-inch pieces
3 tablespoons vegetable oil
5 medium green onions, chopped (⅓ cup)
2 teaspoons sugar
½ teaspoon salt
¼ teaspoon pepper
2 tablespoons white or cider vinegar
8 oz fresh spinach (9 cups)
2 Hard-Cooked Eggs (page 74), sliced

1 In 10-inch skillet, cook bacon over medium heat, stirring occasionally, until crisp. Remove bacon with slotted spoon; drain on paper towels. Drain all but 3 tablespoons bacon drippings from skillet (if fewer than 3 tablespoons remain, add enough vegetable oil to drippings to equal 3 tablespoons).

2 Add oil, onions, sugar, salt and pepper to drippings in skillet. Cook over medium heat 2 to 3 minutes, stirring occasionally, until onions are slightly softened. Stir in vinegar.

3 Place spinach in very large bowl. Pour warm dressing over spinach; toss to coat. Arrange egg slices on top. Crumble bacon and sprinkle on top. Serve immediately.

1 Serving (1½ Cups): Calories 140; Total Fat 11g (Saturated Fat 2.5g; Trans Fat 0g); Cholesterol 75mg; Sodium 150mg; Total Carbohydrate 4g (Dietary Fiber 2g); Protein 5g **Exchanges:** 1 Vegetable, ½ Lean Meat, 2 Fat **Carbohydrate Choices:** 0

Washing Spinach

To wash fresh spinach, remove and discard stems. Place leaves in sink or bowl filled with cool water. Swish with hands in water to rinse dirt from spinach. Lift leaves up to drain off excess water. Repeat until no dirt remains, changing water if necessary.

Spinach-Bacon Salad

Gorgonzola–Toasted Walnut Salad

GORGONZOLA–TOASTED WALNUT SALAD FAST

PREP 20 min TOTAL 20 min • **6 servings**

TOASTED WALNUT DRESSING

⅓ cup olive or vegetable oil

⅓ cup coarsely chopped walnuts, toasted (page 22)

2 tablespoons fresh lemon juice

1 clove garlic

⅛ teaspoon salt

Dash pepper

SALAD

1 to 2 heads radicchio, torn into bite-size pieces (4 cups)

1 to 2 heads Bibb lettuce, torn into bite-size pieces (4 cups)

½ cup crumbled Gorgonzola or blue cheese (2 oz)

½ cup ½-inch pieces fresh chives

⅓ cup coarsely chopped walnuts, toasted (page 22)

1 In blender or food processor, place all dressing ingredients. Cover; blend on high speed about 1 minute or until smooth.

2 In large bowl, toss salad ingredients and dressing. Serve immediately.

1 Serving: Calories 260; Total Fat 24g (Saturated Fat 4.5g; Trans Fat 0g); Cholesterol 10mg; Sodium 230mg; Total Carbohydrate 7g (Dietary Fiber 3g); Protein 5g **Exchanges:** 1 Starch, 5 Fat **Carbohydrate Choices:** ½

GORGONZOLA, PEAR AND TOASTED WALNUT SALAD Core and slice 2 medium ripe pears; add with salad ingredients in Step 2.

CHÈVRE–TOASTED WALNUT SALAD Substitute chèvre (goat) cheese for the Gorgonzola.

MIXED GREENS WITH FRIED CHEESE FAST

Impressive and simple. Crumb-coated warm cheese slices on a simple salad is simply delicious.

PREP 15 min TOTAL 15 min • **4 servings**

5½ oz block Colby–Monterey Jack cheese blend (from 8-oz block)

6 tablespoons Italian dressing (not creamy; for homemade dressing, see page 475)

¼ cup seasoned dry bread crumbs

6 cups bite-size pieces mixed salad greens

1 Cut cheese block crosswise into 12 (¼-inch) slices. In separate small shallow bowls, place 2 tablespoons of the dressing and the bread crumbs. Dip cheese slices into dressing, then coat completely with bread crumbs.

2 Spray 10-inch nonstick skillet with cooking spray; heat over medium heat. Cook cheese slices in skillet 1 to 2 minutes, gently turning once, until light golden brown and cheese is warm. Do not overcook or cheese will melt.

3 Toss salad greens and remaining dressing; divide among 4 plates. Top each salad with 3 pieces of cheese. Serve immediately.

1 Serving: Calories 260; Total Fat 19g (Saturated Fat 8g; Trans Fat 0g); Cholesterol 35mg; Sodium 690mg; Total Carbohydrate 11g (Dietary Fiber 2g); Protein 11g **Exchanges:** 2 Vegetable, 1 High-Fat Meat, 2 Fat **Carbohydrate Choices:** 1

MIXED GREENS WITH FRIED CHEESE AND TOMATOES Add ½ cup grape tomatoes in Step 3 with salad greens and dressing.

Frying Cheese

Cut cheese into 12 (¼-inch) slices. Dip cheese in dressing; coat with bread crumbs.

Cook coated cheese in skillet just until light golden brown and cheese is warm.

MANDARIN SALAD WITH SUGARED ALMONDS

LOWER CALORIE

PREP 20 min TOTAL 30 min • **6 servings**

SUGARED ALMONDS
- ¼ cup sliced almonds
- 4 teaspoons sugar

SWEET-SOUR DRESSING
- ¼ cup vegetable oil
- 2 tablespoons sugar
- 2 tablespoons white or cider vinegar
- 1 tablespoon chopped fresh parsley
- ½ teaspoon salt
- Dash pepper
- Dash red pepper sauce

SALAD
- 3 cups bite-size pieces mixed salad greens or iceberg lettuce
- 3 cups bite-size pieces romaine lettuce
- 2 medium stalks celery, chopped (1 cup)
- 2 medium green onions, thinly sliced (2 tablespoons)
- 1 can (11 oz) mandarin orange segments, drained

1 In 1-quart saucepan, cook almonds and 4 teaspoons sugar over low heat about 10 minutes, stirring constantly, until sugar is melted and almonds are coated; cool and break apart.

2 In tightly covered container, shake all dressing ingredients. Refrigerate until serving.

3 In large bowl, toss salad ingredients, dressing and almonds. Serve immediately.

1 Serving (1⅓ Cups): Calories 170; Total Fat 12g (Saturated Fat 1.5g; Trans Fat 0g); Cholesterol 0mg; Sodium 220mg; Total Carbohydrate 15g (Dietary Fiber 2g); Protein 2g **Exchanges:** ½ Fruit, 2 Vegetable, 2 Fat **Carbohydrate Choices:** 1

CRUNCHY CHICKEN-MANDARIN SALAD
Make salad as directed; divide among 6 plates. Top each serving with a grilled boneless skinless chicken breast, sliced (warm or cold). Sprinkle each salad with 2 tablespoons chow mein noodles.

ITALIAN CHOPPED SALAD

Genoa and cotto salamis are the best-known Italian salamis. Genoa is rich, fatty and studded with white peppercorns; cotto is studded with black peppercorns.

PREP 25 min TOTAL 25 min • **4 servings**

SALAD
- 6 cups chopped romaine lettuce
- 1 cup chopped fresh basil leaves
- 1 cup chopped cooked chicken
- 2 large tomatoes, chopped (2 cups)
- 2 medium cucumbers, chopped (1½ cups)
- 1 package (3 oz) Italian salami, chopped
- 1 can (15 to 19 oz) cannellini beans, drained, rinsed

Making Sugared Almonds

Cook almonds and sugar over low heat about 10 minutes, stirring constantly.

Cook until sugar is melted and almonds are coated; cool and break apart.

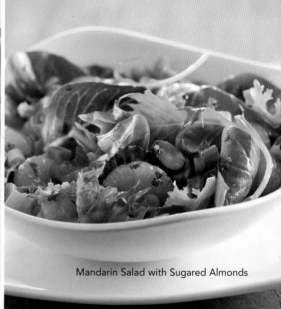

Mandarin Salad with Sugared Almonds

BASIL VINAIGRETTE DRESSING

- ⅓ cup olive oil
- ¼ cup red wine vinegar
- 2 tablespoons chopped fresh or 2 teaspoons dried basil leaves
- 1 teaspoon sugar
- ¼ teaspoon salt

In large bowl, mix all salad ingredients. In tightly covered container, shake dressing ingredients. Pour over salad; toss until coated. Serve immediately.

1 Serving: Calories 560; Total Fat 31g (Saturated Fat 6g; Trans Fat 0g); Cholesterol 45mg; Sodium 740mg; Total Carbohydrate 41g (Dietary Fiber 11g); Protein 27g **Exchanges:** 2 Starch, 2 Vegetable, 2 Lean Meat, 4 Fat **Carbohydrate Choices:** 3

SANTA FE SALAD WITH TORTILLA STRAWS

Fully ripened avocados have a rich, smooth flavor and soft, buttery texture.

PREP 25 min **TOTAL** 40 min • **6 servings**

TORTILLA STRAWS

- 1 flour tortilla (7 or 8 inch)
  Cooking spray
- ¼ teaspoon coarse (kosher or sea) salt
- ¼ teaspoon chili powder

CREAMY AVOCADO DRESSING

- ½ cup ranch dressing
- 1 medium ripe avocado, pitted, peeled and cut into chunks

SALAD

- 2 cups bite-size pieces iceberg lettuce
- 2 cups bite-size pieces romaine lettuce
- 1 large tomato, chopped (1 cup)
- 1 cup diced peeled jicama
- ¾ cup shredded Cheddar cheese (3 oz)
- ¼ cup sliced pitted ripe olives

1 Heat oven to 350°F. Spray tortilla with cooking spray; sprinkle with salt and chili powder. Cut tortilla in half, then cut each half crosswise into ¼-inch strips. Place on ungreased cookie sheet. Bake 10 to 12 minutes or until crisp and golden brown.

2 Meanwhile, place dressing and avocado in blender. Cover; blend on medium speed until smooth and creamy.

3 Place lettuce on shallow serving platter or in large bowl. Top with tomato, jicama, cheese, olives and tortilla straws. Serve with dressing.

1 Serving (1 Cup): Calories 240; Total Fat 20g (Saturated Fat 5g; Trans Fat 0g); Cholesterol 20mg; Sodium 450mg; Total Carbohydrate 11g (Dietary Fiber 3g); Protein 5g **Exchanges:** ½ Starch, 1 Vegetable, 4 Fat **Carbohydrate Choices:** 1

MAKE-AHEAD DIRECTIONS Dressing can be made up to 2 hours ahead of time; cover and refrigerate. Tortilla straws can be made up to 2 days ahead of time. Cool completely, then store in a resealable food-storage plastic bag.

Making Tortilla Straws

Spray tortilla with cooking spray; sprinkle with salt and chili powder. Cut tortilla in half; cut each half crosswise into ¼-inch strips.

Place on cookie sheet; bake until crisp and golden brown.

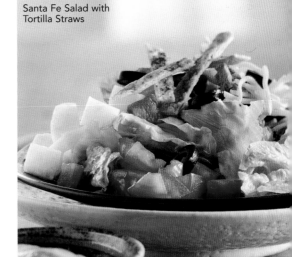

Santa Fe Salad with Tortilla Straws

GREENS WITH PROSCIUTTO, GORGONZOLA AND PEPPERONCINI LOWER CALORIE

Arugula is a bitter, aromatic salad green with a peppery mustard flavor that looks like radish leaves and is sold in bunches with the roots attached. It's very perishable, so wrap it tightly in a resealable food-storage plastic bag and refrigerate no longer than 2 days. Wash it thoroughly before using to remove any grit in the leaves.

PREP 25 min TOTAL 25 min • **6 servings**

- ¼ lb prosciutto (8 to 10 slices), cut into ⅛-inch strips*
- 4 cups bite-size pieces mixed salad greens
- 1 cup bite-size pieces arugula
- 1 small head radicchio, cut into thin strips (1 cup)
- ⅓ cup red wine vinaigrette dressing
- ½ cup crumbled Gorgonzola or feta cheese (2 oz)
- 6 pepperoncini peppers (bottled Italian peppers), drained, if desired

1 In 10-inch nonstick skillet, cook prosciutto over medium-high heat 5 minutes, stirring occasionally. Reduce heat to medium. Cook 5 to 10 minutes longer, stirring frequently, until prosciutto becomes mostly crisp. Drain on paper towels.

2 In large bowl, toss greens and dressing. Sprinkle with prosciutto and cheese. Garnish with pepperoncini peppers.

*Very thinly sliced deli ham can be substituted. Pat ham dry with paper towels before cooking. The ham may not become as crisp and may remain in larger pieces. Another substitution is 6 slices of bacon, crisply cooked and crumbled.

1 Serving: Calories 110; Total Fat 8g (Saturated Fat 2.5g; Trans Fat 0g); Cholesterol 20mg; Sodium 500mg; Total Carbohydrate 4g (Dietary Fiber 1g); Protein 5g **Exchanges:** 1 Vegetable, ½ High-Fat Meat, 1 Fat **Carbohydrate Choices:** 0

BROCCOLI SUNSHINE SALAD

PREP 15 min TOTAL 2 hr 15 min • **6 servings**

- ½ cup mayonnaise or salad dressing (for homemade mayonnaise, see page 483)
- 2 tablespoons cider vinegar
- 1 tablespoon sugar
- 3 cups fresh broccoli florets (8 oz)
- ⅓ cup raisins
- ¼ cup shredded Cheddar cheese (1 oz)
- 4 slices bacon, crisply cooked, crumbled (¼ cup)
- 2 tablespoons chopped red onion
- 2 tablespoons sunflower nuts, if desired

1 In large glass or plastic bowl, mix mayonnaise, vinegar and sugar. Add all remaining ingredients except sunflower nuts; toss until evenly coated.

2 Cover; refrigerate 2 hours to blend flavors. Stir before serving; sprinkle with sunflower nuts.

1 Serving (½ Cup):: Calories 230; Total Fat 19g (Saturated Fat 4g; Trans Fat 0g); Cholesterol 20mg; Sodium 230mg; Total Carbohydrate 12g (Dietary Fiber 2g); Protein 4g **Exchanges:** ½ Other Carbohydrate, 1 Vegetable, 4 Fat **Carbohydrate Choices:** 1

LIGHTER **DIRECTIONS** For 8 grams of fat and 140 calories per serving, use reduced-fat mayonnaise and cheese. Decrease bacon to 2 slices.

Beets

The humble beet is emerging as one of the unsung heroes of the vegetable world. Sweet tasting and rich in nutrition, beets are not only delicious as a side dish but also a beautiful addition to salads. They range in color from deep red to white, with red and golden beets the most widely available varieties.

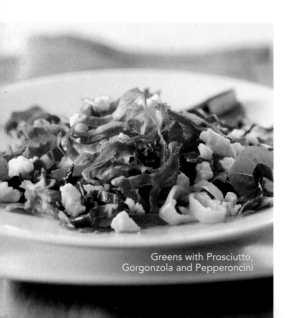

Greens with Prosciutto, Gorgonzola and Pepperoncini

Roasted Beet Salad

ROASTED BEET SALAD

PREP 15 min TOTAL 1 hr 25 min • **4 servings**

- 1½ lb small beets (1½ to 2 inches in diameter)
- 1 tablespoon olive or vegetable oil
- 4 cups bite-size pieces mixed salad greens
- 1 medium orange, peeled, sliced
- ½ cup walnut halves, toasted (page 22), coarsely chopped
- ¼ cup crumbled chèvre (goat) cheese (1 oz)
- ½ cup Fresh Herb Vinaigrette (page 474)

1 Heat oven to 425°F. Remove greens from beets, leaving about ½ inch of stem. Wash beets well; leave whole with root ends attached. Place beets in ungreased 13x9-inch pan; drizzle with oil. Bake uncovered about 40 minutes or until tender.

2 Remove skins from beets under running water. Let beets cool until easy to handle, about 30 minutes. Peel beets and cut off root ends; cut beets into slices. Cut each slice in half.

3 On 4 salad plates, arrange salad greens. Top with beets, orange slices, walnuts and cheese. Serve with dressing.

1 Serving: Calories 410; Total Fat 33g (Saturated Fat 5g; Trans Fat 0g); Cholesterol 5mg; Sodium 440mg; Total Carbohydrate 19g (Dietary Fiber 6g); Protein 7g **Exchanges:** ½ Other Carbohydrate, 3 Vegetable, 6½ Fat **Carbohydrate Choices:** 1

See how to remove skins from **roasted beets:**
Visit bettycrocker.com/BCcookbook

PANZANELLA

Panzanella, or "bread salad," is an Italian classic. Buy a firm-textured bread so the pieces don't become mushy.

PREP 20 min TOTAL 1 hr 20 min • **6 servings**

- 4 cups cubed (1 inch) day-old Italian or other firm-textured bread
- 2 medium tomatoes, cut into bite-size pieces (2 cups)
- 2 cloves garlic, finely chopped
- 1 medium green bell pepper, coarsely chopped (1 cup)
- ⅓ cup chopped fresh basil leaves
- 2 tablespoons chopped fresh parsley
- ⅓ cup olive oil
- 2 tablespoons red wine vinegar
- ½ teaspoon salt
- ⅛ teaspoon pepper

1 In large glass or plastic bowl, mix bread, tomatoes, garlic, bell pepper, basil and parsley.

2 In tightly covered container, shake remaining ingredients. Pour over bread mixture; toss gently until bread is evenly coated.

3 Cover; refrigerate at least 1 hour, but no longer than 8 hours, until bread is softened and flavors are blended. Toss before serving.

1 Serving: Calories 190; Total Fat 13g (Saturated Fat 2g; Trans Fat 0g); Cholesterol 0mg; Sodium 340mg; Total Carbohydrate 15g (Dietary Fiber 2g); Protein 3g **Exchanges:** 1 Starch, 2 Fat **Carbohydrate Choices:** 1

Panzanella

SEVEN-LAYER SALAD

This is an easy and delicious salad to serve family and friends.

PREP 25 min TOTAL 2 hr 25 min • **6 servings**

6 cups bite-size pieces mixed salad greens
2 medium stalks celery, thinly sliced (1 cup)
1 cup thinly sliced radishes
8 medium green onions, sliced (½ cup)
12 slices bacon, crisply cooked, crumbled (¾ cup)
1 cup frozen sweet peas, cooked, drained
1½ cups mayonnaise or salad dressing (for homemade mayonnaise, see page 483)
½ cup grated Parmesan cheese or shredded Cheddar cheese (2 oz)

1 In large glass bowl, layer salad greens, celery, radishes, onions, bacon and peas. Spread mayonnaise over peas, covering top completely all the way to edge of bowl. Sprinkle with cheese.

2 Cover; refrigerate at least 2 hours, but no longer than 12 hours, to blend flavors. Toss before serving, if desired.

1 Serving (1¼ Cups): Calories 580; Total Fat 54g (Saturated Fat 11g; Trans Fat 0g); Cholesterol 55mg; Sodium 790mg; Total Carbohydrate 11g (Dietary Fiber 3g); Protein 12g **Exchanges:** ½ Starch, 1 Vegetable, 1 High-Fat Meat, 9 Fat **Carbohydrate Choices:** 1

LIGHTER DIRECTIONS For 12 grams of fat and 200 calories per serving, substitute ½ cup reduced-fat mayonnaise and 1 cup plain fat-free yogurt for the 1½ cups mayonnaise. Decrease bacon to 6 slices and cheese to ¼ cup.

JICAMA-AVOCADO SALAD WITH JALAPEÑO-CREAM DRESSING

LOWER CALORIE

Jicama, a root vegetable with thin brown skin, stays crisp and crunchy and tastes somewhat like water chestnuts, only moister and sweeter. Another plus? It won't discolor, making it perfect for this salad.

PREP 20 min TOTAL 1 hr 20 min • **4 servings**

JALAPEÑO-CREAM DRESSING
¼ cup mayonnaise or salad dressing
¼ cup sour cream
1 to 2 tablespoons seeded diced fresh jalapeño chiles

1 to 2 tablespoons milk
2 teaspoons finely chopped fresh cilantro
1 teaspoon fresh lime juice

SALAD
Lettuce leaves, if desired
3 cups shredded, peeled jicama
1 large, pitted, peeled and cubed avocado

1 In small bowl, mix all dressing ingredients; blend well. Cover and refrigerate at least 1 hour to blend flavors.

2 To serve, arrange lettuce leaves on individual serving plates or bowls. Top with jicama and avocado. Serve with dressing.

1 Serving: Calories 170; Total Fat 12g (Saturated Fat 3g; Trans Fat 0g); Cholesterol 15mg; Sodium 150mg; Total Carbohydrate 15g (Dietary Fiber 7g); Protein 2g **Exchanges:** ½ Starch, ½ Other Carbohydrate, 2½ Fat **Carbohydrate Choices:** 1

ASPARAGUS-STRAWBERRY SALAD WITH LEMON-HONEY DRESSING FAST LOWER CALORIE

PREP 20 min TOTAL 20 min • **4 servings**

LEMON-HONEY DRESSING
¼ cup fresh lemon juice
2 tablespoons vegetable oil
2 tablespoons honey

SALAD
1 lb fresh asparagus spears, cut into 1-inch pieces (2 cups)
2 cups sliced fresh strawberries

1 In tightly covered container, shake all dressing ingredients; set aside.

2 In 2-quart saucepan, heat 1 inch water to boiling. Add asparagus. Heat to boiling. Boil uncovered 2 to 4 minutes or until crisp-tender. Remove asparagus from boiling water; immediately plunge into ice water until cold to stop cooking. Drain.

3 Arrange asparagus and strawberries on individual serving plates or in bowls; drizzle with dressing.

1 Serving: Calories 150; Total Fat 7g (Saturated Fat 1g; Trans Fat 0g); Cholesterol 0mg; Sodium 0mg; Total Carbohydrate 19g (Dietary Fiber 3g); Protein 2g **Exchanges:** 1 Other Carbohydrate, 1 Vegetable, 1½ Fat **Carbohydrate Choices:** 1

DELICIOUSLY EASY SALAD COMBOS

The possibilities are endless for terrific-tasting, last-minute salads. Look at what you have on hand in the refrigerator or cupboard in a new way for inspiring combinations. And don't forget about the produce aisle and deli counter—both are convenient time-savers offering many options. Here are a few fabulous salad ideas to get you started.

1 Asparagus and Parmesan Salad: Snap off tough bottom ends of asparagus. Starting below tip of asparagus, use vegetable peeler to remove outer layer of spear. Place spears in boiling water in 10-inch skillet; boil 2 minutes. Place in cold water to chill; drain well. Arrange 5 or 6 spears on each individual serving plate; drizzle lightly with olive oil and balsamic vinegar. Sprinkle with kosher salt, freshly ground pepper and shaved or grated Parmesan cheese.

2 Classic Wedge Salad: Cut an ice-cold medium head of iceberg lettuce into 4 to 6 wedges; place on individual serving plates. Top each with about 2 tablespoons blue cheese dressing and 2 tablespoons crisply cooked bacon pieces; serve immediately.

3 Cranberry-Toasted Walnut Slaw: Just before serving, stir ¼ cup dried cranberries and ¼ cup coarsely chopped toasted walnuts (page 22), into coleslaw.

4 Cukes and Tomatoes: On serving platter or individual serving plates, arrange cucumber slices or chunks with tomato wedges or slices. Sprinkle with salt and pepper; drizzle with your favorite dressing or just a splash of vinegar.

5 Greens and Melon Salad: Arrange mixed greens on serving platter or individual serving plates; top each with ½ cup diced watermelon, cantaloupe and honeydew melon. Drizzle with Italian or vinaigrette dressing.

6 Hearts of Palm Vinaigrette: Drain canned or jarred hearts of palm; slice into ¼-inch-thick pieces; drizzle with Italian dressing. Sprinkle with pepper.

7 Honey-Nut Pineapple Slaw: Just before serving, stir ½ cup canned pineapple tidbits (well-drained) and honey-roasted peanuts into coleslaw.

8 Mango, Avocado and Raspberry Salad: On serving platter or individual serving plates, arrange ripe avocado slices and mango slices; drizzle with raspberry vinaigrette dressing. Sprinkle with toasted slivered almonds and pepper.

Heirloom Recipe and New Twist

Potato salad has changed little over the years, but in 1950, in the first edition of this cookbook, the warm potatoes were tossed with French dressing before making the salad. Several years ago, we eliminated that step and think our current salad is equally delicious. The new twist includes sweet potatoes and has a slightly smoky flavor from chipotle chiles that we think you will like.

CLASSIC

CREAMY POTATO SALAD

This classic potato salad recipe is always a favorite for picnics and potlucks. Make it your own by adding a variety of flavors. See Potato Salad Mix-Ins, page 466, for ideas.

PREP 15 min **TOTAL** 4 hr 55 min • **10 servings**

- 6 medium unpeeled round red or Yukon Gold potatoes (2 lb)
- 1½ cups mayonnaise or salad dressing (for homemade mayonnaise, see page 483)
- 1 tablespoon white or cider vinegar
- 1 tablespoon yellow mustard
- 1 teaspoon salt
- ¼ teaspoon pepper
- 2 medium stalks celery, chopped (1 cup)
- 1 medium onion, chopped (½ cup)
- 4 Hard-Cooked Eggs (page 74), chopped
  Paprika, if desired

1 In 3-quart saucepan, place potatoes and just enough water to cover potatoes. Cover and heat to boiling; reduce heat to low.

2 Cook 30 to 35 minutes or until tender; drain. Let stand until cool enough to handle. Peel potatoes; cut into cubes.

3 In large glass or plastic bowl, mix mayonnaise, vinegar, mustard, salt and pepper. Add potatoes, celery and onion; toss. Stir in eggs. Sprinkle with paprika. Cover; refrigerate at least 4 hours to chill and blend flavors.

1 Serving (¾ Cup): Calories 350; Total Fat 28g (Saturated Fat 4.5g; Trans Fat 0g); Cholesterol 105mg; Sodium 480mg; Total Carbohydrate 19g (Dietary Fiber 2g); Protein 5g **Exchanges:** 1½ Starch, 5½ Fat **Carbohydrate Choices:** 1

LIGHTER DIRECTIONS For 13 grams of fat and 210 calories per serving, use reduced-fat mayonnaise and 2 eggs.

See how to make **potato salad:**
Visit bettycrocker.com/BCcookbook

Creamy Potato Salad

Southwest Potato Salad

NEW TWIST

SOUTHWEST POTATO SALAD

Look for sweet potatoes that have a bright red or deep-orange flesh for the most intense color, flavor and moist texture.

PREP 20 min TOTAL 3 hr 15 min • **12 servings**

- 4 medium unpeeled round red or Yukon Gold potatoes (1½ lb)
- 4 small unpeeled sweet potatoes (1½ lb)
- 1¼ cups mayonnaise or salad dressing (for homemade mayonnaise, see page 483)
- 2 tablespoons milk
- 1 teaspoon cumin seed
- ½ teaspoon salt
- 1 to 2 chipotle chiles in adobo sauce (from 7-oz can), finely chopped
- 1 large red bell pepper, chopped (1½ cups)
- 8 medium green onions, sliced (½ cup)

1 In 4-quart Dutch oven or saucepan, place red or Yukon Gold potatoes and sweet potatoes; add just enough water to cover potatoes. Cover and heat to boiling; reduce heat to low.

2 Cook 20 to 25 minutes or until sweet potatoes are tender. Remove sweet potatoes from Dutch oven. Cook red or white potatoes 10 to 15 minutes longer, if necessary, until tender. Drain. Let stand about 15 minutes or until cool enough to handle. Peel potatoes; cut into cubes.

3 In large glass or plastic bowl, mix mayonnaise, milk, cumin seed, salt and chiles. Add potatoes, bell pepper and onions; stir gently to coat. Cover; refrigerate at least 2 hours to chill and blend flavors.

1 Serving (¾ Cup): Calories 260; Total Fat 19g (Saturated Fat 3g; Trans Fat 0g); Cholesterol 10mg; Sodium 260mg; Total Carbohydrate 22g (Dietary Fiber 3g); Protein 2g **Exchanges:** 1½ Starch, 3½ Fat **Carbohydrate Choices:** 1½

DILL POTATO SALAD   LOWER CALORIE

PREP 30 min TOTAL 1 hr 30 min • **8 servings**

DILL DRESSING
- ⅓ cup white vinegar
- ¼ cup olive or vegetable oil
- 1 tablespoon chopped fresh or 2 teaspoons dried dill weed
- 1 clove garlic, finely chopped
- 1 teaspoon sugar
- ½ teaspoon salt
- ½ teaspoon ground mustard
- ¼ teaspoon coarse ground black pepper

SALAD
- 12 oz fresh green beans, trimmed
- 10 to 12 small red potatoes (1½ lb), cut into quarters
- ¼ cup water
- ¼ cup chopped red onion
- 1 small yellow bell pepper, coarsely chopped (½ cup)

1 In tightly covered container, shake all dressing ingredients.

2 Cut beans in half if desired. In 2-quart microwavable casserole, place beans, potatoes and water. Cover; microwave on High 10 to 12 minutes, rotating casserole ½ turn every 4 minutes, until potatoes are tender. Drain.

3 In large glass or plastic bowl, toss potatoes, beans and dressing. Add onion and bell pepper; toss. Cover; refrigerate 1 to 2 hours to chill and blend flavors. Stir before serving.

1 Serving: Calories 150; Total Fat 7g (Saturated Fat 1g; Trans Fat 0g); Cholesterol 0mg; Sodium 160mg; Total Carbohydrate 20g (Dietary Fiber 3g); Protein 2g **Exchanges:** 1 Starch, 1 Vegetable, 1 Fat **Carbohydrate Choices:** 1

Potato Salads

There's no creamy dressing on a vinegar-based potato salad like Dill Potato Salad (above). This type of salad is quite different from the one with a creamy base, but it is also served cold. Then there's Hot German Potato Salad, page 466, which is also vinegar-based but served warm and has a bacon-flavored dressing. They are all delicious, whichever one you choose.

POTATO SALAD MIX-INS

Who would think something as humble as creamy potato salad could create so much passion and debate? Each cook puts a special spin on potato salad, with a fierce loyalty for making it this way or that. What kind of potatoes to use, whether to add mayonnaise or salad dressing, yellow or Dijon mustard, what type of onions to use and even how many hard-cooked eggs are needed can create lively conversation. Start with our wonderful Creamy Potato Salad (page 464) or purchased potato salad, then look to these mix-in ideas to help create your signature style.

Bacon, Ham, Pepperoni or Salami: Stir in ½ to 1 cup diced crisply cooked crumbled bacon or diced ham, pepperoni or salami.

Capers, Olives or Pickles: Stir in 1 tablespoon small drained capers or 2 tablespoons to ¼ cup chopped sweet or dill pickles or pickle relish, or sliced or chopped pitted well-drained olives (any variety).

Fresh Herbs: Stir in 1 to 2 tablespoons chopped fresh herbs such as basil, chives, dill, lemon balm or lemon verbena, parsley, oregano, tarragon, thyme or lemon thyme (thyme is potent, so start with 1 tablespoon and add more if needed to taste). Mix and match any of these herbs or just use a single type of herb.

Fresh Veggies

Pesto

Fresh Veggies: Stir in ½ to 1 cup chopped, cubed or sliced fresh vegetables like bell pepper, broccoli florets, cucumber, radishes, spinach leaves, yellow summer squash, zucchini or any other favorites.

Pesto: Stir in 1 to 2 tablespoons Basil Pesto (page 485) or any variation. If making Creamy Potato Salad (page 464), stir in with the mayonnaise in Step 2.

HOT GERMAN POTATO SALAD

LOWER CALORIE

The tangy sweet-sour dressing, which soaks into the velvety cooked potatoes, and the smoky bacon are what give this salad its characteristic flavor.

PREP 10 min TOTAL 1 hr 5 min • **6 servings**

- 4 medium red or white potatoes, unpeeled (1½ lb)
- 3 slices bacon, cut into 1-inch pieces
- 1 medium onion, chopped (½ cup)
- 1 tablespoon all-purpose flour
- 1 tablespoon sugar
- ½ teaspoon salt
- ¼ teaspoon celery seed
  Dash pepper
- ½ cup water
- ¼ cup white or cider vinegar

1 In 3-quart saucepan, place potatoes and just enough water to cover potatoes. Cover and heat to boiling; reduce heat to low. Cook 30 to 35 minutes or until tender; drain. Let stand until cool enough to handle. Cut potatoes into ¼-inch slices.

2 In 10-inch skillet, cook bacon over medium heat 8 to 10 minutes, stirring occasionally, until crisp. Remove bacon with slotted spoon; drain on paper towels.

3 Cook onion in bacon drippings in skillet over medium heat, stirring occasionally, until tender. Stir in flour, sugar, salt, celery seed and pepper. Cook over low heat, stirring constantly, until mixture is bubbly; remove from heat.

Hot German Potato Salad

4 Stir in water and vinegar. Heat to boiling, stirring constantly. Boil and stir 1 minute; remove from heat. Stir in potatoes and bacon. Heat over medium heat, stirring gently to coat potato slices, until hot and bubbly. Serve warm.

1 Serving (⅔ Cup): Calories 120; Total Fat 2g (Saturated Fat 0.5g; Trans Fat 0g); Cholesterol 0mg; Sodium 270mg; Total Carbohydrate 22g (Dietary Fiber 3g); Protein 3g **Exchanges:** 1 Starch, 1 Vegetable, ½ Fat **Carbohydrate Choices:** 1½

SLOW COOKER DIRECTIONS Cut uncooked potatoes into ¼-inch slices. Cook and drain bacon; refrigerate. Increase flour to 2 tablespoons. Decrease water to ⅓ cup. Spray 3½- to 6-quart slow cooker with cooking spray. In slow cooker, mix all ingredients except bacon. Cover; cook on Low heat setting 8 to 10 hours or until potatoes are tender. Stir in bacon.

CUCUMBER SALAD LOWER CALORIE

Instead of everyday garden cukes, look for the slender English or hothouse cucumbers. They are virtually seedless.

PREP 10 min **TOTAL** 3 hr 10 min • **6 servings**

- 2 medium cucumbers, thinly sliced*
- ⅓ cup cider or white vinegar
- ⅓ cup water
- 2 tablespoons sugar
- ½ teaspoon salt
- ⅛ teaspoon pepper
  Chopped fresh dill weed or parsley, if desired

1 In small glass or plastic bowl, place cucumbers. In tightly covered container, shake remaining ingredients except dill weed. Pour over cucumbers. Cover; refrigerate at least 3 hours to blend flavors.

2 Drain cucumbers before serving. Sprinkle with dill weed.

*If desired, before slicing cucumbers, run the tines of a fork down the length of each cucumber for a decorative look.

1 Serving (½ Cup): Calories 30; Total Fat 0g (Saturated Fat 0g; Trans Fat 0g); Cholesterol 0mg; Sodium 200mg; Total Carbohydrate 7g (Dietary Fiber 0g); Protein 0g **Exchanges:** 1 Vegetable **Carbohydrate Choices:** ½

CREAMY CUCUMBER SALAD After draining cucumbers, stir in ¾ cup sour cream or plain yogurt.

CREAMY COLESLAW LOWER CALORIE

This is a delicious coleslaw to make for any occasion. For variety, you could add ¼ to ½ cup chopped red bell pepper. To serve, garnish with a lemon twist and a little fresh parsley.

PREP 15 min **TOTAL** 1 hr 15 min • **8 servings**

- ½ cup mayonnaise or salad dressing (for homemade mayonnaise, see page 483)
- ¼ cup sour cream
- 1 tablespoon sugar
- 2 teaspoons fresh lemon juice
- 2 teaspoons Dijon mustard
- ½ teaspoon celery seed, if desired
- ¼ teaspoon salt
- ¼ teaspoon pepper
- ½ medium head green cabbage, thinly sliced or chopped (4 cups)
- 1 medium carrot, shredded (½ cup)
- 1 small onion, finely chopped (⅓ cup)

1 In large glass or plastic bowl, mix all ingredients except cabbage, carrot and onion. Add remaining ingredients; toss until evenly coated.

2 Cover; refrigerate at least 1 hour to blend flavors. Stir before serving.

1 Serving (⅔ Cup): Calories 140; Total Fat 13g (Saturated Fat 2.5g; Trans Fat 0g); Cholesterol 15mg; Sodium 200mg; Total Carbohydrate 6g (Dietary Fiber 1g); Protein 1g **Exchanges:** ½ Other Carbohydrate, ½ Vegetable, 2½ Fat **Carbohydrate Choices:** ½

LIGHTER DIRECTIONS For 6 grams of fat and 85 calories per serving, use reduced-fat mayonnaise and sour cream.

TROPICAL CREAMY COLESLAW Add 1 can (8 oz) pineapple tidbits or chunks in juice, drained, with the cabbage, carrot and onion. Just before serving, sprinkle with ½ cup chopped macadamia nuts.

Thinly Slicing Cabbage

To thinly slice cabbage, place a flat side of ¼ head of cabbage on cutting board. Cut into thin slices with a large sharp knife. Cut slices several times to make smaller pieces.

Sweet-and-Sour Coleslaw

SWEET-AND-SOUR COLESLAW

LOWER CALORIE

PREP 15 min TOTAL 3 hr 15 min • **8 servings**

- ½ medium head green cabbage, finely shredded (4 cups)
- 1 large carrot, finely shredded (1 cup)
- 1 medium green bell pepper, chopped (1 cup)
- 4 medium green onions, thinly sliced (¼ cup)
- ½ cup sugar
- ½ cup white wine vinegar, white vinegar or cider vinegar
- ¼ cup vegetable oil
- 1 teaspoon ground mustard
- ½ teaspoon celery seed
- ½ teaspoon salt

1 In large glass or plastic bowl, place cabbage, carrot, bell pepper and onions. In tightly covered container, shake remaining ingredients. Pour over vegetables; stir.

2 Cover; refrigerate at least 3 hours, stirring several times, until chilled and flavors are blended. Stir before serving; serve with slotted spoon.

1 Serving: Calories 140; Total Fat 7g (Saturated Fat 1g; Trans Fat 0g); Cholesterol 0mg; Sodium 170mg; Total Carbohydrate 17g (Dietary Fiber 1g); Protein 1g **Exchanges:** 1 Other Carbohydrate, 1 Vegetable, 1½ Fat **Carbohydrate Choices:** 1

QUICK SWEET-AND-SOUR COLESLAW
Substitute 6½ cups packaged coleslaw mix for the cabbage and carrot; omit bell pepper.

CHINESE CABBAGE SALAD WITH SESAME DRESSING

LOWER CALORIE

Napa is one of several varieties of Chinese cabbage. This long, narrow variety is pale green with leaves that are very crinkly and thickly veined. It has a tender texture and mild flavor.

PREP 15 min TOTAL 2 hr 15 min • **4 servings**

SALAD

- 2 cups finely shredded Chinese (napa) cabbage (8 oz)
- ¼ cup chopped peeled jicama
- ¼ cup chopped green bell pepper
- ¼ cup coarsely shredded carrot

SESAME DRESSING

- 3 tablespoons rice vinegar or white wine vinegar
- 2 teaspoons sugar
- 2 teaspoons sesame seed, toasted (page 22)
- 2 teaspoons soy sauce
- 1 teaspoon dark sesame oil
- ⅛ teaspoon crushed red pepper flakes

1 In medium glass or plastic bowl, toss cabbage, jicama, bell pepper and carrot. In tightly covered container, shake all dressing ingredients. Pour over salad; toss.

2 Cover; refrigerate 2 hours to blend flavors. Stir before serving.

1 Serving: Calories 60; Total Fat 2g (Saturated Fat 0g; Trans Fat 0g); Cholesterol 0mg; Sodium 170mg; Total Carbohydrate 9g (Dietary Fiber 2g); Protein 1g **Exchanges:** 1½ Vegetable, ½ Fat **Carbohydrate Choices:** ½

THREE-BEAN SALAD

PREP 20 min TOTAL 3 hr 20 min • **6 servings**

- 1 cup Italian dressing (for homemade dressing, see page 475)
- 1 tablespoon sugar
- 2 cloves garlic, finely chopped
- 1 can (14.5 oz) cut green beans, drained
- 1 can (14.5 oz) cut wax beans, drained
- 1 can (15 to 16 oz) kidney, black or garbanzo beans, drained, rinsed
- 4 medium green onions, sliced (¼ cup)
- ¼ cup chopped fresh parsley

1 In small bowl, mix dressing, sugar and garlic.

2 In medium glass or plastic bowl, mix remaining ingredients. Pour dressing mixture over salad; toss.

3 Cover; refrigerate at least 3 hours, stirring occasionally, until flavors are blended. Stir before serving; serve with slotted spoon.

1 Serving (¾ Cup): Calories 380; Total Fat 29g (Saturated Fat 4g; Trans Fat 0g); Cholesterol 0mg; Sodium 370mg; Total Carbohydrate 22g (Dietary Fiber 6g); Protein 7g **Exchanges:** 1 Starch, 1 Vegetable, 6 Fat **Carbohydrate Choices:** 1½

LIGHTER DIRECTIONS For 1 gram of fat and 200 calories per serving, substitute purchased fat-free Italian dressing for the Italian dressing.

NORTHERN ITALIAN WHITE BEAN SALAD

PREP **15 min** TOTAL **2 hr 15 min** • **6 servings**

- 2 cans (15 or 19 oz each) cannellini beans, drained, rinsed
- 1 large tomato, seeded, coarsely chopped (1 cup)
- 1 small red bell pepper, chopped (½ cup)
- ½ cup chopped red onion
- ¼ cup chopped fresh parsley
- ¼ cup olive or vegetable oil
- 2 tablespoons chopped fresh or 2 teaspoons dried basil leaves
- 2 tablespoons red wine vinegar
- ½ teaspoon salt
- ⅛ teaspoon pepper
- 12 lettuce leaves

1 In large glass or plastic bowl, carefully mix all ingredients except lettuce.

2 Cover; refrigerate at least 2 hours to blend flavors. Use slotted spoon to spoon onto lettuce.

1 Serving: Calories 360; Total Fat 10g (Saturated Fat 1.5g; Trans Fat 0g); Cholesterol 0mg; Sodium 210mg; Total Carbohydrate 49g (Dietary Fiber 12g); Protein 18g **Exchanges:** 3 Starch, 1 Vegetable, 1 Very Lean Meat **Carbohydrate Choices:** 3

Northern Italian White Bean Salad

CLASSIC TABBOULEH LOWER CALORIE

This traditional Middle Eastern dish is always made with bulgur. It's served cold with a crisp bread.

PREP **10 min** TOTAL **1 hr 40 min** • **6 servings**

- ¾ cup uncooked bulgur
- 1½ cups chopped fresh parsley
- 3 medium tomatoes, chopped (2¼ cups)
- 5 medium green onions, thinly sliced (⅓ cup)
- 2 tablespoons chopped fresh or 2 teaspoons crushed dried mint leaves
- ¼ cup olive or vegetable oil
- ¼ cup fresh lemon juice
- ¾ teaspoon salt
- ¼ teaspoon pepper
   Whole ripe olives, if desired

1 In small bowl, cover bulgur with cold water. Let stand 30 minutes; drain. Press out as much water as possible.

2 In medium glass or plastic bowl, place bulgur, parsley, tomatoes, onions and mint.

3 In tightly covered container, shake remaining ingredients except olives. Pour over bulgur mixture; toss. Cover; refrigerate at least 1 hour to blend flavors. Garnish with olives.

1 Serving (¾ Cup): Calories 170; Total Fat 10g (Saturated Fat 1.5g; Trans Fat 0g); Cholesterol 0mg; Sodium 320mg; Total Carbohydrate 19g (Dietary Fiber 5g); Protein 3g **Exchanges:** 1 Starch, 1 Vegetable, 1 Fat **Carbohydrate Choices:** 1

GARBANZO BEAN TABBOULEH Add 1 can (15 to 16 oz) garbanzo beans, drained and rinsed, and 1 cup chopped green bell pepper with the bulgur in Step 2.

MINTY TABBOULEH Use ¾ cup each chopped fresh mint and parsley for the 1½ cups chopped fresh parsley. Omit the additional 2 tablespoons of mint.

SOUTHWESTERN TABBOULEH Substitute 1 cup chopped fresh cilantro for the parsley. Decrease lemon juice to 2 tablespoons; increase salt to 1 teaspoon. Add 2 teaspoons ground cumin with the remaining ingredients in Step 3.

ALMOST-INSTANT GRAIN SALADS

Grains make splendid salads. Rinse cooked grains with cold water for a fast chill. Then mix them with a few added ingredients and serve immediately or chill for 30 minutes.

Asian Brown Rice Salad: Mix 2 cups cooked brown rice with ½ cup halved fresh snow peas, strings removed, ¼ cup chopped red bell pepper, ¼ cup diced carrot and 2 tablespoons chopped red onion. Whisk together 2 tablespoons rice wine vinegar and ¼ cup purchased peanut sauce; stir into salad. Top with chopped peanuts.

Black Bean and Rice Salad: Mix 2 cups cooked rice with ½ cup chilled cooked corn, ½ cup shredded Cheddar cheese, ½ cup canned black beans, rinsed and drained, ¼ cup sliced ripe olives and ½ cup salsa; top with cubed avocado.

Cobb Couscous Salad

Cobb Couscous Salad: Mix 2 cups cooked couscous, 2 tablespoons bacon bits, 2 cups torn fresh spinach, 1 diced tomato, 1 diced avocado, ¼ cup crumbled blue cheese and 1 cup diced cooked chicken. Drizzle with blue cheese, ranch or Italian dressing. Sprinkle with chopped Hard-Cooked Egg (page 74).

Greek Wheat Berry Salad: Mix 2 cups cooked wheat berries with ¼ cup each crumbled feta cheese, chopped pitted kalamata olives, diced cucumber and chopped plum tomato, 2 tablespoons finely chopped red onion and ½ cup canned garbanzo beans, rinsed and drained. Toss grains mixture with ¼ to ½ cup Greek vinaigrette or Italian dressing.

Quinoa Veggie Salad

Quinoa Veggie Salad: Mix 2 cups cooked quinoa with 1 cup torn arugula leaves, ¼ cup chopped roasted red bell peppers and ¼ cup halved yellow cherry tomatoes. Drain and chop ¼ cup marinated artichoke hearts, reserving oil; add artichokes to salad. Add 2 tablespoons lemon juice, salt and pepper to reserved oil; toss with salad.

WHEAT BERRY SALAD

LOWER CALORIE

Wheat berries are whole kernels of wheat. Look for them in the cereal, bulk foods or natural-foods section of your supermarket. This salad is chewy (from the wheat berries), crunchy and delicious.

PREP 10 min TOTAL 2 hr 40 min • **10 servings**

- ¾ cup uncooked wheat berries
- 3 cups water

  CREAMY VINAIGRETTE DRESSING
- ⅓ cup vegetable oil
- 2 tablespoons mayonnaise or salad dressing
- 2 tablespoons red wine vinegar
- ½ teaspoon salt
- ¼ teaspoon garlic powder
- ⅛ teaspoon pepper

  SALAD
- 1 cup fresh broccoli florets
- 1 cup fresh cauliflower florets
- 1 cup cherry tomatoes, cut in half
- 1 small green bell pepper, chopped (½ cup)
- 4 medium green onions, sliced (¼ cup)
- ½ cup crumbled feta cheese (2 oz)

1 In 3-quart saucepan, soak wheat berries in water 30 minutes. Heat to boiling over high heat. Reduce heat to low. Partially cover; simmer 55 to 60 minutes or until wheat berries are tender. Drain and rinse with cold water.

2 In small bowl, stir all dressing ingredients until well mixed. In large serving bowl, toss wheat berries, salad ingredients and dressing. Cover; refrigerate at least 1 hour.

1 Serving: Calories 160; Total Fat 11g (Saturated Fat 2.5g; Trans Fat 0g); Cholesterol 10mg; Sodium 230mg; Total Carbohydrate 11g (Dietary Fiber 3g); Protein 3g **Exchanges:** ½ Starch, 1 Vegetable, 2 Fat **Carbohydrate Choices:** 1

Wheat Berry Salad

Hearty Soybean and Cheddar Pasta Salad

COBB SALAD

The original Hollywood Brown Derby restaurant, where owner Robert H. Cobb created the Cobb salad, is gone, but this hearty dish remains popular.

PREP 10 min TOTAL 1 hr 10 min • **4 servings**

LEMON VINAIGRETTE DRESSING

- ½ cup vegetable oil
- ¼ cup fresh lemon juice
- 1 tablespoon red wine vinegar
- 1 clove garlic, finely chopped
- 2 teaspoons sugar
- ½ teaspoon salt
- ½ teaspoon ground mustard
- ½ teaspoon Worcestershire sauce
- ¼ teaspoon pepper

SALAD

- 1 medium head (about 1 lb) iceberg lettuce, shredded (6 cups)
- 2 cups cut-up cooked chicken
- 3 Hard-Cooked Eggs (page 74), chopped
- 2 medium tomatoes, chopped (1½ cups)
- 1 medium avocado, pitted, peeled and chopped
- ¼ cup crumbled blue cheese (1 oz)
- 4 slices bacon, crisply cooked, crumbled (¼ cup)

1 In tightly covered container, shake all dressing ingredients. Refrigerate at least 1 hour to blend flavors.

2 Divide lettuce among 4 salad plates or shallow bowls. Arrange remaining salad ingredients in rows on lettuce. Serve with dressing.

1 Serving: Calories 610; Total Fat 49g (Saturated Fat 10g; Trans Fat 0g); Cholesterol 230mg; Sodium 650mg; Total Carbohydrate 12g (Dietary Fiber 4g); Protein 30g **Exchanges:** 2 Vegetable, 4 High-Fat Meat, 3 Fat **Carbohydrate Choices:** 1

HEARTY SOYBEAN AND CHEDDAR PASTA SALAD

Edamame is the Japanese name for fresh green soybeans—tasty little bright green gems that cook quickly and are high in protein.

PREP 20 min TOTAL 1 hr 35 min • **4 servings**

SALAD

- 1 cup uncooked penne pasta (3 oz)
- 1 bag (12 oz) frozen shelled edamame (green) soybeans
- 1 large tomato, coarsely chopped (1 cup)
- 1 small yellow bell pepper, coarsely chopped (½ cup)
- ½ medium cucumber, coarsely chopped (½ cup)
- 6 oz Cheddar cheese, cut into ½-inch cubes (1½ cups)

DRESSING

- ⅓ cup vegetable oil
- ¼ cup red wine vinegar
- 1 teaspoon Italian seasoning
- ½ teaspoon salt
- ¼ teaspoon pepper
- ¼ teaspoon garlic powder

1 Cook pasta and soybeans separately as directed on each package. Rinse with cold water; drain.

2 In large bowl, toss pasta, soybeans, tomato, bell pepper, cucumber and cheese. In small bowl, beat all dressing ingredients with wire whisk until well mixed. Pour over salad; toss.

3 Cover; refrigerate at least 1 hour to blend flavors. Stir before serving.

1 Serving: Calories 710; Total Fat 45g (Saturated Fat 13g; Trans Fat 0g); Cholesterol 45mg; Sodium 780mg; Total Carbohydrate 39g (Dietary Fiber 11g); Protein 37g **Exchanges:** 2 Starch, 3 High-Fat Meat, 2½ Fat **Carbohydrate Choices:** 2½

Cobb Salad

CHICKEN-THYME PENNE

You'll need about 2 pounds of uncooked boneless skinless chicken breasts, which equals 4 cups cubed cooked chicken, to make this dish. Cook them however you want or buy deli rotisserie chicken.

PREP 25 min **TOTAL** 4 hr 25 min • **8 servings**

- 3 cups uncooked penne pasta (9 oz)
- 4 cups cubed cooked chicken
- 2 cups seedless red grapes, halved
- 2 medium stalks celery, sliced (1 cup)
- ⅓ cup chopped onion
- 3 tablespoons olive or vegetable oil
- 2 tablespoons chopped fresh or 2 teaspoons dried thyme leaves, crushed
- 1¼ cups mayonnaise or salad dressing (for homemade mayonnaise, see page 483)
- 1 tablespoon milk
- 1 tablespoon honey
- 1 tablespoon coarse-grained mustard
- 1 teaspoon salt
- 1 cup chopped walnuts, toasted (page 22)

1 Cook and drain pasta as directed on package. Rinse with cold water; drain.

2 In large (4-quart) bowl, mix pasta, chicken, grapes, celery and onion. In small bowl, mix oil and 1 tablespoon of the fresh thyme (or 1 teaspoon of the dried thyme). Pour over chicken mixture; toss to coat.

3 In small bowl, mix mayonnaise, milk, honey, mustard, salt and remaining thyme. Cover chicken mixture and mayonnaise mixture separately; refrigerate at least 4 hours but no longer than 24 hours.

4 Up to 2 hours before serving, toss chicken mixture and mayonnaise mixture. Cover; refrigerate. Just before serving, stir in ¾ cup of the walnuts. Sprinkle salad with remaining walnuts.

1 Serving: Calories 690; Total Fat 46g (Saturated Fat 7g; Trans Fat 0g); Cholesterol 80mg; Sodium 600mg; Total Carbohydrate 41g (Dietary Fiber 4g); Protein 29g **Exchanges:** 2 Starch, 1 Fruit, 3 Medium-Fat Meat, 5½ Fat **Carbohydrate Choices:** 3

TURKEY-BASIL PENNE Substitute cooked turkey for the chicken and fresh basil for the thyme.

Chicken-Thyme Penne

TUNA-MACARONI SALAD

PREP 20 min **TOTAL** 1 hr 20 min • **6 servings**

- 1 package (7 oz) elbow macaroni (2½ cups)
- ½ cup frozen sweet peas, thawed
- 1 can (9 oz) tuna, drained
- 1 cup mayonnaise or salad dressing (for homemade mayonnaise, see page 483)
- 1 cup shredded Cheddar cheese (4 oz), if desired
- ¼ cup sweet pickle relish, if desired
- 2 teaspoons fresh lemon juice
- ¾ teaspoon salt
- ¼ teaspoon pepper
- 1 medium stalk celery, chopped (½ cup)
- 1 small onion, chopped (⅓ cup)

1 Cook macaroni as directed on package, adding peas for last 4 to 6 minutes of cooking; rinse with cold water and drain.

2 In large bowl, mix macaroni and peas with remaining ingredients. Cover; refrigerate at least 1 hour to blend flavors.

1 Serving: Calories 450; Total Fat 30g (Saturated Fat 4.5g; Trans Fat 0g); Cholesterol 35mg; Sodium 780mg; Total Carbohydrate 29g (Dietary Fiber 3g); Protein 15g **Exchanges:** 2 Starch, 1½ Very Lean Meat, 5½ Fat **Carbohydrate Choices:** 2

LIGHTER **DIRECTIONS** For 1 gram of fat and 210 calories per serving, use fat-free mayonnaise, reduced-fat Cheddar cheese and water-packed tuna.

STRAWBERRY MARGARITA CUPS LOWER CALORIE

This recipe is an absolute "wow" and definitely not your 1950s-style gelatin mold! These soft-textured salads would also make a divine dessert.

PREP 10 min TOTAL 4 hr 10 min • **6 servings**

1½ cups boiling water
1 box (8-serving size) wild strawberry-flavored gelatin
1 can (10 oz) frozen margarita mix concentrate, thawed
1 box (10 oz) frozen strawberries in light syrup, thawed
½ cup tequila or water
Sweetened Whipped Cream (page 214), if desired
Fresh strawberries and grated lime peel, if desired

1 In medium bowl, pour boiling water on gelatin; stir until gelatin is dissolved. In blender or food processor, place margarita mix, strawberries with syrup and tequila. Cover and blend on high speed until smooth. Stir strawberry mixture into gelatin.

2 If desired, dip rims of glasses in water, then in sugar. Spoon about ¾ cup mixture into each of 6 margarita glasses or 10-oz custard cups. Refrigerate about 4 hours or until firm.

3 Top with whipped cream, fresh strawberries and lime peel.

1 Serving (¾ Cup): Calories 150; Total Fat 0g (Saturated Fat 0g; Trans Fat 0g); Cholesterol 0mg; Sodium 80mg; Total Carbohydrate 36g (Dietary Fiber 0g); Protein 2g **Exchanges:** 4 Other Carbohydrate **Carbohydrate Choices:** 2½

EASY CRANBERRY-ORANGE MOLD LOWER CALORIE

PREP 10 min TOTAL 4 hr 10 min • **8 servings**

1 can (11 oz) mandarin orange segments, drained, juice reserved
1 box (4-serving size) orange-flavored gelatin
1 can (16 oz) whole berry cranberry sauce
Salad greens, if desired

1 Spray 4-cup mold with cooking spray. Add enough water to reserved mandarin orange juice to measure 1¼ cups. In 1-quart saucepan, heat juice mixture to boiling.

2 In medium bowl, pour boiling mixture on gelatin; stir until gelatin is dissolved. Stir in cranberry sauce until sauce is melted. Stir in orange segments. Pour into mold.

3 Refrigerate about 4 hours or until firm. Unmold; serve on salad greens.

1 Serving: Calories 150; Total Fat 0g (Saturated Fat 0g; Trans Fat 0g); Cholesterol 0mg; Sodium 65mg; Total Carbohydrate 35g (Dietary Fiber 1g); Protein 1g **Exchanges:** 2½ Fruit **Carbohydrate Choices:** 2

Unmolding Gelatin Salads

Dip mold into warm (not hot) water for several seconds. Dip tip of knife in warm water; carefully run knife around top edge of mold to loosen.

Place chilled serving plate on top of mold. Holding both mold and plate firmly, turn upside down onto plate and gently shake to release gelatin. Carefully lift mold from gelatin.

Easy Cranberry-Orange Mold

DRESSING BASICS

ABOUT OIL

Oils add body to dressings and range in flavor from earthy and nutty to neutral or fruity and mildly sweet. Recipes often call for a specific oil designed to complement the ingredients, but feel free to experiment with a different oil or combination of oils.

TYPE OF OIL	DESCRIPTION
Vegetable Oils (often generically labeled as vegetable oil; check label for oil source)	
Canola, Corn, Soybean, Sunflower	Delicate/neutral
Peanut	Mildly buttery
Safflower	Mildly nutty
Olive Oils	
Olive Oil and Light Olive Oil	Delicate/neutral; golden color and mild flavor
Extra-Virgin Olive Oil	Fruity olive flavor that is stronger than regular olive oil; golden to green or bright green color
Nut Oils (highly flavorful; start with a small amount, adding more as needed)	
Almond	Nutty, mildly sweet
Avocado	Nutty, sharp
Hazelnut	Nutty, rich
Walnut	Mildly nutty
Sesame Oil (highly flavorful; start with a small amount, adding more as needed)	
Sesame Oil, light	Nutty, light color
Sesame Oil, dark (also called Asian)	Strong toasted sesame seed flavor; amber color

ABOUT VINEGAR

There are many kinds of vinegar on the market, and they all add lively zest to salad dressings. Most recipes call for one type of vinegar, but you can try a little mixing and matching.

TYPE OF VINEGAR	DESCRIPTION
Balsamic (white grapes)	Rich, sweet, dark brown or white
Cider (fermented apple cider)	Mild apple flavor, golden brown
Fruit (blueberries, raspberries or strawberries steeped in cider or white wine vinegar)	Flavor and color of berry used; mildly sweet
Herb (basil, chives, dill weed or tarragon steeped in white wine vinegar or cider vinegar)	Flavor of herb used
Rice (fermented rice)	Plain and sweetened forms; delicate, sweet flavor
White (distilled grain alcohol)	Strong, pungent and clear
Wine (champagne, sherry, red or white wine)	Flavor of wine used

Use a wire whisk to mix salad dressings.

Fresh Herb Vinaigrette

In tightly covered container or bowl using whisk, shake or mix ½ cup olive oil, 3 tablespoons red or white wine vinegar, 1 tablespoon chopped fresh herbs (basil, marjoram, oregano, rosemary, tarragon or thyme), 1 tablespoon chopped fresh parsley, 1 tablespoon chopped green onion, ½ teaspoon salt and ¼ teaspoon pepper. Makes about ¾ cup vinaigrette.

FRENCH DRESSING

FAST LOWER CALORIE

PREP 5 min TOTAL 5 min • **1½ cups dressing**

1 cup olive or vegetable oil
¼ cup white or cider vinegar
¼ cup fresh lemon juice
½ teaspoon salt
½ teaspoon ground mustard
½ teaspoon paprika

In tightly covered container, shake all ingredients. Shake before serving. Store tightly covered in refrigerator up to 1 week.

1 Tablespoon: Calories 80; Total Fat 9g (Saturated Fat 1g; Trans Fat 0g); Cholesterol 0mg; Sodium 50mg; Total Carbohydrate 0g (Dietary Fiber 0g); Protein 0g **Exchanges:** 2 Fat **Carbohydrate Choices:** 0

RED FRENCH DRESSING Mix together ½ cup of the French dressing and ½ cup ketchup.

THOUSAND ISLAND DRESSING

FAST

PREP 15 min TOTAL 15 min • **1 cup dressing**

1 cup mayonnaise or salad dressing (for homemade mayonnaise, see page 483)
2 tablespoons chopped pimiento-stuffed green olives or sweet pickle relish
2 tablespoons chili sauce or ketchup
1 tablespoon chopped fresh parsley
1 teaspoon finely chopped onion
1 Hard-Cooked Egg (page 74), finely chopped
½ teaspoon paprika

In small bowl, mix all ingredients. Stir before serving. Store tightly covered in refrigerator up to 5 days.

1 Tablespoon: Calories 110; Total Fat 11g (Saturated Fat 2g; Trans Fat 0g); Cholesterol 20mg; Sodium 130mg; Total Carbohydrate 0g (Dietary Fiber 0g); Protein 0g **Exchanges:** 2 Fat **Carbohydrate Choices:** 0

LIGHTER DIRECTIONS For 5 grams of fat and 55 calories per serving, use reduced-fat mayonnaise; substitute 2 hard-cooked egg whites for the hard-cooked whole egg.

RUSSIAN DRESSING Omit olives, parsley and egg. Increase chili sauce to ¼ cup. Add 1 teaspoon prepared horseradish.

HONEY-DIJON DRESSING

FAST

PREP 5 min TOTAL 5 min • **1 cup dressing**

½ cup vegetable oil
⅓ cup honey or real maple syrup
¼ cup fresh lemon juice
1 tablespoon Dijon mustard

In tightly covered container, shake all ingredients. Shake before serving. Store tightly covered in refrigerator up to 1 week.

1 Tablespoon: Calories 90; Total Fat 7g (Saturated Fat 1g; Trans Fat 0g); Cholesterol 0mg; Sodium 25mg; Total Carbohydrate 6g (Dietary Fiber 0g); Protein 0g **Exchanges:** ½ Fruit, 1 Fat **Carbohydrate Choices:** ½

HONEY–POPPY SEED DRESSING Omit mustard. Add 1 tablespoon poppy seed.

ITALIAN DRESSING FAST

PREP 10 min TOTAL 10 min • **1¼ cups dressing**

1 cup olive or vegetable oil
¼ cup white or cider vinegar
2 tablespoons finely chopped onion
1 tablespoon chopped fresh or 1 teaspoon dried basil leaves
1 teaspoon sugar
1 teaspoon ground mustard
½ teaspoon salt
½ teaspoon dried oregano leaves
¼ teaspoon pepper
2 cloves garlic, finely chopped

In tightly covered container, shake all ingredients. Shake before serving. Store tightly covered in refrigerator up to 1 week.

1 Tablespoon: Calories 100; Total Fat 11g (Saturated Fat 1.5g; Trans Fat 0g); Cholesterol 0mg; Sodium 60mg; Total Carbohydrate 0g (Dietary Fiber 0g); Protein 0g **Exchanges:** 2 Fat **Carbohydrate Choices:** 0

LIGHTER ITALIAN DRESSING For 5 grams of fat and 50 calories per serving, substitute ½ cup apple juice for ½ cup of the oil.

CREAMY ITALIAN DRESSING In small bowl, beat ½ cup of the Italian dressing and ½ cup mayonnaise or salad dressing with wire whisk until smooth.

See how to whisk a **salad dressing:**
Visit bettycrocker.com/BCcookbook

RASPBERRY VINAIGRETTE DRESSING FAST LOWER CALORIE

PREP 10 min TOTAL 10 min • **1 cup dressing**

- ½ cup red wine vinegar
- ⅓ cup seedless red raspberry jam
- ¼ cup olive or vegetable oil
- ¼ teaspoon salt

In small bowl, beat all ingredients with whisk until well blended. Stir before serving. Store tightly covered in refrigerator up to 1 week.

1 Tablespoon: Calories 50; Total Fat 3.5g (Saturated Fat 0g; Trans Fat 0g); Cholesterol 0mg; Sodium 40mg; Total Carbohydrate 5g (Dietary Fiber 0g); Protein 0g **Exchanges:** ½ Fruit, ½ Fat **Carbohydrate Choices:** ½

ASIAN DRESSING

FAST LOWER CALORIE

PREP 10 min TOTAL 10 min • **1 cup dressing**

- ⅓ cup rice vinegar, white or cider vinegar
- ¼ cup vegetable oil
- 3 tablespoons soy sauce
- 2 tablespoons dry sherry or apple juice
- 1 teaspoon dark sesame oil
- 1 teaspoon grated gingerroot or ¼ teaspoon ground ginger
- 1 tablespoon sesame seed, toasted (page 22)
- 1 teaspoon sugar

In tightly covered container, shake all ingredients. Shake before serving. Store tightly covered in refrigerator up to 1 week.

1 Tablespoon: Calories 35; Total Fat 3.5g (Saturated Fat 0g; Trans Fat 0g); Cholesterol 0mg; Sodium 170mg; Total Carbohydrate 0g (Dietary Fiber 0g); Protein 0g **Exchanges:** ½ Fat **Carbohydrate Choices:** 0

BUTTERMILK RANCH DRESSING

LOWER CALORIE

PREP 5 min TOTAL 2 hr 5 min • **1¼ cups dressing**

- ¾ cup mayonnaise or salad dressing (for homemade mayonnaise, see page 483)
- 1 clove garlic, finely chopped
- ½ cup buttermilk
- 1 teaspoon parsley flakes
- ½ teaspoon dried minced onion
- ½ teaspoon salt
  Dash freshly ground pepper

In small bowl, mix all ingredients. Cover; refrigerate at least 2 hours to blend flavors. Stir before serving. Store tightly covered in refrigerator up to 5 days.

1 Tablespoon: Calories 60; Total Fat 7g (Saturated Fat 1g; Trans Fat 0g); Cholesterol 0mg; Sodium 110mg; Total Carbohydrate 0g (Dietary Fiber 0g); Protein 0g **Exchanges:** 1½ Fat **Carbohydrate Choices:** 0

LIGHTER DIRECTIONS For 4 grams of fat and 45 calories per serving, use reduced-fat mayonnaise.

BUTTERMILK RANCH–PARMESAN DRESSING Add ⅓ cup grated Parmesan cheese and ½ teaspoon paprika.

BLUE CHEESE DRESSING

LOWER CALORIE

PREP 10 min TOTAL 3 hr 10 min • **1⅔ cups dressing**

- ¾ cup crumbled blue or Gorgonzola cheese (3 oz)
- 1 package (3 oz) cream cheese, softened
- ½ cup mayonnaise or salad dressing (for homemade mayonnaise, see page 483)
- ⅓ cup half-and-half
- 1 teaspoon cider vinegar
- ⅛ teaspoon pepper

1 Reserve ⅓ cup of the blue cheese. In small bowl, mix remaining blue cheese and the cream cheese until well blended. Stir in mayonnaise, half-and-half, vinegar and pepper until creamy. Stir in reserved ⅓ cup blue cheese.

2 Cover; refrigerate at least 3 hours to blend flavors. Stir before serving. Store tightly covered in refrigerator up to 5 days.

1 Tablespoon: Calories 50; Total Fat 5g (Saturated Fat 2g; Trans Fat 0g); Cholesterol 10mg; Sodium 80mg; Total Carbohydrate 0g (Dietary Fiber 0g); Protein 1g **Exchanges:** 1 Fat **Carbohydrate Choices:** 0

LIGHTER DIRECTIONS For 3 grams of fat and 35 calories per serving, decrease blue cheese to ½ cup. Substitute 4 oz (half of 8-oz package) ⅓-less-fat cream cheese (Neufchâtel) for the regular cream cheese and ¼ cup fat-free (skim) milk for the half-and-half. Use reduced-fat mayonnaise.

SAUCES, SEASONINGS & CONDIMENTS

SAUCES

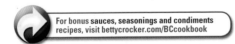

For bonus sauces, seasonings and condiments recipes, visit bettycrocker.com/BCcookbook

FAST = Ready in 20 minutes or less LOWER CALORIE = See Helpful Nutrition and Cooking Information, page 685
LIGHTER = 25% fewer calories or grams of fat MAKE AHEAD = Make-ahead directions SLOW COOKER = Slow cooker directions

← Ingredients for Basil Pesto (page 484), Tropical Fruit Salsa (page 481), Jamaican Jerk Seasoning Rub (page 500), White Wine–Garlic Sauce (page 488)

SAUCE BASICS
From tried-and-true classics and international sauces to twists on the traditional, this chapter showcases a variety of tasty toppings that will make all of your food come alive with flavor . . . and turn something basic into something extraordinary!

THICKENING SAUCES

Different sauces are thickened in different ways. These are the four classic thickening methods:

Roux: A mixture of flour and fat (usually butter) is cooked over low to medium heat until smooth and bubbly and then liquid is added. Some recipes call for cooking the roux until it turns golden to deep brown. Making a roux cooks the flour and prevents foods from taking on a raw flour taste. See White Sauce, page 486, or Mornay Sauce, page 487.

Cornstarch: Cornstarch often is stirred into cold water or other liquid and thoroughly blended before being added to the hot mixture. Sauces thickened with cornstarch become clear and almost shiny. See Sweet-and-Sour Sauce, page 482, or Raspberry Sauce, page 235.

Emulsion: An egg-based sauce is cooked over low heat. If the temperature is too hot, the mixture will overcook and curdle. These sauces must be cooked thoroughly to kill salmonella bacteria. See Hollandaise Sauce, page 487, or Whiskey Sauce, page 228.

Reduction: A liquid such as broth, wine, vinegar or cream is boiled or simmered until the volume is reduced and the mixture is thickened. Evaporation results in a concentration of the flavor. To speed the process of reducing liquids, use a skillet (which has a large surface area) instead of a saucepan. See Gorgonzola- and Mushroom-Stuffed Beef Tenderloin with Merlot Sauce, page 337, or Brandy-Herb Pan Steaks page, 334.

Tips for Perfect Sauces

It's easy to make superbly smooth, lump-free sauces if you follow these tips. Also, exercise a little patience; if you rush it, the sauce may scorch, curdle or separate.

- Gather all of the ingredients before beginning so that you can give your full attention to cooking the sauce.

- Cook sauces over low to medium heat unless a recipe specifies otherwise. Egg-thickened sauces should be cooked over very low heat.

- Use a whisk to mix sauces and stir constantly just until thickened.

- Combine cornstarch or flour with an equal amount of cold water in a small bowl until well blended before adding to hot mixture.

- Sauces can be made ahead and reheated when ready to serve. Slowly reheat over low to medium heat. Egg-thickened sauces should be reheated over very low heat.

Sauces can be made with a variety of ingredients and kitchen utensils.

Heirloom Recipe and New Twist

This amazing classic salsa has been a favorite for many years and is a traditional Southwestern-style sauce. It's full of tomato flavor and perfect any time you want to serve a tasty salsa. But when you are ready for a change, try our new twist, Salsa Verde. Made with tomatillos, it's quick to make, spicy and a wonderful alternative to classic salsa.

SALSA   LOWER CALORIE

Salsa comes from the Spanish word for "sauce." Some salsas are fresh and others cooked. Chiles, give them that characteristic kick. Pico de gallo is another name often used for uncooked salsa like this.

PREP 20 min **TOTAL** 1 hr 20 min • **3½ cups salsa**

- 3 large tomatoes, seeded, chopped (3 cups)
- 1 small green bell pepper, chopped (½ cup)
- 8 medium green onions, sliced (½ cup)
- 3 cloves garlic, finely chopped
- 2 tablespoons chopped fresh cilantro
- 1 tablespoon finely chopped seeded jalapeño chiles
- 2 to 3 tablespoons lime juice
- ½ teaspoon salt

In medium glass or plastic bowl, mix all ingredients. Cover; refrigerate at least 1 hour to blend flavors. Store covered in refrigerator up to 1 week.

¼ Cup: Calories 20; Total Fat 0g (Saturated Fat 0g; Trans Fat 0g); Cholesterol 0mg; Sodium 90mg; Total Carbohydrate 4g (Dietary Fiber 0g); Protein 0g **Exchanges:** Free **Carbohydrate Choices:** 0

BLACK BEAN SALSA Stir in 1 can (15 oz) black beans, drained and rinsed. Makes 5 cups salsa

Tomatoes for Salsa

Look for large juicy tomatoes when you make salsa. Removing the seeds is easy with a small spoon. Hold the quartered tomato over a bowl to catch the seeds and juice as you scoop them out, and use it in the salsa if you like.

Salsa

Salsa Verde

See how to make **salsa**: Visit
bettycrocker.com/BCcookbook

SALSA VERDE FAST LOWER CALORIE

PREP 15 min TOTAL 15 min • **1¼ cups salsa**

- **8 oz tomatillos, husks removed, rinsed, cut in half***
- **2 canned serrano chiles, rinsed and seeded, or 1 fresh serrano chile, seeded**
- **¼ cup chopped red onion**
- **¼ cup chopped fresh cilantro or parsley**
- **¼ teaspoon salt**

In food processor or blender, place all ingredients. Cover; process until well blended. Serve immediately, or cover and refrigerate up to 1 week.

*Small green tomatoes can be substituted.

¼ Cup: Calories 20; Total Fat 0g (Saturated Fat 0g; Trans Fat 0g); Cholesterol 0mg; Sodium 120mg; Total Carbohydrate 4g (Dietary Fiber 1g); Protein 0g **Exchanges: Free Carbohydrate Choices:** 0

Preparing Tomatillos

Open dry husks and pull up toward top of tomatillo. Pull or cut with paring knife to remove husks and stems.

Rinse tomatillo; rub gently to remove sticky film. Cut as desired.

Tomatillos

Tomatillos (tohm-ah-TEE-ohs) are from the same family as tomatoes but are very different. They are green with a flavor that hints of lemon and apples. Tomatillos have a thick skin with a papery covering and a firm texture much like a green tomato.

TROPICAL FRUIT SALSA

LOWER CALORIE

Serve this salsa at room temperature for the fullest flavor. If mangoes and papayas aren't available, try substituting a combination of peaches, nectarines, plums and apricots.

PREP 15 min TOTAL 1 hr 15 min • **3 cups salsa**

- **2 kiwifruit, peeled, chopped (⅔ cup)**
- **1 ripe medium mango, seed removed, peeled, and chopped (1 cup)**
- **1 medium papaya, peeled, seeded and chopped (1½ cups)**
- **1 jalapeño chile, seeded, finely chopped**
- **1 cup fresh pineapple chunks***
- **1 tablespoon finely chopped red onion**
- **1 tablespoon chopped fresh cilantro**
- **2 tablespoons fresh lime juice**

1 In medium glass or plastic bowl, mix all ingredients. Cover; refrigerate 1 to 2 hours to blend flavors.

2 Serve with grilled poultry, pork or seafood.

*2 cans (8 oz each) pineapple chunks in juice, drained, can be substituted.

¼ Cup: Calories 60; Total Fat 0g (Saturated Fat 0g; Trans Fat 0g); Cholesterol 0mg; Sodium 0mg; Total Carbohydrate 14g (Dietary Fiber 2g); Protein 0g **Exchanges:** 1 Fruit **Carbohydrate Choices:** 1

FRESH PEACH SALSA

PREP 20 min TOTAL 1 hr 20 min • **2¼ cups salsa**

- **2 cups chopped fresh or frozen (thawed) peaches**
- **¼ cup finely chopped red bell pepper**
- **2 to 4 tablespoons grapefruit juice**
- **4 teaspoons chopped fresh cilantro**
- **2 medium green onions, chopped (2 tablespoons)**
- **Dash salt**

1 In medium glass or plastic bowl, mix all ingredients. Cover; refrigerate 1 to 2 hours to blend flavors.

2 Serve with poultry, pork or seafood.

¼ Cup: Calories 20; Total Fat 0g (Saturated Fat 0g; Trans Fat 0g); Cholesterol 0mg; Sodium 15mg; Total Carbohydrate 5g (Dietary Fiber 0g); Protein 0g **Exchanges: Free Carbohydrate Choices:** ½

PEANUT SAUCE FAST

PREP 5 min TOTAL 10 min • **1 cup sauce**

- ½ cup creamy peanut butter
- ½ cup water
- 2 tablespoons fresh lime juice
- ½ teaspoon ground coriander
- ½ teaspoon ground cumin
- ⅛ teaspoon salt
- ⅛ teaspoon ground red pepper (cayenne), if desired
- 2 cloves garlic, finely chopped

1 Place peanut butter in medium bowl. Gradually stir in water and lime juice with whisk until smooth and creamy; stir in remaining ingredients. To make a warm sauce, place all ingredients in 1-quart saucepan. Heat over medium heat, stirring with whisk frequently, until smooth and warm.

2 Use sauce immediately, or cover and refrigerate up to 3 days or freeze up to 2 months.

2 Tablespoons: Calories 110; Total Fat 8g (Saturated Fat 1.5g; Trans Fat 0g); Cholesterol 0mg; Sodium 75mg; Total Carbohydrate 4g (Dietary Fiber 0g); Protein 4g **Exchanges:** ½ High-Fat Meat, 1 Fat **Carbohydrate Choices:** 0

CHIMICHURRI SAUCE

Chimichurri is a common condiment in Argentina. Either curly- or flat-leaf (Italian) parsley can be used in this recipe. Flat-leaf parsley has a stronger peppery flavor. Use this sauce to perk up the flavor of grilled meat or poultry.

PREP 10 min TOTAL 2 hr 10 min • **1 cup sauce**

- 1 bunch fresh parsley (about 1 cup firmly packed), chopped
- 2 cloves garlic, finely chopped
- ¾ cup olive or vegetable oil
- ¼ cup white vinegar
- ½ teaspoon salt
- ⅛ teaspoon pepper

In blender or food processor, place all ingredients. Cover; blend on high speed until well blended. Cover; refrigerate 2 hours. Store covered in refrigerator.

2 Tablespoons: Calories 190; Total Fat 20g (Saturated Fat 2.5g; Trans Fat 0g); Cholesterol 0mg; Sodium 150mg; Total Carbohydrate 0g (Dietary Fiber 0g); Protein 0g **Exchanges:** 4 Fat **Carbohydrate Choices:** 0

SWEET-AND-SOUR SAUCE

FAST   LOWER CALORIE

This traditional Asian sauce can range in flavor from not very sweet to quite sweet. Our version is sweet with a tangy hit from the vinegar. Use it on chicken or pork.

PREP 10 min TOTAL 15 min • **1½ cups sauce**

- ½ cup packed brown sugar
- 1 tablespoon cornstarch
- 1 can (8 oz) crushed pineapple in juice, drained, juice reserved
- ⅓ cup white vinegar
- 1 tablespoon soy sauce

1 In 1-quart saucepan, mix brown sugar and cornstarch.

2 Add enough water to reserved pineapple juice to measure ½ cup; stir into sugar mixture. Stir in vinegar and soy sauce. Heat to boiling over medium heat, stirring constantly. Boil and stir 1 minute. Stir in pineapple.

3 Use sauce immediately, or cover and refrigerate up to 2 weeks or freeze up to 6 months.

1 Tablespoon: Calories 25; Total Fat 0g (Saturated Fat 0g; Trans Fat 0g); Cholesterol 0mg; Sodium 40mg; Total Carbohydrate 7g (Dietary Fiber 0g); Protein 0g **Exchanges:** ½ Fruit **Carbohydrate Choices:** ½

Chimichurri Sauce

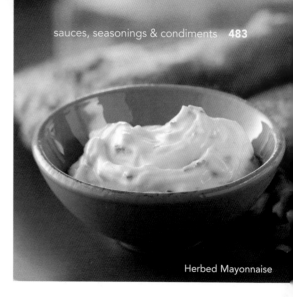

Herbed Mayonnaise

TARTAR SAUCE

Tartar sauce is a favorite to serve with most any type of fish or seafood. If you make it with salad dressing, it will be sweeter.

PREP 5 min TOTAL 1 hr 5 min • **1 cup sauce**

- 1 **cup mayonnaise or salad dressing**
- 2 **tablespoons finely chopped dill pickle or pickle relish**
- 1 **tablespoon chopped fresh parsley**
- 2 **teaspoons diced pimientos, drained**
- 1 **teaspoon grated onion**

In small bowl, mix all ingredients. Cover; refrigerate about 1 hour or until chilled. Store covered in refrigerator up to 5 days.

1 Tablespoon: Calories 100; Total Fat 11g (Saturated Fat 1.5g; Trans Fat 0g); Cholesterol 10mg; Sodium 95mg; Total Carbohydrate 0g (Dietary Fiber 0g); Protein 0g **Exchanges:** 2 Fat **Carbohydrate Choices:** 0

LIGHTER DIRECTIONS For 5 grams of fat and 50 calories per serving, use reduced-fat mayonnaise.

DILL TARTAR SAUCE Stir in 1 tablespoon chopped fresh or 1 teaspoon dried dill weed.

MAYONNAISE FAST

Homemade mayonnaise is deceptively easy to make and it's deliciously lush and decadent. You may never go back to store-bought again. Use it in any recipe calling for mayonnaise.

PREP 10 min TOTAL 10 min • **1¾ cups sauce**

- 1¼ **cups vegetable oil**
- 2 **tablespoons fresh lemon juice**
- 1 **tablespoon Dijon mustard**
- ¼ **teaspoon salt**
- 1 **pasteurized egg***

1 In blender, place ¼ cup of the oil, the lemon juice, mustard, salt and egg; cover and blend until smooth.

2 Leave cover on blender but remove center cap. With blender running at medium-high speed, slowly add remaining 1 cup oil in thin stream through opening in cover. Scrape down sides of container as needed. Store in tightly covered container in refrigerator up to 5 days.

*Pasteurized eggs are uncooked whole eggs that have been heat-treated to kill bacteria that can cause food poisoning and gastrointestinal distress. Because the egg in this recipe is not cooked, be sure to use a pasteurized egg. Look for them in the dairy case at large supermarkets.

1 Tablespoon: Calories 90; Total Fat 10g (Saturated Fat 1.5g; Trans Fat 0g); Cholesterol 10mg; Sodium 35mg; Total Carbohydrate 0g (Dietary Fiber 0g); Protein 0g **Exchanges:** 2 Fat **Carbohydrate Choices:** 0

CURRIED MAYONNAISE Add ½ to 1 teaspoon curry powder to egg mixture before blending.

GARLIC MAYONNAISE Stir 1 garlic clove, minced, into prepared mayonnaise.

HERBED MAYONNAISE Stir 1 tablespoon chopped fresh basil, chervil, chives, cilantro, marjoram, oregano or parsley into prepared mayonnaise. If using dried herbs, use only 1 teaspoon.

CREAMY HORSERADISH SAUCE

FAST LOWER CALORIE

This zesty, tongue-tingling sauce pairs very well with grilled steak or burgers.

PREP 5 min TOTAL 5 min • **¾ cup sauce**

- ½ **cup sour cream**
- ¼ **cup mayonnaise or salad dressing**
- 2 **tablespoons prepared horseradish**
- 2 **teaspoons Dijon mustard**

In small bowl, mix all ingredients. Store covered in refrigerator up to 5 days.

1 Tablespoon: Calories 50; Total Fat 6g (Saturated Fat 1.5g; Trans Fat 0g); Cholesterol 5mg; Sodium 60mg; Total Carbohydrate 0g (Dietary Fiber 0g); Protein 0g **Exchanges:** 1 Fat **Carbohydrate Choices:** 0

Learn to Make Pesto

BASIL PESTO FAST

Pesto is a quick and easy, flavorful sauce that has a multitude of uses. Make it in a snap with basil from your garden or when the beautiful bunches of basil are beckoning you at the farmers' market. Keep some pesto on hand to perk up the flavor of everyday foods.

PREP 10 min **TOTAL** 10 min • **1¼ cups pesto**

2 cups firmly packed fresh basil leaves
¾ cup grated Parmesan cheese
¼ cup pine nuts, toasted if desired (page 22)

½ cup olive or vegetable oil
3 cloves garlic

1 In blender or food processor*, place all ingredients. Cover; blend on medium speed about 3 minutes, stopping occasionally to scrape down the sides with a rubber spatula, until smooth.

2 Use pesto immediately, or cover tightly and refrigerate up to 5 days or freeze up to 1 month (color of pesto will darken as it stands).

If you have a small processor, process half of the basil at a time, then add remaining ingredients and continue as directed.

2 Tablespoons: Calories 160; Total Fat 15g (Saturated Fat 3g; Trans Fat 0g); Cholesterol 5mg; Sodium 140mg; Total Carbohydrate 1g (Dietary Fiber 0g); Protein 4g **Exchanges:** ½ Vegetable, 3 Fat **Carbohydrate Choices:** 0

Keys to Success

- Firmly pack basil leaves in measuring cup to ensure you're using enough basil.
- Scrape down sides of blender or food processor occasionally so that ingredients chop evenly.
- Place plastic wrap directly on surface of pesto to help prevent it from darkening in refrigerator or freezer.
- Thaw frozen pesto in refrigerator or place in resealable food-storage plastic bag with frozen pesto in container of hot water until thawed. Do not microwave to thaw because pesto will lose flavor.

Great Ways to Use Pesto

Pesto adds a burst of fresh flavor to many dishes, transforming a familiar food into something different and new. A little goes a long way, so start off with a small amount, adding more if you like.

Cooked Vegetables: Toss with hot cooked vegetables instead of using butter.

Corn on the Cob: Spread on hot, cooked corn on the cob instead of using butter and salt.

Dip or Spread: Serve with appetizers as a dip or as a spread for bread, crackers, or cut-up raw vegetables.

Mashed Potatoes: Stir into hot mashed potatoes.

Meat or Fish: Brush on chicken, pork, beef, shrimp, scallops or fish during cooking or top cooked meat or fish after cooking.

Pasta, Rice or Couscous: Toss with hot cooked pasta, rice or couscous.

Pasta Salads: Replace a little of the mayonnaise or dressing with pesto in pasta salads.

Pizza: Spread on crust instead of using traditional pizza sauce or add dollops to baked pizza as a topping.

Sandwich Spread: Use instead of mayonnaise or mustard in sandwiches or in addition to your typical spread.

Sauces: Stir into cream sauce or cheese sauce for serving on chicken, pork or pasta.

Scrambled Eggs: Add a spoonful to eggs while beating.

Soups: Stir into soups such as potato, tomato or corn chowder, or serve soup with a dollop of pesto on top.

MORE PESTOS

Here are some great ways to change the flavor of pesto to something new but just as tasty as classic pesto. So if you don't have basil on hand or just want a new flavor combination, try one of these creative mixtures.

Cilantro Pesto

Spinach Pesto

Basil, Roasted Red Pepper and Walnut Pesto

Basil Pesto

Sun-Dried Tomato Pesto

Basil, Roasted Red Pepper and Walnut Pesto: Use food processor. Decrease basil to 1 cup. Decrease oil to ⅓ cup; add ½ cup drained roasted red or yellow bell peppers (from jar). Substitute walnuts for the pine nuts.

Cilantro Pesto: Substitute 1½ cups firmly packed fresh cilantro and ½ cup firmly packed fresh parsley for the basil.

Spinach Pesto: Substitute 2 cups firmly packed fresh spinach for the basil.

Sun-Dried Tomato Pesto: Use food processor. Omit basil. Decrease oil to ⅓ cup; add ½ cup sun-dried tomatoes in oil, undrained.

Making Pesto Cubes

For homemade pesto anytime, freeze pesto in ice cube trays. Once frozen, move pesto cubes to a resealable freezer plastic bag and store in freezer up to 6 months.

See how to make **pesto:** Visit bettycrocker.com/BCcookbook

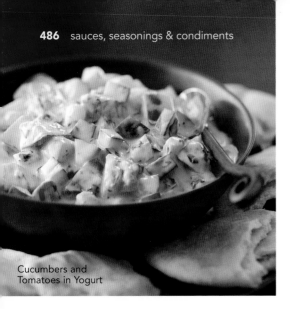

Cucumbers and
Tomatoes in Yogurt

CUCUMBERS AND TOMATOES IN YOGURT LOWER CALORIE

Called raitas *in India, yogurt-based sides like this cool taste buds when paired with spicy food.*

PREP 10 min **TOTAL** 50 min • **2 cups sauce**

- 1 medium cucumber
- 1 medium green onion, chopped (1 tablespoon)
- ½ teaspoon salt
- 1 medium tomato, chopped (¾ cup)
- 1 tablespoon chopped fresh cilantro or parsley
- ¼ teaspoon ground cumin
  Dash pepper
- ½ clove garlic, finely chopped
- 1 cup plain regular or Greek yogurt (8 oz) (for homemade Greek yogurt, see page 254)

1 Cut cucumber lengthwise in half; scoop out seeds. Chop cucumber (about 1 cup). In medium glass or plastic bowl, mix cucumber, onion and salt; let stand 10 minutes. Stir in tomato.

2 In small bowl, mix remaining ingredients except yogurt. Add to cucumber mixture; toss. Cover; refrigerate at least 30 minutes, but no longer than 2 days, to blend flavors.

3 Drain thoroughly. Just before serving, fold in yogurt.

½ **Cup:** Calories 35; Total Fat 0.5g (Saturated Fat 0g; Trans Fat 0g); Cholesterol 0mg; Sodium 320mg; Total Carbohydrate 5g (Dietary Fiber 1g); Protein 2g **Exchanges:** 1 Vegetable **Carbohydrate Choices:** ½

WHITE SAUCE FAST LOWER CALORIE

Also known as béchamel sauce, white sauce has many uses. If you're not partial to canned cream soups, this is a great alternative as a base sauce. Check out the variations to make it thicker or thinner, or to customize the flavor.

PREP 5 min **TOTAL** 10 min • **1 cup sauce**

- 2 tablespoons butter
- 2 tablespoons all-purpose flour
- ¼ teaspoon salt
- ⅛ teaspoon pepper
- 1 cup milk

1 In 1½-quart saucepan, melt butter over low heat. Stir in flour, salt and pepper. Cook over medium heat, stirring constantly, until mixture is smooth and bubbly; remove from heat.

2 Gradually stir in milk. Heat to boiling, stirring constantly; boil and stir 1 minute. Serve immediately.

1 **Tablespoon:** Calories 25; Total Fat 1.5g (Saturated Fat 1g; Trans Fat 0g); Cholesterol 5mg; Sodium 55mg; Total Carbohydrate 1g (Dietary Fiber 0g); Protein 0g **Exchanges:** ½ Fat **Carbohydrate Choices:** 0

THICK WHITE SAUCE Increase butter and flour to ¼ cup each.

THIN WHITE SAUCE Decrease butter and flour to 1 tablespoon each.

CHEESE SAUCE Stir in ¼ teaspoon ground mustard with the flour. After boiling and stirring sauce 1 minute, stir in ½ cup shredded Cheddar cheese (2 oz) until melted. Serve with eggs and vegetables. Makes about 1⅓ cups sauce.

CURRY SAUCE Stir in ½ teaspoon curry powder with the flour. Serve with chicken, lamb or shrimp.

DILL SAUCE Stir in 1 teaspoon chopped fresh or ½ teaspoon dried dill weed and dash ground nutmeg with the flour. Serve with fish.

MUSTARD SAUCE Decrease butter and flour to 1 tablespoon each. After boiling and stirring sauce 1 minute, stir in 3 tablespoons Dijon mustard. Serve with beef, veal, ham or vegetables.

MORNAY SAUCE

FAST **LOWER CALORIE**

Made with equal amounts of Parmesan and Swiss cheeses, Mornay is the perfect sauce to serve with meat, fish, shellfish, eggs or vegetables.

PREP 5 min TOTAL 10 min • **1 cup sauce**

> 2 tablespoons butter
> 1 tablespoon all-purpose flour
> ½ cup half-and-half
> ½ cup chicken broth (for homemade broth, see page 528)
> ¼ cup shredded Parmesan cheese (1 oz)
> ¼ cup shredded Gruyère or Swiss cheese (1 oz)

1 In 1½-quart saucepan, melt butter over low heat. Stir in flour. Cook over low heat, stirring constantly, until mixture is smooth and bubbly; remove from heat.

2 Gradually stir in half-and-half and broth. Heat to boiling, stirring constantly. Boil and stir 1 minute. Remove from heat; whisk in cheeses until melted and sauce is smooth. Serve immediately.

1 Tablespoon: Calories 40; Total Fat 3.5g (Saturated Fat 2g; Trans Fat 0g); Cholesterol 10mg; Sodium 140mg; Total Carbohydrate 1g (Dietary Fiber 0g); Protein 2g **Exchanges:** 1 Fat **Carbohydrate Choices:** 0

VELOUTÉ SAUCE Omit half-and-half and cheeses. Increase broth to 1 cup. Add ⅛ teaspoon black pepper and ⅛ teaspoon ground nutmeg.

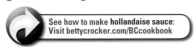 See how to make **hollandaise sauce:**
Visit bettycrocker.com/BCcookbook

HOLLANDAISE SAUCE

FAST **LOWER CALORIE**

Here's the classic hollandaise—lusciously rich, lemony and smooth. Spoon it over vegetables, eggs, fish or seafood for a heavenly touch.

PREP 10 min TOTAL 15 min • **¾ cup sauce**

> 3 egg yolks
> 1 tablespoon fresh lemon juice
> ½ cup cold butter, cut into pieces*

1 In 1½-quart saucepan, vigorously stir egg yolks and lemon juice with wire whisk. Add ¼ cup of the butter. Heat over very low heat, stirring constantly with wire whisk, until butter is melted.

2 Add remaining ¼ cup butter. Continue stirring vigorously until butter is melted and sauce is thickened. (Be sure butter melts slowly so eggs have time to cook and thicken sauce without curdling.) If the sauce curdles (mixture begins to separate), add about 1 tablespoon boiling water and beat vigorously with wire whisk until smooth. Serve immediately.

*Do not use margarine or vegetable oil spread.

1 Tablespoon: Calories 80; Total Fat 9g (Saturated Fat 4.5g; Trans Fat 0g); Cholesterol 75mg; Sodium 55mg; Total Carbohydrate 0g (Dietary Fiber 0g); Protein 0g **Exchanges:** 2 Fat **Carbohydrate Choices:** 0

BÉARNAISE SAUCE Stir in 1 tablespoon dry white wine with the lemon juice. After sauce thickens, stir in 1 tablespoon finely chopped onion, 1½ teaspoons chopped fresh or ½ teaspoon dried tarragon leaves and 1½ teaspoons chopped fresh or ¼ teaspoon dried chervil leaves.

Learn with Betty | HOLLANDAISE SAUCE

Perfect Sauce: This sauce is just the right consistency, smooth without lumps.

Undercooked Sauce: This sauce was not cooked long enough and is too thin.

Overcooked Sauce: This sauce was cooked too long, or heat was too high, and it has curdled.

PEPPERY RED WINE SAUCE

PREP 10 min TOTAL 40 min • **1 cup sauce**

- 6 tablespoons butter
- ½ cup finely chopped shallots (3 medium)
- 1 cup dry red wine (such as Merlot or Zinfandel) or nonalcoholic red wine
- 1 cup beef broth (for homemade broth, see page 530)
- 1 tablespoon balsamic vinegar
- 2 teaspoons Dijon mustard
- 1 teaspoon coarse ground black pepper

1 In 8-inch skillet, melt 2 tablespoons of the butter over medium-high heat. Add shallots; cook 1 minute, stirring frequently. Add wine; heat to boiling over high heat. Reduce heat to medium-high; cook until mixture coats back of metal spoon, 10 to 12 minutes.

2 Stir in broth. Heat to boiling. Reduce heat to medium-high; cook until mixture coats back of metal spoon and is slightly reduced, 8 to 10 minutes longer, stirring constantly.

3 With whisk, beat in remaining 4 tablespoons butter, 1 tablespoon at a time. Reduce heat to low. Beat in vinegar, mustard and pepper.

¼ Cup: Calories 180; Total Fat 18g (Saturated Fat 11g; Trans Fat 0.5g); Cholesterol 45mg; Sodium 440mg; Total Carbohydrate 2g (Dietary Fiber 0g); Protein 1g **Exchanges:** 3½ Fat **Carbohydrate Choices:** 0

WHITE WINE–GARLIC SAUCE

PREP 15 min TOTAL 35 min • **1 cup sauce**

- ¼ cup olive oil
- 4 cloves garlic, finely chopped
- 2 cups dry white wine (such as Chardonnay or Sauvignon Blanc) or nonalcoholic white wine
- ¼ cup white wine vinegar
- ½ cup whipping cream
- ¼ cup chopped fresh parsley
- ½ teaspoon salt
- ½ teaspoon pepper

1 In 10-inch skillet, heat oil over medium-high heat. Add garlic; cook 1 minute, stirring constantly. Add wine and vinegar; heat to boiling over high heat. Reduce heat to medium-high and simmer until mixture coats back of metal spoon, 10 to 12 minutes.

2 Stir in whipping cream; simmer until mixture coats back of metal spoon and is slightly reduced, 3 to 4 minutes longer, stirring constantly. Remove from heat. Stir in parsley, salt and pepper.

¼ Cup: Calories 260; Total Fat 25g (Saturated Fat 9g; Trans Fat 0g); Cholesterol 40mg; Sodium 310mg; Total Carbohydrate 3g (Dietary Fiber 0g); Protein 1g **Exchanges:** ½ Other Carbohydrate, 5 Fat **Carbohydrate Choices:** 0

Making Wine Sauce

Cook until mixture coats back of metal spoon.

Beat in remaining 4 tablespoons butter, 1 tablespoon at a time.

Peppery Red Wine Sauce

HERBED BUTTER SAUCE FAST

Sometimes simple is best, as with this easy butter sauce speckled with fresh herbs. It's sensational drizzled over fish, seafood, poultry or vegetables, or tossed with pasta.

PREP 5 min TOTAL 10 min • **½ cup sauce**

- **½ cup butter, cut into pieces***
- **2 tablespoons chopped fresh or 1 teaspoon dried herb leaves (basil, chives, oregano, savory, tarragon or thyme)**
- **2 teaspoons fresh lemon juice**

In 1-quart saucepan or 8-inch skillet, melt butter over medium heat. Stir in herbs and lemon juice. Use immediately.

Do not use margarine or vegetable oil spread.

1 Tablespoon: Calories 100; Total Fat 12g (Saturated Fat 6g; Trans Fat 0.5g); Cholesterol 30mg; Sodium 75mg; Total Carbohydrate 0g (Dietary Fiber 0g); Protein 0g **Exchanges:** 2½ Fat **Carbohydrate Choices:** 0

HERBED BROWNED BUTTER SAUCE In 1-quart saucepan, heat butter over medium heat just until light brown (see Browning Butter, page 153). Watch carefully because butter can brown and then burn quickly. Continue as directed.

Deglazing for Pan Sauces

Deglazing is a simple technique of pouring cold liquid into a hot pan after cooking meat or vegetables so that you can scrape up all of the delicious bits from the bottom of the pan. Deglazing is used to make pan sauces, such as the recipes at left or in the box at right.

Before you deglaze, here are some tips:

- To add flavor to a sauce, season meat with salt and pepper before cooking in a small amount of oil.
- Make sure there are no burnt bits in the pan to turn your sauce bitter.
- Pour off and discard most of the fat.
- Have the heat at medium-high to high.
- After adding cold liquid to the pan, use a spoon or spatula to scrape brown bits from the bottom of the pan.
- Stir constantly while deglazing.
- Turn down the heat when bits are dispersed.
- Remove the pan from the heat if you are adding alcohol to prevent flaming.
- We suggest seasoning to taste with salt and pepper, but you could add garlic powder, onion powder or dried herbs as desired.

PAN SAUCES

Sauces made in a skillet after cooking meat are called pan sauces. Use the deglazing technique (at left). Add some liquid and seasonings if desired. Cook 3 to 5 minutes or until the sauce is the desired consistency. Here are some flavor ideas to get started.

Balsamic Vinegar Sauce: Cook chicken breasts or pork chops in skillet. Remove meat from pan; cover to keep warm. Add 1 cup thinly sliced onion, 2 cloves garlic, chopped, and 1 tablespoon butter to skillet; cook until very tender, stirring constantly. Stir in ¼ cup balsamic

Balsamic Vinegar Sauce

vinegar, ¼ cup water and 2 teaspoons packed brown sugar. Cook and stir over medium-high heat, scraping bits from bottom of pan. If necessary, add 2 to 4 tablespoons water or more as necessary. Season to taste with salt and pepper.

Red Wine or Brandy Sauce: Cook pork chops or beef steaks in skillet. Remove meat from pan; cover to keep warm. Remove pan from heat. Add about ½ cup red wine or brandy to pan. Cook and stir over medium-high heat, scraping bits from bottom of pan. If desired, add ¼ to ½ cup beef

Brandy Sauce

broth to sauce and season to taste with salt, pepper and dried thyme or marjoram leaves. Cook and stir until slightly reduced. Stir in 1 tablespoon butter if desired.

White Wine or Sherry Sauce: Cook chicken breasts in skillet. Remove chicken from pan; cover to keep warm. Remove pan from heat. Add about ½ cup white wine or dry sherry to pan. Cook and stir over medium-high heat, scraping bits from bottom of pan. If desired add ¼ to ½ cup chicken broth to sauce and season to taste with salt, pepper and dried basil leaves. Cook and stir until slightly reduced. Stir in 1 tablespoon butter if desired.

Cranberry Sauce

CLARIFIED BUTTER

Think you've never heard of clarified butter? Many seafood restaurants serve it hot with lobster and crab. A staple in Indian cuisine, it's known as ghee. Removing the milk solids and evaporating the water in butter give it a nutty flavor, increase its smoking point and extend its storage life. It won't burn at high temperatures, so it can be used for sautéing and stir-frying. Aside from serving it with seafood, it's great brushed over warm Naan (page 128) or pita bread, or drizzled over hot cooked basmati rice.

PREP 20 min TOTAL 30 min • ¾ cup butter

1 lb unsalted butter, cut into 1-inch pieces

1 In 1-quart saucepan, melt butter over low heat. Continue simmering over low heat 15 to 20 minutes, occasionally skimming off milk solids that rise to surface, until butter is clear and deep yellow in color. Do not stir (some of the milk solids will turn brown and sink to bottom of pan).

2 Remove from heat. Cool 5 to 10 minutes; do not stir. Gently pour clarified butter into airtight container, leaving milk solids in saucepan. Discard milk solids. Store covered in refrigerator up to 4 weeks.

1 Tablespoon: Calories 280; Total Fat 31g (Saturated Fat 19g; Trans Fat 1g); Cholesterol 80mg; Sodium 0mg; Total Carbohydrate 0g (Dietary Fiber 0g); Protein 0g **Exchanges:** 6 Fat **Carbohydrate Choices:** 0

CRANBERRY SAUCE

The natural pectin in the cranberries thickens this easy homemade sauce. Be sure to cook the cranberries until they pop so the pectin is released and the sauce gels as it cools.

PREP 15 min TOTAL 3 hr 30 min • 4 cups sauce

4 cups (1 lb) fresh or frozen cranberries
2 cups sugar
2 cups water
1 tablespoon grated orange peel, if desired

1 Wash cranberries; remove any stems and discard any blemished berries.

2 In 3-quart saucepan, heat sugar and water to boiling over medium heat, stirring occasionally. Boil 5 minutes.

3 Stir in cranberries. Heat to boiling; boil about 5 minutes or until cranberries pop. Stir in orange peel. Cover; refrigerate about 3 hours or until chilled. Store covered in refrigerator up to 1 week.

¼ Cup: Calories 110; Total Fat 0g (Saturated Fat 0g; Trans Fat 0g); Cholesterol 0mg; Sodium 0mg; Total Carbohydrate 28g (Dietary Fiber 1g); Protein 0g **Exchanges:** 2 Fruit **Carbohydrate Choices:** 2

Clarifying Butter

Simmer butter over low heat, occasionally skimming off milk solids that rise to surface.

Continue until butter is clear and deep yellow in color.

Carefully pour warm clarified butter into air-tight container, leaving milk solids in saucepan.

FRESH CRANBERRY-ORANGE RELISH LOWER CALORIE

Once you've tasted this fresh relish bursting with sweet-tart flavor, you'll be hooked. You might even find yourself sneaking a spoonful for a little snack.

PREP 20 min TOTAL 24 hr 20 min • **2½ cups relish**

> 3 cups (12 oz) fresh or frozen cranberries
> 1 seedless orange, unpeeled
> 1 cup sugar

1 Wash cranberries; remove any stems and discard any blemished berries. Cut orange into 1-inch pieces with peel. (The peel adds a tangy orange flavor; it won't make the relish bitter tasting.)

2 Place sugar in medium bowl. In food processor, place half of the cranberries and orange pieces. Cover; process about 15 seconds, using short on-and-off motions, or until evenly chopped. Stir cranberry mixture into sugar. Repeat with remaining cranberries and orange pieces.

3 Cover; refrigerate at least 24 hours, but no longer than 1 week to blend flavors.

2 Tablespoons: Calories 50; Total Fat 0g (Saturated Fat 0g; Trans Fat 0g); Cholesterol 0mg; Sodium 0mg; Total Carbohydrate 13g (Dietary Fiber 0g); Protein 0g **Exchanges:** 1 Fruit **Carbohydrate Choices:** 1

FRESH CRANBERRY-ORANGE-GINGER RELISH Stir 1 tablespoon finely chopped crystallized ginger into sugar in Step 2.

RHUBARB SAUCE LOWER CALORIE

Rhubarb varies in sweetness, so add sugar to taste. Serve the sauce as a sweet-tart accompaniment to pork or chicken. Or serve it for dessert, either by itself or over pound cake or ice cream.

PREP 10 min TOTAL 25 min • **3 cups sauce**

> ½ to ¾ cup sugar
> ½ cup water
> 1 lb fresh or frozen rhubarb, cut into 1-inch pieces (3 cups)
> Ground cinnamon, if desired

1 In 2-quart saucepan, heat ½ cup sugar and the water to boiling over medium heat, stirring occasionally. Stir in rhubarb; reduce heat to low. Simmer uncovered about 10 minutes, stirring occasionally, until rhubarb is tender and slightly transparent, adding up to ¼ cup sugar, if desired, for added sweetener.

2 Stir in cinnamon. Serve sauce warm or chilled. Store covered in refrigerator up to 1 week.

½ Cup: Calories 80; Total Fat 0g (Saturated Fat 0g; Trans Fat 0g); Cholesterol 0mg; Sodium 0mg; Total Carbohydrate 19g (Dietary Fiber 1g); Protein 0g **Exchanges:** 1 Fruit, ½ Other Carbohydrate **Carbohydrate Choices:** 1

STRAWBERRY-RHUBARB SAUCE Substitute 1 cup strawberries, cut in half, for 1 cup of the rhubarb. After simmering rhubarb, stir in strawberries; heat just to boiling.

Making Cranberry-Orange Relish

Place half of cranberries and orange pieces in food processor.

Process until evenly chopped; stir in sugar.

Fresh Cranberry-Orange Relish

PEAR-CHERRY CHUTNEY

PREP 1 hr 10 min TOTAL 2 hr 10 min ● **4½ cups chutney**

- 3 **medium firm ripe pears, peeled, cored and coarsely chopped**
- 1 **cup dried cherries**
- ¾ **cup sugar**
- ½ **cup cider vinegar**
- 2 **teaspoons finely chopped gingerroot**
- ½ **teaspoon ground cinnamon**
- ¼ **teaspoon ground cloves**

1 In 2-quart saucepan, mix all ingredients. Heat to boiling; reduce heat to low. Simmer uncovered about 1 hour, stirring frequently, until thickened.

2 Cool 1 hour, stirring occasionally. Serve chutney at room temperature for best flavor. Cover and refrigerate up to 1 week.

¼ **Cup:** Calories 140; Total Fat 0g (Saturated Fat 0g; Trans Fat 0g); Cholesterol 0mg; Sodium 0mg; Total Carbohydrate 33g (Dietary Fiber 2g); Protein 0g **Exchanges:** 2 Other Carbohydrate **Carbohydrate Choices:** 2

PEAR-APRICOT CHUTNEY Substitute chopped dried apricots for the dried cherries.

PEAR-CRANBERRY CHUTNEY Substitute dried cranberries for the dried cherries.

PEAR-RAISIN CHUTNEY Substitute regular or golden raisins for the dried cherries.

LEMON CURD LOWER CALORIE

Fresh lemon juice is recommended for the best flavor in this buttery, sweet and tangy custard. Let the lemons stand at room temperature for at least an hour so they warm up a bit—they'll produce more juice.

PREP 15 min TOTAL 25 min ● **2 cups curd**

- 1 **cup sugar**
- 1 **tablespoon finely shredded lemon peel**
- 1 **cup lemon juice (5 large lemons)**
- 3 **tablespoons cold butter, cut into pieces**
- 3 **eggs, slightly beaten**

1 In 1½-quart saucepan, mix sugar, lemon peel and lemon juice with wire whisk. Stir in butter and eggs. Cook over medium heat about 8 minutes, stirring constantly, until mixture thickens and coats back of spoon (do not boil).

2 Immediately pour into 1 (1-pint) or 2 (1-cup) containers. Store covered in refrigerator up to 1 week.

1 Tablespoon: Calories 45; Total Fat 1.5g (Saturated Fat 0.5g; Trans Fat 0g); Cholesterol 25mg; Sodium 15mg; Total Carbohydrate 7g (Dietary Fiber 0g); Protein 0g **Exchanges:** ½ Fruit, ½ Fat **Carbohydrate Choices:** ½

LIME CURD Substitute lime peel and juice for the lemon peel and juice.

Pear-Cherry Chutney

Cooking Lemon Curd

Cook over medium heat, stirring constantly with wire whisk, until mixture thickens and coats back of spoon.

SEASONING BASICS
Unlock the secret of seasoning the dishes you make with confidence. With a little practice, you can add a pinch of this and a dash of that to create your own signature taste.

WHAT ARE HERBS, SPICES AND SEASONING BLENDS?

- Herbs are the leaves of annual and perennial plants. They are available fresh or dried.

- Spices are the dried fruits, flowers, roots or bark of tropical trees and shrubs. You can purchase whole spices to grind at home or ground spices.

- Seasoning blends combine a variety of spices and herbs to create a full-flavored mix. Examples of such blends include chili powder (ground chile peppers, cloves, coriander, cumin, garlic and oregano) and Italian seasoning (basil, marjoram, oregano, rosemary, sage, savory and thyme).

STORING HERBS, SPICES AND SEASONING BLENDS

Dried Herbs, Spices and Seasoning Blends: Store in airtight containers away from heat, light and moisture. For best flavor, keep whole spices and herb leaves up to 1 year and ground spices and herbs up to 6 months. Older spices and herbs can be used, but the flavors will weaken with age. Chili powder, ground red pepper (cayenne) and paprika should be refrigerated to retain color and flavor.

Fresh Herbs: For basil, cilantro and parsley, cut ½ inch off the bottoms of the stems; place in a jar of water. Loosely cover tops with a plastic bag (see photo at right). Let basil stand at room temperature up to 2 days (refrigeration may turn it black). Refrigerate cilantro and parsley up to 1 week. For other herbs, wrap stems in a damp (not wet) paper towel; place in a resealable food-storage plastic bag. Refrigerate up to 2 weeks.

COOKING WITH HERBS

To capture the best herb flavor in all of your favorite foods, keep these tips in mind:

- Fresh herbs are milder than dried herbs, so follow the "3-to-1" rule. That means, when substituting fresh for dried, use three times more. When substituting dried for fresh, use one-third as much.

- In recipes with long cooking times, robust herbs (such as bay leaves, oregano, thyme, tarragon, rosemary and sage) hold up to the heat and can be added right away. But more mild, delicate herbs (such as basil, marjoram and parsley), especially when fresh, should be stirred in just before serving.

- When experimenting with herbs in a four-serving recipe, start by adding 1 teaspoon of robust fresh herbs, 1 tablespoon of mild fresh herbs or ¼ teaspoon of any dried herbs. You can always add more if desired.

- Before stirring dried herbs into dishes, crush them in your hand to release their flavor and natural oils.

Storing fresh parsley

Thyme

Lemon Thyme

Dill Weed

Cilantro

Sage

Parsley

Mint

Rosemary

Purple Sage

Italian Parsley

Oregano

Bay Leaves

Basil

Chives

Lemon Grass

Tarragon

Marjoram

HERBS

Basil: Sweet, spicy, fragrant. Chop leaves just before using. Use with tomatoes, poultry, eggs, fish or in pasta sauces, pesto, marinades, herb butters.

Bay Leaves: Fresh have more intense flavor and aroma than dried. Use in Greek dishes, soups, stews, under chicken skin or to top fish while cooking. Discard leaves before eating.

Chervil: Mild, parsley-like. Use with eggs, fish, in salads, sauces, soups, stuffing.

Chives: Mild green onion flavor; distinct taste and aroma. Use with potatoes, eggs, fish or in appetizers, soups, salads, biscuits, cornbread.

Cilantro: Similar appearance to Italian parsley but with a lively, pungent smell and taste. Chop leaves; discard stems. Use in salsas and other Mexican, Indian and Indonesian dishes, marinades, salads (sparingly), pasta salads, soups, stews.

Dill Weed: Fresh, peppery, tangy. Chop leaves and tender stems; discard woody stems. Use in herb butters, breads, dips, salads (sparingly), pickles or with potatoes and other vegetables, fish.

Fennel: Anise flavor. Chop leaves and stems. Use as a stuffing for oily fish (like mackerel) or in soups, salads, stuffing or tossed with cooked vegetables. Seeds are used as spice.

Horseradish: Pungent, peppery. Choose firm roots without blemishes; peel and grate before using. Use in sauces or condiments for fish or meat.

Italian Parsley: Also known as flat-leaf parsley, it is more fragrant, less bitter than regular (curly) parsley. Chop leaves; discard stems. Use in Italian, European and Middle Eastern dishes for stronger parsley flavor.

Lemon Grass: Sour lemon flavor, extremely fibrous and stringy. Cut off and discard bulb; remove tough outer leaves. Cut yellow (lower section) into thin slices. Bend, bruise pieces to release lemon flavor (discard after cooking) or process in food processor; cook thoroughly to soften enough to eat. Use in Asian dishes, soups.

Marjoram: Sweet, slightly oregano-like yet delicate flavor; add at the end of cooking. Use with vegetables such as carrots, zucchini, mushrooms, peas, spinach and tomatoes, with poultry, fish, pork, beef, lamb or in stuffing, soups, salads.

Mint: Strong, cool, fresh, sweet. Many varieties, with a range of flavors. Use in Greek or Italian dishes or with cucumbers, peas, potatoes, carrots or lamb.

Oregano: Pungent—use sparingly. Use in Italian dishes, with vegetables, fish, meat, poultry or in sauces, soups.

Parsley: Allows each flavor of a dish to come through. Works well with garlic to temper its flavor. Chop curly leaves; discard stems. Use in sauces, eggs, stuffing, herb butters or with corn, potatoes.

Rosemary: Strong, sweet; hints of pine, lemon—use sparingly. Use in soups, breads, tomato dishes or with vegetables, seafood, poultry, pork, beef, lamb.

Sage: Slightly bitter with subtle musty-mint flavor—use sparingly. Many varieties, in a range of colors and flavors. Used in Mediterranean foods, particularly Italian dishes, stuffing, marinades or with peas, eggplant, lima beans, carrots, poultry.

Savory: Mint-thyme flavor; combines well with other herbs. Use with poultry, fish, meat, vegetables, any kind of bean or in herb butters.

Tarragon: Delicate, anise-like—use sparingly. Use in salads, salad dressings, egg dishes, sauce or with poultry, fish, cheese.

Thyme: Peppery, minty, mild lemon flavor—use sparingly. Many varieties, with a range of colors and flavors. Chop leaves and soft stems; discard woody stems. Use in stews, dressings or with vegetables, poultry, fish, pork, beef, lamb.

SPICES/SEASONINGS

Allspice: Available whole, ground. Cinnamon, clove, nutmeg flavor. Use in baked goods, jerk seasoning, pickling, pies or with fruit.

Anise Seed: Available whole, ground. Sweet licorice flavor. Use in cakes, cookies, breads, fruit dishes.

Caraway Seed: Available whole. Delicate nutty, anise flavor. Use in breads, stews or with vegetables, meats.

Cardamom: Available as whole or split pods, whole or ground seeds. Hints of eucalyptus, camphor and lemon. Use in Indian and Middle Eastern dishes and to flavor coffee or tea.

Celery Seed: Available whole, ground. Strong flavor—use sparingly. Use in soups, salads, salad dressings, meat dishes, pickling.

Cinnamon: Available in sticks, ground. Sweet, woodsy. Use in baked goods, hot drinks, pickling, savory dishes.

Cloves: Available whole, ground. Sweet, peppery. Use in baked goods, pickling, sauces, tea or with fruit, ham, meat.

Coriander: Seeds of the cilantro plant. Available whole, ground. Lemon-sage flavor. Not to be confused with cilantro, which has a different flavor. Use in soups, stews, sausages, ratatouille, pickling, curries.

Cumin: Available whole, ground. Nutty, earthy, with peppery bite. Use in Mexican, Thai, Mediterranean dishes, dry rubs, chilies, stews or with beans, lentils.

Dill Seed: Available whole, ground. Caraway-dill flavor. Not to be confused with dill weed, which has a different flavor. Use in pickling, breads, salad dressings.

Dill Weed (Dried): Dried dill leaves. Not to be confused with dill seed, which has a different flavor. Use in breads, dips, pickling, salads, sauces or with vegetables, fish.

Fennel Seed: Available whole, ground. Sweet anise flavor. Use in breads, cakes, sweet sausages.

Garlic: Available minced, powdered (finely ground), dehydrated, flaked, fresh, or as paste, juice. Slightly musty flavor. Use in appetizers, bread, salads, sauces, soups or with vegetables fish, poultry, meat.

Ginger: Available ground, crystallized, fresh. Spicy-hot, sweet. Use in beverages, baked goods, sauces, soup, Asian dishes, tea or with fruit, vegetables, fish, poultry, meat.

Mustard Seed: Available whole, ground, powdered (finely ground), or as oil. Use seeds in pickling or with vegetables, cooked meats; ground or powdered in sauces, main dishes, salad dressings; oil for stir-fries, salad dressings, marinades.

Nutmeg: Available whole, ground (mace is the covering of the nutmeg seed so can use same way). Sweet, spicy. Use in baked goods, eggnog and other beverages, custards, sauces or with vegetables.

Paprika: Available ground. Ranges from sweet to hot; slightly bitter. Use in casseroles, eggs, salads, soups or with vegetables, fish, meat.

Peppercorns: Black, white and green varieties. Available whole, ground, cracked (green sold packed in brine or dried). Slightly hot with a hint of sweetness (black is the strongest, green is the mildest). Use in savory foods of all kinds.

Poppy Seed: Available whole or ground. Nutty flavor; crunchy texture. Use as filling or topping for cakes, coffee cakes, pastries, breads or in salad dressings.

Red Pepper (Cayenne): Available ground. Very hot, peppery. Use in savory foods of all kinds.

Saffron: Available in threads, powdered. Distinctive flavor, mildly bitter. Use in Indian and Spanish dishes.

Sesame Seed: Seeds available in a variety of colors or as oil. Light, nutty flavor (white seeds milder than black). Use to add flavor and crunch to breads, salads, stir-fries or other Asian dishes.

Star Anise: Available whole, ground. Bitter, more pungent than anise. Key ingredient in five-spice powder. Use in Asian dishes.

Turmeric: Available ground. Fragrant, woodsy. Key ingredient in store-bought curry powder, food color. Use in eggs, pickling, rice, Indian dishes, poultry, seafood.

Sesame Seed

Allspice

Star Anise

Black Sesame Seed

Cumin

Anise Seed

Dill Seed

Cardamom

Mace

Minced Garlic

Ginger

Turmeric

Nutmeg

Dill Weed

Celery Seed

Cinnamon

Coriander

Paprika

Mustard Seed

Cloves

Caraway Seed

Saffron

Poppy Seed

Fennel Seed

TERIYAKI MARINADE LOWER CALORIE

PREP 5 min TOTAL 1 hr 5 min • ½ cup marinade

- ¼ cup water
- 3 tablespoons soy sauce
- 1 tablespoon fresh lemon juice
- 1 tablespoon vegetable oil
- 1 tablespoon packed brown sugar
- ⅛ teaspoon coarse ground black pepper
- 1 clove garlic, finely chopped

1 In shallow glass or plastic dish or resealable food-storage plastic bag, mix all ingredients.

2 Add about 1 pound boneless or 2 to 3 pounds bone-in beef, pork or chicken, turning to coat with marinade. Cover dish or seal bag; refrigerate, turning meat occasionally, at least 1 hour but no longer than 24 hours.

3 Remove meat from marinade; reserve marinade. Cook meat as desired, brushing occasionally with marinade.

4 Remaining marinade must be boiled to be served as a sauce (if not boiled, discard marinade). In 1-quart saucepan, heat marinade to boiling, stirring constantly; boil and stir 1 minute.

1 Tablespoon: Calories 25; Total Fat 1.5g (Saturated Fat 0g; Trans Fat 0g); Cholesterol 0mg; Sodium 340mg; Total Carbohydrate 2g (Dietary Fiber 0g); Protein 0g **Exchanges:** ½ Fat **Carbohydrate Choices:** 0

FAJITA MARINADE LOWER CALORIE

PREP 5 min TOTAL 3 hr 5 min • ½ cup marinade

- ¼ cup vegetable oil
- ¼ cup red wine vinegar
- 1 teaspoon sugar
- 1 teaspoon dried oregano leaves
- 1 teaspoon chili powder
- ½ teaspoon garlic powder
- ½ teaspoon salt
- ¼ teaspoon pepper

1 In shallow glass or plastic dish or resealable food-storage plastic bag, mix all ingredients.

2 Add about 1 pound boneless or 2 to 3 pounds bone-in beef, pork or chicken, turning to coat with marinade. Cover dish or seal bag; refrigerate, turning meat occasionally, at least 1 hour but no longer than 24 hours.

3 Remove meat from marinade; reserve marinade. Cook meat as desired, brushing occasionally with marinade.

4 Remaining marinade must be boiled to be served as a sauce (if not boiled, discard marinade). In 1-quart saucepan, heat marinade to boiling, stirring constantly; boil and stir 1 minute.

1 Tablespoon: Calories 70; Total Fat 7g (Saturated Fat 1g; Trans Fat 0g); Cholesterol 0mg; Sodium 150mg; Total Carbohydrate 0g (Dietary Fiber 0g); Protein 0g **Exchanges:** 1½ Fat **Carbohydrate Choices:** 0

Fajita Marinade
with a flank steak

GARLIC MARINADE LOWER CALORIE

PREP 10 min TOTAL 1 hr 15 min • **¾ cup marinade**

- ¼ cup vegetable oil
- 4 cloves garlic, finely chopped
- 1 tablespoon chopped fresh or 1 teaspoon dried rosemary leaves, crushed
- ½ teaspoon ground mustard
- 2 teaspoons soy sauce
- ¼ cup red or white wine vinegar
- ¼ cup dry sherry or apple juice

1 In 10-inch skillet, heat oil over medium-high heat. Cook garlic in oil, stirring frequently, until golden. Stir in rosemary, mustard and soy sauce; remove from heat. Stir in vinegar and sherry; cool.

2 In shallow glass or plastic dish or resealable food-storage plastic bag, place 1 to 1½ pounds boneless or 3 to 4 pounds bone-in beef, pork or lamb. Pour marinade over meat. Cover dish or seal bag; refrigerate, turning meat occasionally, at least 1 hour but no longer than 24 hours.

3 Remove meat from marinade; reserve marinade. Cook meat as desired, brushing occasionally with marinade.

4 Remaining marinade must be boiled to be served as a sauce (if not boiled, discard marinade). In 1-quart saucepan, heat marinade to boiling, stirring constantly; boil and stir 1 minute.

1 Tablespoon: Calories 45; Total Fat 4.5g (Saturated Fat 0.5g; Trans Fat 0g); Cholesterol 0mg; Sodium 50mg; Total Carbohydrate 0g (Dietary Fiber 0g); Protein 0g **Exchanges:** 1 Fat **Carbohydrate Choices:** 0

BALSAMIC GARLIC MARINADE Substitute balsamic vinegar (½ cup) for the wine vinegar and sherry.

ONION AND GARLIC MARINADE Cook ¼ cup finely chopped onion with garlic until tender. Substitute thyme for the rosemary.

LEMON-HERB MARINADE

LOWER CALORIE

PREP 10 min TOTAL 3 hr 10 min • **⅔ cup marinade**

- ⅓ cup vegetable oil
- 1 teaspoon grated lemon peel
- 2 tablespoons fresh lemon juice
- 1 tablespoon dry vermouth, dry white wine or beef broth
- 1 teaspoon chopped fresh or ¼ teaspoon dried sage leaves
- 1 teaspoon chopped fresh or ¼ teaspoon dried oregano leaves
- ½ teaspoon salt
- ¼ teaspoon coarse ground black pepper

1 In shallow glass or plastic dish or resealable food-storage plastic bag, mix all ingredients.

2 Add up to 2 pounds boneless beef, pork, chicken or turkey, turning to coat with marinade. Cover dish or seal bag; refrigerate, turning meat occasionally, at least 1 hour but no longer than 24 hours.

3 Remove meat from marinade; reserve marinade. Cook meat as desired, brushing occasionally with marinade.

4 Remaining marinade must be boiled to be served as a sauce (if not boiled, discard marinade). In 1-quart saucepan, heat marinade to boiling, stirring constantly; boil and stir 1 minute.

1 Tablespoon: Calories 60; Total Fat 7g (Saturated Fat 1g; Trans Fat 0g); Cholesterol 0mg; Sodium 110mg; Total Carbohydrate 0g (Dietary Fiber 0g); Protein 0g **Exchanges:** 1½ Fat **Carbohydrate Choices:** 0

Marinade Tips

- Mix marinades and marinate foods in glass or plastic containers or food-storage plastic bags because these containers won't react with acidic ingredients like vinegar, wine or lemon juice.

- Use ¼ to ½ cup marinade for each 1 to 2 pounds of food.

- Marinate all foods except fish in the refrigerator up to 24 hours; if you let it marinate longer, food can become mushy. Marinate fish only 15 to 30 minutes or it will become mushy.

SOUTHWESTERN RUB

LOWER CALORIE

Rubs are a simple way to season meats—just sprinkle on the seasoning mixture and rub it into the meat with your fingers. Because this rub has oil in it, it's known as a wet rub rather than a dry rub.

PREP 10 min TOTAL 25 min • **3 tablespoons rub**

- 1 tablespoon chili powder
- 1 teaspoon ground cumin
- ¼ teaspoon salt
- ¼ teaspoon ground red pepper (cayenne)
- 1 large clove garlic, finely chopped
- 1 tablespoon vegetable oil

1 In small bowl, mix all ingredients.

2 Spread rub evenly on 1 pound boneless meat (chicken, pork or beef) or 2½ pounds ½-inch-thick pork chops (about 8). Cover; refrigerate at least 15 minutes but no longer than 24 hours. Cook meat as desired.

1 Teaspoon: Calories 15; Total Fat 1.5g (Saturated Fat 0g; Trans Fat 0g); Cholesterol 0mg; Sodium 75mg; Total Carbohydrate 0g (Dietary Fiber 0g); Protein 0g **Exchanges:** Free **Carbohydrate Choices:** 0

JAMAICAN JERK SEASONING RUB LOWER CALORIE

PREP 10 min TOTAL 25 min • **3 tablespoons rub**

- 1 tablespoon dried minced onion
- 2 teaspoons dried thyme leaves
- 1 teaspoon ground allspice
- 1 teaspoon pepper

- ½ teaspoon salt
- ½ teaspoon ground cinnamon
- ¼ teaspoon ground red pepper (cayenne)

1 In small bowl, mix all ingredients.

2 Spread rub evenly on 1 pound boneless meat (chicken, pork or beef). Cover; refrigerate at least 15 minutes but no longer than 24 hours. Cook meat as desired.

1 Teaspoon: Calories 0; Total Fat 0g (Saturated Fat 0g; Trans Fat 0g); Cholesterol 0mg; Sodium 130mg; Total Carbohydrate 0g (Dietary Fiber 0g); Protein 0g **Exchanges:** Free **Carbohydrate Choices:** 0

BASIL AND LEMON-PEPPER RUB

LOWER CALORIE

PREP 10 min TOTAL 25 min • **2 tablespoons rub**

- 1 tablespoon packed brown sugar
- 1 teaspoon lemon pepper
- 1 teaspoon dried basil leaves
- ½ teaspoon garlic powder
- ½ teaspoon seasoning salt

1 In small bowl, mix all ingredients.

2 Spread rub evenly on 1 pound boneless meat (chicken, pork or fish). Cover; refrigerate at least 15 minutes but no longer than 24 hours. Cook meat as desired.

1 Teaspoon: Calories 10; Total Fat 0g (Saturated Fat 0g; Trans Fat 0g); Cholesterol 0mg; Sodium 170mg; Total Carbohydrate 3g (Dietary Fiber 0g); Protein 0g **Exchanges:** Free **Carbohydrate Choices:** 0

Using Seasoning Rubs

Mix all rub ingredients in bowl.

Spread rub evenly over all sides of meat, working into surface of meat with fingers.

Southwestern Rub on pork chops

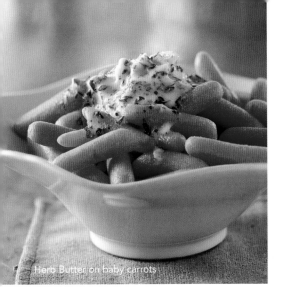

Herb Butter on baby carrots

SAVORY BUTTERS

FAST **LOWER CALORIE**

Add flavor fast with a dollop of one of these easy butters. Top grilled or broiled beef or fish steaks, pork chops or chicken breasts. Or toss with hot pasta, rice or vegetables. And of course, these butters are also great to spread on bread.

PREP 5 min **TOTAL** 5 min • **½ cup butter**

½ cup butter, softened

In small bowl, beat butter and ingredients for one of the flavor variations below with electric mixer on medium speed until light and fluffy. Use immediately, or chill about 1 hour to blend flavors. Store covered in refrigerator up to 1 week.

1 Teaspoon: Calories 35; Total Fat 4g (Saturated Fat 2g; Trans Fat 0g); Cholesterol 10mg; Sodium 25mg; Total Carbohydrate 0g (Dietary Fiber 0g); Protein 0g **Exchanges:** 1 Fat **Carbohydrate Choices:** 0

GARLIC BUTTER Add 1 to 2 cloves garlic, finely chopped, or ¼ to ½ teaspoon garlic powder.

HERB BUTTER Add 2 tablespoons to ¼ cup chopped fresh or 1 to 2 teaspoons dried herb leaves (basil, chives, oregano, savory, tarragon or thyme) and 2 teaspoons fresh lemon juice.

ITALIAN PARMESAN BUTTER Add 2 tablespoons grated Parmesan cheese and ½ teaspoon Italian seasoning.

LEMON-PEPPER BUTTER Add 2 tablespoons finely grated lemon peel, 1 teaspoon fresh lemon juice and ⅛ to ¼ teaspoon pepper.

SWEET BUTTERS **FAST** **LOWER CALORIE**

Muffins, scones, biscuits and that ordinary morning slice of toast would love to be topped with sweetly flavored butter.

PREP 5 min **TOTAL** 5 min • **½ cup butter**

½ cup butter, softened

In small bowl, beat butter with electric mixer on medium speed until light and fluffy; stir in ingredients for one of the flavor variations below with spoon. Use immediately, or chill about 1 hour to blend flavors. Store covered in refrigerator up to 1 week.

1 Teaspoon: Calories 35; Total Fat 4g (Saturated Fat 2g; Trans Fat 0g); Cholesterol 10mg; Sodium 25mg; Total Carbohydrate 0g (Dietary Fiber 0g); Protein 0g **Exchanges:** 1 Fat **Carbohydrate Choices:** 0

ALMOND BUTTER Stir in 1 tablespoon finely chopped almonds, toasted if desired (page 22), and ½ teaspoon almond extract.

HONEY OR MAPLE BUTTER Stir in ½ cup honey or real or maple-flavored syrup.

ORANGE BUTTER Stir in 1 teaspoon grated orange peel and 1 tablespoon orange juice.

PECAN BUTTER Stir in ¼ cup chopped pecans, toasted if desired (page 22), and 2 tablespoons packed brown sugar.

RASPBERRY BUTTER Stir in ½ cup raspberries, crushed, and 1 tablespoon sugar. Or, stir in ¼ cup seedless raspberry jam.

Pecan Butter

CREAM CHEESE SPREADS

FAST **LOWER CALORIE**

PREP 5 min TOTAL 5 min • ⅔ to 1 cup spread

1 package (3 oz) cream cheese, softened

In small bowl, stir cream cheese until smooth and creamy. Add ingredients for one of the flavor variations below; stir with spoon until well blended. Use immediately, or chill about 1 hour to blend flavors. Store covered in refrigerator up to 1 week.

1 Tablespoon: Calories 30; Total Fat 3g (Saturated Fat 2g; Trans Fat 0g); Cholesterol 10mg; Sodium 45mg; Total Carbohydrate 0g (Dietary Fiber 0g); Protein 0g **Exchanges:** 1 Fat **Carbohydrate Choices:** 0

BACON-CHIVE CREAM CHEESE SPREAD
Add 2 tablespoons milk and stir until blended. Stir in ¼ cup shredded Cheddar cheese (1 oz), 2 tablespoons crumbled crisply cooked bacon (2 slices) and 1 tablespoon chopped fresh chives.

HONEY-WALNUT CREAM CHEESE SPREAD
Stir in 2 tablespoons honey, or real or maple-flavored syrup, and ½ cup finely chopped walnuts, toasted if desired (page 22).

MAPLE-CINNAMON CREAM CHEESE SPREAD
Stir in 2 tablespoons real or maple-flavored syrup and ¼ teaspoon ground cinnamon.

OLIVE-WALNUT CREAM CHEESE SPREAD
Add 2 tablespoons milk and stir until blended. Stir in ½ cup finely chopped walnuts, toasted if desired (page 22), and ¼ cup finely chopped pitted kalamata or pimiento-stuffed green olives.

PEANUT BUTTER–CREAM CHEESE SPREAD
Add 2 tablespoons milk and stir until blended. Stir in ¼ cup crunchy peanut butter and 1 tablespoon honey.

Flavored Vinegar
Flavored vinegars can add a distinctive taste to your favorite recipes. Making them yourself not only gives satisfaction but also can be less costly than buying them. Be sure to follow any food safety guidelines for storage. Herbs and fruits can cause vinegar to spoil.

HERB VINEGAR   LOWER CALORIE

PREP 10 min TOTAL 10 days 10 min • **2 cups vinegar**

2 cups white wine vinegar or white vinegar
½ cup firmly packed fresh herb leaves (basil, chives, dill weed, mint, oregano, rosemary or tarragon)

1 In tightly covered glass jar or bottle, shake vinegar and herb leaves. Let stand in cool, dry place 10 days.

2 Strain vinegar; discard herbs. Place 1 sprig of fresh herb in jar to identify flavor, if desired. Store covered at room temperature up to 6 months.

1 Tablespoon: Calories 0; Total Fat 0g (Saturated Fat 0g; Trans Fat 0g); Cholesterol 0mg; Sodium 0mg; Total Carbohydrate 0g (Dietary Fiber 0g); Protein 0g **Exchanges:** Free **Carbohydrate Choices:** 0

BERRY VINEGAR
Substitute 2 cups berries, crushed, for the herbs.

GARLIC VINEGAR
Substitute 6 cloves garlic, cut in half, for the herbs.

LEMON VINEGAR
Substitute peel from 2 lemons for the herbs.

Herb Vinegar, Berry Vinegar, Garlic Vinegar, Lemon Vinegar

SLOW COOKER SUPPERS

For bonus **slow cooker suppers** recipes,
visit bettycrocker.com/BCcookbook

FAST = Ready in 20 minutes or less **LOWER CALORIE** = See Helpful Nutrition and Cooking Information, page 685
LIGHTER = 25% fewer calories or grams of fat **MAKE AHEAD** = Make-ahead directions **SLOW COOKER** = Slow cooker directions

← Chicken Stew with Pepper and Pineapple (page 523), Lamb Dijon (page 510), Jambalaya (page 519), Curried Carrot
Soup (page 522)

SLOW COOKER BASICS

Wouldn't it be great to walk in the front door after a long day to find a hot, hearty meal ready and waiting for you and your family? That homemade dinner dream can be a reality when you rely on the convenience of a slow cooker. Just check out our tips and great recipes, and you're on your way to these easy meals.

SLOW COOKER FEATURES

Manufacturers offer slow cookers in a variety of shapes and sizes, and with an array of features. Most slow cookers range in size from 3½ to 8 quarts. For best results, use the slow cooker size recommended in the recipe. Following are the most common features.

Continuous: The majority of slow cookers are continuous, meaning they cook foods continuously using very low wattage. The heating coils, located in the outer metal shell of the cooker, are on constantly to heat the ceramic insert, which is usually removable. Continuous models have two to four fixed settings: Low (about 200°F), High (about 300°F), Warm (about 140°F) and, in some models, Auto, which shifts from High to Low automatically. All recipes in this book were tested with continuous slow cookers.

Programmable: Programmable models offer one-touch control with multiple time and temperature settings.

Portable: Portable models have locking lids, carrying handles and travel bags to transport the slow cooker.

Multicompartment: Multicompartment units have either two or three 2.5-quart cooking compartments with individual heat settings.

Intermittent: Intermittent cookers have a heating element in the base and a separate cooking container placed on the base. Heat cycles on and off to maintain a constant temperature. The recipes in this cookbook have not been tested in an intermittent cooker. If you have an intermittent cooker, follow the manufacturer's instructions for layering ingredients and selecting a temperature.

SUCCESS WITH SLOW COOKERS

- For easy cleanup, coat the inside of the insert or cooker with cooking spray.
- Slow cookers work most efficiently when they are two-thirds to three-fourths full.
- Always keep the slow cooker covered for the specified cook time. Removing the cover lets heat escape, adding 15 to 20 minutes to the cook time. Only remove the cover if a recipe specifies and only after the first 2 hours of cooking. An exception to this rule: When cooking large cuts of meat, rotate them halfway through cooking for the best results.
- Root vegetables take longer to cook than other vegetables, so cut them into smaller pieces and put them at the bottom of the cooker.
- Make sure raw potatoes are covered with liquid to prevent them from turning dark.

For slow cooker recipes, cut ingredients into uniform sizes for the best results.

- Don't add more liquid than specified. Ingredients may look dry before cooking, but because liquids don't evaporate from a slow cooker, the food will be moist.

- Remove poultry skin and excess fat from meats before cooking to reduce fat in the finished dish.

- Brown meats and poultry in a skillet before cooking to add color and flavor.

- For the best taste, use dried herb leaves instead of ground.

- Most cooked foods can be held up to an hour on the Low or Warm setting without overcooking. Some recipes, like dips and spreads, can be kept on Low or Warm for up to 2 hours. Stir occasionally if needed.

WHEN TO ADD INGREDIENTS

An advantage of slow cooking is that most ingredients can be put into the slow cooker right at the start. But keep in mind there are foods that benefit from being added later on.

- Some herbs (such as basil and oregano) lose flavor when cooked too long. It's best to stir in fresh herbs during the last hour of cooking.

- Ground red pepper (cayenne) and red pepper sauce can become bitter when cooked too long. Use small amounts to start and taste the food during the last hour before adding more.

- Long cook times cause fish and seafood to fall apart and even become tough. Stir in these from-the-sea favorites with 1 hour remaining.

- For the best flavor and color, add tender vegetables (like fresh tomatoes, mushrooms and zucchini) and thawed frozen vegetables during the last 30 minutes of cooking.

- Dairy products, such as milk, sour cream and cheese, can easily curdle so stir them in during the last 30 minutes of cooking.

SLOW COOKER FOOD SAFETY

Slow cookers heat up more slowly and cook at lower temperatures than other cooking appliances. To keep food safe, follow these guidelines:

- Let frozen ingredients thaw completely before cooking.

- Keep perishable foods refrigerated until you're ready to put them into the slow cooker.

- Always cook and drain ground meat before adding to the slow cooker.

- Brown poultry and meats just before placing in the slow cooker and not ahead of time.

- Do not cook whole chickens or meat loaf in a slow cooker. The center of these foods can't reach a safe temperature quickly enough.

- Cut ingredients into specified sizes and layer as directed so that the dish cooks properly during the indicated amount of time. If the power goes out and you're not sure how long the power was off, the food may not be safe. It's best to discard it.

- Place leftovers in shallow containers and refrigerate within 2 hours of cooking. Don't use the insert for storage.

- Slow cookers should not be used for reheating. Instead, heat cooked food in a microwave or conventional oven, or on the stove-top, until hot and then put into a preheated slow cooker to keep warm for serving.

Note

The temperature in the center of food being cooked should reach 130°F to 140°F within 3 to 4 hours or approximately halfway through cook time. At the end of cooking, food must be at least 160°F to 165°F in center and at least 165°F for poultry.

SPICED CORNED BEEF BRISKET WITH HORSERADISH SOUR CREAM

Serve this boldly flavored brisket with boiled new red potatoes and steamed green cabbage.

PREP 10 min TOTAL 8 hr 10 min • **8 servings**

- 1 corned beef brisket (3 to 3½ lb)
- 1 large sweet onion (Bermuda, Maui or Spanish), sliced
- ¾ teaspoon crushed red pepper flakes
- 1 cup reduced-sodium chicken broth (for homemade broth, see page 528)
- 1 tablespoon Worcestershire sauce
- ½ cup sour cream
- 1 tablespoon cream-style prepared horseradish
- 2 tablespoons chopped fresh parsley

1 Remove beef from package; discard liquid and seasoning packet. Trim fat from beef and thoroughly rinse.

2 Spray 5- to 6-quart slow cooker with cooking spray. In slow cooker, place onion and beef; sprinkle with pepper flakes. In small bowl, mix broth and Worcestershire sauce; pour over beef. Cover; cook on Low heat setting 8 to 9 hours or until beef is tender.

3 In small bowl, stir sour cream, horseradish and parsley until well mixed. Slice beef across the grain; serve with horseradish sour cream.

1 Serving: Calories 340; Total Fat 26g (Saturated Fat 9g; Trans Fat 1g); Cholesterol 125mg; Sodium 1480mg; Total Carbohydrate 4g (Dietary Fiber 0g); Protein 23g **Exchanges:** 3½ High-Fat Meat **Carbohydrate Choices:** 0

CARAMELIZED ONION POT ROAST

PREP 25 min TOTAL 8 hr 25 min • **12 servings**

- 1 tablespoon olive or vegetable oil
- 1 boneless beef chuck roast (4 lb), trimmed of excess fat
- 1 teaspoon salt
- ½ teaspoon pepper
- 6 medium onions, sliced
- 1½ cups beef broth (for homemade broth, see page 530)
- ¾ cup beer or nonalcoholic beer
- 2 tablespoons packed brown sugar
- 3 tablespoons Dijon mustard
- 2 tablespoons cider vinegar

1 In 10-inch skillet, heat oil over medium-high heat. Cook beef in oil about 10 minutes, turning occasionally, until brown on all sides. Sprinkle with salt and pepper.

2 Spray 3½- to 6-quart slow cooker with cooking spray. In slow cooker, place onions and beef. Mix remaining ingredients; pour over beef and onions. Cover; cook on Low heat setting 8 to 10 hours or until beef is tender.

3 Using slotted spoon, remove beef and onions from slow cooker. Slice beef across the grain. Skim fat from beef juices if desired; serve juices with beef.

1 Serving: Calories 300; Total Fat 17g (Saturated Fat 6g; Trans Fat 0.5g); Cholesterol 80mg; Sodium 480mg; Total Carbohydrate 8g (Dietary Fiber 1g); Protein 29g **Exchanges:** ½ Other Carbohydrate, 4 Lean Meat, 1 Fat **Carbohydrate Choices:** ½

Caramelized Onion Pot Roast

Trimming Excess Fat from Meat

Trim fat from uncooked beef using a boning, utility or paring knife.

Slicing Meat Across the Grain

Slice cooked beef across the grain for tender non-stringy slices.

BURGUNDY STEW WITH HERB DUMPLINGS LOWER CALORIE

PREP 25 min TOTAL 8 hr 50 min • **8 servings**

2 lb boneless beef bottom or top round, tip or chuck steak, cut into 1-inch pieces
4 medium carrots, cut into ¼-inch slices (2 cups)
2 medium stalks celery, sliced (1 cup)
2 medium onions, sliced
1 can (14.5 oz) diced tomatoes, undrained
1 can (8 oz) sliced mushrooms, drained
¾ cup dry red wine or beef broth
1½ teaspoons salt
1 teaspoon dried thyme leaves
1 teaspoon ground mustard
¼ teaspoon pepper
¼ cup water
3 tablespoons all-purpose flour
Herb Dumplings (page 109)

1 Spray 3½- to 6-quart slow cooker with cooking spray. In slow cooker, mix all stew ingredients except water and flour. Cover; cook on Low heat setting 8 to 10 hours (or High heat setting 4 to 5 hours) or until beef is tender.

2 In small bowl, stir water and flour until well mixed; gradually stir into beef mixture. Cover.

3 Make herb dumplings through Step 1 as directed. Drop dough by 8 spoonfuls onto hot beef mixture. Increase heat setting to High. Cover; cook 25 to 35 minutes or until toothpick inserted in center of dumplings comes out clean.

1 Serving: Calories 280; Total Fat 7g (Saturated Fat 2g; Trans Fat 0.5g); Cholesterol 60mg; Sodium 1010mg; Total Carbohydrate 26g (Dietary Fiber 3g); Protein 27g **Exchanges:** 1 Starch, 2 Vegetable, 2½ Lean Meat **Carbohydrate Choices:** 2

QUICKER BURGUNDY STEW WITH HERB DUMPLINGS Omit herb dumplings. In medium bowl, mix 1½ cups Original Bisquick mix, ½ teaspoon dried thyme leaves and ¼ teaspoon dried sage leaves, crumbled. Stir in ½ cup milk just until moistened. Continue as directed in Step 3.

TEX-MEX ROUND STEAK

One cup of fresh cilantro used in this recipe might seem like a lot, but cooked for a long time, it becomes very mild, blending in the overall flavor of the dish.

PREP 15 min TOTAL 8 hr 15 min • **6 servings**

1 boneless beef round steak (1½ lb), trimmed of excess fat
3 medium stalks celery, thinly sliced (1½ cups)
1 large onion, sliced
1 cup frozen whole kernel corn, thawed
1 cup chopped fresh cilantro
1 jar (20 oz) salsa (for homemade salsa, see page 480)
1 can (15 oz) black beans, drained, rinsed
½ cup beef broth (for homemade broth, see page 530)
1 cup shredded pepper Jack cheese (4 oz)

1 Spray 3½- to 6-quart slow cooker with cooking spray. Cut beef into 6 pieces; place in slow cooker.

2 In large bowl, mix remaining ingredients except cheese; pour over beef. Cover; cook on Low heat setting 8 to 9 hours or until beef is tender. Sprinkle with cheese.

1 Serving: Calories 440; Total Fat 19g (Saturated Fat 9g; Trans Fat 0.5g); Cholesterol 85mg; Sodium 910mg; Total Carbohydrate 30g (Dietary Fiber 7g); Protein 35g **Exchanges:** 2 Starch, 4 Lean Meat, ½ Fat **Carbohydrate Choices:** 2

Cooking Dumplings on Stew

Drop dough onto stew pieces rather than directly into liquid to prevent dumplings from becoming soggy on bottom.

Dumplings are done when toothpick inserted in center of dumplings comes out clean.

BEEF AND POTATOES WITH ROSEMARY LOWER CALORIE

Be sure to use red potatoes in this recipe. They will hold their shape better than russets.

PREP 20 min TOTAL 8 hr 20 min • **8 servings**

- 1 lb medium red potatoes, cut into fourths
- 1 cup ready-to-eat baby-cut carrots
- 3 tablespoons Dijon mustard
- 2 tablespoons chopped fresh or 1½ teaspoons dried rosemary leaves, crumbled
- 1 teaspoon chopped fresh or ½ teaspoon dried thyme leaves
- 1 teaspoon salt
- ½ teaspoon pepper
- 1 boneless beef chuck roast (3 lb), trimmed of excess fat
- 1 small onion, finely chopped (⅓ cup)
- 1½ cups beef broth (for homemade broth, see page 530)

1 Spray 3½- to 6-quart slow cooker with cooking spray. In slow cooker, place potatoes and carrots.

2 Mix mustard, rosemary, thyme, salt and pepper; spread evenly over beef. Place beef on potatoes and carrots; sprinkle with onion. Pour broth evenly over beef and vegetables. Cover; cook on Low heat setting 8 to 10 hours or until beef and vegetables are tender.

3 Using slotted spoon, remove beef and vegetables from slow cooker; place on serving platter. Skim fat from beef juices if desired; serve juices with beef and vegetables.

1 Serving: Calories 350; Total Fat 18g (Saturated Fat 7g; Trans Fat 1g); Cholesterol 95mg; Sodium 710mg; Total Carbohydrate 12g (Dietary Fiber 2g); Protein 33g **Exchanges:** ½ Starch, ½ Vegetable, 4½ Lean Meat, 1 Fat **Carbohydrate Choices:** 1

BEEF AND POTATOES WITH ROSEMARY AND GRAVY To make gravy, skim fat from juices in slow cooker. Measure 1½ cups of the juices; pour into small saucepan. Heat to boiling over medium-high heat. Shake 2 tablespoons cornstarch and ¼ cup cold water in tightly covered jar. Stir cornstarch mixture into beef juices. Cook about 5 minutes, stirring occasionally, until thickened.

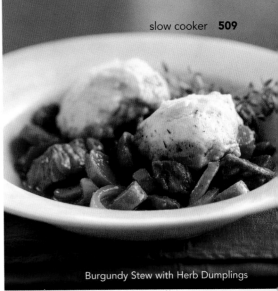

Burgundy Stew with Herb Dumplings

Tex-Mex Round Steak

Beef and Potatoes with Rosemary

LAMB DIJON

Slow cooking is the perfect way to cook less-tender cuts like the lamb stew meat in this recipe.

PREP 25 min TOTAL 8 hr 35 min • **6 servings**

- ¼ cup all-purpose flour
- 1 teaspoon salt
- ¼ teaspoon pepper
- 2 lb lamb stew meat, cut into 1-inch cubes
- 2 tablespoons olive or vegetable oil
- 6 new potatoes (1¼ lb), cubed
- ¼ cup Dijon mustard
- ½ teaspoon grated lemon peel
- 1 tablespoon lemon juice
- 2 teaspoons chopped fresh or ½ teaspoon dried rosemary leaves
- 2 cloves garlic, finely chopped
- 1 can (14.5 oz) beef broth (for homemade broth, see page 530)
- 1 package (10 oz) frozen peas, thawed

1 In resealable food-storage plastic bag, mix flour, salt and pepper. Add lamb; seal bag tightly. Shake until lamb is evenly coated with flour mixture. In 12-inch skillet, heat oil over medium-high heat. Cook lamb in oil about 20 minutes, stirring occasionally, until brown; drain.

2 Spray 3½- to 6-quart slow cooker with cooking spray. Mix lamb and remaining ingredients except peas in slow cooker. Cover; cook on Low heat setting 8 to 10 hours or until lamb is tender.

3 Skim fat from juices in slow cooker. Stir peas into lamb mixture. Cover and cook on High heat setting 10 to 15 minutes or until peas are hot.

1 Serving: Calories 360; Total Fat 14g (Saturated Fat 4g; Trans Fat 0g); Cholesterol 85mg; Sodium 1040mg; Total Carbohydrate 28g (Dietary Fiber 4g); Protein 31g **Exchanges:** 2 Starch, 3½ Lean Meat, ½ Fat **Carbohydrate Choices:** 2

Make It To Go

Want to tote a meal to a gathering? Wrap the slow cooker in a towel or newspaper to keep it warm. Attach rubber bands around the handles to secure it for travel.

Barbecue Beef Sandwiches

BARBECUE BEEF SANDWICHES

For a delicious kick, spread the buns with horseradish sauce.

PREP 20 min TOTAL 7 hr 40 min • **12 sandwiches**

- 1 boneless beef chuck roast (3 lb), trimmed of excess fat
- 1 cup barbecue sauce
- ½ cup apricot or peach preserves
- ⅓ cup chopped green bell pepper
- 1 tablespoon Dijon mustard
- 2 teaspoons packed brown sugar
- 1 small onion, sliced
- 12 kaiser rolls or burger buns, split

1 Spray 4- to 5-quart slow cooker with cooking spray. Cut beef into 4 pieces; place in slow cooker. Mix remaining ingredients except rolls; pour over beef. Cover; cook on Low heat setting 7 to 8 hours or until beef is tender.

2 Remove beef from slow cooker to cutting board; cut into thin slices. Return to slow cooker. Cover; cook 20 to 30 minutes longer or until hot. Fill buns with beef mixture. If desired, serve juices in small individual bowls for dipping.

1 Sandwich: Calories 410; Total Fat 14g (Saturated Fat 5g; Trans Fat 1g); Cholesterol 60mg; Sodium 570mg; Total Carbohydrate 46g (Dietary Fiber 1g); Protein 26g **Exchanges:** 2 Starch, 1 Other Carbohydrate, 2½ Medium-Fat Meat **Carbohydrate Choices:** 3

CHEESEBURGER JOES

LOWER CALORIE

PREP 20 min **TOTAL** 6 hr 20 min • **12 sandwiches**

- 1½ lb lean (at least 80%) ground beef*
- ½ teaspoon garlic-pepper blend
- 1 loaf (8 oz) prepared cheese product, diced (2 cups)
- 2 tablespoons milk
- 1 medium green bell pepper, chopped (1 cup)
- 1 small onion, chopped (⅓ cup)
- 2 cloves garlic, finely chopped
- 12 burger buns, split
  Sliced dill pickles, if desired

1 In 12-inch skillet, place beef; sprinkle with garlic-pepper blend. Cook over medium heat 8 to 10 minutes, stirring occasionally, until beef is brown; drain.

2 Spray 3- to 4-quart slow cooker with cooking spray. Mix beef and remaining ingredients except buns in slow cooker. Cover; cook on Low heat setting 6 to 7 hours. Stir mixture before serving. Serve beef mixture in buns with pickles.

Ground turkey or pork can be substituted.

1 Sandwich: Calories 280; Total Fat 13g (Saturated Fat 6g; Trans Fat 0.5g); Cholesterol 50mg; Sodium 520mg; Total Carbohydrate 21g (Dietary Fiber 1g); Protein 17g **Exchanges:** 1½ Starch, 2 Medium-Fat Meat **Carbohydrate Choices:** 1½

TANGY ITALIAN BEEF SANDWICHES

PREP 10 min **TOTAL** 10 hr 10 min • **12 sandwiches**

- 1 boneless beef sirloin tip roast (3 to 4 lb), trimmed of fat
- ¼ cup packed brown sugar
- 1 bottle (16 oz) Italian dressing (for homemade dressing, see page 475)
- 2 teaspoons Italian seasoning
- 12 hard rolls or burger buns, split

1 Spray 3- to 4-quart slow cooker with cooking spray. If beef is tied, remove strings or netting. Place beef in slow cooker. Sprinkle with brown sugar; pour dressing over beef.

2 Cover and cook on Low heat setting 10 to 12 hours.

3 Remove beef from slow cooker to cutting board. Using 2 forks, shred beef. Return beef to cooker; stir in Italian seasoning. Using slotted spoon to remove beef from cooker, fill each bun with about ⅓ cup beef. Serve with juices for dipping.

1 Sandwich: Calories 420; Total Fat 22g (Saturated Fat 3g; Trans Fat 0g); Cholesterol 65mg; Sodium 630mg; Total Carbohydrate 30g (Dietary Fiber 0g); Protein 27g **Exchanges:** 1½ Starch, ½ Other Carbohydrate, 3 Lean Meat, 2½ Fat **Carbohydrate Choices:** 2

Cheeseburger Joes

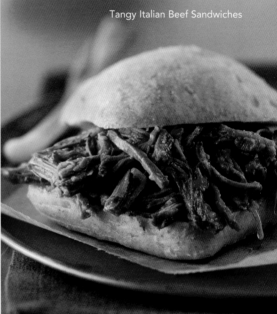

Tangy Italian Beef Sandwiches

Heirloom Recipe and New Twist

This classic sandwich recipe was developed several years ago to mimic a restaurant favorite. Not only is it super-easy to make in the slow cooker, but the flavor is outstanding and this particular recipe is requested often by consumers. It's great to make for a crowd. You'll also love our new twist made with tangy blue cheese and red wine that was developed especially as a party recipe—enjoy!

CLASSIC

FRENCH DIP SANDWICHES

PREP 5 min **TOTAL** 7 hr 5 min • **10 sandwiches**

- 1 boneless beef chuck roast (3 lb)
- 1½ cups water
- ⅓ cup soy sauce
- 1 teaspoon dried rosemary leaves
- 1 teaspoon dried thyme leaves
- 1 clove garlic, finely chopped
- 1 dried bay leaf
- 3 or 4 peppercorns
- 2 loaves (1 lb each) French bread

1 Spray 3½- to 4-quart slow cooker with cooking spray. In slow cooker, place beef (if roast comes in netting or is tied, do not remove). Mix remaining ingredients except bread; pour over beef. Cover; cook on Low heat setting 7 to 8 hours.

2 Skim fat from surface of juices; discard bay leaf and peppercorns. Remove beef from slow cooker; place on cutting board (remove netting or strings). Cut beef into thin slices. Cut each loaf of bread into 5 pieces, about 4 inches long; cut in half horizontally. Fill bread with beef. Serve with broth from cooker for dipping.

1 Sandwich: Calories 400; Total Fat 13g (Saturated Fat 4.5g; Trans Fat 1g); Cholesterol 50mg; Sodium 1050mg; Total Carbohydrate 46g (Dietary Fiber 3g); Protein 25g **Exchanges:** 3 Starch, 2 Medium-Fat Meat **Carbohydrate Choices:** 3

French Dip Sandwiches

Sandwiches To Go

Make this sandwich filling and refrigerate it in a covered container. Then you can quickly heat sandwiches for a quick meal any time.

See how to make French dip sandwiches
Visit bettycrocker.com/BCcookbook

Zinfandel Beef and Blue Cheese Sandwiches

NEW TWIST

ZINFANDEL BEEF AND BLUE CHEESE SANDWICHES

PREP 15 min TOTAL 7 hr 15 min • **10 sandwiches**

- 1 boneless beef chuck roast (3 lb)
- 1 teaspoon salt
- 1 medium onion, thinly sliced
- 1 teaspoon dried rosemary leaves
- 1 teaspoon dried thyme leaves
- 1 clove garlic, finely chopped
- 1 dried bay leaf
- 3 or 4 peppercorns
- 1 cup dry red wine (such as Zinfandel) or nonalcoholic red wine
- ¾ cup beef broth (for homemade broth, see page 530)
- 1 teaspoon Worcestershire sauce
- 10 soft ciabatta rolls or hoagie buns, split and toasted if desired
- 1¼ cups crumbled Stilton or blue cheese

1 Spray 3½- to 4-quart slow cooker with cooking spray. Sprinkle beef with salt. In slow cooker, place beef (if roast comes in netting or is tied, do not remove) and onion. Mix remaining ingredients except rolls and cheese; pour over beef. Cover; cook on Low heat setting 7 to 8 hours.

2 Skim fat from surface of juices; discard bay leaf and peppercorns. Remove beef and vegetables from slow cooker; place beef on cutting board (remove netting or strings). Cut beef into thin slices. Fill rolls with beef; top with onions and sprinkle with cheese. Serve with broth from cooker for dipping.

1 Sandwich: Calories 560; Total Fat 23g (Saturated Fat 10g; Trans Fat 1.5g); Cholesterol 90mg; Sodium 990mg; Total Carbohydrate 49g (Dietary Fiber 2g); Protein 39g **Exchanges:** 3 Starch, ½ Other Carbohydrate, 3 Lean Meat, 1 Medium-Fat Meat, 1½ Fat **Carbohydrate Choices:** 3

ZINFANDEL BEEF AND MOZZARELLA SANDWICHES Substitute mozzarella cheese for the Stilton and serve on French rolls.

SWEET AND TANGY SHORT RIBS

PREP 35 min TOTAL 9 hr 35 min • **6 servings**

RIBS
- 1 tablespoon vegetable oil
- 4 lb beef short ribs, cut into rib sections
- 1 large sweet onion (Bermuda, Maui or Spanish), cut in half, sliced

SAUCE
- 1 bottle (12 oz) chili sauce
- ¾ cup apricot preserves
- 2 tablespoons packed brown sugar
- 2 tablespoons cider vinegar
- 2 tablespoons Worcestershire sauce
- 2 teaspoons ground mustard
- 2 cloves garlic, finely chopped

1 In 12-inch nonstick skillet, heat oil over medium-high heat. Cook ribs in oil (in batches if necessary) 6 to 8 minutes, turning occasionally, until brown on all sides.

2 Spray 4- to 5-quart slow cooker with cooking spray. In slow cooker, place onion and ribs. Cover; cook on Low heat setting 8 hours.

3 In 2-quart saucepan, cook sauce ingredients over low heat 15 to 20 minutes, stirring frequently, until thickened.

4 Drain excess liquid from slow cooker. Pour sauce over ribs. Increase heat setting to High. Cover; cook about 1 hour longer or until meat begins to separate from bones.

1 Serving: Calories 470; Total Fat 20g (Saturated Fat 7g; Trans Fat 1g); Cholesterol 90mg; Sodium 880mg; Total Carbohydrate 47g (Dietary Fiber 4g); Protein 24g **Exchanges:** 3 Other Carbohydrate, 3½ Medium-Fat Meat, ½ Fat **Carbohydrate Choices:** 3

MAKE AHEAD **DIRECTIONS** The sauce can be made up to 1 day ahead. Store covered in the refrigerator; reheat before adding to the ribs.

High-Altitude Slow Cooking

At high altitudes, longer cooking times are necessary for most foods, especially meats, which may take twice as long as specified to get tender. To shorten meat cooking time, try the High setting instead of the Low setting. For vegetables, cut into smaller pieces than specified so they cook more quickly.

Call your local USDA (United States Department of Agriculture) Extension Service office, listed in the phone book under "county government," or go to www.fsis.usda.gov/Fact_Sheets/index.asp for additional information.

PORKETTA POT ROAST

Parsnips are a delicious root vegetable that looks like a thick carrot with creamy-yellow to white flesh. When cooked, parsnips are sweeter than carrots.

PREP 15 min TOTAL 9 hr 15 min • **8 servings**

- 2 teaspoons Italian seasoning
- 1½ teaspoons fennel seed, crushed
- ¾ teaspoon salt
- ½ teaspoon celery seed
- 1 boneless pork shoulder (3 lb)
- 3 medium parsnips, peeled, cut into ¾-inch pieces (3 cups)
- 2 medium sweet potatoes, peeled, cut into ¾-inch pieces (3 cups)
- 12 cloves garlic, peeled, cut in half
- 1½ cups water

1 In small bowl, mix Italian seasoning, fennel seed, salt and celery seed. Pat seasoning mixture evenly onto pork (if pork comes in netting or is tied, do not remove). Heat 12-inch nonstick skillet over medium-high heat. Cook pork in skillet 5 to 10 minutes, turning several times, until brown on all sides.

2 Spray 4- to 5-quart slow cooker with cooking spray. In slow cooker, place parsnips, sweet potatoes and garlic; pour water over vegetables. Place pork on vegetables. Cover; cook on Low heat setting 9 to 10 hours or until pork is tender.

3 Remove pork from slow cooker; place on cutting board (remove netting or strings). Cut pork across grain into slices; serve with vegetables and juices.

1 Serving: Calories 350; Total Fat 20g (Saturated Fat 7g; Trans Fat 0g); Cholesterol 90mg; Sodium 290mg; Total Carbohydrate 16g (Dietary Fiber 3g); Protein 26g **Exchanges:** 1 Starch, 3 Medium-Fat Meat, 1 Fat **Carbohydrate Choices:** 1

GARLIC PORK ROAST

LOWER CALORIE

PREP 20 min TOTAL 8 hr 20 min • **10 servings**

- 1 tablespoon olive or vegetable oil
- 1 boneless pork loin roast (3½ lb), trimmed of excess fat
- 1 teaspoon salt
- ½ teaspoon pepper
- 1 medium onion, sliced
- 3 cloves garlic, peeled
- 1 cup chicken broth (for homemade broth, see page 528) or water

1 In 10-inch skillet, heat oil over medium-high heat. Cook pork in oil about 10 minutes, turning occasionally, until brown on all sides. Sprinkle with salt and pepper.

2 Spray 3½- to 6-quart slow cooker with cooking spray. In slow cooker, place onion, garlic and pork; pour broth over pork. Cover; cook on Low heat setting 8 to 10 hours or until pork is tender. Serve pork with juices.

1 Serving: Calories 200; Total Fat 8g (Saturated Fat 2.5g; Trans Fat 0g); Cholesterol 65mg; Sodium 410mg; Total Carbohydrate 1g (Dietary Fiber 0g); Protein 31g **Exchanges:** 4½ Very Lean Meat, 1 Fat **Carbohydrate Choices:** 0

Browning Large Cuts of Meat

Cook meat in hot oil about 10 minutes, turning occasionally, until brown on all sides.

Porketta Pot Roast

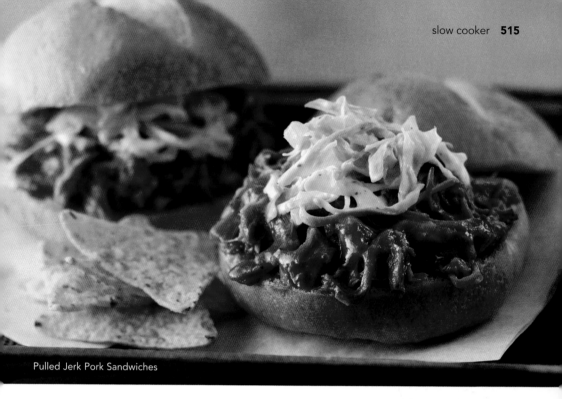

Pulled Jerk Pork Sandwiches

PULLED JERK PORK SANDWICHES

Pulled pork, a favorite style of southern and some southeastern barbecues, refers to the method of preparing the cooked pork by pulling it apart with your fingers or two forks.

PREP 5 min **TOTAL** 8 hr 35 min • **8 servings**

- 1 tablespoon Jamaican jerk seasoning (dry)
- 1 boneless pork shoulder (2½ lb)
- ¼ teaspoon dried thyme leaves
- 1 medium onion, chopped (½ cup)
- 1 cup cola carbonated beverage
- 2 cups barbecue sauce
- 8 burger buns or flour tortillas (9 or 10 inch)
  Creamy Coleslaw (page 467, or purchased), if desired

1 Rub jerk seasoning over pork (if pork comes in netting or is tied, do not remove); sprinkle with thyme. Spray 3½- to 6-quart slow cooker with cooking spray. In slow cooker, place pork and onion; pour cola over pork. Cover; cook on Low heat setting 8 to 10 hours.

2 Remove pork from slow cooker to cutting board (remove netting or strings). Remove

Pulling Pork

Using 2 forks, pull pork into desired size pieces or shreds.

Or, using fingers, pull pork apart into desired size pieces or shreds.

juices from slow cooker and reserve. Using 2 forks or your fingers, shred pork into desired sized pieces; return to slow cooker. Stir in barbecue sauce and ½ cup reserved juices. Increase heat setting to High. Cover; cook 30 to 45 minutes or until heated through.

3 In 2-quart saucepan, heat remaining juices to boiling. Spoon pork into buns; top with coleslaw and serve with juices for dipping.

1 Serving: Calories 420; Total Fat 14g (Saturated Fat 4.5g; Trans Fat 0g); Cholesterol 65mg; Sodium 900mg; Total Carbohydrate 49g (Dietary Fiber 2g); Protein 25g **Exchanges:** 2 Starch, 1 Other Carbohydrate, 3 Lean Meat, 1 Fat **Carbohydrate Choices:** 3

PORK ROAST WITH CREAMY MUSTARD SAUCE

German Spaetzle, page 392, or Potato Gnocchi, page 392, tossed with melted butter and a sprinkle of fresh herbs, would be excellent with this roast.

PREP 15 min **TOTAL** 7 hr 30 min • **8 servings**

- 1 tablespoon vegetable oil
- 1 boneless pork sirloin roast (2½ to 3 lb), trimmed of excess fat
- ¾ cup dry white wine or nonalcoholic white wine
- 2 tablespoons all-purpose flour
- 1 teaspoon salt
- ½ teaspoon pepper
- 2 medium carrots, finely chopped or shredded (1 cup)
- 1 medium onion, finely chopped (½ cup)
- 1 small shallot, finely chopped (2 tablespoons)
- ¼ cup half-and-half
- 2 to 3 tablespoons country-style Dijon mustard

1 In 10-inch skillet, heat oil over medium-high heat. Cook pork in oil about 10 minutes, turning occasionally, until brown on all sides.

2 Spray 3½- to 6-quart slow cooker with cooking spray. Place pork in slow cooker. Mix remaining ingredients except half-and-half and mustard; pour over pork. Cover; cook on Low heat setting 7 to 9 hours or until pork is tender.

3 Remove pork from slow cooker; cover and keep warm. Skim fat from pork juices if desired. Stir half-and-half and mustard into juices. Increase heat setting to High. Cover;

cook about 15 minutes or until slightly thickened. Serve sauce with pork.

1 Serving: Calories 270; Total Fat 13g (Saturated Fat 4.5g; Trans Fat 0g); Cholesterol 90mg; Sodium 460mg; Total Carbohydrate 5g (Dietary Fiber 0g); Protein 31g **Exchanges:** 1 Vegetable, 4 Lean Meat, ½ Fat **Carbohydrate Choices:** ½

SPANISH CHICKEN

PREP 15 min **TOTAL** 6 hr 15 min • **6 servings**

- 1¾ lb boneless skinless chicken breasts or thighs, cut into 1-inch pieces
- 1 lb Italian turkey sausage, cut into 1-inch pieces
- 1 large red bell pepper, chopped (1½ cups)
- 1 large onion, chopped (1 cup)
- 2 cloves garlic, finely chopped
- 1 teaspoon dried oregano leaves
- ½ to 1 teaspoon crushed red pepper
- 1 can (28 oz) diced tomatoes, undrained
- 1 can (6 oz) tomato paste
- 1 can (14 oz) artichoke heart quarters, drained
- 1 can (4 oz) sliced ripe olives, drained
- 2 cups hot cooked rice (page 429)

1 Spray 3½- to 4-quart slow cooker with cooking spray. In slow cooker, mix all ingredients except artichoke hearts, olives and rice. Cover; cook on Low heat setting 6 to 8 hours.

2 Cook rice in water as directed on package. Stir artichoke hearts and olives into mixture in slow cooker; heat through. Serve with rice.

1 Serving: Calories 490; Total Fat 14g (Saturated Fat 3.5g; Trans Fat 0g); Cholesterol 120mg; Sodium 1860mg; Total Carbohydrate 46g (Dietary Fiber 8g); Protein 47g **Exchanges:** 3 Starch, 5 Very Lean Meat, 1 Fat **Carbohydrate Choices:** 3

Spanish Chicken

Spicy Chicken in Peanut Sauce

Mango Chutney Chicken Curry

SPICY CHICKEN IN PEANUT SAUCE

PREP 15 min TOTAL 7 hr 15 min • **4 servings**

- 1 tablespoon olive or vegetable oil
- 8 large chicken thighs (about 3 lb), skin removed
- 1 large onion, chopped (1 cup)
- 2 cans (14.5 oz each) diced tomatoes with green chiles, undrained
- 1 can (14.5 oz) crushed fire-roasted or regular diced tomatoes, undrained
- 2 tablespoons honey
- 1½ teaspoons ground cumin
- 1 teaspoon ground cinnamon
- ⅓ cup creamy peanut butter
- 2 cups hot cooked jasmine or basmati rice (page 429) or couscous

1 In 12-inch nonstick skillet, heat oil over medium-high heat. Cook chicken in oil about 4 minutes, turning once, until brown.

2 Spray 4- to-5-quart slow cooker with cooking spray. In slow cooker, mix onion, diced and crushed tomatoes, honey, cumin and cinnamon. Add chicken; spoon tomato mixture over chicken. Cover; cook on Low heat setting 7 to 8 hours.

3 Stir peanut butter into mixture in slow cooker until melted and well blended. Serve chicken and sauce over rice.

1 Serving: Calories 740; Total Fat 33g (Saturated Fat 8g; Trans Fat 0.5g); Cholesterol 140mg; Sodium 1180mg; Total Carbohydrate 52g (Dietary Fiber 8g); Protein 60g **Exchanges:** 1 Starch, 1½ Other Carbohydrate, 3 Vegetable, 7½ Lean Meat, 2 Fat **Carbohydrate Choices:** 3½

MANGO CHUTNEY CHICKEN CURRY

Serve with small bowls of toppers like toasted shredded coconut, chopped peanuts, raisins and chopped cilantro.

PREP 20 min TOTAL 6 hr 20 min • **4 servings**

- 4 bone-in chicken breast halves (about 3 lb), skin removed
- 1 can (15 oz) garbanzo beans, drained, rinsed
- 1 small onion, thinly sliced
- 1 small red bell pepper, chopped (½ cup)
- 1 cup fresh sugar snap peas
- ¾ cup water
- 2 tablespoons cornstarch
- 1½ teaspoons curry powder
- ¼ teaspoon salt
- ¼ teaspoon pepper
- 1 jar (9 oz) mango chutney
- 4 cups hot cooked rice (page 429) or couscous

1 Spray 3½- to 4-quart slow cooker with cooking spray. In slow cooker, layer chicken, beans, onion, bell pepper and pea pods. Mix remaining ingredients except rice; pour into slow cooker. Cover; cook on Low heat setting 6 to 7 hours or until vegetables are tender and juice of chicken is clear when thickest part is cut to bone (at least 165°F).

2 Serve chicken and vegetables over rice.

1 Serving: Calories 610; Total Fat 7g (Saturated Fat 1.5g; Trans Fat 0g); Cholesterol 75mg; Sodium 380mg; Total Carbohydrate 97g (Dietary Fiber 7g); Protein 39g **Exchanges:** 3½ Starch, 2 Other Carbohydrate, 2½ Vegetable, 3½ Very Lean Meat, ½ Fat **Carbohydrate Choices:** 6½

CHICKEN CHOW MEIN

LOWER CALORIE

PREP 15 min **TOTAL** 6 hr 30 min • **4 servings**

- 1 tablespoon vegetable oil
- 8 boneless skinless chicken thighs (about 1½ lb)*, trimmed of excess fat, cut into 1-inch pieces
- 2 medium carrots, sliced diagonally (1 cup)
- 2 medium stalks celery, coarsely chopped (1 cup)
- 1 medium onion, chopped (½ cup)
- 2 cloves garlic, finely chopped
- 1 can (8 oz) sliced water chestnuts, drained
- 1 cup chicken broth (for homemade broth, see page 528)
- 2 tablespoons soy sauce
- ½ teaspoon finely chopped gingerroot
- 2 tablespoons cornstarch
- 3 tablespoons cold water
- 1 cup sliced fresh mushrooms (3 oz)
- 1 cup snow pea pods (4 oz)
  Chow mein noodles, if desired

1 In 10-inch skillet, heat oil over medium-high heat. Cook chicken in oil about 5 minutes, turning once, until brown.

2 Spray 3½- to 6-quart slow cooker with cooking spray. In slow cooker, place carrots, celery, onion, garlic and water chestnuts; top with chicken. In small bowl, mix broth, soy sauce and gingerroot; pour over chicken. Cover; cook on Low heat setting 6 to 8 hours.

3 In small bowl, mix cornstarch and water until smooth; stir into chicken mixture. Stir in mushrooms and pea pods. Increase heat setting to High. Cover; cook 15 minutes longer. Serve over noodles.

Boneless skinless chicken breasts can be substituted.

1 Serving: Calories 260; Total Fat 9g (Saturated Fat 2.5g; Trans Fat 0g); Cholesterol 60mg; Sodium 810mg; Total Carbohydrate 19g (Dietary Fiber 4g); Protein 25g **Exchanges:** 3 Vegetable, 3 Lean Meat, ½ Fat **Carbohydrate Choices:** 1

HERBED TURKEY AND WILD RICE CASSEROLE **LOWER CALORIE**

PREP 15 min **TOTAL** 6 hr 45 min • **6 servings**

- 6 slices bacon, cut into ½-inch pieces
- 1 lb turkey breast tenderloins, cut into ¾-inch pieces
- 1 medium onion, chopped (½ cup)
- 1 medium carrot, sliced (½ cup)
- 1 medium stalk celery, sliced (½ cup)
- 2 cans (14 oz each) chicken broth (for homemade broth, see page 528)
- 1 can (10¾ oz) condensed cream of chicken soup
- ¼ teaspoon dried marjoram leaves
- ⅛ teaspoon pepper
- 1¼ cups uncooked wild rice, rinsed, drained

1 In 10-inch skillet, cook bacon over medium heat, stirring occasionally, until crisp. Stir in turkey. Cook 3 to 5 minutes, stirring occasionally, until turkey is brown. Stir in onion, carrot and celery. Cook 2 minutes, stirring occasionally; drain.

2 Spray 3½- to 6-quart slow cooker with cooking spray. In slow cooker, beat 1 can of the broth and the soup, using wire whisk, until smooth. Stir in remaining can of broth, the marjoram and pepper. Stir in turkey mixture and wild rice. Cover; cook on High heat setting 30 minutes.

3 Reduce heat to Low setting. Cook 6 to 7 hours longer or until rice is tender and liquid is absorbed.

1 Serving: Calories 340; Total Fat 9g (Saturated Fat 2.5g; Trans Fat 0g); Cholesterol 65mg; Sodium 1190mg; Total Carbohydrate 36g (Dietary Fiber 3g); Protein 30g **Exchanges:** 2 Starch, 1 Vegetable, 3 Very Lean Meat, 1 Fat **Carbohydrate Choices:** 2½

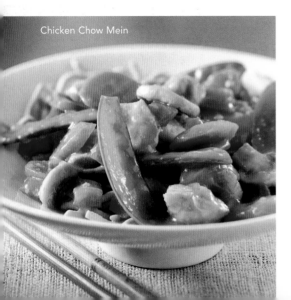
Chicken Chow Mein

JAMBALAYA LOWER CALORIE

PREP 20 min TOTAL 8 hr 20 min • **8 servings**

- 1 large onion, chopped (1 cup)
- 1 medium green bell pepper, chopped (1 cup)
- 2 medium stalks celery, chopped (1 cup)
- 3 cloves garlic, finely chopped
- 1 can (28 oz) diced tomatoes, undrained
- 2 cups chopped fully cooked smoked sausage
- 1 tablespoon parsley flakes
- ½ teaspoon dried thyme leaves
- ½ teaspoon salt
- ¼ teaspoon pepper
- ¼ teaspoon red pepper sauce
- ¾ lb uncooked deveined peeled medium shrimp, thawed if frozen
- 3 cups uncooked regular long grain white rice

1 Spray 3½- to 6-quart slow cooker with cooking spray. In slow cooker, mix all ingredients except shrimp and rice. Cover; cook on Low heat setting 7 to 8 hours (or High heat setting 3 to 4 hours) or until vegetables are tender.

2 Stir in shrimp. Cover; cook about 1 hour longer or until shrimp are pink.

3 Cook rice as directed on package. Serve jambalaya with rice.

1 Serving: Calories 280; Total Fat 10g (Saturated Fat 3g; Trans Fat 0g); Cholesterol 90mg; Sodium 630mg; Total Carbohydrate 30g (Dietary Fiber 2g); Protein 16g **Exchanges:** 1½ Starch, 1½ Vegetable, 1 High-Fat Meat, ½ Fat **Carbohydrate Choices:** 2

FAMILY-FAVORITE CHILI

LOWER CALORIE

Always cook ground meat before adding it to the slow cooker. Getting cold, uncooked ground beef to a safe temperature in the cooker takes too long.

PREP 20 min TOTAL 6 hr 35 min • **8 servings**

- 2 lb lean (at least 80%) ground beef
- 1 large onion, chopped (1 cup)
- 2 cloves garlic, finely chopped
- 1 can (28 oz) diced tomatoes, undrained
- 1 can (15 oz) tomato sauce
- 2 tablespoons chili powder
- 1½ teaspoons ground cumin
- ½ teaspoon salt
- ½ teaspoon pepper
- 1 can (15 to 16 oz) kidney or pinto beans, drained, rinsed
  Shredded Cheddar cheese, if desired

1 In 12-inch skillet, cook beef over medium heat 8 to 10 minutes, stirring occasionally, until brown; drain.

2 Spray 3½- to 6-quart slow cooker with cooking spray. In slow cooker, mix beef and remaining ingredients except beans and cheese. Cover; cook on Low heat setting 6 to 8 hours (or High heat setting 3 to 4 hours).

3 Stir in beans. Increase heat setting to High. Cover; cook 15 to 20 minutes longer or until slightly thickened. Sprinkle with cheese.

1 Serving: Calories 300; Total Fat 12g (Saturated Fat 4.5g; Trans Fat 0.5g); Cholesterol 70mg; Sodium 800mg; Total Carbohydrate 22g (Dietary Fiber 6g); Protein 27g **Exchanges:** 1 Starch, 1 Vegetable, 3½ Lean Meat **Carbohydrate Choices:** 1½

FAMILY-FAVORITE CHILI WITH SMOKED SAUSAGE Reduce ground beef to 1 lb. Add 1 lb cooked smoked beef sausage, cut into ½-inch slices, in Step 2. Substitute shredded smoked Cheddar or smoked Gouda cheese for the shredded Cheddar.

FAMILY-FAVORITE TURKEY CHILI WITH BROWN RICE Substitute ground turkey breast for the ground beef, cooking until no longer pink in Step 1. Serve chili over cooked brown rice. Substitute shredded reduced-fat Cheddar cheese for the shredded Cheddar.

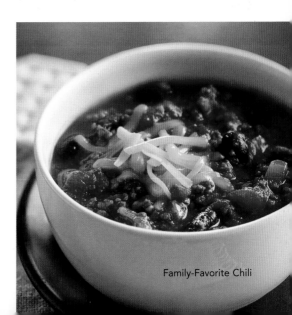

Family-Favorite Chili

CHEESY POTATO-BACON SOUP

Look for bacon that is already cooked at the grocery store—it's a great time-saver. Or pick up a package of microwavable bacon instead.

PREP 15 min **TOTAL** 6 hr 35 min • **6 servings**

- 1 bag (32 oz) frozen southern-style diced hash brown potatoes, thawed
- 1 medium onion, chopped (½ cup)
- 1 medium stalk celery, diced (½ cup)
- 3½ cups chicken broth (for homemade broth, see page 528)
- 1 cup water
- 3 tablespoons all-purpose flour
- 1 cup half-and-half
- 2 cups shredded Cheddar cheese
- 12 slices bacon, crisply cooked, crumbled
- 4 medium green onions, thinly sliced (¼ cup)

1 Spray 3- to 4-quart slow cooker with cooking spray. In cooker, mix potatoes, onion, celery, broth and water. Cover; cook on Low heat setting 6 to 8 hours.

2 In small bowl, mix flour and half-and-half; stir into potato mixture. Increase heat setting to High; cover and cook 20 to 30 minutes longer or until mixture thickens. Stir in cheese until melted; stir in half of bacon. Sprinkle each serving with remaining bacon and green onions.

1 Serving (1½ Cups): Calories 410; Total Fat 15g (Saturated Fat 9g; Trans Fat 0g); Cholesterol 45mg; Sodium 1210mg; Total Carbohydrate 50g (Dietary Fiber 5g); Protein 19g **Exchanges:** 3½ Starch, 1 High-Fat Meat, 1 Fat **Carbohydrate Choices:** 3

EASY BEAN AND KIELBASA SOUP

If your mornings are rushed, slice the sausage and chop the vegetables the night before and store in resealable food-storage plastic bags in the refrigerator.

PREP 15 min **TOTAL** 8 hr 30 min • **8 servings**

- ½ package (20 oz) 15- or 16-dried bean soup mix, sorted, rinsed
- 1 ring (1 lb) fully cooked kielbasa, cut lengthwise in half, then cut crosswise into slices
- 4 medium carrots, chopped (2 cups)
- 3 medium stalks celery, chopped (1½ cups)
- 1 large onion, chopped (1 cup)
- 5 cans (14 oz each) chicken broth (for homemade broth, see page 528)
- 2 tablespoons tomato paste
- 1 teaspoon dried thyme leaves
- ½ teaspoon salt
- ½ teaspoon pepper
- 1 can (14.5 oz) diced tomatoes, undrained

1 Spray 5- to 6-quart slow cooker with cooking spray. In slow cooker, mix all ingredients except tomatoes. Cover; cook on Low heat setting 8 to 10 hours or until vegetables are tender.

2 Stir in tomatoes. Increase heat setting to High. Cover; cook about 15 minutes longer or until hot.

1 Serving: Calories 370; Total Fat 18g (Saturated Fat 6g; Trans Fat 0.5g); Cholesterol 35mg; Sodium 2020mg; Total Carbohydrate 35g (Dietary Fiber 6g); Protein 18g **Exchanges:** 2 Starch, 1 Vegetable, 1½ High-Fat Meat, 1 Fat **Carbohydrate Choices:** 2

Cheesy Potato-Bacon Soup

Easy Bean and Kielbasa Soup

Italian Chicken-Lentil Soup

LENTIL AND CANADIAN BACON SOUP

Canadian bacon is a closer relative to ham than to regular bacon. It's lean and fully cooked. If you prefer ham, use 1½ cups instead of the Canadian bacon.

PREP 20 min TOTAL 8 hr 20 min • **8 servings**

- 1 package (16 oz) dried lentils (2¼ cups), sorted, rinsed
- 2 cans (14 oz each) vegetable broth (for homemade broth, see page 530)
- 1 package (6 oz) sliced Canadian bacon, coarsely chopped
- 2 medium carrots, cut into ½-inch pieces (1 cup)
- 1 medium potato, peeled, cut into ½-inch pieces (1 cup)
- 1 medium onion, chopped (½ cup)
- 1 medium stalk celery, cut into ½-inch pieces (½ cup)
- 4 cups water
- 1 teaspoon dried thyme leaves
- ½ teaspoon salt
- ¼ teaspoon pepper

Spray 3½- to 6-quart slow cooker with cooking spray. In slow cooker, mix all ingredients. Cover; cook on Low heat setting 8 to 9 hours (or High heat setting 3 to 5 hours) or until lentils are tender. Stir well before serving.

1 Serving: Calories 260; Total Fat 2.5g (Saturated Fat 0.5g; Trans Fat 0g); Cholesterol 10mg; Sodium 910mg; Total Carbohydrate 39g (Dietary Fiber 10g); Protein 20g **Exchanges:** 2 Starch, 2 Vegetable, 1 Lean Meat **Carbohydrate Choices:** 2½

ITALIAN CHICKEN-LENTIL SOUP

PREP 15 min TOTAL 5 hr 30 min • **6 servings**

- 4 medium carrots, sliced (2 cups)
- 1 medium zucchini, chopped (2 cups)
- 1 medium onion, chopped (½ cup)
- 1 cup dried lentils (8 oz), sorted, rinsed
- 4½ cups chicken broth (for homemade broth, see page 528)
- ½ teaspoon salt
- ¼ teaspoon pepper
- 1 lb boneless skinless chicken thighs, trimmed of excess fat
- 1 can (28 oz) diced tomatoes, undrained
- 1 cup sliced fresh mushrooms (3 oz)
- ¼ cup chopped fresh or 1 tablespoon dried basil leaves
  Shredded Parmesan cheese, if desired

1 Spray 3½- to 6-quart slow cooker with cooking spray. In slow cooker, mix carrots, zucchini, onion, lentils, broth, salt and pepper; top with chicken. Cover; cook on Low heat setting 5 to 6 hours.

2 Remove chicken from slow cooker to cutting board. Use 2 forks to pull chicken into shreds. Return chicken to slow cooker. Stir in tomatoes and mushrooms. Cover; cook about 15 minutes or until heated through. Sprinkle with basil. Serve with cheese.

1 Serving: Calories 280; Total Fat 4g (Saturated Fat 1g; Trans Fat 0g); Cholesterol 30mg; Sodium 1200mg; Total Carbohydrate 35g (Dietary Fiber 10g); Protein 25g **Exchanges:** 2 Starch, 1 Vegetable, 2½ Very Lean Meat **Carbohydrate Choices:** 2

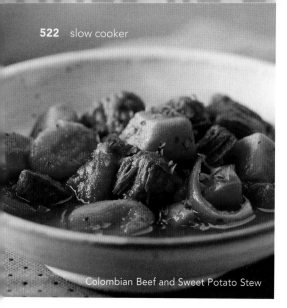
Colombian Beef and Sweet Potato Stew

COLOMBIAN BEEF AND SWEET POTATO STEW

PREP 15 min **TOTAL** 8 hr 15 min • **6 servings**

- 1 lb boneless beef chuck flatiron steak, trimmed of excess fat, cut into 1-inch pieces
- ½ teaspoon salt
- ¼ teaspoon pepper
- 1 tablespoon olive or vegetable oil
- 3 cups 1-inch pieces peeled sweet potatoes
- 2 teaspoons finely chopped garlic
- 2 whole cloves
- 1 dried bay leaf
- 1 cinnamon stick
- 1 large onion, cut into eighths
- 1 can (28 oz) Italian-style tomatoes, undrained
- 8 dried apricots, cut in half
  Chopped fresh parsley, if desired

1 Sprinkle beef with salt and pepper. Heat oil in 10-inch skillet over medium-high heat. Cook beef in oil about 5 minutes, stirring occasionally, until brown.

2 Spray 4- to 5-quart slow cooker with cooking spray. Mix beef and remaining ingredients except apricots and parsley in slow cooker. Cover; cook on Low heat setting about 8 hours or until beef is tender.

3 Stir in apricots. Cover; cook on Low heat setting about 15 minutes or until apricots are softened. Discard cloves, bay leaf and cinnamon stick. Sprinkle stew with parsley.

1 Serving: Calories 260; Total Fat 9g (Saturated Fat 3.5g; Trans Fat 0g); Cholesterol 40mg; Sodium 630mg; Total Carbohydrate 27g (Dietary Fiber 5g); Protein 17g **Exchanges:** ½ Starch, 1 Other Carbohydrate, 1 Vegetable, 2 Lean Meat, ½ Fat **Carbohydrate Choices:** 2

CURRIED CARROT SOUP

LOWER CALORIE

Curry powders vary in flavor but usually are sweet, yet pungent. Spices often included in curry are cardamom, cinnamon, cloves, chiles, nutmeg, cumin, fennel and turmeric. This amazing blend flavors this soup.

PREP 15 min **TOTAL** 7 hr 25 min • **4 servings**

SOUP

- 1⅔ cups chopped onions (about 3 medium)
- 1 tablespoon dried minced garlic
- 2 bags (1 lb each) frozen sliced carrots, thawed
- 1 to 2 tablespoons curry powder
- ⅛ teaspoon crushed red pepper flakes
- ¼ teaspoon salt
- 1 carton (32 oz) reduced-sodium chicken broth (for homemade broth, see page 528)
- 1 cup half-and-half

GARNISHES, IF DESIRED

Chopped dry-roasted peanuts
Chopped fresh cilantro or parsley

1 Spray 3½- to 4-quart slow cooker with cooking spray. In slow cooker, mix all soup ingredients except half-and-half.

2 Cover; cook on Low heat setting 7 to 9 hours.

3 Strain cooked vegetables from cooking liquid, reserving liquid. In blender or food processor, place vegetables. Cover; blend until smooth. Return vegetable puree to slow cooker.

4 Stir in 1½ cups of the reserved liquid and the half-and-half. Cover; cook on Low heat setting about 10 minutes longer or until warm. Garnish each serving with peanuts and cilantro.

1 Serving (1½ Cups): Calories 150; Total Fat 6g (Saturated Fat 3g; Trans Fat 0g); Cholesterol 15mg; Sodium 580mg; Total Carbohydrate 20g (Dietary Fiber 6g); Protein 4g **Exchanges:** ½ Other Carbohydrate, 2 Vegetable, 1½ Fat **Carbohydrate Choices:** 1

CHICKEN STEW WITH PEPPER AND PINEAPPLE LOWER CALORIE

To be sure you get every last drop of the ginger-flavored sauce, spoon the stew over hot cooked rice or noodles. Sprinkle with sliced green onions, toasted coconut or chopped cashews.

PREP 20 min TOTAL 7 hr 35 min ● **4 servings**

- 1 lb boneless skinless chicken breasts, cut into 1½-inch pieces
- 4 medium carrots, cut into 1-inch pieces
- ½ cup chicken broth
- 2 tablespoons soy sauce
- 2 tablespoons finely chopped gingerroot*
- 1 tablespoon packed brown sugar
- ½ teaspoon ground allspice
- ½ teaspoon red pepper sauce
- 1 tablespoon cornstarch
- 1 can (8 oz) pineapple chunks in juice, drained, juice reserved
- 1 medium green bell pepper, cut into 1-inch pieces

1 Spray 3½- to 6-quart slow cooker with cooking spray. In slow cooker, mix all ingredients except cornstarch, pineapple and bell pepper. Cover; cook on Low heat setting 7 to 8 hours (or High heat setting 3 to 4 hours) or until vegetables are tender and chicken is no longer pink in center.

2 In small bowl, mix cornstarch and reserved pineapple juice until smooth; gradually stir into chicken mixture. Stir in pineapple and bell pepper. Increase heat setting to High. Cover; cook about 15 minutes longer or until slightly thickened.

*1 teaspoon ground ginger can be substituted.

1 Serving: Calories 230; Total Fat 4g (Saturated Fat 1g; Trans Fat 0g); Cholesterol 65mg; Sodium 680mg; Total Carbohydrate 23g (Dietary Fiber 3g); Protein 26g **Exchanges:** 1 Fruit, 1 Vegetable, 3½ Very Lean Meat, ½ Fat **Carbohydrate Choices:** 1½

Blending Soups

Always use caution when blending any hot food in a blender or food processor. For either appliance, do not overfill. Blend vegetables in batches if necessary. For a blender, use the low speed and vent it by removing the center area of the cover so that any collected steam can escape.

HEARTY PORK STEW

PREP 25 min TOTAL 6 hr 55 min ● **6 servings**

- 1½ lb boneless pork loin, cut into 1-inch cubes
- 2 cups diced (½-inch pieces) peeled parsnips (3 medium)
- 1½ cups cubed (1-inch pieces) peeled butternut squash
- 3 medium carrots, cut into ¼-inch slices (1½ cups)
- 1 medium onion, chopped (½ cup)
- 1 carton (32 oz) chicken broth (4 cups; for homemade broth, see page 528)
- ½ teaspoon salt
- ½ teaspoon pepper
- 3 tablespoons all-purpose flour
- 3 tablespoons butter, softened

1 Spray 3½- to 6-quart slow cooker with cooking spray. In slow cooker, mix all ingredients except flour and butter. Cover; cook on Low heat setting 6 to 7 hours (or High heat setting 3 to 4 hours) or until pork is no longer pink and vegetables are tender.

2 Mix flour and butter; gently stir into pork mixture, 1 spoonful at a time, until blended. Increase heat setting to High. Cover; cook 30 to 45 minutes longer, stirring occasionally, until thickened.

1 Serving: Calories 290; Total Fat 11g (Saturated Fat 5g; Trans Fat 0g); Cholesterol 65mg; Sodium 960mg; Total Carbohydrate 19g (Dietary Fiber 4g); Protein 27g **Exchanges:** 1 Starch, 1 Vegetable, 3 Lean Meat, ½ Fat **Carbohydrate Choices:** 1

Hearty Pork Stew

LEEK AND PARSNIP VEGETABLE STEW LOWER CALORIE

Leeks have a subtle flavor and are similar to scallions or green onions. After cutting the leeks in half, be sure to rinse them well to remove any grit trapped between the layers.

PREP 20 min **TOTAL** 8 hr 40 min • **8 servings**

- 4 medium red potatoes, cut into ½-inch pieces
- 2 medium leeks, cut in half lengthwise, rinsed and cut into ½-inch pieces (4 cups)
- 4 medium stalks celery, cut into ½-inch pieces (2 cups)
- 3 medium carrots, cut into ½-inch pieces (1½ cups)
- 2 medium parsnips, peeled, cut into ½-inch pieces (1½ cups)
- 1 can (28 oz) whole tomatoes, undrained, cut up
- 1 can (14 oz) chicken broth (for homemade broth, see page 528)
- ½ teaspoon dried thyme leaves
- ½ teaspoon dried rosemary leaves
- ½ teaspoon salt
- 3 tablespoons cornstarch
- 3 tablespoons cold water

1 Spray 4- to 5-quart slow cooker with cooking spray. In slow cooker, mix all ingredients except cornstarch and water. Cover; cook on Low heat setting 8 to 10 hours.

2 In small bowl, mix cornstarch and water until smooth; gradually stir into stew until blended. Increase heat setting to High. Cover; cook about 20 minutes longer, stirring occasionally, or until thickened.

1 Serving: Calories 150; Total Fat 0.5g (Saturated Fat 0g; Trans Fat 0g); Cholesterol 0mg; Sodium 550mg; Total Carbohydrate 31g (Dietary Fiber 5g); Protein 4g **Exchanges:** 5 Vegetable **Carbohydrate Choices:** 2

Jazzing Up Slow-Cooked Dishes

Long slow cooker times often cause colors to dull and flavors to meld. To add some spark to your finished dish, try one of these easy toppers:

- Chopped fresh herbs, whole herb leaves or herb sprigs
- Chopped or sliced avocados, onions, bell peppers, chiles or tomatoes
- Citrus zest or strips
- Cubed, diced, shaved, shredded, crumbled or grated cheese
- Coarsely broken or crushed potato, tortilla or corn chips
- Whole or coarsely crushed croutons (for homemade croutons, see page 455)
- Small-sized savory snack mixes
- Crumbled, crisply cooked bacon
- Toasted or untoasted nuts (see page 22)
- Sour cream or plain yogurt

Leek and Parsnip Vegetable Stew

SOUPS, SANDWICHES & PIZZAS

SOUPS

SANDWICHES AND PIZZAS

FEATURES

For bonus **soups, sandwiches and pizzas** recipes, visit bettycrocker.com/BCcookbook

---

FAST = Ready in 20 minutes or less LOWER CALORIE = See Helpful Nutrition and Cooking Information, page 685
LIGHTER = 25% fewer calories or grams of fat MAKE AHEAD = Make-ahead directions SLOW COOKER = Slow cooker directions

← Grilled Cheese (page 547), Gazpacho (page 537), Pizza made with thin crust (page 543), Cuban Pork Sandwiches (page 547)

SOUP BASICS
Whether clear or creamy, hot or cold, quickly cooked or slowly simmered, these soul-stirring soups are perfect for any meal.

TIPS FOR SUCCESSFUL SOUPS

- Use the pan size specified in the recipe. If the pan is too small, the soup may boil over or the mixture may heat too slowly, resulting in overcooked vegetables and meats.

- To ensure even cooking, cut vegetables so they are similar in size.

- Heat cream or cheese soups slowly. Boiling can cause the soup to separate and curdle.

- To remove the fat that floats to the top, see Skimming Fat, page 528.

- Rice and pasta absorb liquid so you may want to cook them separately and add to the soup just before serving.

STORING AND REHEATING SOUPS

- Refrigerate soups in shallow containers so they cool rapidly. Once completely cooled, cover tightly. Refrigerate most soups with vegetables or meat no more than 3 days. Soups made with fish and shellfish should be eaten within 1 day.

- Most broth-based soups freeze well for up to 6 months. See Chicken Broth at Your Fingertips, page 529.

- Pour soup into freezer containers, leaving ¼- to ½-inch headspace because soups expand as they freeze.

- Soups made with cream may separate after freezing. To freeze this type of soup, add the cream after reheating it thoroughly. Heat again over low heat if necessary.

- Freezing potatoes makes them soft and mealy, so add cooked potatoes when reheating.

- Thaw frozen soups overnight in the refrigerator before reheating. Use right away.

- Reheat broth-based soups over medium heat, stirring occasionally, until hot. Or reheat in the microwave.

- Reheat soups containing milk or cheese over low heat, stirring frequently, until hot. Don't boil or soup may curdle or separate.

- Green bell pepper flavor intensifies after freezing and onion gradually loses flavor, so the seasoning may need to be adjusted to taste during reheating.

- Thick soups become thicker during storage. While reheating, add a little broth, milk or half-and-half until the soup reaches the desired consistency.

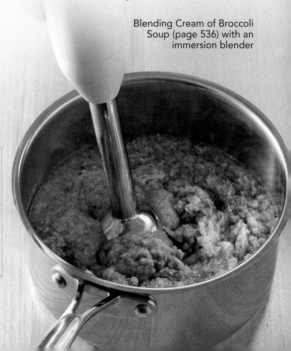

Blending Cream of Broccoli Soup (page 536) with an immersion blender

Immersion Blenders

Immersion blenders are made to go right into pans full of hot mixtures, eliminating the need to puree soup in batches in a blender or food processor. To avoid damaging the motor, submerge the blender just to the top of the stem. Follow the manufacturer's directions before using and washing.

Learn to Make **Chicken Broth**

CHICKEN AND BROTH

No store-bought variety of broth will ever stand up to the flavor and richness of homemade broth. Clear, low-fat, delicious broth is easy to achieve with a little know-how. Chicken noodle soup made from homemade broth will spoil you, and you'll make it again and again.

PREP 25 min **TOTAL** 1 hr 25 min • **4 cups broth and 2½ to 3 cups cooked chicken**

1 cut-up whole chicken (3 to 3½ lb)*	1 medium carrot, cut up
1 teaspoon salt	1 small onion, cut up
½ teaspoon pepper	1 sprig fresh parsley
1 medium stalk celery with leaves, cut up	4½ cups cold water

1 In 4-quart Dutch oven or stockpot, place chicken. Add remaining ingredients; heat to boiling. Skim foam from broth; reduce heat. Cover; simmer about 45 minutes or until juice of chicken is clear when thickest part is cut to bone (at least 165°F).

2 Carefully remove chicken from broth by placing wooden spoon into cavity and lifting with fork or tongs. Cool chicken about 10 minutes or just until cool enough to handle. Strain broth through fine strainer; discard vegetables.

3 Remove skin and bones from chicken. Cut chicken into ½-inch pieces. Skim fat from broth. Use broth and chicken immediately, or cover and refrigerate broth and chicken in separate containers up to 24 hours or freeze up to 6 months.

*3 to 3½ lb chicken parts can be used to make broth.

1 Serving (1 Cup Broth and About ½ Cup Chicken): Calories 240; Total Fat 8g (Saturated Fat 2g, Trans Fat 0g); Cholesterol 90mg; Sodium 990mg; Total Carbohydrate 14g (Dietary Fiber 3g); Protein 29g **Exchanges:** ½ Starch, 1 Vegetable, 3½ Very Lean Meat, 1 Fat **Carbohydrate Choices:** 1

SLOW COOKER DIRECTIONS Decrease water to 3 cups. Increase salt to 1¼ teaspoons. Spray 5- to 6-quart slow cooker with cooking spray. In slow cooker, mix all ingredients. Cover; cook on Low heat setting 8 to 10 hours. Continue as directed in Step 2.

Keys to Success

- Coarsely chop the celery, carrots, and onion. Uneven pieces are fine for broth, as they will be strained out.

- **Bring mixture to a boil, then reduce to a simmer** to prevent additional fat from leaching from chicken bones and causing broth to be cloudy.

- **Skim foam created by simmering chicken in water.** This foam needs to be discarded to achieve a flavorful, broth.

- **Remove skin and bones while chicken is still warm** but just cool enough to handle. Simply peel away skin and pull bones away from meat.

- **Strain broth using fine strainer** or strainer lined with cheesecloth.

- **Discard vegetables from broth.** Vegetables impart flavor and add vitamins and minerals to broth, but they get overcooked and lose flavor in the process.

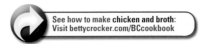

See how to make chicken and broth: Visit bettycrocker.com/BCcookbook

CHICKEN NOODLE SOUP

LOWER CALORIE

PREP 1 hr 25 min **TOTAL** 2 hr • **6 servings**

    Chicken and Broth (at left)
4 **medium carrots, sliced (2 cups)**
4 **medium stalks celery, sliced (2 cups)**
1 **medium onion, chopped (½ cup)**
1 **cup uncooked medium egg noodles (2 oz)**
    Chopped fresh parsley, if desired

1 Refrigerate cut-up cooked chicken. Add enough water to broth to measure 5 cups.

2 In 4-quart Dutch oven or stockpot, heat broth, carrots, celery and onion to boiling; reduce heat. Cover; simmer about 15 minutes or until carrots are tender.

3 Stir in noodles and chicken. Heat to boiling; reduce heat. Simmer uncovered 7 to 10 minutes or until noodles are tender. Sprinkle with parsley.

1 Serving (1 Cup): Calories 240; Total Fat 8g (Saturated Fat 2g; Trans Fat 0g); Cholesterol 90mg; Sodium 990mg; Total Carbohydrate 14g (Dietary Fiber 3g); Protein 29g **Exchanges:** ½ Starch, 1 Vegetable, 3½ Very Lean Meat, 1 Fat **Carbohydrate Choices:** 1

CHICKEN RICE SOUP Substitute ½ cup uncooked regular long-grain white rice for the uncooked noodles. Stir in rice with the vegetables. Cover; simmer about 15 minutes or until rice is tender. Stir in chicken; heat until chicken is hot.

CONFETTI CHICKEN NOODLE SOUP Add ½ cup each frozen sweet peas and corn with noodles and chicken in Step 3. Continue as directed.

QUICK CHICKEN SOUP Make as directed—except substitute 3 cans (14 oz each) chicken broth and 2 cups cut-up cooked chicken or turkey for the chicken and broth.

Skimming Fat

With Fat Separator:
Pour or ladle warm broth into fat separator; let stand a few minutes for fat to rise to surface. Pour out broth carefully, stopping when you get to the layer of fat.

With Spoon:
Refrigerate broth 6 to 8 hours or overnight, until fat hardens on surface. Carefully scoop fat from surface with spoon.

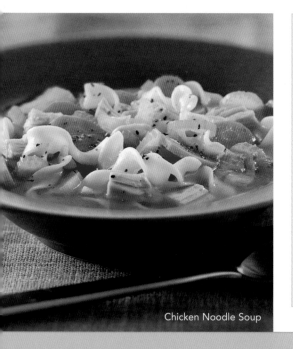

Chicken Noodle Soup

Chicken Broth at Your Fingertips

Make broth when you've got the time. Then keep the broth in the freezer for when you have a recipe that calls for it. Freeze broth in small or large quantities so you'll always be able to thaw just the right amount for your recipe. Label containers with the date and amount, and use within 6 months.

- Freeze in ice cube trays for broth in small amounts. Once frozen, transfer cubes to a resealable plastic freezer bag.

- Freeze in ½- or 1-cup portions in resealable plastic freezer bags or freezer containers to pull out and use when recipes call for more than a tablespoon or two.

- Freeze the entire amount in a large freezer container. This is perfect if you like to make homemade soups and other recipes calling for a lot of broth.

BEEF AND BROTH LOWER CALORIE

PREP 30 min TOTAL 3 hr 45 min • **6 cups broth and 1 cup cooked beef**

- 2 lb beef shank cross cuts or soup bones
- 2 tablespoons vegetable oil, if desired
- 6 cups cold water
- 1 medium carrot, chopped (½ cup)
- 1 medium stalk celery with leaves, chopped (½ cup)
- 1 small onion, chopped (⅓ cup)
- 1 teaspoon salt
- ¼ teaspoon dried thyme leaves
- 5 black peppercorns
- 3 whole cloves
- 3 sprigs fresh parsley
- 1 dried bay leaf

1 Remove marrow from centers of bones. In 4-quart Dutch oven or stockpot, melt marrow over low heat until hot, or heat 2 tablespoons oil. Cook beef shanks in marrow or oil over medium heat until brown on both sides.

2 Add water; heat to boiling. Skim foam from broth. Stir in remaining ingredients; heat to boiling. Skim foam from broth; reduce heat. Cover; simmer 3 hours.

3 Remove beef from broth. Cool beef about 10 minutes or just until cool enough to handle. Strain broth through fine strainer; discard vegetables and seasonings.

4 Remove beef from bones. Cut beef into ½-inch pieces. Skim fat from broth. Use broth and beef immediately, or cover and refrigerate broth and beef in separate containers up to 24 hours or freeze up to 6 months.

1 Cup: Calories 120; Total Fat 3g (Saturated Fat 1g; Trans Fat 0g); Cholesterol 50mg; Sodium 440mg; Total Carbohydrate 2g (Dietary Fiber 0g); Protein 20g **Exchanges:** ½ Vegetable, 2½ Very Lean Meat, ½ Fat **Carbohydrate Choices:** 0

SLOW COOKER DIRECTIONS Decrease water to 5 cups. Increase salt to 1¼ teaspoons. In 10-inch skillet, heat marrow or 2 tablespoons oil over medium heat. Cook beef in marrow or oil until brown on both sides. Spray 3½- to 6-quart slow cooker with cooking spray. In slow cooker, mix remaining ingredients; add beef. Cover; cook on Low heat setting 8 to 10 hours. Continue as directed in Step 3.

VEGETABLE BROTH LOWER CALORIE

Mild vegetables are preferred for a well-balanced neutral flavor. Broccoli, rutabaga, red cabbage or other strong-flavored vegetables would overpower the broth or give it a muddy, objectionable color.

PREP 20 min TOTAL 1 hr 30 min • **8 cups broth**

- 8 cups cold water
- 6 cups coarsely chopped mild vegetables (bell peppers, carrots, celery, leeks, mushrooms*, potatoes, spinach or zucchini)
- 1 medium onion, coarsely chopped (½ cup)
- 4 cloves garlic, finely chopped
- ½ cup fresh parsley sprigs
- 2 tablespoons chopped fresh or 2 teaspoons dried basil leaves
- 2 tablespoons chopped fresh or 2 teaspoons dried thyme leaves
- 1 teaspoon salt
- ¼ teaspoon cracked black pepper
- 2 dried bay leaves

1 In 4-quart Dutch oven or stockpot, mix all ingredients. Heat to boiling; reduce heat. Cover; simmer 1 hour, stirring occasionally.

2 Cool about 10 minutes. Strain broth through fine strainer; discard vegetables and seasonings. Use broth immediately, or cover and refrigerate up to 24 hours or freeze up to 6 months. Stir before measuring.

*Some mushrooms have woody stems that cannot be eaten, but they can be used to flavor the broth and then discarded.

1 Cup: Calories 50; Total Fat 0g (Saturated Fat 0g; Trans Fat 0g); Cholesterol 0mg; Sodium 380mg; Total Carbohydrate 11g (Dietary Fiber 2g); Protein 1g **Exchanges:** ½ Starch, 1 Vegetable **Carbohydrate Choices:** 1

Freezing Broth

Freeze broth in ice-cube trays. Once frozen, put broth into resealable freezer plastic bags and store in freezer.

FISH BROTH LOWER CALORIE

Celery leaves add great flavor to broth. Try adding chopped celery leaves along with the celery stalks called for in soup recipes.

PREP 20 min TOTAL 1 hr • **6 cups broth**

- 1½ **lb fish bones and trimmings**
- 4 **cups cold water**
- 2 **cups dry white wine or clam juice**
- 1 **large stalk celery with leaves, chopped**
- 1 **small onion, sliced**
- 3 **medium fresh mushrooms, chopped**
- 1 **tablespoon lemon juice**
- 1 **teaspoon salt**
- ½ **teaspoon dried thyme leaves**
- 3 **sprigs fresh parsley**
- 1 **dried bay leaf**

1 Rinse fish bones and trimmings with cold water; drain. In 4-quart Dutch oven or stockpot, mix bones, trimmings, 4 cups cold water and remaining ingredients; heat to boiling. Skim foam from broth; reduce heat. Cover; simmer 30 minutes.

2 Cool about 10 minutes. Strain broth through fine strainer; discard skin, bones, vegetables and seasonings. Use broth immediately, or cover and refrigerate up to 24 hours or freeze up to 6 months.

1 Cup: Calories 25; Total Fat 0g (Saturated Fat 0g; Trans Fat 0g); Cholesterol 0mg; Sodium 1200mg; Total Carbohydrate 3g (Dietary Fiber 0g); Protein 0g **Exchanges:** ½ Vegetable **Carbohydrate Choices:** 0

Using Fish Broth

Plan to make fish broth next time you have leftover bones and trimmings from any fish. The broth is great to use for any fish- or seafood-based soup or stew such as:

- Hearty Seafood Stew, page 300
- Jambalaya, page 519
- Manhattan Clam Chowder, page 534
- New England Clam Chowder, page 534
- Oyster Stew, page 533
- Shrimp Creole, page 296

CHICKEN TORTILLA SOUP

LOWER CALORIE

PREP 15 min TOTAL 35 min • **4 servings**

- 3 **teaspoons vegetable oil**
- 4 **soft corn tortillas (5 or 6 inch), cut into 2 x ½-inch strips**
- 1 **medium onion, chopped (½ cup)**
- 2 **cans (14 oz each) chicken broth (for homemade broth, see page 528)**
- 1 **can (10 oz) diced tomatoes with green chiles, undrained**
- 1½ **cups shredded cooked chicken**
- 1 **tablespoon lime juice**
- 1 **tablespoon chopped fresh cilantro or parsley**

1 In 2-quart nonstick saucepan, heat 2 teaspoons of the oil over medium-high heat. Add tortilla strips; cook 30 to 60 seconds, stirring occasionally, until crisp and light golden brown. Remove from saucepan; drain on paper towels.

2 In same saucepan, cook onion in remaining 1 teaspoon oil over medium-high heat, stirring occasionally, until tender. Stir in broth and tomatoes. Heat to boiling; reduce heat. Simmer uncovered 20 minutes. Stir in chicken; heat until hot.

3 Stir in lime juice. Sprinkle tortilla strips on top of soup or spoon soup over tortilla strips. Sprinkle with cilantro.

1 Serving: Calories 230; Total Fat 8g (Saturated Fat 1.5g; Trans Fat 0g); Cholesterol 45mg; Sodium 1100mg; Total Carbohydrate 17g (Dietary Fiber 3g); Protein 22g **Exchanges:** 1 Starch, 2½ Very Lean Meat, 1 Fat **Carbohydrate Choices:** 1

Chicken Tortilla Soup

VEGETABLE-BEEF SOUP

The prep time is long on this recipe, but if you already have the beef broth ready, you are almost there! Serve this hearty soup with fresh bakery Italian rolls to complete the meal.

PREP **3 hr 45 min** TOTAL **4 hr 30 min** • **7 servings**

Beef and Broth (page 530)
1 ear fresh sweet corn or ½ cup frozen whole kernel corn
2 medium potatoes, cubed (2 cups)
2 medium tomatoes, chopped (1½ cups)
2 medium carrots, thinly sliced (1 cup)
2 medium stalks celery, sliced (1 cup)
1 medium onion, chopped (½ cup)
1 cup 1-inch pieces fresh green beans or frozen cut green beans
1 cup shelled green peas or 1 cup frozen sweet peas
¼ teaspoon pepper

1 If necessary, add enough water to beef broth to measure 5 cups. Return strained beef and broth to 4-quart Dutch oven.

2 Cut kernels from ear of corn. Stir corn and remaining ingredients into broth. Heat to boiling; reduce heat. Cover; simmer about 30 minutes or until vegetables are tender.

1 Serving (1½ Cups): Calories 240; Total Fat 9g (Saturated Fat 3.5g; Trans Fat 0g); Cholesterol 45mg; Sodium 640mg; Total Carbohydrate 19g (Dietary Fiber 4g); Protein 20g **Exchanges:** 1 Starch, 1 Vegetable, 2 Lean Meat, ½ Fat **Carbohydrate Choices:** 1

BORSCHT

This recipe for a traditional favorite from Russia and Poland calls for mixed pickling spice, which is available at most grocery stores. It usually includes a fragrant combination of coarse pieces of allspice, bay leaves, cardamom, cinnamon, cloves, coriander, ginger, mustard seed and peppercorns.

PREP **25 min** TOTAL **4 hr 5 min** • **6 servings**

¾ lb boneless beef chuck, tip or round roast, cut into ½-inch cubes
1 smoked pork hock
4 cups water
1 can (10½ oz) condensed beef broth
1 teaspoon salt
¼ teaspoon pepper
4 medium beets, cooked (page 587), or 1 can (15 oz) sliced beets, drained
3 cups shredded green cabbage
2 medium potatoes, peeled, cubed (2 cups)
1 large onion, sliced
2 cloves garlic, finely chopped
1 tablespoon mixed pickling spice
2 teaspoons dill seed or 1 sprig fresh dill weed
¼ cup red wine vinegar
¾ cup sour cream
Chopped fresh dill weed, if desired

1 In 4-quart Dutch oven, place beef, pork hock, water, broth, salt and pepper. Heat to boiling; reduce heat. Cover; simmer 1 hour to 1 hour 30 minutes or until beef is tender.

2 Shred beets, or cut into ¼-inch strips. Remove pork hock from soup; let stand until cool enough to handle. Remove pork from bone; cut pork into bite-size pieces.

3 Stir pork, beets, cabbage, potatoes, onion and garlic into soup. Tie pickling spice and dill seed in cheesecloth bag or place in tea ball; add to soup. Cover; simmer 2 hours.

4 Stir in vinegar. Simmer uncovered 10 minutes. Remove spice bag. Serve soup with sour cream. Sprinkle with fresh dill.

1 Serving: Calories 270; Total Fat 14g (Saturated Fat 7g; Trans Fat 0g); Cholesterol 60mg; Sodium 810mg; Total Carbohydrate 18g (Dietary Fiber 3g); Protein 18g **Exchanges:** 4 Vegetable, 2 Medium-Fat Meat, ½ Fat **Carbohydrate Choices:** 1

Borscht

SLOW COOKER **DIRECTIONS** Decrease water to 3 cups. Shred beets, or cut into ¼-inch strips. Spray 4- to 6-quart slow cooker with cooking spray. In slow cooker, mix all ingredients except vinegar, sour cream and fresh dill. Cover; cook on Low heat setting 8 to 10 hours. Remove pork hock and cut pork as directed in Step 2. Stir pork and vinegar into soup. Cover; cook on Low heat setting 10 minutes. Serve soup with sour cream. Sprinkle with fresh dill.

MINESTRONE WITH ITALIAN SAUSAGE

Top each serving with a little chopped fresh basil or a fresh basil sprig for an extra burst of color and flavor.

PREP 45 min TOTAL 45 min • **7 servings**

- 1 tablespoon olive or vegetable oil
- 1 lb bulk sweet Italian pork sausage
- 2 medium carrots, coarsely chopped (1 cup)
- 1 medium onion, chopped (½ cup)
- 2 teaspoons dried basil leaves
- 2 teaspoons finely chopped garlic
- 5¼ cups beef broth (for homemade broth, see page 530)
- 1 can (14.5 oz) diced tomatoes, undrained
- 1 can (15.5 oz) great northern beans, drained, rinsed
- 1 cup uncooked small elbow macaroni (4 oz)
- 1 medium zucchini, cut in half lengthwise, then cut into ¼-inch slices (1 cup)
- 1 cup frozen cut green beans

1 In 5-quart Dutch oven, heat oil over medium-high heat. Add sausage, carrots, onion, basil and garlic; cook 5 to 7 minutes, stirring frequently, until sausage is no longer pink; drain.

2 Stir broth, tomatoes and great northern beans into sausage mixture. Heat to boiling. Reduce heat to medium-low; cover and cook 7 to 8 minutes, stirring occasionally.

3 Stir in macaroni, zucchini and frozen green beans. Heat to boiling. Cook over medium-high heat 5 to 6 minutes, stirring occasionally, until vegetables are hot and macaroni is tender.

1 Serving (1½ Cups): Calories 380; Total Fat 16g (Saturated Fat 5g; Trans Fat 0g); Cholesterol 25mg; Sodium 1400mg; Total Carbohydrate 38g (Dietary Fiber 6g); Protein 20g **Exchanges:** 2 Starch, 1 Vegetable, 1½ Medium-Fat Meat, 1½ Fat **Carbohydrate Choices:** 2½

MEATLESS MINESTRONE Substitute 1 can (15.5 oz) of great northern beans or your favorite canned beans for the sausage and use vegetable broth instead of beef broth.

OYSTER STEW FAST

PREP 10 min TOTAL 20 min • **4 servings**

- ¼ cup butter
- 1 pint shucked oysters, undrained or fresh shucked oysters in their liquid
- 2 cups milk
- ½ cup half-and-half
- ½ teaspoon salt
  Dash pepper
  Oyster crackers, if desired

1 In 1½-quart saucepan, melt butter over low heat. Stir in oysters. Cook 2 to 4 minutes, stirring occasionally, just until edges curl.

2 In 2-quart saucepan, heat milk and half-and-half over medium-low heat until hot. Stir in salt, pepper and oyster mixture; heat until hot. Sprinkle each serving with oyster crackers.

1 Serving (1 Cup): Calories 290; Total Fat 20g (Saturated Fat 10g; Trans Fat 1g); Cholesterol 115mg; Sodium 700mg; Total Carbohydrate 12g (Dietary Fiber 0g); Protein 14g **Exchanges:** 1 Low-Fat Milk, 1 Medium-Fat Meat, 3 Fat **Carbohydrate Choices:** 1

Shucking Fresh Oysters

Slip tip of oyster knife between top and bottom shells, next to hinge. Carefully run knife around oyster to other side of hinge, using twisting motion, to pry top and bottom shells apart.

Cut muscle attached in middle of oyster to both top and bottom shells to spread apart and separate. Remove top shell from bottom, being careful to not spill oyster juice in bottom shell.

Remove meat from bottom shell by sliding knife inward, under meat, close against surface of bottom shell, to keep meat intact.

NEW ENGLAND CLAM CHOWDER

PREP 10 min TOTAL 30 min • **4 servings**

- 4 slices bacon, cut into ½-inch pieces
- 1 medium onion, chopped (½ cup)
- 1 medium stalk celery, sliced (½ cup)
- 2 cans (6½ oz each) minced or chopped clams, drained, ¼ cup liquid reserved*
- 2¾ cups milk or half-and-half
- 2 medium peeled potatoes, diced (2 cups)
- ¼ teaspoon salt
   Dash pepper
- ¼ cup all-purpose flour
   Chopped fresh parsley, if desired

1 In 3-quart saucepan, cook bacon, onion and celery over medium heat, stirring occasionally, until bacon is crisp and onion is tender; drain.

2 Stir clam liquid, clams, ¾ cup of the milk, the potatoes, salt and pepper into bacon and onion. Heat to boiling; reduce heat. Cover; simmer about 15 minutes or until potatoes are tender.

3 In medium bowl, whisk remaining milk and the flour until smooth and blended. Stir into clam mixture. Heat to boiling, stirring frequently. Boil and stir 1 minute until thickened. Sprinkle each serving with parsley.

*1 pint shucked fresh clams with their liquid can be substituted. Chop the clams and stir in with the potato in Step 2.

1 Serving (1¼ Cups): Calories 240; Total Fat 5g (Saturated Fat 1.5g; Trans Fat 0g); Cholesterol 75mg; Sodium 490mg; Total Carbohydrate 19g (Dietary Fiber 1g); Protein 29g **Exchanges:** ½ Starch, ½ Low-Fat Milk, 1 Vegetable, 3 Very Lean Meat, 1 Fat **Carbohydrate Choices:** 1

MANHATTAN CLAM CHOWDER

Cooks in Rhode Island in the late 1800s liked to throw tomatoes into clam chowder. Sometime in the mid-twentieth century, their creation became known as Manhattan clam chowder. It resembles New England clam chowder but is made with tomatoes instead of milk or cream.

PREP 15 min TOTAL 35 min • **4 servings**

- ¼ cup chopped bacon or salt pork
- 1 small onion, finely chopped (⅓ cup)
- 2 cans (6½ oz each) minced or chopped clams, undrained*
- 2 medium peeled potatoes, diced (2 cups)
- ⅓ cup chopped celery
- 1 cup water
- 1 can (14.5 oz) whole tomatoes, undrained
- 2 teaspoons chopped fresh parsley
- 1 teaspoon chopped fresh or ¼ teaspoon dried thyme leaves
- ¼ teaspoon salt
- ⅛ teaspoon pepper

1 In 2-quart saucepan, cook bacon and onion over medium heat 8 to 10 minutes, stirring occasionally, until bacon is crisp and onion is tender; drain.

2 Stir in clams, potatoes, celery and water. Heat to boiling; reduce heat. Cover; simmer about 10 minutes or until potatoes are tender.

3 Stir in remaining ingredients, breaking up tomatoes with fork. Heat to boiling, stirring occasionally.

*1 pint shucked fresh clams with their liquid can be substituted. Chop the clams and stir in with the potatoes in Step 2.

1 Serving: Calories 230; Total Fat 3g (Saturated Fat 0.5g; Trans Fat 0g); Cholesterol 65mg; Sodium 450mg; Total Carbohydrate 23g (Dietary Fiber 3g); Protein 26g **Exchanges:** 1 Starch, 2 Vegetable, 3 Very Lean Meat **Carbohydrate Choices:** 1½

SLOW COOKER DIRECTIONS In 10-inch skillet, cook bacon (without onion) as directed in Step 1. Spray 2- to 3½-quart slow cooker with cooking spray. In slow cooker, mix bacon, onion and remaining ingredients except clams and thyme. Cover; cook on Low heat setting 9 to 10 hours. Stir in undrained clams and thyme. Increase heat setting to High. Cover; cook 10 to 20 minutes or until hot.

New England Clam Chowder

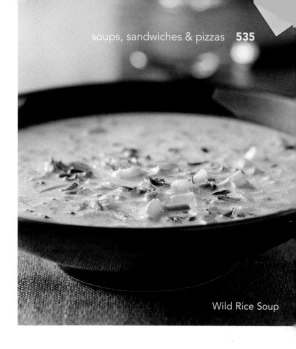

Wild Rice Soup

WILD RICE SOUP

PREP 35 min TOTAL 1 hr 10 min • **7 servings**

- ¼ cup butter
- 4 medium stalks celery, sliced (2 cups)
- 2 medium carrots, coarsely shredded (2 cups)
- 1 large onion, chopped (1 cup)
- 1 medium green bell pepper, chopped (1 cup)
- ¼ cup plus 2 tablespoons all-purpose flour
- 1 teaspoon salt
- ½ teaspoon pepper
- 3 cups cooked wild rice (page 429)
- 2 cups water
- 2 cans (10½ oz each) condensed chicken broth
- 3 cups half-and-half
- ⅔ cup slivered almonds, toasted (page 22), if desired
- ½ cup chopped fresh parsley

1 In 4-quart saucepan or Dutch oven, melt butter over medium-high heat. Cook celery, carrots, onion and bell pepper in butter about 10 minutes, stirring frequently, until crisp-tender.

2 Stir in flour, salt and pepper. Stir in wild rice, water and broth. Heat to boiling; reduce heat. Cover; simmer 15 minutes, stirring occasionally.

3 Stir in half-and-half, almonds and parsley. Heat just until hot (do not boil or soup may curdle).

1 Serving: Calories 360; Total Fat 20g (Saturated Fat 11g; Trans Fat 1g); Cholesterol 55mg; Sodium 1240mg; Total Carbohydrate 33g (Dietary Fiber 4g); Protein 12g **Exchanges:** 2 Starch, 1 Vegetable, ½ Very Lean Meat, 3½ Fat **Carbohydrate Choices:** 2

LIGHTER **DIRECTIONS** For 3 grams of fat and 215 calories per serving, omit butter; spray saucepan with cooking spray before heating. Use fat-free half-and-half.

CHICKEN–WILD RICE SOUP Stir in 4 cups cubed cooked chicken or turkey in Step 3.

Learn with Betty | WILD RICE

Perfect Wild Rice: Many rice kernels have opened, revealing their cream-colored interiors, and are tender, yet chewy.

Undercooked Wild Rice: The rice kernels are firm and chewy and have not opened.

Overcooked Wild Rice: All of the rice kernels have opened and curled. The texture is very soft and mushy.

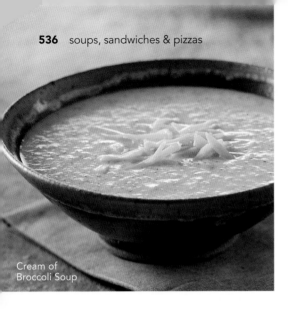

Cream of
Broccoli Soup

CREAM OF BROCCOLI SOUP

LOWER CALORIE

PREP 35 min **TOTAL** 45 min • **8 servings**

1½ lb fresh broccoli
2 cups water
1 large stalk celery, chopped (¾ cup)
1 medium onion, chopped (½ cup)
2 tablespoons butter
2 tablespoons all-purpose flour
2½ cups chicken broth (for homemade broth, see page 528)
½ teaspoon salt
⅛ teaspoon pepper
Dash ground nutmeg
½ cup whipping cream
Shredded cheese, if desired

1 Remove florets from broccoli. Cut stalks into 1-inch pieces, discarding any leaves.

2 In 3-quart saucepan, heat water to boiling. Add broccoli florets and stalk pieces, celery and onion. Cover; heat to boiling. Reduce heat; simmer 7 to 10 minutes or until broccoli is tender (do not drain).

3 In blender, carefully place broccoli mixture. Cover; blend on medium speed 30 to 60 seconds or until smooth. Set aside.

4 In same saucepan, melt butter over medium heat. Stir in flour. Cook, stirring constantly, until mixture is smooth and bubbly; remove from heat. Stir in broth. Heat to boiling, stirring constantly. Boil and stir 1 minute.

5 Stir in broccoli mixture, salt, pepper and nutmeg; heat just to boiling. Stir in whipping cream; heat just until hot (do not boil or soup may curdle). Serve soup topped with cheese.

1 Serving (1 Cup): Calories 110; Total Fat 8g (Saturated Fat 4.5g; Trans Fat 0g); Cholesterol 25mg; Sodium 510mg; Total Carbohydrate 6g (Dietary Fiber 2g); Protein 4g **Exchanges:** 2 Vegetable, 1 Fat **Carbohydrate Choices:** ½

CREAM OF CAULIFLOWER SOUP Substitute 1 medium head cauliflower (about 2 lb), separated into florets, for the broccoli. Add 1 tablespoon lemon juice with the onion in Step 2.

TOMATO-BASIL SOUP

LOWER CALORIE

Fully ripe, juicy tomatoes provide the best flavor for this soup. If your tomatoes aren't completely ripe, you may need to increase the salt and sugar just a bit.

PREP 30 min **TOTAL** 1 hr • **4 servings**

2 tablespoons olive or vegetable oil
1 medium carrot, finely chopped (½ cup)
1 medium onion, finely chopped (½ cup)
1 clove garlic, finely chopped
6 large tomatoes, peeled, seeded and chopped (6 cups)*
1 can (8 oz) tomato sauce
¼ cup thinly sliced fresh or 2 teaspoons dried basil leaves
½ teaspoon sugar
¼ teaspoon salt
Dash pepper

1 In 3-quart saucepan, heat oil over medium heat. Cook carrot, onion and garlic in oil about 10 minutes, stirring occasionally, until tender but not brown.

2 Stir in tomatoes. Cook uncovered about 10 minutes, stirring occasionally, until heated through.

3 Stir in remaining ingredients. Cook uncovered about 10 minutes, stirring occasionally, until hot.

3 cans (14.5 oz each) diced tomatoes, undrained, can be substituted. Omit salt; increase sugar to 1 teaspoon.

1 Serving: Calories 170; Total Fat 8g (Saturated Fat 1g; Trans Fat 0g); Cholesterol 0mg; Sodium 550mg; Total Carbohydrate 22g (Dietary Fiber 6g); Protein 4g **Exchanges:** 4 Vegetable, 1 Fat **Carbohydrate Choices:** 1½

FRENCH ONION SOUP

The long, slow cooking of the onions gives this soup its rich flavor and color. Gruyère cheese is a rich, nutty, buttery-tasting form of Swiss cheese with fewer and smaller holes.

PREP 20 min TOTAL 1 hr 30 min • **4 servings**

- 2 **tablespoons butter**
- 4 **medium onions, sliced**
- 2 **cans (10½ oz each) condensed beef broth**
- 1½ **cups water**
- ⅛ **teaspoon pepper**
- ⅛ **teaspoon dried thyme leaves**
- 1 **dried bay leaf**
- 4 **slices (¾ to 1 inch thick) toasted French bread**
- 1 **cup shredded Gruyère, Swiss or mozzarella cheese (4 oz)**
- ¼ **cup grated Parmesan cheese**

1 In 4-quart nonstick Dutch oven, melt butter over medium-high heat. Stir in onions to coat with butter. Cook uncovered 10 minutes, stirring every 3 to 4 minutes. Reduce heat to medium-low. Cook 35 to 40 minutes longer, stirring well every 5 minutes, until onions are deep golden brown (onions will shrink during cooking).

2 Stir in broth, water, pepper, thyme and bay leaf. Heat to boiling; reduce heat. Cover; simmer 15 minutes. Remove bay leaf.

3 Set oven control to broil. Place toasted bread in 4 ovenproof bowls or individual ceramic casseroles.* Add soup. Sprinkle with cheeses. Place bowls on cookie sheet or in pan with shallow sides.

4 Broil with cheese about 5 inches from heat 1 to 2 minutes or just until cheese is melted and golden brown. Watch carefully so cheese does not burn. Serve with additional French bread if desired.

*Do not use glass containers; they cannot withstand the heat from the broiler and may break.

1 Serving: Calories 360; Total Fat 18g (Saturated Fat 10g; Trans Fat 1g); Cholesterol 50mg; Sodium 1210mg; Total Carbohydrate 28g (Dietary Fiber 3g); Protein 22g **Exchanges:** 2 Starch, 2 High-Fat Meat **Carbohydrate Choices:** 2

GOLDEN ONION SOUP Omit French bread and cheeses; do not broil.

GAZPACHO LOWER CALORIE

PREP 20 min TOTAL 1 hr 20 min • **8 servings**

- 1 **can (28 oz) whole tomatoes, undrained**
- 1 **medium green bell pepper, finely chopped (1 cup)**
- 1 **cup finely chopped cucumber**
- 1 **cup croutons**
- 1 **medium onion, chopped (½ cup)**
- 2 **tablespoons dry white wine or chicken broth**
- 2 **tablespoons olive or vegetable oil**
- 1 **tablespoon ground cumin**
- 1 **tablespoon white vinegar**
- ½ **teaspoon salt**
- ¼ **teaspoon pepper**

1 In blender or food processor, place tomatoes, ½ cup of the bell pepper, ½ cup of the cucumber, ½ cup of the croutons, ¼ cup of the onion and the remaining ingredients. Cover; blend on medium speed 30 to 60 seconds until smooth. Pour into large bowl.

2 Cover; refrigerate at least 1 hour. Serve remaining vegetables and croutons as accompaniments.

1 Serving (½ Cup): Calories 80; Total Fat 4g (Saturated Fat 0.5g; Trans Fat 0g); Cholesterol 0mg; Sodium 320mg; Total Carbohydrate 10g (Dietary Fiber 2g); Protein 2g **Exchanges:** 2 Vegetable, ½ Fat **Carbohydrate Choices:** ½

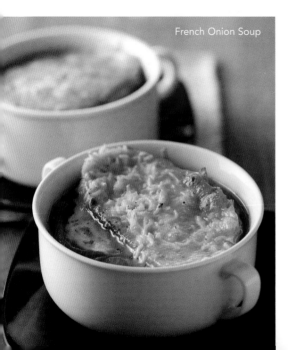
French Onion Soup

BUTTERNUT SQUASH SOUP

This wonderfully rich, thick and flavorful soup became a staff favorite while being tested in our kitchens. Try it with the Maple-Pecan Apple Salsa in the variation, or just sprinkle servings with chopped toasted walnuts, or pumpkin seeds.

PREP 30 min **TOTAL** 45 min • **6 servings**

- 2 **tablespoons butter**
- 1 **medium onion, chopped (½ cup)**
- 1 **butternut squash (2 lb), peeled, seeded and cubed***
- 2 **cups chicken broth (for homemade broth, see page 528)**
- ½ **teaspoon dried marjoram leaves**
- ¼ **teaspoon black pepper**
- ⅛ **teaspoon ground red pepper (cayenne)**
- 1 **package (8 oz) cream cheese, cubed**
  Additional chicken broth or water, if desired

1 In 3-quart saucepan, melt butter over medium heat. Cook onion in butter, stirring occasionally, until crisp-tender.

2 Add all remaining ingredients except cream cheese. Heat to boiling; reduce heat. Cover; simmer 12 to 15 minutes or until squash is tender.

3 In blender or food processor, place one-third each of the soup mixture and cream cheese. Cover; blend on high speed until smooth, scraping down sides of blender if needed. Repeat twice with remaining soup mixture and cream cheese. Return mixture to saucepan. Heat over medium heat, stirring with whisk, until blended and hot (do not boil). Add additional chicken broth if thinner consistency is desired.

*Squash will be easier to peel if you microwave it first. Pierce whole squash with knife in several places to allow steam to escape. Place on paper towel and microwave on High 4 to 6 minutes or until squash is hot and peel is firm but easy to cut. Cool slightly before peeling.

1 Serving: Calories 240; Total Fat 17g (Saturated Fat 10g; Trans Fat 0.5g); Cholesterol 50mg; Sodium 1220mg; Total Carbohydrate 15g (Dietary Fiber 2g); Protein 5g **Exchanges:** 1 Starch, 3½ Fat **Carbohydrate Choices:** 1

SLOW COOKER **DIRECTIONS** In 10-inch skillet, melt butter over medium heat. Cook onion in butter, stirring occasionally, until crisp-tender. Spray 3½- to 4-quart slow cooker with cooking spray. In slow cooker, mix onion and remaining ingredients except cream cheese. Cover; cook on Low heat setting 6 to 8 hours. In blender or food processor, place one-third to one-half of the soup mixture at a time. Cover; blend on high speed until smooth. Return mixture to slow cooker. Stir in cream cheese with wire whisk. Cover; cook on Low heat setting about 30 minutes, stirring occasionally with wire whisk, until cheese is melted and soup is smooth.

BUTTERNUT SQUASH SOUP WITH MAPLE-PECAN APPLE SALSA Make soup as directed. In small bowl, combine ½ cup diced unpeeled apple, ½ cup chopped toasted pecans (page 22), 2 tablespoons real maple syrup and ½ teaspoon ground cinnamon; stir well to coat. Top each bowl of soup with a spoonful of salsa.

Cutting Butternut Squash

Cut 1 inch from top and bottom of squash; peel off skin with vegetable peeler down to darker orange flesh.

Cut squash in half lengthwise. Use spoon to scoop out and discard seeds and membranes. Cut squash into pieces.

Butternut Squash Soup

SPLIT PEA SOUP

Split peas are a variety of legume grown specifically for drying. They are found with dried beans and lentils in the supermarket.

PREP 20 min TOTAL 2 hr 20 min • **8 servings**

- 1 **bag (16 oz) dried green or yellow split peas (2 cups), sorted, rinsed**
- 8 **cups water**
- 1 **ham bone or 2 lb ham shanks or smoked pork hocks**
- 1 **large onion, chopped (1 cup)**
- 2 **medium stalks celery, finely chopped (1 cup)**
- ¼ **teaspoon pepper**
- 3 **medium carrots, cut into ¼-inch slices (1½ cups)**

1 In 4-quart Dutch oven, mix all ingredients except carrots. Heat to boiling, stirring occasionally; reduce heat. Cover; simmer 1 hour to 1 hour 30 minutes.

2 Remove ham bone; let stand until cool enough to handle. Remove ham from bone. Remove excess fat from ham; cut ham into ½-inch pieces.

3 Stir ham and carrots into soup. Heat to boiling; reduce heat. Cover; simmer about 30 minutes or until carrots are tender and soup is desired thickness.

1 Serving: Calories 250; Total Fat 6g (Saturated Fat 2g; Trans Fat 0g); Cholesterol 15mg; Sodium 250mg; Total Carbohydrate 32g (Dietary Fiber 16g); Protein 16g **Exchanges:** 2 Starch, 1 Vegetable, 1 Very Lean Meat **Carbohydrate Choices:** 2

SLOW COOKER DIRECTIONS Decrease water to 7 cups. Spray 4- to 6-quart slow cooker with cooking spray. In slow cooker, mix all ingredients. Cover; cook on Low heat setting 3 to 4 hours or until peas are tender. Remove ham bone and cut ham as directed in Step 2. Stir ham into soup.

Split Peas

Most often used to make tasty soups, split peas can also be used for side dishes and casseroles (see page 444 for cooking time). These yellow or green legumes are high in fiber and have a good amount of protein. They do not require soaking as many other legumes do.

WHITE CHICKEN CHILI

Top servings of this tasty chili with shredded cheese, tortilla chips, chopped green onions, diced tomatoes, chopped fresh cilantro, sliced avocado or sour cream.

PREP 10 min TOTAL 45 min • **6 servings**

- 1 **tablespoon vegetable oil**
- 1 **large onion, chopped (1 cup)**
- 2 **cloves garlic, finely chopped**
- 3 **cups chicken broth (for homemade broth, see page 528)**
- 1 **can (11 oz) white shoepeg or whole kernel sweet corn, drained**
- 1 **can (15.5 oz) great northern beans, drained**
- 1 **can (15.5 oz) butter beans, drained**
- 2 **tablespoons chopped fresh cilantro**
- 2 **tablespoons lime juice**
- 1 **teaspoon ground cumin**
- ½ **teaspoon dried oregano leaves**
- ¼ **teaspoon red pepper sauce**
- ¼ **teaspoon salt**
- 2 **cups chopped cooked chicken breast**

1 In 4-quart Dutch oven, heat oil over medium heat. Cook onion and garlic in oil 4 to 6 minutes, stirring occasionally, until onion is tender.

2 Stir in remaining ingredients except chicken. Heat to boiling; reduce heat. Simmer uncovered 20 minutes. Stir in chicken; simmer about 5 minutes longer or until hot.

1 Serving (1⅓ Cups): Calories 360; Fat 6g (Saturated Fat 1.5g; Trans Fat 0g); Cholesterol 40mg; Sodium 920mg; Total Carbohydrate 46g (Dietary Fiber 11g); Protein 31g **Exchanges:** 2 Starch, 3 Vegetable, 2 Lean Meat **Carbohydrate Choices:** 3

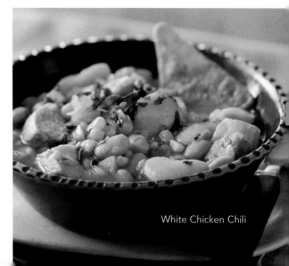

White Chicken Chili

Heirloom Recipe and New Twist

Because this chili recipe has not changed much since it was originally printed in the 1969 edition of the Betty Crocker Cookbook, we think of it as a true classic. It's delicious and you'll make it again and again. Be sure to try our new twist, which is meatless and includes a very tasty pepper-filled salsa that is served on top of the chili. Then for even more inspiration, check out the two variations from Facebook fans.

CLASSIC

CHILI

PREP 25 min **TOTAL** 1 hr 35 min • **4 servings**

- 1 **lb lean (at least 80%) ground beef**
- 1 **medium onion, chopped (½ cup)**
- 1 **clove garlic, finely chopped**
- 1 **can (14.5 oz) diced tomatoes, undrained**
- 1 **can (8 oz) tomato sauce**
- 1 **tablespoon chili powder or ancho chile pepper powder**
- ¾ **teaspoon ground cumin**
- ¼ **teaspoon salt**
- ¼ **teaspoon pepper**
- 1 **can (15 to 16 oz) kidney or pinto beans, drained, rinsed, if desired**

1 In 3-quart saucepan, cook beef, onion and garlic over medium heat 8 to 10 minutes, stirring occasionally, until thoroughly cooked; drain.

2 Stir in remaining ingredients except beans. Heat to boiling; reduce heat. Cover; simmer 1 hour, stirring occasionally.

3 Stir in beans. Heat to boiling; reduce heat. Simmer uncovered about 10 minutes, stirring occasionally, until desired thickness.

1 Serving: Calories 400; Total Fat 14g (Saturated Fat 5g; Trans Fat 1g); Cholesterol 70mg; Sodium 1000mg; Total Carbohydrate 37g (Dietary Fiber 10g); Protein 31g **Exchanges:** 2 Starch, 1 Vegetable, 3 Lean Meat, 1 Fat **Carbohydrate Choices:** 2½

CHILI WITH VEGETABLES Make chili as directed adding 1½ cups frozen mixed vegetables with remaining ingredients in Step 2.

CINCINNATI-STYLE CHILI For each serving, spoon about ¾ cup chili over 1 cup hot cooked spaghetti. Sprinkle each serving with ¼ cup shredded Cheddar cheese and 2 tablespoons chopped onion. Top with sour cream if desired.

See how to make **chili:** Visit bettycrocker.com/BCcookbook

TURKEY AND WHITE BEAN CHILI Make chili as directed except—substitute lean ground turkey for the ground beef and cannellini beans for the kidney beans.

CHILI-TOPPED BAKED POTATOES Bake potatoes, page 589. Cut each baked potato in half lengthwise; mash slightly. Serve scoops of chili over baked potatoes.

> Contributed by **Jennifer Hart-Mora** from **Sacramento, California**

CHUCKWAGON CHILI Omit ground beef. Cut 1 lb lean trimmed beef round steak into ½-inch pieces. Brown with onion and garlic as directed in Step 1. Cook 1 hour to 1 hour 30 minutes or until beef is fork-tender.

> Contributed by **Angie Mitchell** from **Montezuma Station, Indiana**

Chili

THREE-BEAN CHILI AND RICE

This interesting chili recipe was developed in our kitchens for a chili cook-off contest—it won first place. The flavor is amazing and the chili mixture is served over rice, making it very hearty. It's topped with a spicy pepper salsa, which adds even more flavor.

PREP 55 min **TOTAL** 1 hr 30 min • **6 servings**

GARLIC RICE

- 2 tablespoons vegetable oil
- 4 cloves garlic, cut into thin slices
- 2 cups uncooked regular long-grain white rice
- 3 cups water
- 1 teaspoon salt

CHILI

- 1 can (28 oz) diced tomatoes, undrained
- 1 can (15 oz) kidney beans, drained, rinsed
- 1 can (15 oz) black beans, drained, rinsed
- 1 can (15 oz) garbanzo beans (chickpeas), drained, rinsed
- 1 can (15 oz) tomato sauce
- 3 small bell peppers (any color), diced
- 1 Anaheim or jalapeño chile, seeded, chopped
- 2 tablespoons chili powder
- ½ teaspoon salt
- ¼ teaspoon pepper

SALSA CREAM

- 1 container (8 oz) sour cream
- ⅓ cup Three-Pepper Salsa (at right)

1 In 3-quart saucepan, heat oil over medium-high heat. Cook and stir garlic in oil until light golden brown. Add rice; cook 3 minutes, stirring often. Add 3 cups water and 1 teaspoon salt. Heat to boiling over high heat; reduce heat. Cover; simmer 15 minutes or until rice is tender. Remove garlic slices from rice with fork before serving.

2 Meanwhile, in 4-quart Dutch oven or saucepan, mix all chili ingredients. Heat to boiling; reduce heat. Cover; simmer 25 to 30 minutes, stirring occasionally, until bell peppers are tender.

3 In small bowl, mix salsa cream ingredients.

4 To serve, spoon 1 cup rice on one side of large, shallow soup bowl. Spoon 1½ cups chili next to rice. Top with salsa cream and three-pepper salsa, using slotted spoon to serve the salsa.

1 Serving (1 Cup Rice and 1½ Cups Chili): Calories 750; Total Fat 18g (Saturated Fat 6g; Trans Fat 0g); Cholesterol 20mg; Sodium 2000mg; Total Carbohydrate 122g (Dietary Fiber 18g); Protein 26g **Exchanges:** 7½ Starch, ½ Other Carbohydrate, ½ Very Lean Meat, 2½ Fat **Carbohydrate Choices:** 8

THREE-PEPPER SALSA In medium bowl, mix 1 finely chopped red onion and ½ teaspoon salt. Place onion in strainer; rinse with cold water for about 1 minute and drain well. Return onion to bowl. Add 3 medium seeded and finely chopped tomatoes, 1 small seeded and finely chopped poblano chile, 1 small seeded and finely chopped jalapeño chile, 1 small finely chopped yellow bell pepper, 2 tablespoons fresh lime juice, ¼ cup chopped fresh cilantro and 1 tablespoon olive oil; mix well. Add salt and pepper to taste. Refrigerate until serving time.

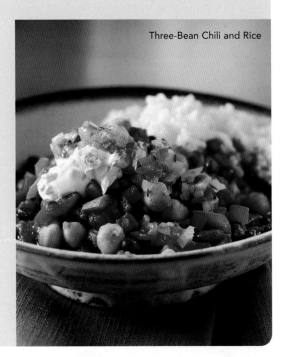

Three-Bean Chili and Rice

CUBAN BLACK BEAN SOUP

PREP 20 min TOTAL 2 hr 35 min • **8 servings**

- 2 tablespoons vegetable oil
- 1 large onion, chopped (1 cup)
- 3 cloves garlic, finely chopped
- 1 bag (16 oz) dried black beans, sorted, rinsed (2 cups)
- 1 cup finely chopped cooked ham
- 3 cups beef broth (for homemade broth, see page 530)
- 3 cups water
- ¼ cup dark rum or apple cider
- 1½ teaspoons ground cumin
- 1½ teaspoons dried oregano leaves
- 1 medium green bell pepper, chopped (1 cup)
- 1 large tomato, chopped (1 cup)
  Chopped Hard-Cooked Eggs (page 74), if desired
  Additional chopped onion, if desired

1 In 4-quart Dutch oven, heat oil over medium heat. Cook 1 cup chopped onion and the garlic in oil 4 to 6 minutes, stirring occasionally, until onion is tender.

2 Stir in remaining ingredients except eggs and additional onion; heat to boiling. Boil 2 minutes; reduce heat. Cover; simmer about 2 hours or until beans are tender. Serve soup topped with eggs and onion.

1 Serving (1½ Cups): Calories 290; Total Fat 6g (Saturated Fat 1g; Trans Fat 0g); Cholesterol 10mg; Sodium 610mg; Total Carbohydrate 40g (Dietary Fiber 14g); Protein 19g **Exchanges:** 2 Starch, 2 Vegetable, 1 Very Lean Meat **Carbohydrate Choices:** 2½

Cuban Black Bean Soup

SENATE BEAN SOUP

How did this soup get its name? It's served every day in the U.S. Senate's restaurant. Some say it's been around since the early twentieth century, but no single story regarding its origins can be corroborated.

PREP 20 min TOTAL 4 hr 35 min • **8 servings**

- 1 bag (16 oz) dried navy beans (2 cups), sorted, rinsed
- 12 cups water
- 1 ham bone or 2 lb ham shanks or smoked pork hocks
- 2½ cups Mashed Potatoes (page 602)
- 1 large onion, chopped (1 cup)
- 2 medium stalks celery, chopped (1 cup)
- 1 clove garlic, finely chopped
- 2 teaspoons salt
- ¼ teaspoon pepper

1 In 4-quart Dutch oven, heat beans and water to boiling. Boil uncovered 2 minutes; remove from heat. Cover; let stand 1 hour.

2 Add ham bone. Heat to boiling; reduce heat. Cover; simmer about 2 hours or until beans are tender. Stir in remaining ingredients. Cover; simmer 1 hour.

3 Remove ham bone; let stand until cool enough to handle. Remove ham from bone. Remove excess fat from ham; cut ham into ½-inch pieces. Stir ham into soup.

1 Serving: Calories 330; Total Fat 10g (Saturated Fat 3g; Trans Fat 1g); Cholesterol 15mg; Sodium 960mg; Total Carbohydrate 45g (Dietary Fiber 9g); Protein 16g **Exchanges:** 3 Starch, 1 Very Lean Meat **Carbohydrate Choices:** 3

SLOW COOKER DIRECTIONS Decrease water to 8 cups and salt to 1½ teaspoons. Spray 4- to 6-quart slow cooker with cooking spray. In slow cooker, mix all ingredients except mashed potatoes. Cover; cook on Low heat setting 8 to 9 hours or until beans are tender. Remove ham bone and cut ham as directed in Step 3. Stir ham and mashed potatoes into soup. Increase heat setting to High. Cover; cook 15 minutes.

SOUTHWESTERN BEAN SOUP Add 1 can (4.5 oz) chopped green chiles, drained, 1 tablespoon chili powder and 1 teaspoon ground cumin with remaining ingredients in Step 2. Top soup with salsa if desired.

PIZZA LOWER CALORIE

PREP 45 min **TOTAL** 1 hr 35 min • **2 pizzas (8 slices each)**

PIZZA CRUST

2½ to 3 cups all-purpose or bread flour
1 tablespoon sugar
1 teaspoon salt
1 package (2¼ teaspoons) regular active or fast-acting dry yeast
3 tablespoons olive or vegetable oil
1 cup very warm water (120°F to 130°F)

PIZZA TOPPING

1 lb lean (at least 80%) ground beef, pork, lamb or turkey
1 large onion or 1 medium green bell pepper, chopped (1 cup)
2 cloves garlic, finely chopped
1 teaspoon Italian seasoning
1 can (8 oz) pizza sauce
2 cups sliced fresh mushrooms (about 5 oz)*
2 cups shredded mozzarella, Cheddar or Monterey Jack cheese (8 oz)
¼ cup grated Parmesan or Romano cheese

1 In large bowl, mix 1 cup of the flour, the sugar, salt and yeast. Add oil and warm water. Beat with electric mixer on medium speed 3 minutes, scraping bowl frequently. Stir in enough remaining flour until dough is soft and leaves sides of bowl. Place dough on lightly floured surface. Knead 5 to 8 minutes or until dough is smooth and springy. Cover loosely with plastic wrap; let rest 30 minutes. Partially bake as directed below for thin or thick crusts.

2 Meanwhile, in 10-inch skillet, cook beef, onion, garlic and Italian seasoning over medium heat 8 to 10 minutes, stirring occasionally, until beef is brown and onion is tender; drain.

3 Spread pizza sauce over partially baked crusts. Top with beef mixture, mushrooms and cheeses.

4 Bake thin-crust pizzas at 425°F for 8 to 10 minutes, thick-crust pizzas at 375°F about 20 minutes, or until cheese is melted.

1 jar (4.5 oz) sliced mushrooms, drained, can be substituted.

1 Slice: Calories 170; Total Fat 8g (Saturated Fat 4g; Trans Fat 0g); Cholesterol 30mg; Sodium 320mg; Total Carbohydrate 13g (Dietary Fiber 1g); Protein 11g **Exchanges:** 1 Starch, 1 Vegetable, 1 High-Fat Meat **Carbohydrate Choices:** 1

FOR THIN CRUSTS Heat oven to 425°F. Grease 2 cookie sheets or 12-inch pizza pans with oil. Sprinkle with cornmeal. Divide dough in half. Pat each half into 12-inch round on cookie sheet using floured fingers. Partially bake 7 to 8 minutes or until crust just begins to brown. Add toppings and bake as directed in Steps 2 through 4.

FOR THICK CRUSTS Grease two 8-inch square pans or 9-inch round pans with oil. Sprinkle with cornmeal. Divide dough in half. Pat each half in bottom of pan using floured fingers. Cover loosely with plastic wrap; let rise in warm place 30 to 45 minutes or until almost doubled in size. Move oven rack to lowest position. Heat oven to 375°F. Partially bake 20 to 22 minutes or until crust just begins to brown. Add toppings and bake as directed in Step 4.

CHEESE PIZZA Omit beef, onion, garlic and Italian seasoning. Increase shredded cheese to 3 cups.

MEAT LOVER'S PIZZA Substitute bulk Italian sausage for the beef. Add 1 cup sliced pepperoni on top of Italian sausage in Step 3.

See how to make **pizza crust**:
Visit bettycrocker.com/BCcookbook

Shaping Pizza Dough

For thin crust, pat each half of dough into 12-inch round on cookie sheet or pizza pan greased with oil and sprinkled with cornmeal.

For thick crust, pat each half of dough in bottom of square or round pan greased with oil and sprinkled with cornmeal. Cover and let rise until almost double in size.

FRESH MOZZARELLA AND TOMATO PIZZA LOWER CALORIE

PREP 35 min TOTAL 3 hr 15 min • **1 pizza (8 slices)**

ITALIAN-STYLE PIZZA CRUST

- 1 package (2¼ teaspoons) regular active or fast-acting dry yeast
- ½ cup warm water (105°F to 115°F)
- 1¼ to 1½ cups all-purpose flour
- ½ teaspoon salt
- ½ teaspoon sugar
- 1 teaspoon olive oil

PIZZA TOPPING

- 4 oz fresh mozzarella cheese, well drained
- 2 plum (Roma) tomatoes, thinly sliced
- ¼ teaspoon salt
  Freshly ground pepper to taste
- ¼ cup thin strips fresh basil leaves
- 1 tablespoon chopped fresh oregano leaves
- 1 tablespoon small capers, if desired
- 1 tablespoon olive oil

1 In large bowl, dissolve yeast in warm water. Stir in half of the flour, the salt, sugar and 1 teaspoon oil. Stir in enough of the remaining flour to make dough easy to handle. Place dough on lightly floured surface. Knead about 10 minutes or until smooth and springy. Grease large bowl with shortening. Place dough in bowl, turning dough to grease all sides. Cover; let rise in warm place 20 minutes. Gently push fist into dough to deflate. Cover; refrigerate at least 2 hours but no longer than 48 hours. (If dough should double in size during refrigeration, gently push fist into dough to deflate.)

2 Move oven rack to lowest position. Heat oven to 425°F. Grease cookie sheet or 12-inch pizza pan with oil. Sprinkle with cornmeal. Pat dough into 12-inch round on cookie sheet or pat in pizza pan using floured fingers. Press dough from center to edge so edge is slightly thicker than center.

3 Cut cheese into ¼-inch slices. Place cheese on dough to within ½ inch of edge. Arrange tomatoes on cheese. Sprinkle with salt, pepper, 2 tablespoons of the basil, the oregano and capers. Drizzle with 1 tablespoon oil.

Fresh Mozzarella and Tomato Pizza

Cutting Basil Leaves

Layer washed fresh leaves in stack. Roll up stack lengthwise into tight roll.

Cut across roll, making thin slices. Fluff slices with fingers to separate into thin strips.

4 Bake about 20 minutes or until crust is golden brown and cheese is melted. Sprinkle with remaining 2 tablespoons basil.

1 Slice: Calories 140; Total Fat 5g (Saturated Fat 2g; Trans Fat 0g); Cholesterol 10mg; Sodium 300mg; Total Carbohydrate 17g (Dietary Fiber 1g); Protein 6g **Exchanges:** 1 Starch, 1 Fat **Carbohydrate Choices:** 1

SHREDDED MOZZARELLA AND TOMATO PIZZA Substitute 2 cups shredded mozzarella cheese (8 oz) for the fresh mozzarella. Sprinkle 1 cup of the cheese over dough. Add remaining ingredients as directed—except sprinkle with remaining 1 cup cheese before drizzling with oil.

Calzones

Filling Calzones

Place filling on half of each dough round to within 1 inch of edge.

Fold dough over filling; pinch edges or press with fork to seal securely.

CALZONES

PREP 45 min TOTAL 1 hr 40 min • **6 servings**

    Pizza Crust (page 543)
2 cups shredded mozzarella cheese (8 oz)
¼ lb salami, cut into thin strips
½ cup ricotta cheese
¼ cup chopped fresh basil leaves
2 plum (Roma) tomatoes, chopped
    Freshly ground pepper
1 egg, slightly beaten

1 Let pizza crust dough rest 30 minutes.

2 Heat oven to 375°F. Grease 2 cookie sheets with shortening or cooking spray.

3 Divide dough into 6 equal parts. On lightly floured surface, roll each part into 7-inch round with floured rolling pin.

4 On half of each dough round, place mozzarella cheese, salami, ricotta cheese, basil and tomatoes to within 1 inch of edge. Sprinkle with pepper. Carefully fold dough over filling; pinch edges or press with fork to seal securely.

5 Place calzones on cookie sheets. Brush with egg. Bake about 25 minutes or until golden brown.

1 Serving: Calories 490; Total Fat 24g (Saturated Fat 9g; Trans Fat 0g); Cholesterol 75mg; Sodium 980mg; Total Carbohydrate 46g (Dietary Fiber 2g); Protein 24g **Exchanges:** 3 Starch, 2 High-Fat Meat, ½ Fat **Carbohydrate Choices:** 3

`LIGHTER` **DIRECTIONS** For 8 grams of fat and 350 calories per serving, use reduced-fat mozzarella cheese and fat-free ricotta cheese; substitute cooked chicken for the salami.

SLOPPY JOES LOWER CALORIE

PREP 10 min TOTAL 35 min • **6 sandwiches**

1 lb lean (at least 80%) ground beef
1 medium onion, chopped (½ cup)
¼ cup chopped celery
1 cup ketchup
1 tablespoon Worcestershire sauce
1 teaspoon ground mustard
⅛ teaspoon pepper
6 burger buns, split

1 In 10-inch skillet, cook beef, onion and celery over medium heat 8 to 10 minutes, stirring occasionally, until beef is brown; drain.

2 Stir in remaining ingredients except buns. Heat to boiling; reduce heat. Simmer uncovered 10 to 15 minutes, stirring occasionally, until vegetables are tender. Spoon into buns.

1 Sandwich: Calories 280; Total Fat 7g (Saturated Fat 1.5g; Trans Fat 0g); Cholesterol 50mg; Sodium 810mg; Total Carbohydrate 35g (Dietary Fiber 2g); Protein 21g **Exchanges:** 2 Starch, 1 Vegetable, 1½ High-Fat Meat **Carbohydrate Choices:** 2

`LIGHTER` **DIRECTIONS** For 3 grams of fat and 235 calories per serving, substitute ground turkey breast for the ground beef; spray skillet with cooking spray before heating.

CREATE A SIGNATURE GRILLED CHEESE SANDWICH

Follow the cooking directions for Grilled Cheese sandwiches (at right), varying the types of breads, cheeses and fillings. Here are a few ideas to get you started.

1 Apple Grilled Cheese: Spread raisin walnut bread with Apple Butter (page 247, or purchased) and top with slices of sharp Cheddar cheese.

2 Caramelized Onion Grilled Cheese: Top sourdough bread with sliced smoked Gouda cheese and Caramelized Onions (page 598).

3 Day-After-Thanksgiving Grilled Cheese: Spread slices of marble rye bread with cranberry mustard; top with sliced turkey, cranberry relish and Havarti cheese.

4 Gouda-Pear Grilled Cheese: Drizzle cinnamon swirl bread with honey; top with thin slices of pear and sliced aged Gouda.

5 Grilled "Hot" Ham and Cheese: Top pumpernickel bread with sliced pepper Jack cheese, sliced deli ham, and well-drained pepperoncini slices.

6 Italian Country Grilled Cheese: Layer sliced ciabatta bread, with sliced fontina cheese, sliced tomato, sliced avocado and crisp bacon slices.

7 Mini Brie-Raspberry Grilled Cheese: Spread French bread slices with raspberry preserves and top with thick slices of Brie cheese.

8 Spanish Grilled Cheese: Spread whole-grain rustic bread with fig jam and top with sliced Manchego cheese.

GRILLED CHEESE FAST

There's plenty of debate about what makes a great grilled cheese sandwich. Some insist on using American cheese, while others use only natural cheeses. Soft bread that squishes down when you take a bite is favored by many, whereas a substantial, sturdy bread is a must for others. The choice is yours—enjoy!

PREP 10 min **TOTAL** 20 min • **4 sandwiches**

- 12 slices American cheese (about 8 oz) or 2 cups shredded Cheddar cheese (8 oz)*
- 8 slices white or whole wheat bread
- ⅓ cup butter, softened

1 Place 3 slices cheese or ½ cup shredded cheese on each of 4 bread slices. Top with remaining bread. Spread 2 teaspoons butter over each top slice of bread.

2 Place sandwiches, buttered side down, in 12-inch skillet. Spread remaining butter over top slices of bread. Cook uncovered over medium heat about 5 minutes or until bottoms are golden brown. Turn; cook 2 to 3 minutes longer or until bottoms are golden brown and cheese is melted.

*If you're using natural cheese, any type of shredded cheese, such as Monterey Jack, Swiss, Gruyère, Jarlsberg or Gouda can be used.

1 Sandwich: Calories 480; Total Fat 35g (Saturated Fat 19g; Trans Fat 1.5g); Cholesterol 95mg; Sodium 1180mg; Total Carbohydrate 26g (Dietary Fiber 0g); Protein 17g **Exchanges:** 2 Starch, 2 High-Fat Meat, 2½ Fat **Carbohydrate Choices:** 2

BACON, TOMATO AND AVOCADO GRILLED CHEESE

Place ¼ cup shredded cheese on each of 4 bread slices. Divide among 4 sandwiches 1 small onion, chopped (⅓ cup), 8 slices bacon, crisply cooked, 1 medium tomato, thinly sliced, and 1 medium avocado, thinly sliced. Top with remaining cheese and bread. Spread butter over top slices of bread. Continue as directed in Step 2.

PESTO-PARMESAN GRILLED CHEESE

Spread Basil Pesto (page 484) or purchased basil pesto lightly over each bread slice before adding cheese in Step 1. Sprinkle butter-topped slices with Parmesan cheese before grilling.

CUBAN PORK SANDWICHES

FAST

PREP 10 min **TOTAL** 20 min • **4 sandwiches**

- 4 burger buns, split
- 4 teaspoons mayonnaise or salad dressing
- 2 teaspoons yellow mustard
- 4 oz cooked roast pork, thinly sliced
- 4 oz cooked ham, thinly sliced
- 4 slices (1 oz each) Swiss cheese
- 12 slices dill pickles
- 3 tablespoons butter, melted

1 For each sandwich, spread one cut side of each bun with 1 teaspoon mayonnaise and the other side with ½ teaspoon mustard. Layer pork, ham, cheese and 3 pickle slices in each bun, folding meats or cheese to fit if necessary. Press sandwiches firmly with palm of hand to flatten to about 1-inch thickness.

2 Heat 12-inch nonstick skillet over medium-high heat. Brush tops of sandwiches with melted butter. Place sandwiches, buttered sides down, in skillet. Brush bottoms with remaining butter. Cook about 6 minutes, turning once, until crisp and brown on both sides.

1 Sandwich: Calories 450; Total Fat 28g (Saturated Fat 12g; Trans Fat 1g); Cholesterol 90mg; Sodium 1140mg; Total Carbohydrate 24g (Dietary Fiber 1g); Protein 27g **Exchanges:** 1½ Starch, 3½ Medium-Fat Meat, 1½ Fat **Carbohydrate Choices:** 1½

Bacon, Tomato and Avocado Grilled Cheese

REUBEN SANDWICHES

History isn't clear as to how the Reuben sandwich got its name. One source says it was named in 1914 for the owner of New York's once-famous Reuben's Delicatessen. Others say Reuben Kay, a wholesale grocer from Omaha, named the sandwich in 1955. Wherever it originated, it's a delicious, hearty deli favorite that's easy to make at home.

PREP 20 min **TOTAL** 40 min • **6 sandwiches**

- 6 tablespoons Thousand Island dressing (page 475) or purchased Thousand Island dressing
- 12 slices regular or marble rye or pumpernickel bread
- 6 slices (1 oz each) Swiss cheese
- 1 can (14 or 14.5 oz) sauerkraut, drained
- ¾ lb cooked corned beef, thinly sliced
- ¼ cup butter, softened

1 Spread 1 tablespoon dressing over each of 6 bread slices. Top with cheese, sauerkraut, corned beef and remaining bread. Spread 1 teaspoon butter over each top slice of bread.

2 Place 3 sandwiches, buttered sides down, in 12-inch skillet. Spread 1 teaspoon butter over top slices of bread. Cook uncovered over low heat about 10 minutes or until bottoms are golden brown. Turn; cook about 8 minutes longer or until bottoms are golden brown and cheese is melted. Remove from skillet; place in warm oven or cover with foil to keep warm. Repeat with remaining sandwiches and butter.

1 Sandwich: Calories 520; Total Fat 33g (Saturated Fat 14g; Trans Fat 1g); Cholesterol 105mg; Sodium 1770mg; Total Carbohydrate 31g (Dietary Fiber 4g); Protein 24g **Exchanges:** 2 Starch, 2½ Medium-Fat Meat, 3½ Fat **Carbohydrate Choices:** 2

LIGHTER **DIRECTIONS** For 11 grams of fat and 335 calories per serving, use purchased fat-free Thousand Island dressing; substitute thinly sliced deli turkey or chicken breast for the corned beef. Omit butter; spray skillet with cooking spray before heating.

RACHEL SANDWICHES Substitute thinly sliced deli turkey breast for the corned beef.

Reuben Sandwiches

GRILLED TURKEY PANINI

PREP 45 min **TOTAL** 50 min • **8 sandwiches**

- ¾ cup mayonnaise
- ¼ cup Basil Pesto (page 484) or purchased basil pesto
- 16 slices crusty Italian bread
- ¼ cup butter, softened
- 8 slices cooked turkey (¾ lb)
- 1 can (14 oz) artichoke hearts, drained, chopped
- 3 medium plum (Roma) tomatoes, sliced
- 8 slices (1 oz each) fontina or provolone cheese

1 In small bowl, mix mayonnaise and pesto.

2 Spread 1 side of each bread slice with butter. Turn slices buttered sides down; spread other side of each slice with 1 tablespoon pesto mixture. Top 8 slices with turkey, artichoke, tomatoes and cheese. Top with remaining bread slices, buttered sides up.

3 Place 3 or 4 sandwiches in sandwich grill or 12-inch skillet; cook over medium heat 3 to 4 minutes (turning once if using skillet), until bread is toasted and cheese is melted. Remove from grill; place in warm oven or cover with foil to keep warm. Repeat with remaining sandwiches.

1 Sandwich: Calories 570; Total Fat 39g (Saturated Fat 14g; Trans Fat 1g); Cholesterol 95mg; Sodium 860mg; Total Carbohydrate 28g (Dietary Fiber 4g); Protein 26g **Exchanges:** 2 Starch, 3 Lean Meat, 5½ Fat **Carbohydrate Choices:** 2

BEEF BURRITOS

PREP 25 min **TOTAL** 30 min • **8 servings**

- 2 cups shredded cooked beef
- 1 cup canned refried beans
- 8 flour tortillas (9 or 10 inch)
- 2 cups shredded lettuce
- 2 medium tomatoes, chopped (1½ cups)
- 1 cup shredded Cheddar cheese (4 oz)

1 In two 1-quart saucepans, heat beef and refried beans separately over medium heat 2 to 5 minutes, stirring occasionally, until hot. Warm tortillas as directed on package.

2 Place about ¼ cup of the beef on center of each tortilla. Spoon about 2 tablespoons beans onto beef. Top with ¼ cup of the lettuce, 3 tablespoons tomatoes and 2 tablespoons cheese.

3 Fold one end of tortilla up about 1 inch over filling; fold right and left sides over folded end, overlapping. Fold remaining end down.

Folding Burritos

Fold one end of tortilla up about 1 inch over filling.

Fold right and left sides over folded end, overlapping. Fold remaing end down.

1 Serving: Calories 390; Total Fat 15g (Saturated Fat 6g; Trans Fat 1g); Cholesterol 45mg; Sodium 530mg; Total Carbohydrate 44g (Dietary Fiber 4g); Protein 20g **Exchanges:** 3 Starch, 1½ Medium-Fat Meat, 1 Fat **Carbohydrate Choices:** 3

CHICKEN BURRITOS Substitute shredded chicken for the beef and Monterey Jack cheese for the Cheddar cheese.

CHICKEN QUESADILLA SANDWICHES

A pancake griddle or large cook-top grill that fits over two burners makes quick work out of cooking many quesadillas at once.

PREP 45 min **TOTAL** 45 min • **4 servings**

- 2 teaspoons vegetable oil
- 1 lb boneless skinless chicken breasts (about 4)
- ¼ cup chopped fresh cilantro
- ¼ teaspoon ground cumin
- 8 flour tortillas (7 or 8 inch)
- 2 tablespoons vegetable oil
- 1 cup shredded Monterey Jack cheese (4 oz)
- 1 can (4.5 oz) chopped green chiles, drained Salsa, if desired

1 In 10-inch skillet, heat 2 teaspoons oil over medium-high heat. Cook chicken breasts, cilantro and cumin in oil 15 to 20 minutes, turning chicken once and stirring cilantro mixture occasionally, until juice of chicken is clear when centers of thickest pieces are cut (at least 165°F). Shred chicken into small pieces; mix chicken and cilantro mixture.

2 Brush 1 side of 1 tortilla with some of the 2 tablespoons oil; place oiled side down in same skillet. Layer with one-fourth of the chicken mixture, ¼ cup of the cheese and one-fourth of the chiles to within ½ inch of edge. Top with another tortilla; brush top of tortilla with oil. Cook over medium-high heat 4 to 6 minutes, turning after 2 minutes, until light golden brown.

3 Repeat with remaining tortillas, chicken mixture, cheese and chiles. Cut quesadillas into wedges. Serve with salsa.

1 Serving: Calories 610; Total Fat 29g (Saturated Fat 10g; Trans Fat 1.5g); Cholesterol 95mg; Sodium 900mg; Total Carbohydrate 49g (Dietary Fiber 2g); Protein 40g **Exchanges:** 2 Starch, 1½ Other Carbohydrate, 3½ Very Lean Meat, 1 High-Fat Meat, 3½ Fat **Carbohydrate Choices:** 3

Beef Burritos

CHICKEN SALAD SANDWICHES

FAST

PREP 15 min TOTAL 15 min • **4 sandwiches**

- 1½ cups chopped cooked chicken or turkey
- 1 medium stalk celery, chopped (½ cup)
- 1 small onion, finely chopped (⅓ cup)
- ½ cup mayonnaise or salad dressing
- ¼ teaspoon salt
- ¼ teaspoon pepper
- 8 slices bread

In medium bowl, mix all ingredients except bread. Spread mixture on 4 bread slices. Top with remaining bread.

1 Sandwich: Calories 430; Total Fat 27g (Saturated Fat 4.5g; Trans Fat 0g); Cholesterol 60mg; Sodium 630mg; Total Carbohydrate 27g (Dietary Fiber 1g); Protein 19g **Exchanges:** 2 Starch, 2 Lean Meat, 4 Fat **Carbohydrate Choices:** 2

LIGHTER DIRECTIONS For 6 grams of fat and 260 calories per serving, use fat-free mayonnaise.

EGG SALAD SANDWICHES Substitute 6 Hard-Cooked Eggs (page 74), chopped, for the chicken.

HAM SALAD SANDWICHES Substitute 1½ cups chopped cooked ham for the chicken. Omit salt and pepper. Stir in 1 teaspoon yellow mustard.

TUNA SALAD SANDWICHES Substitute 2 cans (5 oz each) tuna in water, drained, for the chicken. Stir in 1 teaspoon lemon juice.

Chicken Salad Sandwiches

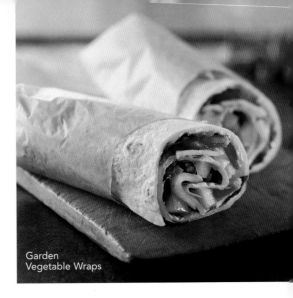
Garden Vegetable Wraps

GARDEN VEGETABLE WRAPS

FAST

PREP 15 min TOTAL 15 min • **4 servings**

- 4 oz (half of 8-oz package) cream cheese, softened
- 4 flour tortillas (9 or 10 inch)
- 1 cup loosely packed fresh spinach
- 1 large tomato, thinly sliced
- ¾ cup shredded carrot
- 8 slices (1 oz each) Muenster or Monterey Jack cheese
- 1 small yellow bell pepper, chopped (½ cup)

1 Spread 2 tablespoons of the cream cheese over each tortilla. Top with spinach and tomato to within 1 inch of edge. Sprinkle with carrot. Top with cheese slices. Sprinkle with bell pepper.

2 Roll up tortillas tightly. Serve immediately, or wrap securely with plastic wrap and refrigerate up to 24 hours.

1 Serving: Calories 480; Total Fat 30g (Saturated Fat 18g; Trans Fat 1g); Cholesterol 85mg; Sodium 670mg; Total Carbohydrate 31g (Dietary Fiber 3g); Protein 20g **Exchanges:** 2 Starch, 2 High-Fat Meat, 2 Fat **Carbohydrate Choices:** 2

GARDEN VEGETABLE HUMMUS WRAP Substitute hummus for the cream cheese.

TURKEY, BACON AND GUACAMOLE WRAP Substitute guacamole for the cream cheese and omit bell pepper. Layer 8 oz sliced cooked turkey and 4 slices bacon on tortillas. Continue as directed.

20 MINUTES OR LESS

For bonus **20 minutes or less** recipes,
visit bettycrocker.com/BCcookbook

FAST = Ready in 20 minutes or less LOWER CALORIE = See Helpful Nutrition and Cooking Information, page 685
LIGHTER = 25% fewer calories or grams of fat MAKE AHEAD = Make-ahead directions SLOW COOKER = Slow cooker directions

← Thai Chicken with Basil (page 557), Asparagus–Turkey Sausage Skillet (page 559), Nut-Crusted Pork (page 565),
Peanut-Sauced Thai Tilapia (page 572)

TWENTY-MINUTE MEAL BASICS

With the fast-to-fix recipes, do-ahead ideas and other time-saving tricks in this chapter, you can easily make a satisfying homemade dinner in twenty minutes or less.

THE QUICK PANTRY

By keeping your pantry, refrigerator and freezer stocked with convenience items, getting dinner on the table in no time is a snap. Some of our favorite staples include:

- Boneless skinless chicken breasts
- Bottled marinades and salad dressings
- Canned beans
- Dried, fresh and frozen pastas
- Frozen vegetables and canned fruits
- Ground beef
- Prewashed and precut fresh produce and salad greens
- Purchased pasta or pizza sauces
- Refrigerated bread products
- Shredded cheese

PREPARING NOW, SAVING TIME LATER

Get a head start on dinners during the week by taking time during the weekend to prep ingredients for future meals or to cook and freeze your family's favorite dishes. Freeze desired amounts in resealable freezer plastic bags. Here are some fast-track ideas to get you started:

- Shape ground beef, turkey or chicken into patties or meatballs; freeze up to 4 months.

Ground beef patties ready for the freezer

- Brown and drain ground beef or sausage. Freeze up to 3 months.
- For stir-fries, cut raw meat and poultry into strips or cubes; arrange in single layer on foil-lined cookie sheet and freeze until firm before placing in resealable plastic freezer bag. Freeze up to 9 months.
- Flatten boneless skinless chicken breasts to ¼-inch thickness for quicker cooking.
- Make Italian Tomato Sauce, page 370, or Marinara Sauce, page 371; freeze up to 1 year. Or prepare Bolognese, page 370, or Creamy Tomato-Vodka Sauce, page 371; freeze up to 6 months.
- Chop, dice or slice fresh veggies such as onions, bell peppers, carrots and celery. Arrange in single layer on foil-lined cookie sheet and freeze until firm before placing in resealable freezer plastic bag. Freeze up to 1 month.

TIPS FOR QUICK COOKING

- For nights that are jam-packed, plan on pulling something from the freezer that's already cooked and just needs to be thawed and reheated (like pasta sauce).
- Pick up a rotisserie chicken from the grocery store. Round out the meal with a loaf of bread from the bakery and precut veggies from the produce section.
- Cut prep time with helpful kitchen gadgets like food processors, flexible cutting mats and kitchen scissors.
- When preparing fresh veggies, cut them into small pieces to shorten cooking time.
- During the last few minutes of cooking pasta, add fresh or frozen veggies to the water instead of preparing them separately.
- For easy cleanup, line cookie sheets and baking pans with foil.

PECAN-MAPLE CHICKEN FAST

PREP 20 min TOTAL 20 min • **4 servings**

- 4 boneless skinless chicken breasts (about 1¼ lb)
- 2 tablespoons butter
- ½ teaspoon salt
- 2 tablespoons real or maple-flavored syrup
- ½ cup pecan halves

1 Between pieces of plastic wrap or waxed paper, gently pound each chicken breast to ¼-inch thickness (page 404).

2 In 12-inch nonstick skillet, melt butter with salt over medium heat. Cook chicken in butter 1 to 2 minutes, turning once, until brown.

3 Stir in syrup and pecans. Cook 8 to 10 minutes, turning chicken once and stirring pecans once or twice, until chicken is no longer pink in center.

1 Serving: Calories 310; Total Fat 19g (Saturated Fat 5g; Trans Fat 0g); Cholesterol 90mg; Sodium 410mg; Total Carbohydrate 9g (Dietary Fiber 1g); Protein 28g **Exchanges:** ½ Other Carbohydrate, 4 Lean Meat, 1½ Fat **Carbohydrate Choices:** ½

CRUNCHY POTATO CHIP CHICKEN FAST

To quickly crush chips, place them in a tightly sealed food-storage plastic bag and crush with a rolling pin or meat mallet.

PREP 20 min TOTAL 20 min • **4 servings**

- 4 cups sour cream and onion–flavored potato chips, crushed (1 cup)
- 1 tablespoon parsley flakes
- 1 egg
- 2 teaspoons Worcestershire sauce
- 2 tablespoons vegetable oil
- 4 boneless skinless chicken breasts (about 1¼ lb)

1 In shallow bowl, mix potato chips and parsley. In another shallow bowl, beat egg and Worcestershire sauce.

2 In 12-inch nonstick skillet, heat oil over medium-low heat. Dip chicken into egg mixture, then coat with potato chip mixture. Cook chicken in oil 10 to 12 minutes, turning once, until deep golden brown and juice of chicken is clear when center of thickest part is cut (at least 165°F).

1 Serving: Calories 300; Total Fat 17g (Saturated Fat 3.5g; Trans Fat 0g); Cholesterol 125mg; Sodium 200mg; Total Carbohydrate 9g (Dietary Fiber 0g); Protein 29g **Exchanges:** ½ Starch, 4 Lean Meat, 1 Fat **Carbohydrate Choices:** ½

SKILLET CHICKEN NACHOS FAST

PREP 20 min TOTAL 20 min • **6 servings**

- 1 tablespoon olive or vegetable oil
- 1¼ lb boneless skinless chicken breasts, cut into ¼-inch pieces
- 1 package (1 oz) taco seasoning mix
- 1 can (8 oz) tomato sauce
- 1 medium red bell pepper, chopped (1 cup)
- 1 can (15 oz) black beans, drained, rinsed
- 1 can (7 oz) whole kernel sweet corn, drained
- 2 cups shredded Mexican cheese blend (8 oz)
- 6 oz tortilla chips (about 42 chips)
- ¼ cup chopped fresh cilantro

1 In 12-inch nonstick skillet, heat oil over medium-high heat. Cook chicken in oil 3 to 5 minutes, stirring occasionally, until no longer pink in center.

2 Stir in taco seasoning mix, tomato sauce, bell pepper, beans, corn and 1 cup of the cheese. Reduce heat to medium; cook 3 to 5 minutes, stirring occasionally, until heated through and cheese is melted.

3 Divide tortilla chips among 6 plates. Spoon chicken mixture evenly over chips. Sprinkle with remaining 1 cup cheese and the cilantro.

1 Serving: Calories 520; Total Fat 24g (Saturated Fat 9g; Trans Fat 0g); Cholesterol 95mg; Sodium 1320mg; Total Carbohydrate 38g (Dietary Fiber 5g); Protein 36g **Exchanges:** 2 Starch, ½ Other Carbohydrate, ½ Vegetable, 4 Very Lean Meat, 4 Fat **Carbohydrate Choices:** 2½

SKILLET BEEF NACHOS Substitute 1¼ lb ground beef for the chicken. In Step 1, cook beef 5 to 7 minutes or until thoroughly cooked. Drain and continue as directed.

Meal Planning

A little time set aside for weekly meal planning pays off. Check your refrigerator and pantry for needed items, then make a list before you shop. There will be fewer last-minute trips to the grocery store.

CHEESY CHICKEN SKILLET DINNER FAST LOWER CALORIE

PREP 20 min TOTAL 20 min • **6 servings**

- 1 teaspoon canola or vegetable oil
- 1¼ lb boneless skinless chicken breasts, cut into ¾-inch pieces
- 2 large carrots, cut into ⅛-inch slices (2 cups)
- 1 medium zucchini, cut into ⅛-inch slices (2 cups)
- 2 tablespoons soy sauce
- 8 medium green onions, sliced (½ cup)
- 2 cups shredded reduced-fat sharp Cheddar cheese (8 oz)

1 Heat 12-inch nonstick skillet over medium-high heat. Add oil; tilt skillet to coat bottom. Add chicken; cook 4 to 5 minutes or until no longer pink in center, stirring frequently. Remove from skillet; cover to keep warm.

2 In same skillet, cook carrots and zucchini 5 minutes or until crisp-tender, stirring frequently. Add chicken and soy sauce; toss until chicken and vegetables are coated with soy sauce. Remove from heat.

3 Sprinkle with onions and cheese. Cover; let stand 2 minutes to melt cheese.

1 Serving: Calories 210; Total Fat 7g (Saturated Fat 2.5g; Trans Fat 0g); Cholesterol 65mg; Sodium 730mg; Total Carbohydrate 6g (Dietary Fiber 1g); Protein 31g **Exchanges:** ½ Other Carbohydrate, 3½ Lean Meat **Carbohydrate Choices:** ½

ITALIAN CHEESY CHICKEN SKILLET DINNER Substitute an Italian cheese blend for the Cheddar cheese.

Convenient Chicken

Boneless skinless chicken breasts are great to have on hand for quick meals. But often they are frozen together and so take longer to thaw. When you bring them home, wrap each chicken breast in plastic wrap and freeze in a freezer plastic bag. When it comes time to thaw, just microwave using the Defrost setting for about 2 to 2½ minutes.

Crunchy Potato Chip Chicken

Skillet Chicken Nachos

Cheesy Chicken Skillet Dinner

Dijon Chicken Smothered in Mushrooms

DIJON CHICKEN SMOTHERED IN MUSHROOMS

FAST   LOWER CALORIE

For a meal that's sure to satisfy, serve this saucy chicken dish with baked potatoes, cooked green beans and Italian rolls.

PREP 20 min **TOTAL** 20 min • **4 servings**

- 4 boneless skinless chicken breasts (about 1¼ lb)
- ¼ cup all-purpose flour
- ½ teaspoon salt
- ¼ teaspoon pepper
- 2 tablespoons olive or canola oil
- ½ cup roasted garlic-seasoned chicken broth (from 14-oz can)
- 1 jar (4.5 oz) sliced mushrooms, drained
- 1½ tablespoons Dijon mustard
  Chopped fresh thyme leaves, if desired

1 Between pieces of plastic wrap or waxed paper, gently pound each chicken breast to ¼ inch thickness (page 404). In shallow pan, stir together flour, salt and pepper.

2 In 12-inch nonstick skillet, heat oil over medium-high heat. Coat both sides of chicken with flour mixture. Cook chicken in oil 6 to 8 minutes, turning once, until chicken is no longer pink in center. Place chicken on serving plate; cover to keep warm.

3 Stir broth into skillet. Heat to boiling over medium-high heat. Stir in mushrooms and mustard. Cook 2 to 3 minutes, stirring frequently, until slightly thickened. Spoon sauce over chicken. Sprinkle with thyme.

1 Serving: Calories 240; Total Fat 11g (Saturated Fat 2g; Trans Fat 0g); Cholesterol 70mg; Sodium 750mg; Total Carbohydrate 8g (Dietary Fiber 1g); Protein 27g **Exchanges:** ½ Starch, 3½ Lean Meat **Carbohydrate Choices:** ½

DIJON PORK SMOTHERED IN MUSHROOMS

Substitute pork tenderloin for the chicken breasts. Cut into 1-inch slices, and flatten as directed in Step 1. Continue as directed, cooking until pork is no longer pink in center.

SPICY SKILLET CHICKEN **FAST**

This is an easy and tasty southwestern-inspired dish. Use your favorite salsa, hot or mild. If you want to try different beans, pinto or kidney are both good substitutes for the black beans.

PREP 20 min **TOTAL** 20 min • **4 servings**

- 2 teaspoons chili powder
- ½ teaspoon salt
- ¼ teaspoon pepper
- 4 boneless skinless chicken breasts (about 1¼ lb)
- 1 tablespoon vegetable oil
- 1 can (15 oz) black beans, drained, rinsed
- 1 can (11 oz) whole kernel corn with red and green peppers, undrained
- ⅓ cup salsa
- 2 cups hot cooked rice (page 429)

1 In small bowl, mix chili powder, salt and pepper. Sprinkle evenly over both sides of chicken.

2 In 12-inch nonstick skillet, heat oil over medium heat. Cook chicken in oil 8 to 10 minutes, turning once, until juice of chicken is clear when center of thickest part is cut (at least 165°F).

3 Stir in beans, corn and salsa. Heat to boiling; reduce heat. Cover; simmer 3 to 5 minutes or until vegetables are hot. Serve with rice.

1 Serving: Calories 500; Total Fat 8g (Saturated Fat 2g; Trans Fat 0g); Cholesterol 75mg; Sodium 870mg; Total Carbohydrate 66g (Dietary Fiber 9g); Protein 40g **Exchanges:** 4 Starch, 1 Vegetable, 4 Very Lean Meat **Carbohydrate Choices:** 4½

Coconut-Curry Chicken

THAI CHICKEN WITH BASIL

FAST **LOWER CALORIE**

Thai fish sauce, or nam pla, is a salty, watery, fermented sauce with a very pungent odor. It is used extensively in Southeast Asian cooking. You may be familiar with its flavor, as it's the key ingredient in the sauce accompanying deep-fried spring rolls served in Thai and Vietnamese restaurants.

PREP 20 min TOTAL 20 min • **4 servings**

- 2 **tablespoons vegetable oil**
- 4 **boneless skinless chicken breasts (about 1¼ lb)**
- 3 **cloves garlic, finely chopped**
- 2 **jalapeño chiles, seeded, finely chopped**
- 1 **tablespoon fish sauce***
- 1 **teaspoon sugar**
- ¼ **cup chopped fresh basil leaves**
- 1 **tablespoon chopped fresh mint leaves**
- 1 **tablespoon chopped unsalted dry-roasted peanuts**

1 In 12-inch skillet, heat oil over medium-high heat. Cut each chicken breast into 4 pieces. Cook chicken, garlic and chiles in oil 8 to 10 minutes, stirring occasionally, until chicken is no longer pink in center.

2 Stir in fish sauce and sugar. Sprinkle with basil, mint and peanuts.

*To substitute for fish sauce, use 3 tablespoons reduced-sodium soy sauce and 1 tablespoon dry sherry.

1 Serving: Calories 230; Total Fat 12g (Saturated Fat 2g; Trans Fat 0g); Cholesterol 75mg; Sodium 290mg; Total Carbohydrate 3g (Dietary Fiber 0g); Protein 28g **Exchanges:** 4 Lean Meat **Carbohydrate Choices:** 0

COCONUT-CURRY CHICKEN

FAST **LOWER CALORIE**

Toasted coconut adds an exotic tropical flavor, but just 2 tablespoons contain 4 grams of fat. This recipe contains just enough coconut to provide great flavor without adding unnecessary fat.

PREP 15 min TOTAL 15 min • **4 servings**

- 1 **tablespoon curry powder**
- ¾ **lb boneless skinless chicken breasts**
- 1 **teaspoon vegetable oil**
- 1 **small onion, cut into thin wedges**
- 1 **small zucchini, cut into ¼-inch slices**
- 1 **medium bell pepper (any color), cut into ¾-inch squares**
- ⅓ **cup reduced-fat unsweetened coconut milk**
- 1 **tablespoon brown bean sauce**
- 1 **teaspoon grated gingerroot**
- ½ **teaspoon salt**
- 2 **tablespoons shredded coconut, toasted (page 18)**

1 Rub curry powder on chicken. Cut chicken into ¾-inch pieces. Let stand 10 minutes.

2 Spray wok or 12-inch skillet with cooking spray; heat over medium-high heat until cooking spray starts to bubble. Add chicken; cook and stir 2 minutes until chicken is no longer pink in center. Move chicken to side of wok.

3 Add oil to center of wok. Add onion, zucchini and bell pepper; cook and stir 2 minutes. Add coconut milk, bean sauce, gingerroot and salt; cook and stir until sauce coats vegetables and chicken and is heated through. Sprinkle with toasted coconut.

1 Serving: Calories 170; Total Fat 6g (Saturated Fat 3g; Trans Fat 0g); Cholesterol 55mg; Sodium 400mg; Total Carbohydrate 8g (Dietary Fiber 2g); Protein 20g **Exchanges:** 1 Vegetable, 2½ Lean Meat **Carbohydrate Choices:** ½

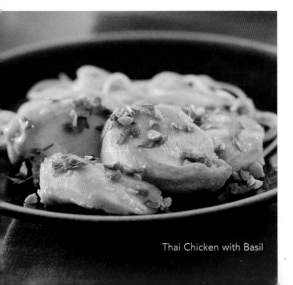

Thai Chicken with Basil

FETTUCCINE WITH CHICKEN AND VEGETABLES FAST

For this recipe, be sure to use Italian dressing that is not creamy style.

PREP 20 min TOTAL 20 min • **4 servings**

- 1 package (9 oz) refrigerated fettuccine
- 2 cups fresh small broccoli florets
- ½ cup Italian dressing (for homemade dressing, see page 475)
- 1 lb uncooked chicken breast strips for stir-fry*
- 1 medium red onion, cut into thin wedges
- ¼ teaspoon garlic-pepper blend**
- ½ cup sliced drained roasted red bell peppers (from 7-oz jar)
  Shredded Parmesan cheese, if desired

1 Cook fettuccine and broccoli together as directed on fettuccine package. Drain; toss with 2 tablespoons of the dressing. Cover to keep warm.

2 In 12-inch nonstick skillet, heat 2 tablespoons of the dressing over medium-high heat. Cook chicken, onion and garlic-pepper blend in dressing 4 to 6 minutes, stirring occasionally, until chicken is no longer pink in center.

3 Stir roasted peppers and remaining ¼ cup dressing into chicken mixture. Cook 2 to 3 minutes, stirring occasionally, until warm. Serve chicken mixture over fettuccine and broccoli. Serve with cheese.

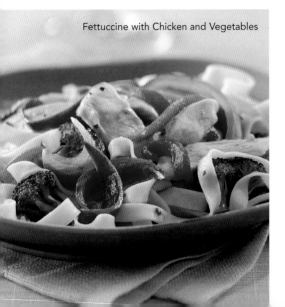

Fettuccine with Chicken and Vegetables

*Boneless skinless chicken breasts, cut crosswise into ¼-inch slices, can be substituted.

**⅛ teaspoon each garlic powder and coarse ground black pepper can be substituted.

1 Serving: Calories 460; Total Fat 17g (Saturated Fat 2g; Trans Fat 0g); Cholesterol 75mg; Sodium 460mg; Total Carbohydrate 42g (Dietary Fiber 4g); Protein 34g **Exchanges:** 2 Starch, ½ Other Carbohydrate, 4 Very Lean Meat, 3 Fat **Carbohydrate Choices:** 3

CREAMY CHICKEN AND VEGETABLES WITH NOODLES

FAST

Choose 2 cups of your family's favorite frozen vegetable to use in place of the mixed vegetables. Broccoli, corn and green beans would all be good choices. Cut-up rotisserie chicken can be used to make this a super-quick, delicious dinner.

PREP 15 min TOTAL 15 min • **4 servings**

- 5 cups uncooked medium egg noodles (10 oz)
- 2 cups frozen mixed vegetables, thawed, drained
- 6 medium green onions, sliced (6 tablespoons)
- 1 container (8 oz) garden vegetable cream cheese spread
- 1¼ cups milk
- 1½ cups cubed cooked chicken
- ½ teaspoon garlic salt
- ¼ teaspoon pepper
- 2 tablespoons canned French-fried onions (from 2.8-oz can), if desired

1 Cook and drain noodles as directed on package.

2 Meanwhile, spray 12-inch skillet with cooking spray; heat over medium heat. Add mixed vegetables and green onions; cook about 4 minutes, stirring frequently, until vegetables are crisp-tender. Stir in cream cheese and milk until blended. Stir in chicken, garlic salt and pepper; cook until hot.

3 Stir noodles into cheese sauce mixture; cook until hot. Sprinkle with French-fried onions.

1 Serving: Calories 620; Total Fat 25g (Saturated Fat 13g; Trans Fat 0.5g); Cholesterol 155mg; Sodium 1130mg; Total Carbohydrate 65g (Dietary Fiber 6g); Protein 32g **Exchanges:** 3 Starch, 1 Other Carbohydrate, 1 Vegetable, 3 Medium-Fat Meat, 1½ Fat **Carbohydrate Choices:** 4

ASPARAGUS–TURKEY SAUSAGE SKILLET FAST

PREP 20 min TOTAL 20 min • **4 servings**

- 1 tablespoon olive or vegetable oil
- 1 package (19.5 oz) lean Italian turkey sausages, casings removed, cut into ½-inch slices
- 1 large onion, coarsely chopped (1 cup)
- 1 cup chicken broth (for homemade broth, see page 528)
- 1 cup water
- 1 cup uncooked orzo or rosamarina pasta (6 oz)
- 1 lb fresh asparagus spears, trimmed, cut into 1-inch pieces
- 2 tablespoons sliced pimientos (from 4-oz jar)

1 In 12-inch nonstick skillet, heat oil over medium-high heat. Add sausage and onion; cook 2 minutes, stirring occasionally.

2 Stir in broth and water. Heat to boiling. Stir in orzo; boil 2 minutes. Add asparagus and pimientos. Reduce heat to medium. Cover; return to boiling. Cook 8 to 10 minutes or until pasta is tender and sausage is no longer pink.

1 Serving: Calories 470; Total Fat 19g (Saturated Fat 4g; Trans Fat 0.5g); Cholesterol 125mg; Sodium 1140mg; Total Carbohydrate 34g (Dietary Fiber 3g); Protein 40g **Exchanges:** 2 Starch, 1½ Vegetable, 1½ Very Lean Meat, 2 Lean Meat, 2½ Fat **Carbohydrate Choices:** 2

CHEESY SPINACH AND CHICKEN PIZZA FAST

PREP 15 min TOTAL 15 min • **6 servings**

- 1 package (14 oz) prebaked original Italian pizza crust or other 12-inch prebaked pizza crust
- 4 oz Havarti cheese, shredded (1 cup)
- 2 cups fresh baby spinach leaves
- 1 cup diced cooked chicken
- 1 cup shredded Cheddar cheese (4 oz)
- ¼ cup chopped drained roasted red bell peppers (from 7-oz jar)
- ½ teaspoon garlic salt

Heat oven to 425°F. Place pizza crust on ungreased pizza pan. Top with remaining ingredients. Bake 8 to 10 minutes or until crust is golden brown.

1 Serving: Calories 390; Total Fat 18g (Saturated Fat 9g; Trans Fat 0g); Cholesterol 60mg; Sodium 660mg; Total Carbohydrate 36g (Dietary Fiber 2g); Protein 20g **Exchanges:** 2 Starch, 1 Vegetable, 2 Medium-Fat Meat, 1 Fat **Carbohydrate Choices:** 2½

PIZZA WITH PIZZAZZ

Start with a purchased pizza crust and choose a topping below (leave a 1-inch border around crust when topping it). Bake on a cookie sheet for 10 minutes at 425°F until golden brown. Use these ideas to top frozen cheese pizzas too.

Autumn Pizza: Top pizza crust with 1⅓ cups caramelized onions. Sprinkle with ¼ cup dried cranberries and 4 ounces crumbled chèvre (goat) cheese. Top with dollops of mashed cooked butternut squash (about 1½ cups) and sprinkle with ½ teaspoon finely chopped rosemary leaves.

Autumn Pizza

Cheesy Barbecue Pizza: Spread 1 cup barbecue sauce evenly over pizza crust. Top with 1½ cups shredded Cheddar cheese, ¼ cup sliced pitted ripe olives and ⅓ cup French-fried onions.

Chicken Caesar Pizza: Top pizza crust with 1½ cups shredded mozzarella cheese and 6 ounces grilled chicken breast strips. Top hot cooked pizza with 4 cups Caesar Salad (page 454).

Mediterranean Pizza

Mediterranean Pizza: Spread pizza crust with 1 cup Basil Pesto (page 484, or purchased pesto). Top with ¼ cup each chopped pitted kalamata olives, artichoke hearts, drained and chopped, and chopped sun-dried tomatoes. Sprinkle with 1 cup shredded mozzarella cheese.

Pizza Bianca: Sprinkle crust with 2 teaspoons freshly grated garlic. Top with 2 cups shredded mozzarella cheese and sprinkle with fresh chopped herbs (thyme, rosemary, basil, parsley).

Salsa Pizza: In 10-inch skillet, brown 1 pound lean ground beef. Add 1¼ cups salsa; spread on pizza crust. Sprinkle with ¼ cup chopped green onions and 1½ cups shredded Colby–Monterey Jack cheese blend.

ASIAN CHICKEN ROLL-UPS

FAST **LOWER CALORIE**

Look for bags of shredded lettuce and carrots in the produce case, or use 3 cups broccoli slaw mix instead.

PREP 15 min TOTAL 15 min • **4 roll-ups**

- 2 tablespoons creamy peanut butter
- 2 tablespoons teriyaki baste and glaze or stir-fry sauce
- 1 tablespoon packed brown sugar
- 1 tablespoon hot water
- 1 teaspoon sesame or vegetable oil
- 4 flour tortillas (8 to 10 inch)
- ½ lb thinly sliced roasted chicken or turkey breast (from deli)
- 1½ cups thinly sliced iceberg lettuce
- 1½ cups shredded carrots
- ½ cup chopped fresh cilantro

1 In small bowl, beat peanut butter, teriyaki glaze, brown sugar, water and oil with wire whisk until blended.

2 Spread about 2 tablespoons peanut butter mixture over each tortilla. Top each with one-fourth of the chicken, about ⅓ cup lettuce, about ⅓ cup carrots and 2 tablespoons cilantro. Roll up tortillas.

1 Roll-Up: Calories 290; Total Fat 10g (Saturated Fat 2g; Trans Fat 0.5g); Cholesterol 25mg; Sodium 540mg; Total Carbohydrate 35g (Dietary Fiber 3g); Protein 16g **Exchanges:** 2 Starch, 1 Vegetable, 1 Lean Meat, 1 Fat **Carbohydrate Choices:** 2

BEEF TENDERLOIN WITH MUSHROOM-WINE SAUCE

FAST **LOWER CALORIE**

Reduce prep time by purchasing presliced mushrooms; just measure and start cooking!

PREP 20 min TOTAL 20 min • **4 servings**

- 1 lb beef tenderloin
- 2 teaspoons chopped fresh or ½ teaspoon dried marjoram leaves
- 2 teaspoons sugar
- 1 teaspoon coarse ground black pepper
- 1 tablespoon vegetable oil
- 1 cup sliced fresh mushrooms (3 oz)
- 1 small onion, thinly sliced
- ¾ cup beef broth (for homemade broth, see page 530)
- ¼ cup dry red wine or nonalcoholic wine
- 1 tablespoon cornstarch

1 Cut beef crosswise into 4 (¾-inch) slices. In small bowl, mix marjoram, sugar and pepper; rub on both sides of beef slices.

2 In 10-inch skillet, heat oil over medium-high heat. Cook beef in oil 3 to 5 minutes, turning once, until of desired doneness. Remove beef to serving platter; keep warm.

3 In drippings in skillet, cook mushrooms and onion over medium-high heat about 2 minutes, stirring occasionally, until onion is crisp-tender.

4 In small bowl, mix broth, wine and cornstarch; stir into mushroom mixture. Cook over medium-high heat about 2 minutes, stirring constantly, until mixture thickens and boils. Boil and stir 1 minute. Pour over beef.

1 Serving: Calories 230; Total Fat 12g (Saturated Fat 3.5g; Trans Fat 0g); Cholesterol 65mg; Sodium 250mg; Total Carbohydrate 6g (Dietary Fiber 0g); Protein 26g **Exchanges:** 1 Vegetable, 3 Lean Meat, 1 Fat **Carbohydrate Choices:** ½

Quick Food Prep

Make mealtime speedier by looking for convenience items at the grocery store. Presliced mushrooms, shredded carrots, precut lettuce and frozen chopped onions and bell peppers are all easy to find when you are shopping.

Asian Chicken Roll-Ups

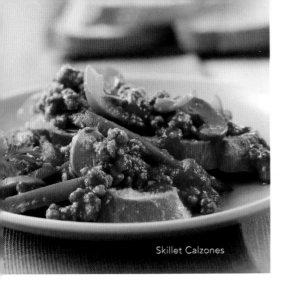

Skillet Calzones

SKILLET CALZONES FAST

No yeast dough is required for this. You make the calzones with crisp slices of bread and cook it on top of the stove. It's an easy weeknight meal.

PREP 20 min TOTAL 20 min • **4 servings**

- 8 **diagonally cut slices (½ inch thick) French bread**
  Cooking spray
- 2 **tablespoons grated Parmesan cheese**
- 1 **lb lean (at least 80%) ground beef**
- 1 **small green bell pepper, sliced**
- 1 or 2 **cloves garlic, finely chopped**
- 1 **can (14.5 oz) diced tomatoes with Italian-style herbs, undrained***
- 1 **can (8 oz) pizza sauce**
- 1 **jar (4.5 oz) sliced mushrooms, drained**

1 Set oven control to broil. Place bread slices on ungreased cookie sheet. Spray bread with cooking spray; sprinkle with cheese. Broil with tops 4 to 6 inches from heat 1 to 2 minutes or until light brown; set aside.

2 In 10-inch skillet, cook beef, bell pepper and garlic over medium-high heat 5 to 7 minutes, stirring occasionally, until thoroughly cooked; drain. Stir in tomatoes, pizza sauce and mushrooms. Cook 1 to 2 minutes or until hot.

3 Place 2 toasted bread slices on each of 4 plates; top with beef mixture.

*Any variety of seasoned diced tomatoes can be substituted.

1 Serving: Calories 460; Total Fat 18g (Saturated Fat 6g; Trans Fat 1.5g); Cholesterol 75mg; Sodium 1040mg; Total Carbohydrate 44g (Dietary Fiber 5g); Protein 29g **Exchanges:** 2 Starch, 2 Vegetable, 3 Medium-Fat Meat, 1½ Fat **Carbohydrate Choices:** 3

BEEF WITH BOW-TIE PASTA FAST

Look for miniature bow-tie pasta (tripolini) for a change instead of the regular bow-ties. Add fresh basil sprigs and Parmesan cheese for a great garnish.

PREP 20 min TOTAL 20 min • **6 servings**

- 1½ **lb boneless beef sirloin steak**
- 3 **cups 2-inch pieces asparagus (1 lb)**
- 2 **medium onions, sliced**
- 1½ **cups beef broth (for homemade broth, see page 530)**
- 4 **cups cooked farfalle (bow-tie) pasta**
- 1 **cup tomato puree (from 28-oz can)**
- 3 **tablespoons chopped fresh or 1 tablespoon dried basil leaves**
- 3 **tablespoons chopped sun-dried tomatoes (not oil-packed)**
- ¼ **teaspoon pepper**
- 2 **tablespoons shredded Parmesan cheese**

1 Trim fat from beef. Cut beef with grain into 2-inch strips; cut strips across grain into ⅛-inch slices. (For easier cutting, partially freeze beef about 1 hour.)

2 Spray 12-inch skillet with cooking spray; heat over medium heat. Add asparagus, onions and 1 cup of the broth. Cook 5 to 7 minutes, stirring occasionally, until liquid has evaporated; remove mixture from skillet.

3 Add beef to skillet; cook about 2 minutes over medium heat, stirring frequently, until beef is no longer pink.

4 Return asparagus mixture to skillet. Stir in pasta, remaining broth and remaining ingredients except cheese. Cook about 2 minutes, stirring frequently, until mixture is hot. Sprinkle with cheese.

1 Serving: Calories 360; Total Fat 6g (Saturated Fat 2g; Trans Fat 0g); Cholesterol 75mg; Sodium 670mg; Total Carbohydrate 39g (Dietary Fiber 4g); Protein 38g **Exchanges:** 1½ Starch, ½ Other Carbohydrate, 2 Vegetable, 3 Very Lean Meat, 1 Lean Meat **Carbohydrate Choices:** 2½

BEEF WITH BOW-TIE PASTA AND FETA
Substitute crumbled feta cheese for the Parmesan cheese, and stir in ¼ cup capers.

ORANGE TERIYAKI BEEF WITH NOOMLES FAST LOWER CALORIE

PREP 20 min TOTAL 20 min • **4 servings**

- 1 lb boneless beef top sirloin, trimmed of fat, cut into thin strips
- 1 can (14 oz) beef broth (for homemade broth, see page 530)
- ¼ cup teriyaki stir-fry sauce
- 2 tablespoons orange marmalade
  Dash ground red pepper (cayenne)
- 1½ cups frozen sugar snap peas
- 1½ cups uncooked fine egg noodles (3 oz)

1 Spray 12-inch skillet with cooking spray. Cook beef in skillet over medium-high heat 2 to 4 minutes, stirring occasionally, until browned. Remove beef from skillet; keep warm.

2 In same skillet, mix broth, stir-fry sauce, marmalade and red pepper. Heat to boiling. Stir in sugar snap peas and noodles; reduce heat to medium. Cover; cook about 5 minutes or until noodles are tender.

3 Stir in beef. Cook uncovered 2 to 3 minutes or until sauce is slightly thickened.

1 Serving: Calories 270; Total Fat 4.5g (Saturated Fat 1.5g; Trans Fat 0g); Cholesterol 80mg; Sodium 1190mg; Total Carbohydrate 27g (Dietary Fiber 2g); Protein 29g **Exchanges:** 1 Starch, 2 Vegetable, 3 Very Lean Meat, ½ Fat **Carbohydrate Choices:** 2

CHEESY HAMBURGER-POTATO SKILLET FAST

PREP 20 min TOTAL 20 min • **4 servings**

- 1 lb lean (at least 80%) ground beef
- 1 bag (20 oz) refrigerated diced cooked potatoes with onions
- 1 can (14.5 oz) diced tomatoes with Italian-style herbs, undrained*
- 1 tablespoon pizza seasoning or Italian seasoning
- 1½ cups shredded pizza cheese blend (6 oz)
- 2 tablespoons chopped fresh parsley

1 In 12-inch nonstick skillet, cook beef and potatoes over medium-high heat 8 to 10 minutes, stirring occasionally, until beef is thoroughly cooked; drain.

2 Stir in tomatoes and pizza seasoning. Cook about 4 minutes, stirring occasionally, until thoroughly heated.

3 Sprinkle with cheese and parsley. Cover; heat about 1 minute or until cheese is melted.

Any variety of seasoned diced tomatoes can be substituted.

1 Serving: Calories 490; Total Fat 26g (Saturated Fat 13g; Trans Fat 1g); Cholesterol 115mg; Sodium 470mg; Total Carbohydrate 31g (Dietary Fiber 4g); Protein 34g **Exchanges:** 2 Starch, 4½ Medium-Fat Meat, ½ Fat **Carbohydrate Choices:** 2

BEEF AND KASHA MEXICANA

FAST LOWER CALORIE

Kasha, also known as buckwheat groats, is native to Russia and is a traditional food. It has a hearty flavor, and its small size makes it ideal in main dishes because it cooks quickly.

PREP 20 min TOTAL 20 min • **6 servings**

- 1 lb extra-lean (at least 90%) ground beef
- 1 small onion, chopped (⅓ cup)
- 1 cup uncooked buckwheat kernels or groats (kasha)
- 1 can (14.5 oz) diced tomatoes, undrained
- 1 can (4.5 oz) chopped green chiles, undrained
- 1 package (1 oz) 40% less-sodium taco seasoning mix
- 2 cups frozen whole kernel corn, thawed
- 1½ cups water
- 1 cup shredded reduced-fat Cheddar cheese (4 oz)
- 2 tablespoons chopped fresh cilantro, if desired
- 2 tablespoons sliced ripe pitted olives, if desired

1 In 12-inch skillet, cook beef and onion over medium-high heat 5 to 7 minutes, stirring occasionally, until beef is thoroughly cooked; drain. Stir in kasha until kernels are moistened by beef mixture.

2 Stir in tomatoes, chiles, taco seasoning mix, corn and water. Heat to boiling. Cover; reduce heat to low. Simmer 5 to 7 minutes, stirring occasionally, until kasha is tender.

3 Sprinkle cheese over kasha mixture. Cover; cook 2 to 3 minutes or until cheese is melted. Sprinkle with cilantro and olives.

1 Serving (1⅓ Cups): Calories 300; Total Fat 8g (Saturated Fat 3.5g; Trans Fat 0g); Cholesterol 50mg; Sodium 720mg; Total Carbohydrate 33g (Dietary Fiber 4g); Protein 23g **Exchanges:** 1½ Starch, ½ Other Carbohydrate, 2½ Lean Meat **Carbohydrate Choices:** 2

BEEF AND KASHA TORTILLAS Spoon mixture onto soft corn or flour tortillas; roll up.

CORNED BEEF SKILLET HASH

FAST

PREP 20 min TOTAL 20 min • **4 servings**

- 2 cups chopped cooked corned beef brisket*
- 1½ cups chopped cooked potatoes (about 1½ medium)
- 1½ cups diced cooked beets (about 12 oz fresh beets)** (page 587)
- ⅓ cup chopped onion
- ½ teaspoon salt
- ¼ teaspoon pepper
- 2 tablespoons vegetable oil
  Chopped fresh parsley, if desired

1 In large bowl, mix all ingredients except vegetable oil and parsley.

2 In 10-inch skillet, heat oil over medium heat. Spread beef mixture in skillet. Cook 10 to 15 minutes, turning occasionally with wide spatula, until brown. Sprinkle with parsley.

One can (12 oz) corned beef can be used for the brisket.

**One can (15 oz) sliced beets, drained and diced, can be used for the cooked beets.*

1 Serving: Calories 370; Total Fat 26g (Saturated Fat 7g; Trans Fat 3g); Cholesterol 65mg; Sodium 1100mg; Total Carbohydrate 19g (Dietary Fiber 3g); Protein 14g **Exchanges:** 1 Starch, 1 Vegetable, 1½ Lean Meat, 4 Fat **Carbohydrate Choices:** 1

CORNED BEEF AND MIXED VEGGIE HASH Substitute 1½ cups frozen mixed vegetables for the beets.

ROAST BEEF HASH Substitute chopped cooked roast beef for the corned beef and omit the beets. Cook as directed.

Hash

Hash just refers to easy dishes made by combining a variety of chopped ingredients to fry. Corned beef hash is the most famous, and cooked until golden brown, it's delicious for supper or breakfast. If you have leftover veggies, go ahead and add them to your hash.

Orange Teriyaki Beef with Noodles

Beef and Kasha Mexicána

PIZZA BURGERS FAST LOWER CALORIE

PREP 20 min TOTAL 20 min • **6 sandwiches**

- 1 lb lean (at least 80%) ground beef
- 1 medium onion, chopped (½ cup)
- 1 small green bell pepper, chopped (½ cup)
- 1 jar (14 oz) or can (15 oz) pepperoni-flavored or regular pizza sauce
- ½ cup sliced ripe olives, if desired
- 6 burger buns, split
- ¾ cup shredded pizza cheese blend (3 oz)

1 In 10-inch skillet, cook beef, onion and bell pepper over medium heat 8 to 10 minutes, stirring occasionally, until beef is thoroughly cooked; drain.

2 Stir in pizza sauce and olives. Heat to boiling, stirring occasionally.

3 Spoon about ½ cup beef mixture on bottom half of each bun. Immediately sprinkle each with 2 tablespoons cheese; cover with top halves of buns. Serve immediately, or let stand about 2 minutes until cheese is melted.

1 Sandwich: Calories 350; Total Fat 16g (Saturated Fat 6g; Trans Fat 1g); Cholesterol 60mg; Sodium 670mg; Total Carbohydrate 29g (Dietary Fiber 2g); Protein 22g **Exchanges:** 2 Starch, 2½ Medium-Fat Meat, ½ Fat **Carbohydrate Choices:** 2

PARMESAN ORZO AND MEATBALLS FAST

PREP 20 min TOTAL 20 min • **4 servings**

- 1½ cups frozen bell pepper and onion stir-fry (from 1-lb bag)
- 2 tablespoons Italian dressing
- 1 can (14 oz) beef broth (for homemade broth, see page 530)
- 1 cup uncooked orzo or rosamarina pasta (6 oz)
- 1 bag (10½ oz) frozen cooked Italian meatballs (about 16 meatballs)
- 1 large tomato, chopped (1 cup)
- 2 tablespoons chopped fresh parsley
- ¼ cup shredded Parmesan cheese

1 In 12-inch nonstick skillet, cook stir-fry vegetables and dressing over medium-high heat 2 minutes. Stir in broth; heat to boiling. Stir pasta and meatballs into vegetables. Heat to boiling; reduce heat to low. Cover and simmer 10 minutes, stirring occasionally.

2 Stir in tomato. Cover and simmer 3 to 5 minutes or until most of the liquid has been absorbed and pasta is tender. Stir in parsley. Sprinkle with cheese.

1 Serving: Calories 480; Total Fat 23g (Saturated Fat 7g; Trans Fat 0.5g); Cholesterol 30mg; Sodium 1120mg; Total Carbohydrate 45g (Dietary Fiber 4g); Protein 23g **Exchanges:** 2½ Starch, ½ Other Carbohydrate, ½ Vegetable, 1 Lean Meat, 1 High-Fat Meat, 2 Fat **Carbohydrate Choices:** 3

PENNE WITH CHEESY TOMATO SAUCE FAST

PREP 20 min TOTAL 20 min • **5 servings**

- 2⅔ cups uncooked penne pasta (8 oz)
- ½ lb bulk Italian pork sausage
- 1 container (15 oz) refrigerated tomato pasta sauce (for homemade sauce, see page 370)
- ¼ cup shredded fresh basil leaves
- ½ cup diced mozzarella cheese (2 oz)
- ¼ cup shredded Parmesan cheese (1 oz)

1 Cook and drain pasta as directed on package, cover to keep warm.

2 While pasta is cooking, in 3-quart saucepan, cook sausage over medium heat about 8 minutes, stirring occasionally, until no longer pink; drain.

3 Stir pasta sauce into sausage. Heat to boiling; reduce heat to medium-low. Stir in basil and mozzarella cheese. Cook 1 to 2 minutes or until cheese is slightly melted. Serve sauce over pasta. Sprinkle with Parmesan cheese.

1 Serving: Calories 430; Total Fat 16g (Saturated Fat 6g; Trans Fat 0g); Cholesterol 35mg; Sodium 880mg; Total Carbohydrate 52g (Dietary Fiber 4g); Protein 19g **Exchanges:** 3 Starch, 1 Vegetable, 1½ High-Fat Meat **Carbohydrate Choices:** 3½

Parmesan Orzo and Meatballs

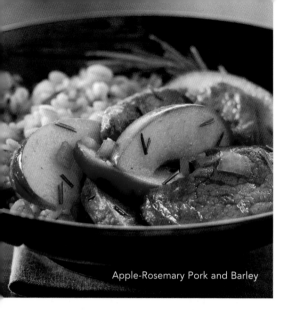

Apple-Rosemary Pork and Barley

APPLE-ROSEMARY PORK AND BARLEY FAST

PREP 20 min TOTAL 20 min • **4 servings**

- 1½ cups apple juice
- ¾ cup uncooked quick-cooking barley
- 2 tablespoons chopped fresh or 2 teaspoons dried rosemary leaves, crushed
- 1 pork tenderloin (¾ lb), cut into ¼-inch slices
- 2 teaspoons canola or soybean oil
- 1 medium onion, chopped (½ cup)
- 1 clove garlic, finely chopped
- ¼ cup apple jelly
- 1 large unpeeled red cooking apple, sliced (1½ cups)

1 In 2-quart saucepan, heat apple juice to boiling. Stir in barley and 1 tablespoon of the rosemary; reduce heat to low. Cover and simmer 10 to 12 minutes until liquid is absorbed and barley is tender.

2 In 10-inch nonstick skillet, heat oil over medium-high heat. Cook pork, onion, garlic and remaining 1 tablespoon rosemary in hot oil about 5 minutes, stirring frequently, until pork is no longer pink in center. Stir in apple jelly and apple slices; cook until hot. Serve over barley.

1 Serving: Calories 400; Total Fat 6g (Saturated Fat 1.5g; Trans Fat 0g); Cholesterol 55mg; Sodium 50mg; Total Carbohydrate 63g (Dietary Fiber 8g); Protein 23g **Exchanges:** 2 Starch, 2 Fruit, 2½ Very Lean Meat, 1 Fat **Carbohydrate Choices:** 4

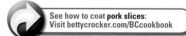

See how to coat pork slices:
Visit bettycrocker.com/BCcookbook

NUT-CRUSTED PORK FAST

PREP 20 min TOTAL 20 min • **4 servings**

- 1 egg, beaten
- ¼ cup honey, or real maple or maple-flavored syrup
- 1 pork tenderloin (¾ to 1 lb), cut into ½-inch slices
- 1 cup chopped pecans
- ½ cup yellow cornmeal
- 1 teaspoon salt
- ½ teaspoon pepper
- 2 tablespoons vegetable oil

1 In large bowl, mix egg and honey. Add pork slices; toss to coat.

2 In food processor, place pecans, cornmeal, salt and pepper. Cover; process until finely chopped. Place pecan mixture in resealable food-storage plastic bag; add pork slices. Seal bag; shake to coat.

3 In 10-inch nonstick skillet, heat oil over medium-high heat. Cook pork in oil 6 to 8 minutes, turning once, until golden brown on outside and no longer pink in center.

1 Serving: Calories 530; Total Fat 32g (Saturated Fat 4.5g; Trans Fat 0g); Cholesterol 105mg; Sodium 640mg; Total Carbohydrate 35g (Dietary Fiber 3g); Protein 25g **Exchanges:** 2 Starch, 2 Lean Meat, 4 Fat **Carbohydrate Choices:** 2

PORK CARNITAS FAST LOWER CALORIE

PREP 20 min TOTAL 20 min • **4 servings**

- 1 pork tenderloin (1 lb), cut into ½-inch slices
- 2 cloves garlic, finely chopped
- 2 tablespoons packed brown sugar
- 1 tablespoon orange juice
- 1 tablespoon molasses
- ½ teaspoon salt
- ¼ teaspoon pepper

1 Heat 10-inch nonstick skillet over medium-high heat. Cook pork and garlic in skillet 6 to 8 minutes, turning occasionally, until pork is no longer pink in center. Drain if necessary.

2 Stir in remaining ingredients. Cook until mixture thickens and coats pork.

1 Serving: Calories 190; Total Fat 4.5g (Saturated Fat 1.5g; Trans Fat 0g); Cholesterol 70mg; Sodium 350mg; Total Carbohydrate 12g (Dietary Fiber 0g); Protein 26g **Exchanges:** 1 Other Carbohydrate, 3½ Very Lean Meat, ½ Fat **Carbohydrate Choices:** 1

Apricot-Glazed Pork Dinner

Couscous and Sweet Potatoes with Pork

APRICOT-GLAZED PORK DINNER FAST

Look for the chili oil in the Asian food area of the supermarket. It's a little spicy and adds great flavor, but regular vegetable oil can be used, too.

PREP 20 min **TOTAL** 20 min • **4 servings**

- 1 cup uncooked regular long-grain white rice
- 1 tablespoon chili oil or vegetable oil
- 1 pork tenderloin (1 lb), cut into ½-inch slices
- 4 cups frozen broccoli, carrots and cauliflower or broccoli florets
- 3 tablespoons apricot preserves
- 1 tablespoon oyster sauce or hoisin sauce

1 Cook rice as directed on package, omitting salt.

2 Meanwhile, in 12-inch skillet, heat oil over medium-high heat. Cook pork in oil 4 to 5 minutes, stirring constantly, until no longer pink in center.

3 Add vegetables. Cook and stir 2 minutes. Stir in preserves and oyster sauce. Cook and stir about 30 seconds or until hot. Serve with rice.

1 Serving: Calories 430; Total Fat 8g (Saturated Fat 2g; Trans Fat 0g); Cholesterol 70mg; Sodium 190mg; Total Carbohydrate 56g (Dietary Fiber 4g); Protein 32g **Exchanges:** 2 Starch, 1 Other Carbohydrate, 2 Vegetable, 3 Lean Meat **Carbohydrate Choices:** 4

COUSCOUS AND SWEET POTATOES WITH PORK FAST

PREP 20 min **TOTAL** 20 min • **4 servings**

- 1½ cups uncooked couscous
- 1 pork tenderloin (1 lb), thinly sliced
- 1 medium sweet potato, peeled, sliced into thin bite-size strips
- 1 cup chunky-style salsa (for homemade salsa, see page 480)
- ½ cup water
- 2 tablespoons honey
- ¼ cup chopped fresh cilantro

1 Cook couscous as directed on package.

2 While couscous is cooking, spray 12-inch skillet with cooking spray. Cook pork in skillet over medium heat 2 to 3 minutes, stirring occasionally, until brown.

3 Stir sweet potato, salsa, water and honey into pork. Heat to boiling; reduce heat to medium. Cover and cook 5 to 6 minutes, stirring occasionally, until potato is tender and pork is no longer pink in center. Sprinkle with cilantro. Serve pork mixture over couscous.

1 Serving: Calories 450; Total Fat 5g (Saturated Fat 1.5g; Trans Fat 0g); Cholesterol 50mg; Sodium 530mg; Total Carbohydrate 70g (Dietary Fiber 4g); Protein 31g **Exchanges:** 3½ Starch, 1 Other Carbohydrate, ½ Vegetable, 2½ Very Lean Meat, ½ Fat **Carbohydrate Choices:** 4½

COUSCOUS AND CARROTS WITH PORK

Substitute 1 cup sliced (¼ inch) carrots for sweet potato. Cook as directed until carrots are tender.

CARIBBEAN PORK AND JASMINE RICE FAST

If you don't have jerk seasoning, make your own by mixing ¼ teaspoon each ground allspice, dried thyme leaves and salt, plus ⅛ teaspoon ground red pepper (cayenne).

PREP 20 min TOTAL 20 min • **4 servings**

- 1 cup uncooked jasmine rice
- 1 pork tenderloin (1 lb), cut into ¼-inch slices
- 1 small red onion, coarsely chopped
- 1 teaspoon Caribbean jerk seasoning
- 1 medium sweet potato, peeled, cut lengthwise in half, then cut crosswise into ⅛-inch slices
- ½ cup water
- 1 cup snow pea pods (4 oz), strings removed
- 1 can (8 oz) pineapple chunks in juice, drained, juice reserved
- ¼ cup lime juice
- 2 tablespoons honey
- 2 teaspoons cornstarch

1 Cook rice as directed on package.

2 Spray 12-inch skillet with cooking spray; heat over medium-high heat. Add pork, onion and jerk seasoning; cook 3 to 4 minutes, stirring frequently until pork is brown.

3 Stir in sweet potato and ½ cup water. Cover and cook over medium heat 5 minutes. Stir in pea pods and pineapple chunks. Cook 2 minutes, stirring occasionally, or until pork is no longer pink in center.

4 Mix reserved pineapple juice, lime juice, honey and cornstarch until smooth; stir into mixture in skillet. Heat to boiling, stirring constantly. Boil and stir 1 minute. Divide rice among 4 bowls. Top with pork mixture.

1 Serving: Calories 420; Total Fat 5g (Saturated Fat 1.5g; Trans Fat 0g); Cholesterol 50mg; Sodium 670mg; Total Carbohydrate 68g (Dietary Fiber 3g); Protein 27g **Exchanges:** 2 Starch, ½ Fruit, 1½ Other Carbohydrate, 1 Vegetable, 1½ Very Lean Meat, 1 Lean Meat **Carbohydrate Choices:** 4½

CAJUN SMOTHERED PORK CHOPS FAST

PREP 15 min TOTAL 15 min • **4 servings**

- 4 bone-in pork loin chops, ½ inch thick (about 1¾ lb)
- 2 teaspoons salt-free extra-spicy seasoning blend
- 2 teaspoons canola oil
- ½ medium onion, sliced
- 1 jalapeño chile, seeded, chopped
- 1 can (14.5 oz) diced tomatoes, undrained

1 Sprinkle both sides of pork chops with seasoning blend. In 12-inch nonstick skillet, heat oil over medium-high heat. Add onion and chile; cook about 2 minutes, stirring occasionally, until slightly tender. Push mixture to one side of skillet.

2 Add pork to other side of skillet. Cook about 3 minutes, turning once, until brown. Add tomatoes. Heat to boiling; reduce heat. Cover; cook 4 to 8 minutes or until pork is no longer pink in center.

1 Serving: Calories 270; Total Fat 13g (Saturated Fat 4g; Trans Fat 0g); Cholesterol 90mg; Sodium 190mg; Total Carbohydrate 6g (Dietary Fiber 1g); Protein 32g **Exchanges:** ½ Starch, 4 Lean Meat **Carbohydrate Choices:** ½

Caribbean Pork and Jasmine Rice

Cajun Smothered Pork Chops

FRESH PASTA PRESTO

Simply cook and drain a 9-ounce package of refrigerated fresh pasta, toss with an easy sauce, add a handful of high-flavor ingredients, and magically you can have dinner on the table in minutes. Sprinkle these pasta dishes with a little shaved, shredded or grated cheese.

Fettuccine with Meatballs: In medium skillet, cook 1 cup chopped bell peppers and 1 cup sliced mushrooms with a little olive oil until peppers are crisp-tender; stir in 2 cups tomato pasta sauce, and frozen cooked meatballs. Serve over hot cooked fettuccine.

Pasta Margherita: Combine hot cooked angel hair (capellini) pasta with 1½ cups halved grape tomatoes, ½ cup diced fresh mozzarella cheese, ½ cup chopped fresh basil and 4 to 5 tablespoons Italian dressing. Serve warm or at room temperature.

Ravioli with Pesto and Asparagus

Ravioli with Pesto and Asparagus: In medium skillet cook 1 pound chopped asparagus with ¼ cup water until crisp-tender; drain. Toss with 1 cup pesto, asparagus and hot cooked ravioli.

Shrimp Linguine

Shrimp Linguine: In medium skillet, cook 2 cups thinly sliced zucchini in a little olive oil until crisp-tender; add 2 cups marinara sauce, a sprinkle of crushed red pepper flakes and 1 pound cooked peeled medium shrimp; heat through. Serve over hot cooked linguine.

Turkey Tortellini: In medium saucepan, heat 2 cups Alfredo sauce, 10 ounces chopped cooked frozen broccoli and 1½ cups chopped cooked turkey breast; stir in hot cooked tortellini.

CREAMY HAM AND FETTUCCINE FAST

PREP 20 min TOTAL 20 min • **4 servings**

- 1 package (9 oz) refrigerated fettuccine
- 1 cup frozen sweet peas, thawed
- 1 tablespoon vegetable oil
- 4 medium green onions, sliced (¼ cup)
- 6 oz thinly sliced cooked ham, cut into ¼-inch strips
- ⅓ cup sour cream
- ¼ cup ranch dressing
- 2 tablespoons milk

1 Cook fettuccine and peas together as directed on fettuccine package.

2 Meanwhile, in 12-inch skillet, heat oil over medium-high heat. Cook onions in oil 1 minute, stirring frequently. Stir in ham. Cook 1 to 2 minutes, stirring frequently, until hot; reduce heat to low. Stir in sour cream, dressing and milk.

3 Drain fettuccine and peas; add to skillet. Cook 2 to 3 minutes, stirring constantly, until hot.

1 Serving: Calories 470; Total Fat 21g (Saturated Fat 6g; Trans Fat 0g); Cholesterol 100mg; Sodium 810mg; Total Carbohydrate 49g (Dietary Fiber 3g); Protein 20g **Exchanges:** 3 Starch, 1½ Medium-Fat Meat, 2½ Fat **Carbohydrate Choices:** 3

LIGHTER DIRECTIONS For 10 grams of fat and 380 calories per serving, omit oil; spray skillet with cooking spray. Use Canadian bacon instead of the ham. Use reduced-fat sour cream and ranch dressing and fat-free (skim) milk.

Slicing Green Onions

Place onions on cutting board. Hold firmly with hand and cut into thin slices starting at white (bulb) end.

Easy Vegetable Chow Mein

ANGEL HAIR PASTA WITH BASIL, AVOCADO AND TOMATOES FAST LOWER CALORIE

PREP 20 min TOTAL 20 min • **6 servings**

- 8 oz uncooked angel hair (capellini) pasta
- 2 tablespoons olive or vegetable oil
- 2 cloves garlic, finely chopped
- ¾ cup chopped fresh basil leaves
- ½ to ¾ large ripe avocado, pitted, peeled and cut into small cubes
- 4 medium tomatoes, cut into small cubes
- ½ teaspoon salt
- ¼ teaspoon pepper

1 Cook and drain pasta as directed on package.

2 Meanwhile, in 3-quart saucepan, heat oil over medium heat. Cook garlic in oil about 5 minutes, stirring occasionally, until garlic is tender but not brown; remove from heat.

3 Stir basil, avocado and tomatoes into garlic in saucepan. Toss vegetable mixture and pasta. Sprinkle with salt and pepper.

1 Serving: Calories 260; Total Fat 8g (Saturated Fat 1g; Trans Fat 0g); Cholesterol 0mg; Sodium 350mg; Total Carbohydrate 38g (Dietary Fiber 4g); Protein 7g **Exchanges:** 2 Starch, 1 Vegetable, 1½ Fat **Carbohydrate Choices:** 2½

ANGEL HAIR PASTA WITH CHICKEN Stir 1 cup shredded cooked chicken into mixture with the tomatoes. Cook just until heated.

ANGEL HAIR PASTA WITH SHRIMP Stir 8 oz cooked medium shrimp into mixture with the tomatoes. Cook just until heated.

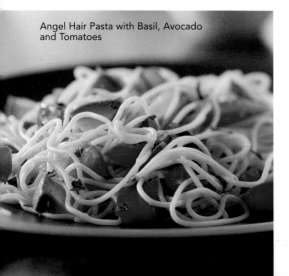

Angel Hair Pasta with Basil, Avocado and Tomatoes

EASY VEGETABLE CHOW MEIN

FAST

Use the frozen vegetable mix suggested in this recipe, or try one of your favorite frozen stir-fry vegetable combinations.

PREP 15 min TOTAL 15 min • **4 servings**

- 1 cup vegetable broth (for homemade broth, see page 530)
- 2 tablespoons cornstarch
- 2 tablespoons stir-fry sauce
- ¼ teaspoon red pepper sauce
- 2 tablespoons vegetable oil
- 2 cloves garlic, finely chopped
- 1 bag (1 lb) frozen stir-fry vegetables
- 2½ cups coleslaw mix (shredded cabbage and carrots)
- 4 cups chow mein noodles

1 In small bowl, mix broth, cornstarch, stir-fry sauce and pepper sauce; set aside.

2 In 12-inch nonstick skillet, heat oil over medium-high heat. Add garlic and frozen vegetables; cook about 5 minutes, stirring frequently, until vegetables are crisp-tender.

3 Stir in coleslaw mix and broth mixture. Cook, stirring constantly, until thickened. Serve over noodles.

1 Serving: Calories 380; Total Fat 21g (Saturated Fat 3g; Trans Fat 0g); Cholesterol 0mg; Sodium 760mg; Total Carbohydrate 43g (Dietary Fiber 5g); Protein 6g **Exchanges:** 2 Other Carbohydrate, 3 Vegetable, 4 Fat **Carbohydrate Choices:** 3

EASY CHICKEN CHOW MEIN Use chicken broth instead of vegetable broth and add 2 cups cubed cooked chicken or turkey with the frozen vegetables in Step 2.

Heirloom Recipe and New Twist

The popularity of easy dishes made with ramen noodles is amazing, and we receive requests daily for these ideas. This recipe is a favorite of our staff and really simple to make. Our new twist is a spicy Thai version of the recipe. The coconut milk gives it a nice creamy consistency and cilantro gives it a great fresh flavor.

CLASSIC

RAMEN SHRIMP AND VEGGIES

FAST   LOWER CALORIE

It's easy to break up the ramen noodles with your hands before opening the package.

PREP 20 min **TOTAL** 20 min • **4 servings**

- 2 teaspoons vegetable oil
- 1 lb uncooked deveined peeled medium shrimp, thawed if frozen, tail shells removed
- 2 cups water
- 1 package (3 oz) Oriental-flavor ramen noodle soup mix
- 1 package (16 oz) fresh stir-fry vegetables (4 cups)
- ¼ cup stir-fry sauce

1 Heat oil in 12-inch nonstick skillet over medium-high heat. Cook shrimp in skillet 2 to 4 minutes, stirring occasionally, until pink. Remove shrimp from skillet; keep warm.

2 In same skillet, heat water to boiling. Break up noodles from soup mix into water; stir until slightly softened. Stir in vegetables. Heat to boiling. Boil 4 to 6 minutes, stirring occasionally, until vegetables are crisp-tender.

3 Stir in seasoning packet from soup mix and stir-fry sauce. Cook 3 to 5 minutes, stirring frequently, until hot. Stir in shrimp.

1 Serving: Calories 210; Total Fat 4.5g (Saturated Fat 1g; Trans Fat 1g); Cholesterol 160mg; Sodium 1160mg; Total Carbohydrate 21g (Dietary Fiber 3g); Protein 22g **Exchanges:** 1 Starch, 1 Vegetable, 2½ Very Lean Meat, ½ Fat **Carbohydrate Choices:** 1½

RAMEN BEEF AND VEGGIES Substitute 1 lb uncooked beef strips for stir-fry (from the meat case) for the shrimp. In Step 1, cook beef 3 to 5 minutes, stirring occasionally, until no longer pink.

See how to make **ramen shrimp and veggies**: Visit bettycrocker.com/BCcookbook

Ramen Shrimp and Veggies

Thai Ramen Shrimp and Veggies

THAI RAMEN SHRIMP AND VEGGIES FAST

Look for the stir-fry vegetables in the produce section of the grocery store.

PREP 20 min TOTAL 20 min • **4 servings**

- 2 teaspoons vegetable oil
- 1 lb uncooked deveined peeled medium shrimp, thawed if frozen, tail shells removed
- 1 can (14 oz) coconut milk (not cream of coconut)
- 2 tablespoons water
- 1 package (3 oz) Oriental-flavor ramen noodle soup mix
- 1 package (16 oz) fresh stir-fry vegetables (4 cups)
- ¼ cup Thai peanut sauce
- 1 tablespoon chopped fresh cilantro
- 1 teaspoon finely grated lime peel
  Crushed red pepper flakes, if desired
- ¼ cup salted peanuts or cashews

1 Heat oil in 12-inch nonstick skillet over medium-high heat. Cook shrimp in skillet 2 to 4 minutes, stirring occasionally, until pink. Remove shrimp from skillet; keep warm.

2 In same skillet, heat coconut milk and water to boiling. Break up noodles from soup mix into coconut milk mixture; stir until slightly softened. Stir in vegetables. Heat to boiling. Reduce heat to medium and cook uncovered 4 to 6 minutes, stirring occasionally, until vegetables are almost crisp-tender.

3 Stir in seasoning packet from soup mix and peanut sauce. Cook, stirring frequently, about 3 minutes or until hot. Stir in cilantro and lime peel; stir in shrimp. Sprinkle with pepper flakes. Garnish with peanuts.

1 Serving: Calories 550; Total Fat 34g (Saturated Fat 21g; Trans Fat 1.5g); Cholesterol 160mg; Sodium 690mg; Total Carbohydrate 35g (Dietary Fiber 5g); Protein 27g **Exchanges:** 1½ Starch, ½ Other Carbohydrate, ½ Vegetable, 3 Very Lean Meat, 6½ Fat **Carbohydrate Choices:** 2

SALSA-SHRIMP TACOS

FAST LOWER CALORIE

PREP 15 min TOTAL 15 min • **6 servings**

- ¾ cup chunky-style salsa
- ½ cup chopped green bell pepper
- ¾ lb uncooked deveined peeled medium shrimp, thawed if frozen, tail shells removed
- 1 box (4.6 oz) taco shells (12 shells)
- ¾ cup shredded Mexican cheese blend (3 oz)
- ¾ cup shredded lettuce
- ¼ cup taco sauce

1 In 10-inch nonstick skillet, heat salsa and bell pepper over medium-high heat, stirring frequently, until warm.

2 Stir in shrimp. Cook 3 to 4 minutes, turning shrimp occasionally, until shrimp are pink.

3 Fill each taco shell with about ¼ cup shrimp mixture. Top with cheese, lettuce and taco sauce.

1 Serving (2 Tacos): Calories 190; Total Fat 9g (Saturated Fat 2g; Trans Fat 2g); Cholesterol 95mg; Sodium 400mg; Total Carbohydrate 16g (Dietary Fiber 1g); Protein 13g **Exchanges:** 1 Starch, 1 Vegetable, 1 Very Lean Meat, 1 Fat **Carbohydrate Choices:** 1

Salsa-Shrimp Tacos

ORANGE-DILL PAN-SEARED TUNA FAST LOWER CALORIE

PREP 20 min TOTAL 20 min • **4 servings**

- 4 tuna, swordfish or other firm fish steaks, ¾ inch thick (4 oz each)
- ½ teaspoon peppered seasoned salt
- 1 small red onion, thinly sliced
- ¾ cup orange juice
- 1 tablespoon chopped fresh or ¼ teaspoon dried dill weed
- 1 tablespoon butter
- 1 teaspoon grated orange peel, if desired

1 Heat 12-inch nonstick skillet over medium-high heat. Sprinkle both sides of tuna steaks with peppered seasoned salt. Place tuna in skillet; reduce heat to medium-low. Cover; cook 6 to 8 minutes, turning once, until fish flakes easily with fork. Remove tuna from skillet; keep warm.

2 In same skillet, cook onion over medium-high heat 2 minutes, stirring occasionally. Stir in orange juice; cook 2 minutes. Stir in dill, butter and orange peel. Cook 1 to 2 minutes or until slightly thickened. Serve over fish.

1 Serving: Calories 210; Total Fat 9g (Saturated Fat 3g; Trans Fat 0g); Cholesterol 50mg; Sodium 240mg; Total Carbohydrate 6g (Dietary Fiber 0g); Protein 27g **Exchanges:** 4 Lean Meat **Carbohydrate Choices:** ½

PEANUT-SAUCED THAI TILAPIA
FAST

PREP 20 min TOTAL 20 min • **4 servings**

- 2 teaspoons canola or vegetable oil
- 1 bag (16 oz) frozen stir-fry vegetables (about 4½ cups)
- 1 tablespoon canola or vegetable oil
- 4 tilapia fillets, ½ inch thick (5 oz each)
- 4 tablespoons Thai peanut sauce

1 In 12-inch nonstick skillet, heat 2 teaspoons oil over high heat. Add frozen vegetables; cook 4 to 5 minutes, stirring frequently, until crisp-tender. Divide vegetables among 4 dinner plates; cover to keep warm.

2 Add 1 tablespoon oil to same skillet; reduce heat to medium-high. Add fish fillets; cook 3 minutes. Turn fish; spread 1 tablespoon peanut sauce over each fillet to cover. Cook about 4 minutes longer or until fish flakes easily with fork. Serve fish with vegetables.

1 Serving: Calories 260; Total Fat 11g (Saturated Fat 1.5g; Trans Fat 0g); Cholesterol 75mg; Sodium 160mg; Total Carbohydrate 9g (Dietary Fiber 3g); Protein 31g **Exchanges:** ½ Fruit, 4½ Very Lean Meat, 1½ Fat **Carbohydrate Choices:** ½

SNAPPER WITH TOMATO-PEPPER SAUCE FAST LOWER CALORIE

Add a small handful of green salad olives to the sauce for a change of flavor. Stir them in with the wine.

PREP 20 min TOTAL 20 min • **4 servings**

- 1 lb red snapper, cod or other medium-firm fish fillets (½ inch thick)
- 1 large tomato, chopped (1 cup)
- 1 small green bell pepper, chopped (½ cup)
- 1 small onion, sliced
- 2 tablespoons finely chopped fresh cilantro or parsley
- ¼ teaspoon salt
- ¼ cup dry white wine or chicken broth
- 2 cups hot cooked rice (page 429), if desired

1 Heat 12-inch nonstick skillet over medium heat. If fish fillets are large, cut into 4 serving pieces. Arrange fish, skin side down, in single layer in skillet. Cook uncovered 4 to 6 minutes, turning once, until fish flakes easily with fork. Remove fish to warm platter; keep warm.

2 In same skillet, cook remaining ingredients except wine and rice over medium heat 3 to 5 minutes, stirring frequently, until bell pepper and onion are crisp-tender. Stir in wine; cook about 1 minute or until hot. Spoon over fish. Serve with rice.

1 Serving: Calories 120; Total Fat 1.5g (Saturated Fat 0g; Trans Fat 0g); Cholesterol 60mg; Sodium 250mg; Total Carbohydrate 5g (Dietary Fiber 1g); Protein 22g **Exchanges:** 1 Vegetable, 3 Very Lean Meat **Carbohydrate Choices:** ½

Cutting Bell Pepper

Cut along inside of each quarter to remove seeds and membranes from inside and stem from top end. Cut each quarter into thin strips. Hold with fingers folded under for safety and chop to desired size.

VEGETABLES & FRUITS

VEGETABLES

FRUITS

CHARTS, FEATURES AND GLOSSARIES

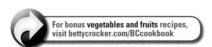

For bonus **vegetables and fruits** recipes,
visit bettycrocker.com/BCcookbook

FAST = Ready in 20 minutes or less **LOWER CALORIE** = See Helpful Nutrition and Cooking Information, page 685
LIGHTER = 25% fewer calories or grams of fat **MAKE AHEAD** = Make-ahead directions **SLOW COOKER** = Slow cooker directions

← Fresh uncooked beets, Asparagus with Parmesan (page 591), Roasted Beets (page 593), Apple-Pear Salad
(page 613)

VEGETABLE BASICS

Whether picked to be part of the main dish or served as a side, vegetables add texture, color, flavor and a bounty of healthful nutrients to any meal. Browse any farmers' market or grocery store, and you will see the vast array of choices available, from standards like carrots and broccoli to more exotic vegetables like colored potatoes and white asparagus. Among the many varieties shown on the following pages (as well as plenty more), you'll find treasures to brighten your table.

BUYING AND STORING FRESH VEGETABLES

- Always select vegetables that look fresh and not withered.

- Choose those that are firm for their variety and ripe. All vegetables should have good color and be bright with no sign of decay or bruising.

- Storage varies but in general fresh vegetables should be used within a few days as they do start to lose flavor, quality and nutritional value if stored too long. See vegetable listings, pages 577 to 585, for recommendations on individual vegetables.

EATING MORE VEGETABLES

These power-packed gems contain a variety of essential nutrients important for good health, and they taste great, too. So be sure to add them to your everyday meals.

- Try substituting veggie snacks instead of high-calorie snacks when you are on the go. Pack a small container with baby carrots, sliced cucumber or bell pepper strips to munch on.

- Add sliced or chopped veggies to sandwiches. Try slices of cucumber in your next turkey sandwich. You'll like the crunch. Chopped celery and carrot are great additions to chicken or tuna salad.

- Add something new the next time you toss a salad. Shelled cooked edamame, roasted peppers, pickled beets, sliced radishes, sugar snap peas and asparagus pieces are all great choices that will add color, flavor and nutrients.

- To bring out the flavor of most vegetables, try roasting them. See the Fresh Vegetable Cooking Chart, pages 586 to 590, for directions.

- Keep frozen vegetables on hand to add to casseroles, soups and stews or just as an extra side dish for any meal. They are picked and frozen while at their peak of freshness so flavor and nutrients are not lost.

- Look for new varieties of old favorites. Baby vegetables are a great example and are often available locally in season.

Baby vegetables: eggplant, zucchini and carrots

American Eggplant

Asian Eggplant

Beefsteak Tomatoes

Heirloom Tomatoes

Yellow Pear Tomatoes

Campari Tomatoes

Cherry Tomatoes

Plum (Roma) Tomatoes

Grape Tomatoes

Tomatillos

Sweet Bell Peppers

Anaheim Chiles

Chipotle Chiles

Jalapeño Chiles

Poblano Chiles

Fresno Chiles

Serrano Chiles

Ancho Chiles

Thai Chiles

Habanero Chiles

Banana Peppers

NIGHTSHADE VEGETABLES

This group also includes potatoes, page 583.

Eggplant: Choose firm, even-colored, unblemished eggplants heavy for size. Caps and stems should be intact with no mold. Refrigerate in plastic bag up to 5 days.

Asian (Chinese, Japanese, Thai): Colors include purple, green, white or striated. Longer, smaller than common eggplant.

Sweet Peppers: Choose shiny, bright-colored, unblemished peppers with firm sides. Refrigerate in plastic bag up to 5 days.

Bell: Available in green, red, yellow, orange, purple, brown.

Banana: Long, yellow, banana-shaped.

Tomatillos: Choose firm, unblemished fruit with tight-fitting husks. Store in paper bag in refrigerator up to 1 month. Remove husks; wash fruit before using.

Tomatoes: Choose firm, unblemished fruit heavy for size. Store at room temperature (refrigerating will cause flavor loss); use within a few days.

Beefsteak: Rich flavor, meaty texture. Good fresh or cooked.

Cherry: Red or yellow; bite-size, great flavor. Use in salads, as garnish or cooked.

Heirloom: Seeds are passed down through generations. Have distinct attributes like exceptional flavor or unusual coloring.

Plum (Roma): Great flavor; fleshy, making them great for sauces and salads as there is less juice than a round tomato. **Grape** tomatoes are baby plum tomatoes.

CHILES

Choose firm chiles; avoid shriveled or soft spots. Store fresh chiles in refrigerator drawer; store dried ones in airtight container in cool, dark place. Typically, the larger the chile, the milder the flavor.

Anaheim: Fresh, canned. Mild; frequently stuffed.

Fresno: Fresh. Medium-size. Similar in flavor to jalapeño and usually red.

Habeñero: Fresh or dried. Range from light green to bright orange. Distinctively hot.

Jalapeño: Fresh or canned. Dark green; hot to very hot. **Chipotle** is a dried, smoked jalapeño.

Poblano: Fresh or canned. Green: flavor ranges from mild to zippy. Reddish-brown: sweeter than green. **Ancho** is a dried Poblano.

Serrano: Fresh. Medium-size. Very hot and green at first, ripening to red or orange.

Thai: Fresh. Small; several colors. Very hot.

Yellow Onion

Red Onion

White Onion

Sweet Onions

Shallots

Cipollini Onions

Garlic

Elephant Garlic

Asparagus

Pearl Onions

White Asparagus

Green Onions (Scallions)

Leek

Shiitake

Porcini

Portabella

Chanterelle

Enoki

White Button

Oyster

Morel

Crimini/ Brown

ONIONS

The onion group of vegetables is often called the Lily family and includes not only onions but also garlic, leeks, shallots and asparagus. They all grow tubers, bulbs or rhizomes.

Asparagus: Spears are green, white, or purple. Choose firm, bright-colored stalks with tight tips. Refrigerate in plastic bag up to 3 days.

Garlic: Made of papery coated sections called cloves. Choose fresh, firm heads of garlic that have no green sprouts.

Leeks: Milder than onions. Look for crisp leaves, unblemished white bulb ends; avoid withered, yellow leaves. Refrigerate in plastic bag up to 5 days. Cut lengthwise; wash thoroughly to remove dirt trapped between layers.

Onions: Choose firm, blemish-free onions with thin skins and no sign of mold or sprouting.

Do not store near potatoes— onions will absorb moisture.

Green (Scallions): Look for bright green, fresh tops, white bulb ends. Refrigerate in plastic bag up to 1 week.

Red, Yellow, White: Store whole in cool (45°F to 60°F), dry, dark place with good ventilation up to 2 months. Once cut, cover with plastic wrap; refrigerate up to 4 days.

Sweet: Very juicy, mild sugary taste without the "burn" associated with other onions. Refrigerate whole in single layer 4 to 6 weeks.

Shallots: Papery skin; more like garlic than onions. Store in cool, dry place up to 2 weeks.

MUSHROOMS

Store unwashed, wrapped in paper towel in a plastic or paper bag. Refrigerate up to 4 days. For fresh, look for firm caps with good color and no soft spots or decay. Wash just before using.

Chanterelle: Fresh, dried. Delicate, nutty flavor; chewy texture. Cook as side dish, or add to soups, sauces, stir-fries.

Dried (Various): More concentrated flavor than fresh. Store in cool, dry place up to 1 year. Rehydrate as directed on package. 1 ounce dried (rehydrated) = 4 ounces fresh.

Morel: Fresh, dried. Smoky, earthy, nutty flavor. Sauté in butter.

Porcini: Often dried. Earthy flavor; firm texture. Popular in French and Italian cooking.

Portabella: Very large, with dense, meaty texture. Grill for sandwiches, sauté, or slice for salads. **Crimini** is a young portabella.

Shiitake: Meaty; strong flavored. Choose plump ones with edges that curl under.

White (Button): Mild, earthy flavor. Small to quite large (for stuffing). Choose firm, white ones with no sign of decay.

580

Savoy
Cabbage

Red Cabbage

Broccoli Rabe
(Rapini)

Kohlrabi

Green
Cabbage

Brussels
Sprouts

Broccoli

Kale

Cauliflower

Napa (Chinese)
Cabbage

Baby Bok Choy

Broccolini

Bok Choy

Mini Cucumbers

Cucumbers

Globe Artichokes

Okra

English Cucumbers

Globe Artichokes

Bi-color Corn

White Corn

Celery

CABBAGE

These are all cruciferous vegetables, part of the cabbage family.

Bok Choy: Mild. Crunchy stalks; tender leaves. Use in salads and stir-fries; as side dish.

Broccoli: Florets and stalks edible. Use raw in salads, or cook. Florets should be tight and not flowering.

Broccolini: Cross between broccoli and Chinese kale. Mildly sweet, slightly peppery; crunchy. Refrigerate up to 10 days. Use raw in salads, crudités; cook crisp-tender as side dish.

Brussels Sprouts: Strong flavor similar to cabbage. Small sprouts will be milder than large ones. Look for those with compact heads. Cook for side dishes.

Cabbage: Choose cabbage with fresh, crisp leaves (firmly packed, if head variety). Refrigerate, tightly wrapped, up to 1 week.

Cauliflower: Mild and usually white. Florets should be firm and compact. Stems usually not eaten. Use raw in salads, or cook.

Kale: Mild cabbage flavor; many varieties, colors. Store in coldest part of refrigerator 2 to 3 days (any longer, and flavor gets very strong). Remove or discard tough center stalk.

Kohlrabi (Cabbage Turnip): Bulbs have mild broccoli–celery root flavor. Leaves have collard green flavor. Use raw; add to soups, stews, stir-fries.

Refrigerate leaves up to 4 days, bulbs up to 10 days.

OTHER VEGETABLES

Artichoke, Globe: Available fresh, canned (hearts and bottoms) in various sizes: jumbo for stuffing and steaming, baby in marinated salads, sautéed, roasted. Refrigerate in plastic bag up to 1 week.

Artichoke, Jerusalem (Sunchoke): Available year-round (season peaks October to March). Choose hard artichokes with smooth skins and no soft spots. Use raw in salads; boiled, steamed, fried. Refrigerate in plastic bag up to 1 week.

Celery: Crisp, mild and stringy stalks. Use raw in salads, or cook.

Corn: White, yellow, bi-colored. Choose bright green, tight-fitting husks; fresh-looking silk; plump, consistently sized kernels. Wrap unhusked in damp paper towels; refrigerate up to 2 days.

English Cucumber: Available year-round (peak is May to August). Virtually seedless. Choose firm cucumbers with smooth skins; avoid shriveled or soft spots. Refrigerate in plastic bag up to 10 days.

Okra: Available fresh year-round in the South (May to October, rest of United States), canned, frozen. Choose tender, unblemished, bright green pods less than 4 inches long. Refrigerate in plastic bag up to 3 days.

Cassava (Yuca)

Parsnips

Rutabaga

Taro

Turnip

Carrots

Gingerroot

Beets

Celeriac

Radishes

Sweet Potatoes

Fennel

Daikon Radish

Fingerling Potatoes

Yukon Gold Potatoes

Purple (or Blue) Potatoes

New/Baby Potatoes

Round Red Potatoes

Russet/Idaho Potatoes

ROOT VEGETABLES

Beets: Colors range from red or purple to white. Choose bright-colored, firm beets with smooth skins. Remove greens as soon as possible; store separately. Greens and roots should be cooked. Refrigerate in plastic bag up to 1 week.

Carrots and Parsnips: Mild sweet flavor. Choose those with no signs of decay or cracking. Refrigerate in plastic bag up to 2 weeks.

Cassava (Yuca): Bland, starchy; absorbs other flavors. Two types: sweet and bitter (which must be cooked before eating). Choose hard, evenly shaped cassava; avoid blemishes, cracks, mold, stickiness. Store in cool, dark place up to 3 days. Use as side dish or in soups.

Fennel: Mild licorice flavor. Bulbs and greens can be eaten raw or cooked. Choose clean, firm bulbs with fresh-looking greens. Refrigerate in plastic bag up to 1 week.

Jicama: A sweet vegetable that looks like a turnip and can be eaten raw; use in salads.

Gingerroot: Peppery, slightly sweet. Choose firm, smooth roots. Refrigerate fresh, unpeeled in plastic bag up to 3 weeks; freeze up to 6 months.

Radish: Mild to peppery flavor. Great in salads, as snacks. Choose firm radishes with bright colors. **Daikon** are much larger; good in salads,

stir-fries. Refrigerate either variety in plastic bag up to 1 week.

Sweet Potato: Available in varieties ranging from pale skin with light yellow flesh to dark orange or red skin and flesh. We often call them yams, but true yams are not related to sweet potatoes. Choose nicely shaped, smooth, firm potatoes with even-colored skins. Store in cool (45°F to 60°F), dry, dark, well-ventilated place up to 2 weeks.

Turnips, Rutabagas, Celeriac: Good roasted, used in stews, baked dishes. Choose firm vegetables with no signs of decay or bruising. Refrigerate in plastic bag up to 2 weeks.

POTATOES

Store red, white or russet potatoes in a cool (45°F to 60°F), dry, dark, well-ventilated place up to 2 weeks. Store the following varieties in same manner up to 1 month.

Fingerling: Small; finger-shaped; range of colors. Mild flavor; fine texture.

Purple: Small with dense texture (like russets). Most of the purple fades during cooking.

Yellow (Yellow Finnish, Yukon Gold): Skin and flesh range from buttery yellow to golden. Mild butterlike flavor, which fades slightly during cooking.

Sweet Dumpling Squash

Hubbard Squash

Buttercup Squash

Sugar Pie Pumpkin

Acorn Squash

Green Zucchini

Delicata Squash

Turban Squash

Carnival Squash

Patty Pan Squash

Yellow Crookneck Squash

Butternut Squash

Spaghetti Squash

Jack Be Little Pumpkin

Yellow Summer Squash

Chayote Squash

Mung Bean Sprouts

Chinese Long Beans

Edamame

Yellow Wax Beans

Green String Beans

Sugar Snap Peas

Snow Peas

Pea Shoots

SQUASH

Summer: Thin, edible skins; soft, edible seeds. Choose firm squash with shiny, unblemished skin. Refrigerate in plastic bag up to 5 days.

Chayote: Mild flavor; requires bold seasoning. Refrigerate in plastic bag up to 1 month. Use raw in salads, or stuff and bake.

Patty Pan: Pale green to yellow.

Winter: Thick, hard skin, seeds. Choose squash heavy for size with dull-colored hard rind (no soft spots). Whole: store in cool (45°F to 60°F), dry, dark place with good ventilation up to 2 months. Cut and peeled: refrigerate in plastic wrap up to 5 days.

Acorn: Green skin; acorn-shaped. Bake halves with filling or remove rind, cut up and roast.

Butternut: Yellow or gold; peanut-shaped. Cook as for acorn squash.

Carnival: Cream, orange or green. Flavor similar to sweet potatoes or butternut squash. Bake or steam.

Delicata: Pale yellow skin with green stripes. Sweet, buttered-corn flavor. Seed cavity is small; lots of edible flesh. Bake or steam.

Sweet Dumpling: Green, white stripes. Sweet; good stuffed with rice or stuffing.

FRESH LEGUMES

Legumes are seed pods that split along both sides when ripe. Choose bright, smooth, crisp pods. Refrigerate in plastic bag up to 4 days.

Edamame (fresh soybeans): Often sold in their fuzzy green pods (avoid blemishes) or frozen. Serve as snack; add to rice, salads, scrambled eggs; mash into guacamole.

Long Beans (Asparagus Bean, Chinese Long Bean, Yard-Long Bean): Same family as black-eyed peas. Milder, less sweet than green beans. Usually cut in half or smaller pieces, then sautéed or stir-fried. Mushy if overcooked.

Mung Bean Sprouts: Tender; great for salads or stir-fries. Refrigerate in plastic bag up to 3 days.

Pea Shoots: The best leaves, tendrils from pea plants. Choose fresh, crisp, young, tender shoots with top leaves. Remove coarse stems. Use raw in salads; steam (without water) as a side dish with lemon or sprinkled with ginger and sugar. Use within 2 days.

Peas (English, Sugar Snap, Snow): English peas must be removed from pods before cooking; sugar snaps and snow peas can be eaten in the pod. All can be eaten raw or cooked; great in salads or side dishes.

FRESH VEGETABLE COOKING CHART

Use the following chart for preparing and cooking vegetables. Store vegetables in a plastic bag in the refrigerator or at room temperature if indicated in the chart. Wash all vegetables well before using. Use fresh vegetables within a few days for the best results.

To Boil: In saucepan, heat 1 inch water to boiling, unless stated otherwise. Add vegetables. Heat to boiling; reduce heat to low. Cook for amount of time in chart; drain.

To Steam: In saucepan or skillet, place steamer basket in ½ inch water (water should not touch bottom of basket). Place vegetables in steamer basket. Cover tightly and heat to boiling; reduce heat to low. Steam for amount of time in chart.

To Sauté: In skillet, cook in butter or oil over medium-high heat for amount of time in chart.

To Bake: Heat oven to 350°F. Place vegetables in oven as directed. Bake for amount of time in chart.

To Roast: Heat oven to 425°F. Toss cut (unless stated otherwise) vegetables with about 1 tablespoon olive oil and season as desired. Place vegetables in baking pan. Roast for amount of time in chart.

To Microwave: Use microwavable dish with cover or use plastic wrap to cover. When using paper towels or plastic wrap in the microwave, use products that are microwave safe. Add 2 tablespoons water unless stated otherwise, to dish with vegetables. Microwave on High, unless stated otherwise, for amount of time in chart; drain. Stir or rearrange vegetables once or twice during cooking. Let vegetables stand* covered for 1 to 2 minutes to finish cooking.

Vegetable with Amount for 4 Servings	Preparation	Conventional Directions	Microwave Directions
Artichokes, Globe (4 medium)	Remove discolored leaves; trim stem even with base. Cut 1 inch off top. Snip tips off leaves. To prevent discoloration, dip in cold water mixed with small amount of lemon juice.	**Steam:** 20 to 30 minutes, adding 2 tablespoons lemon juice to water, until leaves pull out easily and bottom is tender when pierced with knife.	Place 1 or 2 artichokes in dish; add ¼ cup water. Microwave 5 to 7 minutes until leaves pull out easily.
Artichokes, Jerusalem (1 lb)	Leave whole, or cut as desired. To prevent discoloration, toss with cold water mixed with small amount of lemon juice.	**Boil:** Covered 7 to 9 minutes or until crisp-tender. **Steam:** 15 to 20 minutes or until crisp-tender.	Place in dish. Microwave 5 to 7 minutes or until crisp-tender.
Asparagus (1½ lb)	Break off ends as far down as stalks snap easily. For spears, tie stalks in bundles with string, or hold together with band of foil. Or cut stalks into 1-inch pieces.	**Boil:** Uncovered 6 to 8 minutes or until crisp-tender. **Steam:** 6 to 8 minutes or until crisp-tender. **Roast** (whole spears): 10 to 12 minutes.	Place in dish. Microwave 4 to 6 minutes or until crisp-tender.
Beans, Green, Purple Wax and Yellow Wax (1 lb)	Remove ends. Leave beans whole, or cut into 1-inch pieces.	**Boil:** Uncovered 6 to 8 minutes or until crisp-tender. **Steam:** 10 to 12 minutes or until crisp-tender. **Roast** (whole beans): 6 to 8 minutes.	Place in dish. Microwave 8 to 10 minutes or until crisp-tender.
Beans, Lima (3 lb unshelled; 3 cups shelled)	To shell beans, remove thin outer edge of pod with sharp knife or scissors. Slip out beans.	**Boil:** Covered 15 to 20 minutes or until tender.	Place in dish; add ½ cup water. Microwave on High 4 to 5 minutes or until boiling. Microwave on Medium-Low (30%) 20 to 25 minutes or until tender.

Vegetables continue to cook a short time after being microwaved. Most vegetables require a stand time after cooking, which completes the cooking and equalizes the temperature throughout the food.

Vegetable with Amount for 4 Servings	Preparation	Conventional Directions	Microwave Directions
Beets (5 medium)	Cut off all but 1 to 2 inches of tops. Leave whole with root ends attached.	**Boil:** Add water to cover and 1 tablespoon vinegar. Boil, covered, 20 to 30 minutes. **Steam:** 45 to 50 minutes or until tender. **Roast** (before peeling): 35 to 40 minutes.	Place in dish with 2 tablespoons water. Microwave 12 to 16 minutes or until tender.
Broccoli (1½ lb)	Trim off large leaves; remove tough ends of stems. Cut as desired.	**Boil:** Uncovered 4 to 6 minutes or until crisp-tender. **Steam:** 10 to 11 minutes or until crisp-tender.	Place in dish. Microwave 6 to 8 minutes or until crisp-tender.
Brussels Sprouts (1 lb)	Remove discolored leaves; cut off stem ends. Cut large sprouts in half.	**Boil:** Uncovered 8 to 12 minutes or until tender. **Steam:** 8 to 12 minutes or until tender. **Roast:** 12 to 15 minutes.	Place in dish. Microwave 5 to 6 minutes or until tender.
Carrots (6 to 7 medium)	Peel; cut off ends. Leave ready-to-eat baby-cut carrots whole or cut as desired.	**Boil:** Covered 7 to 10 minutes or until tender. **Steam:** 8 to 10 minutes or until tender. **Roast:** 25 to 30 minutes.	Place in dish. Microwave 5 to 9 minutes until crisp-tender.
Cauliflower (1 medium head)	Remove outer leaves and stalk; cut off any discoloration. Leave whole or separate into florets.	**Boil:** Uncovered 8 to 12 minutes or until tender. **Steam:** 8 to 12 minutes or until tender. **Roast:** 15 to 20 minutes.	Place in dish. Microwave 8 to 10 minutes or until tender.
Corn (4 ears)	Husk ears and remove silk just before cooking.	**Boil:** Add water to cover and 1 tablespoon sugar. Boil, unovered, 5 to 7 minutes. **Steam:** 5 to 7 minutes.	Wrap ears in plastic wrap or place in dish. 1 ear: Microwave 2 to 3 minutes. 2 ears: Microwave 3 to 4 minutes.
Eggplant (1 medium)	Remove stems. Peel can be left on or peel if desired. Cut as desired.	**Boil:** Covered 5 to 8 minutes or until tender. **Steam:** 5 to 7 minutes or until tender. **Sauté:** With 2 tablespoons butter, 5 to 10 minutes or until tender.	Place in dish. Microwave 7 to 9 minutes or until tender.
Fennel (3 to 4 medium)	Remove feathery tops and tough or discolored outer ribs; trim base. Cut bulbs into fourths.	**Boil:** Covered 8 to 11 minutes or until tender. **Steam:** 12 to 15 minutes or until tender. **Roast:** 20 to 25 minutes.	Place in dish. Microwave 4 to 5 minutes or until tender.
Greens: Beet, Chicory, Collards, Escarole, Kale, Mustard, Spinach, Swiss Chard and Turnip (1 lb)	Remove root ends and imperfect leaves.	**Steam:** 5 to 8 minutes or until tender.	Beets, Chicory or Escarole: Place in dish. Microwave 8 to 10 minutes, until tender. Collards, Kale, Mustard, Spinach, Swiss Chard or Turnips: Place in dish. Microwave 4 to 6 minutes or until tender.

FRESH VEGETABLE COOKING CHART

Vegetable with Amount for 4 Servings	Preparation	Conventional Directions	Microwave Directions
Kohlrabi (4 medium)	Cut off root ends and tops. Cut as desired.	**Boil:** Covered 15 to 20 minutes or until tender. **Steam:** 8 to 12 minutes or until tender.	Place in dish. Microwave 3 to 5 minutes or until tender.
Leeks (6 medium)	Remove green tops to within 2 inches of white part. Peel outside layer of bulbs. Cut as desired.	**Boil:** Covered 10 to 12 minutes or until tender. **Steam:** 10 to 12 minutes or until tender. **Roast:** 12 to 15 minutes.	Place in dish. Microwave 4 to 5 minutes or until tender.
Mushrooms (1 lb)	Trim off stem ends; do not peel. Leave whole, or cut as desired.	**Sauté:** With 1 tablespoon butter, 4 to 6 minutes, stirring frequently, until tender. **Roast:** 5 to 10 minutes.	Place in dish; add 1 tablespoon butter. Microwave 3 to 4 minutes or until tender.
Okra (1 lb)	Remove ends. Leave whole or cut into slices.	**Boil:** Uncovered 8 to 10 minutes or until tender. **Steam:** 6 to 8 minutes or until tender.	Place in dish; add ¼ cup water. Microwave 5 to 6 minutes or until tender.
Onions, White, Yellow and Red (8 to 10 small)	Peel onions in cold water to prevent eyes from watering. Cut as desired.	**Boil:** Covered 15 to 20 minutes. **Steam:** 15 to 20 minutes. **Sauté:** With 2 tablespoons butter, cook onions cut into ¼-inch slices 6 to 9 minutes or until tender. **Roast:** 30 to 40 minutes.	Place in dish; add ¼ cup water. Microwave 7 to 9 minutes or until tender.
Parsnips (6 to 8 medium)	Peel; cut off ends. Leave whole or cut as desired.	**Boil:** Covered 9 to 15 minutes or until tender. **Steam:** 9 to 15 minutes or until tender. **Roast:** 25 to 30 minutes.	Place in dish. Microwave 5 to 6 minutes or until tender.
Pea Pods, Snow or Chinese (1 lb)	Remove tips and strings.	**Boil:** Uncovered 2 to 3 minutes or until crisp-tender. **Steam:** 3 to 5 minutes or until crisp-tender.	Place in dish. Microwave 6 to 7 minutes or until crisp-tender.
Peas, Sweet (2 lb)	Shell just before cooking.	**Boil:** Uncovered 5 to 10 minutes or until tender. **Steam:** 8 to 10 minutes or until tender.	Place in dish. Microwave 4 to 6 minutes or until tender.
Peas, Sugar Snap (1 lb)	Snip off stem ends and remove strings.	**Boil:** Uncovered 4 to 5 minutes or until crisp-tender. **Steam:** 6 to 7 minutes or until crisp-tender.	Place in dish. Microwave 6 to 7 minutes or until crisp-tender.
Peppers, Bell (2 medium)	Remove stems, seeds and membranes. Leave whole to stuff and bake, or cut as desired.	**Steam:** 4 to 6 minutes or until crisp-tender. **Sauté:** With 1 tablespoon butter, 3 to 5 minutes or until crisp-tender. **Roast:** 15 to 20 minutes.	Place in dish. Microwave 3 to 4 minutes or until crisp-tender.

Vegetable with Amount for 4 Servings	Preparation	Conventional Directions	Microwave Directions
Potatoes, Fingerling (10 to 12)	Leave whole, or cut as desired.	**Boil:** Add water to cover. Boil, uncovered, 15 to 20 minutes or until tender. **Steam:** 18 to 22 minutes or until tender. **Roast:** 25 to 30 minutes.	Place in dish; add ¼ cup water. Microwave 9 to 11 minutes or until tender.
Potatoes, Red and White (6 medium)	Leave whole, or peel and cut as desired.	**Boil:** Add water to cover. Boil, uncovered, 15 to 20 minutes or until tender. **Steam:** 15 to 20 minutes or until tender. **Bake:** Uncovered 1 hour or until tender. **Roast:** 40 to 45 minutes.	Pierce whole potatoes to allow steam to escape. Place on paper towel. 1 or 2 potatoes: Microwave 4 to 6 minutes, until tender. Cover; let stand 5 minutes. 3 or 4 potatoes: Microwave 8 to 12 minutes or until tender. Cover; let stand 5 minutes.
Potatoes, Russet (4 medium)	Leave whole, or peel and cut as desired.	**Boil:** Add water to cover. Boil, uncovered, 15 to 20 minutes or until tender. **Steam:** 18 to 22 minutes or until tender. **Roast:** 30 to 40 minutes.	Pierce whole potatoes to allow steam to escape. Place on paper towel. 1 or 2 potatoes: Microwave 4 to 6 minutes or until tender. Cover; let stand 5 minutes. 3 or 4 potatoes: Microwave 8 to 12 minutes or until tender. Cover; let stand 5 minutes.
Potatoes, Small: Red and White (10 to 12)	Leave whole, or cut as desired.	**Boil:** Add water to cover. Boil, uncovered, 15 to 20 minutes or until tender. **Steam:** 18 to 22 minutes or until tender. **Roast:** 40 to 45 minutes.	Place in dish; add ¼ cup water. Microwave 9 to 11 minutes or until tender.
Potatoes, Sweet (4 medium)	Leave whole, or peel and cut as desired.	**Boil:** Add water to cover. Boil, uncovered, 10 to 15 minutes or until tender. **Steam:** 15 to 20 minutes or until tender. **Bake:** Uncovered 1 hour or until tender. **Roast:** 40 to 45 minutes.	Pierce whole potatoes to allow steam to escape. Place on paper towel. Microwave 9 to 11 minutes, or until tender. Cover; let stand 5 minutes.
Potatoes, Yukon Gold (6 medium)	Leave whole, or peel and cut as desired.	**Boil:** Add water to cover. Boil, uncovered, 15 to 20 minutes or until tender. **Steam:** 18 to 22 minutes or until tender. **Roast:** 25 to 30 minutes.	Pierce whole potatoes to allow steam to escape. Place on paper towel. 1 or 2 potatoes: Microwave 4 to 6 minutes or until tender. Cover; let stand 5 minutes. 3 or 4 potatoes: Microwave 8 to 12 minutes or until tender. Cover; let stand 5 minutes.

FRESH VEGETABLE COOKING CHART

Vegetable with Amount for 4 Servings	Preparation	Conventional Directions	Microwave Directions
Rutabagas (2 medium)	Peel; cut as desired.	**Boil:** Covered 20 to 25 minutes or until tender. **Steam:** 20 to 25 minutes or until tender. **Roast:** 40 to 45 minutes.	Place in dish; add ¼ cup water. Microwave 13 to 15 minutes or until tender.
Squash, Summer: Chayote, Crookneck, Zucchini, Pattypan, Straightneck (1½ lb)	Remove stem and blossom ends, but do not peel. Cut as desired.	**Boil:** Uncovered 5 to 10 minutes. **Steam:** 5 to 7 minutes or until tender. **Sauté:** With 1 tablespoon olive oil, 5 to 10 minutes or until tender.	Place in dish. Microwave 4 to 6 minutes or until almost tender.
Squash, Winter: Acorn, Buttercup, Butternut, Pumpkin, Spaghetti (2 lb)	Cook in halves or pieces with seeds removed.	**Boil:** Peeled and cut up; covered 10 to 15 minutes or until tender. **Steam:** 10 to 15 minutes. **Bake:** Place squash halves cut side up in baking dish. Cover and bake 40 minutes or until tender.	Whole Squash except spaghetti: Pierce with knife in several places to allow steam to escape. Place on paper towel. Microwave uncovered 5 minutes or until squash feels warm to the touch. Cut in half; remove seeds. Arrange halves in dish. Microwave 5 to 8 minutes or until tender. Whole Spaghetti Squash: Pierce with knife in several places to allow steam to escape. Place on paper towel. Microwave uncovered 18 to 23 minutes or until tender. Cut in half; remove seeds and fibers.
Turnips (4 medium)	Cut off tops. Leave whole, or cut as desired.	**Boil:** Covered 20 to 25 minutes. **Steam:** 15 to 20 minutes or until tender. **Roast:** 30 to 35 minutes.	Place in dish. Microwave 6 to 8 minutes or until tender.

ARTICHOKES WITH ROSEMARY BUTTER

To eat a fresh artichoke, remove a leaf, dip it in the butter mixture and draw it between your teeth to scrape off the meaty part. Continue removing leaves until you see the center cone of light green leaves. Cut the leaves from the cone, remove and discard the fuzzy choke to reveal the meaty heart in the center.

PREP 10 min **TOTAL** 45 min • **4 servings**

- 4 medium artichokes
- ½ cup butter
- 1 teaspoon chopped fresh or ¼ teaspoon dried rosemary leaves, crushed
- 1 teaspoon lemon juice

1 Remove any discolored leaves and the small leaves at base of artichokes. Trim stems even with base of artichokes. Cutting straight across, cut 1 inch from tops and discard tops. Cut off points of remaining leaves with scissors. Rinse artichokes with cold water.

2 Place steamer basket in ½ inch water in 4-quart Dutch oven (water should not touch bottom of basket). Place artichokes in basket. Cover tightly. Heat to boiling; reduce heat. Steam 20 to 25 minutes or until bottoms are tender when pierced with knife.

3 Meanwhile, melt butter; stir in rosemary and lemon juice. Pluck out artichoke leaves one at a time. Dip base of leaf into rosemary butter.

1 Serving: Calories 280; Total Fat 23g (Saturated Fat 15g; Trans Fat 1.5g); Cholesterol 60mg; Sodium 280mg; Total Carbohydrate 14g (Dietary Fiber 7g); Protein 4g **Exchanges:** 2 Vegetable, 5 Fat **Carbohydrate Choices:** 1

ASPARAGUS WITH PARMESAN

FAST LOWER CALORIE

Roasting the asparagus enhances the flavor and brings out the natural sweetness. You could use Asiago cheese instead of the Parmesan if you like.

PREP 5 min **TOTAL** 20 min • **4 servings**

- 1½ lb fresh asparagus
- 1 tablespoon olive oil
- 1 tablespoon butter
- 1 medium green onion, sliced (1 tablespoon)
- 1 clove garlic, finely chopped
- ½ teaspoon salt
- ¼ teaspoon freshly ground pepper
- ¼ cup freshly grated or shredded Parmesan cheese

Snapping Ends from Asparagus

1 Snap off tough bottom ends of asparagus. In 3-quart saucepan, heat 1 inch water (salted if desired). Add asparagus. Heat to boiling; reduce heat. Simmer uncovered 4 minutes.

Snap off tough ends of asparagus where they break easily.

2 Meanwhile, heat oven to 375°F. In ungreased 8-inch square pan, place oil, butter, onion and garlic. Heat uncovered in oven 5 minutes.

3 Drain asparagus; spread in oil mixture in pan. Sprinkle with salt, pepper and cheese. Bake uncovered about 10 minutes or until cheese is melted.

1 Serving: Calories 110; Total Fat 8g (Saturated Fat 3.5g; Trans Fat 0g); Cholesterol 10mg; Sodium 430mg; Total Carbohydrate 4g (Dietary Fiber 2g); Protein 4g **Exchanges:** 1 Vegetable, 1½ Fat **Carbohydrate Choices:** 0

GREEN BEANS WITH PARMESAN Substitute fresh whole green beans for the asparagus. Continue as directed.

Preparing Artichokes

Remove discolored leaves, leaves with thorns and small leaves at base of artichoke.

Trim stem even with base of artichoke; cut 1 inch from top of artichoke and discard top.

Using scissors, cut points from remaining leaves; rinse artichokes with cold water.

Heirloom Recipe and New Twist

This all-time favorite recipe is recognized quickly at any gathering, and consumers ask for it again and again. It's quick to make and can be easily doubled, then baked in a 13x9-inch baking dish. You'll see that the new twist is very different, updated for today. We think you will like the switch to fresh green beans and the tangy blue cheese flavor.

CLASSIC

GREEN BEAN CASSEROLE

LOWER CALORIE

We really like this recipe with French-style green beans, but you could also use fresh green beans. Cut 1 pound fresh green beans into 1½- to 2-inch pieces and cook until crisp-tender. Then continue with the recipe as directed.

PREP 10 min **TOTAL** 50 min • **6 servings**

- 1 **can (10¾ oz) condensed cream of mushroom, cream of celery or cream of chicken soup**
- ½ **cup milk**
- ⅛ **teaspoon pepper**
- 2 **cans (14.5 to 16 oz each) French-style green beans, drained***
- 1 **can (2.8 oz) French-fried onions**

1 Heat oven to 350°F. In ungreased 8-inch square (2-quart) glass baking dish, mix soup, milk and pepper. Stir in beans. Sprinkle with onions.

2 Bake uncovered 30 to 40 minutes or until hot in center.

*2 bags (1 lb each) frozen cut green beans can be substituted. Cook as directed on bag for minimum time. Drain; stir into soup mixture.

1 Serving: Calories 160; Total Fat 10g (Saturated Fat 2.5g; Trans Fat 2g); Cholesterol 0mg; Sodium 680mg; Total Carbohydrate 14g (Dietary Fiber 2g); Protein 3g **Exchanges:** ½ Starch, 1 Vegetable, 2 Fat **Carbohydrate Choices:** 1

See how to make **green bean casserole**: Visit bettycrocker.com/BCcookbook

Green Bean Casserole

Blue Cheese–Pecan Green Beans

BLUE CHEESE–PECAN
GREEN BEANS LOWER CALORIE

PREP 15 min **TOTAL** 35 min • **6 servings**

  12 oz fresh green beans, trimmed
  ½ cup pecan halves
  2 tablespoons butter (do not use
     margarine)
  3 oz blue cheese, crumbled (¾ cup)

1 In 2-quart saucepan, place beans in 1 inch water. Heat to boiling; reduce heat. Simmer uncovered 8 to 10 minutes or until beans are crisp-tender; drain. Place in serving bowl; cover to keep warm.

2 Meanwhile, in 1-quart saucepan, cook pecans over medium heat 5 to 7 minutes, stirring frequently until nuts begin to brown, then stirring constantly until nuts are golden brown and toasted. Place in small bowl; reserve.

3 In same 1-quart saucepan, melt butter over low heat. Heat, stirring constantly about 6 minutes or until butter is golden brown. (Once the butter begins to brown, it browns very quickly and can burn, so use low heat and watch carefully.) Immediately remove from heat. Pour over beans; toss to coat. Sprinkle with cheese and reserved pecans.

1 Serving (½ Cup): Calories 170; Total Fat 14g (Saturated Fat 6g; Trans Fat 0g); Cholesterol 20mg; Sodium 230mg; Total Carbohydrate 6g (Dietary Fiber 2g); Protein 5g **Exchanges:** 1 Vegetable, ½ Lean Meat, 2½ Fat **Carbohydrate Choices:** ½

Blue Cheese

Strong-flavored blue cheese adds a nice tang to recipes. The longer this cheese is aged, the stronger the flavor will be. Look for it in pieces that you can crumble, or buy it already crumbled. You could also use Gorgonzola or Stilton cheese instead of the blue cheese.

ROASTED BEETS LOWER CALORIE

A secret kept for too long, fresh beets have been rediscovered and are on their way to stardom. Beets are usually available year-round. If given a choice, pick smaller, young beets for the best flavor.

PREP 10 min **TOTAL** 1 hr 20 min • **6 servings**

  2 lb small beets (1½ to 2 inch)
  ½ teaspoon salt
  ¼ teaspoon coarse ground black pepper
  2 tablespoons regular olive oil
  2 tablespoons chopped fresh basil leaves
  1 tablespoon balsamic vinegar

1 Heat oven to 425°F. Cut off all but 2 inches of beet tops. Wash beets; leave whole with root ends attached. Place beets in ungreased 13x9-inch pan. Sprinkle with salt and pepper. Drizzle with oil.

2 Roast uncovered about 40 minutes or until beets are tender. Let beets cool until easy to handle, about 30 minutes. Peel beets and cut off root ends; cut beets into ½-inch slices.

3 In medium bowl, toss beets, basil and vinegar. Serve warm or at room temperature.

1 Serving: Calories 90; Total Fat 4.5g (Saturated Fat 0.5g; Trans Fat 0g); Cholesterol 0mg; Sodium 270mg; Total Carbohydrate 10g (Dietary Fiber 2g); Protein 2g **Exchanges:** 2 Vegetable, 1 Fat **Carbohydrate Choices:** ½

Cooking Beet Greens

Fresh beet greens are easy to cook. Wash thoroughly, cut the greens and stems from the beets and then cut them into pieces. Heat 1 tablespoon olive oil in a skillet over medium heat. Add the greens and stems and cook uncovered 5 to 10 minutes or until the greens are wilted and stems are crisp-tender, stirring frequently. Season to taste with salt and pepper.

Preparing Beets

Before cooking, cut off all but 2 inches of stems. Wash beets; leave whole with root ends attached.

After cooking, peel beets with paring knife under cold water, removing stems, skins and roots.

SESAME BUTTERED BROCCOLI

FAST LOWER CALORIE

PREP 15 min **TOTAL** 15 min • **4 servings**

- 1½ lb fresh broccoli
- 2 tablespoons butter, melted
- 2 teaspoons soy sauce
- 1 teaspoon sesame seed, toasted (page 22)
- ½ teaspoon sesame oil

1 Remove florets from broccoli. Cut stalks into 1x½-inch pieces, discarding any leaves.

2 In 2-quart saucepan, heat 1 cup water to boiling. Add broccoli; return to boiling. Boil uncovered 4 to 6 minutes or until crisp-tender; drain well. Return broccoli to saucepan; cover to keep warm.

3 In small bowl, mix remaining ingredients. Pour over broccoli; toss to coat.

1 Serving: Calories 100; Total Fat 7g (Saturated Fat 3g; Trans Fat 0g); Cholesterol 15mg; Sodium 220mg; Total Carbohydrate 6g (Dietary Fiber 4g); Protein 3g **Exchanges:** 1 Vegetable, 1½ Fat **Carbohydrate Choices:** ½

BROCCOLI WITH ROASTED RED PEPPERS AND HAZELNUTS

LOWER CALORIE

PREP 30 min **TOTAL** 30 min • **8 servings**

- 5 cups fresh broccoli florets
- 1 tablespoon olive or vegetable oil
- 1 clove garlic, finely chopped
- ¼ cup chopped hazelnuts (filberts)
- ½ cup chopped drained roasted red bell peppers (from 7-oz jar)
- ¼ teaspoon salt

1 In 2-quart saucepan, heat 1 cup water to boiling. Add broccoli. Cover; cook about 1 minute or just until crisp. Drain and immediately place broccoli in ice water.

2 In 12-inch skillet, heat oil over medium heat. Cook garlic and hazelnuts in oil 1 to 2 minutes, stirring frequently, until nuts are lightly toasted.

3 Drain broccoli. Stir broccoli, roasted peppers and salt into nut mixture. Cook about 3 minutes, stirring occasionally, until broccoli is crisp-tender.

1 Serving (½ Cup): Calories 70; Total Fat 4g (Saturated Fat 0g; Trans Fat 0g); Cholesterol 0mg; Sodium 90mg; Total Carbohydrate 5g (Dietary Fiber 2g); Protein 2g **Exchanges:** 1 Vegetable, 1 Fat **Carbohydrate Choices:** ½

CHEESY BACON BRUSSELS SPROUTS **LOWER CALORIE**

This vegetable with the funny name delivers big on flavor. Brussels sprouts look and taste like miniature green cabbages. Remove any discolored outer leaves before cooking.

PREP 25 min **TOTAL** 1 hr 25 min • **10 servings**

- 1¼ lb fresh Brussels sprouts (1 to 1½ inch), cut in half (5 cups)
- 6 slices bacon, cut into 1-inch pieces
- 1 tablespoon butter
- 1 large onion, finely chopped (1 cup)
- 1 tablespoon all-purpose flour
- ¼ teaspoon dried thyme leaves
- ¼ teaspoon pepper
- ¾ cup half-and-half
- 2 teaspoons chicken bouillon granules
- ⅓ cup shredded Parmesan cheese (1½ oz)
- ½ cup shredded Cheddar cheese (2 oz)

1 Heat oven to 350°F. In 3-quart saucepan, place Brussels sprouts and enough water just to cover sprouts. Heat to boiling; boil 6 to 8 minutes or until crisp-tender. Drain and return to saucepan; set aside.

2 In 10-inch skillet, cook bacon over medium heat 6 to 8 minutes, stirring occasionally, until crisp. Remove bacon with slotted spoon; drain on paper towels. Drain bacon drippings leaving 1 tablespoon in skillet.

3 Add butter to bacon drippings. Heat over medium-high heat until butter is melted. Add onion; cook 2 to 3 minutes, stirring frequently, until crisp-tender. Add flour, thyme and pepper; cook and stir until well blended. Gradually stir in half-and-half and bouillon granules. Heat to boiling, stirring constantly; boil and stir 1 minute. Remove from heat; stir in Parmesan cheese.

4 Pour sauce over Brussels sprouts in saucepan; mix gently. Spoon into ungreased 2-quart casserole. Bake uncovered 15 minutes. Sprinkle with bacon and Cheddar cheese. Bake 10 to 15 minutes longer or until hot and bubbly.

1 Serving (½ Cup): Calories 130; Total Fat 8g (Saturated Fat 4g; Trans Fat 0g); Cholesterol 20mg; Sodium 330mg; Total Carbohydrate 8g (Dietary Fiber 3g); Protein 6g **Exchanges:** 1 Vegetable, ½ High-Fat Meat, 1 Fat **Carbohydrate Choices:** ½

CHEESY BACON BROCCOLI Substitute 1¼ lb fresh broccoli, cut into 1½-inch pieces. Bake as directed.

CHEESY BACON GREEN BEANS Omit Brussels sprouts. In Step 1, place 1 bag (1 lb) frozen cut green beans and 2 tablespoons water in 2-quart microwavable casserole. Cover; microwave on High 5 minutes. Drain and continue as directed.

Cheesy Bacon Brussels Sprouts

Preparing Brussels Sprouts

Remove any discolored outer leaves; cut off stems.   Cut large sprouts in half.

SWEET-SOUR RED CABBAGE

LOWER CALORIE

Some like this classic cabbage dish sweet and some prefer it sour. For a sweeter touch, add another tablespoon of brown sugar; for a more sour taste, add an extra tablespoon of vinegar.

PREP 20 min TOTAL 50 min • **8 servings**

- 1 **medium head red cabbage (1½ lb), shredded**
- 4 **slices bacon, diced**
- 1 **small onion, sliced**
- ¼ **cup packed brown sugar**
- 2 **tablespoons all-purpose flour**
- ¼ **cup water**
- 3 **tablespoons white vinegar**
- ¼ **teaspoon salt**
- ⅛ **teaspoon pepper**

1 In 10-inch skillet, heat 1 inch water to boiling. Add cabbage; return to boiling. Boil uncovered about 15 minutes, stirring occasionally, until tender; drain and set aside. Wipe out skillet and dry with paper towel.

2 In same skillet, cook bacon over medium heat 4 minutes, stirring occasionally. Add onion. Cook 2 to 4 minutes, stirring occasionally, until bacon is crisp. Remove bacon and onion with slotted spoon; drain on paper towels. Drain bacon drippings leaving 1 tablespoon in skillet.

3 Stir sugar and flour into bacon drippings. Stir in water, vinegar, salt and pepper until well mixed. Stir in cabbage, bacon and onion. Cook over medium heat 1 to 2 minutes, stirring occasionally, until hot.

1 Serving: Calories 100; Total Fat 4g (Saturated Fat 1.5g; Trans Fat 0g); Cholesterol 0mg; Sodium 160mg; Total Carbohydrate 13g (Dietary Fiber 2g); Protein 3g **Exchanges:** ½ Other Carbohydrate, 1 Vegetable, 1 Fat **Carbohydrate Choices:** 1

SLOW COOKER **DIRECTIONS** Omit Step 1. Cook bacon (without onion) as directed in Step 2; reserve 1 tablespoon bacon drippings. Refrigerate bacon. Increase water to ⅓ cup. Spray 3½- to 4-quart slow cooker with cooking spray. In slow cooker, mix brown sugar, flour, water, vinegar, salt, pepper and reserved bacon drippings. Stir in cabbage and onion. Cover; cook on Low heat setting 6 to 7 hours. Stir in bacon.

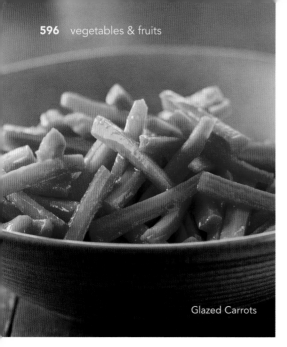

Glazed Carrots

GLAZED CARROTS LOWER CALORIE

Baby-cut carrots are a nice substitute for the julienne-cut carrots in this recipe. Use 1½ pounds.

PREP 20 min TOTAL 35 min • **6 servings**

- 1½ **lb fresh carrots, cut into julienne strips (page 8)**
- ⅓ **cup packed brown sugar**
- 2 **tablespoons butter**
- ½ **teaspoon salt**
- ½ **teaspoon grated orange peel**

1 In 2-quart saucepan, heat 1 inch water to boiling. Add carrots. Return to boiling; reduce heat. Simmer uncovered 6 to 9 minutes or until crisp-tender; drain and set aside.

2 In 12-inch skillet, cook remaining ingredients over medium heat, stirring constantly, until bubbly. Stir in carrots. Cook over low heat about 5 minutes, stirring occasionally, until carrots are glazed and hot.

1 Serving: Calories 130; Total Fat 4g (Saturated Fat 2g; Trans Fat 0g); Cholesterol 10mg; Sodium 260mg; Total Carbohydrate 22g (Dietary Fiber 3g); Protein 1g **Exchanges:** 1 Other Carbohydrate, 1 Vegetable, 1 Fat **Carbohydrate Choices:** 1½

HONEY-GLAZED LEMON CARROTS

Substitute 2 tablespoons honey for the brown sugar and lemon peel for the orange peel.

SAUTÉED CAULIFLOWER WITH BROWNED BREAD CRUMBS

PREP 10 min TOTAL 25 min • **4 servings**

- 1 **medium head cauliflower (2 lb), separated into florets**
- 4 **tablespoons butter**
- 1 **tablespoon Dijon mustard**
- 2 **cups soft bread crumbs (about 3 slices bread)**
- 2 **tablespoons olive oil**

1 In 10-inch skillet, heat 1 inch water (salted if desired) to boiling. Add cauliflower; return to boiling. Boil uncovered 3 minutes or until almost tender. Drain cauliflower in colander and immediately rinse under cold water to stop cooking; set aside.

2 In same skillet, melt 3 tablespoons of the butter over medium heat. Stir mustard into butter; add bread crumbs. Cook 8 to 10 minutes, stirring frequently, until crumbs are golden brown. Remove crumbs to plate.

3 Wipe out skillet with paper towel. In skillet, melt remaining 1 tablespoon butter and the oil over medium-high heat. Stir in cauliflower. Cook about 5 minutes, stirring occasionally, until lightly browned and tender. Sprinkle crumbs over top.

1 Serving (¾ Cup): Calories 420; Total Fat 22g (Saturated Fat 7g; Trans Fat 0.5g); Cholesterol 30mg; Sodium 1270mg; Total Carbohydrate 47g (Dietary Fiber 5g); Protein 10g **Exchanges:** 2½ Starch, ½ Other Carbohydrate, 1 Vegetable, 4 Fat **Carbohydrate Choices:** 3

Sautéed Cauliflower with Browned Bread Crumbs

SPICY COLLARD GREENS WITH BACON LOWER CALORIE

Collard greens are a form of cabbage, but instead of forming a head, they stay in a loose-leaf form. They're an excellent source of vitamins A and C, as well as calcium and iron.

PREP 25 min TOTAL 1 hr 30 min • **4 servings**

- 2 lb collard greens, ribs and stems removed, leaves coarsely chopped (about 8 cups)
- 6 slices bacon, chopped
- 1 medium onion, chopped (½ cup)
- 1 jalapeño chile, seeded, finely chopped
- ½ teaspoon dried thyme leaves
- ½ teaspoon seasoned salt
- ½ teaspoon pepper

1 In 4-quart Dutch oven or saucepan, heat 6 cups water to boiling. Add collard greens; return to boiling. Boil 30 minutes.

2 Meanwhile, in 12-inch skillet, cook bacon over medium-high heat, stirring occasionally, until crisp. Remove bacon with slotted spoon; drain on paper towels. Drain bacon drippings leaving 1 tablespoon in skillet.

3 Heat bacon drippings in skillet over medium heat. Add remaining ingredients; cook 5 minutes, stirring frequently.

4 Drain collard greens. Stir greens and bacon into skillet. Reduce heat to low. Cover; cook about 15 minutes, stirring occasionally, until greens are very tender.

Preparing Collard Greens

Remove thick ribs from centers of collard leaves by holding each leaf with hand and stripping away rib with other hand.

Layer several leaves in stack; roll up and cut into ½- to 1-inch thick slices. Coarsely chop slices.

1 Serving: Calories 130; Total Fat 10g (Saturated Fat 3.5g; Trans Fat 0g); Cholesterol 15mg; Sodium 380mg; Total Carbohydrate 6g (Dietary Fiber 3g); Protein 6g **Exchanges:** 1 Vegetable, ½ High-Fat Meat, 1 Fat **Carbohydrate Choices:** ½

COLLARD GREENS WITH BLACK-EYED PEAS During last 5 minutes of cooking, stir in 1 can (15 oz) black-eyed peas, drained, rinsed.

SCALLOPED CORN LOWER CALORIE

PREP 10 min TOTAL 55 min • **8 servings**

- 2 tablespoons butter
- 1 small onion, finely chopped (⅓ cup)
- ¼ cup finely chopped green bell pepper
- 2 tablespoons all-purpose flour
- ½ teaspoon salt
- ½ teaspoon paprika
- ¼ teaspoon ground mustard
  Dash pepper
- ¾ cup milk
- 1 can (15.25 oz) whole kernel corn, drained*
- 1 egg, slightly beaten
- 1 cup corn flakes cereal or panko crispy bread crumbs
- 1 tablespoon butter, melted

1 Heat oven to 350°F. In 10-inch skillet, melt 2 tablespoons butter over medium heat. Cook onion and bell pepper in butter 2 to 4 minutes, stirring occasionally, until crisp-tender. Stir in flour, salt, paprika, mustard and pepper. Cook, stirring constantly, until smooth and bubbly; remove from heat.

2 Stir in milk. Heat to boiling, stirring constantly. Boil and stir 1 minute; remove from heat. Stir in corn and egg. Pour into ungreased 1-quart casserole.

3 In small bowl, mix cereal and 1 tablespoon butter; sprinkle over corn mixture. Bake uncovered 30 to 35 minutes or until center is set.

*2 cups frozen (thawed) whole kernel corn can be substituted.

1 Serving: Calories 120; Total Fat 6g (Saturated Fat 2.5g; Trans Fat 0g); Cholesterol 40mg; Sodium 300mg; Total Carbohydrate 13g (Dietary Fiber 1g); Protein 3g **Exchanges:** 1 Starch, 1 Fat **Carbohydrate Choices:** 1

CUCUMBER AND KALE SAUTÉ

FAST LOWER CALORIE

Because the center stalk of kale is not tender, remove it before cooking.

PREP 15 min TOTAL 15 min • **4 servings**

- 2 medium cucumbers (about 1 lb)
- 1 tablespoon olive or vegetable oil
- 1 small onion, thinly sliced
- 1 clove garlic, finely chopped
- 2 cups torn kale pieces
- 2 teaspoons chopped fresh or ½ teaspoon dried basil leaves
- ¼ teaspoon salt
  Dash of pepper

1 Peel cucumbers if desired. Cut in half lengthwise and remove seeds. Cut each half crosswise into ¼-inch slices.

2 Heat oil in 12-inch skillet over medium heat. Cook cucumbers, onion and garlic in oil about 4 minutes, stirring occasionally, until cucumbers are crisp-tender. Stir in remaining ingredients. Cook and stir just until kale is wilted.

1 Serving: Calories 70; Total Fat 4g (Saturated Fat 0.5g; Trans Fat 0g); Cholesterol 0mg; Sodium 160mg; Total Carbohydrate 7g (Dietary Fiber 2g); Protein 2g **Exchanges:** 1½ Vegetable, 1 Fat **Carbohydrate Choices:** ½

CUCUMBER AND CHARD SAUTÉ Substitute torn swiss chard for the kale.

ZUCCHINI AND KALE SAUTÉ Substitute 2 medium zucchini for the cucumbers.

CARAMELIZED ONIONS

LOWER CALORIE

Sweet onions have more sugar than other onions, and it's the sugar that caramelizes, giving a deep golden brown color and rich flavor. If you can't find sweet onions, regular yellow onions can be used— just sprinkle about 1 tablespoon of brown sugar over the onions and cook as directed.

PREP 55 min TOTAL 55 min • **7 servings**

- 2 tablespoons butter*
- 3 large sweet onions (Bermuda, Maui, Spanish or Walla Walla), sliced (8 cups)
- ¼ teaspoon salt

1 In 12-inch nonstick skillet, melt butter over medium-high heat. Stir in onions to coat with butter. Cook uncovered 10 minutes, stirring every 3 to 4 minutes.

2 Reduce heat to medium-low. Sprinkle salt over onions. Cook 35 to 40 minutes longer, stirring well every 5 minutes, until onions are deep golden brown (onions will shrink during cooking).

*Do not use margarine or vegetable oil spreads.

1 Serving: Calories 60; Total Fat 3.5g (Saturated Fat 1.5g; Trans Fat 0g); Cholesterol 10mg; Sodium 110mg; Total Carbohydrate 6g (Dietary Fiber 1g); Protein 0g **Exchanges:** 1 Vegetable, ½ Fat **Carbohydrate Choices:** ½

CRANBERRY CARAMELIZED ONIONS Stir in ½ cup dried cranberries during last 5 to 10 minutes of cooking. Serve on turkey or chicken sandwiches.

Learn with Betty | CARAMELIZED ONIONS

Perfect Onions: These onions are deep golden brown in color and will taste caramelizd.

Undercooked Onions: These onions are too light in color and will not taste caramelized.

Overcooked Onions: These onions are too dark with charred edges and will taste burned.

TWICE-BAKED POTATOES

Vary the cheese as you like for these stuffed potatoes. Swiss, Colby and Monterey Jack are all tasty alternatives to the Cheddar cheese.

PREP 15 min TOTAL 1 hr 45 min • **8 servings**

- 4 **large Idaho or russet baking potatoes (8 to 10 oz each)**
- ¼ **to ½ cup milk**
- ¼ **cup butter, softened**
- ¼ **teaspoon salt**
  Dash pepper
- 1 **cup shredded Cheddar cheese (4 oz)**
- 1 **tablespoon chopped fresh chives**

1 Heat oven to 375°F. Gently scrub potatoes, but do not peel. Pierce potatoes several times with fork to allow steam to escape. Bake 1 hour to 1 hour 15 minutes or until potatoes are tender when pierced in center with fork.

2 When potatoes are cool enough to handle, cut in half lengthwise; scoop out inside, leaving ¼-inch shell. In medium bowl, mash potatoes with potato masher or electric mixer on low speed until no lumps remain. Add milk in small amounts, beating after each addition (amount of milk needed to make potatoes smooth and fluffy depends on kind of potatoes used).

3 Add butter, salt and pepper; beat vigorously until potatoes are light and fluffy. Stir in cheese and chives. Fill potato shells with mashed potato mixture.

4 Increase oven temperature to 400°F. Place potatoes on ungreased cookie sheet. Bake about 20 minutes or until hot.

1 Serving: Calories 200; Total Fat 11g (Saturated Fat 6g; Trans Fat 0g); Cholesterol 30mg; Sodium 210mg; Total Carbohydrate 20g (Dietary Fiber 2g); Protein 6g **Exchanges:** 1 Starch, ½ High-Fat Meat, 1½ Fat **Carbohydrate Choices:** 1

MAKE AHEAD DIRECTIONS Make potatoes through Step 3. Wrap tightly and refrigerate up to 24 hours or freeze up to 1 month. Bake as directed in Step 4. Bake refrigerated potatoes 30 minutes, frozen potatoes about 40 minutes.

BACON AND PEPPER TWICE-BAKED POTATOES Stir in ½ cup crumbled crisply cooked bacon (8 slices) and ½ cup diced red bell pepper with the cheese and chives in Step 3.

ITALIAN TWICE-BAKED POTATOES Substitute 1 cup shredded Italian cheese blend for the Cheddar cheese and add ½ teaspoon dried Italian seasoning with the cheese.

Twice-Baked Potatoes

Scooping Potato from Skins

Carefully scoop out the inside of each potato half with soup spoon, leaving a ¼-inch shell.

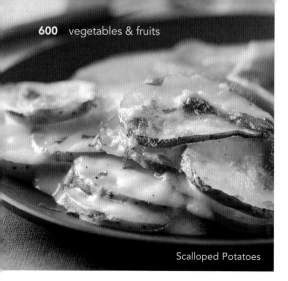

Scalloped Potatoes

SCALLOPED POTATOES

PREP 20 min TOTAL 2 hr 5 min • **6 servings**

- 4 tablespoons butter
- 1 small onion, finely chopped (⅓ cup)
- 3 tablespoons all-purpose flour
- 1 teaspoon salt
- ¼ teaspoon pepper
- 2½ cups milk
- 6 medium peeled or unpeeled potatoes, thinly sliced (6 cups)

1 Heat oven to 350°F. Grease 2-quart casserole with shortening or cooking spray.

2 In 2-quart saucepan, melt 3 tablespoons of the butter over medium heat. Cook onion in butter about 2 minutes, stirring occasionally, until tender. Stir in flour, salt and pepper. Cook, stirring constantly, until smooth and bubbly; remove from heat. Stir in milk. Heat to boiling, stirring constantly. Boil and stir 1 minute.

3 Spread potatoes in casserole. Pour sauce over potatoes. Cut remaining 1 tablespoon butter into small pieces; sprinkle over potatoes.

4 Cover; bake 30 minutes. Uncover; bake 1 hour to 1 hour 10 minutes longer or until potatoes are tender. Let stand 5 to 10 minutes before serving (sauce thickens as it stands).

1 Serving: Calories 260; Total Fat 10g (Saturated Fat 5g; Trans Fat 0.5g); Cholesterol 30mg; Sodium 500mg; Total Carbohydrate 36g (Dietary Fiber 2g); Protein 6g **Exchanges:** 2 Starch, ½ Other Carbohydrate, 1½ Fat **Carbohydrate Choices:** 2½

AU GRATIN POTATOES After stirring in milk and boiling 1 minute in Step 2, stir in 1 cup sharp Cheddar cheese. Cook and stir until cheese is melted. Continue as directed.

ROASTED ROSEMARY-ONION POTATOES LOWER CALORIE

PREP 15 min TOTAL 40 min • **4 servings**

- 1 small onion, finely chopped (⅓ cup)
- 2 tablespoons olive or vegetable oil
- 2 tablespoons chopped fresh or 2 teaspoons dried rosemary leaves, crushed
- 1 teaspoon chopped fresh or ¼ teaspoon dried thyme leaves
- ¼ teaspoon salt
- ⅛ teaspoon pepper
- 4 medium peeled or unpeeled potatoes, cut into 1-inch chunks (4 cups)

1 Heat oven to 450°F. Spray 15x10x1-inch pan with cooking spray.

2 In large bowl, mix all ingredients except potatoes. Add potatoes; toss to coat. Spread potatoes in single layer in pan.

3 Roast uncovered 20 to 25 minutes, turning occasionally, until potatoes are light brown and tender when pierced with fork.

1 Serving: Calories 160; Total Fat 7g (Saturated Fat 1g; Trans Fat 0g); Cholesterol 0mg; Sodium 150mg; Total Carbohydrate 21g (Dietary Fiber 2g); Protein 2g **Exchanges:** 1 Starch, ½ Other Carbohydrate, 1 Fat **Carbohydrate Choices:** 1½

ROASTED ROSEMARY-ONION SWEET POTATOES Substitute 2 to 3 medium sweet potatoes for the potatoes. Bake as directed.

Roasted Rosemary-Onion Potatoes

Potato Pancakes

FRIED POTATOES

PREP 30 min TOTAL 30 min • **4 servings**

> 2 tablespoons vegetable oil
> 4 medium peeled or unpeeled potatoes, thinly sliced (4 cups)
> 1 medium onion, thinly sliced, if desired
> 1½ teaspoons salt
> ¼ teaspoon pepper

1 In 10-inch nonstick skillet, heat oil over medium heat. Add potatoes and onion; sprinkle with salt and pepper.

2 Cover; cook over medium heat 10 minutes, stirring occasionally. Uncover; cook 10 minutes longer, stirring occasionally, until potatoes are brown and tender.

1 Serving: Calories 180; Total Fat 7g (Saturated Fat 1g; Trans Fat 0g); Cholesterol 0mg; Sodium 890mg; Total Carbohydrate 27g (Dietary Fiber 2g); Protein 3g **Exchanges:** 1 Starch, 1 Other Carbohydrate, 1 Fat **Carbohydrate Choices:** 2

HASH BROWN POTATOES

LOWER CALORIE

PREP 45 min TOTAL 45 min • **4 servings**

> 4 medium peeled or unpeeled Idaho or russet baking potatoes (1½ lb)
> ½ teaspoon salt
> ⅛ teaspoon pepper
> 2 tablespoons vegetable oil

1 Shred enough potatoes to measure 4 cups. Rinse well; drain and pat dry.

2 In large bowl, mix potatoes, salt and pepper. In 10-inch nonstick skillet, heat 1 tablespoon of the oil over medium heat. Pack potato mixture firmly in skillet, leaving ½-inch space around edge.

3 Reduce heat to medium-low. Cook about 15 minutes or until bottom is brown. Drizzle remaining 1 tablespoon oil evenly over potatoes. Cut potato mixture into quarters; turn over. Cook about 12 minutes longer or until bottom is brown.

1 Serving: Calories 160; Total Fat 7g (Saturated Fat 1g; Trans Fat 0g); Cholesterol 0mg; Sodium 300mg; Total Carbohydrate 23g (Dietary Fiber 2g); Protein 2g **Exchanges:** 1 Starch, ½ Other Carbohydrate, 1 Fat **Carbohydrate Choices:** 1½

CHEESY HASH BROWN POTATOES After dividing potato mixture into quarters and turning over in Step 3, sprinkle with ½ cup shredded Cheddar cheese (2 oz) during last 2 to 5 minutes of cooking, or cook until cheese melts.

ONION HASH BROWN POTATOES Add 1 small onion, finely chopped (⅓ cup), with potatoes in Step 2.

POTATO PANCAKES LOWER CALORIE

Potato pancakes, or latkes, are eaten traditionally during Hanukkah, but they are great to serve any time. Serve them with sour cream or Applesauce (page 613).

PREP 35 min TOTAL 35 min • **16 pancakes**

> 4 medium Idaho or russet baking potatoes (1½ lb), peeled
> 4 eggs, beaten
> 1 small onion, finely chopped (⅓ cup), if desired
> ¼ cup all-purpose flour
> 1 teaspoon salt
> ¼ cup vegetable oil

1 Shred enough potatoes to measure 4 cups. Rinse well; drain and pat dry.

2 In large bowl, mix potatoes, eggs, onion, flour and salt. In 12-inch skillet, heat 2 tablespoons of the oil over medium heat. Using ¼ cup potato mixture for each pancake, place 4 mounds into skillet. Flatten each with spatula to about 4 inches in diameter.

3 Cook pancakes about 2 minutes on each side or until golden brown. Remove from skillet; cover to keep warm. Repeat with remaining potato mixture; as mixture stands, liquid and potatoes will separate, so stir to mix as necessary. Add remaining oil as needed to prevent sticking.

1 Pancake: Calories 80; Total Fat 5g (Saturated Fat 1g; Trans Fat 0g); Cholesterol 55mg; Sodium 160mg; Total Carbohydrate 7g (Dietary Fiber 0g); Protein 2g **Exchanges:** ½ Starch, 1 Fat **Carbohydrate Choices:** ½

Learn to Make **Mashed Potatoes**

MASHED POTATOES

Nothing says comfort food better than mashed potatoes. Creamy, smooth, fluffy mashed potatoes are easy to achieve with a few tricks you'll learn here. You can choose to peel them or not. For a crowd, try our simple make-ahead, skins-on Slow Cooker Smashed Potatoes.

PREP 10 min **TOTAL** 40 min • **6 servings**

6 medium peeled or unpeeled round red or white potatoes, Yukon Gold potatoes or russet potatoes (2 lbs), cut into quarters

⅓ to ½ cup milk, warmed

¼ cup butter, softened

½ teaspoon salt

Dash pepper

1 In 2-quart saucepan, place potatoes and enough water just to cover potatoes. Heat to boiling; reduce heat. Cover; simmer 20 to 30 minutes or until potatoes are tender when pierced with fork. Drain. Shake pan with potatoes over low heat to dry (this will help make mashed potatoes fluffier).

2 Mash potatoes in pan with potato masher until no lumps remain. Add milk in small amounts, mashing after each addition (amount of milk needed to make potatoes smooth and fluffy depends on kind of potatoes used).

3 Add butter, salt and pepper. Mash vigorously until potatoes are light and fluffy and desired consistency. If desired, dot with small pieces of butter or sprinkle with paprika, chopped fresh parsley or chives.

1 Serving: Calories 200; Total Fat 8g (Saturated Fat 4g; Trans Fat 0g); Cholesterol 20mg; Sodium 260mg; Total Carbohydrate 28g (Dietary Fiber 3g); Protein 3g **Exchanges:** 1 Starch, 1 Other Carbohydrate, 1½ Fat **Carbohydrate Choices:** 2

LIGHTER **DIRECTIONS** For 4 grams of fat and 145 calories per serving, use fat-free (skim) milk and decrease butter to 2 tablespoons.

BUTTERMILK MASHED POTATOES Substitute buttermilk for milk.

CHEESY MASHED POTATOES Stir in 1 cup (4 oz) shredded cheese (Asiago, Cheddar, Monterey Jack or Parmesan) or crumbled cheese (blue or Gorgonzola) with the butter, salt and pepper in Step 3.

CHIPOTLE-CHEDDAR MASHED POTATOES Stir in 1 cup (4 oz) shredded Cheddar cheese and 1 to 2 chipotle chiles in adobo sauce (from 7-oz can), finely chopped, with the butter, salt and pepper in Step 3.

GARLIC MASHED POTATOES Cook 6 cloves garlic, peeled, with the potatoes. Mash garlic with potatoes.

HERBED MASHED POTATOES Stir in 2 tablespoons chopped fresh chives and ½ teaspoon each chopped fresh thyme leaves and rosemary leaves with butter, salt and pepper in Step 3.

HORSERADISH MASHED POTATOES Add 2 tablespoons prepared mild or hot horseradish with butter, salt and pepper in Step 3.

Mashed Potatoes

Keys to Success

- **Shake pan with drained potatoes over low heat to dry them** so mashed potatoes will be fluffier.

- **Mash with potato masher** (to make quick work of mashing potatoes) until no lumps remain.

- **If using an electric hand mixer, beat on low speed for a short amount of time** (see below) to keep potatoes from becoming gummy.

- **Warm milk slightly so that potatoes stay hot while mixing.** This can be done in the microwave or in a small saucepan on the cooktop.

- **Add milk in small amounts, mashing after each addition,** to get fluffy mashed potatoes.

- **Use round red or white potatoes or Yukon Gold potatoes** for mashed potatoes that have a lot of texture with pieces of potato.

- **Use russet potatoes** if you like smooth potatoes with a minimum of lumps.

Mashing Potatoes with a Mixer

- If using a nonstick saucepan or saucepan that is not shiny inside (such as anodized steel, which is dark gray in color), transfer potatoes to a medium bowl after Step 1.

- If using a stainless steel saucepan, mash potatoes right in the saucepan. Beat potatoes for 30 to 60 seconds with electric mixer on low speed as directed in Steps 2 and 3.

SLOW COOKER SMASHED POTATOES LOWER CALORIE

Here's a great way to have mashed potatoes that can be made in advance and kept warm while preparing the rest of your meal.

PREP 15 min **TOTAL** 6 hr 15 min • **12 servings**

- 3 **lb small peeled or unpeeled round white or red potatoes**
- ⅓ **cup water**
- 1 **container (12 oz) chive-and-onion sour cream potato topper**
- 2 **tablespoons ranch dressing and seasoning mix (from 1-oz package)**
- ¼ **cup chopped fresh chives or parsley**
- ⅓ **cup half-and-half**
- 1 **cup shredded Cheddar cheese, if desired**

1 Cut potatoes into halves or fourths as needed to make equal-size pieces. Place in 5- to 6-quart slow cooker. Add water; mix well to coat all pieces.

2 Cover and cook on Low heat setting 5 to 6 hours.

3 Gently mash potatoes with fork or potato masher. Stir in potato topper, dressing mix and chives. Stir in half-and-half and cheese until well mixed. Potatoes will hold on Low heat setting up to 1 hour; stir occasionally.

1 Serving (½ Cup): Calories 140; Total Fat 4g (Saturated Fat 2.5g, Trans Fat 0g); Cholesterol 10mg; Sodium 240mg; Total Carbohydrate 22g (Dietary Fiber 3g, Sugars 3g); Protein 3g **Exchanges:** 1 Starch, ½ Other Carbohydrate, 1 Fat **Carbohydrate Choices:** 1½

See how to make **mashed potatoes:**
Visit bettycrocker.com/BCcookbook

PICKING THE BEST POTATO				
Potato	Boiled	Mashed	Baked	Roasted or Panfried
Fingerling	X			X
Round Red or White	X	X		X
Russet/Idaho		X	X	X
Yukon Gold	X	X		X

ROASTED VEGETABLES

LOWER CALORIE

Pick packaged baby-cut carrots that are all about the same size so they cook evenly and are done at the same time.

PREP 15 min TOTAL 40 min • **10 servings**

- 3 tablespoons olive or vegetable oil
- ½ teaspoon salt
- ⅛ teaspoon pepper
- 1 clove garlic, finely chopped
- 1 cup ready-to-eat baby-cut carrots
- 6 small red potatoes, cut into quarters
- 2 small onions, cut into ½-inch wedges
- 1 small red bell pepper, cut into 1-inch pieces
- 1 medium zucchini, cut lengthwise in half, then cut crosswise into 1-inch slices
- 1 cup grape or cherry tomatoes

1 Heat oven to 450°F. In small bowl, stir oil, salt, pepper and garlic until well mixed. In ungreased 15x10x1-inch pan, toss carrots, potatoes, onions, bell pepper and zucchini with oil mixture until coated.

2 Roast uncovered 20 minutes, stirring once. Stir in tomatoes. Roast about 5 minutes longer or until vegetables are tender and starting to brown.

1 Serving: Calories 110; Total Fat 4.5g (Saturated Fat 0.5g; Trans Fat 0g); Cholesterol 0mg; Sodium 130mg; Total Carbohydrate 16g (Dietary Fiber 3g); Protein 2g **Exchanges:** ½ Starch, 1 Vegetable, 1 Fat **Carbohydrate Choices:** 1

Roasted Vegetables

CANDIED SWEET POTATOES

PREP 10 min TOTAL 35 min • **6 servings**

- 6 medium unpeeled sweet potatoes (2 lb)*
- ⅓ cup packed brown sugar
- 3 tablespoons butter
- 3 tablespoons water
- ½ teaspoon salt

1 In 2-quart saucepan, place sweet potatoes and enough water just to cover potatoes. Heat to boiling; reduce heat. Cover; simmer 20 to 25 minutes or until potatoes are tender when pierced with fork. Drain. When potatoes are cool enough to handle, peel and cut into ½-inch slices.

2 In 10-inch skillet, heat remaining ingredients over medium heat, stirring constantly, until smooth and bubbly. Add potatoes. Gently stir until glazed and hot.

*1 can (23 oz) sweet potatoes, drained and cut into ½-inch slices, can be substituted; omit Step 1.

1 Serving: Calories 220; Total Fat 6g (Saturated Fat 3g; Trans Fat 0g); Cholesterol 15mg; Sodium 250mg; Total Carbohydrate 41g (Dietary Fiber 4g); Protein 2g **Exchanges:** ½ Starch, 2 Other Carbohydrate, 1 Fat **Carbohydrate Choices:** 3

LIGHTER **DIRECTIONS** For 2 grams of fat and 185 calories per serving, decrease butter to 1 tablespoon; use nonstick skillet.

MAPLE-MASHED SWEET POTATOES Substitute ¼ cup real maple syrup for the brown sugar. Sprinkle with ¼ cup chopped pecans when adding potatoes in Step 2.

ORANGE SWEET POTATOES Substitute orange juice for the water. Add 1 tablespoon grated orange peel with the brown sugar.

PINEAPPLE SWEET POTATOES Omit water. Add 1 can (8 oz) crushed pineapple in syrup, undrained, with the brown sugar.

Sweet Potatoes

For the sweetest flavor, buy orange or red sweet potatoes. Light-colored potatoes will not be as tasty and will have a mealy texture. Store sweet potatoes in a cool, dry place, but use within 2 weeks.

FAST VEGGIE SIDES

1 Asparagus with Toasted Nuts and Citrus Zest: Top hot cooked asparagus spears with slivered almonds or pine nuts that have been toasted in melted butter on top of the stove. Sprinkle with grated lemon or orange peel.

2 Broccoli Italian Style: Toss hot cooked broccoli florets with warm zesty Italian dressing; sprinkle with grated Parmesan cheese or shredded Cheddar cheese.

3 Broccoli with Garlic-and-Herb Cream Sauce: Heat garlic-and-herb spreadable cheese in small saucepan over low heat, stirring frequently, until smooth and creamy, adding milk or cream if needed. Spoon over hot cooked broccoli.

4 Cauliflower and Roasted Peppers: Toss hot cooked cauliflower florets with sliced roasted red bell peppers; sprinkle with dried basil and garlic powder.

5 Grape Tomato Sauté: Sauté whole grape tomatoes, jarred chopped garlic and Italian seasoning in olive oil just until tomatoes are hot. Season with salt and pepper to taste.

6 Green Beans with Shaved Asiago: Drizzle hot cooked green beans with olive oil. Then, holding your vegetable peeler over the beans, shave slices of Asiago or Parmesan cheese on top.

7 Herbed Green Beans: Toss hot cooked green beans with salt-free garlic-pepper seasoning, chopped fresh basil and chopped fresh parsley.

8 Maple-Glazed Carrots: Mix together equal amounts of maple syrup and melted butter; toss with hot cooked, well-drained baby-cut carrots.

9 Sugar Snap Peas with Honey Butter: Mix together equal amounts of honey and melted butter; toss with hot cooked, well-drained sugar snap peas. Sprinkle with honey-roasted peanuts.

WILTED SPINACH

LOWER CALORIE

PREP 30 min TOTAL 30 min • **4 servings**

- 2 **tablespoons olive or vegetable oil**
- 1 **medium onion, chopped (½ cup)**
- 1 **slice bacon, cut up**
- 1 **clove garlic, finely chopped**
- ½ **teaspoon salt**
- ¼ **teaspoon pepper**
- ¼ **teaspoon ground nutmeg**
- 1 **lb fresh spinach, stems removed**
- 2 **tablespoons fresh lime juice**

1 In 4-quart Dutch oven or saucepan, heat oil over medium heat. Cook onion, bacon and garlic in oil 8 to 10 minutes, stirring occasionally, until bacon is crisp; reduce heat to low.

2 Stir in salt, pepper and nutmeg. Gradually add spinach. Toss just until spinach is wilted. Drizzle with lime juice.

1 Serving (½ Cup): Calories 110; Total Fat 8g (Saturated Fat 1.5g; Trans Fat 0g); Cholesterol 0mg; Sodium 390mg; Total Carbohydrate 6g (Dietary Fiber 3g); Protein 3g **Exchanges:** 1 Vegetable, 1½ Fat **Carbohydrate Choices:** ½

GLAZED ACORN SQUASH

PREP 10 min TOTAL 1 hr 10 min • **4 servings**

- 2 **acorn squash (1 to 1½ lb each)**
- 4 **tablespoons real or maple-flavored syrup**
- 4 **tablespoons whipping cream or butter**

1 Heat oven to 350°F. Cut each squash in half lengthwise; remove seeds and fibers. Place squash, cut side up, in ungreased 13x9-inch pan.

2 Spoon 1 tablespoon syrup and 1 tablespoon whipping cream into each squash half. Bake uncovered about 1 hour or until tender.

1 Serving: Calories 210; Total Fat 5g (Saturated Fat 3g; Trans Fat 0g); Cholesterol 15mg; Sodium 35mg; Total Carbohydrate 38g (Dietary Fiber 7g); Protein 2g **Exchanges:** 1 Starch, 1½ Other Carbohydrate, 1 Fat **Carbohydrate Choices:** 2½

SLOW COOKER **DIRECTIONS** Use squash that are ¾ to 1 lb each. Cut each squash in half crosswise; remove seeds and fibers. Spray 5- to 6-quart slow cooker with cooking spray. Pour ¼ cup water into slow cooker. Place squash halves, cut side up, in cooker (may be necessary to stack them). Spoon 1 tablespoon

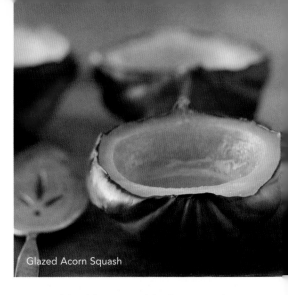

Glazed Acorn Squash

syrup and 1 tablespoon whipping cream into each squash half. Cover; cook on High heat setting 3 to 4 hours or until tender.

APPLE-STUFFED ACORN SQUASH Omit maple syrup and whipping cream. Bake squash halves 30 minutes. In small bowl, mix 1 large tart red apple, diced; 2 tablespoons each chopped nuts and packed brown sugar; and 1 tablespoon melted butter. Spoon into squash halves. Bake about 30 minutes.

GARDEN PATCH SAUTÉ

FAST LOWER CALORIE

PREP 20 min TOTAL 20 min • **6 servings**

- 1 **tablespoon olive or vegetable oil**
- 1 **medium zucchini, cut into ¼-inch slices (1 cup)**
- 1 **medium yellow summer squash, cut into ¼-inch slices (1 cup)**
- 1 **cup sliced fresh mushrooms (3 oz)**
- 1 **cup grape or cherry tomatoes, cut in half**
- 2 **tablespoons chopped fresh chives**
- ½ **teaspoon garlic salt**

1 In 10-inch nonstick skillet, heat oil over medium-high heat. Cook zucchini, yellow squash and mushrooms in oil 4 to 5 minutes, stirring frequently, until crisp-tender.

2 Stir in tomatoes. Sprinkle with chives and garlic salt. Cook 2 to 3 minutes, stirring frequently, just until tomatoes begin to soften.

1 Serving: Calories 40; Total Fat 2.5g (Saturated Fat 0g; Trans Fat 0g); Cholesterol 0mg; Sodium 85mg; Total Carbohydrate 3g (Dietary Fiber 1g); Protein 1g **Exchanges:** ½ Vegetable, ½ Fat **Carbohydrate Choices:** 0

FRUIT BASICS

Whether you like crisp apples or pears, small fragrant berries or large, juicy melons and pineapples, you'll find a selection available at farmers' markets and grocery stores throughout most of the year. Serve fruit often—it's a really healthful way to add sweetness, variety and a wealth of important nutrients to your meals.

BUYING AND STORING FRESH FRUITS

- Purchase fruit that is bright in color, heavy for its size (indicating juiciness) and firm to the touch for the variety. Fresh fruit should not show any sign of decay or have soft spots. For berries, check for mold that can occur in closed containers.

- Fruits such as berries, pineapples, watermelon, cherries and apples will not ripen after purchase so look for ripe fruit at the market.

- Choices such as bananas, pears, peaches, cantaloupe and kiwifruit will ripen after purchase.

- To ripen fruits after purchase, place them in a paper bag at room temperature 1 to 2 days. Don't use a plastic bag as mold can occur.

- The produce experts at your market are good resources when it comes to the ripeness of an individual fruit variety and can help you choose just the right one. Also look to the web for questions on varieties, new and old.

Snack on dried fruit like mangoes, apricots, raisins and apples, each a great choice for a healthful treat.

EATING MORE FRUIT

Fruit is a wonderful natural snack food— sweet, delicious, a tasty energy booster that's loaded with nutrients.

- Add sliced bananas or strawberries to your cereal in the morning.

- Pack a small container of fresh blueberries or raspberries when you are on the go.

- Apples and pears are great for eating out of hand.

- Add sliced peaches or nectarines to your next peanut butter sandwich as a great, fresh substitute for jelly.

- Keep frozen and canned varieties of fruits on hand. Look for frozen fruits without added sugar (you can add your own) and canned fruits in light syrup.

- For quick snacks, purchase melons and pineapple precut and ready to eat.

- Try a fresh orange or grapefruit instead of drinking juice—there's more fiber and fewer calories in the whole fruit.

- Add dried fruit to salads and desserts for a touch of added natural sweetness or eat dried fruit as a snack. Try dried apricots, cherries, cranberries, figs, mangoes, plums and raisins.

Blackberries

Raspberries

Golden Raspberries

Cranberries

Red Currants

Blueberries

Strawberries

Cape Gooseberries

BERRIES

Choose firm, plump berries; avoid mold, mushy or soft spots. Remove any moldy/damaged berries before refrigerating unwashed. Very perishable; use within a few days. Available year-round, but best when in season locally for superior flavor.

Blackberries: Largest wild berry. Best used immediately but can be refrigerated up to 2 days.

Blueberries: Juicy and sweet; range from tiny wild blueberries to large cultivated ones.

Cranberries: Available fresh September to December (avoid discolored, shriveled ones); also frozen, dried. Fresh berries are very tart. Dried are sweetened; use like raisins.

Gooseberries: Varieties include green, white, yellow or red with smooth or fuzzy skins. Limited season (March to June) depending on region; also canned. Great in jams, jellies, desserts.

Raspberries (Red, Golden, Black): Most intensely flavored berry. Red are available year-round; yellow in June to September; black in mid-June to mid-August.

Red Currants: Related to gooseberries. Available June to August in red, black, white. Black typically used for preserves, syrups, liqueurs. Use red/white as snacks or for preserves.

Strawberries: Choose berries that are all red, brightly colored, with bright green tops. Great in salads, desserts, snacks.

Colorado Peaches

Peaches

Pluots

Black Plums

Nectarines

Prune Plums

Red Plums

Sweet Cherries

STONE FRUITS

Choose plump stone fruits; free of bruises, soft or shriveled spots; not excessively hard. Avoid any greening (in lighter-colored fruit). Refrigerate 3 to 5 days.

Nectarines: Sweeter, richer, firmer flesh than peaches. Available mid-spring to late September; peak season is July to August. Choose fragrant fruit that gives to gentle pressure.

Peaches: Fuzzy-skinned varieties range from lightly shaded pink/creamy white to red-shaded yellow. Flesh ranges from pink-tinged white to yellow-gold. U.S. varieties available May to October in most regions (or imports available during off-season). Choose intensely aromatic fruit that gives to gentle pressure.

Plums: Japanese varieties: larger, rounder; juicy; soft flesh; good for eating. European varieties (including prune plums or sugar plums): smaller; less juicy; firmer flesh; good for baking/drying. Plumcots and pluots are varieties of plums crossed with apricots.

Sweet Cherries: Available fresh (choose firm—not hard—cherries), dried, frozen. Stemmed cherries last longer. Eat out of hand or cooked.

Mango

Plantain

Red Plantain

Dates

Coconut

Quince

Mangosteen

Kiwano
(Horned Melon)

Pomegranate

Lychee

Papaya

Carambola
(Star Fruit)

Figs

Guayaba

Kiwifruit

Longan

Dragon Fruit

Pineapple

Cherimoya

Rambutan

Grapefruit

Valencia Orange

Navel Oranges

Lime

Minneola Tangelos

Key Limes

Clementine Oranges

Meyer Lemon

Lemon

TROPICAL FRUITS

Exotic tropical fruits are available at different times of year. Look for new and interesting varieties that are firm, with great color and a fresh aroma.

Cherimoya: Creamy white flesh; sweet custard taste (discard large black seeds). Ripen unwashed at room temperature until fruit yields to gentle pressure. For more intense flavor, chill before serving.

Dragon Fruit: Pink skin (white or red flesh) or yellow skin (white flesh). Kiwi-pineapple flavor; edible seeds. Choose evenly colored skin with few blotches; avoid very dry, brown stem or brown-tipped "leaves." Fruit should yield to gentle pressure. Eat plain, in salads or smoothies.

Kiwano (Horned Melon): Bright, lime-green pulp; banana-cucumber taste; jellylike texture; edible seeds. Golden-orange at peak ripeness. Store at room temperature up to 2 weeks.

Mango: Golden orange flesh with large center seed; very sweet flavor. Chill before serving.

Pineapple: Firm yellow flesh; very fragrant with sweet/tart flavor. Choose firm fruit with no sign of decay and crisp green top.

Plantain: "Cooking banana." Less sweet; more firm than bananas. Popular in Latin American and some Asian and African cuisines. Avoid those with bruises. Green: mild, squash-like flavor. Ripened: soft, spongy texture. Use both types in side dishes. Store at room temperature.

CITRUS

Choose fruit heavy for size, with smooth-textured skin. Store unwashed at room temperature or refrigerate up to 2 weeks.

Blood Orange (Moro Orange): Deep red; sweet, juicy flesh. Peel is smooth or pitted with red blush. Peak season: December to May. Refrigerate up to 2 weeks.

Kumquat: Entirely edible; skin is sweet, pulp is tart. Peak season: December to May. Store unwashed at room temperature up to 2 days or refrigerate up to 2 weeks.

Meyer Lemon: Mild, juicy. Sweeter than common lemons; rind isn't bitter. Peak season: November to May. Refrigerate in plastic bag up to 2 weeks.

Tangelo: Cross between grapefruit and tangerine. Range of sizes. Yellow-orange to deep orange; smooth skin. Sweet-tart; juicy; few seeds. Minneola is most common variety. Peak season: November to March. Refrigerate up to 2 weeks.

Golden Delicious Apple

Red Delicious Apples

Red Bartlett Pears

Cortland Apples

Ginger Gold Apples

Pink Lady Apple

Jonathan Apple

Bosc Pears

Granny Smith Apple

Bartlett Pear

Honeycrisp Apple

Apple Pears

Braeburn Apple

Seckel Pears

Gala Apple

Comice Pear

French Butter Pears

McIntosh Apples

APPLES

Choose firm, smooth-skinned apples without bruises, blemishes or musty smell. Choose apples based on purpose—eating or baking/cooking (see Picking Apples, page 165). Store refrigerated in plastic bag up to 1 month.

Sweet: Crispin/Mutsu (crisp), Fuji (crisp), Gala (crisp), Ginger Gold (crisp), Golden Delicious (crisp), Honey Crisp (crisp), Honey Gold (slightly crisp), Red Delicious (crisp), Regent (crisp)

Slightly Sweet: Fireside (slightly crisp), Prairie Spy (crisp)

Sweet-Tart: Braeburn (crisp), Jonagold (crisp), Jonamac (tender), McIntosh (tender)

Slightly Tart: Cortland (slightly crisp), Ida Red (slightly crisp), Jonathan (tender), Newtown Pippin (crisp), Northern Spy (crisp), Paula Red (slightly crisp), Rome (slightly crisp), Winesap (crisp)

Tart: Granny Smith (crisp), Haralson (tart)

PEARS

Choose blemish-free pears. Ripen at room temperature; store in refrigerator 1 month.

Cooking/Baking Pears: Anjou (Green, Red when slightly ripe), Bosc, French Butter, Seckel

Eating/Salad Pears: Anjou (Green, Red when ripe), Asian, Bartlett, Comice, French Butter

APPLESAUCE FAST LOWER CALORIE

PREP 20 min TOTAL 20 min • **6 servings**

- 4 medium apples (1½ lb), peeled, quartered and cored
- ½ cup water
- ¼ cup packed brown sugar or 3 to 4 tablespoons granulated sugar
- ¼ teaspoon ground cinnamon
- ⅛ teaspoon ground nutmeg

1 In 2-quart saucepan, heat apples and water to boiling over medium heat, stirring occasionally; reduce heat. Simmer uncovered 5 to 10 minutes, stirring occasionally to break up apples, until tender.

2 Stir in remaining ingredients. Heat to boiling. Boil and stir 1 minute. Serve warm or chilled. Store covered in refrigerator.

1 Serving (½ Cup): Calories 90; Total Fat 0g (Saturated Fat 0g; Trans Fat 0g); Cholesterol 0mg; Sodium 0mg; Total Carbohydrate 22g (Dietary Fiber 2g); Protein 0g **Exchanges:** 1 Fruit, ½ Other Carbohydrate **Carbohydrate Choices:** 1½

SPICY FRUIT COMPOTE

PREP 10 min TOTAL 35 min • **6 servings**

- 1 cup orange juice
- ½ cup water
- ⅓ cup maple-flavored syrup, real maple syrup or packed brown sugar
- ½ cup sweetened dried cranberries
- ⅓ cup dried apricots, cut in half
- 2 pears or apples, peeled and cut into bite-size pieces
- 2 tablespoons sugar
- ¼ teaspoon pumpkin pie spice
- 2 cinnamon sticks

1 In 2-quart saucepan, mix all ingredients until blended. Heat to boiling over medium-high heat; reduce heat to low. Simmer uncovered 8 to 12 minutes or until pears are tender.

2 Let stand at room temperature 10 minutes. Remove cinnamon sticks. Serve compote warm or cold.

1 Serving (½ Cup): Calories 180; Total Fat 0g (Saturated Fat 0g; Trans Fat 0g); Cholesterol 0mg; Sodium 10mg; Total Carbohydrate 43g (Dietary Fiber 3g); Protein 0g **Exchanges:** 1 Fruit, 2 Other Carbohydrate **Carbohydrate Choices:** 3

MAKE AHEAD **SPICY FRUIT COMPOTE** Make the compote up to 4 days ahead of time; cover and refrigerate. Serve cold, or reheat in the microwave on High 1 to 2 minutes until warm.

CINNAMON FRUIT COMPOTE Substitute ground cinnamon for the pumpkin pie spice, raisins for the cranberries and dried peaches for the apricots.

APPLE-PEAR SALAD

LOWER CALORIE

PREP 25 min TOTAL 25 min • **8 servings**

- 1 large red apple, cut into quarters, then cut crosswise into thin slices
- 1 large pear, cut into quarters, then cut crosswise into thin slices
- 1 medium stalk celery, cut diagonally into thin slices (½ cup)
- 4 oz Havarti cheese, cut into julienne strips
- 3 tablespoons olive or vegetable oil
- 2 tablespoons frozen (thawed) apple juice concentrate
- 3 tablespoons coarsely chopped honey-roasted peanuts

In medium bowl, mix apple, pear, celery and cheese. In small bowl, thoroughly mix oil and juice concentrate. Pour over apple mixture; toss to coat. Sprinkle with peanuts.

1 Serving: Calories 170; Total Fat 12g (Saturated Fat 4.5g; Trans Fat 0g); Cholesterol 15mg; Sodium 125mg; Total Carbohydrate 11g (Dietary Fiber 2g); Protein 4g **Exchanges:** ½ Fruit, ½ High-Fat Meat, 2 Fat **Carbohydrate Choices:** 1

Spicy Fruit Compote

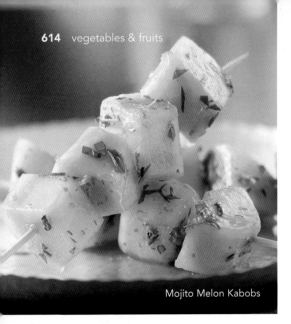

Mojito Melon Kabobs

MOJITO MELON KABOBS

LOWER CALORIE

Mojito typically refers to a cocktail made with lime juice, sugar, mint leaves and rum. We've used those same flavors in these pretty kabobs.

PREP 20 min **TOTAL** 1 hr 20 min • **12 kabobs**

- 2 limes
- 5 cups assorted melon cubes
- ⅓ cup sugar
- ⅓ cup dark rum*
- 3 tablespoons finely chopped fresh mint leaves

1 Grate 2 tablespoons peel from limes. Cut each lime in half crosswise; squeeze halves over small bowl to remove 6 tablespoons juice.

2 Place melon cubes in 1-gallon resealable food-storage plastic bag. Sprinkle lime peel and pour lime juice over melon. Add sugar, rum and mint. Seal bag; turn to coat. Refrigerate at least 1 hour, but no longer than 24 hours, to blend flavors.

3 Discard marinade. To serve, thread 4 or 5 melon cubes on each of 12 (5- or 6-inch) bamboo skewers.

*⅓ cup frozen (thawed) limeade concentrate (from 6-oz can) can be substituted.

1 Kabob: Calories 50; Total Fat 0g (Saturated Fat 0g; Trans Fat 0g); Cholesterol 0mg; Sodium 10mg; Total Carbohydrate 13g (Dietary Fiber 1g); Protein 0g **Exchanges:** 1 Other Carbohydrate **Carbohydrate Choices:** 1

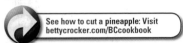

See how to cut a pineapple: Visit bettycrocker.com/BCcookbook

PEACH AND PLUM SALAD

FAST   LOWER CALORIE

PREP 10 min **TOTAL** 10 min • **6 servings**

- 3 medium plums, sliced
- 3 medium peaches, sliced
- ½ cup coarsely chopped walnuts, toasted (page 22)
- ¼ cup raspberry preserves
- 2 tablespoons red wine vinegar or white vinegar
- 1 tablespoon vegetable oil

Arrange plums and peaches on serving plate. Sprinkle with walnuts. In small bowl, mix remaining ingredients; drizzle over fruit.

1 Serving: Calories 170; Total Fat 9g (Saturated Fat 1g; Trans Fat 0g); Cholesterol 0mg; Sodium 0mg; Total Carbohydrate 21g (Dietary Fiber 3g); Protein 2g **Exchanges:** 1 Fruit, ½ Other Carbohydrate, 2 Fat **Carbohydrate Choices:** 1½

BROILED PINEAPPLE

FAST   LOWER CALORIE

PREP 15 min **TOTAL** 15 min • **4 servings**

- 1 can (20 oz) sliced pineapple in juice, drained, or 12 slices (⅜ inch) fresh pineapple
- 1 tablespoon packed brown sugar
- 2 tablespoons lime juice
- 2 tablespoons honey
- ½ cup vanilla fat-free yogurt
- 1 teaspoon honey
- ½ teaspoon grated lime peel

1 Set oven control to broil. Place pineapple slices on ungreased broiler pan. In small bowl, mix brown sugar, lime juice and 2 tablespoons honey; drizzle over pineapple. Broil with tops of pineapple 4 inches from heat 6 to 8 minutes, turning once, until light brown.

2 In another small bowl, mix remaining ingredients. Serve pineapple slices topped with yogurt mixture.

1 Serving (3 Slices Pineapple and 2 Tablespoons Sauce): Calories 150; Total Fat 0g (Saturated Fat 0g; Trans Fat 0g); Cholesterol 0mg; Sodium 20mg; Total Carbohydrate 35g (Dietary Fiber 1g); Protein 2g **Exchanges:** 1 Fruit, 1½ Other Carbohydrate **Carbohydrate Choices:** 2

BROILED GRAPEFRUIT Omit lime. Cut 2 medium grapefruits in half. Place halves on broiler pan. Top each grapefruit half with brown sugar mixture. Serve with yogurt mixture.

VEGETARIAN

CHARTS, FEATURES AND GLOSSARIES

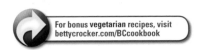

For bonus **vegetarian recipes,** visit
bettycrocker.com/BCcookbook

FAST = Ready in 20 minutes or less **LOWER CALORIE** = See Helpful Nutrition and Cooking Information, page 685
LIGHTER = 25% fewer calories or grams of fat **MAKE AHEAD** = Make-ahead directions **SLOW COOKER** = Slow cooker directions

← Fresh edamame, Southwestern Pot Pie (page 625), Portabella Muffuletta Sandwiches (page 634), Tofu Teriyaki
Noodles (page 627)

VEGETARIAN BASICS

Whether you adhere to a strict vegetarian lifestyle or you simply want to add some versatility to your weekly menus, great-tasting recipes based on vegetables, legumes, grains and pasta can be found here. There's also lots of information on ingredients used in meatless cooking to get you started.

TYPES OF VEGETARIANS

Vegetarian eating varies based on the types of foods allowed or eliminated. Below are brief summaries of the most common vegetarians:

Vegan: Does not eat meat of any kind (beef, pork, poultry, fish or seafood), meat based broths, eggs, dairy or animal-derived products, such as gelatin, honey and lard.

Flexitarian: Mainly sticks to a vegetarian diet but occasionally eats meat.

Ovo-Lacto/Lacto-Ovo: Does not eat meat of any kind or animal-based broth but does eat eggs and dairy products, and some may consume animal-derived products such as gelatin, honey and lard.

Lacto: Does not eat meat but does eat dairy products.

Ovo: Does not eat meat but does eat eggs.

Tips for Working with Tofu

- Tofu is perishable, so check the sell-by date on the package. If unopened, it will keep in the refrigerator up to 5 days. Once opened, use within 2 or 3 days. Store covered with water and change the water daily.

- Tofu can be frozen for up to 5 months. Freeze in the original container or wrap tightly in plastic wrap before freezing.

- Throw out tofu that smells sour.

- Squeeze the liquid from tofu before cooking so that it is denser and easier to cook. This will help it brown better, too. Press the tofu between layers of paper towels or kitchen towels to remove excess moisture.

- Because tofu has little or no fat, it can stick to the pan when stir-frying. To avoid adding too much oil, use a nonstick pan.

- Add volume to scrambled eggs or egg salad by substituting tofu for half the eggs.

TYPES OF TOFU

Sometimes called *bean curd*, tofu is made from soybeans and is processed into a solid block. This versatile food absorbs the flavors of foods easily. Look for tofu refrigerated in the grocery produce department. It's available in flavored and unflavored varieties.

Extra-Firm or Firm Tofu: Higher in protein, fat and calcium than other types of tofu, this solid, dense form of tofu holds its shape in recipes. Use it as a replacement for poultry or pork in casseroles, stews, soups, sandwiches, salads, stir-fries or on the grill.

Soft Tofu: Because this type of tofu is soft in texture and doesn't hold its shape, it's great in dips, dressings, desserts, sauces, smoothies and spreads.

Silken Tofu: Processed in a slightly different way from other tofu varieties, this type has a creamy, smooth, custard-like texture. Use it in dips, dressings, desserts, sauces, smoothies and spreads.

Cook tofu cubes in a small amount of oil until browned, stirring frequently.

SOY FOODS

All the foods below are made from soybeans, which can be an important part of a healthy diet. High-protein powerhouses, soy-based foods can replace meat and poultry sources of protein, helping to reduce the amount of saturated fat in your diet.

Soy Products

Edamame: See page 627.

Miso: Fermented bean paste—a basic flavoring in Japanese cooking. There are many different colors and flavors, ranging from sweet to salty. Use lighter versions in mild soups or sauces, darker versions in highly flavored dishes. Found in Japanese markets or natural food stores. Refrigerate in airtight container up to 1 year.

Soy Cheese: Available as full-fat, low-fat and nonfat versions in many popular cheese flavors. A few may be available at grocery stores, but many are found in health food stores. All are lactose free, but be sure to check labels for added milk protein. Best served chilled or at room temperature; may separate if heated.

Soy Flour: Made from roasted soybeans that are ground into a powder. Look for full-fat soy flour and defatted soy flour, which has had the oils removed during processing. Store in the refrigerator or freezer.

Soy Ice Cream: Dairy-free ice cream available in many flavors.

Soy Mayonnaise: Available in flavors such as plain, Dijon, wasabi. Made from soybean oil.

Soy Milk: Available in aseptic (nonrefrigerated) cartons or refrigerated, or as soy milk powder. Varieties include regular and light versions in plain, chocolate and vanilla. Once opened, refrigerate all soy milk; use within 5 days. Store soy milk powder in refrigerator or freezer.

Soy Nuts: Roasted soybeans available salted or unsalted and in flavors such as wasabi, barbecue and honey roasted.

Soy Pudding: Dairy-free refrigerated pudding available in many flavors.

Soy Yogurt: Available flavors include plain, vanilla and fruit flavors.

Soybean Oil: Clean taste. A cooking oil low in saturated fat, high in omega-3 fatty acids. Many oils sold as "vegetable oil" are made from soybeans, but not all. Read ingredient list to be sure.

Soynut Butter: Available in plain, unsweetened, honey, chocolate flavors. Use like peanut butter; milder "nut" flavor than peanut butter. Some varieties are 30 percent lower in total fat or 50 percent lower in saturated fat than regular peanut butter. Great for those with peanut allergies.

Tamari: Similar to but thicker than soy sauce; unique, mellow flavor.

Tempeh: Fermented cooked soybeans, formed into dense, chewy cakes with nutty, yeast flavor; use as a meat substitute. Holds shape when cooked—great for veggie burgers. When crumbled, great in casseroles. Available fresh or frozen. Refrigerate fresh up to 2 weeks; freeze up to 3 months.

Textured Soy Protein: Available dried, granular or in chunks of compressed, processed soy flour (rehydrate before using) Textured soy crumbles (frozen, ready-to-use crumbles) resemble ground beef and are used to replace ground meat in recipes.

Tofu: See Types of Tofu, page 617.

How Tofu Is Made

To make tofu, soybeans are soaked, cooked, ground and then mixed with a curdling ingredient. The resulting curds are pressed into cakes, which are tofu. Firmness depends on the amount of whey liquid extracted. Tofu is very mild in flavor.

Soy Milk

Chocolate Soy Milk

Soybean Oil

Soy Sauce

Tamari

Soy Yogurt

Soy Mayonnaise

Soy Cheeses

Chocolate Tofu

Edamame (Pods and Shelled)

Flax Tempeh

Tempeh

Vegetable Tempeh

Silken Tofu

Firm Tofu

Red Miso

Chocolate Soy Pudding

Soy Ice Cream (Strawberry)

Textured Soy Protein

Textured Soy Crumbles

White Miso

Brown Miso

Soy Flour

Soynut Butter

Baked Tofu Italian

Baked Tofu Teriyaki

Soy Nuts

POLENTA WITH GARDEN VEGETABLES LOWER CALORIE

Refrigerated polenta can usually be found in the produce or dairy cases of large supermarkets. For this recipe, you can use plain polenta or one of the flavored varieties, such as Italian herb or sun-dried tomato.

PREP 35 min TOTAL 35 min • **4 servings**

- 1 roll (1 lb) refrigerated polenta, cut into ½-inch slices
- 2 tablespoons olive or vegetable oil
- 1 small red onion, cut into thin wedges
- 2 cloves garlic, finely chopped
- 8 oz fresh green beans, trimmed, cut into ¾-inch pieces
- 1 medium red bell pepper, coarsely chopped (1 cup)
- 1½ cups sliced fresh mushrooms (4 oz)
- 1 small yellow summer squash, cut in half lengthwise, then cut crosswise into ¼-inch slices (about 1 cup)
- ½ teaspoon fennel seed, crushed
- ¼ teaspoon salt
- ¼ cup finely shredded mozzarella cheese (1 oz)

1 Cook polenta as directed on package. Meanwhile, in 10-inch skillet, heat oil over medium-high heat. Cook onion and garlic in oil 3 to 5 minutes, stirring occasionally, until crisp-tender.

2 Reduce heat to medium-low. Stir in green beans and bell pepper. Cover; cook 8 to 10 minutes, stirring occasionally, until beans are crisp-tender. Stir in mushrooms, squash, fennel seed and salt. Cover; cook 3 to 5 minutes, stirring occasionally, until squash is crisp-tender.

3 Serve polenta over vegetable mixture. Sprinkle individual servings with cheese.

1 Serving: Calories 200; Total Fat 9g (Saturated Fat 2g; Trans Fat 0g); Cholesterol 0mg; Sodium 460mg; Total Carbohydrate 25g (Dietary Fiber 4g); Protein 6g **Exchanges:** 1½ Starch, 1 Vegetable, 1½ Fat **Carbohydrate Choices:** 1½

POLENTA WITH BROCCOLI AND PARMESAN Substitute 2 cups fresh broccoli florets for the green beans and shredded Parmesan for the mozzarella cheese.

POLENTA WITH CONFETTI VEGETABLES Omit mushrooms, summer squash and fennel. Stir in 1 cup each frozen shelled edamame and frozen corn, and ½ teaspoon dried marjoram leaves in Step 3 with the beans. Continue as directed.

ARTICHOKE-SPINACH LASAGNA

LOWER CALORIE

PREP 20 min TOTAL 1 hr 30 min • **8 servings**

- 1 medium onion, chopped (½ cup)
- 4 cloves garlic, finely chopped
- 1 can (14 oz) vegetable broth (for homemade broth, see page 530)
- 1 tablespoon chopped fresh or 1 teaspoon dried rosemary leaves
- 1 can (14 oz) artichoke hearts, drained, coarsely chopped
- 1 box (9 oz) frozen chopped spinach, thawed, squeezed to drain
- 1 jar (15 to 17 oz) Alfredo sauce
- 9 uncooked lasagna noodles
- 3 cups shredded mozzarella cheese (12 oz)
- 1 package (4 oz) crumbled herb-and-garlic feta cheese (1 cup)
  Rosemary sprigs, if desired
  Lemon wedges, if desired

1 Heat oven to 350°F. Spray 13x9-inch (3-quart) glass baking dish with cooking spray.

2 Spray 12-inch skillet with cooking spray; heat over medium-high heat. Add onion and garlic; cook about 3 minutes, stirring occasionally, until onion is crisp-tender. Stir in broth and 1 tablespoon rosemary. Heat to boiling. Stir in artichokes and spinach; reduce heat. Cover; simmer 5 minutes. Stir in pasta sauce.

3 Spread one-fourth of the artichoke mixture in bottom of baking dish; top with 3 noodles. Sprinkle with ¾ cup of the mozzarella cheese. Repeat layers twice. Spread with remaining artichoke mixture; sprinkle with remaining mozzarella cheese. Sprinkle with feta cheese.

4 Cover and bake 40 minutes. Uncover and bake about 15 minutes longer or until noodles are tender and lasagna is bubbly. Let stand 10 to 15 minutes before cutting. Garnish with rosemary sprigs and lemon wedges.

1 Serving: Calories 350; Total Fat 13g (Saturated Fat 8g; Trans Fat 0g); Cholesterol 40mg; Sodium 950mg; Total Carbohydrate 38g (Dietary Fiber 5g); Protein 20g **Exchanges:** 2 Starch, 1 Vegetable, 1½ Medium-Fat Meat, 1 Fat **Carbohydrate Choices:** 2½

MEDITERRANEAN LASAGNA Stir in ½ cup chopped pitted kalamata, Greek or ripe olives with the pasta sauce.

Polenta with Garden Vegetables

SPAGHETTI AND SPICY RICE BALLS

These rice and oat "meatballs" get a light wheat germ coating, giving them a golden-brown color and a bit of nutty-flavored crunch. Wheat germ is high in oil content, so it can turn rancid quickly; store it in the refrigerator or freezer.

PREP 30 min TOTAL 30 min • **5 servings**

- 2 **cups cooked regular long-grain white or brown rice* (page 429)**
- ½ **cup quick-cooking oats**
- 1 **medium onion, chopped (½ cup)**
- ¼ **cup unseasoned dry bread crumbs**
- ¼ **cup milk**
- 1 **tablespoon chopped fresh or 1 teaspoon dried basil leaves**
- 2 **teaspoons chopped fresh or ½ teaspoon dried oregano leaves**
- ¼ **teaspoon ground red pepper (cayenne)**
- 1 **egg, beaten**
- ½ **cup wheat germ**
- 1 **tablespoon vegetable oil**
- 1 **package (16 oz) spaghetti**
- 2 **cups meatless tomato pasta sauce, heated Finely shredded Parmesan cheese, if desired**

Artichoke-Spinach Lasagna

1 In medium bowl, mix rice, oats, onion, bread crumbs, milk, basil, oregano, red pepper and egg. Shape mixture into 10 balls; roll in wheat germ to coat.

2 In 10-inch skillet, heat oil over medium heat. Cook rice balls in oil about 10 minutes, turning occasionally, until light golden brown. Meanwhile, cook and drain spaghetti as directed on package.

3 Serve rice balls and pasta sauce over spaghetti; sprinkle with cheese.

*Do not use instant rice.

1 Serving: Calories 740; Total Fat 12g (Saturated Fat 2.5g; Trans Fat 0g); Cholesterol 45mg; Sodium 1180mg; Total Carbohydrate 133g (Dietary Fiber 9g); Protein 24g **Exchanges:** 7½ Starch, 1 Other Carbohydrate, 1 Vegetable, 1½ Fat **Carbohydrate Choices:** 9

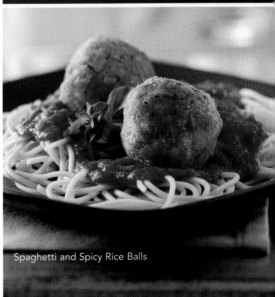

Spaghetti and Spicy Rice Balls

Learn to Make **Eggplant Parmigiana**

EGGPLANT PARMIGIANA

There's no mystery to this dish—the secret is a combination of fresh, young, tender eggplant and a moist cooking technique. When the dish is cooked, it should be bubbly and the eggplant will still be slightly firm but can be easily pierced with a fork. Look below for tips to great eggplant parmigiana that you will be proud to serve anytime.

PREP 1 hr 5 min **TOTAL** 1 hr 40 min • **6 servings**

1 **egg**	¼ cup **olive or vegetable oil**
2 tablespoons **water**	2 cups **tomato pasta sauce** (for homemade sauce, see page 370)
⅔ cup **seasoned dry bread crumbs**	2 cups **shredded mozzarella cheese** (8 oz)
⅓ cup **grated Parmesan cheese**	
2 **small unpeeled eggplants** (about 1 lb each), cut into ¼-inch slices	

1 Heat oven to 350°F. In shallow dish, mix egg and water. In another shallow dish, mix bread crumbs and Parmesan cheese. Dip eggplant in egg mixture; coat with crumb mixture.

2 In 12-inch non-stick skillet, heat 2 tablespoons of the oil over medium heat. Cook half of the eggplant in oil about 5 minutes, turning once, until light golden brown; drain on paper towels. Repeat with remaining oil and eggplant, using additional oil if necessary.

3 In ungreased 11x7-inch (2-quart) glass baking dish, place half of the eggplant, overlapping slices slightly. Spoon half of the sauce over eggplant. Sprinkle with 1 cup of the mozzarella cheese. Repeat with remaining eggplant, sauce and cheese.

4 Bake uncovered about 25 minutes or until sauce is bubbly and cheese is light brown.

1 Serving: Calories 410; Total Fat 23g (Saturated Fat 8g; Trans Fat 0g); Cholesterol 60mg; Sodium 830mg; Total Carbohydrate 35g (Dietary Fiber 5g); Protein 17g **Exchanges:** 1 Starch, 4 Vegetable, 1½ High-Fat Meat, 2 Fat **Carbohydrate Choices:** 2

Keys to Success

- Cover and refrigerate homemade tomato sauce, if making, **overnight** so that flavors can blend.
- **Coat eggplant right before cooking** so the crumb coating stays crispy, as moisture from eggplant slices can soften the coating.
- **Cook eggplant slices one half at a time** to avoid overcrowding in pan. This also helps to keep the coating crispy.
- **Add more oil to pan, if necessary,** to ensure remaining eggplant gets a light golden-brown crust.
- **Cook eggplant in skillet** just before layering the parmigiana so it stays crisp from frying.

Eggplant Parmigiana

EGGPLANT-RAVIOLI PARMIGIANA Cook 1 bag (25 oz) frozen cheese-filled ravioli as directed on package; drain and keep warm. Prepare Eggplant Parmigiana as directed except—arrange half of cooked ravioli over eggplant in dish. Spoon half of sauce over pasta. Sprinkle with 1 cup of the mozzarella cheese. Repeat with remaining eggplant, ravioli, sauce and cheese. Bake as directed.

EGGPLANT-OLIVE PARMIGIANA Prepare Eggplant Parmigiana as directed except—stir ½ cup sliced pitted imported Italian black olives into the 2 cups tomato pasta sauce before spooning over eggplant in dish in Step 3.

> ## Eggplant
>
> Here's a little fact that is not well known. Eggplant is actually not a vegetable at all. It's a fruit—specifically a berry. It's part of the nightshade family, (see page 577) and a relative of the tomato and potato. Whatever we classify it as, this delicious food is available year-round in a variety of colors and sizes. Choose eggplants that are smooth and without blemishes, avoiding any with soft or brown spots. Young eggplants are the most tender and should not need to be peeled. Store eggplants in the refrigerator and use within 5 days—they are highly perishable and become bitter with age.

See how to make **eggplant parmigiana**: Visit bettycrocker.com/BCcookbook

EASY FRIED VEGETABLES

The cooking method used for the eggplant in the Eggplant Parmigiana recipe can be used to fry other vegetables. Serve these tasty morsels as a hearty side dish, in sandwiches or salads, or as appetizers with a great dip.

Start with 1 tablespoon olive oil and add more as needed for frying.

Use the same amount of egg mixture and crumb mixture and the same coating method as given in the Eggplant Parmigiana recipe.

Try substituting grated Asiago or Romano cheese for the Parmesan. Add ½ teaspoon dried basil, oregano or Italian seasoning to the crumb mixture for more flavor. Use a wide spatula for turning so vegetables hold their shape.

Cook until light golden brown. If vegetables start to brown too much, reduce the heat slightly.

Great Dips for Fried Vegetables: Hummus, page 49 (or purchased); Pesto, page 484 (any flavor, or use purchased pesto); Ranch Dip (purchased); Salsa, page 480 (or purchased); Sour Cream and Onion Dip (purchased)

Vegetable	Preparation	Coating	Frying Time in Minutes
Bell Peppers (3 medium)	Cut into rings.	Coat with egg and crumb mixtures.	3 to 5
Onions, White, Yellow or Red (2 to 3 medium)	Slice ¼ inch thick.	Coat with egg and crumb mixtures.	5 to 8
Portabella Mushroom Caps (6 to 8 medium caps)	Use whole.	Coat with egg and crumb mixtures.	3 to 5
Sweet Potatoes (2 medium)	Slice ¼ inch thick.	Coat with egg and crumb mixtures.	5 to 8
Tomatoes (4 medium)	Slice ¼ inch thick.	Coat with egg and crumb mixtures.	2 to 4
Yellow Summer Squash (2 medium)	Slice unpeeled ¼ inch thick.	Coat with egg and crumb mixtures.	3 to 5
Zucchini (2 medium)	Slice unpeeled ¼ inch thick.	Coat with egg and crumb mixtures.	3 to 5

MOUSSAKA LOWER CALORIE

Eggplant has been called the vegetarian's beef because of its meaty texture. Choose firm, even-colored eggplants that are heavy for their size and free of blemishes. Caps and stems should be intact with no mold. Refrigerate unwashed in a plastic bag up to 5 days.

PREP 30 min TOTAL 1 hr 40 min • **4 servings**

   4 frozen soy-protein burgers or
      soy-protein vegetable burgers
   1 medium unpeeled eggplant (about
      1½ lb), cut into ¼-inch slices
   ¼ cup all-purpose flour
   ½ teaspoon salt
   ½ teaspoon pepper
   ¼ teaspoon ground nutmeg
   ¼ teaspoon ground cinnamon
   3 cups milk
   4 oz (half of 8-oz package) cream cheese,
      cut into cubes
   1 can (15 oz) tomato sauce
   2 eggs, beaten

1 Heat oven to 375°F. Grease 3-quart casserole. On large microwavable plate, microwave burgers uncovered on High 2 to 3 minutes, turning once, until thawed. Cut into 1-inch pieces; set aside.

2 In 2-quart saucepan, place eggplant and enough water to cover. Heat to boiling; cook 5 to 8 minutes or until tender. Drain in colander; set aside.

3 In same saucepan, mix flour, salt, pepper, nutmeg, cinnamon and milk. Heat to boiling, stirring constantly. Boil 1 minute,

Moussaka

stirring constantly. Remove from heat. Stir in cream cheese until melted and smooth.

4 Place half of eggplant in casserole. Layer burger pieces, tomato sauce, 1½ cups of the white sauce and remaining eggplant. Stir eggs into remaining white sauce; pour over eggplant.

5 Bake uncovered about 1 hour or until firm. Let stand 10 minutes before serving.

1 Serving: Calories 330; Total Fat 6g (Saturated Fat 2.5g; Trans Fat 0g); Cholesterol 15mg; Sodium 1560mg; Total Carbohydrate 40g (Dietary Fiber 7g); Protein 29g **Exchanges:** 2 Starch, 2 Vegetable, 2½ Very Lean Meat, 1 Fat **Carbohydrate Choices:** 2½

MEDITERRANEAN GRATIN

PREP 15 min TOTAL 40 min • **4 servings**

   1 box (5.6 oz) roasted garlic and olive oil
      couscous mix
   6 cups fresh baby spinach leaves (5 oz)
   2 tablespoons water
   ½ cup drained roasted red bell peppers
      (from 7.25-oz jar), chopped
 1½ teaspoons grated lemon peel
   ¼ teaspoon salt
   1 can (15 to 16 oz) garbanzo beans
      (chickpeas), drained, rinsed
   1 cup crumbled feta cheese (4 oz)
   ½ cup coarsely chopped walnuts
   1 tablespoon olive or vegetable oil

1 Heat oven to 350°F. Spray 11x7-inch (2-quart) glass baking dish or gratin dish with cooking spray.

2 Make couscous as directed on box for version without olive oil. Meanwhile, in 12-inch skillet, place spinach and water. Cover; cook over medium heat 2 to 4 minutes, stirring occasionally, until spinach is wilted.

3 Stir in cooked couscous, roasted peppers, lemon peel, salt, beans and ½ cup of the cheese. Spread mixture in baking dish. In small bowl, mix walnuts, oil and remaining ½ cup cheese. Sprinkle over couscous mixture.

4 Bake uncovered 20 to 25 minutes or until heated through.

1 Serving: Calories 530; Total Fat 23g (Saturated Fat 6g; Trans Fat 0g); Cholesterol 25mg; Sodium 910mg; Total Carbohydrate 61g (Dietary Fiber 11g); Protein 21g **Exchanges:** 3½ Starch, 1 Vegetable, 1 Medium-Fat Meat, 3 Fat **Carbohydrate Choices:** 4

Texas Tater Casserole

TEXAS TATER CASSEROLE

Frozen soy-protein burger crumbles replace the ground beef in this favorite casserole.

PREP 25 min **TOTAL** 1 hr 15 min • **6 servings**

Cooking spray
1 large onion, chopped (1 cup)
1 medium stalk celery, chopped (½ cup)
2 cloves garlic, finely chopped
2 cups frozen soy protein crumbles (from 12-oz package)
2 cans (10¾ oz each) condensed Cheddar cheese soup
1 can (11 oz) whole kernel corn with red and green peppers, drained
½ cup chunky-style salsa
2 teaspoons chili powder
¼ teaspoon pepper
4½ cups (16 oz) frozen potato nuggets (from 32-oz bag)
½ cup shredded taco-seasoned cheese blend (2 oz)

1 Heat oven to 375°F. Generously spray 12-inch skillet with cooking spray. Add onion, celery and garlic to skillet; spray vegetables with cooking spray. Cook over medium heat 8 to 10 minutes, stirring occasionally, until crisp-tender.

2 Stir in veggie crumbles, soup, corn, salsa, chili powder and pepper. Spoon into ungreased 2½-quart casserole. Top with potato nuggets.

3 Bake uncovered 40 minutes. Sprinkle with cheese. Bake 5 to 10 minutes longer or until bubbly and cheese is melted.

1 Serving: Calories 470; Total Fat 21g (Saturated Fat 10g; Trans Fat 4g); Cholesterol 25mg; Sodium 2070mg; Total Carbohydrate 51g (Dietary Fiber 7g); Protein 19g **Exchanges:** 3 Starch, ½ Other Carbohydrate, 1½ Lean Meat, 3 Fat **Carbohydrate Choices:** 3½

SOUTHWESTERN POT PIE

Making this easy dinner on the stovetop is extra-convenient. It's covered with a delicious cornbread topping that's studded with sunflower nuts. Go ahead and serve it right from the pan!

PREP 15 min **TOTAL** 55 min • **4 servings**

2 tablespoons vegetable oil
1 large onion, chopped (1 cup)
2 cups cubed peeled sweet potatoes or butternut squash
2 cups chunky-style salsa (for homemade salsa, see page 480)
½ cup water
¼ teaspoon ground cinnamon
1 can (15 to 16 oz) garbanzo beans (chickpeas), drained
1 cup frozen whole kernel corn
1 pouch (6.5 oz) cornbread and muffin mix
½ cup milk
1 tablespoon roasted sunflower nuts, if desired

1 In 4-quart Dutch oven or saucepan, heat 1 tablespoon of the oil over medium-high heat. Cook onion in oil about 5 minutes, stirring occasionally, until crisp-tender.

2 Stir in sweet potatoes, salsa, water and cinnamon. Heat to boiling; reduce heat. Cover; simmer 20 to 25 minutes or until potatoes are tender. Stir in beans and corn.

3 In medium bowl, mix cornbread mix, milk and remaining 1 tablespoon oil. Stir in nuts. Drop by large spoonfuls onto vegetable mixture. Cover; simmer about 15 minutes or until toothpick inserted into center of dumplings comes out clean.

1 Serving: Calories 590; Total Fat 16g (Saturated Fat 3g; Trans Fat 0.5g); Cholesterol 0mg; Sodium 1230mg; Total Carbohydrate 94g (Dietary Fiber 15g); Protein 17g **Exchanges:** 5 Starch, 1 Other Carbohydrate, 2½ Fat **Carbohydrate Choices:** 6

BLACK BEAN SOUTHWESTERN POT PIE
Substitute 1 can (15 to 16 oz) black beans, drained, for the garbanzo beans.

Tofu Stir-Fry with Black
Bean Sauce

TOFU STIR-FRY WITH BLACK BEAN SAUCE LOWER CALORIE

Black bean sauce is robust in flavor, thin and salty. It is made from fermented black beans, garlic and often star anise. Look for it with other Asian ingredients.

PREP 25 min TOTAL 1 hr 25 min • **5 servings**

- 1   tablespoon olive oil
- 1   large onion, thinly sliced (1 cup)
- 4   cups chopped fresh broccoli
- 1   medium red bell pepper, cut into ½-inch slices, then cut in half (1 cup)
- ⅓   cup black bean garlic sauce (from 7-oz jar)
- 2   tablespoons soy sauce
- 1   tablespoon chili garlic sauce (from 8-oz jar)
- 1   package (12 to 14 oz) firm lite tofu, drained if needed, cut into ¾-inch cubes
- ⅓   cup chopped fresh cilantro
- 5   cups hot cooked basmati rice (page 429)
- ¼   cup honey-roasted or regular sunflower nuts

1 In wok or 12-inch skillet, heat oil over medium-high heat. Cook onion in oil about 2 minutes, stirring occasionally, until crisp-tender. Add broccoli and bell pepper; stir-fry about 2 minutes or until almost crisp-tender.

2 In small bowl, mix black bean sauce, soy sauce and chili garlic sauce. Stir into vegetable mixture to coat. Add tofu; stir-fry 2 to 3 minutes or until thoroughly heated. Stir in cilantro. Serve over rice. Sprinkle with nuts.

1 Serving (1 Cup Tofu Mixture and 1 Cup Rice): Calories 340; Total Fat 10g (Saturated Fat 1.5g; Trans Fat 0g); Cholesterol 0mg; Sodium 540mg; Total Carbohydrate 48g (Dietary Fiber 9g); Protein 14g **Exchanges:** 3 Starch, 1 Vegetable, ½ Medium-Fat Meat, 1 Fat **Carbohydrate Choices:** 3

SWEET-AND-SOUR STIR-FRY

Versatile tofu takes on the flavor of the ingredients it is cooked with. In this recipe, the marinade adds lots of sweet-and-sour flavor to the tofu.

PREP 20 min TOTAL 2 hr 30 min • **4 servings**

- 1   package (12 to 14 oz) firm or extra-firm tofu, drained if needed, cut into 1-inch cubes
- ¼   cup water
- 1   tablespoon cider vinegar
- 1   tablespoon honey
- 2   tablespoons soy sauce
- ½   teaspoon ground ginger
- 1   can (8 oz) pineapple chunks in juice, drained, juice reserved
- 2   teaspoons cornstarch
- 2   tablespoons cold water
- 1   tablespoon sesame oil
- 1   medium onion, chopped (½ cup)
- 2   medium carrots, sliced (1 cup)
- 1   medium green bell pepper, cut into 1-inch pieces (1 cup)
- 4   cups hot cooked rice (page 429) Sunflower nuts, if desired

1 Place tofu in medium glass or plastic bowl. Mix ¼ cup water, the vinegar, honey, soy sauce, ginger and pineapple juice. Pour over tofu; toss gently. Cover; refrigerate 1 to 2 hours.

2 Remove tofu from marinade; reserve marinade. In small bowl, dissolve cornstarch in water; set aside. In wok or 12-inch skillet, heat oil over medium-high heat. Add onion and carrots; stir-fry about 3 minutes or until crisp-tender. Add pineapple, tofu and bell pepper; gently stir-fry 2 minutes.

3 Stir cornstarch mixture into reserved marinade; pour into wok. Cook 2 minutes, stirring occasionally. Reduce heat. Cover; cook 2 minutes. Serve over rice. Sprinkle with nuts.

1 Serving: Calories 390; Total Fat 8g (Saturated Fat 1.5g; Trans Fat 0g); Cholesterol 0mg; Sodium 1090mg; Total Carbohydrate 67g (Dietary Fiber 4g); Protein 13g **Exchanges:** 3 Starch, ½ Fruit, 1 Other Carbohydrate, ½ Lean Meat, 1 Fat **Carbohydrate Choices:** 4½

PEPPER AND SOYBEAN STIR-FRY FAST

We suggest jasmine rice in this recipe, but regular long-grain or brown rice could be served with this stir-fry instead.

PREP 20 min TOTAL 20 min • **4 servings**

- 1 tablespoon vegetable oil
- 1 tablespoon curry powder
- 1 bag (1 lb) frozen bell pepper and onion stir-fry
- 1 bag (12 oz) frozen shelled edamame (green) soybeans
- 4 cloves garlic, finely chopped
- 1 cup canned unsweetened coconut milk (not cream of coconut)
- 2 cups hot cooked jasmine rice (page 429)
- ½ cup salted roasted cashews
  Chopped fresh cilantro or parsley, if desired

1 In wok or 12-inch nonstick skillet, heat oil over medium-high heat. Add curry powder; cook 1 minute, stirring frequently. Stir in stir-fry vegetables, soybeans and garlic. Cook 2 minutes, stirring frequently. Cover; cook about 3 minutes longer or until vegetables are tender.

2 Stir in coconut milk. Reduce heat to medium-low; simmer uncovered 2 minutes, stirring occasionally. Serve over rice. Sprinkle with cashews and cilantro.

1 Serving: Calories 540; Total Fat 28g (Saturated Fat 12g; Trans Fat 0g); Cholesterol 0mg; Sodium 370mg; Total Carbohydrate 53g (Dietary Fiber 11g); Protein 19g **Exchanges:** 2½ Starch, ½ Other Carbohydrate, 1 Vegetable, 1½ Very Lean Meat, 5 Fat **Carbohydrate Choices:** 3½

Edamame

The word *edamame* means "beans on branches," and the bean lives up to its name as it grows in clusters on bushy branches. Edamame are simply soybeans harvested at the peak of ripening. To retain freshness, they are often parboiled and quick-frozen. To eat boiled edamame from the pod, squeeze the seeds directly from the pods into your mouth using your fingers.

TOFU TERIYAKI NOODLES

PREP 20 min TOTAL 40 min • **4 servings**

- 1 cup hot water
- 6 dried black or shiitake mushrooms (½ oz)
- 8 oz uncooked soba (buckwheat) noodles or whole wheat spaghetti
- 1 tablespoon vegetable oil
- 1 large onion, sliced
- 1 package (12 to 14 oz) firm or extra-firm tofu, drained if needed, cut into ¼-inch cubes
- 1 package (8 oz) sliced fresh mushrooms (about 3 cups)
- 8 oz fresh sliced shiitake, crimini or baby portabella mushrooms
- ⅓ cup teriyaki sauce
- ¼ cup chopped fresh cilantro
- 1 tablespoon sesame seed, toasted if desired (page 22)

1 In small bowl, pour hot water over dried mushrooms. Let stand about 20 minutes or until soft; drain. Rinse with warm water; drain. Squeeze out excess moisture from mushrooms. Remove and discard stems; cut caps into ½-inch strips.

2 Meanwhile, cook and drain noodles as directed on package.

3 In 12-inch skillet, heat oil over medium-high heat. Cook onion in oil 3 minutes, stirring frequently. Stir in tofu and all mushrooms; cook 3 minutes, stirring frequently. Stir in teriyaki sauce; reduce heat. Partially cover; simmer about 2 minutes or until vegetables are tender. Stir in noodles, cilantro and sesame seed.

1 Serving (2 Cups): Calories 370; Total Fat 8g (Saturated Fat 1.5g; Trans Fat 0g); Cholesterol 0mg; Sodium 1170mg; Total Carbohydrate 54g (Dietary Fiber 9g); Protein 20g **Exchanges:** 2 Starch, ½ Other Carbohydrate, 3 Vegetable, 1 Very Lean Meat, 1½ Fat **Carbohydrate Choices:** 3½

Draining Tofu

Place tofu between layers of paper towels or clean kitchen towels on cutting board. Gently press down on top of towels to extract water from tofu. Replace damp towels with dry towels. Place bowl or other weight on top of towels. Let stand 15 minutes for tofu to extract additional water.

TOFU STROGANOFF WITH WILD RICE

PREP 35 min TOTAL 1 hr 25 min • **6 servings**

- 2 packages (12 to 14 oz each) firm tofu, drained if needed
- ¼ cup sour cream
- 1 tablespoon tomato paste or ketchup
- 2 cloves garlic, chopped
- 1 teaspoon reduced-sodium soy sauce
- ½ teaspoon salt
- ⅛ teaspoon ground red pepper (cayenne)
- 1 tablespoon olive oil
- 3 medium onions, finely chopped (1½ cups)
- 1 tablespoon butter
- 2 tablespoons reduced-sodium soy sauce
- 4 cups sliced fresh baby portabella mushrooms
- 6 cups hot cooked wild rice (page 429)
- ¼ cup finely chopped fresh parsley
  Freshly ground pepper to taste

1 In blender or food processor, place 1 package of tofu, the sour cream, tomato paste, garlic, 1 teaspoon soy sauce, the salt and red pepper. Cover; blend on high speed 1 to 2 minutes, stopping blender frequently to scrape sides, until smooth. Set aside.

2 Cut remaining package of tofu into 1-inch cubes. In 12-inch skillet, heat oil over medium heat. Cook cubed tofu in oil about 10 minutes, stirring occasionally, until tofu starts to turn light golden brown; remove from skillet.

3 In same skillet, cook onions in butter 4 to 5 minutes, stirring occasionally, until softened. Stir in 2 tablespoons soy sauce and the mushrooms. Cook 3 to 4 minutes, stirring occasionally, until mushrooms are tender.

4 Stir tofu cubes and reserved sauce into mushroom mixture. Cook 5 to 8 minutes, stirring occasionally, until thoroughly heated. Serve over rice. Sprinkle with parsley and pepper.

Cleaning Mushrooms

Gently wipe mushrooms with clean damp paper towel or quickly rinse with water.

1 Serving (1 Cup Tofu Mixture and 1 Cup Rice): Calories 370; Total Fat 12g (Saturated Fat 4g; Trans Fat 0g); Cholesterol 10mg; Sodium 1020mg; Total Carbohydrate 46g (Dietary Fiber 6g); Protein 20g **Exchanges:** 3 Starch, 1½ Very Lean Meat, 1½ Fat **Carbohydrate Choices:** 3

LIGHTER **DIRECTIONS** For 370 calories and 7 grams of fat, use reduced-fat firm tofu and reduced-fat sour cream.

MEXICAN TOFU-RICE SKILLET

PREP 35 min TOTAL 35 min • **4 servings**

- 1 package (12 to 14 oz) extra-firm tofu, drained if needed
- 1 cup frozen whole kernel corn (from 12-oz bag)
- 1 can (14.5 oz) diced tomatoes with green chiles, undrained
- 1 package (5.6 oz) Spanish rice–flavor rice and pasta blend mix in tomato sauce
- 1¼ cups water
- 1 cup shredded Mexican cheese blend (4 oz)
- 1½ cups shredded lettuce
- 1 large tomato, seeded, chopped (1 cup)
- 4 medium green onions, sliced (¼ cup)

1 Place tofu between 2 layers of paper towels; press gently to remove as much water as possible. Cut into ½-inch cubes; set aside.

2 In 12-inch nonstick skillet, mix corn, canned tomatoes, contents of rice mix package and water. Gently stir in tofu. Heat to boiling; reduce heat to low. Cover; simmer 12 to 14 minutes, stirring occasionally, until rice is tender.

3 Remove skillet from heat. Sprinkle cheese over rice mixture. Cover; let stand 4 to 5 minutes or until liquid is absorbed and cheese is melted. Top with lettuce, chopped tomato and onions.

1 Serving: Calories 420; Total Fat 16g (Saturated Fat 6g; Trans Fat 0g); Cholesterol 25mg; Sodium 1060mg; Total Carbohydrate 48g (Dietary Fiber 5g); Protein 23g **Exchanges:** 3 Starch, 1 Vegetable, 1½ High-Fat Meat, ½ Fat **Carbohydrate Choices:** 3

ITALIAN TOFU-RICE SKILLET Substitute 1 can (14.5 oz) diced tomatoes with Italian seasoning for the diced tomatoes with green chiles. Use mozzarella cheese instead of the Mexican cheese blend.

EASY WAYS WITH TOFU

Tofu is one of the most versatile, protein-rich foods for anyone who is looking for ways to eat more plant-based meals. Soft silken tofu lends itself best to desserts and cream sauces, and firm and extra-firm tofu are best used for stir-fries and baking. Here are some ideas for trying your hand at tofu cookery.

1 Asian Tofu Salad: Cut extra-firm tofu into 1-inch cubes. Place cubes in skillet with 2 tablespoons Asian dressing and cook until golden brown, 10 to 12 minutes. Toss tofu with mixed greens, shredded carrot, chopped cucumber, sliced green onions and some additional Asian dressing. Sprinkle with toasted sesame seed.

2 Chocolate-Banana Tofu Mousse: Blend 1 box silken tofu with 2 ripe bananas until smooth. Meanwhile, melt 8 ounces semisweet baking chocolate. Fold chocolate into tofu mixture; add ¼ teaspoon vanilla. Divide mixture among 4 ramekins and chill 1 hour. Garnish with chocolate shavings.

3 Fried Tofu with Peanut Sauce: Cut extra-firm tofu into ½-inch cubes. Dust tofu with nutritional yeast or cornstarch, and fry in olive oil over medium-high heat until slightly browned, about 5 minutes. Toss tofu with about 2 tablespoons peanut sauce and serve over pasta. Sprinkle with sliced green onions.

4 Sesame Baked Tofu: Cut extra-firm tofu into ½-inch slices. Blot with paper towels, pressing down to remove as much liquid as possible. Mix equal parts tamari sauce and sesame oil; brush both sides of tofu generously with mixture. Let tofu stand 10 minutes. Bake uncovered in baking dish at 325°F for about 1 hour, turning halfway through, until glaze has baked in and tofu feels firm to the touch.

5 Tofu Egg Salad: Combine 2 tablespoons mayonnaise with 1 teaspoon Dijon mustard, 1 teaspoon lemon juice, 1 tablespoon sweet pickle relish, 2 tablespoons diced celery and a sprinkle of dried dill weed. In separate bowl, mash about 8 ounces firm tofu with fork. Fold tofu into mayonnaise mixture. Sprinkle with paprika.

6 Tofu Patties: Mash 1 pound extra-firm tofu using fork and combine with ½ cup panko crispy bread crumbs, ½ cup ground walnuts, some chopped green onions, garlic salt and 1 to 2 tablespoons tamari sauce to moisten. Form into patties; fry in skillet sprayed with cooking spray until brown and crisp on both sides.

7 Tofu Spaghetti: At least 1 day before making spaghetti, wrap 1 block firm or extra-firm tofu with plastic wrap and freeze overnight. Thaw tofu before making spaghetti. Squeeze thawed tofu to remove any moisture, using paper towels or clean kitchen towels. Make tomato pasta sauce (page 370). Crumble tofu directly into sauce and cook 15 minutes before serving. Top with chopped fresh parsley and shredded Parmesan cheese. Freezing tofu, then thawing it, makes it more porous so it soaks up sauce and flavor is enhanced.

8 Veggie-Tofu Stir-Fry: Cook cubes of extra-firm tofu in mixture of 2 tableepoons each soy sauce, chili garlic sauce and sweet chili sauce. Cook 5 minutes; add halved grape tomatoes and cook 2 to 3 minutes longer. Add 1 cup fresh baby spinach and cook until just wilted. Top with additional sweet chili sauce if desired. Serve with jasmine rice if desired.

Tempeh Stir-Fry with Yogurt-Peanut Sauce

TEMPEH STIR-FRY WITH YOGURT-PEANUT SAUCE

Tempeh, pronounced TEHM-pay and also spelled tempe, is a fermented, high-protein soybean cake with a chewy texture and slightly nutty flavor. If you can't find it in your supermarket (sometimes it's sold in the freezer case with other vegetarian foods), check a co-op or natural foods store.

PREP 40 min **TOTAL** 40 min • **4 servings**

- ¼ cup creamy peanut butter
- ¼ cup vanilla low-fat yogurt
- 3 tablespoons teriyaki marinade (from 12-oz bottle)
- 1 tablespoon honey
- 2 tablespoons vegetable oil
- 1 package (8 oz) tempeh, cut into 2 x ¼ x ¼-inch strips
- 1 medium onion, cut into thin wedges
- 4 medium carrots, cut into 2 x ¼ x ¼-inch strips (2 cups)
- 12 oz fresh green beans, trimmed, cut in half crosswise (2 cups)
- ¼ cup water
- 1 medium red bell pepper, cut into thin bite-size strips
- 2 cups hot cooked white or brown rice (page 429)
- ¼ cup chopped fresh cilantro

1 In small bowl, beat peanut butter, yogurt, teriyaki marinade and honey with wire whisk until smooth; set aside.

2 In wok or 12-inch skillet, heat 1 tablespoon of the oil over medium heat. Cook tempeh in oil 5 to 6 minutes, turning frequently, until light golden brown. Remove tempeh from skillet.

3 In same skillet, heat remaining 1 tablespoon oil over medium heat. Cook onion in oil 1 minute, stirring occasionally. Stir in carrots, green beans and water. Cover; cook 5 minutes. Stir in bell pepper. Cook 2 to 3 minutes, stirring occasionally, until vegetables are crisp-tender.

4 Stir in tempeh and reserved peanut butter mixture until well mixed. Cook 1 to 2 minutes, stirring occasionally, until hot. Serve over rice. Sprinkle with cilantro.

1 Serving: Calories 490; Total Fat 22g (Saturated Fat 4g; Trans Fat 0g); Cholesterol 0mg; Sodium 600mg; Total Carbohydrate 52g (Dietary Fiber 8g); Protein 20g **Exchanges:** 1½ Starch, 1½ Other Carbohydrate, 2 Vegetable, 1½ Medium-Fat Meat, 2½ Fat **Carbohydrate Choices:** 3½

TEMPEH STIR-FRY WITH NOODLES

Substitute 8 oz cooked angel hair (cannellini) pasta, drained, for the hot cooked rice. Sprinkle each serving with chopped peanuts.

TOFU NUGGETS FAST LOWER CALORIE

Extra-firm tofu holds up to frying and gives these golden-brown nuggets a slightly chewy texture.

PREP 20 min **TOTAL** 20 min • **10 servings**

- 3 tablespoons all-purpose flour
- 6 tablespoons cold water
- ⅔ cup unseasoned dry bread crumbs
- 1 teaspoon salt
  Dash ground red pepper (cayenne)
- 1 package (12 to 14 oz) extra-firm tofu, drained if needed, patted dry, cut into 1-inch cubes
  Vegetable oil for frying
- ⅔ cup barbecue sauce, sweet-and-sour sauce, salsa or ketchup

1 In small bowl, beat flour and water with whisk until smooth. In shallow dish or pie plate, mix bread crumbs, salt and red pepper. Dip tofu cubes in flour mixture; roll in bread crumb mixture to coat.

2 In 10-inch skillet, heat oil (½ inch) over medium-high heat. Cook 15 nuggets in oil about 1 minute, turning once, until golden brown. Drain on paper towels. Repeat with remaining nuggets. Serve hot with barbecue sauce.

1 Serving (4 Nuggets and 1 Tablespoon Sauce): Calories 160; Total Fat 9g (Saturated Fat 1.5g; Trans Fat 0g); Cholesterol 0mg; Sodium 470mg; Total Carbohydrate 14g (Dietary Fiber 0g); Protein 5g **Exchanges:** 1 Starch, 1½ Fat **Carbohydrate Choices:** 1

DELUXE STUFFED-CRUST PIZZA

Here's pizzeria-style pizza that is super-easy to make at home. Using string cheese makes stuffing the edge of the crust very simple.

PREP 25 min TOTAL 45 min • **6 servings**

- 1 tablespoon yellow cornmeal
- 1 loaf (1 lb) frozen 100% whole wheat bread dough, thawed
- 4 sticks (1 oz each) string cheese, cut in half lengthwise
- ¼ cup Italian-style tomato paste (from 6-oz can)
- 1 small onion, cut in half lengthwise, then thinly sliced
- 1 medium bell pepper, thinly sliced
- 1 can (4 oz) mushrooms pieces and stems, drained
- 1 oz sliced veggie pepperoni (from 5.5-oz package), coarsely chopped (¼ cup)*
- 12 pitted kalamata or Greek olives, coarsely chopped (⅓ cup)
- 2 cups shredded mozzarella cheese (8 oz)

1 Heat oven to 400°F. Grease cookie sheet with shortening or cooking spray. Sprinkle cornmeal over cookie sheet.

2 On cookie sheet, press or roll dough into 13-inch round. Arrange string cheese in circle around edge of dough. Carefully roll edge of dough up over string cheese; seal well.

3 Spread tomato paste evenly over dough. Top with onion, bell pepper, mushrooms, pepperoni and olives. Sprinkle with shredded cheese.

4 Bake 15 to 17 minutes or until crust is golden brown and cheese is melted. Cut into wedges to serve.

*2 frozen soy-protein burgers, thawed and cut into ¼-inch pieces, or ½ cup frozen veggie crumbles (from 12-oz package), thawed, can be substituted.

1 Serving: Calories 400; Total Fat 15g (Saturated Fat 7g; Trans Fat 0g); Cholesterol 30mg; Sodium 880mg; Total Carbohydrate 43g (Dietary Fiber 6g); Protein 25g **Exchanges:** 2½ Starch, ½ Other Carbohydrate, 2 Medium-Fat Meat, ½ Fat **Carbohydrate Choices:** 3

DELUXE STUFFED-CRUST TOMATO PIZZA

Omit mushrooms. Slice 2 Italian plum (Roma) tomatoes thinly. Layer tomatoes over olives. Sprinkle with ½ teaspoon dried basil leaves. Continue as directed.

Deluxe Stuffed-Crust Pizza

Making Stuffed Pizza Crust

Arrange string cheese sticks (cut in half lengthwise) around edge of dough.

Carefully roll edge of dough up over cheese; seal well.

VEGGIE AND BEAN BURGERS

PREP 25 min TOTAL 25 min • **4 sandwiches**

- ½ cup fresh broccoli florets
- 2 oz fresh mushrooms (about 4 medium)
- ½ small red bell pepper, cut into large pieces
- ½ cup cooked instant white or brown rice
- 1 can (15 to 16 oz) garbanzo beans (chickpeas), drained, rinsed
- 1 egg
- 1 clove garlic
- ½ teaspoon seasoned salt
- 1 teaspoon dried chopped onion
- ⅓ cup seasoned dry bread crumbs
- 3 tablespoons vegetable oil
- 4 whole wheat burger buns, split
  Toppings (Cheddar cheese slices, lettuce, sliced tomato, sliced onion and mayonnaise), if desired

1 In food processor, place broccoli, mushrooms and bell pepper. Cover; process, using quick on-and-off motions, to finely chop vegetables (do not puree). Remove vegetables from processor to medium bowl; stir in rice.

2 Add beans, egg, garlic and seasoned salt to food processor. Cover; process until smooth. Stir bean mixture, dried chopped onion and bread crumbs into vegetable mixture. Shape mixture into 4 patties, about ½ inch thick.

3 In 10-inch nonstick skillet, heat oil over medium-high heat. Cook patties in oil 8 to 10 minutes, turning once, until brown and crisp. Serve in buns with toppings.

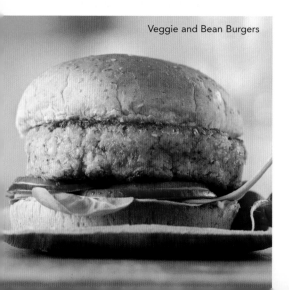

Veggie and Bean Burgers

1 Sandwich: Calories 460; Total Fat 16g (Saturated Fat 2.5g; Trans Fat 0g); Cholesterol 55mg; Sodium 540mg; Total Carbohydrate 61g (Dietary Fiber 9g); Protein 17g **Exchanges:** 3½ Starch, 2 Vegetable, 2 Fat **Carbohydrate Choices:** 4

VEGGIE AND BEAN "MEATBALLS" Heat oven to 400°F. Generously spray 15x10x1-inch pan with cooking spray. Shape vegetable mixture into 16 balls; place in pan. Generously spray tops of balls with cooking spray. Bake about 20 minutes or until crisp. Serve with tomato pasta sauce (any variety) or cheese sauce.

CALIFORNIA BLACK BEAN BURGERS

PREP 25 min TOTAL 25 min • **6 sandwiches**

- 1 can (15 oz) black beans, undrained
- 1 can (4.5 oz) chopped green chiles, undrained
- 1 cup unseasoned dry bread crumbs
- 1 teaspoon chili powder
- 1 egg, beaten
- ¼ cup yellow cornmeal
- 2 tablespoons vegetable oil
- 6 burger buns, split, toasted
- 2 tablespoons mayonnaise or salad dressing
- 1¼ cups shredded lettuce
- 3 tablespoons chunky-style salsa

1 In food processor or blender, place beans. Cover; process on high speed until slightly mashed. Remove beans from food processor to medium bowl. Stir in chiles, bread crumbs, chili powder and egg.

2 Shape mixture into 6 patties, about ½ inch thick. Coat each patty with cornmeal.

3 In 10-inch skillet, heat oil over medium heat. Cook patties in oil 5 to 10 minutes, turning once, until crisp and thoroughly cooked on both sides. Spread bottom halves of buns with mayonnaise. Top with lettuce, patties and salsa. Cover with top halves of buns.

1 Sandwich: Calories 400; Total Fat 11g (Saturated Fat 2g; Trans Fat 0g); Cholesterol 35mg; Sodium 1090mg; Total Carbohydrate 60g (Dietary Fiber 7g); Protein 14g **Exchanges:** 4 Starch, 1 Fat **Carbohydrate Choices:** 4

CALIFORNIA BLACK BEAN BURGERS WITH TOMATOES AND CHEESE Cut 1 medium tomato into 6 slices. Add 1 slice to each sandwich along with 1 slice of mozzarella cheese.

Falafel

WILD RICE–PECAN PATTIES

These patties are deliciously chewy with a toasted pecan crunch. We tested them in the fall and found they're really good on buns with Cranberry Sauce (page 490).

PREP 20 min TOTAL 1 hr 10 min • **4 servings**

- 2 **cups cooked wild rice (page 429)**
- 1 **cup soft bread crumbs (about 1½ slices bread)**
- ½ **teaspoon garlic salt**
- ⅓ **cup chopped pecans, toasted (page 22)**
- 2 **eggs**
- 1 **jar (2.5 oz) sliced mushrooms, drained, finely chopped**
- 1 **jar (2 oz) diced pimientos, drained**
- 2 **tablespoons vegetable oil**

1 In medium bowl, mix all ingredients except oil.

2 In 10-inch skillet, heat oil over medium heat. Scoop wild rice mixture by ⅓ cupfuls into skillet; flatten to ½ inch. Cook about 3 minutes on each side or until light brown. Remove from skillet; cover to keep warm. Repeat for remaining patties.

1 Serving (2 Patties): Calories 360; Total Fat 18g (Saturated Fat 2.5g; Trans Fat 0g); Cholesterol 105mg; Sodium 450mg; Total Carbohydrate 40g (Dietary Fiber 4g); Protein 11g **Exchanges:** 2½ Starch, 1 Vegetable, 3 Fat **Carbohydrate Choices:** 2½

WILD RICE–PECAN SLIDERS In Step 2, scoop rice mixture by 2 to 3 tablespoonfuls into skillet. Cook as directed. Serve on miniature burger buns.

See how to make falafel: Visit bettycrocker.com/BCcookbook

FALAFEL (FAVA BEAN ROUNDS)

LOWER CALORIE

These rounds are made from well-seasoned fava beans and then fried until golden brown. They're perfect served by themselves or in pita bread. If you don't have time to start with dried beans, use two 15- to 16-ounce cans of garbanzo beans, drained and liquid reserved.

PREP 15 min TOTAL 3 hr 45 min • **4 servings**

- 2 **cups water**
- 1 **cup dried fava or garbanzo beans**
- 3 **tablespoons chopped fresh parsley**
- 2 **tablespoons all-purpose flour**
- 2 **teaspoons finely chopped garlic**
- 1 **teaspoon salt**
- 1 **teaspoon ground coriander**
- ¾ **teaspoon ground cumin**
- ¼ **teaspoon baking powder**
- ⅛ **teaspoon ground ground red pepper (cayenne)**
- 1 **egg**
- 1 **small red onion, finely chopped Vegetable oil for frying**

1 In 2-quart saucepan, heat 2 cups water and the beans to boiling. Boil 2 minutes; remove from heat. Cover and let stand 1 hour.

2 Add enough water to cover beans if necessary. Heat to boiling; reduce heat. Cover and simmer 1 to 1½ hours or until tender. Drain, reserving liquid.

3 Mash beans with fork; add 2 to 3 tablespoons reserved liquid if necessary. (Do not puree beans in blender or food processor.) Stir in remaining ingredients except oil (mixture should be thick). Cover and let stand 1 hour.

4 Pinch off 1-inch pieces; shape into rounds and flatten.

5 In 3-quart saucepan, heat oil (2 inches) to 375°F. Fry 4 or 5 rounds at a time in oil 2 to 3 minutes, turning once, until golden brown. Remove with slotted spoon; drain on paper towels.

1 Serving: Calories 230; Total Fat 11g (Saturated Fat 2g; Trans Fat 0g); Cholesterol 55mg; Sodium 650mg; Total Carbohydrate 24g (Dietary Fiber 5g); Protein 9g **Exchanges:** 1 Starch, 1½ Vegetable, ½ Very Lean Meat, 2 Fat **Carbohydrate Choices:** 1½

Italian Grinders

1 Sandwich: Calories 320; Total Fat 10g (Saturated Fat 2.5g; Trans Fat 0g); Cholesterol 0mg; Sodium 1080mg; Total Carbohydrate 40g (Dietary Fiber 6g); Protein 17g **Exchanges:** 2½ Starch, 1½ Lean Meat, 1 Fat **Carbohydrate Choices:** 2½

PORTABELLA MUFFULETTA SANDWICHES FAST LOWER CALORIE

Portabella mushrooms are wonderful large, earthy-flavored flat mushrooms that are perfect for sandwiches. Look for caps that are firm and fresh looking.

PREP **15 min** TOTAL **15 min** ● **2 sandwiches**

OLIVE SALAD
- ¼ cup chopped celery
- 3 tablespoons chopped pimiento-stuffed green olives
- 1 tablespoon reduced-fat mayonnaise or salad dressing

SANDWICHES
- 6 oz fresh portabella mushrooms, cut into ½-inch slices
- 1 to 2 teaspoons olive or vegetable oil
- ⅛ teaspoon garlic powder
- 2 French rolls (6 inch), split
- 2 slices (¾ oz each) provolone or mozzarella cheese
- ½ medium tomato, thinly sliced

1 In small bowl, mix all olive salad ingredients. Set aside.

2 Spray broiler pan with cooking spray. Place mushroom slices on pan. In small bowl, mix oil and garlic powder. Brush half of oil mixture on mushrooms. Broil 4 to 6 inches from heat 5 to 6 minutes or until tender, turning and brushing with remaining oil mixture once halfway through cooking. Remove mushrooms from pan.

3 Place rolls, cut side up, on broiler pan. Broil 4 to 6 inches from heat 30 to 60 seconds or until golden brown. Place cheese on bottom halves of rolls. Top with mushrooms, olive salad and tomato slices. Cover with top halves of rolls.

1 Sandwich: Calories 330; Total Fat 16g (Saturated Fat 5g; Trans Fat 0g); Cholesterol 15mg; Sodium 780mg; Total Carbohydrate 33g (Dietary Fiber 3g); Protein 13g **Exchanges:** 1 Starch, ½ Other Carbohydrate, 2 Vegetable, 1 Medium-Fat Meat, 2 Fat **Carbohydrate Choices:** 2

ITALIAN GRINDERS

LOWER CALORIE

Can't resist the aroma and flavor of a meatball sandwich smothered in sauce with peppers and onions? Then you'll enjoy these sandwiches.

PREP **25 min** TOTAL **25 min** ● **4 sandwiches**

- 4 frozen soy-protein burgers or soy-protein vegetable burgers
- 3 tablespoons grated Parmesan cheese
- 1 teaspoon Italian seasoning
- 4 teaspoons olive or vegetable oil
- 1 small onion, cut in half, sliced
- 1 small red bell pepper, cut into ¼-inch strips
- 1 small green bell pepper, cut into ¼-inch strips
- 4 hot dog buns, split
- ½ cup meatless tomato pasta sauce, heated

1 On large microwavable plate, microwave burgers uncovered on High 2 to 3 minutes, turning once, until thawed. Crumble burgers into medium bowl; mix in cheese and Italian seasoning. Shape mixture into 16 balls.

2 In 10-inch nonstick skillet, heat 2 teaspoons of the oil over medium heat. Cook burger balls in oil, turning frequently, until brown. Remove from skillet; cover to keep warm.

3 In same skillet, heat remaining 2 teaspoons oil over medium heat. Cook onion and bell peppers in oil, stirring frequently, until crisp-tender.

4 Place 4 burger balls in each bun. Top with vegetable mixture. Serve with pasta sauce.

VEGGIE JOES LOWER CALORIE

These vegetarian sloppy joes have all the flavor and texture of the traditional ground beef version. For a new twist, skip the buns and try spooning the mixture over tortilla chips, pasta or rice instead.

PREP 10 min TOTAL 4 hr 10 min • **16 servings**

- 4 cups frozen soy protein crumbles (from two 12-oz packages)
- 1 medium onion, finely chopped (½ cup)
- 1½ cups ketchup
- ½ cup water
- 2 tablespoons packed brown sugar
- 2 tablespoons white vinegar
- 1 tablespoon yellow mustard
- ½ teaspoon pepper
- ¼ teaspoon salt
- 16 burger buns, split

1 Spray 3½- to 4-quart slow cooker with cooking spray. In slow cooker, mix all ingredients except buns.

2 Cover; cook on Low heat setting 4 to 6 hours. (If slow cooker has black liner, do not cook longer than 6 hours or mixture may burn around edge.) Fill each bun with ⅓ cup mixture.

1 Serving: Calories 190; Total Fat 3g (Saturated Fat 0.5g; Trans Fat 0g); Cholesterol 0mg; Sodium 640mg; Total Carbohydrate 30g (Dietary Fiber 3g); Protein 10g **Exchanges:** 1½ Starch, ½ Other Carbohydrate, 1 Very Lean Meat, ½ Fat **Carbohydrate Choices:** 2

MAKE AHEAD DIRECTIONS Make recipe as directed. Freeze desired portions in freezer containers up to 4 months.

BAKED CHIMICHANGAS

LOWER CALORIE

Traditionally deep-fried, this recipe was developed to bake the chimichangas. It's an easy technique and turns them into a lower-calorie entrée.

PREP 20 min TOTAL 30 min • **8 servings**

- 2 tablespoons vegetable oil
- 1 small onion, finely chopped (⅓ cup)
- 1 clove garlic, finely chopped
- 1 can (15 oz) black beans, drained
- 1 medium tomato, seeded, chopped (¾ cup)
- 1 can (4.5 oz) chopped green chiles, drained
- ¼ cup slivered almonds
- ¼ cup raisins
- 1 tablespoon red wine vinegar
- 1 teaspoon chili powder
- ½ teaspoon salt
- ¼ teaspoon ground cinnamon
- ⅛ teaspoon ground cloves
- 8 flour tortillas (8 to 10 inch)
  Guacamole, salsa and sour cream, if desired

1 Heat oven to 475°F. Spray cookie sheet with cooking spray.

2 In 10-inch skillet, heat 1 tablespoon of the oil over medium-high heat. Cook onion and garlic in oil 2 to 3 minutes, stirring occasionally, until onion is crisp-tender. Stir in remaining ingredients except tortillas, garnishes and remaining oil. Heat to boiling; reduce heat to medium. Cook uncovered 5 minutes, stirring occasionally.

3 Spoon about ½ cup mixture down center of each tortilla. Fold sides of each tortilla toward center; fold ends up. Place seam side down on cookie sheet. Brush tops and sides of chimichangas with remaining 1 tablespoon oil.

4 Bake 6 to 8 minutes or until golden brown. Serve with guacamole, salsa and sour cream.

1 Serving: Calories 270; Total Fat 10g (Saturated Fat 1.5g; Trans Fat 0.5g); Cholesterol 0mg; Sodium 900mg; Total Carbohydrate 32g (Dietary Fiber 2g); Protein 12g **Exchanges:** 2 Starch, ½ Vegetable, ½ Medium-Fat Meat, 1 Fat **Carbohydrate Choices:** 2

Veggie Joes

Heirloom Recipe and New Twist

Really cheesy cheese enchiladas—are so good and definitely a favorite of the Betty Crocker Kitchens. The new twist is just a little spicier and filled with the fresh flavors of green salsa, zucchini and cilantro. We think you will like it, too.

CLASSIC

CHEESE ENCHILADAS

PREP 25 min **TOTAL** 50 min • **4 servings**

- 2 cups shredded Monterey Jack cheese (8 oz)
- 1 cup shredded Cheddar cheese (4 oz)
- ½ cup sour cream
- 1 medium onion, chopped (½ cup)
- 2 tablespoons chopped fresh parsley
- ¼ teaspoon pepper
- 1 can (15 oz) tomato sauce
- 1 small green bell pepper, chopped (½ cup)
- 1 can (4.5 oz) chopped green chiles, drained
- 1 clove garlic, finely chopped
- ⅔ cup water
- 1 tablespoon chili powder
- 1½ teaspoons chopped fresh or ½ teaspoon dried oregano leaves
- ¼ teaspoon ground cumin
- 8 soft corn tortillas (5 or 6 inch)
  Additional shredded cheese, sour cream and chopped onion, if desired

1 Heat oven to 350°F. In medium bowl, mix cheeses, sour cream, onion, parsley and pepper; set aside.

2 In 2-quart saucepan, heat tomato sauce, bell pepper, chiles, garlic, water, chili powder, oregano and cumin to boiling, stirring occasionally; reduce heat. Simmer uncovered 5 minutes. Pour into ungreased 9-inch glass pie plate.

3 Dip each tortilla into sauce to coat both sides. Spoon about ¼ cup cheese mixture onto each tortilla. Roll tortillas around filling; place seam side down in ungreased 11x7-inch (2-quart) glass baking dish. Pour remaining sauce over enchiladas.

4 Bake uncovered 25 to 30 minutes or until bubbly. Garnish with additional shredded cheese, sour cream and chopped onion.

1 Serving (2 Enchiladas): Calories 530; Total Fat 34g (Saturated Fat 20g; Trans Fat 1g); Cholesterol 100mg; Sodium 1310mg; Total Carbohydrate 31g (Dietary Fiber 5g); Protein 26g **Exchanges:** 1 Starch, ½ Other Carbohydrate, 1 Vegetable, 3 High-Fat Meat, 2 Fat **Carbohydrate Choices:** 2

Cheese Enchiladas

Cheese Enchiladas Verde

NEW TWIST

CHEESE ENCHILADAS VERDE

PREP 15 min TOTAL 40 min • **4 servings**

- 1½ cups shredded Mexican cheese blend (6 oz)
- 1 small zucchini, shredded (¾ cup)
- ¼ cup chopped fresh cilantro
- ⅓ cup garden vegetable or chives-and-onion cream cheese spread
- 8 soft corn tortillas (5 or 6 inch)
- 1 jar (16 oz) green salsa* (2 cups)
- 1 medium avocado, pitted, peeled and diced
- 4 medium green onions, sliced (¼ cup)

1 Heat oven to 350°F. Spray 11x7-inch (2-quart) glass baking dish with cooking spray.

2 In medium bowl, mix shredded cheese, zucchini and cilantro. Spread about 2 teaspoons cream cheese on each tortilla. Top each with about ⅓ cup shredded cheese mixture to within 1 inch of edge. Roll up tortillas; place seam side down in baking dish. Pour salsa over enchiladas.

3 Cover; bake about 25 minutes or until hot. Top with avocado and onions.

Green salsa is known as salsa verde or green tomatillo salsa. Regular salsa or picante sauce can be substituted.

1 Serving (2 Enchiladas): Calories 490; Total Fat 31g (Saturated Fat 15g; Trans Fat 1g); Cholesterol 65mg; Sodium 550mg; Total Carbohydrate 36g (Dietary Fiber 7g); Protein 17g **Exchanges:** ½ Starch, ½ Fruit, ½ Other Carbohydrate, 2½ Vegetable, 1½ Medium-Fat Meat, 4½ Fat **Carbohydrate Choices:** 2½

Cilantro

Often used in southwestern cooking, cilantro adds a cool touch to food that is often spicy. This herb is fairly strong flavored, so use it in small amounts, adding more as you determine the flavor is good.

See how to make **cheese enchiladas:** Visit bettycrocker.com/BCcookbook

SMOKY CHIPOTLE SOFT TACOS

LOWER CALORIE

The word mole *comes from the Aztec word* molli, *meaning "concoction." It's a tasty, complex sauce with dozens of ingredients, which vary by region and individual cook. In the United States, we're most familiar with dark, rich, red moles.*

PREP 20 min TOTAL 4 hr 20 min • **18 tacos**

- Cooking spray
- 1 large onion, chopped (1 cup)
- 1 Anaheim chile, chopped (⅓ cup)
- 6 cups frozen soy protein crumbles (from two 12-oz packages)
- ¾ cup chili sauce
- 1½ cups water
- ½ cup mole sauce (from 8.25-oz jar)
- 1 tablespoon chopped chipotle chiles in adobo sauce (from 7-oz can)
- 1 teaspoon ground cumin
- ¾ teaspoon salt
- 18 flour tortillas (6 inch)
- 2 cups shredded Cheddar cheese (8 oz)
- 3 medium tomatoes, chopped (2¼ cups)

1 Generously spray 8-inch skillet with cooking spray. Add onion and Anaheim chile; spray onion and chile with cooking spray. Cook over medium heat 4 to 5 minutes, stirring occasionally, until onion is crisp-tender.

2 Spray 3½- to 4-quart slow cooker with cooking spray. In slow cooker, mix onion mixture and remaining ingredients except tortillas, cheese and tomatoes.

3 Cover; cook on Low heat setting 4 to 5 hours. Spoon ⅓ cup mixture down center of each tortilla; top with 1 heaping tablespoon cheese and 2 tablespoons tomatoes. Roll up tortillas.

1 Taco: Calories 250; Total Fat 10g (Saturated Fat 3.5g; Trans Fat 0g); Cholesterol 15mg; Sodium 730mg; Total Carbohydrate 24g (Dietary Fiber 4g); Protein 15g **Exchanges:** 1½ Starch, 1½ Lean Meat, 1 Fat **Carbohydrate Choices:** 1½

Chipotle Chiles

Very smoky flavored, chipotle chiles are dried, smoked jalapeño chiles. Look for them dried or in cans with very spicy adobo sauce. Often, some of the sauce will be used to flavor recipes.

MIDDLE EAST VEGETABLE TACOS LOWER CALORIE

PREP 25 min TOTAL 25 min • **6 servings**

- 1 tablespoon olive or vegetable oil
- 1 medium eggplant (1½ lb), peeled, cut into ½-inch cubes
- 1 medium red bell pepper, cut into ½-inch strips
- 1 medium onion, cut into ½-inch wedges
- 1 can (14.5 oz) diced tomatoes with basil, garlic and oregano, undrained
- ¼ teaspoon salt
- 1 container (8 oz) plain hummus (for homemade hummus, see page 49)
- 1 box (4.6 oz) taco shells (12 shells)
  Plain yogurt or sour cream, if desired

1 In 10-inch nonstick skillet, heat oil over medium-high heat. Cook eggplant, bell pepper and onion in oil 5 to 7 minutes, stirring occasionally, until crisp-tender. Stir in tomatoes and salt. Reduce heat to medium. Cover; cook about 5 minutes or until eggplant is tender.

2 Spread 4 teaspoons hummus on half of inside of each taco shell. Spoon about ½ cup vegetable mixture into each shell. Serve with yogurt.

1 Serving (2 Tacos): Calories 290; Total Fat 12g (Saturated Fat 1.5g; Trans Fat 2g); Cholesterol 0mg; Sodium 600mg; Total Carbohydrate 40g (Dietary Fiber 7g); Protein 7g **Exchanges:** 2 Starch, 2 Vegetable, 2 Fat **Carbohydrate Choices:** 2½

VEGETABLE CURRY WITH COUSCOUS FAST LOWER CALORIE

PREP 15 min TOTAL 15 min • **4 servings**

- 1 tablespoon vegetable oil
- 1 medium red bell pepper, cut into thin strips
- ¼ cup vegetable or chicken broth
- 1 tablespoon curry powder
- 1 teaspoon salt
- 1 bag (1 lb) frozen broccoli, carrots and cauliflower (or other combination)
- ½ cup raisins
- ⅓ cup chutney
- 2 cups hot cooked couscous or rice
- ¼ cup chopped peanuts

1 In 12-inch skillet, heat oil over medium-high heat. Cook bell pepper in oil 4 to 5 minutes, stirring frequently, until tender.

2 Stir in broth, curry powder, salt and vegetables. Heat to boiling. Boil about 4 minutes, stirring frequently, until vegetables are crisp-tender.

3 Stir in raisins and chutney. Serve over couscous. Sprinkle with peanuts.

1 Serving: Calories 330; Total Fat 9g (Saturated Fat 1.5g; Trans Fat 0g); Cholesterol 0mg; Sodium 760mg; Total Carbohydrate 53g (Dietary Fiber 7g); Protein 9g **Exchanges:** 1½ Starch, 1½ Other Carbohydrate, 2 Vegetable, 1½ Fat **Carbohydrate Choices:** 3½

INDIAN LENTIL STEW

Curry powder is made of many spices that might include cardamom, chiles, cinnamon, fennel seed, fenugreek, cumin, turmeric, nutmeg, coriander and cloves.

PREP 55 min TOTAL 55 min • **4 servings**

- 2 tablespoons butter
- 1 large onion, chopped (1 cup)
- 1 tablespoon curry powder
- 2 tablespoons all-purpose flour
- 1 can (14 oz) vegetable broth (for homemade broth, see page 530)
- ¾ cup dried lentils (6 oz), sorted, rinsed
- ½ teaspoon salt
- ½ cup apple juice
- 3 cups 1-inch pieces peeled dark-orange sweet potatoes
- 1 cup frozen sweet peas (from 12-oz bag)
  Sour cream or plain yogurt, if desired
  Chutney, if desired

1 In 3-quart saucepan, melt butter over medium-high heat. Cook onion and curry powder in butter 2 minutes, stirring occasionally. Stir in flour. Gradually add broth, stirring constantly, until thickened.

2 Stir in lentils and salt. Reduce heat to low. Cover; simmer 20 minutes, stirring occasionally.

3 Stir in apple juice, sweet potatoes and peas. Heat to boiling; reduce heat to low. Cover; simmer 15 to 20 minutes, stirring occasionally, until vegetables are tender. Top individual servings with sour cream and chutney.

1 Serving: Calories 360; Total Fat 7g (Saturated Fat 3g; Trans Fat 0g); Cholesterol 15mg; Sodium 790mg; Total Carbohydrate 62g (Dietary Fiber 12g); Protein 14g **Exchanges:** 2½ Starch, 1½ Other Carbohydrate, 1 Very Lean Meat, 1 Fat **Carbohydrate Choices:** 4

INDEX

Index

Note: Page numbers in *italics* indicate photographs.

Helpful Nutrition and Cooking Information

We provide nutrition information for each recipe that includes calories, fat, cholesterol, sodium, carbohydrate, fiber and protein. Individual food choices can be based on this information.

Criteria Used for Calculating Nutrition Information

- The first ingredient was used wherever a choice is given (such as ⅓ cup sour cream or plain yogurt).
- The first ingredient amount was used wherever a range is given (such as 3- to 3½-pound cut-up whole chicken).
- The first serving number was used wherever a range is given (such as 4 to 6 servings).
- "If desired" ingredients and recipe variations were not included (such as sprinkle with brown sugar, if desired).
- Only the amount of a marinade or frying oil that is estimated to be absorbed by the food during preparation or cooking was calculated.

Criteria Used for Calculating Lower-Calorie Recipes

Recipes designated as Lower Calorie were determined using the following guidelines:

- Main dishes: 350 calories or less
- Chilies, stews, plain meats: 250 calories or less
- Soups, breads, side dishes, appetizers: 175 calories or less
- Desserts: 200 calories or less
- Condiments, beverages, dips, sauces, dressings: 80 calories or less

Ingredients Used in Recipe Testing and Nutrition Calculations

- Ingredients used for testing represent those that the majority of consumers use in their homes: large eggs, 2% milk, 80%-lean ground beef and canned ready-to-use chicken broth.
- Fat-free, low-fat or low-sodium products were not used, unless otherwise indicated.
- Solid vegetable shortening was used to grease pans, unless otherwise indicated.

Equipment Used in Recipe Testing

We use equipment for testing that the majority of consumers use in their homes. If a specific piece of equipment (such as a wire whisk) is necessary for recipe success, it is listed in the recipe.

- Cookware and bakeware without nonstick coatings were used, unless otherwise indicated.
- No dark-colored, black or insulated bakeware was used.
- When a pan is specified in a recipe, a metal pan was used; a baking dish or pie plate means ovenproof glass was used.
- An electric hand mixer was used for mixing only when mixer speeds are specified in the recipe directions. If a stand mixer is necessary, the recipe will call for that appliance. When a mixer speed is not given, a spoon or fork was used.

Food Yields and Equivalents

If Recipe States	Amount Needed
FRUITS AND VEGETABLES	
Apples	
1 cup sliced	1 medium
3 medium	1 pound
Apricots or Dates, dried, 1 cup	6 ounces
Asparagus, 16 to 20 spears	1 pound
Bananas, 1 cup sliced or mashed	2 small or 1 medium
Beans, green or wax, 3 cups cut up	1 pound
Broccoli, 2 cups florets	8 ounces
Cabbage (green, red, napa), 4 cups shredded	1 medium head
Carrots/Parsnips, 1 cup shredded or sliced	1½ to 2 medium
Cauliflower, 4 cups florets	1 medium head
Celery, 1 cup sliced	3 stalks
Corn, 1 cup kernels	2 medium ears
Cranberries	
Fresh, 4 cups	1 pound
Dried, 1 cup	4 ounces
Garlic, ½ teaspoon chopped	1 clove
Lemon/Lime	
2 teaspoons peel	1 medium
3 tablespoons juice	
Mushrooms, 3 cups sliced	8 ounces
Onion, ½ cup chopped	1 medium
Orange	
2 tablespoons peel	1 large
½ cup juice	
Peaches/Pears, 2 cups sliced	3 medium
Peppers, Bell, 1 cup chopped	1 medium
Potatoes	
Small red, 10 to 12 small	1½ pounds
White, red, sweet, 1 medium	6 ounces
Strawberries, 4 cups sliced	1 quart
Tomato, 1 cup chopped	1 large
DAIRY AND MEATS	
Bacon, ½ cup crumbled	8 slices, cooked
Butter, ½ cup (8 tablespoons)	1 stick (4 ounces)
Cheese, 1 cup shredded	4 ounces

If Recipe States	Amount Needed
Chicken, 2 to 3 cups, chopped	2 medium whole chicken breasts or 1 rotisserie chicken
Eggs	
Whole, ¼ cup	1 large
Whites, ¼ cup	2 large
Yolks, ¼ cup	3 large
BAKING/PANTRY INGREDIENTS	
Crumbs, crushed	
Bread, dried, 2¼ cups	8 ounces
Bread, fresh, ½ cup	1 slice
Chocolate wafer, 1½ cups	27 cookies
Graham cracker, 1½ cups	21 squares
Saltine cracker, 1½ cups	21 squares
Vanilla wafer, 1½ cups	38 cookies
Flour, 3½ cups	1 pound
Sugar	
Brown, 2¼ cups	1 pound
Granulated, 2¼ cups	1 pound
Powdered, 4 cups	1 pound

Food Substitutions

Food/Amount	Replace With
Baking powder, 1 teaspoon	½ teaspoon cream of tartar plus ¼ teaspoon baking soda
Brown sugar, 1 cup	1 cup granulated sugar plus 2 tablespoons molasses
Buttermilk, 1 cup	1 tablespoon lemon juice or vinegar plus enough milk to make 1 cup
Chocolate	
Unsweetened baking, 1 ounce	3 tablespoons cocoa plus 1 tablespoon melted shortening
Semisweet chips, 1 cup	6 ounces semisweet baking chocolate, chopped
Semisweet baking, 1 ounce	1 ounce unsweetened baking chocolate plus 1 tablespoon sugar or 1 tablespoon cocoa plus 2 tablespoons sugar and 2 teaspoons shortening
Cornstarch, 1 tablespoon	2 tablespoons all-purpose flour
Tomato sauce, 15-ounce can	6-ounce can tomato paste plus 1½ cans water
Yeast, 1 package (.25 ounce)	2¼ teaspoons regular or active dry yeast
Yogurt, plain, 1 cup	1 cup sour cream

Metric Conversion Guide

Volume

U.S. Units	Canadian Metric	Australian Metric
¼ teaspoon	1 mL	1 ml
½ teaspoon	2 mL	2 ml
1 teaspoon	5 mL	5 ml
1 tablespoon	15 mL	20 ml
¼ cup	50 mL	60 ml
⅓ cup	75 mL	80 ml
½ cup	125 mL	125 ml
⅔ cup	150 mL	170 ml
¾ cup	175 mL	190 ml
1 cup	250 mL	250 ml
1 quart	1 liter	1 liter
1½ quarts	1.5 liters	1.5 liters
2 quarts	2 liters	2 liters
2½ quarts	2.5 liters	2.5 liters
3 quarts	3 liters	3 liters
4 quarts	4 liters	4 liters

Note: The recipes in this cookbook have not been developed or tested using metric measures. When converting recipes to metric, some variations in quality may be noted.

Weight

U.S. Units	Canadian Metric	Australian Metric
1 ounce	30 grams	30 grams
2 ounces	55 grams	60 grams
3 ounces	85 grams	90 grams
4 ounces (¼ pound)	115 grams	125 grams
8 ounces (½ pound)	225 grams	225 grams
16 ounces (1 pound)	455 grams	500 grams
1 pound	455 grams	0.5 kilogram

Measurements   Temperatures

Inches	Centimeters	Fahrenheit	Celsius
1	2.5	32°	0°
2	5.0	212°	100°
3	7.5	250°	120°
4	10.0	275°	140°
5	12.5	300°	150°
6	15.0	325°	160°
7	17.5	350°	180°
8	20.5	375°	190°
9	23.0	400°	200°
10	25.5	425°	220°
11	28.0	450°	230°
12	30.5	475°	240°
13	33.0	500°	260°

Equivalent Measures

3 teaspoons	=	1 tablespoon
4 tablespoons	=	¼ cup
5 tablespoons + 1 teaspoon	=	⅓ cup
8 tablespoons	=	½ cup
12 tablespoons	=	¾ cup
16 tablespoons	=	1 cup (8 ounces)
2 cups	=	1 pint (16 ounces)
4 cups	=	1 quart (2 pints/32 ounces)
8 cups	=	½ gallon (4 pints/64 ounces)
4 quarts	=	1 gallon (128 ounces)

Common Abbreviations

degree	° (or dg)	package	pkg
dozen	doz	pint	pt
gallon	gal	pound	lb (or #)
hour	hr	quart	qt
inch	in (or in.)	second	sec
minute	min	tablespoon	Tbsp (or T)
ounce	oz	teaspoon	tsp (or t)

Take Your Cookbook to the Next Level!

We've created an exciting online destination to be a perfect companion to your new edition of the *Betty Crocker Cookbook.*

Throughout the book, look for icons directing you to: **bettycrocker.com/BCcookbook***

See how to make **three-bean casserole:** Visit bettycrocker.com/BCcookbook

From this home page, you'll have access to **85 bonus cooking videos** showing how to make dozens of recipes from the book and demonstrating a variety of useful kitchen tasks.

You'll also have access to **400 bonus recipes** that expand on each chapter in the book with ideas ranging from special holiday appetizers and gluten-free baking to easy weeknight meals and more.

*In Canada, visit: lifemadedelicious.ca/BCcookbook